The **Rough Guide** to

Egypt

written and researched by

Dan Richardson and Daniel Jacobs

with additional contributions by
Michael Kohn, Michael Ackroyd
and Ros Ford

ROUGH GUIDES

NEW YORK • LONDON • DELHI

www.roughguides.com

Contents

◄◄ Lahun Pyramid, ◄ The Eastern Desert

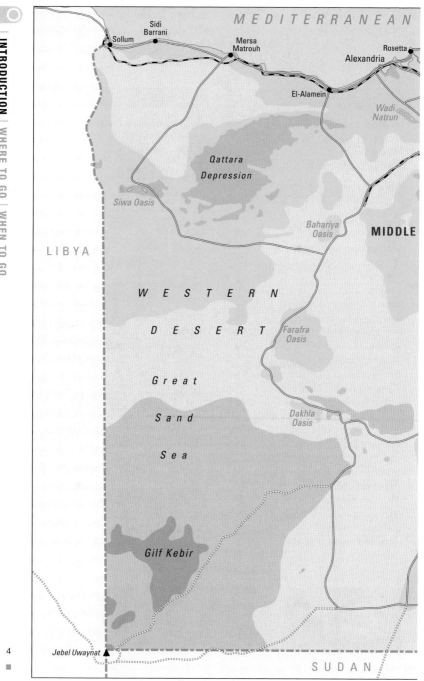

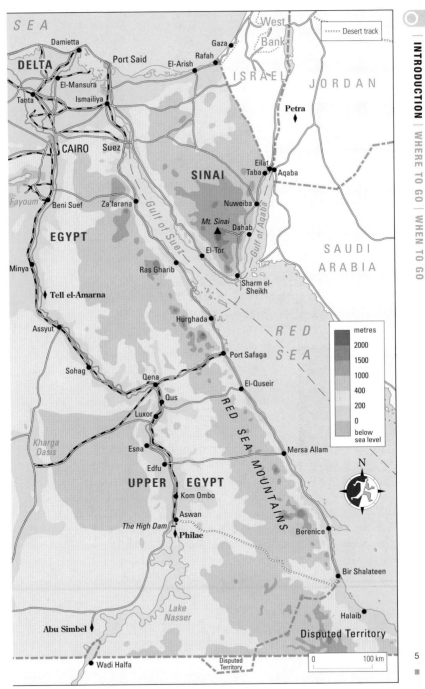

Introduction to
Egypt

Egypt is the oldest tourist destination on earth. Ancient Greeks and Romans started the trend, coming to goggle at the cyclopean scale of the Pyramids and the Colossi of Thebes. At the onset of colonial times, Napoleon and the British in turn looted Egypt's treasures to fill their national museums, sparking off a trickle of Grand Tourists that eventually became a flood of travellers, packaged for their Nile cruises and Egyptological lectures by the enterprising Thomas Cook.

Today, the attractions of the country are not only the monuments of the Nile Valley and the souks, mosques and madrassas of Islamic Cairo, but the natural wonders of the Red Sea, Sinai, and the Eastern and Western deserts: fantastic coral reefs and tropical fish, dunes and rockscapes – plus ancient fortresses, monasteries and rock art.

The land itself is a freak of nature, whose lifeblood is the River Nile. From the Sudanese border to the shores of the Mediterranean, the Nile Valley and its Delta are flanked by arid wastes, the latter as empty as the former are teeming with people. This stark duality between fertility and desolation is fundamental to Egypt's character and has shaped its development since prehistoric times, imparting continuity to diverse cultures and peoples over seven millennia. It is a sense of permanence and timelessness that is buttressed by religion, which pervades every aspect of life. Although the pagan cults of ancient Egypt are as moribund as its legacy of mummies and temples, their ancient fertility rites and processions of boats still hold their place in the celebrations of Islam and Christianity.

6

The result is a multi-layered culture, which seems to accord equal respect to ancient and modern. The peasants (*fellaheen*) of the Nile and Bedouin tribes

INTRODUCTION | WHERE TO GO | WHEN TO GO

of the desert live much as their ancestors did a thousand years ago. Other communities include the Nubians of the far south, and the Coptic Christians, who trace their ancestry back to pharaonic times. What unites them is a love of their homeland, extended family ties, dignity, warmth and hospitality towards strangers. Though most visitors are drawn to Egypt by its monuments, the enduring memory is likely to be of its people and their way of life.

Where to go

Egypt's capital, **Cairo**, is a seething megalopolis whose chief sightseeing appeal lies in its **bazaars** and medieval **mosques**, though there is scarcely less fascination in its juxtapositions of medieval and modern

Fact file

• The Arab Republic of Egypt covers 1,001,450 square kilometres, of which 96.4 percent is **desert**; only the Nile Valley, its Delta and some oases are fertile.

• Egypt's **population** of 75 million is twice that of the next most populous Arab country (Algeria) and a quarter of the population of the Arab world. Its ethnic profile is Eastern Hamitic – Egyptians, Bedouin, Nubians and Berbers account for 99 percent – with tiny minorities of Greeks, Armenians and others. Arabic is universally spoken; Nubian or Siwi locally. Islam is the national **religion**, with some 96 percent followers; almost all the rest are Coptic Orthodox Christians. Average **life expectancy** is 64 years.

• A **republic** since 1952, Egypt is divided into 26 governorates or *muhafazat*. President Hosni Mubarak has been head of state since 1981. The National Democratic Party invariably wins 88 percent of the vote in elections to the People's Assembly (Maglis al-Shaab) and Advisory Council (Maglis al-Shura). Opposition parties and independent MPs are outspoken, but powerless to change anything.

• **Tourism** is Egypt's largest money-earner, followed by tolls on the Suez Canal, and exports of oil, petroleum products, textiles and natural gas.

Coral reefs

While the Nile Valley and the desert shaped its civilization, there's a third dimension to Egypt's environment. The Red Sea sustains an incredibly rich ecosystem of **coral reefs** and tropical fish, ranging from coastal mangrove swamps and coral gardens to deep-sea islands and underwater pillars. Since it was first explored by Jacques Cousteau in the 1960s, this undersea world has become the basis of a whole new tourist industry, with diving resorts all along the Red Sea Coast and south Sinai, and "liveaboards" venturing as far south as Eritrea. See p.708 for details of reef ecology, and p.707 for the essential facts of diving in Sinai; reefs from Hurghada to Mersa Alam are covered on p.782.

life, with fortified gates, villas and skyscrapers interwoven by flyovers whose traffic may be halted by donkey carts. The immensity and diversity of this "Mother of Cities" is as staggering as anything you'll encounter in Egypt, while just outside Cairo are the first of the **pyramids** that range across the desert to the edge of the Fayoum, among them the unsurpassable trio at **Giza**, the vast necropolis of **Saqqara** and the recently reopened pyramids at **Dahshur**. Besides all this, there are superb

▼ Camels in Luxor

museums devoted to Ancient, Coptic and Islamic Egypt, and enough **entertainments** to occupy weeks of your time.

However, the principal tourist lure remains, as ever, the **Nile Valley**, with its **ancient monuments** and timeless river vistas – Nile **cruises** on a luxury vessel or a felucca sailboat being a great way to combine the two. The town of **Luxor** is synonymous with the magnificent temples of **Karnak** and the **Theban Necropolis**, which includes the **Valley of the Kings** where Tutankhamun and other pharaohs were buried. **Aswan**, Egypt's southernmost city, has the loveliest setting on the Nile and a languorous ambience. From here, you can visit the island **Philae temple of Isis** and the rock-hewn colossi at **Abu Simbel**, or embark on a cruise to other temples around **Lake Nasser**. Other sites not to be missed are **Edfu** and **Kom Ombo** between Luxor and Aswan, and **Abydos** and Dendara north of Luxor.

Besides monuments, Egypt abounds in natural wonders. Edged by coral reefs teeming with tropical fish, the **Sinai Peninsula** offers superb **diving** and **snorkelling**, and palm-fringed **beaches** where women can swim unmolested. Resorts along the Gulf of Aqaba are varied enough to suit everyone, whether you're into the upmarket hotels of **Sharm el-Sheikh**, **Na'ama Bay** or **Taba**, or cheap, simple living at **Dahab** and **Nuweiba**. From there it's easy to visit **St Catherine's Monastery** and **Mount Sinai** (where Moses received the Ten Commandments) in the mountainous interior. With more time, cash and stamina, you can also embark on **jeep safaris** or **camel treks** to remote oases and spectacular wadis.

Egypt's **Red Sea Coast** has more reefs further offshore, with snorkelling and diving traditionally centred around **Hurghada**, while barely-touched island reefs further south from **Port Safaga** down to **Mersa Alam** beckon serious diving enthusiasts. Inland, the mountainous **Eastern Desert**

Ali or Aly?

There's no standard system of transliterating Arabic script into Roman, so you're sure to find that the Arabic words in this book don't always match the versions you'll see elsewhere. Maps and street signs are the biggest sources of confusion, so we've generally gone for the transliteration that's the most common on the spot. However, you'll often need to do a bit of lateral thinking, and it's not uncommon to find one spelling posted at one end of a road, with another at the opposite end. See p.859 for an introduction to the Egyptian language.

أنت في أحضان التاريخ

YOU ARE IN THE EMBRACE OF THE HISTORY

The ibis

Images of ibises appear on temples, tombs and billboards all over Egypt. The white-bodied, black-billed Sacred ibis that the ancient Egyptians revered as an incarnation of Thoth, the God of Knowledge, was last seen in Egypt in 1801 and is now only found as far north as Sudan – but in ancient times they were so abundant that literally millions were mummified at Tuna el-Gebel and other sites, despite it being a capital offence to kill one. Another species often depicted in tombs was the Crested ibis, used as the hieroglyph for *Akhu* (part of the soul) and known as the Akhu bird; while the Glossy ibis was painted in black, without its iridescent sheen. Nowadays, the main kinds seen in the Nile Valley are Amboselli's ibis – a near lookalike for the Sacred ibis – and two colourful cousins: the Scarlet ibis resembles a flamingo, but smaller, with blood-red plumage, while the Red-billed ibis has iridescent pink wings and a red beak.

harbours the **Coptic Monasteries of St Paul and St Anthony**, Roman quarries, and a host of pharaonic and **prehistoric rock art**, seen by few apart from the nomadic Bedouin.

While the Eastern Desert is still barely touched by tourism, the **Western Desert Oases** have been on the tourist trail for thirty years and

▼ Cinema hoardings, Downtown Cairo

nowadays host safaris into the wilderness. **Siwa**, out towards the Libyan border, has a unique culture and history, limpid pools and bags of charm. Another option is to follow the "Great Desert Circuit" (starting from Cairo or Assyut) through the four "inner" oases. Though **Bahariya** and **Farafra** hold the most appeal, with the lovely **White Desert** between them, the larger oases of **Dakhla** and **Kharga** also have their rewards once you escape their modernized "capitals". And for those into serious desert expeditions, there's the challenge of exploring the **Great Sand Sea** or the remote wadis of the **Gilf Kebir** and **Jebel Uwaynat**, whose prehistoric rock art featured in the film *The English Patient*. In contrast to these deep-desert locations are the quasi-oases of the **Fayoum** and **Wadi Natrun**, featuring the awesome **Valley of the Whales**, diverse ancient ruins and **Coptic monasteries**.

Moving north to the **Mediterranean**, Egypt's second city, **Alexandria**, boasts a string of beaches to which Cairenes flock in summer, and

The sheesha

The **sheesha** or water-pipe is an integral part of Egyptian life. Wherever you go, you'll see men puffing away on them, whether in cafés or just on the street (though it'll be the café that's supplied them in either case). Women don't smoke them, as smoking isn't considered lady-like in Egypt.

The origin of the *sheesha* is something of a mystery. The name is Persian for "glass", a reference to the vase. Another name is *nargila*, Persian for coconut, which shows what the vase was originally, and both names tell us that the water pipe came to Egypt from Persia. But there were sophisticated water pipes in Persia almost as soon as tobacco arrived in the seventeenth century, and some have suggested that they must have been used there before tobacco arrived, presumably for smoking cannabis. Possibly the Persians got the idea from their trade with East Africa, where water pipes definitely were being used to smoke cannabis long before the arrival of tobacco.

Once strictly an old man's pastime, *sheesha*-smoking has gone through something of a renaissance of late, and flavoured tobacco (apple, strawberry, apricot and mint among other varieties) is now available as well as the traditional *ma'azil*, which is mixed with molasses. The water acts as quite an efficient filter, as you'll see from the state of it after use. Meanwhile, the smell of *ma'azil* is one of the great aromas of Egypt, guaranteed to take you right back there if you ever smell it again.

11

▲ Donkey, Siwa Town

excellent seafood restaurants. Despite being founded by Alexander the Great and lost to the Romans by Cleopatra, the city today betrays little of its ancient glory; however, its magnificent new **library**, the statues raised from **Cleopatra's Palace** and the legendary **Lighthouse of Pharos** are restoring an air of majesty to Alexandria. Famous, too, for its decadence during colonial times, romantics can still indulge here in a nostalgic exploration of the "Capital of Memory", while further along the Mediterranean coast lie the World War II battlefield of **El-Alamein** and the Egyptian holiday resort of **Mersa Matrouh**. For divers, this coastline offers an array of **sunken cities** and wartime **wrecks** to explore.

The Nile **Delta**, east of Alexandria, musters few archeological monuments given its major role in ancient Egyptian history, and is largely overlooked by tourists. However, for those interested in Egyptian culture, the Delta hosts colourful religious **festivals** at **Tanta**, **Zagazig** and other towns. Further east lies the **Canal Zone**, dominated by the Suez Canal

◄ Bakers

12

and its three cities. **Port Said** and **Ismailiya** are pleasant, albeit sleepy places, where you can get a feel of "real Egypt" without tripping over other tourists. **Suez** is grim, but a vital transport nexus between Cairo, Sinai and the Red Sea Coast.

When to go

D eciding on the best time for a visit involves striking a balance between climatic and tourist factors. Egypt's traditional season runs from **late November to late February**, when the Nile Valley is balmy, although Cairo can be overcast and chilly. However, at these times, particularly during the peak months of December and January, the major Nile resorts of Luxor and Aswan get unpleasantly crowded. This winter season is also the busiest period for the Sinai resorts, while Hurghada is active year round.

With this in mind, **March or April** are good compromise options, offering decent climate and fewer visitors. In **May and June** the heat is still tolerable but, after that, Egyptians rich enough to do so migrate to Alex and the coastal resorts. From **July to September** the south and desert are ferociously hot and sightseeing is best limited to early morning or evening – though August still sees droves of backpackers. **October into early November** is perhaps the best time of all, with easily manageable climate and crowds.

Weather and tourism apart, the **Islamic calendar** and its related festivals can have an effect on your travel. The most important factor is **Ramadan**, the month of daytime fasting, which can be problematic for eating and transport, though the festive evenings do much to compensate. See "Public Holidays and Moulids" in the Basics chapter for details of its timing.

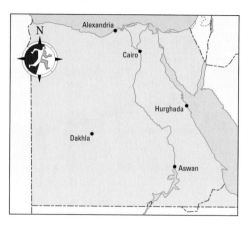

Average daily temperatures

	Jan	Mar	May	July	Sept	Nov
Alexandria *Mediterranean*						
Max/Min (°F)	65/51	70/55	79/64	85/73	86/73	77/62
Max/Min (°C)	18/11	21/13	26/18	29/23	30/23	25/17
Aswan *Southern Nile Valley*						
Max/Min (°F)	74/50	87/58	103/74	106/79	103/75	87/62
Max/Min (°C)	23/10	31/14	39/23	41/26	39/24	31/17
Cairo *Northern Nile Valley*						
Max/Min (°F)	65/47	75/52	91/63	96/70	90/68	78/58
Max/Min (°C)	18/8	24/11	33/17	36/21	32/20	26/14
Dakhla *Western Desert*						
Max/Min (°F)	70/41	82/47	99/68	104/74	96/70	82/53
Max/Min (°C)	21/5	28/8	37/20	40/23	36/21	28/12
Hurghada *Red Sea Coast*						
Max/Min (°F)	70/50	74/61	86/70	90/77	86/74	77/59
Max/Min (°C)	21/10	23/12	30/21	32/25	30/23	25/15

Note that these are average daily maximum and minimum temperatures. Summer peaks in Aswan, Hurghada or Sinai, for example, can hit the 120°s F (low 50°s C) in hot years. The dryness of the air and absence of cloud cover makes for drastic fluctuations, though they do also make the heat tolerably unsticky outside Cairo and the Delta. The Mediterranean Coast can be windy and wet in winter.

31

things not to miss

It's not possible to see everything that Egypt has to offer in one trip – and we don't suggest you try. What follows is a selective taste of the country's highlights: outstanding temples and tombs, vibrant festivals, spectacular desertscapes, and good things to eat, drink and buy. It's arranged in five colour-coded categories, so that you can browse through to find the very best things to see, do and experience. All highlights have a page reference to take you into the guide, where you can find out more.

01 Abu Simbel Page **494** • The monumental sun temple of Ramses II is the most spectacular of the Nubian antiquities that were relocated to higher ground on the shores of Lake Nasser.

03 Abydos Page **347** • One of the most ancient cult-centres in Egypt, its mortuary temple of Seti I contains magnificent bas-reliefs, the finest to have survived from the New Kingdom.

02 Bellydancing Pages **267** & **379** • The centuries-old tradition of *raqs sharqi* (oriental dance) is best seen at clubs frequented by locals, where the dancers and musicians will set your pulse racing.

04 Dunes Pages **557**, **577** & **583** • From the crescent-shaped dunes of Dakhla to the "whalebacks" of the Great Sand Sea or the red dunes of Wadi Hamra, their beauty never fails to captivate.

05 **Red Sea monasteries** Page **769** • Deep in the desert, the monastery of St Paul is one of the oldest in Egypt – if not the world – dating back to the dawn of Christian monasticism.

06 **Jeep or camel safaris** Pages **505**, **542**, **574** & **748** • Make tracks into the canyons of Sinai or the dunes of the Western Desert – overnight trips or major expeditions are easily arranged.

07 **Textiles and clothes** Pages **237**, **343**, **462** & **593** • Kerdassa and Harraniyya outside Cairo, Akhmim, Luxor and Aswan in the Nile Valley, Siwa and Bahariya oases and the Sinai Bedouin, each have their own styles and products – from camel-hair carpets to silk scarves.

08 Ras Mohammed Page **714**
• Egypt's oldest marine nature park boasts spectacular shark reefs and the wreck of the Dunraven.

10 The Pyramids and Sphinx at Giza Page **229** •
The world's most famous monuments have inspired scholarly and crackpot speculations for centuries.

09 Birdwatching Pages **499**, **523** & **673** • The egrets at Wadi Rayan are a magnet for ornithologists, as are sites at Lake Nasser, Lake Manzola and the Sinai Peninsula.

11 Juice bars Page **71** • On almost every street corner in Cairo, you can quench your thirst with whatever's in season, freshly pressed: from oranges and mangoes to strawberries and sugar cane.

12 Aswan Page **453** • Egypt's gateway to Nubia since ancient times, Aswan's islands, bazaars and riverside restaurants can keep you happy for days.

13 Street food Page **69** • Street snacks such as *tamiyya*, *kushari* and *fuul* are tasty, cheap and nourishing.

14 Oases Pages **584**, **551**, **531** & **542** • Explore the palm groves, hot springs and medieval *qasrs* of Dakhla, Siwa, Bahariya and Farafra – ancient oases that are embracing modernity in their own way.

15 Nile cruises Pages **64** & **476** • Enjoy the sunset and the river's scenery from a luxury cruise boat on the Nile.

16 **Dahab** Page **730** • Sinai chill-out zone, renowned for its diving, watersports and laid-back beach cafés. Also a base for camel and jeep safaris into the rugged interior.

17 **The Egyptian Antiquities Museum** Page **125** • A statue of Tawaret, the pregnant hippopotamus goddess of fertility, is just one of the highlights of this amazing collection, which includes Tutankhamun's treasures, monumental statues from the Old Kingdom and the Amarna era, and a dozen royal mummies.

18 **Alexandria** Page **606** • With its dazzling new library, the ruins of Cleopatra's Palace and the Pharos lighthouse emerging from the seabed, this Mediterranean port city founded by Alexander the Great is making waves again.

19 St Catherine's Monastery Page 750 •
Secluded beneath Mount Sinai, St Catherine's harbours the burning bush that appeared to Moses, and other holy relics.

20 Islamic Cairo Page 149 •
City of a thousand minarets, teeming with life, and chock-full of architectural masterpieces and historic monuments. Head for Khan el-Khalili bazaar, or the Citadel.

21 Jewellery Pages 280, 381 & 593 •
There's an endless choice of pharaonic, classical, Islamic and contemporary designs in the bazaars of Cairo, Luxor and Aswan, and oases such as Siwa.

22 Diving and snorkelling Pages 707, 714, 782 & 784 •
Amazing coral reefs, tropical fish and sunken wrecks make the Red Sea a paradise for scuba divers and snorkellers, while Egypt's Mediterranean coast boasts ancient underwater ruins, sunken U-Boats and warships to explore.

23 Valley of the Kings Page 408

• The descent into the Underworld, the Judgement of Osiris and the rebirth of the pharaoh are vividly depicted on the walls and ceilings of the royal tombs.

24 Catacombs of Kom es-Shoqafa Page 628

• The spookiest tombs in Egypt, located beneath the Karmous quarter of Alexandria, their bizarre fusion of pharaonic, Greek and Roman funerary motifs reflects the city's ancient diversity of cultures.

25 Egyptian cuisine Page 70

• Sample an Egypt *mezze*, consisting of many delicious, small dishes – particularly good for vegetarians.

26 **Karnak Temple** Page **385** • Dedicated to the Theban Triad of Amun, Mut and Khonsu, this vast complex reached its zenith during the New Kingdom.

27 **Feluccas** Pages **381**, **474** & **477** • Spend an afternoon sailing to Sehel or Banana island, or embark on a two- or three-day journey upriver from Aswan, visiting the temples at Kom Ombo and Edfu.

29 **Na'ama Bay** Page **721** • Egypt's premier resort, teeming with bars, clubs and luxury hotels, with magnificent coral gardens nearby.

28 **Mount Sinai** Page **753** • This awesome peak is revered as the site where Moses received the Ten Commandments from God.

30 **Karkaday** Pages **71** & **462** • This infusion of hibiscus flowers makes a delicious hot or cold drink with medicinal properties. The flowers are graded by quality in Aswan's bazaar.

31 **The pyramids of Dahshur** Page **251** • Less famous than the Giza trio but no less fascinating – and far less crowded. The Bent pyramid, resting place of Snofru, has a distinctive angled top.

Basics

Basics

Getting there

Although it is possible to get to Egypt by land via Israel or Jordan, most visitors will want to fly. As a major air hub, Cairo is well served by international airlines, with direct scheduled flights from London and New York and a large choice of indirect routes from pretty much everywhere. From the UK, major tourist resorts are also served by charter flights.

Air fares vary with the season: they are highest from June until the end of August, drop during the "shoulder" seasons – April, May, September and October – and you'll get the best prices during the low season, November to March (excluding Christmas and New Year, when prices are hiked up and seats are at a premium). Note also that flying at weekends can sometimes add as much as US$60/£40 to the round-trip fare; price ranges quoted below are for the cheapest round-trip tickets including airport departure tax, and assume midweek travel. Many of them will be subject to restrictions such as fixed dates, which cannot be changed once the ticket is booked, and some may require advance purchase.

You can often cut costs by going through a specialist flight agent – either a consolidator, who buys up blocks of tickets from the airlines and sells them at a discount, or a discount agent, who in addition to dealing with discounted flights may also offer special student and youth fares and a range of other travel-related services such as travel insurance, rail passes, car rentals, tours and the like. Some agents specialize in charter flights, which may be cheaper than anything available on a scheduled flight, but again departure dates are fixed and withdrawal penalties are high. From Britain, you may even find it cheaper to pick up a bargain package deal to Luxor from one of the tour operators listed on pp.31–32.

Unfortunately, the likelihood of finding a courier flight (where you shepherd a parcel through customs in exchange for a heavily discounted ticket) is virtually nil for travel to Egypt. However, if Egypt is only one stop on a longer journey, you might want to consider buying a Round-the-World (RTW) ticket.

Cairo is unlikely to feature on the cheaper "off-the-shelf" RTW itineraries offered by some agents, but can be visited on RTW mileage tickets issued by the airline consortiums Star Alliance and One World Alliance.

Booking flights online

Many airlines and discount travel websites sell tickets online, cutting out the costs of agents and middlemen. Good deals can often be found through discount or auction sites, as well as through the airlines' own websites.

Online booking agents and general travel sites

Ⓦ **www.cheapflights.co.uk** (in UK & Ireland); Ⓦ **www.cheapflights.com** (in US); Ⓦ **www.cheapflights.ca** (in Canada); and Ⓦ **www.cheapflights.com.au** (in Australia). Flight deals, travel agents, plus links to other travel sites.
Ⓦ **www.cheaptickets.com** Discount flight specialists (US only). Also at ☏ 1-888/922-8849.
Ⓦ **www.ebookers.com** Efficient, easy-to-use flight finder, with competitive fares.
Ⓦ **www.etn.nl/discount** A hub of consolidator and discount agent links, maintained by the nonprofit European Travel Network.
Ⓦ **www.expedia.co.uk** (in UK); Ⓦ **www.expedia.com** (in US); and Ⓦ **www.expedia.ca** (in Canada). Discount air fares, all-airline search engine and daily deals.
Ⓦ **www.flyaow.com** Online air travel info and reservations.
Ⓦ **www.geocities.com/thavery2000** An extensive list of airline websites and US toll-free numbers.
Ⓦ **www.hotwire.com** Bookings from the US only. Last-minute savings of up to forty percent on regular published fares. Travellers must be at least 18 and there are no refunds, transfers or changes allowed. Log-in required.

Ⓦ www.kelkoo.co.uk Useful UK-only price-comparison site, checking several sources of low-cost flights as well as other goods and services, according to specific criteria.

Ⓦ www.lastminute.com (in UK) ; Ⓦ www.site59.com (in US); Ⓦ www.lastminute.com.au (in Australia); and Ⓦ www.lastminute.co.nz (in New Zealand). Good last-minute holiday package and flight-only deals.

Ⓦ www.opodo.co.uk Popular and reliable source of low-cost UK air fares. Owned by, and run in conjunction with, nine major European airlines.

Ⓦ www.orbitz.com Comprehensive site, with the usual flight, car hire and hotel deals, but also great follow-up customer service.

Ⓦ www.priceline.co.uk (in UK); and Ⓦ www.priceline.com (in US). Name-your-own-price website that has deals of around forty percent off standard fares.

Ⓦ www.skyauction.com Bookings from the US only. Auctions tickets and travel packages to destinations worldwide.

Ⓦ www.travelocity.co.uk (in UK); Ⓦ www.travelocity.com (in US); Ⓦ www.travelocity.ca (in Canada); and Ⓦ www.zuji.com.au (in Australia). Destination guides, low fares and great deals for car rental, accommodation and lodging.

Ⓦ www.travelshop.com.au Australian site offering discounted flights, packages, insurance and online bookings. Also on ☎ 1800/108 108.

Ⓦ travel.yahoo.com Useful site offering flights and hotel deals, as well as Rough Guide material in its coverage of destination countries and cities across the world.

Ⓦ www.travelzoo.com Great resource for news on the latest airline sales, cruise discounts and hotel deals. Links bring you directly to the carrier's site.

Flights from Britain and Ireland

From London, there are direct scheduled flights to Cairo, Alexandria, Luxor and Sharm el-Sheikh (Sinai), and charters to Luxor, Sharm el-Sheikh and Hurghada (Red Sea coast). There are no direct flights to Egypt from elsewhere in the UK or Ireland: you can either make your own way to London and fly from there, or take an indirect flight via London or a European city, such as Amsterdam, Paris or Frankfurt.

Flying direct to Cairo from London, both EgyptAir and British Airways have daily scheduled flights from Heathrow. BA also flies four times weekly from Heathrow to Alexandria, while EgyptAir also has weekly direct flights to Luxor and to Sharm el-Sheikh. Fares vary according to the time of year (the most expensive being around Christmas) but depend more on the type of ticket – flexibility and duration being the main factors. BA currently charges just under £300 for a low-season return flight to Cairo (fixed-date, no advance purchase required), rising to £420 in high season, although discount agents may sell the same ticket for less. EgyptAir charges from £299 in low season for a similar ticket, and £309 to Luxor, and £319 to Sharm el-Sheikh. At the time of writing, one of the best deals to Egypt is offered by Red Sea Flights (the flight-only division of the dive company Explorer), in the form of direct flights to Sharm el-Sheikh from London Gatwick (three times weekly) and Manchester (once-weekly). They currently use charter airlines, though the flights have scheduled status, which means that they are not subject to the same restrictions as charter flights on things like length of stay, and they are bookable online. Prices vary depending on the specific flight, but start from £188 return, and are almost always a lot lower than those of the established airlines. Other dive companies (see p.32) also offer cheap flight-only deals to Sharm el-Sheikh, though these are usually not advertised, so you'll need to approach the company direct.

Most other major European airlines sell **indirect flights** to Egypt travelling via their own "home" airport on the Continent. Standards vary enormously, from classy KLM to tatty Tarom, with most of the others somewhere in between. At the top end of the scale, prices are much the same as those of BA, though fixed-date or advance-purchase tickets go for well under £300. Most airlines serve only Cairo, but Lufthansa, Olympic and Saudi Arabian also fly to Alexandria. KLM and its subsidiary, KLM City Hopper, have flights from a large number of British airports outside London, as do Lufthansa and Air France, sometimes in combination with a smaller operator. Your best range of choices outside London is from Manchester (served by BA, Air France, Air Malta, Alitalia, CSA, KLM, Lufthansa, Olympic and Swiss), or Birmingham (Alitalia, CSA, KLM, Lufthansa and Swiss, also by Flybe in combination with Air France). **From Scotland**, you've a choice of BA, CSA, KLM and Lufthansa from Edinburgh, or BA and KLM from Glasgow, and from Aberdeen you can fly with BA, KLM or a combination of Régional and Air France. In addition to these choices, BMI offer through tickets from a number of British airports via London in combination with BA.

If a foreign airline flies via somewhere interesting, consider breaking the journey for a **stopover** there; if not, you'll want to spend as little time as possible in the airport (Bucharest is the worst) – a factor that might determine your choice of airline. CSA, Malev and Air Malta are some of the cheapest airlines from London to Cairo and may offer stopovers in Prague, Budapest or Valetta respectively.

Discount agencies or student/youth travel specialists like STA Travel (with a dedicated Africa desk at its London Euston Road branch) can often come up with very good deals, such as return flights to Cairo from £260 in winter, £310 in summer.

It's also possible to get flight-only deals on **charter flights**, though they rarely cost much less than scheduled services, and you are limited to a maximum stay of one month. Charters do, however, fly direct to destinations other than Cairo such as Luxor, Aswan, Hurghada or Sharm el-Sheikh, and they often depart from regional airports as well as from London. Various operators offer special one-off flight deals: check out Soliman, Travel Care, Kuoni, Voyages Jules Verne, Hayes and Jarvis, Thomas Cook, and Libra Holidays (see pp.31–32 for addresses).

In addition to the recommended discount agents listed below, useful sources for finding a flight are classified advertisements in the travel sections of newspapers like *The Independent* and *The Guardian* (Saturday editions), *The Sunday Times* or – in London – *Time Out* and *The Evening Standard*. Bargains are also advertised on Teletext and the Internet, and high-street travel agents are worth checking for deals on package holidays and charter flights.

From Ireland, there are no direct flights to Egypt; the best option is to book a flight or package departing from Britain – either through your local travel agent or via the Internet – and get there on a budget flight. Return fares Dublin–London cost €50–150; Ryanair is usually the cheapest, but flies only to Stansted, Luton and Gatwick, leaving you with a two- to three-hour journey to Heathrow if your onward connection is from there. Aer Lingus, British Midland and British Airways cost a bit more but fly straight to Heathrow, and BA will fly you on to Cairo for a total of €540–1000. Alternatively, Air France can take you from Dublin to Cairo via Paris for €445–665, while Alitalia fly via Italy for €413–448. Other options include CSA, Malév and Iberia, and buying tickets through discount agents such as UsitNOW can often get you a cheaper fare than by approaching the airlines direct. Aer Lingus can also fly you from Dublin or Cork to Amsterdam for an onward connection with KLM, and you can get to Cairo from Shannon via Amman with Royal Jordanian, or from Cork via Prague with CSA. Getting to Cairo **from Belfast** can be awkward, and tickets offered by the airlines are pricey (cheapest is BA at £503–673) and involve two changes of plane. Your best bet is with a discount agent like UsitNOW or Flights4Less, who can organize a combination involving BMI or Flybe to London, then BA or EgyptAir on to Cairo, with fares starting at £460 in winter, £532 in summer.

If you're pushed for time, or want to make things easier, buying a **package holiday** makes a lot of sense. There are still some amazing bargains to be had amongst the basic Luxor-plus-Cairo or Luxor-only packages. Besides these, many smaller independent operators feature felucca trips on the Nile, diving holidays on the Red Sea, or camel trekking in Sinai.

Airlines

Aer Lingus Ireland ☏ 0818/365 000, UK ☏ 0845/084 4444, ☷ www.aerlingus.ie. Several flights a day from Dublin, Shannon and Cork to London, and daily flights from Dublin and Cork to Amsterdam, for onward connections to Cairo.
Air France UK ☏ 0845/359 1000, Ireland ☏ 01/605 0383, ☷ www.airfrance.com. Flights to Cairo via Paris from Aberdeen (codeshare with Régional), Birmingham (codeshare with Flybe), Edinburgh (codeshare with CityJet), Manchester, London, Dublin and Newcastle.

Air Malta UK ☎0845/607 3710, Ireland ☎1800/397400, 🌐www.airmalta.com. London, Dublin and Manchester to Cairo via Malta, often including a stopover in Valletta.

Alitalia UK ☎0870/544 8259, 🌐www.alitalia .co.uk, Ireland ☎01/677 5171, 🌐www.alitalia.ie. London, Dublin, Birmingham and Manchester to Cairo via Rome or Milan.

Austrian Airlines UK ☎0870/124 2625, 🌐www .aua.com. London to Cairo via Vienna.

BMI UK ☎0870/607 0555, Ireland ☎01/435 0011. Flights from several British and Irish airports to London Heathrow for onward connections to Cairo.

British Airways UK ☎0870/850 9850, Ireland ☎1800/626 747, 🌐www.ba.com. London to Cairo direct daily; London to Alexandria direct four times weekly. Connections from most British and Irish airports.

CSA (Czech Airlines) UK ☎0870/444 3747, Ireland ☎01/814 4626, 🌐www.csa.cz. London, Dublin, Birmingham, Cork, Edinburgh and Manchester to Cairo via Prague.

Cyprus Airways UK ☎020/8359 1333, 🌐www .cyprusairways.com. London to Cairo via Larnaca.

EgyptAir UK ☎020/7734 2343, 🌐www.egyptair .com.eg. London to Cairo direct daily; London to Luxor and Sharm el-Sheikh direct once weekly. No alcohol served on flights, though if you take your own they'll supply mixers.

El Al UK ☎020/7957 4100, 🌐www.elal.co.il. London to Cairo via Tel Aviv.

Iberia UK ☎0845/601 2854, Ireland ☎01/407 3017, 🌐www.iberia.com. London, Dublin and Manchester to Cairo via Barcelona or Madrid.

KLM UK ☎0870/507 4074, 🌐www.klm.com. London (Heathrow, Gatwick and City), Dublin, Aberdeen, Birmingham, Bristol, Cardiff, Edinburgh, Glasgow, Humberside, Leeds/Bradford, Manchester, Newcastle, Norwich and Teesside to Cairo via Amsterdam.

Lufthansa UK ☎0845/837 7747, Ireland ☎01/844 5544, 🌐www.lufthansa.com. London, Dublin, Birmingham, Edinburgh and Manchester to Cairo and Alexandria via Frankfurt.

Malév UK ☎0870/909 0577, Ireland ☎01/844 4303, 🌐www.malev.hu. London, Dublin to Cairo via Budapest. One of the better Eastern European airlines.

Olympic Airways UK ☎0870/606 0460, Ireland ☎01/608 0090, 🌐www.olympic-airways.com. London and Manchester to Cairo and Alexandria via Athens.

Red Sea Flights UK ☎0845/644 7090, 🌐www .redseaflights.com. London direct to Sharm el-Sheikh three times weekly; Manchester direct to Sharm el-Sheikh once a week.

Royal Jordanian UK ☎020/7878 6300, Ireland ☎061/474 995, 🌐www.rja.com.jo. London and Shannon to Cairo via Amman.

Ryanair Ireland ☎0818/30 30 30, UK ☎0871/246 0000, 🌐www.ryanair.com. Budget flights to London Stansted from many British and Irish airports (and from Dublin, Knock and Shannon to London Gatwick, and Dublin to Luton) for onward connections to Egypt out of Heathrow or Gatwick.

Saudi Arabian Airlines UK ☎020/7798 9898, 🌐www.saudiairlines.com. London to Cairo and Alexandria via Jeddah or Riyadh.

Swiss UK ☎0845/601 0956, Ireland ☎1890/200515, 🌐www.swiss.com. London, Dublin, Birmingham and Manchester to Cairo via Zurich. From Dublin you may have to change additionally in London on your outward journey, or stopover in Zurich.

Tarom Romanian Airlines UK ☎020/7224 3693, 🌐www.tarom.ro. London to Cairo via Bucharest. Unpredictable, with awful food and one of the worst airports in Europe, but sometimes offers rock-bottom prices.

Turkish Airlines UK ☎020/7766 9300, 🌐www .thy.com. London to Cairo via Istanbul.

Flight and travel agents

Bridge the World UK ☎0870/443 2399, 🌐www .bridgetheworld.com. Good-value flights and packages aimed mainly at backpackers.

ebookers UK ☎0870/010 7000, 🌐www .ebookers.com; Ireland ☎01/241 5689, 🌐www .ebookers.ie. Low fares on an extensive selection of scheduled flights and package deals.

Flightcentre ☎0870/890 8099, 🌐www .flightcentre.co.uk. Discounted fares including UK to Egypt.

Flights4Less UK ☎0871/222 3432, 🌐www .flights4less.co.uk. Good discount air fares and easy-to-use Internet flight selector. Owned by Lastminute .com.

Joe Walsh Tours Ireland ☎01/872 2555, 🌐www .joewalshtours.ie. General budget fares agent which sometimes has cheap flight deals to Egypt.

Lee Travel Ireland ☎021/427 7111, 🌐www .leetravel.ie. Flights and holidays, including discounted air fares from Dublin to Cairo.

North South Travel UK ☎ & ☎01245/608 291, 🌐www.northsouthtravel.co.uk. Friendly, competitive travel agency, offering discounted fares worldwide – profits are used to support projects in the developing world, especially the promotion of sustainable tourism.

Soliman Travel ☎020/7370 5159, 🌐www .solimantravel.co.uk. Well-established Egypt specialists offering package holidays and flight deals including charters.

STA Travel UK ☎0870/160 0599, 🌐www .statravel.co.uk. Worldwide specialists in low-cost flights and tours, often with discounts for students and under-26s.

Trailfinders UK ☏ 0845/058 5858, ⓦ www .trailfinders.com; Ireland ☏ 01/677 7888, ⓦ www .trailfinders.ie. One of the best-informed and most efficient agents for independent travellers.

Travel Bag UK ☏ 0870/890 1456, ⓦ www .travelbag.co.uk. Discount deals including flights from the UK to Egypt.

Travel Care UK ☏ 0870/112 0085, ⓦ www .travelcare.co.uk. Package tours and flights, including late deals, and charter flights to Luxor, Sharm and Hurghada, with a user-friendly website.

UsitNOW Republic of Ireland ☏ 01/602 1904, Northern Ireland ☏ 028/9032 7111, ⓦ www .usitnow.ie. Ireland's main student and youth travel specialists.

World Travel Centre Ireland ☏ 01/416 7007, ⓦ www.worldtravel.ie. Discounted fares including Ireland to Egypt.

Package tours

Tour operators to Egypt come in many shapes and sizes. Mainstream operators offer traditional tours and cruises, as well as flight-plus-hotel packages to Luxor, Aswan and elsewhere which can cost little more than a flight – for example, seven nights in Luxor for around £400 (often less if booked at the last minute) – and share the same advantage of varied departure and destination points. Again, check the websites and newspapers listed below.

Other tour operators include small, independent adventure holiday companies priding themselves on modest-sized groups, adventurous itineraries or special interest activities – for all of which Egypt offers a lot of scope; and diving holiday specialists, who arrange trips to the Red Sea centred around Hurghada or Sharm el-Sheikh, usually inclusive of rental equipment and dives. All prices quoted below are inclusive of flights, unless otherwise stated.

Tour operators

Mainstream tours

Abercrombie & Kent UK ☏ 020/7730 9600, ⓦ www.abercrombiekent.co.uk. Upmarket firm with a number of Egypt tours including some led by Egyptologists; also creates custom packages.

Bales Worldwide UK ☏ 0870/241 3208, ⓦ www .balesworldwide.com. Family-owned company

offering a range of packages from a nine-day "Egypt Discovery" tour (from £699) to a fifteen-day "Splendour of Egypt" tour (from £1298), based in first-class hotels in Cairo, Luxor and Aswan. Tailor-made tours are available too.

Discover Egypt UK ☏ 020/7407 2111, ⓦ www .discoveregypt.co.uk. Charter flights, packages, and tailor-made itineraries featuring Nile cruises and multi-centre holidays.

Hayes & Jarvis UK ☏ 0870/898 9890, ⓦ www .hayes-jarvis.com. Hotel packages in Luxor (from £389), and on the beach at Dahab, Sharm or Hurghada (from £305); also offers two-centre holidays, and Nile cruises from £603.

Kuoni Travel UK ☏ 01306/747002, ⓦ www.kuoni .co.uk. Experienced operator offering a wide variety of packages, including Nile cruises from £659, a week in Luxor from £494, or a seven-day tour to Siwa, Bahariya and Alexandria from £978.

Libra Holidays UK ☏ 0871/226 0446, ⓦ www .libraholidays.co.uk. Seven nights in Luxor (from £409), Sharm el-Sheikh (£369), Hurghada (£399), or cruising the Nile (£559). Red Sea diving holidays are covered in the Goldenjoy Dive brochure.

Peltours UK ☏ 020/8371 5200, ⓦ www.peltours .com. Deluxe 15-day Cairo/Sinai/Nile cruise package from £1244, or four nights in Cairo from £745. Also offers seven days in Taba Heights with a direct charter from £389.

Soliman Travel UK ☏ 020/7370 5159, ⓦ www .solimantravel.co.uk. One of the longest-established tour operators with a large range of packages and tailor-made holidays mainly in five-star accommodation. Nile cruises from £499; seven nights in Luxor from £395; seven-night diving holidays in Hurghada or Sharm el-Sheikh from £399 excluding dive courses; and three-night city breaks to Alexandria or Cairo from £369.

Somak Holidays UK ☏ 020/8423 3000, ⓦ www .somak.co.uk. Offers three-night city breaks in Cairo from £399, a seven-night Luxor package from £499, and a ten-night package including a Nile cruise and three nights in Cairo from £879.

Thomas Cook UK ☏ 0870/750 5711, ⓦ www .thomascook.com. Thomas Cook more or less created tourism in Egypt with his first escorted tour in 1869, and the country remains a speciality. The firm offers a week in Luxor from £407, three nights in Cairo from £345, or twin-centre deals featuring Aswan and Sharm el-Sheikh or Cairo and Hurghada.

Thomson UK ☏ 0870/550 2575, ⓦ www.thomson .co.uk. Reputable high-street tour operator offering two weeks in Hurghada from £499, a week in Luxor from £365, a week in Sharm from £315.

Trade Winds UK ☏ 0870/751 0003, ⓦ www .tradewinds.co.uk. Long-haul package specialist offering four-night Cairo city breaks from £499, a week in Sharm el-Sheikh from £359, or a seven-night Nile cruise from £679.

Voyages Jules Verne UK ☎020/7616 1000, ⓦwww.vjv.co.uk. An interesting selection of upmarket holidays, including a seven-night cruise from Aswan to Luxor from £595 on a paddle steamer that formerly belonged to King Fuad, four-night Cairo city breaks from £395, or a sixteen-night Grand Tour from £1895.

Adventure and specialist tours

Adventures Abroad UK ☎0114/247 3400, ⓦwww.adventures-abroad.com. Canadian-based company offering small group tours to Egypt alone or combined with Israel, Jordan, Syria, etc (even Kenya and Tanzania). Activities include camel rides, trekking and felucca cruises.

Ancient World Tours UK ☎020/7917 9494, ⓦwww.ancient.co.uk. In-depth archeological and historical tours led by experts (tour leaders have included David Rohl – see p.807). Claims to visit more sites in Egypt than any other operator, including several that no one else covers, and some that few tourists ever reach.

Exodus UK ☎0870/240 5550; Ireland ☎01/679 5700; ⓦwww.exodus.co.uk. Its fifteen-day "Egyptian Discoverer" tour features a Nile cruise from Aswan to Luxor, a day in Hurghada and two nights in Cairo (from £881 plus local charges of US$100); other options include a nine-day trip including three days on a felucca (from £651 plus US$85), or a fifteen-day overland tour of Egypt and Jordan (from £1207 plus US$100). Prices include flights.

Explore Worldwide UK ☎0870/333 4001, Ireland ☎01/677 9479, ⓦwww.explore.co.uk. Highly respected small-groups operator with several Egyptian programmes, including a fifteen-day Nile Valley and Red Sea tour with four days on a felucca (from £775), a fifteen-day tour of the Nile and Western Desert (from £805), or eight days snorkelling and camel trekking in the Sinai (from £670). Prices include flights.

Guerba Expeditions UK ☎01373/826611, ⓦwww.guerba.co.uk. Long-established Africa-overland experts with a variety of Egyptian tours, such as eight days in Cairo, Luxor and Aswan from £465, and a thirteen-day "Classic Egypt" tour that includes Sharm el-Sheikh, St Catherine's and Mt Sinai, from £695. Online bookings can be made from Britain, Ireland, Europe, North America and Australasia. Prices do not include flights.

Imaginative Traveller UK ☎0800/316 2717, ⓦwww.imaginative-traveller.com. Offers over thrity tours of Egypt, including fourteen-day Nile Valley and Red Sea trips (from £475/€700 plus US$180); eight days in Alexandria and Siwa Oasis (from £245/€365

plus US$90); and eight-day learn-to-dive packages at Dahab and Hurghada including a PADI Open Water Diving Course (from £355/€525). Online bookings can be made from Britain, Ireland, Europe, North America and Australasia. Prices do not include flights.

Peregrine UK ☎ 01635/872 300. British branch of an Australian firm (see p.37) selling Gecko's adventure tours including an eleven-day "Felucca Safari" visiting Cairo, Aswan and Luxor (from £285 plus air fare) to a fifteen-day "Backroads of Egypt" journey including a Nile trip plus five days spent with Bedouins in the Western Desert (from £450 excluding flights).

Swim with Dolphins UK ☎0845 345 9052, ⓦwww.dolphinswims.co.uk. Luxury liveaboards on the Red Sea (from £679 for seven nights) and Sinai desert adventure safaris (from £497 for seven days). Prices do not include flights. Can be booked online from abroad.

Top Deck Travel UK ☎020/7370 4555, ⓦwww.topdecktravel.co.uk. Youth-oriented tours popular with Australians and New Zealanders include an eight-day "Essential Egypt" tour to Cairo, Luxor and Aswan (£269 plus US$25), an eight-day "Nile Discovery" tour, a fourteen-day "Egypt Explored" tour covering Cairo, Luxor, Aswan and Sinai (£359 plus US$40), and a 21-day "Ultimate Egypt" tour including Cairo, Luxor, Hurghada and Sinai, plus a three-day felucca journey from Aswan to Edfu (£525 plus US$55). Prices do not include flights.

Dive holiday companies

Crusader Travel UK ☎020/8744 0474, ⓦwww.crusadertravel.com. Experienced, specialist agent for diving holidays, which helps clients shop around the tour operators. Also does flight-only charter deals to Sharm, Hurghada and Luxor.

Explorer Tours UK ☎01753/681 999, ⓦwww.explorers.co.uk. Red Sea holidays with PADI courses from £425 including flight and lessons. Their flight-only subsidiary is Red Sea Flights (see p.30).

Oonasdivers UK ☎01323/648 924, ⓦwww.oonasdivers.com. Red Sea diving holidays (from £575 for a package including flight and twelve dives, plus £140 for a PADI open water course), also liveaboards and, for non-divers, the (cheaper) option of a beach holiday at the same resort.

Regaldive UK ☎0870/220 1777, ⓦwww.regaldive.co.uk. Various dive packages at Dahab, El Gouna, Hurghada, Safaga, Sharm el-Sheikh and other bases, including courses for everyone from beginners to advanced, plus mini-safari add-ons and wreck trips. Seven nights in Sharm B&B costs from £349 including flight (plus £170 for a five-day PADI open-water course including equipment rental), but there are sometimes special offers available, starting from £199.

Scubasnacks UK ☎0870/746 1266, ⓦwww
.scubasnacks.co.uk. Seven-day packages based at
Dahab, Hurghada and Sharm el-Sheikh from £349
for flight and hotel, plus around £200 (the exact price
depends on where you'll be based) for a five-day
PADI open-water course. Cheaper special offers are
sometimes available, and there are also liveaboard
diving holidays based on a boat in the Red Sea.

Flights from the US and Canada

The volume of North American travellers to
Egypt is not great, and this is reflected in a
relative dearth of flights. Only EgyptAir flies
direct, from New York: failing that, you'll have
to change planes somewhere on the way.
North American travel agents can arrange
flights with no problem, or – if you're heading to London – you can arrange connections yourself (see "Flights from Britain and
Ireland" pp.28–29). If you are flying to Israel
or Jordan to enter Egypt from there, see
pp.39–40 for information on how to move on
to Egypt.

EgyptAir flies to Cairo four times weekly
from New York (11hr). Official round-trip
fares (instant purchase, non-refundable) start
at US$870 including tax in the low season
(winter), rising to US$1590 in the high season
(summer). Failing that, a number of European
and Middle Eastern airlines serve Cairo from a
much wider range of departure points, though
New York still offers by far the biggest choice
of airlines. From the West Coast, several
airlines fly to Egypt from Los Angeles, but only
British Airways, Air France and Northwest/
KLM fly from San Francisco, British Airways
alone from Seattle. Delta offer flights from
a large number of US cities in combination
with Air France, and United flights connect
with Lufthansa services. All West Coast flights
are routed via the airlines' hub cities, so you
should check that you won't have to wait
overnight for your onward connection. By
shopping around discount agents and flight
consolidators, you should be able to pick
up a round-trip ticket for as little as US$700
in low season, US$1270 high season out
of New York, and $980 (low season) $1800
(high season) from the West Coast.

From Canada there are no direct flights
to Cairo, but many of the European carriers
operate services via their hub cities from
Toronto and Montreal. Fares from discount
agents start at around CDN$1400 in low
season, and CDN$2800 in high season.
Vancouver is served by British Airways via
London, Northwest/KLM via Amsterdam,
and Lufthansa via Frankfurt, with tickets
from discount agents at around CDN$1575
in low season, CDN$3200 in high season.
Air Canada also sells through tickets from
most Canadian cities in combination with
Lufthansa.

Airlines

Aeroflot US ☎1-888/340-6400, Canada
☎416/642-1653, ⓦwww.aeroflot.com. LA, New
York, San Francisco, Seattle and Washington DC to Cairo
via Moscow. A dire airline (take sandwiches) and hardly
the shortest route, but sometimes the cheapest option.

Air Canada ☎1-888/247-2262, ⓦwww
.aircanada.ca. Flights from most Canadian cities to
Cairo and Alexandria via Frankfurt in combination with
Lufthansa.

Air France US ☎1-800/237-2747, Canada
☎1-800/667-2747, ⓦwww.airfrance.com. Flights
to Cairo via Paris from Atlanta, Chicago, Houston,
LA, Miami, Montreal, New York, Philadelphia, San
Francisco, Toronto and Washington DC.

Alitalia US ☎1-800/223-5730, Canada
☎1-800/361-8336, ⓦwww.alitalia.com. Boston,
Chicago, Miami, New York, Toronto and Washington
DC to Cairo via Milan or Rome.

Austrian Airlines ☎1-800/843-0002, ⓦwww
.aua.com. New York, Toronto and Washington DC to
Cairo via Vienna.

British Airways ☎1-800/ AIRWAYS, ⓦwww
.ba.com. Boston, Chicago, Detroit, LA, Miami,
Montreal, New York, Philadelphia, Phoenix, San
Francisco, Seattle, Toronto, Vancouver and Washington
DC to Cairo and Alexandria via London Heathrow.
Flights from Atlanta, Dallas/Fort Worth, Denver,
Houston, Orlando and San Diego involve changing
airports in London; flights from Baltimore involve an
overnight stay in London.

CSA (Czech Airlines) US ☎1-800/223-2365,
Canada ☎416/363-3174, ⓦwww.czechairlines
.com. Montreal, New York and Toronto to Cairo via
Prague.

Delta ☎1-800/241-4141, ⓦwww.delta.com.
Atlanta, Boston, Chicago, Cincinnati, LA, Miami, New
York, San Francisco and Washington DC to Cairo via
Paris in conjunction with Air France. Connections from
most US airports with a change at one of Delta's hubs.

EgyptAir US ☎1-800/334-6787 or 212/315-0900,
Canada ☎416/960-0009, ⓦwww.egyptair.com.eg.
New York to Cairo direct four times weekly.

El Al US ☏1-800/223-6700 or 212/768-9200, ⊛www.elal.com. Chicago, LA, Miami, New York and Toronto to Cairo via Tel Aviv.

Iberia ☏1-800/772-4642, ⊛www.iberia.com. Chicago, New York and Miami to Cairo via Barcelona or Madrid.

Lufthansa US ☏1-800/645-3880, Canada ☏1-800/563-5954, ⊛www.lufthansa.com. Atlanta, Boston, Chicago, Dallas/Fort Worth, Denver, Detroit, Houston, LA, Miami, Montreal, New York, Philadelphia, Portland, San Francisco, Toronto, Vancouver and Washington DC to Cairo and Alexandria via Frankfurt.

Malev Hungarian Airlines ☏1-800/223-6884 or 212/566-9944, ⊛www.malev.hu. New York and Toronto to Cairo via Budapest.

Northwest/KLM ☏1-800/447-4747, ⊛www.nwa.com. Boston, Chicago, Detroit, Houston, LA, Memphis, Minneapolis, Montreal, New York, San Francisco, Seattle, Toronto, Vancouver and Washington DC to Cairo via Amsterdam.

Olympic Airways ☏1-800/223-1226 or 718/896-7393, ⊛www.olympic-airways.com. Montreal, New York and Toronto to Cairo via Athens.

Royal Air Maroc ☏1-800/344-6726, ⊛www.royalairmaroc.com. New York to Cairo via Casablanca.

Royal Jordanian ☏1-800/223-0470 or 212/949-0050, ⊛www.rja.com.jo. Chicago, Detroit and New York to Cairo via Amman.

Saudi Arabian Airlines ☏1-800/4-SAUDIA, ⊛www.saudiairlines.com. New York to Cairo via Riyadh or Jeddah.

Swiss ☏1-877/FLY-SWISS, ⊛www.swiss.com. Boston, Chicago, LA, Miami, Montreal and New York to Cairo via Zurich.

Tarom Romanian Air ☏212/560-0840, ⊛www.tarom.ro. New York to Cairo via Bucharest. Rock-bottom service, but also rock-bottom prices.

Turkish Airlines ☏1-800/874-8875 or 212/339-9650, ⊛www.thy.com. Chicago and New York to Cairo via Istanbul.

United Airlines ☏1-800/538-2929, ⊛www.united.com. Chicago, Denver, LA, San Diego, San Francisco and Washington DC, with connections from most American cities, to Cairo and Alexandria via Frankfurt in combination with Lufthansa.

Discount travel companies

Air Brokers International ☏1-800/883-3273 or 415/397-1383, ⊛www.airbrokers.com. Consolidator and specialist in round-the-world tickets.

Airtech ☏212/219-7000, ⊛www.airtech.com. Standby seat broker; also deals in consolidator fares.

Educational Travel Center ☏1-800/747-5551 or 608/256-5551, ⊛www.edtrav.com. Student/youth discount agent.

Flightcentre US ☏1-866/WORLD-51, ⊛www.flightcentre.us, Canada ☏1-866/WORLD-55, ⊛www.flightcentre.ca. Rock-bottom fares to Egypt and other destinations.

STA Travel US ☏1-800/329-9537, Canada ☏1-888/427-5639, ⊛www.sta-travel.com. Specialist in independent travel; also student IDs, travel insurance, car rental, etc.

Student Flights ☏1-800/255-8000 or 480/951-1177, ⊛www.isecard.com/studentflights. Student/youth fares and student IDs.

TFI Tours ☏1-800/745-8000 or 212/736-1140, ⊛www.lowestairprice.com. Well-established consolidator.

Travel Avenue ☏1-800/333-3335, ⊛www.travelavenue.com. Full-service travel agent that offers discounts in the form of rebates.

Travel Cuts Canada ☏1-888/246-9762, US ☏1-800/592-CUTS, ⊛www.travelcuts.com. Canadian student-travel organization specializing in student fares, IDs and other travel services.

Travelosophy US ☏1-800/332-2687, ⊛www.itravelosophy.com. Discounted and student fares.

Worldtek Travel ☏1-800/243-1723, ⊛www.worldtek.com. Discount travel agency.

Package holidays

There are many operators offering **packages** to Egypt or customized independent tours. Most package holidays concentrate on Cairo and the Pyramids (often with an experienced Egyptologist as the guide), or a Nile Valley cruise, but there are also plenty of others that take in more of the country or offer specialist activities – for example, archeological trips or diving safaris. Check the Sunday travel sections of papers such as the *New York Times* and *Los Angeles Times* for special travel deals. Adventure tours with British firms like Guerba, Imaginative Traveller and Swim with Dolphins (see p.32) can be booked online from the US or Canada.

Tour operators

Mainstream tours

Abercrombie & Kent ☏1-800/323-7308 or 630/954-2944, ⊛www.abercrombiekent.com. Upmarket firm with a number of Egypt tours, some led by Egyptologists, including a fourteen-day "Pharaohs and Pyramids" tour from US$5170 plus air fares, or a twelve-day "Splendors of the Nile" tour from US$4690 plus air fares. Can also create custom packages.

Cox & Kings ☎ 1-800/999-1758, ⓦ www
.coxandkingsusa.com. Upmarket customized tour
operator offering tours such as a twelve-day "Classical
Egypt" package from US$2885 plus air fares to Egypt
and $295 for internal flights.

Egypt Tours ☎ 1-800/52-EGYPT, ⓦ www
.egyptours.com. Tours ranging from a six-night
Highlights tour (from US$2649 including air fare) to
a 21-night "In Depth" trip (from $8614), as well as
combined tours with Jordan and Israel.

Esplanade Tours ☎ 1-800/426-5492, ⓦ www
.esplanadetours.com. Customized itineraries
including city breaks in Cairo, Luxor or Aswan, Nile
cruises and tours. A fourteen-day "Magical Egypt" tour
costs from US$2868 plus air fare.

General Tours ☎ 1-800/221-2216, ⓦ www
.generaltours.com. Escorted tours include a ten-day
"River of the Pharaohs" tour starting at US$2249
including flights, or a 21-day tour of Egypt and Turkey
from US$3389 including air fares.

Globus Journeys ☎ 1-866/755-8581, ⓦ www
.globusjourneys.com. Fully escorted tours to Egypt,
including a twelve-day Grand Tour from US$1734, or
a ten-day Egyptian Splendour tour from US$2329,
prices including air fares.

Homeric Tours ☎ 1-800/223-5570, ⓦ www
.homerictours.com. Deluxe package tours, from an
eight-day "Egyptian Escape" visiting Cairo, Aswan
and Luxor with a four-day Nile cruise from US$1539
including air fare, to a fourteen-day version with an
added Lake Nasser cruise visiting Abu Simbel from
US$2399. Greece extensions available.

Isram World of Travel ☎ 1-800/223 7460,
ⓦ www.isram.com. Eight- to thirteen-day tours,
all including Nile cruises. Eight-day "Jewel of the
Nile" tours with a stay in Cairo, a Nile cruise and an
air-trip to Abu Simbel from US$2080 including air
fare; thirteen-day tours including three days in Sharm
el-Sheikh from US$2555 including air fare; Cairo
city breaks from US$455 plus air fare. Add-ons to
Alexandria, Sinai and/or Jordan possible.

Maupintour ☎ 1-800/255-4266, ⓦ www
.maupintour.com. Ten-day "Ancient Egypt" tours
including a four-day Nile cruise from US$2249 plus
air fare; seventeen-day versions from US$3859
plus air fare; customized add-ons are also available,
including beach stays by the Red Sea.

Ya'lla Tours ☎ 800/644-1595, ⓦ www.yallatours
.com. An interesting range of packages including
"Footsteps of the Holy Family" tour to sites of
biblical significance (nine nights from US$1065),
four-night breaks in Cairo (from US$495), with
optional add-ons to Alexandria and the Fayoum,
or a thirteen-night tour of Egypt and Jordan (from
US$2895). Prices do not include air fares from
the US.

Adventure and specialist tours

Adventure Center ☎ 1-800/228-8747 or
510/654-1879, ⓦ www.adventure-center.com.
A large assortment of itineraries for small groups,
including a Nile cruise, Red Sea diving, temples, the
Pyramids and more, camping or in hotels. Can also
book adventure tours run by UK firm Exodus (see
p.32) and Australian firm Peregrine (see p.37).

Adventures Abroad ☎ 1-800/665-3998 or
604/303-1099, ⓦ www.adventures-abroad.com.
Canadian-based company offering small group tours
to Egypt alone or combined with Israel, Jordan, Syria,
etc (even Kenya and Tanzania). Activities include
camel rides, trekking and felucca cruises.

Archaeological Tours ☎ 1-866/740-5130,
ⓦ www.archaeologicaltrs.com. Small-group
archeological/historical educational tours with
renowned Egyptologist.

GAP Traveller ☎ 1-866/732 5885, ⓦ www
.gapadentures.com. Canadian agents for Exodus
(see p.32).

Insight International Tours ☎ 1-800/582-8380,
ⓦ www.insightvacations.com. A nine-day "Wonders
of Egypt" tour starting at US$1375 plus air fare, or
a twelve-day "Splendours of Egypt" tour starting at
US$1725 plus flight.

Mistress of Magic ⓦ egyptmagic.bizland.com.
New Age tour led by a mystical High Priestess
to uncover "the sacred secrets of Egypt" with
ceremonies, readings and past-life regressions,
visiting Cairo, Luxor, Aswan and Siwa.

Travcoa US ☎ 1-800/992-2003, Canada
☎ 1-800/563-0005, ⓦ www.travcoa.com. All-
inclusive deluxe-accommodation tours including a
twelve-day "Nile Revealed" tour to Cairo, Aswan, Luxor
and Abu Simbel including a five-day luxury Nile cruise
from US$4995 plus air fare.

Wilderness Travel ☎ 1-800/368-2794, ⓦ www
.wildernesstravel.com. Offers a small-group, sixteen-
day tour covering Sinai as well as Cairo, Luxor and
Aswan (from US$4995 excluding flight), or a seven-
day tour (from US$1995 excluding flight), both with an
optional five-day extension to Jordan.

Flights from Australia and New Zealand

Most Australians and New Zealanders visit
Egypt as an extension of a European trip,
usually buying a flight to London, plus an add-
on fare to Cairo. However, you might want
to consider taking in Egypt as a stopover
on a Round-the-World (RTW) ticket, or take
advantage of some very reasonable budget
fares to Cairo from Asia. If you are planning

to travel on to Egypt from Israel or Jordan, see pp.39–40.

There are no direct flights from Australia or New Zealand to Egypt, but a number of European, Middle Eastern and Asian carriers offer indirect flights, changing planes at their hub airports. Travel agents may also be able to put together a ticket using different airlines on different legs of the journey. Prices for a flight to Cairo via Southeast Asia, Europe or the Middle East start at around A$1640/NZ$2140 in low season (summer), A$2400/NZ$2300 in high season (winter).

For the most direct route as well as good standards of comfort and service, your best bet is Singapore Airlines, who fly via Singapore from a good choice of Australian and New Zealand cities. They are often one of the best-priced options too, though from some cities in Australia, Malaysia Airlines may be slightly cheaper. Of the Middle Eastern airlines, Emirates is usually the best and the cheapest, and serves Brisbane, Melbourne and Perth in addition to Sydney and Auckland. A number of European airlines offer flights via Europe, which is only a slightly roundabout route. Austrian is one of the cheapest at present, and KLM is also a possibility. From New Zealand, Air New Zealand can get you to Egypt using a combination of flights with Kuwait, Austrian, KLM and other airlines.

STA Travel is one of the best places to start looking for a ticket if you are under 26 or a student. You can check fares and book online, but it's also worth comparing the price of a RTW ticket, which may offer better value (and sometimes even a lower price) than a straight return, especially from New Zealand.

Airlines

Air New Zealand Australia ☎13/2476, NZ ☎0800/737 000, ⓦwww.airnz.com. Through-tickets from New Zealand to Egypt in combination with other airlines.

Austrian Airlines Australia ☎1800/642 438 or 02/9251 6155, NZ ☎09/522 5948, ⓦwww.aua.com. Sydney and Melbourne to Cairo via Vienna.

EgyptAir c/o Global Aviation, Australia ☎02/9232 6677, ⓦwww.egyptair.com.eg. Flies to Cairo from Bangkok, Mumbai, Tokyo and Osaka, and can usually arrange connecting services from Australia and New Zealand.

Emirates Australia ☎1300/303 777 or 02/9290 9700, NZ ☎09/377 6004, ⓦwww.emirates.com. Auckland, Brisbane, Melbourne, Perth and Sydney to Cairo via Dubai.

Gulf Air Australia ☎02/9244 2199, NZ ☎09/308 3366, ⓦwww.gulfairco.com. Sydney to Cairo via Bahrain.

Korean Air Australia ☎02/9262 6000, ⓦwww.koreanair.com.au; NZ ☎09/914 2000, ⓦwww.koreanair.co.nz. Auckland, Brisbane and Sydney to Cairo via Seoul.

Malaysia Airlines Australia ☎13/2627, NZ ☎0800/777 747, ⓦwww.malaysia-airlines.com. Adelaide, Brisbane, Melbourne, Perth and Sydney to Cairo via Kuala Lumpur.

Qantas Australia ☎13/1313, NZ ☎0800/808 767 or 09/357 8900, ⓦwww.qantas.com. Through-tickets in combination with British Airways via London, Alitalia via Rome or Gulf Air via Bahrain.

Singapore Airlines Australia ☎13/1011, NZ ☎0800/808 909, ⓦwww.singaporeair.com. Adelaide, Auckland, Brisbane, Christchurch, Melbourne, Perth and Sydney to Cairo via Singapore.

Travel agents

Flight Centres Australia ☎13/3133, ⓦwww.flightcentre.com.au; NZ ☎0800/243 544, ⓦwww.flightcentre.co.nz. Online booking and branches across Australia and New Zealand.

OTC Australia ☎1300/855 118, ⓦwww.otctravel.com.au. Deals on flights, hotels and holidays.

STA Travel Australia ☎1300/733 035, ⓦwww.statravel.com.au; NZ ☎0508/782 872, ⓦwww.statravel.co.nz. Worldwide specialist in low-cost flights and tours for students and under-26s, though other customers welcome. Branches throughout Australia and New Zealand, plus online booking.

Trailfinders Australia ☎02/9247 7666, ⓦwww.trailfinders.com.au. Australian branch of the London-based independent travel specialists, well-informed and efficient.

travel.com.au and travel.co.nz Australia ☎1300/130 482 or 02/9249 5444, ⓦwww.travel.com.au; NZ ☎0800/468 332, ⓦwww.travel.co.nz. Comprehensive online travel company, with discounted fares.

Package tours

So far as package holidays go, many Australians and New Zealanders either sign up with a tour in Britain (see pp.31–32), or book a land-only tour and organize their flight separately. There are, however, a few companies that can organize flight-and-tour packages:

see below for details (prices are for land-only deals, though, unless otherwise stated).

Tour operators

Adventure World Australia ☎02/8913 0755, ⓦwww.adventureworld.com.au; NZ ☎09/524 5118, ⓦwww.adventureworld.co.nz. Agents for Explore Worldwide (see p.32).

Adventure Travel NZ ☎09/379 9755, ⓦwww.adventuretravel.co.nz. Sells a variety of different Egypt tours, including Gecko's, Exodus and Explore Worldwide.

Adventures Abroad Australia ☎1800/147 827, NZ ☎0800/800 434, ⓦwww.adventures-abroad.com. Canadian-based company offering small group tours to Egypt alone or combined with Israel, Jordan, Syria, etc (even Kenya and Tanzania). Activities include camel rides, trekking and felucca cruises.

Allways Dive Expeditions Australia ☎1800/338 239, ⓦwww.allwaysdive.com.au. Eleven-day diving trip exploring wrecks and coral reefs around Sharm el-Sheikh and Ras Mohammed from aboard the Wildcat. Price (starting at A$4150) includes return air fares from east coast Australia and seven nights at sea, including all meals and two dives a day.

Insight International Tours Australia ☎1300/727767 or 02/9512 0767, ⓦwww.insightvacations.com/au; NZ ☎09/300 1580, ⓦwww.insightvacations.com/nz. American firm offering a nine-day "Wonders of Egypt" tour starting at A$2099/NZ$2250 plus air fare, or a twelve-day "Splendours of Egypt" tour starting at A$2475/NZ$2650 plus flight.

Made Easy Tours Australia ☎1800/673 337, ⓦwww.madeeasytours.com.au. An eight-day tour to Cairo, Aswan and Luxor including a four-night Nile cruise from A$3090, or combined tours of Egypt and Jordan.

Peregrine Adventures Australia ☎1300/854 444 or 03/9663 8611, NZ ☎0800/448086, ⓦwww.peregrine.net.au. Agents for a number of tour operators, notably UK firm Exodus (see p.32), with a wide range of Egypt tours. Their budget tour brand, Gecko's, offers a variety of adventure tours, from an eleven-day "Felucca Safari" visiting Cairo, Aswan and Luxor (from around A$690/NZ$750) to a fifteen-day "Backroads of Egypt" journey including a Nile trip plus five days spent with Bedouins in the Western Desert (from around A$1100/NZ$1200).

Sun Island Tours Australia ☎1800/257 378, ⓦwww.sunislandtours.com.au. Mainstream holiday packages including Cairo city breaks from A$211 for three days, and Nile cruises from A$1282 for eight days.

Travcoa Australia ☎02/9262 3366, ⓦwww.travcoa.com. Australian branch of the US tour operator (see p.35).

Overland from Britain

Travelling overland from Britain to Egypt only really makes sense if you intend to visit other countries en route. The two most obvious approaches are either by land through Turkey, Syria and Jordan, or **by ferry from Greece**. As the ferry, which calls at Haifa in Israel, has been out of commission for some time due to the political situation in Israel and Palestine, the only current option is to travel **by land through Turkey, Syria and Jordan**. Turkey is accessible by various combinations of train or bus from Britain, and it is even possible to hitch all the way from London to Istanbul, though this is not recommended, given the attendant risks. Note that Syrian visas are best obtained in your home country, as Syrian embassies won't always issue visas to non-residents of the country where they are situated.

In theory, a third route to Egypt is **via Italy, Tunisia and Libya**, though obtaining a Libyan visa is virtually impossible at the best of times. If you do manage to get one, there are regular ferries from Trápani in Sicily to La Goulette, the port for Tunis. From Tunis, you can get a train, bus or service taxi (called a *louage* in Tunisia) down to Sfax or Gabès, both of which have regular *louages* to Tripoli in Libya, where you can pick up a bus or service taxi to Cairo (see p.41).

By sea

The weekly boat service from Piraeus in Greece to Port Said in Egypt via Cyprus and Israel is currently suspended, though it may well resume if the political situation in Israel and Palestine improves substantially. The full journey took three and a half days stopping at the Greek islands of Patmos and Rhodes, then Limassol in Cyprus, and Haifa in Israel, with many Egypt-bound passengers disembarking at Haifa to continue their journey by land. For the latest information on the status of this service, check with Salamis Lines of Cyprus (☎+30-21/0429 4325), or its UK agent Viamare (☎0870/410 6040; ⓦwww.viamare.com).

By rail

It is possible to travel by rail and ferry all the way to Amman in Jordan via Turkey, though once you get beyond Istanbul, it's a very slow option. One of the most cost-effective ways to get as far as Turkey is with a European rail pass. For British, Irish and European residents, the **InterRail pass** is available from main stations and international rail agents in Britain and Ireland (see p.39), and all the countries it covers. In theory it allows unlimited free travel on railways in the countries it covers, half-price in the country it was bought in, but in practice all the trains you'll want to use charge supplements. There are eight zones, and a card covering zone E (France, Belgium, the Netherlands and Luxembourg) and zone G (Italy, Slovenia, Greece and Turkey, including the ferry from Italy to Greece) would get you all the way from Calais to the Syrian border. An all-zone card would cover any other countries you may want to visit en-route, including zone A for Britain and Ireland, although it will probably be cheaper to get to mainland Europe by other means and start using the card when you are there. A two-zone card valid for 22 days costs £215 for under-26s, £303 for over-26s, rising to £295/415 for an all-zone card valid for a month. Officially, you need to have been resident in a participating country for at least six months to buy an InterRail pass. For further details and price updates, see RailEurope's InterRail website at ⓦwww.inter-rail.co.uk.

Non-European residents aren't eligible for InterRail passes, though many agents don't actually check residential qualifications. Non-residents can, however, buy a **Eurail pass**, which should be obtained outside Europe, but can be bought from RailEurope in London by non-residents who were unable to get it at home. Eurail gives unlimited travel in seventeen countries – Austria, Belgium, Denmark, Finland, France, Germany, Greece, Hungary, Ireland, Italy, Luxembourg, the Netherlands, Norway, Portugal, Spain, Sweden and Switzerland – and is valid for more express trains than InterRail, thus saving money on supplements. If you're 26 or over you'll have to buy a first-class pass, available in fifteen-day (US$588), 21-day (US$762), one-month (US$946), two-month (US$1338) and three-month (US$1654) versions. Under-26s can buy a Eurail **Youthpass**, costing US$414 for

fifteen days, US$534 for 21 days, US$664 for one month, US$946 for two months, or US$1160 for three months. You stand a better chance of getting your money's worth out of a Eurail **Flexipass**, which is good for a certain number of travel days in a two-month period. This, too, comes in under-26 and first-class versions: ten days cost US$694 for first-class travel or US$488 for under-26s; and fifteen days, US$914 or US$642. There are also "Saver" versions of all these passes offering a discount of around fifteen percent for two to five people travelling together.

Once in Istanbul, you can get the weekly train to Aleppo in Syria, currently leaving from Istanbul's Haydarpasa station every Thursday morning, and taking around thirty hours: sleeping berths are available. The train is scheduled to continue to Damascus, but does not usually do so; there are, however, five daily trains to Damascus from Aleppo (see the Syrian Railways website at ⓦ www.cfssyria.org/en/national_trips.htm for details). From Damascus you can pick up one of the two weekly trains (currently leaving Mondays and Thursdays) to Amman in Jordan, a nine-hour journey. The Man in Seat 61 website (ⓦwww.seat61.com) has the latest details on the route from London to Amman, as well as extensive information on train travel through Europe. For the onward journey from Amman to Egypt, see p.40.

By bus

It is also possible to travel to Egypt by bus via Europe, Turkey, Syria and Jordan. The first leg, as far as Sofia or Varna in Bulgaria, can be done in one journey from London with Eurolines (£119 one-way, £115 for under-26s), but it's a gruelling 55-hour trip. You would then have to continue on local buses or trains through Turkey and Syria into Jordan (see below). Eurolines also sells fifteen-, thirty- or sixty-day **passes** for unlimited travel between 31 European cities, but the nearest they'll get you to Turkey is Rome, from where you'd need to make your way to an Adriatic port such as Bari or Brindisi, catch a ferry to Greece and continue from there. Between May and October, Busabout offers two-, four-, six-, eight- and twelve-week passes, or a whole-season one, for its own bus services around the Continent, and Flexipasses for any eight, twelve, sixteen or twenty days, with the possibility of adding extra days. Busabout passes can be bought in North America and Australasia as well as in Britain and Europe, though you can only use them as far as Bari or Brindisi, unless you purchase an Athens add-on.

From Greece and Bulgaria, there are regular buses to Istanbul (12hr from Sofia or Thessaloniki, 24hr from Athens), though not every day. From Istanbul, you could take a bus direct to Aleppo (24hr) or Damascus (30hr), but you'd be better off heading for Antakya at the eastern end of Turkey's Mediterranean coastline, from where regular buses leave for Aleppo (4hr) and Damascus (8hr) in Syria. From Damascus, you could take a bus straight through to Cairo via Aqaba (4 weekly; 30hr), but again it's a better idea to do the journey in stages, starting with the seven-hour trip to Amman in Jordan (two daily buses from Damascus). For information on getting from Jordan to Egypt, see p.40.

Overland travel contacts

Through tickets and rail passes in Britain and Ireland

Iarnród Éireann (Continental Rail Desk) Ireland ☏01/703 1885, ⓦwww.irishrail.ie. InterRail and some through tickets.
International Rail UK ☏0870/751 5000, ⓦwww .international-rail.com. InterRail and through tickets to most of Europe.
Northern Ireland Railways Northern Ireland ☏028/9066 6630, ⓦwww.translink.co.uk. InterRail and some through tickets.
Rail Europe UK ☏0870/584 8848, ⓦwww .raileurope.co.uk. InterRail, Eurail and some through tickets.
The Man in Seat 61 ⓦwww.seat61.com. Sound information on trans-European train travel and fares, plus information on trains to Turkey, Syria and Jordan, and on railways in Egypt.

Rail passes in North America

DER Travel ☏1-800/283-2424, ⓦwww.dertravel .com/rail.
CIT Rail ☏1-800/CIT-TOUR, ⓦwww.cit-rail.com.
Rail Europe US ☏1-800/438-7245, Canada ☏1-800/361-7245, ⓦwww.raileurope.com/us. Official Eurail agent in North America.

Rail passes in Australia

CIT World Travel ☏02/9267 1255 or 03/9650 5510, ⓦwww.cittravel.com.au.
Rail Plus ☏1300/555 003 or 03/9642 8644, ⓦwww.railplus.com.au.
Trailfinders ☏02/9247 7666 or 03/9600 3022, ⓦwww.trailfinder.com.au.

Bus tickets and passes

Busabout UK ☏020/7950 1661, US ☏1-800/664 4046, Canada ☏416/322-8468, Australia ☏1300/301 776, NZ ☏09/309 5973, ⓦwww.busabout.com.
Eurolines UK ☏0870/580 8808, ⓦwww .eurolines.co.uk, Ireland ☏01/836 6111, ⓦwww .eurolines.ie.

Getting there from neighbouring countries

If your travels include Israel or Jordan, moving on to Egypt is fairly straightforward. You can either fly – from Tel Aviv or Amman to Cairo – or, more cheaply, use one of the many bus and ferry services. **From Israel and Palestine** the quickest checkpoint for Cairo is the divided border town of Rafah, near the Mediterranean coast; for the resort towns of the Sinai peninsula, it's Taba, near Eilat. Which of these you use – if either of them – will depend on the current political situation in Israel and Gaza: keep your ear to the ground and steer clear of trouble spots. If you are travelling **from Jordan**, you have to go from Aqaba by ferry to Nuweiba in Sinai, or take the fast catamaran to Nuweiba or Sinai's main resort, Sharm el-Sheikh, and then continue your journey by bus. See pp.42–43 for details of Egyptian and Sinai-only visas and for addresses of Egyptian consulates in Israel, Palestine and Jordan.

From Israel or the Gaza Strip

At time of writing the political situation is such that most travellers are avoiding Israel and the Gaza Strip, though direct transport still runs between Israel or Palestine and Egypt. The border crossing between Gaza and Egypt at Rafah, however, is often closed by the Israelis, so most traffic currently uses the Israel/Egypt border crossing at Taba near Eilat.

Entering Egypt via Rafah, you're subject to an Israeli departure tax of NIS118 and an Egyptian entry tax of US$6. Entering via Taba, departure and entry taxes are NIS79 and US$8 respectively.

In the past, a number of firms offered daily bus services from Tel Aviv or Jerusalem to Cairo, but currently the only company operating buses is Mazada Tours (see below), which runs twice a week (Sunday and Thursday) from both Tel Aviv and Jerusalem. One-way tickets are US$44 (plus border taxes totalling US$40), return tickets US$66 (plus US$68), and it's best to book (and confirm return journeys) at least three days in advance. The same company will also get your visa for you on request, but the Egyptian embassy is just around the corner from its office (see p.43 for the address), and it is cheaper to do it yourself.

To reach Rafah under your own steam, take the once-daily Israeli Egged buses from Tel Aviv, Ashqelon and Beersheba. Otherwise the journey involves travelling by service taxi through the Gaza Strip and changing at several points. Whether you can use this route will depend on the current political situation between Israel and the Palestinians and whether the border at Rafah is open, but when things are good, there are service taxis (*sherut* in Hebrew) from Jaffa to the Israel–Gaza border at Erez (Israeli buses from Tel Aviv and Ashqelon will leave you 4km short at Yad Mordecai, and from there to Gaza City and then on to Rafah. You may have to walk or charter a "special" (private taxi) for the 5km from Rafah town to the border post. Once you are across the border, the Egyptian guards will examine your passport and visa (which cannot be issued at Rafah) and demand the entry tax. The exchange office on the Egyptian side is open 24 hours. Rafah and nearby El-Arish in themselves have little to offer apart from bus and service taxi connections to Cairo.

Taba makes a fine jumping-off point for the Sinai coast resorts, St Catherine's Monastery or Cairo. From Eilat, a taxi or a much cheaper #15 bus (which doesn't run on Shabbat) will get you to the Israeli checkpoint at Taba for an exit stamp; you then walk over to the Egyptian side, where proceedings are similar to those at Rafah, except that Sinai-only visas can be obtained on the spot. It usually takes a good hour to cross the border

(longer at holiday times). If you're carrying any Israeli shekels, a few banks in Sharm el-Sheikh and one or two banks and Forex bureaux in Cairo are the only places in Egypt where you can legally exchange them.

Travelling on from Taba (see p.746), there is one bus daily (currently at 3pm) for Dahab (£E22) and Sharm el-Sheikh; (£E26.50); four to Nuweiba (6.30am, 9am, 2pm and 3pm; £E11) and three to Cairo (8am, 10am and 2pm; £E55–75). Taxis take full advantage of the fact that there's no bus to St Catherine's, and also demand premium rates for Nuweiba or places further down the Gulf of Aqaba. Service taxis are a bit cheaper, with per person rates of around £E30 to Nuweiba or Tarabeen, £E50 to Dahab and £E75 to Sharm el-Sheikh. Prices for both drop immediately before the bus departs, and soar once it has departed.

You are not allowed to drive rented cars or 4WDs across the Israeli–Egyptian border. The Israeli Airports Authority website at Ⓦ www.iaa.gov.il/Rashat/en-US/Rashot has further information on both the Rafah and Taba border crossings.

Bus operators

Mazada Tours 141 Rehov Ibn Givrol, Tel Aviv ☎ 03/544 4454; 19 Jaffa Rd, Jerusalem ☎ 02/623 5777, Ⓦ www.mazada.co.il.

Israeli tour operators

ISSTA Lines (Israel Students Travel Company) 113 Rehov Ben Yehuda, Tel Aviv ☎ 03/777 7777, Ⓦ www.issta.co.il. Has branches throughout Israel; the website is unfortunately in Hebrew only.
Neot HaKikar Touring Company 37 Rehov Sherit Israel, Tel Aviv ☎ 03/515 9010, Ⓦ www.neot -hakikar.com. Specializes in Sinai treks.

From Jordan

From Amman, direct buses do the 21-hour journey to Cairo but they are neither very pleasant nor very economical. The main operator is JETT, based on King Hussein Street, 900m north (and uphill) from Abdali station ☎ 06/569 6151. Departures are currently Sat, Sun, Tues, & Thurs 6.30am, though schedules are subject to change, and the journey costs JD42/US$58 one-way including boat fare. Buses should arrive at Sinai bus terminal in Abbassiya, Cairo, but they sometimes terminate at Almaza in Heliopolis (see p.108 for details of transport into town from both these terminals). Plenty of other Abdali-based firms compete, undercutting JETT, though their buses are less comfortable and their services less reliable. One firm worth trying is Afana, next door to JETT and at Abdali station, whose buses leave from Middle East Circle (Duwaar ash-Sharq al-Aswat). Other bus companies around Abdali station operate buses to Cairo (in various states of repair), so if you are serious about saving every penny, it's worth shopping around all the bus and service-taxi offices to compare prices and schedules.

Unless speed is of the essence, however, (in which case flying is a better option), you'd do far better to break the journey at Aqaba or in the Sinai. **From Aqaba**, the quickest route is by land via Eilat in Israel, using local buses. Disincentives are the telltale Taba border stamp, and the hefty exit and entry taxes (totalling around US$40) which are payable at Taba. By sea, the Arab Bridge Maritime Company (see ⓦwww.abmaritime.com.jo for current fares and schedules) operates ferry and catamaran services to Nuweiba, the latter continuing to Sharm el-Sheikh. An Aqaba–Taba service has been talked about for years, but has yet to materialize. You can buy tickets for all sea services from the company's offices in Amman (beside the Royal Jordanian building just off 7th Circle; ⓣ06/585 9554 or 582 4484) and in Aqaba (downtown near the China restaurant; ⓣ03/209 2000), from agents in Aqaba, or up to an hour before departure at the passenger terminal itself, 9km south of Aqaba (open daily 24hr; ⓣ03/201 3891). The terminal is served by local buses from Aqaba's Corniche, or costs an exorbitant JD4 by taxi. There's a duty-free shop by the terminal in case you need a bottle of whisky to take with you.

The ordinary ferry takes three hours to Nuweiba and costs US$22 or JD15. It is scheduled to leave at 1pm and 7pm but is notoriously unpunctual. The ferry will carry bicycles (free), motorbikes (around JD14/US$20), small cars (JD75/US$105) and 4WDs (JD105/US$157). The catamaran, on the other hand, takes just an hour to complete the crossing to Nuweiba, but only carries people (JD21/US$36 to Nuweiba; JD26/US$45 to Sharm). Whether by ferry or by catamaran, a tax of JD6 is payable on departure. On arrival in Nuweiba you can obtain a Sinai-only visa at the port. See p.742 for information on Nuweiba itself, and on travelling in the opposite direction, towards Aqaba.

If you prefer **to fly**, Royal Jordanian (ⓣ06/567 8321) and EgyptAir (ⓣ06/463 0011) operate expensive daily flights from Amman to Cairo, while Royal Jordanian subsidiary Royal Wings (ⓣ06/487 5202, ⓦwww.royalwings.com.jo) flies four times a week from Amman to Sharm el-Sheikh. It also runs seasonal charters to resorts such as Sharm and Hurghada, and may introduce an Amman–Alexandria route in the future. For charter tickets, contact the airline, or Dakkak Tours (ⓣ06/567 0289). For further details, see the *Rough Guide to Jordan*.

From Libya and Sudan

In theory, it is also possible to enter Egypt **from Libya**, by bus or service taxi direct from Tripoli or Benghazi (the service taxi drops you at Midan Opera in central Cairo, the bus at Almaza terminal in Heliopolis), or by taking a bus or service taxi from Benghazi to Al-Burdi, where there are vehicles to the border. On the Egyptian side, you can get a service taxi on to Sollum, from where one bus a day plies the road to Mersa Matrouh.

From Sudan, there's a weekly ferry from Wadi Halfa up Lake Nasser to Aswan, which should connect with the train from Khartoum, though most Western travellers use the service in the opposite direction (see p.479). There is a road from Wadi Halfa to Aswan, and on the coast from Port Sudan to Halaib, but at present the Egyptian authorities will not allow foreigners to enter by land on either of those routes, and you will be turned back if you try. If you are coming north with a vehicle, you will have to arrange to take a barge from Wadi Halfa up to Aswan.

Red tape and visas

Bureaucracy has flourished in Egypt for five thousand years, pervading most aspects of life. Nasser's promise of a civil service job for every graduate has led to a vastly overstaffed, inefficient administration, which you'll come up against when obtaining travel permits or visa extensions, and which may well defeat you if you try to do anything more complicated. Rules change from place to place and individual bureaucrats may interpret them differently, or introduce new regulations, or simply be obstructive through caprice. Remain patient and good-humoured no matter what.

Passports and visas

All visitors to Egypt must hold passports that are valid for at least six months beyond the proposed date of entry to the country. Citizens of most countries, including the UK, Ireland, the USA, Canada, Australia, New Zealand and all European countries, must also obtain tourist visas.

Tourist visas

Regular **tourist visas** are available from Egyptian consulates abroad (see opposite). For most nationalities, including British, Irish, Americans, Canadians, Australians, New Zealanders and all EU citizens, they can also be obtained on arrival at Cairo, Luxor and Hurghada airports. The process is generally painless and cheaper than getting one through a consulate, but bear in mind that visas issued at the airport are only valid for one month. You *cannot* get them at overland border crossings, or at Aswan, Suez or Nuweiba (apart from Sinai-only visas – see opposite). From an embassy or consulate the single-visit and multiple-entry types of visa entitle you to stay in Egypt for three months; the latter allows you to go in and out of the country three times within this period. Don't be misled by statements on the application form that it is "valid for six months"; this simply means that it must be used within six months from the day of issue.

Visa applications can be made in person or by post. Applying in person, you can normally get a visa the same day in Britain, North America, Australia, Israel or Jordan. Always turn up early in the day and expect to pay in cash – postal applications take between seven working days and six weeks to process. When returning the form, you need to include a registered or recorded SAE, your passport, one photo, and a postal or money order (not a personal cheque).

The cost varies according to your nationality, and from place to place. Getting a standard visa on arrival costs US$15, irrespective of your nationality. Abroad, the price varies according to where you buy it, and sometimes your nationality. Some consulates may demand that you pay in US dollars instead of local currency, or ask you to supply extra photos (and maybe glue to stick them down!). It's wise to allow for all these eventualities.

If you don't mind being limited to Sinai, you can obtain special **Sinai-only visas** (free of charge) at Taba on the Israeli–Egyptian border, St Catherine's Monastery or Sharm el-Sheikh airport, or the seaports at Sharm el-Sheikh and Nuweiba. Valid for fourteen days only, this visa restricts you to the Aqaba coast down to Sharm el-Sheikh, and the vicinity of St Catherine's; it is not valid for Ras Mohammed, the mountains around St Catherine's (except for Mount Sinai), or any other part of Egypt. It can't be extended, and there's no period of grace for overstaying. Note that neither regular nor Sinai-only visas are available at Rafah, the other crossing between Israeli-held territory and Egypt.

Egyptian embassies and consulates abroad

For visa applications in person, submit your passport and application in the morning and collect the visa that afternoon (applications cannot be submitted then). Current lists of Egyptian embassies can be found in the English pages of the Egyptian Foreign Ministry website (ⓦwww.mfa.gov.eg), and also on the Arab Net site at ⓦwww.arab.net/egypt/et_embassies.htm.

Australia 1 Darwin Ave, Yarralumla, ACT 2600 ⓣ02/6273 4437 (Mon–Fri 9am–4pm); Level 4, 241 Commonwealth St, Surry Hills, NSW 2010 ⓣ02/9281 4844, (Mon–Fri 9.30am–2.30pm); Level 9, 124 Exhibition St, Melbourne, Vic 3000 ⓣ03/9654 8869 (Mon–Fri 9am–2pm). Single-entry visa A$40, multiple-entry A$50, downloadable visa application form available on line at ⓦwww.egypt.org.au.

Canada 454 Laurier Ave E, Ottawa, ON K1N 6R3 ⓣ613/234 4931/5, ⓦwww.egyptembassy.ca (Mon–Fri 9am–2pm); 1 Pl Ville Marie, Suite 2617, Montreal PQ H3B 4S3 ⓣ514/866 8455/6/7, ⓦwww.egyptianconsulatemontreal.org (Mon–Fri 9.30am–1pm). Single-entry visa CDN$26, multiple-entry CDN$31.

Greece 3 Leoforos Vassilissis Sofias, P.O. Box 106-71, 10671 Athens ⓣ0301/361 8612/3.

Ireland 12 Clyde Rd, Ballsbridge, Dublin 4 ⓣ01/660 6566, ⓦwww.embegyptireland.ie. Single-entry visa €22, multiple-entry €27.

Israel 54 Rehov Basel, Tel Aviv 62744 ⓣ03/546 4152 or 2 (Sun–Thurs 9–11am); 68 Afraty Street, Bnei Betkha, Eilat ⓣ08/637 6882 (Sun–Thurs 10am–2.30pm).

Jordan 14 Riyad Mefleh St, Amman (between 4th and 5th circles, next to Dove Hotel) ⓣ06/560 5202 (daily except Fri 10am–3pm); Al-Wahdat Al-Jarbiyya, Sharia al-Istiqlal, Aqaba ⓣ03/201 6171 or 81 (Sun–Thurs 9am–3pm). Tourist visa JD12, multiple-entry visa JD18.

New Zealand There is no Egyptian embassy or consulate in New Zealand; contact one of the consulates in Australia.

Palestine 204–55 Sharia Omar al-Mukhtar, PO Box 1234, Gaza City ⓣ07/282 4274 or 84 or 94.

South Africa 270 Bourke St, Muckleneuk, Pretoria ⓣ012/343 1590 or 91.

Sudan Sharia al-Gomhuria, PO Box 1126, Khartoum ⓣ01/8377 2190.

UK 2 Lowndes St, London SW1X 9ET ⓣ020/7235 9777, ⓦwww.egyptianconsulate.co.uk. Applications received Mon–Fri 9.30am–12.30pm, collection 2.30–4pm. Single-entry visa £15, multiple-entry £18.

USA 3521 International Court NW, Washington DC 20008 ⓣ202/895-5400, ⓦwww.egyptembassy.us (Mon–Fri 9.30am–1pm); 1110 Second Ave, Suite 201, New York, NY 10022 ⓣ212/759-7120 to 22, ⓦwww.egyptnyc.net (applications Mon–Fri 9am–noon, collection 1.30–2pm); 3001 Pacific Ave, San Francisco, CA 94115–1013 ⓣ415/346-9700, ⓦwww.egy2000.com (Mon–Fri 9.30am–2.30pm); 500 N Michigan Ave, Suite 1900, Chicago, IL 60611 ⓣ312/828-9162 to 4 (Mon–Fri 9.30am–12.30pm); 1990 Post Oak Blvd, Suite 2180, Houston, TX 77056 ⓣ713/961-4915 or 6 (applications 9.30am–12.30pm, collection 2–2.30pm, 2–3 days to issue). Visas cost US$15 for US nationals, US$20–110 for others (though free for South Africans).

Israeli passport stamps

At the time of writing, most Arab countries except Egypt and Jordan will deny entry to anyone whose passport shows evidence of a visit to Israel. This applies in particular to Syria, Lebanon, Libya and Sudan. Although Israeli immigration officials will usually give you an entry stamp on a separate piece of paper if you ask them to, an Egyptian entry stamp at Taba or Rafah in the Sinai will give you away – and the Egyptians insist on stamping your passport. So if you are travelling around the Middle East, be sure to visit Israel *after* you have been to Syria, Lebanon, or wherever. If you enter Egypt from Israel with the intention of travelling on to Libya or Sudan, you are going to have big problems trying to get an onward visa. Even if you have more than one passport, and apply for your Sudanese or Libyan visa on a passport with no Egyptian entry stamp, the embassy will want to know why it doesn't have one. Similarly, if you trade your old passport and get a new one issued by your embassy in Cairo, it is unlikely to pass muster with the Sudanese or Libyan authorities.

Passport precautions

Once in Egypt, you should always carry your passport with you: you'll need it to register at hotels, change money, collect mail, and possibly to show at police checkpoints. If you're travelling for any length of time, you may find it worthwhile to register with your embassy on arrival in Cairo, which will help speed things up if you lose your passport. At the least, it's a wise precaution to photocopy the pages recording your particulars and keep them separately. If you are travelling to areas of the country that require permits, spare sets of photocopies are useful for producing with your application.

Overstaying, extensions and travel permits

Tourists who **overstay** their (regular) visa are allowed a fifteen-day period of grace in which to renew it or leave the country. After this, they're fined £E104 unless they can present a letter of apology from their embassy (which may well cost more).

Visa **extensions** cost around £E12.50, and are obtainable from the Mugamma in Cairo (see p.289) or from passport offices in governorate capitals such as Alexandria, Luxor, Aswan, Suez, El-Tor, Mersa Matrouh and Ismailiya (passport office addresses are detailed under their respective entries). Depending on how long you wish to extend by, and on the whim of the official, you may have to produce exchange or ATM receipts proving that you've cashed sufficient hard currency during your stay, and you'll need to supply one or two photos. Procedures vary slightly from office to office, but shouldn't take longer than an hour outside Cairo.

If you have a single-entry visa and want to leave Egypt and return within the period of its validity, you will need a re-entry visa. Procedures for obtaining these are much the same as for a visa extension, and the cost is around £E14.

Whilst you can travel without restriction through most areas of Egypt, **travel permits** are required for the Red Sea Coast beyond Mersa Alam, for desert travel between Bahariya and Siwa oases (permits available in Siwa), to Ain Della and the Gilf Kebir/Jebel Uwaynat (permits available in Cairo only), as well as sometimes – depending on relations with Libya – between Mersa Matrouh and the border. Permits take from five to fourteen days to process, and Misr Travel (1 Sharia Talaat Harb; ☎02/393 0010, ✉misrtrav@link.com.eg) may be able to help obtain them for some restricted areas;

otherwise you'll need to apply to the military, who are best approached via the tourist police (see p.85). Other border areas may also become problematic, so if you're thinking of visiting such areas, check beforehand. For further information, contact the tourist police in Cairo (see p.85).

Customs

Egyptian **customs** allows you to bring in 200 cigarettes (or 250g of tobacco) and two litres of alcohol. Both Cairo and Luxor airports have duty-free shops for arriving passengers before *and* after customs, and you can buy up to two more litres of spirits and a case of two dozen cans of beer at the duty-free shop after customs clearance on arrival or within 48 hours. If you don't want to buy at the airport, or if you enter by land, you can get the same allowance, for about a dollar a bottle more, at duty-free shops in Cairo, Alexandria, Port Said, Luxor, Aswan, Sharm el-Sheikh, Nuweiba and Hurghada. There is a black market for this duty-free booze, but scams abound (see p.287), so beware.

Though personal effects and cameras are exempt from **duty**, items such as electronic equipment and video cameras should in theory be declared and listed on a Form D. If you lose them during your visit, they will be assumed "sold" when you come to leave and (unless you have police documentation of theft) you will have to pay 100 percent duty. On items with a high resale value (for example, laptop computers or video cameras) you may be required to pay a deposit against possible duty charges, which is refundable on departure. If customs insists on impounding goods, get a receipt and contact your consulate. Customs duty is also likely to be payable on goods posted to you from abroad, which may be impounded at the post office (without notice to you) until it is paid.

Information, websites and maps

In addition to this book, readily available sources of information include the Egyptian Tourist Authority (which has offices abroad and in Egypt), the Internet, travel agencies, hotels and local, often self-appointed, guides (see p.82).

Tourist offices

The Egyptian Tourist Authority (sometimes abbreviated as EGAPT) maintains general information offices in several countries (see below), where you can pick up a range of pamphlets. However, most are simply intended to whet your appetite, and few hard facts can be gained from offices abroad.

In Egypt itself, you'll get a variable response from local tourist offices (addresses are given throughout the guide). The most knowledgeable and helpful ones are in Aswan, Luxor, Alexandria, and the oases of Siwa and Dakhla. Staff in Cairo are also well informed, but may need prodding. Elsewhere, most provincial offices are good for a dated brochure, if nothing else. As often as not, the level of knowledge and the quality of advice you receive may depend on who exactly you speak to: in some cases (detailed in the text), we recommend contacting a specific member of staff who speaks good English and is well informed about hotels, transport and similar matters.

Egyptian tourist offices abroad

Canada 1253 McGill College Ave, Suite 250, Montreal, PQ H3B 2Y5 ☏514/861-4420, ✆eta@total.net.
Greece 10, Amerikis St, 6th floor, 10671 Athens ☏01/360 6906.
South Africa 1st Floor, Regent Palace Building, Mutual Gdns, Cradock Ave, Rosebank, Johannesburg, PO Box 6298 ☏11/880 9602/3.
UK 170 Piccadilly, London W1V 9DD ☏020/7493 5283.
USA 630 Fifth Ave, Suite 1706, New York, NY 10111 ☏212/332-2570, ✆egyptoursp@aol.com; 8383 Wilshire Blvd, Suite 215, Beverly Hills, CA 90211 ☏323/653-8815, ✆egypt@etala.com; 645 N Michigan Ave, Suite 829, Chicago, IL 60611 ☏312/280-4666.

Travel agencies and hotels

Found in towns and cities, travel agencies can advise on (and book) transport, accommodation and excursions, though as private businesses their advice may not be exactly unbiased.

The most ubiquitous agency is Misr Travel, the state-run tourist company, which operates hotels, buses and limos and can make bookings for most things. Its head office is in Cairo (1 Sharia Talaat Harb ☏02/750-0010, ✆tourism@misrtravel.net), with a walk-in office just up the street (7 Sharia Talaat Harb), and branches in Alexandria, Luxor, Aswan, Port Said, Suez, Hurghada, El Arish, Sharm el-Sheikh and Taba. Misr Travel is also represented in London (2nd floor, 308 Regent St, W1B 3AT ☏020/7255 1087) and New York (630 Fifth Ave, Suite 1460, New York, NY 10011 ☏1-800/223-4978 or 212/582-9210-1). American Express and Thomas Cook (see pp.58–59) also offer various travel services besides currency exchange.

Receptionists at hotels can also be a source of information, and maybe practical assistance. In Luxor, Hurghada and some of the Western Desert oases, most *pensions* double as information exchanges and all-round "fixers", as do campsites and back-packers' hotels in Sinai.

Tourist publications

The best guide to **what's on** can be found in the monthly magazine *Egypt Today*, which lists activities, entertainment and exhibitions in Cairo and Alexandria, and events in Luxor and Aswan. Its features cover diverse aspects of Egyptian culture and travel in Egypt. It's sold in Cairo and Alexandria. Selected events are also listed in the daily

Egyptian Gazette, and the weekly English-language edition of *Al-Ahram*, which are more widely available (see also p.77).

Useful websites

Government advice UK Foreign Office Ⓦ www.fco.gov.uk; US State Department Ⓦ travel.state.gov; Canadian Foreign Affairs Department Ⓦ www.dfait-maeci.gc.ca.; Australian Foreign Affairs Department Ⓦ www.dfat.gov.au/geo/egypt/index.html/. The latest information and advice on travel in Egypt put out by Western governments for their citizens, sometimes over-cautious, but well-informed, regularly updated, and always worth reading before making travel plans, and again before departure.

Egyptian National Tourist Organization Ⓦ www.egypttreasures.gov.eg. A good overview of Egypt's tourist attractions, with sections on pharaonic and Coptic Egypt, as well as diving, golf, other sports and even health spas.

Egyptian Tourist Office in the Americas Ⓦ www.egypttourism.org. Aimed at tourists from North America, covering the major sights, and illustrating them with a "slideshow". Handy features include a list of diving centres, sound and light show schedules, a short page of links, and – if it isn't out of date – a calendar of events.

The Official Ministry of Tourism Site Ⓦ www.touregypt.net. Far more informative than the Egyptian National Tourist Organization site, well put-together and jam-packed with useful information, including details of all the main tourist attractions, listings of hotels, nightclubs and Internet cafés, plus travel articles, a virtual dive centre, and even a page that will translate your name into hieroglyphics.

Egypt Links Ⓦ ce.eng.usf.edu/pharos. The biggest list of links to websites about Egypt, covering a huge variety of topics including tourism, art and culture, dive sites, history, politics, business, and towns and regions of the country. Unfortunately this massive garden of sites is not weeded too often, and half of them turn out to be off-line.

Guardian's Egypt Ⓦ www.guardians.net/egypt. An excellent non-commercial site run by an American Egypt enthusiast, and a good one to visit for information on Ancient Egypt and the latest archeological finds. Features include a virtual tour of the pyramids at Giza and Dahshur, inside and out, plus everything you ever wanted to know about mummies, and masses of links.

Rigby's World of Egypt Ⓦ homepage.powerup.com.au/~ancient. A personal website put up by an Australian Egypt enthusiast, with photographs and features including an interesting article on the curse of Tutankhamun, a feature on people's lives in ancient Egypt, translations of ancient Egyptian love poetry, and paintings by the proprietor's artist father, who was also an Egypt enthusiast.

Egyptology Resources Ⓦ www.newton.cam.ac.uk/egypt. If you're serious about Egyptology, this site from the Newton Institute in Cambridge has helpful academic articles and links, plus an Egyptology FAQ, latest Egyptology news, and listings of booksellers, publishers, organizations and museums specializing in Ancient Egypt.

Egyptology On Line Ⓦ www.egyptologyonline.com. A potted Egyptology site for laypeople, with features on famous pharaohs, famous Egyptologists, the main Egyptian gods and the most important pyramids.

Paranormal Egyptology Ⓦ paranormal.about.com/cs/ancientegypt. Links to pages on assorted unorthodox theories about the Sphinx and the Pyramids, from the one that they were part of Atlantis to the one that they were built by Martians.

Egypt Today Ⓦ www.egypttoday.com. One of Egypt's best monthly English-language magazines, with news and features about arts and culture plus reviews of restaurants, films and events.

Al-Ahram Ⓦ weekly.ahram.org.eg. The weekly edition of Al-Ahram, Egypt's main newspaper, online in English, for the latest Egyptian news, and an Egyptian take on the Middle East and the world.

Amnesty International Ⓦ web.amnesty.org/library/eng-egy/index. Amnesty's latest reports on human rights and prisoners of conscience in Egypt – a stark reminder that Egypt is no democracy.

Egyptian Organization for Human Rights Ⓦ www.eohr.org. Further articles about the human rights situation from a Cairo-based NGO.

Digital Freedom Network Ⓦ www.dfn.org. An international anti-censorship site, containing articles from the *Middle East Times* that were cut under government orders – to find them, type "Egypt" into the search box on the left of the screen.

Egyptian Presidency Ⓦ www.presidency.gov.eg. Mubarak's own website, where you can see interior views of his palaces.

Go Red Sea Ⓦ www.goredsea.com. An excellent site on Red Sea diving, with maps and detailed information on dive locations, resorts and hotels, plus a magazine section and online hotel booking.

Egyptian Football Ⓦ www.egyptiansoccer.com. Latest major match results and reports from Egypt's football (soccer) league, plus league tables and information on the country's top clubs and national team.

Weather Report Ⓦ weather.noaa.gov/weather/EG_cc.html. The US government National Weather Service page on Egypt, giving the latest weather conditions in Cairo, Alexandria, Aswan, Hurghada, Luxor, Mersa Matrouh, Port Said, Sharm el-Sheikh and Taba.

Maps

The best general **map** of Egypt is published by Rough Guides on a scale of 1:1,250,000, on durable, tear-proof paper, with roads, railways and contours clearly marked; Freytag & Berndt's (1:1,000,000) is a good second-best, and like the Rough Guide map, it is sold at most good map shops abroad. In Egypt it is published by Al-Ahram, but is not easy to find. Kümmerly & Frey (1:950,000; published in Egypt by Lenhert & Landrock) makes a reasonable alternative, as does the more widespread Bartholomew map (1:1,000,000; also published in Egypt by Lenhert & Landrock), though this shows rather less detail. If you plan to do any serious motoring, the Shell/AA Road Atlas of Egypt covers the country comprehensively, with 1:500,000 maps of the Nile Valley and Delta, and 1:1,000,000 maps of the rest of the country, though it was last updated in 1996. Along with many of the maps mentioned above, it is available from good bookshops in Cairo (see p.286) and sometimes elsewhere in the country.

Taken together, several local **city plans** cover Cairo in comprehensive detail (see pp.109–110). Elsewhere, however, coverage is poor or non-existent. Aside from fairly crude maps of Alexandria, Luxor, Aswan, Hurghada and Port Said, and photocopied handouts in Mersa Matrouh and Siwa Oasis, there are no town plans to be had. Those in this book are as good as any. **Diving maps** of the Red Sea are available in Egypt, but some of these do not cover sites in the Sinai, which for most people is the main diving area.

Full-blown **desert expeditions** require detailed maps that can be obtained in Cairo from the Survey Office (*heyat al-misaha*) on Sharia Abdel Salam Arif at the corner of Sharia Giza (Sun–Thurs 9am–1.30pm; see map p.211 for location), though they may demand an official letter explaining why you need the maps. Geological maps can be obtained without bureaucratic obstruction (but bring your passport) from the Geological Survey and Mining Authority (*misaha wa geologia*) at 3 Sharia Salah Salem, Abbassiya, about 500m south of Midan Abbassiya and Sinai bus terminal (Sun–Thurs 9am–3pm; ☎02/628 8013).

Map outlets

In the UK and Ireland

Stanfords 12–14 Long Acre, London WC2E 9LP ☎020/7836 1321, ⓦwww.stanfords.co.uk. Maps available by mail order, phone or email. Also at 39 Spring Gardens, Manchester M2 2BG ☎0161/831 0250; and 29 Corn St, Bristol BS1 1HT ☎0117/929 9966.
Blackwell's Map Centre 50 Broad St, Oxford OX1 3BQ ☎01865/793 550, ⓦmaps.blackwell.co.uk. Branches in Bristol, Cambridge, Cardiff, Leeds, Liverpool, Newcastle, Reading and Sheffield.
The Map Shop 30a Belvoir St, Leicester LE1 6QH ☎0116/247 1400, ⓦwww.mapshopleicester.co.uk.
National Map Centre 22–24 Caxton St, London SW1H 0QU ☎020/7222 2466, ⓦwww.mapstore .co.uk.
National Map Centre Ireland 34 Aungier St, Dublin 2 ☎01/476 0471, ⓦwww.mapcentre.ie.
The Travel Bookshop 13–15 Blenheim Crescent, London W11 2EE ☎020/7229 5260, ⓦwww .thetravelbookshop.co.uk.
Traveller 55 Grey St, Newcastle-upon-Tyne NE1 6EF ☎ 0191/261 5622, ⓦwww.newtraveller.com.

In the USA and Canada

110 North Latitude US ☎336/369-4171, ⓦwww.110nlatitude.com.
Book Passage 51 Tamal Vista Blvd, Corte Madera, CA 94925; and in the San Francisco Ferry Building ☎1-800/999-7909 or ☎415/927-0960, ⓦwww .bookpassage.com.
Distant Lands 56 S Raymond Ave, Pasadena, CA 91105 ☎1-800/310-3220, ⓦwww.distantlands .com.
Globe Corner Bookstore 28 Church St, Cambridge, MA 02138 ☎1-800/358-6013, ⓦwww.globecorner.com.
Longitude Books 115 W 30th St #1206, New York, NY 10001 ☎1-800/342-2164, ⓦwww .longitudebooks.com.
Map Town 400 5 Ave SW #100, Calgary, AB T2P 0L6 ☎1-877/921-6277 or ☎403/266-2241, ⓦwww.maptown.com.
The Travel Bug Bookstore 3065 W Broadway, Vancouver, BC V6K 2G9 ☎604/737-1122, ⓦwww .travelbugbooks.ca.
World of Maps 1235 Wellington St, Ottawa, ON K1Y 3A3 ☎1-800/214-8524 or ☎613/724-6776, ⓦwww.worldofmaps.com.

In Australia and New Zealand

Mapland 372 Little Bourke St, Melbourne, Vic 3000 ☎03/9670 4383, ⓦwww.mapland.com.au.

Map Shop 6–10 Peel St, Adelaide, SA 5000 ☏08/8231 2033, ⓦwww.mapshop.net.au.
Map World (Australia) 371 Pitt St, Sydney, NSW 2000 ☏03/02/9261 3601, ⓦwww.mapworld .net.au. Also at 65 Northbourne Ave, Canberra, ACT

2601 ☏02/6230 4097; and 1981 Logan Road, Brisbane, Qld 4122 ☏07/3349 6633.
Map World (NZ) 173 Gloucester St, Christchurch, New Zealand ☏0800/627 967, ⓦwww.mapworld .co.nz.

Insurance

Travel insurance can buy you peace of mind as well as save you money. Before paying for a new policy, however, it's worth checking whether you are already covered: some all-risks home insurance policies may cover your possessions when overseas, and many private medical schemes include cover when abroad. In Canada, provincial health plans usually provide partial cover for medical mishaps overseas, while holders of official student/teacher/youth cards in Canada and the US are entitled to meagre accident coverage and hospital in-patient benefits. Students will often find that their student health coverage extends during the vacations and for one term beyond the date of last enrolment.

After exhausting the possibilities above, you might want to contact a specialist travel insurance company. A typical policy usually provides cover for the loss of baggage, tickets and – up to a certain limit – cash or cheques, as well as cancellation or curtailment of your journey. Most exclude so-called dangerous sports unless an extra premium is paid. This can include scuba-diving, and you should be sure if you intend to do any diving that your policy covers you for it:

treatment in a recompression chamber can cost US$1000 a day.

Many policies can be chopped and changed to exclude coverage you don't need – for example, sickness and accident benefits can often be excluded or included at will. If you do take medical coverage, ascertain whether benefits will be paid as treatment proceeds or only after return home, and whether there is a 24-hour medical emergency number. When securing

Rough Guides travel insurance

Rough Guides has teamed up with Columbus Direct to offer you **travel insurance** that can be tailored to suit your needs.

Readers can choose from many different travel insurance products, including a low-cost **backpacker** option for long stays; a **short break** option for city getaways; a typical **holiday package** option; and many others. There are also annual **multi-trip** policies for those who travel regularly, with variable levels of cover available. Different sports and activities (trekking, skiing, etc) can be covered if required on most policies.

Rough Guides travel insurance is available to the residents of 36 different countries with different language options to choose from via our website – ⓦwww.roughguidesinsurance.com – where you can also purchase the insurance.

Alternatively, UK residents should call ☏0800/083 9507; US citizens should call ☏1-800/749-4922; Australians should call ☏1-300/669999. All other nationalities should call ☏+44 870/890 2843.

baggage cover, make sure that the per-article limit – typically under £500/US$900 – will cover your most valuable possession. If you need to make a claim, you should keep receipts for medicines and medical treatment, and in the event you have anything stolen, you must obtain an official theft report from the police (called a *mahdar*).

Health

Despite the potential health hazards of travel in Egypt, the majority of visitors experience nothing worse than a bout or two of diarrhoea. For minor health complaints, a visit to a pharmacy is likely to be sufficient. Egyptian pharmacists are well trained and dispense a wide range of drugs, including many normally on prescription in Europe. If they feel you need a full diagnosis, they can usually recommend a doctor – sometimes working on the premises. Most doctors speak English or French.

Although the change of diet and climate accounts for most health problems, individual responses vary. While some people adapt quickly to the heat and consume local food with impunity, others get sick and stay poorly (children and the elderly are likely to suffer the worst effects). If you're only here for a week or two, it makes sense to be cautious, but longer-staying visitors might prefer to get ill early, acclimatize, and worry less thereafter – a lot depends on your constitution. Bearing this in mind, take whatever precautions seem appropriate.

For comprehensive coverage of the health problems encountered by travellers worldwide, consult the *Rough Guide to Travel Health* by Dr Nick Jones.

Medical resources for travellers

Websites

ⓦ **health.yahoo.com** Information on specific diseases and conditions, drugs and herbal remedies, as well as advice from health experts.
ⓦ **www.cdc.gov** The US government's official site for travel health.
ⓦ **www.fitfortravel.scot.nhs.uk** Scottish NHS website carrying information about travel-related diseases and how to avoid them.
ⓦ **www.istm.org** The website of the International Society for Travel Medicine, with a full list of clinics

specializing in international travel health. Publishes outbreak warnings, suggested inoculations, precautions and other background information for travellers.
ⓦ **www.tmvc.com.au** Contains a list of all Travellers Medical and Vaccination Centres throughout Australia, New Zealand and Southeast Asia, plus general information on travel health.
ⓦ **www.tripprep.com** Travel Health Online provides an online-only comprehensive database of necessary vaccinations for most countries, as well as destination and medical service provider information.

In the US and Canada

Canadian Society for International Health 1 Nicholas St, Suite 1105, Ottawa, ON K1N 7B7 ☎613/241-5785, ⓦwww.csih.org. Distributes a free pamphlet, "Health Information for Canadian Travellers", containing an extensive list of travel health centres in Canada.
Centers for Disease Control 1600 Clifton Rd NE, Atlanta, GA 30333 ☎1-800/311-3435 or 404/639-3534, ⓦwww.cdc.gov. Publishes outbreak warnings, suggested inoculations, precautions and other information for travellers. Useful website plus International Travelers Hotline on ☎1-877/FYI-TRIP.
International Association for Medical Assistance to Travellers (IAMAT) 417 Center St, Lewiston, NY 14092 ☎716/754-4883, ⓦwww .iamat.org, and 1287 St. Clair Avenue West, Suite #1, Toronto, Ontario M6E 1B8 ☎416/652-0137. A non-profit organization supported by donations, it can provide a list of English-speaking doctors in Egypt,

climate charts and leaflets on various diseases and inoculations.

International SOS Assistance Eight Neshaminy Interplex Suite 207, Trevose, PA 19053-6956 ☎1-800/523-8930, ⓦwww.intsos.com. Members receive pre-trip medical referral info, as well as overseas emergency services designed to complement travel insurance coverage.

MEDJET Assistance ☎1-800/963-3538 or ☎205/595-6658, ⓦwww.medjetassistance.com. Annual membership program for travellers ($195 for individuals, $295 for families) that, in the event of illness or injury, will fly members home or to the hospital of their choice in a medically equipped and staffed jet.

Travel Medicine ☎1-800/872-8633, ⓦwww.travmed.com. Sells first-aid kits, mosquito nets, water filters, reference books and other health-related travel products.

In the UK and Ireland

British Airways Travel Clinics 156 Regent St, London W1 (Mon–Fri 9.30am–6pm, Sat 10am–5pm, no appointment necessary; ☎0845/600 2236); 101 Cheapside, London EC2 (Mon–Fri 9am–4.45pm, appointment required; ☎0845/600 2236); ⓦwww.britishairways.com/travel/healthclinintro. Vaccinations, advice from an online database and a complete range of travel healthcare products.

Dun Laoghaire Medical Centre 5 Northumberland Ave, Dun Laoghaire, County Dublin ☎01/280 4996, ⓕ01/280 5603. Advice on medical matters abroad.

Hospital for Tropical Diseases Travel Clinic 2nd floor, Mortimer Market Centre, off Capper St, London WC1E 6AU (Mon–Fri 9am–5pm by appointment only) ☎020/7388 9600, ⓦwww.masta.org. Consultations cost £15, which is waived if you have your injections here, and there's a recorded Health Line (☎0906/133 7733; 50p per min) giving advice on hygiene and illness prevention as well as appropriate immunizations.

Liverpool School of Tropical Medicine Pembroke Place, Liverpool L3 5QA ☎0151/708 9393, ⓦwww.liv.ac.uk/lstm/lstm. Walk-in clinic Mon–Fri 1–4pm; appointment required for yellow fever, but not for other jabs.

MASTA (Medical Advisory Service for Travellers Abroad) Forty regional clinics (call ☎0870/6062782 for the nearest). Also operates a pre-recorded 24-hour Travellers' Health Line (UK ☎0906/822 4100, 60p per min), giving written information tailored to your journey by return of post.

Nomad Pharmacy 40 Bernard St, London, WC1N 1LE; and 3-4 Wellington Terrace, Turnpike Lane, London N8 0PX (Mon–Fri 9.30am–6pm,

☎020/7833 4114 to book vaccination appointment). They give free advice tailored to your travel needs if you go in person, or call the helpline (☎0906/863 3414; 60p per min).

Travel Health Centre Department of International Health and Tropical Medicine, Royal College of Surgeons in Ireland, Mercers Medical Centre, Stephen's St Lower, Dublin 2 ☎01/402 2337. Expert pre-trip advice and inoculations.

Travel Medicine Services PO Box 254, 16 College St, Belfast BT1 6BT ☎028/9031 5220. Offers medical advice before a trip and help afterwards in the event of a tropical disease.

In Australia and New Zealand

Travellers' Medical and Vaccination Centres 27–29 Gilbert Place, Adelaide, SA 5000 ☎08/8212 7522, ⓦwww.tmvc.com.au; 1/170 Queen St, Auckland ☎09/373 3531; 5/247 Adelaide St, Brisbane, Qld 4000 ☎07/3221 9066; 5/8–10 Hobart Place, Canberra, ACT 2600 ☎02/6257 7156; 270 Sandy Bay Rd, Sandy Bay, Tas, Habart; 7005 ☎03/6223 7577, 2/393; Little Bourke St, Melbourne, Vic 3000 ☎03/9602 5788; Level 7, Dymocks Bldg, 428 George St, Sydney, NSW 2000 ☎02/9221 7133; and Shop 15, Grand Arcade, 14–16 Willis St, Wellington ☎04/473 0991.

Preventative medicine

Unless you're coming from an infected area there are no compulsory **inoculations** for Egypt, though you should always be up to date with polio and tetanus. It's also worth being vaccinated against typhoid, which occasionally flares up in parts of Egypt – although the cholera shot is generally acknowledged to be worthless. If you're planning to visit southern Egypt, Sudan or sub-Saharan Africa, the meningitis vaccination is essential, as is yellow fever, which may well be a legal requirement. Though all these vaccinations can be obtained in Cairo (see p.293), it is vital to ensure that sterile needles are used. If necessary, supply your own disposable syringe, sold at pharmacies.

While not an issue for most tourists, visitors planning to stay a long time in Egypt or the Middle East should consider vaccination against hepatitis. The Hepatitis A (Havrix monodose) shot is expensive at about £50/US$90 (though your doctor may provide it free), but with a booster a year later it lasts for ten years. Hepatitis B is transmitted like HIV, through body fluids, so you will be protected from it by the same precautions that you take against HIV infection (see pp.53–54); immunization is only really necessary for medical workers.

Other precautions are fairly obvious, with the most common preventable ailments being heatstroke (see opposite) and **food poisoning**. Rare meat and raw shellfish top the danger list, which descends via creamy sauces down to salads, juices, raw fruit and vegetables – and if slavishly followed would prevent you from eating most of what's on offer. Visitors who insist on washing everything (and only cleaning their teeth) in mineral water are overreacting. Just use common sense, and accustom your stomach gradually to Egyptian cooking. Asking for dishes to be served very hot (*sukhna awi*) will reduce the risk of catching anything. Take prompt care of cuts and skin irritations, since flies can quickly spread infections. Anthisan cream (available abroad) is good for bites, swellings and rashes.

Pharmacies, doctors and hospitals

Pharmacies, found in every town, form the advance guard of Egypt's health service. Pharmacists usually speak English and can dispense most drugs without a prescription. Private **doctors** are equally common, but charge for consultations: expect to pay about £E100 (roughly £9/US$17) a session, excluding the price of any drugs you are prescribed. If you get seriously ill, private **hospitals** are generally preferable to public-sector ones. Those attached to universities are usually well equipped and competent, but small-town hospitals are often abysmal. Many hospitals (*mustashfa*) require a deposit at the very least, and often payment on the spot; you will then have to claim it back from your insurance provider. Despite several good hospitals in Cairo and Alexandria, Egypt is no country to fall seriously ill in. In particular, if you need surgery, it is best to get back home for it if you can.

Health hazards

The **tap water** in Egyptian towns and cities is heavily chlorinated and mostly safe to drink but is unpalatable and rough on tender stomachs. In rural areas, Sinai campsites

and desert rest-houses there's a fair risk of contaminated water. Consequently, most tourists stick to bottled mineral water, which is widely available, tastes better, and won't upset sensitive stomachs. However, excessive fear of tap water is unjustified and hard to sustain in practice if you're here for long. Once your stomach has adjusted, it's usually okay to drink it without further purification (Halazone tablets, iodine crystals, or by boiling).

What you should avoid is any contact with stagnant water that might harbour **bilharzia** (schistosomiasis) flukes. Irrigation canals and the slower stretches of the River Nile are notoriously infested with these minute worms, which breed in the blood vessels of the abdomen and liver (the main symptom is blood in the urine). Don't drink or swim there, nor walk barefoot in the mud, or even on grass that's wet with Nile water. But it's okay to bathe in the saline pools of the desert oases.

Heat and dust

Many visitors experience problems with Egypt's intense heat, particularly in the south. Because sweat evaporates immediately in the dry atmosphere, you can easily become dehydrated without realizing it. **Dehydration** is exacerbated by both alcohol and caffeine. Drink plenty of other fluids (at least three litres per day; twice as much if you're exerting yourself) and take a bit of extra salt with your food. Wear a hat and loose-fitting clothes (not synthetic fabrics), and a high-factor sunscreen to protect yourself from sunburn, especially during summer. Try to avoid going out in the middle of the day and wear a T-shirt when snorkelling, as the sun burns you even quicker in the water.

Heat exhaustion – signified by headaches, dizziness and nausea – is treated by resting in a cool place and drinking plenty of water or juice with a pinch of salt. An intense headache, heightened body temperature, flushed skin and the cessation of sweating are symptoms of **heatstroke**, which can be fatal if not treated immediately. The whole body must be cooled by immersion in tepid water, or the application of wet towels. Seek medical assistance. If walking for long distances in the sun, it is vital to carry drinking water and wear a sunhat; a cotton sunhat can also be drenched with water, wrung to stop it dripping, and worn wet so that the evaporation of the water cools your head – you'll be amazed at how quickly it dries out.

Less seriously, visitors from cooler climates may suffer from **prickly heat**, an itchy rash caused by excessive perspiration trapped beneath the skin. Wearing loose clothing, keeping cool and bathing often will help relieve the symptoms until your body acclimatizes.

In non-air-conditioned environments, you might employ the traditional Egyptian method of sprinkling water on the ground to cool the surrounding area by evaporation – it also levels the dust.

Desert **dust** – or grit and smog in Cairo – may cause your eyes to itch and water. Contact lens-users should wear glasses instead, at least part of the time. If ordinary eye drops don't help, try antihistamine decongestant eye drops such as Vernacel, Vascon-A or Optihist. Persistent irritation may indicate trachoma, a contagious infection which is easily cured by antibiotics at an early stage, but eventually causes blindness if left untreated. Its prevalence in Egypt explains the number of older folk with cloudy eyes and the ophthalmologists in every town.

Spending time in the desert, you might find that your sinuses get painfully irritated by wind-borne dust. Covering your nose and mouth with a scarf helps prevent this, while olbas oil or a nasal decongestant spray (available at pharmacies) can relieve the symptoms.

Diarrhoea and worse...

Almost every visitor to Egypt gets **diarrhoea** at some stage. Unless you're stricken by cramps, the best initial treatment is to simply adapt your diet, using drugs only as a last resort. Plain boiled rice and vegetables are the best things to eat, and you should try to avoid greasy or spicy food, caffeine, alcohol, and most fruit and dairy products (although some say that bananas and prickly pears can help, while yoghurt provides a form of protein that your body can easily absorb). Most importantly, keep your bodily fluids topped up by drinking plenty of bottled water (perhaps mixed with a rehydration sachet or, failing that, salt and sugar). Drugs like Imodium or Lomotil will plug you up,

undermining your body's efforts to rid itself of infection, but can be handy as a stop-gap measure if you have to travel. Avoid Enterovioform, which is still available in Egypt despite being suspected of damaging the optic nerve. Antinal (nifuroxazide) is widely prescribed against diarrhoea in Egypt, and available over the counter in pharmacies, but should not be used for more than a couple of days. Don't give any of these quite powerful drugs to children. Also note that having diarrhoea can make drugs less effective if taken orally (contraceptive pills for example), as they pass straight through your system without being absorbed.

If symptoms persist longer than a few days, or if you develop a fever or pass blood in your faeces, get medical help immediately, since diarrhoea can also be a symptom of serious infection. Accompanied by vomiting and fever, it may indicate **typhoid**, which responds well to antibiotics. Rarer is **cholera**, which requires urgent treatment with antibiotics and rehydration fluids; it is marked by a sudden onset of acute diarrhoea and cramps, and tends to occur in epidemics rather than isolated cases. Except for the "rice-water shits" typical of cholera, similar symptoms occur with bacilliary **dysentery**, which is treated with antibiotics. Amoebic dysentery is harder to shift and can cause permanent damage if untreated. The normal remedy is the heavy-duty antibiotic metronidazole (Flagyl), which should only be taken under medical supervision.

Rabies and malaria

Rabies is endemic in Egypt, where many wild animals (including bats, sometimes found in temples, tombs and caves) carry the disease. Avoid touching *any* strange animal, wild or domestic. Treatment must be given between exposure to the disease and the onset of symptoms; once these appear, rabies is invariably fatal. If you think you've been exposed, return home and seek help immediately.

Currently resurgent throughout Africa, **malaria**, spread by the anopheles mosquito, could become a problem in Egypt in the future, but isn't currently a threat – it does exist during the summer months in the Fayoum, but not to the extent that warrants the use of malaria pills, although you should take extra steps to avoid mosquito bites while you are there (use repellent and cover bare skin, especially feet and ankles, after dusk – see below). Consult your doctor, or enquire at a Medical Advisory Service in the UK (see p.50) for the latest information on malaria risk and prevention. The first signs of infection are muscular soreness and a low fever; four to eight days later, the characteristic bouts of chills and fever appear. If you suspect that you have it, seek treatment immediately.

Mosquitoes and bugs

Even without the risk of malaria, **mosquitoes** can make your life a misery. Horribly ubiquitous over the summer, these blood-sucking pests are never entirely absent. The only solution is total war, using fans, mosquito coils, rub-on repellent, and perhaps a plug-in Ezalo device, sold at pharmacies. A lot of people in Egypt use citronella oil, obtainable from many pharmacies, as a mosquito repellent, but tests have shown it to be much less effective than repellents containing DEET (diethyltoluamide), which are the ones recommended by medical authorities. X-gnat skin gel is an effective natural alternative. You can also reputedly make yourself less attractive to mosquitoes by taking Vitamin B-12 tablets, starting before you leave home. The theory is that after two weeks of 50mg per day, your blood begins to smell bad to them, but again, medical authorities in general are sceptical. The best guarantee of a bite-less night's sleep is to bring a mosquito net to hang from above your bed (if you bring the sort that can be suspended from a single point, you can usually find ways of tying a string across the room to hang it from, but don't forget to pack a long enough piece of string). Mosquitoes favour shady, damp areas, and anywhere around dusk. Feet are the part of the body that most attracts them, and you should always be sure to put repellent on your ankles if they are uncovered when you go out in the evening.

Equally loathsome – and widespread – are **flies**, which transmit various diseases. Only insecticide spray or air conditioning offers any protection. Some cheap hotels harbour fleas, scabies, mites, giant roaches and other bugs. Consult a pharmacist if you find yourself with a persistent skin irritation.

Scorpions and snakes

The danger from scorpions and snakes is minimal, as most species are nocturnal, hide during the heat of the day, and generally avoid people. However, you shouldn't go barefoot, turn over rocks or stick your hands into dark crevices anywhere off the beaten track. Whereas the sting of larger, darker **scorpions** is no worse than a bad wasp sting, the venom of the pale, slender-clawed *Buthridae* is highly toxic. If stung, cold-pack the affected area and seek medical help immediately.

Egypt has two main types of poisonous snake. Vipers vary in colour from sandy to reddish (or sometimes grey) and leave two fang punctures. The horned **viper**, Egypt's deadliest snake, is recognizable by its horns. Cobras are recognizable by their distinctive hood and bite mark (a single row of teeth plus fang holes). The smaller Egyptian **cobra** (coloured sandy olive) is found throughout the country; the longer black-necked cobra (which can spit its venom up to three metres) only in the south. Be somewhat reassured that snakes come out to drink usually at night, and hibernate in the winter. All snake-bites should be washed immediately. Stay calm, as panicking sends the venom through your bloodstream more quickly, and get immediate medical help.

HIV and AIDS

Despite a TV campaign, the level of **AIDS** awareness is low, and most Egyptians still perceive it as a Western problem. Tourists likewise may not think of Egypt as the sort of country that would have an AIDS problem, but the few hundred cases reported here are almost certainly the tip of an iceberg. Prostitution, homosexuality and extra-marital sex in general are so clandestine and taboo that levels of education about them are low, and few Egyptian men take any precautions. As throughout the world, the need for extreme caution, and safe sex, cannot be over-stressed. This particularly applies to Western women having a fling in places like Luxor (see box pp.364–365), who may not be aware of just how much of an industry that is. Anyone of either sex or orientation, contemplating any kind of casual affair, whether with Egyptians or with fellow tourists, should always carry **condoms** and insist on using them. Likewise, be absolutely sure that any injections, tattooing or acupuncture is done with sterile instruments, and that barbers use a new blade if you go to them for a shave. It's also best to avoid having a blood transfusion in Egypt if at all possible. Pharmacies in cities plus a few shops in Hurghada and Sinai are the only places in Egypt to sell condoms (*kabout*) – either Egyptian-made *Tops* (liable to rip) or US imports (thick and short). It's best to bring your own supply.

Women's health

Travelling in the heat and taking antibiotics for an upset stomach make women much more susceptible to vaginal infections. The best precautions are to wash regularly with mild soap, and wear cotton underwear and loose clothing. **Yeast infections** can be treated with Nystatin pessaries (available at pharmacies), "one-shot" Canesten pessaries (bring some from home if you're prone to thrush), or douches of a weak solution of vinegar or lemon juice. Sea bathing can also help. Trichomonas is usually treated with Flagyl, which should only be taken under medical supervision.

Sanitary protection is available from pharmacies in cities and tourist resorts, but seldom anywhere else, so it's wise to bring a supply for your trip.

Bring your own **contraceptives**, since the only forms widely available in Egypt are old-fashioned, high-dosage pills, the coil, and not too trusty condoms (see above). Cap-users should pack a spare, and enough spermicide and pessaries. If you're on the pill, beware that persistent diarrhoea can render it ineffective.

Costs, money and banks

Once you've arrived, Egypt is an inexpensive and good-value destination – except perhaps for Sinai and Hurghada, which are pricier than other parts of the country. As a rule, though, providing you avoid luxury hotels or tourist-only services, costs for food, accommodation and transport are low by European standards. The currency is the Egyptian pound (£E), which is divided into a hundred piastres (pt).

Average costs

Accommodation ranges from about £3–8/US$5–15 a night for a double room in a basic, unclassified hotel to £70–160/US$120–300 in Egypt's most luxurious establishments. On a limited budget, you can expect to get a decent double room in a one- or two-star hotel for £7–20/US$15–35. The occasional splurge in a three-star hotel, with a pool, will cost £20–70/US$35–120 for a double room off season, or £30–100/US$55–180 at peak periods. To some extent, all these costs are affected by where you are and when. Though low-budget options exist, the cost of hotels is higher in Cairo, Sinai and Hurghada throughout the year; in Alexandria during the summer; and in Luxor and Aswan over winter.

The price of a **meal** reflects a similar span, but the basic Egyptian staple of *fuul* and *taamiya* (beans and felafel) or *kushari* (noodles, rice and lentils with hot sauce) can be had in a local eatery for about 50p/90¢. Egyptian pizzas, chicken or kebabs cost about £1–4/US$2–7, and European-style meals in restaurants from around £5/US$9.

Locally manufactured **drinks** are reasonably cheap – a bottle of Stella beer costing about 60p/US$1, native spirits or wines under £5/US$9 – but imported booze in hotels and restaurants, which are generally the only outlets serving alcohol, is more expensive than back home (though you can buy it cheaply in duty-free shops). Everyday items tend to be pricier in Sinai, Hurghada and the desert oases, where goods have to be trucked in from distant centres.

Unless you take domestic flights or rely heavily on private taxis, **transport** is likewise cheap. You can rent a car for £30/US$50 a day, not including fuel (which costs roughly the same per litre as mineral water). The cost of buses, trains and collective taxis is generally absurdly low. For instance, the 885km journey from Cairo to Aswan costs £7.50/US$14 by train in first class, £4.50/US$8.50 in air-conditioned second class, and £6.50/US$12 by bus. In fact, these train fares are high by Egyptian standards as tourists may only use specific air-conditioned trains on this route (see p.60) – if you could use ordinary second- and third-class trains, the fares would cost less than half that.

Hidden costs

Although Egypt is generally fairly cheap, there are some hidden costs that can bump up your daily budget. Most restaurant and hotel bills are liable to a **service charge** plus **local taxes** (Luxor and Hurghada have the highest), which increase the final cost by 17–25 percent (unless already included in the price, or irrelevant, as in really cheap hotels and cafés). Visiting the Pyramids and the monuments of the Nile Valley entails spending a lot on **site tickets** (£2–7/US$4–12), unless you have a student card (see p.56) entitling you to a fifty percent discount. The custodians of tombs and temples and the medieval mosques of Islamic Cairo also expect to be tipped. For more on admission prices, see p.82.

A harder aspect to come to terms with is that you'll be confronted with real poverty. As a tourist, you're not going to solve any problems, but with an average Egyptian's wage at about £E500 a month (around £50/US$90), and a lot of people earning less than that, even a small tip can make a difference to individual family life. For Egyptians, giving money and goods to the needy is a natural act – and a requirement of Islam. As a presumed-rich *khawaga* (the Egyptian term for a foreigner), you will be expected to be liberal with **baksheesh**, which can be divided into three main varieties.

The most common is tipping: a small reward for a small service, which can encompass anyone from a waiter or lift operator to someone who unlocks a tomb or museum room at one of the ancient sites. The sums involved are often paltry (see below) – and you needn't feel railroaded into giving more; but try to strike a balance between defending your own wallet and acquiescing gracefully when appropriate. There's little point in spoiling your mood and offending people over what are trifling sums for a Western tourist but often an important part of people's livelihood in Egypt.

Typical tips might be 50pt–£E1 for looking after your shoes while you visit a mosque (though congregants don't usually tip for this), £E2–5 to a custodian for opening up a door to let you enter a building or climb a minaret. In restaurants, you do not usually leave a percentage of the bill: typical tips (regardless of whether the bill claims to include "service") are as little as 50pt in an ultra-cheap place such as a *kushari* joint, £E2 in a typical cheap restaurant, or £E5 in a smarter establishment. Customers also usually give tips of 50pt in a café, and sometimes 10–25pt in a juice bar.

A second common type of *baksheesh* is more expensive: rewarding the bending of rules – many of which seem to have been designed for just that purpose. Examples might include letting you into an archeological site after hours (or into a vaguely restricted area), finding you a sleeper on a train when the carriages are "full", and so on. This should not be confused with bribery, which is a more serious business with its own etiquette and risks – best not entered into.

The last kind of *baksheesh* is simply almsgiving. The disabled are traditional recipients of such gifts, and it seems right to join locals in giving out small change. Children, however, are a different case, pressing their demands only on tourists. If someone offers some genuine help and asks for an *alum* (pen), it seems fair enough, but to yield to every request might encourage a cycle of dependency that Egypt could do without.

Since most Egyptian money is paper, often in the form of well-used banknotes that can be fiddly to separate out, it can make life easier if you keep small bills in a separate "*baksheesh* pocket" specifically for the purpose. If giving *baksheesh* in foreign currency, give notes rather than coins (which are useless to Egyptians). Bringing a wad of one-dollar bills can be useful for this.

Youth and student discounts

Full-time students are eligible for the **International Student Identity Card** (ISIC), which entitles the bearer to special air, rail and bus fares and discounts at museums, theatres and other attractions. For Americans there's also a health benefit, providing up to US$3000 in emergency medical coverage and US$100 a day for up to sixty days' hospital care, plus a 24-hour hotline to call in the event of a medical, legal or financial emergency. The card costs £7 in the UK, €13 in Ireland, US$22 in the USA, CDN$16 in Canada, Aus$18 in Australia, or NZ$20 in New Zealand. You can also buy an ISIC card at the Medical Scientific Centre in Cairo for £E50 – but you still require a valid student ID card or proof of student status (see p.290 for further details). It is possible to buy a card without any student ID at some of the budget hotels in Cairo, but this unofficial practice has been cracked down on in recent years, and obvious non-students brandishing dodgy student cards for reductions at archeological sites may end up having to explain themselves to the tourist police. A genuine ISIC card entitles to you to a fifty-percent discount on most of Egypt's museums and sites, a thirty-percent discount on rail fares and around fifteen percent on ferries.

An alternative available to anyone under 26 is the **International Youth Travel Card**, which costs the same and entitles holders to the same discounts (within Egypt) as the ISIC card. This card is also available for £E50 from the Medical Scientific Centre in Cairo (see above).

Teachers qualify for the **International Teacher Identity Card**, at the same price, offering similar discounts. All these cards are available from youth travel specialists such as Council Travel, STA, UsitNOW and Travel CUTS (see Travel Companies in Getting There for details). Basically, it's worth

flashing one or the other at every opportunity to see what you can get.

Prices and inflation

Most of the prices in this book are given in local currency (see below). The main exceptions to this rule – air fares, top-flight accommodation and dive or safari packages – are given in US$ and increasingly in Euros, depending on what the establishments themselves quote. Despite this, you can almost always pay in Egyptian pounds, which will be calculated according to the exchange rate at the time.

Many of these price indications will change, so prices quoted in the guide can't be taken for granted. However, the cost for tourists in real terms probably won't rise much compared to local prices, and might even decrease if your own currency is riding high.

Although Egyptian inflation is currently running at around three percent, it's unevenly distributed. Prices for luxury goods and services (ie, most things in the private sector) rise faster than the cost of public transport, petrol and basic foodstuffs, which is held down by subsidies that the government dare not abolish.

Money

Egypt's basic unit of **currency** is the Egyptian pound (called a *ginay* in Arabic, and written as £E or LE). It has been sliding of late against hard currencies, and currently rates at around £E11 to the pound sterling, £E6 to the US dollar, and £E7.75 to the euro. It is divided into 100 piastres, called '*urush* (singular '*irsh*) in Arabic and written as ◝ (abbreviated by Westerners to pt).

Egyptian **banknotes** bear Arabic numerals on one side, Western numerals on the other, and come in denominations of 5pt, 10pt, 25pt, 50pt, £E1, £E5, £E10, £E20, £E50 and £E100. There are also variously sized coins to the value of 5pt, 10pt, 20pt, 25pt and 50pt; some 25pt coins have a hole in the middle.

Many of the notes in circulation are so ragged that merchants refuse them. Trying to palm off (and avoid receiving) decrepit notes can add spice to minor transactions, or be a real nuisance. Conversely, many vendors won't accept high-denomination notes (£E20 upwards) due to a shortage of change. While some offer sweets in lieu of coins, others round prices up. Try to hoard coins and small-value notes for tips, fares and small purchases.

Carrying your money

Arriving in Egypt, it is useful to have at least three days' survival money in **cash**, although you will not need local currency if arriving by air, as bank kiosks offering normal rates are open round the clock at the airport. Arriving by land or sea, you should have no trouble changing money at the border. It is illegal, and unnecessary, to import or export more than £E1000 in local currency.

US dollars, euros and English sterling notes are easy to **exchange** almost anywhere – though due to forgeries, banks are often unwilling to accept US$100 notes issued before 1992, or in less than mint condition. Aside from ordinary spending, hard cash (usually US$) may be required for visas, border taxes and suchlike. In Cairo, Forex bureaux (see p.288) will also change Canadian, Australian, Cypriot, Jordanian and Libyan currency (though notes must be in mint condition), and some banks will change all but the last – branches in five-star hotels are your best bet. Do not bring New Zealand dollars, or Scottish or Northern Irish sterling banknotes, which are not accepted by banks or Forex bureaux. Sudanese pounds likewise cannot be changed in Egypt except perhaps on arrival by boat at Aswan, and Israeli shekels can only be changed at the Taba border crossing, and at one or two banks (in five-star hotels) and some Cairo Forex bureaux.

The rest of your money should, ideally, be spread around different forms and currencies for the sake of security. You may wish to carry the bulk of it in a well-known brand of **travellers' cheque**, with credit cards and/or **Eurocheques** for backup. It is worth bearing in mind, however, that a number of banks now have ATM facilities, which enable you to draw directly from your bank account using a credit or debit card (see opposite). Note too that by taking cash in one currency and cheques in another, you can choose to exchange whichever offers the better rate.

American Express, Barclays, Citibank and Bank of America travellers' cheques are accepted by most banks and exchange offices. Thomas Cook cheques are usually good, though they may present problems in untouristy places – and, like Amex in Egypt, have a reputation for delaying refunds. Any other brand will prove more trouble than it's worth. Eurocheques backed by a Eurocard can be cashed at most branches of the Banque Misr. Cashing International Girocheques at major post offices entails an incredible rigmarole.

Credit, debit and ATM cards

Credit cards are accepted at major hotels, top-flight restaurants, some shops and airline offices, but virtually nowhere else. American Express, MasterCard and Visa are the likeliest to be accepted. Beware of people making extra copies of the receipt, to fraudulently bill you later; insist that the transaction is done before your eyes. American Express cardholders can cash personal cheques at the main Amex branches (see p.58).

In big cities, tourist resorts and major towns, branches of the main banks have **ATMs** (hole-in-the-wall cash machines) that allow you to draw cash using Visa, MasterCard, Plus or Cirrus cards. The ATMs are usually situated outside the banks, inside airports and some shopping centres, so you can use them at any time. By using ATMs you get trade exchange rates, which are somewhat better than those charged by banks for changing cash. Your card issuer may well add a foreign transaction fee, but that is usually lower than the banks' commissions (though it's worth checking before you leave, as some banks, especially in the US, charge quite high fees). Note also that there is a daily limit on ATM cash withdrawals, usually £E4000. On **credit cards**, all cash advances and ATM withdrawals are treated as loans, with interest accruing daily from the date of withdrawal. **Debit cards** do not have this problem and are less likely to incur transaction fees, but always check with your issuer before departure. It's wise to make sure your card is in good condition, and before you leave home, make sure that your card and PIN will work overseas. Where there is no ATM, cash advances on Visa and MasterCard can be obtained at most branches of the Banque Misr on the same basis.

A kind of compromise between plastic and travellers' cheques is **Visa Travel Money**, a disposable prepaid debit card with a PIN that you can use in ATMs worldwide. For more details, see the "Debit cards" section at ⓦwww.international.visa.com.

Emergency numbers for lost cards and travellers' cheques

American Express ℡02/570-3411 or 570-3153.
Diners Club ℡02/738-2638 or 578-3355.
MasterCard/Thomas Cook ℡02/797-1179 or 796-2966.
Visa ℡02/796-2877 or 797-1148.

Banks and exchange

The best exchange rates for cash can be found at **Forex bureaux** (private money changers found in large towns and tourist resorts), though they don't always take travellers' cheques, and will offer worse rates than the banks if they do. However, they are open longer hours and transactions are faster than in Egyptian **banks** (of which the main ones include Bank of Alexandria, Banque Misr, Banque du Caire and National Bank of Egypt), where forms are passed among a bevy of clerks and counters.

Such extended transactions are less likely at foreign banks (found only in Cairo and Alexandria) or branches in hotels, but there are plenty of exceptions in practice. If you're carrying American Express or Thomas Cook travellers' cheques (or cash) it's often quicker to do business at their own local branches (see opposite).

Opening hours for Egyptian banks are generally Sunday to Thursday 8.30am to 2pm, or 9.30am to 1.30pm during Ramadan. Branches in five-star hotels may open longer hours, sometimes even 24/7. For arriving visitors, the banks at Cairo airport and the border crossings from Israel are open 24 hours daily, and those at ports whenever a ship docks.

From time to time there is a **black market** in foreign currency, but it seems to have gone into abeyance of late. It is always extremely clandestine, and even when it operates you are best advised to avoid illegal street money changers, who are very likely to be rip-off artists or agents provocateurs.

Commission and receipts

Commission is not generally charged on straight exchanges, but there might be 40pt stamp duty, which you can either pay on the spot or have them deduct from the amount issued. Even if you're not planning to use them, it's wise to keep all receipts until you leave Egypt.

Rather than going through the hassle of re-exchanging Egyptian pounds into hard currency, it's better to spend it all before leaving (you can't use it at Cairo Airport's duty-free shop, but you can in the café). In theory you can change back up to £E1000 on departure if you have currency **receipts** to prove that you obtained it legally, but in practice you will find that airport banks rarely have any hard currency in stock. If you really need to change back any currency before leaving, a Forex bureau is your best bet.

American Express and Thomas Cook

American Express has several offices in Cairo and branches in Alexandria, Luxor and Aswan. All of them can hold client mail and cash Amex travellers' cheques, paying out in Egyptian pounds. Money may be wired to any branch, most of which also allow Amex cardholders to buy travellers' cheques, or cash personal cheques.

Amex's old-established rival, **Thomas Cook**, will cash most brands of travellers' cheque and sell its own cheques (in whatever hard currency you buy them with). Thomas Cook are also agents for MoneyGram and can pay out cash (in Egyptian pounds or US dollars) wired to them via MoneyGram from abroad (see opposite).

American Express offices

Cairo: (downtown) 15 Sharia Qasr el-Nil ℡02/574-7991/2/3/4/5/6, ⓕ578-4003; and Nile Hilton Hotel ℡02/578-5001/2, ⓕ578-5003; (Giza) 10th Floor, Nile Tower, 21 Sharia Giza ℡02/570-3411, ⓕ570-3146; (Heliopolis) 72 Sharia Omar Ibn al-Khattab ℡02/418-2144, ⓕ290-9157.
Alexandria: 34 Sharia el-Moskar el-Romani, Roushdi ℡03/541-0177, ⓕ545-7363.
Aswan: Cataract Hotel ℡097/306-983, ⓕ302-909.
Luxor: Winter Palace Hotel ℡095/378-833, ⓕ372-862.

Thomas Cook offices

Cairo: (downtown) 17 Sharia Mahmoud Bassiouny ℡02/574-3955, ℻576-2750; airport Terminal 1 ℡02/265-3147; Semiramis Intercontinental Hotel ℡02/795-8544; (suburbs) 10 26th July St, Mohandiseen ℡02/346-7187; 7 Sharia Baghdad, Heliopolis ℡02/417-3511; 33 Sharia Nabil el Wakkad, Heliopolis ℡02/419-4082; 88 St 9, Station Sq, Ma'adi ℡02/359-1419; and 3 Sharia Abul Feda, Zamalek ℡02/735-9223.
Alexandria: 15 Midan Saad Zaghloul ℡03/484-7830.
Aswan: 59 Sharia Abtal el-Tahrir, Corniche el-Nil ℡097/304-011.
Luxor: New Winter Palace Hotel, ℡095/372-402.
Port Said: 43 Sharia el-Gumhorriya ℡066/227-559.
Hurghada: 8 Sharia El Sheraton ℡065/443-500.
Sharm el-Sheikh: Gafy Mall, Gafy Land ℡062/600-211 or 2.

Wiring money to Egypt

Having **money wired** from home using one of the companies listed below is generally easy enough but not cheap, and should be considered a last resort. It's also possible to have money wired directly from a bank in your home country to a bank in Egypt, although this is much less reliable because it involves two separate institutions. If you go this route, your home bank will need the address of the branch bank where you want to pick up the money and the address and telex number of the Cairo head office, which will act as the clearing house; money wired this way normally takes two working days to arrive, and costs around £25/US$40/CDN$54/A$52/NZ$59 per transaction.

Money-wiring companies

MoneyGram UK ℡00-800/8971 8971, Ireland and New Zealand ℡00800/666 3947, US ℡1-800/666 3947, Canada ℡1-800/933-3278, Australia ℡0011800/666 3947, ℺www.moneygram.com.
Western Union UK ℡0800/833 833, Republic of Ireland ℡66/947 5603, US and Canada ℡1-800/325 6000, Australia ℡1800/173 833, New Zealand ℡0800/005 253, ℺www.westernunion.com (customers in the UK, US and Canada can send money online).

Getting around

Egyptian public transport is, on the whole, pretty good. There is an efficient rail network linking the Nile Valley, Delta and Canal Zone, and elsewhere you can travel easily enough by bus or collective (service) taxi. On the Nile you can indulge in feluccas or cruise boats, and in the desert there's the chance to test your camel-riding prowess. For those in a hurry, EgyptAir provide a network of flights.

By rail

Covering a limited network of routes, **trains** are best used for long hauls between the major cities, when air-conditioned services offer a comfier alternative to buses and taxis. For shorter journeys, however, trains are slower and less reliable. There's a crucial distinction between relatively fast **air-conditioned** (a/c) trains (including **wagons-lits** services) and the snail-like non-a/c local-stop services. For reasons of security, the authorities want tourists to use only specially designated a/c trains between Cairo and Upper Egypt, so railway clerks have been instructed not to sell tickets for other trains (see p.84). Most tourists abide by this but, if you have good reasons not to, it may be possible to get an Egyptian to buy your ticket, or to board a non-a/c train without a ticket, and buy one from the conductor.

Students with ISIC cards (see p.56) get thirty-percent reductions on all fares except sleepers and wagons-lits. Train **timetables** for the most popular routes are posted online at ⓦtouregypt.net/trains.htm.

A/c trains

Air-conditioned trains nearly always have two classes of carriage. The most comfortable option is **first class** (*daraga oola*), which has a/c, waiter service, reclining armchairs and no standing in the aisles. Unfortunately for those trying to sleep, they also screen videos until midnight. Air-conditioned **second class superior** (*daraga tania mumtaaza*) is less plush and more crowded – but at two-thirds the price of first class it's a real bargain. Occasionally a/c trains will be first or second class only.

Travelling between Cairo, Luxor and Aswan, foreigners are only allowed to use four "**tourist trains**" (three with seats, plus one sleeper train), whose compartments are guarded by plain-clothes cops toting Uzis. The regular **sleepers** attached to some services along the Nile Valley used to be an economical way of travelling overnight to Luxor or Aswan, but the only sleeper trains that tourists are now permitted to use are the far costlier *wagons-lits* (see opposite). An ordinary first- or a/c second-class carriage, however, should be comfortable enough to allow sleeping on an overnight journey, at a fraction of the cost.

Seats are **reservable** up to seven days in advance. There is occasional double booking but a little *baksheesh* to the conductor usually sorts out any problem. One common difficulty is that return bookings can't be arranged at the point of origin, so if you're travelling back to Cairo from Aswan/Luxor (or vice versa), it's best to book a seat the day you arrive. Most travel agencies sell first-class tickets for a small commission, saving you from having to queue.

To give an idea of **fares**, a first-class ticket from Cairo to Aswan costs about £7.50/US$14; a/c second-class £4.50/US$8.50.

Non-a/c trains

Non-air-conditioned trains divide into **ordinary second class** (*daraga tania aadia*), which has padded bench seating, and **third class** (*daraga talata*), which is just wooden benches and open doors and windows for ventilation. Both classes are invariably crowded, the rolling stock is ancient and often filthy, and schedules fanciful. Few foreigners use them, and the only reason to do so for a long journey is to save money. Over short distances, however, some might enjoy the funky disorder, with peasants and vendors getting on and off at every stop.

There is no advance booking for seats on these services and you needn't queue for a ticket at the station. You simply walk on and buy a ticket from the conductor, paying a small penalty fee (50pt–£E2).

Wagons-lits

The ban on using regular sleepers persuades many tourists to cough up for snazzier *wagons-lits*, which may comprise an entire train, or be limited to a couple of carriages tacked on to a regular service. For anyone on a low budget the fare is hefty (currently US$53 per person from Cairo to Luxor or Aswan in a two-person cabin, $74 in a cabin to yourself), though it's still cheaper than a flight. Passengers get a comfortable two-bed cabin with a sink, breakfast in bed, a dining car, a bar and sometimes a disco.

Booking of *wagons-lits* is best done through branches of Thomas Cook or American Express, or in Cairo at the cash-only reservations centre (daily 9am–3pm; ☎02/574-9474) in Ramses station. Alternatively, you can book online with Wagons Lits (ⓦwww.sleepingtrains.com) or Hamis Travel by Ramses Station (☎02/574-9275, ⓦwww.hamis.com.eg).

By bus

Inter-city **buses** are an inexpensive way to travel, and often preferable to trains. Besides being quicker for short trips along the Nile Valley, buses serve areas beyond the rail network, such as Sinai, the oases, Abu Simbel and Hurghada. Travelling in Egypt for any length of time, you are likely to make considerable use of the various networks.

Bus services

Egypt's bus network is divided between three main operators, based in Cairo. The

Upper Egypt Bus Company serves all points along the Nile Valley, the Fayoum and inner oases, and the Red Sea Coast as far down as El-Quseir. Sinai and the Canal Zone are covered by the **East Delta Bus Company**, whose livery is orange and white. The **West Delta Bus Company**'s blue vehicles serve Alexandria, Mersa Matrouh, Siwa Oasis and the Nile Delta. As bus services are deregulated, other operators such as **El Gouna** are entering the field.

Major routes are plied by **air-conditioned** (a/c) buses – which are usually new(ish) and fast – while local routes usually have **non-a/c** ones, generally old rattletraps. The former are invariably more expensive, but whether their a/c actually works depends on the bus company and the route.

Key routes (from Cairo to Alexandria, Sharm el-Sheikh and Hurghada) are also covered by the **Superjet** company, whose a/c buses have toilets, videos and expensive snacks. Their red, black and gold livery explains their nickname, the "Golden Arrows" or "Golden Rockets". Superjet is a subsidiary of the **Arab Union Transport Company**, which operates international services to Libya, Jordan, Syria and Saudi Arabia.

Terminals and bookings

Though most towns have a single bus depot for all destinations, cities such as Cairo, Alexandria, Port Said and Ismailiya have several **terminals** (detailed in the guide). English- or French-speaking staff are fairly common at the larger ones, but rare in the provinces. **Schedules** – usually posted in Arabic only – change frequently, so information in this guide should be verified in person. Hotels in Sinai and the oases, and the tourist offices in Luxor, Aswan and the oases can also supply information.

At city terminals, **tickets** are normally sold from kiosks, up to 24 hours in advance for a/c or long-haul services. In the provinces, tickets may only be available an hour or so before departure, or on the bus itself in the case of through-services, which are often standing-room only when they arrive. Passengers on a/c services are usually assigned a seat (the number is written in Arabic on your ticket), but seats on "local" buses are taken on a first-come/first-served basis.

By service taxi

Collective **service taxis** (known as *servees*) are one of the best features of Egyptian transport. They operate on a wide variety of routes, are generally quicker than buses and trains, and fares are very reasonable. On the downside, maniacal driving on congested roads calls for strong nerves and a certain fatalism. Accidents are not uncommon.

The taxis are usually big **Peugeot saloons** carrying seven passengers or **microbuses** seating a dozen people. Most business is along specific routes, with more or less non-stop departures throughout the day on the main ones, while cross-desert traffic is restricted to early morning and late afternoon. You just show up at the terminal (locations are detailed, city by city, in the guide) and ask for a service taxi to your destination. As soon as the requisite number of people (or less, if you're willing to pay extra) are assembled, the taxi sets off. As fewer people travel after dark in winter, you might have to wait a while for a ride to a distant town; catching a service taxi to somewhere nearer, and then another one to your final destination, could be quicker. Fridays are bad for travel, too.

On established routes service taxis keep to **fixed fares** for each passenger (detailed in the guide). You can ascertain current rates by asking at your hotel (or the tourist office) or observing what Egyptians pay at the end of the journey.

Alternatively, you can **charter a taxi** for yourself or a group – useful for day excursions or on odd routes. You will have to bargain hard to get a fair price (see entries in the guide).

Driving, biking and hitching

Driving in Egypt is not for the faint-hearted or inexperienced motorist. Cities, highways, backroads and *pistes* each pose a challenge to drivers' skills and nerve. Pedestrians and carts seem blithely indifferent to heavy traffic. Though accidents are less frequent than you'd think, the crumpled wrecks alongside highways are a constant reminder of the hazards of motoring.

Although driving on the right is pretty much universal, other **rules of the road** vary.

Traffic **in cities** is relentless and anarchic, with vehicles weaving to and fro between lanes, signalling by horn. Two beeps means "I'm alongside and about to overtake." A single long blast warns "I can't (won't) stop and I'm coming through!" Extending your hand, fingers raised and tips together, is the signal for "Watch out, don't pass now"; spreading your fingers and flipping them forwards indicates "Go ahead." Although the car in front usually has right of way, buses and trams always take precedence.

On **country roads** – including the two-lane east- and west-bank "highways" along the Nile Valley – trucks and cars routinely overtake in the face of incoming traffic. The passing car usually flashes its lights as a warning, but not always. Most roads are bumpy, with deep potholes and all manner of traffic, including donkey carts and camels. Beware, especially, of children darting into the road. If you injure someone, relatives may take revenge on the spot. Avoid driving **after dark**, when Egyptians drive without lights, only flashing them on to high beam when they see another car approaching. Wandering pedestrians and animals, obstructions and sand drifts present extra hazards. During spring, flash floods can wash away roads in Sinai. On **pistes** (rough, unpaved tracks in the desert or mountains) there are special problems. You need a good deal of driving and mechanical confidence – and shouldn't attempt such routes if you don't feel your car's up to scratch. **Desert driving** is covered in detail on p.506.

One danger to be aware of is that of **unexploded mines** left over from the Middle East's many conflicts. These exist in several parts of the country and have taken the lives of a number of tourists. Because of this, off-road driving is best avoided, especially in the Sinai and along the Red Sea coast. Minefields are usually surrounded by barbed wire (often old and rusty), but are not generally signposted.

Police checkpoints – signposted in English as "Traffic Stations" – occur on the approach roads to towns and oases and along major trunk routes. Foreign motorists are usually waved through, but you might be asked to show your passport or driving licence. In Middle Egypt the checkpoints are militarized, and Egyptian vehicles may be searched for weapons.

The official **speed limit** outside towns is 90km per hour (100km on the Cairo–Alexandria Desert Road), but on certain stretches it can be as low as 30km per hour. Road signs are similar to those in Europe, but speed limits are posted in Arabic numerals, which it would be wise to learn (see box, p.114). The **minimum age** for driving in Egypt is 25 years; the **maximum age** limit is 70 years. Foreigners require an International Driving Licence (obtainable from motoring organizations; see opposite).

Car rental

Renting **a car** pays obvious dividends if you are pushed for time or plan to visit remote sites (you cannot bring rented cars across the border), but whether you'd want to drive yourself is another matter (see above) – it's not much more expensive to hire a car and driver.

Any branch of Misr Travel (see p.45), and numerous local tour agencies, can fix you up with a car and **driver**. An alternative is simply to negotiate with local taxi drivers (see p.65).

For a **self-drive car**, visitors can make arrangements abroad through Hertz, Avis or Budget, or directly with local car rental companies in Egypt (addresses given where relevant in the guide). It's worth shopping around for the best deal, since rates and terms vary considerably. At the cheaper end of the market, you can get a car with unlimited mileage for about £30/US$50 a day. Of the international agencies, Hertz currently offers the best rates. Most companies require a hefty deposit, and not all accept credit cards.

Before making a reservation, be sure to find out if you can pick up the car in one city and return it in another. Generally, this is only possible with cars from Hertz, Avis or Budget, found in the main cities and tourist centres. And before setting out, make sure the car comes with spare tyre, tool kit and full documentation – including insurance cover, which is compulsory issue with all rentals.

Car rental agencies

Avis UK ☎ 0870/606 0100, ⊛ www.avis.co.uk; Ireland ☎ 021/428 1111, ⊛ www.avis.ie; US ☎ 1-800/230-4898, ⊛ www.avis.com; Canada

☎1-800/272-5871, ⓦwww.avis.com; Australia ☎13/6333 or ☎02/9353 9000, ⓦwww.avis.com .au; New Zealand ☎0800/655 111 or 09/526 2847, ⓦwww.avis.co.nz.

Budget UK ☎01442/276 266, ⓦwww.budget .co.uk; Ireland ☎09/0662 7711, ⓦwww.budget .ie; US ☎1-800/527-0700, ⓦwww.budget.com; Canada ☎1-800/472-3325, ⓦwww.budget.com; Australia ☎1300/362 848, ⓦwww.budget.com .au; New Zealand ☎0800/652227 or 09/976 2222, ⓦwww.budget.co.nz.

Europcar UK ☎870/607 5000, ⓦwww.europcar .co.uk; Ireland ☎01/614 2800, ⓦwww.europcar .ie; US & Canada ☎1-877/940-6900, ⓦwww .deltaeuropcar.com; Australia ☎1300/131390, ⓦwww.deltaeuropcar.com.au.

Hertz UK ☎0870/848 4848, ⓦwww.hertz.co.uk; Ireland ☎01/676 7476, ⓦwww.hertz.ie; US ☎1-800/654-3131, ⓦwww.hertz.com; Canada ☎1-800/263-0600, ⓦwww.hertz.com; Australia ☎13/3039 or ☎03/9698 2555, ⓦwww.hertz .com.au; New Zealand ☎0800/654 321, ⓦwww .hertz.co.nz.

Motoring organizations

American Automobile Association (AAA) US ☎1-800/AAA-HELP, ⓦwww.aaa.com

Australian Automobile Association Australia ☎02/6247 7311, ⓦwww.aaa.asn.au

Automobile Association (AA) UK ☎0870/600 0371, ⓦwww.theaa.co.uk

Automobile Association of Ireland (AA) Ireland ☎01/617 9999, ⓦwww.aaireland.ie

Canadian Automobile Association (CAA) Canada ☎613/247 0117, ⓦwww.caa.ca

New Zealand Automobile Association New Zealand ☎0800/500 444, ⓦwww.nzaa.co.nz

Royal Automobile Club (RAC) UK ☎0800/550 055, ⓦwww.rac.co.uk

Motorbikes and bicycles

Motorcycling could be a good way to travel around Egypt, but the red tape involved in bringing your own bike is diabolical (ask your national motoring organization and the Egyptian consulate for details). It's difficult to rent a machine except in Luxor or Hurghada. Bikers should be especially wary of potholes, sand and rocks, besides other traffic on the roads.

Useful for getting around small towns and reaching local sites or beaches, **bicycles** can be rented in Luxor, Aswan, Hurghada, Siwa Oasis and other places for a modest sum. Cycling in big cities or over long distances is not advisable. Traffic is murderous, the heat brutal, and foreign cyclists are sometimes stoned by children (particularly in the Delta). If you're determined to cycle the **Nile Valley**, the new east bank expressway that runs down as far as Aswan is the safer route.

Most towns have a wealth of general **repair shops**, well used to servicing local bikes and mopeds. Though unlikely to have the correct spare parts for your make of bike, they can usually sort out some kind of temporary solution.

Fuel and breakdowns

Petrol (*benzene*) and diesel stations are plentiful in larger towns but few and far between in rural and desert areas. Always fill your tank to the limit. Replace oil/air filters regularly, lest impurities in the petrol, and Egypt's ubiquitous dust, clog up the engine.

Egyptian **mechanics** are usually excellent at coping with breakdowns, and all medium-sized towns have garages (most with a range of spare parts for French, German and Japanese cars). But be aware that if you break down miles from anywhere you'll probably end up paying a lot to get a truck to tow you back.

If you are driving your own vehicle, there is also the problem of having to re-export any car that you bring into the country (even a wreck). You can't just write off a car; you'll have to take it out of Egypt with you.

Vehicle insurance

All car-rental agreements must be sold along with third-party liability insurance, by law. Though accident and damage insurance should be included in the package, always make sure. In the case of an **accident**, get a written report from the police and from the doctor who first treats any injuries, without which your insurance may not cover the costs. Reports are written in Arabic.

Driving your own vehicle, you will need to take out **Egyptian insurance**. Policies are sold by the Al-Chark and Misr insurance companies; offices are found in most towns and at border crossings. Premiums vary according to the size, horsepower and value of the vehicle.

Hitching

Hitching is largely confined to areas with minimal public transport (where anything that moves is considered fair game) or trunk routes (where hopefuls wait by the roadside for passing service taxis or scheduled buses). Since you'll probably end up paying anyway, there's no point in hitching unless you have to. Indeed, foreigners who hitch where proper transport is available may inspire contempt rather than sympathy. As few tourists have their own car in Egypt, you can't expect much help from that quarter, either. Women should never hitch without a male companion.

In the countryside and the desert, where buses may be sporadic or non-existent, it is standard practice for **lorries** (*camions*) and **pick-up trucks** (*bijous*) to carry and charge passengers. You may be asked to pay a little more than the locals, or have to bargain over a price, but it's straightforward enough. Getting rides from tractors is another possibility in rural areas.

Also noteworthy are **pilgrim convoys**, bound for the monasteries of Wadi Natrun, St Paul or St Anthony, or remoter sites to celebrate a festival such as the moulid of St Damyanah (p.671) or Sheikh al-Shazli (see box, p.803).

By air

Egyptian domestic air fares are average by international standards, but probably too expensive for most low-budget travellers. In general, it's only worth flying if your time is very limited, or for the view – the Nile Valley and Sinai look amazing from the air.

EgyptAir, the national airline, enjoys a near monopoly so it has no incentive to offer discounts. **Air Sinai** was specially created to serve the Sinai and Israel, in order to protect EgyptAir from the withdrawal of landing rights in other Arab countries, but is really just the same outfit under another name. Details of flights and the addresses of local offices appear in the text.

Fares are calculated in US$ but payable in Egyptian currency, backed by an exchange receipt. As a rough guide to prices, a one-way economy-class ticket from Cairo to Luxor costs about £70/US$125. In the winter season, you would be lucky to get any kind of flight between Cairo and Luxor, Aswan, Abu Simbel or St Catherine's Monastery, without booking at least a week ahead. Always reconfirm 72 hours prior to the journey, as overbooking is commonplace.

By boat

The colonial tradition of **Nile cruises**, familiar from films and novels, has spawned an industry deploying 240 steamers. Before the 1997 Luxor massacre, most cruise boats were booked months in advance by tour companies and it was difficult for individuals to make bookings in Egypt – but now it's much easier: see the box on pp.476–477 for more details.

There are also some excellent cut-price offers available. Package deals from abroad cost as little as £600/US$1000 for a week's cruise (see pp.31–32, 34–35 and 37 for tour company details); while in Egypt you can arrange a four-day trip on the spot for around £160/US$300 (see box on pp.476–477; all prices are per person, in a twin cabin). Prices escalate dramatically with the luxury quotient. Most boats start off in Luxor, sailing down to Aswan (others start here), with stops at Esna, Edfu and Kom Ombo, over three to five days.

If you're looking for a cruise in Egypt, shop around and don't necessarily go for the cheapest deal – some boats leave a lot to be desired in terms of hygiene and living conditions. The luxurious boats with swimming pools can be wonderful, but you need to pick with care. If at all possible, try to look around the vessel first. The best deals are available from local agents (or directly from the boats) in Luxor and Aswan. Particularly beware of overpriced trips sold by touts and some hotels in Cairo (see box, p.119). The most reliable cruises are generally those sold in association with package holidays.

Feluccas, the lateen-sailed boats used on the Nile since antiquity, still serve as transport along many stretches of the river. Favoured by tourists for sunset cruises, they allow you to experience the changing moods of the Nile while lolling in blissful indolence.

Many visitors opt for longer **felucca cruises**, stopping at the temples between Aswan and Luxor – heading downriver from Aswan. While it's easy to arrange a cruise yourself (see box, pp.474–475), several tour operators also offer packages.

Local **ferries**, which are generally cheap, battered and crowded, cross the Nile and the Suez Canal at various points. There are also smarter tourist ferries between Luxor and the West Bank, but it's more fun to use the ordinary boats.

Long-distance services are confined to the Red Sea and the Gulf of Aqaba, where the slow boats of yore have been superseded by a deluxe high-speed **catamaran** that zips over from Hurghada to Sharm el-Sheikh three times a week, in just ninety minutes. The US$40 (£22) fare isn't much more than is charged by the last of the old boats (which take over five hours), and is worth it to avoid the long overland journey via Suez, which requires the best part of a day. Another catamaran runs from Nuweiba to the Jordanian port of Aqaba.

City transport

Most Egyptian towns are small enough to cover on foot, especially if you stay in a hotel near the centre. In larger cities, however, local transport is definitely useful. Learn to recognize Arabic numerals and you can take full advantage of the cheap **buses**, **minibuses** and **trams** that cover most of Alexandria and Cairo (which also has river taxis and an excellent metro). Bus and tram routes are detailed under individual entries in the guide.

Equally ubiquitous are four-seater **taxis** (black and white in Cairo, black and yellow in Alexandria), which often pick up extra passengers heading in the same direction. As meters are rarely used (or work), the trick is to know the fare and pay on arrival, rather than ask or haggle at the beginning. Above all, don't confuse these cabs with larger special taxis (usually Peugeot 504s or Mercedes), which cost three times more and prey on tourists. If you do rent a special, establish the price – and bargain it down – before you get in. The section on Cairo taxis (p.112) contains some more advice.

Founded in 1934, the **Brooke Hospital for Animals** now has clinics in Cairo, Luxor, Edfu, Aswan, Alexandria and Mersa Matrouh, as well as in Jordan, India and Pakistan. They provide free treatment for any animal brought to the clinic, and rescue abandoned ones. Tourists are asked to help by admonishing drivers who gallop their horses, and not travelling more than four to a carriage. Boycotting the worst offenders may work, but it would be wrong to judge all owners of neglected animals harshly, for many simply can't afford to take their horses off the streets. Tourists are welcome to visit the Brooke clinics in Egypt, and donations can be sent to the Brooke Hospital for Animals, Broadmead House, 21 Panton St, London SW1Y 4DR ☎020/7930 0210. Another charity working in the same field is **Animal Care in Egypt** (ACE), which has a clinic in Luxor. Details of their work appear on ⓦwww.ace-egypt.org.uk.

You will also come across **caleches** – horse-drawn buggies, also known as hantours. These are primarily tourist transport, and you'll be accosted by drivers in Alexandria, a few parts of Cairo, and most of all in Luxor and Aswan. Fares are high by local taxi standards and, despite supposed tariffs set by the local councils, are in practice entirely negotiable. In a few small towns, mostly in Middle Egypt, hantours remain part of local city transport. Ask locals the price of fares before climbing on board, or simply pay what you see fit at the end. Some of the horses and buggies are in pristine condition; others painful to behold. Tourists can help by boycotting drivers who abuse their animals, and by contributing to the Brooke Hospital for Animals (see box above).

Accommodation

The main tourist centres offer a broad spectrum of accommodation, with everything from luxury palaces – familiar from movies such as *Death on the Nile* – to homely *pensions* and flea-ridden dives. Even in high season, in Cairo, Sinai or the Nile Valley, you should be able to find something in your preferred range. Elsewhere, the choice is generally more limited, with only basic lodgings available in most of the desert oases.

Hotels

Egyptian hotels are loosely categorized into **star ratings**, ranging from five-star deluxe class down to one-star. Below this range, there are also unclassified hotels and *pensions*, some of them tailored to foreign backpackers, others mostly used by Egyptians.

Standards vary within any given category or price band – and from room to room in many places. The categorizations tend to have more meaning in the higher bands; once you're down to one or two stars, the differences are almost negligible.

Deluxe hotels are almost exclusively modern and chain-owned (Sofitel, Mövenpick, Hilton, etc), with swimming pools, bars, restaurants, air conditioning and all the usual international facilities. **Four-star** hotels can be more characterful, including some famous (and reconditioned) names from the old tradition of Egyptian tourism: places like the Old Cataract in Aswan and the Winter Palace in Luxor. Again, all hotels in this class are air conditioned, with a pool, café and restaurant, etc. They merge into **three-star** hotels, among which there is again the odd gem, though most are 1970s-style towers, now becoming a little shabby. Facilities like plumbing and air-conditioning get a lot less reliable, too.

Down on the **two- and one-star** level, you rarely get air conditioning, though better places will supply fans, and old-style buildings with balconies, high ceilings and louvred windows are well designed to cope with the heat. Conversely, these places can be distinctly chilly in winter, as they rarely have any form of heating.

Some of the cheaper hotels are classified as **pensions**, which makes little difference in terms of facilities, but tends to signify family ownership and a friendlier ambience. Cairo, in particular, has some wonderful *pensions*.

At the cheap end of the scale, in the most popular tourist towns, like Luxor and Hurghada, you also get **"student hotels"**, specifically aimed at backpackers. They are often quite well run and equipped, if a bit cramped. In some very cheap establishments however, standards of cleanliness may be suspect, and bedding limited to one sheet and a blanket.

Booking and charges

Bookings for the **four- and five-star hotels** are best made through the central reservations office of the chain owning the hotel, or by fax. Simply turning up at a ritzy hotel, or even phoning ahead, you may find a reluctance to book you in, with staff even sometimes claiming the hotel is full. Many rely on tour groups for their business and are not very interested in individual travellers. You may alternatively prefer to book as part of a **package**, through one of the companies detailed on pp.31–32, 34–35 and 37. Package tourists get greatly reduced rates, while modest **discounts** may also be available to independent travellers who book from abroad.

At **mid-range hotels**, it is worth trying to book ahead if you want to stay in a particular place in Cairo, Alex, Aswan or Luxor. Elsewhere – and at all the **cheaper hotels** – most people just turn up. Phoning may itself prove unrewarding (see p.74).

Most hotels levy a **service charge** (12 percent) plus **local taxes** (2–15 percent) on top of their quoted rates. **Breakfast** is often obligatory and may or may not be included in the room rate. It's not usually anything

B

Accommodation price codes

All the establishments listed in this book have been graded according to the categories listed below.

Prices given are for the **cheapest double room** in each establishment in high season (winter in Upper Egypt and Sinai, summer in Alexandria), including tax. Bear in mind, however, that Cairo is generally more expensive for accommodation of all types than most other places in Egypt; thus, a category **①** place in Cairo may be pretty dire, while a room in Siwa Oasis at the same price may be quite comfortable. For places that offer **dorm beds** or charge on a singles basis, rates per person are given in £E.

For the purposes of ready reckoning, we have taken the exchange rate as *roughly* US$1 = £E5.85. Please note that most hotels in categories **⑥** to **⑨** quote rates in US$, but will accept payment in £E.

① under £E50/US$8.50. The rate for a basic room in a no-star hotel. Singles are rare, solo travellers may have to share with strangers or pay for a double room.

② £E50–100/US$8.50–17. A reasonable unclassified or one-star hotel or *pension*, containing a mixture of rooms with shared and private facilities, and in most cases comfortable enough for a shortish stay.

③ £E100–150/US$17–25.50. Mostly one- or two-star hotels, with the odd three-star place: the facilities may amount to no more than in the previous category, or be considerably better, depending on the age and location of the hotel.

④ £E150–200/US$25.50–34. Largely three-star places, some rather aged, but there are many new ones in Hurghada, Luxor and Aswan. Rooms should have a/c, a phone, TV and fridge. There's almost certain to be a restaurant on the premises, and possibly a disco.

⑤ £E200–300/US$34–50. Posher three-star places, which in Luxor, Sinai or Hurghada could well have a pool.

⑥ £E300–450/US$50–75. The border line between three- and four-star hotels, where you can usually take a pool and a/c for granted, although the odd place with neither may charge such rates for half- or full-board accommodation.

⑦ £E450–880/$75–150. At this level, prices are posted in US$, and you're talking somewhere pretty classy, four-star or relatively low-priced five-star. There are scores along the Red Sea Coast, where the deal may include half-board.

⑧ £E880–1500/US$150–250. A deluxe hotel, with a gym, shops, several restaurants, a/c, room service and all the trimmings.

⑨ £E1500/$250 upwards. The very ritziest five-star hotels and holiday villages.

to get excited about. **Extra charges** most commonly turn up at mid-range hotels, which may add on a few pounds for a fan or air conditioning or a TV that doesn't work or may only show Egyptian channels. Throughout this book we have indicated prices according to the categories above.

International booking for luxury hotel chains

Four Seasons UK & Ireland ☎00800/6488 6488; US & Canada ☎1-800/819-5053; Australia ☎1800/142 163; New Zealand ☎0800/449 286; ⓦwww.fourseasons.com.

Intercontinental UK ☎0800/028 9387; Ireland ☎1800/709 300; US & Canada ☎1-800/327-0200; Australia ☎1-800/221 335; New Zealand ☎0800/442 215; ⓦwww.intercontinental.com.
Hilton UK ☎0870/590 9090; Ireland 1800/409 633; US & Canada ☎1-800/HILTONS; Australia ☎1800/222 255 or 02/9287 0707; New Zealand ☎0800/448 002; ⓦwww.hilton.com.
Hyatt UK ☎0845/888 1234; Ireland ☎1800/481034; US & Canada ☎1-888/591 1234; Australia ☎13/1234; New Zealand ☎0800/441234; ⓦwww.hyatt.com.
Marriott UK ☎0800/221 222; Ireland ☎1800/409929; US & Canada ☎1-888/236-2427; Australia ☎1800/251 259 or ☎02/9251 5522;

New Zealand ☎ 0800/441035; ⊛ www.marriott
.com.
Meridien UK ☎ 0800/028 2840; Ireland
☎ 1800/409090; US & Canada ☎ 1-800/543-
4300; Australia ☎ 1-800/622 240; New Zealand
☎ 0800/454 040; ⊛ www.lemeridien.com.
Oberoi UK ☎ 0800/181123; Ireland ☎ 00800/1234
0101; US & Canada ☎ 1-800/223-6800; Australia
☎ 1800/222 033; New Zealand ☎ 0800/441 016;
⊛ www.oberoihotels.com.
Sheraton UK, Ireland & New Zealand
☎ 00800/3253 5353; US & Canada ☎ 1-800/625-
5144; Australia ☎ 1800/073 535; ⊛ www.sheraton
.com.

Hotel touts

"Fishing" for guests (as Egyptians call it) is
common practice in the main tourist centres,
where new arrivals are approached by hotel
touts at train and bus stations, airports and
docks. Though some actually work in the
hotel they're touting, most are simply hustling
for commissions and quite prepared to use
trickery to deliver clients to "their" establishment – swearing that other places are
full, or closed, or whatever. In some cases,
the hotel being touted may be agreeable,
or even the best deal going; all too often,
however, it's the grotty or overpriced places
that depend on touts. In any case, their
commission will usually be added to your
bill – another reason to avoid using them. In
Cairo especially, some of these places exist
purely for the purpose of housing foreigners
so that they can be sold overpriced excursions or souvenirs.

By studying the hotel listings and town
plans in this book, you should be able to
detect most scams. Advice for travellers
flying into Cairo appears on p.119.

Hostels

Egypt's youth hostels are cheap but their
drawbacks are considerable. A daytime

lock-out and nighttime curfew are universal
practice; so, too, is segregating the sexes
and (usually) foreigners and Egyptians
(which you might appreciate when riotous
groups are in residence). The most salubrious hostels are in Cairo, Sharm el-Sheikh
and Ismailiya. These, however, are far from
where the action is, as are grungier places in
Alexandria, Luxor and Sohag. Only Aswan's
hostel is central.

It seems to be up to individual hostels
whether you need a **Hostelling International (HI) card**, and their rules change
constantly. If admitted, non-HI members
are usually charged £E2 extra per night, and
may be granted automatic membership after
six days. For more information, contact the
Egyptian Youth Hostel Association in Cairo
(1 Sharia el-Ibrahimy, Cairo; ☎ 02/796-1448,
ⓔ eyha@link.net; annual membership £E25).
Addresses for all hostels appear in the text.
There are also a few **YMCA hostels**, which
admit anyone. The Y in Assyut is the best,
positively luxurious and excellent value
– though it is unlikely that many tourists will
visit Assyut.

Camping

Egypt is not established camping territory.
Such campsites as there are in the country
tend to be **on the coast**, often shadeless
and with few facilities, catering for holidaying
Egyptian families. You'd have to be desperate to stay at these places.

Rather better are the occasional **campsites
attached to hotels**, which may offer ready-
pitched tents with camp beds, plus use of
the hotel shower and toilet facilities. As for
camping wild, you should always check with
the authorities about any coastal site – some
beaches are mined, others patrolled by the
military. In the oases it's less of a problem,
though any land near water will belong to
someone: so again, ask permission.

Eating and drinking

Egyptian food combines elements of Lebanese, Turkish, Syrian, Greek and French cuisines, modified to suit local conditions and tastes. Dishes tend to be simple and wholesome, made only with fresh ingredients, and therefore vary with the seasons. Nubian cooking, found in southern Egypt, is spicier than food in the north; in Alexandria, Mediterranean influences prevail. Cairo offers every kind of cuisine in the world.

Eating out falls into two camps. At a local level, there are cafés and diners and loads of street stalls, which sell one or two simple dishes. More formally and expensively, restaurants cater to middle-class Egyptians and tourists. The latter have menus (most cafés don't) offering a broader range of dishes, and sometimes specializing in foreign cuisine. They will also invariably add a service charge and taxes to your bill, which usually increases the total by about seventeen percent. You are also expected to **tip** – conventions for which are byzantine. Basically, you tip in proportion to the size of the bill; below ten percent in expensive places, more where the sums involved are trifling. In juice bars and diners, customers simply put 10–25pt on a plate by the exit (see also p.55).

Cafés and street food

The staples of the Egyptian diet are bread ('aish, which also means "life"), fuul and taamiya. **Bread** is eaten with all meals and snacks and comes either as pitta-type 'aish shamsi (sun-raised bread made from white flour) or 'aish baladi (made from coarse wholewheat flour).

Native beans or **fuul** (pronounced "fool") can be prepared in several ways. Boiled and mashed with tomatoes, onions and spices, they constitute fuul madammes, which are often served with a chopped boiled egg for breakfast. A similar mixture stuffed into 'aish baladi constitutes the pitta-bread sandwiches sold on the street.

Deep-fried patties of green beans mixed with spices are called **taamiya** (or sometimes **felafel**) and are again served in pitta bread, often with a snatch of salad, pickles

and **tahina** (a sauce made from sesame paste, tahini).

A common appetizer is **torshi**, a mixture of pickled radishes, turnips, gherkins and carrots; luridly coloured, it is something of an acquired taste, as are pickled lemons, another favourite.

Another cheap café perennial is **makarona**, a clump of macaroni baked into a cake with minced lamb and tomato sauce inside. It's rather bland but very filling. Similarly common is **kushari**, which is a mixture of noodles, rice, macaroni, lentils and onions, in a spicy tomato sauce (another sauce, made of garlic, is optional). These are sold in tiled stand-up diners, also called kushari.

More elaborate, and pricier, are **fatir**, which can be either sweet or savoury. These are a cross between pizza and pancake, consisting of flaky filo pastry stuffed either with white cheese, peppers, mince, egg, onion and olives, or with raisins, jams, curds or just a dusting of icing sugar. They are served at café-like establishments known as fatatri.

Most **sandwiches** are small rolls with a minute portion of basturma (pastrami) or cheese. Other favourites include: grilled liver (kibda) with spicy green peppers and onions; tiny shrimps; and mokh (crumbed sheep's brains).

Lastly, there are **shawarma** – slices of marinated lamb, stuffed into pitta bread and garnished with salad and tahina – somewhat superior to the doner kebabs sold abroad, though foreigners often assume they are the same.

On the **hygiene** front, while cafés and tiled eateries with running water are generally safe, street grub is highly suspect unless it's peelable or hot.

Restaurant meals

The classic Egyptian restaurant or café meal is either a lamb **kebab** or **kofta** (spiced mince patties), accompanied or preceded by a couple of dips. The dips usually comprise **hummus** (made from chickpeas), *tahina* and **babaghanoug** (*tahina* with aubergine).

In a basic place, this is likely to be all that's on offer, save for a bit of salad (usually lettuce- and tomato-based), *fuul* and bread. However, you may also find other grilled meats. **Chicken** (*firakh*, pronounced "frakh" in Upper Egypt) is a standard, both in cafés and as takeaway food from spit-roast stands. **Pigeon** (*hamam*) is common too, most often served with *freek* (spicy wheat) stuffing. There's not much meat on a pigeon, so it's best to order a couple each. In slightly fancier places, you may also encounter pigeon in a **tageen** or *ta'gell*, stewed with onions, tomatoes and rice in an earthenware pot.

More expensive restaurants feature these same dishes, plus a few that are more elaborate. Some may precede main courses with a larger selection of dips, plus olives, stuffed vine leaves and so on – a selection known, as in Greek, as **mezze**. Soups, too, are occasionally featured, most famously **molukhiyya**, which is made from stewing the herb Jew's mallow in chicken stock – a lot tastier than its disconcertingly slimy appearance suggests. Two common main dishes are **mahshi**, comprising stuffed vegetables (tomatoes, aubergines, etc), and **torly**, a mixed vegetable casserole with chunks of lamb, or occasionally beef (which in reality may be donkey, water buffalo or camel meat).

Fish (*samak*) is featured on restaurant menus in Alexandria, Aswan, the Red Sea Coast and Sinai. It is invariably grilled or fried, served with salad and chips, and usually very tasty. There are many types, ranging from snapper to Nile perch; you're usually invited to pick your own fish from the ice box and it'll then be priced by weight. You may also find squid (calamari), shrimps (*gambari*) and octopus (*kaborya*).

One confusion you'll often run up against is the notion that **pasta**, **rice**, **chips** (French fries) and even **crisps** (potato chips) are interchangeable. Order rice and you'll get chips, and your querying of the matter will be regarded as inexplicable.

Vegetarian eating

Most Egyptians eat vegetables most of the time – meat and fish are seen as luxuries. However, the concept of **vegetarianism** is totally incomprehensible to most people. It is possible to tell people that you are vegetarian (*ana nabati* in Arabic) but they may still not understand what you are getting at, and even if you do get across the idea that you don't eat meat (you could try telling people it's against your religious beliefs), you're as likely as not to be offered chicken or fish as a substitute.

Cheese, cakes and nuts

You can supplement regular cooked meals with a variety of fare available from corner shops, delicatessens, patisseries and street stalls.

There are two main types of Egyptian **cheese**: *gibna beyda* (white cheese), which tastes like Greek feta, and *gibna rumi* (Roman cheese), a hard, sharp, yellow cheese. For breakfast you will often be given imported processed cheeses such as La Vache qui Rit ("The Laughing Cow" – a popular nickname for President Mubarak).

Nut shops (*ma'la*) are a high-street perennial, offering all kinds of peanuts (*fuul sudani*) and edible seeds. *Lib abyad* and *lib asmar* are varieties of pumpkin seeds, *lib battikh* come from watermelon, and chickpeas (hummus) are roasted and sugar-coated or dried and salted; all of these are sold by weight. Most nut shops also stock candies and mineral water.

Cakes are available at patisseries (some of which are attached to quite flash cafés) or from street stalls. The classics will be familiar to anyone who has travelled in Greece or Turkey: baklava (filo pastry soaked in honey and nuts) – called *basbousa* in Upper Egypt; *katif* (similar but with shredded wheat); and a variety of milk- or cornflour-based puddings, like *mahallabiyya* (sweet rice or cornflour, topped with pistachio nuts) and most famously *Umm Ali* (corn cake soaked in milk, sugar, coconut and cinnamon and served hot).

Fruits in Egypt are seasonal and wonderful. In winter there are oranges, bananas and pomegranates, followed by strawberries in March. In summer you get mangoes, melons, peaches, plums and grapes, plus a brief season (Aug–Sept) of prickly pears (cactus fruit). Fresh dates are harvested in late autumn. Only apples are imported, and thus expensive. All are readily available at street stalls, or can be drunk as juices at juice bars (see opposite).

Drinks

As a predominantly Muslim country, Egypt gives alcohol a low profile. Drinks consist primarily of tea, coffee, fruit juices and familiar brands of soft drinks. Invitations to drink tea (*shurub shai?*) are as much a part of life in Egypt as they are in Britain, although the drink itself is served quite differently. Many Egyptian men accompany it with a *sheesha* (see box opposite).

Tea, coffee and karkaday

Egypt's national beverage, **tea** (*shai*), is generally made by boiling the leaves, and served black and sugared to taste – though an increasing number of cafés use tea-bags and may supply milk. Tea with milk is *shai bi-laban*, tea-bag tea is *shai libton* – to avoid it ask for loose-leaf tea (*shai kushari*). Tea with a sprig of mint (*shai bi-na'ana*) is refreshing when the weather is hot.

Coffee (*'ahwa*) is traditionally of the "Turkish" kind, served in tiny cups or glasses and pre-sugared as customers specify: *saada* (unsugared), *'ariha* (slightly sweetened), *mazboot* (medium sweet) or *ziyaada* (syrupy). In some places you can also get it spiced with cardamom (*'ahwa makhaweka*). Most middle-class or tourist establishments also serve **instant** coffee, with the option of having it with milk (*'ahwa bi-laban*). Increasingly, however, five-star hotels and other upmarket places are investing in espresso machines.

Beverages are widely consumed in traditional **coffee houses** or **tearooms** (called *'ahwa*), which are exclusively male territory. Foreign women won't be turned away but may feel uneasy, especially if unaccompanied by a man. For a more relaxed tea or coffee, try one of the middle-class places (in larger towns), which are often attached to patisseries, and where Egyptian women may also be found.

The **sheesha**, or waterpipe, is inseparable from Egyptian café society. It takes a special kind of tobacco mixed with molasses, which has a distinctive taste and aroma. Posh coffee houses may also stock apple-flavoured tobacco and provide disposable plastic mouthpieces for their clients' waterpipes. A *sheesha* is normally shared among friends, but you can decline to partake without causing offence. Don't call it a "hubbly bubbly", as the term in Egypt specifically refers to hashish, which is illegal. See box on p.11 of the colour section for more.

A third drink, characteristic of Egypt, is **karkaday** (or *karkadé*), a deep-red infusion of hibiscus flowers. Most popular in Luxor and Aswan, it is equally refreshing drunk hot or cold. Elsewhere, they may use dehydrated extract instead of real hibiscus, so it doesn't taste as good. You may also enjoy other **infusions** such as *helba* (a bright yellow infusion of fenugreek), *yansoon* (aniseed) or *'irfa* (cinnamon).

On cold winter evenings you might enjoy **sahleb**, a thick, creamy drink made from milk thickened with ground orchid root, with cinnamon and nuts sprinkled on top. In hot weather Egyptians imbibe **rayeb** (soured milk), which is something of an acquired taste.

Fruit juices and soft drinks

Every main street has a couple of stand-up **juice bars**, recognizable by their displays of fruit. Normally, you order and pay at the cash desk before exchanging a plastic token for your drink at the counter.

Juices made from seasonal fruit include *burtu'an* (orange), *mohz* (banana; with milk *mohz bi-laban*), *manga* (mango), *farawla* (strawberry), *gazar* (carrot), *rumaan* (pomegranate), *subia* (coconut) and *'asab* (the sickly sweet, creamy, light-green juice of crushed sugar cane). You can also order blends; *nus w nus* (literally "half and half") usually refers to carrot and orange juice, but other combinations can be specified.

Street vendors also ladle out iced *'asiir limoon* (strong, sweet lemonade), bitter-sweet liquorice-water, and deliciously refreshing *tamar hindi* (tamarind cordial).

Despite this profusion of cheap fresh juices, the usual brands of **soda** are widely available, including Coca-Cola, Fanta, Sprite and 7-Up (called "Seven"), all in both bottles and cans. Bottled sodas are normally drunk on the spot; you'll have to pay a deposit on the bottle to take one away.

Mineral water

Bottled **mineral water** (*mayya ma'adaniyya*) is widely available, particularly Baraka ("Blessing"; the company is owned by Nestlé); the brands Siwa and Hyat (from Siwa Oasis) are less widely distributed. Baraka comes in 1.5-litre, one-litre and half-litre bottles. If tourists request water, it is assumed that they mean mineral water unless they specifically ask for tap water (*mayya baladi*), which is safe to drink in major towns and cities, but too chlorinated for the average visitor's palate; people with sensitive stomachs should definitely stick to bottled water. When buying mineral water, it is wise to check that the seal is intact; unsuspecting tourists may be palmed off with tap water – a favourite trick in the backpackers' resort of Dahab.

Alcohol

Alcohol can be obtained in most parts of Egypt, but the range of outlets is limited. In the Western Desert oases or Middle Egypt its sale is severely restricted or entirely prohibited. If there are no bars, hotels or Greek restaurants are the places to try; if you can't see anyone drinking it, there's none to be had. When you do manage to locate a drink, keep in mind that the hot, dry climate makes for dehydration, and agonizing hangovers can easily result from overindulgence. Public drunkenness is totally unacceptable in Egypt. In deference to the non-drinking Muslim majority, the sale of alcohol is prohibited on the Prophet Mohammed's birthday and the first and last days of Ramadan (if not during the whole month).

Beer, whose consumption goes back to pharaonic times, is the most widely available

form of alcohol. Native Stella beer is a light lager (4 percent ABV) in half-litre bottles, which is okay if it hasn't sat in the sun for too long, and also in cans. To check that bottled beer hasn't gone flat, invert the bottle before opening and look for a fizzy head. Stella retails in most places for £E6–10, though discos may charge as much as £E20 and cruise boats even more. In competition with Stella, a new brand called Sakkara has hit the market, a similarly light lager (4 percent) that most foreigners seem to prefer. Premium or "export" versions of both Stella and Sakkara (4.7 percent) are available, which have a slightly fuller flavour. There are also Egyptian versions of Carlsberg, Löwenbrau and Meister, none of which is worth the extra cost, and kamikaze (7 percent) versions of Sakkara and Meister, which are worth avoiding. Marzen, a dark bock beer, appears briefly in the spring; Aswali is a dark beer produced in Aswan. Imported beer is the most expensive (£E15–20) and only appears in bars, flash hotels and restaurants. There is also Birrel, a non-alcoholic beer.

A half-dozen or so **Egyptian wines** are produced near Alexandria and have improved a lot since French specialists started supervising production. The most commonly found are Omar Khayyam (a very dry red), Cru des Ptolémées (a decent dry white) and Rubis d'Egypte (an acceptable rosé). A new range of wines called Obélisque emerged in 1999, whose Rouge des Pharaohs is pretty good, though the rosé and white are less so. In most restaurants all these wines retail for about £E30 a bottle (but more like £E45 on a cruise boat). The latest addition to the wine scene is Chateau des Rêves, a classy red with complex flavours, which goes for £E70–100 and is best left to breathe for a while before drinking.

For serious drinking, Egyptians get stuck into spirits, usually mixed with sodas or fruit juice. The favoured tipple is **brandy**, known by the slang name of *jaz* (literally, "bottle"), which comes under three labels: Ahmar (the cheapest), Maa'tak (the best) and Vin (the most common). **Zibiba** is similar to Greek ouzo, but drunk neat. Avoid vile Egyptian-made **gin** and **whisky**, whose labels are designed to resemble famous Western brands; in fact they may even contain wood alcohol and other poisons, and can be dangerous if drunk to excess. Imported spirits are sold at **duty-free shops** in the main resorts for modest sums (Johnny Walker Red Label US$12; Stolichnaya vodka US$10). Beware of touts conning you into buying them duty-free liquor for resale on the black market (see p.287). In line with drinking trends in the West, a new vodka-based alcopop called ID is now available. It comes in various flavours and is sold at liquor stores and in some bars and duty-free shops.

Communications

Communications in Egypt are generally less reliable than they are in the West, but you should have no trouble sending ordinary letters or postcards, making phone calls or sending email. Receiving mail and sending packages is a little more complicated, but all that means in practice is that it will take a little longer and require a bit more patience, although some mail does fail to get through.

Mail

Airmail letters between Egypt and Western Europe (including Britain and Ireland) generally take around a week to ten days, and two to three weeks for North America or Australasia. Sending mail from Egypt, it speeds up the delivery if you get someone to write the name of the country in Arabic. As a rule, around fifteen percent of correspondence (in either direction) never arrives; letters containing photos or other items are especially prone to go astray.

It's best to send letters from a major city or hotel; blue **mailboxes** are for overseas airmail, red ones for domestic post. Airmail (*bariid gawwi*) **stamps** can be purchased at post offices, hotel shops and postcard stands, which may charge 5–10pt above the normal rate (£E1.50 for a postcard/letter to anywhere in the world). **Registered mail,** costing £E1 extra, can be sent from any post office. Selected post offices in the main cities also offer an **Express Mail Service** (48hr delivery, costing £E128.70 for up to 500 grammes to the British Isles, £E136.40 to North America, or £E146.30 to Australia or New Zealand). Private **courier** firms such as DHL and UPS are limited to a few cities, and a lot more expensive.

To send a **parcel**, take it unsealed to a major post office for customs inspection, weighing and wrapping. The procedure – explained in the Cairo section (p.294) – is much the same throughout Egypt.

Post office hours are generally daily except Fri 8am–6pm (Ramadan 9am–3pm), though central offices may stay open until 8pm. Almost invariably, offices are closed on Fridays.

Poste restante

Receiving letters **poste restante** (general delivery) is a bit of a lottery, since post office workers don't always file letters under the initials you might expect. Ask for all your initials to be checked (including *M* for Mr, Ms, etc), and, if you're half expecting anything, suggest other letters as well. To have mail sent to you, it should be addressed (preferably with your surname underlined and/or highlighted) to *Poste Restante* at the central post office. To pick up mail, you'll need your passport.

A better option is to have mail sent to a major **hotel** (anything with three or more stars should be reliable) or c/o **American Express** (branches in Cairo, Alexandria, Luxor and Aswan; see p.58 for addresses), though the latter service is officially only for Amex travellers' cheque- or cardholders. Note that parcels sent c/o American Express will be held at the post office (in the case of Cairo, at the branch on Sharia Mohammed Farid).

Telecommunications

All towns and cities have at least one 24-hour **telephone and telegraph office** (*maktab el-telephonat*, or *centraal*) for calling long-distance and abroad. Many of these feature orange direct-dial phones that take phonecards (you'll need one for at least £E20 or £E30 to make an international call), enabling you to avoid the old system of booking calls through the exchange (which entailed giving the number to a clerk and paying for the call in advance, either for a set amount of time or £E30–40 for an open line, and settling the bill afterwards). Expect to queue and hang around a while. It's also possible to book (and prepay) a call that is routed through to your hotel or some other number. Alternatively, you can **make calls through a hotel** with a trunk or direct international line (most places with three or more stars have them), which entails paying up to 100 percent above the normal rate. Always ascertain the rate first.

Regular **phone boxes** really only serve for local calls, which cost 10pt (though some kiosks only accept the old 5pt coins). You can also make local calls on semi-public phones owned by shopkeepers or hoteliers, who charge 25–50pt. **Phonecard booths** (Menatel, Ringo or Egypt Telecom) are becoming increasingly common – shops which sell the cards usually display the companies' signs. Menatel (£E10 and £E15) is the main company, and charges 10pt for the first minute and 9pt for subsequent minutes for local calls, 40pt and 30pt for long-distance, 80pt and 66pt to a mobile or pager in Egypt, £E4.20 and £E1.30 to North America, £E4.80 and £E1.50 to the British Isles and Europe, and £E6.20 and £E2 to Australia and New Zealand. It offers discounts for higher-value cards, and its latest rates can be found on its website at ⓦ www.menatel.com.eg.

Better still, cards which have a scratch-off panel with a PIN number underneath can be used from any phone by dialling a toll-free number, then the **PIN number** on the card, and finally the number you wish to call. The card just carries the PIN number – you don't actually insert it into the phone. These usually work out cheaper than ordinary phonecards, but are only available intermittently, from the 24-hour telephone offices.

Dialling

Overloaded exchanges and antiquated equipment make **local calls** a hit-and-miss affair, especially during peak hours. Even dialling slowly, you'll often get a wrong number. The **ringing tone** is a double purr, similar to the one used in Britain; the **engaged** (busy) tone consists of two-second bursts of tone separated by one second's silence. A persistent whine or silence indicates that the number is unobtainable or the local exchange is overloaded.

Long-distance calls within Egypt must be prefixed by a two- or three-digit area code number (listed under the appropriate chapters in this book) and are best made from a phonecard kiosk or arranged through your hotel or a telephone office.

International calls can be made using phonecards at Menatel, Ringo or Egypt Telecom kiosks, or you can go to a telephone office, where calls are booked and paid for in advance, and can either be taken in a booth or directed to an outside number such as a hotel. A call to the British Isles, Canada or Europe costs £E4.37 a minute during peak hours (8am–8pm local time); to the USA it's less at £E3.75, to Australia or New Zealand more at £E5.62; outside peak time prices are around twenty percent less.

Direct dialling involves punching 00 for an international line, then the country code, the area code (leaving out the initial zero in calls to most countries outside North America), and finally the subscriber number.

If you have a **telephone charge card** from your phone company back home, you can use it from any international public telephone, and the call will be charged to your account. The benefit of calling cards is mainly one of convenience, as rates aren't necessarily cheaper than calling from a public phone. Check that the issuing company's charge card works from Egypt, as not all do.

Dialling abroad from Egypt

Australia 00-61+ area code (without initial zero) + number
Canada 001+ area code + number
Ireland 00-353 + area code (without initial zero) + number

New Zealand 00-64 + area code (without initial zero) + number
UK 00-44 + area code (without initial zero) + number
US 001+ area code + number

Dialling Egypt from abroad

Australia 0011-20 + area code (without initial zero) + number
Canada 011-20 + area code (without initial zero) + number
Ireland 00-20 + area code (without initial zero) + number
New Zealand 00-20 + area code (without initial zero) + number
UK 00-20 + area code (without initial zero) + number
USA 011-20 + area code (without initial zero) + number

Numbers for charge card calls

BT ☏ 02/365-3644
AT&T ☏ 02/510-0200
MCI ☏ 02/795-5770
Sprint ☏ 02/796-4777
Canada Direct ☏ 02/365-3643
Telecom NZ ☏ 02/365-3764

Emergencies and information

Directory enquiries ☏ 140 or 141
International operator ☏ 120
Police ☏ 122
Tourist police ☏ 126
Ambulance ☏ 123
Fire department ☏ 125

Mobile phones

If you want to use your **mobile phone** in Egypt, you'll need to check with your phone provider whether it will work abroad and what the call charges are. Unless you have a tri-band phone, it is unlikely that a mobile bought for use in the US will work in Egypt – for details of which mobiles will work, contact your mobile service provider.

In the UK, for all but the very top-of-the-range packages, you'll have to inform your phone provider before going abroad to get **international access** switched on. You may get charged extra for this depending on your existing package. You are also likely to be charged extra for incoming calls in Egypt, as the people calling you will be paying the usual rate. If you want to retrieve **messages** while you're away, you'll have to ask your provider for a new access code, as your home one is unlikely to work abroad.

Of Egypt's two mobile phone networks, **Mobinil** have roaming agreements with O2, Vodafone, Orange, T-mobile and Hutchinson 3G in the UK; O2 and Vodafone in Ireland; Cingular, T-mobile and AT&T in the US; Microcell (Fido) in Canada; and Vodafone and Telstra in Australia. **Vodafone Egypt** have roaming agreements with O2, Vodafone, Orange, T-mobile and Hutchinson 3G in the UK; O2, Vodafone and Meteor in Ireland; Cincinnati Bell, Cingular, T-mobile and AT&T in the US; Rogers and Microcell (Fido) in Canada; Telstra, Vodafone and Singtel Optus in Australia; and Vodafone in New Zealand.

If you're planning to use your phone a lot in Egypt, especially for local calls, it's worth getting on to one of the **Egyptian networks**. To do this, get your mobile "unlocked" by a dealer before leaving home; then, once in Egypt, go to a Mobinil or Vodafone retailer (they're everywhere) and buy a sim card. Both firms have deals going for visitors to the country, typically offering an Egyptian mobile number for a month for around £E70–85, including £E5 of free calls, with top-up cards at values from £E10 to £E200 (plus 15 percent tax and a small mark-up for the retailer) available on almost every street corner. Especially in the Western Desert and on the Mediterranean coast, Mobinil tends to have better coverage than Vodafone, but for optimum coverage in remote areas, you can get a deal that allows you access to both networks.

Telegrams and faxes

Telegrams can be sent from any telephone office and are charged per word (including the address).

Most hotels with three or more stars have **fax machines**, making this the best way to reserve a room from abroad. The procedure is the same as for phoning from abroad (see above; individual fax numbers appear in the text). Faxes can be sent from (and received at)

The commonest **mobile phone prefixes** in Egypt are 010 and 012.

certain telephone offices in the main cities; you can also have them sent to American Express offices, who'll hold them like client mail but won't notify the recipient. See p.295 for details of fax points in Cairo.

Email and Internet access

The Internet is growing fast in Egypt as elsewhere, both in terms of access points and in the number of Egyptian websites. New servers are constantly being added to cope with demand, even as competing websites merge or disappear altogether. Useful Egyptian **websites** are listed on p.46. The biggest index of Egyptian sites is at ce .eng.usf.edu/pharos.

Internet access is available in almost all the main tourist destinations, with Internet cafés sprouting everywhere and hotels providing computers for guests to use. The charge for access is usually £E5–10 an hour, although five-star hotels may charge up to £E50.

One of the best ways to keep in touch while travelling is to sign up for a free Internet email address that can be accessed from anywhere, such as YahooMail (accessible through ⓦwww.yahoo.com) or Hotmail (ⓦwww.hotmail.com), which is more popular but can be slow. Once you've set up an account, you can log into the same website to pick up and send mail from any Internet café or hotel with Internet access.

The media

Various British, US, French and German newspapers are available in Cairo, Alexandria, Luxor and Aswan, as are *Newsweek* and *Time* magazines. Elsewhere, however, you'll be lucky to find even the *Egyptian Gazette* (see opposite).

If you have a short-wave radio, you can pick up the **BBC World Service**, which is broadcast on various frequencies depending on the time of day. The main ones are 1323KHz (especially in the south), 9410KHz, 6195KHz and 12,095KHz (especially in the morning), and 7320KHz (especially in the afternoon). Full details of programmes and frequencies – which change from time to time – can be found on the BBC website at ⓦwww.bbc.co.uk/worldservice. Reception is best in the north.

The **Voice of America** broadcasts 24 hours on a number of frequencies including 15,615KHz and 17,555KHz (especially in the morning), 9685KHz, 15,255KHz and 11,835KHz (especially in the afternoon), and 1593KHz (especially at night). Full details of schedules and frequencies can be found online at ⓦwww.voa.gov. Both services carry news on the hour. **Radio Canada** can be picked up at 10pm–midnight in winter,

11pm–1am in summer, on 5850kHz (details at ⓦwww.rcinet.ca).

Cairo has two privately run **music stations** which are worth a listen: Nogoum Radio (100.6FM) plays mainly Arabic pop music, while Nile One (104.2FM) plays Western pop. In addition, the state-owned Music Programme (89.0FM) plays folk and classical music, while the European Programme (94.5FM) has the news in English at 7.30am, 2.30pm and 8pm daily.

Television

Egypt has a plethora of terrestrial **television** channels, all state-controlled. Local football matches and Koranic recitations account for the bulk of programming, so it's not worth paying extra for a TV set in your hotel room unless it receives cable or satellite TV – and even then, chances are that half the channels will be Turkish or Kuwaiti.

Channels 1, 2 and 3 often screen American films (generally after 10pm or during Ramadan between midnight and 4.30am), and **Nile TV** has English subtitles on most programmes, most notably with classic old Egyptian movies, plus news in English and French. In addition to these, some hotels receive **satellite** channels like BBC World, CNN, Star Plus, Prime Sports, EuroNews or MTV. Daily TV **schedules** appear in the *Egyptian Gazette*, whose Monday edition lists all the movies for the forthcoming week.

The press

The Egyptian press encompasses a range of daily papers and weekly magazines, chiefly published in English, French or Arabic. All are fairly heavily censored.

The **English-language** *Egyptian Gazette* (on Saturday, the *Egyptian Mail*) carries agency reports, articles on Middle Eastern affairs and tourist features, but it's pretty lightweight and you can read the whole thing in a few minutes flat. For more serious journalism, look out for the English weekly edition of *Al-Ahram* (see below), which has interesting opinion pieces on politics, sociology and international affairs. The **French-language** counterparts of the *Egyptian Gazette/Egyptian Mail* are *Le Journal d'Egypte* and *Le Progrès Egyptien*; there is also a French edition of *Al-Ahram*, called *Hebdo*.

Of the **Arabic** press, Egypt's oldest newspaper, *Al-Ahram* ("The Pyramids"), founded in 1875, reflects official thinking, as do *Al-Akhbar* and *Al-Gomhouriya*. Other dailies with a party affiliation include the conservative *Al-Wafd* ("The Delegation"); the socialist *Al-Ahaly* ("The Nation"), and *Al-Da'wa* ("The Call"), the journal of the Muslim Brotherhood.

Public holidays and festivals

Egypt abounds in holidays and festivals of all kinds, both Muslim and Christian, national and local. Coming across a local moulid can be one of the most enjoyable experiences Egypt has to offer, with the chance to witness music, dancing and other entertainments.

Even if you're not interested in such festivals, it's important to be aware of **Ramadan**, when all Muslims (which means ninety percent of Egyptians) observe a total fast from sunrise to sunset for a month. This can pose big problems for travellers but the celebratory evenings are again good times to hear music and to share in hospitality.

Islamic holidays

Most Islamic holidays and festivals follow the Islamic calendar. This is lunar-based, so dates vary each year in relation to the Western calendar. You may find it useful to get hold of an annual prayer calendar from a local Islamic cultural centre in your own country.

The twelve **months** are Moharrem (30 days), Safar (29 days), Rabi el-Awwal (30 days), Rabi el-Tani (29 days), Gumad el-Awwal (30 days), Gumad el-Tani (29 days), Ragab (30 days), Sha'ban (29 days), Ramadan (30 days), Shawwal (29 days), Zoul Qiddah (30 days) and Zoul Hagga (29 days – or 30 days in leap years).

See overleaf for the estimated starting dates of Moharrem (which begins on Ras el-Sana el-Hegira) for the next few years. Note that a day in the Islamic calendar begins at sundown, as a consequence of which Islamic festivals start on the evening before you'd expect.

Ramadan

Ramadan, in a sense, parallels the Christian Lent. The ninth month of the Islamic calendar, it commemorates the time in which the Koran was revealed to Mohammed. In contrast to the Christian West, though, the Muslim world observes the fast rigorously.

What **the fast** involves is abstention from food, drink and smoking during daylight hours, and abstinence from sex throughout the month. Strict Muslims will even refrain from swallowing, lest they "drink" their own saliva.

With all opening times and transport schedules going haywire, and most local cafés and restaurants closing during the day (or remaining open, but not selling food), Ramadan is in many respects a bad time to travel. (We have given the Ramadan opening times where available throughout the text.) It is certainly no time to try camel trekking in the Sinai – no guide would undertake the work – and it is probably safer to travel by bus during the mornings only, as drivers will be fasting, too. (Airline pilots are forbidden to observe the fast.)

But there is a compensation in witnessing and becoming absorbed in the pattern of the fast. At sunset, signalled by the sounding of a siren and the lighting of lamps on the minarets, an amazing calm and sense of well-being fall on the streets, as everyone eats *fuul* and *taamiya* and, in the cities at least, gets down to a night of celebration and entertainment. Throughout the evening, urban cafés – and main squares – provide venues for live music and singing, while in small towns and poorer quarters of big cities, you will often come across ritualized *zikrs* – trance-like chanting and swaying.

If you are a **non-Muslim** outsider you are not expected to observe Ramadan, but it is good to be sensitive about not breaking the fast (particularly smoking) in public. In fact, the best way to experience Ramadan – and to benefit from its naturally purifying rhythms – is to enter into it. You may not be able to last without an occasional glass of water, and you'll probably breakfast later than sunrise, but it is worth an attempt – and you'll win local people's respect.

Other Islamic holidays

At the end of Ramadan comes the feast of **Eid el-Fitr**, a climax to the festivities in Cairo, though observed more privately in the villages. Equally important in the Muslim

calendar is **Eid el-Adha** (aka Eid el-Kabir or *Corban Bairam* – the Great Feast), which celebrates the willingness of Ibrahim (Abraham) to obey God and sacrifice his son. The Eid el-Adha is followed, about three weeks later, by **Ras el-Sana el-Hegira**, the first day of the month of Moharrem, which marks the Muslim new year.

Both eids are traditional family gatherings. At the Eid el-Adha every household that can afford it will slaughter a sheep. You see them tethered everywhere, even on rooftops, for weeks prior to the event. The slaughtering is often done on the streets.

The fourth main religious holiday is the **Moulid el-Nabi**, the Prophet Mohammed's birthday. This is widely observed, with processions in many towns and cities.

Moulids

Moulids are the equivalent of medieval European saints' fairs: popular events combining piety, fun and commerce. Their ostensible aim is to obtain blessing (*baraka*) from the saint, but the social and cultural dimensions are equally important. Moulids are an opportunity for people to escape the monotony of their hard-working lives in several days of festivities, and for friends and families from different villages to meet. Farming problems are discussed, as well as family matters – and marriage – as people sing, dance, eat and pray together.

The largest events draw crowds of over a million, with companies of *mawladiya* (literally, "moulid people") running stalls and rides, and music blaring into the small hours. Smaller, rural moulids tend to be heavier on the practical devotion, with people bringing their children or livestock for blessing, or the sick to be cured.

Dates...

With the exception of the Moulid el-Nabi (the Prophet's Birthday – see above), which is celebrated throughout Egypt, most moulids are localized affairs, usually centred around the mosque or tomb (*qubba*) of a holy man or woman. Most are scheduled according to the Islamic calendar, so dates vary from year to year when reckoned by the Western calendar.

Islamic holidays

Islamic religious holidays are calculated on the lunar calendar, so their dates rotate throughout the seasons (as does Ramadan's). Exact dates in the lunar calendar are impossible to predict – local Islamic centres can supply the current year's calendar only – but approximate dates for the next few years are:

	2005	2006	2007	2008	2009	2010
Eid el-Adha	Jan 20	Jan 9 & Dec 30	Dec 19	Dec 8	Nov 26	Nov 15
Ras el-Sana el-Hegira	Feb 9	Jan 30	Jan 19	Jan 8 & Dec 27	Dec 16	Dec 5
Moulid el-Nabi	April 20	April 10	Mar 30	Mar 18	Mar 7	Feb 24
1st of Ramadan	Oct 4	Sept 23	Sept 12	Aug 31	Aug 20	Aug 9
Eid el-Fitr	Nov 3	Oct 23	Oct 12	Sept 30	Sept 19	Sept 8

Public holidays

January 7 Coptic Christmas
April 25 Sinai Liberation Day
May 1 Labour Day
June 18 Evacuation Day
July 23 Revolution Day
Aug 15 Flooding of the Nile
October 6 Armed Forces Day
October 23 Suez Liberation Day
December 23 Victory Day

In addition to these, **Coptic Easter Sunday** (Sham al-Nassim) is a movable public holiday, which will be celebrated on 23 April 2006, 8 April 2007, 27 April 2008, 19 April 2009, and 4 April 2010.

To complicate matters further, certain moulids start (or finish) on a particular day (eg a Tuesday in a given month), rather than on any specific date. However, a minority of festivals occur at the same time every year, generally following the local harvest. If you're planning to attend a moulid, it's wise to verify the (approximate) dates given in this guide by asking local people or the tourist office.

...and spectacles

At the heart of every moulid is at least one **zikr** – a gathering of worshippers who chant and sway for hours, striving to attain a trance-like state of oneness with God.

Frequently, the zikr participants belong to one of the **Sufi brotherhoods**, which are differentiated by coloured banners, sashes or turbans, and named after their founding sheikh. The current incumbent of this office may lead them in a **zaffa** (parade) through town, and in olden times would ride a horse over his followers – a custom known as "the Treading".

Luxor's own festival features a parade of boats; elsewhere, the procession may be led by camels or floats. Accompanying all this are **traditional entertainments**: mock stick fights, conjurers, acrobats and snake charmers; horses trained to dance to music; and, sometimes, belly dancers. Music and singing are a feature of every moulid and locals often bring tape recorders to provide sounds for the rest of the year. If you are lucky enough to catch one of the major events, you'll get the chance to witness Egyptian popular culture at its richest.

The largest moulids are in Cairo, Tanta and Luxor. **Cairo** hosts three lengthy festivals in honour of El-Hussein, Saiyida Zeinab and the Imam el-Shafi'i (held during the months of Rabi el-Tani, Ragab and Sha'ban, respectively), plus numerous smaller festivals (see box on pp.272–273). Following the cotton harvest in October, the Moulid of El-Bedawi in **Tanta** starts a cycle of lesser **Nile Delta festivals** that runs well into November (see p.271). Equally spectacular is the Moulid of Abu el-Haggag in **Luxor**, held during the month of Sha'ban (p.380).

Coptic festivals

Egypt's Christian Coptic minority often attend Islamic moulids – and vice versa. **Coptic moulids** share some of the social and market functions of their Islamic counterparts and, similarly, at their core is the celebration of a saint's name-day. As you'd expect, the major Christian events of the year are also celebrated.

The dates of **Christmas** (January 6/7), **Epiphany** (January 19) and the **Annunciation** (March 21) are as specified in the Julian calendar used by the Orthodox Church, but **Easter** and its related feast days are reckoned according to the solar Coptic calendar, and therefore differ from both the Orthodox and Western dates by up to one month.

Major **saints' day events** include the Moulid of St Damyanah (May 15–20), the Feast of the Apostles Peter and Paul (July 12), and various moulids of the Virgin and St George during August. Many of these are held at monasteries in Middle Egypt, the Delta and the Red Sea Hills.

Lastly, a Coptic festival (of pharaonic origin) celebrated by all Egyptians is the **Sham el-Nessim**, a coming-of-spring festival which provides the excuse for mass picnics in parks and on riverbanks throughout the country. Its name literally means "Sniffing the Breeze".

Sports and outdoor pursuits

Egypt's main spectator sport is football (soccer). As far as participation sports go, both horse- and camel-riding are popular, but the big draw for visitors is snorkelling and diving amid the Red Sea's magnificent coral reefs. Other aquatic activities, such as water skiing, parasailing and windsurfing, are available on the Mediterranean coast. Despite Egypt's relative lack of greenery, golf is also possible, with several courses around Cairo as well as at Sharm el-Sheikh, Soma Bay, El Gouna and Luxor: full details are available at ⓦwww.touregypt.net/golfcourses.htm.

Football

Football (*kurat 'adem*) is Egypt's national sport. The two Cairo-based rivals, **Ahly** and **Zamalek**, are the major teams and contributed most of the country's 1998 squad which won the African Nations Cup and the Arabic Super-Cup. Clashes between the two teams can be intense – and have occasionally led to rioting – but games are in general relaxed: see p.276 for the details of games, tickets and stadium addresses. Should their team win, thousands of jubilant supporters drive around Cairo honking horns and waving flags attached to lances – beware of being run over or impaled.

Two other teams currently on the rise are **Ismaily** from Ismailiya and **Masry** from Port Said, while **Santa Katerina** is a team composed entirely of Sinai Bedouin who train by running up Mount Sinai twice a day. You can find detailed information about all aspects of Egyptian football at ⓦwww.egyptiansoccer.com.

Horse-, donkey- and camel-riding

Around the Pyramids and the major Nile sites, donkeys, horses and camels are all available for rental. **Horses** are fun if you want to ride across stretches of sand between the Pyramids or gallop in the desert in Sinai. **Donkeys** are best used for visiting the Theban Necropolis, where they traverse mountains that you'd never cross on foot, and enliven the trip no end. Elsewhere they have less appeal, but you might rent a *caretta* (donkey-drawn taxi cart) to explore the pools and ruins in Siwa Oasis. The Arabic word for donkey is *humár* (plural *hameer*); a donkey-guide is called a *hámar*.

Camels (the dromedary, or one-humped Arabian camel) make for pretty rigorous but exhilarating riding, and you'll probably want to try them at least once. They are good for short rides around Aswan, to the monastery of St Simeon, for example, but where they really come into their own is in Sinai or the Western Desert oases, where you can go trekking up *wadis* or across dunes that horses could never cope with. Trips – lasting anything from a half-day to a week – are easily arranged with local operators, or as part of "adventure holiday" packages before you set off.

Camel-riding is a real art, which gets a little easier on the body with experience. The mounting is done for you but be sure to hold on to the pommel of the saddle as the camel raises itself in a triple-jerk manoeuvre. Once on, you have a choice of riding it like a horse or cocking a leg around the pommel, as the Bedouin do. Be sure to use a lot of padding around the pommel: what begins as a minor irritation can end up leaving your skin rubbed raw.

Beware also of being palmed off with a male (bull) camel that's in heat – they can be quite vicious. Bad signs are an inflated mouth sac, aggressive behaviour towards its mates, and lots of noise and slobbering. When enraged, camels can launch a fierce attack – they've been known to grip someone's neck and shake them like a rag doll, or crush the bones in a leg.

Snorkelling, diving and angling

Anybody who can swim can **snorkel**, and Egypt's Red Sea resorts have some of the world's most spectacular coral reef wildlife, much of which requires nothing more than a mask and snorkel to see. For those who want to take it more seriously, Egypt is a very good place – and a relatively inexpensive one – to learn how to **dive**, or to go diving if you are already qualified. Dive centres are detailed throughout our chapters on the Sinai and the Red Sea Coast, but see in particular pp.707–711 for more on diving and snorkelling in Egypt.

If you do come to Egypt to dive, you are in for a treat, as the Red Sea has some of the world's most spectacular **coral and reef wildlife**, putting even places like the Caribbean, the Indian Ocean and the South Pacific in the shade. Facilities are well-developed, and in Hurghada and Sinai, dive safaris are a booming industry. Private charter boats (called "liveaboards") take divers to remote reefs, on trips lasting from several days to two or three weeks. Most are pre-booked by groups, which may not welcome individuals joining them at the last moment, so it's better, and cheaper, to buy a package deal at home (see pp.31–32, 34–35 and p.37 for lists of operators). Read the "Sinai" and "Red Sea Coast" chapters for an idea of the dive sites on offer.

For **fishing**, the place to come is not the Red Sea but Lake Nasser, the artificial lake behind the Aswan Dam, which is well stocked with massive and plentiful Nile perch, carp and tilapia. Fishing trips can be arranged in Aswan (see p.483) or booked online through African Angler (🕸www.african-angler.co.uk), or its agents in the UK (Go Fishing Worldwide ☎020/8742 1556; Safari Plus ☎01306/883204; and Tailor Made Holidays ☎020/8398 7424), North America (Travel Egypt ☎1-877/778-3497 or 678/319-9556) and Australia (Angling Adventures ☎1800/033 094 or 03/5221 7308), or with the firm itself in Egypt (☎097/230-9748 or 010/342-410).

Monuments and sites

The price of admission to Egypt's monuments skyrocketed in the 1990s, and entry costs now form a significant part of travel expenses. At major sites like the Theban Necropolis you could spend £35/US$65, taking into account such costly one-offs as Tutankhamun's tomb and the tomb of Nefertari – not to mention extra charges for the right to take photos inside tombs or use a video camera. However, visitors with an ISIC student card (see p.56) qualify for fifty-percent reductions on the price of admission tickets (though not photo permits).

Guides

Official **guides** can be engaged through branches of Misr Travel, American Express and Thomas Cook, local tourist offices and large hotels. You can also hire them on the spot at the Antiquities Museum in Cairo and the Pyramids of Giza. They normally charge a fixed hourly rate, which can be shared among a group of people, though a tip would also be expected.

Such professional guides can be useful at **major sites**, like the Valley of the Kings, where they will be able to ease your way through queues at the tombs. If you feel intimidated by the culture, too, you might welcome an intermediary for the first couple of days' sightseeing. In general, however, there's no special need to employ anyone: they tend to have enough work already with tour groups.

Far more common are **local, self-appointed guides**, who fall into two main categories. At ancient sites, there are always plenty of hangers-on, who will offer to show you "secret tombs" or "special reliefs" or just present themselves in tombs or temples, with palms outstretched. They don't have a lot to offer you, and encouragement makes life more difficult for everyone following. You can usually get rid of them by reading aloud from a guidebook.

The other kind – most often encountered in a small town or village – are people, often teenagers, who genuinely want to help out foreigners, and maybe practise their English at the same time. Services offered could be escorting you from one taxi depot to another, or showing you the route to the souks or to a local site. The majority of people you meet this way don't expect money – children included – and you could risk offence by offering. If people want money from you for such activities, they won't be shy about asking.

An official version of this kind of guiding is offered by members of the **Tourist Friends Association**, who often approach lost-looking foreigners at bus and train stations, and will swiftly produce their identity cards. They are generally students, very friendly and helpful, and not on the make. Be courteous even if you don't want their help.

Ancient monuments

Egypt's **ancient sites and monuments** are maintained by the **Supreme Council of Antiquities** (SCA; formerly known as the Egyptian Antiquities Organization or EAO). Most are kept open on a daily basis, with caretakers on hand to unlock tombs and point you towards the salient features. Local opening hours are detailed in individual entries; for a few hints on *baksheesh*, see pp.55–56 and p.151.

If you're a committed Egyptologist and want to visit sites that are under excavation or closed for repairs, you may want to contact the local branch of the SCA for a **special permit**. This is usually quite routine and you'll just be given a scrawled note in Arabic to show to the guards on site.

Religious buildings

Most of the **mosques** and their attached **madrassas** (Islamic colleges) that you'll want to visit are in Cairo, and, with the exception of the El-Hussein and Saiyida Zeinab mosques, are classified as "historic monuments". They are open routinely to non-Muslim visitors, although anyone not worshipping should avoid prayer times, especially the main service at noon on Friday. Elsewhere in the country, mosques are not used to seeing tourists and locals may object to your presence. Tread with care and if at all possible ask someone to take you in.

At all mosques, **dress** is important. Shorts (or short skirts) and exposed shoulders are out, and in some places women may be asked to cover their hair (a scarf might be provided). Above all, remember to remove your **shoes** upon entering the precinct. They will either be held by a shoe custodian (small *baksheesh* expected) or you can just leave them outside the door, or carry them in by hand (if you do this, place the soles together, as they are considered unclean).

Egyptian **monasteries** (which are Coptic, save for Greek Orthodox St Catherine's, in Sinai) admit visitors at all times except during the Lenten or other fasts (local fasts are detailed in the guide where appropriate). Similar rules of dress etiquette to those for mosques apply, though unless you go into the church itself you don't need to remove your shoes.

Cultural hints

If you want to get the most from a trip to Egypt, it is vital not to assume that anyone who approaches you expects to profit from the encounter. Too many tourists do, and end up making little contact with an extraordinarily friendly people.

Behaviour and attitude on your part are important. If some Egyptians treat tourists with contempt, it has much to do with the way the latter behave. It helps everyone if you can avoid rudeness or aggressive behaviour in response to insistent offers or demands. And be aware, too, of the importance of **dress**: shorts are socially acceptable only at beach resorts (and for women only in private resorts or along the Aqaba coast) shirts (for both sexes) should cover your shoulders. Many tourists ignore these conventions, unaware of how it demeans them in the eyes of the Egyptians.

Photography needs to be undertaken with care. If you are obviously taking a photograph of someone, ask their permission – especially in the more remote, rural regions where you can cause genuine offence. You may also find people stop you from taking photos that show Egypt in a "poor" or "backward" light. On a more positive front, taking a photograph of (and later sending it to) someone you've struck up a friendship with, or exchanging photographs, is often – in the towns at least – greatly appreciated. As ever, be wary of photographing anything militarily sensitive (bridges, train stations, dams, etc.).

When **invited to a home**, it's normal to take your shoes off before entering the reception rooms. It is customary to take a gift: sweet pastries (or tea and sugar in rural areas) are always acceptable.

One important thing to be aware of in Egypt is the different functions of the two hands. Whether you are right- or left-handed, the **left hand** is used for "unclean" functions, most importantly wiping your bottom, but also doing things like putting on and taking off shoes. This means that it is considered unhygienic to eat with your left hand. You can hold things like bread in your left hand in order to tear a piece off with your right hand, but you should never put food into your mouth with your left hand, and certainly never put it into the bowl when eating communally. You should also avoid passing things to people or accepting them with your left hand.

Crime and personal safety

During the 1990s, Egypt's image as a safe country to visit was shattered by a wave of terrorism, culminating in the 1997 Luxor massacre. As a result of this and a further wave of terrorist attacks in 2004 and 2005, security at all tourist sites is extremely heavy, giving first-time visitors an unnerving impression.

Petty crime

While relatively few in number, **pickpockets** are skilled and concentrate on tourists. Most operate in Cairo, notably in queues and on the crowded buses to the Pyramids. To play safe, keep your valuables in a **money belt** or a pouch under your shirt (leather or cotton materials are preferable to nylon, which can irritate in the heat). Overall, though, **casual theft** is more of a problem. Campsites, hostels and cheap hotels often have poor security, making it unwise to leave valuables there. At most places, you can deposit them at the reception (always get a receipt for cash).

If you are **driving**, it goes without saying you should not leave anything you cannot afford to lose visible or accessible in your car.

Terrorism

Between 1992 and 1997, Islamist militants murdered tourists, police and government officials in a series of bombings and shootings. Middle Egypt became a no-go zone for foreigners and tourism expired nationwide after the Luxor massacre. Egyptians were so revolted by the atrocity that even the *Gamaat Islamiya* disowned it as an act by wayward members, and their imprisoned leadership announced an end to violence in 1998. Meanwhile, thousands were detained under the emergency laws until the state saw fit to release them, and the combination of force and inducements seemed to work in ending that spate of attacks.

The lull only lasted until October 2004, however, when it was shattered by bomb attacks at Taba and Ras al-Shaitun in Sinai that killed 34 people; 2005 saw further incidents including a stabbing and two bomb attacks in Khan el-Khalili and Abdel Mouneem Riyad bus station in Cairo, in which four people were killed, including one of the bombers. These were followed in July by Egypt's worst terror attacks to date, a series of simultaneous suicide car-bombs on a hotel, car park and market in Sharm el-Sheikh and Na'ama Bay, which between them killed around eighty people – both Egyptians and Western tourists.

Most Egyptians, of course, were horrified at these atrocities, but some hardcore extremists are clearly prepared to carry out such actions. Needless to say, the authorities are taking the situation very seriously, and are determined to eradicate the terrorists while giving tourists maximum protection. There are armed police at all tourist sites, stations and checkpoints, scanners in hotels, and plainclothes agents in bars and bazaars. More relevant to visitors' movements, travel restrictions apply in the Nile Valley (see box on p.310).

Along the Nile Valley, tourists can only travel on special **train** services designated for tourists, which have plainclothes guards riding shotgun. Tourist buses between Cairo and Israel, and from Aswan to Luxor or Abu Simbel, must travel in a **convoy** (*kol*) with a police escort. Perversely, there is no formal ban on visiting once "risky" areas, but the local police will certainly keep a close eye on you and may insist on accompanying you to sites like Abydos or Dendara.

One way to reduce the risk of trouble is to **respect local customs** (in public, anyway). The less you stand out and cause offence, the smaller the chance of attracting any hostility. By going with the swim of society, you'll gain a measure of protection. In the event of **real trouble**, hit the deck or get off the streets immediately.

It goes without saying that certain subjects – Palestine, Israel and Islam, for instance – should be treated diplomatically should they come up in conversation. Some Egyptians are keen to discuss them, others not.

The police

Egypt has a plethora of police forces whose high profile in Cairo (which has more cops per thousand citizens than any other capital in the world) and at checkpoints on trunk roads strikes first-time visitors as a sign of recent trouble, although it has actually been the rule since the 1960s. Whereas Egyptians fear police brutality, foreign visitors are usually treated with kid gloves and given the benefit of the doubt unless drugs or espionage are suspected.

The **Municipal Police** handle all crimes and have a monopoly on law and order in smaller towns. Their uniform (khaki in winter, tan or white in summer) resembles that of the **Traffic Police**, who wear striped cuffs. Both get involved in accidents and can render assistance in emergencies. However, relatively few officers speak anything but Arabic.

If you've got a problem or need to report a crime, always go to the **Tourist and Antiquities Police**. The ordinary ranks wear the regular khaki police uniform with a "Tourist Police" armband; officers wear black uniforms in winter and white in summer. Found at tourist sites, museums, airports, stations and ports, they are supposedly trained to help tourists in distress, and speak a foreign language (usually English). In practice, the odds of getting such an officer are fifty-fifty – but it's worth trying them first. The more senior the officer, the better the chance they'll speak English.

The fourth conspicuous force is the **Central Security** force (dressed all in black and armed with Kalashnikovs), who guard embassies, banks and highways. Though normally genial enough, this largely conscript force will shift rapidly from tear gas to live rounds when ordered to crush demonstrations or civil unrest. If you find yourself getting caught up in anything, clear out quick. Ordinarily, though, they are nothing to worry about.

To guard vital utilities, there are also Electricity, Airport and **River Police** forces; the last is responsible for overseeing felucca journeys between Aswan and Luxor, though the formalities are usually handled by the captain of the boat rather than the passengers.

The **Military Intelligence** (the Mukhabarat) is only relevant to travellers who wish to visit remote parts of the Western Desert or go down beyond Mersa Alam on the Red Sea coast, for which you need permission (details in the text). Their offices in Mersa Matrouh and the oases are signposted in English and quite tourist-friendly, whereas in Sinai they have secret agents stationed in Dahab, Nuweiba, Na'ama Bay and Sharm el-Sheikh, whose brief includes watching Israeli tourists and Egyptians who visit Israel.

Finally there is the **State Security**, who may take an interest in tourists in border areas or Middle Egypt, but are generally irrelevant as far as most tourists are concerned. All of these forces deploy **plainclothes agents** who hang around near government buildings and crowded places, dressed as vendors or peasants – hence their nickname, the "Galabiyya Police". Aside from the sport of spotting agents in Cairo (where they dress quite snappily), tourists needn't think about them – though in hotels or bars, you might be disconcerted to find yourself chatting with a guy who suddenly announces that he's a cop. There are lots of them around.

Addresses and phone numbers of local police stations appear in the text.

Drugs

Most of Egypt's hashish came from Lebanon until the destruction of that country's industry by the Syrians at the end of the 1980s, when it was replaced by *bango* (marijuana) from Sudan. Since then, Egypt's own marijuana industry, based in the Sinai (see p.733), has seen a vast increase in both quantity and quality, supplemented by hashish from Morocco and the small-scale return of hash from Lebanon. A small amount of opium is also produced in the Sinai.

Despite a tradition of use stretching back to the thirteenth century, Egypt was one of the first countries in modern times to ban cannabis, back in 1879. The prohibition was not strictly enforced under President Sadat (who reputedly smoked dope himself), but the country now has draconian anti-drugs laws that make hanging or life imprisonment mandatory for convicted smugglers and dealers (which could be interpreted to mean somebody caught with a few sachets of the stuff), and the law against cannabis is much more strictly enforced than it ever used to be. Mere possession or use merits a severe prison sentence and a heavy fine, plus legal costs, upwards of US$1000. Despite this, hashish and *bango* are still consumed by those who can afford it. Perversely, *bango* is popularly considered a worse drug than hashish, possibly because it is cheaper and therefore more commonly used by members of society's lower strata; few people seem to be aware that both drugs come from the same plant.

Penalties for drug offences have recently been increased, with prison sentences even for possession of cannabis, and 25 years' hard labour or even the death penalty for trafficking, which includes bringing any illegal drug into the country. In practice, the least you can expect if caught with a smoke is immediate deportation and a ban from ever visiting the country again. You may be able to buy your way out of trouble, but this should be negotiated discreetly and as soon as possible, while the minimum number of officers are involved: once you are taken in, it will be a lot more difficult. Needless to say, your embassy will be unsympathetic. The best advice is to steer well clear of all illegal drugs while you are in the country.

Foreign consulates in Egypt

If you do find yourself in trouble – or simply need a visa – there are **embassies** or **consulates** for most nationalities in Cairo (see pp.291–292). Britain and several other European countries also maintain consulates in Alexandria (p.639) and Luxor (p.382). Consulates can advise on legal matters and replace missing passports, but are unsympathetic towards drug offenders and will not make loans to penniless travellers (though they may repatriate you as a last resort).

Working and studying

Cairo offers the best work possibilities in Egypt for teaching English as a foreign language or journalism, while the American University in Cairo (AUC) is a rewarding if expensive place to study Arabic, Middle Eastern affairs or Egyptology. To a lesser extent, opportunities to teach or study also exist in Alexandria. Elsewhere, you might find work as a tour rep or salesperson at one of the main resorts, as a diving instructor in Hurghada or Sinai, or a bellydancer in a hotel nightclub.

Teaching English

Teaching in Egypt largely means working in Cairo or Alexandria, where there are many private language schools, generally catering to adults. There's quite a big market for people wanting to learn both conversational and business English. Try contacting one of the following:

British Council 192 Corniche el-Nil, Aguza, Cairo ☎02/300-1666; 11 Sharia Mahmoud Abou El Ela, Kafr Abdou, Roushdi Alexandria ☎03/545-6512, ⓦwww.britishcouncil.org.eg. A degree and RSA TEFL certificate are required for jobs at the British Council, which recruits most of its staff in Britain (check ⓦwww.britishcouncil.org /teacherrecruitment.htm for a current list of vacancies, or call ☎020/7389 4931). Vacancies do occur locally from time to time, however. Pays good rates.

International Language Institute (ILI) 2 Sharia Mohammed Bayoumi, Heliopolis, Cairo, ☎02/418-9212 or 291-9295, ⓔili@idsc.net.eg. Affiliated to International House. ILI require an RSA TEFL certificate and a university degree. High turnover of staff, so a good chance of work. Rates are slightly lower than at the British Council.

Journalism

Cairo has been the launch pad for several **journalistic** careers, for it is easy to place work with the local English-language media. *Egypt Today* takes travel articles and photos, while the *Egyptian Gazette* may need subeditors from time to time. International press agencies may also accept material and possibly employ stringers.

Diving instructors

Divers with Divemaster or Instructor certificates can often find work with diving centres in Hurghada or Sinai, which may also take on less qualified staff and let them learn on the job, at reduced rates of pay or in return for free tuition. Dive centres commonly turn a blind eye to the lack of a work permit, or might procure one for a valued worker. As with language schools, you should be wary about surrendering your passport, and ask other foreigners working in the same job about the potential drawbacks.

Bellydancing

Foreign **bellydancers** are much in demand in nightclubs in Cairo, Alexandria, Luxor and Hurghada. The work can be well paid, but you have to be careful: financial or sexual exploitation are real hazards. Aside from work, many foreign dancers come to Egypt to improve their art or buy costumes. Finding a teacher is surprisingly difficult, as there are no schools as such; instruction takes place in people's homes and the addresses are hard to obtain. If you're interested, start making enquiries at the specialist shops in Cairo, where you can buy costumes, music tapes and videos of top performers (see p.282).

Tourism

Though most jobs in **tourism** are restricted to Egyptian nationals, and locally based companies usually insist on a work permit, you can sometimes fix up a season's work with a foreign tour operator abroad as a rep or tour guide. See the lists on pp.31–32, 34–35 and p.37 for companies to approach.

In Sinai, Hurghada and Luxor there may be a demand for people with foreign languages to sell dive courses or work on hotel reception desks. The most useful languages to have are German, French, Italian, Japanese or Russian (the last only on the Red Sea and Sinai coasts). Ask around dive centres or upmarket hotels if you're interested.

Studying

The **American University in Cairo** (113 Sharia Qasr el-Aini, near Midan Tahrir ☏02/797-5055, ⊛www.aucegypt.edu) offers year-abroad and non-degree programmes, a summer school and intensive Arabic courses. A full year's tuition (two semesters and summer school) costs roughly US\$18,000. US citizens may apply to the Stafford Loan Program, at Office of Admissions, 420 Fifth Ave, 3rd Floor, New York, NY 10018-2729 (☏212/730-8800, ⊛www.aucegypt.edu).

Foreign students may also attend one- or two-term programmes at three **Egyptian universities**: Cairo, Ain Shams and Al-Azhar. These are valid for transferable credits at most American and some British universities. In the US, contact the Egyptian Cultural and Educational Bureau, 1303 New Hampshire Ave NW, Washington DC 20036 (☏202/296-3888, ⊛www.eceb-usa.org) or AmidEast, 1730 M St NW Suite 1100, Washington DC 20036 (☏202/776-9600, ⊛www.amideast.org).

A number of schools in Cairo (see p.292) offer courses in **Arabic language**, both in colloquial Egyptian Arabic (the language people speak on the street) and Modern Standard Arabic (the language newspapers are written in). The American University (see above) offers twelve-week intensive courses with 72 hours' tuition at US\$500, and the International Language Institute in Sahafayeen (see p.292 for contact details) offers forty hours' tuition over four weeks for US\$300. The lowest-priced courses are those offered by ECIC (see p.292 for contact details), at £E951 for an eight-week course with 48 hours' tuition.

Travellers with disabilities

Disability is common in Egypt; many conditions that would be treatable in the West, such as cataracts, cause permanent disabilities here because people can't afford the treatment. Disabled people are unlikely to get jobs (though there is a tradition of blind singers and preachers), so the choice is usually between staying at home being looked after by your family, and going out on the streets to beg for alms. For the disabled traveller, this has its advantages; disability and disfigurement do not get the same embarrassed reaction from Egyptians that they do from able-bodied Westerners. Disability carries no stigma, it is simply God's will, to be accepted and made light of – as Egyptians say, *Allah karim* (God is generous).

On the other hand, things are not made easy for disabled people, and the streets are full of all sorts of obstacles that would be hard for a blind or wheelchair-using tourist to negotiate independently. If you walk with difficulty, you will find street obstacles and steep stairs hard going. Queuing, and the heat, will take it out of you if you have a condition that makes you tire quickly. A light, folding camp-stool could be invaluable if you have limited walking or standing power. In that case, it's a good idea to avoid arriving in the summer months, when the scorching sun can really take it out of you – travelling in the spring, autumn or even winter will be a lot less gruelling.

For those who use a wheelchair, the **monuments** are a mix of the accessible and the impossible. Most of the major temples are built on relatively level sites, with a few steps here and there – manoeuvrable in a wheelchair or with sticks if you have an able-bodied helper. Your frustrations are likely to be with the tombs, which are almost always a struggle to reach – often sited halfway up cliffs, or down steep flights of steps. In the Valley of the Kings, for example, the only really straightforward tomb is that of Ramses VI. The Pyramids of Giza are fine to view but not enter, though the sound and light show is wheelchair accessible; Saqqara is difficult, being so sandy. Abu Simbel should be reasonably OK, provided you can cope with the very rough surfaces. If you opt for a Nile cruise, bear in mind that you'll be among a large throng of people and will need to be carried on and off the boat if you depend on a wheelchair (often by people who don't understand English), an experience you may well not relish.

When choosing a hotel, if you use a chair, it's worth trying to choose a place within wheeling distance of the sites you wish to visit. In general, a place in the centre of town is best if possible, and in Aswan, it's not a good idea to stay on the islands if you use a wheelchair, because of the hassle getting on and off the ferries.

Cairo is generally bad news, especially Islamic Cairo, with its narrow, uneven alleys and heavy traffic, but with a car and helper, you could still see the Citadel and other major monuments. There's a lift in the Egyptian Antiquities Museum, and newer metro stations have elevator access from street level to the platforms, though none of the older ones do, which unfortunately includes all those in the city centre. A number of hotels, all five-star, have rooms adapted for wheelchair users (these include the *Cairo Marriott*, *Conrad*, *Four Seasons*, *Grand Hyatt*, *Mena House Oberoi*, *Nile Hilton*, *Ramses Hilton* and *Semiramis Intercontinental*, all reviewed on pp.117–118).

Some **diving** centres in Sinai and Hurghada accept disabled students on their courses, and the hotels in these resorts tend to be wheelchair-friendly.

Taxis are easily affordable and quite adaptable; if you rent one for the day, the driver is certain to help you in and out, and perhaps even around the sites you visit. If you employ a guide, they may well also be prepared to help you with steps and other obstacles.

Planning a holiday

There are **organized tours and holidays** specifically for people with disabilities, and some companies, such as Discover Egypt, offer packages tailor-made to your specific needs; see the listings below for contacts. Egypt specialists include the recently formed Egypt for All (see below), who run a wide range of tours for people with disabilities, including diving holidays, desert safaris, felucca trips and Nile cruises, with programmes ranging from one-day excursions to two-week holidays. If you want to be more **independent**, it's important to become an authority on where you must be self-reliant and where you may expect help, especially regarding transport and accommodation. It is also vital to be honest – with travel agencies, insurance companies and travel companions.

People with a pre-existing medical condition are sometimes excluded from travel **insurance** policies, so read the small print carefully. To make your journey simpler, ask your travel agent to notify airlines or bus companies, who can cope better if they are expecting you, with, for example, a wheelchair provided at airports, and staff primed to help. A medical certificate of your fitness to travel, provided by your doctor, is also extremely useful; some airlines or insurance companies may insist on it.

Make sure that you have extra supplies of **drugs** – carried with you if you fly – and a prescription including the generic name in case of emergency. It's also a good idea to carry spares of any clothing or equipment that might be hard to find; if there's an association representing people with your disability, contact them early in the planning process.

Contacts for travellers with disabilities

In the UK and Ireland

Accessible Sun Avionics House, Naas Lane, Gloucester GL2 2SN ☎01452/729739, minicom ☎01452/725802, ⊛www.accessiblesummersun .co.uk. Holidays for people with disabilities and their companions, including Nile cruises and Red Sea beach holidays.
Holiday Care 2nd floor, Imperial Building, Victoria Rd, Horley, Surrey RH6 7PZ ☎0845/124 9971,

minicom ☎0845/124 9976, ⊛www.holidaycare .org.uk. Provides an information sheet on North Africa, including a brief list of accessible accommodation in Egypt. Information on financial help for holidays available.
Irish Wheelchair Association Blackheath Drive, Clontarf, Dublin 3 ☎01/818 6400, ⊛www.iwa.ie. Useful information provided about travelling abroad with a wheelchair.
Tripscope Alexandra House, Albany Rd, Brentford, Middlesex TW8 0NE ☎0845/7585 641, ⊛www .tripscope.org.uk. This registered charity provides a national telephone information service offering free transport and travel advice for people with a mobility problem.

In the USA and Canada

Access-Able ⊛www.access-able.com. Online resource for travellers with disabilities.
Directions Unlimited 123 Green Lane, Bedford Hills, NY 10507 ☎1-800/533-5343 or 914/241-1700. Travel agency specializing in bookings for people with disabilities.
Mobility International USA 451 Broadway, Eugene, OR 97401 ☎541/343-1284, ⊛www .miusa.org. Information and referral services, access guides, tours and exchange programmes. Annual membership US$35 (includes quarterly newsletter).

In Australia and New Zealand

ACROD (Australian Council for Rehabilitation of the Disabled) PO Box 60, Curtin ACT 2605 ☎ 02/6282 4333 (also TTY). Provides lists of travel agencies and tour operators for people with disabilities.
Disabled Persons Assembly 4/173–175 Victoria St, Wellington ☎04/801 9100 (also TTY). ⊛www.dpa.org.nz. Resource centre with lists of travel agencies and tour operators for people with disabilities.

In Egypt

Egypt For All 344 Sharia Suda, Mohandesin ☎012/311-8975, ⊛www.egyptforall.com. Runs a wide program of tours and excursions for disabled visitors to Egypt.
Farida Tours Cairo ☎02/290-7075, 290-7722, 414-0508, ⊛www.faridatours.com. Can customize trips to Egypt for travellers with disabilities.
Misr Travel (See p.45 for details.) Can be helpful with transport and accommodation arrangements.
Peace Tourism 4 Sharia Ismail Sabry, Heliopolis, Cairo ☎02/637-3833, ℉635-1919, ⊛www .peacetourism.com. Can offer the same sort of assistance as Misr Travel.

Women travellers

The biggest problem women travellers face in Egypt is the perceptions that Egyptian men have. Unless accompanied by husbands, women tourists are seen as loose, willing to have sex at the most casual opportunity, and – in Egyptian social terms – virtually on a par with prostitutes. While Hollywood films are partly to blame for this view, the root cause is the vast disparity between social norms in Islamic and Western countries.

Many women visitors do a range of things that no respectable Egyptian woman would consider: dressing "immodestly", showing shoulders and cleavage; sharing rooms with men to whom they are not married; drinking alcohol in bars or restaurants; smoking; even travelling alone on public transport, without a relative as an escort. While well-educated Egyptians familiar with Western culture can take these in their stride, less sophisticated ones are liable to assume the worst. Tales of affairs with tourists, and the scandalous Russians of Hurghada, are common currency among Egyptian males. In Sinai, however, unaccompanied women experience few hassles, except from construction workers from "mainland" Egypt.

Without compromising your freedom too greatly, there are a few steps you can take to improve your image. Most important and obvious is **dress**: loose opaque clothes that cover all "immodest" areas (thighs, upper arms, chest) and hide your contours are a big help, and essential if you are travelling alone or in rural areas (where covering long hair is also advisable). On public transport (buses, trains, service taxis), try to sit with other women – who may often invite you to do so. On the Cairo metro and trams in Alexandria there are carriages reserved for women. If you're travelling with a man, wearing a wedding ring confers respectability, and asserting that you're married is better than admitting to being "just friends".

As anywhere, looking confident and knowing where you're going is a major help in avoiding hassle. It's also a good idea to avoid making eye contact with Egyptian men (some women wear sunglasses for the purpose), and it is best to err on the side of standoffishness, as even a friendly smile may be taken as a come-on. Problems – most commonly hissing or groping – tend to come in downtown Cairo and in the public beach resorts (except Sinai's Aqaba coast, or Red Sea holiday villages, which are more or less the only places where you'll feel happy about sunbathing). In the oases, where attractions include open-air springs and hot pools, it's okay to bathe – but do so in at least a T-shirt and leggings: oasis people are among the most conservative in the country.

Your reaction to **harassment** is down to you. Some women find that verbal hassle is best ignored, while others may prefer to use an Egyptian brush-off like *khalás* (finished) or *úsqut* (be quiet). If you get groped, the best response is to yell *áram!* (evil!) or *sibnee le wadi* (don't touch me), which will shame any assailant in public, and may attract help. Groping an Egyptian woman would be judged totally unacceptable behaviour, so there's no reason why you should put up with it, either. Some women find that it occasionally helps to clout gropers, if only to make themselves feel better.

Many women in relationships with Egyptian men enter into so-called Orfi **marriages** (aka "Dahab marriages"), arranged by a lawyer, to circumvent the law that prohibits unmarried couples from sleeping under the same roof or public displays of affection. These allow couples to rent a flat without hassle from the Vice Squad (thereby also providing cover for potential prostitution) and can be annulled without a divorce. They don't confer the same

See p.54 for advice on women's health issues while travelling in Egypt.

legal rights as a full marriage in a special registry office (Sha'ar el-Aqari) in Cairo, which is the only kind that allows women to bring their spouse to their own country or gives them any rights in child-custody disputes. Women can bolster their position by insisting on a marriage contract (pre-nuptial agreement). A useful factsheet, Notes on Marrying an Egyptian, is available from the British Embassy in Cairo. Note that, whatever you may be told, foreign women don't need to be married to an Egyptian to buy property or become a partner in a business. If you are considering this, however, it's vital to find a good lawyer, preferably one who has worked abroad and is familiar with Western ways.

On the positive side, spending time with **Egyptian women** can be a delight, if someone decides to take you under their wing. The difficulty in getting to know women is that fewer women than men speak English, and that you won't run into women in cafés or tourist facilities. However, public transport can be a good meeting ground, as can shops and, best of all, local schools (Egypt has a high proportion of women teachers). If asking directions in the street, it's always better to ask a woman than a man.

Female genital mutilation

A little-known and shocking fact about Egyptian women is that the vast majority of them – up to 97 percent according to one survey – have been subjected to a horrific and illegal operation known euphemistically as "female circumcision", and more correctly as female genital mutilation (FGM). In this procedure, typically carried out on little girls aged between seven and ten, the clitoris and sometimes all or part of the inner vaginal lips are cut off with a scalpel, knife or sharp object. The justification is that it reduces the girl's sexual desire, thus protecting her chastity and her family's or husband's "honour". Obviously, it prevents the victim from ever enjoying sex.

FGM is an African rather than an Islamic practice, and in Egypt it is performed by Copts as much as by Muslims. Nonetheless, spurious religious reasons are given to justify it, including two disputed *hadiths* (quotations from Mohammed), dismissed by the Muslim Women's League as "non-authentic".

In 1951, the Egyptian Fatwa Committee decreed that FGM was desirable because it curbs women's sex drive, and in 1981 the Sheikh of al-Azhar Mosque and University said that it was the duty of parents to have their daughters genitally mutilated.

The good news is that things have changed a little bit since then. Firstly, FGM is increasingly performed by qualified medical practitioners under anaesthetic, and this now applies in six out of ten cases, though of course that means that forty percent of victims still have the operation performed by a barber or similarly non-qualified person, and without anaesthetic. Secondly, it is now, at least in theory, illegal – the government banned it in 1996 after a CNN documentary exposed the practice, to Egypt's great shame abroad, and the Supreme Court threw out an attempt by Islamic fundamentalists to have the ban declared unconstitutional. On the other hand, the law is rarely enforced, and it would be hard for the government to enforce it, even if they really wanted to. Thirdly, the incidence of FGM is beginning to decline: a survey in 2000 found that 78 percent of 11- to 19-year-olds had been victims of FGM compared to 83 percent in 1995, and that support for the practice among Egyptian women had fallen from 82 percent to 75 percent; but yes, three-quarters of Egyptian women questioned, despite having suffered it themselves, felt that it was a good thing, and over three-quarters of teenage girls have been subjected to it. As for the religious authorities, both the current Sheikh of al-Azhar and the Coptic pope have stated that FGM is not a religious requirement, though of course that falls well short of a condemnation.

The Assyut Childhood and Development Association, supported by UNICEF, have begun an FGM abandonment programme in Middle Egypt, and gradually awareness is spreading, but the sad fact remains that Egypt has one of the highest rates of FGM in the world, and the practice is not going to disappear in a hurry. Meanwhile, bear in mind that almost all the women you will meet in Egypt have been victims of this barbaric and horrifying abuse of their human rights, and that most of them will have the same thing done to their own daughters.

Travelling with children

Children evoke a warm response in Egypt and are welcome more or less everywhere. It's not unusual to see Egyptian children out with their parents in cafés or shops past midnight. The only child-free zones tend to be bars and clubs frequented by foreigners. Most hotels can supply an extra bed and breakfast (which should be supplemented for variety). Pharmacies sell formula milk, baby food and disposable nappies, and the last two may also be stocked by corner stores in larger towns. Things worth bringing are a mosquito net for a buggy or crib and a parasol for sun protection.

From an adult minder's standpoint, most hazards can be minimized or avoided by taking due precautions. Traffic is obviously dangerous, while stray animals (possible disease carriers), fenced-off beaches (probably mined – see p.95), elevators with no inner doors (keep small hands away!), and poisonous fish and coral in the Red Sea (see p.711) are other potential hazards.

Children (especially young ones) are more susceptible than adults to **heatstroke** and **dehydration** and should always wear a sunhat, and high-factor sunscreen on exposed skin. Certainly for the first few days, if swimming at a beach resort, they should do so in a T-shirt.

The other thing that children are very susceptible to is an **upset tummy** and, while this is to be expected to some extent, especially with an unfamiliar diet, bear in mind that diarrhoea can be much more dangerous to a child than it is to an adult. If diarrhoea strikes, keep your child on a sensible diet (boiled vegetables, yoghurt, bananas), and be sure to maintain their salt and fluid levels, by giving them plenty of mineral water, preferably with oral rehydration salts ("Rehydran", available very cheaply at most pharmacies and worth carrying).

Incidentally, if children balk at unfamiliar **food**, outlets of all major American fast-food chains, as well as the British chain Wimpy, are always close at hand as a last resort. Egyptian sweets are unlikely to appeal much to Western kids, but ice cream is cheap and ubiquitous, as is rice pudding.

On a more positive note, there are plenty of aspects to life in Egypt that children should enjoy, among them camel, horse and donkey rides, but choose carefully – AA Stables in Cairo for example (see p.274) has a good reputation. Activities such as felucca rides, snorkelling and visiting a few of the great monuments can also be enjoyable. All the main resorts have discos and sports facilities, and the hotel pool is bound to be a big favourite with younger holidaymakers. We've listed a number of activities in Cairo that will especially appeal to younger travellers (see pp.276–277).

Senior travellers

A lot of retired people visit Egypt, which is hardly surprising considering that a visit here has been many people's lifelong dream. However, this is not a country to rush around in, even if you had the inclination to do so, nor is it likely to be, unless you are very intrepid indeed, a country where you will want to rough it.

Luckily, your money will go a lot further in Egypt than it would at home, so a bit of luxury should not be beyond your reach, and you can afford to do things the easy way. There is no need to fight your way onto city buses for example, when you can take a taxi for a dollar, or hire one for a whole day, should you so wish, for around £10/US$18. Nor need you stay in a cheap city hotel when as little as £25/US$40 will get you a double room with breakfast in a very nice three-star establishment like the *Grand* or the *Victoria* in Cairo, for example.

Especially if you intend to visit a number of widely spread-out sites, it is definitely worth taking it easy and using **taxis** to get around. This particularly applies if you plan to go to a number of the pyramid sites around Cairo (say, Giza, Saqqara and maybe Dahshur), or sites on the west bank of the Nile at Luxor. If you do not, the heat can really take it out of you in a surprisingly short time. Don't underestimate the sun, which can be absolutely roasting, and always take a sunhat and sufficient drinking water.

Most older people visiting Egypt prefer to take a **package tour** than travel independently, and while there is absolutely no reason why you should not travel on your own, a package tour does make it very much easier. When choosing a package, it is worth considering one that is specifically aimed at travellers of a certain age, and particularly if you are single or widowed, it can be a whole lot more sociable. **Saga Holidays** (UK ℡0800/096 0078 or ℡44 1303 771190, ⊛www.saga.co.uk; US & Canada ℡1-800/343-0273, ⊛www .sagaholidays.com) is the biggest and most established specialist in holidays for the over-50s, and offers various options ranging from an eleven-day "Land of the Pharaohs" tour to beach holidays at Sharm el-Sheikh. Of the tour operators listed on pp.31–32, 34–35 and p.37, the more upmarket firms are the ones most likely to appeal to mature readers.

Gay and lesbian travellers

As a result of sexual segregation, male homosexuality is relatively common in Egypt, but attitudes towards it are schizophrenic. No Egyptian will declare himself gay – which has connotations of femininity and weakness – and the dominant partner may well not consider himself to be indulging in a homosexual act. Rather, it is tacitly accepted as an outlet for urges that can't otherwise be satisfied: few men can afford marriage until their thirties, and boys have little other means of gaining sexual experience. Despite this, people are mindful that homosexuality is condemned in the Koran and the Bible, and reject the idea of Egypt as a "gay destination" (although male prostitution is an open secret in Luxor and Aswan). The common term for gay men in Egyptian Arabic is *hawal*, though it does have derogatory connotations, as do slang terms such as *ma'aza* and *agila*.

Homosexuality as such is not illegal in Egypt, but that does not stop the authorities from persecuting gay men, usually on charges of "habitual debauchery". Indeed, the last few years have seen a massive increase in the persecution of gay Egyptian men, which hit the headlines worldwide when Egyptian police raided the Queen Boat floating discoteque in May 2001. The disco was frequented by heterosexual couples as well as by gay Egyptian and foreign men, but only Egyptian men alone or with male partners were arrested. Most were eventually tried for "habitual debauchery", and two for "contempt of religion". Those convicted received sentences of one to five years in jail. Foreigners seem to be safe from such persecution, but if you have a gay relationship with an Egyptian man, be aware that discretion is vital to avoid putting him in serious danger.

One result of all this is that **meeting places** for gay men have gone underground, and places that are well-known as gay locales have become dangerous for gay Egyptians. **Lesbians** do not face this kind of state harassment, but they have never been visible in Egyptian society, and there is almost no public perception of lesbianism. As a Western woman, your chances of making contact are virtually zilch.

As emphasized under "Health" (see pp.53–54), AIDS is a real threat in Egypt, despite the minuscule number of reported cases. There is some awareness of AIDS amongst Egyptians but most are steadfast in seeing it as a "disease for foreigners" and the concept, let alone the practice, of "safe sex" has yet to emerge.

A few **websites** deal with gay issues in Egypt. The Globalgayz Egypt page at ⓦ www.globalgayz.com/g-egypt2.html has articles about the current situation, and the International Gay and Lesbian Human Rights Commission website at ⓦ www.iglhrc.org posts any new information about civil rights for gay people in Egypt. Gay Egypt at ⓦ www.gayegypt.com offers more in the way of practical advice and contacts, but don't log on to it in Egypt, where it is monitored by the Security Police, who have been known to use Internet contacts to entrap gay Egyptians.

Contacts for gay and lesbian travellers

Madison Travel UK ☎ 01273/202 532, ⓦ www.madisontravel.co.uk. Established travel agents specializing in gay- and lesbian-friendly packages to popular destinations including Luxor.

GayGuide.net ⓦ gayguide.net/Africa/Egypt. A webpage on gay travel to Egypt – there isn't a great deal here, but it's worth a look before you book.

International Gay & Lesbian Travel Association US & Canada ☎ 1-800/448-8550 or 954/776-2626, ⓦ www.iglta.org. Trade group that can provide a list of gay- and lesbian-owned or -friendly travel agents, accommodation and other travel businesses, though they don't currently have very much on Egypt.

Spartacus Gay Guide US & Canada ☎1-800/548-3855, UK ☎ 020/8829 3000, Australia ☎ 02/9699 3507. International gay guide with information on meeting and cruising spots for gay men, but nothing much for lesbians; on sale at gay and alternative bookshops.

Directory

ABU AND UMM Literally "father of" and "mother of", *Abu* and *Umm* are used both as honorific titles and also figuratively as a nickname, picking out the salient character-istic of a person or object. They can also be used metaphorically, as in *Umm al-Dunya* ("Mother of the World"), a common descrip-tion of Cairo.

ADDRESSES The words for street (*sharia*), avenue (*tariq*) and square (*midan*) always precede the name. Whole blocks often share a single street number, which may be in Arabic numerals (see also p.114). Elsewhere, street numbers may not be used at all.

CIGARETTES The vast majority of Egyptian men smoke, and offering cigarettes around is common practice. The most popular brand is Cleopatra (£E2.50; £E2.75 in a crush-proof pack). Locally produced versions of Marlboro, Rothmans and Camel (typically retailing at around £E7.50) have a much higher tar content than their equivalents at home; the genuine article can be found in duty-free shops. Matches are *kibreet*; a ciga-rette lighter is a *wallah*. Respectable women don't generally smoke, and certainly not in public, though nowadays wealthier young women may be seen smoking *sheesha* in Cairo's posher establishments.

ELECTRICITY The current in Egypt is 220V, 50Hz. North American travellers with appliances designed for 110V should bring a converter. Most sockets are for round-pronged plugs, so you'll also need an adapter. Brief power cuts are quite common in Egypt.

LAUNDRY In Egypt no one goes to the laundry: if they don't do their own, they send it out to a *mahwagi*. Wherever you are staying, there will either be an in-house *mahwagi*, or one close by to call on. Some low-budget hotels in Luxor, Aswan and Hurghada allow guests to use their washing machine for a small charge, or gratis. You can buy washing powder at most pharma-cies. Dry cleaners are confined to Cairo, Aswan and Hurghada.

MINEFIELDS These still exist from World War II along the Mediterranean coast, and from Israeli conflicts in the interior of Sinai and along the Red Sea coast (detailed in chapters 3, 4, 7 and 8). Don't take any risks in venturing into fenced-off territory, unless locals go there often.

SPELLINGS Arabic is notoriously hard to transliterate into Roman script. The existence of several systems, and the popular familiarity

Metric weights and measures

1 kilo = approx 2.2lb; 1lb = approx 454g/0.454kg; 1oz = approx 28.3g.
1 centimetre = approx 0.394 inches;
1 inch = approx 2.5cm;
1 foot = approx 30cm.
1 metre = approx 1.094 yards or 39 inches; 1 yard = approx 0.914m.
1 kilometre = approx 0.621 miles;
1 mile = approx 1.609km;
5 miles = approx 8km.
1 litre = approx 1.76 UK pints;
1 UK pint = approx 0.568 litres;
1 UK gallon = approx 4.54litres.
1 litre = approx 2.11 US pints;
1 US pint = approx 0.473 litres;
1 US quart = approx 0.946 litres.
1 litre = approx 0.264 US gallons;
1 US gallon = approx 3.785 litres.

Useful things to bring

- **Alarm clock** For getting up to catch early-morning buses.
- **Binoculars** Perfect for observing reliefs high up on temple facades – or birdlife.
- **Clothes** Egypt is deeply conservative – the more modest your dress the less hassle you will attract. Northern Egypt can be cold and damp in the winter, while the desert gets freezing at night, even in spring and autumn, so a warm sweater is invaluable, as are a solid pair of shoes: burst pipes are commonplace, and wandering around muddy streets in sodden sandals is a miserable experience.
- **Earplugs** Help muffle the noise of videos on long-distance buses and trains, if you're trying to sleep.
- **Film** Kodak and Fuji film is available in most towns and major resorts, but it may be old stock, so bring adequate supplies. For photography in dark alleyways, tombs and hidden corners, fast film (400–800 ASA) is useful, while for good landscape photographs, slow film is a must. For cautions on taking photographs, see p.83.
- **Mosquito net** The best guarantee of a mozzie-free night's sleep in the oases and the Nile Valley. Alternatively, buy a plug-in device (such as Ezalo) at any Egyptian pharmacy.
- **Plug** Few hotels (even relatively upmarket ones) have sink plugs, so pack an omnisize plug.
- **Sleeping bag** A decent bag is invaluable if you're planning to sleep out in the desert in spring or autumn, or in any low-budget hotel over winter. In the summer, a sheet sleeping bag or silk sleeping bag liner is handy if you're staying at cheap hotels, where just one (not necessarily clean) sheet is provided.
- **Snaps** of your family, home town, football team (or whatever) help bridge the language barrier. Locals will proudly show you their own.
- **Torch/flashlight** For exploring dark tombs, and for use during power cuts.

of certain spellings, make consistency a nightmare. Egyptians themselves employ English spelling loosely; basically, you get accustomed to different variations on the same Arabic name.

TIME Egypt is on GMT+2 in winter, which means it is two hours ahead of the British Isles, seven hours ahead of the US East Coast (EST), eleven hours ahead of the US West Coast (PST), six hours behind Western Australia, eight hours behind East Australia and ten hours behind New Zealand. Clocks move forward for Daylight Saving Time on the last Friday in April, and the swap to DST in Egypt or your home country can add or subtract an hour from the time difference. Time in Egypt is a more elastic concept than Westerners are used to. In practice, "five minutes" often means an hour or more; *bahdeen* ("later") the next day; and *bukkra* ("tomorrow") an indefinite wait for something

that may never happen. Besides hinting that it won't, *inshallah* ("God willing") can be a polite way of backing away from unwanted commitments – a game which foreigners can also play. Remember, too, that Western abruptness strikes Egyptians as rude; never begrudge the time it takes to say *Salaam aleikum*, or return a greeting.

TOILETS Public ones are almost always filthy, and there's never any toilet paper (though someone may sell it outside). They're usually known as *Toileta*, and marked with WC and Men and Women signs. Expect squat toilets in bus stations, resthouses and fleapit hotels; on sit-down toilets, beware of pranging yourself on the nozzle of the curly waterpipe, intended to assist the ablutions of devout Muslims. Though it's wise to carry toilet paper (£E1 per double roll in pharmacies) at all times, paper tissues, sold on the streets (50pt), will serve at a pinch.

Guide

Guide

Cairo and the Pyramids

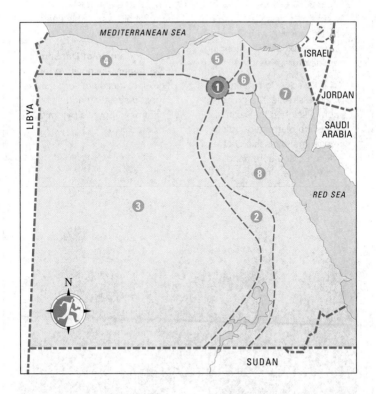

CHAPTER 1 # Highlights

✱ **The Egyptian Antiquities Museum** One of the world's truly great museums, containing a massive collection of ancient statues, sarcophagi, frescoes, reliefs, and incredible treasures from the tomb of Tutankhamun. Unmissable. **See p.125**

✱ **Islamic Cairo** Salah al-Din's medieval city is Cairo's true heart, teeming with life and chock-a-block with stunning architecture. **See p.149**

✱ **The Citadel** Dominating Cairo's skyline, the great fort commissioned by Salah al-Din boasts a plethora of quirky museums, a classic Ottoman mosque, and commanding views of the city. **See p.176**

✱ **Old Cairo** A compact quarter containing the city's most ancient Coptic churches and its oldest synagogue. **See p.191**

✱ **The Pyramids of Giza** The sole surviving wonder of the ancient world, and still stunning to this day. If you only travel to one tourist sight in the whole world, this should be it. **See p.229**

✱ **The Pyramids of Dahshur** Still largely unknown to tour groups, these are some of the most fascinating and significant of all Egypt's pyramids. **See p.251**

△ Cairo

Cairo and the Pyramids

The twin streams of Egypt's history converge just below the Delta at **Cairo**, where the greatest city in the Islamic world sprawls across the Nile towards the **Pyramids**, those supreme monuments of antiquity. Every visitor to Egypt comes here, to reel at the Pyramids' baleful mass and the seething immensity of Cairo, with its bazaars, mosques and Citadel and extraordinary Antiquities Museum. It's equally impossible not to find yourself carried away by the streetlife, where medieval trades and customs coexist with a modern, cosmopolitan mix of Arab, African and European influences.

Cairo has been the largest city in Africa and the Middle East ever since the Mongols wasted Imperial Baghdad in 1258. Acknowledged as *Umm Dunya* or **"Mother of the World"** by medieval Arabs, and as Great Cairo by nineteenth-century Europeans, it remains, as Jan Morris writes in *Destinations*, "one of the half-dozen supercapitals – capitals that are bigger than themselves or their countries … the focus of a whole culture, an ideology or a historical moment". As Egypt has been a prize for conquerors from Alexander the Great to Rommel, so Cairo has been a fulcrum of power in the Arab world from the Crusades unto the present day. The *ulema* of its thousand-year-old Al-Azhar Mosque (for centuries the foremost centre of Islamic intellectual life) remains the ultimate religious authority for millions of Sunni Muslims, from Jakarta to Birmingham. Wherever Arabic is spoken, Cairo's cultural magnetism is felt. Every strand of Egyptian society knits and unravels in this febrile megalopolis.

Egyptians have two names for the city, one ancient and popular, the other Islamic and official. The foremost is **Masr**, meaning both the capital and the land of Egypt – "Egypt City" – an *ur*-city that endlessly renews itself and dominates the nation, an idea rooted in pharaonic civilization. (For Egyptians abroad, "Masr" refers to their homeland; within its borders it means the capital.) Whereas Masr is timeless, the city's other name, **Al-Qahira** (The Conqueror), is linked to an event: the Fatimid conquest that made this the capital of an Islamic empire that embraced modern-day Libya, Tunisia, Palestine and Syria. The name is rarely used in everyday speech.

Both archetypes still resonate and in monumental terms are symbolized by two dramatic **landmarks**: the **Pyramids of Giza** at the edge of the Western Desert and the great **Mosque of Mohammed Ali** – the modernizer of Islamic Egypt – which broods atop the Citadel. Between these two

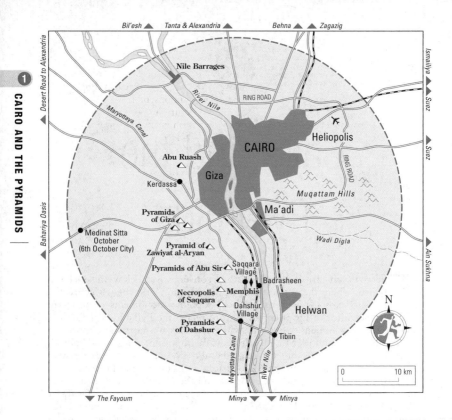

monuments sprawls a vast city, the colour of sand and ashes, of diverse worlds and time zones, and gross inequities. All is subsumed into an organism that somehow thrives in the terminal ward: medieval slums and Art Deco suburbs, garbage-pickers and marbled malls, donkey carts and limos, piousness and "the oaths of men exaggerating in the name of God". Cairo lives by its own contradictions.

This is a city, as Jan Morris put it, "almost overwhelmed by its own fertility". Its **population** is today estimated at around eighteen million and is swollen by a further million commuters from the Delta and a thousand new migrants every day. Today, one-third of Cairene households lack running water; a quarter of them have no sewers, either. An estimated half a million people reside in squatted cemeteries – the famous **Cities of the Dead**. The amount of green space per citizen has been calculated at thirteen square centimetres, not enough to cover a child's palm. Whereas earlier travellers noted that Cairo's air smelt "like hot bricks", visitors now find throat-rasping air **pollution**, chiefly caused by traffic. Cairo out-pollutes LA every day of the week: breathing the atmosphere downtown is reputedly akin to smoking thirty cigarettes a day.

Cairo's genius is to humanize these inescapable realities with **social rituals**. The rarity of public violence owes less to the armed police on every corner than to the *dowshah*: when conflicts arise, crowds gather, restraining both parties, encouraging them to rant, sympathizing with their grievances and then finally urging *"Maalesh, maalesh"* ("Let it be forgiven"). Everyday life is sweetened by flowery gestures and salutations; misfortunes evoke thanks for Allah's dispensation (after all, things could be worse!). Even the poorest can be respected for piety; in the mosque, millionaire and beggar kneel side by side.

Extended-family values and neighbourly intervention prevail throughout the *baladi* quarters or **urban villages** where millions of first- and second-generation rural migrants live, whilst arcane structures underpin life in Islamic Cairo. On a city-wide basis, the colonial distinction between "native quarters" and *ifrangi* (foreign) districts has given way to a dynamic stasis between rich and poor, westernization and traditionalism, complacency and desperation. In the closing decade of the twentieth century, the city's tolerance was further strained by a series of natural and man-made calamities. In October 1992, up to a thousand people died in an **earthquake**, when shoddily built high-rises and hovels collapsed across the city. Cairo's image took a worse battering abroad after the shooting of seventeen Greek tourists in 1996 and the fire-bombing of a German tour bus a year later – although the tourists didn't take long to make a cautious return. Every year its polarities intensify, safety margins narrow and statistics make gloomier reading. The abyss beckons in prognoses of **future trends**, yet Cairo confounds doomsayers by dancing on the edge.

A brief history

Cairo is an agglomeration of half a dozen cities, the earliest of which came into existence 2500 years *after* ancient **Memphis**, the first capital of pharaonic Egypt, was founded (c.3100 BC) across the river and to the south. During the heyday of the Old Kingdom, vast necropolises developed along the desert's edge as the pharaohs erected ever greater funerary monuments, from the first Step Pyramid at **Saqqara** to the unsurpassable **Pyramids of Giza** (for more on this part of the history, see pp.225–226). Meanwhile, across the Nile, there flourished a sister-city of priests and solar cults known to posterity as **Ancient Heliopolis** (see p.222).

It took centuries of Persian, Greek and Roman rule to efface both cities, by which time a new fortified town had developed on the opposite bank. **Babylon-in-Egypt** was the beginning of the tale of cities that culminates in modern Cairo, the first chapter of which is described under "Old Cairo" (see p.194). Oppressed by foreign overlords, Babylon's citizens almost welcomed the army of Islam that conquered Egypt in 641. For strategic and spiritual reasons, their general, Amr, chose to found a new settlement beyond the walls of Babylon – **Fustat**, the "City of the Tent" (see "Old Cairo", p.203), which evolved into a sophisticated metropolis while Europe was in the Dark Ages.

Under successive dynasties of khalifs who ruled the Islamic Empire from Iraq, three more cities were founded, each to the northeast of the previous one, which itself was either spurned or devastated. When the schismatic Fatimids won the khalifate in 969, they created an entirely new walled city – **Al-Qahira** – beyond this teeming, half-derelict conurbation. **Fatimid Cairo** formed the nucleus of the later, vastly expanded and consolidated capital that Salah al-Din (Saladin) left to the Ayyubid dynasty in 1193. But the Ayyubids' reliance on imported slave-warriors – the Mamlukes – brought about their downfall: eventually, the Mamlukes simply seized power for themselves, ushering in a new era.

Mamluke Cairo encompassed all the previous cities, Salah al-Din's Citadel (where the sultans dwelt), the northern port of Bulaq and vast cemeteries and rubbish tips beyond the city walls. Mamluke sultans like Beybars, Qalaoun, Barquq and Qaitbey erected mosques, mausoleums and caravanserais that still

Finding your way around this chapter

ennoble what is now known in English as "Islamic Cairo". The like-named section of this chapter relates their stories, the Turkish takeover, the decline of **Ottoman Cairo** and the rise of Mohammed Ali, who began the modernization of the city. Under Ismail, the most profligate of his successors, a new, increasingly **European Cairo** arose beside the Nile (see "Central Cairo", p.124). By 1920, the city's area was six times greater than that of medieval Cairo, and since then its residential suburbs have expanded relentlessly, swallowing up farmland and desert. The emergence of this **Greater Cairo** is charted under "Gezira and the West Bank" and "The northern suburbs".

Arrival, orientation and information

Setting foot in a big city can be a daunting experience, but you needn't worry about Cairo. Being overcharged by a taxi driver and spending your first night in a second-rate hotel is the worst that can happen to newcomers. Hustlers might try to lure you into overpriced perfume shops, but elaborate swindles are rare and robbery with violence is unheard of.

Cairo International Airport has two main terminals, roughly 3km apart. **Terminal 1** (known as the old airport) is used by Egyptian carriers, El Al and most Arab, African and Eastern European airlines. Western European, East Asian and Gulf airlines use **Terminal 2** (aka the new airport). For **airport information** call ☏02/265-5000 (Terminal 1) or ☏02/291-4255 (Terminal 2). You'll find 24-hour currency exchange as well as **ATMs** that accept Visa, Plus, Cirrus and MasterCard at both terminals.

Emerging from customs, you'll be waylaid by taxi drivers who'll swear that they're the only way of **getting into town**. Usually, this isn't so, but you might prefer going by **taxi** anyway. Cab drivers will probably demand £E60, but Cairenes pay a lot less than that – to get a taxi into town for £E30–40 or so, head out beyond the airport car park and pick up a taxi outside its precincts (taxis pay a fee to enter the airport premises, so they'll obviously add at least that to the bill if you take your cab from there). A favourite ploy of airport taxi drivers is to swear blind the hotel you want to go to is closed, full or a terrible place. They then take you to another hotel where they pick up a hefty commission, which will be added to the cost of your room.

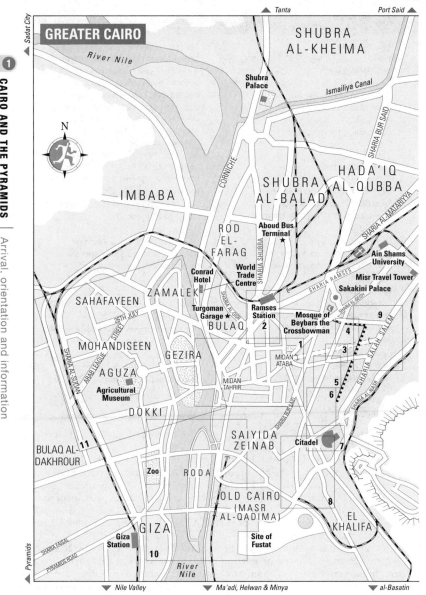

GREATER CAIRO

Tanta

Port Said

River Nile

SHUBRA
AL-KHEIMA

Shubra
Palace

Ismailiya Canal

N

Sadat City

HADA'IQ
AL-QUBBA

IMBABA

SHUBRA
AL-BALAD

Corniche

ROD
EL-
FARAG

Aboud Bus
Terminal

Sharia Shubra

Ain Shams
University

Sharia Almatariyya

Misr Travel Tower

Sakakini Palace

Conrad
Hotel

World
Trade
Centre

ZAMALEK

Sharia Ramses

Sharia al-Geish

SAHAFAYEEN

Turgoman
Garage

Ramses
Station

2

Mosque of
Beybars the
Crossbowman

9

BULAQ

4

26th July
Street

MOHANDISEEN

GEZIRA

1

MIDAN
ATABA

3

Sharia Salah Salem

AGUZA

Arab League

Agricultural
Museum

MIDAN
TAHRIR

Sharia al-Nasr

5

6

DOKKI

Sharia al-Sudan

Sharia Bur Said

BULAQ AL-
DAKHROUR

11

SAIYIDA
ZEINAB

Citadel

7

Zoo

RODA

OLD CAIRO
(MASR
AL-QADIMA)

8

EL
KHALIFA

Sharia Faisal

GIZA

Giza
Station

10

Pyramids Road

Site of
Fustat

River
Nile

Pyramids

Nile Valley

Ma'adi, Helwan & Minya

al-Basatin

On one side of Terminal 1's forecourt is the parking area for **buses** and **minibuses** into the centre. The most comfortable of the bus services is the a/c bus #356 (£E2), which stops at Terminal 2 before continuing to Midan Ramses and Abdel Mouneem Riyad terminal by Midan Tahrir in downtown Cairo. This service runs from about 7am to 11pm, as does minibus #27 (50pt),

Virgin's Tree ▲ & Obelisk ▲ *Ismailiya*

MATARIYYA   EL-ZEITUN

Buses for Cairo   Terminal 1

Cairo International
Airport

Terminal 2

SHARIA AL-HIGAZ

HELIOPOLIS
(MASR AL-GADIDA)

Merryland

MIDAN
TRIOMPHE

Qubba
Palace

MIDAN
ISMAILIYA

SHARIA
AL-AHRAM

MIDAN
ROXI

SHARIA MERGHANI

Urubah
Palace

SHARIA AL-'URUBAH

Almaza Bus
Terminal

NOUZHA

SHARIA AN-NOZHA

ILI

Heliopolis
Sporting Club

Baron
Empain's
Palace

Nasser's Tomb

SUEZ DESERT ROAD

▶ Suez

October
War Panorama

ABBASSIYA

Cairo Stadium

SHARIA AL-NASR

Sadat's Tomb

MEDINET
NASR

Sinai Bus
Terminal

SHARIA
RAMSES

MAP ENLARGEMENTS
1 Central Cairo (see pp.126-127)
2 Around Ramses Station (p.148)
3 Around Khan el-Khalili & al-Azhar (p.154)
4 To the Northern Gates (p.158)
5 Between Al-Azhar & the Bab Zwayla (p.165)
6 Between Bab Zwayla & The Citadel (p.172)
7 The Citadel (p.177)
8 Around Ibn Tulun & S. Cemetery (p.182)
9 The Northern Cemetery (p.188)
10 Old Cairo & Roda Island (pp.192-193)
11 Gezira & The West Bank (pp.210-211)

M u q a t t a m   H i l l s   Petrified
Forest

0   2 km

which follows the same route. After hours, your choice is between bus #400 (25pt), which plies the same route round the clock, though it is less comfortable and takes somewhat longer to get downtown – easily over an hour in rush hour, about forty minutes at night. There is another 24-hour service – bus #948 – to Midan Ataba, on the northern edge of downtown. Note that **touts** work the buses, posing as friendly locals to try to get you into hotels that pay them a commission. The airport terminals are connected to each other by a free EgyptAir **shuttle bus**, running all through the night. Besides the above options, there's a **limousine taxi service** next to Terminal 1's Misr Travel stand; prices are fixed and posted, though higher than regular taxi rates.

Most buses from Jordan and Sinai arrive at the old **Sinai Bus Terminal** (aka Abbassiya Station), 4km from the centre. Taxis outside grossly overcharge newcomers (the fare into town is £E5–8) and try the same tricks as cabbies at the airport (see p.105) to inveigle you into hotels that pay commission; if you want to take a cab, your best bet is to cross the street outside the terminal (Sharia Ramses) and hail a cab that's passing. Alternatively, cross the street and catch a bus or minibus from the bus stop 100m to your right – buses #28, #310 and #710, and minibuses #1 and #998 serve Midan Ramses; buses #27 and #998, and minibus #30 serve both Midan Ramses and Midan Tahrir. However, if you turn left outside the terminal and walk 300m on past the flyover to the hospital, you have an even wider choice of buses and minibuses to Ramses, Tahrir and Ataba. Tickets on the buses and minibuses plying these routes cost 25pt–£E1.

Coming from Jordan or Libya on a Superjet bus, you'll arrive at their terminal in **Almaza**, at the back end of Heliopolis. A taxi into town from here will cost £E15–20, but the terminal is served by bus #15 to Midan Ramses and buses #39 and #796 to Ramses and Tahrir. Alternatively, 300m north of the terminal along Sharia Abu Bakr al-Siddiq, under the flyover, you can pick up a tram (the Heliopolis Metro; see p.223) from the stop across the tracks and to your right, which goes along Sharia Merghani direct to Midan Ramses: make sure you get the right tram, though – it's the long green one, not the short yellow one.

Certain buses from Alexandria and the Delta, plus Superjet services from Sinai will drop you at **Turgoman Garage**, in Bulaq. Transport from Turgoman into downtown Cairo is somewhat disorganized; the simplest option is to take a taxi (£E2–3 to Midan Ramses, £E3–5 to Midan Tahrir), unless you fancy walking, in which case it's straight ahead out of the gate and 600m down Sharia el Kolali to Midan Ramses (see map p.148), or right out of the gate and on down Sharia Shahan to Orabi metro station (see map p.126).

Other bus companies coming from Alexandria and the Delta and Upper Egypt arrive at **Aboud Terminal** in Shubra. By far the easiest way into town from here is to climb up the steps to the main road where minibus service taxis await to take you straight to Sharia Orabi by Ramses train station (see below and the map on p.148).

All **trains** into Cairo stop at **Ramses Station** (see map on p.148). There are hotels nearby, but most visitors prefer to head downtown by metro (Mubarak Station is beneath Midan Ramses), taxi (£E3–5), or a bus along Sharia Ramses. Alternatively, it's a fifteen-minute walk down Sharia Ramses, taking a left at Sharia Emad el-Din or Sharia Orabi, into the main downtown area, where most of the budget hotels are located.

Orientation

Greater Cairo consists of two metropolitan governorates: **Cairo**, on the east bank of the Nile, and **Giza**, across the river. The **River Nile** (*Bahr el-Nil*, or simply *El-Nil*) is the prerequisite of their existence and fundamental to basic orientation. Bear in mind that it flows northwards through the city, so that "downriver" means north, and "upriver" south, a reversal of the usual associations. The city's waterfront is dominated by the **islands** of Gezira and Roda and the **bridges** that connect them to the **Corniche** (embankment) on either side of the Nile. There are four major divisions of the city:

• **Central Cairo** spreads inland to the east of the islands. Its **downtown** area – between Ezbekiya Gardens and **Midan Tahrir** – bears the stamp of Western planning, as does **Garden City**, the embassy quarter further south. At the northern end of central Cairo (beyond the downtown area) lies **Ramses Station**, the city's main train terminal. Most of the banks, airlines, cheap hotels and tourist restaurants lie within this swathe of the city.

• Further east sprawls **Islamic Cairo**, encompassing **Khan el-Khalili** bazaar, the Gamaliya quarter within the **Northern Walls**, and the labyrinthine Darb al-Ahmar district between the **Bab Zwayla** and the **Citadel**. Beyond the latter spread the eerie **Cities of the Dead** – the Northern and Southern cemeteries.

• The Southern Cemetery and the populous **Saiyida Zeinab** quarter merge into the rubbish tips and wasteland bordering the **ruins of Fustat** and the **Coptic quarter** of **Old Cairo**, further to the south. From there, a ribbon of development follows the metro out to **Ma'adi**, Cairo's plushest residential suburb, and **Helwan**, the city's heaviest industrial centre. Except for stylish **Heliopolis**, the **northern suburbs** likewise hold little appeal for visitors.

• Across the river on the **west bank**, the residential neighbourhoods of **Aguza** and **Dokki** aren't as smart as nearby **Mohandiseen** or the high-rise northern end of **Gezira** island, known as **Zamalek**. The **Imbaba** district, just to the northeast, was once notable for its weekly **camel market**, but this has now moved slightly further out to Bil'esh. The dusty expanse of **Giza** (which lends its name to the west bank urban zone) is enlivened by **Cairo Zoo** and the nightclub-infested **Pyramids Road** leading to the **Pyramids of Giza**.

Information

Cairo's downtown **tourist office**, at 5 Sharia Adly (daily 8.30am–7pm; ☏02/391-3454), can supply a rather useless free map and out-of-date brochures, but little in the way of hard facts. There are also tourist offices at both airport terminals: Terminal 1 (open 24hr; ☏02/265-4760); Terminal 2 (open 24hr; ☏02/265-2223). Tourist information is also available at Ramses Station (daily 8am–8pm; ☏02/579-0767), Manial Palace (daily 8am–3pm; ☏02/531-5587), Giza train station (daily 9am–3pm; ☏02/570-2233), and the Giza Pyramids (daily 8am–5pm; ☏02/383-8823).

Should the need arise, an alleyway to the left of the Sharia Adly office gives access to the headquarters of the **tourist police** (open 24hr; ☏02/395-9116). Whether they're helpful or a waste of time largely depends on who you encounter. Other tourist police stations can be found at Ramses Station (☏02/579-0767), the Giza Pyramids (☏02/385-0259), Khan el-Khalili (☏02/590-4827) and the Manial Palace (☏02/363-6707).

Maps and addresses

Cairo's more interesting areas are mapped in detail alongside their descriptions in this chapter. These – and the general plan on pp.126–127 – should suffice for most sightseeing needs, but if you require a more detailed **map**, the *New Handy Map of Cairo* is generally the best, with a street index and an inset covering Heliopolis. Cairo City Key's *Detailed Map of Greater Cairo* comes second, with maps of Heliopolis and Ma'adi on the back, though it doesn't have a street index or extend out to Medinet Nasr. Alternatives include the Cairo Engineering and Manufacturing Company's *Cairo Tourist Map*, which extends out to Heliopolis, and Lenhert & Landrock's map of the same name, which is better for downtown. The free "souvenir" map issued by the tourist office conveys the city's general layout, but can't be relied upon for navigation. Of more use for longer stays are the American University in Cairo's (AUC) *Cairo: The Practical Guide Maps* (£E30), which contains a useful set of maps; the weighty and currently out-of-print *Cairo A–Z* (£E40); and the *Cairo City Key* (£E40). The best place to buy maps is at a bookshop such as Lenhert & Landrock (44 Sharia Sherif) and Shorouk (1 Midan Talaat Harb).

It helps to memorize a few **geographical terms**. *Sharia* means "street" and always precedes the name (for example, Sharia Talaat Harb); narrower thoroughfares may be termed *Darb*, *Haret*, *Sikket* or *Zuqaq*, instead of Sharia. *Midan* denotes a square or open space. *Bab* signifies a medieval gate, after which certain quarters are named (for example, Bab el-Khalq); *Kubri* a bridge; and *Souk* a market. However, some of these words have more than one English transliteration (for example, *Sharia* is also spelt *Sharic* and *Chareh*) or may be inconsistently transliterated. **Street names** are posted in English (or French) and Arabic in central Cairo and Zamalek; almost everywhere else in Arabic only, or not at all. The same goes for **numbers**, rendered in Western and Arabic numerals (see p.114), or just the latter; a single number may denote a whole block with several entrance passageways – something to remember when you're following up addresses.

Don't expect Cairenes themselves to relate to maps; they comprehend their city differently. That said, however, people are remarkably helpful to visitors, going out of their way to steer them in the right direction; offer profuse thanks, but never *baksheesh*, which will offend in this situation.

City transport

Getting around Cairo is relatively straightforward; Midan Tahrir is the main transport hub, with several other terminals in the centre connecting up the city (see "Buses", p.113). The metro is simple to use, and taxis are inexpensive once you understand their system. Familiarize yourself with Arabic numerals (see box on p.114) and you can also use buses and minibuses, which reach most parts of the city.

You might as well resign yourself to the fact that everyone here drives like participants in the Paris–Dakar Rally, but accidents are surprisingly rare, all things considered. The streets are busy from 8am to midnight, and, unless you enjoy sweltering in traffic jams, it's best to try and avoid travelling during **rush hours** (7–10am & 4–7pm), when the streets are choked.

The metro

Cairo's **metro** (the first in the Arab world) works like nothing else in the city: clean and efficient, with a well-enforced ban on littering and smoking. Trains run every few minutes from 5am to midnight; outside of the rush hours (as above) they're no more over-crowded than in other cities around the world. The front carriage of each train is reserved for women, worth keeping in mind if you're a lone female traveller.

Stations are signposted with a large "M"; signs and route maps appear in Arabic and English. **Tickets** are purchased in the station (55pt for a short hop, 75pt for longer journeys); twin sets of booths cater for passengers heading in opposite directions, sometimes with separate queues for either sex. Hang on to

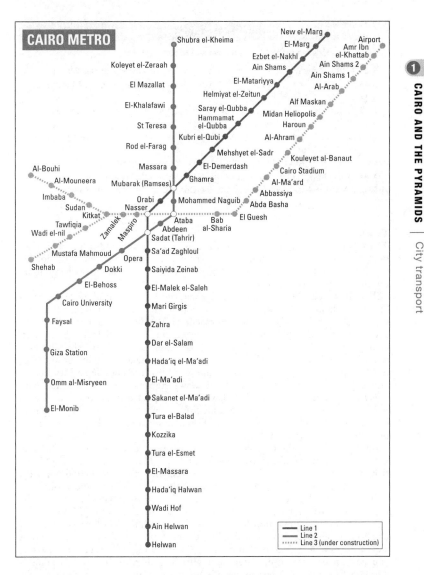

CAIRO METRO

Shubra el-Kheima
Koleyet el-Zeraah
El Mazallat
El-Khalafawi
St Teresa
Rod el-Farag
Massara
Mubarak (Ramses)
Orabi
Nasser

Al-Bouhi
Al-Mouneera
Imbaba
Sudan
Kitkat
Tawfiqia
Wadi el-nil
Mustafa Mahmoud
Shehab
Dokki
El-Behoss
Cairo University
Faysal
Giza Station
Omm al-Misryeen
El-Monib

Zamalek
Maspiro
Opera

New el-Marg
El-Marg
Airport
Amr Ibn
el-Khattab
Ezbet el-Nakhl
Ain Shams
Ain Shams 2
El-Matariyya
Ain Shams 1
Helmiyat el-Zeitun
Al-Arab
Saray el-Qubba
Alf Maskan
Hammamat
el-Qubba
Midan Heliopolis
Kubri el-Qubi
Haroun
Al-Ahram
Mehshyet el-Sadr
Kouleyet al-Banaut
El-Demerdash
Cairo Stadium
Ghamra
Al-Ma'ard
Mohammed Naguib
Abbassiya
Abda Basha
El Guesh
Ataba
Bab
al-Sharia
Abdeen
Sadat (Tahrir)
Sa'ad Zaghloul
Saiyida Zeinab
El-Malek el-Saleh
Mari Girgis
Zahra
Dar el-Salam
Hada'iq el-Ma'adi
El-Ma'adi
Sakanet el-Ma'adi
Tura el-Balad
Kozzika
Tura el-Esmet
El-Massara
Hada'iq Halwan
Wadi Hof
Ain Helwan
Helwan

— Line 1
— Line 2
······ Line 3 (under construction)

your ticket to get through the automatic barriers at the other end. Travelling without a ticket will result in a fine (£E50).

Line One connects the northeastern suburb of **El-Marg** with the southern industrial district of **Helwan** (via Mubarak, Sadat, Saad Zaghoul, Saiyida Zeinab, Mar Girgis and Maadi), with Line Two running from **Shubra** in the north to **El Monib** (via Mubarak, Ataba, Sadat, Gezira and Giza). The new stations on Line Two are wheelchair accessible, but stations on Line One are not. Line Three is still under construction, but will eventually run from the airport via the city centre (Ataba and Nasser) to Zamalek and Mohandiseen.

Useful metro stations

From a tourist's standpoint, there are seven **crucial stations**:

MUBARAK, beneath Midan Ramses, is for reaching or leaving Ramses Station.

NASSER, two stops on, leads onto 26th July Street near the top end of Talaat Harb (take the High Court exit).

SADAT, the most used (and useful) station, is set beneath Midan Tahrir, and doubles as a pedestrian underpass.

SAIYIDA ZEINAB, two stops beyond, lies midway between that quarter and the northern end of Roda Island.

EL-MALEK EL-SALEH, the next stop is useful for exploring parts of Old Cairo.

MARI GIRGIS is the best stop for Coptic Cairo and Amr's Mosque.

GEZIRA/OPERA connects directly into the Opera Complex in south Gezira.

Taxis

The most common type of **taxi** is the four-seater black-and-white taxi (Fiats or Ladas), which in peak hours may carry passengers collectively. Occasionally you'll come across a seven-seater Peugeot 504 version, which may charge more on the grounds that it is bigger.

To **hail a cab**, pick a major thoroughfare with traffic heading in the right direction, stand on the kerb, and wave and holler out your destination (for example, "Mohandiseen") as one approaches; if the driver's interested he'll stop and wait for you. State your destination again, in more detail. If the driver starts talking money, say "*maalesh*" (forget it) and look for another cab; otherwise jump in. Don't be alarmed by the circuitous routes taken to avoid bottlenecks, nor by other people getting in along the way. Near the end, direct him to stop where you want (bearing in mind one-way systems and other obstacles) with "*hina/hinak kwayes*" (here/there's okay). Don't expect drivers to speak English or know the location of every street; identify a major landmark or thoroughfare in the vicinity and state that instead. If your destination is obscure or hard to pronounce, get it written down in Arabic.

Ideally, you know the correct **fare** and just hand over the money confidently, with a tip if you feel like it, say "*itfuddel, shukran*" (here you are, thank you) and that's the end of it. If the driver protests, either he's trying it on and will back down if you invoke the police, or you've misjudged the fare and should pay more with good grace. Fares are determined by market rates rather than by meters (which are rarely switched on). Cairenes normally pay a £E2 minimum; £E3–5 for a downtown hop (for example, Midan Tahrir to Al-Azhar, Zamalek or Mohandiseen); and more if heading further out, especially to a prosperous area (for example £E15 to Heliopolis or the Pyramids). For each extra person, you pay 25 percent again. After midnight, fares increase by 50–100 percent. Though foreigners can get away with **local rates**, drivers expect you to pay over the odds, especially if you are well dressed or staying in an expensive hotel: say £E5 minimum, £E5–8 across downtown or the Nile, and £E15–20 further out. The airport and the Pyramids are special cases (see p.105 and p.229). Fares given in the text are for a single person at **tourist rates**, unless indicated otherwise. Remember that taxi drivers don't generally deal with change so it's best to have the exact fare ready.

A second type of taxi is the pricier **limousines**, usually Mercedes or Peugeot 406s. Operated by firms such as Limo Misr (☎02/685-6125) and Target Limousine (☎02/588-0095), they are stationed at five-star hotels and at the airport, with fixed but expensive fares, and rentable by the day as well as for set routes. A limo for the day (16 hours and 100km) costs £E1050 for a Mercedes, £E380 for a Peugeot.

Service taxis

Service taxis travel a set route (see box below for some of the most useful) and can be flagged down anywhere along it if there is space aboard. In town they are invariably microbuses, known as *arrabeya bil nafar* or just *servees*, and are more like buses than taxi cabs. Cairo has some 60,000 service taxis which transport over a million Cairenes to work every day, causing appalling pollution, traffic jams (because they'll stop anywhere) and accidents. **Fares** range from 50pt to £E1 per person, according to the distance travelled (inter-city versions, which are usually Peugeot saloons, are covered at the end of this chapter; see p.301). They are especially useful for longer-distance journeys such as from town to the pyramids. Their main terminals are at **Abdel Mouneem Riyad** (behind the Egyptian Museum and in front of the *Ramses Hilton* hotel), and behind and around **Ramses station**. For Saqqara and Dahshur, they leave from a yard off Maryotteya Canal near its junction with Pyramids Road (down the east bank of the canal and first left), the junction itself being easily reached by service taxi from Ramses or Abdel Mouneem Riyad.

Buses

Cairo's **buses** are battered, exhaust-spewing workhorses, active from 5.30am to 12.30am daily (6.30am–6.30pm & 7.30pm–2am during Ramadan). Fares are cheap enough to be affordable by everyone, so buses are usually full and over-flow during the 7–10am and 4–7pm rush hours, when passengers hang from doorways or each other and clamber in and out through windows. Though many foreigners are deterred from using buses by the crush, not to mention the risk of pickpockets and gropers, there's no denying that the network reaches virtually everywhere. Because buses tend to make slow progress against the traffic, however, service taxi microbuses (see above) are generally a better option, where available.

Buses should have **route numbers** in Arabic on the front, side and back (see box overleaf). Those with a slash through the number (represented in this guide as, for example, #13/) may follow different routes from buses with the same number unslashed; some route numbers even have two slashes. **Bus stops** are not always clearly signposted (look for metal shelters, plaques on lampposts or crowds waiting), and buses often just slow down instead of halting, compel-ling passengers to board and disembark on the run. Few bus stops give any

---

Useful service taxi routes

ABDEL MOUNEEM RIYAD (in front of *Ramses Hilton*) to the Pyramids (*Haram*), Faisal (near the Pyramids), Midan Giza, Mohandiseen, Bulaq, Bulaq al-Dakrour, Imbaba, Ma'adi and Helwan.

RAMSES (behind the station) to Abbassiya, Medinet Nasr, al-Basatin, Ma'adi and Helwan; (Sharia al-Gala) to Aboud terminal, Midan Giza and the Pyramids; (al-Fath Mosque) to Dirasa and the Citadel entrance (via Ataba and Al-Azhar).

MIDAN ATABA to Dirasa (via Al-Azhar), and sometimes to the Pyramids.

MIDAN GIZA to Ramses, the Pyramids and Badrasheen (for Saqqara).

MARYOTTEYA CANAL (Pyramids Road) to Tahrir, Ramses and sometimes Ataba; (yard down side street off the east bank) to Abu Sir and Saqqara, Dahshur.

Arabic numerals

Though **Arabic numerals** may seem confusing at first, they are not hard to learn and with a little practice you should soon be able to read bus numbers without any problems. The one and the nine are easy enough; the confusing ones are the five, which looks like a Western zero, the six, which looks like a Western seven, and the four, which looks like a three written backwards. In practice, once you've got the hang of it, the trickiest are the two and the three, which are sufficiently similar to be easily confused.

1	١		6	٦
2	٢		7	٧
3	٣		8	٨
4	٤		9	٩
5	٥		0	٠

indication of which buses they are served by or where they are going to, let alone any information in English, so you will just have to ask people on each bus that stops whether it is going to your destination. Except at terminals, you must enter through the rear door (which is often removed to facilitate access); at official stops, you're supposed to exit from the front. Conductors sell **tickets** (the flat fare on most routes is 25pt, 50pt on longer routes, £E1 on newer, more comfortable vehicles, and £E2 on air-conditioned buses) from behind a crush-bar by the rear door. The front of the bus is usually less crowded, so it's worth squeezing your way forwards; start edging towards the exit well before your destination.

New blue-and-white **a/c buses** are now being introduced on some routes for those who want to travel in comfort and avoid the crowds (flat fare £E2). At the moment, they serve only prosperous suburbs such as Heliopolis and Medinet Nasr and tourist sites like the Pyramids, but other routes will supposedly be added in the future.

Most buses start from (or pass through) at least one of the main city-centre nucleii at Midan Tahrir, Abdel Mouneem Riyad terminal (behind the Antiquities Museum), Midan Ramses or Midan Ataba. At each of these locations, there are several bus stops, and where exactly you pick up your bus will depend on which direction it is going in and whether it starts there or is simply passing through. If possible, ask the conductor "*Rayih...?*" (Are you going to...?) to make sure.

Minibuses

During the early 1980s, **minibuses** were introduced along many of the existing bus routes. Besides making better headway through traffic and actually halting

Useful bus routes

Abdel Mouneem Riyad and Midan Ramses to: Airport #356, #400 (24hr), minibus #27; Abbassiya and Heliopolis (Midan Roxi) #400, #400/, #500, minibuses #27, #35, #35/.

Abdel Mouneem Riyad to: Citadel (Bab Gabal) minibus #105; Saiyida Zeinab and Ibn Tulun Mosque #72//, #102, #160; Immam al-Shafi'i minibus #154; Manashi #214; Muqattam Hills #951; Pyramids #30, #355, #357, #900; Sphinx #997; Haraniyya #337; Badrasheen #987.

at stops, they are far more comfortable and never crowded, as standing is not permitted. Tickets (25pt–£E1) are bought from the driver. Minibuses should not be confused with service taxis (usually smaller microbuses, see p.113). There are minibus **terminals** alongside the big bus stations in Midan Tahrir (by the *Nile Hilton* and near Arab League/Omar Makram Mosque) and Midan Ataba, and minibuses usually use the same bus stops as ordinary buses.

Trams and river-taxis

As the metro and minibus systems expand, Cairo's original **tram network** (built in colonial times) is being phased out. The Heliopolis tram system remains in use throughout that area (see "The northern suburbs", p.223, for details), but all the other lines into town have been withdrawn. Like buses, the trams are cheap and battered, sometimes with standing room only; their Arabic route numbers are posted above the driver's cab.

The most relaxing way to reach Old Cairo is by river-taxi. **River-taxis** (aka waterbuses) leave from the Maspero Dock outside the Television Building, 600m north of the Antiquities Museum. Boats run every hour from 7am until 4pm to Old Cairo via Giza and Roda (other services, and all after 4pm, run only as far as El Gama'a Bridge; frequencies may be slightly different during Ramadan); you can buy tickets (50pt flat fee) at the dock. On Fridays and Sundays, they also run up to the Nile Barrages at Qanatir (£E5 each way; see "Excursions from Cairo", p.295).

Driving

The only thing scarier than **driving in Cairo** is cycling, which is tantamount to suicide. Dashes, crawls and finely judged evasions are the order of the day; donkey carts and jaywalkers trust in motorists' swift reactions. Any collision draws a crowd. Minor dents are often settled by on-the-spot payoffs, but should injury occur, it's wise to involve a cop right away. Multi-storey car parks, such as the one on Midan Ataba, are ignored as motorists park bumper-to-bumper along every kerb, leaving their handbrakes off so vehicles can be shifted by the local *minairdy* (street parking attendant), whom they tip £E1 or so. Given all this, it's no surprise that few foreigners drive in Cairo. If you are brave enough to drive yourself, see p.62 for details on **renting a car**, or better still, a car with a driver, which costs around $20 a day more.

Car rental agencies

Avis 16A Sharia Maamal el-Sukar, Garden City ☎02/794-7400, ✉ruavais@rusys.eg.net; airport Terminal 1 ☎02/265-4249 and Terminal 2 ☎02/265-2429; and at the *Nile Hilton* hotel. **Budget** 22 Sharia al-Mathaf al-Zira'i, Dokki ☎02/762-0518; airport Terminal 2 ☎02/265-2395. **Hertz** 195 26th July St, Aguza ☎02/347-4172, ✉reservations@hertzegypt.com; airport Terminal 2 ☎02/265-2430; and at the *Ramses Hilton* hotel.

Walking

The one advantage of Cairo's density is that many places of interest are within **walking** distance of Midan Tahrir or other transport interchanges. You can walk across downtown Cairo from Tahrir to Midan Ataba in fifteen to thirty minutes; the same again brings you to Khan el-Khalili in the heart of Islamic Cairo. Starting from here or the Citadel, the fascinating medieval quarter can really only be explored on foot.

Arguably, walking is the best way to experience the city's pulsating streetlife. Though pavements are congested with vendors and pedestrians, they weave gracefully around each other, in contrast with the bullish jostlings of Western capitals. The commonest irritants are rubbish, noxious fumes and puddles, uneven pavements and gaping drains; in poorer quarters, the last two may not even exist. Women travellers must also reckon with gropers, who strike chiefly along Talaat Harb and around the Khan. Close proximity to a male escort confers some immunity, but the best solution is to develop an instant response (see "Women travellers", p.90).

To make faster headway you can walk along the edge of the road – obviously, always facing oncoming traffic. **Traffic** is heavy from 8am to midnight, and ceases for a few hours before dawn. Its daytime flow only diminishes during Ramadan celebrations, major football matches, and the midday prayer on Fridays, when many side streets are carpeted over and used as outdoor mosques.

At all times, **crossing the road** takes boldness. Drivers will slow down to give people time to dart across, but dithering or freezing midway confuses them and increases the risk of an accident. A prolonged horn burst indicates that the driver can't or won't stop. Remember that motorists obey police signals rather than traffic lights, which were only installed in the 1980s and have still to acquire any real local credibility.

Accommodation

Cairo is packed with **accommodation** to suit every tourist's taste and budget. When tourism is at its normal level, most hotels are busy or full throughout December and January, while the cheaper ones are flooded with backpackers over the summer. When tourism is down, however – as it invariably is following any kind of ruction in the Middle East – you can be certain of a vacancy almost anywhere. Consequently, **hotel touts** compete more fiercely than ever (see box, p.119). At the airport they may masquerade as blazered "tourist officials" and are keen to book you into the most expensive hotel that will wash (say, £E150/US$25 a night for backpackers); downtown, they're more likely to be touting budget hotels. Taxi drivers are also in on the game and may claim a split from both parties. Yet **finding a room** needn't be traumatic if you take control of the situation. All you need to do is hop on a bus or hail a taxi and begin visiting downtown hotels.

Hotels and pensions

Cairo's hotels reflect the city's diversity: deluxe chains overlooking the Nile; functional high-rises; colonial piles and homely *pensions* with the same raddled facades as bug-infested flophouses. **Standards** vary within any given price range or star rating – and from room to room in many places. Try to inspect the facilities (a/c denotes air conditioning) before checking in. Also establish the price and any service tax or extra charges (which should be posted in reception) at the outset. Guests at deluxe hotels or certain budget places such as the *Ismailia House*, *Luna* and the *Pensione Roma* can avail themselves of **laundry services** charged at piece rates; in budget places, prices should be around £E4 for a dress, £E2 for a skirt, shirt or trousers, and 50pt for socks or underwear. Elsewhere, hotel receptionists or building janitors can probably put you in touch with the local *makwagi*, who does washing and ironing also at piece rates.

Hotels with three or more stars require payment in US$, or Egyptian currency backed by an exchange receipt. Officially, rates are the same all year, with an annual rise in early October.

Deluxe and four-star hotels – city-wide

All the international chains are represented in Cairo, which has over thirty hotels with a four- or five-star (deluxe) rating. Though package tourists may get hefty reductions, the regular rates for such places start at around US$150 for a double. Our **city-wide selection** boasts fine locations, superlative facilities or splendid decor; none of the deluxe or four-star hotels include breakfast in their price. All the hotels below are marked on the map on pp.126–127, unless otherwise stated.

Cairo Marriott Sharia Saraya al-Gezira, off 26th July St, Zamalek ☎02/735-8888, ✉reservation @cairomarriott.com (see map on p.210; for international reservations, see pp.67–68). Modern guest rooms built around a lavish palace constructed to house Napoleon's wife Empress Eugénie; choose between garden rooms or slightly pricier tower rooms with a better view. There are fine restaurants and bars, a casino, nightclub (summer only) and pool, rooms have fast Internet connections and the hotel is wi-fi enabled throughout; non-residents can drink or dine in the *khedival* salons and billiard room. Good value compared with other hotels in this bracket. ❽

Conrad 1191 Corniche el-Nil, Bulaq ☎02/580-8000, ⓦwww.conradhotels.com (see map on p.106; international reservations via Hilton, see pp.67–68). Run by the Hilton chain, this new hotel is a little way out of town, but calmer and more sedate than its city-centre counterparts, with some of the most comfortable rooms in Cairo. Its standards of service and understated luxury give a feeling of being an oasis of tranquility amidst the hubbub. It has international dining, palm trees in the lobby, a pool and health club, but no disco or nightclub. ❽

El-Gezirah southern end of Gezira Island ☎02/737-3737, ✉H5307@accor.com (see map on p.211). Overlooking the Nile from the southern end of Gezira Island, and formerly part of the Sheraton chain, though now run by Sofitel, it has a pool, casino and bank, Middle Eastern and Italian restaurants, *Rumours* piano bar, and the expensive *Juliana* disco (see p.269). The thick carpets and deluxe fittings in the guest rooms are slightly more worn than you would expect in a five-star, but the prices are also a little bit lower. ❼

Four Seasons 1089 Corniche el-Nil, Garden City ☎02/791-7000, ⓦwww.fourseasons.com (for international reservations, see pp.67–68). Sleek, sophisticated and luxurious to a fault, this branch of the Four Seasons chain is better suited to Western tastes than its gaudier sister establishment opposite the zoo in Giza (see map on pp.67–68). The rooms have a classic charm with little extras like a DVD player and high-speed Internet terminal. ❾

Grand Hyatt ☎02/365-1234, ⓦcairo.grand .hyatt.com (see map p.192; for international reservations, see pp.67–68). A superior five-star at the northern tip of Roda Island, though best accessed via its own bridge from Garden City, with stylish rooms in a sumptuous new wing (north-facing ones offer killer views of central Cairo and the Nile), with all the facilities you'd expect – sauna, health club, business centre, two pools – plus no fewer than twelve restaurants, including a revolving restaurant with panoramic views on the 40th floor (see p.212). ❽

Helnan Shepheard Hotel Corniche el-Nil, ☎02/792-1000, ⓦwww.helnan.com. Five-star, Nile-side version of the famous nineteenth-century establishment that stood on Midan Opera. Rebuilt on the present site in 1957, it still retains a certain 1950s feel, despite various refurbishments, not to mention its takeover by the Scandinavian Helnan chain. The guest rooms are done out with royal blue carpets and dark wood furnishings, and rooms on the quieter side facing the Muqattam Hills are cheaper than those facing the Nile. Facilities include two restaurants, a casino and the *Castle* disco (see p.269), but no swimming pool. ❼

Mena House Oberoi ☎02/383-3222, ⓦwww .oberoihotels.com (for international reservations, see pp.67–68; see map on p.230). Set in lush grounds near the Giza Pyramids (of which some rooms have a view), this one-time *khedival* hunting lodge witnessed Roosevelt and Churchill initiate the D-Day plan, and the formal signing of the peace treaty between Israel and Egypt. Its renovated arabesque halls and nineteenth-century rooms are delightful; the modern Mena Gardens annexe isn't as lovely, though the rooms are plush enough. Facilities include the *Moghul* restaurant (the best Indian restaurant in Egypt; see p.263), pool, golf course and tennis courts. ❽

Nile Hilton ☎02/578-0444 or 0666, ⓦwww .hilton.com (for international reservations, see pp.67–68). Sited between Midan Tahrir and the Nile, this refurbished 1950s building is one of the first landmarks you'll get to recognize in Cairo, and boasts the biggest hotel rooms in town. It also contains a range of cafés and restaurants: the

Taverne du Champs de Mars, Ibis Café, Da Mario, Rotisserie Belvedere and rooftop *Pyramids Bar*. River-facing doubles cost slightly more than rooms overlooking Tahrir. ❼

Ramses Hilton ☏ 02/577-7444, ⓦ www.hilton .com (for international reservations, see pp.67–68). Cairo's tallest hotel, and rooms on the upper stories give excellent views over the city and as far as the Pyramids. All the facilities you could want are here, including six restaurants, a fitness centre, business centre, casino, pool and rooftop cocktail bar, and the rooms are luxurious to a fault, but the *Ramses* still plays second fiddle to its sister, the *Nile Hilton*, and the standard of

service here is somewhat inferior, though prices are twice as high. ❾

Semiramis Intercontinental ☏ 02/795-7171, ⓦ www.cairo.intercontinental.com (for international reservations, see pp.67–68). The spacious, elegant rooms in this smart Nileside hotel just south of Midan Tahrir have all the usual facilities – minibar, wall safe, satellite TV, a/c, balcony – and there's a gym, a pool, the *Haroun al-Rashid* nightclub (see p.267), and eleven restaurants offering cuisine from around the world. Rooms on the upper floors give excellent views, and in fact the views over Cairo from the slightly cheaper city-side rooms are better than those from the Nile side. ❾

Mid-range and cheap places: hotels and pensions

The mid-range of the budget spectrum chiefly consists of **three-star hotels** whose rooms have private bathrooms and a/c, perhaps also fridges, phones and TV. If facilities fall short of what's advertised (and charged for), you're entitled to raise a stink. However, a couple of places in the centre are (more or less) refurbished colonial edifices whose old-world charm makes up for any lack of modern gadgetry.

Budget travellers usually go for the **cheap hotels and pensions** on the upper floors of downtown office buildings. Designed to exclude sunlight and circulate air during summer, the unheated ones can be a damp and draughty in winter, while during the summer, mosquitoes can be a problem. By way of compensation, some feature Art Deco rooms with sweeping balconies, and all can provide bottled water, tea and soft drinks. Most are reached from street level via an alleyway and/or lobby serving the entire building; a few are locked at midnight, so if you arrive late at night you'll have to roust the doorman (*bowab*), who will probably expect some modest *baksheesh* for his trouble. Riding the elevators can feel like playing Russian roulette, but we've never heard of a serious accident.

The following rundown is by no means exhaustive, focusing as it does on places that are cheap, agreeable or conveniently located (a few combine all these assets). The hotels are listed according to location, the areas corresponding to descriptive sections (and maps) in this chapter; the downtown ones are all shown on the map on pp.126–127, mostly keyed in by number. Breakfast is included in the price unless otherwise stated.

Downtown – between Tahrir and Ezbekiya

Talaat Harb, Mahmoud Bassiouni and Qasr el-Nil streets offer the widest range of **budget** hotels. A few are excellent, a few really squalid, but the majority fall somewhere in between. Richer tourists can choose between comfortable modern hotels or a number of vintage establishments redolent of prewar high society. The hotels below are all marked on the map on pp.126–127.

Amin 38 Midan Falaki ☏ 02/393-3813. Very reasonable rooms with fans on the 6th, 7th and 10th floors; it's worth paying £E5 more for a room with private bathroom and constant hot water – the shared facilities aren't so clean. Opposite Bab al-Luq market. Breakfast not included. ❶

Berlin 2 Sharia el-Shawarby ☏ & Ⓕ 02/395-7502, Ⓔberlinhotelcairo@hotmail.com. A small hotel on the 4th floor, just off Qasr el-Nil, with lofty double and triple rooms, each with its own shower stall, quiet split-unit a/c, plus Art Nouveau-style fittings, and friendly and helpful management. Services include

Hotel touts and excursion rackets

There's a racket going on in Cairo, of which newly arrived tourists are the victims. It starts at the airport and bus terminals, and you need to be aware of it if you are to avoid it. The aim is to steer tourists into hotels which will pay a commission to the person bringing them, usually a taxi driver or street tout. The commission will of course be added to your bill. The same hotels may then try to sell you overpriced tours to Luxor and Aswan, or steer you into perfume or papyrus shops, taking a commission in turn on all sales. Some of them are less than subtle in their sales techniques. Most places in Cairo are reputable and above board, but it pays to know that some are not, and how to avoid those places and their scams.

As soon as you arrive at Cairo airport, and before you even clear customs, you may be approached by "travel agents" wearing official badges with their photo, on which the only thing written in English is the words "Ministry of Tourism". This does not mean, despite what these people may tell you, that they work for the ministry of tourism, simply that they have a licence to operate in the airport. They will probably try to dissuade you from going to the hotel you had in mind, and they may even appear to call the hotel to check if there is room. A voice on the other end of the phone may say, "Sorry, we are full today." Don't believe it. Nor should you believe these "travel agents" if they tell you that your hotel has closed or is no good. Similarly, do not believe taxi drivers (especially the taxi drivers who accost you before you leave the airport), or any "friendly stranger" who gets talking to you on the bus into town, or in the street in downtown Cairo, if they ask where you are going and then proceed to tell you that the hotel you want has closed, or is dirty or expensive, "but I know a better one." If a taxi driver tells you that the hotel you want has closed, take another taxi. If you are already on your way into town, ask to be dropped off at Midan Tahrir or on Sharia Talaat Harb and walk the rest of the way. Other touts may approach you on the street and try to steer you into a different hotel from the one of your choice. Some of them hang around downstairs below popular hotels when certain flights have just come in and may even claim to be the manager! Remember, while you have your baggage with you, you are an obvious new arrival and you will attract every tout in town.

A number of hotels that work with touts also subject their guests to a sales campaign with the aim of getting them to buy papyruses, perfumes, horse and camel trips and, most of all, excursions to Luxor and Aswan. These hotels will take a cut of whatever the tourist pays. Most hotels in town will of course sell sightseeing tours, either within Cairo or further afield, and these tours will be advertised in reception, but no reputable hotel will use sales techniques to persuade their guests to buy such tours, nor overcharge to the extent that some do. In places where sales techniques are used, the tour will almost certainly be priced well over the odds, and large parts of it will be spent visiting papyrus and perfume shops (often referred to as "museums") rather than the sites you came to see.

The tour that is usually sold and adapted by dubious operators is that of Amigo Tours in Aswan, which is frequently sold to unsuspecting tourists with a mark-up of 300 percent or more. Nor is it only in budget hotels that travel desks sell Amigo Tours trips with a huge mark-up – some quite reputable hotels are at it too.

Our advice is: first of all, never stay in a hotel that is recommended by a taxi driver or street tout in preference to the one you have already decided on. Secondly, never buy any tour without first shopping around. Thirdly, check out of any hotel that starts putting pressure on you to buy a tour, or that allows in touts who will try to take you to papyrus or perfume shops. And fourthly, don't pay for more than one night upfront, so that you can leave if necessary the next day.

For more on touts, see p.139.

laundry, Internet access (£E5 per hour), airport pick-ups, and their own drivers to take you round the pyramid sites or elsewhere at decent rates. ❷

Carlton 21 26th July St ☎02/575-5022, ⓔcarltonhotelcairo@yahoo.com. Built in 1935 and still retaining some wood-panelled period charm, albeit rather worn around the edges. Modern facilities include a/c, and pricier deluxe rooms have satellite TV and a minibar. There's a restaurant on the 7th floor and a very pleasant rooftop garden with coffee shop. ❸

Cosmopolitan 1 Sharia Ben Talaab, off Qasr el-Nil ☎02/392-3956, ⓕ393-3531. This refurbished and rather grand monumental *belle époque* building has a European restaurant, English-style bar, bank and international calls facility, but avoid the tours sold at the travel desk. All rooms have a/c and private baths. ❻

Crown 9 Sharia Emad el-Din ☎020/591-8374, ⓔcrowncairo@yahoo.com. Sufferers of bad backs may appreciate the firmness of the beds at this 4th floor city hotel, but others may find them hard. The better rooms have a/c and private bathroom, but all are pretty decent though plain. Breakfast not included. ❶

Dahab 26 Sharia Bassiouny ☎02/579-9104, ⓦwww.dahabhotel.net. A Dahab tourist camp transported – surprisingly convincingly – to a downtown roof, this place has clean but poky rooms, dorm beds (£E10) and lots of backpackers. Friendly staff and plenty of vegetation make it a pleasant hang-out, where facilities include a Bedouin-style café, communal kitchen, laundry service and 24-hour hot water. Unfortunately, it is infested with touts, who lie in wait at the entrance and are allowed in by the management to prey on guests. Breakfast not included. ❶

Garden City House 26 Sharia Kamal al-Din Salah ☎02/354-4969, ⓦwww.gardencity.plus.com. Refurbished 3rd-floor *pension* on the edge of the Garden City, behind the *Semiramis*. Some rooms have Nile views, some have en-suite bathrooms, and some have a/c. On the downside, the location is rather noisy. ❷

Grand 17 26th July St ☎02/575-7801 to 5, ⓔgrandhotel@link.net. Characterful and very comfortable Art Deco edifice featuring original lifts and furniture, a fountain, *Valley of the Kings* restaurant (see p.259), coffee shop and old-fashioned, homely rooms with immaculately varnished wooden floors, attached to large, spotless and bright tiled bathrooms. Entrance in the alley off Sharia Talaat Harb. Very good value. ❺

Happyton 10 Sharia Ali el Kassar ☎02/592 8671/6. Two-star hotel with en-suite rooms with a/c. The rooms are all well kept but vary in size, with some

of them quite large. There's no bar as such, but you can buy beer in the lobby and drink it on the roof terrace. A TV in your room costs £E8 a night extra, so specify if you don't want one; a/c costs £E10. ❷

Ismailia House 1 Midan Tahrir ☎02/796-3122, ⓔismahouse@hotmail.com. Advance booking is advisable for this cool, clean and cheerful 7th-floor haven, with singles, doubles, triples and dorm beds (£E17), 24-hr hot water and plenty of communal areas to hang out in. The Tahrir-facing rooms are noisy at night but have great views. ❷

Lotus 12 Sharia Talaat Harb ☎02/575-0627, ⓦwww.lotushotel.com. Reception on the 7th floor, reached via an arcade. Clean, with friendly staff, a restaurant and a bar, but avoid buying tours here. Some rooms with a/c and private baths. Hot water 6–10am and 6–10pm. ❷

Luna 27 Talaat Harb ☎02/396-1020, ⓔlunapension@hotmail.com. Well-kept hotel with friendly, helpful staff, and large, clean, a/c rooms, some en suite. It's worth asking for the Egyptian breakfast (*fuul* and *felafel*) in preference to the Continental. Free airport pick-up if you stay four days or more. ❷

New Hotel 21 Sharia Adly ☎02/392-7065, ⓕ392-9555. A reasonable mid-range place with a 24-hr café and slightly worn, carpeted rooms, some with a/c and en-suite shower and toilet. ❷

Odeon Palace 6 Sharia Abdel Hamid Said ☎02/577-6637, ⓕ576-7971. Three-star tower with lots of wood panelling and a comfortable lived-in feel, as well as a restaurant and 24-hour roof garden bar, just off Sharia Talaat Harb; breakfast not included. ❺

Orient Palace 14 26th July St ☎02/393-9375 or 6. A friendly place, with the cheapest singles in town (£E15), but rather dingy rooms in general. On the 10th floor (use the right-hand elevator), with a rooftop café. ❶

Pensione Roma 169 Sharia Mohammed Farid – entrance around the side of the Gattegno department store ☎02/391-1088 or 391-1340, ⓕ579-6243. The stylish 1940s ambience, immaculately maintained by Madame Cressaty, comes highly recommended and it's a wise idea to book in advance (call at 9am or the night before). Constant hot water, shared and private bathrooms; laundry service. ❷

Select 19 Sharia Adly, beside the synagogue ☎02/393-3707. Quiet, Palestinian-run establishment, with simple, mostly triple rooms and hot-water bathrooms, 8 floors up in a 1930s building with period touches. ❷

Sultan ☎02/577-2258, **Safary** ☎02/577-8692, ⓔsafaryhotel12003@yahoo.com and **Venice** ☎02/575-1477, 4 Sharia Tawfiqia. Trio of ultra-cheapies in a building opening onto a colourful market street near Midan Orabi, very handy for inexpensive eating and groceries, and just the right distance away from the centre of downtown. All are very friendly, and offer hot water and use of kitchen facilities, but none is especially clean. The *Safary*, which has dorm beds only (the other two offer poky singles and doubles as well as dorms), is popular with Japanese backpackers, despite being the least appealing of the three. Dorm beds £E8–10. Prices do not include breakfast. ❶

Tulip 3 Midan Talaat Harb ☎02/393-9433, ⓔtuliphotel@yahoo.com. Decent old-style place facing *Groppi's*. The rooms, some en suite, are bright and cheerful and the beds have firm mattresses. ❷

Windsor 19 Sharia Alfi Bey ☎02/591-5810, ⓕ592-1621, ⓦwww.windsorcairo.com. Colonial hotel that retains much character, and one of the nicest bars in Cairo (the *Barrel Lounge*, see p.265), but has definitely seen better days and is rather overpriced (trading on the fact that Michael Palin slept here when filming a travel documentary). The patron's father, Ramses Wissa Wassef, founded Harraniyya's weaving school (see p.237). All rooms have a/c and satellite TV; all but the very cheapest have private bathroom. Offers fifteen percent discount for *Rough Guide* readers, but avoid buying tours here. ❺

Downtown – nearer Ramses Station

These places are a little further from the centre, but still within striking distance, and handy if arriving late or leaving early from one of the terminals around Midan Ramses. They're marked on the map on p.148.

Big Ben 33 Sharia Emad el-Din ☎02/590-8881. Singles, doubles and triples with fans, soft beds and some with private bath – a few even have balconies with a view of the mosque next door. Take the left-hand elevator in the foyer to the 7th floor. Breakfast not included. ❷

Fontana off Midan Ramses ☎02/592-2321, ⓕ592-2145. Comfortable and well kept, with a small rooftop swimming pool, bar, restaurant, patisserie, and disco or bellydancing in its nightclub (see p.268). The rooms have TV, fridge and a/c, and some have views of the Citadel. ❺

New Cicil 29 Sharia Emad el-Din, 4th floor ☎02/591-3859. A clean-ish place with a mainly Egyptian clientele, fans in the rooms, and shared hot-water bathrooms. Breakfast not included. ❶

Venus Hotel 38 Sharia Ramses ☎02/577-5186. The best budget option near Ramses, the rooms are clean and comfortable although they are small; some are en suite with a/c, and the staff are friendly, though you're dependent on the lift as the hotel's on the 12th floor. There's also a TV lounge, laundry service and luggage store. ❷

Victoria 66 Sharia el-Gumhorriya ☎02/589-2290 to 94, ⓔinfo@victoria.com.eg. A three-star 1930s hotel once frequented by George Bernard Shaw. Lots of wood panelling, large a/c rooms (many with mahogany furniture), bar, restaurant and spacious, comfortable lounge area make this one of the best deals in town. Bank and hairdresser on the premises; international calls. Takes Amex, Master-Card and Visa. ❺

Islamic Cairo

Islamic Cairo rubs shoulders with its medieval past: noises, smells and insects penetrate one's room, while outside the quarter's values and customs demand recognition. Excluding numerous bug-ridden dives around Saiyida Zeinab and Khan el-Khalili, three hotels are worth considering. They're marked on the map on p.154.

El-Hussein Muski ☎02/591-8089, ⓕ591-8479. Entered via a passage into *Fishawi's*, rooms overlooking the square are harangued by Cairo's loudest muezzins, while the upper floors shake from wedding parties in its rooftop restaurant (great views, awful food). Sleep is impossible during festivals (bring earplugs), when the square bops all night, but if you don't mind the noise, a balcony overlooking the square gives you a ringside view. Reservations advisable. ❷

El Malky 4 Sharia el-Hussein ☎02/589-1093, ⓕ589-6700. Behind the Saiyidna Hussein Mosque,

with a mainly Muslim clientele, this is a well-kept hotel that's clean and good value. It's well located in the heart of Islamic Cairo but out of the noise and bustle, with carpeted, a/c, en-suite rooms, generally comfortable though the beds are a bit on the hard side. ❷

Radwan Muski ☎02/786-5180 or 2, ⓔsaid19480@yahoo.com. In an excellent location just across the Muski from the *El-Hussein*, so equally noisy, but with smaller rooms, less character and sporadic hot water, though bathrooms are en suite. Not advisable for women alone. Breakfast not included. ❷

Zamalek

The northern half of Gezira Island is quieter and fresher than central Cairo, except along 26th July Street, where buses and service taxis shuttle between downtown and the west bank, with an elevated roadway for through traffic. Besides its *Cairo Marriott* and *El-Gezirah* (see p.117), the island has a few modern **three-star hotels**, plus a couple of **cheaper options**. Below are our top choices; all are keyed on the map on pp.210–211.

El-Nil Zamalek 21 Sharia Aziz Abaza ☎02/735-1846, ℗735-0220. Spacious rooms with bath, phone, TV and a/c in this modern riverside two-star, some with a balcony overlooking the Nile. ❹

Longchamps 21 Sharia Ismail Muhammed, 5th floor ☎02/735-2311, ⓦwww.hotellongchamps.com. Spotless, quiet and well-run three-star hotel with a/c, satellite TV, Internet connection and a fridge in all rooms, plus a pleasant terrace and meals available. It's advisable to book at least a couple of weeks ahead, but if it's full, the *Horus House* downstairs isn't a bad fallback option. ❻

Mayfair 9 Sharia Aziz Osman, 1st floor above ground ☎02/735-7315, ⓦwww.mayfaircairo.com. Immaculate, comfortable en-suite a/c rooms, all with balconies, in a quiet location, with a great Art Deco entrance lobby, a breakfast terrace overlooking the street, and a ten percent discount for *Rough Guide* readers, but avoid buying tours here. ❷

Pension Zamalek 6 Sharia Salah al-Din ☎02/735-9318, ⓔpensionzamalek@msn.com. Very much a European-style *pension*: clean, quiet and secluded with a pleasant family atmosphere, and one bathroom to every two rooms. ❸

Hostels and camping

Hostelling and camping offer meagre rewards by comparison with downtown hotels, and any gains in clean air or seclusion tend to be negated by the extra travel involved in sightseeing from an outlying base.

That said, the **HI youth hostel** near the El-Gama'a Bridge on Roda Island (☎02/364-0729, ℗368-4107; see map on pp.192–193) is readily accessible by #82 minibus from Tahrir. Buses #355 and #357 also run nearby, or you can catch a river-taxi to the Giza University stop and walk back across the bridge. There is a choice between three-person dorms (£E20.25 per bed including breakfast) or cheaper six- to eight-person ones (£E15.25) and it's open year-round. Non-HI members pay £E2 extra, or can take out membership for £E25. Doors are closed midnight to 8am, so no carousing unless you aim to make a full night of it.

Salma Camping in Harraniyya, outside Giza (☎02/381-5062 or 010/145-7316), attracts tourists with camper-vans or bikes. Camping or caravanning, it costs £E15 per person, including free hot showers with no extra tent or vehicle charge. Alternatively, you can rent a hut or even a double room at £E50 a night for two people; breakfast is not included, but there is use of a kitchen. Despite its friendly staff, bar, delightful garden and view of the Pyramids, the site's distance from everywhere but the Wissa Wassef School (next door) is bound to cause difficulties, though it is obviously handy for the Pyramid sites at Giza, Abu Sir and Saqqara. It's reached by turning off Pyramids Road towards Saqqara at Maryotteya Canal (1km before the pyramids), and then after 4km taking a sign-posted turn-off at Harraniyya village; continue for 100m, and the site is about 100m away on your right. Buses and service taxis run from town to the junction of Maryotteya Canal with Pyramids Road, where you can catch regular service taxis to the Harraniyya turn-off.

Long stays and flat-hunting

Should you decide to stay a while, it's worth remembering that many hotels reduce their rates by ten percent after fifteen days' occupation. Depending on demand for rooms and your rapport with the management, it may be possible to negotiate further discounts for **long stays at pensions**.

In the longer term, however, it's better **to rent an apartment**; a base with a phone makes working or socializing in Cairo a lot easier. Prices are a lot lower in winter than in summer, but given the range of localities and amenities, expect to look at half a dozen places before settling on one. Check the small ads in *Egypt Today*, the *Egyptian Gazette* and *Community Times* and expat community newssheets such as the *Maadi Messenger* or *British Community News*, and look at noticeboards at English-language institutes and cultural centres (see p.292), the *Bon Appetit* café in Sharia Mohammed Mahmoud (see p.258), and the American University. It's also possible to see what's available and check prices online via the websites of firms like E-dar (Ⓦwww .e-dar.com) and Gomhoria (Ⓦwww.algomhoria.com). Foreigners working or studying in Cairo often seek flatmates or want to sublet during temporary absences. With luck, you can move into a fully furnished flat with little ado. As a general guide to **prices**, you can rent a flat in the centre for around £E1000 per month per person, or a houseboat for two moored on the Nile at Aguza for £E2000.

Another way involves using a *simsar* (flat agent), who can be found in any neighbourhood by making enquiries at local shops and cafés. Unless you spend a long, fruitless day together, he's only paid when you settle on a place; ten percent of your first month's rent is the normal charge. Flat agencies in Ma'adi levy the same commission on both tenant and landlord. Additional "key money" is illegal, but often demanded.

Before agreeing to **sign a lease**, **check** plumbing, water pressure, sockets, lighting, phone, stove and water-heater (*buta* gas cylinders need changing), and ask if power or water cuts are regular occurrences. Also determine whether utilities (phone, gas, electricity) and services (the *bowab*, garbage collector) are included in the rent and are paid up to date when you move in (ask to see receipts if necessary). All the flat's contents should be accurately noted on an inventory, and the responsibility for repairs and the size of the deposit established. A flat without a phone isn't likely to acquire one, whatever the landlord promises.

Cairo's **residential neighbourhoods** range from smart Western enclaves to countrified *baladi* quarters. Quietly spacious **Ma'adi**, thirty minutes by metro from the centre, is home to most of Egypt's American community and mega-wealthy natives. **Zamalek**, favoured by embassies and European expats, is likewise costly, but always has vacancies. Another focus for the foreign community is **Heliopolis**, a self-contained suburb where palatial Art Deco flats jostle with air-conditioned high-rises. Rents here are lower than in downtown Cairo, where few flats are available at any price unless you move into **Bulaq** or the Qasr al-Aini side of **Garden City**.

Across the Nile, middle-class **Dokki** merges into *baladi* market quarters, while **Mohandiseen** parades blocks of flats and shopping centres along its shiny boulevards. Single males with a grasp of Arabic and Egyptian ways might enjoy living in **baladi quarters** (Islamic Cairo, Bulaq, Imbaba), which are cheap and cheerful, unhygienic and noisy. Foreigners are expected to contribute to the incessant drama of local life and do (verbal) battle when necessary – personal privacy doesn't exist in these urban villages. If you are planning to stay in Cairo for a while, the AUC's regularly updated *Cairo: the Practical Guide* contains much valuable wisdom on the subject of apartment rental and of Cairo living in general.

The City

With so much to see (and overlook, initially), you can spend weeks in **CAIRO** and merely scratch the surface. But as visitors soon realize, there are lots of reasons why people don't stay for long. The city's density, climate and pollution conspire against it, and the culture shock is equally wearing. Tourists unfamiliar with Arab ways can take little for granted, regular visitors expect to be baffled, and not even Cairenes comprehend the whole metropolis. The downside weighs especially on newcomers, since it's the main tourist sites that generate most friction. A day at Khan el-Khalili bazaar can feel like a course in sales resistance and *baksheesh* evasion. Generally, however, Cairenes are the warmest, best-natured city dwellers going. They have to be to live in such a pressure cooker without exploding. Their sly wit and prying render pretension and secrecy impotent; their spirited ingenuity transcends horrendous conditions. Potential riots are defused by tolerance and custom; a web of ties resists alienation. Once you have something of the measure of this, Cairo feels an altogether different and more enjoyable place.

Central Cairo

Most people prefer to get accustomed to **central Cairo** before tackling the older, Islamic quarters, for even in this Westernized downtown area known as *wust al-Balad*, the culture shock can be profound. Beyond the sanctuary of the luxury hotels beside the Nile, crowds and traffic jostle for space in the fume-laden air; whistling cops direct weaving taxis and limousines, donkey carts and buses; office workers rub shoulders with *baladi* folk, Nubians and soldiers. The pavements and shadowy lobbies of cavernous Art Deco or Empire-style apartment buildings are a lifetime's world for many vendors and doormen – both major contributors to Cairo's grapevine. Above the crumbling pediments and hoardings, pigeon lofts and extra rooms spread across the rooftops – a spacious alternative to the streets below, forming a city above the city centre.

Cairo's museums

Although Cairo has more than a dozen museums, most visitors limit themselves to the big three, devoted respectively to **Egyptian Antiquities** (see opposite), **Coptic** (see p.196) and **Islamic Art** (see p.168). Of these, the Antiquities Museum is the most popular and by far the largest, necessitating at least two visits to do it any kind of justice. The Coptic and Islamic Art museums can each comfortably be seen in a couple of hours and make fitting adjuncts to exploration of their quarters of the city, though at time of writing both were closed.

On a practical note, unless you're planning to buy a photo permit, it's best to leave your **camera** at the hotel. Otherwise you'll have to check it in at the entrance to all three main museums, a process which occasionally leads to the wrong camera being returned to the wrong owner. For the smaller and more distant museums, given temporary closures and erratic opening hours, it's worth telephoning before setting out.

The area is essentially a lopsided triangle, bounded by **Ramses Station**, **Midan Ataba** and **Garden City**, and for the most part it's compact enough to explore on foot. Only the Ramses quarter and the further reaches of Garden City are sufficiently distant to justify using transport. At the heart of central Cairo is the broad, bustling expanse of **Midan Tahrir** (for an account of the square, see p.138); aside from being the city's main transport terminal, Tahrir's most famous landmark is the domed **Museum of Egyptian Antiquities**, which houses the finest collection of its kind in the world.

The Museum of Egyptian Antiquities

At the northern end of Midan Tahrir, the **Museum of Egyptian Antiquities** (daily 9am–6.45pm; during Ramadan 9am–4pm; £E40, students £E20, no cameras allowed) feels almost as archaic as the civilization it records. Founded in 1858 by Auguste Mariette, who excavated the Serapeum at Saqqara and several major temples in Upper Egypt (and was later buried in the museum grounds), it has long since outgrown its present building, which now scarcely provides warehouse space for the pharaonic artefacts. Allowing one minute for each, it would take about nine months to view its 136,000 exhibits. Forty thousand more items lie crated in the basement, where many have sunk into the soft ground, necessitating excavations beneath the building itself. A new Grand Egyptian Museum, which will house some or all the exhibits in the present one, is already under construction by the pyramids of Giza, and is due to open in around 2015. Meanwhile, for all the chaos, poor lighting and captioning of the old museum, the richness of the collection makes this one of the world's few truly great museums, and one that no visitor to Cairo should miss.

A single visit of three to four hours suffices to cover the Tutankhamun exhibition and a few other **highlights**. Everyone has their favourites, but a reasonable shortlist might include, on the ground floor, the Amarna galleries (**rooms 3 and 8**), the cream of statuary from the Old, Middle and New kingdoms (**rooms 42, 32, 22 and 12**) and the Nubian funerary cache (**Room 44**); on the upper floor, the Fayoum Portraits (**Room 14**) and model figures (**rooms 37, 32 and 27**), and, of course, the Mummy Room (**Room 56**) – though it costs extra.

Before you enter the museum, check the pond in front of the main entrance: the water lilies growing here are the now-rare blue lotus, a psychoactive plant used as a drug by the Ancient Egyptians – which they are depicted using (by dipping the flowers into their wine) on several frescoes and reliefs.

Once inside the museum you'll probably be offered a **guided tour**, which generally lasts two hours (at around £E60 an hour), though the museum deserves at least six. The guides are extremely knowledgeable and they do help you to make sense of it all – if you are in a small group it really isn't that expensive. Alternatively, you can rent headphones with a **recorded commentary** (£E20) in English, Arabic or French, and numbers to press on a handset for each of the items covered. However, as the exhibits were already numbered on at least two different systems, the addition of new numbers for the digital commentary complicates matters still further, leading to some items now having three different numbers, and often no other labelling (in such cases, we have identified exhibits by their most prominent number). The best published **guide** to the museum's contents is the AUC's *Illustrated Guide to the Egyptian Museum* (£E150), with lavish illustrations of the museum's top exhibits. It doesn't list the exhibits in order, but there is a room-by-room picture index at the back to help you find what you are looking at in the text, and it is certainly an excellent souvenir of the museum.

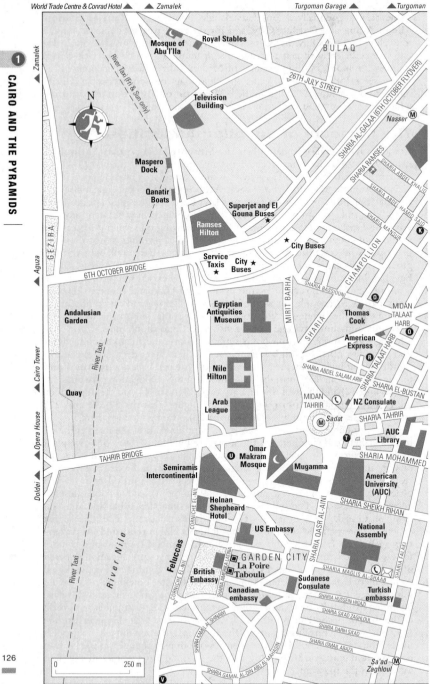

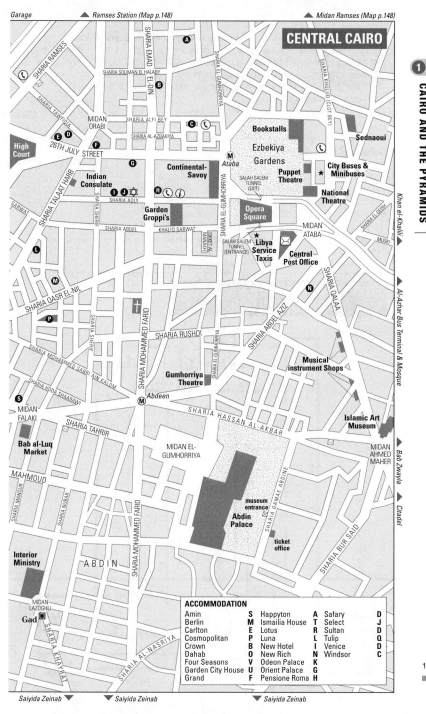

Garage ▲ Ramses Station (Map p.148) ▲ Midan Ramses (Map p.148)

CENTRAL CAIRO

Khan el-Khalili ▶

Al-Azhar Bus Terminal & Mosque ▶

Bab Zwayla ▶

Citadel ▶

SHARIA RAMSES
SHARIA EMAD EL-DIN
SHARIA EL-GUMHORRIYA
SHARIA KHULUG (CLOT BEY)
SHARIA TAWFIQIA
SHARIA SOLIMAN EL HALABY
SHARIA ALFI BEY
MIDAN ORABI
SHARIA AL-AZBAKIYA
Bookstalls
Sednaoui
Ezbekiya Gardens
High Court
26TH JULY STREET
Ataba
Puppet Theatre
City Buses & Minibuses
SHARIA TALAAT HARB
Continental-Savoy
SALAH SALEM TUNNEL (EXIT)
National Theatre
SHARIA EL GEISH
Indian Consulate
SHARIA ADLY
SHARIA SHERIF
Garden Groppi's
KHALIG SARWAT
Opera Square
MIDAN ATABA
MUSKI
SARWAT
SHARIA ABDEL
SINKET AL-MANAKH
SALAH SALEM TUNNEL (ENTRANCE)
Libya Service Taxis
Central Post Office
SHARIA QASR EL-NIL
SHARIA SHERIF
SHARIA MOHAMMED FARID
SHARIA DALAA
SHARIA RUSHDI
SHARIA EL-GUMHORRIYA
SHARIA ABDEL AZIZ
SHARIA MOHAMMED SABRI AIN KALOM
Musical instrument Shops
SHARIA HODA SHAARAWI
Gumhorriya Theatre
Abdeen
Islamic Art Museum
MIDAN FALAKI
SHARIA HASSAN AL-AKBAR
MIDAN AHMED MAHER
SHARIA TAHRIR
Bab al-Luq Market
MIDAN EL-GUMHORRIYA
SHARIA GAMAE ARDINE
MAHMOUD
SHARIA MANSUR
SHARIA NUBAR
SHARIA MOHAMMED FARID
SHARIA BUR SAID
museum entrance
Abdin Palace
ticket office
Interior Ministry
A B D I N
MIDAN LAZOGHLI
Gad
SHARIA AL-NASRIYA
SHARIA KHAYRAT

ACCOMMODATION

Amin	**S**	Happyton	**A**	Safary	**D**
Berlin	**M**	Ismailia House	**T**	Select	**J**
Carlton		Lotus	**R**	Sultan	**Q**
Cosmopolitan	**P**	Luna	**L**	Tulip	**D**
Crown	**B**	New Hotel	**I**	Venice	**Q**
Dahab	**O**	New Rich	**N**	Windsor	**C**
Four Seasons	**V**	Odeon Palace	**K**		
Garden City House	**U**	Orient Palace	**G**		
Grand	**F**	Pensione Roma	**H**		

127

Saiyida Zeinab ▼ ▼ Saiyida Zeinab ▼ Saiyida Zeinab

> On your way to the museum, beware of a "friendly local" who may accost you and try to persuade you that the museum is closed for a couple of hours. Instead, he will invite you to spend the time enjoying "Egyptian hospitality" at a local papyrus shop (or "papyrus museum" as he will probably call it). Needless to say, you will have then to endure an hour's worth of time-wasting hard-sell, and the papyri will be outrageously overpriced.

The museum's first-floor **café-restaurant** is entered via the souvenir shop from outside the museum.

Ground floor

Exhibits are arranged more or less chronologically, so that by starting at the entrance and walking in a clockwise direction round the outer galleries you'll pass through the Old, Middle and New kingdoms, before ending up with the Late and Greco-Roman periods in the east wing. This approach is historically and artistically coherent but rather plodding. A snappier alternative is to proceed instead through the Atrium – which samples the whole era of

pharaonic civilization – to the superb Amarna gallery in the northern wing; then backtrack to cover sections that sound interesting, or instead head upstairs to Tutankhamun.

To suit either option, we've covered the ground floor in six sections: the Atrium, Old, Middle and New kingdom galleries, the Amarna gallery, and the East Wing. Whichever approach you decide on, it's worth starting with the Atrium foyer (**Room 43**), where the dynastic saga begins.

The Rotunda and Atrium

The **Rotunda**, inside the museum entrance, kicks off with **monumental sculptures** from various eras, notably (in the four corners) three colossi of Ramses II (XIX Dynasty) and a statue of Amenhotep, son of the XVIII Dynasty royal architect Hapu. Also here, hidden away in the northwest corner, are sixteen small wooden and stone statues of a 24th-century BC official named Iby showing him at various stages in his life. Just to the left of the door as you enter sits the limestone **statue of King Zoser** (#106), installed within its *serdab* beside his Step Pyramid at Saqqara in the 27th century BC, and removed by archeologists 4600 years later. Those who regard Zoser's reign as the start of the Old Kingdom categorize the preceding era as the Early Dynastic or **Archaic Period**.

The actual forging of dynastic rule is commemorated by a famous exhibit in **Room 43**, as you enter the Atrium. The **Palette of Narmer**, a decorative version of the slate palettes used to grind kohl, records the unification of the Two Lands (c.3100 BC) by a ruler called Narmer or Menes. One side of the palette depicts him wearing the White Crown of Upper Egypt, smiting an enemy with a mace, while a falcon (Horus) ensnares another prisoner and tramples the heraldic papyrus of Lower Egypt. The reverse face shows him wearing their Red Crown to inspect the slain, and ravaging a fortress as a bull; dividing these tableaux are mythical beasts with entwined necks, restrained from conflict by bearded men, an arcane symbol of his political achievement. Two XII Dynasty **funerary barques** from the pyramid of Senusert III at Dahshur stand on either side of the room.

Descending into **Room 33**, which is the museum's atrium, you'll find **pyramidions** (pyramid capstones) from Dahshur, and more sarcophagi from the New Kingdom. Overshadowing those of Tuthmosis I and Queen Hatshepsut (before she became pharaoh), the **sarcophagus of Merneptah** (#213) is surmounted by a figure of the king as Osiris and protectively embraced from within by a relief of Nut, the sky goddess. But Merneptah's bid for immortality failed: when discovered at Tanis in 1939, his sarcophagus held the coffin of Psusennes, a XXI Dynasty ruler whose gold-sheathed mummy now lies upstairs.

At the centre of the Atrium is a **painted floor from the royal palace at Amarna** (XVIII Dynasty). A river brimming with ducks and fish is framed by reeds where waterfowl and cows amble, a fine example of the lyrical naturalism of the Amarna period. For more of this revolutionary epoch in pharaonic history, head upstairs past the **colossal statues of Amenophis III, Queen Tiy and their three daughters**, which serenely presage Akhenaten and Nefertiti in the northern wing.

But first you must pass through **Room 13**, containing Merneptah's Victory Stele on the right, also called the **Israel Stele**. Its name derives from the boast "Israel is crushed, it has no more seed", from among a list of Merneptah's conquests at the temple of Karnak – the sole known reference to Israel in all the records of Ancient Egypt. Partly on the strength of this, many believe that

Merneptah, son of Ramses II, was the Pharaoh of the Exodus (XIX Dynasty) – although this view has come under increasing criticism of late (see box on p.201). The other side carries an earlier record of deeds by Amenophis III (Akhenaten's father) in the service of Amun, whom his son later repudiated. Hidden away on the other side of the room is a **model of a typical Egyptian house**, as excavated at Amarna, the short-lived capital of Akhenaten and Nefertiti – who are honoured with their own gallery in rooms 8 and 3 just ahead (see p.132).

Old Kingdom Galleries

The southwest corner of the ground floor is devoted to the **Old Kingdom** (c.2700–2181 BC), when the III–VI dynasties ruled Egypt from Memphis and built the Pyramids. Lining the central aisle of **rooms 46–47** are funerary statues of deceased VIPs and servants (the custom of burying retainers alive ended with the II Dynasty). In Room 47, the **panel from Userkaf's temple**, by the north side of the doorway to Room 48, is the first known example of natural scenes being used as decoration within a royal funerary edifice: a pied kingfisher, purple gallinule and sacred ibis are clearly recognizable. On the north side of Room 47, six **wooden panels** from the tomb of **Hesy-Re** portray this senior scribe of the III Dynasty, who was also the earliest known dentist. Room 47 also displays statuettes of *shabti* (worker) figures, depicted preparing food (#52 and 53). To the north and south are three **slate triads of Menkaure flanked by Hathor** and the goddess of the Aphroditopolis nome, from the Mycenius valley temple at Giza. The pair of alabaster **lion tables** by the fourth pillar on the north side were probably used for sacrifices or libations towards the end of the II Dynasty.

Among the more striking exhibits in Room 46 are **statuettes** of the dwarf Khnumhotep, Overseer of the Wardrobe, a man with a deformed head and a hunchback afflicted by Pott's disease (#54 and 65).

Fragments of the **beard of the Sphinx** are at the end of the hall (**Room 51**), to the left below the stairs (#6031). The British Museum in London possesses another metre-long chunk; the beard was probably five metres long before it was shot to pieces by Mamluke and Napoleonic troops during target practice. Also in Room 51, a sculptured head of V Dynasty pharaoh Userkaf (#6051) represents the earliest known larger-than-life-size statue in the world.

At the entrance to **Room 41**, **reliefs** from a V Dynasty tomb at Maidum (#25) depict a desert hunt and other rural activities. Another panel (#59), from a V Dynasty tomb at Saqqara, shows grain being weighed out, milled and graded, as well as glass being blown and statues carved. The women on these reliefs wear long chemises, the men loincloths or sometimes nothing (revealing them to be circumcized, according to Egyptian custom). **Room 42** boasts a superb **statue of Chephren**, his head embraced by Horus (#31). Carved from black diorite, whose white marbling emphasizes the sinews of his knee and clenched fist, the statue comes from Chephren's valley temple at Giza. Equally arresting on the left is the wooden **statue of Ka-aper** (#40), a plump figure with an introspective gaze, which Arab diggers at Saqqara called "Sheikh al-Balad" because it resembled their own village headman. One of the two newly restored wooden statues to the right (#123 and 124) could well be of the same man. The **statue of a scribe** (#43), poised for notation with an open scroll across his knees, is also memorable.

On the walls of **Room 31** are sandstone reliefs from Wadi Maraghah, near the ancient turquoise mines of Sinai. Twin limestone **statues of Ra-Nufer** signify his dual role as Memphite high priest of Ptah and Sokar; aside from their wigs and kilts, they look virtually identical. Both were created in the royal workshops, possibly by the same artist.

Room 32 is dominated by life-size seated **statues of Prince Rahotep and Princess Nefert**, from their *mastaba* at Maidum (IV Dynasty). His skin is painted brick-red, hers a creamy yellow – a distinction common in Egyptian art. Nefert wears a wig and diadem and swathes herself in a diaphanous wrap; the prince is simply clad in a waist cloth. Look out for the **tableau of the dwarf Seneb and his family** on the left (#39). Embraced by his wife, this Overseer of the Wardrobe seems contented; his naked children hold their fingers to his lips. In the second niche on the left-hand wall hangs a perfectly observed, vividly stylized mural, known as the **Maidum Geese** (III/IV Dynasty). Although the heyday of the Old Kingdom is poorly represented by a **statue of Ti**, also on the left (#49), its twilight era boasts, just by the doorway, the first known metal sculptures (c.2300 BC): two **statues of Pepi I and his son**, made by hammering sheets of copper over wooden armatures (though these were away for restoration at the time of writing).

In **Room 37**, next door, the **furniture of Queen Hetepheres** has been expertly reconstructed from heaps of gold and rotten wood. As the wife of Snofru and mother of Cheops, she was buried near her son's pyramid at Giza with a sedan chair, gold vessels and a canopied bed. Also in the room, in a cabinet of its own, is a tiny **statuette of Cheops**, the only known likeness of the Great Pyramid pharaoh.

Middle Kingdom Galleries

With **Room 26** you enter the **Middle Kingdom**, when centralized authority was restored and pyramid-building resumed under the XII Dynasty (c.1991–1786 BC). A relic of the previous era of civil wars (termed the First Intermediate Period) sits on the right, glum-faced. Endowed with hulking feet to suggest power, and black skin, crossed arms and a curly beard to link it to Osiris, this **statue of Mentuhotpe Nebhepetre** was buried near his funerary shrine at Deir el-Bahri and discovered by Howard Carter – whose horse fell through the roof. If the Mummy of Dagi were still around, it could use the pair of "eyes" painted inside its sarcophagus across the hall (#34) to espy two statues of Queen Nofret wearing a sheath dress and a Hathor wig, flanking the entrance to Room 21.

The statuettes at the back of **Room 22** are striking for the uncharacteristic expressiveness of their faces, in contrast to the manic staring eyes of the wooden statue of Nakhti on the right. Also in the room are likenesses of Amenemhet III and Senusert I, but your attention is grabbed by the **burial chamber of Harhotpe** from Deir el-Bahri, in the middle of the room and covered inside with pictorical objects, charms and texts. Surrounding the chamber are ten limestone **statues of Senusert** from his pyramid complex at Lisht, stiffly formal in contrast to his cedarwood figure in the case to your right as you enter the room (#88). The sides of these statues' thrones bear variations of the *sema-tawy* symbol of unification: Hapy the Nile-god, or Horus and Seth, entwining the heraldic plants of the Two Lands.

This basic imperative of statecraft might explain the unique **double statue of Amenemhat III** (#508) in **Room 16**. Personified as the Nile god bringing his people fish on trays, the dual figures may represent Upper and Lower Egypt, or the living king and his deified *ka*. On the left, five **lion-headed sphinxes with human faces** watch your exit from the Middle Kingdom; the anarchic Second Intermediate Period and the Hyksos invasion go uncommemorated.

New Kingdom Galleries

With **Room 11** you pass into the **New Kingdom**, an era of renewed pharaonic power and imperial expansion under the XVIII and XIX dynasties (c.1567-1200 BC). Egypt's African and Asian empires were forged by Tuthmosis III, who had long been frustrated while his unwarlike stepmother, Hatshepsut, ruled as pharaoh. From one of the Osiride pillars of her great temple at Deir el-Bahri comes a commanding crowned **head of Hatshepsut** (#94), while on the left of the room stands an unusual *ka* statue of Pharaoh Hor (#75), mounted on a sliding base to signify his posthumous wanderings. In **Room 12** you'll find a grey schist statue of **Tuthmosis III** (#62) and other masterpieces of XVIII Dynasty art. At the back of the room, the **Hathor Shrine** from Tuthmosis III's ruined temple at Deir el-Bahri contains a statue of the goddess in her bovine form, emerging reborn from a papyrus swamp. Tuthmosis stands beneath her cow's head, and is suckled as an infant in the fresco behind Hathor's statue, overshadowed by a star-spangled ceiling. To the right of the shrine is a block statue (#418) of Hatshepsut's vizier, Senenmut, with the queen's daughter Neferure, with a smaller statue of the same duo in the second recess on the right. The relationship between the queen, her daughter and her vizier has inspired much speculation. From the same period comes a section of the Deir el-Bahri "**Punt relief**" (in the second niche on the left), showing the Queen of Punt, who suffered from elephantiasis, and her donkey, observed by Hatshepsut during her expedition to that fabled land.

To the right of the Punt relief stands a grey granite **statue of the god Khonsu** with a sidelock denoting youth and a face thought to be that of the boy pharaoh Tutankhamun, which was taken from the temple of the moon-god at Karnak. Flanking this statue and the Punt relief, two **statues** of a man named **Amenhotep** portray him as a young scribe of humble birth and as an octogenarian priest, honoured for his direction of massive works like the Colossi of Memnon.

Before turning the corner into the northern wing, you encounter two **lion-headed statues of Sekhmet**, found at Karnak. **Sphinxes** with the heads of Hatshepsut and her family dominate **Room 6**, where some of the reliefs along the southern wall come from the Tomb of Maya at Saqqara. The tomb was uncovered in the nineteenth century but subsequently lost until its rediscovery in 1986. **Room 8** is largely an overflow for the Amarna Gallery (see below) but also contains a monumental **dyad of Amun and Mut**, smashed to pieces by medieval limestone quarriers and lovingly pieced together from fragments long lost in the vaults of the museum and at Karnak, where it originally stood. Those pieces that could not be fitted into the jigsaw are displayed in a case just behind it.

To the left of the stairs in **Room 10**, note the painted **relief** on a block from Ramses II's temple at Memphis (#769), which shows him subjugating Egypt's foes. In a motif repeated on dozens of temple pylons, the king grabs the hair of a Libyan, Nubian and Syrian, and wields an axe. Ramessid pharaohs who never fought a battle were especially keen on such reliefs. The room ends with a pun (#6245): a **statue of Ramses II** as a child, finger to mouth, holding a plant while protected by the sun-god *Re* or *Ra*, which combines with the word for child (*mes*) and the word for the plant (*su*) to form his name. From Room 10 you can follow the New Kingdom into the East Wing (covered opposite), or climb the stairs to the Tutankhamun galleries on the upper floor.

The Amarna Gallery

Room 3 and much of the adjoining **Room 8** focus on the **Amarna period**: a break with centuries of tradition which barely outlasted the reign of Pharaoh

Akhenaten (c.1379–1362 BC) and Queen Nefertiti. Rejecting Amun and the other deities of Thebes, they decreed the supremacy of a single god, the Aten; built a new capital at Amarna in Middle Egypt to escape the old bureaucracy; and left enigmatic works of art that provoke a reaction.

Staring down from the walls of **Room 3** are four **colossi of Akhenaten**, whose attenuated skull and face, flaring lips and nostrils, rounded thighs and belly are suggestive of a hermaphrodite or a primeval earth goddess. Because these characteristics are carried over to the figures of his wife and daughters on certain **steles** (in the left-hand niche and the cases in front of it) and tomb reliefs, it has been argued that the Amarna style pandered to some physical abnormality in Akhenaten (or the royal family) – the captions hint at perversions. Others retort that the famous head of Nefertiti, in Berlin, proves that it was just a stylistic device. Another feature of Amarna art was its note of intimacy: a **stele of the royal family** (#167 in Room 8) portrays Akhenaten dandling their eldest daughter, Meritaten, whilst Nefertiti cradles her sisters. For the first time in Egyptian art, breakfast was depicted. The Amarna focus on this world rather than the afterlife infused traditional subjects with new vitality – witness the freer brush strokes on the fragments of a **marsh scene**, displayed around the walls of Room 3. To the left of the entrance to the room, display case A contains some of the **Amarna Letters** (others are in London and Berlin), recording pleas for troops to aid the pharaoh's vassals in Palestine, the impact of his death, and Nefertiti's search for allies against those who pressed Tutankhamun to reverse the Amarna revolution. Originally baked into earthen "envelopes" for delivery, these cuneiform tablets were stored in the Foreign Office archives at Amarna.

Akhenaten's carnelian-, gold- and glass-inlaid **coffin** is in Room 8, the upper half displayed alongside the gilding from the bottom part of the coffin. This gilding disappeared from the museum at some time between 1915 and 1931, but resurfaced in Switzerland in the 1980s. It has now been restored and mounted on a Plexiglas cast in the presumed shape of the original coffin.

The East Wing

As an inducement to follow the New Kingdom into the East Wing, **Room 15** holds a sexy statue of the wife of Nakht Min (#71). Inside **Room 14** is a huge alabaster **statue of Seti I**, whose sensitive facial modelling recalls Nefertiti's head. Originally, it would have worn a *nemset* headdress like the one on Tutankhamun's funerary mask. More striking, however, is the restored pink granite triple statue of Ramses III being crowned by Horus and Set, representing order and chaos respectively.

Waning with the XX Dynasty and expiring with the XXI, the New Kingdom was followed by the so-called **Late Period** of mostly foreign rulers. From the same period, in the middle of the room, comes an alabaster **statue of Amenirdis the Elder**, whom the pharaoh made divine votaress of Amun to watch over the Theban priesthood (**Room 30**). Dressed as a New Kingdom queen, Amenirdis wears a falcon headdress crowned with *uraei*, originally topped by a Hathor crown bearing a solar disc and horns. Of the diverse **statues of deities** in **Room 24**, it's Taweret (or Tweri), the pregnant-hippopotamus goddess of childbirth, that most visitors remember.

Rooms 34 and **35** cover the **Greco-Roman Period** (332 BC onwards), when Classical art engaged with Ancient Egyptian symbolism. The meld of styles is typified by the bizarre **statues and sarcophagi** down the corridor in **Room 49**, especially that of Alexander II at the threshold of the room. Room 44, on your way, is used for temporary exhibitions.

Upper floor

The upper floor is dominated by the Tutankhamun galleries, which occupy the best part of two wings. Once you've seen Tut's treasures, everything but the Mummy Room and the display of masterpieces seems lacklustre – even though the other galleries feature artefacts just as fine as those downstairs. Come back another day and check them out.

Tutankhamun Galleries

The funerary impedimenta of the boy-king **Tutankhamun** numbers 1700 items and fills a dozen rooms. Given the brevity of his reign (1361–1352 BC) and the paucity of his tomb in the Valley of the Kings, one's mind boggles at the treasure that must have been stashed with great pharaohs like Ramses or Seti. Tutankhamun merely fronted the Theban counter-revolution that effaced Amarna and restored the cult of Amun and its priesthood to their former primacy. However, the influence of Amarna is apparent in some of the **exhibits,** which are laid out roughly as they were packed into his tomb: chests and statues (**Room 45**) preceding furniture (**rooms 40, 35, 30, 25, 20, 15**

EGYPTIAN ANTIQUITIES MUSEUM: UPPER FLOOR

and 10), shrines (**rooms 9–7**) and gold appurtenances (**Room 3**). Adjacent to this are jewellery (**Room 4**) and other treasures from diverse tombs (**rooms 2 and 13**). Most visitors make a beeline for the last four (2, 3 and 4 close fifteen minutes early), ignoring the sequence just outlined. If that includes you, skip ahead through the following rundown.

When Howard Carter's team penetrated the sealed corridor of the tomb in 1922 (see p.413), they found an antechamber stuffed with caskets and detritus ransacked by robbers, and two life-size **ka statues of Tutankhamun** (flanking the doorway to **Room 45**), whose black skin symbolized his rebirth. Just beyond are golden **statues of Tutankhamun**, mostly depicting him hunting with a harpoon.

Room 35 is dominated by a **gilded throne** with winged-serpent arms and clawed feet (#179). Its seat back shows the royal couple relaxing in the rays of the Aten, their names given in the Amarna form – dating it to the time when Tutankhamun still observed the Amarna heresy. Among the other worldly goods that the boy pharaoh carried with him into the next world are an ebony and ivory **gaming set** for playing *senet*, a game similar to draughts (#49), and a host of **shabti figures** to fulfil any tasks the gods might set him (flanking the door to Room 34).

Room 30 has a case of "**Prisoners' Canes**" (#187), whose ebony- and ivory-inlaid figures symbolize the unity of north and south. A bust of the boy king emerging from a lotus (#118) shows the continued influence of the Amarna artistic style during Tutankhamun's reign. The "**ecclesiastical throne**" (#181) in **Room 25** is a prototype for episcopal thrones of the Christian Church. Its seat back is exquisitely inlaid with ebony and gold, but looks uncomfortable. More typical of pharaonic design are the wooden *Heb* chair and footstools, and an ornate commode.

The king's clothes and unguents were stored in two magnificent **chests**. On the lid and sides of the "Painted Chest" (#186) in **Room 20**, he is depicted hunting ostriches and antelopes and devastating ranks of Syrians in his war chariot, larger than life; the end panels show him trampling other foes in the guise of the sphinx. In contrast to the warlike figures of Tutankhamun elsewhere in the gallery, the lid of the "Inlaid Chest" bears a gentle, Amarna-style vignette of Ankhesenamun (daughter of Nefertiti and Akhenaten) offering lotus, papyrus and mandrake to her husband, framed by poppies, pomegranates and cornflowers. The **golden shrine** covered in repoussé scenes of conjugal harmony once held statues of Tut and his wife Ankhesenamun that were stolen in antiquity.

From ivory headrests in **Room 15**, it's a natural progression to **gilded beds** dedicated to the gods whose animal forms are carved on their bedposts (#183, 221 and 732 in **Room 10**). Beyond these in **Room 9** is a **shrine of Anubis** (#54), carried in the pharaoh's cortege: the protector of the dead depicted as a vigilant jackal with gilded ears and silver claws. Next along, four alabaster canopic jars in an alabaster chest (#176) contained the pharaoh's viscera, and were themselves contained in the next exhibit, a golden **canopic chest** protected by statues of the goddesses Isis, Nephthys, Selket and Neith (#177). Ranged along **rooms 7 and 8** are four boxy **gilded shrines**, which fitted one inside another like Russian dolls, enclosing Tutankhamun's sarcophagus.

The always packed-out **Room 3** contains **Tutankhamun's gold**, some of which may be on tour abroad. Assuming it's in Cairo, the centrepiece is his haunting **funerary mask**, wearing a *nemset* headdress inlaid with lapis lazuli, quartz and obsidian. The middle and innermost layers of his mummiform **coffin**, adorned with the same materials, show the boy king with his hands clasped in the Osiride position, protected by the cloisonné feathers of Wadjet,

Nekhbet, Isis and Nephthys. On Tutankhamun's mummy (which remains in his tomb at the Valley of the Kings) were placed scores of **amulets**, a cloisonné **corselet** spangled with glass and carnelian, gem-encrusted **pectorals** and a pair of golden **sandals** – all displayed here.

The **Jewellery Room** next door is almost as overpowering. A VI Dynasty golden **head of a falcon** (once attached to a copper body) from Hieraconpolis rates as the star attraction, but there's stiff competition from the **crown and necklaces of Princess Khnumyt** and the **diadem and pectorals of Princess Set-Hathor**. Buried near the latter at Dahshur were the **amethyst belt and anklet of Mereret**, another XII Dynasty princess. The ceremonial **axe of Ahmosis**, commemorating his expulsion of the Hyksos from Egypt, was buried in the tomb of his mother, Queen Ahhotep. From the same cache (found by Mariette in 1859) came a hinged bracelet of lapis lazuli and the bizarre **golden flies** of the Order of Valour – bug-eyed decorations for bravery.

From the XXI–XXII Dynasty, when northern Egypt was ruled from the Delta, comes the Treasure of 787, displayed in **Room 2**. Of the three royal caches unearthed by Montet in 1939, the richest was that of Psusennes I, whose electrum coffin was found inside the sarcophagus of Merneptah (which is downstairs). His gold necklace is made from rows of discs, in the New Kingdom style.

Between **Room 8** and the Atrium stand two wooden **chariots**, found in the antechamber of Tutankhamun's tomb. Intended for state occasions, their gilded stucco reliefs show Asiatics and Nubians in bondage; pharaonic war chariots were lighter and stronger.

Having finished with Tut, you can either head down the western wing to the Mummy Room, or tackle the other galleries (see below).

Mummies

The southern end of the museum's upper floor harbours two rooms full of mummies. **Room 53** exhibits **mummified animals and birds** from necropolises across Egypt, evincing the strength of animal cults towards the end of the pagan era, when devotees embalmed everything from bulls to mice and fish.

Modern Egyptians regard these relics of ancestral superstition with equanimity, but the exhibition of human remains offended many – hence Sadat's closure of the famous **Mummy Room** (previously Room 52) in 1981. Since then, the Egyptian Museum and the Getty Institute have been working to restore the badly decomposed royal mummies. The results of their work are now displayed in Room 56, where you have to buy another ticket (£E70, students £E35; closes 6.30pm) to see them. Altogether eleven royal mummies are displayed here (clearly labelled and arranged chronologically anticlockwise around the room), including the mortal remains of some of the most famous pharaohs, in particular the great conquerors of the XIX Dynasty, Seti I and his son Ramses II, the latter looking rather slighter in the flesh than the massive statues of him at Memphis and elsewhere. Also here is Ramses's son, Merneptah, whom many believe to be the pharaoh of the biblical exodus (see box p.201). Unless you have a keen interest in mummies, it isn't really worth the high price you have to pay to see them.

All the mummies are kept in sealed cases at controlled humidity, and most of them look remarkably peaceful – Tuthmosis II and Tuthmosis IV could almost be sleeping – and many still have hair. Queen Henuttawi's curly locks and handsome face suggest Nubian origin. In deference to the deceased, no guiding is allowed, and the low hum of *sotto voce* chatter is only broken by the attendant periodically calling for "Silence, please!" The mummies were found in the royal cache at Deir el-Bahri (see p.425) and in a spare chamber in the tomb of Amenophis II (see p.418), where they had been reburied during the XXI Dynasty to protect them from grave robbers. For a description of the mummification process, see p.410; and for a graphic demonstration of the hollowness of a mummy, take a look up Ramses V's right nostril – from this angle you'll be able to see straight out through the hole in his skull.

The other galleries

To view the other galleries in approximate chronological order you should start at **Room 43** (overlooking the Atrium) and proceed in a clockwise direction, as on the ground floor. However, since most visitors wander in from Tut's galleries, we've described the western and eastern wings from that standpoint.

Starting with the **western wing**, notice the "**Heart Scarabs**" that were placed upon the throats of mummies, bearing a spell that implored the deceased's heart not to bear witness against him or her during the Judgement of Osiris (**Room 6**). **Room 12**'s hoard of **objects from XVIII Dynasty royal tombs** includes the mummies of a child and a gazelle (Case I); priestly wigs and wig boxes (Case L); two leopards from the funerary cache of Amenophis II (#3842); and the chariot of Tuthmosis IV (#4113). **Room 17** holds the **contents of private tombs**, notably that of Sennedjem, from the Workmen's village near the Valley of the Kings. With skills honed on royal tombs, Sennedjem carved himself a stylish vault; its door (#215) depicts him playing *senet*. The sarcophagus of his son Khonsu carries a design showing the lions of Today and Yesterday supporting the rising sun, while Anubis embalms his mummy under the protection of Isis and Nephthys.

While the corridor displays **canopic chests and coffins**, the inner rooms feature **Middle Kingdom models**. From Meketre's tomb at Thebes come marvellous domestic figures and tableaux in **Room 27**: a woman carrying wine jars on her head (#74), peasants netting fish from reed boats (#75), and cattle being driven past an estate-owner (#76). In **Room 32** compare the fully crewed model boats in Case F with the unmanned solar barques for voyaging through eternity in Case E. Model-soldier buffs will delight in the phalanxes of Nubian archers and Egyptian pikemen from the tomb of Prince Mesehti at Assyut, in **Room 37**.

The museum's **southern wing** is best seen at a trot. The middle section contains a **model of a funerary complex** showing how the pyramids and their temples related to the Nile (**Room 48**), and the cubic **leather funerary tent** of an XXI Dynasty queen, decorated in red-and-green checkered squares (#3848, by the southeast stairway in Room 50). More striking are two exhibitions in the central section: **recent finds and forgotten treasures**, which are showcased outside Room 54; and in Room 43, **objects from the tomb of Yuya and Thuya**. The finest of these are Thuya's gem-inlaid gilded mask, their mummiform coffins and statues of the couple. As parents of Queen Tiy (wife of Amenophis III), they were buried in the Valley of the Kings; their tomb was found intact in the late nineteenth century. Hidden away by the entrance to Room 42 is a panel of blue faïence tiles from Zoser's burial hall at Saqqara (#17).

Also in Room 48, on the east side by the banister over the Rotunda, is a display case (#144) containing a stone head of Akhenaten's mum Queen Tiy that prefigures the Amarna style, and "dancing dwarves" modelled on equatorial pygmies. The same case also holds a beautiful, very lifelike wooden statuette of a Nubian woman, possibly Queen Tiy, with her hair in braids, looking strikingly modern.

If approached from the north, the **eastern wing** begins with **Room 14**, containing a couple of mummies and the superbly lifelike but sadly ill-lit "**Fayoum Portraits**" found by archeologist Flinders Petrie at Hawara. Painted in encaustic (pigments mixed into molten wax) while their sitters were alive, the portraits were glued onto Greco-Roman mummies (100–250 AD). The staggering diversity of Egypt's pantheon by the late pagan era is suggested by the **statues of deities** in **Room 19**. The tiny statuettes are worth a closer look, especially those of the pregnant hippo goddess Sekhmet (in Case C), Harpocrates (Horus as a child), Ibis-headed Thoth and the dwarf god Ptah-soker (all in Case E), and the almost Mexican-looking Bes (in Case P). In the centre of the room, look out for the gold and silver image of Horus in Case V, apparently the case for a mummified hawk.

Next door and the room after are devoted to **ostraca and papyri**. Ostraca were limestone flakes or potshards, on which were scratched sketches or ephemeral writing; papyrus was used for finished artwork and lasting **manuscripts**. Besides the *Book of the Dead* (**rooms 1 and 24**) and the *Book of AmDuat* (depicting the Weighing of the Heart ceremony; #6335 on the south side of **Room 29**), note the *Satirical Papyrus* (#232 in Cabinet 9 on the north side), showing mice being served by cats. Painted during the Hyksos period (see p.811), the cats represent the Egyptians, the mice their rulers, who came from countries that were part of Egypt's former empire, implying that rule of Egyptians by foreigners is not the natural order. Room 29 also displays a scribe's writing kit and an artist's paints and brushes (by the doorways at either end), while the next door **Room 34** contains musical instruments and statuettes of people playing them. In the corridor (**Room 33**), two interesting seats are displayed: an Amarna toilet seat in Case O by the door, and in Case S, a seat used for childbirth looking remarkably similar to those used today. **Room 39** has some Greco-Roman glassware, mosaics and statuettes, while **Room 44** displays Mesopotamian-like faïence panels from the palaces of Ramses II and III.

Midan Tahrir and around

The centre of modern Cairo is a concrete assertion of national pride, which threatens to burst as it pumps traffic around the city. Created on the site of Britain's Qasr el-Nil Barracks after the 1952 revolution, **Midan Tahrir** (Liberation Square) embodies the drawbacks of subsequent political trends. During the 1960s, two bureaucratic monoliths and several transport depots responsible for much of Egypt and all of Greater Cairo were concentrated here, as Nasser adopted Soviet-style centralization. A decade later, Sadat rejected his mentor's "Arab Socialism" in favour of an *Infitah* (Open Door) to Western capitalism, causing private car ownership to soar almost as fast as Cairo's population. Impending gridlock was only averted by digging a metro, in spite of which, buses and roads are still grossly overcrowded.

The entrances to **Sadat metro station** serve as pedestrian underpasses linking these depots and buildings with the main roads leading off Tahrir. Despite clear labelling in English, it's easy to go astray in the maze of subways and surface at the wrong location. Many Cairenes prefer to take their chances crossing by road – a nerve-wracking experience for newcomers. Though some **landmarks** are obvious, rooftop billboards and neon signs flanking the end of streets like Talaat Harb or Qasr el-Nil (beside the *Cleopatra Hotel*) also help with orientation. To watch the square over tea, try one of the Arab cafés between Talaat Harb and El-Bustan; the café nearest to Sharia Talaat Harb, the *Wadi el-Nil*, was bombed by Islamic radicals in 1993.

Tahrir landmarks

Abutting the grounds of the Antiquities Museum to the south, the blue-and-white **Nile Hilton** – the first modern "international" hotel built along the Corniche – stretches down to where the Tahrir Bridge runs between guardian lions towards Gezira Island. The tan-coloured edifice just beyond the *Hilton*, built during the 1960s to serve as the secretariat of the Arab League, now stands as a vestige of the time when Egypt was acknowledged leader of the "progressive" Arab cause. After Sadat's treaty with Israel, the headquarters of the **Arab League** moved to Tunis and most of its members severed relations with Egypt.

Tout trouble

Common on the streets of downtown Cairo, especially Talaat Harb, are **touts**, who pose as friendly strangers and attach themselves to tourists. They are petty crooks and confidence tricksters, not by any means all young, whose aim is either to work various scams on you, to persuade you to buy overpriced tours (see p.119), or to steer or follow you into shops, where they will tell the shopkeeper in Arabic that they are your guide and entitled to a commission on whatever you buy, added to your bill of course. And we are not just talking ten percent. In general, touts favour particular perfume and papyrus shops with whom they regularly work, but they can go with you into any shop, and in general the shopkeeper will go along with them to avoid trouble – you will be gone next week after all, but the tout will still be around.

Touts tend to come up behind you to start a conversation. Each has their own line. Some will compliment you on your clothing, others will simply ask what you are looking for – if anyone asks you this when you are not obviously looking for anything, you can be sure it's a tout. Once they've gained your confidence they can be very hard to shake off. Should you make the mistake of telling one of them your name and hotel, you may find them turning up there asking for you, or you may even be greeted on the street by name by a different tout (who may even say, "Don't you remember me?" as if you had met before), since they often work in teams.

Trouble is, Cairo is full of friendly people who greet you on the street with no ill intent whatsoever. "Welcome in Egypt" is a common refrain, and it usually means just that. So how do you tell who's a tout and who's just being friendly? The first rule of thumb is, whoever it is, there's no need to be rude: just smile and say hello, or nod or wave, but never slacken your pace. Just carry on walking. An ordinary Egyptian will not be offended. A tout will probably try to stop you by demanding to know why you are in such a hurry, or why you are angry or upset, or they may accuse you of being rude. Similarly, ordinary Egyptians do not usually walk up behind you to strike up a conversation, but will call to you as you pass, though touts may also do this. In general you can get rid of touts by being noncommittal. If asked where you are going for example, you can reply airily, "Nowhere." Sometimes you may get abuse for this, but it is better than getting one of them attached to you. As a last resort, bear in mind that it is illegal for touts to harass tourists, and you can expect ordinary Egyptians to take your side if you have any serious problems. It is not usually necessary, however, to be rude or have an argument: so long as you are aware of the situation from the start, you should be able to get rid of them relatively quickly.

Touts favour **specific areas**. One such is Sharia Talaat Harb, especially between Midan Tahrir and Midan Talaat Harb, where outside *Felfela* is a favourite place, as are road junctions (where they will often accost you while crossing the street). Other places sometimes worked by touts include the Ghuriya and Spice Bazaar in Islamic Cairo (see p.164), and the road from there to Bab Zuweila, and some also work Sharia Tahrir on Gezira Island. People who greet you in areas with few tourists, on the other hand, are most unlikely to be touts, and indeed ordinary Egyptians are much more likely to take an interest in you in such areas.

Mubarak's policy of rapprochement was finally rewarded in 1992, when the League returned to Cairo and, with it, posses of limos and gun-toting guards. Further down the Corniche, roughly opposite the new **Helnan Shepheard Hotel**, was the site of the Thomas Cook landing stage, where generations of tourists embarked on Nile cruises and General Gordon's ill-fated expedition set off for Khartoum in 1883.

Across the Tahrir Bridge ramp from the Arab League building, Egypt's Ministry of Foreign Affairs is less conspicuous than the **Omar Makram Mosque**, where funeral receptions for deceased VIPs are held in brightly coloured marquees. But dominating the southern end of Midan Tahrir is a concave office block that inspires shuddering memories: **the Mugamma**. A "fraternal gift" from the Soviet Union in the 1960s, this Kafkaesque warren of gloomy corridors, dejected queues and idle bureaucrats houses the public departments of the Interior, Health and Education ministries, and the Cairo Governorate. How many of the 50,000 people visiting *El-Mugamma* each day suffer nervous breakdowns from sheer frustration is anyone's guess; an African supposedly flung himself through a window several years ago (for advice on handling the Mugamma, see p.289). On the corner of Sharia Qasr al-Aini, opposite the Mugamma, a handsome pseudo-Islamic facade masks the old campus of the **American University in Cairo** (entered via Sheikh Rihan Street; the Library is one block northeast). Responsible for publishing some of the best research on Egypt in the English language, the AUC is also a Western-style haven for wealthy Egyptian youths and US students doing a year abroad, its shady gardens and preppy ambience seeming utterly remote from everyday life in Cairo. Visitors might experience a premonitory shiver that Iran's gilded youth probably looked pretty similar before the Islamic Revolution. Egyptian Marxists and Islamic fundamentalists regard the AUC as a tool of US and Zionist imperialism.

Five or so minutes' walk north from the main AUC entrance, near the University Library at **Midan Falaki** (or walk along Sharia Tahrir from the square), you'll find a pedestrian bridge of the kind that circumvented Midan Tahrir before its subways were dug. Off to the right, a broad street awash with fruit and vegetable stalls runs alongside **Bab al-Luq market**. Not a place for the squeamish, and overpriced compared to other markets, it's still an interesting spot to watch haggling and gossiping over trussed poultry or tea and *sheeshas*. It also holds a number of extremely cheap eating places. A coffee merchant's store across on the north side fills the square with the fine aroma of cardamom-spiced *'ahwa mahaweka*.

Moving on from Tahrir you can continue south and east to explore the Garden City and the Abdin quarter (see opposite), or walk back to the square and take either Sharia Talaat Harb or Qasr el-Nil to head for the shops and restaurants of downtown Cairo (see pp.143–145).

Garden City and the Abdin quarter

Spreading south from the square towards Old Cairo and the Islamic districts are two very different, yet historically interlinked, quarters. Deluxe hotels follow the Corniche towards Roda Island, separating the old diplomatic quarter from the Nile just as Sharia Qasr al-Aini divides the leafy winding streets of **Garden City** from the grid of blocks where Egypt's ministries and parliament are located. Like a spider in its web, the ex-royal, now presidential Abdin Palace lends its name to the convoluted **Abdin quarter** that merges into Saiyida Zeinab.

Since Garden City and Abdin meet around Midan Tahrir, both can claim to host Egypt's **National Assembly** (*Maglis al-Shaab*). During the late 1980s,

Cairenes were agog over abusive exchanges and fisticuffs in parliament, as the hardline minister Zaki Badr replied to allegations of torture, wrongful arrest and bugging by the **Interior Ministry**, sited a couple of blocks to the west in Abdin. Badr has long since gone, but the ministry's repressive activities continue: Amnesty International reports cases of torture from Alexandria to Aswan. The road on which both buildings stand is barricaded at either end against suicide car bombers, floodlit at night and perpetually guarded by machine-gunners.

Garden City

When Ibrahim Pasha's al-Dubbarah Palace was demolished in 1906, British planners developed the site for diplomatic and residential use, laying down crescents and cul-de-sacs to create the illusion of lanes meandering through a **Garden City**. Until the Corniche road was ploughed through, embassies and villas boasted gardens running down to the Nile; nowadays, fishermen's shacks and vegetable plots line the river's edge.

Aside from the traffic, it's a pleasant walk along the Corniche towards Roda Island, past a cluster of **feluccas** available for Nile cruises (see p.274). Further inland, Art Deco residences mingle with heavily guarded **embassies** (for addresses, see pp.291–292). Despite being outsized by the US – whose embassy here is the largest in the world – the British enjoy grander buildings with more spacious grounds, a legacy of their pre-eminence in the days of Lord Cromer and Sir Miles Lampson. The main artery, running south from Tahrir towards Old Cairo, is **Sharia Qasr al-Aini**, which goes from riches to rags, banks and villas yielding to cheap backstreet eating places near the Sayala Bridge. A bygone "Palace of the Spring" lends its name to the mixed neighbourhood between Garden City and the slaughterhouse district (see "Old Cairo", p.205), and to Cairo's largest public **hospital**, erected in the 1960s, where Yusuf Idris practised as a doctor before devoting himself to writing. **Roda Island** and the mainland **further south** are described under "Old Cairo" (see pp.191–207).

The Abdin Palace

With hindsight, several rulers must have regretted that Ismail moved the seat of state from the Citadel to what is now the **Abdin quarter**, where tenements surrounded the palace enclave long ago. The neighbourhood is still chiefly

---

War stories

During World War II, much of Garden City was commandeered by military organizations. At GHQ – which rapidly outgrew "Grey Pillars" to fill an entire neighbourhood – **R.A. Bagnold** proposed the formation of the Long Range Desert Group, whose daring raids (with David Stirling's SAS) behind enemy lines were the genesis of a martial legend.

On Sharia Rustrum, the Middle Eastern headquarters of the **SOE** (Special Operations Executive) plotted operations from Yugoslavia to Libya, involving Fitzroy McLean, Evelyn Waugh and Patrick Leigh Fermor, among others. At no.13 Sharia Ibrahim Pasha Naguib, novelist **Olivia Manning** and her husband Reggie (the model for Guy Pringle in *Fortunes of War*) lived beneath Stirling's brother, Peter, who hosted wild parties in a flat crammed with captured ammunition.

British sang-froid only cracked once, when the Afrika Korps seemed poised to seize Alexandria and advance on Cairo. On **"Ash Wednesday"** (July 1, 1942) GHQ and the Embassy burned their files, blanketing Garden City with smoke. Half-charred classified documents were wafted aloft to fall on the streets, where peanut vendors twisted them into little cones.

residential and working-class, and divided from the Saiyida Zeinab quarter by **Sharia Bur Said** (Port Said), which marks the course of the Khalig al-Masri canal that was filled in after the Aswan Dam reduced Cairo's dependency on Nile floodwater.

When Khedive Ismail began building the European-style **Abdin Palace** in the 1860s, a worldwide scarcity of cotton had raised the value of Egypt's export crop to £25 million a year, and his own civil list was double that of Queen Victoria. After prices slumped and creditors gathered, the palace was bequeathed to his successors together with vast debts that reduced them – and Egypt – to near vassal status.

The nadir of humiliation came in February 1942, when British armoured cars burst through the palace gates and Ambassador Lampson demanded that King Farouk sack the prime minister or abdicate himself. It was this that resolved Nasser to assemble the Free Officers, seize power and redeem Egypt. Ten years later, as Farouk displayed his long-awaited son at a magnificent reception, rioters burned downtown Cairo within earshot of the palace; six months afterwards, the Free Officers deposed him and declared a Republic.

Another mass protest – against Sadat's abolition of subsidies on bread and other essentials in January 1977 – took place outside the palace on **Midan el-Gumhorriya** (Square of the Republic). Chanting "Thieves of the *Infitah*, the people are famished", crowds overwhelmed Central Security and rampaged against symbols of wealth and authority until the subsidies were restored. Still the state headquarters of Egypt's president, the Abdin Palace is flanked to the north by the Cairo Governorate building. During Ramadan a large tent is pitched in the middle of the square, in which virtuoso performers recite the Koran.

The Palace Museum

At the back of the Palace grounds is the **Abdin Palace Museum** (daily except Fri 9am–3.30pm; £E10, students £E5, camera £E10), devoted to a collection of guns and other weaponry. The entrance is behind the palace in Sharia Gamae Abdine, and tickets are sold just across the street. A souvenir booklet (£E15) is available at the entrance, though its commentary is not especially useful.

Begin by walking through the palace grounds, past assorted historical cannons, to **Mubarak's Hall**, which contains an assortment of antique and contemporary weapons presented to President Mubarak by foreign leaders, most notably a set of gold-plated automatic rifles given by former Iraqi dictator Saddam Hussein. From here you cross a courtyard, past more cannons and gatling guns and a shrine to local saint Sidi Badran, which predates the palace and was restored under King Fouad.

This brings you to the **Arms museum**, entered between two suits of armour. Pavilion 2, on the right, is filled with **daggers**, including Rommel's, engraved with the slogan "Alles für Deutschland" (everything for Germany), and some gruesome-looking multi-bladed daggers used by India's Hindu rajputs against the Muslim Mughals in the eighteenth century. Back in the main room, you pass Mamluk breastplates, chain mail and non-ballistic weaponry including swords and maces before getting down to the real business of the day, namely **guns**. While many of these will be of interest only to serious weapons enthusiasts, there are some that will catch anybody's eye, among them an 1852 Beckwith percussion rifle with six revolving barrels, various sets of duelling pistols in presentation cases complete with accessories, and a display of unusually shaped revolvers. Nearby is a particularly mean-looking Apache-Dolene pin-fire revolver which doubles as a knuckleduster and a blade. In the same display case, a twenty-chamber Belgian revolver from the early twentieth century was no doubt handy for prolonged games of Russian roulette.

The next section of the museum is devoted to **medals and decorations** from around the world, but especially from early twentieth-century Europe. Also here, and a lot more interesting, are a set of Napoleonic enamel snuff and tobacco boxes, and King Farouk's personal *sheesha* pipes, plus a vial made from a giant crab claw, and a pair of particularly busty porcelain busts. From here you move on to the **Gifts museum** containing presents given to the president by various Egyptian organizations and foreign dignitaries, including (in gallery four) an abalone and mother-of-pearl Dome of the Rock from Yasser Arafat, and a silver plate bearing the images of President Mubarak's wife Suzanne and Akhenaten's wife Nefertiti set against a map of Middle Egypt. The **Historical Documents** room, with treaties and decrees dating back to the nineteenth century, displays some fascinating letters of condolence sent to King Farouk on the death of his father King Fouad by the likes of Adolf Hitler, Japan's Emperor Hirohito, and Britain's ill-fated King Edward VIII.

The last part of the museum is devoted to **silverware, glassware and crockery**, including ewers, plates, fruit bowls, candlesticks and cutlery. The highlights are the assorted dinner sets used by the Egyptian royal family, and a tea set belonging to King Fouad, complete with what would be a traditional English-style pair of teacups and saucers, except that they are made of solid silver instead of the more customary bone china.

Downtown Cairo

The layout of **downtown Cairo** goes back to the 1860s, when Khedive Ismail had it rebuilt in the style of Haussmann's new Paris boulevards to impress dignitaries attending the inauguration of the Suez Canal. Cutting an X-shaped swathe through the area are the main throughfares of **Talaat Harb** and **Qasr el-Nil** (each about 1km long), which contain most of the city's budget hotels, airlines and travel agencies. Almost every visitor gravitates here at least once, while many spend a lot of time checking out the restaurants, shops and bars.

Although overshadowed by Talaat Harb and Qasr el-Nil, four streets running east off the northern end of Talaat Harb are equally integral to downtown Cairo: **Sharia Abdel Khaliq Sarwat**, **Sharia Adly**, **26th July Street** and **Sharia Alfi Bey**.

Talaat Harb

Fifty years ago, Suleyman Pasha Street was lined with trees and sidewalk cafés, a gracious ornament to the Europeanized city centre built in the late nineteenth century. Since being renamed **Sharia Talaat Harb** (though many Cairenes still call it Suleyman Pasha), the street's once elegant facades have been effaced by grime and neglect, tacky billboards and glitzy facings – yet its vitality and diversity have never been greater. Overflowing the pavements, thousands of Cairenes window-shop, pop into juice bars and surge out of cinemas. Imelda Marcos would drool over the profusion of shoe shops, some devoted to butterfly creations fit only for a boudoir. In the shadows of Western-style affluence, beggars lie with palms outstretched and barefoot urchins hump garbage pails onto donkey carts – an accepted part of Cairo's streetlife.

Almost every tourist seeks a break from the crowds and culture shock at one of three places along the initial stretch of Talaat Harb. **Felfela's Restaurant**, just around the corner of Hoda Shaarawi, is followed shortly by the **Café Riche**, where the Free Officers supposedly plotted their overthrow of Egypt's monarchy;

another version maintains that they communicated over the telephone in **Groppi's**, a famous coffee house on **Midan Talaat Harb**, at the intersection with Qasr el-Nil. Here stands a statue of Talaat Harb (1876–1941), nationalist lawyer and founder of the National Bank.

Up to this point traffic runs both ways, but thereafter northbound vehicles are restricted to Qasr el-Nil; because the streets cross over, it's easy to take the wrong one by mistake if you're on foot. Between Midan Talaat Harb and 26th July Street, Talaat Harb abounds in takeaways, **cinemas** and cheap **hotels**. Number 34, next door to the Miami Theatre, is the **Yacoubian Building**, immortalized in Alaa Al Aswany's bestselling 2002 novel of the same name (see p.854), though the real building differs somewhat from the fictional version.

Qasr el-Nil

Although the racecourse that once ran beside **Sharia Qasr el-Nil** disappeared last century, northbound traffic tries to rival bygone derbys, and the shops, though functional enough, play second fiddle to Talaat Harb's. Heading up from Tahrir you'll pass American Express and the l'Orientaliste Bookshop before coming upon a stall devoted to foreign newspapers and magazines, outside *Groppi's*.

Two blocks beyond Midan Talaat Harb, a side street on the right allows a glimpse of the carmine-and-gold Art Nouveau **Cosmopolitan Hotel**, an elegant leftover from colonial times. Kalashnikov-toting police and Central Security troops are ubiquitous in downtown Cairo, but never threatening.

Harbouring bookshops, bars and health clubs, some of the **backstreets** here also serve as **outdoor mosques**. For midday prayers on Fridays, the street running into Abdel Khaliq Sarwat is carpeted with green mats where the faithful perform a succession of *rekas*, swaying their heads, raising their hands and prostrating themselves while reciting parts of the Koran.

Sharia Abdel Khaliq Sarwat and Sharia Adly

Other than the Khan el-Khalili bazaar, **Sharia Abdel Khaliq Sarwat** – the first major street you reach after the Midan Talaat intersection – has the city's highest concentration of **jewellers**, particularly around the Midan Opera end, where a street of goldsmiths called Sikket al-Manakh leads off to the south. Because their marked prices are higher, canny shoppers can use them as benchmarks when haggling for lower rates in the Khan (see p.280).

The vast Edwardian neo-Gothic apartment block at the junction of Abdel Khaliq Sarwat and Mohammed Farid frowns its northern face upon **Sharia Adly**. Heading east along this street you'll find a buff, temple-like edifice with Central Security guards posing on a Cecil B. de Mille-like stairway. The arborial reliefs on its columns represent the Tree of Manna whence Heaven's bounty fell upon the Israelites, for the building is Cairo's last working **synagogue**. Discreetly open on Saturday mornings, its opulent marbled interior receives few worshippers these days, the city's Jewish community having dwindled to around fifty, all aged. For Rosh HaShana and Passover a rabbi is flown in from Tel Aviv; otherwise, there's only the melancholy custodian and his Christian friend.

One block along is Cairo's main **tourist office**, with the **tourist police** sited above; for details of both, see p.109. Across the road, **Garden Groppi's** spacious patio and panelled salon are in contrast to the *Groppi's* on Midan Talaat Harb. During World War II, this was one of the few posh establishments open to ordinary British troops – "other ranks", as they were called – who the military top brass had decided should not mix socially with officers. Its high prices nonetheless ensured that officers, Egyptian *pashas* and their fur-draped

Levantine mistresses predominated. Nowadays it's frequented by courting couples, journalists and bourgeois matrons.

Another colonial institution that bit the dust still survives in moribund form north of Sharia Adly's termination at Midan Opera. Before World War I, tourists could buy "anything from a boa constrictor to a fully grown leopard" outside the grandiose **Continental-Savoy Hotel** – where one scandalized missionary insisted on providing trousers to cover the genitals of a performing baboon. Orde Wingate, the eccentric military genius who liberated Abyssinia from Italian rule for Emperor Haile Selassie, attempted suicide in his room here.

26th July Street and Sharia Alfi Bey

The busiest, widest thoroughfare of downtown Cairo is **Sharia Setta w'Ashreen Yulyu** – more easily rendered as **26th July Street** – which runs all the way from Ezbekiya Gardens across the Nile to Zamalek. Formerly called Fouad I, after Ismail's son, its current name commemorates the date of King Farouk's abdication in 1952, following a bloodless coup by the Free Officers three days earlier, though quite a few people still call it Sharia el-Malik Fouad.

As well as a slew of hotels – most noticeably the *Grand* – this stretch of the street features a bevy of sleazy **nightclubs** (see p.268), a couple of liquor stores, and almost as many shoe shops and pavement hawkers as Talaat Harb. Behind the Cicurel department store, expropriated from its Jewish owner in 1957, is a vintage Cairene restaurant, *El Haty*.

Better still for eating and drinking is **Sharia Alfi Bey**, two blocks north – known by locals as the Cairene Champs-Élysées. At one end is **Midan Orabi**, frequented round-the-clock by Cairenes noshing on felafel and kebabs bought from one of the many takeaways here. Walking down from here you'll find the *Alfi Bey* restaurant, opposite a dirt-cheap 24-hour *taamiya* joint called *Akher Saa* (next door to the Nile Christian Bookshop), and further along the street a wonderfully relaxed bar inside the *Windsor Hotel*. Opposite the hotel entrance are two funky Arab cafés. Though perfectly safe late at night, the backstreets that link these thoroughfares retain an aura of illicit goings-on. When Lawrence Durrell and his wife were evacuated from Greece to Cairo in 1941, they discovered that their refugee hotel here doubled as a brothel.

Midan Opera and Midan Ataba

During the 1860s, when Cairo's centre was rebuilt (see p.143), an Opera House was also constructed; symbolically, the building faced west, overlooking **Midan Opera** and the modern city rather than Islamic Cairo. Although the opening night saw a lavish production of *Rigoletto*, it was surpassed a year later by the anniversary celebrations, when an opus that had been specially commissioned to have an imperial Egyptian theme was first performed – Verdi's *Aida*. An equestrian statue of Ibrahim Pasha, by Cordier, honours Ismail's father. Though still the sprucest bit of greenery in central Cairo, the square lost its namesake when the Opera House burned down in 1971; a multi-storey car park now occupies the site.

Almost a century after Ismail mortgaged Egypt to foreign creditors, anti-colonial resentments exploded here on "**Black Saturday**" (January 26, 1952). The morning after British troops had killed native policemen in Ismailiya, demonstrators were enraged to find an Egyptian police officer drinking on the terrace of *Madame Badia's Opera Casino* (where the Opera Cinema stands today). A scuffle began and the nightclub was wrecked; rioting spread quickly, encouraged by the indifference of Cairo's police force. As ordinary folk looted, activists sped around in jeeps torching foreign premises. Similarly, during the bread riots of 1977, nightclubs and boutiques were specifically targeted by the radical Islamic group *Al-Taqfir w'al-Higrah* (Repentance and Holy Flight).

Midan Ataba

Behind Midan Opera car park, a minibus depot and split-level thoroughfares render **Midan Ataba** just as Yusuf Idris described it in *The Dregs of the City*: "a madhouse of pedestrians and automobiles, screeching wheels, howling klaxons, the whistles of bus conductors and roaring motors". Originally called the Square of Green Steps, Ataba should rightly be renamed the Square of Flyovers.

There is one attraction, however, that you might want to visit, the **Post Office Museum** on the second floor of the Central Post Office (daily except Fri 8am–1pm; 50pt; tickets sold in the post office at the commemorative stamps office, then go upstairs through the guarded entrance on the east side of the building). The museum houses exhibits from Egypt's postal service through the ages, with stamps galore (including the rare Suez Canal commemorative issue), Egypt's oldest mailboxes, and a picture of the Sphinx and Pyramids composed entirely of stamps bearing an image of the same.

The minibus terminal is around the back of the multi-storey car park; for local **transport** details, see pp.114–115. From Midan Ataba you can also take a number of **walking routes into Islamic Cairo** (see pp.149–191).

Ezbekiya Gardens and north to Ramses

The **Ezbekiya Gardens**, to the north of Opera and Ataba squares, were laid out in the 1870s by the former chief gardener of Paris, forming a twenty-acre park. Subsequent extensions to 26th July Street reduced them to trampled islands amidst a sea of commerce and traffic, but the western half has now been enclosed to preserve its magnificent banyan tree, while much of the eastern side remains a pitch for hawkers of Islamic arts, gewgaws and incense, as well as a market for second-hand books. Beyond the clothes stalls on the east side stands the **Cairo Puppet Theatre** (see p.277).

In medieval times a lake fed by the Nasiri Canal and surrounded by orchards existed here, but in 1470 the Mamluke general Ezbek built a palace, inspiring other beys and wealthy merchants to follow suit. During the French occupation Napoleon commandeered the sumptuous palace of Alfi Bey, and his successor Kléber promoted Western innovations such as windmills, printing presses, and a balloon launch which embarrassingly failed. Another novelty was *Le Tivoli* club, where "ladies and gentlemen met at a certain hour to amuse themselves" – unheard of in a society where men and women socialized separately.

During Mohammed Ali's time, visitors could still witness Cairenes celebrating the Prophet's Birthday here (12 *Rabi al-Awwal*) with unrestrained fervour. Sufi dervishes entranced by *zikrs* lay prostrate to be trampled by their mounted sheikh in the famous *Doseh* (Treading) ceremony. However, snake-swallowing had already been ruled "disgusting and contrary to their religion" by the sheikh of the Sa'adiya, and under British rule popular festivals were discouraged and dispersed around the city. Nowadays, El-Hussein and other squares are more active during the *Moulid al-Nabi*.

Though nothing remains of them today, two bastions of colonialism once overlooked Ezbekiya from a site bounded by Alfi Bey and El-Gumhorriya, where Scottish pipers once played. Here, *Shepheard's Hotel* (founded in 1841) flourished alongside the Thomas Cook Agency, which pioneered tourist "expeditions" in the 1870s. Rebuilt more grandly in 1891, *Shepheard's* famous terrace,

Moorish Hall, Long Bar and Ballroom (featuring "Eighteenth Dynasty Edwardian" pillars modelled on Karnak) were destroyed by Black Saturday rioters in 1952 (see p.145).

Between Ezbekiya and Ramses

When Mohammed Ali created a military high road to link the Citadel with Cairo's new railway station, and named it after the French physician Antoine Clot – whom he ennobled for introducing Western ideas of public health to Egypt – nobody foresaw that **Sharia Clot Bey** (spelt Klot Bek on newer street signs) and the fashionable area north of Ezbekiya would degenerate into a vice-ridden "Open Land". By World War I, however, the quarter was full of honky-tonk bars, backstreet porn shows and brothels; shacks and plush establishments alike paying tribute to Ibrahim el-Gharby, the fearsome transvestite "King of the *Wasa'a*". In the Mahfouz novel and classic Egyptian movie *The Beginning and the End*, the main character's hash-dealing brother set up shop here. During World War II, activities centred around Wagh el-Birket, known to troops as "**the Berka**": a long street with curtained alleys leading off beneath balconies where the prostitutes sat fanning themselves. Only after the killing of two Australian soldiers (who were notorious for throwing women and pianos out of windows) was the Berka closed down in 1942.

Nowadays the area is shabbily respectable, with cheap shops and cafés. Any bus heading up it from the gardens towards Ramses will take you past the hulking nineteenth-century **Cathedral of St Mark**, now superseded by the new Coptic cathedral in Abbassiya. The derelict Moorish pile at the Ramses end of **Sharia el-Gumhorriya** (which runs up from the west side of the gardens) was the original premises of *Al-Ahram* (The Pyramids), the first – if not still the foremost – newspaper in the Arab world.

Ramses Station and around

The Ramses Station area is the northern ganglion of Cairo's transport system. Splayed flyovers and arterial roads haemorrhage traffic onto darting pedestrians, keeping **Midan Ramses** busy round the clock. Its main focus is **Ramses Station** itself, a quasi-Moorish shoebox to which a major **post office** and the **Egyptian Railways Museum** are appended. The museum (Tues–Sun 8am–1pm; £E10, £E20 on Fri & public holidays, camera £E10), at the east end of the station, houses model steam engines, stations, engineering works and even the odd airplane, plus a couple of real steam locomotives, most notably Khedive Ismail's private train.

In ancient times, when the Nile ran further east, Ramses was the site of *Tendunyas*, the port of Heliopolis. Renamed *Al-Maks* (the Customs Point) by the Arabs, it was incorporated within Cairo's fortifications by Salah al-Din, whose Iron Gate was left high and dry as the Nile receded westwards, and was pulled down in 1847 to make way for the station. The square takes its name from a nine-metre-high red granite **Colossus of Ramses II**, moved here from Memphis in 1955. By the end of the twentieth century, however, the statue had become so corroded by pollution that it was decided to move it. Despite lobbying by local Egyptologists, who wanted it returned to its original site, it is due to be relocated to the junction of Pyramids Road and the Alexandria Desert Road, out by the Giza Pyramids.

Near Ramses Station is one of the main intercity **bus terminals** – Turgoman Garage (see p.299) – plus departure points for service taxi microbuses to destinations in and around Cairo (see p.113) and to the Canal Zone (see p.301). You may also find microbuses to Alexandria and the Delta here. For most of the

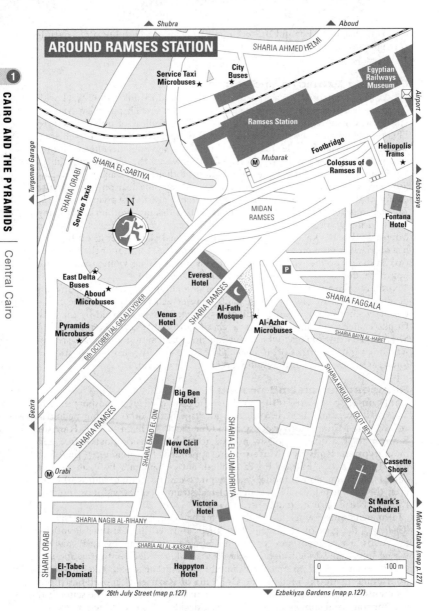

AROUND RAMSES STATION

▲ Shubra   ▲ Aboud

SHARIA AHMED HELMI

Service Taxi
Microbuses ★

City
Buses
★

Egyptian
Railways
Museum

✉ Airport ▶

Ramses Station

▲ Turgoman Garage

SHARIA EL-SABTIYA

SHARIA ORABI
Service Taxis

Ⓜ Mubarak

Footbridge

Heliopolis
Trams ★

Colossus of
Ramses II ●

▶ Abbassiya

N

MIDAN
RAMSES

Fontana
Hotel

Everest
Hotel

P

East Delta
Buses ★
Aboud ★
Microbuses

6th OCTOBER (AL-GALA') FLYOVER

SHARIA RAMSES

Al-Fath
Mosque ☪

SHARIA FAGGALA

Venus
Hotel

Al-Azhar ★
Microbuses

SHARIA BAYN AL-HARET

Pyramids ★
Microbuses

▲ Gezira

SHARIA RAMSES

Big Ben
Hotel

SHARIA EMAD EL-DIN

New Cicil
Hotel

SHARIA EL-GUMHORRIYA

SHARIA KHULUD (CLOT BEY)

Cassette
Shops

Ⓜ Orabi

✝ St Mark's
Cathedral

▶ Midan Ataba (map p.127)

Victoria
Hotel

SHARIA NAGIB AL-RIHANY

SHARIA ORABI

SHARIA ALI AL-KASSAR

0 ———— 100 m

El-Tabei
el-Domiati

Happyton
Hotel

▼ 26th July Street (map p.127)   ▼ Ezbekiyza Gardens (map p.127)

microbuses to destinations in greater Cairo, you'll have to cross the humpbacked iron bridge to the north side of the station. Just below the bridge, there used to be an army surplus market, but it was removed to prevent fundamentalists from donning uniforms in order to impersonate military officers. Overlooking Midan Ramses from its southern end, the terrace café of the otherwise rather down-at-heel fifteenth-floor *Everest Hotel* is open round the clock and offers a superb vista over the square.

Islamic Cairo

> The core of the city itself was circumscribed by the river and hills of refuse, the castle, the aqueduct and the abandoned slums. Most of the bazaars lay in the densely packed quarters of the North-East, nestling in amongst and parasitic upon the rubble of the old Fatimid palaces, and behind the commercial streets one found small courtyards and large tenements, into which were crowded communities of closely knit creeds and tribes. ... The city was like a disordered mind, an expression of archaic wishes and half-submerged memories of vanished dynasties.
>
> Robert Irwin, *The Arabian Nightmare*

Islamic Cairo sustains fantasy and confounds certainty. Few foreigners enter its maw without equal measures of excitement and trepidation. Streets are narrow and congested, slimy underfoot with donkey shit and burst water mains, overhung with latticed balconies. Mosques, bazaars and medieval lanes abound; the smell of *sheeshas* and frying offal wafts through alleys where muezzins wail "*Allahu Akbar!*" (God is most great) and beggars entreat "*Ya Mohannin, ya Rabb*" (O Awakener of Pity, O Master) – as integral to streetlife as the artisans and hawkers. The sights, sounds, smells and surprises draw you back time after time, and getting lost or dispensing a little *baksheesh* is a small price to pay for the experience.

You can have a fascinating time exploring this quarter of the city without knowing anything about its history or architecture, but to describe Islamic Cairo one has to refer to both. Islamic architecture has its own conventions, terminology and stylistic eras, which we've attempted to summarize in the glossary on p.867. The potted history section provides a general context, with many of the personalities and events mentioned in more detail under the appropriate monument. Most of these are named after their various founders; modern-day Islamic fundamentalists shun them as *mesjid el-derar* – mosques built for self-glorification.

The 1992 **earthquake** caused a lot of damage in Islamic Cairo, though this has led to a great many of the mosques and monuments being gradually returned to their former glory after years of neglect, often with financial aid from organizations like the American Research Center and the World Monuments Fund. Unfortunately, however, this means that many of the Islamic Cairo's monuments are currently closed to the public. Even so, there is plenty to keep you busy, and you can happily spend days, even weeks, exploring the area without running out of new things to see.

A brief history of Islamic Cairo

Islamic Cairo is the sum total of half a dozen cities whose varied names, ages and locations make for an unusually complex urban history. One helpful constant is that new cities have invariably been constructed to the north of the old, for quite simple reasons: an east–west spread was constrained by the Muqattam Hills and the Nile (which ran further east than nowadays), while the prevailing northerly wind blew the smoke and smell of earlier settlements away from newer areas.

Thus when the Muslim troops of Amr conquered Egypt for Islam in 641 AD, they sited their city, **Al-Fustat**, just north of Coptic Babylon (see "Old Cairo", p.203). Here it grew into a powerhouse of religious conversion, surpassing Alexandria as Egypt's leading city, though remaining a mere provincial capital in the vast Islamic empire ruled from Damascus by the khalifs, whose only direct contact occurred when the last of the **Umayyads** (661–750) fled to Al-Fustat, and then burned it. Their successors, the **Abbasids** (750–935), ordered the city to be rebuilt further north, and so *Medinet al-Askar* (City of Cantonments)

Approaching and exploring Islamic Cairo: practicalities

The best (if not only) way **to explore Islamic Cairo** is by walking. Basically, you decide on a starting point that's readily accessible from downtown Cairo, and then follow an itinerary on foot from there. The most obvious **starting points** are Khan el-Khalili, the Bab Zwayla and the Citadel; see the beginning of each of these sections for details on getting there by public transport (also see the bus/minibus information on pp.113–115). If you want to walk from the downtown area, there are four approaches to Islamic Cairo from **Midan Ataba** (see p.146), using the Ataba post office and fire station for orientation.

THE MUSKI is the classic approach to **Khan el-Khalili**: a narrow bazaar, identifiable by the crowds passing between the *El-Mousky* hotel and a clump of luggage stalls. For more details, see "Around Khan el-Khalili and Al-Azhar", p.153.

SHARIA AL-AZHAR. Overshadowed by a flyover running from Midan Ataba to the heart of Islamic Cairo, Sharia al-Azhar – which runs parallel to the Muski – buzzes with traffic and cottage industries. Buses and minibuses push their way through the crowds and traffic, across one of Cairo's few remaining tram routes at the Bur Said overpass, taking you on to the **Al-Azhar Mosque**, just south of **Midan el-Hussein**. By walking back from the square along the Muski to the junction with Sharia al-Muizz, you can go south to **Bab Zwayla**.

SHARIA QALAA (formerly Boulevard Mohammed Ali), across from the fire station. This street runs directly to the **Citadel** (2km). When nineteenth-century ruler Khedive Ismail's Minister of Public Works ordered the thoroughfare to be ploughed through the old quarter, he asked rhetorically: "Do we need so many monuments? Isn't it enough to preserve a sample?" The stretch down to Midan Ahmed Maher – where the **Islamic Arts Museum** is located – features musical instrument shops, all-night stalls and cafés. In pre-revolutionary times, brothels and hashish dens infested the stepped lanes that rise between its tenements.

SHARIA EL-GEISH. Also topped by a flyover, "Army Street" runs out towards Abbassiya and Heliopolis. The main reason for venturing beyond the Paper Market is to visit the Mosque of Beybars the Crossbowman on Midan Zahir, and the Sakakini Palace beyond.

Many of the **itineraries** given on the following pages can be linked up or truncated; the main limitations on how much you can see are time and your own stamina. It makes sense to read up on an area before striking out on foot. The streets of Islamic Cairo are labyrinthine and, while getting lost among them can result in the richest experiences, some visitors prefer to be shown round by a **guide**. The tourist office can put you in touch with authorized guides, and unofficial ones may accost you on the street.

Most of Islamic Cairo's **monuments** are self-evident and often identified by little green plaques with Arabic numbers; these correspond to the numbers on Lehnert & Landrock's map of Cairo and the listings in the exhaustive *Islamic Monuments in Cairo: A Practical Guide*, published by the AUC. Although the area **maps** printed in this book should suffice, the AUC book and four fold-out maps published by SPARE (the Society for the Preservation of the Architectural Resources of Egypt) show even more detail.

Likewise, certain **books** can provide further detail and evocative accounts of time and place. Edward Lane's *The Manners and Customs of the Modern Egyptians* illuminates life during Mohammed Ali's time. The changes wrought last century underlie Naguib Mahfouz's *Midaq Alley* and *Cairo Trilogy*. Mamluke Cairo is the setting for

came into being. More important in the long term was the Abbasid reliance on Turkish-speaking warriors, who were granted fiefdoms throughout the empire, including Egypt.

Robert Irwin's surreal *The Arabian Nightmare*, whereas its fevered demise haunts *Zayni Barakat* by Gamal al-Ghitani. Life in the Cities of the Dead is captured in *Down to the Sea* by Gamil Attiyah Ibrahim. For straight – but never dull – history, try James Aldridge's *Cairo* or Desmond Stewart's *Great Cairo, Mother of the World*. All of these works are reviewed under "Books" in Contexts (pp.845–846) and a selection is available at bookstores such as Al-Shorouk on Midan Talaat Harb, the Anglo-Egyptian Bookshop at 169 Sharia Mohammed Farid and the AUC bookstore at the back of the main campus. Al-Shorouk, AUC and Lenhert & Landrock (44 Sharia Sherif) are the best places to look for the SPARE maps, which are not always easy to come by.

The buildings you will most want to visit are **mosques**, **madrassas** (theological schools) and **wikalas** (caravanserais, see p.867). On occasion, former private **mansions** are also open to the public. Most mosques and religious buildings no longer charge any **entrance fee** – these were abolished after complaints by Muslim visitors who felt that they should not have to pay to pray. This has not stopped certain unscrupulous custodians and other opportunists from attempting on occasion to charge visitors for entry. If somebody tries to charge you for entering a mosque, demand an official ticket – if they have none, the charge is spurious and you should refuse to pay it. **Opening hours** are roughly 9am to 7pm daily, though they may well open up later, depending on when the guardian turns up, and they may close an hour or two earlier in winter. During Ramadan, when everybody wants to be at home by sunset in order to eat, you will not be able to visit after about 4pm. Entry charges and opening hours are only given in the text when they differ significantly from the above. You will also not be welcome during **prayer times** and the Friday noon assembly, which lasts over an hour but should be finished by 2.30pm. A couple of mosques are permanently closed to non-Muslims (as indicated in the text).

Although entry charges have been abolished for visiting mosques, custodians generally expect **baksheesh**. Egyptians pay 50pt for looking after shoes, though you may wish, as a tourist, to be more generous. Someone who opens a place up, takes you into a tomb or lets you up a minaret rates £E5–10 (which you should pay after your visit). Excessive demands should be politely resisted, and asking for change is awkward, so bring the right bills.

How you **dress** is important. Wearing shorts automatically diminishes prestige in Egyptian eyes, and women wearing halter-necks, skimpy T-shirts, miniskirts, etc, will attract gropers and the disapproval of both sexes. Mosques balk at admitting the "immodestly" dressed, and for Muslims and unbelievers alike it's obligatory to remove shoes (or don overshoes) to avoid sullying the sacred precincts. Comfortable, easy-to-slip-off footwear is recommended; sandals offer scant protection against manure and leaking drains. Women may feel more comfortable with a male companion, and covering their hair and shoulders with a shawl or headscarf.

It shouldn't need saying that intimate **behaviour** in public is a definite no-no – in March 2005, a mentally disturbed Egyptian attacked two tourists with a knife in Khan el-Khalili, simply for kissing while posing for a photo. By remaining courteous and alert, you minimize the risk of hassles on the crowded streets. An effective yet graceful way of brushing off hustlers is to intone *"la shukran"* (no thank you) while smiling, touching your heart (a gesture of sincerity) and hurrying on. But never begrudge the effort of politeness, nor mistake every approach for a sales ploy. Ordinary Egyptians enjoy welcoming *khawagas* with the right attitude as much as they like watching arrogant tourists get misdirected and cheated.

In 870, encouraged by popular discontent, the Abbasids' viceroy in Egypt asserted his independence and went on to wrest Syria from their control. Like his predecessors, Ahmed **Ibn Tulun** founded a new city, reaching from

Medinet al-Askar towards a spur of the Muqattam. Inspired by the imperial capital of Samarra, it consisted of a gigantic congregational mosque, palace and hippodrome, surrounded by "the Wards" (*Al-Qitai*) or military quarters after which the city was named. However, when the Abbasids invaded Egypt in 905, Al-Qitai was razed and ploughed under, sparing only the great Mosque of Ibn Tulun, which stands to this day.

The city regained a shadow of its former importance under the **Ikhshidids** (935–969), who seceded from the later Abbasid khalifs. But the impetus for its revival, and that of the Islamic empire, came from Tunisia, where adherents of Shia Islam had created their own theocracy, ruled by a descendant of Ali and Fatima – the dynasty of **Fatimids**. Aiming to seize the khalifate, they hit upon Egypt as an ill-defended yet significant power base, and captured it with an army of 100,000 in 969. The Fatimid general, Gohar (Jewel), a converted Greek, immediately began a new city where the dynasty henceforth reigned (969–1171).

By this time distinctions between the earlier cities had blurred, as people lived wherever was feasible amidst the decaying urban entity known as **Masr** (which also means "Egypt"). The Fatimids distanced themselves from Masr by building their city of **Al-Qahira** (The Conqueror) further north than ever, where certain key features remain. It was at the Al-Azhar Mosque that Al-Muizz, Egypt's first Fatimid ruler, delivered a sermon before vanishing into his palaces (which, alas, survive only in name); the Mosque of Al-Hakim commemorates the khalif who ordered Masr's destruction after residents objected to proclamations of his divinity. You can also see the great Northern Walls and the Bab Zwayla gate, dating from Al-Gyushi's enlargement of Al-Qahira's defences. But as the Fatimid city expanded, Fustat began disappearing as people scavenged building material from its abandoned dwellings; a process that spread to Masr, creating great swathes of *kharab*, or derelict quarters.

The disparate areas only assumed a kind of unity after **Salah al-Din** (Saladin to the Crusaders) built **the Citadel** on a rocky spur between Al-Qahira and Masr, and walls which linked up with the aqueduct between the Nile and the Citadel, so as to surround the whole. Salah al-Din promoted Sunni, not Shia, Islam and built madrassas to propagate orthodoxy; he ruled not as khalif, but as a secular sultan ("power"). His successors, the **Ayyubids**, erected pepperpot-shaped minarets (only one remains, on Sultan Ayyub's Madrassa and Mausoleum; see p.158) and the magnificent tombs of the Abbasid Khalifs and Imam al-Shafi'i (which still exist) in the Southern Cemetery, but they made the same error as the Abbasids: depending on foreign troops and bodyguards. When the sultan died heirless and his widow needed help to stay in power, these troops, the Mamlukes, were poised to take control.

The **Mamlukes** were a self-perpetuating caste of slave-warriors, originally from Central Asia but later drawn from all over the Near East and the Balkans. Their price in the slave markets reflected the "value" of ethnic stock – 130–140 ducats for a Tartar, 110–120 for a Circassian, 50–80 for a Slav or Albanian – plus individual traits: sturdy, handsome youths were favoured. Often born of concubines and raised in barracks, Mamlukes advanced through the ranks under amirs who sodomized and lavished gifts upon their favourites. With the support of the right amirs, the most ruthless Mamluke could aspire to being sultan. Frequent changes of ruler were actually preferred, since contenders had to spread around bribes, not least to arrange assassinations. The Mamluke era is divided into periods named after the garrisons of troops whence the sultans intrigued their way to power: the Qipchak or Tartar **Bahri Mamlukes** (1250–1382), originally stationed by the river (*bahr* in Arabic); and their Circassian successors, the **Burgi Mamlukes** (1382–1517), quartered in a tower (*burg*) of the Citadel.

Paradoxically, the Mamlukes were also renowned as aesthetes, commissioning mosques, mansions and *sabil-kuttabs* that are still the glory of today's Islamic Cairo. They built throughout the city, from the Northern to the Southern Cemetery, and the Citadel to the Nile, and although urban life was interrupted by their bloody conflicts, the city nevertheless maintained civilized institutions: public hospitals, libraries and schools bequeathed by wealthy Mamlukes and merchants. The caravanserais overflowed with exotica from Africa and the spices of the East, and with Baghdad laid waste by the Mongols, Cairo had no peer in the Islamic world, its wonders inspiring many of the tales in the *Thousand and One Nights*.

But in 1517 the **Ottoman Turks** reduced Egypt from an independent state to a vassal province in their empire, and the Mamlukes from masters to mere overseers. When the French and British extended the Napoleonic War to Egypt they found a city living on bygone glories: introspective and archaic, its population dwindling as civil disorder increased. Eighteenth-century travellers like R.R. Madden were struck by "the squalid wretchedness of the Arabs, and the external splendour of the Turks", not to mention the lack of "one tolerable street" in a city of some 350,000 inhabitants.

The city's renaissance – and the ultimate shift from Islamic to modern Cairo – is owed to **Mohammed Ali** (1805–48) and his less ruthless descendants. An Ottoman servant who turned against his masters, Mohammed Ali effortlessly decapitated the vestiges of Mamluke power and raised a huge mosque and palaces upon the Citadel. Foreigners were hired to advise on urban development, and Sharia Qalaa (Blvd Mohammed Ali) was ploughed through the old city. As Bulaq, Ezbekiya and other hitherto swampy tracts were developed into a modern, quasi-Western city, Islamic Cairo ceased to be the cockpit of power and the magnet for aspirations. But as visitors soon discover, its contrasts, monuments and vitality remain as compelling as ever.

Around Khan el-Khalili and Al-Azhar

Khan el-Khalili bazaar and the Mosque of Al-Azhar form the commercial and religious heart of Islamic Cairo and the starting point for several walking tours. **To get there from downtown Cairo** you can take a taxi, bus, or walk. Taxis (which usually go via the Al-Azhar flyover) shouldn't cost more than £E5, although drivers often try to overcharge tourists bound for Midan el-Hussein – the main square adjoining Khan el-Khalili that's best given as your destination. For details of the buses from downtown, see pp.113–114.

Approaching on foot: the Muski

Walking **from Midan Ataba** there are two basic routes: along Sharia al-Azhar (beneath the flyover), which takes ten to fifteen minutes; or via the Muski, a more interesting, slightly longer approach. It's best to go one way and return by the other.

The Muski is a narrow, incredibly congested street running eastwards from Midan Ataba; look for the faded Arabic sign of the *El-Mousky Hotel* on the corner. Worming your way through the crowds – past windows full of wedding gear, tape decks and fabrics, and vendors peddling everything from salted fish to socks – beware of mopeds and other traffic thrusting up behind. Barrow-men still yell traditional warnings – "*Riglak!*" (Your foot!), "*Dahrik!*" (Your back!), "*Shemalak!*" (Your left side!). Itinerant drinks-vendors are much in evidence: although the *saqi* (water-sellers) have been made redundant by modern plumbing, *susi* dispensing liquorice-water and *sherbutli* with their silver-spouted lemonade bottles remain an essential part of streetlife.

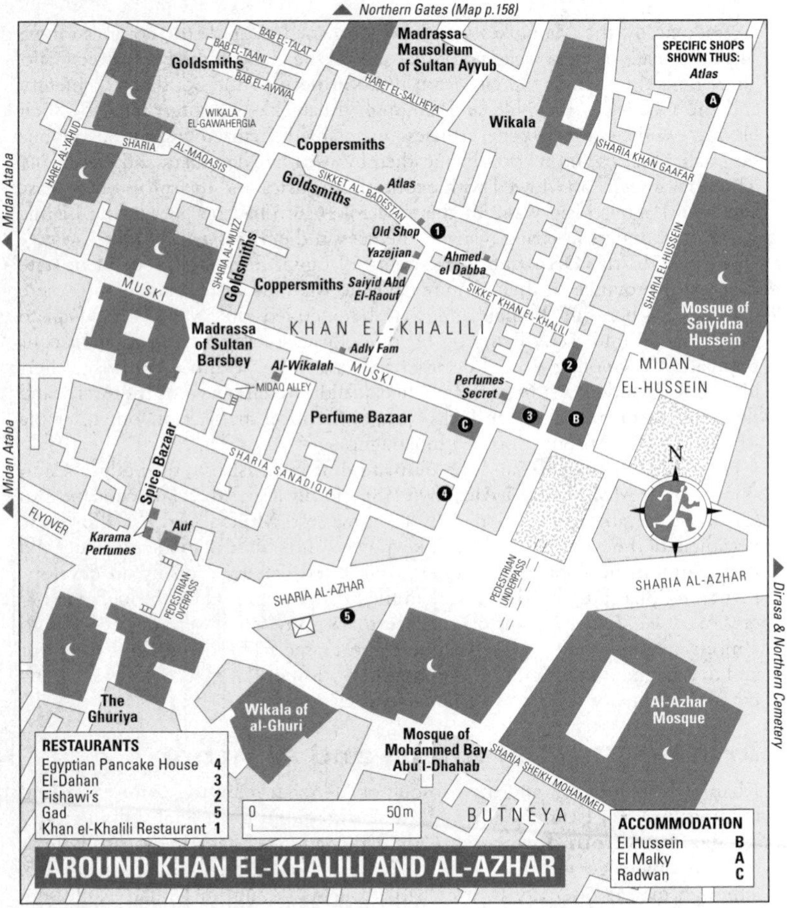

▲ Northern Gates (Map p.158)

AROUND KHAN EL-KHALILI AND AL-AZHAR

RESTAURANTS
Egyptian Pancake House 4
El-Dahan 3
Fishawi's 2
Gad 5
Khan el-Khalili Restaurant 1

ACCOMMODATION
El Hussein B
El Malky A
Radwan C

Halfway along the Muski you'll cross Sharia Bur Said, which you cannot cross directly (you'll have to take a right and dodge under the flyover). Beyond here the Muski turns touristy, with hustlers emerging as it nears Khan el-Khalili.

Midan el-Hussein

Midan el-Hussein, framed by an eclectic mix of architecture, is a central point of reference. To the north stands the tan-coloured **Mosque of Saiyidna Hussein**, where the Egyptian president and other dignitaries pray on special occasions; it's a sacred place, off-limits to non-Muslims. Its cool marble, green and silver interior guards the relic of a momentous event in Islamic history: the **head of Hussein**. The grandson of the Prophet Mohammed, Hussein was killed in Iraq in 680 by the Umayyads, who had earlier been recognized as Mohammed's successors against the claims of his son-in-law, Ali, Hussein's father, whom they had murdered. This generational power struggle over the khalifate caused an enduring schism within Islam. The Muslim world's Sunni ("followers of the way") majority not only recognized the khalifate but forbade the office to anyone of Ali's line. Conversely, the Shia ("partisans of Ali") minority refused to accept any khalif but a descendant of Ali, and revered Hussein as a martyr. In predominantly Sunni Muslim Egypt, he's nevertheless regarded as a popular saint, ranked beside Saiyida Zeinab, the Prophet's granddaughter.

Hussein's annual moulid is one of Cairo's greatest **festivals** – a fortnight of religious devotion and popular revelry climaxing on the *leyla kebira* or "big night", the last Wednesday in the Muslim month of Rabi al-Tani. Here the Sufi brotherhoods parade with their banners and drums, and music blares all night, with vast crowds of Cairenes and *fellaheen* from the Delta (each of whose villages has its own café and dosshouse in the neighbourhood). El-Hussein is also a focal point during the festivals of Moulid al-Nabi, Eid al-Adha, Ramadan and Eid al-Fitr, all well worth seeing. A balcony room at the *El-Hussein Hotel* provides a perfect vantage point, but don't expect to get any sleep. Ablaze with neon lights (including green "Allahs"), the minarets boom sleepers into wakefulness around dawn with their amplified muezzins – and that's on ordinary nights of the year.

The Khan el-Khalili bazaars

Above all, the **Khan el-Khalili** quarter pulses with commerce, as it has since the Middle Ages. Except on Sundays, when most shops are shut, everything from spices to silk is sold in its bazaars. What follows is primarily a guide to the sights; for hard facts about merchandise, dealers and bargaining, see "Shopping", pp.278–287. Generically speaking, all the bazaars around here are subsumed under the name Khan el-Khalili – after Khalil, a Master of Horse who founded a caravanserai here in 1382. However, the Khan itself is quite compact, bounded by Hussein's Mosque, Sharia al-Muizz and the Muski, with two medieval lanes (Sikket al-Badestan and Sikket Khan el-Khalili) penetrating its maze-like interior.

Most of the shop fronts conceal workshops or warehouses, and the system of selling certain goods in particular areas still applies, if not as rigidly as in the past. **Goldsmiths**, jewellers and souvenir-antique shops mostly congregate along the lanes, which retain a few arches and walls from Mamluke times. When you've tired of wandering around, duck into **Fishawi's** via one of the passages off the Muski or the square. Showing its age with tobacco-stained plaster and cracked gilded mirrors, this famous café has been open day and night every day of the year for over two centuries, an evocative place to sip mint tea, eavesdrop, and risk a *sheesha*.

South off the Muski, along Sharia al-Muizz, you'll find the Souk al-Attarin or **Spice Bazaar**, selling dried crushed fruit and flowers besides more familiar spices. On the corner of the same street, screened by T-shirt and *galabiyya* stalls, stands the **Madrassa of Sultan al-Ashraf Barsbey**, who made the spice trade a state monopoly, thus financing his capture of Cyprus in 1426.

Sharia Sanadiqiya (off Sharia al-Muizz) will take you into the **Perfume Bazaar**, a dark, aromatic warren sometimes called the Souk es-Sudan because much of the incense is from there; in the last century, Baedeker's *Guide for Travellers* also noted "gum, dum-plant nuts" and "ill-tanned tiger-skins" amongst the merchandise. Mamluke sultans appointed a *Muhtasib* to oversee prices, weights and quality. Empowered to inflict summary fines and corporal punishments, he was also responsible for public morals – "enjoining what is right and forbidding what is wrong". The first passage on your left off Sharia Sanadiqiya leads up a flight of steps to a tiny cul-de-sac. This is Zuqaq al-Midaq, or **Midaq Alley**, immortalized by Naguib Mahfouz in his novel of the same name, and made into a film, which was shot here. There is no street sign apparent; it's kept in the tiny (and easy to miss) café, where they'll ask if you want to photograph it — for *baksheesh*, of course.

Al-Azhar Mosque

To the southwest of Midan el-Hussein, a pedestrian underpass leads towards the **Mosque of Al-Azhar** (pronounced "Al-*Az*har"), whose name can be translated as "the radiant", "blooming" or "resplendent". Founded in 970, as soon as the enclosure walls of Fatimid Al-Qahira were completed, Al-Azhar claims to be the world's oldest university (a title disputed by the Kairaouine Mosque in Fez, Morocco). For more than a millennium, though, Al-Azhar has provided students from all over the Muslim world with free board and with an education that, despite Nasserite reforms, remains largely as it was during the classical Islamic era. *Muqawrin* study every facet of the Koran and Islamic jurisprudence (*fiqh*); logic, grammar and rhetoric; and how to calculate the phases of the lunar Muslim calendar. Much of this involves listening in a circle (*halqa*) at the feet of a sheikh, and rote memorization; but with greater knowledge, students may engage in Socratic dialogue with their teachers, or instruct their juniors.

Given this, and the Sheikh al-Azhar's status as the ultimate theological authority for Egyptian Muslims, it's unsurprising that the mosque has always been politically significant. Salah al-Din changed it from a Shi'ite hotbed into a bastion of Sunni orthodoxy, while Napoleon's troops savagely desecrated it to demonstrate their power. Omitting any mention of this, a nineteenth-century Baedeker guide (see p.844) cautioned visitors to this "fountain-head of Mohammedan fanaticism... not to indulge in any gestures of amusement or contempt". A nationalist stronghold from the nineteenth century onwards, Al-Azhar was chosen by Nasser as the venue for his speech of defiance during the Suez invasion of 1956. When Saudi King Fahd prayed here with Mubarak in 1989 it symbolized Egypt's return to the conservative Arab fold; yet, paradoxically, many of Al-Azhar's 90,000 students revere the blind fundamentalist sheikh Omar Abd al-Rahman, currently serving a life sentence in the US for his part in the 1993 bombing of the ill-fated New York World Trade Center.

The **mosque** itself (open for tourists Mon–Thurs & Sun 8am–5pm, Fri 8–11am & 3–5pm; open for prayer daily 8am–9pm) is an accretion of centuries and styles, harmonious if confusing. You come in through the fifteenth-century **Barber's Gate**, where students traditionally had their heads shaved, onto a great **sahn** (courtyard) that's five hundred years older, overlooked by three minarets. The *sahn* facade, with its rosettes and keel-arched panels, is mostly Fatimid, but the latticework-screened *riwaqs* (residential quarters) of the **madrassas** (theological schools) on your right-hand side date from the Mamluke period. Unfortunately, these are rarely opened for visitors, but you can walk into the carpeted, alabaster-pillared **qibla liwan** (prayer hall), where the *mihrab*, or prayer niche facing Mecca, is located.

The **roof** and minarets (closed to visitors at time of writing, but worth asking) offer great views of Islamic Cairo's timeless vista of crumbling, dust-coloured buildings that could have been erected decades or centuries ago, the skyline bristling with dozens of minarets.

Butneya

The warren of lanes and tenements behind Al-Azhar — an area known as **Butneya** — could be described as Cairo's "Thieves' Quarter", except that racketeering and drugs are more important. Until 1988, the main business was hashish: sold from "windows" and "green doors", it could be smoked with impunity in *ghorzas* (literally "stitches", small and hidden places) throughout the quarter. Local drugs barons like Kut Kut and Wilad Nasare entered Cairene folklore for their ostentatious wealth and devotion to their neighbourhood; Mustafa Marzuaa built a fifteen-room villa, with video recorders in every room, smack in the middle. After the great crackdown in December 1988, when scores of corrupt officials were arrested, the drugs "mafiosi" decamped to the suburbs, leaving Butneya to local racketeers. Some gangs cream the profits from organized garbage collection and begging; others extort money from shops or restaurants, and one gang even specializes in weddings: families pay them to stay away rather than risk disturbances – to hire bouncers would be a shameful admission of family weakness.

None of this should affect foreigners who stay outside the quarter (though you might be offered hashish, or even regaled with stories of the "good old days" when slabs were carved up on tables outdoors). In any case, the well-defined tourist trail leads elsewhere. Leaving Al-Azhar by the Barber's Gate, you can turn left down an alley to reach the Wikala of al-Ghuri and other monuments described in the next-but-one walking tour; or return to Midan el-Hussein and check out the following itinerary.

To the Northern Gates and back again

As described below, this itinerary covers an array of monuments from different eras, occupying the one-time heart of Fatimid Cairo. Although one can walk the route – from Midan el-Hussein to the Northern Gates and back again – within an hour, checking out the interiors of all the monuments could take half a day or more, so you might wish to be selective. If your time is limited, it's probably best to concentrate on the three big attractions: the Qalaoun–Al-Nasir–Barquq complex, Al-Hakim's Mosque and the Beit al-Sihaymi.

Midan el-Hussein to Bayn al-Qasrayn

Starting from Midan el-Hussein (see the map p.154), walk 200m west along the Muski to a crossroads with two mosques, and then turn right onto the northern extension of **Sharia al-Muizz**. Here, jewellers' shops overflowing from the Goldsmiths Bazaar soon give way to vendors of pots, basins and crescent-topped finials, after whom this bit of street is popularly called *Al-Nahaseen*, the **Coppersmiths Bazaar**.

In Fatimid times this bazaar was a broad avenue culminating in a great parade ground between khalifal palaces – hence its name, **Bayn al-Qasrayn** (Between the Two Palaces), which is still used today although traces of the palaces are long gone. Robert Irwin writes evocatively of the place as it was during the Mamluke era, when it was customary "for the men and even a few of the women to promenade in the cool twilight. Later, when respectable people had gone back to their homes, the streets were left to the lamplighters, carousing mamlukes, prostitutes and the sleepers." More recently, the street has given its name to the first novel of Naguib Mahfouz's *Cairo Trilogy*, where it is usually translated as "Palace Walk".

To the right of the bazaar, a minaret poking above a row of stalls gives away the unobtrusive **Madrassa and Mausoleum of Sultan Ayyub**, more interesting for its historical associations than anything else. Its founder, the last Ayyubid sultan, was responsible for introducing Mamlukes, or foreign slave troops (originally Qipchaks, from an ethnic group related to the Tartars, who lived in Russia's lower Volga region), an act pregnant with consequences for Egypt. As related under "Cities of the Dead" (p.186), the sultan's widow's daring bid for power made the Mamlukes aware that they were kingmakers – whence

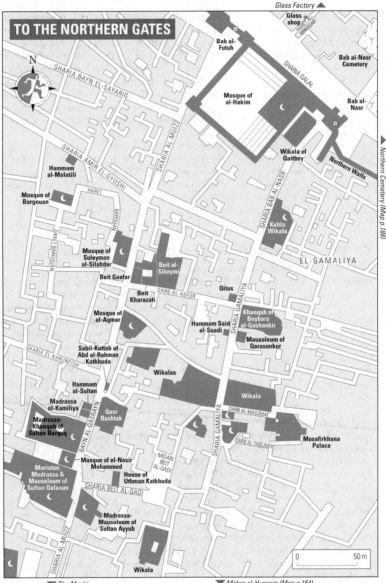

TO THE NORTHERN GATES

Glass Factory ▲

Glass shop

Bab al-Futuh

Bab al-Nasr Cemetery

Mosque of al-Hakim

Bab al-Nasr

SHARIA BAYN EL-SAYARIG

SHARIA GALAL

N

Hammam al-Malatili

SHARIA AMIR EL-GYUSHI

HARET

SHARIA AL-MUIZZ

Wikala of Qaitbey

Northern Walls

▶ Northern Cemetery (Map p.188)

Mosque of Bargouan

BARGOUAN

SIKKET BARGOUAN

SHARIA BAB AL-NASR

Kahla Wikala

Mosque of Suleyman al-Silahdar

Beit al-Sihaymi

EL-GAMALIYA

Beit Gaafar

Beit Kharazati

DARB AL-ASFUR

Qitus

Mosque of al-Aqmar

Hammam Said al-Suadi

SHARIA GAMALIYA

Khanqah of Beybars al-Gashankir

Sabil-Kuttab of Abd al-Rahman Katkhuda

SHARIA EL-KHRUNFISH

Mausoleum of Qarasunkur

Wikalas

Hammam al-Sultan

Wikala

Madrassa al-Kamiliya

DARB AL-MASSMAT

Qasr Bashtak

Madrassa-Khanqah of Sultan Barquq

BAYN AL-QASRAYN

SHARIA GAMALIYA

DARB AL-TABLAWY

Musafirkhana Palace

Mosque of el-Nasir Mohammed

MIDAN BEIT AL-QADI

House of Uthman Katkhuda

Maristan, Madrassa & Mausoleum of Sultan Qalaoun

SHARIA BEIT AL-QADI

Madrassa-Mausoleum of Sultan Ayyub

SHARIA AL-MUIZZ

Wikala

0   50 m

▼ The Muski

▼ Midan el-Hussein (Map p.154)

it was a short step to ruling Egypt themselves, as they did from 1250 onwards. From an architectural standpoint, Ayyub's madrassa (built 1242–50) was the first to incorporate all four *mahhabs* (rites) of Sunni Islam and to be linked to its founder's mausoleum, thus serving as the prototype for the Mamlukes' great mosque-madrassa-mausoleum complexes. Beneath the minaret, whose *mabkhara* (incense burner) or "pepperpot" crown is the sole example of this Ayyubid motif left in Cairo, an alleyway with a gate (on the left) leads into the court-yard of what used to be the madrassa. A sixteenth-century *sabil-kuttab* (Koranic school and fountain) protrudes from the wall between the minaret and Ayyub's domed mausoleum (usually locked), further up the street.

The Qalaoun-Al-Nasir-Barquq complex

Across the road from the *madrassa*, the medieval complex of buildings endowed by the sultans **Qalaoun**, **Al-Nasir** and **Barquq** forms an unbroken and quite breathtaking 185-metre-long facade. Founded by three of the most significant of the Mamlukes, each of these building groups was designed to serve several functions, yet to form a harmonious whole. Unfortunately, all of them were severely damaged in the 1992 earthquake, and parts of them are still undergoing restoration, but it's worth trying to visit as much as is now open.

The Qalaoun Complex

Influenced by the Syrian and Crusader architecture its founder had encoun-tered while fighting abroad, **Sultan Qalaoun's Maristan, Madrassa and Mausoleum** arguably inaugurated the Burgi Mamluke style, which is typified by lavish ornamentation and execution on a grand scale. If modern visitors are impressed by the fact that these structures were completed in thirteen months (1284–85), Qalaoun's contemporaries were amazed. Unfortunately, at time of writing, the complex was undergoing heavy restoration work and closed to public access.

The **Maristan** provided free treatment for every known illness (including cataract removals), storytellers and musicians to amuse the patients, and money to tide them over following their discharge. A modern eye clinic now occupies the site of Qalaoun's hospital, of which only three *liwans* remain; to see them, walk down the tree-shaded lane that starts opposite the *sabil-kuttab* mentioned above.

Further up the street, a main door clad in bronze with geometric patterns gives access to a corridor running between the madrassa and the mausoleum. The damaged **Madrassa** (entered to the left off this corridor) has a sanctuary *liwan* recalling the three-aisled churches of northern Syria, with Syrian-style glass mosaics around its prayer niche.

But the real highlight of the ensemble is Qalaoun's **Mausoleum**, across the corridor. First comes an atrium court with a *mashrabiya* doorway, surmounted by a beautiful stucco arch worked with interlocking stars, floral and Koranic motifs, as intricate as lace. Beyond is the tomb chamber, thirty metres high, with its soaring dome pierced by stained-glass windows in viridian, ultramarine and golden hues. Elaborately coffered, painted ceilings overhang walls panelled in marble, with mother-of-pearl mosaics spelling out "Mohammed" in abstract calligraphy. Until this century the *mihrab* was credited with healing powers, so supplicants could be seen "rubbing lemons on one of its pilasters, and licking up the moisture", while a stick hanging from the tomb's railings was used "to cure fools or idiots by striking them on the head".

Qalaoun himself was a handsome Qipchak, purchased for one thousand dinars during Ayyub's reign. He rose through the ranks due to the patronage of Sultan Beybars al-Bunduqdari, whose seven-year-old son he eventually deposed in 1279. Qalaoun's sonorous titles *Al-Mansour* and *Al-Alfi* ("the Thou-sand", after his high price) were mocked by his name, which sounds comical in Arabic; it's supposedly derived from the Mongolian word for "duck", or an obscure Turkish noun meaning "great ransom" or "rich present". A tireless foe of the Crusaders – he died en route to Acre fortress in 1290, aged 79 – Qalaoun imported Circassians to offset Qipchak predominance amongst the Mamlukes, and founded a dynasty that ruled for almost a century (barring hiccups).

The Al-Nasir Complex

Qalaoun's second son, responsible for the **Mosque of Al-Nasir Mohammed** next door, had a rough succession. Only nine years old when elected, he was deposed by his regent, then restored but kept in miserable conditions for a decade by Beybars al-Gashankir. He finally had Beybars executed and subsequently enjoyed a lengthy reign (1293–1340, counting interregnums), which marked the zenith of Mamluke civilization.

The building of thirty mosques, the great aqueduct and a canal north of Cairo attests to Al-Nasir's enthusiasm for public works (matched apparently by his devotion to horses and sheep). The **minaret** is a superb ensemble of stuccoed *kufic* and *naskhi* inscriptions, ornate medallions and stalactites, probably made by Moroccan craftsmen. Al-Nasir is actually buried in Qalaoun's mausoleum, and his own son occupies the **mausoleum** intended for him.

At the time of writing, the complex was undergoing restoration work, but due to open in the near future.

The Barquq Madrassa and Khanqah

Now restored to full glory following severe earthquake damage, the adjacent **Madrassa and Khanqah of Sultan Barquq** appears in a much-reproduced nineteenth-century drawing by Owen Carter, which also depicts the Sabil-Kuttab of Ismail Pasha, opposite Al-Nasir's mosque. Its broad facade, divided into shallow recesses, echoes Qalaoun's madrassa, although Barquq's complex (1384–86) has the taller dome. It also boasts a minaret, which you can ascend (second door on the right in the entrance passage and over the roof) for excellent views of Islamic Cairo, though it's a good idea to bring a torch as parts of the spiral staircase are very dark.

Barquq was the first Circassian sultan (1382–98), a Burgi Mamluke who seized power by means of intrigue and assassination. His name, meaning "plum" in Arabic, appears on the raised boss in the centre of the bronze-plated doors, behind which a vaulted passageway leads to an open court. The **madrassa**'s sanctuary *liwan* (on the right as you enter) has a beautiful blue and gold ceiling supported by porphyry columns of pharaonic origin; upstairs are the cells of the Sufi monks who once inhabited the **khanqah** (monastery). To the north of the *qibla liwan*, a splendid domed mausoleum upheld by gilded pendentives contains the tomb of Barquq's daughter.

Mansions and Sabil-Kuttabs

The domestic architecture of the Mamlukes was no less sophisticated: perfectly adapted to Cairene conditions, it offered greater comfort than contemporary European homes – for the well-to-do, at least. An example close at hand is the **House of Uthman Katkhuda**, so called after an eighteenth-century resident, although the mansion itself dates from 1350. You'll find it on Sharia Beit al-Qadi, which runs eastwards opposite Qalaoun's mausoleum; it's halfway along the north side of the street at no.9, but currently closed for restoration. The entrance leads into the *qa'a*, a narrow, sixteen-metre-high reception hall with a handsome fountain and wainscotting, cooled by a north-facing *malqaf*, or air scoop, on the roof.

Back on Sharia al-Muizz, walk past Barquq's complex (beyond which the street is known as Bayn al-Qasrayn, meaning "between the two palaces" – see p.157) and cross the road, turning into a muddy alleyway on the right, where a door on the left (just before the archway straight in front of you) opens onto the fourteenth-century **Qasr Bashtak**. Here the *qa'a* is upstairs, with *mashrabiya*-screened galleries that permitted ladies to witness the amir's parties, and similar devices overlooking the street. Amir Bashtak was married to Al-Nasir's daughter, so he could afford a five-storey palace with running water on every floor; alas, only a section has survived. The entrance to Qasr Bashtak is round the side on Darb Kermez, just before the bend, but it is currently closed for restoration.

Back on Bayn al-Qasrayn and situated on a fork in the road just beyond the Qalaoun, Al-Nasir and Barquq complex, the **Sabil-Kuttab of Abd al-Rahman Katkhuda** rises in tiers of airy wooden fretwork above solid masonry and grilles at street level. Founded by an eighteenth-century amir who wished to make amends for roistering, this is an Ottoman-influenced example of a type of building once widespread throughout Cairo, intended to provide the "blessings" of water and education, mentioned in the Holy Koran. Thus, local people could draw water from the *sabil* (public fountain) on the ground floor (where the Ka'ba at Mecca is depicted in Syrian tilework), while their sons learned Koranic precepts in the *kuttab* upstairs. (Girls were deemed unworthy of schooling.) An old proverb suggests that teaching methods were simple: "A boy's ear is on his back – he listens when he is beaten."

By taking the left-hand fork at the *sabil-kuttab* and walking 70m north you reach the **Mosque of Al-Aqmar**, on the right (open daily from 8am until just after the last prayer, which is about 7.30pm in winter, 9.30pm in summer). Newly restored, its most salient feature is the facade, whose ribbed shell hood, keel arches and stalactite panels were the first instance of a decorated mosque facade in Cairo. Built between 1121 and 1125 by the Fatimid khalif's grand vizier, the mosque gets its name – "the moonlit" – from the glitter of its masonry under lunar light. Notice the intricate medallion above the door; the way that the street level has risen well above the mosque's entrance; and the "cutaway" corner up the road, designed to facilitate the manoeuvring of loaded camels.

One block further north, turn right into **Darb al-Asfur**. This whole street has now emerged from years of major restoration work, which has left it in such a pristine state that it no longer seems part of the surrounding district. In fact it looks more like a modern imitation than a genuine Gamaliya street. The first three houses on the left are all open to the public (daily 9am–5pm; £E20, students £E10), entered through the broad wooden door of no.19, **Beit al-Sihaymi**, which is the finest of the three. Its rooms surround a lovely courtyard filled with bird noises and shrubbery, overlooked by a *maq'ad* or loggia, where males enjoyed the cool northerly breezes; the ground-floor reception hall with its marble fountain was used during winter, or for formal occasions. The *haramlik* section, reserved for women, is equally luxurious, adorned with faïence, stained glass, painted ceilings and delicate latticework. From here, you pass through the similarly restored early eighteenth-century **Beit Gaafar**, to emerge via the smaller, nineteenth-century **Beit Kharazati** on the corner at no.25. The three houses offer a unique chance to see what lies behind the walls of these old-city streets, and view the interior of a traditional wealthy Cairene's home, although the family life that once filled it is missing.

Returning to the main street and continuing north brings you to the **Mosque of Suleyman al-Silahdar**, recognizable by its "pencil" minaret, a typically Ottoman feature. Built in 1839, the mosque reflects the Baroque and Rococo influences that reached Cairo via Istanbul during Mohammed Ali's reign – notably the fronds and garlands that also characterize *sabil-kuttabs* from the period. Shortly afterwards the street widens into a triangular square, beyond which it's busy with the colourfully painted carts of garlic- and onion-sellers who roll in through the mighty gate ahead.

Al-Hakim's Mosque and the Northern Gates

The **Mosque of Al-Hakim**, abutting the Northern Walls, commemorates one of Egypt's most notorious rulers. **Al-Hakim bi-Amr Allah** (Ruler by God's Command) was only eleven years old when he became the sixth Fatimid khalif, and fifteen when he had his tutor murdered. His reign (996–1021) was capricious and despotic by any standards, characterized by the persecution of Christians, Jews and merchants and by a rabid misogyny: Al-Hakim forbade women to leave their homes (banning the manufacture of women's footwear to reinforce this) and once had a group of noisy females boiled alive in a public bath. His puritanical instincts were also levelled at wine, chess and dancing girls – all of which he prohibited – and all the city's dogs were exterminated as their barking annoyed him. Merchants found guilty of cheating during Al-Hakim's inspections were summarily sodomized by his Nubian slave, Masoud, while the khalif stood upon their heads – comparatively restrained behaviour from a man who once dissected a butcher with his own cleaver.

In 1020, followers proclaimed Al-Hakim's divinity in the Mosque of Amr, provoking riots which he answered by ordering Fustat's destruction, watching it burn from the Muqattam Hills, where he often rode alone at night. However, legend ascribes the conflagration to Al-Hakim's revenge on the quarter where his beloved sister, **Sitt al-Mulk** (Lady of Power), took her lovers. Only after half of Fustat-Masr was in ruins was she examined by midwives and pronounced a virgin, whereupon he surveyed the devastation and asked, "Who ordered this?" Allegedly, it was his desire for an incestuous marriage that impelled her to arrange Al-Hakim's "disappearance" during one of his nocturnal jaunts, though his body was never found.

By governing as regent for the child-khalif Zahir and dying peacefully in her bed, Sitt al-Mulk forfeited the eternal fame that later accrued to Shagar al-Durr, renowned as the only female ruler of Egypt since Cleopatra (see p.186). Meanwhile, Al-Hakim's follower Hamza Ibn Ali, and his disciple, Mohammed al-Durzi, persuaded many foreign Muslims that Al-Hakim was a manifestation of God similar to the Christian Messiah. This idea is the origin of the **Druze** faith, whose tightly knit communities still exist in Syria, Lebanon and Israel, and who subscribe to doctrines of which the details are secret. Conversely, the Copts maintain that Al-Hakim experienced a vision of Jesus, repented, and became a monk.

At all events, though, his huge **mosque** was thereafter shunned or used for profane purposes until 1980, when it was restored by a sect of Isma'ili Shi'ites from Brunei who venerate Al-Hakim. The sect's addition of brass lamps, glass chandeliers and a new *mihrab* outraged purists, but the original wooden tie-beams and stucco frieze beneath the ceilings remain. From the roof, you can gaze over Bab al-Nasr Cemetery (see opposite) and admire the mosque's minarets, which resemble bastions and are its only original features. One advantage of modernization is that the courtyard has some degree of wheelchair access, though there is still the odd step to negotiate.

The Northern Gates

In times past, the annual pilgrim caravan returning from Mecca would enter Cairo via the **Bab al-Futuh** (Open Gate), drawing huge crowds to witness the arrival of the *Mahmal*. This decorative camel litter once carried Ayyub's widow on her pilgrimage, but thereafter it symbolized rather than signified the sultan's participation. Islamic pageantry is still manifest during the **Moulid of Sidi Ali al-Bayoumi**, in early October, when the Rifai brotherhood parades behind its mounted sheikh with scarlet banners flying. The procession starts from El-Hussein, passes through the Bab al-Futuh and north along Sharia Husseiniya, where locals bombard the sheikh and his red-turbanned followers with huge sweets called *aruah*.

From Al-Hakim's Mosque, you can gain admission to a **prison** in the dark interior of the **Northern Walls**, whose custodian will point out archers' slits and bombardiers' apertures, shafts for pouring boiling oil onto enemies entering through the Bab al-Futuh below, and bits of pharaonic masonry (featuring Ramses II's cartouche and a hippo) filched from Memphis. The ceiling of the 200-metre tunnel is vaulted, which allowed mounted guards passage through. At its end lies a grim and cavernous judgement room where the condemned, if found guilty, were hanged immediately, their corpses unceremoniously dumped through a hole in the floor, into the waters of the moat.

Erected in 1087 to replace the original mud-brick ramparts of Fatimid Al-Qahira, the walls were intended to rebuff the Seljuk Turks, but never put to the test, although they later provided a barracks for Napoleonic, and then British, grenadiers. The French attempted to rename the bastions of Bab al-Futuh and the next gate along, **Bab al-Nasr** (Gate of Victory), and titles such as "Tour Julien" and "Tour Pascal" are still inscribed on them. Bab al-Nasr can be reached, like Bab al-Futuh, from the roof of Al-Hakim's Mosque. The gate's inscription – "No deity but Allah; Mohammed is the Prophet of God" – includes a defiant Shi'ite addition, "And Ali is the Deputy of God". It was after entering this gate in 1517 that the victorious Ottoman sultan Selim the Grim had eight hundred Mamlukes decapitated and their heads strung on ropes on Gezira Island. Directly opposite the gate lies **Bab al-Nasr Cemetery**, nowadays so overbuilt with houses that you can hardly see the tombs. At the top end of Haret al-Birkhader, one of the small streets off Sharia Galal opposite Bab al-Futuh, is a traditional **glass factory** where they hand-blow Muski glass, and are usually happy for tourists to pop in and have a look: if you can't find it, ask for directions in their shop at no.10.

From Bab al-Nasr you could catch a taxi or walk 1500m east, following the Walls and then Sharia Galal, to reach Barquq's complex in the Northern Cemetery (see p.190). Alternatively, minibus #10 runs from here in one direction to Dirasa, and the other way to Midan Ramses via the Mosque of Beybars (see p.220) and Midan Ataba.

Heading back along Sharia Gamaliya

Re-entering Islamic Cairo along Sharia Bab al-Nasr you pass into **El-Gamaliya**, whose name derives from the old camel road, Sharia Gamaliya, off which the quarter's alleys run; in one of them, Nobel prize-winning author Naguib Mahfouz was born in 1911. Immediately to your right stands the sturdy fifteenth-century caravanserai or **Wikala of Qaitbey**, largely derelict within following damage in the 1993 earthquake, though most of the facade remains intact. Such caravanserais naturally clustered near the city gates, and the facades of three more *wikalas* (the last reduced to a mere portal) are visible beyond a small domed mausoleum on the other side of Sharia Gamaliya.

Beyond these *wikalas* stands the **Khanqah of Beybars al-Gashankir**, with its unmistakably bulbous dome and stumpy minaret (daily 1–7pm; entry free but *baksheesh* expected). Founded in 1310, and thus the oldest Sufi monastery in Cairo, the *khanqah* is entered via a "baffled" corridor that excludes street noises from the inner courtyard. Without tiles or mosaics, the courtyard escapes severity by the variety of its windows: ribbed, S-curved or keel-arched in styles derived from the Fatimid era. Al-Gashankir's tomb (off the corridor) is spectacular by comparison, with sunbeams falling through stained glass onto marbled walls inset with radiating polygons, and his cenotaph within its ebony *mashrabiya* cage. Sultan for one year only, Beybars was dubbed *Al-Gashankir* (the Taster) to distinguish him from Beybars al-Bunduqdari (the Crossbowman), a mightier predecessor.

Opposite the *khanqah* on the corner of Darb al-Asfur (see p.161), is a *sabil*, **Qitus**, built in 1630 and, like the rest of the street, now lovingly restored, though not open to the public. Continuing south along Sharia Gamaliya for 100m, you'll pass a ruined *wikala*, a fifteenth-century mosque built above shops (whose rent finances the mosque's maintenance), and then another couple of mosques. Immediately after this, turn left into Darb al-Tablawy, an alleyway that bends left around a high stone wall to reach the **Musafirkhana Palace**. Though semi-derelict and undergoing slow restoration, this eighteenth-century mansion (where Khedive Ismail was born) retains beautiful *mashrabiyas*, decorative ceilings, a fountain in the reception hall, and a peaceful atmosphere rarely disturbed by visitors. Though it is still closed to the public at the time of writing, the custodian may let you in for a small tip if you can locate him.

Returning to the main street, you'll find that it narrows and forks as it runs south. Precise directions are difficult, but by turning right at one fork and passing through a medieval-looking gate, you should emerge onto a square with shops selling scrap metal and weighing machines, behind the El-Hussein Mosque.

Between Al-Azhar and the Bab Zwayla

Some of the most arresting sights in Islamic Cairo cluster between **Al-Azhar Mosque** and the medieval gate known as the **Bab Zwayla** – a fairly brief itinerary (20–60min) that can be followed in either direction. We've described the sequence of places starting from Al-Azhar and finishing at the gate, but you could equally well start at the Bab Zwayla (a short walk from the Islamic Art Museum) and work north from there. Be aware that this section of the old city, and particularly the area around the Al-Ghuri complex, is a popular hang-out for **touts** (see p.139).

Bab Zwayla is also the starting point for **longer walking tours** of the Qasaba and Darb al-Ahmar, winding up beneath the Citadel, as described in the section following; so you could also take this itinerary in reverse from there.

The Wikala, Mosque-Madrassa and Mausoleum of Al-Ghuri

The **Wikala of Al-Ghuri** is Cairo's best-preserved merchants' hostel (twenty such squatted or derelict structures remain, out of the 200 active in 1835). Its upstairs rooms have been converted into artists' studios (officially closed for restoration at time of writing, though the custodian will show you around for a small consideration). With its stables and lock-ups beneath tiers of spartan rooms, the *wikala* is uncompromisingly functional, yet the rhythm of *ablaq* (striped) arches muted by the sharp verticals of shutters, and the severe masonry lightened by *mashrabiyas* and a graceful fountain, achieves elegance.

Although it was built (in 1505) just as the new Cape route to the East Indies was diminishing Cairo's role as a spice entrepôt, the *wikala* doubtless witnessed the kind of scenes described in *The Arabian Nightmare*:

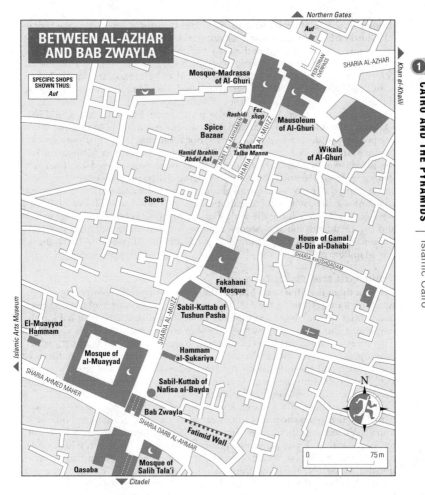

BETWEEN AL-AZHAR AND BAB ZWAYLA

SPECIFIC SHOPS
SHOWN THUS:
Auf

Northern Gates

Auf

SHARIA AL-AZHAR

Khan el-Khalili

PEDESTRIAN OVERPASS

Mosque-Madrassa
of Al-Ghuri

Rashidi   Fez
shop

Spice
Bazaar

HARET AL-TAHHANIN

SHARIA AL-MUIZZ

Mausoleum
of Al-Ghuri

Shahatta
Talba Manna

Wikala
of Al-Ghuri

Hamid Ibrahim
Abdel Aal

Shoes

House of Gamal
al-Din al-Dahabi

SHARIA KHUSHQADAM

Fakahani
Mosque

SHARIA AL-MUIZZ

Sabil-Kuttab of
Tushun Pasha

Islamic Arts Museum

El-Muayyad
Hammam

Mosque of
al-Muayyad

Hammam
'al-Sukariya

SHARIA AHMED MAHER

Sabil-Kuttab of
Nafisa al-Bayda

Bab Zwayla

SHARIA DARB AL-AHMAR

Fatimid Wall

N

0   75 m

Qasaba

Mosque of
Salih Tala'i

Citadel

The Muhtasib stood immovable, flanked by two huge Turks who carried lanterns on great staves. Black slaves staggered under trunks of merchandise that were being fought over. A party of men were unsuccessfully trying to persuade a camel to leave by the same gate that it had come in by. A sheep was being roasted in the centre of the compound.

Located on a side street off Sharia al-Azhar, the *wikala* can be reached by turning left on leaving the Mosque of Al-Azhar, then following the alley round past a market; or you can visit it after seeing the **Ghuriya –** the mausoleum and mosque-madrassa of Al-Ghuri. Boldly striped in buff and white, this pair of buildings forms a set piece at the junction of Sharia al-Muizz and the Al-Azhar high road, plainly visible from the footbridge. To the right (west) of the bridge stands the **Mosque-Madrassa**, now restored to its full glory. The rooftop offers glimpses of the Spice Bazaar and a grand view of the neighbourhood – the door is diagonally opposite the entrance to the main part of the mosque, but is often closed, so you may have to ask a custodian for access. Across the way is Al-Ghuri's **Mausoleum** (closed for restoration), originally topped by a green-tiled dome, which collapsed in the early twentieth century. On the other side of the mausoleum is the Al-Ghuri Palace, which has become an adult educational centre. Currently closed for restoration, it held an exhibition area and a theatre with a splendid ceiling, where performances by whirling dervishes were held, though these have now moved to the Citadel (see p.271).

Sixty years old when he became the penultimate Mamluke sultan in 1500, **Qansuh al-Ghuri** remained vigorous into his seventies, playing polo, writing poetry and discoursing with Sufis – not forgetting traditional pursuits like building, intrigue and arbitrary justice. Though not averse to filching marble for his mosque-madrassa, Al-Ghuri wished to be remembered for his strict enforcement of Koranic precepts: sentencing a dervish accused of "atheism, sorcery, and the use of milk for his ablutions and intimate toilet" to be paraded naked on a camel, and then hanged; and berating his judges for laxity. Al-Ghuri was killed in 1516 fighting the Turks outside Aleppo; his body was never found and his intended tomb was occupied by his luckless successor, Tumanbey (see opposite). Gamal al-Ghitani's novel *Zayni Barakat* is a fictionalized account of this Mamluke twilight.

Towards the Bab Zwayla

In olden times the **Sharia al-Muizz**, the street between the Ghuriya buildings, was roofed over, forming the Silk Bazaar where carpets were sold, the subject of a famous drawing by David Roberts. Nowadays, shops along here sell mostly household goods, making fewer concessions to tourism than Khan el-Khalili. The street is named after the conquering Fatimid khalif and it was the chief thoroughfare of Islamic Cairo, running from the Northern Gates down towards the Citadel, and meeting another main road – the Darb al-Ahmar – at the Bab Zwayla. Traditionally, each stretch of Al-Muizz had its own name, usually derived from the merchandise sold there.

On the west side of the street, less than 50m south of Al-Ghuri's Mosque, is the last **fez workshop** in Cairo, kept alive by sales to five-star hotels and tourists. Various qualities are available, the cheapest going for just £E10. The fez, or *tarboush fassi*, was originally a mark of Ottoman allegiance, which came to represent the secular, Westernized effendi, as opposed to the turbaned traditionalist. Under Nasser it fell from fashion, stigmatized as a badge of the old regime. Waiters and entertainers are the main wearers nowadays, but demand is so small that the craft of fez-making seems unlikely to survive.

Some 200m south, you'll find the "Fruit Seller" or **Fakahani Mosque**, whose arabesque-panelled doors are all that remain of the twelfth-century original after its reconstruction in 1735. The nearby **House of Gamal al-Din al-Dahabi**, at no.6 Sharia Khushqadan (aka "Haret Hoche Kadam"), was the home of seventeenth-century Cairo's foremost gold merchant. Its magnificent interior is still under restoration but is nonetheless open to the public (daily 9am–9pm; £E10, students £E5), and full of beautiful stone inlay work and ornate wooden ceilings, especially in the first-floor portico overlooking the main courtyard.

South of the Fakahani Mosque, Sharia al-Muizz curves around the Rococo facade of the 1820 Ottoman-built **Sabil-Kuttab of Tusun Pasha**, adorned with wrought-iron sunbursts, garlands and fronds. Shortly afterwards the street passes between two buildings structurally adjacent to the Bab Zwayla, whose formidable outline dominates the view ahead. To your left, the wall of a *mashrabiya*-fronted *wikala* is preceded by an unobtrusive door (next to a jewellers' shop) that fronts the eighteenth-century **al-Sukanya Hammam**, a traditional bathhouse that is currently being restored so closed to the public. The fires that heated the water here were also used to cook *fuul madammas* (broad beans) for the neighbourhood's breakfast. The traditional extra allure of such baths was described by Flaubert in 1839: "You reserve the bath for yourself (five francs including masseurs, pipe, coffee, sheet and towel) and you skewer your lad in one of the rooms." Flaubet described the masseurs as "naked *kellaas* … turning you over like embalmers preparing you for the tomb". The reputation of bathhouses as gay brothels has endured, though it is hoped that the restoration of this and three other hammams in Islamic Cairo will mark their return to fashion as legitimate places to enjoy a steam bath.

Across the way, the **Mosque of Al-Muayyad** – also known as the "Red Mosque" for the colour of its exterior – occupies the site of a prison where its founder was once incarcerated for plotting against Sultan Barquq. Plagued by lice and fleas, he vowed to transform it into a "saintly place for the education of scholars" once he came to power. When he did, 40,000 dinars were dutifully lavished on the mosque's construction (1415–22). The building is entered via a nine-tiered stalactite portal with a red-and-turquoise geometric frame around its bronze door, but is closed for repairs at present. Off the vestibule lies a mausoleum where Al-Muayyad and his son are buried in befittingly sized cenotaphs. The kufic inscription on Al-Muayyad's reads: "But the god-fearing shall be amidst gardens and fountains: Enter you them, in peace and security" – which seems appropriate for the mosque's courtyard, half filled with palms and open to the sky. Beneath the roofed section a thickly carpeted sanctuary precedes the *qibla* wall, niched and patterned with polychrome marble and mosaic. Its minarets are built atop the turrets of Bab Zwayla, the neighbouring city gate. Another old bathhouse, the **Hammam al-Muayyad,** can be found down a small alley behind the mosque, but it has been derelict for a while and doesn't look like being restored any time soon.

Bab Zwayla

The Al-Muayyad's minarets, added four hundred years after the turrets were built, make **Bab Zwayla** look far mightier than the Northern Gates. The gate itself was constructed when the Fatimid city's defences (including sixty gates) were reinforced during the 1090s, using Anatolian or Mesopotamian Christian architects and Egyptian labour. Originally the main south gate, Bab Zwayla later became a central point in the Mamluke city, which had outgrown the Fatimid walls and pushed up against Salah al-Din's extensions. Nevertheless, the practice of barring the gates each night continued well into the nineteenth century, maintaining a city within a city. There's a strikingly medieval passage just on the north side of the gate, but the full awesomeness of the Bab itself is best seen from the south side. Note the barbells high up on the western gatetower: a relic of medieval keep-fit enthusiasts.

The gate was named after Fatimid mercenaries of the Berber al-Zwayla tribe, quartered nearby, whom the Mamlukes displaced. Through the centuries it was the point of departure for caravans to Mecca and the source of the drum rolls that greeted the arrival of senior "Amirs of One Hundred". Dancers and snake charmers also performed here, and from the fifteenth century onwards punishments provided another spectacle. Dishonest merchants might be hung from hooks or ropes; garrotting, beheading or impalement were favoured for common criminals; while losers in the Mamluke power struggles were often nailed to the doors. It was here that Tumanbey, the last Mamluke sultan, was hanged in 1517, after a vast crowd had recited the *Fatah* and the rope had broken twice before his neck did. However, Bab Zwayla's reputation was subsequently redeemed by its association with Mitwalli al-Qutb, a miracle-working local saint said to manifest himself to the faithful as a gleam of light within the gatehouse.

The **western gatetower**, the **turret** and the **minarets** are now open to the public (daily 8am–5pm; £E10, students £E5) and can be visited via a door just next to the al-Muayyad Mosque. Finds from the site are on display, as well as votive offerings left by local residents for Mitwalli al-Qutb. You can also climb to the top of the two minarets for great views over Islamic Cairo and a bird's-eye perspective over the al-Muayyad and Salih Tala'i mosques below.

A whole slew of places to the south of the Bab are covered by the next itinerary (see p.171), but it's worth mentioning an alternative: namely, heading westwards along Sharia Ahmed Maher **towards the Islamic Art Museum** (see below). En route you'll pass stalls selling waterpipes and braziers, a nineteenth-century *sabil-kuttab* and a fifteenth-century mosque. Minibuses #68 and #75 run to the museum, but it's probably quicker to walk (about ten minutes). The neighbourhood between Bab Zwayla and the Abdin district is known as the **Bab el-Khalq quarter**, after a long-since-vanished medieval gate. On your right off Sharia Ahmed Maher, just before Sharia Bur Said (the entrance to the museum is off this street), is Darb es-Saada, a street of carpenters' workshops, which backs onto a local remand prison. Relatives of the inmates can often be seen on unofficial visits, lining the street and calling up to the windows of the cells.

The Museum of Islamic Art

Like so many things in Islamic Cairo, the **Museum of Islamic Art** at the junction of Sharia Ahmed Maher, Sharia Bur Said and Sharia Qalaa, 600m west of Bab Zwayla (see map p.165), is currently closed for refurbishment. However, it's worth checking with the tourist office if it has reopened (daily 9am–3pm, Friday closed for prayer: May–Sept 12.30–2pm, Oct–April 11.30am–1pm; £E30, students £E16), as it is an unmissable collection: bear in mind, though, that the layout and location of exhibits may have changed from those described below.

The museum is best visited midway through an exploration of Islamic Cairo, since the historic architecture lends meaning to the museum's artefacts, which, in turn, enhance your appreciation of the old city. It was the ruinous state of many of its mosques and mansions that impelled Khedive Tewfiq and the historians Herz and Cresswell to establish an Islamic collection in 1880. Pieces were stored in Al-Hakim's Mosque until 1902, when a museum was created on the ground floor of the imposing neo-Mamluke *Dar al-Kutub* (National Library) which houses it today.

Because Sunni Muslims extended the Koranic strictures against idolatry to any images of humans or animals, these are largely absent. Instead of paintings and statues, there are exquisite designs based on geometry, Islamic symbolism, plant motifs and Arabic calligraphy – a totally different aesthetic. You'll also notice that dates are given as AH – After the Hegira (Mohammed's flight from Mecca) – the starting point of Islamic chronology (622 AD by Western reckoning).

Touring the museum

The exhibition starts with some of the museum's most **recent acquisitions** in **Room 1**. Surrounded by Ottoman mosaics of polychrome marble, a single display case in **Room 2** contains objects from the **Umayyad period** (661–750). Among them is a bronze ewer with a spout in the form of a crowing cockerel, which probably belonged to the last Umayyad khalif of the Arab

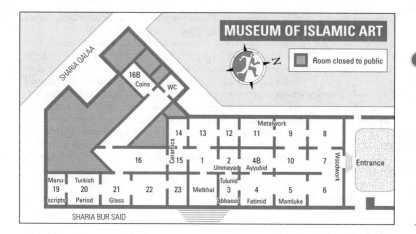

MUSEUM OF ISLAMIC ART

Room closed to public

SHARIA QALAA

16B
Coins
WC

Metalwork

14 13 12 11 9 8

Ceramics

16 15 1 2 4B 10 7
Ummayad Ayyubid

Woodwork

Entrance

Manu- Turkish Tulunid
19 20 21 22 23 Metkhal 3 4 5 6
scripts Period Glass Metkhal Abbassid Fatimid Mamluke

SHARIA BUR SAID

Empire, Marwan II, who was slain near Abu Sir. On his death, the Ummayads were succeeded by the Abbasid dynasty, who moved the capital of the khalifate from Damascus to Baghdad.

Brassware from the **Abbassid** period in **Room 3** includes the figure of a deer, not an animal much associated with the Middle East. Also here are ninth- and tenth-century Persian imitations of Chinese ceramics, showing how Chinese art influenced the Islamic world. The examples of **stucco** on the walls here show how it was developed into a high art form under the Abbassids, and especially in Iraq. From being deeply cut and crisply textured with relatively naturalistic vines and acanthus scrolls, stucco panels became increasingly abstract and flowing, no longer carved but moulded. Meanwhile under **Tulunid** rule in Egypt (868–905), three different styles from Samarra were also imitated in wood; compare the stucco panels with the woodwork from Al-Qitai.

Passing through a huge door from Sultan Qalaoun's *Maristan* into **Room 4**, you enter the **Fatimid era** (969–1171). As Shi'ites, the Fatimids had no doctrinal objection to depicting animals and birds (a theme popular amongst their co-religionists in Persia), as attested by **panels from the Western Palace**. Also exhibited are inlaid ivory and jewellery, rock crystal, painted **glassware**, and early **lustre ware** ceramics from Fustat. On the southern wall, **frescoes** from a Fustat bathhouse depict people and animals, not yet taboo at this time in Islamic art.

Room 4B (part of the main hall) is a lovely composite of Mamluke columns, an Ottoman fountain and floor, and intricate *mashrabiya* work from the **Ayyubid** period (1171–1250).

From Room 4, you enter **Room 5** under a collection of Ottoman-period stained-glass "moon windows" set in open plasterwork. Also in the doorway (on the right), a stone medallion once embedded in the wall of a building depicts a two-headed eagle and fire-breathing bull amongst a confusion of animal forms that all seem to belong to one body. The room itself covers the **Mamluke period** (1250–1517) and centres upon a lovely sunken mosaic fountain. Round about are displayed **mosque lamps** and stucco *mihrabs*; woven and printed textiles of linen and cotton; inlaid metalwork, polychrome pottery and a wooden **cenotaph from the El-Hussein Mosque**. At the far end of the room is a wooden door from the Mosque of Sultan Ayyub, bearing square *kufic* and cursive *naskhi* inscriptions. The **glassware** here is noticeably more sophisticated, painted with ornate calligraphy.

A pair of doors from the Al-Azhar Mosque leads into **Room 6**, the first of three rooms devoted to **woodwork**, whose evolution paralleled that of stuccos. The deeply incised, naturalistic forms of Umayyad woodcarving gave way to interlocking arches and concentric circles under the Abbassids, followed by bevelled, stylized birds and animals in Tulunid times. Gradually confined to small areas during the Fatimid era, figures were then progressively simplified into arabesques by Ayyubid craftsmen. However, representational art could still be found under the early Mamlukes, as evinced by a **frieze from Qalaoun's Maristan**, which shows hunting, music and dancing. Also featured in Room 6 are carved panels from the Western Palace, the original *mihrab* from Saiyida Ruqayya's Mashrad, and a portable prayer niche for use on military campaigns.

Room 7, opposite the entrance, contains a series of *mashrabiyas*, and a high-lighted **object of the month**. Hanging from the ceilings of rooms 7 to 11 are examples of the brass lanterns traditionally hung in mosques, though out of use in these days of electricity.

Room 8's treasures include three wooden **minbars** (pulpits), a panelled ceiling and a case of pieces originally inlaid in the geometric designs of *minbars*, ceilings, doors and furniture. The objects in the room's other display cases include wooden combs, ivory boxes, and a beautiful bone-inlaid panel depicting a hawk attacking a hare. Among the wooden panels on the wall, a frieze in Hebrew commemorates the building of a synagogue in the twelfth century by one Ibrahim el-Amshati.

Wooden panels overspill into **Room 9**, where caskets inlaid with ivory and mother-of-pearl rather show up the shoddy workmanship of the goods nowadays sold to tourists in the Khan. Bronze **mirrors** and brass lamps inaugurate the museum's **metalwork** section, but the room's most striking pieces are a Persian brass candlestick in the form of two intertwined snakes and, among the **figurines** by the west wall, a little man on a horse saying "Look, no hands!". What looks like a horse-headed cigar-cutter in the same case is in fact a chopper for betel nut, a stimulant much used in India and Southeast Asia, but not in the Middle East.

Room 10, next door, reflects Ottoman tastes in interior design. Beneath an **exquisitely coffered ceiling**, guests could socialize around a graceful fountain, secretly overlooked by the women of the household. The furnishings in here date from the seventeenth and eighteenth centuries.

From Mosul in Iraq came the technique of inlaying copper or silver into bronze, which was to characterize Egyptian **metalwork**. A brass-plated door from the Mosque of Salih Tala'i stands at the entrance to **Room 11**. Inside you'll find candlesticks and caskets; incense burners inlaid with gold and silver (some with Christian symbols); a fourteenth-century hand-warmer; and a case of astrolabes, used by Muslim navigators.

Room 12 contains a fraction of the Mamluke **Armoury** (most of which was taken to Istanbul by Selim the Grim). Case 7, on the left of the door to Room 11, holds the swords of Mehmet II and Suleyman the Magnificent (the respective conquerors of Constantinople and the Balkans). Daggers on the west wall include one with an exquisite enamelled Persian scabbard of the fifteenth or sixteenth century.

Room 13 takes us back to the Fatimid period, with a display of lustreware decorated with people and animals in the northeasterly of the room's four main display cases. The relatively primitive nature of this decoration is shown up by the metallic blue Mina'i ware in the southwest case. In the northwest case, and on the west wall, tiny glass vessels are the ancestors of today's ornate perfume bottles.

Room 14 contains more ceramics, mainly Persian, including blue wall-tiles. Ceramics in Room 15 include tiles found at Fustat that originated in Tunisia, Andalusia and Christian Europe, showing the extent of the city's commercial reach, and including blue Delft tiles from Holland. Also here are stone moulds used for casting metal ornaments.

The dominant exhibit in Room 16 is a blue-tiled nineteenth-century Turkish fireplace. At the southern end of the room, a section of an old kuttab (Koranic school) from Rosetta incorporates a niche for the teacher to sit beneath its *murqana*'d ceiling. Among the ceramics, notice the *ahlaq* (chokes) that were inserted in the necks of Fatimid water jars to regulate their flow, fretted with bird, animal and calligraphic motifs. The room also contains stucco *mihrabs* and nineteenth-century Turkish prayer rugs. A diversion from Room 16 takes you down a passage whose walls are decked with stone inscriptions, to Room 16B, used to display coins, weights, medals and glass seals, but currently closed.

At the museum's southern end, Room 19 showcases calligraphy and book-binding, including Persian and Indian illustrated manuscripts, but primacy is accorded to the word of God, with numerous medieval Korans from the collection of King Farouk. The first mass-produced, totally standardized Korans were made in Egypt following Napoleon's introduction of the printing press; Cairo is still the main publishing centre of the Arab world.

Room 20 is stuffed with Ottoman material, including seventeenth- and eighteenth-century wall-tiles depicting the Kaaba at Mecca, Islam's holiest site, and the Prophet's Mosque at Medina, Mohammed's burial place. Among the room's less pious offerings is a beautifully made *sheesha* pipe from Istanbul.

Room 21 is devoted to Egyptian glass. Various techniques perfected in ancient times continued to be used; lustreware (a Fatimid speciality) and enamelled glass were the chief innovations in the Islamic period. Among the mosque lamps and eighth- to fourteenth-century perfume jars, a large hour-glass stands out as the most prominent exhibit.

Amongst the Persian objects of the ninth to seventeenth centuries in Room 22 are three ceramic figurines of animals: a camel with a litter on its back by the west wall and a lion by the east wall, both in cobalt blue; plus, by the east wall, a hoopoe glazed in turquoise.

Like the neighbouring *metkhal* (entrance hall), Room 23 is used for temporary exhibitions.

Between the Bab Zwayla and the Citadel

There are two basic walking routes between the Bab Zwayla and the Citadel: via the Qasaba, Sharia al-Muizz and Sharia Qalaa; or following the old Darb al-Ahmar (after which this quarter of Islamic Cairo is named). It's possible to get the best of both worlds by combining the Darb al-Ahmar with a detour into the Qasaba and Saddlemakers Bazaar, located on the other route: a total distance of about 1500m. Assuming you're starting from the Bab Zwayla as in the itinerary below, it's logical to visit the Qasaba before embarking on the Darb al-Ahmar; whereas the reverse holds true if you're coming from the Citadel. Starting with the "Blue Mosque" of Aqsunqur on Sharia Bab al-Wazir (the Citadel end of Darb al-Ahmar), you can backtrack through the text from there.

From the Bab Zwayla into the Qasaba

Emerging from the Bab Zwayla, you'll see a cluster of Islamic monuments across the street, which is often flooded by burst water mains. On the right-hand corner stands a Sufi establishment, the Zawiya of Farag ibn Barquq

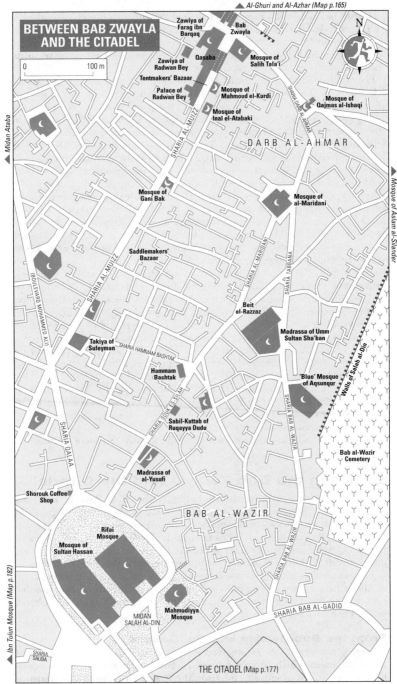

▲ Al-Ghuri and Al-Azhar (Map p.165)

BETWEEN BAB ZWAYLA AND THE CITADEL

0   100 m

N

Zawiya of Farag ibn Barqaq

Bab Zwayla

Qasaba

Mosque of Salih Tala'i

Zawiya of Radwan Bey

Tentmakers' Bazaar

Palace of Radwan Bey

Mosque of Mahmoud el-Kurdi

Mosque of Qajmas al-Ishaqi

Mosque of Inal el-Atabaki

DARB AL-AHMAR

◄ Midan Ataba

Mosque of Gani Bak

Mosque of al-Maridani

SHARIA AL-MUIZZ

SHARIA DARB AL-AHMAR

► Mosque of Aslam al-Silander

Saddlemakers' Bazaar

SHARIA AL-MARIDANI

SHARIA TABBANA

SHARIA AL-MUIZZ

(BOULEVARD MOHAMMED ALI)

Beit el-Razzaz

Madrassa of Umm Sultan Sha'ban

Takiya of Suleyman

SHARIA HAMMAM BASHTAK

Hammam Bashtak

'Blue' Mosque of Aqsunqur

Walls of Salah al-Din

Sabil-Kuttab of Ruqayya Dudu

SHARIA SOUK ES-SILAH

Bab al-Wazir Cemetery

Madrassa of al-Yusufi

SHARIA BAB AL-WAZIR

Shorouk Coffee Shop

SHARIA QALAA

BAB AL-WAZIR

Rifai Mosque

Mosque of Sultan Hassan

◄ Ibn Tulun Mosque (Map p.182)

SHARIA BAB AL-WAZIR

SHARIA BAB AL-GADID

Mahmudiyya Mosque

MIDAN SALAH AL-DIN

SHARIA SALIBA

THE CITADEL (Map p.177)

▼ Southern Cemetery (Map p.182)

(currently closed for restoration), whose inlaid marble lintels and *ablaq* panels may be hidden by stalls. Opposite the *zawiya*, the **Mosque of Salih Tala'i** withdraws behind an elegant portico with five keel arches – a unique architectural feature. The shops around its base (whose rents contributed to the mosque's upkeep) were once at street level, but this has risen well over a metre since the mosque was built in 1408. The shops have been restored, but are as yet unoccupied. The last of Cairo's Fatimid mosques, the building shows an assured use of the motifs that were first employed on the Mosque of Al-Aqmar: ribbed and cusped arches and panels, carved tie beams and rosettes. Notice the capitals, plundered from pre-Islamic buildings, and the "floriated kufic" script around the arches.

Straight ahead lies the **Qasaba**, where colourful fabrics, appliqué and leather-work are piled in dens ranked either side of a gloomy, lofty passageway, still shored up by beams after the 1992 earthquake. Erected by Ridwan Bey in 1650, this is one of the best-preserved examples of a covered market left in Cairo. It is popularly known as the Khiyamiyya, or **Tentmakers Bazaar**, as colourful printed fabrics are used here to make tents for moulids and weddings and to screen unsightly building work – a big improvement on tarpaulins. Printed fabric is sold by the metre, quite cheaply; labour-intensive appliqué work is much pricier (see "Shopping", p.281).

Beyond the Qasaba

Emerging from the southern end of the Qasaba, **Sharia al-Muizz** extends its path between two mosques and the facade of Ridwan Bey's former palace, beyond which the monuments thin out as vegetable stalls and butchers congest the narrow street. By Mamluke times most of the older quarters here were semi-derelict, merging into the "Tartar Ruins" near the Citadel. The Tartars, recruited by Sultan Kitbugha (1296–96), were despised by other Mamlukes as horse-eaters and billeted in a quarter that's long since disappeared. About 150m on you'll pass the **Mosque of Gani Bak**, a protégé of Sultan Barsbey, who was poisoned by rivals at the age of 25. Beyond, a few stalls selling donkey- and camel-wear constitute what remains of the Souk es-Surugiyyah, or **Saddle-makers Bazaar**, formerly the centre of Cairo's leather industry.

Assuming you don't turn back here to pursue the Darb al-Ahmar, it's a fairly mundane 350-metre walk to Al-Muizz's junction with **Sharia Qalaa**. The Sultan Hassan and Rifai mosques below the Citadel are plainly visible at the boulevard's southern end, 300m away. Alternatively, use bus services in the opposite direction to reach the Islamic Arts Museum, 1km up Sharia Qalaa. Some of the buses continue on to Midan Ataba, others to Abdin or Al-Azhar.

Along the Darb al-Ahmar

An alternative, more picturesque route towards the Citadel follows the "Red Road", or **Darb al-Ahmar**, which is plied by two minibus routes: #68 from Midan Ramses, and #75 from Midan Tahrir. Originally a cemetery beyond the southern walls of the Fatimid city, this quarter became a fashionable residential area in the fourteenth century, as Al-Nasir developed the Citadel. The thoroughfare acquired its present name in 1805, when Mohammed Ali tricked the Mamlukes into staging a coup before slaughtering them. Stuffed with straw, their heads were sent to Constantinople as a sign of his power; six years later the surviving Mamlukes fell for another ruse, and were massacred in the Citadel (see p.176).

Start by walking 150m east from Salih Tila'i's Mosque near the Bab Zwayla. On the corner where the Darb turns south, the **Mosque of Qajmas al-Ishaqi** looms over workshops sunk beneath street level. A marble panel with swirling leaf forms in red, black and white surmounts the entrance to a vestibule with a gilded ceiling; left off this is the mosque itself. Notice the sinuous decorations on the *mihrab* (incised grooves filled with red paste or bitumen) and the fine panelling on the floor near the *qibla* wall (ask the custodian to lift a mat). Best of all are the stained-glass windows in the tomb chamber occupied by one Abu Hurayba. A raised passage connects the mosque with a *sabil-kuttab* across the street; both were built in the 1480s.

A short detour: Al-Silahdar's Mosque

If you're not pushed for time, consider detouring off the Darb to visit the **Mosque of Aslam al-Silahdar**. From Qajmas's Mosque, walk through the tunnel around the side and on past a shrine where the street forks (either one will do); Al-Silahdar's Mosque lies 250m ahead. The marble panel outside is typical of exterior decoration during the Bahri Mamluke period; inside, the layout is that of a cruciform **madrassa**. Students used to live in rooms above the north and south *liwans*, behind an ornate facade of stucco mouldings and screened windows. The mosque's founder was a Qipchak Mamluke who lost his position as swordbearer after Sultan al-Nasir believed rumours spread by his enemies, and imprisoned him, only to reinstate Aslam as *silahdar* ("sword-bearer") six years later. To return to the Darb, either retrace your steps or take the street running southwest off the square, which joins the Darb further south, beyond Al-Maridani's Mosque.

South along the Darb Al-Ahmar

South from the Qajmas Mosque, the Darb al-Ahmar passes the **Mosque of Al-Maridani**, built in 1340 and still a peaceful retreat from the streets. The mosque is usually entered via its northern portal, offset by a stalactite frieze with complex patterns of joggled voussoirs and *ablaq* panels. Inside, a splendid *mashrabiya* screen separates the open courtyard from the *qibla riwaq*, whose stained-glass windows and variegated columns (Mamluke, pre-Islamic and pharaonic) can be glimpsed through the lattice. Because it was economical with wood and minimized the effect of warping in a hot, dry climate, *mashrabiya*-work was an ideal technique for Egyptian craftsmen. Architecturally speaking, the minaret marks the replacement of the Ayyubid "pepperpot" finial by a small dome on pillars, which became the hallmark of Mamluke minarets. Below the dome and above the *minbar*, arboreal forms in stucco may allude to the Koranic verse, "A good word is as a good tree – its roots firm, its branches in heaven".

Leaving via the southern entrance, you'll need to turn left to rejoin the Darb – or **Sharia Tabbana** as it's called at this point. Roughly 200m on, past a small Turkish mosque, stands the hulking **Madrassa of Umm Sultan Sha'ban**, currently closed to the public due to restoration work. Umm ("Mother of") Sha'ban was the concubine of a son of Al-Nasir, whose own son erected the madrassa (1368–69) as a gesture of gratitude after he became sultan at the age of ten; murdered in 1376, he preceded her to the grave and was buried here since his own madrassa was unfinished. A wealth of *murqanas* and *ablaq* rims the entrance, which is flanked by a *sabil* and a drinking trough. Watering animals was meritorious in the eyes of Islam; the Prophet himself had seen a prostitute give water to a thirsty dog, and promised her, "For this action you shall enter paradise". Behind the mosque, and entered through the neighbouring doorway (no.56), lurks the **Beit al-Razzaz**, a rambling, derelict palace, also currently closed for restoration.

Further along the street, now called **Sharia Bab al-Wazir** after the Gate of the Vizier that once stood here, lies the **"Blue Mosque"** or **Mosque of Aqsun-qur**, which is directly accessible via #68 minibus from Midan Ramses and the Bab Zwayla, or #75 from Midan Tahir, but is currently closed for restoration. When originally built in 1347, the mosque was plainer, its *ablaq* arches framing a *sahn*, now battered and dusty, with a palm tree and chirping birds. The Iznik-style tiles (imported from Turkey or Syria) were added in the 1650s by Ibrahim Agha, who usurped and redecorated the fourteenth-century mosque. The indigo and turquoise tiles on the *qibla* wall – with cypresses, tulips and other floral motifs either side of the magnificently inlaid *mihrab* – were added at the same time. Along with similar tiles around the tomb of Ibrahim Agha in the mosque's southwest corner, they were probably made in Damascus, and explain the mosque's name and its popularity with tourists.

The marble *minbar*, inlaid with salmon, plum, green and grey stone, is from the original building. The recently restored circular minaret, also original, affords a superb **view** of the Citadel, and on a clear day you can even make out the Pyramids on the far side of the city.

The mosque's founder, Shams al-Din Aqsunqur, intrigued against the successors of Sultan al-Nasir, his father-in-law – whose son Al-Ashraf Kuchuk (Little One) was enthroned at the age of six, "reigned" five months, and was strangled by his brother three years later. The reign of Al-Kamil Sha'ban (not to be confused with Sha'ban II, who erected the madrassa) lasted a year, ending in a palace coup and the crowning of his brother-in-law, Muzaffar Hadji. Recalling how Aqsunqur had manipulated Kuchuk (who's buried just inside the mosque's entrance) and deftly organized the coup against Sha'ban, Muzaffar promptly had him garrotted.

From this mosque, Bab al-Wazir gradually slopes up to meet the approach road **to the Citadel**. If that's your destination, turn left and keep climbing.

A couple of hundred metres west of the blue mosque, the **Hammam Bashtak** was a bathhouse serving the Darb al-Ahmar quarter, many of whose tenements lack washing facilities, but like most of Islamic Cairo's traditional steam bathhouses, it is currently closed. Its elaborate portal is worth a second glance, however, the ribbed keel arch bearing the napkin symbol of a *jamdar* or "Master of Robes". In Mamluke society, this position ranked below the "Men of the Sword" (cabinet ministers, chosen from the Amirs of One Hundred), but was on a par with the sultan's Taster, Cup-Bearer, Slipper-Holder and Polo-Stick Keeper. Several Mamlukes who became sultans included their former rank (or slave price) among their titles.

To reach the Citadel from the hammam, walk 300m down **Sharia Souk es-Silah** (formerly the Weapons Bazaar, now a second-hand ballbearings market), past the neglected gingerbread facade of the **Sabil-Kuttab of Ruqayya Dudu** at no.41, and the **Madrassa of al-Yusufi**, whose founder was a Cup-Bearer.

The Citadel and around

The Citadel is the natural focus of a visit to Islamic Cairo; the area just below it, around Midan Salah al-Din, features two of the city's greatest monuments – the **Sultan Hassan** and **Rifai mosques**. To do justice to these, and to the Citadel itself, you need a good half a day.

To reach the Citadel area, you can either catch a taxi from downtown (£E5–8) or a bus (see p.114 for bus routes) – if you've got the energy, it's also an interesting walk. Any of these approaches will leave you beneath the Citadel, either on Midan Salah al-Din or lower down behind the Sultan Hassan and Rifai mosques. Note, however, that the actual **entrance** to the Citadel is over a kilometre's walk from Midan Salah al-Din, which is where most Cairenes will assume you want to go if you just ask for the Citadel (*al-Qalaa* – usually pronounced "al-'Alaa").

Depending on how much time you have, you may only want to visit the Citadel, but it is well worth stopping in Midan Salah al-Din to take in the arresting mix of sounds and the views (see below). For information on moving on from the Citadel and connecting up with other walking itineraries, see p.181.

Midan Salah al-Din

Humdrum traffic islands and monumental grandeur meet beneath the Citadel on **Midan Salah al-Din**, where makeshift swings and colourful tents are pitched for local moulids. With an audience of lesser mosques on the sidelines, the scene is set for a confrontation of the square's two behemoths, given voice when the **muezzins** call. Both the **Rifai** and **Sultan Hassan mosques** have powerfully voiced muezzins whose duet echoes off the surrounding tenements. This amazing aural experience is best enjoyed from one of the seats on the sidewalk outside the **Shorouk coffee shop**, behind the two mosques on the corner of Sharia Sultan Hassan and Sharia Qalaa. From this vantage point you can survey both mosques, built so close as to create a knife-sharp, almost perpetually shadowed canyon between them. The dramatic angles and chiaroscuro, coupled with the great stalactite portal on this side of the Rifai, make this facade truly spectacular, although the view from the Citadel itself takes some beating. A few centuries ago, all this area would have been swarming with mounted Mamlukes, escorting the sultan to polo matches or prayers.

The Citadel

The Citadel (daily 8am–5pm; mosques closed Fri except for prayer; museums refuse entry 30min before closing; £E35, students £E20) presents the most dramatic feature of Cairo's skyline: a centuries-old bastion crowned by the needle-like minarets of the great Mosque of Mohammed Ali. The entrance at Bab al-Gabal is on the opposite side of the Citadel, a good kilometre's walk from Midan Salah al-Din, but can be reached by minibus #154 from Abdel Mouneem Riyad terminal near Midan Tahrir, or by service taxi microbuses from Ramses and Ataba along Sharia Salah Selim.

The whole fortified complex was begun by **Salah al-Din**, the founder of the Ayyubid dynasty – known throughout Christendom as Saladin, the Crusaders' chivalrous foe. Salah al-Din's reign (1171–93) saw much fortification of the city, though it was his nephew, Al-Kamil, who developed the Citadel as a royal residence, later to be replaced by the palaces of Sultan al-Nasir.

The main features of the Citadel as it is today, however, are associated with **Mohammed Ali**, a worthy successor to the Mamlukes and Turks. In 1811 he feasted 470 leading Mamlukes in the Citadel palace, bade them farewell with honours, then had them ambushed in the sloping lane behind the **Bab al-Azab**, the locked gate (now closed to the public) opposite the Akhur Mosque. An oil painting in the Manial Palace on Roda Island depicts the apocryphal tale of a Mamluke who escaped by leaping the walls on his horse; in reality he survived by not attending the feast.

On entering the Citadel, you keep the wall to your right and follow it round into the southern courtyard of the **southern enclosure**, most of whose buildings are currently closed for restoration, among them the former **Mint**. A

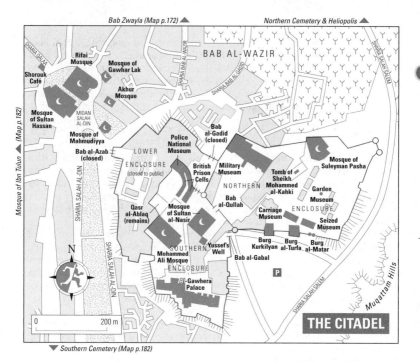

BAB AL-WAZIR

Rifai Mosque
Mosque of Gawhar Lak
Shorouk Café
Akhur Mosque
Mosque of Sultan Hassan
MIDAN SALAH AL-DIN
Mosque of Mahmudiyya
Bab al-Azab (closed)
Police National Museum
Bab al-Gadid (closed)
LOWER ENCLOSURE (closed to public)
British Prison Cells
Military Museum
NORTHERN ENCLOSURE
Tomb of Sheikh Mohammed al-Kahki
Mosque of Suleyman Pasha
Garden Museum
Qasr al-Ablaq (remains)
Mosque of Sultan al-Nasir
Bab al-Qullah
Carriage Museum
Seized Museum
Yussef's Well
Burg Kurkilyan
Burg al-Turfa
Burg al-Matar
SOUTHERN ENCLOSURE
Mohammed Ali Mosque
Bab al-Gabal
Bab al-Gabal
Al-Gawhera Palace
Muqattam Hills

Mosque of Ibn Tulun ▲ (Map p.182)

SHARIA SALAH AL-DIN

SHARIA SALAH AL-DIN

N

0   200 m

THE CITADEL

passage from the courtyard's north side leads through to the central courtyard; to the left of this passage, stairs lead up to the back of the Citadel's most dominant structure, the Mosque of Mohammed Ali.

Mohammed Ali's monuments

The **Mohammed Ali Mosque**, which so ennobles Cairo's skyline, disappoints at close quarters: its domes are sheathed in tin, its alabaster surfaces grubby. Nonetheless, it exudes *folie de grandeur*, starting with the ornate clock given by Louis Philippe (in exchange for the obelisk in the Place de la Concorde, Paris), which has never worked; and the Turkish Baroque ablutions fountain, resembling a giant Easter egg. Inside the mosque, whose lofty dome and semi-domes are decorated like a Fabergé egg, the use of space is classically Ottoman, reminiscent of the great mosques of Istanbul. A constellation of chandeliers and globe lamps illuminates Thuluth inscriptions, a gold-scalloped *mihrab* and two *minbars*, one faced in alabaster, the other strangely Art Nouveau. Mohammed Ali is buried beneath a white marble cenotaph, behind a bronze grille on the right of the entrance. The mosque itself was erected between 1824 and 1848, but the domes had to be demolished and rebuilt in the 1930s.

Due south of Mohammed Ali's Mosque is the entrance to what remains of his **Al-Gawhara Palace**, where he waited while the Mamlukes were butchered. Also known as the Bijou ("Jewelled") Palace, its French-style salons contain a dusty display of nineteenth-century dress, royal furniture and tableware. Its most notable exhibit, however, is a mother-of-pearl model of Jerusalem's Dome of the Rock. Somewhere in this vicinity is the spot where St Francis of Assisi attempted to preach Christianity to the Ayyubid ruler Al-Kamil.

Medieval remains

For an idea of the Citadel's appearance before Mohammed Ali's grandiose reconstruction programme, descend from the Mohammed Ali Mosque's front entrance into the Citadel's central courtyard. On your right, at the end of the passage from the southern courtyard, is the **Mosque of Sultan al-Nasir** (also called the Mosque of Ibn Qalaoun, after Al-Nasir's father). Unlike other Citadel mosques, this one is open to sightseers on Fridays as it is not used for prayers.

The Mamlukes and the Mongols of Persia enjoyed good relations when the mosque was constructed (1318–35), and a Tabriz master mason probably designed the corkscrew minarets with their bulbous finials and faïence decorations, if not the dome, which also smacks of Central Asia. Since Selim the Grim carted its marble panelling back to Turkey, the mosque's courtyard has looked ruggedly austere, with rough-hewn pillars supporting *ablaq* arches linked by Fatimid-style tie-beams – although the *mihrab* itself is a feast of gold and marble. Notice the stepped merlons around the parapet, and the blue, white and silver decorations beneath the sanctuary *liwan*.

If you leave the mosque, turn right and walk clockwise around it, you'll find a wasteland with barbicans at the far end. There, a locked gate prevents admission to **Yussef's Well**, which spirals down 97m to the level of the Nile, whence water percolates through fissures in the bedrock. Dug by prisoners between 1176 and 1182, this so-called "Well of the Snail" had its steps strewn with soil to provide a footing for the donkeys that carried up water jars. The Citadel's infamous Jubb dungeon, "a noisome pit where foul and deadly exhalations, unclean vermin and bats rendered the pitchy darkness more horrible", was blocked up by Al-Nasir in 1329, but reactivated under the latterday Mamluke sultans.

The Police National Museum

On the northwestern side of the central enclosure, a gate leads through to another courtyard, at whose northern end is the **Police National Museum**. As you pass through the gateway, the door to your right (with a plaque that reads "Citadel's Prison Museum") leads to **cells** that were used when the Citadel was a prison. Famous detainees included Anwar Sadat, arrested by the British for wartime espionage (see p.215), as well as Sayed Kuttub, the Islamist idealogue executed for treason in 1966, whose ideas inspired the Muslim Brotherhood and the likes of Osama Bin Laden. Although the cells are currently closed to the public, they are being cleaned up in preparation for future opening.

The quirky **exhibition** in the museum covers some of Egypt's most sensational murders and assassinations, although the most infamous of all – Anwar Sadat's – is conspicuously absent. The main hall features portraits of interior ministers since 1878, and its rooms (going round clockwise) begin with one on Pharaonic Egypt, including weapons of the time and an explanation of the conspiracy to assassinate Ramses III. The next room, incongruously labelled "Islamic Period", shows photos taken after the assassination of Lord Moyne by members of the maverick Zionist paramilitary group, the Stern Gang, in Zamalek in 1944. Also featured here are 1940s Assyut gangster Al-Khott, and female serial killers Rayya and Sakina, whose grizzly murders of nearly thirty young girls for their jewellery led to the duo's execution in 1921. The next room has a scale model of Ismailiya barracks illustrating the 1952 Battle of Ismailiya (see p.685) that galvanized public opinion against the British occupation. The incident is further illustrated with photos and artefacts. The "Forgery and Counterfeiting" room contains the death mask of murderer Mahmoud Amin Mahmoud Soleiman, as well as a press for counterfeiting banknotes; forged coins and bills further illustrate the theme. Fake ancient coins appear in the "Confiscations" room, along with ancient artefacts seized from smugglers attempting to export them illegally.

There is a superb **view** of the entire city from the terrace outside the Police Museum, where you'll also find **toilets** and a **café**. At the southern end, in a pit, are the **excavated remains of the Qasr al-Ablaq**, or Striped Palace of Sultan al-Nasir. For many of the hapless boy-sultans chosen by the Mamlukes, the palace amounted to a luxury prison, and finally an execution cell. Nevertheless, the Citadel remained the residence of Egypt's rulers for nearly 700 years, and Mohammed Ali prophesied that his descendants would rule supreme as long as they resided here. Ismail's move to the Abdin Palace did indeed foreshadow an inexorable decline in their power.

The Northern Enclosure

Passing through the Bab al-Qullah, you'll enter the Citadel's northern enclosure, open to visitors despite a military presence. Straight ahead, beyond a parade of Soviet- and US-made tanks from four Arab–Israeli Wars, Mohammed Ali's old Harim Palace is occupied by the **Military Museum**. This vast exhibition devotes more space to ceremonial accoutrements than the savage realities of war, and even pacifists should enjoy the main salon, with its spectacular trompe l'oeil. While in a military vein, it's worth recalling that the Citadel fell to Mohammed Ali after he stationed cannons on the Muqattam heights. The military electronics that festoon them now are a reminder that strategic ground seldom loses its utility.

By turning right at the barracks near the enclosure entrance and following the lane around, you'll come out into a compound with a formal garden. This "**Garden Museum**" is unshaded but decorated with assorted columns, the odd nineteenth-century gateway, and – its centrepiece – the top of a minaret from the 1441 mosque of Qaitbey al-Jatkasi. To its south is the **Carriage Museum**, with its row of horseheads. Inside are six royal carriages and two picnic buggies, one of them an infant prince's; the largest state carriage – heavy with gold – was presented as a gift to Khedive Ismail by Emperor Napoleon and Empress Eugénie.

Just beyond is the small **Seized Museum** (currently closed for refurbishment), displaying various pharaonic, Roman, Coptic and Islamic antiquities recovered from smugglers before they left Egypt. Exhibits in the first room include, in the first display case on the right, the mummy of an ibis before which sits a little man in supplication, plus whole sarcophagi from the late Pharaonic period. The second room contains Coptic icons, antique manuscripts, glassware and pistols, all charmingly labelled "misdemeanor no. 738", "misdemeanor no. 1296" and the like.

Behind here are two of the many bastions along the Citadel's ramparts, each with evocative names. Although the derivation of **Burg Kirkilyan** (Tower of the Forty Serpents) is unknown, the **Burg al-Matar** (Tower of the Flight Platform) probably housed the royal carrier pigeons. Neither can be entered, but it's worth visiting a neglected treasure at the other end of the compound. A cluster of verdigris domes and a pencil-sharp minaret identify the **Mosque of Suleyman Pasha** as an early sixteenth-century Ottoman creation, borne out by the lavish arabesques and rosettes adorning the interior of the cupola and semi-domes. Inside, cross the courtyard to find a **mausoleum** where the tombs of amirs and their families have *tabuts* indicating their rank: turbans or hats for the men, floral-patterned *lingam*-like rods for the women. Adjacent to the courtyard is a **madrassa** where students took examinations beneath a *riwaq* upheld by painted beams.

The Mosque of Sultan Hassan

The **Mosque of Sultan Hassan** (daily except Fri 8am–10pm, Fri 8am–1pm & 2.30–5pm; £E12, students £E6) stands on Midan Salah al-Din, facing the Citadel. Raised at the command of a son of Al-Nasir, the Sultan Hassan Mosque was unprecedentedly huge in scale when it was begun in 1356, and some design flaws soon became apparent. The plan to have a minaret at each corner was abandoned after the one directly above the entrance collapsed, killing 300 people. Hassan himself was assassinated in 1391, two years before the mosque's completion. After another minaret toppled in 1659, the weakened dome collapsed; and if this wasn't enough, the roof was also used as an artillery platform during coups against sultans Barquq (1391) and Tumanbey (1517). But the mosque is big enough to withstand a lot of battering: 150m long, covering an area of 7906 square metres, its walls rise to 36m and its tallest minaret to 68m.

The mosque is best seen when the morning sun illuminates its deep courtyard and cavernous mausoleum, revealing subtle colours and textures disguised by shadows later in the day. Entering beneath a towering stalactite hood, you're drawn by instinct through a gloomy domed vestibule with *liwans*, out into the central **sahn** – a stupendous balancing of mass and void. Vaulted **liwans** soar on four sides, their height emphasized by hanging lamp chains, their maws by red-and-black rims, all set off by a bulbous-domed ablutions fountain (probably an Ottoman addition). Each *liwan* was devoted to teaching a rite of Sunni Islam, providing theological justification for the cruciform plan the Mamlukes strove to achieve regardless of the site. At Sultan Hassan, four **madrassas** have been skilfully fitted into an irregular area behind the *liwans* to maintain the internal cruciform.

Soft-hued marble inlay and a band of monumental *kufic* script distinguish the sanctuary *liwan* from its roughly plastered neighbours. To the right of the *mihrab* is a bronze door, exquisitely worked with radiating stars and satellites in gold and silver; on the other side is **Hassan's mausoleum**. Cleverly sited to derive *baraka* from prayers to Mecca, while overlooking his old stamping grounds, the mausoleum is sombre beneath its restored dome, upheld by stalactite pendentives. Around the chamber runs a carved and painted *Thuluth* inscription, from the Throne verse of the Koran. Note also the ivory-inlaid *kursi*, or Koranic lectern.

The Rifai and Amir Akhur mosques

Adjoining Sultan Hassan, the **Rifai Mosque** (daily except Fri 8am–10pm, Fri 8am–1pm & 2.30–5pm; £E12, students £E6) is pseudo-Mamluke, built between 1869 and 1912 for Princess Khushyar, the mother of Khedive Ismail. With the royal entrance now closed, you enter on the side facing Sultan Hassan. Straight ahead in a sandalwood enclosure lies the **tomb of Sheikh Ali al-Rifai**, founder of the Rifai *tariqa* of dervishes, whose moulid occurs during the sixth month of the Muslim calendar, *Gumad el-Tani*. Off to your left are the *mashrabiya*-screened **tombs of King Fouad** (who reigned 1917–36), his mother, the last **Shah of Iran** and **King Farouk** of Egypt (who likewise died in exile). The monumental sanctuary (on the left) is impressive, but after Ismail's chief eunuch had overseen its forty-four columns, nineteen types of marble, eighteen window grilles costing £E1000 apiece, and £E25,000 dispersed on gold leaf, dowdiness was scarcely possible: what it lacks is the power of simplicity embodied by the mosques of Ibn Tulun and Sultan Hassan.

Finally, facing the Citadel, you can't miss the **Mosque of Amir Akhur** (on the left), with its bold red-and-white *ablaq*, breast-like dome and double minaret finial, incorporating a *sabil-kuttab* at the lower end of its sloping site.

On from the Citadel

Of the various routes you could take from the Citadel, the shortest (covered below) takes you to the awesome Mosque of Ibn Tulun, whilst the longest ones (requiring transport, and covered on pp.186–187) involve the Cities of the Dead. The route along the Darb al-Ahmar/Sharia Bab al-Wazir from the Bab Zwayla is covered on pp.171–175; you could pick up the trail at the Blue Mosque (p.175) and follow the text in reverse.

The Mosque of Ibn Tulun and the Saiyida Zeinab quarter

Two aspects of Islam are strikingly apparent in the great **Mosque of Ibn Tulun** and the quarter of the city named after Egypt's beloved saint, **Saiyida Zeinab**. The mosque evokes the simplicity of Islam's central tenet, submission to Allah, whereas the surrounding neighbourhoods are urban stews seething with popular cults. **Zeinab's moulid** is the wildest festival in Cairo, sucking 500,000 people into a pulsing vortex around her mosque, 1km west of Ibn Tulun's. Its high-octane blend of intense devotion and sheer enjoyment is also characteristic of **other moulids** honouring Saiyida Nafisa, Ruqayya and Aisha, whose shrines lie between Ibn Tulun and El-Khalifa (the Southern Cemetery).

The following section covers only Ibn Tulun, Saiyida Zeinab and sites along Sharia Saliba, which are shown in relation to the Citadel and Southern Cemetery on the **map** on p.182. Conceivably, you could visit all of them in a single day – though a more leisurely approach would allow you more time to take them in.

Approaches to the quarter

Buses #72// and #160/ provide the easiest access to Saiyida Zeinab **from Midan Tahrir**, running through the quarter past its namesake shrine and within sight of Ibn Tulun's Mosque, towards the Citadel, and on to the Mausoleum of Al-Shafi in the Southern Cemetery. Alternatively, bus #840 runs **from Midan Ataba**. There is also a **metro station** within five to ten minutes' walk from Midan Saiyada Zeinab.

Alternatively, the fifteen-minute walk **from the Mosque of Sultan Hassan** to Ibn Tulun takes you along **Sharia Saliba**, past a prison that serves as a barometer of law and order: whenever there's been a crackdown you can see several arms thrust from each cell window. Next comes the lofty **Sabil-Kuttab of Qaitbey**, with its bold red, white and black facade, now beautifully restored and housing an Islamic Civilization Library. Further along, beyond the **Khanqah of Shaykhu** (currently under restoration), Sharia el-Khalifa turns off **towards the Southern Cemetery**, as described in the following section, "Cities of the Dead". By ignoring this and carrying on past the nineteenth-century *sabil* of **Umm Abbas**, with its blue-and-red panels and gilt calligraphy, you'll see the huge walls of Ibn Tulun's Mosque on the left. Its entrance is that way, too. The portal on the main street belongs not to Ibn Tulun but to the adjoining recently restored **Madrassa of Sarghatmish**. The courtyard, resplendent in white marble inlaid with red, black and green porphyry, is absolutely stunning, with a cool, light feel that makes a pleasant change from the rather heavy architecture of Cairo's classic mosques. It centres around a fountain surmounted with an *oba* (canopy), and surrounded by the cell-like quarters formerly used by its students. The Sarghatmish who had the madrassa built, a Mamluke commander assassinated on the orders of Sultan Hassan in 1358, is interred in an adjoining chamber.

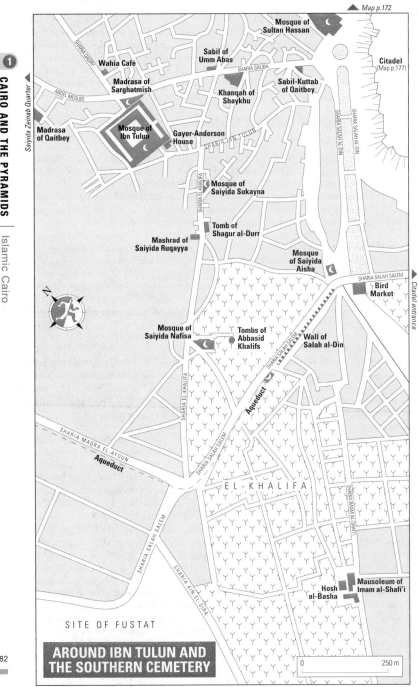

▲ Map p.172

Mosque of Sultan Hassan

Citadel (Map p.177)

Sabil of Umm Abas

SHARIA SALIBA

Wahia Café

◄ Saiyida Zeinab Quarter

SHARIA QADRY

ABDEL MEGUID

Madrasa of Sarghatmish

Khanqah of Shaykhu

Sabil-Kuttab of Qaitbey

SHARIA SALAH AL-DIN

Madrasa of Qaitbey

Mosque of Ibn Tulun

Gayer-Anderson House

SHARIA IBN TULUN

SHARIA EL-KHALIFA

Mosque of Saiyida Sukayna

Tomb of Shagur al-Durr

Mashrad of Saiyida Ruqayya

Mosque of Saiyida Aisha

SHARIA SALAH SALEM

Bird Market

Citadel entrance ►

N

Mosque of Saiyida Nafisa

Tombs of Abbasid Khalifs

Wall of Salah al-Din

SHARIA SALAH SALEM

Aqueduct

SHARIA EL-KHALIFA

SHARIA SALAH SALEM

SHARIA MAGRA EL-AYOUN

Aqueduct

E L - K H A L I F A

SHARIA MAGRA AL-SHAFI

SHARIA SALAH SALEM

Mausoleum of Imam al-Shafi'i

Hosh al-Basha

SHARIA AIN EL-SIRA

SITE OF FUSTAT

AROUND IBN TULUN AND THE SOUTHERN CEMETERY

0   250 m

The Mosque of Ibn Tulun

Ibn Tulun's Mosque (daily 8am–5pm; no entry fee) is a rare survivor of the classical Islamic period of the ninth and tenth centuries, when the Abbassid khalifs ruled the Muslim world from Iraq. Their purpose-built capital, Samarra, centred upon a congregational mosque where the entire population assembled for Friday prayer, and this most likely provided the inspiration for the Ibn Tulun. You enter the mosque via a **ziyada**, or enclosure, designed to distance the mosque from its surroundings; to the left stands the Gayer-Anderson House (see overleaf). It's only within the inner walls that the vastness of the mosque becomes apparent: the courtyard is 92 metres square, while the complex, measuring 140m by 122m, covers six and a half acres.

Besides its sheer size, the **mosque** impresses by its simplicity. Its vast courtyard, open to the sky, has the grandeur of a desert where all of Allah's worshippers are prostrated equally beneath the sun. Ibn Tulun's architects understood the power of repetition – see how the merlons echo the rhythm of the arcades – but also restraint: small floral capitals and stucco rosettes seem at first glance to be the only decorative motifs. Beneath the arcades you'll find a sycamore-wood frieze over two kilometres long, relating roughly one-fifth of the Koran in *kufic* script. The severely geometric *mida'a*, an inspired focal point, was added in the thirteenth century, when the *mihrab* was also jazzed up with marble and glass mosaics – the only unsuccessful note in the complex.

The **minaret** (entered from the mosque's outer courtyard, but currently closed) is unique for its exterior spiral staircase, which gives the structure a helical shape. Supposedly, Ibn Tulun twisted a scrap of paper into a spiral, and then justified his absent-minded deed by presenting it as the design for a minaret. But the great minaret at Samarra (itself influenced by ancient Babylonian ziggurats) seems a likelier source of inspiration. When the minaret re-opens, expect to pay *baksheesh* to climb it, and for looking after your shoes or providing shoe covers, but resist excessive demands, especially if you are told (falsely) that they are official charges.

Ibn Tulun and Al-Qitai

It was from Iraq that the Abbassids made **Ahmed Ibn Tulun** governor of Fustat in 868, and smarted as he declared his independence. Ibn Tulun (the "Son of Tulun", a Turkish slave) founded the Tulunid dynasty that ruled Egypt until 905, and established a new city to the northeast of Fustat. According to legends, Noah's Ark had come to rest on this site when the Flood receded; Moses confronted the pharaoh's magicians here; and Abraham had been ready to sacrifice his son on a nearby hillock. Unperturbed by this, nor by the existence of Christian and Jewish cemeteries on the site, he dictated the construction of **Al-Qitai**, called "the Wards" after its division into military cantonments.

Ibn Tulun's performance on the polo field filled his doctors with foreboding, for in sickness he "refused to follow their orders, flouted their prescribed diet, and when he found himself still sinking, he had their heads chopped off, or flogged them till they died". But under his soft-living successor the Al-Qitai midan was converted into a garden with a quicksilver lake, where the insomniac Khomaruya lolled on an airbed guarded by a blue-eyed lion. The Tulunids could afford such luxury, for their annual revenue amounted to 4,300,000 dinars.

When the Abbassids subsequently reconquered Egypt in 905, they destroyed everything here but the mosque, which became derelict. Exploited as a makeshift caravanserai and a hideout for bodysnatchers during the terrible famine of 1200, it was belatedly restored in 1296 by Sultan Laghin, who had hidden there as an amir suspected of murdering the sultan.

The Gayer-Anderson House

From the *ziyada* of the Ibn Tulun Mosque a sign directs you to the **Gayer-Anderson House** (daily 9am–4pm; £E30, students £E15), otherwise known as the Beit al-Kritiliya ("House of the Cretan Woman"), which abuts the southeast corner of the mosque.

Gayer-Anderson was a retired British major who, during the 1930s and 1940s, refurbished two mansions dating from the sixteenth and eighteenth centuries, filling them with Oriental bric-a-brac. Amongst the many paintings here is a self-portrait of Gayer-Anderson wearing a pharaonic headdress. **Tours** of the house (the buildings are linked by a passage on the third floor) are conducted by charming curators. There are Persian, Chinese and Queen Anne rooms, and an amazing guest bedroom named after Damascus, whence its opulent wooden panelling originated. Women can sneak through a camouflaged *dulap* (wall cupboard) into the screened gallery overlooking the *salamlik*, as in olden days. With its polychrome fountain, decorated ceiling and kilim-covered pillows, this is the finest reception hall left in Islamic Cairo. It was the set for a tryst and murder in the James Bond film *The Spy Who Loved Me*.

Saiyida Zeinab

The backstreets west of Ibn Tulun harbour another gem of Islamic architecture in the **Madrassa of Qaitbey**. Ignore the dust and grime and tip the curator to unlock the building, whose mosaic floors and *minbar* are superb examples of fifteenth-century craftsmanship.

Real aficionados can also track down other monuments in the area, as detailed in the AUC's *Islamic Monuments in Cairo* guide. Otherwise, ride further west into the densely populated **Saiyida Zeinab quarter**, where Islamic and modern Cairo merge in a confusion of tenement blocks and **markets**. Midan Lazoghli, on the edge of the Abdin quarter, hosts a daily car spares and repairs souk, while a **bird market** is held beneath an overpass in the direction of Qasr al-Aini Hospital on Mondays and Thursdays – hence its name, the Souk Itnayn w Khamibs.

Like Saiyida Zeinab metro station, the market is on the quarter's periphery, where it merges with Garden City and Old Cairo (see map p.192). To the northeast of the slaughterhouse district and the Al-Abdin Mosque, at 2 Sharia Bayram el-Tonsi, is the **Brooke Hospital for Animals**. Founded by Dorothy Brooke in 1934, the hospital treats infirm donkeys and other beasts of burden free of charge, purchases the incurables and puts them out to grass. Egyptians find the whole idea bizarre but appreciate the service; a stream of patients wends its way up the street. The hospital welcomes visitors (daily 9am–4pm; ☎02/364-9312).

The quarter's highlight is the annual **Moulid of Saiyida Zeinab**, which features parades of Sufi orders by day and nocturnal festivities that attract half a million people. Ecstatic devotion and pleasure rub shoulders (and other parts of the anatomy, if you're a woman) in this seething, mostly male crowd, transfixed by the music and spectacles. To see the *zikrs*, snake charmers, conjurers, nail-swallowers and dancing horses performing, you'll have to force your way through a scrum of people and tents – don't bring any valuables. The fifteen-day event takes place during Ragab, the seventh month of the Muslim calendar.

The focal point for these celebrations is the **Mosque of Saiyida Zeinab** (closed to non-Muslims), off Sharia Bur Said. Born in 628 AD, Zeinab, the Prophet's granddaughter, emigrated to Fustat after the Umayyads slew her brother, Hussein, and died there shortly afterwards. For Egyptian Muslims – especially women – Zeinab is a protectress whose *baraka* ("blessing") is sought in matters of fortune and health; in other words, a popular saint. Although the

Koran forbids the deification of mortals, the human urge to anthropomorphize religious faith seems irresistible. Every Muslim nation has its own "saints" (chosen by popular acclaim rather than a supreme authority) and respects bloodlines descended from the Prophet or his immediate kin. For the Shia, the martyrdom of Ali and Hussein is a parable of their own oppression, while Zeinab (whose moulid attracts foreign Shia) is honoured as their closest kinswoman.

Before heading back into town, you might want to try one of Saiyida Zeinab's many cheap but renowned **eating places**, for more on which see p.260. To return to downtown Cairo from here, catch a bus or minibus from Sharia Khayrat opposite Zeinab's Mosque, or ask for directions to the nearest metro entrance (ten minutes' walk). From Saiyida Zeinab or Saad Zaghloul (which is as near) you can take the metro north to Tahrir or Ramses, or south to Old Cairo (Mari Girgis station).

Cities of the Dead

It's thought that at least 500,000 Cairenes live amid the **Cities of the Dead**: two vast cemeteries that stretch away from the Citadel to merge with newer shantytowns below the Muqattam. The Southern Cemetery, sprawling to the southeast of Ibn Tulun's mosque, is only visible from the Muqattam, or at close quarters. The Northern Cemetery, by contrast, is an unforgettably eerie sight, with dozens of mausoleums rising from a sea of dwellings along the road from Cairo Airport.

Although tourists generally – and understandably – feel uneasy about viewing the cemeteries' splendid **funerary architecture** with squatters living all around or in the tombs, few natives regard the Cities of the Dead as forbidding places. Egyptians have a long tradition of building "houses" near their ancestral graves and picnicking or even staying there overnight; other families have simply occupied them. By Cairene standards these are poor but decent neighbourhoods, with shops, schools and electricity, maybe even piped water and sewers. The saints buried here provide a moral touchstone and *baraka* for their communities, who honour them with **moulids**.

Though generally not a dangerous quarter, it's best to exercise some caution when **visiting**. Don't flaunt money or costly possessions, and be sure to dress modestly; women should have a male escort, and will seem more respectable if wearing a headscarf. By responding to local kids (who may request *baksheesh*) with the right blend of authority and affection, you can win the sympathy of their elders and seem less of an intruder; react wrongly, and you might be stoned out of the neighbourhood. You'll be marginally less conspicuous on Fridays, when many Cairenes visit their family plots; but remember that mosques can't be entered during midday prayers. At all events, leave the cemeteries well before dark, if only to avoid getting lost in their labyrinthine alleys – and don't stray to the east into the inchoate (and far riskier) slums built around the foothills of the Muqattam.

The Southern Cemetery (Al-Qarafah al-Kubra)

The older and larger **Southern Cemetery** is broadly synonymous with the residential quarter of **El-Khalifa**, named after the Abbassid khalifs buried amidst its mud-brick tenements. The area is noted for drug dealing and quite unsafe after dark. Although the Abbassid tombs aren't half as imposing as those of the Mamlukes in the Northern Cemetery, one of the approach routes passes several shrines famous for their moulids, while another moulid is held at the beautiful **Mausoleum of Imam al-Shafi'i**, best reached by bus as a separate excursion. For this reason, we've described two different routes into what Egyptians call "the Great Cemetery" (Al-Qarafah al-Kubra).

Sharia Saliba to the Tomb of the Abbassid Khalifs

This walking route passes through one of the oldest poor neighbourhoods in Cairo, where it's thought that people started settling around their saints' graves as early as the tenth century. None of the tombs is remarkable visually, but the stories and moulids attached to them are interesting. The trail begins where **Sharia el-Khalifa** turns south off Sharia Saliba, just after the Khanqah of Shaykhu (see map p.182).

Heading south along this narrow street, full of commerce and capering children, you'll be pestered past a succession of tombs. The second on the left, within a green-and-white mosque, is that of **Saiyida Sukayna**, a daughter of Hussein, whose moulid (held during Rabi el-Tani) is attended by several thousand locals and features traditional entertainments like dancing horses and stick-twisters.

Such saintly graves invariably acquired an oratory (*mashrad*) or mosque, unlike the **Tomb of Shagar al-Durr**, 100m further on: a derelict edifice sunk below street level. Shagar al-Durr (Tree of Pearls) was the widow of Sultan Ayyub, who ruled as sultana of Egypt for eighty days (1249–50) until the Abbassid khalif pronounced "Woe unto nations ruled by a woman", compelling her to marry Aybak, the first Mamluke sultan, and govern "from behind the *mashrabiya*". In 1257 she ordered Aybak's murder after learning that he sought another wife, but then tried to save him; the assassins cried, "If we stop halfway through, he will kill both you and us!" Rejecting her offer to marry Qutuz, their new leader, the Mamlukes handed Shagar al-Durr over to Aybak's former wife, whose servants beat her to death with bath clogs and threw her body to the jackals. Now totally gutted, her locked tomb once contained a *tabut* inscribed: "Oh you who stand beside my grave, show not surprise at my condition. Yesterday I was as you, tomorrow, you will be like me."

Slightly further down and across the street, three shrines are grouped within a compound entered via a green-and-white doorway. The **Mashrad of Saiyida Ruqayya**, on the left, commemorates the stepsister of Saiyida Zeinab, with whom she came to Egypt; the name of her father, Ali, adorns its rare Fatimid *mihrab*, and the devotion she inspires is particularly evident during Ruqayya's moulid.

Ruqayya's devotion doesn't, however, compare with that accorded to the **Mosque of Saiyida Nafisa**, 100m to the south, past the market square. This, Egypt's third-holiest shrine, is closed to non-Muslims, though visitors can still appreciate the good-natured crowd that hangs around after Friday noon prayers, or Nafisa's moulid, usually held in the middle of the month of Gumad al-Tani (see p.273). Honoured during her lifetime as a descendant of the Prophet, a *hafizat al-Qur'an* (one who knows the Koran by heart) and a friend of Imam al-Shafi'i, Nafisa was famed for working miracles and conferring *baraka*. Her shrine has been repeatedly enlarged since Fatimid times – the Southern Cemetery possibly began with devotees settling or being buried near her grave – and the present mosque was built in 1897.

If you walk through the passage to its left, turn right at the end and then right again, you should find yourself outside the compound enclosing the **Tombs of the Abbassid Khalifs** (open 24hr). Having been driven from Baghdad by the Mongols, the khalifs' surviving relatives gratefully accepted Beybars' offer to re-establish them in Egypt, only to discover that they were "No longer Commander of the Faithful, but Commander of the Wind". Beybars appropriated the domed mausoleum (usually kept locked) for his own sons; the khalifs were buried outdoors in less than grandiose tombs. Notice the beautiful foliate *kufic* inscription on the cenotaph of Khadiga, under the wooden shed. In 1517 the last Abbassid khalif was formally divested of his office, which the Ottomans assumed in 1538 and Ataturk abolished in the 1920s.

An alternative route back towards the Citadel passes the **Mosque of Saiyida Aisha**, whose **moulid** occurs during Sha'ban. To get there, retrace your steps to the market square south of Ruqayya's shrine and take the road leading off to the right. It's roughly 500 metres' walk to Aisha's Mosque. From there, Sharia Salah Salem runs southwest alongside the medieval **Wall of Salah al-Din**, and northeast to the Citadel entrance at Bab al-Gabal, while Sharia Salah al-Din leads north to Midan Salah al-Din. If you happen to be here on Friday, consider making a detour to the **bird market** (Souk al-Asafeer or Souk al-Gom'a), held on a side street to the south of the Salah Salem overpass.

The Mausoleum of Imam al-Shafi'i

Imam al-Shafi'i, revered as the founder of one of the four rites of Sunni Islam, occupies a great mausoleum 2km from the Citadel. Aside from catching a taxi from there (for about £E3–5), the mausoleum is accessible by bus #81 or #89 from Midan Ataba, or bus #160 from Midan Ramses, or more comfortable #154 minibuses from Abdel Mouneem Riyad, which turn off Sharia Imam al-Shafi'i, 100m beforehand. If you miss the turn-off, ride on to the terminal, have a glass of tea with the driver, and get dropped at the corner on the way back.

Recognizable by its graceful dome, crowned by a metal boat like a weather vane, the **Mausoleum of Imam al-Shafi'i** lurks beside a mosque at the end of the street (free but *baksheesh* appropriate). The largest Islamic mortuary complex in Egypt, it was raised in 1211 by Al-Kamil, Salah al-Din's nephew, a propagator of Sunni orthodoxy like the Imam himself, who died in 820. Al-Shafi'i's teak cenotaph – into which the faithful slip petitions – lies beneath a magnificent dome perched on stalactite squinches, painted red and blue, with gilt designs. The walls are clad in variegated marble, dating from Qaitbey's restoration of the building in the 1480s. In times past, the boat on the roof was filled with birdseed and water; boats are vehicles of spiritual enlightenment in Islamic symbolism, while birds are associated with souls.

Al-Shafi'i's **moulid** attracts many sick and infirm people, seeking his *baraka*. The festival occurs in Sha'ban, the eighth month of the Muslim calendar, but the starting date varies. Normally it's the first Wednesday of the month; however, if this falls on the first or second day of Sha'ban, the moulid is delayed until the following Wednesday. Either way, it ends on Wednesday evening the following week. More prosaically, the street leading northwards to the mausoleum from the Al-Basatin quarter is used for scrap, clothing and livestock **markets** every Friday morning.

By walking clockwise around the block in which the Imam's mausoleum is located, you'll find a five-domed complex directly behind it. Inside the courtyard are clumps of cenotaphs decorated with garlands and fronds, topped by a turban, fez or other headdress to indicate the deceased's rank. These constitute the **Hosh al-Basha**, where Mohammed Ali's sons, their wives, children and retainers are buried. The conspicuously plain cenotaph belongs to a princess with radical sympathies, who abhorred ostentation. The body of King Farouk himself, who died in exile, now reposes in the Rifai Mosque. In a separate room, forty statues commemorate the 470 Mamlukes butchered by Mohammed Ali in the Citadel (see p.176).

The Northern Cemetery (Al-Qarafat al-Sharqiyyah)

The finest of Cairo's funerary monuments – erected by the Burgi Mamlukes from the fourteenth to sixteenth centuries – are spread around the **Northern Cemetery**. The majority of tourists who venture in from Sharia Salah Salem are content to see three main sites, plus whatever crops up in between, over an hour or so.

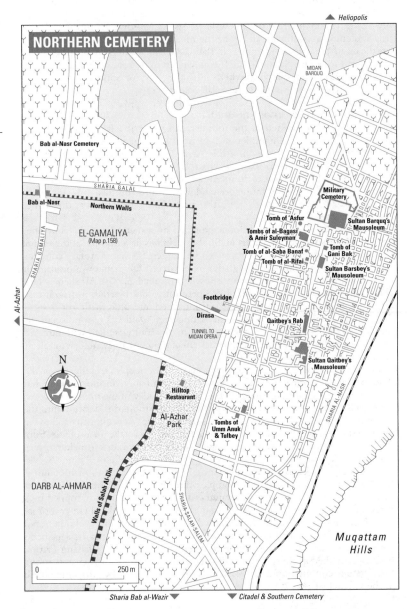

NORTHERN CEMETERY

▲ Heliopolis

MIDAN BARQUQ

Bab al-Nasr Cemetery

SHARIA GALAL

Bab al-Nasr   Northern Walls

SHARIA GAMALIYA

EL-GAMALIYA
(Map p.158)

◄ Al-Azhar

Military Cemetery

Tomb of 'Asfur

Sultan Barquq's Mausoleum

Tombs of al-Bagasi & Amir Suleyman

Tomb of Gani Bak

Tomb of al-Saba Banat

Tomb of al-Rifai

Sultan Barsbey's Mausoleum

Footbridge

Dirasa

Qaitbey's Rab

TUNNEL TO MIDAN OPERA

N

Sultan Qaitbey's Mausoleum

SHARIA AL-NASR

Hilltop Restaurant

Al-Azhar Park

Tombs of Umm Anuk & Tulbey

Walls of Salah Al-Din

DARB AL-AHMAR

SHARIA SALAH SALEM

Muqattam Hills

0   250 m

Sharia Bab al-Wazir ▼   ▼ Citadel & Southern Cemetery

Aside from catching a taxi (ask for the *Qarafat al-Sharqiyyah* – Eastern Cemetery – in Arabic), the surest way of **getting there** is to walk from Al-Azhar. This will take around fifteen minutes, following the dual carriageway Bab al-Ghuriyab past university buildings and uphill to its roundabout junction with Salah Salem. Although the tombs of Anuk and Tulbey are amongst the nearby mausoleums, you might prefer to head 250m north along the highway to Dirasa – also accessible by minibus #102 **from Midan Tahrir** or minibus #10 **from Ramses and Ataba** – and then cut east into the cemetery. That way you start with Qaitbey's Mausoleum (a known point on the circuit), whose ornate dome and minaret are clearly visible. Dirasa can also be reached by service taxi microbus from Midan Ramses, and there will be a metro station here when the new cross-town line finally opens (see map on p.111).

Sultan Qaitbey's Mausoleum

Sultan Qaitbey was the last strong Mamluke ruler and a prolific builder of monuments from Mecca to Syria; his funerary complex (depicted on £E1 notes) is among the grandest in the Northern Cemetery. His name means "the restored" or "returned", indicating that he nearly died at birth; as a scrawny lad, he fetched only fifty dinars in the slave market. The rapid turnover in rulers after 1437 accelerated his ascent, and in 1468 he was acclaimed as sultan by the bodyguard of the previous incumbent, an old comrade-in-arms who parted from Qaitbey with tears and embraces. His 28-year reign was only exceeded by Al-Nasir's, and Qaitbey remained "tall, handsome and upright as a reed" well into his eighties, still attentive to citizens' complaints at twice-weekly *diwaniyyas*.

An irregularly shaped complex built in 1474, the **Mausoleum of Sultan Qaitbey** (daily 9am–5pm) is dynamically unified by the bold stripes along its facade, which is best viewed from the north. The trilobed portal carries one's eye to the graceful **minaret**, soaring through fluted niches, stalactite brackets and balconies to a teardrop finial. Inside, the **madrassa** *liwans*, floors and walls are a feast of marble and geometric patterns, topped by elaborately carved and gilded ceilings, with a lovely octagonal roof lantern. Qaitbey's **tomb chamber** off the *qibla liwan* is similarly decorated, its lofty dome upheld by squinches. One of Mohammed's footprints, brought over from Mecca, is also preserved in the tomb chamber. Ask to climb the minaret for a close view of the marvellous stone carving on the dome's exterior. A raised star-pattern is superimposed over an incised floral one, the two designs shifting as the shadows change. From this minaret vantage point you could also plot a course to Barsbey's complex, further up the narrow, winding street.

The Barsbey and Barquq complexes

As the street jinks northwards from Qaitbey's Mausoleum it passes (on the left) the apartment building that Qaitbey deeded to provide income for the building's upkeep and employment for poor relations. Such bequests could not be confiscated, unlike merchants' and Mamlukes' personal wealth, which partly financed the **Mausoleum of Sultan al-Ashraf Barsbey** (daily 9am–8pm), 200m beyond the building. Based on a now-ruined *khanqah*, the complex was expanded to include a mausoleum and mosque-madrassa (1432) after Barsbey's funerary pile near Khan el-Khalili was found lacking. If there's a curator around, ask him to lift a mat hiding the marble mosaic floor inside the long mosque, which also features a superb *minbar*. At the northern end, a great dome caps Barsbey's tomb, its marble cenotaph and mother-of-pearl-inlaid *mihrab* softly lit by stained-glass windows, added at a later date. The stone carving on the dome's exterior marks a transition between the early chevron patterns and the fluid designs on Qaitbey's Mausoleum.

Barsbey was the sultan who acquired young Qaitbey at a knockdown rate. He himself had been purchased in Damascus for eight hundred dinars, but was "returned to the broker for a filmy defect in one of his blue eyes". Unlike other sultans who milked the economy, Barsbey troubled to pay his Mamlukes regularly and the reign (1422–38) of this well-spoken teetotaller was characterized by "extreme security and low prices". Fifty metres up the street, another finely carved dome surmounts the **Tomb of Gani Bak**, a favourite of Barsbey's, whose mosque stands near the Saddlemakers Bazaar.

The third – and oldest – of the great funerary complexes can be found 50m further north, on the far side of a square with a direct through road onto Sharia Salah Salem. Recognizable by its twin domes and minarets, the **Mausoleum of Sultan Barquq** (daily 9am–8pm) was the first royal tomb in a cemetery that was previously noted for the graves of Sufi sheikhs. Its courtyard is plain, with sere, stunted tamarisks, but the proud chevron-patterned domes above the sanctuary *liwan* uplift the whole ensemble. Barquq and his son Farag are buried in the northern tomb chamber, his daughters Shiriz and Shakra in the southern one, with their faithful nurse in the corner. Both are soaring structures preceded by *mashrabiyas* with designs similar to the window screens in Barquq's madrassa, "Between the Two Palaces". The sinuously carved *minbar* was donated by Qaitbey to what was then a Sufi *khanqah*; stairs in the northwest corner of the courtyard lead to a warren of dervish cells on the upper floors, long since deserted.

The complex was actually erected by Farag, who transferred his father's body here from the madrassa on Sharia al-Muizz. Farag was crowned at the age of ten and deposed and killed in Syria after thirteen years of civil strife: it's amazing that the mausoleum was finally completed in 1411.

Depending on your route out, you might pass the minor **tombs of Barsbey al-Bagasi and Amir Suleyman**, or those of **Princess Tulbey and Umm Anuk**, nearer Bab al-Ghuriyab and visible from the highway.

Al-Azhar Park

Across Sharia Salah Salem from the northern cemetery, its entrance about 200m south of Dirasa, and 500m north of the Citadel's Bab Gadid, is the new and very welcome, thirty-hectare **Al-Azhar Park** (winter daily except Fri 10am–10pm, Fri 10am–11.30pm; summer daily 10am–1am; £E10). Funded by a US$45m grant from the Aga Khan Trust, the park was built on the site of a filthy and rather dangerous stretch of waste ground, used as a rubbish dump and the haunt of junkies. Now all that has changed: in its place is a beautiful and scrupulously kept recreational area for families and residents that has provided local employment and given one of Cairo's most deprived areas a new lease of life. Scattered around the park's lawns and fountains are trees, plants and shrubs from around the world, all labelled, while the western boundary includes a 1300-metre stretch of Ayyubid city wall, most of it newly uncovered during construction of the park, and whose bastions will be open to the public when work is complete. The park also contains a lakeside café and a classy restaurant (see p.261), with its high point offering a 360-degree panoramic view over Islamic Cairo from the Muqqatam hills past the Citadel, the Sultan Hassan and Rifai mosques, the Blue Mosque, the Qajmas al-Ishaqi Mosque, Bab Zwayla, the al-Ghuri complex, the Qalaoun and Barquq complexes and the Suleyman al-Silhadar Mosque to the Northern Gates: the vista is especially impressive at night when they are all illuminated. The park also incorporates three emergency reservoirs for times of drought and is part of a regeneration project for the Darb al-Ahmar area including workshops, a credit union, a school and a community centre, all much needed in one of Cairo's poorest and most run-down neighbourhoods.

Old Cairo, Roda Island and the southern suburbs

The southern sector of the city is divisible into three main areas, the most interesting of which is **Old Cairo** (Masr al-Qadima), the historic link between Egypt's pharaonic and Islamic civilizations. Here, the fortress-town of **Babylon**, where the Holy Family is thought to have taken refuge, developed into a powerhouse of native Christianity which today remains the heart of Cairo's **Coptic community**. Featuring several medieval churches, the superb **Coptic Museum** and an atmospheric synagogue, it totally eclipses the site of **Fustat** – Egypt's first Islamic settlement, of which little remains but the much-altered **Mosque of Amr** – or the largely uninteresting **southern suburbs** of Ma'adi and Helwan.

Connected by bridge to Old Cairo – and so covered in this section, too – is **Roda Island**, which boasts a venerable Nilometer and the wonderfully kitsch Manial Palace. The Nilometer is best visited in combination with Coptic Cairo, but the palace is more easily accessible from central Cairo.

Approaching Old Cairo: transport links

Depending on whether it's broadly or narrowly defined, **Old Cairo** covers everything south of Garden City and Saiyida Zeinab – from the slaughterhouse district beside the Mamluke Aqueduct out to the ancient Jewish cemetery of Al-Basatin – or a relatively small area near the Mari Girgis metro station, known to foreigners as **"Coptic Cairo"**. Cairenes themselves distinguish between the general area of *Masr al-Qadima* and specific localities such as *Fumm al-Khalig* (Mouth of the Aqueduct) or *Qasr el-Sham'ah* (the erstwhile fortress of Babylon). Most tourists concentrate on Coptic Cairo, followed by a brief look at the Mosque of Amr.

The Coptic quarter is rapidly accessible by taking the **metro** from downtown Cairo to the **Mari Girgis** station (four stops from Midan Tahrir in the Helwan direction; 50pt). Another possibility is the **river-taxis** (aka water buses; 50pt) that leave from the Maspero Dock (see p.115), zigzagging southwards upriver. Note, however, that not all of them run as far as Mari Girgis, and services end at 3pm. The Mari Girgis stop is the fifth one; to reach the Coptic quarter from there, head inland, turn left and then cross the tracks at the end of the road. **Taxis** from downtown Cairo are reluctant to accept less than £E10, while **buses** from Tahrir and **minibuses** from Midan Ataba to Amr's Mosque are usually packed on the outward journey but fine for getting back. To reach other points, see the directions below.

Coptic Cairo

Coptic Cairo recalls the millennial interlude between pharaonic and Islamic civilization and the enduring faith of Egypt's Copts (see pp.194–195). Though not a ghetto, the quarter's huddle of dark churches suggests a mistrust of outsiders – an attitude of mind that has its roots in the Persian conquest and centuries of Greek or Roman rule.

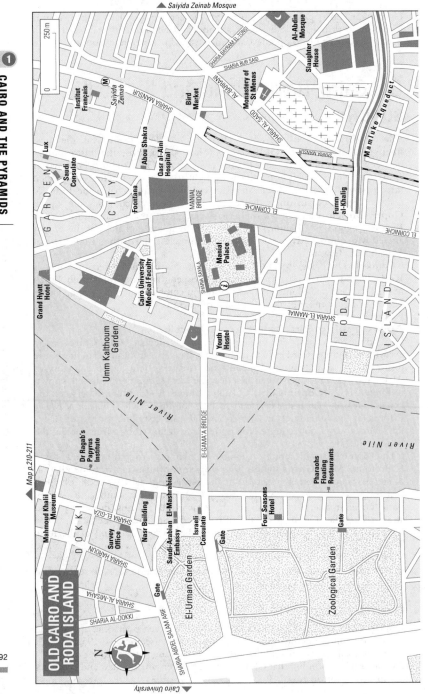

▲ Saiyida Zeinab Mosque

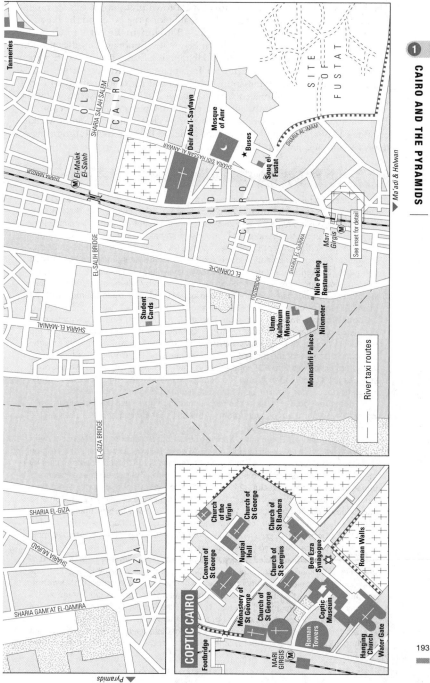

Tanneries

SHARIA SALAH SALEM

OLD CAIRO

Deir Abu'l-Sayfayn

Mosque of Amr

★ Buses

Souq el Fustat

SITE OF FUSTAT

SHARIA SIDI HASSAN AL ANWAR

SHARIA AL-IMAM

M El-Malek El-Saleh

SHARIA MANSUR

OLD CAIRO

Mari Girgis M

See inset for detail

SHARIA EL-QADWA

▼ Ma'adi & Helwan

EL-SALIH BRIDGE

EL CORNICHE EL NIL

FOOTBRIDGE

Nile Peking Restaurant

Student Cards

SHARIA EL-MANIAL

Umm Kathoum Museum

Monastirli Palace

Nilometer

River taxi routes

EL-GIZA BRIDGE

SHARIA MURAD

SHARIA EL-GIZA

GIZA

SHARIA GAMI'AT EL-QAMIRA

▼ Pyramids

COPTIC CAIRO

Church of the Virgin

Church of St George

Church of St Barbara

Convent of St George

Nuptial Hall

Church of St Sergius

Ben Ezra Synagogue

Monastery of St George

Church of St George

Coptic Museum

Roman Walls

Footbridge

MARI GIRGIS M

Roman Towers

Hanging Church

Water Gate

Perhaps as early as the sixth century BC, a town grew up in this area, built around a fortress intended to guard the canal linking the Nile and the Red Sea. Some ascribe the name of this settlement – **Babylon-in-Egypt** – to Chaldean workmen pining after their home town beside the Euphrates; another possible derivation is **Bab il-On**, the "Gate of Heliopolis". Either way, it was Egyptian or Jewish in spirit long before Emperor Trajan raised the existing fortress in 130 AD. Resentful of Greek domination and Hellenistic Alexandria, many of Babylon's inhabitants later embraced Christianity, despite bitter persecution by the pagan Romans. Subsequently, after the emperor Constantine's conversion, the community was further oppressed by Byzantine clerics in the name of Melkite orthodoxy. Thus when the Muslim army besieged Babylon in 641, promising to respect Copts and Jews as "People of the Book", only its garrison resisted.

The Copts

While most Egyptians are Muslims, about ten percent of the population are Coptic Orthodox Christians. **The Copts** share a common national culture with their Muslim compatriots, but remain acutely conscious of their separate identity. Because inter-communal marriages are extremely rare, it's often said that the Copts are "purer" descendants of the ancient Egyptians than the Muslims – overlooking the infusions of Nubian, Greek, Jewish and Roman blood that occurred centuries before the Arab conquest. Though some maintain that they have higher cheekbones or almond-shaped eyes, Copts are rarely recognizable other than by tokens of their faith (wearing a cross around their neck, or tattooed on their wrist) or by forenames such as Maria, Antunius (Antony), Girgis (George) and Ramses.

Coptic Christianity differs from the Eastern Orthodox and Roman churches over doctrine and ritual. The Coptic Orthodox Church and its pope (chosen from the monks of Wadi Natrun) are totally independent from the Vatican, which only recently agreed to disagree for the sake of ecumenical harmony. The Coptic Bible (first translated from Greek in c.300 AD) antedates the Latin version by a century. While Coptic services are conducted in Arabic, portions of the liturgy are sung in the old Coptic language descended from ancient Egyptian, audibly prefiguring the Gregorian chants of Eastern Orthodoxy. However, the Coptic influence goes well beyond music, for it was in Egypt that the monastic tradition, the cult of the Virgin and – arguably – the symbol of the cross originated.

Christianity reached Egypt early: tradition holds that **St Mark** made his first convert (a Jewish shoemaker of Alexandria) in 45 AD. From Jews and Greeks the religion spread to the Egyptians of the Delta – which teemed with Christian communities by the third century – and thence southwards up the Nile. The persecution of believers began under Emperor Decius (249–51) and reached its apogee under Diocletian, whom the Copts accuse of killing 144,000 Christians; the Coptic Church dates its chronology from his accession (284). During this **Era of Martyrs** many believers sought refuge in the desert. Paul of Thebes, Antony and Pacome – the sainted **"Desert Fathers"** – inspired a multitude of hermits and camp followers whose simple communities became the first **monasteries**.

The Christian faith appealed to Egyptians on many levels. Its message of resurrection offered ordinary folk the eternal life that was previously available only to those who could afford elaborate funerary rituals. And much of the new religion's **symbolism** fitted old myths and images. God created man from clay, as did Khnum on his potter's wheel, and weighed the penitent's heart, like Anubis; Confession echoed the Declaration of Innocence; the conflict of two brothers and the struggle against Satan echoed the myth of Osiris, Seth and Horus. Scholars have traced the **cult of the Virgin** back to that of the Great Mother, Isis, who suckled Horus. The resemblance

The Roman fortress

Almost opposite the **Mari Girgis** (St George) metro station you'll see the twin circular **towers** of Babylon's western gate. In Trajan's day, the Nile lapped the base of this gate and was spanned by a pontoon bridge leading to the southern tip of Roda. Today, Babylon's foundations are buried under ten metres of accumulated silt and rubble, so the churches within the compound and the streets outside are nearly at the level of the fortress's ramparts. The right-hand tower is ruined, exposing a central shaft buttressed by masonry rings and radial ribs, which enabled it to withstand catapults and battering rams. Atop the other tower stands the Orthodox Church of St George (see p.199). Both towers are encased in alternating courses of dressed stone (much of it taken from pharaonic temples) and brick, a Roman technique known as *opus mixtum* or "mixed work".

between early **Coptic crosses** and pharaonic *ankhs* has also led some to argue that Christianity's principal symbol owes more to Egypt than Golgotha.

Although Emperor Constantine converted to Christianity and legalized his adopted faith throughout the empire (313–30), Byzantine converts known as **Melkites** continued to oppress the Copts. Political tensions were expressed in bitter theological disputes between **Arius** and **Athanasius** of Alexandria, which the Nicene Council (325) failed to resolve. When the Copts rejected the compromise verdict of the Council of Chalcedon (451) that Christ's human and divine natures were both unmixed and inseparable, and insisted that his divinity was paramount, they were expelled from the fold for this **Monophysite heresy** (monophysite meaning "single nature", a misrepresentation of their stance on Christ's divinity).

The association between Coptic Christianity and proto-nationalism was plain to Egypt's foreign rulers. "Copt" derives from the Greek word for Egypt, *Aigyptos*, truncated to *gibt* in Egyptian Arabic. Most Egyptians remained Christian long after the Arab conquest (640–41) and were treated justly by the early Islamic dynasties. Mass **conversions to Islam** followed harsher taxation, abortive revolts, punitive massacres and indignities engendered by the Crusades, until the Muslims attained a nationwide majority (probably during the thirteenth century, though earlier in Cairo). Thereafter Copts still participated in Egyptian life at every level, but the community retreated inwards and its monasteries and clergy stagnated until the nineteenth century, when Coptic reformists collaborated with Islamic and secular nationalists bent on overhauling Egypt's institutions.

In recent decades the Coptic community has undergone a **revival** under the dynamic leadership of its current pope, **Shenouda III**. The monasteries have been revitalized by a new generation of highly educated monks; community work and church attendances flourish as never before. Undoubtedly, this Coptic solidarity also reflects alarm at rising Islamic fundamentalism: what frightens the Copts is the state's strategy of wooing Islamist opinion by discriminating against non-Muslims. Merely to open a new church requires presidential permission; in 1998, one in Ma'adi was closed by security forces backed up by armoured cars. Over 200 converts to Christianity have been arrested under the National Security Act, and in 1999, sectarian Muslim mobs murdered 21 Copts at El-Qusiya in Middle Egypt (see p.340) while local police, already accused of torturing local Coptic residents, stood by and did nothing – some accounts even accuse them of participating.

Fortunately, it's relatively few Muslims who actively support this kind of sectarian repression – which is at least a source of comfort for Egypt's six million Copts and 200,000 **Christians of other denominations** (Greek Orthodox, Maronite, Armenian, Catholic, Anglican and Baptist).

Once the Coptic Museum hs reopened, you should be able to walk from it through the fortress's inner courtyard and down into the old **Water Gate** beneath the Hanging Church. The gate is partly flooded and, though its arches and walls are visible from precarious walkways, the interior is only accessible by a stairway behind the three stone piers supporting the back of the church (bring a torch). It was through this gate that the last Byzantine viceroy, Melkite bishop Cyrus, escaped by boat under cover of darkness before Babylon surrendered to the Muslims.

While exploring the Coptic quarter, you'll also notice various sections of Babylon's Roman **walls**, rebuilt during the fourth and fifth centuries.

The Coptic Museum

Nestled between the Hanging Church and the Roman towers of Babylon, the **Coptic Museum** is one of the highlights of Old Cairo. At the time of writing it was closed for renovation, but it is due to reopen soon (daily 9am–5pm; Ramadan daily 9am–3pm; £E30, students £E15), though bear in mind the museum's layout and the items on show in each room may have changed from the description below. Its peerless collection of Coptic artefacts is enhanced by the beautiful carved ceilings, beams and stained-glass domes inside its *mashrabiya*'d wings, which enclose peaceful gardens. A gateway from its grounds gives access to the courtyard of the Hanging Church (see p.199).

Founded in 1908 under the patronage of Patriarch Cyril V and Khedive Kamil, the museum was intended to save Christian antiques from the ravages of neglect and foreign collectors, but soon widened its mandate to embrace secular material. With artefacts from Old Cairo, Upper Egypt and the desert monasteries, the museum traces the evolution of Coptic art from Greco-Roman times into the Islamic era (300–1000 AD). Notwithstanding debts to pharaonic and Greco-Roman culture, its spirit was refreshingly unmonumental: Stanley Stewart (see p.845) calls it "realistic, at times humorous", and notes that Coptic art reflected "plebian or agricultural concerns". It often seems homespun compared to pharaonic and Islamic craftsmanship and, appropriately enough, its finest expression was in textiles.

Though spread over three floors, the collection can be seen in detail within a couple of hours, or covered at a trot in half that time.

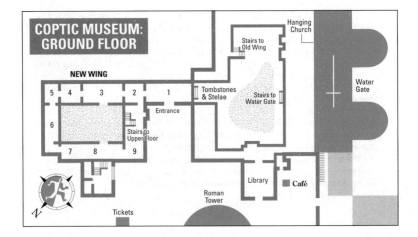

Entering the museum grounds from Mari Girgis street, the **New Wing**, built in 1937, is straight ahead. The **ground floor** is arranged in chronological order in an anticlockwise direction, starting with Room 1. The other exit from this room leads into a garden containing tombstones and funerary steles, from where you can access stairs that lead down to the Water Gate beneath the Hanging Church and up into the old wing.

Centred upon a fountain from one of the old houses of the quarter, **Room 1** displays **pagan reliefs and statues** of figures from Classical mythology. Their squat proportions and oversized heads make Aphrodite, Daphnae, Pan, Leda and the Swan look more African than Greco-Roman. The tendency to superimpose two flat layers, and the motif of a broken pediment with a shell, were both characteristic of proto-Coptic art. Artefacts in **Room 2** evince a **shift towards Christian symbolism** from the third century onwards. Pharaonic *ankhs* (see p.312) are transmuted into looped crosses, while true crosses appear on the shell pediments and coexist with Horus hawks on a basket-weave capital.

Coptic artistry reached its zenith between the sixth and ninth centuries, as exemplified by the **stone carvings and frescoes from Bawit Monastery**, near Assyut. In the middle of the righthand wall of **Room 3** is a splendid apse niche depicting Christ enthroned between the creatures of the Apocalypse and the moon and sun; below, the Virgin and Child consort with Apostles whose homely faces can still be seen in any Egyptian city today. In **Room 4**, whose contents are described as "Miscellaneous", notice the eagle on the right, an early Christian symbol of resurrection (as was the peacock). **Room 5** is also filled with miscellaneous objects, its centrepiece a painted capital carved with sinuous acanthus leaves, a motif borrowed from the Greeks and Romans but apparently devoid of symbolic meaning for the Copts.

Entering **Room 6**, dedicated to **objects from the Monastery of St Jeremiah** at Saqqara, you walk between an avenue of capitals with acanthus leaves and grapevines that mingle with pharaonic palm fronds and lotus motifs. At the end is the earliest known example of a stone pulpit, possibly influenced by the *heb-sed* thrones of Zoser's funerary complex. The fresco to its right, like the Bawit apse, subtly identifies the Virgin Mary with Isis. Other instances of recycled iconography can be seen around the corner in **Room 7**: a frieze of the grape harvest (a theme favoured by pharaonic nobles) and a small sphinx-like lion figure between two stylized versions of itself.

Room 8 moves on to **Biblical scenes** (Abraham and Isaac, Christ with angels) and **friezes** of animals offset in plant rondels – a motif that was later adopted by Fatimid woodcarvers. Entering **Room 9** you'll encounter on your right a tenth-century panel from Umm al-Birgat (in the Fayoum), depicting Adam and Eve before and after the Fall, for which he blames her in the latter scene while a serpent relishes the denouement. In the centre of the hall is an elaborate papyrus and lotus basket-weave capital, hollowed out to form a **baptismal font**.

Climbing the staircase to the **upper floor**, you come to casefuls of *ostraca* (inscribed shards of pottery, stone, bone and wood) and manuscripts produced by monastic scriptoria, including several papyrus sheets from the **Gnostic Gospels of Nag Hammadi**, whose 1200 pages shed light on the development of early Christianity and its mystic tradition. The Gospels (translated from Greek into Coptic) were probably buried during the purges against Gnostics in the fourth and fifth centuries; farmers unearthed the sealed jar in 1945 (see p.353).

Proceeding clockwise from **Room 10**, a 1600-year-old towel by the doorway to Room 11 – and next to the oldest book ever to be found complete with its

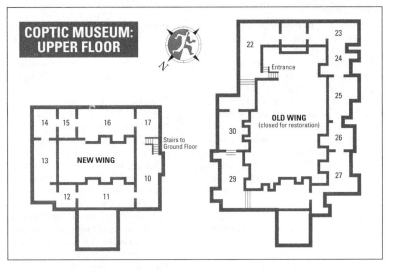

cover – presages a host of **textiles**. From the third or fourth century onwards, Coptic weavers (chiefly women) developed various techniques to a pitch of sophistication. Tapestry and pile-weave designs blended human and bird forms with plant motifs; tunics were appliquéd with bands and rondels. In **Room 12** there's a magnificent silk robe embroidered with pictures of the Apostles, dating from the eighteenth century.

Room 13 displays Alexandrian-style **ivorywork** and cruder efforts from Upper Egypt, alongside a selection of **icons** from Old Cairo, Aswan and Kharga Oasis. Some believe that the change from murals to painted icons resulted from the need to hide sacred treasures from hostile interlopers. The next three rooms showcase **metalwork**, ranging from crosses and censers to musical instruments and tools. In **Room 15** are patriarchal crowns, a lamp emblazoned with both a Christian cross and an Islamic crescent, and an eagle from the Fortress of Babylon.

The upper floor concludes with an exhibition in **Room 17** of **Nubian paintings** salvaged during the 1950s and 1960s from villages about to be drowned by Lake Nasser. Like Isis-worship in ancient times, Christianity persisted as the dominant religion in Nubia for several centuries after it had waned in Egypt. The figures are darker, with larger eyes and rounder heads than the Copts.

Old Wing

Entered via stairs from the sculpture garden, the **Old Wing** boasts even finer ceilings and *mashrabiyas*. On the left as you enter **Room 22** are the original **fourth-century altar** and a Fatimid-era dome from the Church of St Sergius. In the other direction lie two halls full of Nubian wall paintings, plus a pair of lunettes (semicircular paintings) from Bawit Monastery (**Room 23**). Rounding the corner, an original screen from the Church of St Barbara inaugurates the **woodwork** section. Fragments in the following alcove show a similar mixture of Hellenistic mythology, pharaonic symbolism and Coptic naturalism to the stone-carving in the other wing, while later pieces feature human activities. A **panel depicting Christ's entry into Jerusalem**, taken from the Hanging Church, is the high point of **Room 25**.

Sharing **Room 26** with Coptic toys and domestic utensils are several **mummy portrait panels**, latter-day versions of the Roman "Fayoum Portraits" displayed in the Museum of Egyptian Antiquities (see p.138). In the far right-hand corner is a remarkable **Early Coptic crucifix** (one of the few in existence), which combines a beardless Christ with a Horus hawk and sun disc. Byzantine and Sassanid (Persian) influences underlie the **friezes** of hunting scenes and fabulous creatures – motifs which continued into Islamic times until the Sunni restoration. The episcopal chairs in the annexe to **Room 27** are similar to the reception thrones used by wealthy amirs.

The last quarter of the wing displays **pottery**, arranged by type or form rather than antiquity. Ancient motifs such as fish, ducks and plants are widely employed. At the end of **Room 29** are **Pilgrims' flasks** showing St Menas between two camels (see p.643). Amongst the later work in **Room 30** are lustreware pieces like those made by Muslim potters at Fustat, but here emblazoned with a Coptic fish or cross. The annexe beyond contains a small collection of **glassware**.

The Hanging Church

Built directly above the water gate, the **Hanging Church** (*Al-Mu'allaqah*, "The Suspended" in Arab ic; daily 9am–5pm: Coptic Mass Fri 8–11am & Sun 7–10am) can be reached via an ornate portal on Mari Girgis street. Ascending a steep stairway, you enter a nineteenth-century vestibule displaying cassettes and videos of Coptic liturgies and papal sermons. Above this are the monks' quarters; beneath it lies a secret repository for valuables, only discovered last century. Through the door and to the right, a glass panel in the floor of the church allows you to see that the church is indeed "suspended" bridge-like above the water gate.

The main **nave** – whose ceiling is ribbed like an upturned boat or ark – is separated from its side aisles by sixteen pillars, formerly painted with images of saints. Behind the marble pulpit, beautifully carved screens hide three **haikals** (altar areas) from the congregation. Accentuated by inlaid bone and ivory, their star patterns are similar to those found in mosques. Both pulpit and screens date from the thirteenth century, but the church was founded at least six hundred years earlier and may even have originated in the fourth century as a chapel for the soldiers of the bastion. Amongst its relics, the church once claimed to own an olive stone chewed by the Virgin Mary, to whom *Al-Mu'allaqah* is dedicated. The thirteen pillars holding up the pulpit represent Jesus and the twelve disciples: as is customary in Coptic churches, one of the pillars is black, for Judas, and another, perhaps rather unfairly, is grey for "doubting" Thomas.

The Monastery of St George and into the Old Quarter

Returning to the Coptic Museum and heading north, go through the first gateway beyond the Coptic Museum entrance (ignoring any demands for cash from "doormen") to reach the precincts of the **Monastery of St George**, now the seat of the Greek Orthodox Patriarchate of Alexandria. The monastery itself rarely admits tourists, but it's worth looking into the neighbouring **Church of St George** (daily 8.30am–4pm). The only round church in Egypt (that shape because it is built atop one of the old Roman gateway towers), its dark interior is perfumed with incense and pierced by sunbeams filtered through stained glass. A (barred) flight of steps descends into the bowels of the Roman tower, once believed to be "peopled by devils". The present church was built in 1904 after a fire destroyed the original tenth-century structure. Notwithstanding the church's Orthodox allegiance, its **Moulid of Mari Girgis** (on St George's Day – April 23) is one of the largest Coptic festivals in Cairo.

Further up the main road, a **subterranean gateway** leads into the oldest part of Old Cairo, whose cobbled lanes flanked by high-walled houses wend between **medieval churches and cemeteries**. In 1929, Evelyn Waugh wrote disparagingly of a "constricted slum" whose Coptic residents hardly differed from their Muslim neighbours: "the only marked sign of their emancipation from heathen superstition was that the swarm of male and juvenile beggars were here reinforced by their womenfolk, who in the Mohammedan quarters maintain a modest seclusion". Since the late 1970s, the quarter has been gradually sanitized and tarted up for tourists, and now seems quite spruce compared to Islamic Cairo.

The most interesting of the churches is reached through the first gate on the left, after you pass through the subterranean gateway. This is the Coptic **Convent of St George** (*Deir Mari Girgis*; daily 9am–4pm), whose main building, still a nunnery, is closed to visitors. However, you can usually walk down into a lofty hall that once belonged to a Fatimid mansion and into the chapel beyond, with its tall, narrow wooden doors, which boasts a cedarwood casket containing relics of St George. To the left of this building, though not always open, is a small room used for the "**chain-wrapping ritual**", symbolizing the saint's persecution by the Romans. Several of the nuns speak English and welcome questions about their faith; they might even be prepared to wrap you in chains for a souvenir photo.

Upon leaving the convent, walk on to the end of the lane, where it meets another thoroughfare. At this intersection, turn right around the corner to the Church of St Sergius, or head left to explore the quarter's northern reaches.

North to the churches of St George and the Virgin

The north part of the Coptic quarter contains nothing special, but its solitude is refreshing and you might enjoy wandering around the overgrown **cemeteries** – so far unsquatted Cities of the Dead.

Fifty metres up the road from the intersection, an alley to the right leads to yet another **Church of St George**, founded in 681 by Athanasius the Scribe. From the original foundation only the Hall of Nuptials survived a conflagration in the mid-nineteenth century, after which the current structure was erected.

Beyond it, at the end of the road, stands the smaller **Church of the Virgin**, also known as Qasriyyat al-Rihan ("Pot of Basil") after the favourite herb of the Orthodox Church. Because Al-Hakim's mother was of that faith, the church was given to the Greek community for the duration of his reign, but later returned to the Copts. Largely rebuilt in the eighteenth century, it's chiefly notable for several icons painted by John the Armenian in 1778.

The churches of St Sergius and St Barbara

Heading right from the intersection beyond the convent, you pass a tourist bazaar before reaching the **Church of St Sergius** (*Abu Serga*; daily 8am–4pm), whose site below street level attests to its great age. Probably founded in the fifth century and continuously rebuilt since medieval times, *Abu Serga* retains the basilical form typical of early Coptic churches. The low ceiling and the antique columns topped with Corinthian capitals support the women's gallery, where you can inspect its thirteenth-century *haikal* screen and bits of frescoes and mosaics in the central apse. Steps to the right of the altar descend into a **crypt** where the Holy Family are believed to have stayed. A Coptic **festival** (June 1) commemorates their sojourn.

From St Sergius, you can wander along to the end of the lane where another thoroughfare leads to the Church of St Barbara (to the left) and Ben Ezra Synagogue (on the right).

The eleventh-century **Church of St Barbara** (Fri & Sun 8am–4pm, Mon–Thurs & Sat 8am–8pm) replaced an earlier Church of SS Cyrus and John, which was razed during Al-Hakim's assault on Fustat. Unlike others in the quarter, its wooden-vaulted roof is lofty, with skylights and windows illuminating a nave flanked by Arabic arches with Fatimid tie-beams. Nor would its **minbar**-esque pulpit and inlaid **haikal** screen look amiss in a mosque. The western sanctuary contains the relics of **Sitt Barbara**. Tradition holds that she was the daughter of a pagan merchant who was murdered for preaching Christianity in the third century, but sceptics might note that her belated recognition followed another questionable case (see p.756).

The Jews of Egypt

Egypt's Jewish community is dying out: fewer than two hundred *Yahud* remain in Alexandria, Old Cairo and the Jewish Old People's Home in Heliopolis. The three synagogues that still exist will probably become empty memorials within a decade or so – a melancholy end to a story that begins in the **Old Testament**. The book of Genesis relates how the descendants of Abraham escaped famine in Canaan (Palestine) by migrating to Egypt at the behest of Joseph, the pharaoh's favourite. Settling in the "Land of Goshen", they "multiplied and waxed mighty" until a new pharaoh enslaved them to build "the treasure-cities, Pithom and Raamses". Their flight from Egypt to the Promised Land is described in Exodus.

Squaring this with ancient Egyptian **history** presents difficulties. Whereas numerous sites are suggestive of Pithom and Raamses, there's no mention of the Exodus in pharaonic records. Assuming the Old Testament is based on genuine history, the Jews probably arrived sometime in the Ramessid era (c.1320–1237 BC), while the Exodus is generally ascribed to the reign of Merneptah (1236–1223 BC). There's some evidence for the Prophet Jeremiah's foundation of a new community at Babylon-in-Egypt after the destruction of Jerusalem (585 BC), but there is no firm historical ground until the second century BC, when it is known that the Ptolemies encouraged an influx of Jews into Alexandria.

In contrast to the Alexandrian fusion of Greek and Jewish culture, the Jews of Babylon were more akin to native Egyptians. Mutual sympathies were strengthened by the **Jewish revolt** against Roman rule (115–17 AD) and the Coptic belief in the **Egyptian exile of the Holy Family**. Babylon's Jewish community would have been a natural haven for Mary, Joseph and the baby Jesus when Herod's wrath made Palestine too dangerous (it's harder to see why they should have hidden out near Assyut, as is also claimed).

As "People of the Book", Egypt's Jews were treated about as well (or badly) as the Copts **during the Islamic period**, acting as small traders, gold- and silversmiths, moneychangers or moneylenders. In Mohammed Ali's day, E.W. Lane (see p.844) estimated that they numbered about five thousand. The British, however, introduced a new element: Jews who came as Europeans and shared the Brit-colonial disdain for the natives. Most of these new arrivals were merchants or professionals and settled in Alexandria or Cairo. A few families of *haute Juiverie* – the Menasces, Rolos, Hararis and Cattauis – were financiers who moved in royal circles. These **foreign Jews** lamented post-revolutionary restrictions on business and left en masse before and after the Suez Crisis (1956).

Meanwhile, native Jews were torn between Egypt and **Israel** as each war eroded their security. By the time of the 1967 war their numbers had declined from 75,000 to 2600 (mostly living in Cairo), though the capital still had 26 working synagogues, until mobs attacked them for the first time during the conflict. Thereafter, all but a few hundred Jews emigrated, leaving the poor, now aged, community that remains today.

The Ben Ezra Synagogue

Down the road, behind a wrought-iron fence, the **Ben Ezra Synagogue** (daily 9am–4pm) is a unique relic of Cairo's ancient Jewish community. Bereft of its former host of worshippers (see the box on p.201), the synagogue would have crumbled away were it not for the efforts of one "Rabbi" Cohen, who shamelessly overcharged for souvenir postcards to fund repairs for twenty years, until the American Jewish Congress and the Egyptian government stepped in to restore it. Today it is as good as new.

In form, the synagogue resembles a basilical church of the kind that existed here between the fourth and ninth centuries. Sold to the Jews in order to pay taxes raised from the Copts to finance Ibn Tulun's Mosque, this church was either demolished or incorporated within the synagogue, which Abraham Ben Ezra, the Rabbi of Jerusalem, restored in the twelfth century. The inlaid marble and gilded stalactite niche date from around then, but most of the graceful mouldings and floral swirls are the result of nineteenth-century repairs, which unearthed a huge cache of medieval manuscripts, including a sixth-century Torah written on gazelle hide (now dispersed around Western libraries).

Nevertheless, Jewish and Coptic traditions invest the site with ancient significance. Here, the pharaoh's daughter found Moses in the bulrushes; Jeremiah gathered survivors after Nebuchadnezzar destroyed Jerusalem; and the temple named after him provided a haven for the Holy Family, who lived amongst the Jews of Babylon for three months. Moreover, the Copts believe that Peter and Mark pursued their apostolic mission in Egypt, whence Peter issued the First Epistle General. The rest of Christendom disagrees, however, arguing that the Biblical reference to Babylon (I Peter 5:13) is only a metaphor for Rome.

Around the back of the synagogue are a newly restored chunk of the Roman walls and a derelict Jewish Refuge founded by one Ralph Green.

The Mosque of Amr, Deir Abu'l-Sayfayn and Fustat

To get a feel for what happened after Babylon and Egypt surrendered to Islam, return to Mari Girgis Street and follow it northwards, past the turning for Fustat and a small bus depot, to the **Mosque of Amr**. Though it was altered several times and doubled in size in 827, this boasts direct descent from Egypt's first-ever mosque, built in 641. A simple mud-brick, thatch-roofed enclosure without a *mihrab*, courtyard or minaret, it was large enough to contain the Muslim army at prayer. At its inauguration, **Amr Ibn al-As** told his 3500 Arab warriors:

The Nile floods have risen. The grazing will be good. There is milk for the lambs and kids. Go out with God's blessing and enjoy the land, its milk, its flocks and its herds, and take good care of your neighbours, the Copts, for the Prophet of God himself gave orders for us to do so.

Until the fratricidal struggle between Sunni and Shia, this injunction was honoured: aside from paying a poll tax, non-Muslims enjoyed equal rights. It was Ibn Tulun and Al-Hakim who introduced the discrimination (or worse), that later rulers either foreswore on principle or practised for motives of bigotry, fear or greed. But on an everyday level, citizens of each faith amicably coexisted within the city of Fustat-Masr, as they do in modern Cairo.

The site of the mosque was indicated by Allah, who sent a dove to nest in Amr's tent while he was away at war; on returning he declared it sacrosanct, waited until the dove's brood was raised, then built a mosque. The existing building follows the classic congregational pattern, arched *liwans* surrounding a pebbled *sahn* centred on an ablutions well. Believers pray or snooze on fine carpets in the sanctuary *liwan*, whose original *mihrab* is misaligned towards Mecca. When Amr introduced a pulpit, he was rebuked by Khalif Omar for raising himself above his Muslim brethren. The *mashrabiya*'d **mausoleum** of his son, Abdullah, marks the site of Amr's house in Fustat. A nearby column bears a gash caused by people licking it until their tongues bled, to obtain miraculous cures. The pair of columns on the left as you come in are said to part to allow the truly righteous to squeeze through, and another was whipped from Mecca by Omar. From the mosque's **well**, it is said, a pilgrim retrieved a goblet dropped into the Well of Zemzem in the Holy City.

Deir Abu'l-Sayfayn

If the Coptic quarter hasn't satisfied your curiosity about medieval churches, pay a visit to **Deir Abu'l-Sayfayn** (daily 8am–5pm), northwest of Amr's Mosque. This high-walled enclosure is entered via a humble wooden door, as the original iron-bound door is now in the Coptic Museum. Within the compound are several churches including the fourth-century Church of Anba Shenouda (currently undergoing renovation, but open to the public). First mentioned in the tenth century (when it served as a sugar-cane warehouse) and totally rebuilt after the burning of Fustat, the neighbouring **Church of St Mercurius** claims older antecedents. Beneath its northern aisle lies a tiny crypt where St Barsum the Naked lived with a snake until his death in 317; a special Mass is held here on his nameday (September 10).

A doorway beside the crypt stairway leads through into the rest of the complex. The Upper Church, reached by steps, contains five disused chapels. Of more interest are the Small Church with its *haikal* dedicated to St James the Sawn-asunder, and the early seventh-century **Church of St Shenute**, featuring beautiful cedarwood and ebony iconostases. From the same period comes the diminutive, icon-packed **Church of the Holy Virgin**, beyond which stands the **Convent of St Mercurius**, still inhabited by nuns. The liturgy is celebrated in all the churches (Wed 8am–noon, Fri 7–11am & Sun 6–10am). Adjacent to Deir Abu'l-Sayfayn are extensive Protestant and Maronite **cemeteries**, including a military cemetery for Commonwealth servicemen killed in the Second World War.

The remains of Fustat and Cairo's zebaleen

Behind the Amr Mosque, smouldering rubbish tips and hovels sprawl beneath a pall of smoke, seemingly as far as the Citadel. The hundred-year-old shantytown on the site of ancient Fustat looks – and smells – daunting, but is actually a success story in Third World terms. Its US-sponsored health centre is the most conspicuous example of many recent improvements in a community that used to be at the bottom of the Cairene heap. Should you care to explore, a twenty-minute walk alongside the shantytown will bring you to the **remains of Fustat**. Bring water, a few stones to deter dogs, and above all tread carefully – much of the site consists of centuries-old rubbish tips and kilns, prone to caving in. The foundation walls and water system (still being excavated by the American University) hardly do justice to Fustat's past, though the pottery shards that blanket the site are evocative; some fine early medieval and imported Chinese ware found here can now be seen in the Museum of Islamic Arts (see p.168).

Originally a cluster of tribal encampments around Amr's Mosque, Fustat (City of the Tent) evolved into a mud-brick beehive of multi-storey dwellings with rooftop gardens, fountains, and a piped water and sewage system unequalled in Europe until the eighteenth century. As the Abbassids, Tulunids and Ikhshidids also built their own cities ever further to the northeast, a great conurbation known as **Fustat–Masr** was formed. Its decline began in Fatimid times, as the noxious potteries encouraged migration towards Al-Qahira; thieves moved in and dereliction spread like cancer. In 1020, the mad khalif Al-Hakim ordered his troops to sack Fustat-Masr for reasons worthy of Caligula (see p.162). Yet even in 1168, what remained was so vast that Vizier Shawar decided to evacuate and burn it rather than let the Crusaders occupy the old city beyond Al-Qahira's walls. Set ablaze with 10,000 torches and 20,000 barrels of naphtha, Fustat smouldered for 55 days.

Today the Fustat shantytown is inhabited by seventeen thousand people whose filthy work keeps Cairo tolerably clean. Whole families of **potters** slave over beehive kilns, churning out domestic ware for *baladi* households and piping for sewers and water mains. Even more important are the *zebaleen* or **rubbish-gatherers**. These families collect and sift Cairo's rubbish for anything edible or recyclable. All the glass, cardboard, metal, rags and leather are sold as raw materials to over five hundred factories. Though previously regarded as an embarrassment by the authorities, the *zebaleen* have made an indispensable contribution to Cairo's ecology, recognized by the award of a prize at the World Earth Summit and an official government contract in 1991. Community amenities are being improved through self-help projects with foreign backing, in a development programme that could be a model for others in the Third World.

On the corner of Sharia al-Imam, the road leading down into Fustat, and Sharia Hassan al-Anwar, the newly constructed **Souq el Fustat** (daily 10am–10pm) is a small market for handicrafts and objets d'art made by local artisans, who get subsidized rents on the shops in exchange for teaching handicraft skills to local children. An Egyptian Civilization Museum is being constructed on an adjacent plot, and is due to open in 2008, with exhibits illustrating the history of civilization in Egypt from pharaonic times to the present.

Fustat is served by bus #83 from Midan Ramses. Otherwise, **to return to central Cairo**, walk to Mari Girgis or El-Malek el-Saleh metro station, or head back to the Amr's Mosque and catch a bus (#27 and #134/ to Midan Tahrir, #27 and #825 to Ataba, #27, #83, #94 and #134/ to Ramses).

North to the Aqueduct

Travelling between Coptic and central Cairo by bus or taxi, you'll catch sight of the great **Aqueduct** that carried water to the Citadel. Originally a mere conduit supported by wooden pillars, it was solidly rebuilt in stone by Sultan al-Nasir in 1311 and subsequently extended in 1505 by Al-Ghuri to accommodate the Nile's westward shift, to a total length of 3405m. River water was lifted by the **Burg al-Saqiyya**, a massive hexagonal water-wheel tower near the Corniche. On its western wall can be seen Al-Ghuri's heraldic emblem and slots for engaging the six oxen-powered water wheels, which remained in use until 1872.

The site of this tower is known as **Fumm al-Khalig** ("Mouth of the Canal"), after the waterway that once ran inland to meet the walls of Fatimid al-Qahira. This Khalig Masri ("Egyptian Canal") supplied most of Cairo's water during Mamluke and Ottoman times, and was also linked to the ancient Nile Delta–Red Sea waterway, re-dug by Amr and Al-Nasir. In an annual ceremony to mark the Wafa el-Nil, or Nile flood, the dike that separated it from the river was breached, sending fresh water coursing through the city. Pleasure boats were launched onto the lakes near Bab al-Luq and Ezbekiya, while fireworks heralded nocturnal revelries. But the taming of the Nile spelt the end of this practice, and after piped water was introduced early last century the canal was filled in to create Bur Said and Ramses streets.

Further inland

From the Fumm al-Khalig roundabout, Sharia al-Sadd al-Barrani runs up to Saiyida Zeinab (2km) past a swathe of **Christian cemeteries**. Within the northernmost cemetery, high walls enclose the **Monastery of St Menas** (*Deir Abu Mina*), whose sunken basilical church has been endlessly rebuilt since 724. Having returned the holy remnants of St Menas to his desert monastery (see p.643), the church now gives pride of place to the relics of saints Behnam and Sarah, who were martyred by their own father. The monastery receives very few visitors and has no set opening hours.

Further south, the Aqueduct bestrides a medieval slum centred around a huge **slaughterhouse** and reeking **tanneries**. To outsiders, stark poverty seems all-pervasive; yet among those who live here, social distinctions are keenly felt. A slaughterhouse worker and his boss will both wear bloodstained *galabiyyas* during working hours, and possibly live on the same street – but the former can only speculate on what riches the latter keeps indoors. Conversely, people will salvage designer-label bags and boxes to flaunt on the streets as if they were returning with a purchase.

Unlike the tanneries of Morocco, this is hardly on the tourist trail, although French writer Gustave Flaubert spent an afternoon here in 1850, shooting birds of prey and "wolf-like dogs". However, the odd tourist has been known to attend Saturday evening *zikrs* outside the **Mosque of Sidi Ali Zein al-Abdin**, on the periphery of the quarter of Saiyida Zeinab (see p.184).

Roda Island

The narrow channel between **Roda Island** and the mainland is bridged in such a way that the island engages more with Garden City than with Old Cairo – a reversal of historic ties. As its much-rebuilt **Nilometer** suggests, it was the southern end of Roda that was visited by ferries en route between Memphis and Heliopolis, and Roman ships bound for Babylon-in-Egypt. However, nothing remains of the Byzantine fortress that defied the Muslim invasion, nor the vaster Ayyubid *qasr* where the Bahri Mamlukes were garrisoned, since Roda reverted to agricultural use as Cairo's focus shifted northeastwards. The island's main sight, the **Manial Palace**, re-established a fashion for palatial residences early this century, though it wasn't until the 1950s that Roda experienced a building explosion similar to Zamalek's.

Approaching the sights

With Roda's tourist attractions sited 3km apart, choice of **transport** is a major consideration. The Nilometer is best reached on foot from Old Cairo via the footbridge from the Corniche. You can take a minibus or service taxi down the Corniche from the centre to Old Cairo; alternatively Mari Girgis metro station is just two blocks southeast of the footbridge. Should you decide to settle for only one site, make it the palace, which is easily accessible from central Cairo. Aside from a taxi (£E4–5), a #58 minibus is the fastest way of getting there from Midan Tahrir (Abdel Mouneem Riyad terminal), or minibus #56 from Ramses: alight on Sharia Sayala, near the palace gates. Walking takes about half an hour from downtown Cairo, and on hot days can leave you totally bushed.

The first bridge, coming from downtown, leads to the **Grand Hyatt Hotel**, a deluxe five-star job with some of the best views in Cairo. The next crossing,

Qasr al-Aini Bridge, leads down to **Cairo University Medical Faculty**. By walking 150m south from here you can reach the palace gates without crossing the Manial Bridge, used by traffic heading for Giza. Cairo's **youth hostel** overlooks the El-Gama'a Bridge, 500m further west.

The Manial Palace

The **Manial Palace** (daily 9am–4.30pm; £E20, students £E10) is a Cairo must. Built in 1903, its fabulously eclectic architecture reflects the taste of King Farouk's uncle, Prince Mohammed Ali, author of *The Breeding of Arabian Horses* and the owner of a flawless emerald that magically alleviated his ill health (so legend has it). Each of the main buildings manifests a different style – Persian, Syrian, Moorish, Ottoman and Rococo – or mixes them together with gay abandon.

Having bought your ticket, make a beeline for the **Reception Palace** just inside the gateway. Its magnificent *salamlik*, adorned with stained glass, polychrome tiles and ornate woodcarving, prepares you for the opulent guest rooms upstairs; the finest is the Syrian Room, which was quite literally transplanted from Damascus. On the stairs you'll notice a scale model of Qaitbey's Mausoleum, made entirely of mother-of-pearl.

Leaving the Reception Palace and turning right, you come upon a pseudo-Moroccan tower harbouring the prince's **mosque**, whose lavish decor is reminiscent of the great mosque of his namesake in the Citadel. Further along, the grotesque **Hunting Museum** features scores of mounted ibex heads, gorgeous butterflies and ineptly stuffed fowl, a hermaphrodite goat, a table made from elephants' ears and a vulture's claw candlestick.

The **Prince's Residence**, deeper into the banyan-shaded garden, is richly decorated in a mixture of Turkish and Occidental styles. The drab-looking building out back contains a long **Throne Hall** whose red carpet passes life-size royal portraits hung beneath a sunburst ceiling. Around the outside of this hall are the skeletons of the prince's horse and camel, and a stairway to the upper level (often closed). If accessible, visitors can admire its Obsidian Salon and the private apartments of the prince's mother, enriched by a silver four-poster bed from the Abdin Palace. Lastly, follow the signs to the **Private Museum**, a family hoard of manuscripts, carpets, glassware and silver plate – notice the huge banqueting trays.

The Nilometer and Umm Kalthoum Museum

The southern tip of Roda Island, most easily accessed via a footbridge from the Corniche west of Mari Girgis and Old Cairo, features a new **museum** dedicated to the life and work of Egypt's most popular singer, **Umm Kalthoum** (daily 10am–5pm; £E2). Through audiovisual clips, photos, press cuttings and a filmshow, the museum attempts to recreate the life of this giant of Arabic music (see p.840). Though she died in 1975, her songs, invariably backed by an orchestra of violins, remain massively popular throughout the Arab world. Exhibits include 78rpm wax records, letters from Egyptian and other Arab heads of state including Nasser, Sadat and King Farouk, and, most poignantly, her trademark pink scarf and dark glasses. Unfortunately, however, all explanation is in Arabic only.

In the same compound is the **Nilometer** (daily 9am–5pm; £E6, student £E3). From ancient times into the present century, Egyptian agriculture depended on the annual **flooding of the Nile**. Crop yields were predicted and taxes were set according to the river's level in August, as measured by Nilometers. A reading of 16 *ells* (8.6m) foretold the valley's complete irrigation; significantly more or less meant widespread flooding or drought. Public rejoicing followed the announcement of the Wafa el-Nil ("Abundance of the Nile"), while any other verdict caused gloom and foreboding.

Although the southern tip of Roda has probably featured a Nilometer since pharaonic times, the existing one dates from 861 and its Turkish kiosk is actually a modern replica, built in 1947 and recently restored. Descending well below the level of the Nile, its stone-lined shaft was connected to the river by three tunnels (now sealed) at different heights – the uppermost is still accessible. Around the shaft's interior are Koranic verses in *kufic* script, extolling rain as God's blessing; its central column is graduated into 16 *ells* of roughly 54cm each. The Nilometer is often locked, but its caretaker will turn out for rare visitors.

The neighbouring **Monastirli Palace** is a Rococo confection dating from 1850. Built as a conference centre, the palace has now been transformed into an International Music Centre, with a theatre, exhibition hall and library, but is open to tourists only one Sunday a month (£E5; ⓦwww.manasterly.com).

The southern suburbs

South of Old Cairo, a ribbon of development follows the east bank of the Nile down to Helwan. Though easily reached by metro, these **southern suburbs** hold little attraction for tourists, notwithstanding Ma'adi's popularity as an expatriate residential area. However, even the least-favoured quarters cast some light on various facets of Egyptian life.

Al-Basatin: the Jewish cemetery

A case in point is the **Jewish cemetery of Al-Basatin**, 3km beyond El-Khalifa (minibus #54 or bus #160/ from Midan Tahrir, or microbus from behind Ramses station). The cemetery was given to Cairo's Jewish community by Ibn Tulun in 822, and was divided equally between rabbinical Jews and the dissident Karaite sect. In the 1960s and 1970s, all the graves were stripped of their marble, and squatters occupied the mausoleums, though Al-Basatin has few of these compared to the Muslim and Coptic cemeteries. The 1980s saw an agreement by the elders of Cairo's depleted Jewish community to accept US$80,000 in return for allowing a highway to be ploughed through the cemetery. When foreign rabbis intervened, the whole affair acquired diplomatic overtones and turned into a massive legal wrangle. In the end the government reached an agreement with an American Jewish organization to rehouse the squatters, restore the cemetery and build a flyover to carry the ring road over it.

Ma'adi and the quarries of Tura

With its Corniche boutiques and takeaways, and acres of villas set amidst luxuriant grounds, **Ma'adi** is unmistakably wealthy. Besides native millionaires and Gulf Arabs, most of Egypt's American community lives here, and it's also home to some of the city's trendy but expensive **restaurants**, such as the Thai *Bua Khao*, at 9 Road 151 (daily 11.30am–11pm; ☎02/358-0126), a handful of Chinese restaurants, including a branch of the city-wide *Peking* chain at 29 Sharia al-Nasr/Road 257 (daily noon–1am; ☎02/516-4218), and an Indian, the *Bukhara*, 43 Sharia Misr Helwan (daily noon–1am; ☎02/380 5999). There's also a branch of Zamalek's pasta parlour *Dido's Al Dente* at 1 Road 270 (daily 10am–2am; ☎02/520-2255), and a posh patisserie, *La Poire*, in the Pico Building at 24 Sharia Wadi el-Nil (daily 7am–11pm).

The **Military Hospital**, on the Corniche further north, is the largest of its kind in the Middle East. It was here that the ex-Shah of Iran died of cancer, and President Sadat was rushed by helicopter from the blood-soaked reviewing stand in Medinet Nasr. As a young officer during World War II, Sadat was actually stationed in Ma'adi when he became embroiled in a Nazi spy ring (see p.215). Ma'adi is directly accessible from Tahrir or Ramses by microbus service taxi or metro (25min).

Further south amidst the Muqattam foothills, the **quarries of Tura** have yielded fine limestone since pharaonic times (it was here that pyramid casing blocks were quarried), and now also produce cement.

Helwan

The once-fashionable spa of **Helwan** is now grossly polluted by a gigantic **iron- and steelworks** that exploits power from the Aswan Dam and iron ore from the Western Desert. The steelworks wreak eco-death on a nineteenth-century **Japanese Garden** (daily: winter 9am–10pm; summer 9am–midnight; £E2, video £E10) – complete with Buddhas and a pagoda – five blocks east from Helwan metro station (turn left as you exit); ask for *Ganenit el-Arbaine Harami*. One hundred metres south of Ain Helwan metro station (one stop back up the line from Helwan station) on the west side of the tracks, a tacky but fun **Waxworks Museum** (*methaf sham*; daily 9am–3.30pm; £E2) portrays such moments in Egyptian history as the death of Cleopatra and Salah al-Din's meeting with Richard the Lionheart. The sulphurous **Ain Helwan Baths** (daily 24hr; free) are less than 100m northwest of Ain Helwan station.

Gezira and the west bank

Flowing northwards through Cairo, the Nile divides into channels around the two major islands of Roda and Gezira. **Gezira**, the larger island, is further from the centre than Roda and notably more spacious and verdant than the rest of Cairo.

Across the island, elevated highways bear cross-town traffic to diverse **districts on the west bank** of the Nile, collectively known as **Giza** and administered as a separate governorate from Cairo. Moving south through its neighbourhoods, **Imbaba** is a working-class district and former site of Cairo's main camel market – a world apart from the adjoining **Aguza**, with its Corniche nightlife, and even more from the Dallas-style pretensions of **Mohandiseen**. Further south and east is **Dokki**, whose wealthy enclaves give way to *baladi* market quarters, the green lungs of Cairo's zoo and scattered university faculties, before the dusty expanse of Giza city extends to the Pyramids. Giza's **transport** and utilities are functionally integrated with Cairo's.

Gezira and Zamalek

Gezira (literally "island") dominates the waterfront from Garden City to Bulaq, its three sets of bridges spanning the Nile. Nearly 4km long and 1km wide, the island is big enough to encompass two distinct zones. The southern half, featuring the Opera House complex, parks, a viewing tower and famous sporting clubs, is Gezira proper. **Zamalek** (pronounced "Zah-*mah*-lek"), further north, is pure real estate – apartments, villas, offices and embassies – with a Westernized ambience and nightlife. Both seem so integral to Cairo that it's hard to envisage their absence, yet the island itself only coalesced in the early 1800s and remained unstable until the first Aswan Dam regulated the Nile's flood in the 1900s: for more on the history and architecture of Gezira and Zamalek, check out Samir Raafat's website at ⓦwww.egy.com/landmarks.

Almost a third of the island belongs to the **Gezira Sporting Club** (see p.276), laid out by the British Army on land given by Khedive Tewfiq. The club's main pursuits were horse racing and polo, imbued with an extraordinary mystique. "It is on the Gezira polo grounds that the officers of the Cavalry Brigade are tested for military efficiency and fitness for command", wrote C.S. Jarvis in the 1920s. Diplomats and selected upper-crust Egyptians also belonged to the club and, after Nasser decided against expropriation following the revolution, it soon acquired members from the new elite. The hefty membership fees still restrict access to its golf course, tennis courts, stables, gardens and pet cemetery; non-members are resolutely excluded.

Approaches to Gezira and Zamalek: the bridges

The **6th October Bridge**, high above the Sporting Club, is more of a direct link between Aguza and central Cairo than a viable approach to Gezira (though there are stairs down to both banks of the island). However, it does overlook the offices and former ground (now used only for training) of **Ahly FC**, one of Egypt's top football teams, whose name means "National".

It's the southern bit of **Gezira**, however, that's most accessible and worth seeing. Despite heavy traffic, it's enjoyable to walk across the **Tahrir Bridge** (200m from Midan Tahrir), catching the breeze and watching barges and feluccas on the river. Gaining the island, you can strike 200m northwards past the *El-Borg Hotel* and turn left down an avenue to reach the Cairo Tower (10min), or follow the traffic heading for Dokki, which brings you to the Cairo Opera House and several museums (5–10min). Alternatively, you can take a *caleche* (a horse-drawn carriage seating up to five people) on a circuit of Gezira – a short trip, around the Cairo Tower area, will cost around £E25, while a longer circuit, all the way round the Gezira Sporting Club, works out at about £E40; *caleches* can be picked up on Sharia al-Gezira at the corner of Sharia el-Borg, or on Sharia Tahrir just before the Gala'a Bridge.

To get to **Zamalek**, save yourself a long walk from central Cairo and grab a taxi (which shouldn't cost more than £E5). Buses from Midan Tahrir to Zamalek will drop you on Sharia Gabalaya on the western side of the district, and there's no lack of minibuses heading west along **26th July Street** from Midan Ataba and Midan Ramses. Having traversed the island, the highway crosses the **Zamalek Bridge** onto the west bank, where Midan Sphinx funnels traffic into Mohandiseen (see p.214). When the new Metro line opens there will be a station in the north of the island called, unsurprisingly, Zamalek.

Cairo Tower

Rising 187m above Gezira, the **Borg al-Qahira** or **Cairo Tower** offers a stupendous view of the seething immensity of Cairo (daily: winter 8am–11pm; summer 9am–1am; £E50, video permit £E20); the entrance is to the north of the tower in Sharia el-Borg. Built between 1957 and 1962 with Soviet help, the tower combines pharaonic and socialist realist motifs within a latticework shaft of poured concrete that blossoms into a lotus finial.

On the fourteenth floor is an overpriced "Egyptian-style" restaurant (set menu payable with tower ticket: £E90 for entry and meal) that – when it's working – revolves for a 360° view; above it is a similarly styled cafeteria serving tolerable tea (entry plus drink is £E70), with a viewing room – complete with telescopes – upstairs from here. The real attraction, though, provided by the café, restaurant and a **viewing platform** at the top, is the **panoramic vista of Cairo**. East across the river, the blue-and-white *Nile Hilton* and the antenna-festooned Television Building delineate an arc of central Cairo. Beyond lies the medieval

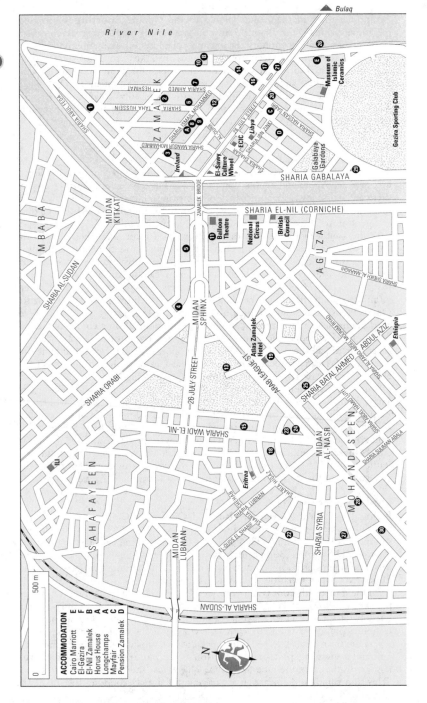

ACCOMMODATION

Cairo Marriott	E
El-Gezira	F
El-Nil Zamalek	B
Horus House	A
Longchamps	A
Mayfair	C
Pension Zamalek	D

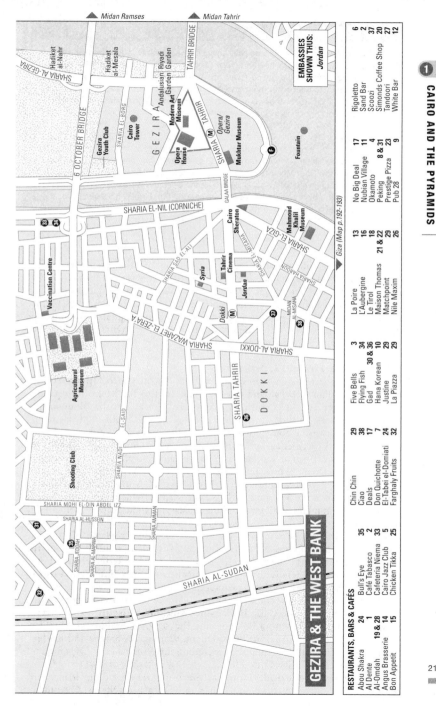

GEZIRA & THE WEST BANK

EMBASSIES SHOWN THUS: *Jordan*

RESTAURANTS, BARS & CAFÉS

Abou Shakra	24	Bull's Eye	35
Al Dente	1	Café Tabasco	2
Al-Omdah	19 & 28	Cafeteria Niema	33
Angus Brasserie	14	Cairo Jazz Club	5
Bon Appetit	15	Chicken Tikka	25

Chin Chin	29	Five Bells	29
Ciao	38	Flying Fish	34
Deals	17	Gad	30 & 36
Don Quichotte	7	Hana Korean	10
El-Tabei el-Domiati	24	Justine	29
Farghaly Fruits	32	La Piazza	32

La Poire	13	No Big Deal	17
L'Aubergine	16	Nubian Village	11
Le Tirol	18	Okamoto	4
Maison Thomas	21 & 22	Peking	8 & 31
Matchpoint	29	Prestige Pizza	23
Nile Maxim	26	Pub 28	9

Rigoletto	6		
Sand Bar	2		
Scoozi	37		
Simonds Coffee Shop	20		
Tandoori	27		
White Bar	12		

Giza (Map p.192-193)

Cairo's best views

The Cairo Tower, with its sporadically revolving restaurant, is just one of several high points where you can take in a view over Cairo. The newer and more reliably revolving restaurant at the *Grand Hyatt* hotel (see p.117) is high enough, and well enough placed, to offer what must rate as the very best Cairo view, encompassing the Pyramids, the Citadel, the Nile and most of downtown. The rooftop bar at the *Nile Hilton* (see pp.117–118) is a close competitor, with great views of Tahrir Square that only the front rooms at the *Ismailia House* hotel can equal, and beyond the square you can see as far as the Citadel and the Muqattam Hills. The Citadel itself (see p.176) offers a good view over Islamic Cairo, while some of Islamic Cairo's minarets give you a vista as far as the Pyramids on a clear day if they are open (the Qalaoun complex and the Blue Mosque are among the best; the al-Muayyad minarets atop Bab Zwayla also give a pretty good view). But the best and widest view over Islamic Cairo is from the high point in al-Azhar Park (see p.190). Finally, for a vista over the chaos and mayhem that calls itself Midan Ramses, the terrace café of the *Hotel Everest* (see p.148) is the place.

quarter, bristling with minarets below the Citadel and the serene Muqattam Hills. Roda Island and deluxe hotels dominate the view south (upriver); to the north are Zamalek, Shubra and the Nile Delta. Westwards, the city extends to meet the desert, with the Pyramids visible on the horizon on clear days. Come a while before sunset to witness Cairo transformed by nightfall, as a thousand muezzins call across the water. Below the tower is the *Legends* nightclub (see p.269), which has bellydancing every night.

The Opera House complex

Fans of postmodernist architecture should check out the **Cairo Opera House**, which is near Tahrir Bridge and directly connected to the Metro (the station is called "Opera", but is confusingly marked as "Gezira" on the Metro map). Outwardly Islamic in style, its interior melds pharaonic motifs with elements of the Baroque opera houses of the nineteenth century: an audacious blend of Oriental and Occidental by Japanese architect Koichiro Shikida. A US$30 million gift from Japan, it was built in 1988, belatedly replacing the old building on Midan Opera, which burned down in 1971. Off to the right as you walk towards the Opera House is the **Modern Art Museum** (daily except Mon 10am–1.30pm & 5–10pm; £E10, students £E5), which displays paintings, sculptures and graphics by Egyptian artists since 1908; there is always something new on show.

Following Sharia Tahrir towards the west bank, you'll pass the old Gezira Exhibition Grounds, whose dilapidated pavilions formerly housed the **Gezira Museum** (objets d'art collected by the royal family) and a **Planetarium** – both closed for long-term renovation – and a **Museum of Egyptian Civilization**, illustrating national history from pharaonic to modern times, also closed, but due to reopen in a new venue at Fustat in 2008 (see p.204). Across the road to the south, just before the Galaa Bridge, the **Mukhtar Museum** (daily except Mon 9am–2pm & 5–9pm; £E5) honours the sculptor Mahmoud Mukhtar (1891–1934), who is buried in the basement. Working in bronze and marble, he created several patriotic sculptures, including the *Renaissance of Egypt* monument that welcomes drivers into Dokki.

The 27-storey **El-Gezirah Hotel** at the southern tip of the island can be reached by slip roads from the Tahrir and Galaa bridgeheads. On public holidays, a **fountain** in the middle of the Nile between Gezira and Roda shoots an immense jet of water into the sky.

Zamalek

Originally a very British neighbourhood, despite its Continental grid of tree-lined boulevards, **Zamalek** still has bags of social cachet: renting a flat here is the Cairene equivalent of moving into Manhattan. Unlike most parts of Cairo, the quarter feels very private; residents withdraw into air-conditioned high-rises or 1930s apartment buildings, and with so many foreign companies and **embassies** in the area (see p.291), most of the streets are lifeless after dark.

Somewhat paradoxically, Zamalek also features some of the trendiest **night-spots** in Cairo. Near the Aguza side of the Gezira Sporting Club on Sharia Hassan Sabry, the *Four Corners* complex contains, among others, a deluxe French restaurant, *Justine* (see p.261); there are more bars and restaurants to be found in the *Marriott Hotel*. Other places congregate north of the 26th July flyover. Middle-class Cairenes and expats favour *Pub 28*, at the junction of Shagar al-Durr and Hassan Assim streets, and *Harry's Bar* at the *Marriott*. A younger crowd congregates at *Deals* bar and the neighbouring café on Sharia Sayed el-Bakry, and the *Sand Bar* and *Tabasco Café* on Sharia al-Marashli.

Zamalek by day has less to offer, though children may enjoy the **aquarium grotto** in **Gabalaya Gardens** (daily 9am–4pm; 35pt; see p.275), entered from Sharia Gabalaya. For more cultural pursuits, head for the other end of Sharia al-Gezira as it curves around the northeastern edge of the Sporting Club. Here, a graceful nineteenth-century villa now houses the Museum of Islamic Ceramics (see below); the **Mahmoud Khalil Museum** that was formerly housed here is now in Dokki (see p.216). The modern annexes of the adjacent **Cairo Marriott Hotel** screen what was originally a "madly sumptuous palace" built for Napoleon's wife Empress Eugénie, later sold to wealthy Copts in lieu of Ismail's debts and turned into a hotel. Non-residents can wander in and loll amidst *khedival* splendour for the price of a drink.

Although Zamalek is pretty young by Egyptian standards, it isn't without its history. The portions of Sharia Shagar al-Durr and Sharia Mansur Moham-med south of 26 July Street were once home to nineteen **Edwardian villas** constructed by the British government in 1906–7 to house important official employees. Of the nine still standing, the grandest is at 20 Sharia Ibn Zinki (on the corner of Mansur Mohammed) with its imposing triple-arched portico. Further south, the *Four Corners* complex occupies the site of a villa where the UK's senior representative in wartime Egypt, **Lord Moyne**, was shot in 1944, along with his driver, by members of a far-right Zionist paramilitary group called the Stern Gang. A more recent Zamalek murder, which shocked the Middle East as much, was that of Tunisian singer **Zikra** in November 2003 at her swanky apartment on Sharia Mohammed Mazhar. She was killed by her husband, apparently in a fit of jealousy, after refusing his demand that she give up her career. Having produced two pistols and a machine gun, he pumped Zikra with 25 rounds, then shot two of their friends, and finally himself. Thousands attended the singer's funeral.

Museum of Islamic Ceramics

Housed in a white-domed villa close to the *Cairo Marriott*, the **Museum of Islamic Ceramics** (daily except Fri 10am–1.30pm & 5–9pm; £E25, students £E12) is one of Cairo's most agreeable museums. Built by Prince Amru Abrahim in the late nineteenth century, the structure itself is worth a look for its elaborate marble inlays and floors, while the collection inside contains pieces from Egypt, Persia, Syria, Turkey, Morocco, Iraq and even Andalusia (Muslim Spain), ranging from the seventh century to the present. The illustrated guidebook (£E25) explains each piece in English and also gives a thorough account of the history of Islamic ceramics. Downstairs there's an art gallery (same hours; free) that exhibits original paintings and sculptures as well as prints by modern Egyptian artists such as Asraf and Alzamzami. All the works exhibited are for sale.

Imbaba

From Midan KitKat, 300m north of Zamalek Bridge, Sharia al-Sudan arcs through the **Imbaba** district, whose overspill covers the site of the "**Battle of the Pyramids**" where Napoleon's army routed the Mamlukes on July 21, 1798, prior to taking Cairo. Unfortunately for Napoleon – who dreamed of "founding a religion, marching into Asia riding an elephant", bearing "the new Koran that I would have composed to suit my needs" – his strategic ambition to disrupt British power in India was literally scuppered when Nelson sank his fleet at Abu Qir Bay. Within eighty years, the Suez Canal had cemented the link between naval power, control of Egypt and Britain's empire "East of Suez"; a bond later reinforced by aviation. Although flying boats on the famous Cape-to-Cairo run used the Nile, most Imperial Airways flights used **Imbaba Airport**, now a flying school.

Mohandiseen

Laid out during the 1960s to house Egypt's new technocrats, Medinat Mohandiseen ("Engineers' City"), as the suburb was initially called, responded to an influx of business and media folk during the Sadat era by shortening its name to just **Mohandiseen** and emulating America. Nowhere else in Cairo can you cruise down a boulevard glittering with boutiques and junk food outlets, squint and imagine that you're in LA. Even the palm trees seem to hail from Hollywood, rather than the Nile. But around midday on Fridays, the illusion is ruptured as herds of camels are driven through Mohandiseen en route to the slaughterhouse, bringing traffic to a standstill.

Sharia Orabi runs northwest for 1.5km (strictly speaking, this area is called Sahafeyeen), but other than the **International Language Institute** (ILI), two blocks from the Al-Sudan ring road, it has no more to offer than the continuation of 26th July Street. Most of the action occurs along Mohandiseen's main axis, **Arab League Street** (Sharia Gameat al-Dowal al-Arabiya), also known as "The Mall", which is bisected by palms and shrubbery for its three-kilometre length. Due to its orientation, you can look down it on a clear day (admittedly rare in Cairo) and see the Pyramids of Giza in the distance. During summer Cairene families picnic here – an indication of how few green spaces are available. The avenue's main landmark is the **Atlas Zamalek Hotel**, 500m past Midan Sphinx. Fast food joints – both home-grown chains and international franchises – proliferate along the way to Midan al-Nasr, the centre of a radial grid of streets harbouring a dozen **embassies**.

To **reach the quarter** from central Cairo, you can catch buses from Midan Falaki, Midan Tahrir, Midan Ataba or Midan Ramses that end up on Sharia al-Sudan near Midan Lubnan. Alternatively, to get to Midan al-Nasr on Arab League Street, you can take buses from Falaki or Tahrir (Arab League Building), Ramses or Ataba (see p.114 for bus numbers). A faster way is to jump in a service taxi microbus at Ramses or the corner of 26th July Street with Sharia al-Gala and get whisked across Zamalek to Midan Sphinx or Arab League Street (but make sure of the destination of the microbus).

Beyond the Al-Sudan ring road lies **Bulaq al-Dakhrour**, an unplanned sprawl of ramshackle dwellings built by migrant *fellaheen* from Upper Egypt and the Delta. Bulaq al-Dakhrour ends at the **Maryotteya Canal**, beyond which the village of **Kerdassa** (see p.237) precedes another canal before the strip of luxury hotels (*Mövenpick, Pyramids Park, Sofitel, Oasis*) along the Desert Road to Alexandria.

Aguza and Dokki

A 100-metre-wide channel separates Zamalek and Gezira from the west bank districts of **Aguza and Dokki**. Being mainly residential and devoid of major "sights", they're only worth considering as a quieter place to stay than central Cairo, or for their nightlife, though in their time these prim-looking neighbourhoods generated as much scandal as the Clot Bey and Abdin quarters once did.

Aguza

Wedged between Mohandiseen and the Nile, **Aguza** ("Old Woman") stretches its legs **along the Corniche**. At the northern end of Sharia el-Nil, near the Zamalek Bridge, are the **Balloon Theatre** – a regular venue for the National and Reda dance troupes – and Egypt's **National Circus** (see p.277). Further south at no.192 is the **British Council**, a fulcrum of expat life and a sought-after place of employment (see p.86 and p.292). A popular stopover for taxi drivers and nightclubbers is the 24-hour *Cafeteria Niema*, opposite the Police Hospital near the 6th October Bridge.

Fifty years ago the Corniche was a popular mooring place for houseboats, which saw their share of scandal. One was occupied by a famous belly dancer, Hekmet Fathy, who used to entice Allied staff officers aboard to inveigle secrets from them on behalf of the Nazis. Also involved was a young Egyptian officer, Anwar Sadat, who attempted to convey messages to Rommel and was subsequently jailed by the British for treason. Post-revolutionary Egypt was austere by comparison, but hardly innocent. In 1988 the government tried to suppress the memoirs of Eitimad Khorshid, a *femme fatale* who cut a swathe through the Nasserite establishment of the 1950s, and promised to reveal all in what became an underground bestseller.

To reach any of the above locations, catch a taxi via the 6th October Bridge, an elevated extension of which pushes 500m inland towards the **Agricultural Museum** (daily except Mon 9am–1pm; 10pt) in the grounds of the Ministry of Agriculture; the entrance is on the south side of the estate. A group of six pavilions – some closed for renovation, others that could themselves almost be museum pieces – these solemnly dingy museums of yesteryear contain exhibits on ancient farming techniques, with stuffed animals and models of native village life. There are also quirky items such as prettily arranged displays of insects and a rather horrific demonstration of various animal diseases. One of the pavilions houses the **Cotton Museum** (closed Thurs & Fri), which gives the rundown on Egypt's main cash crop. For most visitors, however, the pleasant grounds are more of a draw than the dusty old museums. The Ministry of Agriculture marks the point where Aguza merges into Dokki.

Dokki

The social geography of **Dokki** (usually pronounced "Do'i", with a glottal stop in the middle) is more complex than Aguza's. Broadly speaking, the rich occupy the land nearest the river and the Dokki Sporting Club, with a phalanx of private hospitals, VD clinics and covert bordellos separating their villas and apartments from the poorer market quarter to the southwest.

Coming over the Galaa Bridge from Gezira Island, you'll see Mahmoud Mukhtar's **Renaissance of Egypt statue** and the twin towers of the **Cairo Sheraton**, which is the departure point for **buses to Tel Aviv and Jerusalem** (see p.300). From here, Sharia al-Sad al-Ali itself continues on to meet Suleyman Gohar, Dokki's vibrant **market quarter**. For **cinemas** and **restaurants**, look along Sharia Tahrir and Sharia al-Misaha, radiating west and southwest from the Galaa Bridge.

Two main roads head south from the *Sheraton*. Running one block inland, **Sharia el-Giza** passes the **Russian Embassy** and the former residence of President Sadat, where his widow, Jihan, still lives in guarded seclusion (photography is prohibited in this area). Another once-famous resident of Dokki was Field Marshal Amr, a long-time friend and ally of Nasser's who supposedly committed suicide after being accused of plotting a coup against him, and was posthumously scapegoated for Egypt's defeat in the 1967 war.

The main feature of interest on Sharia el-Giza, however, is the **Mahmoud Khalil Museum** (daily except Mon 10am–6pm; ☎02/336-2376; £E25, students £E12; wheelchair access), two blocks south of the *Sheraton*, housed in the refurbished mansion where Khalil, a pre-war politician and Agriculture Minister, lived with his French-born wife, Emeline Hector. Together they built up this magnificent collection of art and sculpture, mostly French Impressionist and post-Impressionist works by the likes of Monet, Renoir, Gauguin and Pissarro, but also featuring artists such as Van Gogh, Delacroix and Rodin. There are information sheets on the artists in various languages, but the computer screens that tell you about the Khalils and their home are, unfortunately, in Arabic only.

Running parallel to Sharia el-Giza is the Corniche, **Sharia el-Nil** (now officially Sharia Gamal Abdel Nasser). Three boats moored 200m south of the *Cairo Sheraton* house **Dr Ragab's Papyrus Institute** (daily 9am–9pm; free), where the ancient craft of papyrus-making (which died out in the tenth century AD but was revived in modern times by Dr Ragab) is demonstrated. Although it's more of a papyrus emporium than a museum (and pricey to boot), you are not harassed to buy.

Beyond the Papyrus Institute are Cairo's **Rowing Club** and **Yacht Club**, both citadels of privilege. A few blocks nearer Giza, the Nasr Building contains two excellent Swiss-owned **restaurants**: *Le Chalet* and *Le Château*.

Dokki is well served by buses #109, #194, #203, #529, #566, #791 and #814 from in front of the Arab League Building on Midan Tahrir, which run down Sharia Tahrir. Dokki metro stop is also on Sharia Tahir, and reasonably close to both the Mahmoud Khalil Museum and Dr Ragab's Papyrus Institute.

Giza

In pharaonic times **Giza** lay en route between Heliopolis and Memphis and probably also housed the skilled corps of pyramid-builders. As Memphis declined during the Christian era, so Giza flourished, thanks to its proximity to the Fortress of Babylon, across the river; Amr's reopening of the ancient Delta–Red Sea canal subsequently boosted its prosperity under Muslim rule. Giza's apogee coincided with the reign of Salah al-Din – the Moorish traveller Ibn Jubayr described it as a "large and important burgh with fine buildings" – when its Sunday market attracted vast crowds. But the area's vulnerability to floods caused stagnation, and it wasn't until Ismail laid the Pyramids Road, drained swamps and built a palace in the 1860s that Giza became fashionable again. By Nasser's time, however, expansion was proceeding virtually unchecked. As Giza's population topped a million, a tide of high-rise hovels, tacky nightclubs and roaring flyovers devoured crumbling villas, erstwhile farmland and desert, right to the Giza Plateau beneath the Pyramids.

The zoo and Midan Giza can be reached by **bus** from Tahrir (#30, #355 and #357, minibuses #82 and #83), Ramses (#30 and minibus #83) and Ataba (#6, #9, #106 and #109), and also from Ramses and Abdel Mouneen Riyad by service taxi microbus; alternatively, they are not far from Faysal and Giza metro stations.

Around Cairo Zoo and University

The extensive grounds which Deschamps laid out for Ismail's palace are now divided into Cairo's **Zoological Garden** – which is packed on Fridays and public holidays, but fun to visit at other times (see p.277) – and the smaller **El-Urman Garden**: along with the **floating restaurants** near the **El-Gama'a Bridge**, they're marked on the "Old Cairo and Roda Island" map (see pp.192–193). The bridge is named after **Cairo University**, which was founded in 1908 as a counterweight to traditionalist Al-Azhar but has never been any the less political. Access to its scattered faculties is controlled by Central Security, so foreigners may need a letter of introduction (or at least their passports) to pass beyond its gates. Aside from making student friends, morbid curiosity might inspire a visit to the Agricultural Faculty, near the bottom of Sharia Gameat al-Qahira. Occupying a former palace of Mohammed Ali, its basement holds remnants of his torture chamber.

Midan Giza and Pyramids Road

West of the **El-Giza Bridge** and south of the university belt, Cairo's second largest **bus and taxi terminal** agitates **Midan Giza**. Its seething ranks include buses to the Pyramids; minibuses to Tahrir, Ramses and Heliopolis; and service taxis to Fayoum City, Beni Suef and the Red Sea Coast. A few minutes' walk south is **Giza Station**. More flyovers funnel traffic onto the **Pyramids Road** (Sharia al-Ahram), which runs the gauntlet of **nightclubs** and tourist bazaars for 8km. It was outside a hotel on this avenue that seventeen Greek tourists were shot dead by Islamic radicals, who mistook them for a group of Israelis, in spring 1996. A couple of kilometres before the Pyramids of Giza, Sharia al-Ahram crosses two canals in quick succession, which lead south to Saqqara and Dahsur; service taxi microbuses for both can be found by the first of these two canals, Maryotteya. See pp.225–253 for details of both these and the Giza pyramid site.

The northern suburbs

During the last century, Cairo's **northern suburbs** swallowed up villages and farmland and expanded far into the desert to form a great arc of residential neighbourhoods stretching from the Nile to the Muqattam. **Heliopolis**, with its handsome boulevards and Art Deco villas, is still favoured above the satellite suburbs that have mushroomed in recent decades, and retains a sizeable foreign community. Otherwise, tourists usually only venture into **Abbassiya** for the Sinai Bus Terminal, or to visit the Coptic Patriarchate and Sakakini Palace; and you have to be fanatically keen to bother hunting down the Virgin's Tree in **Matariyya**,

Sadat's tomb in **Medinet Nasr**, or Mamluke edifices in **Bulaq**. See the "Greater Cairo" map on pp.106-107 for a guide to the location of these areas.

Bulaq, Shubra and Rod el-Farag

Bulaq and its neighbours **Shubra** and **Rod el-Farag** (northwest of central Cairo) are run-down and overcrowded, averaging 170,000 residents per square kilometre – ten times the density of Garden City – and have a predominantly *baladi* ambience. More or less bereft of "sights", these quarters might appeal to visitors fascinated by ordinary Cairene life. **Getting there**, bus #134 serves Shubra from Tahrir and Ramses. However, Shubra and Rod el-Farag are best reached by metro. Bulaq was less accessible at the time of writing, as roadworks on 26th July Street in Bulaq have meant that buses and service taxis must make a diversion, though the new elevated roadway should make the journey faster when completed.

Bulaq

Immediately east of the 6th October flyover (see the "Central Cairo" map on pp.126–127) lies the oldest of the northern suburbs, **Bulaq**, whose name derives from the Coptic word for "marsh". During medieval times, the westward shift of the Nile turned a sandbank into an island, which merged with the east bank as the intervening channel silted up. As the Fatimid port of Al-Maks was left high and dry, Bulaq became the new anchorage in the 1350s, rapidly developing into an entrepôt after Sultan Barsbey re-routed the spice trade and encouraged manufacturing. When Mohammed Ali set about establishing a foundry, textiles factory and modern shipyards here in the 1820s, Bulaq was the obvious site. Unfortunately, the Ottomans permitted free trade, enabling British manufacturers to undersell local industries and force Egypt back into its dependency on cotton exports to the Lancashire mills.

Since then, small workshops and apartment buildings have taken over Bulaq, while world affairs are handled in two towering landmarks along the Corniche: the **Television Building** and the **Cairo Plaza**. Inland of the latter is a onetime hostel for members of the Rifai order, next to the **Mosque of Sinan Pasha**, a sixteenth-century hybrid of Mamluke and Ottoman styles. More revered by locals for its namesake's *baraka* is the fifteenth-century **Mosque of Abu'l'Ila**, on 26th July Street just west of the Corniche. Nearby stand the former **royal stables of Mohammed Ali**, which at one time housed the Royal Carriage Museum (now in the Citadel, see p.179).

Shubra

Two million Cairenes live in the sprawling beehive known as **Shubra**, the older part of which is called Shubra al-Balad to distinguish it from the newer outgrowth beyond the Ismailiya Canal, dubbed Shubra al-Kheima. Originally an island (its name, "Elephant", supposedly comes from a ship that ran aground), Shubra became attached to the mainland about the same time as Bulaq, but was given over to orchards and villages until the nineteenth century. In 1808, Mohammed Ali built a summer palace here that caused Europeans to snigger ("The taste, alas! of an English upholsterer"), where he later died insane. Other palaces were erected by Ismail, who also laid a carriage road to the original residence, planted with sycamore-fig and acacia trees, where Cairenes promenaded.

The 1891 edition of *Murray's Handbook* deemed **Sharia Shubra** "the most republican promenade in the world. No description of vehicle, nor manner of animal, biped or quadruped, is excluded, and the Khedive and his outriders are jostled and crossed in a most unseemly fashion by files of bare-boned and sore-covered mules and donkeys, whipped in by ragged urchins." Nowadays the avenue seems thoroughly proletarian, for Shubra has long since evolved from a garden suburb into densely packed quarters where educated Copts and Muslims rub shoulders with poor rural migrants.

Though self-help projects have improved some of the bleak low-rise estates in Shubra al-Kheima, dire poverty inclines a minority towards radical Islam, and reinforces the traditional superstitions that most Cairenes at least half-believe. *Baladi* folk turn instinctively to **magic**, whereas educated people will exhaust rational solutions before resorting to a sheikh or sheikha. What psychologists might regard as mental illnesses are treated as cases of demonic possession, possibly caused by deliberate cursing. (One method of hexing is to recite the 33rd *sura* of the Koran backwards.) While certain moulids feature public **exorcisms**, most are private, especially those with pagan elements. Joseph McPherson, Cairo's secret police chief in the 1920s, witnessed a *zaar* where celebrants whirled to ancient and Muslim incantations, cymbals clashed, and a ram, ganders, doves and rabbits were sacrificed, their blood being daubed on the participants, whose frenzy increased:

Sometimes they bent their bodies back, till they formed a writhing and vibrating bow, resting on the ground by the heels and back of the head, whilst the muscles of their bodies carried on the dance with unbelievable contortions.

When all concerned believe in the ritual's spiritual efficacy, the desired result is frequently achieved.

Rod el-Farag

During the 1950s, a slice of Shubra al-Balad was developed as a separate residential and commercial district, named "Farag's Orchard" after its previous role. The name remains appropriate, since **Rod el-Farag** hosts Cairo's largest **fruit and vegetable market**, Abu el-Farag. Like the others, it's the exclusive preserve of one or two cabals of wholesalers. In Rod el-Farag's case, they hail from the villages around the capital, whereas elsewhere *Saiyidis* from Upper Egypt may control trade. The modern **Port of Cairo** is another local source of wealth with a shady underside.

Abbassiya, Hada'iq al-Qubba and Medinet Nasr

In practice, the demarcation lines between these northeastern districts (which subdivide into other quarters) and Heliopolis are blurred by sheer density, overcrowding and interlocking transport networks.

Abbassiya

The sprawling **Abbassiya** district gets its name from a palace built by Mohammed Ali's grandson, Pasha Abbas I, who dreaded assassination during his brief reign (1848–54) and kept camels saddled there for rapid flight into the desert – to no avail, for he was murdered by his servants. Previously, the area was called Ridaniya and was the site of the last battle between the Mamlukes and the invading Ottoman Turks, who went on to take Cairo. Nearer the centre, the British established the Abbassiya Barracks (where the nationalist leader Orabi surrendered after his defeat at Tell el-Kebir), which vastly expanded during wartime. Like the Army GHQ (still located in Abbassiya), it was later seized by the Free Officers in a bloodless coup against Egypt's monarchy on the night of

22 July, 1952. Cairenes awoke next day to learn of a "revolution" led by General Naguib – a nominal figurehead, since it was Nasser who had engineered it and secretly controlled affairs until his public emergence as leader.

Abbassiya's Janus profile juxtaposes spacious institutions and crowded slums, marshalling yards and hospitals. Its main thoroughfare, Sharia Ramses, divides the oil-depot zone of Al-Sharabiyya from Gamra and El-Sakakini, two residential market quarters. On Sharia Sakakini, near Ghamra metro station, the ornate Rococo **Sakakini Palace**, built in 1898 for an Italian nobleman, is being restored and due to open to the public soon. In the meantime, it is still worth a look if you are in the area for its outrageously kitsch facade, and if you are lucky, you may persuade the caretaker to let you see the marvellous interior with its huge mirrors, murals, painted ceilings and antique elevator.

At the end of Sharia Sakakini, on Midan al-Zahir, the thirteenth-century **Mosque of Beybars the Crossbowman**, built in 1268 and covering ten thousand square metres, is one of Cairo's biggest mosques, and the first to be built outside the city's walls. Ceasing to be used for prayer in the sixteenth century, it was subsequently used as a military storehouse by the Ottomans, a barracks by Napoleon and a slaughterhouse by the British. Restoration started in the early 1990s but soon petered out, and the southeast side is now again in use as a mosque. The rest of it can be visited by tourists in the meantime. Its sturdy walls enclose a vast open courtyard, surrounded by a rather heavy arcade. A more conspicuous edifice is the curvaceous **Coptic Cathedral of St Mark**, the seat of the Coptic Patriarchate since it was raised in the 1970s. Visitors interested in joining pilgrim excursions to the Red Sea Monasteries should contact officials in the adjacent Church of SS Peter and Paul (*Al-Batrussiya*), at 222 Sharia Ramses.

Other landmarks include the **Misr Travel Tower**, housing the Ministry of Tourism, 500m from the **Sinai Bus Terminal** near the junction of Salah Salem and Al-'Urubah, and a similar distance from the Engineering Faculty of **Ain Shams University**. Round about are sited numerous clubs (*nady*) and training schools belonging to professional unions, the police and military.

To get to Abbassiya, buses (including #130, #400, #400/, #500, #828 and #955) and minibuses (including #27, #35 and #35/) run from Tahrir's Abdel Mouneem Riyad terminal via Midan Ramses.

Hada'iq al-Qubba: Nasser's Tomb

Northeast of Abbassiya along Sharia al-Khalifa al-Ma'mun (a continuation of Sharia Abbassiya), a modern mosque stands beside a dusty shrine containing the **Tomb of Gamal Abdel Nasser**. When Nasser died in September 1969, a million Egyptians followed his bier through the streets of Cairo and the whole Arab world mourned. His cult was subsequently downplayed by Sadat (who feared comparisons) and in recent years most of the visitors to Nasser's shrine have been foreign admirers or gloating Israelis. Whatever Egyptians may think about Nasser's son, Khalid – who was finally acquitted of involvement in Thawraat Masri (Egypt's Revolution), a Libyan-backed group that attacked US and Israeli targets in the 1980s – his father's legend remains a potent one. Saddam Hussein's claim to be Nasser's "spiritual heir" was only the latest attempt by an Arab leader to metaphorically wrest the sword from the stone.

The tomb lies on the edge of **Hada'iq al-Qubba**, a district named after Ismail's **Qubba Palace**. Its four hundred rooms were inherited by Khedive Tewfik and later contained King Farouk's vast collection of rare stamps, coins and other treasures, ranging from medieval Korans to a Fabergé thermometer. Now a presidential residence used for state conferences, it was here that the Shah of Iran spent the last days of his exile. The palace's walled grounds can be seen along the #420 bus route from Abbassiya; it and Nasser's tomb are best reached by Metro (Saray el-Qubba station and Kubri el-Qubi station respectively).

Medinet Nasr

During the 1960s and 1970s a whole new satellite-suburb was created on the site of the Abbassiya Rifle Ranges, and many government departments were relocated to this "Victory City". But unless you've got business with the Inland Revenue or Transport Ministry, there's little in **Medinet Nasr** worth noting. Travellers coming in from Suez will pass the Olympic-size **Cairo Stadium** at one end of Sharia al-Nasr, where Cairo football clubs Ahly and Zamalek usually play their home matches, and where international ties and cup finals are also held (see p.276).

Alongside the boulevard is a landscaped parade ground centred on a pyramid-shaped **Victory Memorial** to the 1973 October War (see p.688). In 1981, Islamic radicals infiltrated the 6th October anniversary parade and blasted the reviewing stand with machine guns and grenades, fatally wounding President Sadat (Mubarak, who stood beside him, was unharmed). **Sadat's Tomb** is beneath the Victory Memorial.

North of Sadat's Tomb and the Victory Memorial, on Sharia al-Oruba, the huge **October War Panorama**, opened in 1989, stands surrounded by a display of military hardware. It was built on a suggestion made to Hosni Mubarak by Kim Il Sung of North Korea when the Egyptian president visited that country in 1983. Construction was supervised by North Korean technicians, and it shows: the building looks like a pavilion in some Communist theme park of the 1950s and is decorated with Maoist-style reliefs, but instead of East Asian peasants and workers striding purposefully forward, it's Egyptian soldiers in front of the Pyramids. Every day it holds five showings (daily except Tues 9.30am, 11am and 12.30pm, plus in winter 5pm and 6.30pm, summer 6pm and 7.30pm; £E10, camera £E2) that start with two rather silly dioramas illustrating the opening round of the October War, and culminate in a really quite impressive three-dimensional panorama of the war in Sinai, during which the audience is rotated around 360° to take it all in. The commentary (in Arabic, with an English version available via headphones) explains the action with such phrases as "the glorious minutes passed rapidly", and the whole thing is so over-the-top in its triumphalism that you might almost think the Egyptians had actually won the October War.

Heliopolis (Masr al-Gadida)

By the end of the nineteenth century, the doubling of Cairo's population and the exponential growth of its foreign community had created a huge demand for new accommodation, which fired the imagination of a Belgian entrepreneur. Baron Empain proposed creating a garden city in the desert, linked to the downtown area by an overground metro: a commercial venture attractive to investors, since Empain's company would collect both rents and fares from commuting residents of **Heliopolis**. Laid out by Sir Reginald Oakes in radial grid patterns, the suburb's wide avenues were lined with apartment blocks ennobled by pale yellow Moorish facades and bisected by shrubbery. Named after the ancient City of the Sun near Matariyya (see p.222), Heliopolis soon acquired every facility from schools and churches to a racecourse and branch of *Groppi's*.

Wealthy Egyptians settled here from the beginning; merely prosperous ones moved in as foreigners left in droves throughout the 1950s. Meanwhile, poorer

Ancient Heliopolis, the Ennead and the cult of Re

Although Anthony Trollope scoffed "Humbug!" when he saw what little remained in 1858, the site of **ancient Heliopolis**, near modern Matariyya, originally covered perhaps five square kilometres. The City of the Sun (called *On* by its founders, but better known by its Greek appellation) evolved in tandem with Memphis, the first capital of Dynastic Egypt (see p.248). As Memphis embodied the political unification of Upper and Lower Egypt, so Heliopolis incarnated its theological aspect, syncretizing diverse local cults into a hierarchical cosmogony that proved more influential than other creation myths of the Old Kingdom.

Cosmogony

In the **Heliopolitan cosmogony**, the world began as watery chaos (Nun) from which Atum the sun-god emerged onto a primal mound, spitting forth the twin deities Shu (air) and Tefnut (moisture). They engendered Geb (earth) and Nut (sky), whose own union produced Isis, Osiris, Seth and Nephthys. Later texts often regarded this divine **Ennead** (Nine) as a single entity, while the

▼ Shu, Nut and Geb

universe was conventionally represented by the figures of Shu, Nut and Geb. Meanwhile (for reasons unknown), the primal deity Atum was subsumed by Re or Ra, a yet mightier aspect of the sun-god.

Re manifested himself in multiple forms: as hawk-headed Re-herakhte (Horus of the Horizon); the beetle Khepri (the rising sun); the disc Aten (the midday sun); and as Atum (the setting sun). The Egyptians believed that Re rose each morning in the east, traversed the sky in his solar barque and sank into the western land of the dead every evening, to voyage through the Duat (netherworld) during the night, emerging at sunrise. This journey inevitably linked Re to the Osirian myth, and from the V Dynasty onwards it became de rigueur for pharaohs to claim descent from Re by identifying themselves with Horus and Osiris. The **cult of Re** was exclusive, for only the pharaoh and priesthood had access to Re's sanctuary, whose daily rituals were adopted by other divine cults and soon became inextricably entangled with Osiris-worship (see "Karnak" and "Abydos", Chapter 2). Ordinary folk – whose participation was limited to public festivals – worshipped lesser, more approachable deities.

▶ Re

Remains

Having been eclipsed by Karnak and Amun-worship during the New Kingdom, Heliopolis was devastated by the Persians in 525 BC. Once rebuilt, however, its intellectual reputation attracted fifth-century BC luminaries such as Plato, Eudoxus (who probably invented the sundial after studying Egyptian astronomy) and Herodotus. But as Alexandria became the new focus for science and religion, Heliopolis inexorably declined; the first-century geographer Strabo found it nearly desolate and the Romans totally ignored it. Today, the only tangible reminders of its existence are **Senusert's obelisk** and the **Spring of the Sun**, where Atum supposedly washed himself at the dawn of creation.

quarters started growing up around Heliopolis, ending its privileged isolation from Greater Cairo. During the 1970s, air-conditioned towers began to replace spacious villas, the racecourse was turned into a fun park, and burger joints proliferated. Today, visitors come for the restaurants and nightlife, or to admire the stylish architecture along its central boulevards; many foreigners also rent apartments or work in Heliopolis, which is nowadays called "New Cairo" (Masr al-Gadida).

Transport: the Heliopolis metro

Depending on your starting point, choice of transport, and whether it's rush hour, Heliopolis is between fifteen- and thirty-minutes' ride from downtown Cairo. You can get there by **bus** (#400, #400/ and #500) or **minibus** (#27, #35 and #35/) from Tahrir and Ramses but, especially during the rush hour, these are slower than the suburb's **original tram system**, known as the **Heliopolis metro**, which begins at Midan Ramses. From there, its three tram lines follow the same track through Abbassiya, diverging shortly before Midan Roxi. Each has its own colour-coded direction boards:

• The **Abd al-Aziz Fahmi line** (destination written in blue) runs past Midan Roxi and along Sharia al-Ma'had al-Ishtiraki and Sharia al-Higaz, past Merryland and Heliopolis Hospital, to Midan Heliopolis, where it turns off up Abd al-Aziz Fahmi towards Ain Shams.

• More centrally, the **Nouzha line** (destination written in red) veers off Sharia Merghani near the Heliopolis Sporting Club, and follows Al-Ahram and Osman Ibn Affan to Midan Triomphe, then heads up Sharia Nouzha to Midan al-Higaz.

• Initially running alongside the Nouzha line, the **Merghani line** (destination in white on yellow) follows the street of that name past the International Language Institute (ILI) to Midan Triomphe, and out towards the Armed Forces Hospital.

Sights and activities

Nouzha-line, red-coded trams run through the heart of Heliopolis, whose finest **architecture** lines the boulevards between Sharia Merghani and Abu Bakr al-Saddiq. Stay on board to review Sharia al-Ahram's parade of handsome arcades topped with Andalusian balconies and pantiles, or alight near the **Heliopolis Sporting Club** and walk around the corner of the **Urubah Palace** onto Sharia Ibrahim. Other side streets have more of a 1920s feel, with crisply graceful Art Deco apartments. But the most famous landmark lies off Sharia al-'Urubah, further southeast. Resembling a Hindu temple, **Baron Empain's Palace** originally boasted a revolving tower that enabled its owner to follow the sun throughout the day. The now derelict structure (dubbed "Le Baron" by locals) can be glimpsed from some of the airport-bound buses.

Not far away – and accessible by Merghani tram – the **International Language Institute** (ILI) offers Arabic classes and also employs many foreigners as teachers (see p.86 and p.292). Along the Merghani tram route, too, are the Heliopolis and Heliolido **sporting clubs**, with tennis and squash courts, swimming pools and gymnasiums. The Heliopolis Sporting Club only admits foreigners in the summer and seems snootier than the Heliolido. Northeast of the latter, **Merryland** contains a boating lake and funfair, a small zoo and an overpriced café – nothing to get excited about, but it's nice to be surrounded by greenery – and it's a safe place for children to play. Abd al-Aziz Fahmi trams continue on past Merryland, up Al-Higaz towards Midan Heliopolis.

Matariyya and beyond

Northwest of Heliopolis, several former villages have evolved into ramshackle *baladi* suburbs. **El–Zeitun** (the Olives) merits a footnote in history as the site of Sultan Selim's defeat of the Mamlukes in 1517 and of conspiratorial gatherings of Free Officers during the early 1950s. The adjacent **Helmiya** quarter gets its name from yet another *khedival* palace built last century. But for actual sights you have to venture even further out, into Matariyya.

The modern suburb of **Matariyya** traces its antecedents way back to the Old Kingdom and claims later acquaintance with the infant Christ. As evidence of the former, the neighbourhood's Midan al-Misallah displays a 22-metre-high, pink granite **Obelisk of Senusert I**. One of a pair raised to celebrate the pharaoh's Jubilee Festival (c.1900 BC), it originally stood outside the Temple of Re, erected by Amenemhat I, Senusert's father, who founded the XII Dynasty. Another pair, belonging to the XVIII Dynasty ruler Tuthmosis III, was moved by the Romans to Alexandria, whence it ended up in New York's Central Park and on London's Embankment. However, the significance of this site and its cult of the sun-god are far older, dating back to the earliest dynasties.

Cairo's metro makes this sector of the northern suburbs readily accessible from the centre. Matariyya metro station is eleven stops from Tahrir, in the direction of El-Marg; the neighbourhood can also be reached by tram from Heliopolis.

The Spring of the Sun, Virgin's Tree and Ain Shams

Nowadays, the **Spring of the Sun** waters a famous Christian relic, the **Virgin's Tree**. Located 500m south of the obelisk, this gnarled sycamore-fig is supposedly descended from a tree whose branches shaded the Holy Family during their Egyptian exile. Tradition has it that they rested here between Bilbeis and Babylon-in-Egypt (see p.201) and Mary washed the clothes of the baby Jesus in the stone trough that still lies beside the tree. Early this century, "Christian souvenir-hunting was so bad that the owner of the sycamore tied a knife to the tree and put up a notice begging people not to hack at it any more with axes, and to leave some of it for others" (Aldridge). Now enclosed within a compound, it grows near the **Church of the Virgin**, a modern building on the site of far older churches.

The spring's Arabic name has attached itself to the **Ain Shams** quarter, one metro stop beyond Matariyya. Densely populated and solidly working-class, the neighbourhood is regarded by the police as a hotbed of Islamic fundamentalism.

The Lake of the Pilgrims

Still further out, beyond El-Marg, caravans once prayed beside the **Lake of the Pilgrims** (Birket el-Hagg) before embarking on their journey to Mecca. Today, alas, the "covered litters of the female pilgrims and the picturesque corps of mounted *Bashi-Bazouks*" no longer "moves slowly forward on its desert route". Instead, the barren wastes outside Cairo have for several decades harboured rocket ranges, chemical weapons factories and other **military installations**, rendering vast tracts off-limits. Ironically, much of this research was undertaken in collaboration with Iraq, Egypt's main Arab ally before the Gulf War, during which they fought on opposite sides.

Bil'esh Camel Market

Formerly in Imbaba, but now held 60km north of the city at **Bil'esh**, is Cairo's Friday **Camel Market**, a weekly feast of drama and cruelty. Beaten into defecating ranks, the hobbled camels are assessed by traders who disregard their emaciation – caused by a month-long trek from northwestern Sudan to Aswan, followed by an overnight truck ride to Cairo – and concentrate on other features.

Strength and speed are discernible in the legs, chest, eyes, ears and position of the hump, while teeth reflect age; the clearly knackered are evaluated for their meat and hide. During rutting season, signs of irritation (an inflated mouth sac, ferocious slobbering and gurgling) often herald a kick or bite from an enraged bull camel. Docile females are generally preferred as mounts. They're also exchanged for goats and other livestock, while Bishari herdsmen and Egyptian merchants gossip over tea, unperturbed by throat-slittings and disembowelments near the piles of saddlery and tack. In an adjacent compound is a furniture and bric-a-brac market, not unlike a car-boot or yard sale.

Lasting from dawn till early afternoon every Friday, the Souk el-Gamal (pronounced "Gah*mell*") is busiest between 6am and 8.30am. To get there by taxi will cost around £E60–80 for the round trip. Alternatively, you can catch the #214 bus from Abdel Mouneem Riyad to Manashi by the Nile Barrage at Qanatir (45min) and take a service taxi microbus from there. Alternatively, you can take a succession of service taxi microbuses from Sharia Sabtiya, off Midan Ramses, changing vehicles at Warraq and Manashi. Going back into town, you may be able to find a microbus that will take you all the way to Ramses.

The Pyramids

All things dread Time, but Time dreads the Pyramids.

Anonymous proverb

For millions of people **the Pyramids** epitomize Ancient Egypt: no other monument is so instantly recognized the world over. Yet comparatively few foreigners realize that at least 97 pyramids are spread across seventy kilometres of desert, from the outskirts of Cairo to the edge of the Fayoum. The mass of **theories, claims and counterclaims** about how and why the Pyramids were built contributes to the sense of mystery that surrounds them. Some of the recent contributions to this debate include *The Orion Mystery* (1994), in which Robert Bauval asserts that the orientation of the Giza Pyramids corresponds to the three stars in Orion's Belt, and the "ventilation" shafts in the Geat Pyramid were aligned with Orion's Belt and Alpha Draconis. Graham Hancock took this a stage further in *Fingerprints of the Gods* (1995), arguing that the entire pyramid field corresponded to an astronomical map. In later books he says that the Sphinx and Pyramids are far older than reckoned and recall a vanished ur-civilization that was destroyed in 12,000 BC, having left its stamp on Angkor Wat, the Maya and Easter Island. Egyptologists have since been lining up to refute these theories; meanwhile you can read up on the latest crop – including some involving Martians – on the Internet through links at Ⓦparanormal .about.com/cs/ancientegypt.

Most visitors are content to see the great **Pyramids of Giza** and part of the sprawling necropolis of **Saqqara**, both easily accessible from Cairo (tours to Saqqara often include a visit to the ruins of the ancient city of **Memphis**).

Only a minority ride across the sands to **Abu Sir**, or visit the **Dahshur** pyramid field (see the map opposite for the location of all these sites). Still further south, the dramatic "Collapsed Pyramid" of **Maidum** and the lesser Middle Kingdom pyramids of **Hawara**, **El-Lisht** and **Lahun** are easier to reach from the Fayoum, so for the sake of convenience we've covered them in Chapter 3 (see p.526). The pyramid at **Abu Ruash**, to the west of Cairo, inaccessible and little more than a pile of sand, is only of interest to specialists, as are the remains of a previously unknown pyramid unearthed nearby (if you do want to find them, service taxis from Mansureya Canal by Pyramids Road serve the nearby Abu Ruash industrial area).

If you are really determined, and very energetic, it is possible to visit the pyramid sites at Giza, Abu Sir, Saqqara and Dahshur all in one day starting very early (say 7.30am from town). To do this, you will need to find a taxi driver who will take you, wait at each, and finally bring you back. Make sure the driver understands exactly what you want, and negotiate hard. In principle, you should be able to visit all four sites for around £E100, or Giza, Saqqara and Dahshur for £E80, but even £E120–150 would not be an unreasonable rate, it being a whole day's work for the driver. Some hotels (the *Berlin*, for example) have their own drivers who are used to taking tourists on such excursions. Alternatively, you could opt for a guided tour (see p.241) that takes in both Giza and Saqqara in one day.

The Pyramids in history

The derivation of the word "pyramid" is obscure. *Per-em-us*, an Ancient Egyptian term meaning "straight up", seems likelier than the Greek *pyramis* – "wheaten cake", a facetious descriptive term for these novel monuments. Then again, "obelisk" comes from *obeliskos*, the ancient Greek for "skewer" or "little spit".

Whatever, the Pyramids' sheer **antiquity** is staggering. When the Greek chronicler Herodotus visited them in 450 BC, as many centuries separated his lifetime from their creation as divide our own time from that of Herodotus, who regarded them as ancient even then. For the Pyramid Age was only an episode in three millennia of pharaonic civilization, reaching its zenith within two hundred years and followed by an inexorable decline, so that later dynasties regarded the works of their ancestors with awe. Fourteen centuries after the royal tombs of the Old Kingdom were first violated by robbers, the Sa'te (XXVI) Dynasty collected what remained, replaced missing bodies with surrogates, and reburied their forebears with archaic rituals they no longer comprehended.

The Pyramid Age began at Saqqara in the 27th century BC, when the III Dynasty royal architect Imhotep enlarged a *mastaba* tomb to create the first **step pyramid**. As techniques evolved, an attempt was made to convert another step pyramid at Maidum into a true pyramid by encasing its sides in a smooth shell, but it seems that the design was faulty and the pyramid collapsed at some time under its own weight (see p.527). According to one theory, this happened during construction of what became the Bent Pyramid at Dahshur, necessitating a hasty alteration to the angle of its sides (see p.252). The first sheer-sided **true pyramid**, apparently the next to be constructed, was the Red Pyramid at Dahshur (see p.251), followed by the Great Pyramid of Cheops at Giza (see p.231), which marked the zenith of pyramid architecture. After two more perfect pyramids at Giza, fewer resources and less care were devoted to the pyramid fields of Abu Sir and South Saqqara, and the latterday pyramids near Fayoum Oasis, and no subsequent pyramid ever matched the standards of the Giza trio.

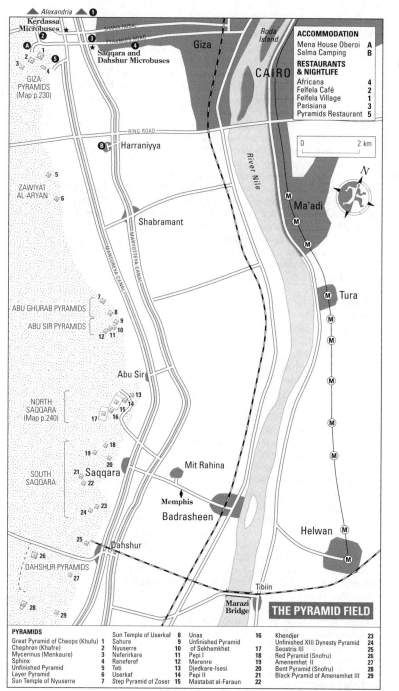

▲ *Alexandria* ▲ ❶

Kerdassa
Microbuses ★
SHARIA FAISAL
❷
PYRAMIDS ROAD
Ⓐ 1
Ⓐ 2 ❸
2 ★ **Saqqara and**
3 4 **Dahshur Microbuses**
Ⓑ 5 ❹

Giza

Roda
Island

GIZA
PYRAMIDS
(Map p.230)

CAIRO

RING ROAD

Ⓑ **Harraniyya**

0   2 km

River Nile

N

ZAWIYAT 5
AL-ARYAN 6

Shabramant

Ⓜ **Ma'adi**
Ⓜ
Ⓜ

ABU GHURAB PYRAMIDS 7
8
9
ABU SIR PYRAMIDS 10
12 11

MANSURIYA CANAL
MARYOTEYA CANAL

Ⓜ **Tura**
Ⓜ
Ⓜ

Abu Sir

13
NORTH 14
SAQQARA 15
(Map p.240) 17 16

Ⓜ

18
19
20
21
SOUTH 22
SAQQARA 24 23

Saqqara

Mit Rahina

Ⓜ

25
Dahshur
26
DAHSHUR PYRAMIDS
27

Memphis

Badrasheen

Helwan Ⓜ

28
29

Tibiin

Marazi
Bridge

THE PYRAMID FIELD

Ⓜ

PYRAMIDS

Great Pyramid of Cheops (Khufu)	**1**	Sun Temple of Userkaf	**8**	Unas	**16**
Chephren (Khafre)	**2**	Sahure	**9**	Unfinished Pyramid	
Mycerinus (Menkaure)	**3**	Nyuserre	**10**	of Sekhemkhet	**17**
Sphinx	**4**	Neferirkare	**11**	Pepi I	**18**
Unfinished Pyramid	**5**	Raneferef	**12**	Merenre	**19**
Layer Pyramid	**6**	Userkaf	**13**	Djedkare-Isesi	**20**
Sun Temple of Nyuserre	**7**	Step Pyramid of Zoser	**14**	Pepi II	**21**
		Teti	**15**	Mastabat al-Faraun	**22**

Khendjer	**23**
Unfinished XIII Dynasty Pyramid	**24**
Seostris III	**25**
Red Pyramid (Snofru)	**26**
Amenemhet II	**27**
Bent Pyramid (Snofru)	**28**
Black Pyramid of Amenemhet III	**29**

The Pyramids' **enigma** has puzzled people ever since they were built. Whereas the Ancient Greeks vaguely understood their function, the Romans were less certain; medieval Arabs believed them to be treasure houses with magical guardians; and early European observers reckoned them the Biblical granaries of Joseph. The nineteenth century was a golden era of discoveries by Belzoni, Vyse, Petrie, Mariette, Maspero and Lepsius, which all suggested that the Pyramids were essentially containers for royal tombs and nothing else. It was also the heyday of Pyramidologists like Piazzi Smyth and David Davidson, who averred that their dimensions in "pyramid inches" proved the supremacy of Christianity and the Jewish origin of the pyramid-builders.

Archeologists now agree that the Pyramids' **function** was to preserve the pharaoh's **ka**, or double: a vital force which emanated from the sun-god to his son, the king, who distributed it amongst his subjects and the land of Egypt itself. Mummification, funerary rituals, false doors for his **ba** (soul) to escape, model servants (*shabti* figures) and anniversary offerings – all were designed to ensure that his *ka* enjoyed an afterlife similar to its former existence. Thus was the social order perpetuated throughout eternity and the forces of primeval chaos held at bay, a theme emphasized in tomb reliefs at Saqqara. On another level of **symbolism**, the pyramid form evoked the primal mound at the dawn of creation, a recurrent theme in ancient Egyptian cosmogony, echoed in megalithic *benben* and obelisks whose pyramidal tips were sheathed in glittering electrum.

Although the limestone scarp at the edge of the Western Desert provided an inexhaustible source of building material, finer stone for casing the pyramids was quarried at Tura across the river, or came from Aswan in Upper Egypt. Blocks were quarried using wooden wedges (which swelled when soaked, enlarging fissures) and copper chisels, then transported on rafts to the pyramid site, where the final shaping and polishing occurred. Shipments coincided with the inundation of the Nile (July–November), when its waters lapped the feet of the plateau and Egypt's workforce was released from agricultural tasks.

The fifth-century BC Greek historian Herodotus relates that a hundred thousand slaves took a decade to build the causeway and earthen ramps, and a further twenty years to raise the Great Pyramid of Cheops. Archeologists now believe that, far from being slaves, most of the workforce were actually peasants who were paid in food for their three-month stint (papyri enumerate the quantities of lentils, onions and leeks), while a few thousand skilled craftsmen were employed full-time on its **construction**. One theory holds that a single ramp wound around the pyramid core, and was raised as it grew; when the capstone was in place, the casing was added from the top down and the ramp was reduced. Other ramps (recently found) led from the base of the pyramid to the quarry. Apparently, pulleys were only used to lift the plug blocks that sealed the corridors and entrance; all the other stones were moved with levers and rollers. It is estimated that during the most productive century of pyramid-building, some 25 million tons of material were quarried.

Whether or not the ancient Egyptians deemed this work a religious obligation, the massive levies certainly demanded an effective bureaucracy. Pyramid-building therefore helped consolidate the state. Its decline paralleled the Old Kingdom's, its cessation and resumption two anarchic eras (the First and Second Intermediate Periods) and the short-lived Middle Kingdom (XII Dynasty). By the time of the New Kingdom, other monumental symbols seemed appropriate. Remembering the plundered pyramids, the rulers of the New Kingdom opted for hidden tombs in the Valley of the Kings.

The Pyramids of Giza

Of the Seven Wonders of the ancient world, only the **Pyramids of Giza** have withstood the ravages of time. "From the summit of these monuments, forty centuries look upon you", cried Napoleon; "A practical joke played on History", retorted another visitor. The Great Pyramid of Cheops has inspired more learned and crackpot speculation than any monument on earth. For millions of people, the Giza Pyramids embody antiquity and mystery. Burdened with expectations, however, you may find the reality disappointing. Resembling small triangles from afar and corrugated mountains as you approach, their gigantic mass can seem oddly two-dimensional when viewed from below. Far from being isolated in the desert as carefully angled photos suggest, they rise just beyond the outskirts of Giza City. During daytime, hordes of touts and tourists dispel any lingering mystique, as do the Sound and Light shows after dark. Only at sunset, dawn and late at night does their brooding majesty return.

Visiting the Pyramids

The site is directly accessible from Cairo by the eleven-kilometre-long Sharia al-Ahram (Pyramids Road) built by Khedive Ismail for Napoleon's consort, the Empress Eugénie. Though heavy traffic can prolong the journey, **getting there** is straightforward. Taxi drivers often quote upwards of £E20, but the proper fare is around £E15 for a one-way trip from town. A cheaper option is to take a/c bus #355 or #357 (£E2), or ordinary bus #900 (25pt), all from behind Ramses train station or on Midan Tahrir; minibus #183 from Midan Ataba (50pt); or a microbus service taxi from Ramses or Abdel Mouneem Riyad (75pt; drivers heading for the Pyramids shout, "Al-Ahram, al-Ahram".). Bus #30 from Midan Ramses also runs more or less all the way to the site. An easier one-day, minimum-effort way to visit the Giza Pyramids, while also taking in Saqqara, is to go on a guided tour (see p.241).

Opposite the **Mena House** is a **tourist office** (daily 8am–5pm; ☎02/383-8823). To visit **the site** during opening hours (daily: winter 8am–4pm; summer 8am–5pm) you must buy a ticket (£E40, students £E20) covering the site, the Sphinx and Chephren's Valley Temple – though tickets aren't rigorously checked. Extra **tickets** (only sold at the attractions themselves) are required for entry to the Great Pyramid of Cheops (£E100), the Solar Boat Museum (£E35), Chephren's Pyramid (£E20) and the Pyramid of Mycerinus (currently closed). Visiting after hours will probably cost more, depending on your evasion and/or negotiation skills. Beware of con men posing as ticket collectors or "special guides", who offer commentary along the lines of "Cheops Pyramid very old" – ignore them, or threaten to call the tourist police if necessary. Also ignore horse and camel touts on the way in who try to tell you that their stables are "government". Such nuisances are supposedly set to disappear under the "Giza Plateau Conservation Project", which will include an Imax cinema, cultural centres and more sites open to the public and, with the plateau effectively cut off from Nazlat al-Samman village, will exclude cars and touts.

Plan on spending half a day at the Pyramids, which are best entered early in the morning before the heat and crowds become unbearable (tour buses start arriving from 10.30am), or in the late afternoon – by 5pm most tour groups have left and people have yet to arrive for the nightly **Sound and Light Show**. There are three one-hour shows every night accompanied by a rather crass, melodramatic commentary in different languages. For schedules, which vary

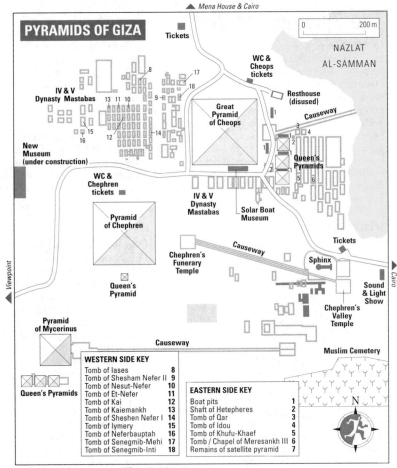

▲ Mena House & Cairo

PYRAMIDS OF GIZA

Tickets

NAZLAT

AL-SAMMAN

WC & Cheops tickets

Resthouse (disused)

Causeway

8

17

18

IV & V Dynasty Mastabas   13 11 10

9

Great Pyramid of Cheops

New Museum (under construction)

15

16

12

14

WC & Chephren tickets

Queen's Pyramids

3

4

1

2

5

6

1

IV & V Dynasty Mastabas

Solar Boat Museum

Pyramid of Chephren

Causeway

Tickets

Chephren's Funerary Temple

Sphinx

Sound & Light Show

Queen's Pyramid

Chephren's Valley Temple

Pyramid of Mycerinus

Causeway

Muslim Cemetery

Queen's Pyramids

Viewpoint

▶ Cairo

0   200 m

N

WESTERN SIDE KEY

Tomb of Iases	8
Tomb of Shesham Nefer II	9
Tomb of Nesut-Nefer	10
Tomb of Et-Nefer	11
Tomb of Kai	12
Tomb of Kaiemankh	13
Tomb of Sheshen Nefer I	14
Tomb of Iymery	15
Tomb of Neferbauptah	16
Tomb of Senegmib-Mehi	17
Tomb of Senegmib-Inti	18

EASTERN SIDE KEY

Boat pits	1
Shaft of Hetepheres	2
Tomb of Qar	3
Tomb of Idou	4
Tomb of Khufu-Khaef	5
Tomb / Chapel of Meresankh III	6
Remains of satellite pyramid	7

▼ Abu Sir & Saqqara

seasonally, call ☎02/385-2880 or 386-3469, or check *Egypt Today*, or ⓦwww.sound-light.egypt.com or ⓦwww.egyptsandl.com. Seats cost £E60, plus £E35 for a video camera; the Arabic version costs £E11, though non-Arab nationals are not allowed to buy tickets for it. Hundreds of Egyptians enjoy a free show from vantage points such as past the Muslim cemetery, eschewing the seats on the terrace facing the Sphinx (which is wheelchair accessible). Bring a sweater, since nights are cold even in summer.

Behind the grandstand is a row of stables **renting horses and camels** that are generally in no better shape than the animals touted around the site by Nagama Bedouin. They usually demand £E50 for a brief camel ride, and you should beware of those offering rides at £E10 per hour – they have a tendency to lead you far out into the desert and then announce that the £E10 rate was only for the outward journey and it will be £E50 per hour to get back. As the site is small enough to cover on foot, riding is more of an experience than a timesaver, and haggling with these guys just might ruin your visit, but if you do want to ride a horse or camel, we suggest getting in touch with a reputable operator such as AA or KG (see p.274).

In Baedeker's day, it was de rigueur for visitors to climb the Great Pyramid: while two Bedouin seized an arm apiece and hauled from above, a third would push from below. **Climbing the pyramids** is now forbidden and it is undoubtedly very dangerous, although attempts are still made. Though **going inside** is quite safe, anyone suffering from claustrophobia or asthma should forget it. Clambering through all three shafts in the Great Pyramid will make your leg muscles ache the following day.

As site plans suggest, the Pyramids' **orientation** is no accident. Their entrances are aligned with the Polar Star (or rather, its position 4500 years ago); the internal tomb chambers face west, the direction of the Land of the Dead; and the external funerary temples point eastwards towards the rising sun. It is also claimed that the trio of pyramids represents the three stars in Orion's belt. Less well preserved are the causeways leading to the so-called valley temples, and various subsidiary pyramids and *mastaba* tombs. The entire site is being renovated by the Supreme Council for Antiquities (SCA) and continues to yield surprises: notably the recent discovery of a possible secret chamber within the Great Pyramid, which some think will contain treasures as stunning as those from Tutankhamun's tomb; a previously unknown small pyramid by the southeastern corner of Cheops', with the oldest pyramidion (capstone) yet discovered; and tunnels under the seats in front of the Sphinx, whose age and purpose are so far unknown.

The Great Pyramid of Cheops (Khufu)

The oldest and largest of the Giza Pyramids is that of the IV Dynasty pharaoh **Khufu** – better known as **Cheops** – who probably reigned between 2589 and 2566 BC. Called the "Glorious Place of Khufu" by the ancient Egyptians, it originally stood 140m (roughly 480ft) high and measured 230m along its base, but the removal of its casing stones has reduced these dimensions by three metres. The pyramid is estimated to weigh six million tons and contain over 2,300,000 blocks whose average weight is 2.5 tons (though some weigh almost 15 tons). This gigantic mass actually ensures its stability, since most of the stress is transmitted inwards towards its central core, or downwards into the underlying bedrock. Until recently, the pyramid was thought to contain only three chambers: one in the bedrock and two in the superstructure. Experts believe that its design was changed twice, the subterranean chamber being abandoned in favour of the middle one, which was itself superseded by the uppermost chamber. By the time archeologists got here, their contents had been looted long ago, and the only object left

▲ Cheops

in situ was Khufu's sarcophagus. However, in April 1993, a German team of scientists using a robot probe accidentally discovered a door with handles supposedly enclosing a fourth chamber, apparently never plundered by thieves, which might contain the mummy and treasures of Cheops himself. The head of the Supreme Council of Antiquities, Dr Zawi Hawas, argues that there is no chamber, and that the "door" was a device for smoothing the inside of the shaft – but until investigations resume, the truth will not be known.

Inside the Great Pyramid

To keep down humidity inside the pyramid, **the number of visitors** allowed to enter is limited to 150 in the morning and 150 in the afternoon, so it is wise

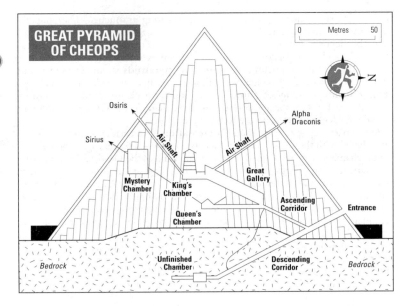

to buy **tickets** (£E100, students £E50, no cameras allowed) as early as possible. In the morning, tour groups tend to snap up all of them before anyone else can get a look in; it is generally less difficult to get the afternoon tickets, especially if you can be at the ticket office as soon as they go on sale at 1pm.

You enter the pyramid via an opening created by the treasure-hunting Khalif Ma'mun in 820, some distance below the original entrance on the north face (now blocked). After following this downwards at a crouch, you'll reach the junction of the ascending and descending corridors. The latter – leading to an unfinished chamber below the pyramid – is best ignored or left until last, and everyone heads up the 1.6-metre-high **ascending corridor**. According to medieval Arab chroniclers, intruders soon encountered an "idol of speckled granite" wreathed by a serpent which "seized upon and strangled whoever approached", but latterday visitors are merely impeded by the 1:2 gradient of the passage, which runs for 36m until it meets another junction.

To the right of this is a **shaft** that ancient writers believed to be a well connected to the Nile; it's now recognized as leading into the subterranean chamber and thought to have been an escape passage for the workmen. Straight ahead is a horizontal passage 35m long and 1.75m high, leading to a semi-finished limestone chamber with a pointed roof, which Arabs dubbed the "**Queen's Chamber**". Petrie reckoned this was the *serdab*, or repository for the pharaoh's statue, while the eccentric Davidson saw it as symbolizing the ultimate futility of Judaism. Either way, there's no evidence that a queen was ever buried here. In the northern and southern walls are two holes made in 1872 for the purpose of discovering the chamber's ventilation shafts; it was through one of these that the robot probe discovered the "secret chamber", at the end of a 65m passageway only twenty centimetres high and the same distance wide, which is aligned with the Dog Star, Sirius (representing the goddess Isis).

However, most people step up into the **Great Gallery**, the finest section of the pyramid. Built of Muqattam limestone, so perfectly cut that a knife blade can't be inserted between its joints, the 47-metre-long shaft narrows to a corbelled roof 8.5m high. (Davidson believed that its length in "pyramid inches" corresponded to the number of years between the Crucifixion and the outbreak of World War I.) The incisions in its walls probably held beams that were used to raise the sarcophagus or granite plug blocks up the steep incline (nowadays overlaid with wooden steps). Though no longer infested by giant bats, as nineteenth-century travellers reported, the Great Gallery is sufficiently hot and airless to constitute something of an ordeal, and you'll be glad to reach the horizontal antechamber at the top, which is slotted for the insertion of plug blocks designed to thwart entry to the putative burial chamber.

The **King's Chamber** lies 95m beneath the apex of the pyramid and half that distance from its outer walls. Built of red granite blocks, the rectangular chamber is large enough to accommodate a double-decker bus. Its dimensions (5.2 by 10.8 by 5.8 metres) have inspired many abstruse calculations and whacky prophecies: Hitler ordered a replica built beneath the Nuremberg Stadium, where he communed with himself before Nazi rallies. To one side of the chamber lies a huge, lidless **sarcophagus** of Aswan granite, bearing the marks of diamond-tipped saws and drills. On the northern and southern walls, at knee height, you'll notice two air shafts leading to the outer world, aligned with the stars of Orion's Belt and Alpha Draconis (representing Osiris and the hippo goddess Rer respectively).

Unseen above the ceiling, five **relieving chambers** distribute the weight of the pyramid away from the burial chamber; each consists of 43 granite monoliths weighing 40 to 70 tons apiece. These chambers can only be reached by a ladder from the Great Gallery, and then a passage where Colonel Vyse found Khufu's name inscribed in red (the only inscription within the Giza Pyramids), but the flow of people normally rules this out.

On your way back down, consider investigating the 100-metre-long **descending corridor**, which leads to a crudely hewn **unfinished chamber** beneath the pyramid. There's nothing to see, but the nerve-wracking descent is worthy of Indiana Jones.

Subsidiary tombs

East of the Great Pyramid, it's just possible to discern the foundations of Khufu's funerary temple and a few blocks of the causeway that once connected it to his valley temple (now buried beneath the village of Nazlat al-Samman). Nearby stand three ruined **Queens' Pyramids**, each with a small chapel attached. The northern and southern pyramids belonged to Merites and Hensutsen, Khufu's principal wife (and sister), and the putative mother of Chephren, respectively; the middle one may have belonged to the mother of Redjedef, the third ruler of the dynasty. Between that and the Great Pyramid, the remains of a fourth satellite pyramid have recently been discovered, including its capstone, the oldest yet found, but the pyramid's purpose is so far unknown.

Just northeast of Queen Merites' pyramid is a **shaft** where III Dynasty pharaoh Snofru's wife Queen Hetepheres' sarcophagus was found, having been stashed here following lootings at its original home in Dahshur. To the east of it are the tombs of Qar and his son Idou, which contain life-size statues of the deceased and various reliefs. To the east of Queen Hensutsen's pyramid are the tombs of Cheops' son Khufu-Khaef, and Chephren's wife (also Hetepheres' daughter) Meres-ankh, the best preserved of all the tombs on the Giza plateau, complete with statues in the niches and reliefs showing scenes of daily life, with much of the paintwork intact. To get into these tombs, ask at the custodian's hut beside Hetepheres' shaft; naturally, the custodian will appreciate a tip for opening up.

To the west of the Great Pyramid lie dozens of **IV and V Dynasty masta-bas**, where archeologists have uncovered a 4600-year-old mummified princess, whose body had been hollowed out and encased in a thin layer of plaster – a hitherto unknown method of mummification. Here are more **tombs** that until 1995 had been closed to the public since their discovery in the nineteenth century. In general, these are less interesting than those on the eastern side of the Great Pyramid, but that of Neferbauptah – almost parallel with the west side of Chephren's pyramid – has a dinosaur fossil preserved in the fifth block from the right of the second row up on its north side. Should you want to enter any of these tombs, ask at the Inspectorate office to the north. Beware of deep shafts with no fences around them.

The Solar Boat Museum

Perched to the south of the Great Pyramid, across the road from another cluster of *mastabas*, is a humidity-controlled pavilion (daily: winter 9am–4pm; summer 9am–5pm; £E35, students £E20) containing a 43-metre-long **boat** from one of the five boat pits sunk around Khufu's Pyramid. (Another boat has been located by X-rays and video cameras, but for the present remains unexcavated.)

When the pit's limestone roofing blocks were removed in 1954, a faint odour of cedarwood arose. Restorer Hagg Ahmed Yussef subsequently spent fourteen years rebuilding a graceful craft from 1200 pieces of wood, originally held together by sycamore pegs and halfa-grass ropes. Archeologists term these vessels "solar boats" (or barques), but their purpose remains uncertain – carrying the pharaoh through the underworld (as shown in XVII–IX Dynasty tombs at Thebes) or accompanying the sun-god on his daily journey across the heavens are two of the many hypotheses.

The Pyramid of Chephren (Khafre)

Sited on higher ground, with an intact summit and steeper sides, the middle or **Second Pyramid** seems taller than Khufu's. Built by his son **Khafre** (known to posterity as Chephren), its base originally covered 214.8 square metres and its weight is estimated at 4,883,000 tons. As with Khufu's Pyramid, the original rock-hewn burial chamber was never finished and an upper chamber was subsequently constructed. Classical writers such as Pliny believed that the pyramid had no entrance, but when Belzoni located and blasted open the sealed portal on its north face in 1818, he found that Arab tomb robbers had somehow gained access nearly a thousand years earlier, undeterred by legends of an idol "with fierce and sparkling eyes", bent on slaying intruders. In March 1993, several tourists were injured by an explosion inside Chephren's Pyramid, probably caused by a bomb.

▲ Chephren

Inside the pyramid (£E20, students £E10, no current limit on numbers, no cameras allowed), you can follow one of the two entry corridors downwards, and then upwards, into a long horizontal passage leading to Chephren's **burial chamber**, where Belzoni celebrated his discovery by writing his name in black letters. This ebullient circus strongman-turned-explorer went on to find Seti I's tomb in the Valley of the Kings, and died searching for the source of the River Niger. Set into the chamber's granite floor is the sarcophagus of Khafre, who reigned c.2558–2533 BC. The square cavity near the southern wall may have marked the position of a canopic chest containing the pharaoh's viscera.

Chephren's Funerary Complex and the Sphinx

The funerary complex of Chephren's Pyramid is the best-preserved example of this typically Old Kingdom arrangement. When a pharaoh died, his body was ferried across the Nile to a riverside valley temple where it was embalmed by priests. After the process was complete, mourners gathered here to purify themselves before escorting his mummy up the causeway to a funerary (or mortuary) temple, where further rites preceded its interment within the pyramid. Thereafter, the priests ensured his *ka*'s afterlife by making offerings of food and incense in the funerary temple on specific anniversaries.

Chephren's **funerary temple** consists of a pillared hall, central court, niched storerooms and a sanctuary, but most of the outer granite casing has been plundered over centuries and the interior may not be accessible. Amongst the remaining blocks is a 13.4-metre-long monster weighing 163,000 kilos. Flanking the temple are what appear to be boat pits, although excavations have yielded nothing but pottery fragments. From here you can trace the foundations of a **causeway** that runs 400m downhill to his valley temple, near the Sphinx.

The **valley temple** lay buried under sand until its discovery by Mariette in 1852, which accounts for its reasonable state of preservation. Built of limestone and faced with polished Aswan granite, the temple faces east and used to open onto a quay. Beyond a narrow antechamber you'll find a T-shaped hall whose gigantic architraves are supported by square pillars, in front of which stood diorite statues of Chephren. Contrary to the widely accepted theory, a few scholars believe that mummification occurred at Memphis or Chephren's mortuary temple, this edifice being reserved for the "Opening of Mouth" ceremony, whereby the *ka* entered the deceased's body.

The Sphinx

This legendary monument, whose enclosure is entered through the Valley Temple, is carved from an outcrop of soft limestone that was supposedly left standing after the harder surrounding stone was quarried for the Great Pyramid; however, since the base stone was too soft to work on directly, it was clad in harder stone before finishing. Conventional archeology credits Chephren with the idea of shaping it into a figure with a lion's body and a human head, which is often identified as his own (complete with royal beard and *uraeus*, see p.312), though it may represent a guardian deity. Some thousand years later, the future Tuthmosis IV is said to have dreamt that if he cleared the sand that engulfed the **Sphinx** it would make him ruler; a prophecy fulfilled, as recorded on a stele that he placed between its paws. All these notions went unchallenged until 1991, when two American geologists argued that the Sphinx was at least 2600 years older than had been imagined: its bedrock was heavily weathered and eroded by water, probably during the Nabtian Pluvial era (3000–1200 BC). This argument is dismissed by Supreme Council of Antiquities director Zawi Hawas, who cites an analysis of the Sphinx's bedrock by the Getty Institute, which concludes that the erosion was caused by the action of mineral salts within the plateau and/or the wind. The controversy delighted the maverick Egyptologist John West, who has long claimed that Egyptian civilization was the inheritor of a more Ancient, lost culture – the mythical Atlantis. The name "Sphinx" was actually bestowed by the Ancient Greeks, after the legendary creature that put riddles to passers-by and slew those who answered wrongly; the Arabs called it Abu el-Hol (the Awesome or terrible one).

Used for target practice by Mamluke and Napoleonic troops, the Sphinx lost much of its beard to the British Museum and was sandbagged for protection during World War II. Early modern repairs did more harm than good, since its porous limestone "breathes", unlike the cement that was used to fill its cracks. There is also the problem of chemical pollutants from sewage and fires in the neighbouring settlement of Nazlat al-Samman. A more recent long-term **restoration project** (1989–98) involved hand-cutting ten thousand limestone blocks, to refit the paws, legs and haunches of the beast; the missing nose and beard have not been replaced, deliberately.

Three **tunnels** exist inside the Sphinx, one behind its head, one in its tail and one in its north side. Their function is unknown, but none of them go anywhere. Other tunnels have been unearthed in the vicinity of the Sphinx; again, we don't know who built them or what they were for, but one suggestion is that they were created by later ancient Egyptians looking for buried treasure.

During Sound and Light shows, the Sphinx is given the role of narrator.

The Pyramid of Mycerinus (Menkaure)

Sited on a gradual slope into undulating desert, the smallest of the Giza Pyramids speaks of waning power and commitment. Though started by Chephren's successor, **Menkaure** (called Mycerinus by the Greeks), it was finished with unseemly haste by his son Shepseskaf, who seemingly enjoyed less power than his predecessors and depended on the priesthood. Herodotus records the legend that an oracle gave Mycerinus only six years to live, so to cheat fate he made merry round the clock, doubling his annual quantum of experience. Another story has it that the pyramid was actually built by Rhodophis, a Thracian courtesan who charged each client the price of a building block (the structure is estimated to contain 200,000 blocks).

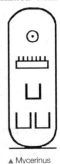
▲ Mycerinus

Because its lower half was sheathed in Aswan granite, this is sometimes called the Red Pyramid (a name also applied to one of Snofru's pyramids at Dahshur). Its relative lack of casing stones is due to a twelfth-century sultan whose courtiers persuaded him to attempt the pyramid's demolition, a project he wisely gave up after eight months. Medieval Arab chroniclers frequently ascribed the Giza Pyramids to a single ruler, who supposedly boasted: "I, Surid the king, have built these pyramids in sixty-one years. Let him who comes after me attempt to destroy them in six hundred. To destroy is easier than to build. I have clothed them in silk; let him try to cover them in mats." The **interior** (currently closed to the public) is unusual for having its unfinished chamber in the superstructure and the final burial chamber underground. Here Vyse discovered a basalt sarcophagus later lost at sea en route to Britain, plus human remains that he assumed were Menkaure's, but which are now reckoned to be a XXVI Dynasty replacement and rest in the British Museum.

The complex also features three subsidiary pyramids, a relatively intact funerary temple, and a causeway to the now-buried valley temple. Northwest of the latter lies the sarcophagus-shaped **Tomb of Queen Khentkawes**, an intriguing figure who appears to have bridged the transition between the IV and V dynasties. Apparently married to Shepseskaf, the last IV Dynasty ruler, she may have wed a priest of the sun-god after his demise and gone on to bear several kings who were buried at Saqqara or Abu Sir (where she also built a pyramid).

The best **viewpoints** for a vista over the pyramids are south of Mycerinus' pyramid. Most tourists gather (along with horse and camel touts and knick-knack sellers) along the tarmac road some 400m west of the pyramid, which is

Kerdassa and Harraniyya

These two villages have no connection with the Pyramids, but tour groups often pay one or both of them a visit. **KERDASSA**, roughly due west of Imbaba (but accessible by microbus from the junction of Pyramids Road with Sharia Mansureya), is where most of the scarves, *galabiyyas* and shirts in Cairo are made, plus carpets, which are sold by the metre. Although no longer a place for bargains, it's still frequented by collectors of ethnic textiles, particularly Bedouin robes and veils (the best-quality ones retail for hundreds of dollars). In times past, Kerdassa was also the starting point of the camel trail across the Western Desert to Libya.

Folks on guided tours (see p.241) are inevitably taken to **HARRANIYYA**, the site of the famous **Wissa Wassef Art Centre** (daily 10am–5pm; ☎02/381-5746, ⊛wissa -wassef-arts.com). Founded fifty years ago by Ramses Wissa Wassef, an architect who wanted to preserve village crafts and alleviate rural unemployment, the centre teaches children to design and weave carpets, and has branched out into batik work and pottery. Supervised by his widow and the original generation of students, pupils produce beautiful tapestries, which now sell for thousands of dollars and are imitated throughout Egypt. You can see them at work (except at lunchtime and on Fridays), and admire a superb collection in the museum designed by Hassan Fathy, a master-piece of mud-brick architecture. To reach the Art Centre under your own steam, take a taxi or minibus 4km south along the Saqqara road (Maryotteya Canal, west bank) from Pyramids Road, or catch bus #334 from Abdel Mouneem Riyad terminal, and get off at Haraniyya.

particularly popular in the late afternoon when the sun is in the right direction. In the morning, however, photos are better taken from the southeast, though it can often be hazy early on. For the best view of the Pyramids close together, the ridge to the south of Mycerinus' pyramid is the place to head for.

The Pyramids of Zawiyat al-Aryan

The **Zawiyat al-Aryan pyramid field** lies roughly midway between Giza and North Saqqara and about 3.5km from the Sun Temples of Abu Ghurab at Abu Sir (see p.239). Both its pyramids are sanded over and scarcely worth a detour, but Egyptologists still ponder their place in the evolution of pyramid-building.

The northerly **Unfinished Pyramid** makes extensive use of granite, suggest-ing that it might hail from the IV Dynasty, but never got beyond its foundations and enclosure wall – unfinished blocks and stone chippings are scattered all around. To the southeast lies a **Layer Pyramid** built of small stone blocks, which seems to have been intended as a step pyramid and thus presumably belongs to the III Dynasty.

Should you have a special urge to see these pyramids, your best bet is either to stop off here on a horse- or camel-ride from the Pyramids of Giza, or else take a service taxi microbus from Maryotteya Canal at Pyramids Road to the nearby village of Shabramant and walk from there.

The Pyramids of Abu Sir

This necropolis of V Dynasty (c.2494–2345 BC) pharaohs covers an arc of desert beyond the village of **ABU SIR**. The mortuary complexes here are smaller than the Giza Pyramids of the previous dynasty, suggesting a decline in royal power; their ruinous state and the effort required to reach them also mean that few tourists come here. Those who do often feel that Abu Sir's splendid isolation compensates for its monumental shortcomings. The site is currently closed to the public (when it opens, its hours and prices should be 9am–4pm daily in winter, 9am–5pm in summer; £E20, students £E10), but if you have a special interest, you may be able to persuade the custodian to let you in and look around.

Getting there

The Pyramids of Abu Sir are a ten-minute walk from the village of the same name, which can be reached by service taxi microbus from Maryotteya Canal at Pyramids Road or by taxi from Saqqara (£E5–8). The boldest option, however, is to visit them **en route between Giza and Saqqara** by horse or camel, spending three hours in the saddle. Making a round trip **from North Saqqara** (see below) is less demanding, but still requires commitment. With the Pyramids clearly visible 6km away, you can either walk (1hr 30min–2hr) or conserve energy by renting a horse or camel from near the refreshments hut (£E60–100 for the round trip).

The pyramid complexes

The four pyramid complexes are ranged in an arc that ignores chronological order. At the southern end of the pyramid field a low mound marks the core of the unfinished **Pyramid of Neferefre**, whose brief reign preceded Nyuserre's. As the core is composed of locally quarried limestone and was never encased in finer Tura masonry, no causeway was ever built. However, the desert may yet disgorge other structures: during the 1980s, Czechoslovak archeologists uncovered another pyramid complex, thought to belong to Queen Khentkawes, the mother of Sahure.

Dominating the view north is the much larger **Pyramid of Neferirkare**, the third ruler of the V Dynasty, who strove to outdo his predecessor, Sahure. If finished, it would have been 70m high – taller than the third pyramid at Giza – but Neferirkare's premature demise forced his successor to hastily complete a modified version using perishable mud-brick. Although too dangerous to climb, its summit commands a view of the entire pyramid field, from the three at Giza and the four at Saqqara to the Red and Bent pyramids at Dahshur, and even the Collapsed Pyramid of Maidum on the distant horizon. The valley temple and grand causeway of Neferirkare's Pyramid were later usurped to serve the **Pyramid of Nyuserre**, further north. A battered mortuary temple with papyriform columns mocks the original name of this dilapidated pyramid, "The Places of Nyuserre are Enduring"; the pharaohs who followed him preferred burial at Saqqara. A cluster of *mastabas* to the northwest includes the **Tomb of Ptahshepses**. Currently entered via a rickety ladder, the tomb's most curious feature is the double room off the courtyard, which may have held solar boats. If so, the only other known example of this in a private tomb is that of Kagemni in North Saqqara. Ptahshepses was Chief of Works to Sahure, the first of the V Dynasty kings to be buried at Abu Sir.

The **Pyramid of Sahure** is badly damaged, but its associated temples have fared better than others in this group. A 235-metre-long causeway links the ruined valley temple to Sahure's mortuary temple on the eastern side of the pyramid. Though most of its reliefs (which were the first to show the king smiting his enemies, later a standard motif) have gone to various museums, enough remains to make the temple worth exploring. It's also possible to crawl through a dusty, cobwebbed passage to reach the burial chamber within the pyramid (whose original name was "The Soul of Sahure Gleams"). Just to the north of the causeway, a series of fascinating reliefs shows scenes from the building of a pyramid, notably of workers dragging a pyramidion (capstone) covered with white gold, while dancers celebrate the pyramid's completion.

The Sun Temples of Abu Ghurab

Just northeast of Abu Sir is the site known as **Abu Ghurab** (if you are riding between Giza and Saqqara, you could ask the guide to stop here). Its twin temples were designed for worship of Re, the sun-god of Heliopolis, but their Jubilee reliefs and proximity to a pyramid field suggest a similar function to Zoser's *heb-sed* court at Saqqara.

Unlike the ruinous **Sun Temple of Userkaf**, 400m from Sahure's Pyramid, the more distant **Sun Temple of Nyuserre** repays a visit. At its western end stood a colossal *benben* or megalith as tall as a pyramid, symbolizing the primordial mound – of which only the base remains. Approached from its valley temple by a causeway, the great courtyard is centred on an alabaster altar where cattle were sacrificed. From the courtyard's vestibule, corridors run north to storerooms and south to the king's chapel. The "Chamber of Seasons" beyond the chapel once contained beautiful reliefs; to the south you can find the remnants of a brick model of a solar boat.

North Saqqara

While Memphis (see p.248) was the capital of the Old Kingdom, Egypt's royalty and nobility were buried at **Saqqara**, the limestone scarp that flanks the Nile Valley to the west – the traditional direction of the Land of the Dead. Although superseded by the Theban necropolis during the New Kingdom, Saqqara remained in use for burying sacred animals and birds, especially in Ptolemaic times, when these cults enjoyed a revival. Over three thousand years it grew to cover seven kilometres of desert – not including the associated necropolises of Abu Sir and Dahshur, or the Giza Pyramids. As such, it is today the largest archeological site in Egypt. Its name – usually pronounced "sa'-'ah-rah" by Cairenes, with the Qs as glottal stops – probably derives from Sokar, the Memphite god of the dead, though Egyptians may tell you that it comes from *saq*, the Arabic word for a hawk or falcon, the sacred bird of Horus.

Besides the pyramids and *mastabas* seen by visitors, Saqqara has an incalculable wealth of monuments and artefacts still hidden beneath the windblown sands. In 1986, the **tomb of Maya**, Tutankhamun's treasurer, was discovered, stuffed with precious objects (it won't be open to the public for some time). Yet aside from Zoser's Pyramid, the site was virtually ignored by archeologists until Auguste Mariette found the Serapeum in 1851.

The Saqqara necropolis divides into two main sections: **North Saqqara** – the more interesting area (covered here) – and **South Saqqara** (see p.250). North Saqqara boasts a score of sights, so anyone with limited time should be selective. The **highlights** are Zoser's funerary complex, the Serapeum, and two outstanding *mastabas*; if time allows, add other tombs to your itinerary. To take in the whole site you would need several days.

Getting there and other practicalities

North Saqqara lies 21km south of the Giza Pyramids as the camel trundles, or 32km from Cairo by road, being roughly opposite Helwan on the east bank of

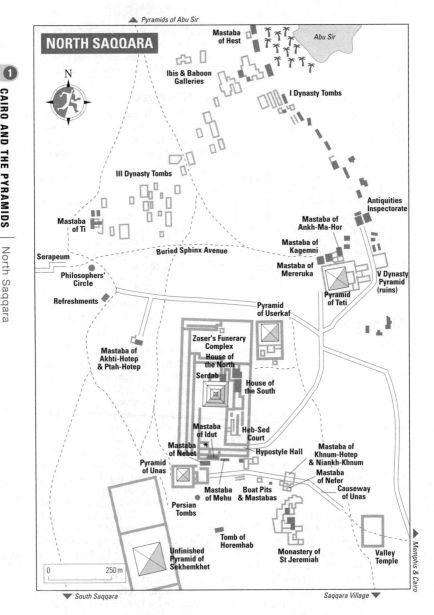

the Nile. Getting there **by public transport**, the quickest method (about an hour) is to take a bus or service taxi to Pyramids Road, get off at Maryotteya Canal (about 1km before the Pyramids), head down the east bank of the canal and take the first left, leading to a yard where you'll find service taxi microbuses to Saqqara. An alternative route is to take bus #330 from Midan Giza to Saqqara village, or bus #987 from Midan Ramses or Midan Tahrir to El-Badrasheen, and then a minibus to Saqqara, by way of Memphis. A final option is to take the metro to Helwan station (30min; 75pt), then a minibus to Tibiin, near the Marazi Bridge (15min; 65pt); another service taxi across to El-Badrasheen on the west bank (15min; 50pt); and finally one to Saqqara as above (15min; 35pt). One disadvantage of all these methods is that they leave you in Saqqara village, still over a kilometre from the site entrance, though the service taxi from Maryotteya will drop you off nearer the site entrance if you ask. Getting back to Cairo, it is wise not to leave too late, or you may not find transport in Saqqara village, and will have to either pay well over the odds for a taxi, or walk another 5km to El-Badrasheen (or at least to the Maryotteya Canal) to pick up a bus or microbus back to Cairo.

To save time and energy for the site, you could take a **tour**, such as the ones run by the affable Salah Mohammed Abdel Hafiez (☎02/298-0650, mobile ☎012 3138446, ⓔsamo@link.net). The tours leave around 8am in summer, 9am in winter. You'll be driven in an a/c minibus to Memphis, North Saqqara, the Wissa Wassef tapestry school at Harraniyya and the Pyramids of Giza – all accompanied by an English-speaking Egyptologist – before returning to Cairo at about 4pm in winter, 5pm in summer. Be sure to ask to see the Mastaba of Ti during your trip. The price of the tour (£E50) doesn't include admission tickets, but *Rough Guide* readers who book direct get a £E5 discount, with a free airport transfer to your hotel on arrival also thrown in. Thomas Cook, Misr Travel and American Express also run tours to Saqqara for upwards of £E160 per person. Another option is to rent a **private taxi** for the day (£E60–80 for just Giza and Saqqara, £E80–120 if you add on Dahshur), splitting the cost between however many people you can assemble. Be sure to specify which sites are included and how long you expect to stay when you negotiate with the driver.

Lastly, you could plump for riding **across the desert from the Pyramids of Giza by horse or camel** (3hr). Although touts swear that the route takes you through the desert, past Zawiyet al-Aryan, the Sun Temples of Abu Ghurab and the Pyramids of Abu Sir, they often guide you along a more direct village track on the edge of the cultivated area, supposedly due to military restrictions. Either way, the journey will leave you stiff for days afterwards (see p.81 for the rudiments of camel-handling). Most people opt for a one-way ride (£E90–120 for a horse, £E120–150 for a camel); return trips cost twice that, plus a negotiable sum for waiting time (around £E300–400 in all). Be warned that some guides threaten to abandon travellers in the middle of nowhere unless they receive hefty *baksheesh*; it's usually safe to call their bluff, but better to use a reputable firm such as AA or KG (see p.274).

Even if you don't emulate Lawrence of Arabia, bear in mind **conditions** at Saqqara. Over winter, the site can be swept by chill winds and clouds of grit; during the hottest months walking around is exhausting. Beware of deep pits, which aren't always fenced off. Bring at least one litre of water apiece, as vendors at Memphis and the refreshments tent at North Saqqara are grossly overpriced, like every restaurant along the Saqqara road; a packed lunch is also a good idea.

Though **opening hours** are daily 8am to 4pm in winter, 8am to 5pm in summer, guards start locking up the tombs at least half an hour early. A kiosk on the approach road sells **tickets** (£E35, students £E20). It's a good idea to check at the kiosk which tombs are open – especially those further afield – as they often close due to restoration work. Some guards encourage unauthorized snapping in the tombs in the expectation of *baksheesh*, but aside from this you're not obliged to give anything unless they help with lighting or provide a guided tour. If you don't want a running commentary, make this clear at the outset.

To reduce foot-slogging around the site, consider **renting a camel** (£E40–50 per hour), **horse** (£E30–40 per hour) **or donkey** (£E25 per hour) from around the step pyramid or outside the refreshments hut near the Serapeum.

Zoser's funerary complex

The funerary complex of King Zoser (or Djoser) is the largest in Saqqara, and its **Step Pyramid** heralded the start of the Pyramid Age. When Imhotep, Zoser's chief architect, raised the pyramid in the 27th century BC, it was the largest structure ever built in stone – the "beginning of architecture", according to one historian. Imhotep's achievement was to break from the tradition of earthbound *mastabas*, raising level upon level of stones to create a four-step, and then a six-step pyramid, which was clad in dazzling white limestone. None of the blocks was very large, for Zoser's builders still thought in terms of mud-brick rather than megaliths, but the concept, techniques and logistics all pointed towards the true pyramid, finally attained at Giza.

Before it was stripped of its casing stones and rounded off by the elements, Zoser's Pyramid stood 62m high and measured 140m by 118m along its base. The original entrance on the northern side is blocked, but with permission and keys from the site's Antiquities Inspectorate you can enter via a gallery on the opposite side, dug in the XXVI Dynasty. Dark passageways and vertical ladders descend 28m into the bedrock, where a granite plug failed to prevent robbers from plundering the burial chamber of this III Dynasty monarch (c.2667–2648 BC).

Surrounding the pyramid is an extensive **funerary complex**, originally enclosed by a finely cut limestone wall, 544m long and 277m wide, now largely ruined or buried by sand. False doors occur at intervals for the convenience of the pharaoh's *ka*, but visitors can only enter at the southeastern corner, which has largely been rebuilt. Beyond a vestibule with simulated double doors (detailed down to their hinge pins and sockets) lies a narrow colonnaded corridor, whose forty "bundle" columns are ribbed in imitation of palm stems, which culminates in a broader **Hypostyle Hall**.

From here you emerge onto the **Great South Court**, where a rebuilt section of wall (marked ★ on our site plan) bears a **frieze of cobras**. Worshipped in the Delta as a fire-spitting goddess of destruction called Wadjet or Edjo, the cobra was adopted as the emblem of royalty and always appeared on pharaonic headdresses – a figure known as the *uraeus*. Nearby, a deep shaft plummets into Zoser's **Southern Tomb**, decorated with blue faïence tiles and a relief of the king running the *heb-sed* race. During the Jubilee festival marking the thirtieth year of a pharaoh's reign, he had to sprint between two altars representing Upper and Lower Egypt and re-enact his coronation, seated first on one throne, then upon another, symbolically reuniting the Two Lands. Besides demonstrating his vitality, the five-day festival confirmed the renewal of his *ka* and the obedience of provincial dignitaries.

Although the festival was held at Memphis, a pair of altars, thrones and shrines were incorporated in Zoser's funerary complex to perpetuate its efficacy on a cosmic timescale. The B-shaped structures near the centre of the Great Court are the bases of these altars; the twin thrones probably stood on the platform at the southern end of the adjacent **Heb-Sed Court**. Both shrines were essentially facades, since the actual buildings were filled with rubble. This phoney quality is apparent if you view them from the east: the curvaceous roof line and delicate false columns wouldn't look amiss on a yuppie waterfront development. Notice the four **stone feet** beneath a shelter near the northern end of the court.

Beyond this lies the partially ruined **House of the South**, whose chapel is fronted by proto-Doric columns with lotus capitals, and a spearhead motif above the lintel. Inside you'll find several examples of XVIII–IXX Dynasty tourist graffiti, expressing admiration for Zoser or the equivalent of "Ramses was here" – banalities which one scornful ancient graffitist likens to "the work of a woman who has no mind". Continuing northwards, you'll pass a relatively intact row of casing stones along the eastern side of Zoser's Pyramid. The **House of the North** has fluted columns with papyrus capitals; the lotus and the papyrus were the heraldic emblems of Upper and Lower Egypt.

On the northern side of the pyramid, a tilted masonry box or **serdab** ("cellar" in Arabic) contains a life-size statue of Zoser gazing blindly towards the North and circumpolar stars, which the ancients associated with immortality; seated thus, his *ka* was assured of eternal life. Zoser's statue is a replica, however, the original having been removed to Cairo's Antiquities Museum (see p.129). The ruined mortuary temple to the right of the *serdab* is unusual for being sited to the north rather than the east of its pyramid, and for the underground tunnel which originally led to Zoser's burial chamber.

South of the complex

South of Zoser's funerary complex are several tombs and other ruins, dating from various dynasties. During the Old Kingdom, nobles were buried in subterranean tombs covered by large mud-brick superstructures; the name *mastaba* (Arabic for "bench") was bestowed upon them by native workmen during excavations last century. Three such edifices stand outside the southern wall of Zoser's complex, although two of them are currently closed. The open one, the **Mastaba of Idut**, has interesting reliefs in five of its ten rooms. Among the fishing and farming scenes, notice the crocodile eyeing a newborn hippo, and a calf being dragged through the water so that cows will ford a river. The chapel contains a false door painted in imitation of granite, scenes of bulls and buffaloes being sacrificed, and Idut herself. Idut was the daughter of Pharaoh Unas, whose pyramid stands just beyond the **Mastaba of Nebet**, his queen. If accessible, its reliefs are also worth seeing: in one scene, Nebet smells a lotus blossom.

The Pyramid of Unas

Although its frontal aspect resembles a mound of rubble, the **Pyramid of Unas** retains many casing stones around the back, some carved with hieroglyphs. A low passageway on the northern side leads into its **burial chamber**, whose alabaster walls are covered with inscriptions listing the rituals and prayers for liberating the pharaoh's *ba*, and the articles for his *ka* to use in the afterlife. These **Pyramid Texts** are the earliest known example of decorative writing within a pharaonic tomb, and formed the basis of the New Kingdom *Book of the Dead*. They speak of the pharaoh becoming a star and travelling to Sirius and other constellations. Painted stars adorn the ceiling, while the sarcophagus area is surrounded by striped, checked and zigzag patterns. Thomas Cook & Sons sponsored the excavation of the tomb by Gaston Maspero in 1881.

Unas was the last pharaoh of the V Dynasty, so his pyramid follows those of Abu Sir, which evince a marked decline from the great pyramids of Giza. Given the duration of pharaonic civilization, it's sobering to realize that only 350 years separated the creation of the Step Pyramid from this sad reminder of past glories. Originally, it was approached by a one-kilometre-long

▲ Unas

causeway enclosed by a roof and walls. Reliefs inside the short reconstructed section depict the transport of granite from Aswan, archers, prisoners of war, and a famine caused by the Nile failing to rise. The ruins of a valley temple face the ticket office below the plateau.

To the south of the causeway are two gaping, brick-lined **boat pits** that may have contained solar barques like the one at Giza, or merely symbolized them, since nothing was found when the pits were excavated.

Other tombs and ruins

A stone hut to the south of the Unas Pyramid gives access to a spiral staircase that descends 25m underground, to where three low corridors lead into the vaulted **Persian Tombs**. Chief physician Psamtik, Admiral Djenhebu and Psamtik's son Pediese were all officials of the XXVII Dynasty of Persian kings founded in 525 BC, yet the hieroglyphs in their tombs invoke the same spells as those written two thousand years earlier. The dizzying descent and claustrophobic atmosphere make this an exciting tomb to explore. Though often locked, it's not "forbidden" as guards sometimes pretend, hoping to wangle excessive *baksheesh*.

Further to the southeast lies the recently rediscovered **Tomb of Horemheb**. Built when he was a general, it became redundant after Horemheb seized power from Pharaoh Ay in 1348 BC and ordered a new tomb to be dug in the Valley of the Kings, the royal necropolis of the New Kingdom. Many of the finely carved blocks from his original tomb are now in museums around the world. Another set of paving stones and truncated columns marks the nearby **Tomb of Tia**, sister of Ramses II. The **Tomb of Maya**, Tutankhamun's treasurer, was found nearby in 1986 and is still under excavation. Due east lie the sanded-over mud-brick ruins of the **Monastery of St Jeremiah**, which the Arabs destroyed in 960, four hundred years after its foundation. Practically all of the monastery's carvings and paintings have been removed to the Coptic Museum in Old Cairo. Just to its north, on the causeway of Unas, are four *mastabas* belonging to nobles.

It's indicative of how much might still be hidden beneath the sands at Saqqara that the **unfinished Pyramid of Sekhemkhet** was only discovered in 1950. Beyond his monuments, nothing is known of Sekhemkhet, whose step pyramid and funerary complex were presumably intended to mimic those of his predecessor, Zoser, and may also have been built by Imhotep. The alabaster sarcophagus inside the pyramid (which is unsafe to enter) was apparently never used, but the body of a child was found inside an auxiliary tomb.

From Sekhemkhet's pyramid and the monastery it's roughly 700m to the nearest part of South Saqqara.

Around the Pyramids of Userkaf and Teti

While neither of these pyramids amounts to much, the *mastabas* near Teti's edifice contain some fantastic reliefs. If you're starting from Zoser's complex, it's only a short walk to the pulverized **Pyramid of Userkaf**, the founder of the V Dynasty, whose successors were buried at Abu Sir (see p.237). From here, a track runs northwards to the **Pyramid of Teti**, which overlooks the valley from the edge of the plateau. Excavated by Mariette in the 1850s, it has since been engulfed by sand and may be closed; in one of the funeral chambers (accessible by a sloping shaft and low passageway), the star-patterned blocks of its vaulted roof have slipped inwards.

Although most of the VI Dynasty kings who followed Teti chose to be buried at South Saqqara, several of their courtiers were interred in a **"street of tombs"** beside his pyramid, which was linked to the Serapeum by an Avenue of Sphinxes (now sanded over). To do justice to their superbly detailed reliefs takes well over an hour, but it's rare to find all of them open.

The Mastaba of Mereruka

The largest tomb in the street belongs to **Mereruka**, Teti's vizier and son-in-law, whose 32-room complex includes separate funerary suites for his wife Watet-khet-hor, priestess of Hathor, and their son Meri-Teti. In the entry passage, Mereruka is shown playing a board game and painting at an easel; the chamber beyond depicts him hunting in the marshes with Watet-khet-hor (the frogs, birds, hippos and grasshoppers are beautifully rendered), along with the usual farming scenes. Goldsmiths, jewellers and other artisans are inspected by the couple in a room beyond the rear door, which leads into another chamber showing taxation and the punishment of defaulters. A pillared hall to the right portrays them watching sinuous dancers; a room to the left depicts offerings, sacrifices and birds being fed, with a *serdab* at the far end.

△ Teti

Beyond the transverse hall, with its tomb shaft, false door and reliefs of grape-treading and harvesting, lies the main offerings hall, dominated by a statue of Mereruka emerging from a false door. The opposite wall shows his funeral procession; around the corner are boats under full sail, with monkeys playing in their rigging. To the left of the statue, Mereruka is supported by his sons and litter-bearers, accompanied by dwarves and dogs; on the other side, children frolic while dancers sway above the doorway into Meri-Teti's undecorated funerary suite.

To reach **Watet-khet-hor's suite**, return to the first room in the *mastaba* and take the other door. After similar scenes to those in her husband's tomb, Watet-khet-hor is carried to her false door in a lion chair.

The Mastabas of Kagemni and Ankh-ma-hor

East of Mereruka's tomb and left around the corner, the smaller **Mastaba of Kagemni** features delicate reliefs in worse shape. The pillared hall beyond the entrance corridor shows dancers and acrobats, the judgement of prisoners, a hippo hunt and agricultural work, all rich in naturalistic detail. Notice the boys feeding a puppy and trussed cows being milked. The door in this wall leads to another chamber where Kagemni inspects his fowl pens while servants trap marsh birds with clap-nets; on the pylon beyond this he relaxes on a palanquin as they tend to his pet dogs and monkeys. As usual in the offerings hall, scenes of butchery appear opposite the false door. On the roof of the *mastaba* (reached by stairs from the entrance corridor) are two boat pits. As vizier, Kagemni was responsible for overseeing prophets and the estate of Teti's pyramid complex.

The **Mastaba of Ankh-ma-hor** is also known as the "Doctor's Tomb" after its reliefs showing circumcision, toe surgery and suchlike, as practised during the VI Dynasty. If the tomb is open it's definitely worth a look, unlike the sand-choked **I Dynasty tombs** that straggle along the edge of the scarp beyond the **Antiquities Inspectorate**.

Two outstanding mastabas

If your time is limited, these are the tombs to visit: the **Double Mastaba of Akhti- and Ptah-Hotep** lies 200m off the road to the refreshments hut, while the **Mastaba of Ti** is 500m in the other direction and easiest to get to from the Serapeum (see opposite).

The Mastaba of Akhti-Hotep and Ptah-Hotep

This *mastaba* belonged to **Ptah-Hotep**, a priest of Maat during the reign of Unas's predecessor, Djedkare, and his son **Akhti-Hotep**, who served as vizier, judge and overseer of the granaries and treasury. Though smaller than Ti's *mastaba*, its reliefs are interesting for being at various stages of completion, showing how a finished product was achieved. After the preliminary drawings had been corrected in red by a master artist, the background was chiselled away to leave a silhouette, before details were marked in and cut. The agricultural scenes in the entrance corridor show this process clearly, although with the exception of Ptah-Hotep's chapel, none of these reliefs was ever painted.

Off the pillared hall of Akhti-Hotep is a T-shaped chapel whose inside wall shows workers making papyrus boats and jousting with poles. More impressive is the chapel of his father, covered with exquisitely detailed reliefs. Between the two door-shaped steles representing the entrance to the tomb, Ptah-Hotep enjoys a banquet of offerings, garbed in the panther-skin of a high priest. Similar scenes occur on the facing wall, whose upper registers show animals being slaughtered and women bringing offerings from his estates. The left-hand wall swarms with activity, as boys wrestle and play *Khaki la wizza* (a leapfrog game still popular in Nubia); wild animals mate or flee from hunting dogs, while others are caged. A faded mural above the entrance shows the priest being manicured and pedicured at a time when Europe was in the Stone Age.

The Mastaba of Ti

Discovered by Mariette in 1865, this V Dynasty tomb has been a rich source of information about life in the Old Kingdom. A royal hairdresser who made an advantageous marriage, **Ti** acquired stewardship over several mortuary temples and pyramids, and his children bore the title "royal descendant".

Ti makes his first appearances on either side of the doorway, receiving offerings and asking visitors to respect his tomb **[a]**. The reliefs in the courtyard have been damaged by exposure, but it's possible to discern men butchering an ox **[b]**, Ti on his palanquin accompanied by dogs and dwarves **[c]**, servants feeding cranes and geese **[d]**, and Ti examining accounts and cargo **[e]**. His unadorned tomb (reached by a shaft from the courtyard) contrasts with the richly decorated interior of the *mastaba*.

Near his son's false door, variously garbed figures of Ti **[f]** appear above the portal of a corridor where bearers bring food and animals for the sustenance of his *ka* **[g]**. Beyond a doorway **[h]** over which Ti enjoys the marshes with his wife, funerary statues are dragged on sledges above scenes of butchery, and his Delta fleets are arrayed **[i]**. Potters, bakers, brewers and scribes occupy the rear wall of a storage room **[j]**, while dancers shimmy above the doorway to Ti's chapel.

In the harvesting scene, notice the man twisting a donkey's ear to make it behave **[k]**. Further along, Ti inspects shipwrights shaping tree trunks, and sawing and hammering boards **[l]**. Goldsmiths, sculptors, carpenters, tanners and market life are minutely detailed **[m]**, like the musicians who entertain Ti at his offerings table **[n]**. Peer through one of the apertures and you'll see a cast of his statue inside its *serdab*. The original is in the Egyptian Museum in Cairo.

▲ Feeding cranes

Reliefs on the northern wall depict fishing and trapping in the Delta **[o]**; Ti sailing through the marshes while his servants spear hippopotami **[p]**; harvesting papyrus for boat-building; and ploughing and seeding fields **[q]**. The scene of

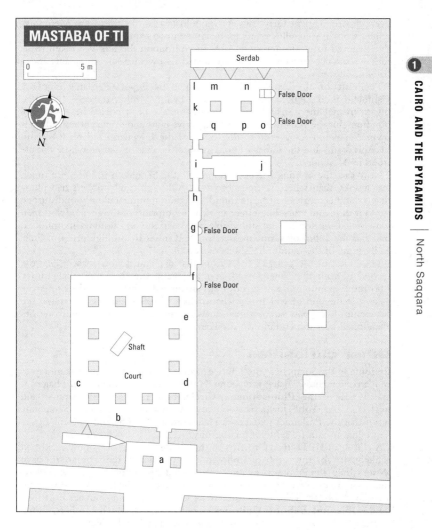

MASTABA OF TI

0   5 m

N

Serdab

l   m   n
k   ☐ False Door
q   p   o   ☐ False Door

i   j

h

g ◯ False Door

f ◯ False Door

e

Shaft

c   Court   d

b

a

hunting in the marshes is also allegorical, pitting Ti against the forces of chaos (represented by fish and birds) and evil (hippos were hated and feared).

The Serapeum

Saqqara's weirdest monument lies underground near a derelict building down-hill from the refreshments tent. Discovered by Mariette in 1851, the rock-cut galleries of the **Serapeum** held the mummified corpses of the Apis bulls, which the Memphites regarded as manifestations of Ptah's "blessed soul" and identified with Osiris after death.

Having been embalmed on alabaster slabs at Memphis, the bulls were interred in sarcophagi weighing up to seventy tons apiece. Meanwhile, the priests began searching for Ptah's reincarnation amongst the sacred herd. Once a new bull had been chosen, it spent forty days at Nilopolis (across the river from Memphis), where women were allowed to approach it *only* to expose their vulvas (a practice believed to ensure fertility). After the full moon the bull was taken to its future residence in Memphis, where it had its own priestly attendants and a harem of cows.

The **cult of the Apis bulls** was assailed by Egypt's Persian conqueror, Cambyses, who stabbed one to disprove its divinity, whilst Artaxerxes I avenged his nickname "the donkey" by having a namesake beast buried here with full honours. But the Ptolemies encouraged native cults and even synthesized their own. "Serapeum" derives from the fusion of the Egyptian Osarapis (Osiris in his Apis form) and the Greeks' Dionysus into the cult of *Serapis*, whose temple stood in Alexandria.

Now that the lighting has been improved, the Serapeum galleries are much less spooky than when Mariette broke in. Although tomb robbers had plundered them centuries before, he found a single tomb miraculously undisturbed for four thousand years. The finger mark and footprints of the ancient workman who sealed the tomb were still visible, and Mariette also found a mummified bull and the coffin of Khamenwaset, son of Ramses II and high priest of Ptah. Sadly, none of the mummified bulls remains *in situ*.

The oldest of the galleries dates from that era, and is now inaccessible; the second is from the Saite period, and the main one from Ptolemaic times. Enormous granite or basalt **sarcophagi** are ranged either side of the Ptolemaic gallery, at the end of which is a narrow shaft whereby robbers penetrated the Serapeum. The finest sarcophagus squats on the right, while another one lies abandoned near the entrance to the Ramessid gallery.

Other curiosities

En route to the Serapeum you'll notice a concrete slab sheltering broken statues of Plato, Heraclitus, Thales, Protagoras, Homer, Hesiod, Demetrius of Phalerum and Pindar – the **Philosopher's Circle**, now rather rubbish-strewn and neglected. The statues formerly stood near a temple that overlaid the Serapeum, proof that the Ptolemies juxtaposed Hellenistic philosophy and Ancient Egyptian religion with no sense of incongruity.

A cluster of **III Dynasty tombs** to the east of Ti's *mastaba* is now reckoned a likely site for the tomb of Imhotep, as yet undiscovered. The architect of Zoser's Step Pyramid was revered throughout pharaonic history and eventually became a demigod, credited with powers of healing; the Ptolemies associated him with Asclepius, the Greek god of medicine. Further northeast lie the **Ibis and Baboon Galleries** sacred to Thoth, which Flaubert visited in the 1840s: "We go down into a hole and then crawl along a passageway almost on our stomachs, inching over fine sand and fragments of pottery; at the far end the jars containing ibises are stacked like blocks of sugar at a grocer's, head to foot."

Memphis

Most tour excursions to Saqqara include a flying visit to the scant **remains of Memphis** in the village of **MIT RAHINA**. Sadly, these hardly stir one's imagination to resurrect the ancient city effaced over centuries by Nilotic silt, which now lies metres below rustling palm groves and oxen-ploughed fields. Although something of its glory is evident in the great necropolises

The cults of Ptah and Sokar

In pre-Dynastic times, **Ptah** was the Great Craftsman or Divine Artificer, who invented metallurgy and engineering. However, the people of Memphis esteemed him as the Great Creator who, with a word, brought the universe into being – a concept that never really appealed to other Egyptians. Like most creator gods, he was subsequently linked with death cults and is shown dressed in the shroud of a mummy. The Greeks equated him with Hephaestus, their god of fire and the arts.

Another deity closely associated with Memphis is **Sokar**, originally the god of darkness but subsequently of death, with special responsibility for necropolises. He is often shown, with a falcon's head, seated in the company of Isis and Osiris. Although his major festival occurred at Memphis towards the end of the inundation season, Sokar also rated a shrine at Abydos, where all the Egyptian death gods were represented.

▲ Ptah

ranged across the desert, and the countless objects in Cairo's Antiquities Museum, to appreciate the significance of Memphis you have to recall its history.

The city's foundation is attributed to Menes, the quasi-mythical ruler (known also as Narmer – and possibly a conflation of several rulers) who was said to have unified Upper and Lower Egypt and launched the I Dynasty around 3100 BC. At that time, Memphis was sited at the apex of the Delta and thus controlled overland and river communications. If not the earliest city on earth, it was certainly the first imperial one. Memphis was Egypt's capital throughout the Old Kingdom, regained its role after the anarchic Intermediate Period, and was never overshadowed by the parvenu seat of the XII Dynasty. Even after Thebes became capital of the New Kingdom, Memphis still held sway over Lower Egypt and remained the nation's second city until well into the Ptolemaic era, only being deserted in early Muslim times after four thousand years of continuous occupation.

Alas for posterity, most of this garden city was built of mud-brick, which returned to the Nile silt whence it came, and everyone from the Romans onwards plundered its stone temples for fine masonry.

Nowadays, leftover statues and steles share a garden (daily: winter 8am–4pm; summer 8am–5pm; £E25, students £E15) with souvenir kiosks. The star attraction, found in 1820, is a limestone **Colossus of Ramses II**, similar to the one that used to stand in Midan Ramses, but laid supine within a concrete shelter. A giant **alabaster sphinx** weighing eighty tons is also mightily impressive. Both these figures probably stood outside the vast Temple of Ptah, the city's patron deity.

By leaving the garden and walking back along the road, you'll notice (on the right) several alabaster **embalming slabs**, where the holy Apis bulls were mummified before burial in the Serapeum at Saqqara. In a pit across the road are excavated chambers from Ptah's temple complex; climb the ridge beyond them and you can gaze across the cultivated valley floor to the Step Pyramid of Saqqara.

South Saqqara

Like their predecessors at Abu Sir, the pharaohs of the VI Dynasty (c.2345–2181 BC) established another necropolis – nowadays called **South Saqqara** – which started 700m beyond Sekhemkhet's unfinished pyramid and extended for over three kilometres. Unfortunately for sightseers, the most interesting monuments are those furthest away across the site; renting a donkey, horse or camel (£E30–50 for the round trip) will minimize slogging over soft sand. It is also possible to walk from Saqqara village: just keep heading west until you emerge from the palm trees. If you stop to ask directions, bear in mind that, whatever you say (even if you say it in Arabic), the villagers will almost certainly assume you are looking for the Step Pyramid, and direct you accordingly.

Once you reach the site, two tracks run either side of several pyramids before meeting at the Mastabat al-Faraun. The western one is more direct than the route that goes via Saqqara village, set amidst lush palm groves 2km from North Saqqara's ticket office. There is no official entrance fee to the site, and you probably won't see another tourist. Apart from the tranquillity, however, what you get here, with the pyramids of North Saqqara clearly visible to your north, and those of Dahshur to your south, is the feeling of being in the midst of a massive pyramid field, somewhere very ancient and vast.

The site

Heading south along either track, you'll pass a low mound of rubble identified as the **Pyramid of Pepi I**. The name "Memphis", which Classical authors bestowed upon Egypt's ancient capital and its environs, was actually derived from one of this pyramid's titles. To the southwest, another insignificant heap indicates the **Pyramid of Merenre**, who succeeded Pepi. French archeologists are excavating the latter's pyramid, but neither site is really worth a detour.

Due west of Saqqara village, sand drifts over the outlying temples of the **Pyramid of Djedkare-Isesi**. Known in Arabic as the "Pyramid of the Sentinel", it stands 25m high and can be entered via a tunnel on the north side. Although a shattered basalt sarcophagus and mummified remains were found here during the 1800s, it wasn't until 1946 that Abdel Hussein identified them as those of Djedkare, the penultimate king of the V Dynasty. Far from being the first ruler to be entombed in South Saqqara, Djedkare was merely emulating the last pharaoh of the previous dynasty, whose own mortuary complex is uniquely different, and the oldest in this necropolis.

Built of limestone blocks, Shepseskaf's mortuary complex resembles a gigantic sarcophagus with a rounded lid; another simile gave rise to its local name, **Mastabat al-Faraun** – the Pharaoh's Bench. If you can find a guard, it's possible to venture through descending and horizontal corridors to reach the burial chamber and various storerooms. The monument was almost certainly commissioned by Shepseskaf, who evidently felt the need to distance himself from the pyramid of his father, Mycerinus. However, the archeologist Jequier doubted that the complex was ever used for any actual burial and Shepseskaf's final resting place remains uncertain.

Northwest of here lies the most complete example of a VI Dynasty mortuary complex, albeit missing casing stones and other masonry that was plundered in medieval times. The usual valley temple and causeway culminate in a mortuary temple whose vestibule and sanctuary retain fragments of their original reliefs. Beyond this rises the **Pyramid of Pepi II**, whose reign supposedly lasted 94 years, after which the VI Dynasty expired. A descending passage leads to his rock-cut burial chamber, whose ceiling and walls are inscribed with stars and Pyramid Texts. These also appear within the subsidiary pyramids of Pepi's queens, Apuit and Neith, which imitate his mortuary complex on a smaller scale. Various nobles and officials are buried roundabouts.

Dahshur

The **Dahshur pyramid field** (daily: winter 8am–4pm; summer 8am–6pm; last ticket sold an hour before closing; £E20, students £E10) contains some of the most impressive of all the pyramids, and some of the most significant in the history of pyramid-building. The easiest way **to get to Dahshur** is by taxi, but there are also service taxi microbuses to Dahshur village from Maryotteya Canal by Pyramids Road (the same yard as for Saqqara; see p.250) and from Saqqara village. Infrequent service taxis run the 2km to the site entrance from Dahshur village, but most people will find it easier to walk or take a private taxi. The latter is quite a good idea since not only is the site a good couple of kilometres from the village, but it is also extremely spread out: it's another kilometre from the gate to the Red Pyramid, and another from there to the Bent Pyramid, so walkers should be prepared to cover quite a distance. A taxi should cost £E2 from the village to the Red Pyramid, but somewhat more if you also want to be driven around the site and back. **Getting back to Cairo** should not be left too late or you may find yourself stranded with the nearest public transport 5km away in Saqqara – transport from Dahshur tends to dry up at around 5pm.

The pyramids are in two groups. To the east are three **Middle Kingdom complexes**, dating from the revival of pyramid-building (c.1991–1790 BC) that culminated near the Fayoum. Though the pyramids proved unrewarding to nineteenth-century excavators, their subsidiary tombs yielded some magnificent jewellery (now in the Antiquities Museum). To the north, the pyramids of XII Dynasty pharaohs Seostris III and Amenenkhet II are little more than piles of rubble, but the southernmost of the three, the **Black Pyramid** of Amenemhet III (Joseph's pharaoh in the Old Testament, according to some), is at least an interesting shape: though its limestone casing has long gone, a black mud-brick core is still standing (its black basalt capstone is in the Antiquities Museum). More intriguing, however, are the two **Old Kingdom pyramids** further into the desert, which have long tantalized archeologists with a riddle. Both of them are credited to **Snofru** (c.2613–2588 BC), father of Cheops and founder of the IV Dynasty, whose monuments constitute an evolutionary link between the stepped creations of the previous dynasty at North Saqqara and the true pyramids of Giza.

The Red Pyramid

The first pyramid you come to if you follow the road past the ticket office is Snofru's northern **Red Pyramid**, which is named after the colour of the limestone it was built from. Despite its lower angle (43.5°) and height (101m), Snofru's Red Pyramid clearly prefigures Cheops's edifice, which is also the only pyramid that exceeds it in size, Snofru's Red Pyramid being larger than Chephren's Pyramid at Giza. It was probably Snofru's third attempt (see p.252) at pyramid building, but he was not laid to rest in any of the three burial chambers here – all were unused.

The Red Pyramid's **interior** is now open to the public, and you can climb up and descend into it to check out its three rather musty chambers. Electric lighting has been installed to illuminate them, but it sometimes fails, so it's a good idea to bring a torch or flashlight if you have one. The first two chambers are roughly parallel to each other, but the third is on a higher level and perpendicular to the other two. One definite advantage of visiting the interior of this pyramid rather than those at Giza is that you will very probably be alone to absorb the rather eerie, if fetid, atmosphere.

The Bent Pyramid

From the Red Pyramid, a track leads south to the pyramid where Snofru was buried, the **Bent Pyramid**, which is not only the most intriguing of all the pyramids, but, because of its state of preservation, also the most breathtaking. What makes Snofru's final resting place different from all the other pyramids is its change of angle towards the top: it rises more steeply (54.3°) than the Red Pyramid or Giza pyramids for three-quarters of its height, before abruptly tapering at a gentler slope – hence its name. The explanation for its shape, and why Snofru should have built two pyramids only a kilometre apart, is a longstanding conundrum of Egyptology.

▲ Snofru

Mindful of the truism that a pharaoh required but one sanctuary for his *ka*, many reasoned that the Bent Pyramid resulted from a change of plan prompted by fears for its stability, and when these persisted, a second, safer pyramid was built to guarantee Snofru's afterlife. But for this theory to hold water, it's necessary to dismiss Snofru's claim to have built a *third* pyramid at Maidum as mere usurpation of an earlier structure; and the possibility that its sudden collapse might have caused the modification of the Bent Pyramid must likewise be rejected on the grounds that he needed only one secure monument.

In 1977, a professor of physics at Oxford University reopened the whole debate. Arguing that Snofru did, indeed, build the "Collapsed Pyramid" at Maidum, whose fall resulted in changes to Dahshur's Bent Pyramid, Kurt Mendelssohn overcame the "one pharaoh–one *ka*–one pyramid" objection by postulating a pyramid production line. As one pyramid neared completion, surplus resources were deployed to start another, despite the satisfaction of the reigning king's requirements. The reason for continuous production was that building a single pyramid required gigantic efforts over ten to thirty years; inevitably, some pharaohs lacked the time and resources. A stockpile of half-constructed, perhaps even finished, pyramids was an insurance policy on the afterlife.

Egyptologists greeted Mendelssohn's theory with delight or derision, but unlike the Great Pyramids, or the lives of Hatshepsut, Nefertiti and Akhenaten, the enigma of Snofru's pyramids has never excited much public interest. Nevertheless, of all the pyramids, the Bent Pyramid is probably the most visually stunning. The reason it seems so impressive lies in the fact that, although its corners have fallen away at the base, the pyramid's limestone casing is still largely intact, giving a clear impression of what it once looked like – smooth and white. All the Old Kingdom pyramids were originally clad in limestone, their surfaces smooth like this one, but they have almost all been stripped, the stone burned for lime. The Bent Pyramid escaped that fate because its narrower angle made it harder to remove the facing, though this has disappeared from much of the base.

In fact, the removal of the lowest courses of limestone cladding enables you to see not only how closely the blocks were slotted together, but something else too. On the ground at the northwest corner of the pyramid, pits and grooves have been carved into the bedrock. These were used to dress the pyramid, and presumably were carved before the pyramid was begun, indicating that construction began with the marking out of a base on the cleared bedrock. This is even clearer on the small satellite pyramid immediately to its south.

The Bent Pyramid is unusual in one final respect: it has two entrances, one on its west side as well as the more conventional one in its north face. The reason for this is unknown. To its south is a subsidiary queen's pyramid, possibly belonging to Snofru's wife Hetepheres (though some say Snofru himself was buried here). If it did belong to her, she didn't stay there too long: after robbers had entered both of Snofru's pyramids at Dahshur, Hetepheres' sarcophagus was moved to Giza for safekeeping, and hidden down a shaft next to the Great Pyramid of her son Cheops. The interior of the Bent Pyramid is unlikely to be open to the public in the near future, but you can see inside it on the Guardian's Egypt website at Ⓦwww.guardians.net/egypt.

Consumers' Cairo

As befits its size, Cairo has the most varied culinary scene, shopping and nightlife in North Africa. Much of it is new, having developed in the Sadat era after decades of Nasserite austerity, and for those who can afford it, conspicuous consumption is very much the order of the day. As a visitor, you're well catered for, whether you're into sailing on the Nile, watching a belly dancer, or absorbing a whole world of popular culture at Cairo's religious festivals. All of this is fun to discover but more mundane practicalities can involve hassles and bureaucracy, mysteries and intricacies which we've tried to unravel beginning with "Money" on p.288.

Eating and drinking

The culinary scene in Cairo has diversified enormously since the 1970s, making it possible to eat anything from *sukiyaki* to Kentucky Fried Chicken. Don't fall into the trap of eating only in tourist restaurants, however, or thinking that Egyptian food doesn't rise beyond *kofta* and kebab. You can satisfy most tastes if you know where to look. The options range from Arab cafés offering a few simple dishes to extravagant "food weeks" at deluxe hotels (advertised in *Egypt Today*). Though few natives would agree with them, foreigners are generally pleasantly surprised by the cost of eating out in Cairo. Nearly all the downtown coffee houses, restaurants, cafés and bars are keyed to the map on p.254; for places in Zamalek and on the west bank, see the map on p.210. Drinking, though somewhat limited, is also quite affordable – see p.264.

Coffee houses, patisseries and juice bars

Cairene males have socialized in **coffee houses** or **tearooms** (*'ahwa*) ever since the beverage was introduced from Yemen in the early Middle Ages (for

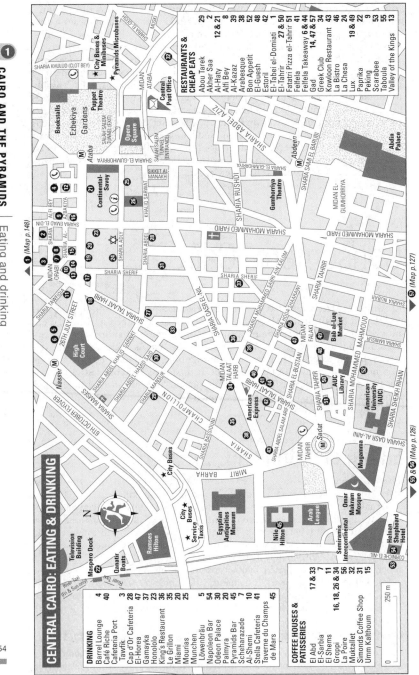

CENTRAL CAIRO: EATING & DRINKING

DRINKING

Barrel Lounge	4
Café Riche	40
Cafeteria Port	
Tawfik	3
Cap d'Or Cafeteria	28
El-Horea	47
Gamayka	37
Honololo	23
King's Restaurant	36
Le Grillon	35
Miami	20
Mourias	25
Munchen	
Löwenbräu	5
Napoleon Bar	54
Odeon Palace	30
Palmyra	20
Pyramids Bar	45
Scheharazade	7
Al-Shemi	10
Stella Cafeteria	41
Taverne du Champs	
de Mars	45

COFFEE HOUSES & PATISSERIES

El Abd	17 & 33
El-Sarbia	7
El Shems	11
Groppi	16, 18, 26 & 34
La Poire	56
Muktallet	32
Simonds Coffee Shop	31
Umm Kalthoum	15

RESTAURANTS & CHEAP EATS

Abou Tarek	29
Akher Saa	2
Al-Haty	12 & 21
Alfi Bey	8
Al-Kazaz	39
Arabesque	38
Bon Appetit	52
El-Guesh	48
Estoril	42
El-Tabei el-Domiati	1
El-Tahrir	27 & 50
Fatatri Pizza el-Tahrir	51
Felfela	41
Felfela Takeaway	6 & 44
Gad	14, 47 & 57
Greek Club	34
Kowloon Restaurant	43
La Bistro	46
La Chesa	24
Lux	19 & 49
Paprika	22
Peking	9
Scarabee	53
Taboula	55
Valley of the Kings	13

a rundown on coffee and tea drinking and preparation, see p.71). Although professional *qasas* (storytellers) have largely been supplanted by broadcast or taped music, other traditional diversions such as backgammon and dominoes are still popular, and smokers remain loyal to their waterpipes. Most *'ahwas* are shabby hole-in-the-wall places, with chairs overlooking the street, while a few – such as *Fishawi's* and *Al-Shataranj* – are large and more sophisticated, with high ceilings and tall mirrors (these often also sell pastries, see below). Certain *'ahwas* are the haunt of hobbyists – chess players at *Al-Shataranj* in Saiyida Zeinab and *El-Horea* in Midan Falaki, stamp collectors at the *Muktallat* at 14 Souq al-Khudar off Midan Ataba – or rural migrants (oasis folk frequent *Al-Wahia* on Sharia Qadry, off Sharia Bur Said), but most have an eclectic clientele. One or two are distinguished by their decor, notably the incredibly kitsch *El Shems* in the passage by 4 Sharia Tawfiqia, and the *Umm Kalthoum* café on Sharia al-Azbakiya behind *Alfi Bey* restaurant, which is done out with memorabilia of the singer and other stars of her day. **All-night** *'ahwas* can be found around Midan Ramses and Sharia Qalaa; those around the Saiyida Zeinab end of Sharia Mohammed Farid and Sharia el-Nasireya show videos (sometimes in English) throughout the night. There are also modern all-night coffee shops in the *Intercontinental*, *Nile Hilton* and other deluxe hotels.

Until very recently, it was unusual for **women** to frequent *'ahwas*, and unheard of to see them puffing away on a *sheesha*, but times change, and younger, less inhibited women can now be seen in certain establishments with a water pipe to their lips. Their presence still tends to be confined to upmarket venues, and female smokers prefer milder blends of tobacco – apple-flavoured *bitufaah*, for example, rather than molasses-soaked *ma'azil* – but little by little, the gender barrier is coming down. Establishments where women can enjoy a *sheesha* without drawing stares include the terrace of the *Nile Hilton* hotel, the rooftop bar of the *Odeon Palace* hotel, and the Arab League Street branch of *Al-Omdah* in Mohandiseen (see p.262).

For daytime snacks, the upmarket coffee houses and tearooms (more akin to Western cafés than traditional *'ahwas*) serve selections of pastries, rice pudding, crème caramel and suchlike – the most famous are the branches of *Groppi's* (see overleaf). As well as being great places to stop off during the day, they also provide a welcome alternative to the monotony of standard hotel **breakfasts** (rolls and jam and/or cheese spread). Another option is to try one of the breakfast **buffets** offered by a range of deluxe hotels and open to non-residents (see listings pp.256–257). One of the best places for **rice pudding**, topped if you like with *basbousa* (a cake-like confection made with nuts and syrup), is *Foontana* on Sharia Handusa opposite the north side of Qasr el-Aini Hospital (see map p.192 – sign in Arabic only, but look for the honey pots in the window).

To take away or consume on the spot, however, it's cheaper to buy at **patisseries**, where traditional pastries such as baklava and *burma* (the latter being slices of syrup-drenched shredded wheat around a pistachio or hazelnut core) are normally sold by the kilo. Good patiseries to try are *El Abd* at 25 Talaat Harb, and on the corner of 26 July and Sherif, and *El-Sarkia* on Sharia Alfy Bey. Even more renowned is the city-wide chain *La Poire*, of which the original and most central branch, at 1 Sharia Amerika Latina (near the British Embassy in Garden City), offers home-made baklava (£E38 per kilo) and eclairs (£E4 each); other branches inclulde Mohandiseen (opposite the *Atlas Hotel*), Giza (Sharia el-Nil, 100m south of the Gama'a Bridge), and Heliopolis (92 Sharia al-Higaz, near Midan Heliopolis).

Every main street has a couple of tiled stand-up **juice bars** (usually open 8am–10pm), recognizable by their displays of fruit, where you can pick up a

Groppi's coffee house

Synonymous with Cairo's erstwhile European "café society", the classic **Groppi** chain now has five locations. The coffee itself is terrible in all of them, but the pastries are great. The once-palatial branch on Midan Talaat Harb has lost much of its charm since renovation, but the pastries are just as tasty, and its a/c salon restful (daily 7am–11.30pm). The panelled interior of *Garden Groppi's* on Sharia Adly (daily 7am– midnight) hasn't changed much since World War II – when soldiers in the lower ranks weren't allowed in – but its patio is a letdown. There's a far nicer terrace attached to *Groppi's in Heliopolis*, at 21 Sharia al-Ahram (daily 7am–midnight). Lacking the style of the others are two with the same name, *Groppi's Al'Americaine* at 44 Sharia Emad el-Din (daily 7am–midnight) and Sharia Talaat Harb (daily 8am–midnight), both on the corner of 26th July Street. All have an £E8 minimum charge.

glass of freshly squeezed juice – a great way to get the appetite going before breakfast. The ones near the *Café Riche* and *Felfela* charge more than most, but they're never expensive. The best one in Cairo is *Farghaly Fruits*, 71 Arab League Street, in Mohandiseen. In many places, you have to order and pay at the cash desk before exchanging a plastic token for your drink at the counter. You'll also see a number of **nut shops** (*ma'la*) on the main thoroughfares, offering all kinds of peanuts (*fuul sudani*), edible seeds, and often candies and mineral water, too. See p.70 for more on the various types of juices and nuts. **Ice cream** in Cairo is usually not very good, though you may find interesting flavours like guava and mango decent places is *Rigoletto* in Zamalek, with delicious ice cream at £E3.25 a scoop.

Coffee houses and buffet breakfasts

As *'ahwas* are numerous, pretty standard, and do not sell food, the listings below concentrate on more Western-style coffee houses and tearooms.

Downtown

Everest Hotel (see map p.148) 15th Floor, Midan Ramses, south side. The terrace café of an otherwise unremarkable cheap hotel, whose coffee isn't the best in town, but you can take a tea or fruit juice and enjoy a view over Midan Ramses and as far as the Citadel and the Muqattam Hills. Daily 24hr.

Ibis Café on the ground floor of the *Nile Hilton*. Breakfast buffet is open daily 5–10.30am (£E56); there's also an unlimited all-day salad bar (£E48). Daily 24hr.

Simonds Coffee Shop 29 Sharia Sherif. A downtown branch of Zamalek's French-style café (see opposite) with a vintage *Gaggia* espresso machine and pastries. Daily 9am–9pm

Islamic Cairo and Saiyida Zeinab

Al-Shataranj 26 Midan Saiyida Zeinab. A meeting place for chess players; the top ones move on to *El-Horea* on Midan Falaki (see p.255).

Fishawi's behind the *El-Hussein Hotel* in Khan el-Khalili (marked on map on p.154). Cairo's oldest tea house has been managed by the same family – and remained perpetually open – since 1773. Cracked mirrors, battered furniture, haughty staff and wandering vendors; imbibe the atmosphere with a pot of mint tea and a *sheesha*. Prices are posted up in Arabic, but if you can't read it, expect to be overcharged. Daily 24hr.

Naguib Mahfouz Coffee Shop 5 Sikket al-Badestan. Upmarket a/c tourist café in the heart of the bazaar, serving snacks, coffee, mint tea and orange juice. Part of the *Khan el-Khalil Restaurant* (marked on map on p.154). Daily 10am–2am.

Zamalek

All the below are marked on the map on p.210.

Café Tabasco 18b Sharia el-Marashly ☎02/735-8465. A sophisticated, Western-style coffee house, wi-fi enabled, where the TV is on (usually Eurosport) but not obtrusive, there are magazines to read, and you can get coffee, juices, herb teas and food (salad, *mezze*, sandwiches, pasta, pizza and ice cream). A good place to hang out, and within Zamalek they even deliver.

No Big Deal Sharia Sayed el-Bakri, nest to *Deals* bar. Small, Californian-style coffee shop, with infusions (and not just *yansoon* and *karkaday*), home-made cakes, and such exotic beverages as Earl Grey tea. Pleasant, but somehow not very Egyptian. Daily 9am–2am.

Rigoletto Yamaha Centre, 3 Sharia Taha Hussein. Espresso, cappuccino, cheesecake and delicious ice cream (£E3.25 a scoop). £E5 minimum charge to eat in. Daily 9am–midnight.

Simonds Coffee Shop 112 26th July St, near the Hassan Sabry intersection. The original French-style coffee shop, with cappuccino, hot chocolate, lemonade, fresh croissants and *ramequins* (cheese puffs). Daily 7am–10pm.

Pyramids of Giza

Khan el-Khalili Coffee Shop in the *Mena House Oberoi*. Luxurious a/c cafeteria near the Pyramids. Skip the paltry Continental breakfast and have the £E78 "special". The "Oberoi" version includes fruit juice, pancakes and croissants; the "Egyptian" one yoghurt with honey and *fuul* with eggs. Also snacks and main meals including such unlikely dishes as mulligatawny soup, nasi goreng and chicken Madagascar. Daily 24hr. Breakfast served 5am–11am.

Restaurants and street food

Restaurants, cafés and street food comprise a culinary spectrum rather than distinctly separate categories. **Restaurants** run the gamut from *nouvelle cuisine* salons to backstreet kebab houses and open-fronted tiled diners. The ones devoted to *kushari* (£E3–5 a bowl) or *fuul* and *taamiya* (£E1.50 with salad and pickles) provide the cheapest nutritious meals going. A third type of outlet purveys *fatir*, or Egyptian pizzas, which are tastier and cheaper (£E6–10 depending on size and ingredients) than most Western-style pizzas in Cairo.

Despite the blurred line between hole-in-the-wall eateries and outright **street food**, running water remains a crucial factor – anywhere without it is risky. Markets and terminals offer the best outlets; a number of places off Ramses, Orabi, Ataba, Falaki, Lazoghli and Giza squares and midway down Sharia Qalaa function **all night**.

△ *Fishawi's* tea house in the Khan el-Khalili bazaar, Cairo

At the other end of the gastro-cultural spectrum, every hotel rated three stars or above has at least one restaurant and coffee shop (maybe 24hr) that's accessible to non-residents. If familiar food and no hassle are top priority, **hotel dining** is usually a safe bet. For those who need them, there are several branches of *McDonald's, Pizza Hut* and *KFC* around the centre as well as in Mohandiseen and Heliopolis. Surprisingly to Westerners, these chains are considered posh eating places by Cairenes, who may even dress up to go to them.

Between these extremes there's a huge variation in **standards** of cleanliness and presentation, and whether somewhere seems okay or grotty depends partly on your own values. We've tried to present a cross section of what's available in various parts of the city. The majority of places listed have **menus** in English or French and staff who understand both, but others deal only in Arabic; fortunately, many of them display what's on offer, so you only have to point (for information on tipping, see p.69). **Vegetarians** should have no trouble feeding themselves, but alongside the felafel and *kushari* joints, *Felfela* caters well for vegetarians, as does *L'Aubergine* in Zamalek, which actually started off as an all-veg establishment.

The following listings have all been graded according to the categories below: **inexpensive** means that you can get a full meal (starter, main course and soft drink) for £E30 or less, **moderate** means that a full meal costs £E30–75, and **expensive** will set you back over £E75 for a full meal. Many restaurants sell seafood and *kofta* and kebab by weight: a quarter of a kilo is one portion, while a full kilo is usually enough for three to four people. Increasingly, restaurants in Cairo, from fast-food joints through to posh eateries, offer **home delivery** (or hotel delivery, if your hostelry will allow it). Phone numbers are given for those places, and for establishments where a **reservation** is advisable.

Downtown Cairo

Aside from Egyptian restaurants, which range from very upmarket establishments to cheaper *kushari* diners (see "Really cheap downtown options" opposite), downtown Cairo has a fair number of different international cuisines to choose from, with several French, Levantine (Syrian/Lebanese), Italian, Chinese and Korean eating places, and others offering a variety of Western dishes. All the below are marked on the map on p.254 unless otherwise stated.

Al-Haty 3 Sharia Halim, off 26th July St, behind the *Windsor Hotel*. Vintage decor, with mirrors and fans. The fare is inexpensive, traditional and good value, including *mezze*, stuffed vine leaves (*dolma* – though they never seem to actually have them), roast lamb (*moza*), *kofta* and kebab. The chargrilled half-chicken is good. No alcohol. Daily noon–11.30pm. There is another, more elegant branch with low tables and something approaching classic decor in the passage off no.8, on the other side of 26th July St, open daily 11am to 11pm.

Alfi Bey 3 Sharia Alfi Bey. Another vintage restaurant run by strict Muslims. Founded in 1938, its panelling, chandeliers and gilt furniture have been there ever since. Best for lamb dishes, chicken, or pigeon stuffed with rice and liver; good value and moderate prices. Daily 1pm–1am.

Arabesque 6 Sharia Qasr el-Nil ☎02/574-8677. French and Levantine cuisine, strong on soups and

meat dishes, but chiefly remarkable for its "oriental" decor and contemporary art gallery rather than the quality of the food. Wine and beer are served. Moderate. Daily noon–4pm & 7.30pm–1am (Ramadan 5pm–midnight).

Bon Appetit Sharia Mohammed Mahmoud, opposite the AUC Library. Downtown branch of the Mohandiseen café-restaurant (see p.262), this one favoured by students from the AUC, with a free notice board advertising accommodation, Arabic lessons and sometimes even work. Moderate. Daily 8am–11pm.

El-Guesh (aka Sayed Emara) 32 Midan Falaki, on the corner of Tahrir and Falaki streets. A family place serving *kofta* and kebab, stuffed pigeon, or more exotic offerings such as kidney and testicles. Inexpensive. Daily 11am–11pm.

Estoril 12 Sharia Talaat Harb – in the passage ☎02/574-3102. Good Franco-Levantine food in quiet surroundings, with a vintage bar meriting a Bogart. "Eat undescribable and unpronounceable dishes at the oldest restaurant in downtown Cairo" as its blurb says, though the dishes are French and Lebanese standards, and the restaurant only dates from 1959. Moderate. Daily noon–midnight.

Felfela 15 Sharia Hoda Shaarawi. A tourist favourite, offering inexpensive, diverse veggie and meaty Egyptian dishes in a long, hall with funky decor. Sells beer. Service can be a little snooty if you're scruffily dressed, and there's nothing you can get here that wouldn't be cheaper elsewhere. Daily 8am–midnight. *Felfela's* takeaway, around the corner on Talaat Harb (daily 7am–midnight), with another branch opposite the High Court on 26th July St (daily 6am–1.30am), does *shawarmas* and *taamiya* sandwiches, though again you'd pay less elsewhere.

Gad 13 26th July St. The modern and very popular takeaway downstairs is always crowded, as is the upstairs where you can get a sit-down meal. Excellent inexpensive standards – *taamiya*, *fuul*, *shawarma* and burgers – plus delicious specialities such as *kibda skanderani* (Alexandrian-style liver with chilli), wonderful baked-on-the-premises Syrian-style pitta bread (*'aish shaami*), and some of the best *fatirs* in town. If you can make yourself understood on the phone, they also deliver (℡02/576-3353 or 3583). Branches at Midan Falaki, Sharia al-Azhar, Midan Lazoghli, Dokki, Mohandiseen, and opening up all over Cairo. The main branch is open daily 24hr, smaller ones may have shorter hours (typically 9am–2am).

Greek Club above *Groppi's* on Midan Talaat Harb – entrance on Sharia Bassiouni. The cuisine is not particularly Greek, but the food isn't bad (fried squid and chips makes a change from the usual, or there are kebabs), and the summer terrace is pleasant. Moderate prices but you have to pay a temporary membership fee (£E5) to eat here. Serves alcohol, including ouzo. Evenings only, 6pm–1.30am.

Kowloon Restaurant entered via the *Hotel Cleopatra* on the corner of Midan Tahrir and Sharia

el-Bustan ℡02/575-9831. Expensive but superb Korean and Chinese food cooked by Korean chefs. The menu includes several pork dishes and the place is popular with East Asian expats. Mon–Sat 11am–11pm.

La Bistro 8 Sharia Hoda Shaarawi ℡02/392-7694. A bright, clean little place serving reasonably good French food (sea bass in mustard sauce, beef tournedos in red wine sauce, crêpes, chocolate mousse), though the blue-and-white decor is a little jarring and the Muzak excruciating. Moderate. Daily noon–midnight.

La Chesa 21 Sharia Adly ℡02/393-9360. Salubrious, Swiss-managed café serving good Western food, including fondues and Zurich-style veal slices in mushroom sauce, as well as Swiss breakfasts (£E22), scrumptious pastries and great coffee. Expensive but worth it. Daily 7am–midnight.

Paprika 1129 Corniche el-Nil, just south of the TV Building ℡02/578-9447. Based on a mix of Hungarian and Egyptian food, this place does tasty paprika-based dishes and *mezze*. Its speciality is goulash. Frequented by media folk (including Omar Sharif) and footballers, it's especially busy at weekends. Expensive. Daily 11am–1am.

Peking 14 Sharia Saray el-Azbakiya, off 26th July, near the *Windsor Hotel* ℡02/591-2381, ⱳwww.peking-restaurants.com. The poshest Chinese in town, though not prohibitively expensive. It's nowhere near as authentic as the *Kowloon*, and the music is a bit much, but they do takeouts and delivery, and boast branches in Zamalek, Mohandiseen and Heliopolis, plus a floating restaurant (see p.263). Moderate. Daily noon–midnight.

Valley of the Kings on the 1st floor of the *Grand Hotel*. Complete with elegant fountain and stained-glass windows overlooking 26th July St. Good European, Egyptian and Levantine cuisine, with dishes such as fish kebab or rabbit *molukhiyya*, and special meal-deals for £E30 or £E35, though they don't always have everything that's on the menu. Moderate. Daily noon–midnight.

Really cheap downtown options

There are hundreds of *kushari* diners in downtown Cairo, with *Abou Tarek* generally considered the best, though *Lux* and *El-Tahrir* have been contenders in their time. Most other really cheap eats are concentrated around Midan Orabi (especially along the first block of Sharia al-Azbakiya, the small street between the two patisseries) and Midan Falaki (especially on Sharia Mansur, outside Bab al-Luq market). They are not listed individually here, but worth a peruse. All of the following fall into the lower end of the inexpensive price band; you can fill up for well under £E10.

Abou Tarek 40 Sharia Champollion, at the corner of Sharia Maarouf ⱳwww.aboutarek.com. Clean

a/c diner on two floors, serving the best *kushari* in Cairo, with rice pudding for afters. You can't miss it as it's lit up like a Christmas tree. Daily 7am–11.30pm.

Akher Saa 8 Sharia Alfi Bey, next to the Nile Christian Bookshop. A very popular 24hr *fuul* and takeaway with a sit-down restaurant attached. Not a bad place for breakfast either – *fuul*, omelette, bread and *tahina* for £E5.50. *Fuul* or falafel "sandwiches" in pitta to take away are 60pt a piece.

Al-Kazaz 38 Sharia Abo Alaam. Clean, inexpensive 24hr diner, just off Midan Talaat Harb. Tasty *shawarma*, *taamiya* and other fried food, served in a tiny a/c dining room upstairs. You'd be hard-pressed to spend more than £E10.

El-Tabei el-Domiati 31 Sharia Orabi, north of Midan Orabi. Pick'n'mix *mezze* are the best thing in this souped-up *fuul* and *taamiya* diner, though it also does reasonable Egyptian puddings. The takeaway sandwiches, though, are less good. Also has a branch at the bottom of a horrible shopping mall on Talaat Harb and Abdel Hamid Said – you probably won't fancy eating there, but you can buy

salads to take out. If you can make yourself understood on the phone, they also deliver (℡02/577-6699). Daily 7am–1am.

El-Tahrir Sharia Tahrir between Midan Tahrir and Midan Falaki. An old established place, with a second branch at 19 Sharia Abdel Khaliq Sarwat, just off Sharia Talaat Harb. A serious rival to *Abou Tarek*, though most serious *kushari*-freaks agree it plays second fiddle nowadays. Daily 5am–1am.

Fatatri Pizza el-Tahrir Sharia Tahrir, one block east of Midan Tahrir (look for the marble facade on the south side). *Fatirs* (with meat and egg) and crustier versions topped with hot sauce, cheese and olives make a delicious meal for around £E6–10. Also pancake-*fatirs* filled with apple jam and icing sugar. Daily 24hr.

Lux 26th July St, near the corner of Sharia Sherif. Traditional in style and the original holder of the Cairo *kushari* title, with offshoots at 68 Sharia Qasr al-Aini in the Garden City and on the south side of Midan Falaki, but nothing like as good these days as *El-Tahrir* or *Abou Tarek*. Daily 6am–2am.

Garden City and Roda Island

Abou Shakra 69 Sharia Qasr al-Aini, opposite the hospital ℡02/531-6111, Ⓦwww.aboushakra .com (see map on p.192). Decorated in marble and alabaster, this famous, strictly Muslim establishment specializes in *kofta* and kebab sold by weight (£E62 per kilo), to eat in or take out. It's rather refined, though the food isn't as good as in rougher establishments such as *el-Dahan* or *Rifai* in Islamic Cairo. Daily noon–midnight (7pm–midnight during Ramadan).

Revolving Restaurant Grand Hyatt Hotel, Roda Island ℡02/365-1234 (see map on p.192). Formal dress is required, though you can get away with reasonably casual wear, so long as it's smart, and children under 12 are barred at this tip-top French

restaurant with the best view in Cairo. Lunch is a set menu (£E175 including service and tax), dinner is à la carte, when you can start with the likes of snails provençal or seafood bisque, follow with lobster in mustard sauce or duck with apple sauce, and finish with three varieties of crême brulée. Expensive, *naturellement*. Daily 12.30–3pm & 7pm–1am.

Taboula 1 Sharia Amerika Latina, Garden City ℡02/792-5261 (see map on p.192). One of Cairo's best Lebanese restaurants, with very grand decor, a massive choice of *mezze*, various preparations of *kofta*, and Lebanese *fattehs* (dishes made with fried pitta pieces). Expensive but not outrageous. Does takeaways and home delivery. Daily noon–2am.

Islamic Cairo and Saiyida Zeinab

Although every main street and square in **Islamic Cairo** features poky eating places serving cheap grub, most tourists stick to the four places in Khan el-Khalili detailed below. But for those inured to flies and roaches, there are discoveries to be made, like the hole-in-the-wall near the market on Sharia Qalaa, which does freshly grilled shrimp sandwiches. If you are prepared to wander into **Saiyida Zeinab**, you can find some excellent, and low-priced, traditional Egyptian food, especially at night; a trio of places are listed here.

Egyptian Pancake House Between Midan el-Hussein and Al-Azhar (see map on p.154). Made-to-order *fatirs* filled with meat, egg, cheese, coconut, raisins, jam or honey (or any combination thereof). Soft drinks only. Inexpensive. Daily 24hr.

El-Dahan On the Muski, beneath the *El-Hussein Hotel* (see map on p.154). An excellent kebab house, where a quarter kilo of mixed kebab with salad and *tahina* costs £E24.50. There's also roast goat, but no alcohol. Daily 11am–1am.

El-Gahsh A block along Sharia Abdel Meguid from Midan Saiyida Zeinab, on the way to Ibn Tulun Mosque (look for the mule-cart cartoon sign). It may not look much, but this insalubrious little take-away diner is generally held to do the best *fuul* in Cairo. At night, they lay out tables in the neighbouring streets and you can eat loads for around £E5, or just get a *fuul* sandwich for 50pt. Daily 24hr.

El-Hussein On the roof of the *El-Hussein Hotel* (see map p.154). Fantastic views over Islamic Cairo, with inexpensive but not very good food. If you want to be adventurous, try the "crumbs in soup with gelatinic meat", the latter being *bamouza*, which is cow- or sheep-foot jelly. They also have juices, teas and *sheeshas*. Used for wedding parties at least two nights a week. Daily 7am–midnight.

Haram Zeinab On the corner of Sharia Abdel Meguid and Midan Saiyida Zeinab (next to *Al-Shataranj*, the chess players' coffee house). A small place serving excellent *fatirs* at slightly lower prices than you'd pay downtown. Daily 24hr.

Hilltop Restaurant Al-Azhar Park, Sharia Salah Salem (see map on p.154). Classy Egyptian eating, subtle background music, grills and kebabs, and on Thursday, Friday and Saturday evenings, an £E80 eat-all-you-can buffet with soups, salads, half-a dozen main dishes to sample, and a gluttonous choice of afters. And the toilets are spotless. Expensive. Daily 1–6pm & 7–11pm.

Khan el-Khalili Restaurant 5 Sikket al-Badestan (see map on p.154). Expensive, a/c café/restaurant managed by the *Mena House Oberoi*, near the old gate 40m west of El-Hussein's Mosque. Western and Egyptian snacks (£E9.50–16) and meals (main dishes £E39–65) are served in the dining room (evening minimum charge £E30, plus £E1.20 "entertainment tax") as well as ice cream (£E16). Daily 10am–2am.

Rifai 37 Midan Saiyida Zeinab, opposite Saiyida Zeinab Mosque (hidden up an alley by the Sabil Kuttab of Sultan Mustapha). A renowned nighttime *kofta* and kebab joint – people are known to drive from Heliopolis for a takeout. A quarter-kilo of *kofta* and kebab with tahina, *labana*, salad and a glass of salad juice with chilli (careful now!) will set you back the princely sum of £E21. Daily 7pm–6am.

Zamalek

As befits a high-rent, cosmopolitan neighbourhood, Zamalek boasts several upmarket restaurants devoted to foreign cuisine, plus **trendy nightspots** like *Matchpoint* and *Pub 28* (see "Drinking" p.265), the latter of which does good food too. Most of them are within ten minutes' walk of 26th July Street. All are keyed on the map on p.210, as is the Zamalek branch of downtown Chinese *Peking* (23b Sharia Ismail Mohammed ☎02/736-3894).

Al Dente (Didos) 26 Sharia Bahgat Ali ☎02/735-9117. Quite justified in its claim to serve the best pasta in town (choice of spaghetti, fettuccine, penne or fusili with a range of sauces, £E5.50–18), this little place also has excellent salads and specialities such as Portuguese-style fish. Does home delivery anywhere in central Cairo. Daily 11am–1am.

Angus Brasserie 34 Sharia Yehia Ibrahim, inside the *New Star Hotel* ☎02/735-1865. Steaks, notably fillet steak with a choice of mustard, blue cheese or mushroom topping, plus European veal, fish and squid dishes and crêpes for dessert. Moderately priced but only open for dinner. 5pm–12.30am daily.

Don Quichotte 9a Sharia Ahmed Heshmat ☎02/735-6415. Tiny, elegant restaurant serving great cuisines of the world. The speciality of the house is *coquille bonne femme* (seafood in white wine sauce), and puddings include chocolate soufflé. Expensive. Reservations advisable. Daily noon–2am.

Five Bells corner of Adil Abu Bakr and Ismail Mohammed, north of the Zamalek Bridge ☎02/735-8970. It's worth dressing up for this swish Italianate joint, complete with garden and fountain. Specialities include meat fondue, grill-it-yourself charbonnade, and fish with squid and prawns in a choice of red or white sauce. Expensive but good. Daily noon–2am.

Hana Korean Restaurant Sharia Mohammed Mahzar, next to the *El-Nil Zamalek Hotel* ☎02/738-2972. Small, friendly place offering various Asian dishes. A huge portion of *sukiyaki* (do-it-yourself stir-fry seafood soup) costs £E38. Also does deliveries. Daily noon–11pm.

Justine 4 Hassan Sabry, in the *Four Corners* complex, 2 blocks south of Gabalaya Gardens ☎02/737-2119. Probably the finest and one of the most expensive restaurants in Cairo (count on £E100–200 per person including wine). French cuisine, soft lighting, music and formal dress. Daily 1–3pm & 8–11pm. On the same floor (same phone number also) are: La Piazza, a stylish, but less expensive Italian restaurant (pasta dishes £E29–41, main courses £E39–54), which is open daily 12.30pm–12.30am; the moderate–expensive

Chin Chin Chinese restaurant, whose specialities include Szechuan-style fish and roll-it-yourself crispy duck in pancakes with hoisin sauce (daily 7.30–11.30pm); and Matchpoint video snack bar (see p.265).

L'Aubergine 5 Sharia Sayed el-Bakri. Moderately priced with an adventurous menu, changed weekly and featuring a good variety of vegetarian dishes, such as artichoke strudel and halloumi-stuffed eggplant. The food is usually very good though some of the more ambitious dishes may disappoint. There's also a bar upstairs (see p.265). Daily 10am–11pm. Breakfast served 10am–2pm.

Maison Thomas 157 26th July St opposite the Marriott Hotel ☎02/735-7057. Deli-diner-takeout-delivery place serving freshly made baguettes and pizzas (both around £E19–27) as well as light meals (£E28–34). They make their own pork sausages and mozzarella, as well as doing bacon-and-egg breakfasts (8am–12.30pm; £E20). They will deliver to anywhere in central Cairo – even beer at £E5 a bottle. Branches in Heliopolis, Mohandiseen and Ma'adi. Daily 24hr.

Zamalek Restaurant 118 26th July St, near the intersection with Sharia al-Aziz Osman. Cheap takeaway and sit-down diner for taamiya, fuul and tahina (meals £E4–6). Daily 7am–2am.

Mohandiseen, Aguza and Dokki

Mohandiseen has no shortage of fast-food outlets and chic restaurants, mostly situated along or just off Arab League Street (Sharia Gameat al-Dowal al-Arabiya, also nicknamed "The Mall") and Sharia Batal Ahmed Abdel Aziz, while cheap eating places abound in market quarters like Suleyman Gohar in Dokki. The west bank also has branches of several well-known Cairo chains, such as the Indian-influenced Chicken Tikka, at 47 Sharia Batal Ahmed Abdel Aziz (☎02/346-0393); the popular downtown Chinese restaurant Peking (26 Sharia al-Atebba ☎02/749-6713); downtown fast-Egyptian-food-favourite Gad (47a Arab League St ☎02/335-7237); Zamalek deli Maison Thomas (29 Sharia Shehab ☎02/306-6139); pick'n'mix mezze diner El-Tabei el-Domiati (17 Arab League St ☎02/304-1124); and the famous Garden City kebab and kofta restaurant Abou Shakra (17 Arab League St ☎02/344-4767). All of the above restaurants will deliver within Mohandiseen/Dokki/Zamalek, and are keyed on the map on p.210, as are those listed below.

Al-Omdah 6 Sharia al-Gaza'ir, around the corner from the Atlas. Pukka Egyptian food (kushari £E3–5; kofta and kebab £E65 per kilo) and a/c amidst a sea of plastic fast-food joints. Daily 10am–2am, with takeout downstairs. There's a snazzier-looking branch at 17 Arab League Street, popular with Gulf Arabs, with outdoor dining and sheeshas, though the service isn't as good.

Bon Appetit 21 Sharia Wadi el-Nil. Moderately priced café-restaurant with baguette sandwiches, salads, pasta, even chicken Kiev, plus all kinds of espresso-based coffees and ice-cream-based desserts including cassata and banana split. Daily 9am–1am.

Cafeteria Niema 172 Corniche el-Nil, Aguza. The best takeaway fuul and taamiya sandwiches in Cairo – so taxi drivers swear. Hamburgers and shawarma rolls £E2.75. Daily 24hr.

Ciao 10 Midan al-Misaha, Dokki ☎02/335-2482. Reasonable pizzas, albeit with beef and turkey slices instead of ham and pepperoni, are the main attraction at Dokki's leading Italian restaurant. Moderate, with pizzas and pasta dishes at £E12–22 and an £E8 salad bar. Daily noon–11pm.

Flying Fish 166 Corniche el-Nil, Aguza ☎02/749-3234 (see map p.210). Another Omar Sharif hang-out, this excellent and very classy seafood restaurant has specialities such as stuffed fish, squid and lobster (the latter priced by the kilo depending on season); also does home delivery. Expensive. Daily noon–1am.

Nubian Village Midan Sphinx. The main Nubian specialities here are spicy kofta and hot drinks (karkaday, of course, plus hot ginger and herbal teas called hargel and haleban). Otherwise, the menu is typical Egyptian with a few European dishes, but good, and moderately priced, though there's a £E10 minimum charge. Daily 9am–3am.

Le Tirol 38 Sharia Gazirit al-Arab, just west off Sharia Wadi el-Nil ☎02/344-9725. Austrian-style chalet decor and tasty Central European cuisine, expensive, with a lot of beef and veal dishes, a smoked ham platter and, at lower prices, pasta and pizzas. Serves alcohol; also does home delivery. Daily noon–1am.

Okamoto 7 Sharia Ahmed Orabi, off Midan Sphinx ☎02/346-5264. Excellent Japanese food, well worth the high prices; serves sake. Expensive.

Daily noon–2pm & 6–10pm, closed Tue. Last orders 30min before closing.

Prestige Pizza 43 Gazirit al-Arab, just east of Sharia Wadi el-Nil ☎02/347-0383. A smart Italian restaurant with a more casual pizzeria attached for a choice of ambience – and price; also home delivery. Moderate to expensive. Daily noon–2am.

Scoozi 16 Midan al-Misaha ☎02/748-8668. Lebanese restaurant and takeaway with hefty sandwiches, great *mezze*, *kubbe* and grills, moderate prices and home delivery. Daily 10am–2am.

Tandoori 11 Sharia Shehab, 2 blocks west of Arab League St ☎02/748-6301. Run by an ex-employee of the *Mogul Room*, serving good Indian cuisine. Try the tandoori chicken, curried lamb (*kema*) or prawns (*jhinga*). Moderately priced though takeouts and deliveries cost less. Also has some European and Egyptian dishes. No alcohol. Daily noon–midnight.

Giza and the Pyramids area

There are plenty of cheap eating places around Midan Giza, while overpriced kebab restaurants and hotel dining loom large along the Pyramids Road. Visitors with children should enjoy the **outdoor family restaurants** – such as *La Rose* or *Felfela Village* – beside the Maryotteya Canal (bring mosquito repellent), or the floating restaurants near the El-Gama'a Bridge (see below). The Giza restaurants listed below are marked on the map on p.210, while the Pyramids restaurants are on the map on p.230.

El-Mashrabiah 4 Sharia Ahmed Nessim, opposite the El-Urman Garden, Giza ☎02/748-2801. Elegant Moorish decor and excellent Middle Eastern and Egyptian food. Fairly expensive salads, lamb, *kofta* and turkey dishes. No alcohol. Expensive. Daily 12.30pm–1.30am (Ramadan till 3.30am).

Felfela Café 27 Alexandria Desert Road, 300m from junction with Pyramids Road ☎02/383-0234. An offshoot of *Felfela's*, whackily adorned with fake birds and trees, with a similar menu and prices to the downtown branch. Moderate. Daily 8.30am–midnight.

Felfela Village Maryotteya Canal ☎02/384-1515 or 1616. On a canal that crosses Pyramids Road, 1km north on the east bank, this rambling outdoor complex features a zoo and playground and a show with camel rides, acrobats, puppets and belly dancers – even dancing horses. The show (1–7.30pm) is presented daily in summer, Fri and Sun only in winter. Restaurant open daily 10am–7pm. Moderate.

Le Chalet in the Nasr Building, Giza. Swiss-run, clean and pleasant, with fine views of the Nile.

Offers salads and pasta, hot meat or fish platters and delectable pastries and ice creams; also a children's menu. Moderate. Daily 8.30am–midnight. The plush **Le Chateau** restaurant upstairs offers rich – and expensive – main courses and scrumptious desserts; expect a lot of corporate diners. Daily noon–12.30am. Reservations advisable for both on ☎02/761-0165 or 777-1005, orders for home delivery on ☎02/748-5321.

The Moghul Room in the *Mena House*. Cairo's top Indian restaurant but open evenings only (lunchtime curries are served in the Khan el-Khalili across the hall). As the name suggests, non-veg north Indian Mughal dishes are the mainstay here, notably rogan josh (lamb curry with tomato), but they also do veg curries and southern dishes such as vindaloo; they usually go easy on the chilli, so tell them if you want it spicy. Expensive. Daily 7pm–midnight.

Pyramids Restaurant 9 Sharia Abu el-Hol. A plain honest-to-goodness chicken and kebab house with normal *baladi* prices (quarter-kilo *kofta* and kebab £E12, chicken £E16, salad and *tahina* cost extra), despite the plethora of tourists. Daily 10am–2am.

Floating restaurants

Floating restaurants can be an agreeable way to enjoy the Nile, but as cruise schedules change, it is wise to phone and check, and it's worth booking, too. The price quoted is per person.

Nile Maxim ☎02/738-8888. Docked in front of the *Marriott* (see map on p.210), runs dinner cruises with live Egyptian music and bellydancing (daily except Wed 6pm, 8.30pm & 11.15pm, Wed 7.30pm & 10.30pm), with an à la carte menu (main dishes around £E175–235 with free salad bar and dessert), and on Fridays there's a lunchtime buffet with folkloric show for £E85 all-inclusive.

Nile Peking ☎02/53-6388, ⓦwww.peking-restaurants.com. Moored opposite the Nilometer,

200m west of Mari Girgis metro station, this is the floating branch of the citywide *Peking chain* of Chinese restaurants (see p.259). It sails daily 7.30pm–9.30pm, also Wed & Thurs 10.30pm–12.30am, and Fri 3–5pm. The Wednesday late cruise features a bellydancing show. Food is à la carte when moored, with a choice of fourteen set menus (£E50–100, including one vegetarian menu) when sailing. There is also an on-deck café serving afternoon tea. Alcohol is served, and there's a bar with DJs.

The Nile Pharaoh & Golden Pharaoh ☎02/570-1000. Pair of mock-pharaonic barges complete with scarab friezes, picture windows, and golden lotus flowers or figures of Horus mounted on the stern and prow. Moored 1km south of the El-Gama'a Bridge (see map p.192) and operated by *Oberoi Hotels*, they cruise for lunch (2.30–4.30pm; £E95), sunset (Fridays and public holidays in summer only 5.15–7.15pm; £E140) and dinner (7.15–9.15pm, 8–9.45pm & 10pm–midnight; £E140; or 10.30pm–12.30am; £E130). You should check in half an hour before sailing. The first three dinner cruises feature music and a bellydancer, while the lunch and last dinner cruises have live "oriental" (ie Middle Eastern) music. There's also a Friday buffet brunch in summer (11.30am–4.30pm, sailing 2.30–3.30pm; £E55).

Scarabee ☎02/794-3444. Docked on the Corniche near *Helnan Shepheard Hotel*. Not as posh as the other floating restaurants. the *Scarabee* offers two dinner cruises nightly (8–10pm & 10.30pm–12.30am; £E132) with an "oriental" floor show, bellydancer and a dance band, plus Friday buffet lunch cruises (2.30–4.30pm; £E79) with a band and magician; other days, the boat remains docked for lunch (2.30–4pm; à la carte).

Drinking

As throughout Egypt, the sale of alcohol in Cairo is banned during Ramadan and other major Muslim festivals, and drinking is limited to indoor locations at all times. Besides restaurants and hotels, there are various **bars** to choose from. The cheapest of these are rather rough male-only hard-drinking dens. Others are chiefly meeting places for men and prostitutes (the only Egyptian women found there). The more upmarket bars often have a minimum charge, often unadvertised (usually around £E10–20).

Inevitably, there's also some overlap between bars and nightclubs (covered under "Nightlife and entertainment" on p.266).

Downtown

Spit-and-sawdust **drinking dens**, usually open until around midnight – certainly not recommended for women on their own, and even with a male escort you'd be the object of much attention – include the *Stella Cafeteria* on the corner of Sharia Talaat Harb and Sharia Hoda Shaarawi, by *Felfela's* takeout; the *Cap d'Or Cafeteria* at 31 Sharia Abdel Khaliq Sarwat; the *Cafeteria Port Tawfik* in Midan Orabi on the corner of Sharia Orabi; the *Mourias* at 4 Sharia Adly; and a couple at 9 Sharia Alfi Bey. Beer (Stella is £E5–7 in most of these) is usually served with free nibbles and lots of drunken bonhomie. Another type of bar that women definitely won't want to frequent are the exceedingly sleazy **red-light bars**, of which there are several in the downtown area, most notably the *Honololo* opposite the *Pensione Roma* on Sharia Mohammed Farid, which has live music some nights, and the *Al-Shemi* opposite the *Grand Hotel*, in a passage off Sharia Talaat Harb and 26th July Sreet. There's also the *Munchen Löwenbräu* behind *Felfela's* takeaway on 26th July Street, and *King's Restaurant* on Sharia Ibrahim el-Kabari (off Sharia Qasr el-Nil, 20m east of Midan Talaat Harb), which serves kebab as well as beer and whisky. Women should be able to get a fairly hassle-free drink in all the bars listed below, except *Gamayka*, though in *El Horea*, *Grillon*, *Hard Rock Café* and *Odeon Palace*, you may feel happier with a male escort. All the drinking places mentioned above and listed below are marked on the map on p.254, except where otherwise stated.

Barrel Lounge On the first floor of the *Windsor Hotel*, Sharia Alfi Bey. Faded Anglo-Egyptian decor and charming ambience. Foreigners can buy alcohol during Ramadan. Native rum or brandy (best mixed with Coca-Cola) is the cheapest drink, followed by Stella and *zibiba*. Daily 10am–1am.

Café Riche 17 Sharia Talaat Harb. Once a hangout for artists and intellectuals, practically every Arab revolutionary of the last century has visited at least once – including Saddam Hussein – and although now strictly for tourists, it still oozes history. Have a chat with the owner, who can give you the full story; he was a pilot during the wars with Israel. Daily 8am–midnight.

El-Horea Midan Falaki. A mirrored, very 1930s café that's hardly changed since then, and serves beer as well as tea, coffee and *sheesha* pipes. Chess players meet here in the evening and people gather to watch them play – though drinking isn't allowed round the boards. Daily 8am–2am.

Gamayka Sharia el-Bank el-Ahly, a small street off Sheria Sharif. Named after the island of Jamaica (the owner's sister went there once), this cosy little dive is really just an ordinary bar, but a cut above the harder drinking dens mentioned above, and you can have a *sheesha* with your beer (Stella at £E7.50). Daily 24hr.

Hard Rock Café in the *Grand Hyatt* hotel (marked on map on p.192). The Cairo branch of the international chain, popular with bright young things, and rather pricey by local standards (£E50 minimum charge), is mostly notable for having Gamal

Abdel Nasser's 1957 Ford suspended above the tables amidst the usual pop paraphernalia. Daily noon–4am, with a DJ from midnight.

Le Grillon 8 Sharia Qasr el-Nil, down a small passage between Qasr el-Nil and Sharia Bustan. A cosy, carpeted bar that also serves mediocre food and has a smoking garden in case you want a *sheesha*. Daily 11am–2am.

Napoleon Bar in the *Helnan Shepheard* hotel. One of the most comfortable bars in town, with Napoleonic prints on the walls, wood panelling and live music every night. Foreigners can buy alcohol here during Ramadan. Daily 10am–3am.

Odeon Palace Hotel 6 Sharia Abdel Hamid Said. The 24-hour rooftop bar here is a popular and very pleasant location for a bit of after-hours rooftop drinking, with a *sheesha* if you like.

Pyramids Bar on the roof of the *Nile Hilton*. Quite a sleek and suave drinking locale, but what you really come here for is the view over Midan Tahrir and the Nile, and over the rooftops of town to the Citadel. Daily 9am–1am, with a £E35 minimum charge after sunset.

Taverne du Champs de Mars ground floor, *Nile Hilton*. Come evening this spendidly ornate *fin-de-siècle* Brussels tavern – its interior brought over from Belgium and reconstructed here – becomes a music bar, and has traditionally been a gay meeting place (though this may actually make it dangerous for gay contacts). Draught Sakkara beer is £E23 a pint, and they also serve bar snacks and have live music in the evenings. Daily noon–1.30am.

Zamalek

All the place listed below are marked on the map on p.210.

Deals 5 Sharia Sayed el-Bakri. One of Cairo's most congenial drinking spots, and one of the few with any kind of atmosphere, small, homely and popular with expats and Egyptians alike, with pop videos, a range of cold beers, tasty and well-presented bar snacks, and no hassling of women. Now has branches in Mohandiseen (2 Sharia Gol Gamal, cozy and intimate) and Heliopolis (40 Sharia Baghdad). Daily 4pm–2am.

Harry's Bar and **Piano Bar** in the *Marriott Hotel*. Both are extremely popular with expats and open daily noon–2am. *Harry's* has a happy hour 6–7pm and is known for its karaoke nights. The *Piano Bar* is more refined, and, as its name suggests, has live piano music to enhance the ambience.

Matchpoint in the *Four Corners* complex, 4 Sharia Hassan Sabry. A pseudo-American video snack bar, frequented by rich young Cairenes attending the AUC. Officially couples only, though if you're smartly dressed and behave respectably there shouldn't be a problem. Daily 1pm–1am.

Pub 28 28 Shagar al-Durr. A bar that's also popular as a place to eat, with a few different beers plus English cold cuts, *mezze*, grills and good steaks. Daily noon–2am.

Rive Gauche *Hotel el-Nil Zamalek*, 21 Sharia Aziz Abaza. Up a flight of stairs with a "carpet" painted onto them, this is a large space with a high ceiling, pale blue lighting, smoochy music and a Parisian feel. The atmosphere is laid-back and there's a choice of seating from bar stools to sofas. Daily 11pm–3am.

Sand Bar 13a Sharia al-Marashli. Quite a cool locale, clean and airy (even the toilets are immaculate), with varied but mostly jazzy music, bar snacks and draught Sakkara. Daily 2pm–2am.

White Bar 25 Sharia Hassan Assem. American-style bar with minimalist decor and a big video screen (though what's showing doesn't match what's playing). Daily 2pm–2am.

Nightlife and entertainment

For current information about **what's on** at cinemas, concert halls and night-clubs, get hold of the daily *Egyptian Gazette* (£E1; on Saturday, the *Egyptian Mail*), the monthly *Egypt Today* (£E12), or the weekly English edition of *Al-Ahram* newspaper (£E1).

Music

Aside from discos and the Opera House, you're unlikely to hear much Western music outside of tourist restaurants – Egyptians prefer music from the Arab world. For contemporary music, by far the liveliest **time of year** is after the school and university exams, from late June to November; you'll need an Arabic-speaking friend to tell you what's happening as none of it is advertised in the foreign press. Note that Egyptians make a clear distinction between a **disco**, where you dance to records, and a **nightclub**, where you have dinner and watch a floorshow; should you wish to go "clubbing", it's a disco, not a nightclub, that you want.

Contemporary and dance music

Contemporary Egyptian music can be categorized as either *Shaabi*, the urban folk music of *baladi* Cairo, blending traditional *mawals* (laments) with raunchy, satirical lyrics; or *Al-Jeel*, a fusion of Nubian, Libyan and Bedouin rhythms with a disco beat, reflecting the tastes of upwardly mobile Cairene youth.

Though both sounds are played everywhere, live acts are more elusive. *Shaabi* stars now perform at nightclubs along Pyramids Road, at rich weddings and private parties. Hotel nightclubs, open-air concerts at the Gezira and Heliopolis clubs or Cairo University (usually during summer vacation) are likelier venues for *Al-Jeel* stars. Up-and-coming performers might appear at downtown nightclubs.

The music accompanying these dancers is so-called **oriental dance music**, whose golden age was the 1940s and 1950s. Purists distinguish between classical *raqs sharqi* and music influenced by Umm Kalthoum or Western jazz – the torrid sounds associated with bellydancing and pre-revolutionary Cairo. Oriental dance music is also played at weddings.

Folk, classical Arab and religious music

During the Nasser era, numerous troupes were established to preserve Egyptian folk music and dance in the face of urbanization. Folk music does not command a wide following today, but traditional rural numbers like *The Gypsy Dance* or *The Mamluke* performed by the **National Troupe** and the **Reda Troupe** can often be seen at the **Balloon Theatre** on the Corniche in Aguza (☎02/347-1718; see map p.210), which also stages performances of religious and other traditional music.

Another place that often hosts performances of Arabic folk and classical music is the **Abdel Monem el Sawy Culture Wheel** by Zamalek Bridge on Zamalek (☎02/736-6178, ⓦwww.culturewheel.com; see map p.210), which holds regular concerts at low prices, advertised on its website. Performances are also held at the **Gumhorriya Theatre** at 12 Sharia al-Gomhorriya (☎02/390-7707; see map p.127), which are advertised in the weekly English-laguage edition of *al-Ahram*.

All the moulids listed on pp.272–273 feature **religious music** (the reading or chanting of the Koran), while few everyday sounds are more evocative than the call to prayer. Outstanding muezzins inspire local pride and professional jealousy. (In a celebrated court case it was ruled that no copyright existed on any expression of the Koran, since Allah created it.) The duets between the Rifai and Sultan Hassan mosques, and the muezzin near the *Pension Roma*, are superb.

Bellydancing and nightclubs

A Marxist critique of **bellydancing** would point the finger at imperialism, and with good reason. The European appetite for exotica did much to create the art form as it is known today: a sequinned fusion of classical *raqs sharqi* (oriental dance), stylized harem eroticism and the frank sexuality of the *ghawazee* (public dancers, many of whom moonlighted as prostitutes during the nineteenth century). The association with prostitution has stuck ever since, notwithstanding the fact that most dancers today are dedicated professionals, and the top stars wealthy businesswomen. When Fifi Abdou (see below) bought an apartment in the deluxe Giza Towers, other tenants, such as the Saudi royal family, protested that she lowered the tone of the place. The Sheikh of Al-Azhar has even decreed that pilgrimages to Mecca undertaken by dancers and actresses are invalid unless they renounce their jobs. "They should give up their sins and return to God", he declared. Even though customers are strictly forbidden to touch the dancers, no matter how much they pay in tips, the increasing social stigma attached to bellydancing is deterring young Egyptian women from entering the profession, with the result that most up-and-coming bellydancers today are foreigners, and home-grown talent is getting thin on the ground.

For all that, Cairo nonetheless remains the most important bellydancing centre internationally, and every summer, usually in late June or early July, it hosts the world's premiere bellydancing event, the **International Oriental Dance Festival**, usually based at the *Mena House Oberoi* hotel. For the latest information on the festival, which features classes and workshops in the daytime and performances in the evenings, plus extra events such as bellydancing costume shows, check Ⓦ www.raqiahassan.net.

Five-star venues

If you want to see top acts, the place to go is the nightclub of one of the **five-star hotels**. All of these provide a delicious four-course meal to tide you through the warm-up acts until the star comes on sometime between midnight and 3am. There's usually a minimum rate or flat charge (£E100–250) for the whole deal. Reservations and smart dress are required. The top venue at present is the *Haroun al-Rashid* at the *Semiramis Intercontinental*, especially on Thursdays when Dina (see below) performs. The nightclub is open Wed–Sun 7–10.30pm for the early show (minimum charge £E180 including dinner), 11.30pm–4am for the late show (£E345 minimum charge including dinner): don't expect to see the main act until at least 1am. Other good options include the *Casablanca* restaurant at the *Cairo Sheraton* in Dokki (Ⓣ02/336-9800 or 331-1360), where Soraya (see below) performs, and the floating restaurants (see p.263), in particular the *Nile Pharaoh* (Ⓣ570-1000) and *Nile Maxim* (Ⓣ02/735-8888).

Of the **dancers** at these five-star venues, the big name nowadays is **Dina**, who performs at the *Semiramis Intercontinental Hotel* on Thursdays. Other names to look out for are the Brazilian **Soraya**, currently performing nightly at the *Cairo Sheraton*, and the Australian **Caroline**, usually seen on the *Nile Pharaoh* (call venues for specific times). If you get the chance, there are a couple of other dancers to look out for, though both perform very rarely, having pretty much retired. **Fifi Abdou,** who exemplified the *bint balad*, or streetwise village girl in the big city, included circus tricks, vulgar posturing and rapping in her act. Now in her sixties, with several trips to the US for plastic surgery under her belt, Fifi only makes very occasional appearances. Another well-known name, **Lucy**, also more or less in retirement, puts in the odd impromptu performance at the *Parisiana* club (see below), which she runs with her husband.

Cheaper venues

A step down from this are the somewhat sleazy, rip-off nightclubs **along Pyramids Road**, where the entertainments are varied and sometimes good, but the food is usually poor. **Cheaper places**, with no food to speak of, lurk downtown. Most of these are far from pleasant and, if you intend to check them out, you need to be aware of how they operate.

Most open their doors at around 10pm, but none of them really gets going until at least midnight. Most have an entry fee or minimum charge, sometimes both, but be warned that many will also endeavour to rip you off with **hidden charges and sharp practices**. Napkins, for example, may be placed on your table and then charged on your bill. Waitresses may pour your drinks and add a charge for this, or demand *baksheesh*. Nibbles are placed on your table unordered, but they are far from free, and will cost you dear unless you are quick to refuse them. You need to be on your toes and stay relatively sober to keep refusing these extras, as the clubs count on customers getting too drunk to notice them. They may also add spurious taxes, or simply refuse to give change – even for a £E50 note. Such practices have driven most Egyptian customers away, and a lot of these clubs are now pretty much dead, certainly midweek, only livening up, if at all, on Thursday nights and public holidays. The dancers who perform any time before the small hours of the morning are almost uniformly awful; if it's late enough and you're lucky, you might catch one who has a little rhythm. Women are unlikely to enjoy themselves at most of these places as the atmosphere is generally sleazy, drunken, lecherous and male. The only two **exceptions** in the list below are the *Palmyra* and the *Cancan*, where women can go, in a group or accompanied by men, and have a good time.

Cancan in the *Fontana Hotel* off Midan Ramses ☏ 02/592-2321. A lower-priced version of the nightclubs in the five-star hotels, and a lot more reputable than most cheap Cairo nightclubs. It operates on two days of the week only, and starts a lot earlier than most venues, but it's sufficiently upmarket to be a safe and respectable option and one where women can feel comfortable if accompanied. Sun & Thurs 9pm–2am. Minimum charge £E25–30.

Miami In the passage at 16 26th July St. A small and spectacularly seedy venue, where the usual tricks are practised, though not to excess – just keep refusing the snacks and the napkins. The musicians are not bad as these places go. The *New Miamy* (*Goe's*), in the same passage, is similar. Daily 11.30pm–4am. Entry £E5. Stella £E10. No minimum charge.

Palmyra In the passage at 16 26th July St, next door to the *Miami*. One of the few cheap venues that does not try to rip off its customers with spurious charges, a good-natured place where you can feel safe for a night out without having to keep your wits about you, and where the dancers actually make a bit of an effort, and interact with the audience. They even occasionally have other variety acts such as acrobats. Daily 11pm–4am. Entry £E35 including one beer. Stella £E11 thereafter. No minimum charge.

Parisiana Pyramids Road, north side, just east of Maryotteya Canal ☏ 02/383-3911. Run by bellydancer Lucy and her husband, this is just about the only halfway decent nightclub on Pyramids Road, and somewhat more upmarket than places in town. It's also pricier – £E250 including dinner – but only because it is open all night. Daily midnight–7am.

Scheharazade 1 Sharia Alfi Bey. The venue itself is a marvellous old vaudeville-style music hall, but unfortunately the establishment that runs it is as sleazy as they come. The usual tricks with nibbles and change refusal are played, and waiters may even try to insist that snacks (lowest price £E20) are compulsory with every beer. The *Arizona* opposite is to be avoided at all costs. Daily 11pm–6am.

Discos

Cairo has a fair number of **discos** (the term "nightclub" is only used in its old-fashioned sense of a sit-down venue with a meal and floorshow) but nowhere to rave about. The music is usually last year's hits back home or current Egyptian stuff; light shows are unsophisticated. But dance floor manners are good, boozy boors are at a minimum and casual dress is acceptable at all but the ritziest places. More problematical is the trend towards a **couples–only policy**. Though you might imagine this is to prevent women from being swamped, locals say that it's to stop discos from becoming gay haunts (see below) or pick-up joints for prostitutes. In practice, women can usually get into discos without escorts, but men without women will have more difficulty. Call first to avoid disappointment.

Gay venues

There are no **gay** discos as such in Cairo, and the city's gay community remains in shock following the 2001 arrests at the *Queen Boat* (see p.94). In the past, venues such as *Harry's Bar* at the *Marriott* hotel and the *Taverne du Champs de Mars* in the *Nile Hilton* have been meeting places for gay men, but fear is so prevalent in the gay community at present that there are no really safe meeting places. Anywhere that becomes known as a gay venue is equally likely to be the haunt of undercover cops and blackmail artists (gay foreigners are unlikely to be arrested, but could easily be victims of blackmail or robbery if they pick up the wrong person). Most venues carefully avoid any reputation as a gay nightspot, and events that begin to attract a gay crowd (1980s retro nights are a likely bet) are quickly closed. There are absolutely no venues for **lesbians** in Cairo, and you would be unlikely to even spot an all-female couple. Further information on gay meeting places in Cairo, along with advice on how to handle the current situation, can be found online at ⓦwww.gayegypt.com/centralcairo.html, but you are advised not to log onto this site in Egypt as it is closely monitored.

Unless otherwise specified, all of the venues below are open nightly.

Hotel venues

Most of the **hotel discos** cater to rich foreigners and Westernized Egyptians, and none of them is very exciting. Current venues include *Juliana* in the *El-Gezirah* (daily 2–5am; minimum charge £E200), *The Castle* in the *Helnan Shepheard* (daily midnight–4am; minimum charge £E50; couples only), and *The Saddle* in the *Mena House* (10pm–3am; no minimum charge; couples only). Not a fetish club despite its name, *Latex* in the *Nile Hilton* (daily 10pm–5am; minimum charge £E100) has themed nights, with Middle Eastern sounds on Tuesdays, Latino on Wednesdays, current hits and Arabic pop on Thursdays, house on Fridays, R 'n' B on Saturdays, and singles' night on Sundays.

Cheaper venues

Less fastidious, **cheaper venues** include the *Fontana Hotel* disco (daily except Sun & Thurs when there is bellydancing instead, 6pm–midnight; minimum charge £E16), and *Legends* at the base of the Cairo Tower (daily 10pm–6am; minimum charge £E25), which attracts a mainly young and well-heeled clientele.

Africana, about halfway along Pyramids Road in Giza (daily 11pm–4am; £E40 entry including a beer), plays mostly **African and reggae music** to a largely African crowd, but it has been growing progressively more seedy, is frequented by prostitutes, and doesn't really get going until at least 1am.

The city's best music venue is *Cairo Jazz Club* at 197 26th July St in Mohandiseen (daily 10am–3am; ☎02/345-9939; no minimum charge, but

£E16.50 "entertainment tax" is added to your first round bill), which often has live musicians, and also serves food. The lighting is soft, the seating comfortable and the crowd friendly. As its name suggests, it is dedicated mainly, though not exclusively, to **jazz music**.

A couple of **bars** also have dance floors, including the *Hard Rock Café* at the *Grand Hyatt Hotel* (see p.265; daily noon–4am, DJ from midnight; minimum charge £E50), and the *Bull's Eye* at 32 Sharia Jeddah in Mohandiseen (daily 6pm–2am; minimum charge £E30).

Cinemas

Most of the older **cinemas** in downtown Cairo are Art Deco relics of the 1930s and 1940s, purpose-built for foreigners and trashed by rioters on "Black Saturday" in 1952 (see p.145). Never properly refurbished and now distinctly seedy, they still attract huge, virtually all-male audiences, who cat-call at anything remotely risqué. Lurid hoardings portray grotesquer versions of Hollywood mega-heroes, or the stock characters beloved of *baladi* films (indomitable matriarch, broken patriarch, star-crossed lovers, the hussy and the villain).

Though **foreign movies** are shown throughout the year, there's most choice during winter and Ramadan; see listings in the *Egyptian Gazette* or *al-Ahram*. Because the films are subtitled in Arabic, audiences chatter and vendors hawk snacks, drowning out the soundtrack – you have to sit near the front to hear anything. However, the last few years have seen an explosion of expensive new cinemas, most in shopping centres: Al-Tahrir Cinema on Sharia Tahrir, in Dokki (☏02/335-4726; £E15–25); MGM on the top floor of the Maadi Grand Mall (☏02/519-5388; closed Saturdays; £E20); and Ramses Hilton Centre, opposite the hotel (☏02/574-7436; £E20–25). All have plush seats, stereo sound, a/c (turned to arctic setting), and prohibit chattering and smoking. At these cinemas it's advisable to book in advance: elsewhere it's usually okay to buy tickets (£E10–15) an hour or so beforehand. During Ramadan, however, you'll have to get there earlier, as evening performances (the Metro Cinema on Talaat Harb, and the Al-Tahrir screen a different movie every night) draw full houses and massive queues for tickets, with no reserved seats.

To some extent, all films suffer from **censorship**, which can leave the plot in shreds. The only chance to view uncensored foreign movies is during the **Cairo International Film Festival**, usually held in autumn or December. Full details can be found on the festival website at ⓦwww.cairofilmfest.com.

Opera, ballet and theatre

The **Cairo Opera House** on Gezira (☏02/739-8132 or 739-8144, ⓦwww .operahouse.gov.eg) is the chief centre for performing arts. Its main hall hosts performances by prestigious foreign acts (anything from Kabuki theatre to Broadway musicals) and the **Cairo Ballet Company** (Sept–June). The smaller hall is used by the **Cairo Symphony Orchestra**, which gives concerts there every Saturday from September to mid-June. During July and August all events move to the marble-clad open-air theatre where a programme of youth concerts includes everything from Nubian folk-dancing to Egyptian pop to jazz. Programme listings appear in *Egypt Today* and the *Al-Ahram* weekly, and are available in more detail from the ticket office. Tickets to all concerts (£E35–75) should be booked several days beforehand (daily 10am–3pm & 4–8.30pm). A jacket and tie are compulsory for men attending events in the main hall.

Another venue for Western-style performing arts is the **AUC Theatre** at the Falaki Academic Center on Sharia Falaki, between Sharia Mohammed

Mahmoud and Sharia Rihan (☎02/797-6373, ✉pva@aucegypt.edu), where most plays are performed in English. They are usually advertised on campus, or on notices at the entrance to the Falaki Academic Center, though you'll need official ID such as a passport to get in. For those who understand Arabic, the choice includes everything from serious heavyweight plays at the **National Theatre** on Midan Ataba (☎02/591-7783), to comedy just behind it at the **Thalia Theatre** (☎02/593-7948).

Religious festivals and weddings

Though few foreign visitors frequent them, Cairo's **religious festivals** are quite accessible to outsiders – and a lot of fun. Many begin with a *zaffa* (parade) of Sufis carrying banners, drums and tambourines, who later perform marathon *zikrs*, chanting and swaying themselves into the trance-like state known as *jazb*. Meanwhile, the crowd is entertained by acrobats, stick dancers, dancing horses, fortune-tellers and other side shows.

Whereas most festivals are specifically Muslim (see the box overleaf) or Christian (see p.272), people of both faiths attend the birthday or name-day celebrations of holy persons with *baraka* (the power of blessing) – known as **moulids**. Aside from the crowds (don't bring valuables, or come alone if you're a woman), the only problem is ascertaining festival **dates**. Different events are related to the Islamic, Coptic or secular calendars, and sometimes to a particular day rather than a certain date, so details below should be double-checked with Egyptian friends or the tourist office. As a rule, all the longer moulids climax in a *leyla kebira* (literally "big night") on the

---

Whirling dervishes

The *Mowlawiyya* are Egyptian adherents of a Sufi sect founded in Konya, Turkey, during the mid-thirteenth century, and known to Westerners as the **Whirling Dervishes**. Their Turkish name, *Mevlevi*, refers to their original Master, who extolled music and dancing as a way of shedding earthly ties and abandoning oneself to God's love. The Sufi ideal of attaining union with God has often been regarded by orthodox Muslims as blasphemous, and only during Mamluke and Ottoman times did the Whirling Dervishes flourish without persecution.

In modern Egypt the sect is minuscule compared to other Sufi orders, and rarely appears at moulids, but a tourist version of the famous whirling ceremony is currently staged at the Citadel while the permanent venue, Ghuriya cultural centre in Al-Ghuri's Mausoleum, undergoes restoration. If the *Mowlawiyya* are in Cairo, **performances** are held on Mondays, Wednesdays and Saturdays starting at 8pm in summer, 7pm in winter; arrive early to get a good seat, and at least half an hour before the performance in any case. The performances are free, sponsored by the government, and last for about an hour. Photos are permitted but not videos – if you bring a video camera along you'll have to leave the battery at the desk.

Each element of the **whirling ceremony** (*samaa*) has symbolic significance. The music symbolizes that of the spheres, and the turning of the dervishes that of the heavenly bodies. The gesture of extending the right arm towards heaven and the left towards the floor denotes that grace is being received from God and distributed to humanity without anything being retained by the dervishes. Their camelhair hats represent tombstones; their black cloaks the tomb itself; their white skirts shrouds. During the *samaa* the cloaks are discarded.

Note that since the Muslim calendar moves back approximately eleven days a year against the Western (Gregorian) calendar, the equivalent Gregorian months given will only be valid for the next few years.

MOHARRAM (Jan/Feb to Feb/March). New Year begins on **Ras el-Sana el-Hegira**, the first day of Moharram (see p.79 for dates). The initial ten days of this first month are blessed, especially the eve of the tenth day (*Leylat Ashura*), which commemorates the martyrdom of Hussein at Karbala. Until this century, it witnessed passionate displays by Cairo's Shia minority – the men would lash themselves with chains. Nowadays, Sunni Muslims observe the next day (*Yom Ashura*) with prayers and charity; the wealthy often feed poor families, serving them personally to demonstrate humility. But aside from *zikrs* outside Hussein's Mosque, there's little to see.

SAFAR AND RABI AL-AWWAL (March/April to May/June). In olden days the **return of the pilgrims** from Mecca (*Nezlet el-Hagg*) occasioned great festivities at the Bab al-Futuh towards the end of Safar, the second month. Nowadays, celebrations are localized, as pilgrims are feasted on the evening of their return, their homes festooned with red-and-white bunting and painted with *Hadj* scenes. However, it's still customary to congregate below the Citadel a week later and render thanksgiving *zikrs* in the evening. Previously, these gatherings blended into the **Prophet's birthday** (*Moulid al-Nabi*) celebrations during the next month, Rabi al-Awwal, which run from the third day to the night of the twelfth, the last being its great day (see p.79 for dates). The eve of the twelfth – known as the Blessed Night (*Leylat Mubarak*) – witnesses spectacular processions and fireworks, with *munshids* (singers of poetry) invoking spiritual aid while crowds chant "*Allahu Hei! Ya Daim!*" (God is Living! O Everlasting!). Midan el-Hussein, the Rifai Mosque and Ezbekiya Gardens are the best vantage points.

RABI EL-TANI (May/June to June/July). During the fourth month, Rabi al-Tani, the **Moulid of El-Hussein** gathers pace over a fortnight, its big day usually a Tuesday, its *leyla kebira* on Wednesday night. Hussein's Mosque in Khan el-Khalili is surrounded by crowds chanting "*Allah Mowlana!*" (God is our Lord!), dozens of *zikrs* and amplified *munshids*, plus all the usual side shows. Also in this month is the smaller **Moulid of Saiyida Sukayna** – at her mosque on Sharia el-Khalifa (see map p.186).

GUMAD EL-TANI (Aug/Sept to Sept/Oct). On a Thursday or Friday in the middle of the sixth month, Gumad el-Tani, Sufis of the Rifai order attend the **Moulid of Al-Rifai** at his mosque below the Citadel. Those carrying black flags belong to the mainstream Rifaiyah; subsects include the Awlad Ilwan (once famous for thrusting nails into their eyes and swallowing hot coals) and the Sa'adiya (snake charmers, who used to allow their sheikh to ride over them on horseback). Dervishes are less evident

last evening or the eve of the last day – the most spectacular and crowded phase.

Coptic festivals

It should be emphasized that **Coptic festivals** are primarily religious, with fewer diversions than Muslim ones. Unless you're into church services, the "moveable" feasts centred around Easter (which follows the Coptic calendar rather than the Western one), Christmas (January 7), Epiphany (January 19) and the Feast of Annunciation (March 21) have little to offer.

However, there's more to enjoy at two festivals in Old Cairo: the **Moulid of Mari Girgis** at the round Church of St George (April 23, St George's at the **Moulid of Saiyida Nafisa** (on a Wed or Thurs mid-month, or a Tues towards the end of the month), but the event is equally colourful.

RAGAB (Sept/Oct–Oct/Nov). The seventh month is dominated by the great **Moulid of Saiyida Zeinab**, Cairo's "patron saint", which lasts for fifteen days and attracts up to a million people on its big day and *leyla kebira* (a Tues & Wed in the middle of the month). A much smaller, "local" event is the **Moulid of Sheikh al-Dashuti** on the 26th day of Ragab, at his mosque near the junction of Faggala and Bur Said streets, 1km northwest of the Bab al-Futuh. The eve of the 27th is observed by all Muslims as the *Leylat el-Mirag* or of Ascension, with *zikrs* outside the Abdin Palace and principal mosques.

SHA'BAN (Oct/Nov to Nov/Dec). During the eighth month, Sha'ban, the week-long **Moulid of Imam al-Shafi'i** enlivens his mausoleum in the Southern Cemetery (see p.187) from one Wednesday to the next. The eve of the 15th is believed to be the time when Allah determines the fate of every human over the ensuing year, so the faithful hope to gain *baraka*.

RAMADAN (Nov/Dec to Dec/Jan) **AND EID AL-FITR**. The sighting of the new moon on the *Leylat er-Ruyeh* (Night of Observation) marks the onset of **Ramadan**, a month of fasting from sunrise to sunset, with festivities every night (see p.77 for more, and p.79 for dates). *Zikrs* and Koranic recitations draw crowds to El-Gumhorriya and El-Hussein squares, while secular delights are concentrated around Ezbekiya and other areas. The *Leylat el-Qadr* (Night of Power) on the eve of the 27th of the month was traditionally marked by Whirling and Howling Dervishes at Mohammed Ali's Mosque at the Citadel. The end of Ramadan heralds the three-day **Eid al-Fitr** or "Little Feast" (see p.79 for dates), when people buy new clothes, visit friends, mosques, shrines and family graves. In the past, this was followed by the procession of the *kisweh* (the brocaded cloth which covers the sacred Ka'ba at Mecca), a prelude to the departure of the pilgrims around the 23rd day of *Shawwal*. Given modern transport, however, most pilgrims now depart in the following month, *Zoul Qiddah*, with local send-offs that counterpoint the *Nezlet al-Hagg*.

ZOUL HAGGA (Dec/Jan to Jan/Feb). The twelfth month, Zoul Hagga, is notable for the "Feast of Sacrifice" or **Eid al-Adha** (the "Great Feast", **Corban Bairam**), which tales place throughout the city. It involves the mass slaughter of sheep and other livestock on the 10th, commemorating Ibrahim's willingness to sacrifice Isma'il to Allah (the Muslim version of the story of Abraham and Isaac).

MOULID OF SIDI ALI AL-BAYOUMI. Last but not least, there's another colourful parade of Dervishes at the **Moulid of Sidi Ali al-Bayoumi**, the Rifai sects proceeding from El-Hussein's Mosque to the Bab al-Futuh and thence into the Husseiniya quarter. Unlike most Muslim festivals, this is unrelated to the Islamic calendar, happening in early **October**.

Day) and the **Moulid of the Holy Family** at the Church of St Sergius (June 1). Moreover, all Egyptians observe the ancient pharaonic-Coptic spring festival known as **Sham el-Nessim** (literally "Sniffing the Breeze"), when families picnic on salted fish, onions and coloured eggs in gardens and cemeteries.

Weddings

There's nothing bashful about Cairo **weddings** or the curiosity of spectators. On Thursday nights the city resounds with convoys of honking cars conveying guests to Nile-side hotels and casinos; and with ululations, drums and tambourines welcoming the newlyweds (often preceded by a bellydancer), whom relatives shower with rose petals. In poorer quarters all the bridal furniture and wedding guests are first displayed to admiring neighbours.

At the reception itself, the couple sit receiving congratulations ("*Alf mabrouk*" is the formal salutation) while relatives and friends perform impromptu dances. Guests may be segregated, allowing both sexes to let their hair down: women can dance and smoke, men indulge in spirits (or hashish, in private homes). Although it's not uncommon for foreign onlookers to be invited into middle-class or *baladi* wedding parties, rich ones are predictably exclusive.

Activities and kids' stuff

The two classic tourist activities are riding in the desert near the Pyramids and sailing on the Nile in a felucca. Trips further afield are covered at the end of this chapter under "Excursions from Cairo" (see p.295).

Riding in the desert

Notwithstanding the pitfalls mentioned on p.230, **riding in the desert** is a fantastic experience. Unless you relish haggling, authorized stables are a safer bet than footloose Bedouin operators; in either case, check to see that your horse is in good condition and well looked-after. Stables behind the Sound and Light grandstand near the Sphinx include AA (☎012/373-1803 or 02/385-0531), which has very reasonable rates and is good for children, and KG Stables round the corner (☎02/385-1065).

Felucca sailing

Something as restful as **sailing on the Nile in a felucca** can hardly be termed an activity. Since the boatman does all the work, the only effort involved is negotiating rental rates. Most of the feluccas moored along the river bank opposite the *Helnan Shepheard* and the northern tip of Roda can seat eight people and charge £E50 per hour. Bring a picnic and lots of mosquito repellent. For rather less cost, you can join one of the boats just south of Maspero Dock, which do round trips to the Nile Barrages at Qanatir (£E6 per person). Shorter jaunts are available on boats from the quay just north of Tahrir Bridge on Gezira Island (£E2 for 30min). For an even cheaper no-frills ride on the Nile, catch a river-taxi (50pt) from the Maspero Dock to Giza or Old Cairo or up to Qanatir (£E5 each way).

Parks

Cairo is incredibly densely populated, with few green spaces. Even in prosperous Mohandiseen, local residents use the central reservations of the main boulevards for sitting out or picnicking, and most of Cairo's parks charge admission fees, though these are usually small.

The city's most impressive park by far is the new **Al-Azhar Park** on Sharia Salah Salem opposite the Northern Cemetery (winter daily except Fri 10am–10pm, Fri 10am–11.30pm, summer daily 10am–1am; £E10; see p.190). Also in Islamic Cairo, **Saiyida Park**, in Saiyida Zeinab (on Sharia Qadry, one block off Sharia Bur Said; daily 8am–10pm), is a public landscaped garden in traditional Arabic style not far from the Ibn Tulun Mosque, a very welcome green lung in one of the most crowded parts of town, and a good place for a breather after a day's sightseeing.

In **Gezira**, there are a number of small gardens open to the public, including the **Andalusian Garden** just south of Sharia el-Borg (upper section, daily

9am–5pm; £E10; lower section daily, winter 9am–10pm, summer 9am–11pm; £E2), and the **Riyadi Garden** next door, by the river (daily: winter 9am–10pm; summer 9am–11pm; £E2), complete with Cleopatra's Needle-style obelisk. Between them and the 6th October Bridge is another garden, the **Hadiket al-Mesala** (daily 9am–11pm; £E2) and, to its north, the **Hadiket al-Nahr** (daily 9am–9pm; same ticket). On the other side of the island, **Gezira Youth Centre** (daily 8am–10pm; £E2) is used by local residents as a park. The adjoining Gezira Sporting Club has a massive green space, but keeps its fees high and its doors resolutely closed to non-members (day membership costs £E20, or £E30 on Fridays and public holidays).

Further afield, the grounds of the **Agriculture Museum** in **Aguza** (daily except Mon 9am–1pm; 10pt; see p.215) are rather more enticing than the museum itself. On Roda Island, there's the **Umm Kalthoum Garden** north of el-Gema'a Bridge (daily: winter 9am–9pm, summer 9am–midnight; £E2), while the **El-Urman Gardens** on Sharia Abdel Salam Aref near the zoo in **Giza** (daily: winter 8.30am–3.30pm; summer 8.30am–5pm; 30pt, camera 50pt, video £E20; see map p.211) is a stately remnant of the Khedival Gardens laid out by the French. Other options include Gabalaya Gardens in Zamalek, the zoo in Giza, and Merryland in Heliopolis, all covered on p.213, and the **Japanese Garden** in **Helwan** (daily: winter 9am–10pm; summer 9am–midnight; £E2, video £E10; see p.208).

Swimming pools

Swimming pools take on an extra allure in Cairo, whose only "public" pool is the open-air, untended spa at Ain Helwan (in effect open 24hr and free; see p.208). The Heliolido (☏02/258-0070) off Midan Roxi costs £E40 a day, while the nearby Heliopolis Sporting Club (☏02/417-0061, 62 or 63) on Sharia Merghani has a larger pool and admits foreigners over the summer (bring your passport), but the entrance fee (£E25) doesn't include use of the facilities (eg additional £E50 to use the pool). The Olympic-size pool at the Ahli Club by the Opera House on Sharia Om Kalthoum is for more serious swimmers and also has women-only sessions (monthly membership costs US$50).

Hotel pools are more accessible, the best being the *Semiramis Intercontinental* (£E110), *Cairo Marriott* (£E110) and the *Atlas Zamalek* on Arab League Street in Mohandiseen (covered by the hotel restaurant's minimum charge: Mon–Thurs £E25, Fri–Sun £E30). The rooftop pool of the *Fontana Hotel*, off Midan Ramses (£E25), is OK for dipping but hardly big enough for a swim.

Hammams

A totally different experience is available at traditional **hammams** (bathhouses), whose nondescript facades conceal gloomy warrens of sweatrooms and tubs. Some baths serve men in the morning and women in the afternoon; others assign them separate days, or only admit one sex. With no mixed bathing, Egyptian women can ignore taboos and talk frankly; foreigners may be adopted into their circle, which usually includes children being scrubbed. Male baths have been linked to gay prostitution since Ottoman times, so many men avoid them, with the result that most of the old bathhouses in Cairo have became very rundown and are now closed. The only bathhouse still open in Islamic Cairo is **Hammam al-Malatili** at 40 Sharia Emir el-Gyushi (women 10am–5pm, men 7pm–9am; see map p.158), dating from the sixteenth century, though the fifteenth-century Hammam al-Sultan on Sharia Muizz opposite Qasr Bashtak (see map p.172) is due to reopen soon after restoration. Also currently closed for restoration are the Hammam al-Sukariya on Sharia al-Muizz opposite al-Muayyad Mosque (see map p.165) and Hammam Said al-Suadi on Sharia Gamaliya (see map p.158). Another good option is the **Hammam el Arbaa**, at 5 Sharia el-Ansari (aka Sharia al-Hammamat), off Sharia Bulaq al-Gadid, which runs north from 26 July Street opposite the Abu'l'Ila Mosque, in the Wikalet al-Balah district of Bulaq (☎02/577-9705; daily women 1–4pm, men 6pm–1am).

Cleaner, but more expensive and less traditional venues include the **saunas** and **Turkish baths** at the *Nile Hilton* (£E60) and the *Ramses Hilton* (£E150).

Sports: participatory and spectator

Keeping fit in Cairo is difficult but not impossible. The expat Hash House Harriers (Ⓦwww.cairohash.com) is one of several clubs organizing **street running**, best done on Gezira, Roda or the west bank Corniche, before 8am or after 10pm to avoid heavy traffic and air pollution. Alternatively, by paying £E2 to enter the Youth Club under the Giza side of the 6th October Bridge (daily 8am–10pm), you can "stray" into the Gezira Sporting Club – just keep away from the built-up area near the running track, where guards check for tickets.

Although the Gezira Sporting Club's extensive facilities are only available to members and guests (see above), anyone can use the **gymnasiums** in the *Ramses Hilton* (£E40) and *Nile Hilton* (£E60) hotels; or call the Community Services Association, 4 Road #21, Ma'adi (☎02/358-5284), which runs a fitness centre with a weight room.

Of the city's spectator sports, **football** (soccer) is the most exciting. During the season (Sept–May), premier league teams Ahly and Zamalek take on challengers like Ismailiya, Mahalla and Masri at the Cairo Stadium in Medinet Nasr (Fri: usually 3pm in winter; 7pm in summer; £E3–15). The most exciting fixture of the season is the local derby between Ahly and Zamalek, when rivalry runs high and tickets sell out well in advance. Riot police with machine guns are regularly in attendance at matches since football riots, though infrequent, can be extremely bloody.

Cairo and the surrounding region have a number of **golf** courses, of which the most central is the 18-hole course at the Gezira Sporting Club (☎02/735-6000; £E75 plus day membership of £E20–30). The *Mena House Oberoi* by the Pyramids (☎02/383-3222 or 3444) also has an 18-hole course (£E230 a day for non-residents), and there are a couple more around the ring road out past Heliopolis: the 27-hole course at Katameya Heights (☎02/758-0512 or 17, Ⓦwww.katameya.com/indexnet.htm), and an 18-hole course at the *JW Marriott Hotel* (☎02/408-5041). You'll find further information on Cairo's golf courses at Ⓦwww.touregypt.net/golfcourses.htm.

Chiefly for children

Besides the following places, most children (and adults) should enjoy felucca and camel rides, the Pyramids Sound and Light show, and theme restaurants like *Felfela Village* on Maryotteya Canal at Giza (see p.263). Because of Cairo's density, most of the parks and pleasure grounds are on the islands or the west bank (see above).

The Aquarium and zoo

The **Aquarium Grotto** in Gabalaya Gardens in Zamalek (daily 9am–4pm; 35pt) displays assorted live and preserved tropical fish amidst a labyrinth of passageways and stairs that children will love to explore. The entrance is on Sharia Galabaya, on the western side of the park.

Alternatively, the larger **Cairo Zoo** in Giza (daily 9am–5pm; 30pt, camera 25pt, also 25pt to walk across the hippo pond) can easily be reached from downtown by bus (#355 and #357 from Tahrir, #30 and #83 from Ramses, #6, #9, #106 and #109 from Ataba). As zoos go, it's reasonably humane, with quite large enclosures for most animals – the main exception is the lion house. You are greeted on entry by an impressive display of flamingoes, and children will enjoy helping to feed the camels or the elephants. Try to avoid Fridays and public holidays, when the zoo is packed with picnicking families, and don't bother with the small museum of stuffed reptiles (25pt).

Dr Ragab's Pharaonic Village

Reached by half-hourly boats from the Corniche 2km south of the Giza Bridge at 3 Sharia Bahr al-Azam, **Dr Ragab's Pharaonic Village** (daily: winter 9am–6pm; summer 9am–9pm; £E70 at the gate, £E60 at the Papyrus Centre; ☎02/571-8675, ⓦ interoz.com/Egypt/Village) is a kitsch simulation of ancient Egypt on Jacob Island, upriver from Roda in Dokki. During the three-hour tour, visitors survey the Canal of Mythology (flanked by statues of gods) and scores of costumed Egyptians performing tasks from their floating "time machines", before being shown around a replica temple and nobleman's villa, and no less than ten mini-museums, dedicated to Hellenic, Coptic and Islamic civilization, ancient arts, mummification and (a little incongruously) Nasser, Sadat and Napoleon. All in all, it's a fun visit, and quite educational, demonstrating such activities as how papyrus is made and how the ancient Egyptians put on their make-up. Unfortunately, the Pharaonic Village is not served by public transport, and is best reached by taxi (£E8–10 from downtown).

The circus and the puppet theatre

Those who enjoy animals performing tricks, acrobats, clowns and trapeze artists should visit the **National Circus** (☎02/347-0612) in Aguza, next to the Balloon Theatre near the Zamalek Bridge. Performances run from 8pm to 11pm daily except Wednesday, with extra matinées (5pm to 7.30pm) on Thursday and Friday; the box office is open 3–11pm on Thursday and Friday, and 5–11pm from Saturday to Tuesday (tickets £E10–30). Another traditional diversion is the **Cairo Puppet Theatre** (Fri 10.30am, Thurs & Fri 7.30pm; ☎02/591-0954) in Ezbekiya Gardens, which stages *Sinbad the Sailor*, *Ali Baba* and other favourites, or campy musicals (Oct–May).

Rides and games

Fun rides and games are on offer at the **Cookie Amusement Park** near the Giza Pyramids, 400m up Mansoreya Canal from Pyramids Road (daily 10am–11.30pm; £E2.50), with dodgems, roundabouts and a big slide, and the larger **Sinbad Amusement Park** near Cairo Airport, which has bumper cars, a small roller coaster and lots of rides for tots (☎02/624-4001 or 2; daily, winter 10–11pm, summer 4pm–3am; £E3 entry plus £E3–5 per ride). **Merryland** on Sharia al-Higaz, off Midan Roxi in Heliopolis, is a safe environment to play, with a merry-go-round, pedalo lake and small zoo (daily: winter 9am–midnight; summer 24hr; 50pt at weekends, £E1 Fri & public holidays). Further out of the city, in 6th October City, 38km southwest of Cairo beyond the Giza pyramids, is a larger amusement park, **Dreampark** (ⓦ www.dreamparkegypt.com; daily except Fri 4pm–midnight, Fri noon–9pm, Ramadan 9pm–2am), with bigger and better rides and a view of the pyramids from the top of the two roller coasters.

Shopping

Shopping in Cairo is a time-consuming process, which suits most locals fine. Cairenes regard it as a social event involving salutations and dickering, affirmations of status and servility; smoothly impersonal transactions are not an ideal. Excluding government stores, there are basically three types of retail outlet. **Department stores** (generally open daily 10am–2pm & 6–10pm) have fixed prices and the tedious system where you select the goods and get a chit, pay the cashier and then claim your purchases from a third counter. **Smaller shops**, usually run by the owner, stay open till 9 or 10pm and tend to specialize in certain wares. Although most of them have fixed prices, tourists who don't understand Arabic price tags or Egyptian currency are liable to be overcharged in certain places (around the Khan el-Khalili bazaar and Talaat Harb, especially). If you know the correct price, attempts can be thwarted by handing over the exact sum (or as near as possible).

In **bazaars** and **markets** haggling prevails, so it's worth window-shopping around fixed-price stores before **bargaining** for lower rates in bazaar stalls. When asked for a quote, merchants often riposte: "What do you think?" Suggest an absurdly low sum to make them respond and don't be fazed by mockery – it's all part of the game. Buyers' tactics include stressing any flaws that might reduce the object's value; talking of lower quotes received elsewhere; feigning indifference or having a friend urge you to leave. Avoid being tricked into raising your bid twice in a row, or admitting your estimation of the object's worth (just reply that you've made an offer). Providing you don't make an offer they're willing to accept, it's okay to terminate a lengthy session without buying anything.

During **Ramadan** (see p.77), **shopping hours** go haywire, as some places close all day and operate through the night, while others open later and close earlier. Given that people splurge after sundown, Cairo's boutiques and bazaars are as busy then as Western stores before Christmas.

Markets

Although the bazaars deal in more exotic goods, Cairo's **markets** provide an arresting spectacle, free of the touristy slickness that prevails around the Khan el-Khalili bazaar in Islamic Cairo. Watch how people bargain over the humblest items (often recycled from other products), a paradigm of free enterprise in the gutter. What isn't apparent are the customs, guilds and rackets that govern business, as exemplified by the vast wholesale market at Rod el-Farag (see p.219), whence **fruit and vegetables** are distributed throughout the city. Street markets in central Cairo can be found at Bab al-Luq, halfway up Sharia Orabi, at the eastern end of Sheikh al-Rihan, and along Sharia Qalaa – all of which do business through the night, accompanied by local coffee houses. With the kilo price displayed on stalls in Arabic numerals, you shouldn't have to bargain unless they try to overcharge. Elsewhere **haggling** is de rigueur.

Second-hand clothing can be found in the *canto* section of the **Imam al-Shafi'i Market**, which straggles for 1km along the road leading from Al-Basatin to the Imam's mausoleum in the El-Khalifa district. Other parts of this Friday morning market sell scrap, grain, poultry, sheep and cattle. Cairo's **Bird Markets** (10am–2.30pm) are named after the days on which they're held: Souk al-Hadd (Sun; Giza Station), Souk al-Gom'a (Fri; by the Salah Salem overpass, south of the Citadel, see map p.182) and Souk Itnayn w Khamis (Mon & Thurs; in the Abu Rish area of Saiyida Zeinab, see map p.182). On Sharia el-Geish near Midan Ataba there's a daily **Paper Market**, selling all types of paper, dyed leather and art materials, and for **fabrics** (from hand-loomed silk to cheap offcuts), **tools** and much else, you can't beat the daily **Wikalat al-Bulah**, on Sharia Abu'l'lla in the Bulaq district. There's also a **camel market** at Bil'esh (see p.224).

Souvenirs and antiques

Scores of shops in the Khan and central Cairo purvey **souvenirs**, mostly kitsch reproductions of pharaonic art – scarabs, statuettes of deities, busts of Nefertiti, eyes of Horus – which are cheaper to buy at source in Luxor or Aswan.

Sheets of **papyrus** painted with scenes from temples or tombs are equally ubiquitous. A lot of it used to be made from banana leaves, unlike which **genuine** papyrus will withstand crumpling without cracking (though the paint won't). Nowadays, however, so much papyrus is grown for the trade that it is no cheaper to use banana leaf anyway, and the real scam lies in selling printed papyrus as hand-painted. Most of the papyri on sale are printed or partly printed, even if they have a signature. Prices range from around £E2 to £E80 and beyond, depending on size, intricacy, the quantity of gold paint used and where you're buying: around the Pyramids, in big hotels and the Khan, papyrus is sure to be extremely overpriced and most unlikely to be hand-painted. If you've got the stomach to bargain them down, itinerant street vendors give better deals. You can sometimes see **papyrus-making** demonstrated at Dr Ragab's Papyrus Institute (p.211), one of the few places where you can be sure of buying a genuine, hand-painted article.

Copies of **prints** by David Roberts and other nineteenth-century illustrators also make nice souvenirs. For cheap poster-size or postcard editions, check out Reader's Corner and Lehnert & Landrock (see p.286). Old Egyptian **stamps**, **coins** and **postcards** can also be found at Salon el Ferdaos 33 Sharia Abdel Khaliq Sarwat, among other places.

Selling fake *antikas* (with spurious certificates) is an old tradition. Genuine pharaonic, Coptic or Islamic **antiques** cannot be exported without a licence from the Department of Antiquities. Old reproductions and foreign-made antiques are a safer bet. Dealers in the Khan include Old Shop and Ahmed el Dabba (both at 5 Sikket al-Badestan; see map p.154).

Film and processing

Outside of big hotels, you can buy **film** fairly cheaply. Photo Greenwich at 16 Sharia Adly (daily 9am–8pm; ☎02/360-6990) and the Kodak Shop at 20 Sharia Adly (daily 9am–9pm) sell Kodachrome and Agfa film for £E11–16 and also offer **photo-processing** and **printing**. Both charge £E3 per film plus 75pt per print for developing if you want it in an hour, less if you can wait a day. Another reliable place for developing is Mitry Colour, 3rd floor, 127 Sharia Ramses, at the corner of Sharia Khan el-Khouly (Mon–Sat 10am–10pm, Sun 10am–7pm), which charges £E3 for developing and 85pt per print if you want it done in an hour, or £E1.50 and 65pt if you can wait until the next day.

Brass and copper ware

Egyptian craftsmen have been turning out **brass and copper ware** for over a thousand years, and aside from the tourist trade there's still a big domestic market for everything from banqueting trays to minaret finials. Amongst the items favoured as souvenirs are candlesticks, waterpipes, gongs, coffee sets, embossed plates and inlaid or repoussé trays (the larger ones are often mounted on stands to serve as tables). All of these are manufactured and sold within the Khan, particularly along the stretch of Sharia al-Muizz just before Qalaoun's complex, known as the **Coppersmiths Bazaar** (*Souk al-Nahhasin*).

Although the Khan offers the best range of decorative pieces, it's cheaper to buy **Turkish coffeepots** and hookah pipes between the Ghuriya and the Bab Zwayla, along Ahmed Maher, or from workshops on Sharia Khulud and other streets around Ramses. Be sure that anything you intend to drink out of is lined with tin or silver, since brass and copper react with certain substances to form toxic compounds. Test **waterpipes** for leaky joints and remember to call them *sheeshas* or *narghiles* rather than *hubbly bubblies* (which signifies hashish-smoking). Shops on Sharia al-Muizz just north of the Barquq complex specialize in water-pipes, backgammon boards and other coffee house sundries; a passage on the left just before the Sabil-Kuttab of Abd al-Rahman is full of shops selling pipes. Prices range from £E15 to £E120, depending on the size; the ones with stainless steel rather than brass fittings are better made and more durable.

Gold and silver jewellery

Most Egyptians still regard **jewellery** as safer than money in the bank; for women, in particular, it constitutes a safety net in case of divorce or bereavement. Pharaonic, Coptic and Islamic motifs, Bedouin, Nubian and oasis designs, work from Syria, Jordan, Yemen and Arabia – Cairo's jewellers stock them all, and can also make pieces to order.

Gold and silver are sold by the gram, with a percentage added on for workmanship. Bullion prices fluctuate but Egyptian wages remain low. The current ounce price of gold is printed in the daily *Egyptian Gazette*; one troy ounce equals about 31 grams. Barring antiques, all **gold** work is stamped with Arabic numerals indicating its purity: usually 21 carat for Bedouin, Nubian or *fellaheen* jewellery; 18 carat for Middle Eastern and European-style charms and chains. Sterling **silver** (80 or 92.5 percent) is likewise stamped, while a gold camel in the shop window indicates that the items are **gold-plated brass**.

Jewellery

Downtown jewellers are concentrated along Sharia Abdel Khaliq Sarawt and Sikket al-Manakh, near Midan Opera. In Islamic Cairo, the **Goldsmiths Bazaar** (Souk es-Sagha) covers Sharia al-Muizz between the Muski and Sultan Qalaoun's complex, and infiltrates the heart of the Khan via Sikkets al-Badestan and Khan el-Khalili. There are also several good **silversmiths** in the Wikala al-Gawarhergia.

The most popular souvenirs are gold or silver **cartouches**, with given names in hieroglyphics. The price depends on the quantity of metal used and whether the characters are engraved or glued on. A reliable jeweller who specializes in these is Yazejian, in the little lane opposite the *Khan el-Khalili Restaurant* on Sikket al-Badestan in Khan el-Khalili (see map on p.154). The price of the cartouche will depend on the size, which in turn will depend to a large extent on the number of syllables in the name you want to have put on it, but expect to pay around £E400–600.

Carpets, tent-making, appliqué and basketwork

Pure wool kilims and knotted carpets are an expensive (and bulky) purchase in any country, so serious buyers are advised to read up on the subject before spending hundreds of pounds on one. As most Egyptian **kilims** (pile-less rugs) and **knotted carpets** have half as many knots (16 per centimetre) as their Turkish counterparts, they should be significantly cheaper – especially the ones made from native wool rather than the high-grade imported stuff used in finer kilims. Prices posted in downtown stores like Omar Effendi (11 Sharia Adly/42 Sharia Sherif) or Sednaoui (on Clot Bey, 100m up from Midan Ataba) can give you an idea of what to aim for in the bazaar.

Tapestries and rugs

More affordable – and ubiquitous – are the **tapestries and rugs** woven from coarse wool and/or camel hair. These come in two basic styles. Bedouin rugs carry geometric patterns in shades of brown and beige and are usually loosely woven (often purely from camel hair). The other style, deriving from the famous Wissa Wassef School at Harraniyya (see p.237), features colourful images of birds, trees and village life. Beware of stitched-together seams and gaps in the weave (hold pieces up against the light) and unfast colours – if any colour wipes off on a damp cloth, the dyes will run when the rug is washed.

While the suburban village of Kerdassa (p.237) replicates every style imaginable, the only authorized outlet for genuine Wissa Wassef Harraniyya tapestries and batiks is **Senouhi**, on the fifth floor of 54 Sharia Abdel Khaliq Sarwat (Mon–Fri 10am–5pm, Sat 10am–1pm; ℡02/391-0955). Crammed with carpets, jewellery, Bedouin embroidery, modern paintings, and some very high quality bric-a-brac, this small store is a fascinating place to browse, and its delightful owner is happy to show you around. The best site in the bazaar is Haret al-Fahhamin (see "Spices and perfume", p.285), where you can compare Rashidi and Shahatta Talba Manna (both at no.11) with Hamid Ibrahim Abdel Aal (no.5). Unfortunately, none of them is recognizably signposted (or even numbered), so you'll have to ask for directions to the right shop, though their locations are shown on our map (p.165).

Tent-making and appliqué

The traditional Cairene crafts of tent-making and appliqué work are still practised in half a dozen tiny workshops inside the Qasaba, near the Bab Zwayla – hence its sobriquet, the **Tentmakers Bazaar** (Souk al-Khiyamiyya; see map p.172). Colourful **appliqué work** comes in various forms: some designs are pictorial, based on pharaonic motifs or romantic Arab imagery; others are abstract, delicate arabesques (which tend to be dearer). Prices vary according to size and intricacy. A zippered pillowcase or cushion cover costs £E20–30; larger pieces, to be used as hangings, go for upwards of £E100, with bedspread-size ones starting at roughly £E450. A much cheaper alternative is the riotously patterned **printed tent fabric** used for marquees at moulids, or to screen unsightly building work. This costs about £E12 per metre, cut from a bolt of cloth roughly 1.6m wide; offcuts are cheaper still.

Another cheap souvenir is palm-frond **basketwork**, mostly from the Fayoum and Upper Egypt. Fayoumi baskets (for sewing, shopping or laundry) are more practical, but it's hard to resist the woven platters from Luxor and Aswan, as vibrantly colourful as parrots. You may also find baskets from Siwa Oasis, trimmed with tassels.

Clothing, bellydancing costumes and leatherwork

As a cotton-growing country with a major textiles industry, Egypt is big on retail **clothing**. Smartly dressed Cairenes are forever window-shopping along

Talaat Harb and 26th July Street (downtown), Sharia al-Ahram (Heliopolis) and Arab League Street (Mohandiseen), to name only the main clusters of **boutiques** (open till 9/10pm). Staider threads can be had in **department stores** like Chemla and Cicurel on the downtown section of 26th July Street, or Omar Effendi at 2 Talaat Harb (daily 10am–2pm & 5–9pm) and 11 Sharia Adly/42 Sharia Sherif (daily 10am–9pm). The cheapest outlets for clothes are **street vendors** along the Muski.

Egyptian clothes

Although few tourists can wear them outdoors without looking silly, many take home a caftan or *galabiyya* for lounging attire. Women's **caftans** are made of cotton, silk or wool, generally A-line, with long, wide sleeves and a round or mandarin collar (often braided). Men's **galabiyyas** come in three basic styles. *Ifrangi* (foreign) resembles a floor-length tailored shirt with collar and cuffs; the *Saudi* style is more form-fitting, with a high-buttoned neck and no collar; *baladi galabiyyas* have very wide sleeves and a low, rounded neckline. The fixed prices in downtown shops should be beatable by hard bargaining **in the Khan**, where there are also two fixed-price stores. Auf (pronounced "oaf"), on the north side of Sharia al-Azhar by the pedestrian bridge (see map p.154), stocks a wide assortment of ready-mades at reasonable prices, including black dresses with Bedouin-style embroidery. Atlas, on Sikket al-Badestan, does made-to-order garments in handwoven fabrics with intricate braidwork, and can make slippers to order too (allow several weeks; keep all receipts). Their cheapest caftans and *galabiyyas* are dearer than most garments in other shops.

Another fetching item is the heavy, woven, fringed or tassled black **shawls** worn by *baladi* women, which are sold along the Muski for upwards of £E20, depending on their size and composition (nylon or silk); check for any snags or tears in the weave. If you want to go the whole hog, invest in a *melaya*, the flowing black ankle-length wraps that *baladi* women wear over their house dresses when they go outdoors.

Bellydancing costumes

Cairo is the cheapest place in the world to buy bellydancing costumes, and many foreign dancers come here just to buy all the gear. Forget the rubbish sold to tourists and look for one of the tiny specialist emporiums in Khan el-Khalili. The best one is Al-Wikalah at 73 Sharia Gawhar al-Qayid off the Muski (see map on p.154). There's a woman to help fit the costumes, and anything they don't have in stock they can make within a few days. Lavishly beaded and sequinned bras and hipbands, with a skirt and veil, cost £E1500–3000; the more you buy, the lower the price. If you're really serious, go to Amira el-Khattan, 27 Sharia Basra, Mohandiseen (☎02/749-0322), where a full tailor-made costume will set you back about US$300–400. For bellydancing tapes and videos of the great artistes, pay a visit to Es-Sawy, on the left of the passage just before you reach *Fishawi's*. If you're interested in lessons, Miss Raqia Hassan (☎02/748-2338) in Dokki comes recommended by several dancers who are now professional.

Leatherwork

Egyptian **leatherwork** is nice and colourful, if not up to the standards of its Turkish rival. You can get an idea of the range of products from several shops along Sikket Khan el-Khalili. Leather jackets cost upwards of £E100. Cheaper wallets, handbags and pouffes (tuffets) are sold throughout the Khan and central Cairo. Camel saddles are no longer produced in the Saddlemakers Bazaar, but you will find a couple of places still making them on Sharia Ahmed Maher, opposite the side wall of the Al-Muayyad Mosque (see map on p.172). A leather camel saddle will set you back around £E400.

Glass, ceramics and precious stones

Primitive factories on Haret al-Birkedar just outside the Northern Gates still produce **Muski glass**, a form of hand-blown glassware popular in medieval times, which is nowadays made from recycled bottles. Recognizable by its air bubbles and extreme fragility, Muski glass comes in five main colours (navy blue, turquoise, aquamarine, green and purple) and is fashioned into inexpensive glasses, plates, vases, candle holders and ashtrays – sometimes painted with arabesque designs in imitation of enamelled Mamluke glassware. In the bazaar, the main stockist is Saiyid Abd al-Raouf (8 Sikket Khan el-Khalili; see map p.154), but it's better to go to the factory, where you can see the glass being blown and also get a better price. The main one is called Al-Daour and can be found by leaving the walled city through Bab al-Futuh, crossing the main road (Sharia Galal) and finding Haret al-Birkedar about 20m to your right behind the first row of shops; the factory, where you can see the glass being blown, is more or less at the end of it, and there's a retail outlet near the beginning of the street at no.10 (see map on p.158).

A very different kind of glassware is the elegant handmade **perfume bottles** sold in the bazaars. The cheaper ones are made of glass and are as delicate as they look (£E3–10). Pyrex versions cost about twice as much and are a little sturdier (they should also be noticeably heavier). A reasonable and hassle-free place to buy them in the bazaar is Perfumes Secret just off the Muski in the lane opposite the *Radwan Hotel* (see map p.154).

Pottery and alabaster

Robust **household pottery** is sold outdoors near the Mosque of Amr in Old Cairo and along the Corniche between Cairo and Ma'adi. For more refined **ceramics**, check out downtown department store Senouhi (see p.281), or Ceramica Cleopatra (36 Sharia Batal Ahmed Abdel Aziz) and Ceramica el Gawhara (35 Sharia Lubnan), both in Mohandiseen. Vases and sculptures made from **alabaster** are ubiquitous in Cairo's tourist marts, but you can get better deals at source, in Luxor.

Precious stones

Although nothing can substitute for experience, it's worth relating a few tips about **precious stones**, which Egypt imports from all over, having exhausted its own supply through centuries of mining. Most emeralds in Egypt are of poor quality (good ones are clear, dark green); very large or transparent rubies (from India and Burma) are almost certainly fake; and real sapphires should be opaque. True amber will float when put in salt water. Pearls (from the Gulf Emirates and Japan) should feel like glass if tapped against your teeth; German onyx should be opaque and make a sharp sound if dropped onto glass; and genuine turquoise (from Sinai, Iran or the USA) should contain streaks and impurities. To test the authenticity of Brazilian topaz, amethyst or aquamarine, place them on a sheet of white paper – genuine ones should have only two shades within the stone.

Mashrabiya and inlay work

With little demand for the huge latticed screens that once covered nearly every window in Cairo, modern **mashrabiya work** is usually confined to decorative screens and table stands (see "Brass and copper ware", p.279). Generally made of imported red birch or oak, they consist of scores or hundreds of turned wooden beads, joined by dowels and glue, without nails. The technique is also applied to Koran stands (which make splendid magazine racks), the fancier ones being embellished with mother-of-pearl, bone and other inlays.

Inlaid **boxes** come in all sizes, from cigar holders to multi-drawer jewellery caskets. Small boxes cost upwards of £E10; prices increase with size and quality of workmanship. Senhoui (see p.281) has some higher-quality inlaid boxes than those you'll find in the bazaar. **Backgammon boards** (*thowla* – pronounced "dow-la") come in two broad varieties: very simple, with minimal (often poor-quality or plastic) inlay, for around £E35; and larger sets made of hardwoods, intricately inlaid with mother-of-pearl, bone or ivory. A multiple box set can cost £E140 or more.

Many backgammon sets have chessboards on the back; **chesspieces** in every style and material are widely available, but good backgammon counters are hard to find. Now that Egypt has stopped legal imports, fresh supplies of **ivory** (whose sale is not illegal) are smuggled in from Sudan and Kenya, where poachers are decimating elephant herds. If that's not sufficient reason to boycott ivory products, almost all Western countries prohibit their importation. Inlaid or carved **bone** makes an acceptable, cheaper substitute.

Contemporary art

Contemporary art is not something that most people think of buying when they visit Egypt, but as you'll know if you've visited Gezira Island's Modern Art and Mahmoud Mukhtar museums (see p.212), there are some fine artists working in Egypt today, who do exhibit around town. One of the best places to see (and buy) work by contemporary Egyptian painters and sculptors is the Zamalek Art Gallery on the second floor at 11 Sharia Brazil in Zamalek (daily except Fri 10.30am–9pm; ☎02/735-1240, ⓦwww.zamalekartgallery .com), which displays works by some of the most talented new and established Egyptian artists. Also in Zamalek is the Espace Karim Francis, on the third floor of Baehelers Mansions at 157 26th July Street (daily except Mon 4–11pm; ☎02/736-2183, ⓦwww.karimfrancis.com), whose website displays a good sample of its artists' work, while ECIC at 11 Sharia Shagar al-Durr (☎02/736-5410) and Abdel Monem el Sawy Culture Wheel by Zamalek Bridge (☎02/736-6178, ⓦwww.culturewheel.com) both host exhibitions by up-and-coming new talents.

Downtown galleries worth checking out include the Townhouse Gallery at 10 Sharia Nabrawy, off Sharia Champollion (daily except Thurs 10am–2pm & 6–9pm; ☎02/576-8086, ⓦwww.thetownhousegallery.com), and the Mashrabia Gallery for Contemporary Art on the first floor at 8 Sharia Champollion (daily except Fri 11am–8pm; ☎02/578-4494), both of which exhibit work by foreign as well as Egyptian artists. There's also a downtown branch of Espace Karim Francis at 1 Sharia al-Sherrefein, off Sharia Qasr el-Nil, 100m east of Midan Talaat Harb (daily except Fri 2–9pm).

Spices and perfume

As the world's main spice entrepôt from Fatimid times until the eighteenth century, Cairo remains the largest market for perfumes and spices in the Arab world, with some of its business still conducted in bazaars.

Spices and herbs

The Muski end of the **Spice Bazaar** is generally disappointing, with tourist tat impinging on old shops like Donia al-Henaur (incense, spices, candles) and Khedar al-Attar (herbal cures), between the Madrassa of Barsbey and Sharia al-Azhar. However, at the other end of the Souk al-Attarin, a narrow lane behind the Mosque-Madrassa of Al-Ghuri (see map p.165) – the **Haret al-Fahhamin** – is a welter of vivid colours and aromas, mingling with the dirt and stench of ages. Here, piled high and named in Arabic, *'irfa* (cinnamon) and *simsim* (sesame) are still evocative of distant lands. What is sold as saffron (*za'faraan*) is in fact safflower, which is why it seems ridiculously cheap compared with what you'd pay for the real thing back home – real saffron consists of fine red strands only, with no orange or yellow in it at all.

Some shop owners are also **herbalists** (*etara*), whose traditional remedies for every ailment from impotence to constipation are widely used. There are several *etara* on Al-Fahhamin and outside Barsbey's madrassa, but the most famous establishment is Abdul Latif Mahmoud Harraz (39 Sharia Ahmed Maher), opposite a *sabil* 200m west of Bab Zwayla in the Bab el-Khalq quarter, which has been run by the same family since 1885.

Incense and perfume

Just as herbal medicine blends into folk magic (many stalls purvey amulets), both make use of **incense**. The Spice and Perfume bazaars offer the widest range of musks and resins, but you can also find Sudanese vendors squatting beside aromatic cones and medicinal roots in the Ezbekiya Gardens.

Alongside the northern half of the Souk al-Attarin lies a warren of covered alleys that forms the **Perfume Bazaar**. Egypt produces many of the **essences** used by French perfumiers, which are sold by the ounce to be diluted 1:9 in alcohol for perfume, 1:20 for eau de toilette and 1:30 for eau de cologne. Local shops will duplicate famous perfumes for you, or you can buy brand imitations (sometimes unwittingly – always scrutinize labels). Almost all the perfume shops overcharge and cheat – around Talaat Harb especially, but also in the Khan. Boasting that their "pure" essence is undiluted by alcohol, crooked salesmen will omit to mention that oil has been used instead, which is why they rub it into your wrist to remove the sheen. In fact, if you know what you want and you know its name in Arabic, you can buy it from source: the shop the perfume sellers all get their supplies from (note the queue of Egyptian customers) is Karama Perfumes at the corner of Sharia al-Muizz with the Muski, or better still, the shop of the same name two doors up al-Muizz. They may still try to overcharge tourists, but essential oils such as rose or jasmine, for example, should cost around 50pt a gram.

Musical instruments and recordings

Cairo is a good place to buy **traditional musical instruments** such as the *kanoon* (dulcimer), *oud* (lute), *nai* (flute), *rabab* (viol), *mismare baladi* (oboe), *tabla* (drum), *riq* and *duf* (both tambourines; the latter is played by Sufis). All of them are made and sold by half a dozen shops on the west side of **Sharia Qalaa** between Midan Ataba and the Islamic Art Museum (see map p.172), which also deal in Western instruments and cheaper imitations from China.

Traditional instruments are also sold by itinerant vendors, especially during moulids, when a favourite buy is a hand-held dummy that claps its cymbals together when squeezed (known as a *Shoukoukou* after the famous comic monologist).

As the centre of the Arab music world and a melting pot for every tradition (see "Music" pp.839–843), Cairo is a superb place to buy recordings. You won't find anything on vinyl in Cairo, but authorized **cassettes**, and pirated versions of them, are sold from kiosks where it's quite acceptable (indeed, advisable) to listen before buying. Given that non-Arabic labelling is minimal, it helps to recognize labels like *Sout el-Beiruit* (a green cedar-pine logo; Gulf and Levantine music), *SLAM!* (mostly *Al-Jeel* music) and the *Shaabi* imprint *Fel Fel Phone* (which has a retail outlet on Sharia Khulud, near Midan Ramses; see map p.148). The kiosks on Ezbekiya chiefly stock religious and folk cassettes (often cheap, inferior copies). For quality recordings of Umm Kalthoum, Abdel Wahaab and orchestral music, visit Sono Cairo on Sikket Ali Labib Gabr, between Qasr el-Nil and Talaat Harb (opposite the Radio Cinema). **CDs** are less widely available, but there's a good selection of Arabic music on CD at Deals Music Store next to *Deals* bar on Sharia Sayed el-Bakri in Zamalek (daily noon–midnight), and at Diwan bookshop (see below).

Books and newspapers

Egypt is the world's largest publisher of Arabic books and newspapers, so those who know the language can find almost any type of **Arab literature** in Cairo. Aside from magazine and paperback stalls along the downtown thoroughfares, good sources include Dar al-Kitab al-Masri wal-Loubnani (on the first floor of 33 Sharia Qasr el-Nil) and Dar al-Maaref (27 Sharia Abdel Khaliq Sarwat); for Islamic heritage books, try Dar el-Tarath (22 Sharia Gumhorriya) and Ezbekiya Gardens.

Unlike most other places in Egypt, Cairo also has plenty of **books in foreign languages** (chiefly English, French and German). Generally, bookshops charge the original cover price for imported editions – usually at an unfavourable rate. For a huge range of material on all things Egyptian, plus novels, travel guides and dictionaries, visit the American University in Cairo Bookshop at the back of the main campus (daily except Fri 9am–6pm; entrance on Sharia Mohammed Mahmoud), though you'll need ID. There's another branch of the AUC bookshop in Zamalek at 16 Sharia Mohammed Ibn Thakib (Sat–Mon 10am–6pm, Tues–Thurs 10am–7pm, Fri 1–7pm). Another good place for fiction, Egyptology and local literature is Shorouk (1 Midan Talaat Harb), who also sell books online (Ⓦ www.e-kotob.com). Other good downtown bookshops are Lehnert & Landrock (44 Sharia Sherif) and the Anglo-Egyptian Bookshop (169 Sharia Mohammed Farid), which specializes in Arab politics, history and culture, but has an excellent all-round collection. Al-Ahram (165 Sharia Mohammed Farid) also sells books in English. Most of these downtown bookshops are closed on Sunday. In Zamalek, there are a trio of bookshops worth checking: the biggest is Diwan at 159 26th July Street, on the corner of Sharia Ishaq Yaakoub (daily 9am–11.30pm), with a wide selection of books, CDs and DVDs, and a coffee shop. Two smaller places are along Sharia Shagar al-Durr: the Zamalek bookshop opposite *Pub 28*, and Romancia on the corner of Sharia Ismail Mohammed, which has a better selection of maps.

The best place for **second-hand books** is the book market in the north-east corner of Ezbekiya Gardens by Midan Ataba, many of whose titles are in English. Other places selling second-hand books in English include the news-stand opposite the AUC entrance on Sharia Mohammed Mahmoud, and one outside the Algerian embassy on Sharia Brazil in Zamalek (mostly pulps).

Newspapers and magazines

Foreign newspapers and magazines can be found in the bookshops of the five-star hotels or downtown at the stall on Qasr el-Nil, outside *Groppi's*.

The best downtown newsstand is on Sharia Mohammed Mahmoud, opposite the AUC entrance and by *McDonald's*, which carries British dailies (usually one day late), the *International Herald Tribune*, *USA Today* and even sometimes the *New York Times*, plus a few foreign-language novels. The two bookshops on Sharia Shagar al-Durr in Zamalek also stock British papers. When buying weekend editions of British papers, note that colour supplements are sold separately. If you need the latest news you can always check the website of your favourite daily on line. You can sit and read English-language Indian newspapers for free at the Indian embassy visa office, 2nd floor, 37 Sharia Talaat Harb.

Booze and cigarettes

For those who enjoy tippling in their room or want a cache for consumption in "dry" parts of Egypt, there are several places which sell alcohol.

Downtown **liquor stores**, run by Greek or Maronite Christians, maintain a low profile; furtive Muslim customers are served at once, with hardly a word exchanged. The biggest concentration of stores is around the junction of Sharia Talaat Harb with 26th July Street. Outlets include: Orphanides, at 4 Sharia Emad el-Din, and opposite the High Court on 26th July Street; Corinthos (sign in Arabic only) on 26th July, 20m west of Sharia Talaat Harb; Nicolakis, on the corner of Sharia Talaat Harb and Sharia Suq al-Tawfiqia; Gianacus, below the *Hotel Claridge* at 41 Sharia Talaat Harb. All stock Egyptian beer, wine, *zibib*, *raki*, brandy and dubious lookalike brands such as *Johnny Wadie Whisky* (Red and Black labels) and *Gardan's Gin*: checking out the windows can be fun, but you wouldn't want to drink these lookalike brands. Most liquor stores are **open** from mid-afternoon till 8pm, Monday to Friday, and close down entirely during Ramadan and other major Muslim festivals.

Liquor regulations entitle foreigners to buy up to three litres of imported spirits (or two bottles of spirits plus a two-dozen-can carton of beer) at **duty-free prices** within 24 hours of arrival in Egypt, in addition to the two litres you are allowed to bring in from abroad. You can buy these either at the airport, at the Egypt Free Store on Arab League Street in Mohandiseen (who may allow you to make the purchase up to 48 hours after arrival), or at the *Sheraton* in Dokki, but you'll need your passport, as you'll get a stamp in it saying what you've bought.

There is a black market for duty-free booze (Johnny Walker Black Label is the most sought-after brand) if you have – or can be bothered to seek out – a buyer. However, **beware** of Egyptians who accost you in the street asking if you'll buy them some duty-free booze "for my sister's wedding". Buying alcohol for someone else is fine, but under no circumstances should you allow a stranger to be involved in the actual transaction inside the store. The paperwork for any duty-free purchase is filled out in Arabic, and some travellers have discovered on leaving Egypt that a TV or video has been bought duty-free with their passport. Being unable to produce the item for customs officials, they've had to pay duty on it, just as if they'd purchased and then sold it while in Egypt.

With **cigarettes** available on every corner, only smokers addicted to certain foreign brands need hunt down specialist outlets. Babik, in the passage by 39 Sharia Talaat Harb, and Smoker's Corner, on Midan Talaat Harb, sell numerous brands of cigarette papers and other smokers' requisites. Refilling stalls all over the city can recharge your lighter (even if it's "non-refillable") for 50–75pt, or change flints for 25pt.

Money

Though rates of exchange vary slightly, **banks** are chiefly distinguished by their opening hours and relative (in)efficiency. All the main banks are well represented in Cairo, and most of them open Sunday through Thursday, 8.30am to 2pm (9.30am to 1.30pm or thereabouts during Ramadan).

Aside from Thomas Cook or American Express (see below), it's usually quickest to **exchange money** or **travellers' cheques** at the **24-hour** Bank Misr exchange bureaux in the *Nile Hilton* and the *Ramses Hilton*, and outside the *Helnan Shepheard*; or at branches in other major hotels, which are open daily till 8pm. However, none of the banks will change New Zealand dollars, or Scottish and Northern Irish sterling banknotes, and most will not change Israeli shekels (Bank Misr at the *Nile Hilton* is an exception).

An increasing number of **ATMs** (Bank Misr, National Bank of Egypt, NSGB, HSBC and others) now accept cashcards and credit cards, especially on the streets around Sharia Talaat Harb in the downtown area, but also in Zamalek, Mohandiseen, along Sharia Tahrir in Dokki, and in most commercial areas. Malls and five-star hotels also have them. Most ATMs will take Visa, Master-Card, Cirrus, Electron and Plus, but it's a good idea to use machines in tourist areas as these are less likely to reject or swallow foreign cards, and it will be easier to explain what has happened if they do.

Forex

Faster and often giving a better rate for cash than banks, **private exchange bureaux** – known as **Forex** – are usually open daily. Unlike banks, they will usually change Cyprus pounds, Jordanian and Libyan dinars and sometimes Israeli shekels, though not Sudanese pounds, New Zealand dollars, nor Scottish and Northern Irish sterling banknotes. Some will accept travellers' cheques, but at a worse rate than banks, and they may demand to see receipts. Downtown Forex bureaux include Horus at 9 Sharia Alfi Bey, and others at 6 Sharia el-Bustan, 29 Sharia Emad el-Din by the *New Cicil Hotel*, on the corner of Sharia Qasr el-Nil and Sharia Sherif, three on Qasr el-Nil by Sharia el-Gumhoriyya, and one on Sharia Mohammed Sabri at the corner of Sharia Mansur.

American Express

Aside from its overpriced tours and travel services, **American Express** (Amex for short) can be useful to travellers. The main office at 15 Sharia Qasr el-Nil (daily except Fri 9am–4pm; during Ramadan 9am–2.30pm; ☎02/574-7991, 2, 3, 4, 5 or 6, ⊕578-4003) is the best place to send money or letters, although the mail service (closed Fri) is only available to holders of Amex travellers' cheques or cards. As a rule, it's quicker to change foreign currency or Amex cheques here than in commercial banks. Refunds for lost or stolen cards or travellers' cheques can take weeks, though they claim it's the next day. Amex is acutely suspicious of fraud, which is widespread in Cairo.

Other Amex branches can be found in the *Nile Hilton* (☎02/578-5001), on the 10th floor of the Nile Tower at 21 Sharia Giza in Giza (☎02/570-3411), and 72 Sharia Omar Ibn al-Khattab in Heliopolis (☎02/418-2144). Most branches will allow cardholders to draw out emergency cash on a personal cheque, and will also pay out US$ for Amex travellers' cheques.

Thomas Cook

The modern-day descendant of the world's first tourist company, **Thomas Cook** can change foreign currency and most brands of travellers' cheques into

Egyptian money. Their central branch at 17 Sharia Bassiouni (daily 8am–5pm; ☎02/574-3955, ⓕ576-2750) also sells travellers' cheques in return for dollars or sterling, and will change travellers' cheques for hard currency. However, they have a bad reputation when it comes to lost or stolen travellers' cheques; you may have to kick up a fuss – or even demonstrate outside – to get a full refund.

There are **other branches** of Thomas Cook in the **Semiramis Intercontinental** (☎02/795-8544), at the airport (terminal 1, ☎02/265-3147), in Heliopolis (7 Sharia Baghdad ☎02/417-3511; and 33 Sharia Nabil el Wakkad ☎02/419-4082), Mohandiseen (10 26th July St ☎02/346-7187), Zamalek (3 Sharia Abul Feda, ☎02/735-9223) and Ma'adi (88 Street 9, Station Square ☎02/359-1419).

Money transfers

There are several ways of **transferring money from abroad**. Transfers using MoneyGram (see p.59) can be picked up at any office of Thomas Cook, either in Egyptian pounds or, with a 1-percent commission charge, in US dollars. MoneyGram's other agent in central Cairo is Sphinx Trading, 2 Sharia Sherif. Western Union transfers (see p.59) can be picked up at branches of Misr America Bank (most centrally at 4D Sharia el-Gumhoriyya or 19 Sharia Qasr el-Nil), or at branches of Intel Business Associates (1079 Corniche el-Nil, Garden City ☎02/797-1385 or 6, open daily except Fri 9am–9pm).

In order to send money by bank transfer, you will probably have to open an account with a bank in Cairo first. Banks with good international connections include Barclays on Sharia Qasr al-Aini (☎02/366-3725, ⓕ795-2746), and Bank of America, 106 Sharia Qasr al-Aini (☎02/354-7528, ⓕ355-5023), with a good reputation for transfers from the US.

If you wish to use money received at banks to **buy travellers' cheques** at Thomas Cook or Amex, you must produce a Certificate of Transaction (which you have to request at the issuing bank) rather than an ordinary exchange receipt, proving that your Egyptian currency was legally acquired.

Bureaucracy

Most foreigners are no longer required to register with the authorities when entering Egypt; however, any **bureaucratic matters** involving visa extensions, travel permits and the like are almost certain to induce frustration. There's little choice but to relax and go with the flow – we've included some guidelines here to help ease your way through the ordeal.

Visa extensions at the Mugamma

Extending your visa entails visiting the **Mugamma**, that bureaucratic behemoth on Midan Tahrir (daily except Fri 8am–2pm). Display patience and good humour when dealing with the Mugamma; only stage a tantrum or nervous breakdown as a last resort. To avoid the crush, arrive first thing in the morning or during the evening shift. Unless you're certain which numbered "window" is currently appropriate (details below may become outmoded), check with the **information** desk upstairs on the first floor, before going through the door on your left.

For a **tourist visa extension**, go to window #38 – accessed via entrance 4 on the same floor – and pick up a form. You need to provide a passport photo plus a photocopy of the page in your passport with your photo and personal details, and also the page which carries your original visa – there are copying facilities on the ground floor. Take your form to window #47 to get a stamp (£E8), and then back to window #38 where your new visa will be issued. This may be done the same day or the next day, or it may take as long as two weeks, depending on your nationality and the length of stay you ask for. **Re-entry visas** are handled at windows #1–4. They cost £E13.10–16.10 depending on how many entries you need, and you should apply before 1pm, collecting the visa the following day at 2pm. In case of lost or stolen passports (see below), replacement entry stamps are obtainable from rooms #1 and #2; however, these may not pass muster with the Libyan or Sudanese consulates.

Travel permits for restricted areas

Permits to travel in restricted areas (off-*piste* in the deep desert; on minor Delta and Sinai roads; between Mersa Alam and the Sudanese border) are usually issued by Military Intelligence (Mukaharabat 26), whose office is in Sharia Manshia el-Bakry in Heliopolis. Rather than apply to them directly, however, your first approach should be to Misr Travel at 1 Sharia Talaat Harb, who may be able to help you obtain certain permits, or to the Tourist Police at 5 Sharia Adly. You will need to show that you have a good reason for wanting to be in the area in question. Applications will require two photos and photocopies of the identifying pages of your passport and your Egyptian entry visa, plus justification for your journey. Processing takes anywhere between four and fourteen days. You should not need any special permit to travel directly from Mersa Matrouh to the Libyan border, for example if taking a bus or service taxi to Benghazi or Tripoli, but this does sometimes change so it is wise to check first.

Student cards

ISIC student cards, as well as youth (under-26) and teacher cards, are obtainable at Egyptian Student Travel Services, 23 Sharia el-Manial on Roda Island (☎02/531-0330, ⓦwww.estsegypt.com; daily except Fri 8am–8pm, Fri 9am–6pm). You can get there by walking from El-Malek el-Suleh metro. The card costs £E65, and you'll need one passport photo as well as proof of student status – a letter or ID card from your own university is best. Beware of any offers to obtain student cards without proof of scholarly status: the cards are likely to be forgeries, and the tourist police may not be amused if you try to use them at archeological sites.

Passport photos, photocopying and translations

Passport photos can be obtained from the studio in room #99 on the ground floor of the Mugamma (eight colour photos for £E15), or from photo booths in places like the *Nile Hilton* and even some metro stations. Mitry Colour, 3rd floor, 127 Sharia Ramses, at the corner of Sharia Khan el-Khouly (Mon–Sat 10am–10pm, Sun 10am–7pm), charges £E15 for eight photos while you wait, but only £E5 for a dozen photos plus one large print if you are prepared to come back the next day to collect them. The Kodak Shop, 20 Sharia Adly (daily 9am–9pm), has a digital camera and charges £E18 for twenty photos ready in five minutes – and you can have as many poses as you want.

Several shops along 26th July Street and Sharia Mahmoud (near the AUC Library) advertise **photocopying** services. For **translations**, contact Fouad Nemah, 2nd floor, 37 Sharia Qasr el-Nil (☎02/392-2124; ⓔfouad _nemah@hotmail.com), or 14a Sharia Sherif, Heliopolis (☎02/450-6219; both offices open Mon–Thurs & Suns 9.30am–3pm).

Embassies, foreign visas and missing passports

Cairo is a major centre for acquiring visas, and travellers embarking on trans-African or Middle Eastern journeys, or long-distance flights, would do well to sort things out here. Most embassies and consulates are in Garden City, Zamalek, Dokki or Mohandiseen. Since everyday business is handled by consulates rather than embassies, we've listed the former only if there are two separate addresses.

For those applying for **foreign visas**, a few countries require you to provide a **letter of recommendation** – which basically approves your visa application – from your own embassy. For some nationalities they're free, while others have to pay through the nose for them. Americans should note that their embassy may decline to issue letters of recommendation for its citizens to visit countries whose governments are considered hostile to the US.

Lost or stolen passports should be reported to the police as soon as possible. You'll receive a slip of paper indicating the police file number; take this and two photos plus any personal ID to your consulate to apply for a new passport. Then bring this and the police report to the Mugamma for verification of entry (see p.289). You'll also need to obtain a new Egyptian visa.

Australia 11th floor, World Trade Centre, 1191 Corniche el-Nil, Bulaq; 200m north of the 26th July Bridge ☎02/575-0444, ✉austremb@dfat.gov.au, out-of-hours emergency number ☎012/213-7232. Letters of recommendation £E30. Mon–Wed & Sun 8.30am–noon & 1.30–4pm, Thurs 8.30am–1.30pm.

Canada 26 Sharia Kamel el-Shenawi, Garden City ☎02/794-3110, ⓦwww.canada-eg.com (see map p.192). Letters of recommendation £E250. Mon–Thurs & Sun 9am–2pm.

Eritrea 6 Sharia el-Fellah, Mohandiseen ☎02/303-3503 (see map p.210). Visas cost £E260 plus one passport photo; no letter of recommendation required. Mon–Thurs & Sun 8–11am.

Ethiopia 2 Midan al-Misaha, Dokki ☎02/335-3696 (see map p.211). One photo, but no letter of recommendation required. Visas (US$20 single-entry, US$30 multiple-entry) are issued in 24hr. Mon–Thurs & Sat 9am–noon.

Ireland 7th floor, Abu el-Feda Tower, just north of the Zamalek Bridge, Zamalek ☎02/735-8264 (see map p.210). Free letters of recommendation. Mon–Thurs & Sun 9am–noon.

Israel 6 Mohammed al-Durri, Giza, near the El-Gama'a Bridge ☎02/761-0458 (see map p.192). Look for the security guards at the entrance or the Israeli flag flying aloft. Most foreigners can obtain tourist visas at the border. Mon–Thurs & Sun 10.30am–12.30pm.

Jordan 6 Sharia Gohini, Dokki, 2 blocks west of the Sheraton ☎02/749-9912, ⓕ760-1027 (see map p.211). Most nationalities can obtain their visa at the Eilat–Aqaba border, or on arrival by boat at Aqaba, or at Amman airport. Mon–Thurs 9.30am–2pm.

Libya 7 Sharia Saleh el-Ayoub, Zamalek ☎02/735-1269, ⓕ735-0072 (see map p.210). Visas generally only issued to Egyptian residents, but they may be open to persuasion if you have an invitation from someone in Libya. A photo and a photocopy of the relevent pages of your passport are required, but letters of recommendation and translation of your passport details apparently are no longer necessary. Daily except Tues & Fri 10am–noon.

New Zealand c/o Emeco Travel Services, 4th floor, 2 Sharia Talaat Harb ☎02/574-9360 (see map p.126). Letters of recommendation £E66. Mon–Thurs & Sun 9am–5pm.

Palestine 33 Sharia el-Nahda, Dokki ☎02/338-4761. Mon–Thurs & Sun 8am–4pm.

Saudi Arabia 2 Sharia Ahmed Nessim, Giza ☎02/ⓕ760-4560, ⓕ760-4590 (see map p.211).

Sudan 1 Sharia Mohammed Fahmi el-Sayed, Garden City (see map p.192) ☎02/794-9661. Two photos, $100 (in US dollars only) and a letter of recommendation needed (the US embassy is unlikely to issue this for travel to Sudan); one-month visas usually issued the same day. Mon–Thurs & Sun apply 9–11am, collect 2–3pm.

Syria 18 Sharia Abdel Raheem Sabry, Dokki ☎02/749-5210, ⓕ335-8232 (see map p.211). Currently issuing visas to Egyptian residents only, so get your Syrian visa at home. Mon–Thurs & Sun 9am–2pm.

UK 7 Sharia Ahmed Ragheb, Garden City ☎02/794-0852, ⓕ794-3065, ⓦwww .britishembassy.org.eg (see map p.126). Sniffily refuse to issue letters of recommendation, but will do you a letter to say so (that hopefully will serve the same purpose) for £E145. Mon–Thurs & Sun 9.30am–1.30pm.

USA 5 Sharia Amerika Latina, Garden City ☎02/797-2301, ℉797-3602, emergencies ☎797-3300 (see map p.126). Lost or stolen

passports replaced for US$85; limited passports issued for travel to Israel on request. Letters of recommendation are free, but the embassy may refuse to issue them for travel to countries it considers unsafe, in particular those with regimes opposed by the US government. Mon–Thurs & Sun 8am–noon (open for phone enquiries 8am–4.30pm).

Cultural centres, clubs and language courses

Cultural centres are useful for catching up on home news and making contacts. Most have libraries – some open to all, others requiring membership – and some offer free lectures, and paid language courses, though usually for the language of their own country rather than Arabic. If you want to **learn Arabic**, there are some good schools in Cairo that teach the two different types: Modern Standard Arabic (MSA) is what the newpapers are written in, and is essentially the written form of the language; while Egyptian Colloquial Arabic is what people speak on the street, and is not usually written. It differs substantially from the Arabic spoken in other countries, though people in most of the Arab world should understand the Egyptian form. A few schools offer the option to study both MSA and Egyptian Colloquial Arabic, or check the noticeboards at AUC and at *Bon Appetit* in Sharia Mohammed Mahmoud (see p.258) to find a **private tutor**.

Cultural centres

American Research Center in Egypt 1st floor, 2 Midan Simon Bolivar, Garden City ☎02/794-8239. Organizes lectures and day-trips.
British Council 192 Corniche el-Nil, Aguza, near the Circus ☎02/300-1666, ⓦ www.britishcouncil.org.eg. Large library (annual membership £E200), including videos, cassettes and Internet access. Also sponsors visiting cultural acts. Daily except Fri 8am–8pm.
Egyptian Centre for International Cultural Cooperation (ECIC) 11 Sharia Shagar al-Durr, Zamalek ☎02/736-5410, ℮ eg_center@hotmai.com.

Organizes Arabic classes, exhibitions, recitals and occasional tours. Daily except Fri 10am–5pm.
Maulana Azad Indian Cultural Centre Mamor el Shay el Hendy, of Sharia Talaat Harb by no.21 ☎02/393-3396. Has a library open to all (for reading – borrowing for members only). Also offers yoga classes. Mon–Thurs & Sun 10am–5.30pm.
Netherlands–Flemish Institute 1 Sharia Mahmoud Azmi, Zamalek ☎02/738-2527. English lectures about Egypt (Sept–June) on Thurs at 6pm – try to turn up early. Open Mon–Fri 9am–2pm.

Language schools

AUC Public Service Division room #110, 28 Sharia Falaki ☎02/797-6872 or 3, ℮ arabcace@aucegypt.edu. Well respected and extremely central, though their language-teaching methods may not be quite so up-to-date as at Kalimat or the ILI.
Egyptian Centre for International Cultural Cooperation (ECIC) (see above). Classes are cheaper here than at the other language schools listed.

International Language Institute (ILI) 2 Sharia Mohammed Bayoumi, off Sharia Merghani, Heliopolis ☎02/418-9212 or 291-9295, ℮ ili@idsc.net.eg. Approved by International House in London, which means that they use the latest language-teaching techniques.
International Language Institute (ILI) 4 Sharia Mahmoud Azmi, Sahafayeen (north of Mohandiseen) ☎02/346-3087, ⓦ www.arabicegypt.com. No connection with the Heliopolis ILI, but also

IH-approved with the latest techniques. Offers combined MSA and Egyptian Colloquial courses. **Kalimat Language and Cultural Centre** 22 Sharia al-Koroum, behind Mohammed Mustafa Mosque, Mohandiseen ☎02/761-8136, ⓦwww .kalimategypt.com. Set up by former-British-Council teachers of Arabic.

Health care

For minor complaints, consult the nearest **pharmacy**: pharmacists can prescribe a wide range of drugs, including antibiotics. There are a number of 24-hour pharmacies, including: Al-Esa'af, 27 26th July St, at the junction with Sharia Ramses ☎02/574-3369; Atalla, 13 Sharia Sherif, at the junction with Sharia Mohammed Sabri ☎02/393-9029; El-Ezaby in Ramses station ☎02/575-6272 (and with branches citywide); and Abdallah, 2 Sharia Tahar Hussein, Zamalek ☎02/738-1988. In cases of emergency, these pharmacies will also deliver medicines, usually for free.

There are English- or French-speaking **private doctors** all over Cairo; evenings (7–10pm) are generally the best time to get hold of them. A consultation with a reasonably upmarket, English-speaking doctor normally costs around £E100, which doesn't include drugs, but should cover a follow-up visit. Some practices that are used to foreign patients include: Dr Naguib Badir at the Anglo-American Hospital, next to the Cairo Tower on Gezira Island (general practice; ☎02/735-6162, 3, 4 or 5); Dr Doss or Dr Emad Rushdi, *Nile Hilton Hotel* clinic (☎02/578-0444); and Dr Magdy Francis (☎02/749-0818). If you need a **dentist**, try Dr Avedis Djeghalian, 6 Sharia Abdel Hamid Said (☎02/577-7909), or Dr Emad Zaghloul (☎02/345 5429), at Midan Loubnan in Mohandiseen.

Hospitals require a cash deposit of at least £E150 (it can go as high as £E1000) to cover the cost of treatment; medical insurance is not always accepted (though you can reclaim expenses later). The following are well equipped and used to foreigners: Anglo-American Hospital by Cairo Tower, Gezira ☎02/735-6162, 3, 4 or 5; Al-Salam International Hospital, on the Corniche in Ma'adi ☎02/524-0077; and Cairo Medical Centre, on Sharia al-Ansari, just off Sharia Higaz by Midan Roxi, Heliopolis ☎02/450-9800. For any of these hospitals, take a taxi if you can; otherwise use the private **Al-Salam ambulance service** (same phone numbers as the hospital). **Public ambulances** offer free transport to whichever hospital is the nearest: call ☎123.

There are two or three places that provide **vaccinations** against cholera, yellow fever and other diseases. The main one is the Egyptian Organization for Biological Products and Vaccines (Vacsera), at 51 Sharia Wazart el-Zaraa (☎02/761-1111; daily 24hr), 100m north of the 6th October Bridge/Agricultural Museum intersection – take the first right inside the gate, then go round the side of the building on the left. It has English-speaking doctors and vaccines against cholera (£E6), typhoid (£E6) and meningitis (£E55); they can give yellow fever vaccinations (£E70), but they cannot issue the certificate you'll need to prove that you've had the jab if travelling to countries south of the Sahara. There's also another branch of Vacsera in Midan Giza opposite the metro station. The Public Health Vaccination Centre (daily except Fri 10am–7pm), at the rear of the lobby of the largely disused *Hotel Continental-Savoy* on Midan Opera, is highly efficient, with no red tape or fuss, and does yellow fever jabs for £E64.50, including the certificate, and cholera (£E10.50), but no others.

Post and telecommunications

The **central post office** is on Midan Ataba (daily except Fri 8am–8pm, during Ramadan 9am–3pm), with branches (daily except Fri 8am–6pm, during Ramadan 9am–3pm) citywide, including one on Sharia Tahrir by Midan Falaki, one on Sharia Ramses by the junction with 26th July Street, one in Ramses station, and one on Sharia al-Azhar near Al-Azhar Mosque. Mail can be sent to Ataba's **poste restante** or general delivery office (daily except Fri 7am–7pm, Ramadan 8am–4pm; Poste Restante, Post Office Ataba, 11511 Cairo). The entrance for the poste restante counter is in Sharia al-Bedak, round the corner from the main entrance, to the right of the building as you look at it – go to the last door, signposted "Private boxes", and it's inside at counter #10. They hold mail for a month, with no charge to collect – just be sure to bring your passport. They are prone to file letters under the wrong name, but it helps if your surname is underlined and highlighted on anything sent to you. Problems are less likely to occur if you have mail sent **c/o American Express** on Sharia Qasr el-Nil (see p.288); however, this service is only for holders of Amex cards or Amex travellers' cheques.

Although letters posted in the lobby of the *Nile Hilton* are said to arrive faster than those dropped in ordinary mailboxes (painted blue for overseas mail), **airmail letters** can still take two weeks to reach the British Isles, and three weeks to the US. However, Ataba's **express mail service** – opposite the Poste Restante – (daily except Fri 8am–7pm) promises worldwide delivery in three to four working days; items under 500 grams cost £E128.70 to Britain or Ireland, £E136.40 to North America, or £E146.30 to Australia or New Zealand. Any post office can send **registered letters**. You can also buy **stamps** from hotel shops or cigarette kiosks, which charge about 5pt above normal rates (£E1.50 for a postcard/letter to anywhere in the world).

Parcels can only be mailed abroad from the Ramses Square post office, round the back (the north side of the building), in an office marked "Export Section for Foreign Parcels" (daily except Fri 9am–2.30pm). Your package should be taken in unsealed, submitted to customs for inspection, packaged up (this is done for you on the premises for £E5), and finally weighed and dispatched. Current airmail prices for a 10kg package are: £E505 to the UK or Ireland, £E767 to the USA, £E733 to Canada, £E931 to Australia, and £E1030 to New Zealand. Surface mail is much slower (2–6 months), and saves you little money unless you are sending something very heavy (in which case a shipping agent would be better). To **receive a parcel**, you'll need to go to the main entrance (east side) of the same building, fourth floor, and be aware that you may well be charged **import duty** (for example, as much as £E60 on a pair of contact lenses).

A faster, more reliable, but pricier way of sending and receiving packages is by **courier**. International courier companies with offices in Cairo include DHL, 38 Abdel Khaliq Sarwat (☎02/302-9801, ⓦwww.dhl.com/wrd/eg.html), also with branches in Garden City and Heliopolis; and UPS, c/o Loutfy Mansour, 8 Road 78, Ma'adi (☎02/750-8555).

Phones

Cairo's telephone system keeps on being restructured, and the first three digits of Cairo phone numbers (indicating the local exchange) are liable to change. **International calls** can be made using phonecards (see Basics, p.74) in Menatel cardphones at street corners citywide, at Cairo's main **telephone and telegraph offices** (open 24hr), and other locations. There are four main offices: at 8 Sharia Adly; alongside the *Windsor Hotel* on Alfi Bey; on Sharia

Ramses, opposite Sharia Tawfiqia; and 13 Midan Tahrir (the smallest). There are others in Midan Ataba and further afield, sometimes worth trying if you want to avoid queuing; for example, the one on Sharia Maglis al-Shad, by the National Assembly (ten minutes south of Midan Tahrir). Calls are booked and paid for in advance, and can either be taken in a booth or directed to an outside number such as a hotel.

Faxes

Faxes can be sent and received at the four downtown telephone offices (open 24hr) and the EMS office by Ataba post office (daily except Fri 8am–9pm). The EMS office is slightly cheaper to send faxes (British Isles or North America £E5 for the first minute, £E3.25 thereafter; Australia and New Zealand £E6 for the first minute, £E4.95 thereafter), than the phone offices (£E5 per minute to the British Isles or North America; £E6.50 to Australia or New Zealand), but to receive a fax costs £E1.10 at EMS, and 60pt at the telephone offices. American Express clients can receive faxes free at their office. EMS and the phone offices will inform you of your fax's arrival if your name and phone number are at the top of the page. Fax numbers: Amex ⓕ02/574-7997; EMS ⓕ02/390-4250; downtown telephone offices at Sharia Adly ⓕ02/393-3909, Sharia Ramses ⓕ02/578-0977, Alfi Bey ⓕ02/589-7635, Midan Tahrir ⓕ02/578-0979.

Internet and email

Internet offices open and close with dazzling frequency, and the newest ones are likely to offer the lowest rates. You should have no trouble finding offices that charge £E5 an hour, and connections at all of them are reasonable, though few have fast broadband connections. Downtown, Hany at 16 Abdel Khaliq Sarwat is open 24/7 and currently charges only £E3 an hour. Alternatives include 4U at 6 Midan Talaat Harb (daily 8am–midnight; £E5/hr), and Five Stars at 3 Sharia Talaat Harb (daily 8am–2am; £E4/hr). In Zamalek there's an Internet café at the Zamalek Center, 25 Sharia Ismail Mohammed (daily 8am–midnight; £E4/hr). Some hotels also offer cheap Internet connections for their guests.

Excursions from Cairo

The Nile Valley – most people's target after Cairo – is too distant for **day excursions** from the city. Elsewhere, however, you can choose between a jaunt to the seaside or remoter pyramids, a river trip or desert monasteries – and still be back in Cairo the same night. The notes below are an outline of possibilities and are intended (with the exception of the entries on the Nile Barrages and Muqattam Hills) to be used in conjunction with the full accounts in other chapters.

Those without the time to organize their own excursions might consider taking a set or **tailor-made tour** organized by a reputable travel agent or tour company (and there are plenty of disreputable ones about, so beware). Those worth trying include Noga Tours (28 Sharia Quday Shubra ⓣ02/203-9310, ⓦwww.first24hours.com) and Eastmar Tours (in the passage of 13 Sharia Qasr el-Nil ⓣ02/574-5024, ⓦwww.eastmar-travel.com).

The Nile Barrages at Qanatir

Roughly 20km downriver from Cairo, the Nile divides into two great branches which define the Delta, whose flow is controlled by the **Nile Barrages** at

Qanatir. Decoratively arched and turreted, this splendid piece of Victorian civil engineering is surrounded by shady parks and lush islets – an ideal spot for a picnic.

Originally conceived by Mohammed Ali's French hydro-engineer, Mougel Bey, the Barrages were later realized as part of the nationwide hydrological system designed by Sir Colin Scott-Moncrieff. At the eastern end of the 438-metre-long Rosetta Barrage lies the *Istarahah al-Qanatir* or **Presidential Villa** that Islamic Jihad once considered attacking with an anti-aircraft cannon from the garden of one of their member's homes, across the river. Egypt's **State Yacht** (originally King Farouk's, on which he sailed into exile) is often moored at the quay.

Providing you don't come on Friday, when the area is ridiculously crowded, the Barrages make a pleasant excursion. Qanatir is accessible by bus #210 from the Abdel Mouneem Riyad terminal on Midan Tahrir, or by ferry from the Maspero Dock in front of the Television Building. Ferries leave hourly (6am–6pm; £E5) and take two hours; or you can take a pleasure boat (daily round trips departing around 9am; £E6) to the south of Maspero Dock; the bus journey is less appealing. Travelling by felucca is very slow, since the mast has to be lowered at every bridge.

The Muqattam Hills and Wadi Digla

The **Muqattam Hills**, rising beyond Cairo, are seldom visited by tourists but readily accessible by #951 bus from Abdel Mouneem Riyad, or #401 from Midan Ataba. Zigzagging up the hillside past caves and quarries, ruined shrines and guarded outposts, buses terminate at **Medinet Muqattam**, an upmarket suburb whose avenues are flanked by villas and casinos. The Muqattam Corniche, circling the edge of the plateau, offers spectacular views across the Citadel and most of Cairo – an unforgettable vista at sunset.

People planning desert expeditions might consider a few training runs below the Muqattam. Victorian travellers used to engage a dragoman to lead them to the **Petrified Forests** – two expanses littered with broken, fossilized trunks, thought to date from the Miocene Period. The larger one (marked on our map of Greater Cairo) is really only accessible with a guide, but would-be explorers can easily find the "Little Forest" on the Jebel el-Khasab plateau, north of the Digla–Ain Sukhna road.

The **Digla–Ain Sukhna road** turns east off the Nile Valley expressway near a *zebaleen* village beyond Ma'adi. Roughly 25km from the turn-off, you'll pass the Jebel el-Khasab on the left; if you keep on, you'll notice various tracks leading off to the right, which eventually converge on a main desert track running east–west. By following it west, back towards Digla, you'll pass through several meandering *wadis* before the way is blocked by **Wadi Digla**. This miniature canyon is good for **rock-climbing** and **bird-watching**; bring water, food and shade.

The Fayoum

Fayoum Oasis, 100km southwest of Cairo, is another place to escape. Though Fayoum City holds little appeal, you can walk from its centre into lush countryside within half an hour. Irrigated by water wheels and canals, the Fayoum was a major centre during the Middle Kingdom, Ptolemaic and Roman times, as evinced by various ruins around its periphery. While some involve bumpy rides into the desert, others are reasonably accessible from Fayoum City by local bus or service taxi, with a pleasant walk to the site itself. The **ruins of Karanis** lie just off the Fayoum–Cairo road; the dramatic **"Collapsed Pyramid"** of

Maidum is a short ride from El-Wasta. Both sites are usually deserted, in blissful contrast to Giza and Saqqara. Either makes a good day excursion, but you should bring food and drink and be on your way by mid-morning. Service taxis from Midan Giza, or from Sharia Orabi near Ramses station, are the fastest way of reaching Fayoum City (2hr): see p.514 for details. The Maidum pyramid (see p.527) can be reached by service taxi from El-Wasta station, which is served by trains that leave pretty much hourly from Ramses, stopping at Giza station (where there are also a few extra services), and taking between an hour and a quarter and an hour and a half to reach El-Wasta.

Alexandria and the Monasteries of Wadi Natrun

A three-hour journey from Cairo, Egypt's second city and summer capital embraces the Mediterranean with its sweeping Corniche. **Alexandria** has little to show for its ancient glory (personified by Cleopatra) or former decadence (celebrated by Lawrence Durrell), but its fresh seafood and cool breezes are delightful. Aside from a quick spin through the Greco-Roman museum and a literary pilgrimage around the haunts of Durrell, E.M. Forster and the poet Constantine Cavafy, Alexandria's attractions include a Royal Jewellery Museum housed in a spectacularly over-the-top mansion, and the rather spooky Catacombs of Kom es-Shoqafa. With the discovery of Cleopatra's Palace on the ocean floor in Alex's Eastern Harbour (see p.626 for details), there may soon be even more to occupy visitors. Alex can be reached by bus from Aboud terminal (departures every 45min), train from Ramses station (2hr 10min on the *Turbino*), or service taxi from either of those (Aboud has more departures): for details, see p.300.

The Desert Road to Alex passes the turn-off for the fortified **Monasteries of Wadi Natrun**, which have long provided the Coptic Church's spiritual leadership. When not undergoing periodic fasts, the monks welcome pilgrims and other visitors. The most accessible of the monasteries are **Deir Anba Bishoi** and **Deir al-Suryani**, 10km from the rest stop on the highway (which can be reached by bus or service taxi from Cairo). To visit all four, it's best to rent a taxi or car for the day, either in Cairo or at the rest stop, which is roughly midway between Alexandria and Cairo. For more on Wadi Natrun and how to get there, see p.509.

Unless you start very early or have a car, it's not really feasible to visit both Alexandria and the monasteries in one day.

Ismailiya, Ain Sukhna and the Red Sea Monasteries

The canal city of **Ismailiya** is verdantly peaceful, with handsome promenades and colonial-era villas – a nice place to stroll or bicycle, also favoured by Egyptians as a honeymoon destination. Its museum and Garden of Stelae attest to ancient canals that once linked the Delta with the Red Sea; the House of Ferdinand de Lesseps commemorates the founder of the Suez Canal, one of the world's crucial waterways. Outside town you can watch boats slip between the desert on either side. Along the eastern embankment runs the Bar-Lev Line, a fortified Israeli barrier that was stormed on the first day of the 1973 war. Ismailiya itself can be reached by bus from Turgoman Garage or service taxi from Sharia Orabi near Ramses station (2–3hr). For details, see Chapter Six (p.687).

Cairenes with transport visit **Ain Sukhna** on the Gulf of Suez for its **beaches** and offshore coral reefs. If you fancy swimming and **snorkelling**, it's worth renting a car for the day rather than switching buses at Suez and having to hitch back. Bring food and drink (plus snorkel if required), since they're not obtainable there. Don't wander into areas ringed by barbed wire, which are still mined. Ain Sukhna is approachable via Suez (3hr) or by the Digla–Ain Sukhna desert road. Further south and high inland are the **Red Sea Monasteries** of St Paul and St Anthony. With a car, you could combine a visit to St Anthony's with a swim at Ain Sukhna, but unless you leave at the crack of dawn it's impossible to get to both monasteries and return the same night. All three places are described in Chapter Eight (pp.769–772).

Travel details

Cairo is the linchpin of Egypt's transport network and its main link to the outside world. Many parts of the country are accessible from the capital by several forms of transport, while numerous airlines compete over flights to Europe, Africa and Asia.

Trains

All trains depart from **Ramses Station** (*Mahatat Ramses*), a cavernous beehive seemingly designed to bemuse. Almost all trains to points south halt at Giza Station, 15min after leaving Ramses. Entering Ramses Station from Midan Ramses, you'll find the **tourist information office**, tourist police and sleeper booking offices on the left; to your right are platforms 1–4, serving Alexandria, the Delta and Canal Zone. Tickets for air-conditioned services to these destinations are sold at the far end of the main hall, directly opposite the main entrance from Midan Ramses, but if you want to use a slow, non-air-conditioned train, you'll find the ticket office outside, through the doorway to the left of the a/c ticket office.

To the right of the a/c ticket office is the doorway through to platforms 8–11, where southbound trains depart for Middle and Upper Egypt. All tickets for trains on this route, bar sleepers, are sold from offices alongside the furthest platform, #11, accessible via an underpass. Note that foreigners travelling to Upper Egypt are only allowed to use certain services (see p.310).

Opposite platform 4, a round **information kiosk** (☎ 02/575-3555) should in theory be able to advise on departures, schedules and any problems you may have with ticket buying, but you may need to fall back on the tourist office (☎ 02/579-0767) if no one in the information booth can speak English.

There is a **left luggage** (baggage deposit) office by platform 1, open 24/7 and charging £E2.50 per item per day.

Tickets

Buying tickets is rarely easy. In addition to there being separate offices for northbound services (by platform 4) and southbound services (by platform 11), each section has separate windows for 1st class/2nd class superior seating (which is reservable and has a/c) and ordinary 2nd class/3rd class (which isn't and doesn't), and these may change locations. You have to find the right queue and get your requirements (it helps to have them written down in Arabic) across to clerks who may not give a damn. Tickets can be booked up to a week in advance and should be booked at least a day in advance; 1st and 2nd class superior seats sell out first. The peak seasons for travel are winter (for Upper Egypt) and summer (for Alexandria).

Card-carrying **students** are eligible for 30-percent reductions on all trains except sleepers, which must be booked at their own counters in the main hall. Prices given below are full adult fares.

Regular services

At present, full train **timetables** are not available in leaflet or booklet form, but are posted up, in Arabic only, at various points around the station. Unless you can read Arabic, you will have to ask for help from the information office or from friendly passers-by. All services are individually numbered, and the number should be written on your ticket when you reserve a seat. Foreigners are not encouraged to buy ordinary 2nd or 3rd class tickets, and are not allowed to use ordinary services to Upper Egypt (see p.310).

There are two kinds of services to **Alexandria**: air-conditioned and not. Thirteen trains a day are air-conditioned, which also means fast with limited stops, and require reservations. These air-conditioned trains come in three varieties: Turbini, Spanish and French. The three daily non-stop Turbini trains are the best (currently departing at 10.10am, 4.10pm and 9.10pm; 2hr 10min), followed by the four daily Spanish trains, which are also non-stop (2hr 10min). Slightly cheaper than the Spanish and Turbini services are the six daily French trains, which stop at Benha, Tanta and Damanhur, reaching Alexandria in two and a half hours. Lastly, there are some forty non-air-conditioned trains to Alexandria every day, composed of 2nd and 3rd class carriages only. These trains don't need reservations, cost a fraction of the price of the air-conditioned services, stop everywhere, and can take as long as four hours to reach Alexandria.

Direct services to **Mersa Matrouh** only run in summer: there's a thrice-weekly sleeper (see below), and a daily a/c service leaving early in the morning. Failing this, it is far better to travel by bus from Cairo or Alex than to endure the interminable journey in ordinary 2nd or 3rd class from Alexandria.

Apart from the sleeper service (see below), there are nine daily departures for **Aswan** (14–17hr) and five more for **Luxor** (11–12hr). At present, however, tourists are only authorized to use three of these trains (departing at 7am, 10pm and 12.30am). Foreigners travel in special coaches guarded by armed plainclothes policemen, and are not allowed to buy tickets for any other train. Originally this was for protection from "terrorists", but it did tend to make the tourist trains potential targets for snipers, who occasionally took pot-shots at them on their way through Middle Egypt. Although the danger now seems to have passed, the rule still applies. Fares for ordinary seats (not sleeping berths) are £E67 in 1st class and £E42 in 2nd for Luxor, £E81 and £E49 for Aswan.

Sleeper services

In addition to regular services, there are daily **sleeper services** (8pm) to Upper Egypt, which include a bar and disco on the train. The cost per person for a double cabin including dinner and breakfast is US$53 one-way to Luxor or Aswan (you can stop over at Luxor and continue to Aswan on the same ticket). Solo travellers can reserve the entire cabin for US$74, or consent to share it with a stranger of the same sex and pay the normal fare. From mid-June until mid-September, there are also three weekly sleeper trains to Mersa Matrouh (Mon, Wed & Sat 11pm, arriving 6am).

You can book at the sleeper office, next to the tourist office, until 6pm on the day of departure, but you are best off reserving a sleeper a few days in advance if possible. This can be done at the station, by phone or fax with Abela, who operate the sleeper trains (℡02/738-3682 or 4, 𝔽738-3681), or online at 𝔚www.sleepingtrains .com, where you can also check the latest fares

and schedules. Tickets can also be booked through Hamis Travel, whose office is just outside the station, in the building by the third-class ticket office for Alexandria (℡02/574-9275, 𝔽574-9276). As well as taking Visa and MasterCard, they also accept euros, though they prefer Egyptian pounds or US dollars, and they will take bookings online (𝔚www.hamis.com.eg). Their staff tend to be somewhat more helpful than those in the station sleeper office. Bookings can also be made at the Carlson Wagon Lit office by the *Helnan Shepheard* hotel, where they cost slightly more.

Inter-city buses

Inter-city buses reach most parts of Egypt, often faster than trains. Services depart from four main terminals: Turgoman Garage (especially to the Canal Zone), Aboud (especially to Alexandria and the Delta), Sinai Terminal (aka Abbassiya Terminal; services to the Sinai and also to Jordan and Syria) and El Moneeb (especially to Middle Egypt). A number of buses that start at Aboud and Turgoman may stop at El Mouneeb or Sinai Terminal, and at Almaza Terminal in Heliopolis (see "International buses" p.301). A few buses also leave from Sharia al-Galaa near the *Ramses Hilton* hotel, and one or two services from Aboud may be picked up off Sharia Orabi near Ramses station. Some destinations may be served by buses from more than one departure point, notably Alexandria (Aboud, Turgoman and the *Ramses Hilton*), Hurghada (*Ramses Hilton*, Aboud and El Moneeb), Sharm el-Sheikh (Sinai and Turgoman), and Fayoum, Beni Suef and Minya (Turgoman and El Moneeb).

Unless stated otherwise, all services below run daily, though schedules are liable to change. None of the operators will take bookings over the phone – tickets must be purchased in person from the terminal (or, in the case of Mansura and Damietta, from the old Koulali terminal off Sharia Orabi).

Turgoman Garage

Turgoman Garage in Bulaq – 600m west of Ramses Station on Sharia Shanan – handles the majority of bus departures to destinations within Egypt and beyond. It is not really served by local public transport, but it's an easy walk from Ramses station or from Sharia Ramses by Orabi metro. A taxi from Midan Tahrir should cost around £E3, and certainly not more than £E5.

The first booth is for East Delta services to **Suez** (every 30min 6am–8.30pm; 2hr; £E7), **Ismailiya** (every 20min 6am–8pm; 2hr; £E7) and Port Said (approximately hourly 6.15am–10pm; 3hr; £E16). The second booth sells tickets for East Delta services to **Mansura** (hourly 6am–8pm; 2hr; £E8.50–9) and **Damietta** (16 daily; 3hr 30min; £E14–15). These latter two can also be picked up in town at the old Koulali terminal by Sharia Orabi north of Sharia Ramses (☎02/576-6514; see map p.148), and both destinations are in any case better served from Aboud (see below).

The third booth is for West Delta buses to Alexandria (1–2 per hour 5am–11.30pm; 3hr; £E18) and **Mersa Matrouh** (4 daily; 6hr; £E40). The booth after that is run by the Middle Delta Bus Co, serving **Tanta** (16 daily; 1hr 30min; £E6.50) and **Mahalla** (16 daily; 2hr; £E7.50), but again there are more frequent departures to these places from Aboud.

At the far end of the concourse, you'll find the Superjet office, whose smart a/c buses run from here to **Hurghada** (3 daily; 5–6hr; £E57) and **Sharm el-Sheikh** (3 daily; 5hr; £E68). Superjet buses to Alexandria run from Sharia Kalaa by the *Ramses Hilton* hotel (see below).

Aboud Bus Terminal

The **Aboud Bus Terminal**, 3km north of Ramses station, up Sharia Ahmed Helmi by the Sharia Shubra intersection, is now the main terminal for buses and service taxis to Alexandria and the Delta, and buses to Middle and Upper Egypt. It is most easily reached by service taxi microbus from Ramses station (75pt). A taxi will cost around £E3 from Ramses station, £E5–6 from downtown.

The Delta is served by three companies, of which the West Delta Bus Co (☎02/431-6742) runs buses to **Alexandria** (every 45min 7.30am–8.30pm; 3hr; £E12) and **Damanhur** (hourly 7am–11pm; 2hr; £E9), while Middle Delta Bus Co serves **Tanta** (half-hourly 6.30am–9pm; 1hr 30min; £E5–6), **Mahalla el-Kubra** (2hr 30min; half-hourly; £E6–7) and **Kafr el-Sheikh** (3hr; half-hourly; £E6–7). East Delta Bus Co covers **Benha** (every 30min 6am–8pm; 1hr; £E2.50), **Zagazig** (every 20min 6.30am–9.30pm; 1hr 30min; £E5), **Faqus** (every 45min 7.30am–8.15pm; 2hr; £E8), **Mansura** (half-hourly 7am–7.30pm; 2hr £E9), **Damietta** (half-hourly 7am–7.30pm; 3hr 30min; £E15) and, in summer (June–Sept), **Ras el-Bahr** (every 45min; 3hr; £E17).

For destinations southwards up the Nile Valley, the Upper Egypt Bus Co (☎02/431-6723) has departures to **Fayoum** (every 15min 6am–8pm; 2hr; £E8), **Minya** (hourly 6am–1.30am; 4hr; £E15), **Mellawi** (every two hours 7.15am–1.30am; 4hr 30min; £E17), **Assyut** (hourly 7am–1am; 6–7hrs; £E12–15), **Sohag** (every 90 minutes 7am–1am; 8–9hrs; £E30), **Qena** (hourly 7am–1am; 9–10hrs; £E30), **Luxor** (1 daily; 9hr; £E60) and **Aswan** (1 daily; 12hr; £E70). The last two destinations, however, are probably more comfortable by train.

Sinai (Abbassiya) Terminal

The **Sinai Bus Terminal**, 4km from the centre in Abbassiya, is the main terminal for buses to the Sinai. It can be reached by bus from Abdel Mounem Riyad (#27 and #998, and minibus #30) or Midan Ramses (#28, #310 and #710, and minibuses #1 and #998), with more buses to Midan Abbassiya, a short walk away. A taxi will cost £E5–8 from downtown.

Buses are operated by the East Delta Bus Co, and serve **El-Arish** (3 daily; 5hr £E26.50–37), **Taba** (3 daily; 10hr; £E55–75), **Dahab** (4 daily; 9hr; £E62–75) and **Sharm el-Sheikh** (10 daily; 5hr; £E42–60). There are also Superjet services to Sharm from Turgoman Garage (see p.299).

El Moneeb Bus Terminal

The **El Moneeb Bus Terminal**, under a flyover 300m north of El-Monib metro station, is the terminal for the Upper Egypt Bus Co's services to Middle Egypt and the western desert oases (but not Siwa, which is reached from Mersa Matrouh or Alexandria). Here you'll find departures for **Fayoum City** (half-hourly; 2hr; £E4.50), **Beni Suef** (28 daily; 2hr; £E6) and **Minya** (6 daily; 4hr; £E12), as well as **Bahariya** (5–6 daily; 6hr; £E20), **Frafra** (2 daily; 8–10hr; £E27) and **Dakhla** (2 daily; 14–16hr; £E40). Superjet services to Hurghada and Upper Egypt services to Luxor and Aswan also call here.

Ramses Hilton departures

In addition to the West Delta services from Turgoman and Aboud, Superjet runs deluxe buses to **Alexandria** (hourly 6am–11pm; 3hr; £E24) from Sharia al-Galaa near the *Ramses Hilton* hotel (see map p.126). A couple of doors down, El Gouna runs seven daily buses to **Hurghada** (5–6hr; £E55).

International buses

International buses are highly vulnerable to political upheavals, so all the current departure times and fares below are subject to change – double-check everything before departure, including the availability of foreign visas (see p.291).

Despite the current political situation in Israel and Palestine, there are still services to **Tel Aviv** and **Jerusalem** – an 11–12hr journey via El-Arish and Rafah, skirting most of the Gaza Strip, though often rerouted via Taba. At time of writing there are only two buses a week, departing from the *Cairo Sheraton* in Dokki (Sun & Thurs 5.30am; $45 one-way, $65 return, plus border taxes of around US$20 each way). For tickets and information, contact Misr Travel at the *Cairo Sheraton*, ☎02/335-5470.

More useful to tourists at present are East Delta's four weekly services to **Amman** in Jordan and **Damascus** in Syria, travelling via the Nuweiba–Aqaba ferry. Buses leave the Sinai Terminal (Sun, Mon, Wed & Thurs at 7.30am), and the fare is US$51 plus £E50 to Amman (15hr), US$65 plus £E50 to Damascus (30hr). Superjet also runs twice weekly (Sun & Tues 5am; US$70 plus £E50) buses to Amman from their terminal at Almaza at the far end of Heliopolis. Almaza Terminal can be reached by buses #39 and #796 from Abdel Mouneem Riyad, buses #15, #39 and #796 from Midan Ramses, or on the Heliopolis Metro (the Merghani line, with the destination in white on a yellow background), from Ramses to the junction of Sharia Merghani with Sharia Abu Bakr al-Siddiq, following the latter street 300m south to the terminal.

Also from the Almaza Terminal, Superjet runs three buses a week (Sun, Tues & Thurs 7am; £E260) to **Benghazi** (17hr) and **Tripoli** (36hr) in Libya.

Inter-city service taxis

If you don't mind a slightly cramped and definitely hair-raising journey, **service taxis** (*servees*), whether Peugeots, microbuses or minibuses, are usually the fastest way to reach a host of destinations. Their biggest advantage is that they leave as soon as they're full; just turn up, and you'll probably be away in 15min (morning and late afternoon are prime times).

Drivers drum up custom by shouting out their destinations; anybody can point you towards the right vehicle for your destination. Fares generally work out 20–30 percent above the bus fare, though they are occasionally cheaper. Drivers are unlikely to overcharge you, but watch what Egyptians pay and you can hardly go wrong. If you're alighting halfway (for example, at Wadi Natrun, along the Desert Road to Alex), it's normal to pay the full fare.

For **Alexandria and the Delta**, the best place to pick up a service taxi is Aboud terminal, where you'll find vehicles to Alex, Baltim, Benha, Damanhur, Damietta, Faqus, Kafr el-Sheikh, Mahalla, Mansura, Tanta and Zagazig, with very frequent departures and a direct route out of town. Vehicles to several of these destinations, in particular Alex and Tanta, can sometimes be picked up around Ramses rail station too, especially during rush hours, but they may take a roundabout route getting out of town, and end up taking rather longer than taxis from Aboud.

Service taxis for **Suez** and **Ismailiya** leave from Sharia Orabi near Ramses station (see map p.148).

For **Fayoum**, the best place to pick up a service taxi is at Midan Giza (see p.217 for local bus connections), though you can also get them from Sharia Orabi near Ramses station (see map p.148).

For **Bahariya**, service taxis leave from opposite El Mouneeb bus station, where you'll also find more service taxis to Fayoum, and also to Beni Suef and Middle Egypt.

International service taxis

In addition to domestic runs, there are international service taxis to **Libya**. These are run by Wikala Suessi on Midan Opera (☏02/395-4480; see map on p.127), and leave daily from there at around 8pm bound for Benghazi and Tripoli. It's wise to book your place a day or two ahead if possible.

Depending on the current political situation, it is also possible to get to **Palestine and Israel** by service taxi in stages. The most direct route, to the Gaza Strip, is inadvisable at time of writing due to the situation in Palestine, and in any case the Israelis periodically close the border stranding Gaza residents in Egypt. Should things settle down, you can take a service taxi from Sharia Orabi near Ramses station (see map p.148) to Suez, where you should be able to get one to the Rafah border crossing. On the other side of the border, you may have to take a "special" (ie, a private taxi) to Khan Yunis, where there are service taxis to Gaza City and thence to the Israeli border at Erez. If you do this, you will need to set out early to avoid being stranded at Khan Yunis, where there is no accommodation. There is also transport from Rafah directly into Israel. Alternatively, there is a bus from Suez (currently departing at 7am) to the Israeli border at Taba.

Domestic flights

EgyptAir (for information ☏ 02/635-0260 or 70) has flights to Abu Simbel (2 daily, both very early morning; 2hr 45min; £E1275), Alexandria (6 weekly, more in summer; 50min; £E330), Assyut (2 weekly; 1hr; £E478), Aswan (5–8 daily; 1hr 20min; £E908), Hurghada (4 daily; 1hr; £E744), Luxor (5–8 daily; 1hr 5min; £E715), and Sharm el-Sheikh (4–6 daily; 55min; £E744). EgyptAir's Cairo offices (generally open daily 9am–5pm) include: 6 Sharia Adly (☏02/392-7649); 9 Sharia Talaat Harb (☏02/393-2836); *Nile Hilton* (☏02/579-3049); *Cairo Sheraton*, Dokki (☏02/335-4863); Zamalek Club Fence, 26th July Street (☏02/347-2027); and 22 Sharia Ibrahim al-Lakani, Heliopolis (☏02/290-8453), as well as the airport terminal 1 (☏02/635-3861) and terminal 2 (☏02/418-2818).

Tickets and terminals

During winter, EgyptAir flights to the Nile Valley or Hurghada are often fully booked by groups – reserve as far in advance as possible, or hope to get a cancellation on stand-by. Tickets must be purchased in Egyptian currency backed by an exchange receipt, and return tickets cost double the one-way fare. Students may qualify for a reduction, but since EgyptAir enjoys a monopoly it rarely offers big discounts.

Domestic flights leave from terminal 1, the "old airport" (*al-mataar al-qadima*), which can be reached by bus, minibus or taxi (£E40 is the going rate, though drivers may demand more – you should get away with paying £E30 if you get off just outside the airport precincts). Both airport terminals are served by air-conditioned bus #356, minibus #27 and 24-hour bus #400, all from Abdel Mouneen Riyad terminal (in front of the *Ramses Hilton*) and Midan Ramses, and also by 24-hour bus #948 from Midan Ataba. During rush hour, and especially by bus, the journey can take well over an hour, so always allow plenty of time. It's safer of course to take a cab than to rely on bus services.

International flights

Many airlines make Cairo a stopover between the Near and Far East, or between Europe and sub-Saharan Africa, ensuring a competitive market in fares, student and youth discounts – but also heavy demand for flights. Don't leave buying tickets until the last moment. Especially during August, you should book weeks in advance on Eastern European airlines (which often have the cheapest flights to Western Europe, the British Isles and North America) or for popular long-haul destinations like Nairobi and Delhi.

All reservations should be reconfirmed 72 hours before departure. Also check which terminal you are flying from – most Western airlines use terminal 2, the "new airport" (*al-mataaa al-gadida*), while EgyptAir and most East European airlines use terminal 1, the "old airport" (*al-mataaa al-qadima*). Both can be reached by bus (see p.105), or more reliably by taxi.

Agents and tickets

It's worth shopping around agents, such as Spring Tours (3 Sharia Sayed el-Bakry, Zamalek ☎ 02/736-5972, ⓦ www.springtoursegypt.com) and Travco (112 26th July St, Zamalek ☎ 02/737-1737, ⓦ www.travco-eg.com), who may offer discounts and can often find seats when the airline itself swears that none exist. Although some agents and airlines may accept credit card payments for tickets, don't bank on it.

Student and youth discounts

To qualify for student discounts (20–50 percent) you must have a valid ISIC card and be under an age limit (24–31 years, depending on the airline or agency). Another age limit (24–26) determines eligibility for youth discounts, which don't require an ISIC card. There are rarely any student/youth discounts on flights to sub-Saharan Africa, India and the Far East.

Airline offices

Most of the airline offices are in central Cairo; some are represented by local travel agents.

Air Canada c/o Imperial Travel Center, 26 Sharia Bassiouni ☎ 02/575-8939, ⓔ itcsales@itcgroup .com. Daily 9am–5pm.

Air France 2 Midan Talaat Harb ☎ 02/575-8899, ⓕ 02/577-1744, ⓦ www.airfrance.com/eg. Daily except Fri 8.30am–4.30pm.

Air Sinai *Nile Hilton* arcade ☎ 02/576-0750. Daily 9am–5pm.

Alitalia *Nile Hilton* arcade ☎ 02/578-5823, 4 or 5, ⓔ caiupaz@alitalia-egypt.com. Daily except Sat 9am–4pm.

Austrian Airlines 5th floor, 4D Sharia Gezira, Zamalek ☎ 02/735-2777, ⓕ 738-2815, ⓦ www .aua.com.eg. Mon–Thurs & Sun 8.30am–4pm.

British Airways corner of Sharia Bustan and Midan Tahrir ☎ 02/578-0741, 2, 3, 4, 5 or 6, ⓕ 574-7674. Daily except Fri 8.30am–4.30pm.

ČSA Czech Airlines 9 Talaat Harb ☎ 02/393-0416, ⓔ cai@czechairlines.com. Mon–Thurs & Sun 8am–4pm.

Cyprus Airways c/o Apollo Tours, 10 Sharia Talaat Harb ☎ 02/579-7300, 7400 or 7500, ⓔ apollotours@link.net. Daily except Fri 9am–4pm, Fri 10am–1pm.

Delta 17 Sharia Ismail Mohammed, Zamalek ☎ 02/736-2039. Daily except Fri 8.30am–5pm.

EgyptAir (see "Domestic flights" p.301).

El Al 1st floor, 5 Sharia el-Makrizi, just south of Zamalek Bridge, Zamalek ☎ 02/736-1795. Daily except Fri 8.30am–5pm.

Emirates 18 Sharia Elbatal Ahmed Abdelaziz, Mohandeseen ☎ 02/336-1555. Daily except Fri 8.30am–5pm.

Iberia 15 Midan Tahrir ☎ 02/579-5700, ⓦ www.iberia.com.eg. Mon–Thurs & Sun 8.30am–4.30pm.

KLM 11 Sharia Qasr el-Nil ☎ 02/580-5700, ⓦ www.klm.com.eg. Mon–Thurs & Sun 8.30am–4.30pm.

Korean Air Room 26, 2nd floor, Nile Hilton arcade ☎ 02/576-8488, ⓕ 576 4099. Daily except Fri 9am–4pm.

Lufthansa 6 Sharia Sheikh el-Marsafi, Zamalek ☎ 02/739-8339, ⓦ www.lufthansa.com.eg. Mon–Thurs & Sun 8.30am–4.30pm. Also represents Air New Zealand, United and Thai.

Malaysia Airlines Room 13, 1st floor, *Nile Hilton* arcade ☎02/579-9714 or 5. Daily except Fri 9am–4.30pm (Ramadan 9.30am–3pm).

Malev 3rd floor, 5 Sharia Talaat Harb ☎02/391-5083, ✉cairo@malev.hu. Mon–Thurs & Sun 9am–4pm.

Olympic Airways 23 Sharia Qasr el-Nil ☎02/393-1318, ⓕ391-0574. Daily 8.30am–4pm.

Royal Air Maroc 9 Sharia Talaat Harb (entrance in Sharia el-Bustan) ☎02/392-2956, ⓕ393-4574. Daily except Fri 9am–4pm.

Royal Jordanian 6 Sharia Qasr el-Nil ☎02/575-0905, ⓕ576-7005. Daily 9am–4pm.

Saudi Arabian Airlines 5 Sharia Qasr el-Nil ☎02/577-7867, ⓕ574-2804. Daily 9am–7pm.

Singapore Airlines *Nile Hilton* arcade ☎02/575 0276, ⓕ574-7084. Mon–Thurs & Sun 8.30am–4.30pm, Fri 9am–3pm.

Sudan Airways 1 Sharia Abdel Salam Arif ☎02/578-7145, ⓕ575-9946. Daily 8am–7pm.

Swiss 4 Mamar Behlar (between Talaat Harb and Qasr el-Nil) ☎02/396-1737. Mon–Thurs & Sun 8.30am–4.30pm.

Syrianair 25 Sharia Talaat Harb ☎02/392-8284, ⓕ391-0805. Daily except Fri 9am–4pm.

Nile cruises and ferry services

Although luxury **cruises** operated by the *Hilton*, *Sheraton* and *Mena House Oberoi* remain prohibitively expensive, budget travellers may consider less ritzy boats run by agencies such as Eastmar Tours (in the passage of 13 Sharia Qasr el-Nil; ☎02/574-5024, 🌐www.eastmar-travel .com), which charges – depending on season – US$85–150 a night per person for a 4- to 7-night cruise. Be aware, however, that better deals could well be available from local agents in either Luxor or Aswan. For information on Nile cruises, see pp.476–477, and for more on cruises and **sailing on a felucca** – a funkier and much cheaper experience – see pp.474–475.

International Fast Ferries runs the **Hurghada–Sharm el-Sheikh catamaran** and has a Cairo office on the second floor at 46 Sharia Suriya in Mohandiseen (☎02/789-8927 or 8). Tickets can also be purchased from downtown travel agents such as De Castro Tours (12 Sharia Talaat Harb ☎02/574-3213, ✉decastrotours@link.net).

Arab Bridge Maritime, who run **ferries from Nuweiba and Sharm el-Sheikh to Aqaba** in Jordan (see p.742 for details), has an office at 7 Sharia Abdel Khalaq Sarwat ☎02/419-8657.

For details of the **ferry service from Aswan to Wadi Halfa** in Sudan, see p.479; for information on **ferries from Suez to Jeddah** in Saudi, see p.683.

The Nile Valley

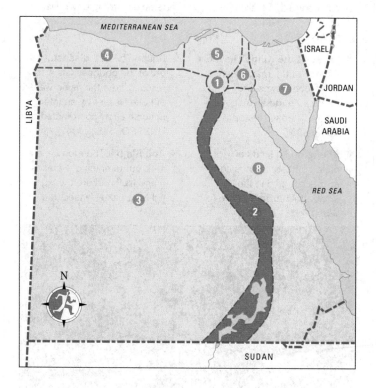

CHAPTER 2 **Highlights**

＊ **Abydos** The carvings in Seti I's mortuary temple are among the greatest produced by pharaonic civilization. See p.347

＊ **Karnak Temple** It took 1300 years to construct this vast cult centre that's as large as ten great cathedrals. See p.385

＊ **Valley of the Kings** The most famous of the magnificent burial complexes and mortuary temples that make up the Theban Necropolis. See p.408

＊ **Shopping** All kinds of handicrafts, souvenirs and spices are sold in the wonderful bazaar at Aswan. See p.462

＊ **Nubian music and dancing** Exuberant and haunting by turns, they are best enjoyed on Sehel or Elephantine Island. See p.470

＊ **Feluccas** A timeless way to view the Nile's scenery and temples, sailing downriver from Aswan to Edfu. See p.474

＊ **Philae** The island sanctuary of the goddess Isis was rescued from the rising waters of Lake Nasser by an international effort coordinated by UNESCO. See p.484

＊ **Abu Simbel** The monumental rock-cut temples of Ramses II and Nefertari are the highlights of Lake Nasser. See p.494

△ The Temple of Isis, Philae

The Nile Valley

Egypt has been called the gift of the Nile, for without the river it could not exist as a fertile, populous country, let alone have sustained a great civilization five thousand years ago. Its character and history have been shaped by the stark contrast between the fecund **Nile Valley** and its Delta (covered in Chapter 5), and the arid wastes that surround them. To the ancient Egyptians, this was the homeland or *Kemet* – the Black Land of dark alluvium, where life and civilization flourished as the benign gods intended – as opposed to the desert that represented death and chaos, ruled by Seth, the bringer of storms and catastrophes.

Kemet's existence depended on an annual miracle of rebirth from aridity, as the Nile rose to spread its life-giving waters and fertilizing silt over the exhausted land during the season of inundation. Once the flood had subsided, the *fellaheen* (peasants) simply planted crops in the mud, waited for an abundant harvest, and then relaxed over summer. While empires rose and fell, this way of life persisted essentially unchanged for over 240 generations, until the Aswan Dam put an end to the inundation in 1967 – a breathtaking period of continuity considering that Jesus lived less than ninety generations ago.

This continuity and ancient history is literally underfoot. Almost every Nile town and village is built upon layers of previous **settlements** – pharaonic, Ptolemaic, Roman and Coptic – whose ancient names, modified and Arabized, have often survived. When treasure-hunting "archeologists" first turned their attention to the ancient temples and tombs in the 1830s, they had to sift through metres of sand and debris before reaching their goal. Yet the centuries of burial preserved a panoply of ancient bas-reliefs and carvings that would otherwise have been defaced by Coptic or Muslim iconoclasts, who hacked away at the pagan gods on the accessible friezes, pillars and ceilings, and plundered masonry for their own churches and mosques.

After a century and a half of excavation by just about every Western nation – and by the Egyptians since independence – the Nile's **monuments** constitute the greatest open-air museum in the world. Revealed along its banks are several thousand **tombs** (Thebes alone has more than 900) and scores of **temples**: so many, in fact, that most visitors feel satiated by just a fraction of this legacy.

To enjoy the Valley, it's best to be selective and mix sightseeing with felucca rides on the river, roaming around bazaars and camel markets, or attending the odd moulid. Most visitors succeed in this by heading straight for **Upper Egypt**, travelling by train or air to **Luxor** or **Aswan**, then making day-trips to the sights within easy range of either base – most notably the cult temple at **Edfu** – in addition to exploring the New Kingdom temples and tombs of **Karnak** and the **Theban Necropolis** from Luxor. Further north, **Middle Egypt**

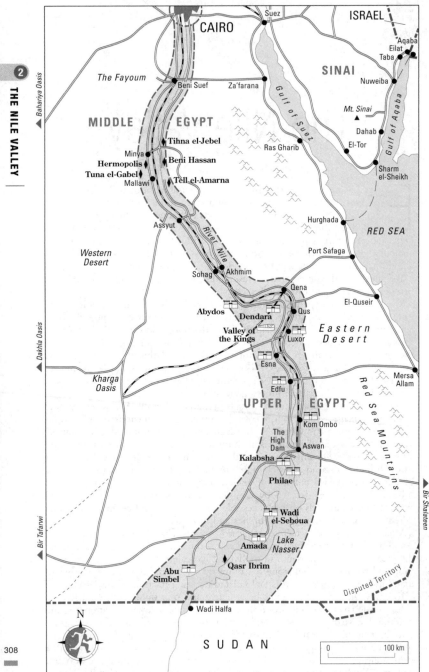

②

THE NILE VALLEY

suffered a series terrorist attacks by Islamic militants during the 1990s, when most tourists simply made day-trips to the temples of **Dendara** and **Abydos**: now, however, adventure travel groups are again visiting the tombs of **Beni Hassan** and the ruins of Akhenaten's capital at **Tell el-Amarna**.

And lastly, a word on the **terms from Egyptology** that fill this chapter: many may be unfamiliar and need a fuller explanation than a glossary allows (see p.867). Hence the boxes at intervals in the text: on statehood and symbolism on p.312; temple architecture under "Abydos" (pp.348–349); funerary beliefs and practices under "The Valley of the Kings" (pp.410–411); and gods and goddesses under their respective cult temples (see the main index for a list).

The river, its gods and pharaohs

The **Nile** is the world's longest river (6695km), originating in the highland lakes of Uganda and Ethiopia, which give rise to the White and Blue Niles. These join into a single river at Khartoum in Sudan, which flows northwards over a series of cataracts through the Nubian desert, before forming Egypt's Nile Valley and Delta, through which it travels 1545km to the Mediterranean Sea. The river's northward flow, coupled with a prevailing wind towards the south, made it a natural highway.

As the source of life, the Nile determined much of ancient Egyptian **society and mythology**. Creation myths of a primal mound emerging from the waters of chaos reflect how villages huddled on mounds till the flood subsided and they could plant their crops. Even more crucially, the need for large-scale irrigation works in the Valley and the consequent mobilization of labour may have engendered the region's system of centralized authority – in effect, the state.

Both the Valley and its Delta were divided into **nomes** or provinces, each with a nomarch or governor, and one or more **local deities**. As political power ebbed and flowed between regions and dynasties, certain of the deities assumed national significance and absorbed the attributes of lesser gods in a perpetual process of religious mergers and takeovers. Thus, for example, Re, the chief god of the Old Kingdom, ended up being assimilated with Amun, the prime divinity of Thebes during the New Kingdom. Yet for all its complexity, Ancient Egyptian religion was essentially practical and intended to get results. Its pre-eminent concerns were to perpetuate the beneficent sun and river, maintain the righteous order personified by the goddess Maat, and achieve resurrection in the afterlife.

Abundant crops could normally be taken for granted, as prayers to Hapy the Nile-god were followed by a green wave of humus-rich water around June. However, if the Nile failed to rise for a succession of years there ensued the "years of the hyena when men went hungry". Archeologists reckon that it was

Travel restrictions and routes into the Nile Valley

Setting out from Cairo, you are faced with a variety of **approaches to the Valley,** but you need to bear in mind certain **travel restrictions**. Egypt is still trying to recover from the fall-out from the **terrorist attacks** on tourists that began in Middle Egypt in 1992 and climaxed with the massacre at Luxor five years later, which cast first the region and then the whole country as "hazardous" on the travel advisory sites of the US State Department and Britain's Foreign Office (see p.46). To win back tourists and reassure its allies, the government crushed the Islamist insurgency and struck a deal whereby Egypt would be re-classified as a **safe country** if they came up with a cohesive security system instead of *ad hoc* responses. The fact that no terrorist acts have occurred in the Valley since the jailed leaders of Al-Jihad urged their followers to renounce violence in 1998 has not yet led to any relaxation in this regime.

The system relies on police checkpoints to filter traffic and ensure that tourists respect the **travel restrictions** listed below (note that these **don't apply** in other parts of Egypt). Officially, tourists can visit any place in the Valley providing they get there in a way that stays within the rules, but in reality it can be hard, if not impossible, to reach some places. Whereas tourists are unbothered by controls within the security "bubble" of Luxor and Aswan, in **Middle Egypt** the police insist on **escorting** them on excursions, or around town, and even confine them to their hotel after dark. While you have little choice but to comply and should certainly never get angry, the system is sufficiently inconsistent and fallible enough that you can sometimes persuade them to cut you some slack.

Bear in mind that you're a privileged visitor but also a nuisance to the **police**, who want you off their turf as soon as possible and preferably into another governorate's territory. Most of the cops are young conscripts, bored and starved of home comforts, so a little humour or a gift (not money) can make a big difference. Confusingly, each governorate fine-tunes the rules for their territory without reference to its neighbours, sometimes resulting in weird inconsistencies.

The following rules and exceptions **specifically apply to the Nile Valley**:

• **Trains** Travelling from Cairo's **Ramses station to Luxor or Aswan**, tourists may only use three regular trains (guarded by plainclothes cops with Uzis) or the deluxe *wagons-lits* service (which has a restaurant and bar). Clerks will simply refuse to sell tickets for other trains. The journey is quite comfortable if you travel in 1st or a/c 2nd class on the three "tourist" trains, so a *wagon-lit* is something of an unnecessary extravagance. If you do want to try your chances on another train, you could try boarding and paying the conductor, but there's sure to be a fuss and the outcome is doubtful. The same restrictions apply to the return journey to Cairo, or onwards from Luxor. In **Middle Egypt**, however, you can usually buy a ticket for any train at the station kiosk with no difficulty, while travelling from Aswan to Luxor (but not the other way) you're allowed to use six trains, not just the three authorized for long-distance travel.

• In **Upper Egypt**, **tourist buses, hired taxis and cars driven by foreigners** must travel in **convoys** escorted by the police. There are three daily between Luxor and Aswan and Luxor and Hurghada; two from Aswan to Abu Simbel, and one from Luxor to Abydos. While local drivers know where and when the convoy departs,

famine – caused by overworking of the land, as well as lack of the flood waters – that caused the collapse of the Old and Middle Kingdoms, and subsequent political anarchy. But each time some new **dynasty** arose to reunite the land and re-establish the old order. This remarkable conservatism persisted even under foreign rule: the Nubians, Persians, Ptolemies and Romans all continued building temples dedicated to the old gods, and styled themselves as pharaohs.

foreigners should always check with the tourist office, since schedules or muster points can change. Arrive at least fifteen minutes early. There are **no scheduled convoys** through Middle Egypt; adventure tour groups make their own arrangements with each governorate, and individuals hoping to drive from Cairo should ask the Ministry of the Interior or the tourist office for advice.

• **Buses** leave from Cairo's **Aboud, El Moneeb** and **Turgoman terminals**. There are several daily a/c services to Luxor and Aswan that are routed via the Red Sea Coast rather than Middle Egypt, thereby avoiding convoy restrictions, but though the journey time is roughly the same, they're a lot less comfortable than 1st- or 2nd-class trains. Non-a/c buses to Beni Suef, Minya, Assyut and Sohag in Middle Egypt do exist, but tourists are only supposed to use ones travelling in a scheduled convoy (which *don't* exist in this region; see above). If you do reach Middle Egypt (by train), then local cops may tolerate you using inter-city buses within the region or heading south to Luxor, from which point on you may use any bus – providing there aren't more than four tourists aboard the vehicle. Even this limit doesn't seem to apply to buses to Hurghada. Since few tourists are using buses at present, in practice you can probably rely on being able to catch any bus – though finding a seat may be another matter, as many arrive already full of Egyptians (standing is allowed).

• **Service taxis** leave from **Aboud**, bound for Minya or Assyut, from where there are connections further south – but at present, tourists aren't allowed to use service taxis anywhere along the Nile Valley, and the police are quite vigilant about enforcing this. However, as the rule isn't always observed between Luxor and Aswan (though it is *in* Luxor and Aswan), and as this is potentially a great way of getting around, we've included some details of routes under town accounts, in case the restriction is lifted.

• **Planes** are the fastest, most expensive way to travel from one end of the Nile Valley to the other, and are not subject to any police restrictions. Depending on the level of tourism, there can be from two to a dozen flights a day to Luxor, Aswan and Abu Simbel, affording amazing views over the Valley's green belt of cultivated land. Tourists can also fly from Aswan to Abu Simbel, and Luxor to Sharm el-Sheikh in Sinai.

• **Package tours** may appeal to visitors with little time or inclination for independent travel, but first-timers often end up buying overpriced tours that involve substandard hotels and excursions. Many readers and hoteliers in Luxor and Aswan have complained of being misled by Amigo Tours, which has touts in many hotels and at the airport and station in Cairo; they also warn against using Hamis Travel. If you *do* want a tour, talk to Salah Mohammed (see p.241) or Eastmar Travel in Cairo – the latter also arranges cruises between Luxor and Aswan and the temples on Lake Nasser, and has branch offices in both Luxor and Aswan.

• Prices for **Nile cruises** have never been lower, whether you shop around on the Internet before you leave (see "Getting There" on p.31, p.34 and p.37), at travel agents in Cairo, Luxor and Aswan, or – cheapest of all – on the boats moored at Aswan, which is also the point of departure for **felucca** rides to Kom Ombo and Edfu (see the boxes on pp.474–475 and pp.476–477 for details).

For details of **ticket buying**, **prices**, **departure** and **journey times**, see "Travel Details" on p.298 at the end of the Cairo chapter.

The Two Lands: pharaonic symbols and cartouches

Much of the symbolism of Ancient Egypt referred to the union of the **Two Lands**, the **Nile Valley** (Upper Egypt) and its **Delta** (Lower Egypt), whose establishment marked the onset of the Old Kingdom (c.3100 BC) – unless you buy the theory advanced by one Egyptologist that the Two Lands were actually the east and west banks of the Nile (which seems unlikely).

Each Land had its own deity – the Delta had **Wadjet**, the cobra goddess, while the Valley had **Nekhbet**, the vulture goddess. With union, their images were combined with the sun-disc of the god Re to form the **winged sun-disc**, which

▲ winged sun-disc

often appeared on the lintels of temple doors. Another common image was that of the Nile-god, **Hapy**, binding together the **heraldic plants** of the Two Lands, the papyrus of the Delta and the lotus of the Valley.

Much the same process can be observed in the evolution of **pharaonic crowns**. At state rituals, the pharaoh customarily wore first the **White Crown** of Upper Egypt and then the **Red Crown** of Lower Egypt, although by the time of the New Kingdom (c.1570 BC) these were often subsumed into the **Combined Crown**. Pharaonic crowns also featured the **uraeus** or fire-spitting cobra, an incarnation of Wadjet believed to be a guardian of the kings.

▲ Happy binding the two lands

Another image that referred to the act of union (an act which had to be repeated at the onset of the Middle and New Kingdoms) was the **Djed column**, a symbol of steadfastness. Additional symbols of royal authority included the **crook** (or staff) and the **flail** (or scourge), which are often shown crossed over the chest – in the so-called Osiride position – on pharaonic statues. A ubiquitous motif was the **ankh**, symbolizing breath or life, which pharaohs are often depicted receiving from gods in tombs or funerary texts.

However, the archetypal symbol of kingship was the **cartouche**, an oval formed by a loop of rope, enclosing the hieroglyphs of the pharaoh's **nomen and prenomen**. Traditionally a pharaoh's title consisted of five names: four adopted on accession to the throne (Horus name, Nebty name, Golden Horus name and prenomen) and a birth name (nomen), roughly corresponding to a family name. The prenomen was introduced by a group of hieroglyphs meaning "He who belongs to the sedge and the bee" and was nearly always compounded with the name of Re, the sun-god. The nomen – the name by which pharaohs are known to posterity – was likewise introduced by an epithet, "Son of Re".

White crown   Red crown   Combined crown   Uraeus   Djed column   Crook   Flail   Ankh

The people of the Nile Valley

Although the Nile Valley and its Delta represents a mere four percent of Egypt's surface area, it is home to 95 percent of the country's population. While Cairo and Alexandria account for about a quarter of this, the bulk of the people still live in small towns and villages and, as in pharaonic times, the **fellaheen** or peasant farmers remain the bedrock of Egyptian society.

Most **villages** consist of flat-roofed mud-brick houses, with chickens, goats, cows and water buffalo roaming the unpaved streets, and elaborate multi-storey pigeon coops (the birds are eaten and their droppings used as fertilizer). The plastered outside walls of the houses are often painted light blue (a colour believed to ward off the Evil Eye), and if the householder has made the pilgrimage to Mecca, they will be decorated with characteristic *Hadj* scenes (recalling the journey with images of ships and charter jets, lions and the sacred Kaaba). Children begin work at an early age: girls feed the animals, fetch water and make the dung patties which are used for fuel (though primus stoves are increasingly popular), while by the age of nine or ten, boys are learning how to farm the land that will one day be theirs.

Rural life might appear the same throughout the Nile Valley, but its character changes as you go further south. The northern part of the Valley is wider and greener, unconstrained by the desert hills; its people have a reputation for being quietly spoken and phlegmatic, notwithstanding a recent turn towards Islamic radicalism. By contrast, Egyptians characterize the **Saiyidis** of Upper Egypt as mercurial in character, alternating between hot-blooded passion and a state known as *kismet* – a kind of fatalistic stasis. To non-Saiyidis, they are also the butt of jokes mocking their stubbornness and stupidity. A further ethnic contingent of the southern reaches of the Valley are the black-skinned **Nubians**, whose traditional homeland stretching far into Sudan was submerged by Lake Nasser in the 1960s.

Nile wildlife

The exotic Nile wildlife depicted on ancient tomb reliefs – hippos, crocodiles, elephants and gazelles – is largely a thing of the past, though you might just see a croc near Aswan. However, the Valley has a rich diversity of **birds**. Amid the groves of palms (dates all along the Valley and dom palms south of Assyut), fruit and flame trees, sycamores and eucalyptus, and fields of *besoom* (Egyptian clover) and sugar cane, you can spot hoopoes, turtle- and laughing-doves, bulbuls, bluethroats, redstarts, wheatears and dark-backed stonechats; purple gallinules, egrets and all kinds of waders are to be seen in the river; while common birds of prey include a range of kestrels, hawks and falcons.

Middle Egypt

It was nineteenth-century archeologists who coined the term **Middle Egypt** for the stretch of river between Cairo and the Qena Bend; in native usage and current administration there's no such area, unlike Upper and Lower Egypt, which are ancient divisions. Nevertheless, it's a handy label for a region that's subtly distinct from Upper Egypt, further south (in this guide, the Middle Egypt account ends at Sohag; the sites to the south – at Abydos and Dendara – are dealt with in the Upper Egypt account as the best access to them is from Luxor). Owing little to tourism, the towns are solidly provincial, with social conservatism providing common ground for those wanting to preserve peaceful relations between the Muslim majority and Middle Egypt's Coptic community (about twenty percent of the local population, roughly double the national average). During the 1990s this was badly strained by Islamic militants, whose attacks on Copts, the security forces and tourists made the region a no-go zone for foreigners. Though adventure tour groups are returning, few independent travellers have followed, and the restrictions intended to ensure tourists' security can be off-putting even though the risk of danger has receded.

Even before this, most tourists rated Middle Egypt a low priority, as towns like **Minya** and **Sohag** lack the romance of Aswan or the stupendous monuments of Luxor, for all that the local antiquities have fascinated scholars. The rock tombs of **Beni Hassan** and the necropolis of **Tuna al-Gabel** are well-preserved relics of Middle Kingdom artistry and Ptolemaic cult-worship, while the desolate remains at **Tell el-Amarna** stand as an evocative reminder of the "heretic" Pharaoh Akhenaten. All these sites may now be visited again, albeit with a police escort and subject to certain travel restrictions (see pp.310–311).

Beni Suef

Beni Suef is one of Egypt's poorest governorates, with high unemployment due to a shortage of arable land. Many villagers actively welcome the siting of five **cement factories** on the east bank, despite the pollution they cause, as the only other work is quarrying for marble in the **Sannur Caves** – a job that has killed or crippled scores of men, and damaged alabaster formations, supposedly protected by law. Hopes for a better life rest on exploiting the **natural gas** fields beneath the Western Desert, with the new Kuraymat power-station as the hub of a future grid of pipelines running to October 6th City, Assyut, Qena and Aswan. Another contributor to environmental pollution is the airbase that hosts Egypt's "Top Gun" **fighter pilots school**, whose students dogfight in the skies above the governorate.

There's no reason to visit the ramshackle capital of **BENI SUEF**, 120km from Cairo, except to switch transport for the Red Sea Coast, the Fayoum or the Pyramid of Maidum. Should this mean **staying** overnight, your best option is the two-star *Semiramis Hotel* (℡082/322-092, ℻326-017; ❷) behind the **telephone** and **post** offices, just north of the **train station**. By carrying on to a bridge and turning right, you'll find a **bank** on Sharia Sa'ad Zaghloul. Alternatively, cross the canal and carry on for 200m then turn right, and you'll reach the depot for **minibuses** and pick-ups to El-Wasta, from where a service taxi can get you within range of the Pyramid of Maidum (see p.527). Hourly **buses** to Minya and the Fayoum, and one daily to Za'farana on the Red Sea – running past the turn-off for St Anthony's Monastery (see p.769) – leave from the bus station on Sharia Bur Said, 400m south of (and on the other side of the canal from) the train station. For **eating**, there's a choice between kebab or chicken at the *Semiramis*, or the *kushari, fuul* or *taamiya* outside the station.

Forgotten cities: Herakleopolis and Oxyrhynchus

Though nothing remains of them, two ancient cities once flourished along this stretch of the Nile Valley.

Herakleopolis is marked by a huge mound of rubble near the village of Ihnasya el-Medina, 15km from Beni Suef. Founded early in the Old Kingdom and long the capital of the twentieth nome, its rise coincided with the decline of the VIII Dynasty, which barely controlled the region around Memphis by 2160 BC. While anarchy reigned throughout the Two Lands, **Achthoes**, the nomarch of Herakleopolis, forged a new dynasty. Although his successors

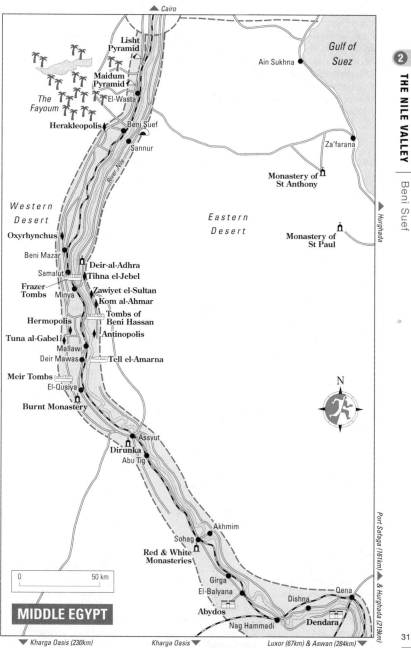

▲ Cairo

Gulf of
Suez

Lisht
Pyramid

Ain Sukhna

Maidum
Pyramid

El-Wasta

The
Fayoum

Za'farana

Herakleopolis

Beni Suef

Sannur

Monastery of
St Anthony

River Nile

Western
Desert

Eastern
Desert

▶ Hurghada

Oxyrhynchus

Monastery of
St Paul

Beni Mazar

Deir-al-Adhra

Samalut

Tihna el-Jebel

Frazer
Tombs

Minya

Zawiyet el-Sultan

Kom al-Ahmar

Hermopolis

Tombs of
Beni Hassan

Tuna al-Gabel

Antinopolis

Mallawi

Deir Mawas

Tell el-Amarna

Meir Tombs

El-Qusiya

Burnt Monastery

N

Assyut

Dirunka

Abu Tig

Port Safaga (161km) ▶ & Hurghada (219km) ▼

Akhmim

Sohag

Red & White
Monasteries

Girga

El-Balyana

Dishna

Qena

Abydos

Dendara

Nag Hammadi

0   50 km

MIDDLE EGYPT

▼ Kharga Oasis (230km)   Kharga Oasis ▼   Luxor (67km) & Aswan (284km) ▼

never achieved control of southern Egypt, their reassertion of centralized authority in the north paved the way for the XII Dynasty and the Middle Kingdom.

Of similarly academic interest, **Oxyrhynchus**, 9km northwest of Beni Mazar, was the capital of the nineteenth nome. It's noted for the discovery of numerous papyri – including third-century fragments of the gospels of Matthew and John; portions of plays by Sophocles, Euripides and Meander; and summaries of the lost books of Livy. More frivolously, it deserves to be remembered for revering the elephant-snout fish – perhaps the weirdest totemic creature on record.

Minya, Mallawi and surrounding sites

The best archeological sites in Middle Egypt are around **Minya**, 229km from Cairo, and **Mallawi**, 47km further south. This area was the epicentre of the conflict between Islamic militants and the security forces in the mid-1990s, when canefields were burned to deny the militants cover, and armoured cars patrolled the streets of Minya and Mallawi. Since the militants were flushed out or ceased fighting in 1998 there have been no reported acts of violence, and locals point out that, even in the worst years, no tourists were attacked in Minya. Even so, the police are omnipresent and expect tourists to conform to security restrictions. This generally means **visiting the sites in private taxis**, with a police escort, rather than using local buses or service taxis – which makes trips more expensive – although for **inter-city travel** you may use any train up or down the Valley, and there's always a chance that you'll be able to pick up a bus or service taxi when the police aren't looking, or when they decide to turn a blind eye just to get you off their turf as fast as possible.

The main attractions are the rock tombs of **Beni Hassan**, roughly midway between the towns; these contain the finest surviving murals from the Middle Kingdom. Nearer to Mallawi are the ruins of **Hermopolis** and its partially subterranean necropolis, **Tuna al-Gabel**, while the rock-cut temples of **Tihna el-Jebel** and the Coptic **Monastery of the Virgin** lie across the river to the north of Minya. The major site of **Tell el-Amarna**, 12km south of Mallawi on the east bank, is covered separately on p.326.

All **trains** between Cairo and Luxor stop at Minya. There are **buses** from Cairo's Aboud and El Moneeb terminals (5hr) and **service taxis** (4hr) from the adjacent depot or Midan Giza. **Drivers** have a choice between the congested, scenic Agricultural Road that hugs the west bank of the Nile; the new Desert Road, further west, which mainly avoids the towns en route; or the older Desert Road along the east bank of the Nile, linked by a bridge to Minya.

Minya

Known as the "Bride of Upper Egypt" (*Arous al-Sa'id*), **MINYA** derives considerable charm from its elegant villas built by Italian architects for Greek and Egyptian cotton magnates – now picturesquely decaying amidst overgrown gardens – and from its people, known in Egypt for their warmth and honesty. The only sign that it was once embroiled in a struggle between Islamic militants and the security forces are the concrete gun-towers at strategic locations – nowadays mostly unmanned. The security regime has sufficiently relaxed that **tourists** may wander about town without an escort, but the police will want to know where you're staying and to accompany you on any excursions to the surrounding sites.

Outside the train station, Midan al-Mahatta is a square redolent of an ex-colonial *ville* in North Africa. From here **Sharia Gumhorriya** leads to the palm-shaded **Midan Tahrir**, the hub of small-town life. Minya's **bazaar** stretches southwards along Sharia el-Hussein as far as **Midan Sa'a** (Clock

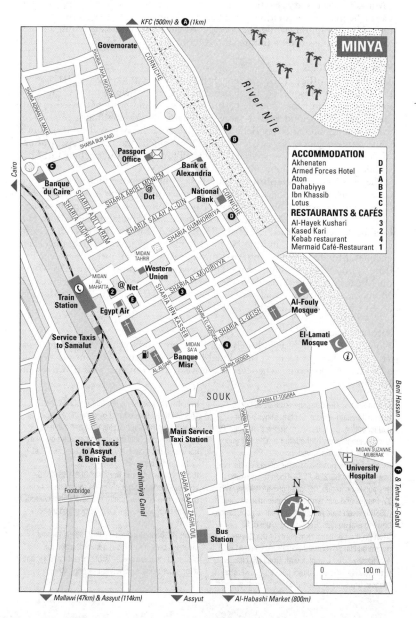

Square), bustling from mid-morning to midnight, as is the adjacent **Sharia Ibn Khasseb**, lined with Coptic jewellers and pharmacies. The **Corniche** is quiet by comparison, with a **park** affording views of the striated hills of the Eastern Desert across the Nile, where the town's name is spelt out in huge white letters, Hollywood style. Further north, pulsating multi-coloured lights cascade down from a water tower, 300m beyond the Governorate building.

Minya's annual **City Festival** on March 8 features a military band on the Corniche in commemoration of the fierce local resistance to British rule during the 1919 revolution; while the weekly **Al-Habashi Market** (Mon) in the south of town has been a fixture since Ottoman times.

Practicalities

The **tourist office** (daily except Fri 9am–5pm; ☎086/273-1521) beside the El-Lamati Mosque on the Corniche is keen to help, with the English-speaking Hussein Farag (mobile ☎010 1299479, ✉lindshussien@aol.com) and his sidekick Mahmoud Abd el-Samir (mobile ☎010 3371388) able to arrange excursions to sites such as Beni Hassan (see p.321). They will even accompany you as a guide (for £E150 per day), in which case the **tourist police** (☎086/236-4527) will waive the rule that all tourists must be accompanied by a policeman on excursions outside town.

There's a 24-hour **telephone office** beside the station, which sells Menatel cards for use in booths around town. The main **post office** (daily except Fri 8am–2pm), one block north of Sharia Abdel Moniem, has a **passport office** (daily except Fri 8am–2pm) on the floor above that can extend visas. Both the local banks (daily except Fri 8.30am-2pm) have ATMs: Banque Misr does cash advances on Visa cards, and the National Bank of Egypt will change travellers' cheques. Money may be transferred through Western Union (daily except Fri 9am–7pm) on Sharia Gumhorriya. The University **hospital** (☎086/236-6743) on Midan Suzanne Mubarak is the best in the region. Dot on Sharia Abdel Moniem, and Net in an alley behind Midan al-Mahatta, both offer **Internet** access (daily 11am–midnight).

Accommodation

None of the old-fashioned hotels near the train station want foreign guests, so visitors are limited to the places listed below. Most have cops outside, who'll ask where you're going whenever you leave and become nervous if you're out late after dark.

Akhenaten on the Corniche ☎086/236-5918, ✉kingakhenaton@hotmail.com. Minya's best budget option. En-suite a/c rooms with satellite TV, and a splendid view of the Nile from its sixth-floor restaurant. Large breakfast included. ❷

Armed Forces Hotel across the bridge on the east bank ☎ & ℱ086/236-6283. Open to civilians, this palatial complex has spacious a/c rooms with TV, fridges and sun terraces; its enormous suites (US$65) sleep four. Amenities include a pool, sauna, bowling and squash. Breakfast included. ❺

Aton on the Corniche 1km north of the Governorate building ☎086/234-2993, ℱ234-1517. A modestly sized complex with small a/c chalets with satellite TV, and a dinky pool on its riverside terrace. Breakfast included. ❺

Dahabiyya moored on the Nile ☎086/236-0096. This old houseboat owned by a Coptic evangelical organization has four cabins with narrow beds, washbasins and heaters, sharing a bathroom with hot water. The boat is a bit shabby but clean and quite atmospheric. ❶

Ibn Khassib 5 Sharia Ragab ☎086/236-4535. Very old-fashioned but clean, its rooms have high ceilings and antique furniture; some also have a/c, TV and bathrooms. There's a garden and a seedy bar. ❶

Lotus 1 Sharia Bur Said ☎086/236-5411. In a quiet-ish part of town, ten minutes' walk from the centre. Decent a/c rooms with showers and TV, and a top-floor restaurant serving alcohol. ❷

Eating, drinking and entertainment

If it's not too windy, you can enjoy the view of the Nile over a plate of chicken or spaghetti Bolognese aboard the *Mermaid Café-Restaurant*, moored alongside the Corniche. Other **restaurants** with a view are on the top floors of the *Akhenaten* and *Lotus* hotels – though food is better at the restaurant in the *Armed Forces Hotel*. For cheaper eats, try *Al-Hayek Kushari*, or the nameless kebab restaurant in the bazaar, where customers share a table. Failing that, there's a *KFC* outlet 500m beyond the Governorate building. Ice cream and cakes are served at the sparklingly clean *Kased Kari* patisserie on Midan al-Mahatta.

Of the three hotels serving **alcohol**, the *Ibn Khassib* is the cheapest source of Stella (£E8.50), Egyptian wine (£E20 for a small bottle) and brandy, followed by the restaurant in the *Lotus*; a beer on the Nile-side terrace at the *Aton* costs £E14.50. For entertainment, pay £E6 to enter the manicured grounds of the *Armed Forces Hotel*, whose amenities include **bowling** (daily 9am–midnight; £E10), **squash** (£E12), a **sauna** and **jacuzzi** (£E4 per person), a fair-sized **swimming** pool (£E12), a **cinema**, a children's playground and sun-loungers overlooking the river.

Transport

Though microbuses (25pt) and taxis (£E2) are widely used for getting around, Minya is compact enough for walking, with its local and long-distance transport depots fairly close together. As in other towns in Middle Egypt, the police prefer you to use **trains** to reach Cairo, Assyut, Luxor or Aswan, and don't seem to mind which of the dozen or so daily services you catch. At present, foreigners may also use inter-city **buses** to Assyut (hourly; 3hr) and Cairo (every 2hr; 5hr), leaving from the bus station on Sharia Sa'ad Zaghloul, but not **service taxis**. Should this change, the main depot and a smaller one serving Samalut are on Sa'ad Zaghloul; minivans to Assyut and Beni Suef leave from a terminal across the canal.

Around Minya: the east bank

Minya's bridge provides easy access to the **east bank** of the Nile, where several ancient sites and Coptic shrines can be visited on an **excursion** arranged by the tourist office. This costs £E50 per car for the places covered below, or £E100 if you also visit Beni Hassan (see p.321) – in which case it's best to see this first and work your way northwards afterwards.

North of Minya: The Frazer Tombs and Tihna el-Jebel

Six kilometres north of Minya, a turning east onto a side road leads towards some cliffs, where fallen rocks as big as houses mark the start of a path to the **Frazer Tombs** (daily 9am–5pm; free). Named after their excavator, Gary Frazer, these V and VI Dynasty rock-cut tombs are reached by sunken passage-ways. The two that are open to visitors once belonged to two dignitaries both named Nika-Ankh. The first contains damaged statues of Nika-Ankh, his wife, their children and grandson, interspersed by hieroglyphs. The effigies in the second tomb are better preserved; note the finely carved pleats on the kilt of Nika-Ankh's statue.

Two kilometres further north, another spur road runs to the village of **TIHNA EL-JEBEL** ("Below the Hill"), beside mounds of earth and the mud-brick **ruins** of the pharaonic town of *Dehenet* (Forehead), known to the Greeks as *Acoris*. A long stairway once flanked by altars and statues leads to a craggy massif with two unfinished **rock-cut temples** dedicated to Amun and Suchos (the Greek name for the crocodile-god Sobek). In the penultimate chamber of the first temple are two niches that originally held mummified crocodiles: if you carefully circumvent a deep shaft right outside, you can see a remaining croc in a chamber beyond the second temple. Further round the cliff-face, a chapel to the goddess Hathor is so high it seems unbelievable that it was ever used for offerings.

Deir al-Adhra: the Monastery of the Virgin

Beyond Tihna the main road hugs the base of the cliffs, where men cut limestone boulders into kerb-stones, and a flight of 166 steps ascends to the cliff-top village of **Gabel et-Teir** (Bird Hill), nowadays also accessible by road. The village is renowned for its **Monastery of the Virgin** – called **Deir al-Adhra** in Arabic – otherwise once known as the Monastery of the Pulley, after a hoist that was the only means of access before stairs were cut into the cliff.

A simple nineteenth-century edifice encloses a **rock-hewn church**, reputedly founded in 328 AD by Helena, mother of the Byzantine emperor Constantine. Its sanctity derives from a tiny **cave** where the Holy Family is believed to have hidden for three days, that now contains an icon of the Virgin credited with miraculous powers. Similar tales surround an icon of St Damyanah and the Forty Virgins (see p.672) and a baptismal font carved into one of the church's Greco-Roman columns. Usually only visited by local villagers, the church receives thousands of pilgrims during the week-long **Feast of the Assumption**, which takes place forty days after the Coptic Easter: during the festival, minibuses run here directly from Minya.

South of Minya: the Church of Aba Hur, Zawiyet el-Sultan and Kom al-Ahmar

Four kilometres south of Minya, the road to Beni Hassan runs past the predominantly Coptic village of **AL-SAWADAH**, where a sign in English welcomes visitors to the **Church of Aba Hur**. You can't miss the modern church that stands in front of a tunnel leading to its subterranean rock-hewn namesake. A blacksmith's son who was born in 310 AD and originally named Baghoura, Aba Hur became a hermit at the age of twenty and took up residence in a disused Ptolemaic temple a year later; his faith under torture converted the Roman governor of Pelusium to Christianity. Should you arrive at prayer-time the saint's shrouded body can be seen behind the iconostasis, wreathed in incense smoke. On July 6, hordes of pilgrims attend the **Moulid of Aba Hur**, camping out in the cemetery beyond Al-Sawadah.

Called **Zawiyet el-Sultan** (after the next village) or Zawiyet el-Mayyiteen ("Corner of the Dead"), this vast **cemetery** consists of thousands of domed mausolea in confessional enclaves, the Coptic ones topped by a forest of crosses. Local people can direct you to the **Hosh al-Basha** in the Muslim section, an austere edifice with an inlaid door, containing the tomb of **Hoda Shaarawi**, an early-twentieth-century feminist who campaigned for women's liberation and was the first woman to publicly remove her veil (in Cairo's Ramses station). Traditionally, locals visit their ancestral tombs during the Muslim months of Shawwal, Ragab and Zoul-Hagga, at the time of the full moon.

Beyond this the road passes **Kom al-Ahmar** (Red Mound), the site (daily 9am–5pm; free) of ancient *Hebenu*, capital of the Oryx nome. The name Hebenu comes from the ancient Egyptian word *hbn*, meaning to kill with a knife, and refers to the revenge of the god Horus on his father's murderer, Seth. The site's most interesting feature is a ruined III Dynasty **pyramid** whose symbolic tomb was never used as such, unlike another tomb dating from the New Kingdom, containing the defaced funerary statue of a local nomarch, Nefer-Skheru. The site was once crowned by a Greco-Roman temple reached by a flight of steps, to the right of which lies a chunk of masonry carved with the face of an unidentified Ptolemaic queen.

Beni Hassan, Speos Artemidos and Antinopolis

Some 20km south of Minya, barren cliffs on the east bank harbour the **rock tombs of Beni Hassan** (daily 8am–5pm; £E20), named after an Arab tribe that once settled hereabouts. The vivid murals in this necropolis shed light on the Middle Kingdom (2050–1800 BC), a period when provincial dignitaries showed their greater independence by having grand burials locally, rather than at Saqqara. Beni Hassan is also memorable for the stark contrast between the fertile banks of the Nile and the desert. A path links the tombs to the isolated temple of **Speos Artemidos**, 3km away.

At present, the only way of visiting the tombs is by **private taxi** from Minya, escorted by a policeman or a guide from the tourist office (which can provide a taxi for £E50). A new road along the east bank enables cars to get there directly in 25 minutes. Alternatively, you can combine Beni Hassan with Tuna al-Gabal and Hermopolis in a longer excursion, travelling via Abu Qirkus on the west bank and taking a ferry across the Nile. In this case, the taxi will drop you at the ferry stage 3km from Abu Qirkus and wait for your return from Beni Hassan; the **ferry** (daily 8am–5pm) takes fifteen minutes and costs £E6 for up to six people, or 50pt each for more than six.

The ticket office at Beni Hassan is 300m from the landing stage, with a rest-house selling soft drinks. A guard will accompany you up the steps to the tombs and unlock them: a tip is expected at the end. As at all the sites in the Nile Valley, there is a heavy police presence.

The tombs of Beni Hassan

Although most of Beni Hassan's 39 tombs are unfinished, the four shown to visitors evince a **stylistic evolution** during the XI–XII Dynasties. Their variously shaped chambers represent a transitional stage between the lateral *mastaba* tombs of the Old Kingdom and the deep shafts in the Valley of the Kings, gradually acquiring porched vestibules and sunken corridors to heighten the impact of the funerary effigies at the back. The actual mummies were secreted at the bottom of shafts, accompanied by funerary texts derived from the royal burials of the Old Kingdom. Pharaonic iconography and contemporary reportage are blended in the **murals**, whose innovative wrestling scenes presaged the battle vistas of the New Kingdom. Though battered and faded in parts, their details reward careful study; the following descriptions are keyed to the tomb plans on p.322. To prevent further fading, **photography** is no longer allowed inside the tombs.

Tomb of Kheti (#17)

Of the many chambers hewn into the cliff-side, the first you'll come to is the **Tomb of Kheti**, which retains two of its papyrus-bud columns, painted in places – the colours are quite fresh. Like most tombs of Ancient Egyptian dignitaries, its images are arranged in "registers" (rows), whose height above floor level reflects their spatial relationship. Thus, Nile scenes go below those involving the Valley, above which come desert vistas, the highest ones most distant.

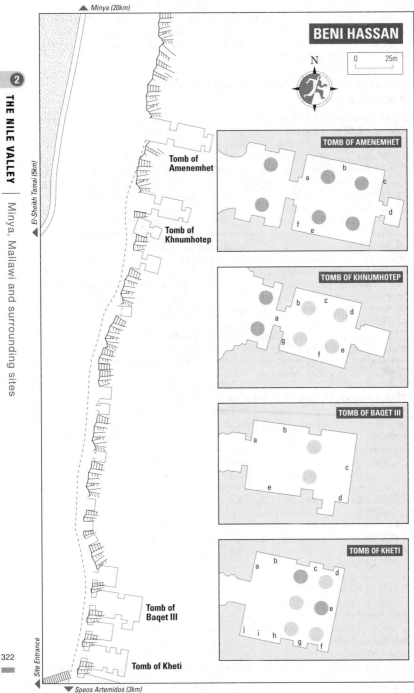

In the murals, hippopotami watch the papyrus harvest [a], as desert creatures are hunted [b] above registers of weavers, dancers, artists and *senet*-players (*senet* was a game a bit like draughts) observed by Kheti and his wife [c], to whom minions bring offerings of gazelles and birds [d].

The rear (east) wall features a compendium of wrestling positions [e], thought to emphasize efforts to defend Egypt against invaders from the east; a now-vanished scene of warriors storming a fortress once explicitly made the point. Don't miss the man standing on his head and in other yoga positions, between the scenes of wine-making [f] and herding cattle [h]. Ploughing [i] is another task overseen by Kheti in his role as nomarch, or governor, attended by his dwarf and fan-bearers [g]. Notice Kheti's boats, and bulls locking horns, in the corner [j].

Tomb of Baqet III (#15)

Kheti inherited the governorship of the Oryx nome from his father, buried in the **Tomb of Baqet III**. Its imagery is similar to that in Kheti's tomb, with some scenes better preserved, others not. While the mural of papyrus-gathering in the marshes [a] is quite faded, the desert hunt [b] is rich in details: notice the copulating gazelles near the left-hand corner. Ball players, women spinning and fullers beating cloth appear below. Nearly 200 wrestling positions are shown on the rear wall [c], with a lovely pair of birds above the funerary niche [d]. The south wall [e] is covered with episodes from the life of this XI Dynasty nomarch. In the second register from the top, his underlings count cattle and beat tax defaulters with sticks.

Tomb of Khnumhotep (#3)

Columned porticos and a niche for statues (which replaced the Old Kingdom *serdab* or secret chamber) are hallmarks of the XII Dynasty tombs, 150m north. The **Tomb of Khnumhotep** is framed by proto-Doric columns and hiero-glyphs praising this nomarch, who was also governor of the Eastern Desert. His funeral cortege appears inside the entrance [a]. Servants weigh grain and scribes record its storage in granaries [b], while beneath the desert hunt [c], Semitic Amus from Syria in striped tunics pay their respects, their alien costumes, flocks and tribute all minutely detailed – the governor is shown accepting eye paint.

In the niche, images of his children are visible on the walls but only the plinth of his statue remains. Elsewhere are vivid scenes of Khnumhotep netting birds, hunting with a throwing stick [d], and spearing fish from a punt in the marshes [e]. After the usual offerings [f], he inspects boat-building timber from a litter and then sails to Abydos [g]. Higher and lower registers portray bare-breasted laundrywomen, weavers and other artisans. The hieroglyphic text beneath these scenes has yielded clues about the political relationship between the nomarchs and pharaohs of the XII Dynasty.

Tomb of Amenemhet (#2)

The **Tomb of Amenemhet** belongs to Khnumhotep's predecessor, whose campaign honours are listed beside the door near a text relating the death of Senusert I. Proto-Doric columns uphold a vaulted ceiling painted with check-ered reed-mat patterns. A mural [a] of armourers, leatherworkers (at the top) and weavers (below) precedes the customary hunting scene [b], beneath which Amenemhet collects tribute from his estates. Note the scribes berating default-ers on the second register from the bottom. Below the wrestling and siege tableaux, boats escort him towards Abydos [c]. The niche [d] contains mutilated effigies of Amenemhet, his mother and his wife Heptet, who sits at her own table to receive offerings **[e]**. Fish are netted and spit-roasted above a painted false door flanked by scenes of music making, cattle fording and baking **[f]**.

Speos Artemidos

The cliffside path at Beni Hassan affords a fine view of the Nile and the abrupt transition from cultivation to desert. If the police let you, follow it for 2.5km past the Tomb of Kheti and turn 500m up a *wadi* to find the small rock-hewn **temple of Speos Artemidos**. Begun by Queen Hatshepsut, whose claims to have restored order after Hyksos misrule are inscribed above its door (but typically usurped by Seti I), the temple has only roughed-out Hathor-headed columns, and its sanctuary – dominated by a statue of the lion-goddess Pakht – is largely unfinished. However, scenes of Hatshepsut making offerings to the gods have been executed in the hall. Just before the site there's a small **grotto** (*speos*), whence comes the temple's Greek name. Further into the desert are early Christian **hermit cells**, after whom the *wadi* was called the Valley of the Anchorites.

Antinopolis

The ancient city of **Antinopolis**, 10km south of Beni Hassan, deserves a mention for its origins alone. Touring Egypt with his lover Antinous in 130 AD, the Roman emperor Hadrian was warned by an oracle to expect a grievous loss, whereupon Antinous drowned himself in the Nile to prevent a greater calamity befalling his master. In grief, Hadrian deified the youth and founded a city in his honour before continuing south to Thebes with his unloved wife Plotina. Today, little remains but some fine red-granite columns; most of the **ruins** were used to build the neighbouring village of Sheikh Abadah, or turned into cement in the nineteenth century.

Hermopolis and Tuna al-Gabel

Across the river on the west bank are two further sites whose remains are less dramatic than their mythical associations. According to one tradition, Creation began on a primordial mound near **Hermopolis**, where two giant stone baboons recall the long-vanished Temple of Thoth. More impressive is the city's necropolis, **Tuna al-Gabel**, where thousands of sacred baboons and ibises were buried in catacombs in the desert.

Due to travel restrictions, both sites are only accessible **by private taxi**, escorted by a policeman or tour guide. A taxi organized by Minya's tourist office costs £E50, or £E100 combined with Beni Hassan or Tell el-Armana. Although the sites appear close on a map, crossing the Nile and getting around are time-consuming, so you should reckon on six or seven hours to see either Beni Hassan or Tell el-Armana, in conjunction with Tuna al-Gabel and Hermopolis – it's not feasible to do them all in a single day excursion.

The ruins of Hermopolis

The pulverized ruins of Hermopolis spread beyond the village of **ASHMU-NEIN**, 8km from Mallawi. Turning right off the village high street you'll come to an outdoor **museum** (free) of antique stone-carvings, fronted by two **giant sandstone baboons** that once sported erect phalluses (hacked off by early Christians) and upheld the ceiling of the Temple of Thoth. Built by Ramses II using masonry from Tell el-Amarna, the temple stood within an enclosure covering 640 square metres, the spiritual heart of the city of the moon-god.

Hermopolis was a cult centre from early Dynastic times, venerated as the site of the primeval mound where the sun-god emerged from a cosmic egg. Like

Thoth and the Hermopolitan Ogdoad

In Egyptian mythology, **Thoth** was the divine scribe and reckoner of time, the inventor of writing and the patron god of scribes. His cult probably originated in the Delta, but achieved the greatest following in Middle Egypt; later, by association with Khonsu, he acquired the attributes of the moon-god and mastery over science and knowledge. Though usually depicted with a man's body and the head of an ibis (his sacred bird), Thoth also assumed the form of a great white baboon, invariably endowed with an outsize penis. Baboons habitually shriek just before dawn, and the Egyptians believed that a pair of them uttered the first greetings to the sun from the sand dunes at the edge of the world.

▲ Thoth

Thoth's role is rather more complex in relation to the Hermopolitan cosmogony, which ordained that the chaos preceding the world's creation had four characteristics, each identified with a pair of gods and goddesses: primordial water (*Nun/Nanuet*), infinite space (*Heh/Hehet*), darkness (*Kek/Keket*) and invisibility (*Amun/Amunet*). From this chaos arose the primeval mound and the cosmic egg whence the sun-god was hatched and proceeded to organize the world. While stressing the role of this **Hermopolitan Ogdoad** (company of eight), Thoth's devotees credited him with laying the cosmic egg in the guise of the "Great Cackler", so it's difficult to know who got star billing in this Creation myth. By the New Kingdom it had generally succumbed to the version espoused at Heliopolis (see p.222), but Thoth's cult continued into Ptolemaic times.

Heliopolis (which made similar claims) its priesthood evolved an elaborate cosmogony, known as the Hermopolitan Ogdoad (see box above). Though Ancient Egyptians called the city *Khmunu*, history remembers it as **Hermopolis Magna**; its Ptolemaic title reflects the Greek association of Thoth with their own god Hermes. However, none of the mounds of rubble that remain seem credible as the site of Creation, and there's little to see except 24 slender granite **columns**, further south. Re-erected by archeologists who mistook the ruins for a Greek *agora*, they previously supported a fifth-century Coptic basilica, but originally belonged to a Ptolemaic temple.

Tuna al-Gabel

From Ashmunein, a tarmac road continues to the village of **TUNA EL-GABEL**, which takes its name from the ancient **necropolis** (daily 8am–5pm; £E12) 5km further on into the desert. Along the way, notice the **boundary stele** on a distant cliff, marking the edge of the agricultural land that was claimed by Tell el-Amarna, across the river (see below). The name "Tuna" may derive from the Ancient Egyptian *Ta-Wnt* (the hare) or *ta-hnt* (meaning a place where many ibis birds gather). For millennia it was a cult-centre where pilgrims gave homage to Thoth by paying the priests to embalm ibises – over two million were sacrificed, mostly bred for the chop. Today this necropolis is awash with sand, wind-rippled drifts casting its angular mausolea into high relief, but obscuring other features.

Past the rest-house at the entrance (which sells drinks and has smart toilets), a path to the right leads to the **catacombs**, which some believe stretch as far as Hermopolis. The accessible portion consists of rough-hewn corridors with blocked-off side passages, where the mummified baboons, which were sacred to Thoth, and ibises were stacked (a few bandages remain). A shrine near the ladder contains a baboon fetish and a pathetic-looking mummy. You can also see the limestone sarcophagus of a high priest of mummification.

Further along the main track are several mausolea excavated by Gustav Lefebvre in 1920. The finest is the **Tomb of Petosiris**, High Priest of Thoth (whose coffin is in the Cairo Antiquities Museum), dating from 350 BC. Its vestibule walls depict traditional activities such as brick-making, sewing and reaping (left), milking, husbandry and wine-making (right) – with all the figures wearing Greek costume. Inside the tomb are colourful scenes from the *Book of Gates* and the *Book of the Dead*. The most vivid scene (on the right-hand wall near the back) shows nine baboons, twelve women and a dozen cobras, each set representing a temporal cycle. Notice the Nubians at the bottom of the opposite wall.

Another mausoleum contains the **Mummy of Isadora**, a young woman from Antinopolis who drowned in the Nile around 120 BC. Victims of the life-giving river acquired posthumous sanctity, but due to slapdash mummification and an infestation of termites her mummy is no longer fit to show.

In the desert off to the right you'll spot some **columns** from the Temple of Thoth that once dominated the site. You can also see the brick superstructure of a **well** that used to supply the necropolis and its sacred aviary with fresh water, drawn up from 70m below the desert by a huge **waterwheel**. A spiral staircase gives access to the well-head.

Mallawi

MALLAWI has gone to the dogs ever since Minya supplanted it as the regional capital in the 1960s. Many streets are still unpaved, and hovels are more prevalent than villas. To Egyptians, it is best known as the birthplace of President Sadat's assassin, Khalid al-Islambouli, and his brother Shawky, who fought with the Afghan *mujahadin* and later formed his own terrorist group in Egypt. Mallawi bore the brunt of the state's counter-insurgency campaign in the mid-1990s, which crippled its economy. Needless to say, the local police want foreigners to pass through as quickly as possible, but will tolerate a visit to the small **museum** on Sharia Banque Misr (daily except Wed 9am–4pm; £E6), exhibiting artefacts from Hermopolis and Tuna al-Gabel, and maybe a quick look at the derelict Hindu-Gothic-style **feudal palace** on a parallel street a few blocks away.

Practicalities

Should tourists ever be allowed to use local **transport**, it's worth knowing that Mallawi's terminals are dispersed on either side of the Ibrahimiya Canal that runs through the middle of town. On the east bank are the train station and, further south, the depot for service taxis to all points south of Mallawi. Northbound taxis leave from a depot 200m north of the canal bridge. On the other side of this is the main drag, Sharia Essim, along which buses and service taxis shuttle between Minya and Assyut. Across the road from the station on Sharia Bank Misr (aka Sharia Gala'a) is a **restaurant** serving *kofta* and a Banque Misr (Mon–Thurs & Sun 8am–2pm). To reach the **post office** (daily except Fri 8.30am–2pm), follow the dirt road to the left of the bank and turn left after 100m.

Tell el-Amarna

TELL EL-AMARNA is the familiar name for the site where **Pharaoh Akhenaten** and **Queen Nefertiti** founded a city dedicated to a revolutionary idea of God, which later rulers assailed as heretical. During their brief reign, Egyptian art cast off its preoccupation with death and the afterlife to revel in human concerns; bellicose imperialism gave way to pacifistic retrenchment;

and the old gods were toppled from their pedestals. The interplay between personalities, beliefs and art anticipates the Renaissance – and their story beats Shakespeare for sheer drama.

The interest of the **site** (see p.330 for access details) is chiefly romantic, for what remains is hardly comparable to the great temples further up the Nile. Only the faintest outline of the city is discernible, while the reliefs in its rock-cut tombs have been badly mutilated (initially by reactionaries, who defaced the images of Akhenaten and his deity). Nonetheless, it strikes some visitors as intensely evocative: a place of mystery whose enchantment grows the more one knows about it.

The story of Akhenaten and Nefertiti

Few figures from ancient history have inspired as much conjecture as Akhen-aten and Nefertiti, as scholars dispute even fundamental aspects of their story – let alone the interpretation of the events.

The tale begins with Pharaoh **Amenophis III**, who flouted convention by making Tiy, his Nubian concubine, Great Wife, despite her lack of royal blood. **Queen Tiy** remained formidable long after Amenophis entered his dotage and their eldest son ascended the throne as **Amenophis IV**. Some believe this event followed his father's death, others that mother and son ruled jointly for twelve years. To square the former theory with the period of his reign (c.1379–1362 BC) and his demise around the age of thirty means accepting that Amenophis Jr embarked on his religious reformation between the ages of 9 and 13. It seems an unusually early age, though a marriage at 13 is quite likely.

The origins of Amenophis's wife, **Nefertiti**, are obscure. Her name – meaning "A Beautiful Woman Has Come" – suits the romantic legend that she was a Mesopotamian princess originally betrothed to Amenophis III. However, others identify her as Amenophis III's child by a secondary wife, or as the daughter of his vizier **Ay**, whose wife, **Tey**, was almost certainly Nefertiti's wet nurse. The pharaonic custom of sister–brother and father–daughter marriages allows plenty of scope for speculation, but the fair-skinned bust of Nefertiti in the Berlin Museum suggests that she wasn't Tiy's child, at any rate. (Amid all the fuss about Cleopatra being black, nobody seems to have noticed that Queen Tiy – and therefore her son, Amenophis IV – were indubitably so.)

Early in his reign, Amenophis IV began to espouse the **worship of Aten** (see p.328), whose ascendancy threatened the priesthoods of other cults. The bureaucracy was equally alarmed by his decree that the spoken language should be used in official documents, contrary to all tradition. To escape their influence and realize his vision of a city dedicated to Aten, the pharaoh founded a **new capital** upon an empty plain beside the Nile, halfway between Memphis and Thebes, which he named **Akhetaten**, the "Horizon of the Aten".

It was here that the royal couple settled in the fifth year of their reign and took Aten's name in honour of their faith. He discarded Amenophis IV for **Akhenaten** (Servant of the Aten) and vowed never to leave the city, while she took a forename meaning "Beautiful are the Beauties of the Aten", styling herself **Nefernefruaten–Nefertiti**. Her status surpassed that of any previous Great Wife, approaching that of Akhenaten himself. Bas-reliefs and stelae show her participating in state festivals, and her own cartouche was coupled with Aten's – an unprecedented association. Tableaux from this period depict an idyllic royal family life, with the couple embracing their daughters and banquet-ing with Queen Tiy. Yet some believe that Tiy tried to persuade Akhenaten to return to Thebes and Amun-worship, and took against Nefertiti because of her fervent Atenism.

Many scholars herald **Aten-worship** as a breakthrough in human spirituality and cultural evolution: the world's first monotheistic religion, and thus representing "a peak of clarity which rose above the lowlands of superstition".

Aten was originally just an aspect of the sun-god (the "Globe" or "Disc" of the midday sun), ranking low in the Theban pantheon until Amenophis III privately adopted it as a personal deity. Then Akhenaten publicly exalted Aten above other gods, subsuming all their attributes into this newly omnipotent being. Invocations to Maat (truth) were retained, but otherwise the whole cast of underworld and celestial deities was jettisoned. Morbid Osirian rites were also replaced by paeans to life in the joyous warmth of Aten's rays (which are usually shown ending in a hand clasping an *ankh*), as in this extract from the *Hymn to Aten*:

When you rise from the horizon the earth grows bright; you shine as the Aten in the sky and drive away the darkness; when your rays gleam forth, the whole of Egypt is festive. People wake and stand on their feet, for you have lifted them up ... Then the whole of the land does its work; all the cattle enjoy their pastures, trees and plants grow green, birds fly up from their nests and raise their wings in praise of your spirit. Goats frisk on their feet and all the fluttering and flying things come alive.

Similarities between the *Hymn* and *The Song of Solomon* (supposedly written 500 years later) have encouraged speculation about the influence of Atenism on early Jewish monotheism. In *Moses and Monotheism*, Freud argued that Moses was an Egyptian nobleman and the Biblical Exodus a "pious fiction which a remote tradition has reworked in the service of its own biases". Conversely, a book by Ahmed Osman advances the theory that Akhenaten's deity derived from tales of the Jewish God related to him by his maternal grandfather Yuya, the Joseph of the Old Testament (see p.421).

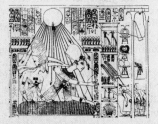

▲ Nerfertiti and Akhenaten

Equally intriguing is the artwork of the Amarna period and the questions it raises about Akhenaten. **Amarna art** focused on nature and human life rather than the netherworld and resurrection. Royal portraiture, previously impersonally formalized, was suffused by naturalism (a process which began late in the reign of Amenophis III, as evinced by the stele depicting the obese king listlessly slumped beside Tiy). While marshes and wildlife remained a popular subject, they no longer implicitly associated birds and fish with the forces of chaos. The roofless Aten temples made new demands on sculptors and painters, who mixed sunk- and bas-relief carving to highlight features with shifting shadows and illumination.

Most striking is the rendering of **human figures**, especially Akhenaten's, whose attenuated cranium, curvaceous spine and belly, and matronly pelvis and buttocks (evident on the colossi in the Cairo Museum) have prompted speculation that the pharaoh may have suffered from Marfan's syndrome – a rare genetic disorder that leads to feelings of alienation and a slight oddness in physical appearance – or was possibly a hermaphrodite. Some argue that the Amarna style was essentially an acquiescence to Akhenaten's physiognomy, others that such distortions were simply a device that could be eschewed, as in the exquisite bust of Nefertiti. Advocates of the "Akhenaten was sick" theory point out that this was the only time when vomiting was ever represented in Egyptian art; however, Amarna art also uniquely depicted royalty eating, yet nobody asserts that other pharaohs never ate.

There's no sign that their happiness was marred by his decision to take a second wife, **Kiya**, for dynastic ends; nor of the degenerative condition that supposedly afflicted Akhenaten in later life. However, the great ceremony held at Akhetaten in their twelfth regnal year marked a turning point. Whether or not this was Akhenaten's true coronation (following his father's death), he subsequently launched a **purge against the old cults**. From Kom Ombo to Bubastis, the old temples were closed and their statues disfigured, causing widespread internal unrest. Although this was quelled by Akhenaten's chief of police, **Mahu**, his foreign minister apparently ignored pleas from foreign vassals menaced by the Hittites and Habiru, and the army was less than zealous in defending Egypt's frontiers. Akhenaten was consequently blamed for squandering the territorial gains of his forefathers.

What happened in the last years of Akhenaten and Nefertiti's reign is subject to various interpretations. The consensus is that Nefertiti and Akhenaten became estranged, and he took as co-regent **Smenkhkare**, a mysterious youth married to their eldest daughter, **Meritaten**. While Nefertiti withdrew to her Northern Palace, Akhenaten and his regent lived together at the other end of the city; the poses struck by them in mural scenes of the period have prompted suggestions of a homosexual relationship. Whatever the truth of this, it's known that Smenkhkare ruled alone for some time after the **death of Akhenaten** (c.1362 BC), before dying himself. Nefertiti's fate is less certain, but it's generally believed that she also died around the same time. To date, none of their mummies have been found (or, rather, definitely identified).

In the late 1970s, a novel solution to the puzzle of Smenkhkare's identity and the **fate of Nefertiti** was advanced by Julia Samson of the Petrie Museum in London. Samson argued that Smenkhkare *was* Nefertiti, who, far from being spurned by Akhenaten, finally achieved pharaonic status, adopting Smenkhkare as her "throne name". Since the faces on the stelae depicting Akhenaten and his co-regent have been obliterated, only their cartouches identify them; and previous hypotheses have never satisfactorily explained why Smenkhkare's should be coupled with "Nefernefruaten", Nefertiti's Aten-name. Conversely, the youth shown with a princess isn't identified as her husband, nor by name, but he does wear the royal *uraeus*, or cobra. Unfortunately, this figure looks too old to be the famous boy-king who succeeded Smenkhkare at the age of 9 – known to posterity as **Tutankhamun**. Tut's own genealogy is obscure (some hold that his parents were Amenophis III and his half-sister Sitamun; others favour Ay and Tey, or Akhenaten and Kiya), but it's certain that he was originally raised to worship Aten, and named Tutankh*aten*. By renouncing this name for one honouring Amun, he heralded a return to Thebes and the old gods, fronting a **Theban counter-revolution** executed by Vizier Ay and General Horemheb.

Some think this was relatively benign while Tut and his successor Ay ruled Egypt, blaming **Horemheb** and Seti I for a later and ruthless extirpation of Atenism. Certainly, in time-honoured tradition, Seti plundered the abandoned city of Akhetaten for masonry to build new temples, ordered its site cursed by priests to deter reoccupation, and excised the cartouches of every ruler tainted with the "Amarna heresy" from their monuments and the List of Kings. So thorough was this cover-up that Akhenaten and Nefertiti remained unknown to history until the nineteenth century.

The site of Akhetaten

The **remains of Akhenaten's city** are spread across a desert plain girdled by an arc of cliffs. Away from the palm groves beside the Nile, the site is utterly

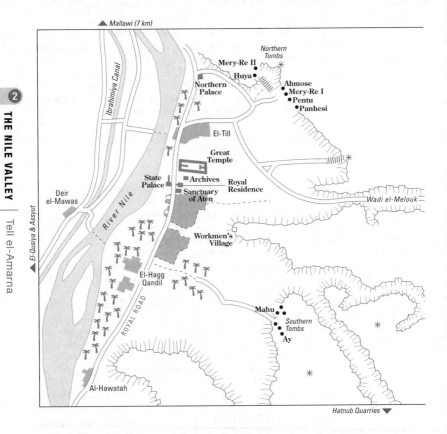

desolate, a tawny expanse of low mounds and narrow trenches littered with potshards. These fragments of pale terracotta, cream and duck-egg blue-glazed pottery seem more tangible links to the city's past than its vestigial remains. Because the city was created from scratch and deserted soon after Tut moved the court back to Thebes, its era of glory lasted only twelve years, and much of the building was never completed, so don't expect to find imposing ruins or statues, as everything of value has been removed to museums. However, over a century of archeological research has identified the city's salient features, assisted by pictures found in contemporary tombs.

Visiting Tell el-Amarna

Tell el-Amarna lies on the east bank of the Nile, 12km from Mallawi and roughly halfway between Minya and Assyut. While tour groups are now visiting, independent travellers are still rare and presently only allowed access **by private taxi** from Minya or Assyut (£E50 return), accompanied by a police escort or tour guide.

The east bank road from Minya peters out 15km beyond Beni Hassan, so access to Tell el-Amarna is via the west bank, using a car ferry 7km from Mallawi. To visit both sites on the same day (£E100 by taxi), you must double back to Minya, or use another car ferry between El-Sheikh Tamai (4–5km south of Beni Hassan) and the west bank, before proceeding to Mallawi to cross

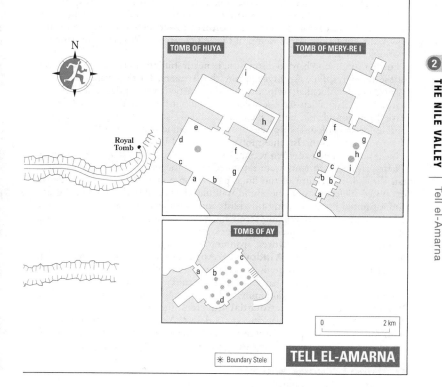

back over to the eastern side. Mallawi's landing stage has a choice of craft: a car ferry (£E16 per vehicle with passengers; retain the ticket for the return journey); a green motor-launch (£E6 for up to six people, or 50pt each for more than six); and an occasional blue tourist boat.

Landing at **EL-TILL,** you'll be greeted by children selling colourful basketwork. **Tickets** for the **site** (daily 8am–5pm; £E1) can be bought here at a kiosk, which also has a **car with a driver** (£E50) for anyone arriving without their own vehicle. They will also assign a policeman to escort you to the main ticket office near the Northern Tombs, and a custodian to ride with you to the Royal Tomb if you wish to visit it. The main office sells separate **tickets** for the Northern and Southern Tombs (£E20) and the Royal Tomb (£E16).

The City

The dirt track running south from El-Till follows the old **Royal Road** that formed ancient Akhetaten's main axis, and is known locally as the *Sikket es-Sultan*, the Road of the Sultan. Alongside is a Muslim cemetery, which overlies part of a rectangle stretching eastwards towards the ridge. This was once the **Great Temple of Aten**, whose northern wall incorporated the Hall of Foreign Tribute where emissaries proffered treasure (as depicted in tombs). Unlike traditional temples, which got darker as one approached the sanctuary, Aten's was roofless, admitting the rays of its namesake. It's thought that Horemheb ordered the temple's destruction after Akhenaten's death, and Ramses II quarried its foundations for his temples at Hermopolis, across the Nile. Today, replicas of a complete and partial lotus-bundle **column** tower incongruously above the low walls, erected by Barry Kemp of the Tell el-Amarna Project, who has been working here for decades.

Further south (and hard to distinguish beneath shifting sands) are the remnants of the Foreign Office **Archives**, where the **Amarna Letters** were discovered. Written in the Akkadian script used for diplomatic correspondence with Asiatic states, these clay tablets have revealed much about the period. Over 360 letters have been found, but more were undoubtedly lost, leaving an incomplete puzzle for archeologists to piece together and argue over. David Rohl believes that some refer to the Israelite monarchs Saul and David.

Next come three excavated rectangles that were once the **Royal Residence**. Their private apartments were separated from the stately reception halls that ran through the centre of the huge palace compound. When Flinders Petrie excavated Nefertiti's suite, he found wall tiles decorated with fruit and flowers, and a painted floor depicting fish, birds and insects (later smashed by a farmer who resented tourists walking across his fields). Across the Royal Road stood an even larger **State Palace**, with a dock for the royal barge. Both palaces were connected by a covered "flyover" spanning the road (part of one pylon remains), into which was set the **Window of Appearances**, whence Nefertiti and Akhenaten showered favoured courtiers with gold collars and other rewards.

To the south of their residence lay the **Sanctuary of Aten**, probably used for private worship by the royal family, and the home of the High Priest, Panehsi. Beyond spread the city's **residential quarters**; the richest homes beside the road, the poorest hovels backing onto desert. Also in this quarter was the workshop of the sculptor Tuthmosis, where the famous bust of Nefertiti was uncovered in 1912, before being smuggled to Berlin's Ägyptisches Museum.

Outlying palaces and stelae

The best-preserved outline of an Amarna building is Nefertiti's **Northern Palace** or summer residence, 1500m from El-Till. Low walls and hollows delineate rooms and courtyards grouped around a garden which once contained a pool that cooled the palace by evaporation. Like all Amarna residences, it was divided into public and private quarters, with north-facing doors to catch the prevailing wind. Rooms were plastered and painted, lit by oil lamps hung from pegs or set in niches, and warmed by braziers over winter. Fitted toilets and bathrooms also featured in the homes of the well-to-do. A magnificent painted floor depicting wildfowl and fish was found here, and is now in the Cairo Antiquities Museum. Unlike traditional marsh scenes, Amarna tableaux rarely feature hunting, suggesting that Akhenaten abjured the sport of kings.

In summer, Akhenaten and Nefertiti would ride in their electrum-plated chariot to the other end of the Royal Road, where another palace called Maru-Aten stood near the modern-day hamlet of Al-Hawatah. Alongside this **Southern Palace** lay a pleasure lake surrounded by trees and shrubs, which fed smaller pools within the palace. The walls of its columned hall were painted with flowers and inlaid with figures and Aten symbols. It was here that Petrie found hundreds of glazed pieces and flakes of paint adhering to blocks that bore Meritaten's cartouche superimposed over another, assumed to be that of Nefertiti – the rather shaky basis upon which archeologists devised the theory of Nefertiti's rejection in favour of Smenkhkare. In 1974, however, John Harris re-examined the fragments and concluded that the hidden cartouches really belonged to Kiya, whose existence had been unknown to earlier scholars. From this point on, Samson developed her theory that Nefertiti and Smenkhkare were one and the same (see p.329).

Akhetaten's periphery was defined by **boundary stelae** carved high up on the cliffs (marked ★ on our map); erected over successive years, their inscriptions and family portraits have enabled archeologists to deduce many events during Akhenaten's reign. Fine alabaster for the temples and public buildings was dragged from the **Hatnub Quarries**, 10km southeast of the city (only accessible by donkey or 4WD car). On the way up the *wadi* are the remains of workmen's huts and pottery from diverse periods.

The Northern Tombs

Some visitors are content to see just the **Northern Tombs**, 4km from El-Till. Bring a **torch** to spotlight uneven floors and to study the reliefs and paintings (now less clear than the copies made by Norman de Garis Davies in the 1900s). Tombs #1 and #2 lack electric lighting and are only shown to visitors who insist. **Photography** is not allowed in any of the tombs.

Tomb of Huya (#1)

As Steward to Queen Tiy and Superintendent of the Royal Harem, **Huya** is shown praying at the entrance, beside a *Hymn to Aten* **[a]**. In the following banqueting scene **[b]**, involving Tiy, the royal couple and two princesses, it may be significant that the dowager queen is merely drinking (which was acceptable by Theban standards of decorum), whereas the Amarna brood tuck in with gusto (an act never hitherto portrayed of royalty). Across the way they imbibe wine, *sans* princesses **[c]**, followed by a royal procession to the Hall of Tribute, where emissaries from Kush and Syria await Akhenaten and Nefertiti **[d]**.

On the rear wall, Akhenaten decorates Huya from the Window of Appearances (notice the sculptor's studio, lower down **[e]**), who displays his awards **[f]** on the other side of the portal, the lintel of which portrays three generations of the royal family, including Amenophis III. Along the east wall, Akhenaten leads Tiy to the temple built for his parents **[g]**. Huya's mummy was stashed in a burial shaft **[h]** below the transverse hall, beyond which is a shrine painted with offerings, containing an unfinished statue of Huya **[i]**.

Tomb of Mery-Re II (#2)

The last resting place of **Mery-Re II**, Overseer of the Two Treasuries, is similar in shape to Huya's tomb, but was constructed late in Akhenaten's reign, since his cartouches have been replaced by Smenkhkare's, and Nefertiti's by Meritaten's. Beyond the entrance (whose adoration scene and *Hymn to Aten* are largely destroyed), the inner walls portray Nefertiti straining a drink for the king, who is seated beneath a sunshade (to your left); and Mery-Re receiving a golden crown, followed by a warm welcome from his household (right). The rear wall bears an unfinished scene of Mery-Re being rewarded by Smenkhkare and Meritaten, drawn in black ink.

Tomb of Ahmose (#3)

This battered tomb is one of the four that visitors usually see. The entrance walls show **Ahmose**, Akhenaten's fan-bearer, praying to Aten, with a now-illegible inscription enjoining the deity to ensure "that there is sand on the shore, that fishes in the stream have scales, and cattle have hair. Let him sojourn here until the swan turns black and the raven white". Inside, you can just discern Ahmose carrying an axe and a fan, his official regalia. On the left-hand wall are bas-reliefs of shield-bearers and pikemen, crouched and moving, followed by an outsized horse and chariot outlined in red pigment (presumably intended to represent Akhenaten leading his army into battle, which never happened). In the transverse hall are two false doors, a deep vertical shaft, and a defaced, life-size statue of Ahmose in a niche.

Tomb of Mery-Re I (#4)

High Priest **Mery-Re I** (father of Mery-Re II) rated a superior tomb, with a coloured cornice around its entrance **[a]** and false columns of painted flowers at the rear of the vestibule **[b]**. Reliefs of Mery-Re and his wife, Tenro, at prayer flank the portal **[c]** into the main chamber, which retains two of its original papyrus-bud columns. Proceeding clockwise round the room, one sees Mery-Re's investiture with a golden collar **[d]**, the royal family leaving the palace **[e]**, and Akhenaten in a chariot (his face and the Aten symbol have been chiselled out, as usual). Scenes of offerings **[f]** and Aten-worship **[g]** flank the left side of doorway into the unfinished rear chamber, which lacks any decoration. More interesting is the eastern wall **[h]**, depicting Akhenaten and the Great Temple (which has helped archeologists visualize the city's appearance). Notice the sensitive relief of blind beggars awaiting alms, low down in the corner **[i]**.

Tombs of Pentu (#5) and Panehsi (#6)

The third tomb in this cluster belongs to **Pentu**, the royal physician. Its papyrus-bundle columns retain traces of paint with chariots visible on the right-hand wall, but there's little else to see. It's better to head 300m south along the cliff path to the isolated tomb of **Panehsi**, overseer of the royal herds and granaries. Unlike most of the others, its decorative facade has remained intact, but the interior has been modified by Copts who used it as a chapel. To the left of the entrance, the royal family prays above their servants. The painted, apse-like recess in the main chamber is probably a Coptic addition – notice the angel's wings. In one corner of the inner chamber, steps spiral down into an underground sarcophagus chamber containing broken urns. Lower down the cliff are strata of rubble and potshards – vestiges of a medieval Coptic village.

▲ Akhenaten

The Royal Tomb

Since a new road was laid in 2004 it has been an easy ten-minute drive to the subterranean **Royal Tomb**, in a desolate ravine 5.5km from the plain. A custodian will ride with you to unlock the tomb and fire up the generator to provide lighting. Dug into the bed of the *wadi* (which now has drainage canals to carry flash floods away), the tomb was the first from the XVIII Dynasty to run directly from a corridor to a burial chamber. Its burial scene and text were virtually obliterated by Amun's priests, and no mummies were ever found there, but in a chamber off the first descending passage, fragmentary bas-reliefs (now being clumsily "restored") depict the funerary rites of one of the royal daughters (either Meketaten or Ankesbaten), and a granite sarcophagus bearing Tiy's cartouche was found, suggesting this might have been a family vault. No one knows whether Akhenaten and Nefertiti were interred in the main burial chamber beyond a deep pit (and perhaps dragged out to rot a few years later) or somewhere else. Some believe that the mysterious mummy found in Tomb #55 in the Valley of the Kings is Akhenaten's (see p.421).

The Southern Tombs

From El-Hagg Qandil beyond the ancient Workmen's Village, a poorly surfaced road runs between palm-groves to the **Southern Tombs**, scattered over seven low hills in two clusters: #7–15 and #16–25. Amarna notables buried here include Tutu, the foreign minister, and Ramose, Steward of Amenophis III, but the ones to see are Ay and Mahu.

Tomb of Ay (#25)

Ay's Tomb was never finished, since he built himself a new one at Thebes after the court returned there under Tutankhamun, but such carvings as were executed show the Amarna style at its apogee and the ceiling of its central aisle is painted with a fetching checkerboard pattern.

Both sides of the tomb's vestibule **[a]** are decorated. On the left, the king and queen, three princesses, Nefertiti's sister Mutnedjmet and her dwarves lead the court in the worship of Aten. Across the way is a superb relief of Ay and his wife Tey rendering homage and the most complete text of the famous *Hymn to Aten*; every fold of their skirts and braid in their hair are meticulously depicted. The really intriguing scenes, however, are in the main chamber. On the left side of the entrance wall, Ay and Tey are showered with decorations from the Window of Appearances, acclaimed by fan-bearers, scribes and guards **[b]**. Palace life is depicted in ink or sunk-relief: a concubine has her hair done, while girls play the harp, dance, cook and sweep. The depth of bowing by courtiers is the most servile ever found in Egyptian art **[c]**. Along the rear wall are a ruined door-shaped stele **[d]** and a stairway leading to an unfinished burial shaft.

Ay and Tey are mysterious figures, honoured as "Divine Father and Mother", but never directly identified as being royal. Some reckon Ay was a son of Yuya and Thuya, Akhenaten's maternal grandparents; others that Tey was Nefertiti's wet-nurse, or that both conceived Tutankhamun. Certainly, Ay was vizier to Amenophis III, Akhenaten and Tutankhamun, and reigned briefly himself (1352–1348 BC). He was ultimately buried in the Western Valley of the Theban Necropolis (see p.421).

Tomb of Mahu (#9)

Ten minutes' walk away, the **Tomb of Mahu**, Akhenaten's chief of police and frontier security, opens with a rough-cut transverse hall featuring a scene of Mahu standing before the vizier with two intruders whom he accuses of being "agitated by some foreign power", as minions heat irons in a brazier for their torture (to the left as you enter). Further in are two more chambers at different levels, linked by a winding stairway – mind your head on the low ceiling.

Assyut and around

Every country has at least one city which is universally loathed by all but those who live there. In Egypt, Assyut holds this honour.

Douglas Kennedy, *Beyond The Pyramids*

ASSYUT (pop. 402,000) was the first part of Middle Egypt to become a no-go zone for tourists in the 1990s, as local **Islamic militants** targeted foreigners as well as the security forces in their war against the state. The city endured nearly a decade of curfews and arrests as the conflict spread south before fizzling out, leaving Assyut with an overwhelming police presence and the mother of bad reputations. So it's not surprising that Assyut's citizens – and the Christian population especially – rejoiced at the nightly **apparitions** of the Virgin Mary that occurred (so people swear) in September 2000, in the form of a light above the tower of the Church of St Mark. Another cause for optimism is the upturn in the economy, due to private and state investments in factories and businesses – and the success of the town's **football** team Assyut Cement, sponsored by the cement factory across the river. Residents are more ambivalent about the fame of Assyut-born sex bomb **Ruby** – whose pop-videos make Britney Spears look like a nun – and local Mafioso **Izzat Hanafi** (see box below). Volatile, god-fearing and decrepit, Assyut is Naples on the Nile or Palermo with chadors.

For tourists, Assyut's attractions are limited to a few monasteries and tombs within the governorate, the odd historic monument being restored in the old quarter, and the city's **Governorate Festival** (April 18), which commemorates the defeat of French forces by local villagers in 1799 and is marked by folklore shows and a flotilla of boats on the Nile. However, few visitors feel comfortable being accompanied by plainclothes **police** – and maybe even a motorcycle escort, too – though, bizarrely, while police shadow foreigners everywhere by

Assyut's militant tradition

In the late 1970s, **Assyut University** became a stronghold of **Islamic Societies** (*Gama'at Islamiya*) bent on turning Egypt into an Islamic republic. They managed to get music and co-ed drama banned, and cafeterias segregated by sex; violations of their standards were liable to be punished by club-wielding militants. The authorities turned a blind eye until 1981, when President Sadat cracked down on religious extremism after years of tolerating it as a counterweight to the Left.

In response, members of the secret group **Al-Jihad** (Holy Struggle) assassinated Sadat in Cairo and stormed Assyut police headquarters the following day, hoping to launch a revolution. Two days of rioting ensued, causing 55 deaths. Among those later indicted at the mass "Trial of the Jihad 302" was the blind university theologian **Sheikh Omar Abd el-Rahman**, their "spiritual leader". Acquitted but exiled to the Fayoum, the Sheikh later moved to the US, where in 1995 he was sentenced to life imprisonment for conspiring to blow up the World Trade Center. By that time many of his followers had joined forces with al-Qaida (see p.833), whose own attack on the Twin Towers on September 11 was reputedly undertaken in Abd el-Rahman's name. In 2001 his son, Ahmed, was captured by US forces in Afghanistan, fighting with the Taliban.

The 1997 Luxor massacre (see p.423) was also related to the sheikh and Assyut; the splinter group responsible consisted of six students from Assyut University, and a letter found on one of the terrorists claimed that they meant to seize hostages in a bid to bargain for Abd el-Rahman's release from prison.

The insurgency and economic depression of the 1990s fostered organized crime in the city. Local crime boss **Izzat Hanafi** was based 10km upriver from Assyut, in the village of **El-Nekheila**, where he ran his drugs plantations and illicit weapons and antiquities rings. In March 2004, 6000 police and 200 armoured cars surrounded the village where Hanafi was protected by gunmen and dozens of cooking-gas cylinders wired to explode. After a six-day siege, during which Hanafi threatened to kill 160 hostages (many of whom were his supporters) and shot up a train to prove that he meant business, troops moved in and arrested him, seizing half a tonne of *bango* and 50 kilos of opium. Residents alleged that up to seventy people died in the fighting; the police stated that only a single gang member was killed. The government has since built a school and hospital to alleviate local resentment and stationed a large police garrison to ensure that El-Nekheila doesn't slip back into the hands of criminals.

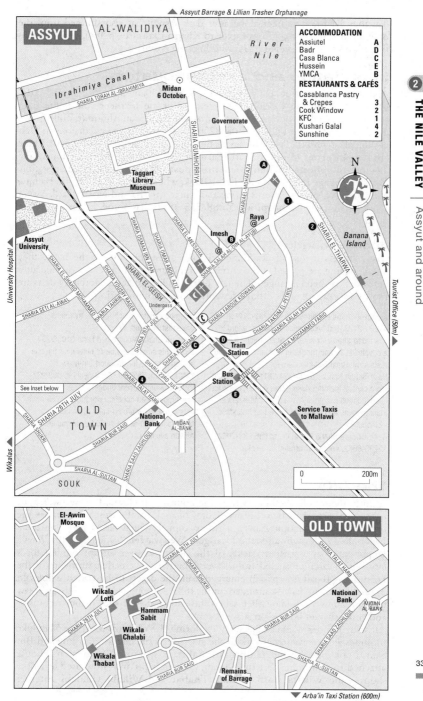

▲ Assyut Barrage & Lillian Trasher Orphanage

ASSYUT

AL-WALIDIYA

River Nile

Ibrahimiya Canal

SHARIA TORAH AL-IBRAHIMIYA

Midan
6 October

Governorate

SHARIA GUMHORRIYA

Taggart
Library
Museum

SHARIA EL-MASSARA

SHARIA EL-MOHAFAZA

Ⓐ

Ⓘ

Raya
@

Imesh

Ⓑ

@

Ⓩ

SHARIA EL-THARWA

Banana
Island

SHARIA OSMAN IBN AFAN

SHARIA OMAR ABDEL AZIZ

SHARIA SALAH AL-DIN AL-AYUBI

Assyut
University

SHARIA EL-SHAHID MOHAMMED

SHARIA YOUSSY FAHER

SHARIA TAHRIR

SHARIA SETI AL-AWAL

SHARIA EL-GEISH

Underpass

SHARIA FAROUK KIDWANI

SHARIA TAKSIM EL-PETROL

SHARIA SALAH SALEM

SHARIA MOHAMMED FARID

Ⓒ

Ⓓ Train
Station

Bus
Station

Ⓔ

Service Taxis
to Mallawi

SHARIA 26TH JULY

SHARIA 23RD JULY

SHARIA KITSHABA

Ⓒ

Ⓐ

SHARIA TALAT HARB

See Inset below

OLD
TOWN

SHARIA 26TH JULY

SHARIA SHUKRI

National
Bank

MIDAN
AL-BANK

SHARIA BUR SAID

SHARIA SAAD ZAGHLOUL

SHARIA AL-SULTAN

SOUK

Wikalas ◄

University Hospital ◄

Tourist Office (50m) ►

0   200m

ACCOMMODATION

Assiutel	A
Badr	D
Casa Blanca	C
Hussein	E
YMCA	B

RESTAURANTS & CAFÉS

Casablanca Pastry & Crepes	3
Cook Window	2
KFC	1
Kushari Galal	4
Sunshine	2

N

OLD TOWN

El-Awim
Mosque

SHARIA 26TH JULY

SHARIA SHUKRI

SHARIA TALAT HARB

Wikala
Lotfi

Hammam
Sabit

Wikala
Chalabi

Wikala
Thabat

SHARIA 26TH JULY

National
Bank

MIDAN
AL-BANK

SHARIA BUR SAID

SHARIA SAAD ZAGHLOUL

SHARIA AL-SULTAN

Remains
of Barrage

SHARIA BUR SAID

▼ Arba'in Taxi Station (600m)

day, they let them wander alone after dark. Assyut has also suffered from the opening of a direct road from Luxor to Kharga Oasis (see p.384), which means that it's no longer necessary to travel there via Assyut.

Information and accommodation

Assyut's **tourist office** (daily except Fri & Sat 8.30am–3pm; ☎088/231-0010, ℻230-5110) on the Corniche will send someone to meet you at the train station, given a day's notice, while the manager Ramadan Abdou (mobile ☎012 3462601) or Madam Fikhry (☎088/230-5110) can arrange excursions to Deir el-Muharraq and the Meir Tombs or the convent at Dirunka (see p.340). There are two **Internet** cafes on Sharia Salah al-Din (*Imesh* is open 24 hours); the 24-hour **telephone exchange** and main **post office** are near the train station. You can change **money** on Midan al-Bank, where National Bank and Banque Misr have ATMs; the latter does cash advances on Visa and MasterCard. Assyut University's Ga'ama **hospital** (☎088/233-4811) has some English-speaking doctors.

Accommodation

Many **hotels** in Assyut don't want foreign guests because of the hassle they entail: **police** are posted at the entrance and tourists can only step outside after an escort has been arranged. The few places willing to accept foreign guests are mostly overpriced and within a few blocks of the train station.

Assiutel Sharia el-Tharwa ☎088/231-2121, ℻231-2122. The best choice if you can afford it, this faded three-star hotel on the Corniche has a/c, satellite TV and fridges in its rooms, a bar and restaurant. Breakfast included. ❺
Badr Sharia Nahda ☎088/232-9811, ℻232-2820. More central than the *Assiutel* but noisier, this once decent option has gone to the dogs under new management, and no longer has a bar. Breakfast included. ❹
Casa Blanca Sharia Khashaba ☎086/233-7662, ℻233-6662. Another overrated three-star

charging way too much for gloomy rooms. Breakfast included. ❹
Hussein Sharia Mohammed Farid ☎088/234-2532. This small, fairly basic hotel near the bus station is handy for transport but noisy. ❷
YMCA Sharia Salah al-Din al-Ayubi ☎088/232-3218. The only decent budget option, its old section has simple clean doubles with fridges; £E5 more gets you a larger a/c en-suite room behind the basketball court at the back. Genial manager Attiyah speaks English. ❶

The City

A dusty metropolis seething with traffic pouring off elevated freeways, **Assyut** has largely erased its own history. Scores of rock tombs west of town are the only sign of pharaonic Sawty, a nome capital which the Greeks renamed Lycopolis (Wolftown) after the local god, **Wepwawet**, "Opener of the Ways". Represented as a wolf or jackal of the desert, he was an apt symbol for a city which later prospered from slavery, for it was here that survivors of the Forty Days Road (see p.572) emerged from the desert to be traded wholesale. Trafficking may have continued until 1883, although Amelia Edwards saw nothing amiss a decade earlier, when she enthused over the "quaint red vases" and "bird-shaped bottles" in Assyut's souks.

If your minder doesn't object, try exploring the **old town**, where Mamluke mosques and caravanserais lurk in the side streets off sharias 26th July and Bur Said. Look out for the **Hammam Sabit,** a working Ottoman bathhouse attached to a mosque, near three medieval merchants' inns now used as workshops – the **Wikala Lotfi**, **Wikala Thabat** and **Wikala Chalabi**. Another feature reminiscent of Islamic Cairo is the remains of a Nile **Barrage** built during the time of Mohammed Ali.

Alternatively, cross the railway tracks via the underpass and stroll along Sharia Salah al-Din al-Ayubi, where each evening Assyutis **promenade** past fairy-lit boutiques to a breezy **Corniche** lined with private clubs hosting weddings and other functions. From here, you can take pleasure **cruises** (May–Nov; £E5–10) to **Banana Island** (*Gezira el-Mohz*) – a lush picnic spot that's also accessible by felucca – and the **Assyut Barrage**, 2km downriver, built by the British between 1898 and 1903.

This era also saw the founding by American missionaries of a boy's college (now the co-ed Al-Salaam School), off Midan 6th October: its Taggart Library **museum** (daily except Fri & Sun 8am–3pm; free) displays such curios as mummified dogs and fish, and pharaonic soldiers' dog-tags. Across the river, the **Lillian Trasher Orphanage** (*Malga Trasher*) is the largest, best-known institution of its kind in Egypt (there's another famous one in Tanta, funded by pop star Mohammed Tharwat). Founded in 1911 by Florida-born Lillian Trasher, who came to Egypt at the age of 23 and died in her adopted homeland in 1961, the orphanage is a source of pride for Assyut's Copts, and visitors are welcome (as are donations). Microbuses (50pt) from the centre stop nearby, or you can get a taxi (£E3).

Eating and drinking

To **eat** familiar food in a sterile environment, head for the Corniche, where *Cook Window* and the nearby *Sunshine Restaurant* have a choice of burgers, pizza and *shawarma*, augmented by *KFC's* usual fare, further up – all stay open till midnight. In the centre of town, *Casablanca Pastry and Crepes* does takeaway pizzas and pancakes (savoury or sweet), or you can dig in at *Kushari Galal* on Sharia Talat Harb (open till 1am or later). There are coffeehouses and juice-bars all over the centre of town, but since the *Badr Hotel* went teetotal, you can only **drink** alcohol in the bar of the *Assuitel* (which gets mildly lively on Thursday nights) – though illicit *shebeens* reportedly flourish in villages around Assyut.

Moving on from Assyut

The police prefer tourists to leave town by train, so they don't restrict them to any particular service. About nine **trains** a day run to Cairo (5–7hr), stopping at Mallawi (2hr), Minya (3hr) and Beni Suef (5hr) along the way, and a dozen trains call at Sohag (2hr), Qena (4hr) and Luxor (6hr) en route to Aswan (12hr). Tourists may not be allowed to use the **buses**, which run more or less hourly to Cairo (6–7hr; £E25) and Sohag (2hr; £E8); every two hours to Minya (2–3hr; £E8); twice daily to Qena (noon & 1pm; 4hr; £E15); Alexandria (7am & 7pm; 10hr; £E35) and Hurghada (9am & 8pm; 8hr; £E25); and once to Sharm el-Sheikh (3pm; 12hr; £E40), Luxor and Aswan (at 8am; 6–9hr; £E25–40). Additionally, there are four buses daily to Kharga (4hr; £E8) between 7am and 10pm, two of which run on to Dakhla Oasis (7–8hr; £E20). While the train and bus stations are both central, **service taxis** leave from the Arba'in terminal beside the El-Mallah Canal on the edge of the old quarter (£E5 by taxi from the centre). Although taxis run to every town along the Valley from Minya to Qena, foreigners may only take them to Kharga Oasis (4hr; £E8). For details of twice-weekly **flights** to Cairo (Sun & Thurs), contact EgyptAir (℡088/231-5228; daily except Fri 9am–3pm) in the governorate building.

Around Assyut

In the vicinity of Assyut are two **monasteries** that testify to the roots Christianity put down in this region in the fourth century. Copts believe that these and other sites were actually visited by the **Holy Family** during the four years that Mary, Joseph and the infant Jesus stayed in Egypt to escape King Herod's massacre of the first-born. Although the Bible says little about this period, details of their wanderings were revealed in a dream to Patriarch Theophilus in AD 500, and Copts have made much of this tradition ever since. Indeed, most tourism in the Assyut region involves Copts from other parts of Egypt, making pilgrimages on holy days – although Assyut's tourist office hopes to lure foreigners with the little-visited **Meir Tombs**.

Dirunka: the Convent of the Virgin

Copts believe that the Holy Family sought refuge in caves at **DIRUNKA**, 12km outside Assyut – as did later Christians. From such troglodyte origins, the present **Convent of the Virgin** (aka *Deir el-Adhra,* or Santa Maria) on the site has grown into what resembles a fortified campus – cynics might say a refuge for Assyut's Coptic population, should the worst ever occur.

The expansion is justified by the nearly one million pilgrims who attend the **Moulid of the Virgin** (August 15–30). This occasions the parading of icons around the spacious cave church where they stand for most of the year. Coptic altars face east because it's from there that Jesus will return, but also because He is "the sun" of their religion. Pilgrims are photographed against a huge portrait of the Virgin, or the verdant plain overlooked by the convent's terrace, below which is a Coptic village where nuns operate a dispensary. About fifty nuns and monks live in the convent.

As the police might wish to escort visitors and may frown on you travelling by minibus (50–75pt) from Assyut, a private taxi (£E30 round-trip with 1hr waiting) is the best way of **getting there**, and saves you a fifteen-minute uphill slog from the roadside. If you don't retain your taxi, returning minibuses can be flagged down on the main road.

En route to Dirunka you'll pass a range of barren hills riddled with the **Tombs of the Nobles** (normally locked, but sometimes accessible by prior arrangement with the tourist office). Mostly from the Middle Kingdom, they provide virtually the only record of events during the First Intermediate Period (2160–2050 BC). The Tomb of Djefaihapy I contains some of the oldest surviving legal documents anywhere (required reading for Egyptology students), while hundreds of votive stelae and figurines were found in the Tomb of Djefaihapy III, that was uniquely used as a popular shrine long after his death.

El-Qusiya: the Burnt Monastery and the Meir Tombs

It's the police who decide whether foreigners can enter the area around El-Qusiaya. If you get the go-ahead, the tourist office can arrange an excursion **by private taxi** to both the Burnt Monastery and the Meir Tombs for £E100, which enables you to get around far more easily than relying on local service taxis or pick-up trucks to and from El-Qusiya.

EL-QUSIYA, 42km north of Assyut, is an agricultural town of 40,000 people, three-quarters of them Copts. In 1998, state security police investigating the murder of two Coptic youths tried to pin the blame on their families using torture to extract confessions and, after this failed, hauled in ever more relatives and associates – up to 1200 in a month – until Bishop Wissa alerted the world's media. Although arrests ceased after his intervention, Wissa was charged under the emergency laws with "endangering national unity", and no police officers were ever punished. While human rights activists stressed that police brutality and abuse of power were a problem throughout Egypt, for Muslims and Copts alike, this doesn't explain what happened a year later. On New Year's Eve, 1999, a fatal quarrel between a Coptic merchant and a Muslim customer was followed by a wave of shootings and arson that left twenty Copts and one Muslim dead and dozens injured, which the police did nothing to stop for two days. No convincing explanation for why and how it happened has emerged; one fatuous "solution" suggested – but not adopted – was to rename the town "Peace Village", since El-Qusiya can mean "Emnity" in classical Arabic.

Some 5km out of town, the **Burnt Monastery** (*Deir el-Muharaaq*) stands near the desert's edge. Its tinderbox surroundings explain the name and protective walls; the crenellated inner rampart is still blackened from a conflagration that occurred during the **Moulid of the Virgin** (June 21–28) over a decade ago. Except on fast days, visitors are shown around the thriving modernized establishment. Many of the hundred students at its Theological College will become monks when they turn 25. Within the compound are grouped the Abbot's residence, a fourth-century keep and two churches. Believers maintain that the **cave sanctuary** of the **Church of the Anointed** (*El-Azraq*) once hid the Holy Family for six months and ten days, and that the church was one of the first in the world, foretold in the Old Testament as "an altar to the Lord in the midst of the land of Egypt" (Isaiah 19:19–21). It's also said that what is now the altar stone was once used to block the cave's entrance. When an abbot ordered its replacement, the mason's hand was paralysed and a vision of Jesus appeared, intoning "Leave it alone." The icon of the Virgin and Child is said to be painted by St Luke; the apostles in the **Church of St George** come from Ethiopia. Remember to remove your shoes before entering the churches.

The **Meir Tombs** are further north, 6km from the village of Meir (or Mayr), reached by a secondary road. This rock-hewn necropolis belonged to the nomarchs of the fourteenth nome, whose capital Qis or Cusae was the ancestor of El-Qusiya. Nine of its seventeen tombs are open to the public (daily except Thurs & Fri 9am–5pm; £E16). Tombs #1 and #2 are inscribed with 720 deities, defaced by the Christian hermits that once resided there; while in tomb #4 you can see the original grid drawn on the wall to help the artists execute their designs. Best of all are the splendid desert hunting scene in the tomb of **Senbi-Sa-Ukh-hotep**, and the women's fashions of the XII Dynasty depicted in Chancellor **Ukh-hotep**'s tomb. Model boats from these tombs are exhibited in the Luxor Museum.

Sohag

Set on a rich agricultural plain bounded by the hills of the Eastern and Western deserts, **SOHAG** (pronounced "So*haj*") is an industrious town of 132,000 with a large Christian community and a small university. Before the conflict in Middle Egypt, Sohag made a nice, relaxed stopover and a base for visits to the nearby **Red and White monasteries**, or Abydos Temple, further away (see p.344). Tourism nose-dived in the 1990s, but the government is now trying to woo back visitors by building an archeological museum and excavating further remains to display alongside a colossal statue of an ancient Egyptian princess in **Akhmim**, across the river. A few tour operators have begun to feature Sohag on their itineraries again, but independent travellers have yet to follow. As in other cities in Middle Egypt, anyone coming here should get in contact with the tourist office beforehand, to smooth out any potential hassles with the local police.

Hopefully, the new **Sohag Museum** on the east bank of the Nile will be ready by 2006, to become a showcase for some five thousand artefacts found within the governorate, from the Middle Kingdom until Greco-Roman times. It's envisaged that the collection will grow as excavations in Akhmim unearth the temple of Ramses II and other New Kingdom structures. Meanwhile, Akhmim remains the centre of attention and Sohag's attractions are episodic. Its weekly Souk el-Itnayn (so-called because it occurs on Monday, 6am–noon) is a massive **animal market**, held just off the Girga road, while the whole town celebrates the **Moulid of Al-Aref** – Sohag's patron saint – a few weeks before the nationwide feast of Eid al-Adha, outside the mosque that bears his

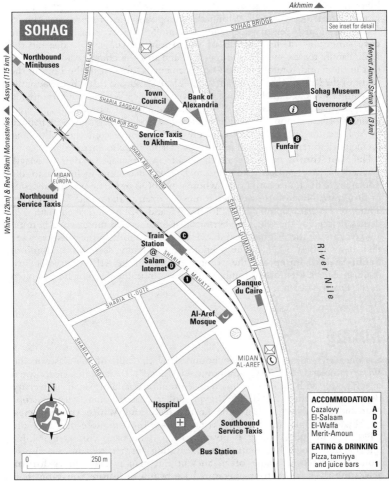

name. Among other deeds, Al-Aref is remembered for hiding Murad Bey, the only Mamluke to escape the infamous massacre at the Citadel in Cairo, who fled to Upper Egypt. **City Day** (April 10) commemorates a local victory over Napoleon's troops in 1799, at the battle of Juhaina.

Practicalities

Sohag's **tourist office** (daily except Fri & Sat 8.30am–3pm; ☎093/460-4913, ext. 268) in the governorate building, can fill you in on the progress of the museum and excavations at Akhmim, while helpful staff – namely Hassan Rifat (mobile ☎010 3342824) or Mahmoud Ashour (☎093/460-4453) – can arrange excursions by taxi to the monasteries and fix **accommodation**, since tourists who just turn up might be turned away by hotels on the pretext that they're full. The slender, garishly illuminated *El-Waffa* (❷) behind the station has a/c rooms with bathrooms (be sure to get one on the river-facing side) that are far superior to the poky old *El-Salaam* (☎093/433-3317; ❶) on Sharia El-Mahatta. Of the two rundown three-stars across the Nile, the *Cazalovy* (☎093/460-1185; ❷) is preferable to the *Merit-Amoun* (☎093/460-1985, ☎460-3222; ❷).

All the hotel **restaurants** are best avoided, which leaves you with a small, friendly pizza place, a juice-bar and the usual *fuul* and *taamiya* outlets on Sharia al-Mahatta. Or you could buy a spit-roast chicken to take back to your hotel.

The main **post** and **telephone office** is on the Corniche (aka Sharia el-Gumhorriya), where there are also two banks (daily except Fri 9am–2pm). There's a second telephone office in the station (24hr), with *Salam* **Internet** (24hr) nearby, on Sharia el Mahatta. The **hospital** (☎093/332-007) is opposite the bus station, while the **police** (☎122) are by the mosque on the eastern side of the Nile bridge.

As in Assyut, the police prefer you to travel by **train** to Luxor (4hr), Cairo (8–10hr) or anywhere else, and set no restriction on which train you take. If you are allowed to use them, you have a choice between seven **buses** daily to Minya and Cairo (5am–10pm), and one a day to Luxor and Aswan, leaving at 6am, plus regular buses and **service taxis** to Qena, from where others run on to Luxor. Assyut (1hr 30min) is the furthest destination for northbound service taxis, while Qena (1hr) is the normal limit for southbound vehicles. Besides the depots for northbound and southbound taxis, there are separate ones for **local** service taxis to Akhmim (near the town council) and the White Monastery (west of the bus station), which tourists might be able to use.

Akhmim

Until the twentieth century, guidebooks ranked Sohag as less important than **AKHMIM**, across the Nile – a place reckoned "the oldest city in Egypt" by the sixteenth-century Moorish geographer-historian Leo Africanus. Akhmimis have built on the rubble of their ancestors since pre-Dynastic times, so the whole town rests on a mound of remains, with a maze-like street plan essentially unchanged since the Middle Ages. The town's name derives from the Coptic *Khmim*, itself derived from the name of an ancient local fertility god, Khente-Min, who was often represented by a giant phallus. Egyptologists also associate the town with the Akhmim Tablet, a kind of worksheet for scribes, defining mathematical units.

Its **weaving** tradition is equally old: the pharaohs were buried in shrouds of Akhmim silk. Early last century, imported textiles closed hundreds of local workshops and concentrated production into four factories, which used power looms from Rochdale in England. The hand-weaving tradition was only preserved by a missionary-inspired **Women's Cooperative** (*Rahabaat*), founded in the 1920s, whose tapestries are now sold as highly priced works of art. The weavers forgo celebrity and high earnings in order not to irritate their menfolk, so visitors are unwelcome – but another small factory, employing men, can be visited. It's the house with the green door across the road from the post office near Meryut Amun's statue. You can **buy** silk and cotton textiles cut from bolts of cloth in the factory shop.

Akhmim's most visible attraction is an eleven-metre-high limestone **statue of Meryut Amun** (daily 9am–5pm; free), found in 1981 during excavations to build a school. Her statue is memorably vivid, with curled hair and rouged lips, but Meryut Amun herself is an enigma. History records her as a daughter of Ramses II, whom the pharaoh incestuously married after the death of her mother, Nefertari, and the cartouches on the statue's base support that identification. Other theories, however, date the statue to the earlier Amarna period, evidenced by its almond-shaped eyes, protruberant belly and Amarna-style pleating, plus the fact that thirteen inscribed blocks from the Amarna era were unearthed beneath the statue.

The answer may lie nearby, where the SCA is excavating a **temple of Rameses II**. A 700-tonne seated **colossus** of the deified pharaoh and his daughters has been partly exposed near what might have been the entrance to the temple (possibly his largest monument after Abu Simbel). Much more will be discovered once the Muslim cemetery that overlays the site has been relocated. But antiquities are being unearthed at building sites all over town and smuggled abroad: in 2004, a New York art dealer was convicted for buying a funerary stele from Akhmim.

The service taxis that shuttle you to Akhmim from Sohag (25pt) are lovely **vintage cars** from the 1930s and 1940s. They drop you at an intersection in Akhmim's centre known as "Setta Aziza"; from here, follow a road leading north towards the market and the Al-Amri Mosque, to find Meryut Amun's statue a bit further on.

Monasteries near Sohag

The **Red and White monasteries** (daily 8am–8pm) to the south of Sohag are both small and dilapidated, yet their near-desolation seems more evocative of the early Christians who sought God in the desert than busier establishments like Dirunka. Only a handful of acolytes tend the chapels, timeworn stones and plastic medallions attesting to the thousands of Copts who visit them during Shenoudi's moulid in the first two weeks of July, when dozens of minibuses shuttle in the pilgrims.

Although local service taxis run to the White Monastery (12km), the police will insist that you take a **private taxi** (arranged by the tourist office for £E30-40), which enables you to also visit the Red Monastery, 4km further on. There's no admission charge for the monasteries, but *baksheesh* is expected.

The White Monastery

Across the plain from Sohag, high limestone walls enclose the **White Monastery** (*Deir al-Abyad*). Named for the colour of its masonry (mostly taken from pharaonic or Roman buildings), and supposedly founded by St Helena on her way back from Jerusalem, the monastery once possessed the greatest Coptic library in Egypt (now dispersed among 23 museums worldwide) and was home to over two thousand monks. Today it has only four residents, and its courtyard is flanked by ruined cloisters and cells. Despite its fortress-like walls – which are much thicker at the base and topped with a Cavetto cornice in the ancient

Egyptian style – the monastery was often sacked by marauders. When Denon passed by with Napoleon's troops in 1798, it was still smouldering after a raid by the Mamlukes.

Remove your shoes before entering the **Church of St Shenoudi**, a lofty basilica admitting breezes and birdsong, observed by a stern-faced Christ Pantokrator. Note the monolithic granite pulpit halfway along the northern wall, Roman columns in the apses, and pharaonic hieroglyphics on the outer rear wall.

The monastery is also known as *Deir Anba Shenouda* after its fifth-century founder, who enforced the monastic rule with legendary beatings – on one occasion, fatally. Shenoudi condemned bathing as an upper-class luxury maintained by the sweat of the poor; early monks cleansed themselves by rolling naked in the sand. During **Shenoudi's moulid** (which reaches its climax on July 14), childless women roll down nearby hills in sacks, hoping to obtain divine intervention.

The Red Monastery

Down the road past walled Coptic and Muslim cemeteries, a straggling village conceals the **Red Monastery** (*Deir al-Ahmar*) in an unobtrusive cul-de-sac. Built of dark red brick, the monastery is attributed to St Bishoi, a penitent armed robber who became Shenoudi's disciple (retaining his club as a reminder); hence its other sobriquet, *Deir Anba Bishoi*.

The monastery's principal **church** is darker than Shenoudi's, its blackened tenth-century murals less remarkable than the finely carved tiers of niches. Whereas purloined Roman columns and the White Monastery's pharaonic-style corvetto cornice betray artistic debts, the intricate floral capitals inside the outer gate show that Coptic architecture soon transcended mere imitation. In the courtyard's far corner squats the smaller **Red Church**, whose inner sanctum is barred to women. Notice the intricate peg-locks on the doors.

Upper Egypt

In antiquity, **Upper Egypt** started at Memphis and ran as far south as Aswan on the border with Nubia. Nowadays, with the designation of Middle Egypt, borders are a bit hazy, though the **Qena Bend** is generally taken as the region's beginning and **Aswan** is still effectively the end of the line.

Within this stretch of the Nile is the world's most intensive concentration of ancient monuments – temples, tombs and palaces constructed from the onset of the Middle Kingdom (c.1990 BC) up until Roman and Byzantine times. The greatest of the buildings are the **cult temples** of **Abydos**, **Dendara**, **Karnak**, **Esna**, **Edfu**, **Kom Ombo**, **Philae** and **Abu Simbel**, each conceived as "homes" for their respective deities and an accretion of centuries of building. Scarcely less impressive are the multitude of tombs in the **Theban Necropolis**, most famously in the **Valley of the Kings**, across the river from **Luxor**, where Tutankhamun's resting place is merely a hole in the ground by comparison with those of such great pharaohs as Seti I and Ramses II.

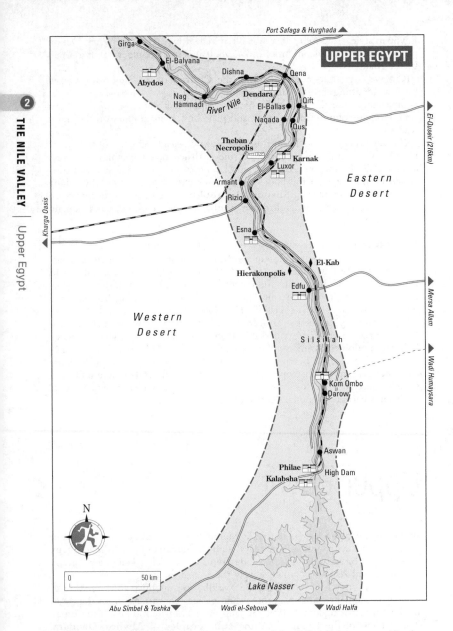

Upper Egypt map showing locations including Girga, El-Balyana, Abydos, Dishna, Qena, Nag Hammadi, Dendara, El-Ballas, Qift, Naqada, Qus, Theban Necropolis, Karnak, Luxor, Armant, Rizig, Esna, El-Kab, Hierakonpolis, Edfu, Silsilah, Kom Ombo, Darow, Aswan, Philae, High Dam, Kalabsha. Eastern Desert, Western Desert, Lake Nasser. Directional markers to Port Safaga & Hurghada, El-Quseir (216km), Mersa Allam, Wadi Humaysara, Kharga Oasis, Abu Simbel & Toshka, Wadi el-Seboua, Wadi Halfa. Scale 0–50 km.

Monuments aside, Upper Egypt marks a subtle shift of character, with the desert closing in on the river, and dom palms growing alongside barrel-roofed houses, designed to reflect the intense heat. One of the greatest pleasures to be had here – indeed one of the highlights of any Egyptian trip – is to absorb the riverscape slowly from the vantage point of a **felucca** (see pp.474–475). This is easily arranged in Aswan, whence you can sail downriver with no fear of being becalmed. Nile **cruise boats** provide a more luxurious experience, calling at the main sites between Luxor and Aswan (see pp.476–477). While cruises can be booked at short notice in either city, better deals are available in Aswan.

Abydos

As Muslims endeavour to visit Mecca once in their lifetimes and Hindus aspire to die at Benares, the Ancient Egyptians devoutly wished to make a pilgrimage to **ABYDOS**, cult centre of the god Osiris. Those who failed to make it hoped to do so posthumously; relatives brought bodies for burial, or embellished distant tombs with scenes of the journey to Abydos (represented by a boat under sail, travelling upriver). Egyptians averred that the dead "went west", for the entrance to the underworld was believed to lie amidst the desert hills beyond Abydos. By bringing other deities into the Osirian fold, Abydos acquired a near monopoly on death cults, which persisted into Ptolemaic times. Its superbly carved **Temple of Seti I** has been a tourist attraction since the 1830s, and many rate its artwork as the finest in Egypt.

Getting there from Luxor or El-Balyana

A shambolic daily **convoy** of visitors to Abydos and Dendara leaves Luxor at 8am. Thomas Cook, American Express and other agencies offer **coach excursions** to one or both sites, but schedules are erratic and the cost is far higher than hiring a **private taxi**. The official rates for a return trip to Dendara and Abydos are £E275 for a five-seater taxi, £E475 for a microbus seating eight, and £E1100 for a minibus carrying twelve, while Luxor hotels such as *Happy Land* will take three or four people for £E225–250 (group rate).

The police don't seem to mind people travelling independently by public transport via the town of **EL-BALYANA**, 10km from Abydos. The unofficial rule for **buses** is that there mustn't be more than four tourists aboard the vehicle, so it pays to be early for the 11am or 1.15pm bus: tickets are sold by the driver. **Trains** are less reliable for the outward journey, as not all stop at El-Balyana, but you can use any train that does to return to Luxor (allow plenty of time to get through the security check at the station). The aim of El-Balyana's **police** is to get you to Abydos and back to Luxor as quickly as possible, so anyone arriving by bus or train will be put in a local taxi and escorted to the temple (about £E20 one-way).

The **site of Abydos** (daily 8am–5pm; £E20) is reached by a well-surfaced country road which terminates at the village of **AL-ARABA EL-MADFUNA**, beside the ruins. Near the entrance to Seti I's temple are soft-drink stalls and a Banque Misr kiosk that opens erratic hours. If the police don't object, you may be able to **stay** at the *Seti I Resthouse* (☎093/494-0444; ❶), which has basic clean rooms with hot water, but no food except for biscuits.

As for the temple, be sure to bring a **torch** to see its darkened reliefs properly. In the interests of "security", visitors are constantly followed by a custodian – even to the washroom!

The Temple of Seti I

While the temples of Karnak and Deir el-Bahri at Luxor are breathtaking conceptions executed on a colossal scale, it is the exquisite quality of its

▲ Seti I

bas-reliefs that distinguishes Abydos' **Temple of Seti I**. The reliefs are amongst the finest works of the New Kingdom, harking back to Old Kingdom forms in an artistic revival that mirrored Seti's political efforts to consolidate the XIX Dynasty and recover territories lost under Akhenaten. The official designation of Seti's reign (1318–1304 BC) was "the era of repeating births" – literally a renaissance.

It was in fact Seti's son, Ramses II (1304–1237 BC), who completed the recon-quest of former colonies and the construction of his father's temple at Abydos. Strictly speaking, the building was neither a cult nor a funerary temple in the ordinary sense (see the box below for an overview of temple architecture), for its chapels contained shrines to a variety of deities concerned with death, resurrection

Ancient Eqyptian temple architecture

From earliest times, two distinct types of temple evolved in Egypt: **cult temples**, dedicated to the principal god of the region, and **mortuary temples**, devoted to the worship of the dead king. Cult temples were regarded as the *pr-ntr* or "house of the god", whose effigy was cosseted with daily rituals and periodically taken to visit its divine spouse in another temple. Such centres were elaborate from the start, unlike mortuary temples, which began as two-roomed structures attached to the king's pyramid and joined to a valley temple by a causeway, only being divorced from their tombs and burgeoning into massive complexes during the New Kingdom.

Most of the great temples of the Nile Valley embody centuries of work by succes-sive kings and dynasties, some of whom added major sections while others merely decorated a wall or carved their name on another pharaoh's statue. Built from stone, to last forever, their general form and layout hardly changed over millennia, and were still being imitated during Ptolemaic and Roman times.

Temple layout

Because each temple was envisaged as a progression from this world into the realm of divine mysteries, halls got darker and lower and doors narrowed as they approached the sanctuary. In accordance with this convention, additional halls or pylons had to increase in size as they grew more distant from the sanctuary. As a corollary of this, the architecture is generally older the further in you venture.

Temples were seldom accessible to commoners, being set within enclosures surrounded by lofty mud-brick walls. These **precincts** often contained priestly residences, workshops and storehouses, along with a **Sacred Lake** for ritual ablutions. In Ptolemaic and Roman times, they also usually featured a **Birth House** or *Mamissi*, which emphasized the king's divine antecedents. Entering the temple proper meant passing through a series of gated **pylons** whose towers bore giant reliefs of the pharaoh making offerings to the gods and smiting Egypt's enemies. A few also boasted graceful **obelisks** whose tips were sheathed in gold or electrum (an alloy of gold and silver). Between the pylons were open **courts**, often flanked with **colonnades** of Osiride pillars and guarded by **colossi** of a pharaoh or deity.

Another pylon (or a screen wall surmounted by open columns) divided the court from a **Hypostyle Hall**, whose forest of columns was intended to resemble a papy-rus thicket, dimly illuminated by shafts of sunlight penetrating apertures in the roof. Beyond lay a series of **vestibules** or antechambers (often preceded by a smaller Hypostyle Hall), climaxing in the **sanctuary** where the deity's effigy and sacred boat reposed. Smaller rooms and **chapels** for storing valuables or worshipping subsidiary deities were grouped off the halls and behind the sanctuary. Some temples also had a **rooftop shrine** or kiosk for celebrating the resurrection of Osiris and revitalizing the divine effigy at New Year.

and the netherworld, and one dedicated to Seti himself. Its purpose was essentially political: to identify the king with these cults and with his putative "ancestors", the previous rulers of Egypt, thus conferring legitimacy on the Ramessid Dynasty, whose ancestors had been mere Delta warriors a few generations earlier.

The temple's spell has endured through the ages, as New Age pilgrims follow in the footsteps of Dorothy Eady – known as **Umm Seti** (Mother of Seti) – who lived at Abydos for 35 years until she died in 1981, believing herself to be the reincarnation of a temple priestess and lover of Seti I. Her book *Abydos – The Holy City in Ancient Egypt* is sold in Luxor, while her trances and prophetic gifts are related in Jonathan Cott's biography, *The Search for Omm Sety*.

Decoration

Virtually every temple wall is covered in **reliefs**, either carved proud (bas-reliefs, the most delicate and time-consuming method), recessed into the surface (sunk-reliefs) or simply incised (the quickest form to execute). They are arranged in rows called "registers", counted from the bottom of the wall upwards. Doorway lintels are always adorned with a winged sun-disc, symbolizing the Two Lands whose heraldic plants are a common motif. Some Ptolemaic temples also feature astronomical ceilings depicting heavenly bodies and creatures of the zodiac. Since reliefs were generally painted in bright colours, temples must once have looked far gaudier than their present state suggests.

Also striking are the variegated **columns**, which evolved from two basic types. Square-sectioned pillars were sometimes faced with a statue of the pharaoh as a god (usually Osiris – hence the term Osiride pillars) or crowned with the head of the goddess Hathor (perhaps surmounted by a sistrum, her sacred instrument). A wider variety derived from plant forms, with different permutations of shafts and capitals. The palm column had a plain shaft and leafy capital; the papyrus column chevron markings and a flowering or closed bud capital; while a cluster of rounded stems gave the lotus column its distinctive "bundle" appearance. By Ptolemaic times, capitals resembled Baroque bouquets and the established forms were mixed to create composite columns.

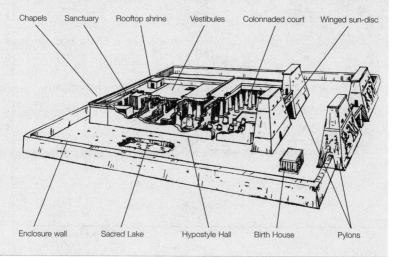

Chapels   Sanctuary   Rooftop shrine   Vestibules   Colonnaded court   Winged sun-disc

Enclosure wall   Sacred Lake   Hypostyle Hall   Birth House   Pylons

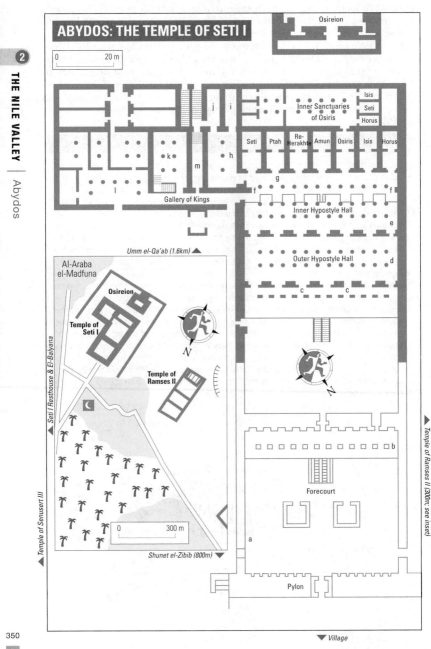

ABYDOS: THE TEMPLE OF SETI I

0   20 m

Osireion

Inner Sanctuaries
of Osiris

Isis
Seti
Horus

Seti   Ptah   Re-
Herakhte   Amun   Osiris   Isis   Horus

j   i

k

m

h

l

g

f   f

Gallery of Kings

Inner Hypostyle Hall

e

Umm el-Qa'ab (1.6km) ▲

Outer Hypostyle Hall

d

Al-Araba
el-Madfuna

c   c

Osireion

Temple of
Seti I

N

Temple of
Ramses II

N

▲ Temple of Senusert III   ◀ Seti I Resthouse & El-Balyana

0   300 m

Shunet el-Zibib (800m) ▼

b

Forecourt

a

Temple of Ramses II (300m; see inset) ▶

Pylon

350

▼ Village

The forecourt and Hypostyle Halls

The temple's original **pylon** and **forecourt** have almost been levelled but you can still discern the lower portion of a scene depicting Ramses II's dubious victory at Qadesh **[a]**, women with finely plaited tresses **[b]**, and Seti making offerings to Osiris (in a niche, nearby). From the damaged statues currently stored in the upper, second court, your eyes are drawn to the square-columned **facade**, where tiny birds inhabit fissures in the wall behind pillars covered with scenes of Ramses greeting Osiris, Isis and Horus **[c]**. Originally, the temple was entered by seven doors (corresponding to the shrines within), but Ramses ordered all except the middle one blocked up. The upper part of the facade has been crudely rebuilt in concrete.

The ponderous sunk-reliefs in the **outer Hypostyle Hall**, completed by Ramses after Seti's death, suggest that he used second-rate artists, having redeployed Seti's top craftsmen on his own (now destroyed) temple. The entrance wall portrays Ramses measuring the temple with the goddess Selket and presenting it to Horus on Seti's behalf, while on the wall to your right Ramses offers a falcon-headed box of papyrus to Isis, Horus and Osiris, and is led to the temple by Horus and Wepwawet (the jackal-headed god of Assyut) to be doused with holy water (represented by the interlinked signs for life and purity) **[d]**. On one of the roof-lintels is a cartouche which has achieved mythical status on the Internet; purportedly, it shows a helicopter and a submarine – though archeologists deride the "**Abydos helicopter**" as a simple case of palitation (the superimposition of one cartouche upon another, combining with erosion to produce an unusual shape), and the digitally enhanced image on the Web is far clearer than the murky original.

The deeper **inner Hypostyle Hall** was the last part of the temple decorated before Seti's death, and some sections were never finished, but others are exceptional. On the right-hand wall Seti stands before Osiris and Horus – who pour holy water from garlanded vases – and makes offerings before the shrine of Osiris, who is attended by Maat and Ronpet (the goddess of the year) in front, with Isis, Amentet (goddess of the west) and Nephthys behind **[e]**. Seti's profile is a stylized but close likeness to his mummy (in the Cairo Antiquities Museum). The east and west walls are of sandstone, the north and south of limestone. Two projecting piers **[f]** near the back of the hall depict Seti worshipping the *Djed* column while wearing the crown of Upper or Lower Egypt. The reliefs along the rear wall – showing him being anointed and crowned by the gods – are still brightly coloured. Best of all is a scene of Seti kneeling before Osiris and Horus, with the sacred persea tree in the background, which appears above head height on the wall between the sanctuaries of Ptah and Re-Herakhte **[g]**.

The sanctuaries

The finest **bas-reliefs** at Abydos are inside the sanctuaries dedicated to Seti and six deities. Though retaining much of their original colouring (showing how most temple reliefs once looked), their graceful lines and subtle moulding are best appreciated on the unpainted reliefs. Seti's classical revival eschewed both Amarna expressionism and the bombastic XVIII Dynasty imperial style, which his son embraced and raised to new heights of megalomania. The seven sanctuaries are roofed with false vaults carved from rectangular slabs, and culminate in false doors (except for Osiris's chamber, which leads into his inner sanctuaries).

To Ancient Egyptians, these chambers constituted the abode of the gods, whom the king (or his priests) propitiated with daily rituals, shown on the walls. Having opened the shrine, the pharaoh offers the god sacrifices and washes and dresses its statue, which is then purified and presented with gifts. After further

The cult of Osiris

Originally the corn-god of Busiris in the Delta, **Osiris** attained national significance early in the Old Kingdom, when he was co-opted into the Heliopolitan Ennead. According to legend, Re (or Geb) divided the world between Osiris and his brother Seth, who resented being given all the deserts and murdered Osiris to usurp his domain. Although the god's body was recovered by **Isis**, the sister-wife of Osiris, Seth recaptured and dismembered it, burying the pieces (and feeding the penis to a crocodile, in one version). Aided by her sister Nephthys, Isis collected the bits and bandaged them together to create the first mummy, which they briefly resurrected with the help of Thoth and Anubis. By transforming herself into a hawk, Isis managed to conceive a child with Osiris before he returned to the netherworld to rule as lord and judge of the dead. Secretly raised to manhood in the Delta, their child **Horus** later avenged his father and cast Seth back into the wilderness (see p.447).

▲ Osiris

As the reputed burial place of the torso (or head) of Osiris, **Abydos** was the setting for two annual **festivals**. The "Great Going Forth" celebrated the search for and discovery of his remains, while the Osiris Festival re-enacted his myth in a series of Mystery Plays. In one scene, the god's barque was "attacked" by minions of Seth and "protected" by **Wepwawet**, the jackal-headed god of Assyut. This marked the final stage in a process of religious mergers, for it was Wepwawet who supplanted **Khentamenty**, the original death-god of Abydos, as the "Foremost of the Westerners", before his own assimilation into the cult of Osiris. The total identification of Abydos with **death cults** was completed by its association with **Anubis**, the jackal-headed god of embalming, always present in funerary scenes.

offerings before the god's barque, he scatters sand on the floor, sweeps away his footprints and withdraws, leaving the deity alone till next morning.

An exception to this rule is the **Sanctuary of Seti**, which emphasizes his recognition by the gods, who lead him into the temple and ceremonially unite the Two Lands along the northern wall. Below the barque near the back of the left-hand wall, Seti receives a list of offerings from Thoth and the High Priest Iunmutef, wearing the leopardskin and braided sidelock of his office. Finally, Seti leaves the temple, his palanquin borne by the souls of jackal-headed deities from the Upper Egyptian town of Nekhen and hawk-headed gods from the Delta capital of Pi-Ramses.

The fine unpainted reliefs of Seti and seated deities in Re-Herakhte's chamber make interesting comparison with similar painted scenes in the sanctuaries of Ptah, Amun, Osiris and Isis. On the side wall just outside the Sanctuary of Horus, the pharaoh presents Maat to Osiris, Isis and Horus, a XIX Dynasty motif symbolizing righteous order and the restoration of royal legitimacy.

The **inner sanctuaries of Osiris** boast three side chapels whose colours were still fresh and shiny in the 1980s, but are now blackened by mould – a rapid rate of deterioration affecting many of the temples and tombs in the Nile Valley.

The southern wing

From the inner Hypostyle Hall you can enter the southern wing of Seti's temple. The portal nearest his sanctuary leads into the columned **Hall of Sokar and Nefertum**, two deities of the north representing the life-giving forces of the earth and the cycle of death and rebirth, who were integrated into the Osirian cult by Seti's time. The niches along the left-hand wall once contained Osiride statues. Reliefs across the way **[h]** depict Seti receiving a hawk-headed Sokar, and Nefertum in both his human and leonine forms (crowned with a lotus blossom). In the **Chapel of Sokar [i]**, Osiris appears in his bier and returns to life grasping his penis (near the back of the right-hand wall), while Isis hovers over him in the form of a hawk on the opposite wall. You'll need a torch to see inside the **Chapel of Nefertum**, next door **[j]**.

The other portal leads through into the **Gallery of Kings**, so called after the list of Seti's predecessors carved on the right-hand wall. For political reasons, the Hyksos pharaohs, Hatshepsut, Akhenaten and his heirs have all been omitted, and Seti has recorded his own name as *Menmare Osiris-Merneptah* (rather than *Menmare Seti-Merneptah*) to distance himself from his namesake Seth, the killer of Osiris. Nonetheless, the list has proved immensely useful to archeologists, naming 34 kings (chiefly from the VI, VII, XII, XVIII and XIX dynasties) in roughly chronological order. Seti and his son Ramses stand facing the list of their "ancestors", which begins with Menes (Zoser).

With the **Sanctuary of the Boats [k]** and the **Hall of Sacrifices [l]** off-limits, the best course beyond here is to follow the side corridor **[m]** past a vivid relief of Seti and Ramses harnessing a bull and running to greet Wepwawet, then go out through a rear door to the Osireion, behind the temple.

The Osireion and other remains

The **site of Abydos** covers a huge area, with ruins and mounds scattered across the edge of the desert. Few visitors have the time to wander far even if the police would let them, but it's worth investigating the structure directly behind Seti's temple.

When Flinders Petrie excavated Abydos in the early twentieth century, he uncovered numerous *mastabas* which he belived to be royal tombs, but which later Egyptologists held to be cenotaphs or Osirian burial places – dummy tombs, built to promote a closer association between the pharaoh's *ka* and Osiris, while his mummy reposed elsewhere. Seti's Cenotaph, known as the **Osireion**, is the only one now visible, albeit half-buried and rendered partly inaccessible by stagnant water. Built of massive blocks, it once enclosed a room containing a mound surrounded by a moat (symbolizing the first land

The Gnostic Gospels

The **Nag Hammadi Codices** – better known as the **Gnostic Gospels** – were found near the town, below the caves of Jebel et-Tur, in 1945. The gospels are fourth-century Coptic translations of second-century Greek originals, although the Gospel of Thomas might date from 50–100 AD, and therefore be as early as – or even older than – the gospels of Matthew, Mark, Luke and John.

The Gnostics (from *Gnosis*, Greek for "knowledge") were early mystics who believed that God could only be known through self-understanding and that the world was illusory. Regarding self and the divine as one, they saw Jesus as a spiritual guide rather than the crucified son of God, pointing to his words in the Gospel of Thomas: *"If you bring forth what is within you, what you bring forth will save you. If you do not bring forth what is within you, what is within you will destroy you."* But the official church thought otherwise and condemned Gnosticism as a heresy; hence the burial of these codices (some of which can be seen today in Cairo's Coptic Museum).

arising from the waters of Chaos at the dawn of Creation), where a pseudo-sarcophagus awaited resurrection.

Some 300m northwest is a ruined **Temple of Ramses II**, Seti's father, where fragments of scenes of the Battle of Qadesh (see p.497) can be discerned on the enclosure walls and pillared courtyard.

Other sites further afield give insights into **predynastic history**. The German Archeological Institute (Ⓦwww.dainst.org) has been excavating the Early Dynastic royal cemetery at **Umm el-Qa'ab** since 1977, and more recently funerary enclosures at **Shunet el-Zebib**. The complex of Khasekhemwy, last king of the II Dynasty, who died about 2686 BC, was surrounded by walls up to 11m high and 5.5m thick, 122m long and 65m wide. Dr Gunter Dreyer believes that the pyramids at Saqqara evolved from the enclosure of sunken brick-lined tombs at Abydos, where hieroglyphic writing predating Saqqara's has been found, suggesting the existence of a predynastic king Hor or Horus, who conquered the Delta and united the Two Lands a century before Narmer. In 1991, six **Solar Boats** were found buried within Khasekhemwy's enclosure, which are thought to date from the reign of the I Dynasty ruler Aha (c.2920–2770 BC). All this raises the possibility that the Early Dynastic burials attributed to Saqqara may have occurred at Abydos instead, and that an intact royal tomb might one day be found here.

Nag Hammadi and Dishna

At **NAG HAMMADI** (pronounced "Naja Ham*maadi*"), 40km south of El-Balyana, the Nile sweeps into the "**Qena Bend**", and the main road and train tracks transfer from the west bank to the other side of the river. Other than its historic association with the Gnostic Gospels (see box on p.353), Nag Hammadi is only notable for its cement factory and the *Aluminium* **hotel** (℡096/581-320; ❺), 3km south of town. Across the river, **DISHNA** looks like any small farming town in the Valley, but is infamous throughout Egypt for its **vendettas**. While blood-feuds are common in Upper Egypt, the one between two villages here lasted generations, obliging every adult male to carry a gun at all times. The police seldom left their fortified post and never got involved in fights: after dark, gunmen roamed freely and held up cars on the highway. Peace was only achieved after mediation by eminent sheikhs in 2004, though even now the police sometimes suspend traffic to the east bank after dark. During the day, however, the road is perfectly safe and Dishna folk are actually renowned for their hospitality to guests – their hostility is reserved for their neighbours.

Dendara and Qena

The **Temple of Hathor** at **Dendara** lacks the sublime quality of Seti's edifice at Abydos, but its astronomical ceiling and rooftop sanctuaries offer a unique insight into the solar rituals at other cult sites where they have not survived. Dendara also shows how Egypt's Greek and Roman rulers identified themselves with the pharaohs and deities of Ancient Egypt by copying their temples, rituals and icongraphy down to the last hieroglyphic – though they did tinker with a few details of reliefs and murals. Goddesses and queens became bustier, and the feet of royalty were shown with all their toes (instead of only the big toe, as the Ancient Egyptians did).

Most tourists visit Dendara in conjunction with Abydos, travelling in a convoy from Luxor – which limits you to only 45 minutes at each site. To stay longer

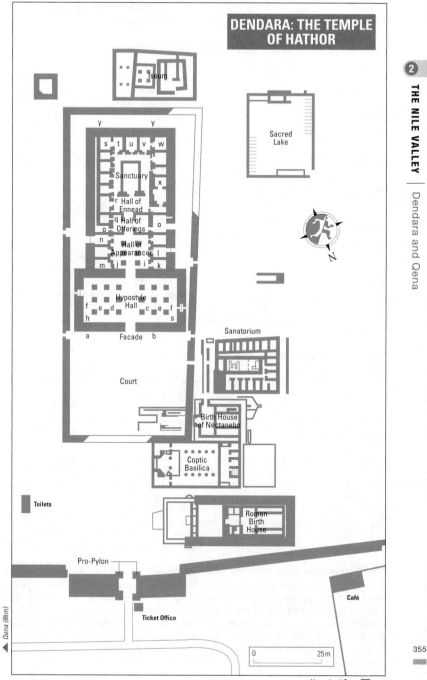

DENDARA: THE TEMPLE OF HATHOR

Iseum

Sacred Lake

y   y

s t u v w

Sanctuary

x

r Hall of Ennead

q Hall of Offerings

o   o

n

Hall of Appearances

l

m j   i   k

Hypostyle Hall

f e d   c e f

h   s

a   Facade   b

Sanatorium

Court

Birth House of Nectanebo

Coptic Basilica

Toilets

Roman Birth House

Pro-Pylon

Café

Ticket Office

0   25m

Qena (8km) ◄

Happyland Camp ▼

at Dendara you'll have to get there by public transport via **Qena** (8km away), which is a bit of a hassle under the current travel restrictions.

Dendara – the Temple of Hathor

Across the Nile from Qena, fields of onions and clover recede towards the cliffs of the Western Desert and the Temple of Hathor near the village of **DENDARA**. One of the few Egyptian temples with an intact and accessible rooftop, it offers fantastic views of the surrounding countryside. The **site** (daily 7am–6pm; £E20) deserves at least an hour and a half, and you'll need a **torch** to illuminate its darker recesses. Visitors who value atmosphere over comfort can **stay** in the basic and rather overpriced rooms at the *Happyland Camp* (❷), outside the temple's enclosure wall: advance bookings can be made via the *New Palace Hotel* in Qena (see p.360). There's also a **café**, serving soft drinks only.

Getting to Dendara from Luxor

The daily **convoy** to Dendara and Abydos leaves Luxor at 8am and returns in the afternoon. Thomas Cook, American Express and other agencies offer **coach excursions** to one or both sites, but schedules are erratic and the cost is far higher than hiring a **private taxi** (see p.384 for taxi rates to Dendara). Alternatively, the *Lotus Boat* and *Tiba Star* run **day cruises** from Luxor to Dendara on Tuesdays, Fridays and Sundays: tickets are sold through American Express (£E250), Thomas Cook (£E280) and the *Iberotel* (see p.384) three days in advance. The only reason to travel **by public transport via Qena** is to stay longer at the temple than the convoy allows. Under current travel restrictions it's an awkward journey, but if the ban on using service taxis is lifted, it's an easy approach (see p.360 for details).

The Temple of Hathor

Although there have been shrines to Hathor, the goddess of joy, at Dendara since predynastic times, the existing **Temple of Hathor** is a Greco-Roman creation, built between 125 BC and 60 AD. Since the object of the exercise was to confer legitimacy on Egypt's foreign rulers, it emulates the pharaonic pattern of Hypostyle Halls and vestibules preceding a darkened sanctuary, "a progression from the light of the Egyptian sun to the mystery of the holy of holies" (T.G.H. James).

The temple **facade** is shaped like a pylon, with six Hathor-headed columns rising from a screen. Here and inside, Hathor appears in human form rather than her bovine aspect (see opposite). Because this section was built during the reign of Tiberius, its reliefs depict Roman emperors making offerings to the gods, namely Tiberius and Claudius before Horus, Hathor and their son Ihy **[a]**, and Tiberius as a sphinx before Hathor and Horus **[b]**. Nineteenth-century engravings show the temple buried in sand almost to the lintel of its portal, which explains why its upper sections bore the brunt of Coptic iconoclasm.

The Hypostyle Hall

Entering the **Hypostyle Hall** with its eighteen Hathor-headed columns, you'll need to let your eyes grow accustomed to the gloom before examining its famous **astronomical ceiling**, which retains much of its original colouring. This is not a sky chart in the modern sense, but a symbolic representation of the heavenly bodies, the hours of the day and night, and the realms of the sun and moon. Although the Qena Bend dictates a north–south orientation rather than the customary east–west axis (since temples always faced the Nile), the

Worshipped from the earliest times as a cow goddess, **Hathor** acquired manifold attributes – body of the sky, living soul of trees, goddess of gold and turquoise, music and revelry – but remained essentially nurturing. Her greatest role was that of wet nurse and bedmate for **Horus**, and giver of milk to the living pharaoh. In her human aspect (with bovine ears and horns), the goddess paid an annual visit to Horus at his temple in Edfu. Escorted by priests and cheered by commoners, her barque proceeded upriver, where Horus sailed out to meet her on his own boat. After much pomp and ritual, the idols were left alone to reconsummate their union while the populace enjoyed a **Festival of Drunkenness**, which led the Greeks to identify

▲ Hathor

Hathor with their own goddess of love and joy, Aphrodite. However, drunkenness at other times drew condemnation, as in this timeless rebuke to a lager lout: "You trail from street to street smelling of beer, you have been found performing acrobatics on a wall, people run from your blows. Look at you beating on your stomach, reeling and rolling about on the ground covered in your own filth!"

ceiling maintains the traditional dichotomy between the northern and southern halves of the sky.

Above the central aisle, a row of flying vultures and winged discs separates the left-hand bays representing the southern heavens from those to the right, dedicated to the northern sky. Here, the first row **[c]** begins with the Eye of Re in its barque, above which appear the fourteen days of the waning moon. Beyond the full moon in the centre come the fourteen stages of the waxing moon (each with its own deity), culminating in the full disc worshipped by Thoth, and lastly the moon as Osiris, protected by Isis and Nephthys. Souls in the form of jackals and birds adorn Re's barque as it journeys across the sun's register **[d]**.

Following these are two bands **[e]** showing the planets, the stars of the twelve hours of the night, and the signs of the zodiac (adopted from Babylonia). The end rows **[f]** are dominated by Nut, who gives birth to the sun at dawn and swallows it at dusk. On one side, the rising sun Khepri (the scarab beetle) is born **[g]**; on the other, the sun shines down on Hathor **[h]**.

The Hall of Appearances

The Ptolemaic section of the temple begins with the columned **Hall of Appearances**, where Hathor consorted with fellow deities before her voyage to Edfu (see overleaf). With a torch, you can examine reliefs on the entrance wall depicting offerings **[i]**, and the foundation of the temple and its presentation to the gods **[j]**. Notice the "blank" cartouches, which attest to the high turnover of rulers in late Ptolemaic times, when stonemasons were loath to inscribe the names of Ptolemies who might not last for long – there were times when they wouldn't even know who actually reigned in Alexandria. Nonetheless, rituals continued at Dendara, where the priests kept holy objects of precious metal in the Treasury **[k]** and drew water for purification ceremonies from a well reached by the so-called Nile Room **[l]**.

Corresponding chambers across the hall include the laboratory **[m]**, where perfumes, incense and unguents were mixed and stored (notice the reliefs showing recipes, and bearers bringing exotic materials from afar); and another room for storing valuables. A liturgical calendar listing festivals celebrated at the temple appears on the inner side of its doorway [n].

The Hall of Offerings and the Hall of Ennead

Beyond lies the **Hall of Offerings**, the entrance to the temple proper, with twin **stairways** to the roof (see below) up which sacrificial animals were led [o]. A list of offerings appears on the rear wall [p], across the way from a relief showing the king offering Hathor her favourite tipple [q].

Next comes the **Hall of the Ennead**, where statues of the gods and kings involved in ceremonies dedicated to Hathor once stood. Her wardrobe was stored in a room to your left, where reliefs show the priests carrying the chests that held the sacred garments. Just outside the sanctuary you can see the text of the Hymns of Awakening. The **Sanctuary** housed Hathor's statue and ceremonial barque, which priests carried to the riverside and placed upon a boat that worshippers towed upriver to Edfu for a conjugal reunion with Horus. Reliefs depict the daily rituals (described under Abydos; see p.351) and the king presenting Maat to Hathor, Horus and Harsomtus (rear wall).

Side chapels

Two corridors with side chapels run alongside (and meet behind) the sanctuary. Above the doorway into the Corridor of Mysteries, Hathor appears as a cow within a wooden kiosk mounted on a barque [r]. Past the chapels of Isis, Sokar and the Sacred Serpent, you'll find the "Castle of the Sistrum" (Hathor's musical instrument), where niches depict her standing on the sky, and the coronation of Ihy as god of music [s]. This is entered via the darkened *Per-Nu* chapel [t], whence Hathor embarked on her conjugal voyage to Edfu during the New Year festival (which fell on July 19 in ancient times).

The New Year procession began from the *Per-Ur* chapel [u], where nowadays a shaky ladder ascends to a small chamber containing reliefs of Hathor, Maat and Isis. In the *Per-Neser* chapel [v], one of the custodians will lift a hatch and guide you down into a low-ceilinged **crypt** carved with cobras and lotuses (*baksheesh* expected). The chapel itself shows Hathor in her terrible aspect as a lioness, for by Ptolemaic times she had assimilated the leonine goddess Sekhmet and the feline goddess Bastet. The temple's most valuable treasures were stored underneath the Chapel of Re [w].

If you haven't already stumbled upon it, return to the Hall of the Ennead, bear left through an antechamber and then right, to find the "Pure Place" [x] or **New Year Chapel**, whose ceiling is covered by a relief of Nut giving birth to the sun, which shines on Hathor's head. It was here that rituals were performed prior to Hathor's communion with the sun on the temple's roof. Check out the rooftop shrines (see below) before leaving the temple and walking round to the rear wall, where two defaced reliefs [y] of Cleopatra and her son Caesarion feature in a procession of deities. The chubby face below the Hathor crown is so unlike the beautiful queen of legend that most people prefer to regard this as a stylized image rather than a lifelike **portrait of Cleopatra**.

Rooftop sanctuaries

From either side of the Hall of Offerings, a stairway ascends to the roof of the temple; the scenes on the walls depict the New Year procession, when Hathor's statue was carried up to an open kiosk on the rooftop to await the dawn. Touched by the rays of the sun, Hathor's *ba* (soul) was revitalized for the coming year. Besides the sun kiosk there are two suites of rooms dedicated to the death and resurrection of Osiris, behind the facade of the Hypostyle Hall.

Although such **rooftop sanctuaries** were a feature of most temples, those at Dendara are uniquely intact.

The one on the left (as you face south) is notable for the reliefs in its inner chamber, which show Osiris being mourned by Isis and Nephthys, passing through the gates of the netherworld, and finally bringing himself to erection to impregnate Isis, who appears as a hovering kite.

The other suite contains a plaster cast of the famous **Dendara Zodiac** ceiling filched by Lelorrain in 1820 and now in the Louvre. Upheld by four goddesses, the circular carving features a zodiac which only differs from our own by the substitution of a scarab for the scorpion and the inclusion of the hippo goddess Tweri. The zodiac was introduced to Egypt (and other lands) by the Romans, who copied it from Babylonia. Mind your head on the low doorway.

Best of all is the magnificent **view** of the temple and the countryside from the rooftop. Also notice the **graffiti** left by French troops in 1799, including the names of their commander Desaix and the artist Denon, who sketched frenziedly at Denadara as the Mamlukes drew nearer, melting down bullets for lead when he ran out of pencils.

Outlying buildings

Surrounding the temple are various other structures, now largely ruined. Ptolemaic temples were distinguished by the addition of *mamissi* or Birth Houses, which associated the pharaoh with Horus, the deified king. When the Romans surrounded the temple with an enclosure wall, it split in two the **Birth House of Nectanebo** (XXX Dynasty), compelling them to build a replacement. The **Roman Birth House** has some fine carvings on its south wall, and tiny figures of Bes and Tweri on the column capitals and architraves. Between the two *mamissi* lies a ruined, fifth-century **Coptic Basilica**, built with masonry from the adjacent structures; notice the incised Coptic crosses.

As a compassionate goddess, Hathor had a reputation for healing and her temple attracted pilgrimages from the sick. In the **Sanatorium** here patients were prescribed cures during dreams, probably induced by narcotics. Water for ritual ablutions was drawn from a **Sacred Lake** now drained of liquid and full of palm trees and birds.

Nearby stands a ruined **Iseum** used for the worship of Isis and Osiris, built by Cleopatra's mortal enemy, Octavian, after he became Emperor Augustus.

Qena

Despite being the provincial capital, **QENA** (pronounced "*Ge*na") has long played second fiddle to Luxor in terms of tourism and investment, a grievance which might explain why it was the site of the first attack on tourists, in 1992. (The killers were traced to a nearby village, whose entire population was evicted, and their homes demolished, for "harbouring terrorists".) Yet its reputation as a militant Islamic stronghold sat oddly with its renown as a hotbed of vice in the mid-nineteenth century, when many of the professional singers whom Mohammed Ali exiled from Cairo for their "indecent" dances and prostitution settled here, and much of the fundamentalism seems to have evaporated since an energetic, honest governor (sadly rare in Egypt), Adel Labeeb, improved civic amenities. Nowadays, locals are proud of Qena's clean streets and leafy promenades and the fact that people from Luxor come here to enjoy its decorous café society.

For foreigners, the main impression is of hundreds of portraits of Mubarak on the roads, as the convoy proceeds towards Dendara, or a view of the guarded government zone beside the Nile, where cruise boats dock. Further inland, once-graceful colonial villas give way to low-rise flats that resemble rejects from Eastern Europe, or maze-like souks that defy cartographers to produce an accurate map of the town. Fortunately, everything one needs to know about is easily found, using the two mosques on the main drag as landmarks. The older mosque (with one minaret) contains the tomb of a twelfth-century sheikh, who is honoured by the **Moulid of Abdel Rahim al-Qenawi**, on the 14th day of Sha'ban. Qena's **National Day** (March 8) festival commemorates a series of battles in 1799, when local villages sank a French flotilla of a dozen vessels.

Due to the Qena Bend, the banks of the Nile lie north and south, rather than east and west of the river: the town is on the north bank, with a bridge to Dendara on the south bank.

Getting to Qena and from Qena to Dendara

At present, independent travellers can only reach **Qena** by bus or train. There are six **buses** a day from Luxor (£E5), which end up at the terminal outside the train station, and others originating elsewhere, which drop (and pick up) passengers at the bridge over the canal, 200m further west. **Trains** from Luxor are faster (40min), but you may be restricted to certain services and not all trains stop in Qena anyway.

Either way, you'd still have to get across town and out **to the temple**. Chances are the police will insist you hire a **private taxi** (£E20) on the spot – but if they don't, you could use **local service taxis** (pick-ups) from the depot at a crossroads near the Nile, 2km away. Pick-ups for Dendara village (50pt) leave from the road to the Nile bridge, or you can take one bound for Nag Hammadi and get off soon after passing beneath a massive bridge that carries the new railway between Port Safaga and Kharga Oasis. The signposted side road to Dendara (1km) is 200m along, on the left.

Qena practicalities

Don't count on **staying** in Qena, where hotels have been told to remove signs in English to discourage foreigners. The shabby *New Palace* (☎096/322-509; ●), behind the Mobil garage, is the best of a bad lot, though less appealing than sleeping at Dendara (see p.356). **Eating** is slightly better: the *Restaurant Hamdi*

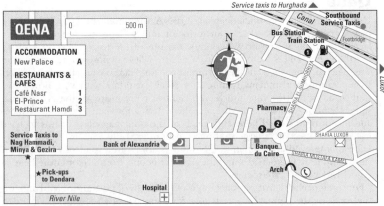

serves full meals (£E10-15) of soup, chicken or *kofta*, rice and vegetables, as does *El-Prince* (which also occasionally sells beer), while *Café Nasr* does cheaper veggie dishes.

There are two **banks** (daily except Fri 8am–2pm) for changing cash and travellers' cheques. The **post office** (daily except Fri 8.30am–2pm) and the 24-hour **telephone exchange** are a short walk from the main intersection, while the **police** can be found in the train station.

Qena is a **transport** hub for the Nile Valley and the Red Sea Coast. There are no restrictions on foreigners using the a/c Superjet buses to Cairo (7am & 8pm; £E37–40), or the regular buses to Hurghada and Suez (hourly; £E22–45), or Port Safaga, El-Quseir and Mersa Allam (3 daily; £E10–19), but Nile Valley towns like Assyut, Sohag and Minya are better reached by train. Many of these destinations are also accessible by service taxis, leaving from different depots, though tourists can't use them at present.

Between Qena and Luxor

Currently, the police make it difficult for tourists to visit any of the sites **between Qena and Luxor** which once attracted people as "undiscovered" locations. Private taxis are meant to stay with the convoy to Dendara, and even if you could find a service taxi willing to take you, you'd be turned back at the checkpoints around the Luxor security zone – which effectively rules out visiting Naqada or Garagos on the west bank. And while El-Madamud, Qus and Qift are accessible by bus from Luxor, most travellers are content to glimpse them en route to the Red Sea Coast.

Were restrictions to be lifted, however, service taxis from Luxor or Qena (£E3–4) run to most places mentioned below, and ferries cross the Nile between El-Ballas and Qift, and Naqada and Qus. There are no bridges until south of Luxor.

Along the east bank

Crowded with traffic for Luxor, the east bank road passes through **QIFT**, ancient *Kebt* or *Koptos*, a mining depot which became a commercial entrepôt once a route to the coast was found. Nowadays well-paved, with resthouses and petrol stations, but some perilous hairpin bends, the 216-kilometre-long **road to El-Quseir** on the Red Sea is described on p.796.

South towards Luxor, a factory for converting *bagasse* (the waste product of sugar refining) into paper presages the large town of **QUS**, which was second only to Cairo during Fatimid and Mamluke times, when it served as a place of

The primal alphabet

During ancient times there was a road between Abydos and Luxor through the Western Desert, which followed the **Wadi el-Hol**. In 1999 a team under John Darnell of Yale University identified two **rock inscriptions** there as the earliest known examples of a **phonetic alphabet**. The alphabet was previously thought to have been developed by Semitic-speaking people in ancient Palestine around 1600 BC, but the Wadi el-Hol inscriptions date from two or three centuries earlier. Darnell believes that Semitic merchants living in Egypt developed a "shorthand" based on Egyptian hieroglyphics. For example, "A" was the pictogram for a bull's head, turned upside down; the semitic for bull is *Aleph*, the first letter of the Hebrew alphabet, pronounced with the same "aah" sound as the Latin letter. It is possible that other symbols may be the precursors of the letters "L", "M", "T" and "R".

exile for deposed sultans. A relic of its former status is the eleventh-century **Al-Amri Mosque**, containing a fine arabesque *mihrab* and teak *minbar*.

Further south, near Khuzam, a side road leads to the Coptic community of **GARAGOS**, which produces artistic **ceramics** and **textiles**. As Garagos is hard to reach by public transport, visitors previously arrived in hired taxis, which the Coptic staff in Luxor's tourist office would happily arrange. Nearing Luxor, you pass by **EL-MADAMUD**, which harbours a **ruined Temple of Mont** whose Ptolemaic–Roman avenue of sphinxes and monumental gateway belie its Old Kingdom origins. The site's overgrown desolation is all the more evocative for being totally undisturbed by tourists.

Along the west bank

EL-BALLAS, 23km from Qena, has manufactured white earthenware jars since antiquity; they are sold at Qena's **pottery** market alongside the town's own traditional wares – the porous water jars that women carry on their heads from childhood. South of here lay ancient Ombos, whose crocodile-worshipping residents never forgave the people of Dendara for eating one: a grudge reaffirmed at every Festival of Drunkenness (see box on p.357).

Further south, the predominantly Coptic village of **NAQADA** lends its name to two **pre-Dynastic cultures** that are reckoned to have existed between around 4000 and 3000 BC: Naqada I (early) and Naqada II (late). However, the reason to come here is to see the huge **Pigeon Palace**, built by a monk just over a century ago. Located in a field 200m west of the main road, the mud-brick *Qasr el-Hamam* enables ten thousand birds to recuperate from their flight over the Western Desert; food is provided – and in turn the keepers eat their resident charges. There are frequent service **taxis** between Naqada and Gezira, across the Nile from Luxor, but tourists can't use them.

Luxor

LUXOR (population 421,000) has been a tourist mecca ever since Nile steamers began calling in the nineteenth century to view the remains of Thebes, ancient Egypt's New Kingdom capital, and its associated sites – the concentration of relics in this area is overwhelming. The town itself boasts **Luxor Temple**, a graceful ornament to its waterfront and "downtown" quarter, while a mile or so north is **Karnak Temple**, a stupendous complex built over 1300 years. Across the river are the amazing tombs and mortuary temples of the **Theban Necropolis**, and as if this wasn't enough, Luxor also serves as a base for trips to Esna, Edfu, Dendara and Abydos temples, up and down the Nile Valley.

In a town where **tourism** accounts for 85 percent of the economy, it's hardly surprising that you can't move without being importuned to step inside a shop, rent a *caleche*, or have your shoes shined. Hassled and overcharged at every turn, some tourists react with fury and come to detest Luxor. Provided you keep your cool and sense of humour, it's possible to find genuine warmth here. Once you get to know a few characters and begin to understand the score, Luxor becomes a funky soap opera with a cast of thousands. Cool feluccca guys and bazaar hustlers, nervous rich tourists and piastre-pinching backpackers – their dealings and misunderstandings are almost as intriguing as the monuments. Read the box on pp.364–365 for an idea of how things are.

Most foreigners come between October and February (especially Christmas and New Year), when the **climate** is cooler than you might imagine, with chilly nights and early mornings. Around the end of March the temperature shoots up 10°C, making April the nicest time of the year to visit, though the weather remains agreeable until May, after which the daytime heat is brutal till late October, when the temperature plummets. During the summer tourism is well down, and the locals have time to sleep by day and party at night.

A little history

The name Luxor derives from the Arabic *El-Uqsur* – meaning "the palaces" or "the castles" – a name which may have referred to a Roman *castrum* or the town's appearance in medieval times, when it squatted amidst the ruins of **Thebes**. This, in turn, was the Greek name for the city known to the ancient Egyptians as *Weset*, originally an obscure provincial town during the Old Kingdom, when Egypt was ruled from Memphis. After power ebbed to regional overlords in the First Intermediate Period, Weset/Thebes gained ascendancy in Upper Egypt under Mentuhotpe II (c.2100 BC), who reunited Egypt under the Middle Kingdom. Though this dissolved into anarchy, the town survived as a power base for local princes who eventually liberated Egypt from the Hyksos invaders, reunited the Two Lands and founded the XVIII Dynasty (c.1567 BC).

As the capital of the **New Kingdom**, whose empire stretched from Nubia to Palestine, Thebes' ascendancy was paralleled by that of **Amun**, whose cult temple at Karnak became the greatest in Egypt. At its zenith under the XVIII and XIX dynasties, Thebes may have had a population of around a million; Homer's *Iliad* describes it as a "city with a hundred gates". Excluding the brief **Amarna Period** (c.1379–1362 BC), when the "heretic" Akhenaten moved the capital northwards and forbade the worship of Amun, the dynasty's – and city's – supremacy lasted some five hundred years. Even after the end of the Ramessid line, when the capital returned to Memphis and thence moved to the Delta, Thebes remained the foremost city of Upper Egypt, enjoying a final fling as a royal seat under the **Nubian** rulers of the XXV Dynasty (c.747–645 BC).

Though Thebes persisted through **Ptolemaic** into **Roman** times, it retained but a shadow of its former glory, and might have been abandoned like Memphis were it not for Christian settlements. During Muslim times its only claim to fame was the tomb of Abu el-Haggag, a twelfth-century sheikh. However, Napoleon's expedition to Egypt awakened foreign interest in its **antiquities**, which were gradually cleared during the nineteenth century and have drawn visitors ever since.

To be fair, not every visitor to Luxor has been unequivocally impressed by its ancient monuments: during the filming of *Death on the Nile*, Hollywood icon Bette Davis famously remarked that "In my day we'd have built all this at the studio – and better".

Arrival, orientation and information

Arriving in Luxor can be stressful, especially at the **train station**, where you're mobbed by hotel touts thrusting cards under your nose and bad-mouthing rival establishments. (A few hotels such as *Happy Land* and *Little Garden* make a point of not employing touts.) As most places are less than fifteen minutes' walk away, it is fine to strike out towards your preferred option without further ado. Much the same goes if you arrive **by bus** at the depot just north of Luxor Temple, where you may prefer to catch a minibus, *caleche* or taxi if you're heading for the southern part of town around Television Street. Travellers who've come up **from Aswan by felucca** are dependent on private taxis from Edfu or Kom Ombo, whose drivers will rendezvous with hustlers at the checkpoint

Luxor's tourism scene

Since many visitors fly directly to Luxor, it's worth outlining some features of the local tourism scene. For starters, the number of visitors has slumped by forty percent since September 11, and although package tourists are gradually trickling back, the ongoing violence in Israel/Palestine has choked off the stream of overland travellers that used to be a major part of the tourist trade. As a consequence, hotels have been cutting back on maintenance and offering discounts, while *caleche* drivers are quoting fares they would have sneered at in the past.

Perhaps now more than ever it is important to consider financial transactions **from the locals' standpoint** rather than expecting to get the cheapest price as a matter of right. Hoteliers, felucca captains and salesmen earn good money one day, then little or nothing for ages – even in good times, and during high season. The hotel touts who swear that your place of choice is closed or dirty know that most hotels in Luxor are half empty – so every guest counts. At **no-star hotels**, the price often depends on how full they are, how many there are of you, and at what time you arrive – it's negotiable. Be fair and realistic, even if you're on a tight budget. To get a double room with a shower and toilet for £E25–30 is a good deal by any standards; trying to force them to go any lower is really taking advantage.

Where such hotels make their money is by surcharges on **taxi, caleche or donkey tours**. Although it's wise not to take the first deal offered, also bear in mind that the lowest price may not necessarily be a good deal: you could end up with someone who's so bad that they have to undercut better guides in order to get any work. The easiest way to spoil your day is to ask what someone else paid; if you're happy with what you've done and can afford it, why worry about what amounts to the price of a cup of tea or coffee back home?

It also helps to take a relaxed attitude towards **street hustlers** and react to such lines as "Hey – remember me?", "You've dropped your wallet", or "I know what you need" with a humorous rebuff (*Fil mish mish* – "In your dreams" – works well). You'll actually get hassled *less* once they recognize that you know the score – including the old ploy of asking you to translate a letter from abroad, as a way to lure you into conversation.

south of Luxor and steer you to their hotels. If you're not being met at **Luxor Airport**, the cost of a taxi into town is officially £E20–25 depending on the size of the car and your destination, but it's hard to settle with a driver for less than £E50.

Orientation

Luxor spreads along the east bank of the Nile, its outskirts encroaching on villages and fields. For a general layout of the town along with Karnak and the Theban Necropolis, see the **map** on p.399; a detailed street plan appears on pp.366–367. **Orientation** in central Luxor is simplified by a relatively compact tourist zone defined by three main roads. **Sharia al-Mahatta** runs 500m from the train station towards Luxor Temple, where it meets **Sharia el-Karnak**, the main drag heading north to Karnak Temple (2.5km). Karnak is also accessible via the riverside **Corniche**, though tourists generally stick to the 1.5km stretch between Luxor Museum and the *Winter Palace Hotel*. The "circuit" is completed by a fourth street, known as **Sharia al-Souk** after its bazaar. In the last two decades Luxor has expanded south towards the village of Awmia, with dozens of hotels and other facilities along **Sharia Khalid Ibn Walid** (running 3km from the *Novotel* to the *Sheraton*) and **Television Street** (named after its TV tower), which now constitute extensions of the tourist zone.

That said, it's best to be forewarned about a few **scams**. Watch out for the hustlers on Sharia al-Souk who approach tourists offering to exchange euros or dollars, and rip them off by sleight of hand. The **black market** in duty-free booze – which tourists are asked to buy on the pretext that it's needed for "My brother's wedding" but is actually re-sold to bars or hotels – still goes on, though the practice has been curbed by the 48-hour limit on duty-free purchases. A bigger problem for tourists is that tour guides, touts, taxi and *caleche* drivers get **commission** on every transaction they facilitate – which is deftly added to your bill. Don't go shopping in the bazaar with a driver or a guide, or pay for a tour through middlemen, when you could deal directly with a tour operator.

Over the past decade, **sex tourism** has quietly become a way of life in Luxor, a "hidden" industry that turns many of the stereotypes of the sex trade inside out. Egyptian women and foreign heterosexual males are left on the sidelines as local men and boys get together with foreign women and gays in feluccas, bars and discos. Thousands of women have holiday romances in Luxor every year and word has got home, encouraging others to come. The exchange of sex for cash usually occurs under the guise of true love, with misled women spending money on their boyfriends or "husbands" until their savings run out and the relationship hits the rocks – but enough foreigners blithely rent toyboys and settle into the scene for locals to make the point that neither side is innocent. Morality aside, it isn't just their money that foreigners are risking or that Egyptians are bringing home to their families. HIV now exists on both sides of the river and **AIDS** could easily spread fast if nothing is done. Yet locals are in denial about the problem and tourists hardly aware that it even exists. The authorities are also cracking down on paedophiles, with several arrested every month.

Hissed invitations and whiffs of smoke by the Nile attest to a smoking subculture that's stronger in Luxor than anywhere else in Egypt except Dahab. **Bango** (marijuana) and **hashish** are easy to obtain if one knows where to ask, and smoking shouldn't cause any problems if it's done discreetly; several low-budget hotels have a liberal atmosphere in this respect.

Information

Once you've found somewhere to stay, it's a good idea to visit the **tourist office** (daily 8am–8pm; Ramadan 8am–sunset; ☏095/237-2215 or 237-3294) south of Luxor Temple to discover the latest official rates for taxis, *caleches*, feluccas or any other service you might be interested in. Confusingly, there are two offices next door to each other; you want the one signposted "Egyptian Tourist Authority", not "Luxor City Information". There's also a branch at the airport (☏095/237-2306), open 24 hours during winter, and another at the train station (generally open daily 8am–8pm).

The **tourist police**'s "front" office lies across the way from the tourist office, while their headquarters is upstairs, around the back of the building (daily 24hr; ☏095/237-3845 or 237-6620). They also have a branch in the station (daily 8am–8pm). The regular **police** are based off Sharia el-Karnak, north of Luxor Temple, and supplemented on the streets by a host of plain-clothes agents known as the "*galabiyya* police", plus uniformed Central Security troops – so you're never far from a cop of some kind if you need one. Whatever your problem, it's always best to go to the tourist police first. For *really* serious matters, contact Colonel Hafiz Hussein – known as "Hafiz Bey" – in his office in the Nile Shopping Centre near Luxor Temple (mobile ☏010 5801686).

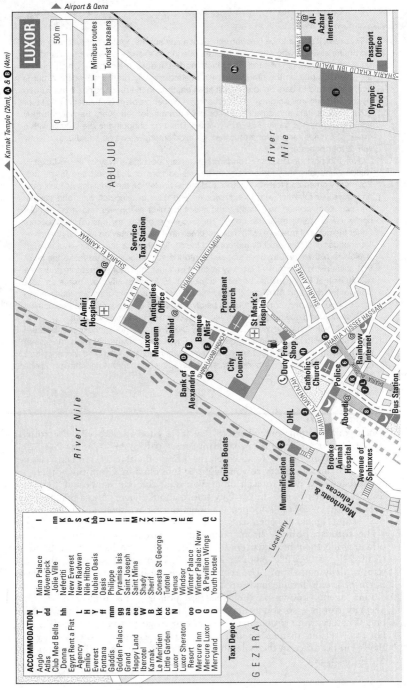

LUXOR

▲ Airport & Qena

▲ Karnak Temple (2km), Ⓐ & Ⓑ (4km)

0 ——— 500 m

- - - Minibus routes
▓ Tourist bazaars

ACCOMMODATION

Anglo	I	Mina Palace	T
Atlas	dd	Mövenpick	
Club Med Bella	hh	Jolie Ville	
Donna		Nefertiti	mm
Egypt Rent a Flat	L	New Everest	K
Agency		New Radwan	P
Emilio	H	Nile Hilton	S
Everest	Y	Nubian Oasis	A
Fontana	ff	Oasis	bb
Gaddis	mm	Philippe	U
Golden Palace	gg	Pyramisa Isis	F
Grand	aa	Saint Joseph	ii
Happy Land	ee	Saint Mina	M
Iberotel	W	Shady	Z
Karnak	B	Sherif	X
Le Meridien	kk	Sonesta St George	ii
Little Garden	cc	Tutotel	V
Luxor	N	Venus	J
Luxor Sheraton		Windsor	E
Resort	oo	Winter Palace: New	R
Mercure Inn	O	Winter Palace: New	
Mercure Luxor	G	& Pavillion Wings	Q
Merryland	D	Youth Hostel	C

GEZIRA

Taxi Depot

Local Ferry

River Nile

Cruise Boats

Motorboats & Feluccas

ABU JUD

SHARIA EL-KARNAK

Service Taxi Station

Al-Amiri Hospital ✚

Luxor Museum

Antiquities Office

Shahid @

Bank of Alexandria

Banque Misr

SHARIA LABIB HABACHI

City Council

Protestant Church

St Mark's Hospital ✚

DHL

Duty Free Shop

Catholic Church

Mummification Museum

Brooke Animal Hospital

Avenue of Sphinxes

Police

Aboud@

Rainbow Internet

Bus Station

SHARIA YUSSEF HASSAN

SHARIA AHMES

SHARIA AL-MONTAZAH

SHARIA TUTANKHAMUN

River Nile

SHARIA KHALID IBN WALID

Al-Azhar Internet @

SHARIA ST JOSEPH

Olympic Pool

Passport Office

River Nile

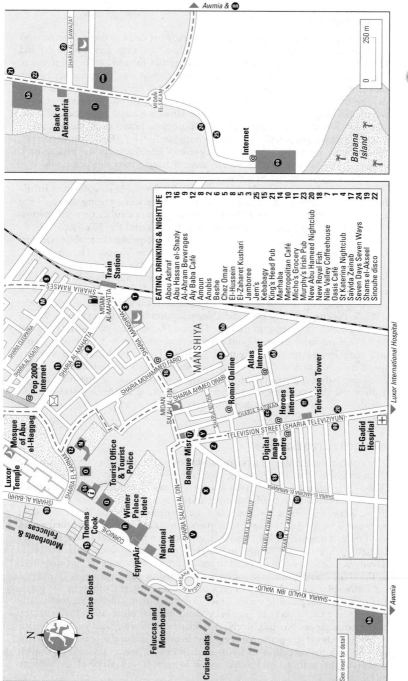

EATING, DRINKING & NIGHTLIFE

Abou Ashraf	13
Abu Hassan el-Shazly	16
Al-Ahram Beverages	9
Aly Baba Café	12
Amoun	8
Anubis	2
Beshe	6
Chez Omar	5
El-Hussein	8
El-Zaharet Kushari	5
Jamboree	3
Jem's	25
Kebabagy	15
King's Head Pub	21
Marhaba	14
Metropolitan Café	10
Micho's Grocery	11
Murphy's Irish Pub	23
New Abu Hameed Nightclub	20
New Royal Fish	18
Nile Valley Coffeehouse	7
Oasis Café	1
St Katerina Nightclub	4
Sayida Zeinab	17
Seven Days Seven Ways	24
Shams el-Akseel	19
Sinouhe disco	22

Awmia &

Luxor Temple

Mosque of Abu el-Haggag

Train Station

MANSHIYA

Tourist Office & Tourist Police

Winter Palace Hotel

National Bank

EgyptAir

Thomas Cook

Bank of Alexandria

Banque Misr

Digital Image Centre

Television Tower

El-Gadid Hospital

Luxor International Hospital

Awmia

Banana Island

Pop 2000 Internet

Romio Online

Atlas Internet

Heroes Internet

Internet

0   250 m

See inset for detail

Transport

Although you can easily explore central Luxor **on foot**, it takes some time to get used to the traffic (a balletic mix of bikes, cars, carts and minibuses) and being importuned at every step. **Caleches** are fun to ride and useful if you're burdened with luggage, but a bit pricey for regular use. Fares are set by the authorities but drivers charge whatever they can get. Expect an argument if you pay the official rate (£E5 for a ride within Luxor; £E10 for 1hr tour); rides to Karnak are a special case (see p.386). The Brooke Animal Hospital (see p.65) asks tourists to dissuade drivers from galloping their horses or taking more than four passengers. **Taxis** serve for trips to outlying hotels (£E5–9) or the airport, but are fairly superfluous around the centre (£E3–5), except for getting back from a disco. As with *caleches*, you'll have to haggle over the price, which is bound to exceed the cost of public transport.

Surprisingly few visitors take advantage of the fleet of blue-and-white **minibuses** that shuttle between outlying points, constantly passing through the centre along Sharia el-Karnak. Northbound minibuses either turn off towards the taxi depot (*mogaf*), or run straight on to Karnak and the *Nile Hilton*. Heading in the opposite direction, they terminate at the public hospital (*moustashfa*) far down Television Street, or at Awmia, out near the *Sheraton*. The *moustafsha*-bound ones detour inland via the train station, while Awmia buses stick to Sharia Khalid Ibn Walid. The tactic is to wave down any minibus heading in the right direction, shout "*mogaf*", "*Hilton*", "*moustafsha*" (or whatever), and hop in if they're going there. There's a flat fare of 25pt on all routes.

While cycling in Luxor isn't advisable, many tourists rent **bicycles** to use on the west bank, for getting around the Theban Necropolis (see p.401). They can be carried on local ferries. Shops on Sharia al-Mahatta and Television Street, and many low-budget hotels, rent them from £E10 a day. Most bikes are one-speed only and may well be defective in some respect (though bikes at *Happy Land* get daily maintenance), so it's always wise to check the machine and do a short test ride. A passport or other ID is generally required as security. You can also rent 150cc **motorbikes** from several places, including the *New Everest Hotel*, for about £E50 a day.

Accommodation

The cost and availability of **accommodation** varies with the time of year and fluctuations in tourism. Officially, there are just "high" (Nov–May) and "low" (June–Oct) **seasons**. In practice, prices rise or fall depending on **demand**, which is affected both by the number of tourists and competition from cruise boats. When tourism is healthy, peak time coincides with the Egyptian school vacation (Dec 10–Jan 10), but in a depressed market, hotels will cut their prices even then, if necessary. Many low-budget places employ **hotel touts**, who refer to netting tourists as "fishing" and happily poach them from rivals. If you've already decided on a hotel it's best to ignore offers to accompany you anywhere, as the touts' commission is usually quietly added to your bill.

As some places calculate prices on a per-person basis, and others by the room, the scope for **bargaining** varies. Three-star hotels may waive taxes, particularly new places that haven't yet got many customers, or older ones threatened by better competitors. No-star hotels rarely charge tax anyway, and will often shave a few pounds off the price. As **breakfast** is pretty much the same everywhere, you needn't pay attention to lavish descriptions of what's on offer – though a **restaurant** with a good cook and a licence to sell **alcohol** are definite advantages.

Staff are crucial, too, as hotels that were good can become bad (or vice versa) just because the manager or receptionist changes – especially low-budget hotels leased on one-year contracts. Some years ago, a spate of sexual assaults on **women travellers** were reported at two particular hotels; nobody was ever prosecuted but the perpetrators seem to have been warned off, for no assaults have been reported since 2001.

The following hotels are all in **Luxor; places on the west bank** are detailed on p.405.

Inexpensive hotels

Inexpensive hotels (under £E100 for a double) and real cheapos (£E25-ish) are concentrated around **Yussef Hassan**, **Al–Mahatta** and **Television** streets. The biggest selection is around Television Street, no more than fifteen minutes' walk from Luxor Temple or the station. Despite its littered backstreets, this is an up-and-coming area that's safe to stay in and quieter than the centre of town (which has fewer low-budget options). Unless stated otherwise, you should be sure of getting hot water and breakfast.

Anglo Sharia al-Mahatta ☎ & ℱ 095/238-1679. Being so close to the train station is a big drawback, but the rooms are a/c and en-suite (if a bit claustrophobic), and the hotel has an alcohol licence. ❶

Atlas Off Sharia Ahmed Orabi ☎ 095/237-3514. About five minutes' walk from the station, this hotel has simple rooms (£E25) with fans or a/c and private baths. Guests can use the washing machine for a fee. Breakfast not included. ❶

Everest Sharia Nozha, off Television St ☎ 095/237-3260 or mobile ☎ 010 5649180 ℯ everesthotel@hotmail.com. Large clean-ish rooms with fans or a/c, many with baths (£E30). Free washing machine and scruffy rooftop. Used by Egyptian groups. ❶

Fontana Sharia Radwan, off Television St ☎ 095/238-0663. A longtime backpackers' favourite: clean and well furnished, with a noticeboard, library and free washing machine; it's worth paying £E10 more for an a/c room with a bathroom. Prices for rooms and tours go up and down like a yo-yo, so compare notes with other guests before agreeing to anything. Sells ISIC cards. ❶

Grand Off Sharia Mohammed Farid ☎ 095/238-2905, ℯ grandhotelluxor@yahoo.com. This quiet no-star has simple rooms with fans (£E20) or a/c (£E5 extra), decent bathrooms and a rooftop terrace. Hires bikes. ❶

Happy Land Sharia el-Kamrr ☎ 095/237-1828, ℱ 237-1140, ℯ happylandluxor@hotmail.com. An established travellers' favourite, known for its cleanliness, honesty and fixed prices. They don't send touts to the station. All rooms with fans, some a/c and en-suite, plus a six-bed dorm (£E12.50 a bed); towels, loo roll and mosquito-zappers are provided. Breakfast includes cornflakes and fruit.

A/c rooftop breakfast terrace with CNN news. Cheap Internet (£E8/hr), bike rental, and trips to Dendara and Abydos, Edfu and Kom Ombo, and the west bank. ❶

Merryland Sharia Nefertiti, between the temple and the museum ☎ & ℱ 095/238-1746. Though clean and quiet, with a fab view of the Nile from its rooftop, the claustrophobic rooms and lack of a pool make this place inferior to its nearby three-star rivals, the *Windsor* and *Philippe*. ❷

Nefertiti Off Sharia el-Karnak ☎ & ℱ 095/237-2386, ⓦ www.nefertitihotel.com. This small central hotel has clean a/c rooms with bath, a rooftop overlooking Luxor Temple, a pool table, mini-gym and Internet (£E10/hr). Breakfast is above average. ❷

New Everest Off Sharia al-Mahatta ☎ 095/237-0017 or mobile ☎ 010 5278297. A shabby, friendly backpackers' den on a quiet sidestreet in the centre. Has a chilled-out rooftop, library, free washing machine, and beer for sale. Rooms have fans and shared bathrooms. Rents motorbikes. ❶

Nubian Oasis Sharia Mohammed Farid ☎ 095/236-2671 or mobile ☎ 012 2929445. At this hotel you can get a basic double with a bathroom for only £E20 – but don't expect much else. Associated with the *Nubian Oasis Hotel* in Aswan. ❶

Oasis Sharia Mohammed Farid mobile ☎ 010 5494647. Though its lobby looks better than upstairs, the rooms are spacious, with fans and shared facilities on two floors and a/c and private bathrooms on another, for £E10 per person. They're keen to sell excursions to the west bank and Valley temples, safaris to the oases or rides to Hurghada. Manager Tito also rents apartments in New Karnak (see p.372). ❶

Saint Mina Sharia Cleopatra ☎ & ℱ 095/237-6568, ℯ minahotel@hotmail.com. Friendly, clean hotel on a quiet backstreet in the Coptic quarter; its small, simple a/c rooms have bathrooms or share facilities with two other rooms. ❶

Shady Television St ☎ 095/238-1337, ⓕ 237-4859, ⓔ shady-hotel@hotmail.com. This hotel (whose name is pronounced "Shar-dy") has small a/c en-suite rooms, a pool out back, a big rooftop with sunloungers, and Internet access (£E10/hr). ❷

Sherif Sharia Badr, off Television St ☎ 095/237-0757 or mobile ☎ 012 7369633, ⓔ sheriefhotel@yahoo.co.uk. Shabby, clean-ish backstreet hotel, with naïve murals, a washing machine, a rooftop, and bicycles and motorbikes for rent. A private bathroom costs £E10 extra. ❶

Venus Sharia Yussef Hassan ☎ 095/237-2625 or mobile ☎ 012 1713599, ⓔ venushotel@hotmail .com. This classic backpackers' hotel off the bazaar is quite noisy but funky, with a louche bar and a rooftop with a liberal atmosphere. Its rooms (£E30–40) are mostly a/c, with clean sheets, showers, and tiny balconies. Internet (£E10/hr); ISIC cards (£E60). The only hotel in Luxor which still organizes donkey trips (£E55) to the west bank – call Tayer on his mobile for details. ❶

Mid-range hotels

Mostly rated with three stars, Luxor's mid-range hotels feature private bathrooms, a/c, phone and TV in the rooms, and a restaurant, bar and maybe also a pool on the premises. There the similarity may end, however, as each differs in its location, decor, atmosphere, clientele and rates. Although breakfast is included in the deal, don't expect anything fancier than you'd get in a low-budget hotel.

Emilio Sharia Yussef Hassan ☎ 095/237-6666, ⓕ 237-0000. Centrally located and popular with European tour groups – reservations advisable. Comfy rooms with video channel, minibar and satellite TV; rooftop pool, bar and disco. Accepts DC, MC, JCB and Visa cards. ❻

Gaddis Sharia Khalid Ibn Walid, 1km south of Midan el-Mesaha ☎ 095/238-2838, ⓕ 238-2837, ⓔ gaddislxr@yahoo.com. Established three-star hotel with a small pool, bar and disco. Recent reports, however, have complained of dirty rooms and cold meals. Takes all major cards. ❺

Golden Palace 600m down Television St ☎ 095/238-2972, ⓕ 238-2974. Shabby, comfy rooms reached by a dodgy lift, and a kidney-shaped pool with faux-Babylonian décor, across the road from the *New Abu Hameed* nightclub (see p.379). They'll usually take far less than the price posted at reception. ❺

Karnak *Sharia Hilton*, 4km from downtown Luxor, 1.5km from Karnak Temple ☎ 095/237-6155, ⓕ 237-4155, ⓦ www.lxr.com.eg/karnakhtl. A decent three-star block with a fair-sized pool, across the road from the *Nile Hilton*. Accessible by public minibus via Karnak Temple. ❻

Little Garden Sharia Radwan ☎ 095/238-9038 or mobile ☎ 012 1038441, ⓦ www.littlegarden.com. A no-star hotel resembling a two-star one; spacious and dazzlingly clean, with comfy a/c rooms (a private terrace costs £E5 extra), a rooftop with sunbeds and showers, and a garden. Free transfer from the airport for pre-booked guests; no touting at the train station. ❸

Luxor Sharia el-Karnak, near Luxor Temple ☎ 095/238-0018 or mobile ☎ 010 1176627. Still known to locals as the *Wena*, this decrepit Edwardian pile was the set for a BBC docu-drama about Howard Carter. Its Arabesque lobby and billiard room have been refurbished and the high-ceilinged rooms, vast garden and pool are set to follow. Check it out. ❹

Mercure Inn Sharia el-Karnak, near Luxor Temple ☎ 095/238-0721, ⓕ 237-0051, ⓦ www.accor -hotels.com. Cosy rooms with fridge and satel-lite TV, in large grounds with a decent-sized pool. Used by Goldenjoy and Kuoni. Locals still call it the *Egotel*. All major credit cards. Breakfast not included. ❻

Mina Palace On the Corniche near Luxor Temple ☎ 095/237-2074, ⓕ 238-2194. Old-fashioned a/c rooms overlooking the Nile; the "06" ones have an extra balcony facing the temple. Its rooftop and terrace are nice drinking spots if you can endure the slow service. ❸

New Radwan Sharia Manshiya ☎ & ⓕ 095/238-5501. Decent a/c rooms, but the pool is a bit murky, and the location noisy. Laundry service; sells beer. ❸

Philippe Sharia Labaib Habachi, near the Corniche ☎ 095/237-2284, ⓕ 238-0050. Clean, carpeted rooms with fridges and a rooftop pool and sun terrace make this a favourite with adventure tour operators, but independent travellers may find the hotel rather impersonal, despite its good reputation. ❺

Saint Joseph Sharia Khalid Ibn Walid ☎ & ⓕ 095/238-1707, ⓔ sihiev2002@hotmail.com. This three-star block has clean, slightly dark rooms with all the usual amenities (reserve ahead for a Nile-facing one on the top floor), and a rooftop with a pool, bar and view of the Theban Hills, where they hold Saturday night Saiyidi parties with snake-dancing and a buffet (£E55 per person). ❺

Tutotel Sharia Salah al-Din ☎ 095/237-7990, Ⓕ 237-2671, Ⓔ gm.tutotel@partner-hotels.com. A small four-star with a rooftop pool and popular basement disco, charging far less than its larger rivals on Sharia Khalid Ibn Walid. ❺

Windsor Sharia Nefertiti, near the Corniche ☎ 095/237-5547, Ⓕ 237-3447, Ⓦ www .windsorluxor.com. While its rooms are better than those at the *Philippe* and its roof terrace has a finer view, the pool is in a courtyard, and tiny, so they charge less. ❸

Upmarket hotels

Luxor's **upmarket hotels** mostly deal with tour groups or rich Egyptians, who pay far less than the advertised rack-rates by booking in advance. Look for discount rates on the Internet; you can save twenty percent in high season and a lot more during summer, when even walk-in enquirers can easily negotiate low prices. Most places charge premium rates for Nile-view rooms; the prices below are for the least expensive (garden- or street-facing) rooms in high season. Non-residents may use hotel restaurants, if not other facilities, too.

Club Med Bella Donna Sharia Khalid Ibn Walid, 700m beyond the *Iberotel* ☎ 095/238-4000, Ⓕ 238-0879, Ⓔ louvcrec01@clubmed.com. Stylish, self-contained resort on the banks of the Nile, where all the guests and staff speak French. Accommodation on a B&B, half- or full-board basis, with discounts for children. ❽

Iberotel Midan el-Mesaha, 1km south of Luxor Temple ☎ 095/238-0925, Ⓕ 238-0972. This former *Novotel* (still widely known as that) has a large atrium, pool and terrace overlooking the Nile; a Nile-view room costs US$20 extra. ❼

Le Meridien Sharia Khalid Ibn Walid, 2km from the temple ☎ 095/236-6999, Ⓕ 236-5666, Ⓦ www .lemeridien.com. Awash with fake marble, Luxor's newest five-star overlooks a heated swimming pool beside a Nile terrace. Disabled access throughout. Lebanese restaurant. All major cards. ❼

Luxor Sheraton Resort Sharia Khalid Ibn Walid, 4km south of the temple ☎ 095/237-4544, Ⓕ 237-4941, Ⓦ www.sheraton.com/luxor. Good facilities and service, but it's not worth paying premium rates for "Nile-view" rooms. Accessible by a free bus from the Luxor Museum seven times daily. ❼

Mercure Luxor Corniche el-Nil, between Luxor Temple and the museum ☎ 095/238-0944, Ⓕ 237-4912, Ⓦ www.accor-hotels.com. Still known to locals as the *Etap*, this anodyne four-star is used by Viking and Kuoni, but anyone paying rack rates will get more for their money at the *Pyramisa Isis* or the *Sheraton*. ❼

Mövenpick Jolie Ville Crocodile Island, 5km south of Luxor ☎ 095/237-4855, Ⓕ 237-4936, Ⓦ www.movenpick-luxor.com. Comfy bungalows in luxuriant grounds, tennis courts, a pool and children's playground. Hourly buses to the *New*

Winter Palace in town, and a motorboat three times daily. All major cards. ❽

Nile Hilton 4km north of downtown Luxor and 1.5km from Karnak Temple ☎ 095/237-4933, Ⓕ 237-6571, Ⓦ www.hilton.com. Club-class, Nile-view and garden-facing rooms, in an enclave beside the river, with tennis courts, a giant chessboard and other diversions. Hourly courtesy bus from the *Mercure Luxor* (see above). All major cards. ❽

Pyramisa Isis Sharia Khalid Ibn Walid ☎ 095/237-2750, Ⓕ 237-2923, Ⓦ www.pyramisaegypt.com. Five-star complex set in lush grounds with wonderful views of the river. Owned by a relative of President Mubarak; the presidential suite costs US$795. Italian and Chinese restaurants; large swimming pool; Internet access. Visa cards only. ❼

Sonesta St George Sharia Khalid Ibn Walid ☎ 095/238-2575, Ⓕ 238-2571, Ⓦ www.sonesta .com. The most lavishly decorated five-star hotel on the street, with oodles of marble, Japanese and Italian restaurants and a heated pool by the Nile. Amex, MasterCard, Visa. ❽

Winter Palace On the Corniche, 100m from Luxor Temple ☎ 095/238-0422, Ⓕ 237-4087, Ⓦ www .accor-hotels.com. The doyen of Luxor's hotels, founded in 1887, has played host to heads of state, Noël Coward and Agatha Christie (parts of *Death on the Nile* were written and filmed here). Now part of the Sofitel chain, it combines old-fashioned elegance with modern facilities. Rooms overlook the Nile or a huge garden with a pool (from US$235 for a standard garden view up to US$1125 for the royal suite). The adjacent *New Wing* and *Pavilion Wing* (❼) are half the price but lack character, though they share the same facilities; the Pavilion Wing is the better of the two. Buffet breakfast (£E85) not included. Amex, MasterCard and Visa. ❽

Renting an apartment and hostelling

Renting an apartment in Luxor is relatively easy, and many regular visitors prefer this to staying at a hotel, for more privacy or to save money. Guy Mauviel's Egypt Rent a Flat **agency** (℡095/236-0205 or mobile ℡010 6142722, ⓦwww.egypt-rentaflat.com; daily except Sun 10.30am–2.30pm & 5-9pm) on Sharia Sidi Mahmoud, in the bazaar quarter, has dozens of properties in Luxor and the west bank, from two-bedroom apartments (from €69 per week, €218 per month) to deluxe mansions (negotiable). Alternatively, try **landlords** such as Tito (mobile ℡010 5494647), who has two a/c flats in New Karnak near the *Hilton*, each with four double rooms, two bathrooms, a kitchen, lounge and satellite TV, for £E80 a night or around £E1000 a month.

With hotels around Television Street so cheap, you won't save money staying at the **youth hostel** (℡095/237-2139) near the Luxor Museum, even if you could endure its noise and daytime lock-out. Packed out with Egyptian teenagers in winter and closed over summer, it has gender-segregated dorms with bunks (for Egyptians only) and "lux" rooms with three beds, for £E22 a head; HI membership is obligatory, but there's no age limit.

Luxor Temple

Luxor Temple (daily: Oct–April 6am–9pm; May–Sept 6am–10pm; Ramadan 6am–6.30pm & 8–11pm; £E35, student £E20, tripod camera £E20) stands aloof in the heart of town, ennobling the view from the waterfront and tourist bazaar with its grand colonnades and pylons, which are spotlit at night. Though best explored by day – when its details can be thoroughly examined in a couple of hours – you should come back after dark to imbibe its atmosphere and drama with fewer people around. For a general guide to **temple architecture**, see pp.348–349.

The temple's dedication and construction

Dedicated to the **Theban Triad** of Amun-Min, Mut and Khonsu (see p.387), Luxor Temple was the "Harem of the South" where Amun's consort Mut and their son Khonsu resided. Every spring a flotilla of barques escorted Amun's effigy from Karnak Temple to this site for a conjugal reunion with Mut in an *Optet* or fertility festival noted for its public debauchery.

Whereas Karnak is the work of many dynasties, most of Luxor Temple was built by two rulers during a period when New Kingdom art reached its apogee. The temple's founder was **Amenophis III** (1417–1379 BC) of the XVIII Dynasty, whose other monuments include the Third Pylon at Karnak and the Colossi of Memnon across the river. Work halted under his son Akhenaten (who erased his father's cartouches and built a sanctuary to Aten alongside the temple), but resumed under Tutankhamun and Horemheb, who decorated its court and colonnade with their own reliefs. To this, **Ramses II** (1304–1237 BC) of the XIX Dynasty added a double colonnaded court and a great pylon flanked by obelisks and colossi. Despite additions by later pharaohs and the rebuilding of its sanctuary under Alexander the Great, the temple has a coherence that reproaches Karnak's inchoate giganticism. When the French army first sighted it in 1799, the troops spontaneously presented arms.

The clarity of its **reliefs** is due to the temple having been half-buried by sand and silt, and overlaid by Luxor itself. Nineteenth-century visitors found a "labyrinthine maze of mud structures" nesting within its court; colonnades turned into granaries where dishonest merchants were hanged by their ears.

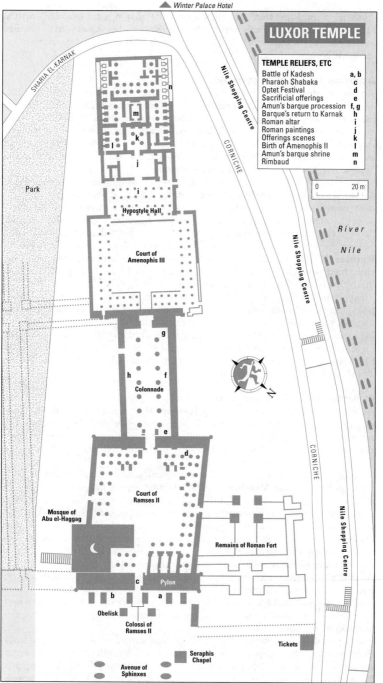

▲ Winter Palace Hotel

LUXOR TEMPLE

TEMPLE RELIEFS, ETC

Battle of Kadesh	a, b
Pharaoh Shabaka	c
Optet Festival	d
Sacrificial offerings	e
Amun's barque procession	f, g
Barque's return to Karnak	h
Roman altar	i
Roman paintings	j
Offerings scenes	k
Birth of Amenophis II	l
Amun's barque shrine	m
Rimbaud	n

0   20 m

SHARIA EL-KARNAK

Nile Shopping Centre

CORNICHE

River

Nile

Park

Hypostyle Hall

Court of
Amenophis III

g

h   f

Colonnade

N

e

d

Mosque of
Abu el-Haggag

Court of
Ramses II

Remains of Roman Fort

Nile Shopping Centre

CORNICHE

c   Pylon

b   a

Obelisk

Colossi of
Ramses II

Tickets

Seraphis
Chapel

Avenue of
Sphinxes

Mummification Museum ▼

373

"So stirs a mini-life amid the debris of a life that was far grander", wrote Flaubert. When the French wanted to remove an obelisk, and archeologists to excavate the temple, they had to pay compensation for the demolition of scores of homes.

Approaching the temple

The ticket office is on the Corniche side, where the gradual slope inside the entrance obscures the fact that the site lies several metres below street level – a measure of the debris that accumulated here over centuries. At the end of the ramp, to your left, is a restored **Chapel of Seraphis** dedicated by the Roman emperor Hadrian on his birthday in AD 126. Beyond this, the courtyard opens into an **Avenue of Sphinxes** with human faces that once led to Karnak Temple – a XXX Dynasty addition by Nectanebo I.

The temple gateway proper is flanked by massive pylons and enthroned colossi, with a single **Obelisk** soaring 25m high. Carved with reliefs and originally tipped with electrum, this was one of a pair until its mate was removed in 1835, taken to France and re-erected on the Place de la Concorde. The four dog-faced baboons at the base of each obelisk also sported erect phalluses until prudish Frenchmen hacked them off. Behind loom three of the six **colossi of Ramses II** that originally fronted the pylon (four seated, two standing). The enthroned pair have Schwarzenegger physiques and double crowns; reliefs of the Nile-god binding the Two Lands adorn their thrones.

The **Pylon** is 65m wide and once stood 24m high. It is notched for flag-poles and carved with scenes of Ramses' supposed victory over the Hittites at Qadesh. You can see Ramses consulting his commanders in the Egyptian camp **[a]**, before charging his foes and battling them until reinforcements arrive **[b]**. Centuries later, Nubian and Ethiopian kings left their mark: notice the relief of Pharaoh Shabaka running the *heb* race before Amun-Min, high up on the left as you walk through the pylon **[c]**.

Courts and colonnades

Beyond the pylon lies the **Court of Ramses II**, surrounded by a double row of papyrus-bud columns, once roofed over to form arcades. The courtyard is set askew to the temple's main axis, doubtless to incorporate the earlier **barque shrines** of Tuthmosis III, dedicated to Khonsu (to the right as you enter), Amun (centre) and Mut (nearest the river).

Incongruously perched atop the opposite colonnade (which is still bricked up to its capitals), the **Mosque of Abu el-Haggag** is a much-rebuilt Fatimid edifice bearing the name of Luxor's patron saint, whose demolition the townsfolk refused to countenance when the temple was excavated. Its interior juxtaposes Islamic motifs with pharaonic hieroglyphs; if suitably dressed and respectful, non-Muslims might be invited in to see them if they ask at the top of the stairway from Sharia el-Karank, outside the grounds.

Remaining in the temple, you can locate the lower half of a frieze depicting Amun's procession approaching the temple during the Optet festival, when the god was presented with lettuces, symbolizing his fertility **[d]**. Ramses makes offerings to Mut and Mont (the Theban war god), observed by his queen and seventeen of the hundred or so sons that he sired over ninety years. Notice the bullocks in the corner of the wall.

The portal itself is flanked by black granite statues of Ramses, their bases decorated with bound prisoners from Nubia and Asia. Beyond lies the older section of the temple, inaugurated by the lofty **Colonnade of Amenophis III**, with its processional avenue of giant papyrus columns whose calyx capitals still support massive architraves. Its scale is so vast that you can hardly take it in. On the walls are more damaged scenes from the Optet festival, intended to be "read" in an anticlockwise direction. After sacrifices to the boats at Karnak **[e]**, Amun's procession **[f]** arrives at Luxor Temple **[g]**, returning to Karnak 24 days later **[h]**. The pharaoh shown here is Tutankhamun, who had the colonnade decorated, but the cartouches honour his successor, Horemheb.

At the end of the colonnade lies the great **Court of Amenophis III**, surrounded on three sides by colonnades of papyrus-bundle columns with bud capitals – the most elegant form devised by the Ancient Egyptians. Its decorations include artwork from the time of Alexander and Philip of Macedon, with some traces of colour still visible on the eastern colonnade. The southern one merges into a **Hypostyle Hall** with 32 papyrus columns, serving as a vestibule to the temple proper. Between the last two columns on the left of its central aisle **[i]** is a Roman altar dedicated to Emperor Constantine, before his conversion to Christianity. On either side of the hall's rear wall, Amenophis makes offerings to the gods.

The inner sanctums

Beyond the hall lies a columned **portico** or antechamber, whose central aisle was flanked by the barque shrines of Mut and Khonsu. Roman legionaries later plastered over the pharaonic reliefs and turned it into a chapel where local Christians were offered a choice between martyrdom or obeisance to the imperial cults. Paintings of Roman emperors are visible near the top of the walls, and around the niche on the south wall **[j]**; elsewhere the stucco has fallen away to reveal Amenophis offering sacrifices to Amun. In the smaller, four-columned **Hall of Offerings**, beyond, reliefs show the pharaoh leading sacrificial cows and presenting incense and sceptres **[k]**.

More interesting reliefs occur in the **Birth Room** of Amenophis III, whose north wall **[l]** emphasizes his divine paternity, since he was not of direct royal descent. The ravaged lower register shows Amun, Hathor and Queen Mutemuia embracing; and Thoth leading Amun (disguised as Tuthmosis IV) into the queen's bedchamber, where the accompanying hieroglyphic caption states, "his dew filled her body". Examined from left to right, the middle register depicts Thoth foretelling Amenophis's birth; Mutemuia's pregnancy and confinement; Isis presenting the child to Amun; and the god cradling his son. Along the top register, Amenophis and his *ka* are nurtured by deities and presented to Amun; in the far right corner, Amenophis becomes pharaoh.

If the Birth Room is inaccessible from the Hall of Offerings you can reach it via the next hall, which Alexander the Great converted into the **Sanctuary of Amun's Barque** by removing four columns and installing a granite shrine **[m]**. Though its "doors of acacia inlaid with gold" are no more, some of the reliefs on the walls bear traces of their original colouring.

The remaining chambers to the south constituted the private apartments of the gods, reached by a transverse hall. However, this section of the temple is badly damaged and really only notable for the name *Rimbaud*, carved high up on the wall near the river **[n]**. Rimbaud spent the last sixteen years of his life roaming the Near and Far East; while living in Ethiopia he was feared dead, so Verlaine published his poems (all written by the age of 21), which took Paris by storm and inspired the Decadent movement.

Outside the walls, assorted pharaonic, Roman and Christian **stonework** is stored near the spot where, in 1989, workers uncovered a cache of 26 New Kingdom statues, sixteen of which are now on show in the Luxor Museum.

Mummification Museum

At the northern end of the Nile Shopping Centre below the Corniche, Luxor's **Mummification Museum** (daily: winter 9am–2pm & 4–9pm, summer 9am–2pm & 5–10pm; £E55, student £E30) devotes more space to the beliefs surrounding death and the afterlife than to the actual practice of mummification (see pp.410–411). It does, however, display a spoon and spatula used to remove the deceased's brain, which was discarded by the Egyptians as an unimportant organ, unlike the viscera, which were preserved in canopic jars. A statue of Anubis, the jackal god of mummification, watches over the collection of reptile and bird mummies and a well-preserved XXI Dynasty official, Maserharti. Photography is not allowed in the museum. On Saturdays at 7pm there is a free **archeological lecture** by such experts as Kent Weeks (studying tomb KV5 in the Valley of the Kings), Houry Souralzin (excavating the mortuary temple of Amenophis III) and Zbigniew Szafranski (of the Polish Mission at Deir el-Bahri).

Luxor Museum

Luxor Museum (daily: winter 9am–2pm & 4–9pm; summer 9am–2pm & 5–10pm; £E55, student £E30), at the northern end of the Corniche, complements the town's monumental assets with a superb collection of statues and funerary goods from the Theban Necropolis and various temples. The museum is wheelchair-accessible, well laid out and labelled in English, though some names are rendered differently from those in this book (for example: Amenhotep for Amenophis). Photography is not allowed inside the museum, but illustrated guides are on sale at the bookshop.

To the right as you enter is a ramp down to the sunken **Cachette Hall**, displaying sixteen of the statues found beneath Luxor Temple in 1987. It's uncertain whether they were hidden at the start of the Roman occupation or nine hundred years earlier, when Egypt was invaded by the Assyrians, who sacked Thebes in 664 BC. They include an alabaster sphinx of Tutankhamun; Amenophis III and Horus enthroned, in basalt; a headless cobra poised to strike in the name of the Nubian pharaoh Taharqa; Horemheb kneeling before the god Atum; and a processional effigy of Amenophis III, its rose quartzite left unpolished to highlight the texture of his kilt, armbands and Combined Crown.

The **first level** opens with a sensitive-faced statue of the adolescent Tutankhamun and a gilded head of the cow deity Mehit-Weret from his tomb in the Valley of the Kings. A colossal head of Amenophis III, found on the west bank in 1957, leads you on to a raised level showcasing more works in stone. Compare the careworn face of Sesostris II and the watchfulness of bureaucrat Yamo-Nedjeh with the serenity of the boy Tut beside the crocodile god Sobek, or the diorite head of Sekhmet from a colossal statue in the Precinct of Mut at Karnak.

A new extension entitled "Thebes Glory" displays artefacts related to the **New Kingdom war machine** (see box on p.691). Tut's war chariot, a relief of Amenophis II target-shooting, and royal bows (some recurved and composite) show how the Egyptians mastered the tactics and technology of the Hyksos invaders. A statue of Horemheb and his wife from their unfinished tomb at Memphis, a granite head of Ramses II and a super-sized alabaster Seti I recall the hard men of the XVIII and XIX dynasties. Notice the head of Nakhtim, a general under Tut and Ay (whose son he might have been), ousted by Horemheb; and the effigy of Nebre, commander of a Mediterranean fort, holding a staff topped by the war-goddess Sekhmet.

Best of all, there are two **royal mummies**. That of **Ahmosis I** has a surprisingly delicate physique for the ruler who expelled the Hyksos. His gold-and-electrum axe (found at Dra' Abul Naga on the west bank) and a gold collar with Flies of Valour, from the tomb of Queen Ahhotep (who may have led the Theban army when Ahmose was a child), are exhibited nearby. The other mummy was returned to Egypt from a museum at Niagara Falls, and might belong to **Ramses I** (see p.420).

On the **top level** are model boats from the Meir Tombs at Assyut, gilded *shabti* figures from Tut's tomb, and architects' tools from the Workmen's Village at Deir el-Medina. Between two haunting heads of **Akhenaten** from his Aten temple at Karnak is a **wall** from the same temple, made of small blocks known as *talatat*, that were later used as filler for the Ninth Pylon, wherein they were discovered in the 1960s. Reassembled, the painted sunk-reliefs depict Akhenaten's *Sed* festival, with the king and Queen Nefertiti in a litter surrounded by fan-bearers. Their figures have the strange physiognomy associated with Akhenaten's reign (see box on p.328).

Eating and drinking

Luxor's culinary scene is less diverse than Cairo's, but there's no shortage of places to eat. Upmarket **hotel restaurants** offer a/c, good service and cuisines such as Chinese (at the *Pyramisa Isis*), Japanese (at the *Sonesta St George*), Italian or French (most places). Elsewhere you'll mainly find pizzas, kebabs, omelettes and other tourist fodder. Menus are generally written up outside and most waiters know English, so it's easy to order. Be prepared for the additional service charges and tax (up to 22 percent), though many places don't actually levy them.

All the usual **street food** can be found along El-Karnak, Ramses and Yussef Hassan streets. A 24-hour **bakery** near the corner of Sharia al-Mahatta and the souk turns out pretzels and rolls, while *Twinky*, at the station end of Sharia el-Manshiya, sells sticky confectionery. If you're **self-catering**, there's no shortage of small **grocery shops** (*ba'als*) selling canned goods, cheeses, olives, fruit yogurts and juices, which can be combined with fresh fruit and bread from the souk to make a wholesome meal, while mini-markets on Television Street stock a wider range of imported goods.

Most of the **restaurants** below are inexpensive by Western standards, and open from mid-morning (or earlier) till 9–10pm (or later), though the range of meals diminishes as the evening wears on. Unless otherwise stated, they don't sell **alcohol**. We've only listed **cafés** that sell food, but there are scores of local coffee houses where you can sample exotic beverages – try *helba*, a bright yellow tea made from fenugreek. The poolside *gelateria* in the *Mövenpick Jolie Ville* serves the best **ice cream** in Luxor.

Additionally, there are some excellent places to eat on the **west bank**, near the ferry landing stage in Gezira. See p.406 for details.

Abou Ashraf Sharia al-Mahatta. Brightly lit take-away and sit-down diner, serving roast chicken, *kofta*, *shawarma* and *kushari*, with a counter of sweet pastries for dessert. Inexpensive, but prone to creative accountancy. Open till midnight.

Abu Hassan el-Shazly Sharia el-Manshiya. A kerbside *kofta* joint amidst the spice and hardware souk. Authentically *baladi*; if you enjoy bazaar-watching and badinage, it's worth trying. *Abu Hagger*, almost next door, tends to deter foreigners with its Damien Hirst-like displays of cow haunches.

Aly Baba Café Sharia el-Karnak. Its elevated view of Luxor Temple and the garden of the *Luxor Hotel* makes amends for the overpriced drinks and snacks. Waiters call "Hey you" to solicit custom.

Amoun Sharia el-Karnak, in the tourist bazaar. Touristy, yes, but good value and tasty (*kofta* excepted). The menu includes seafood, grills, pizzas and veggie options, and delicious fruit drinks.

There's a/c indoors, but most people sit outside to watch the street life. Open till midnight or later.

Anubis By the Mummification Museum. Its Nile terrace is a winner, but the food doesn't match the setting or the cost (£E60–80, excluding drinks), so you could just sink a beer or a non-alcoholic cocktail and shoot some pool to loud hip-hop music.

Chez Omar Sharia Yussef Hassan. A vine-shaded outdoor café behind the *El-Zaharet Kushari* (see below), serving Egyptian snacks and soft drinks; an indoor branch across the way sells spit-roast chicken and pigeon. Popular with French tourists.

1896 Restaurant *Winter Palace Hotel*, Corniche el-Nil ☎095/238-0422. Its colonial décor and starchy service are more alluring than than its Continental cuisine (set dinner for £E20). Smart dress and reservations required.

El-Hussein Sharia el-Karnak. In the heart of the tourist bazaar, next door to the *Amoun* (see p.377) with identical menu and prices, though the food and service are not so good. It's easier to find a seat, however, and is a good spot for people-watching.

El-Zaharet Kushari Sharia Yussef Hassan. Owned by the *Venus Hotel* across the street, this cheery garden place is the only outdoors *kushari* diner in Luxor. You can fill up for £E5. Daily 24-hours.

Jamboree Sharia el-Montazah, near the Brooke Animal Hospital. Aimed at unadventurous Brits, it serves filled jacket potatoes, Cajun chicken and toned-down Egyptian dishes (£E30–55). Its saving grace is a roof terrace with a side-view of Luxor Temple. Daily 10.30am–2.30pm & 6–11pm.

Jem's Sharia Khalid Ibn Walid, near Midan al-Salam ☎ & ⓕ 095/238-3604, ✉ahmed@jemsluxor.co.uk. It's worth reserving a table at this agreeably kitsch upstairs restaurant, serving delicious seafood, pizzas, salads and other Euro-Oriental dishes. The *mezze* (£E30) are a meal in themselves. Sells beer and wine. Daily 9am–midnight (or later).

Kebabagy Nile Shopping Centre, near Luxor Temple. At the southern end of the riverside mall below the Corniche, *Kebabagy* serves kebabs, seafood, pizzas and ice cream on a terrace beside the cruise-boat moorings, at affordable prices.

Marhaba Above the tourist office. With a rooftop terrace overlooking the Theban Hills, the view is great, but staff seem content to dish up indifferent grills and *mezze* to tour groups. Alcohol served.

Metropolitan Café Nile Shopping Centre, below Luxor Temple. Like *Kebabagy* (see below), there's a view across the Nile and fresh breezes from the river, which may be spoilt by diesel-belching cruise boats. The café serves pizzas (£E25–35), club sandwiches, ice creams and beer (£E18) on outdoor wicker tables.

Miyako *Sonesta St George Hotel*, Sharia Khalid Ibn Walid ☎095/238-2575. Luxor's only Japanese restaurant is worth a splurge. Set meals of meat (£E125) or seafood (£E180), à la carte grills (£E55–120), sushi (£E25–40) or sashimi (£E40–100); the Miyako special (£E150) features sushi, sashimi and maki. Smartish dress expected. Serves alcohol. Most cards accepted. Daily 5–11pm.

New Royal Fish Off Television St. Simple, clean and a/c, it serves tasty meals of Red Sea fish or *calamari* with rice, chips, salad and *tahina*, for £E15–35. Daily 8am–midnight.

Oasis Café Sharia Labaib Habachi ⓦwww .oasiscafeluxor.com. Tuck into a muffin and a latte, a steak platter or club sandwich at this restful retreat (think *Casablanca*) with recorded jazz and 1940s vocals, art exhibitions, and foreign-language magazines. Daily brunch 10am–4pm. No cards. Daily 10am–10pm.

Pink Panda *Pyramisa Isis Hotel*, Sharia Khalid Ibn Walid ☎095/237-2750. One of Luxor's poshest restaurants, specializing in Szechuan cooking. Appetizers £E20–26, soups £E10, main dishes £E34–54. Sells alcohol. Most credit cards accepted. Daily noon–11pm.

Saiyida Zeinab Television St. Handy if you're staying in the area, this tiny diner does great *kushari*: a filling meal or a snack, depending on which size portion you order (£E3–5). Open till 1am or later.

Seven Days Seven Ways Sharia Khalid Ibn Walid, near Midan al-Salam, mobile ☎010 2007389. A haven for expat Brits, serving caff food and Sunday roast (5.30pm, 7.30pm & 9pm; £E28; reservation required). The *Royal Oak Pub* and *Showtime Lounge* (both 4pm–2am), upstairs, are for boozing or watching sports and film channels on TV. Daily 9am–11pm.

Shams el-Akseel Sharia el-Kmarr, off Television Street. A nearly round-the-clock *shawarma*, burger, salad, *fuul* and *taamiya* takeway with a few tables upstairs. Daily 6am–2am.

Drinking and duty-free shops

If you don't mind paying £E25–35 plus tax, the classiest place to **drink** a cold Stella beer is the Nile-side terrace of the *Sheraton*, *Pyramisa Isis*, or *Sonesta St George*, which all have fabulous views. In the centre of town, the Nile Shopping Centre below the Corniche has two places serving beer but the view (and fresh air) may be spoilt by cruise boats moored alongside. Otherwise, hotel **bars** are seldom anything special, but there are a couple of fun **pubs** (see below).

Cheap imported booze can be bought at **duty-free shops** within 48 hours of arrival, in the arrivals lounge at Luxor airport and the duty-free shop on the street behind the *Emilio Hotel* (daily 10am–3pm & 7pm–midnight). You'll need your passport, in which the transaction(s) will be noted. Otherwise, fall back on Egyptian beer, wine or spirits (often labelled to resemble imported brands), sold at low-profile **outlets** like Beshe on Sharia al-Souk, Al-Ahram Beverages on Sharia Ramses or Micho's Grocery on Sharia al-Mahatta. They tend to open from 10am to midnight, and as most are run by Christians, they close during Easter as well as Ramadan.

King's Head Pub Sharia Khalid Ibn Walid. Though the king in question is Akhenaten, this place looks and feels like an English pub, offering toasted sandwiches, soups, chips and a Sunday lunch of roast beef and Yorkshire pud. Its beer and cocktails are as cheap as anywhere, there's billiards and satellite TV, and women can drink un-hassled. Owner Gomaa Abu el-Fadl is a novelist, journalist and activist who enjoys a deep conversation. Open daily noon–2am (later if there are customers).

Murphy's Irish Pub Sharia al-Gawazat, off Sharia Khalid Ibn Walid. A preppy, polished-wood refuge with pool, cocktails, pop hits and satellite TV. Daily noon–2am (or later).
Venus Bar *Venus Hotel*, Sharia Yussef Hassan. A downtown bar with Alexandrian bargirls for its *baladi* regulars and table-football and TV sports for tourists. It closes earlier than most unless the hotel is busy.

Nightlife

While the **Sound and Light Show at Karnak Temple** is among Egypt's finest (see p.386), Luxor's nightlife is a paler shadow of Hurghada's, if only because most tourists are too tired from sightseeing to fancy clubbing. Many **discos** are empty, and even at the most popular ones Egyptian males outnumber foreigners. The *Sabil* disco (from 10.30pm) in the *Mercure Luxor* has the hottest DJ, plus a bellydancer from 12.30am, and levies a cover charge of £E30 (including one drink). The basement *Regina* disco in the *Tuthotel* on Sharia Salah al-Din has a reputation for punch-ups and restricts entry to mixed-sex couples, while its rival *Sinouhe*, on Sharia Khalid Ibn Walid, rarely gets going before 2am (when revellers leave the *King's Head*). Both are open till 5am every night, with no minimum charge.

Most top hotels feature a **bellydancer** who struts her stuff for half an hour or so. At some this is just an interlude in the disco, at others, part of a show of **Sayidi music** and **folk dancing** (stick-fights or whirling dervishes). Outsiders can enjoy them for free (but must buy drinks) at the *Pyramisa Isis* disco (Sun & Wed 10.30pm), the patio of *Le Meridien* (nightly 7.30–10.30pm), or the *Hilton's Rababa* nightclub, which has separate Saiyidi (Wed & Sun 9pm), Nubian (Tues & Fri 9pm) and bellydancing (Mon & Thurs 9pm) shows.

The alternative is to visit a **real Egyptian nightclub**, where the decor is seedy, the clientele raucous (women are best off going with male companions), and the music brilliant. You have to stay through till dawn to savour the build-up, as the dancers tease local businessmen into throwing £E100 notes around, which are collected in a box at the end of each act and split equally among the dancer, the bandleader and the club. Rival big-spenders often come to blows over a woman and exit the club with their cronies, leaving the next dancer bereft of profitable customers. Luxor has two such clubs: *St Katerina*, off Sharia Ahmes in the centre, and *New Abu Hameed* on Television Street. The dancing starts at 1am and runs through till 5am if enough patrons are still spending. It's best to go with an Egyptian friend to get past the doorman who might claim there's an entry charge, or to argue if they add it to your bill – there isn't one; you should only pay for drinks (£E10–12 for Stella beer, £E100 upwards for spirits).

For locals who can't afford such pleasures, the main diversions are playing backgammon (*thowla*) or dominoes in **coffee houses.** Though café life is exclusively masculine, foreign women usually feel comfortable in the *Nile Valley* coffee house opposite the tourist bazaar on Sharia el-Karnak, which is identifiable by a huge portrait of the singer Oum Kalsoum. Most places stay open as long as there are customers; Sharia Ramses has several all-nighters.

Festivals

Provided the whole year's programme of tourist events isn't abruptly cancelled – as in 2002 and 2003 – wintertime visitors have a chance of witnessing the **West Bank marathon** (February 16), starting and finishing at Deir el-Bahri – the tourist office will have details. In 2005, plans to stage Mozart's **opera Aïda** at Luxor Temple went awry, but if it happens in years to come the event is sure to be spectacular, with tickets priced €70–140. There are also plans to revive the **Gourna Festival** of Saiyidi music, last held in 2001 on the west bank, featuring musicians such as Sheikh Ahmed Berrin.

Popular religious festivals, or **moulids**, take place each year, according to the Islamic calendar. Most are local affairs attended by a few thousand people, but there is also a huge carnival attracting half a million *fellaheen* from Upper Egypt. They generally occur during the two months of the Muslim calendar preceding Ramadan; locals can rarely tell you the exact date, but always know when one is due. Foreigners are welcome to attend, but beware of pickpockets.

The largest and most famous is the **Moulid of Abu el-Haggag** (pronounced "Hajjaj"), honouring Luxor's patron sheikh, whose mosque overlooks the temple. **Yussef Abu el-Haggag** (Father of the Pilgrimage) was born in Damascus (c.1150), moved to Mecca in his forties and finally settled in Egypt, where he founded a *zawiyah* in Luxor and met with other Sufi sheikhs such as Al-Mursi and Al-Shazli. Many of his descendants still live in the area, and the tradition of venerating local sheikhs is strong in villages around Luxor. During the festival, giant floats move through the densely packed streets, some dedicated to trades (the *caleche* drivers' bears a carriage), others to the sheikh himself. The parading of a large **boat** (or even three boats) is often compared to the solar barque processions of pharaonic times, though in Islamic symbolism boats represent the quest for spiritual enlightenment. Vast crowds attend the *zikrs* outside Abu el-Haggag's Mosque, and revel in traditional entertainments. There are **stick fights** (*tahtib*) to the music of drums and *mizmars* (a kind of oboe), and **horse races** (*mirmah*) where the riders gallop hell for leather, halting in a flurry of dust just before they plough into the crowd. The festival runs 1st–14th of Sha'ban, ending two weeks before the start of Ramadan. During **Ramadan** itself, townsfolk compensate for its daytime rigours by gathering to hear *zikrs* and dance outside Abu el-Haggag's Mosque in the evenings.

Sheikh Ali Musa of Karnak was actually born in another village, and when he died the villagers demanded that his body be buried there instead. The Karnakis said, "Let the sheikh decide", so his coffin was borne to the crossroads, whereupon it turned to face Karnak and was taken back in triumph. His moulid lasts a week, its *leyla kebir* (Big Night) falling on the 6th of Rageb. You can't miss the music, swings and lights around his tomb, near the entrance to Karnak village.

About the same time, on the other side of town, Awmia village honours its own **Sheikh Ahmed al-Adasi** – who is known for appearing in the dreams of Egyptians working in Italy and Morocco – with a week-long festival, whose curtain raiser is a day of stick fights, horse and **camel races** on a nearby wasteground. For the moulid itself, Awmia's main street is enclosed by a tent, where *munshids* sing at ear-splitting volume; further in are fairground rides and a tent of Sufis in a *zikr*. Following the *leyla kebir* on the 14th of Rageb, there's a final day of celebrations called *Ed-Dara*, when camels and horses are paraded through the streets and villagers throw candies at each other.

Other moulids occur across the Nile, at Gurna Ta'rif (p.404) and Riziq (p.440).

Shopping: bazaars and markets

The streets around Luxor Temple are infested with **tourist bazaars** whose salesmen use every trick in the book to lure you into their shops. Don't go shopping with a *caleche-* or taxi-driver, or you'll end up paying him commission on whatever you buy. Despite fierce competition you must bargain hard, as merchants rely upon fresh-off-the-plane tourists to pay way over the odds. Fixed-price shops are rare, but can provide a rough benchmark for bargaining at other places. **Gold and silver** are usually sold by weight and so prices should be roughly fixed; El Safa Bazar on Sharia Labaib Habachi is friendly and honest, while Radwan Bazaar opposite the *Pyramisa Isis Hotel* offers a vast choice of styles. **Crafts** include humble hand-made clay pots used for cooking, sold for as little as £E5 outside the police station; bowls hand-carved from lemon, orange or tamarisk wood in the village of Hegaza; and gorgeous handmade silks, linens and cottons from Akhmim in Middle Egypt. The above crafts, as well as Bedouin carpets and embroidery, are sold at the Fair Trade Center (daily 9am–10pm; ☎095/238-7015, ⓦ www.egyptfairtrade.com) opposite the bus station, which markets the work of nine Egyptian handicrafts cooperatives. **Alabaster** and **papyrus** are generally cheaper to buy on the west bank, where the Nefertari Papyrus Institute is one of the few fixed-price shops.

In Luxor, **curio and carpet shops** have long displaced food, spices and clothing stalls from Sharia al-Souk to Sharia Ahmes or Sharia al-Adasi, but on Tuesdays there's still a large **fruit and veg market** on Sharia al-Souk and on Sharia el-Madina el-Minawra, near Television Street. Luxor's weekly **livestock market** is smaller and less camel-oriented than the Souk el-Gamal at Darow, near Aswan, or Cairo's market at Bil'esh, but just as rough on the nerves of animal lovers. The name of the route to the site – Sharia es-Salakhana, "Slaughterhouse Street" – says it all. The market is held every Tuesday (7–11am) in the village of El-Hebel, 4km outside Luxor. To reach El-Hebel by bicycle, follow Sharia Mustafa Kamel across the train tracks, turn right down Es-Salakhana and simply follow the stream of traffic.

Most non-tourist shops close for a **siesta** (2–5pm).

Activities

Sailing on the river in a **felucca** is a relaxing way to spend an afternoon, while a sunset cruise is the perfect way to end the day. Expect to pay at least £E40 an hour for a boat carrying two people, £E50 upwards for a craft seating six or seven. The favoured destination is **Banana Island** (*Gezira el-Mozh*), a lush peninsula 4km upriver, whose owner charges visitors £E5 each to land. It's enjoyable to wander through the cool, shady groves of mature banana trees, with their vaulting fronds and pendant flowers; the trail ends at a souvenir shop where you can get a drink. The round trip takes between two and three hours depending on the wind, or about half-an-hour each way by **motorboat**

(*zobak*). You should be able to rent one for £E40 an hour by negotiating directly with boatmen. The best felucca and *zobak* captains are allocated berths below Luxor Temple and the *Winter Palace*; less skilled ones tie up nearer the *Mercure Luxor* and *Iberotel*.

Luxor's public Olympic **swimming** pool on Sharia Khalid Ibn Walid (daily 9am–5pm; £E10) is the largest in town, but lacks the sunbeds and amenities found at hotels whose pools are open to non-residents. The *Windsor, Emilio* and *Shady* charge £E10; the *Mercure Inn,* £E30; the *Mercure Luxor,* £E50. At others there's a minimum charge per person for food and drinks: £E20 at the *Hilton,* £E40 at *Club Med.* Non-residents are usually allowed to use the **tennis** courts at the *Hilton,* while **horse-riding** on the west bank can be arranged through stables in Gezira (see p.402). **Golf**-lovers can play the 18-hole desert course at the luxurious Royal Valley Golf Club (mobile ☏012 2465037, ⓦ www.golfluxor .com), out near the airport. For **meditation** or spiritual healing, contact Iris Meijer (mobile ☏010 1891319, ⓦ www.energiesofegypt.com).

Finally, if money is no object, there's the luxury of drifting over the Necropolis in a **hot-air balloon**, which affords an awesome view of the temples, villages and mountains; to get the best photographic results use 200 or 250 ASA film. Cruising at 300 metres, you can smell the cooking fires and donkeys and overhear conversations below, in an eerie silence punctuated by the roar of the balloon's gas-burners. The course is determined by meteorological conditions and the skill of the pilot, so each flight is different – but you'll probably spend about an hour aloft. The three companies operating in Luxor (*Magic Horizon Balloons* ☏095/236-5060 or mobile ☏012 2261697, ⨍238-6651, ⓦ www .magic-horizon.com; *Hod Hod Soliman* ☏ & ⨍095/237-0116; and *Balloons Over Egypt* ☏095/237-6515) are fully insured and CAA-approved, and offer two or three flights daily in season (Oct–May), subject to cancellation at short notice. Call the companies directly for a quote rather than pay a commission by booking through any of the hotels that advertise balloon trips. The deal should include an early-morning transfer from your hotel to the launch site, and refreshments.

Listings

American Express In the arcade outside the *Winter Palace.* Changes money and travellers' cheques, makes cash advances and transfers, sells cheques for Amex cardholders and holds mail for clients (daily 8am–8pm; ☏095/237-8333, ⨍237-2862, ✉luxor@aexp.com).

Banks and exchange The Forex Bureau (daily 8am–8pm) on Sharia el-Karnak, near the tourist bazaar, has better rates and faster service than Luxor's banks. There are ATMs outside Banque Misr (daily 8.30am–9pm, Fri closed between 11.30am & 3pm) and the Bank of Alexandria (daily except Fri & Sat 8am–2pm, 10am–1.30pm during Ramadan) on Sharia Labaib Habachi, and the National Bank of Egypt (daily: winter 8.30am–9pm, summer 8.30am–10pm) on the Corniche.

Barbers Men can get a sharp haircut and shave plus the full facial exfoliation that Egyptians prefer at a barber shop near the *New Royal Fish* restau-rant off Television St, for £E20–30.

Books and newspapers Gaddis (Mon–Sat 9am–10pm), in the bazaar near the tourist office, is the finest bookshop in Upper Egypt, with heaps of Egyptology, repro prints, guide books and novels. Aboudi (daily 8.30am–9.30pm) in the bazaar on Sharia el-Karnak comes a close second, while the best place for postcards is on the corner of Sharia al-Souk and Yussef Hassan. A kiosk on the grass verge near the tourist office sells foreign newspapers.

British Consul (Honorary) Mr Ehab A.A. Gaddis can help British citizens in the event of trouble. Contact him at the "consulate" at the *Gaddis Hotel* on Sharia Khalid Ibn Walid (daily 9am–3pm; ☏095/238-2838).

Dentist Dr Moneer el-Shaoly, on Sharia al-Mahatta ☏095/237-3710.

Doctors Dr Hosam el-Arab's clinic on Television Street (Tues, Thurs & Sun 7am–11pm, Fri 10am–3pm; ☏095/237-0032 or mobile ☏010 6944022,

@hosam_elazab@yahoo.com) will treat patients with insurance without charging upfront. Other practitioners include Dr Makrus Faoze, Sharia al-Adasi ☎095/238-2614 or mobile ☎012 3400729; dermatologist Dr Selim Fakhri ☎095/237-2028; and urologist Dr Samy Fakhri ☎095/237-4964.

EgyptAir In the arcade outside the *Winter Palace* (daily 8am–8pm; ☎095/238-0580 or 238-0581). See "Flights" on p.385.

Hospitals Luxor International off Television St (☎095/238-7192) is the best in Upper Egypt, with consultants from Cairo and annual surgical visits by Sir Magdi Yacoub, but day-to-day care is rough and ready and the hospital is hardly up to European standards. Even so, it's preferable to the El-Gadid (☎095/382-698) on Television St, the St Mark (☎095/237-0465) on Sharia el-Karnak, or the Al-Amiri (☎095/237-2025) near Luxor Museum. Foreigners pay £E120 for an ambulance call-out; dial ☎123.

Internet cafés Downtown, *Pop 2000* on the corner of Sharia al-Souk and *Rainbow Internet* on Sharia Yussef Hassan, are cheaper than *Aboudi* in the tourist bazaar on Sharia el-Karnak. Rates are lower (£E5–6/hr) around Television St, at *Atlas Internet*, *Heroes Internet* and *Romio Online*, or *Al-Azhar Internet* off Sharia Khalid Ibn Walid. Staying at the *Sheraton* or *Hilton*, you can pay £E25/hr on the premises, or find a cheaper café just outside. Most are open daily 10am–11pm.

Passport office Sharia Khalid Ibn Walid (Mon–Thurs & Sat 8am–2pm; ☎095/238-0885). Visa extensions cost £E12 and require one photo plus a photocopy of your passport. Some English spoken.

Pharmacies Exist all over town and have a rota for working nights, posted in Arabic. Many close for a siesta, and on Sundays. Basem & Nasr, in the Nile Shopping Centre, boast of selling Viagra over the counter.

Photo processing Places in the tourist bazaar can develop and print in an hour or two, while the Digital Image Centre (daily 9am–midnight) on Television St will burn photos onto a CD for £E40.

Post office At the temple end of Sharia al-Mahatta (Mon–Thurs & Sun 8am–2pm), with a branch in the station (daily 8am–8pm) and another next to the telephone exchange on Sharia el-Karnak (daily 8am–8pm). Street post boxes are only emptied when they're full, so it's better to post letters from a top-notch hotel. *Don't* use the *poste restante*; have letters sent c/o American Express or the *Winter Palace*. It's less hassle to send packages with DHL, which shares an office with Western Union on the Corniche near the *Mina Palace Hotel* (daily 8am–6pm).

Telephone calls The cheapest way to call abroad is with a Menatel, Nile or Ringo phonecard (£E15–50), sold at shops and kiosks and usable in booths all over town – though finding one in a quiet location can be a challenge. Alternatively, there are private telephone offices offering faster connections than the 24-hour state telecom office off Sharia el-Karnak, and hotels with a private line that get away with charging £E35 (minimum 3min) for international calls. Off-peak hours are 8pm–8am.

Thomas Cook Outside the *Winter Palace*. Changes currency, sells travellers' cheques, does tours and reservations, but won't transfer funds (daily 8am–8pm; ☎095/237-2402, 🖷237-6502).

Excursions from Luxor – and moving on

With Karnak Temple and the Theban Necropolis (see following sections) in the immediate vicinity, it'll be a while before you start considering **excursions** to other sites up and down the Nile Valley. However, the **temples of Esna, Edfu and Kom Ombo** are spaced along the way to Aswan, and bolder tourists may also hanker after **Abydos** and **Dendara**, around Qena. Any of these sites makes a feasible day excursion from Luxor.

Travel restrictions for foreigners are strictly enforced but rather illogical, insofar as some places are readily accessible by one form of transport but not by another, and certain journeys can be made in one direction but not the other way. All tourist coaches, taxis and private cars are obliged to travel in a **convoy** to **Aswan** (leaving Luxor at 7am, 11am and 3pm), which is scheduled to allow stops at Edfu and Kom Ombo (Esna is often omitted), while vehicles heading north towards **Dendara** and **Abydos** are restricted to a single convoy, leaving at 8am. There are also convoys to **Hurghada**, at 8am, 2pm and 6pm. However, almost all these places may also be reached by public buses that run at other times, so you needn't feel entirely bound by convoy schedules. Another oddity is that tourists travelling to Aswan by train are supposedly limited to three services, but no such restriction applies to trains from Aswan to Luxor.

Many hotels offer **excursions by minibus or taxi**, priced on a sliding scale according to the number of people. *Happy Land* (see p.369) can do **Edfu** and **Kom Ombo** terminating in Aswan (£E180 for two; £E330 for up to eleven), or **Abydos** and **Dendara** returning to Luxor (£E225-250 for three or four), which beats the official rates for Edfu and Kom Ombo or Abydos and Dendara for four (£E275), eight (£E475) or twelve (£E1100) people. The *Atlas, Fontana* and *Oasis* hotels are also competitive. **Day cruises** to Dendara on the *Lotus Boat* or *Tiba Star* (Tues, Fri & Sun) involve five hours on the river and an hour at the temple: tickets (£E250–280) are sold by American Express, Thomas Cook and the *Iberotel*, and should be bought three days in advance.

With the road to **Kharga Oasis** now open, a few operators offer **small-group safaris** as far as the White Desert (see p.544). The cost per person depends on the size of the group, and includes meals and camping gear. In Luxor, Abu el-Naga Gabriel (mobile ☎012 4689271, ✉luxorsafari@yahoo .com) charges £E70–90 a day for the oases, or US$100 a day for an 18-day expedition to the Gilf Kebir and Jebel Uweinat (p.573). On the west bank, try Azab Safari (☎095/231-1014) at the *Restaurant Mohammed*, or Hamada El-Khalifa at the *Nile Valley Hotel* (mobile ☎012 7964473, ⊛www.nile-valley .nl). Otherwise, you should be able to hire a **taxi** to drive to Kharga for about £E500.

Moving on to other points in Egypt may be affected by seasonal factors such as Ramadan or Egyptian school holidays.

Buses

The inter-city **bus station** is just off Sharia el-Karnak, to the north of Luxor Temple. It's fairly easy to obtain information at the ticket kiosk, but tickets are usually bought on the bus. There's an **unwritten rule** that no more than four tourists can travel on the same bus unless it goes in a convoy, but it doesn't seem to be strictly enforced – or at least, not on buses heading for the Red Sea. Services to **Aswan** (7.15am, 9.30am, 11am & 3.30pm; 4hr; £E15) are only nominally a/c and often arrive full from Qena, so you're better off taking the train (see below). Buses to **El-Balyana** (11am & 1pm; £E7) and **Qena** (6.30am, 8am, 10.30am, 2.30pm, 7pm & 9pm; £E5) are equally uncomfortable, but run most of the way to Abydos or Dendara. Of the seven daily a/c services to **Port Safaga** (£E20–25; 4hr), **Hurghada** (£E25–30; 4–5hr) and **Suez** (£E31–42; 10hr), the 7pm and 9pm buses carry on to **Cairo** (£E85; 12–15hr), while the 8pm bus goes to **Port Said** (£E70; 12hr). Avoid buses that travel the narrow desert road to Safaga after dark, as accidents are common. In winter, this includes the 5pm bus to **Sharm el-Sheikh** (£E100; 15–17hr) and **Dahab** (£E110; 16-18hr), which takes hours longer than advertised and stops at costly roadside cafeterias.

Trains

For security reasons, foreigners can only buy tickets for four trains to **Cairo** (12–14hr). On #981 (departing at 9.15am), #1903 (at 9.15pm) and #997 (at 11.10pm), a/c 1st (£E62–67, student £E40–45) and 2nd class (£E35–40, student £E27–32) seats are comfortable enough to sleep in, so there's no need to take the *wagon-lit* train #85 at 9.30pm (US$73/£E53; payment in dollars or euros only). The overnight services are more popular than the daytime one. A similar restriction applies to trains to **Aswan** (3hr; 1st class £E25–30, student £E18–23; 2nd class £E16–21/£E13–17), but here the #996 (7.15am) and #1902 (9.30am) are busier than the #980 (5pm). Additionally, there's a little-used third-class train to **Kharga Oasis** in the Western Desert (Thurs 7am;

7–11hr; £E11), that may not run for weeks on end due to sand dunes on the tracks. It's far easier to reach Kharga by road (see opposite).

Service taxis

Currently, the **service taxi depot** on Sharia el-Nil is of no use to foreigners, who are forbidden to take service taxis. However in the event that restrictions are lifted, they'll prove a quick and easy way of reaching most sites in Upper Egypt. The twelve-seater minivans wait beneath a sign in English for each destination, departing as soon as they're full. Journey times and per-person prices are: **Esna** (1hr; £E3), **Edfu** (1hr 30min; £E5), **Kom Ombo** (2hr 30min; £E8) and **Aswan** (3hr 30min; £E10).

Flights

Flight schedules vary seasonally; get the latest from **EgyptAir** (daily 8am–8pm; ☎095/238-0580) near the *Winter Palace*. Destinations include **Cairo** (daily; £E757), **Aswan** (daily; £E359), **Sharm el-Sheikh** (Tues, Thurs & Sat; £E531), **Frankfurt** (Sat; £E2857), **Paris** (Sun; £E2857) and **London** (Mon; £E2857); all fares quoted are one-way; returns cost double. Book as far ahead as you can, or try for last-minute cancellations. There may also be vacant seats on **charter flights to Europe** (except during the Easter holiday). Ask reps at the airport and big hotels, or travel agencies in Luxor. Travellers who overstay the four-week limit on charter return tickets may not get past check-in at the airport.

Luxor Airport (☎095/374-655) is 6km east of town (£E20–25 by taxi).

Karnak

The temple complex of **Karnak** beats every other pharaonic monument bar the Pyramids of Giza. Built on a leviathan scale to house the gods, it comprises three separate temple enclosures, the grandest being the **Precinct of Amun**, dedicated to the supreme god of the New Kingdom – a structure large enough to accommodate ten great cathedrals.

Karnak's magnitude and complexity is due to 1300 years of aggrandizement. From its XII Dynasty core, Amun's temple expanded along two axes – towards the river and the **Temple of Mut** – while its enclosure wall approached the **Precinct of Mont**. Though Pharaoh Akhenaten abjured Amun, defaced his images and erected an Aten Temple at Karnak, the status quo ante was soon restored at the behest of Amun's priesthood.

At the zenith of its supremacy Karnak's wealth was staggering. A list of its assets during the reign of Ramses III includes 65 villages, 433 gardens, 421,662 head of cattle, 2395 square kilometres of fields, 46 building sites, 83 ships, and 81,322 workers and slaves. The Egyptologist T.G.H. James likened it to an industrial giant "which generated a mass of business subsidiary to the practice of the cults and a huge army of officials and working people". Yet ordinary folk were barred from its precincts and none but the pharaoh or his representative could enter Amun's sanctuary. The whole area was known to the ancient Egyptians as *Ipet-Isut*, meaning the most perfect or esteemed of places.

Visiting Karnak

The **site** of Karnak covers over 100 acres, 2.5km north of central Luxor. The only part that's readily accessible is the Precinct of Amun (daily: winter

6am–5.30pm; summer 6am–6.30pm; £E40, students £E20; tripod camera £E20), which hosts nightly Sound and Light shows. This alone covers almost 62 acres, requiring at least two hours for a quick look round, three or four hours for a closer examination. As there's little shade, make sure you wear a hat and bring water. Usually the temple is busy with tour groups in the morning, but almost deserted from mid-afternoon onwards, so if you can stand the heat, that's the best time to come. A café by the Sacred Lake sells tea and soft drinks, and toilets can be found near the grandstand and the open-air museum. A separate ticket (£E20), sold at the ticket kiosk outside Karnak, is required for the open-air museum.

There are two **approaches** from town: via the Corniche, which turns inland further north, or along Sharia el-Karnak, roughly following the **Avenue of Sphinxes** that once connected Luxor and Karnak temples, past the towering **Gateway of Euergetes II** and the precinct's **enclosure wall**. You could cycle or walk, but it's best to conserve your energy for the site. The cheapest way there (and back) is by local **minibus** (25pt per person): services returning to Luxor follow the road nearest the river. The official rates for a one-way **taxi** (£E10) or **caleche** (£E10) ride provide a benchmark for haggling with drivers; for a **return** trip (£E30 including two hours waiting time), be sure to agree a price first, and remember their licence number.

Expect to pay slightly more for rides to the **Sound and Light Show** (£E55, students £27; sold at the Karnak ticket office). The first half consists of a four-stop tour through the temple, ineffably grander when gloomy and spotlit. Although the second half – when you view the ruins from a grandstand beyond the lake – drags on too long, the whole experience is unforgettable. *Caleches* cram in extra passengers for the homeward journey, and race back for a second load. There are three or four shows each night, at least one of them in English. Schedules are posted in the tourist office, and on Ⓦ www.sound-light .egypt.com. Go for the later ones to avoid an aural conflict with local muezzins around sunset.

The Temple of Amun

The great **Temple of Amun** seemingly recedes towards infinity in an overwhelming succession of pylons, courts and columned halls, obelisks and colossi. Compared by T.G.H. James to "an archeological department store containing something for everyone", it bears the stamp of dozens of rulers, spanning some thirteen centuries of ancient history. Half-buried in silt for as long again, the ruins were subsequently squatted by *fellaheen*, before being cleared by archeologists in the mid-nineteenth century. The Karnak thus exposed was far more ruinous than today, with columns and colossi lying amidst piles of rubble and frogs croaking from the swampy enclosure. Since major repairs in the nineteenth century, the temple has been undergoing slow but systematic restoration, epigraphic study and (in some places) excavation.

Making sense of its convoluted layout isn't easy, with the ruins getting denser and more jumbled the further in you go. To simplify **orientation**, we've assumed that the temple's alignment towards the Nile corresponds with the cardinal points, so that its main axis runs east–west, and the subsidiary axis north–south.

It's worth following the main axis all the way back to the **Festival Hall**, and at least seeing the **Cachette Court** of the other wing. A break for refreshments by the lake is advisable if your itinerary includes the **open-air museum** or the **Temple of Khonsu**, off the main circuit.

Entering the temple

Walking towards the Precinct of Amun from the ticket office, and crossing over a dry moat, you'll pass the remains of an **ancient dock**, whence Amun sailed for Luxor Temple during the Optet festival. Before boarding a full-size boat, his sacred barque rested in the small **chapel** to the right, which was erected (and graffitied by mercenaries) during the brief XXIX Dynasty. Beyond lies a short **Processional Way** flanked by ram-headed sphinxes (after Amun's sacred animal) enfolding statues of Ramses II, which once joined the main avenue linking the two temples.

Ahead of this rises the gigantic **First Pylon**, whose yawning gateway exposes a vista of receding portals, dwarfing all who walk between them. Composed of regular courses of sandstone masonry, the 43-metre-high towers are often attributed to the Nubian and Ethiopian kings of the XXV Dynasty, but may have been erected as late as the XXX Dynasty (when Nectanebo I added the enclosure wall). Although the northern tower is unfinished and neither is decorated, their 130-metre width makes this the largest pylon in Egypt. High up on

Amun and the Theban Triad

Originally merely one of the deities in the Hermopolitan Ogdoad (see p.325), **Amun** gained ascendancy at Thebes shortly before the Middle Kingdom, presumably because his cult was adopted by powerful local rulers during the First Intermediate Period. After the expulsion of the Hyksos (c.1567 BC), the rulers of the XVIII Dynasty elevated Amun to a victorious national god, and set about making Karnak his principal cult centre in Egypt.

As the "Unseen One" (whose name in hieroglyphic script was accompanied by a blank space instead of the usual explicatory sign), Amun assimilated other deities into such incarnations as **Amun-Re** (the supreme Creator), **Amun-Min** (the "bull which serves the cows" with a perpetual erection) or ram-headed **Auf-Re** ("Re made Flesh"), who sailed through the underworld revitalizing the souls of the dead, emerging reborn as Khepri. However, Amun most commonly appears as a human wearing ram's horns and the twin-feathered *atef* crown.

His consort, **Mut**, was a local goddess in predynastic times, who became linked with Nekhbet, the vulture protectress of Upper Egypt. Early in the XVIII Dynasty she was "married" to Amun, assimilated his previous consort Amunet and became Mistress of Heaven. She is customarily depicted wearing a vulture headdress and *uraeus* and the Combined Crown of the Two Lands.

Amun and Mut's son **Khonsu**, "the Traveller", crossed the night sky as the moon-god, issued prophecies and assisted Thoth, the divine scribe. He was portrayed either with a hawk's head, or as a young boy with the sidelock of youth.

Karnak was the largest of several temples consecrated to this **Theban Triad** of deities.

▲ Amun

▲ Mut

▲ Khonsu

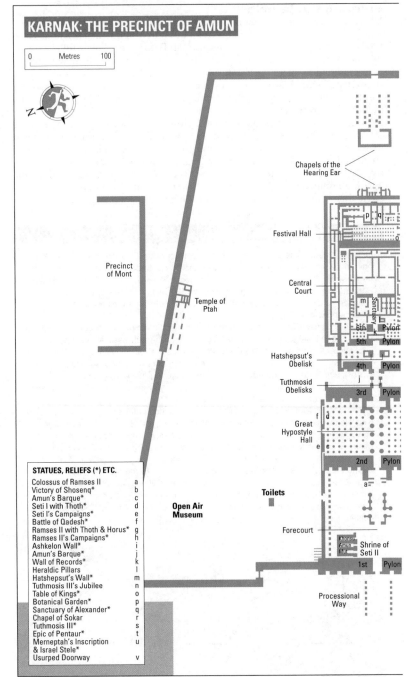

KARNAK: THE PRECINCT OF AMUN

0   Metres   100

Chapels of the
Hearing Ear

Festival Hall

Precinct
of Mont

Temple of
Ptah

Central
Court

Sanctuary

6th Pylon
5th Pylon

Hatshepsut's
Obelisk

4th Pylon

Tuthmosid
Obelisks

3rd Pylon

Great
Hypostyle
Hall

2nd Pylon

Toilets

Open Air
Museum

Forecourt

Shrine of
Seti II

1st Pylon

Processional
Way

STATUES, RELIEFS (*) ETC.

Colossus of Ramses II	a
Victory of Shoseng*	b
Amun's Barque*	c
Seti I with Thoth*	d
Seti I's Campaigns*	e
Battle of Qadesh*	f
Ramses II with Thoth & Horus*	g
Ramses II's Campaigns*	h
Ashkelon Wall*	i
Amun's Barque*	j
Wall of Records*	k
Heraldic Pillars	l
Hatshepsut's Wall*	m
Tuthmosis III's Jubilee	n
Table of Kings*	o
Botanical Garden*	p
Sanctuary of Alexander*	q
Chapel of Sokar	r
Tuthmosis III*	s
Epic of Pentaur*	t
Merneptah's Inscription	u
& Israel Stele*	
Usurped Doorway	v

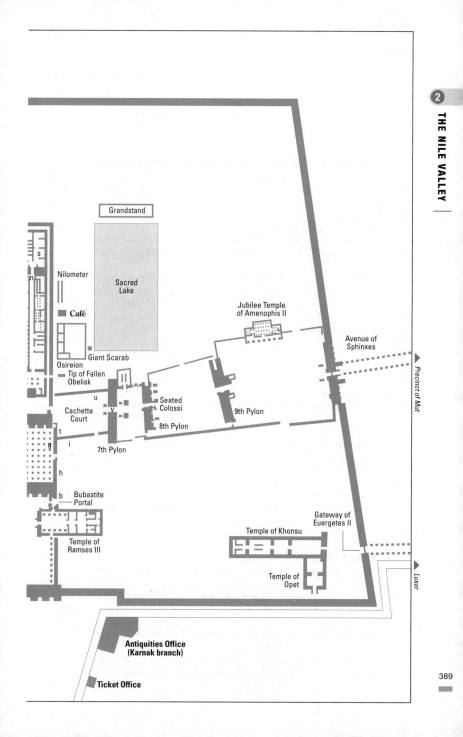

Grandstand

Nilometer

Sacred
Lake

■ Café

Osireion

Giant Scarab

Tip of Fallen
Obelisk

Jubilee Temple
of Amenophis II

Avenue of
Sphinxes

Precinct of Mut

Cachette
Court

Seated
Colossi

9th Pylon

8th Pylon

7th Pylon

Bubastite
Portal

Gateway of
Euergetes II

Temple of Khonsu

Temple of
Ramses III

Temple of
Opet

Luxor

Antiquities Office
(Karnak branch)

Ticket Office

the right as you walk through the pylon, Napoleonic surveyors have inscribed Karnak's vital statistics and the distances to other temples in Upper Egypt.

The **Forecourt** is another late addition, enclosing three earlier structures. In the centre stands a single papyriform pillar from the **Kiosk of Taharqa** (an Ethiopian king of the XXV Dynasty), thought to have been a roofless pavilion where Amun's effigy was placed for its revivifying union with the sun at New Year. Off to the left stands the so-called **Shrine of Seti II**, actually a way station for the sacred barques of Amun, Mut and Khonsu, built of grey sandstone and rose granite.

The Temple of Ramses III to the Second Pylon

The first really impressive structure in the precinct is the columned **Temple of Ramses III**, which also held the Theban Triad barques during processions. Beyond its pylon, flanked by two colossi, is a festival hall with mummiform pillar statues, behind which are carvings of the annual festival of Amun-Min. A Hypostyle Hall precedes the darkened barque shrines of the temple, whose dedication reads in part: "I built and sheathed it with sandstone, bringing great doors of fine gold; I filled its treasuries with offerings that my hands had brought."

Though the pink granite **Colossus of Ramses II** beside the vestibule to the Second Pylon **[a]** is an immediate attention-grabber, it's worth detouring round the side of his temple to pass through the **Bubastite Portal**, named after the XXII Dynasty that hailed from Bubastis in the Delta. En route you'll pass some holes in the Second Pylon, where in 1820 Henri Crevier uncovered a host of statues and blocks from the demolished Aten Temple (including the colossi of Akhenaten in the Luxor and Cairo museums), which Horemheb used as in-fill for his pylon.

Pass through the Portal and turn left to find the **Shoshenk relief**, commemorating the triumphs of the XXII Dynasty Pharaoh Shoshenk. Traditionally, scholars have identified him as the Biblical Shishak (I Kings 14: 25–26) who plundered Jerusalem in 925 BC, thus establishing a crucial link between the chronologies of Ancient Egypt and the Old Testament – an orthodoxy challenged by David Rohl's book, *A Test of Time* (see p.807). Although Shoshenk's figure is almost invisible, you can still see Amun, presiding over the slaughter of Rheoboamite prisoners in Palestine **[b]**. The scenes further along the wall are best seen after visiting the Great Hypostyle Hall.

To reach this, return to the forecourt and pass through the **Second Pylon**, one of several jerry-built structures begun by Horemheb, the last king of the XVIII Dynasty. The cartouches of Seti I (who completed the pylon) and Ramses I and II (Seti's father and son) appear just inside the doorway.

The Great Hypostyle Hall

The **Great Hypostyle Hall** is Karnak's glory, a forest of titanic columns covering an area of 6000 square metres – large enough to contain both St Peter's Cathedral in Rome and St Paul's Cathedral in London. Its grandeur is best appreciated early in the morning or late in the afternoon, when diagonal shadows enhance the effect of the columns. In pharaonic times the hall was roofed with sandstone slabs, its gloom interspersed by sunbeams falling through windows above the central aisle.

The hall probably began as a processional avenue of twelve or fourteen **columns**, each 23m high and 15m round (requiring six people with outstretched arms to encircle their girth). To this, Seti I and Ramses II added 122 smaller columns in two flanking wings, plus walls and a roof. All the columns consist of semi-drums, fitted together without mortar. The central ones have calyx capitals that once supported a raised section of the roof incorporating clerestory windows (the stone grilles of several remain in place), elevated above the papyrus-bud capitals of the flanking columns. Some of the lintels are still painted, as in ancient times.

Their **carvings** show the king making offerings to Theban deities, most notably Amun, who frequently appears in a sexually aroused state. Some Egyptologists believe that the temple priestesses kept Amun happy by masturbating his idol, and that the pharaoh did his bit to ensure the fertility of Egypt by ejaculating into the Nile during the Optet festival. Similar cult scenes decorate the side and end walls of the hall, which manifest two styles of carving. While Seti adorned the northern wing with bas-reliefs, Ramses II favoured cheaper sunk-reliefs for the southern wing. You can compare the two styles on the Hypostyle Hall's entrance wall, which features nearly symmetrical scenes of Amun's barque procession.

In Seti's **northern wing**, the procession begins on the north wall with a depiction of Amun's barque, initially veiled, then revealed **[c]**. Thoth inscribes the duration of Seti's reign on the leaves of a sacred persea tree **[d]** just beyond the doorway. By walking out through this door you'll come upon **Seti I's battle scenes**, whose weathered details are best observed in the early morning or late afternoon. One section **[e]** relates the capture of Qadesh from the Hittites in Syria (lower rows), and Seti's triumphs over the Libyans (above). Depicted elsewhere **[f]** are his campaigns against the Shasu of southern Palestine and the storming of Pa-Canaan, which the Egyptians "plundered with every evil".

Returning to the Hypostyle Hall, you can find similar reliefs commissioned by Ramses II in the **southern wing**, retaining traces of their original colours. Beyond the barque procession on the inner wall, Ramses is presented to Amun and enthroned between Wadjet and Nekhbet, while Thoth and Horus adjust his crowns **[g]**. On the outer wall are **Ramses II's battle scenes**, starting with the second Battle of Qadesh (c.1300 BC) **[h]**. Though scholars reckon it was probably a draw, Ramses claimed total victory over the Hittites. The text of their **peace treaty** (the earliest such document known) appears on the outer wall of the Cachette Court **[i]**.

This is known as the **Ashkelon Wall** after one of the four battle scenes flanking the treaty; another may depict a fight with the Israelites. Rohl argues that the enemy chariots in this scene contradict established chronology, since the Israelites didn't develop them until King Solomon's reign, but Ramses is conventionally supposed to have been the Pharaoh of the Oppression in the time of Moses, centuries earlier. Other clues from the Ashkelon Wall, Shoshenk's reliefs (see above) and the Israel Stele (see p.394) led Rohl to surmise that the Biblical Shishak was not Shoshenk, but Ramses II, and that the established synchronicity between Biblical and Egyptian history is three centuries out, due to an overestimation of the duration of the Third Intermediate Period (dynasties XXI–XXV). See p.807 in the Contexts section for more about Rohl's New Chronology hypothesis.

Pylons and obelisks

Beyond the XIX Dynasty Hypostyle Hall lies an extensive section of the precinct dating from the XVIII Dynasty. The **Third Pylon** that forms its back wall was originally intended by Amenophis III to be a monumental gateway to the temple. Like Horemheb forty years later, he demolished earlier structures to serve as core filler for his pylon. Removed by archeologists, these blocks are now displayed – partly reassembled – in the open-air museum. Two huge reliefs of Amun's barque appear on the far wall of the pylon **[j]**.

The narrow court between the Third and Fourth pylons once boasted four **Tuthmosid obelisks**. The stone bases near the Third Pylon belonged to a pair erected by Tuthmosis III, chunks of which lie scattered around. Of the pink-granite pair erected by Tuthmosis II, one still stands 23m high, with an estimated weight of 143 tonnes. Once tipped with glittering electrum, the finely carved obelisk was later appropriated by Ramses IV and VI, who added their own cartouches.

At this stage it's best to carry on through the **Fourth Pylon** rather than get sidetracked into the Cachette Court on the temple's secondary axis (see p.394). Beyond the pylon are numerous columns which probably formed another hypostyle hall, dominated by the rose-granite **Obelisk of Hatshepsut**, the only woman to rule as pharaoh. To mark her sixteenth regnal year, Hatshepsut had two obelisks quarried in Aswan and erected at Karnak, a task completed in seven months. The standing obelisk is more than 27m high and weighs 320 tons, with a dedicatory inscription running its full height. Its fallen mate has broken into sections, now dispersed around the temple. After Hatshepsut's death, the long-frustrated Tuthmosis III took revenge, defacing her cartouches wherever they occurred and hiding the lower part of her obelisks behind walls – which inadvertently protected them from further vandalism during the Amarna Period.

The carved **tip** of Hatshepsut's fallen obelisk can be examined near the Osireion and Sacred Lake. On the way there, you'll pass a granite bas-relief of Amenophis II target-shooting from a moving chariot, protruding from the **Fifth Pylon**. Built of limestone, this pylon is attributed to Hatshepsut's father, Tuthmosis I. Beyond it lies a colonnaded courtyard with Osiride statues, built by one of the Tuthmosid pharaohs and possibly part of a large inner court surrounding the original Middle Kingdom temple of Amun.

Though the **Sixth Pylon** has largely disappeared, a portion either side of the granite doorway remains. Its outer face is known as the *Wall of Records* **[k]** after its list of peoples conquered by Tuthmosis III: Nubians to the right, Asiatics to the left. Beyond the latter is a text extolling the king's victory at Megiddo (Armageddon) in 1479 BC. By organizing tribute from his vanquished foes rather than simply destroying them, Tuthmosis III was arguably the world's first imperialist.

Around the Sanctuary

The section beyond the Sixth Pylon gets increasingly confusing, but a few features are unmistakable. Ahead stand a pair of square-sectioned **heraldic pillars**, their fronts carved with the lotus and papyrus of the Two Lands, their sides showing Amun embracing Tuthmosis III **[l]**. On the left are two **Colossi of Amun and Amunet**, dedicated by Tutankhamun (whose likeness appears with them) when orthodoxy was re-established after the Amarna Period. There's also a seated **statue of Amenophis II**.

Next comes a granite **Sanctuary** built by Philip Arrhidaeus, the cretinous half-brother of Alexander the Great, on the site of a Tuthmosid-era shrine which similarly held Amun's barque (whose pedestal is still *in situ*). The interior bas-reliefs show Philip making offerings to Amun in his various aspects, topped by a star-spangled ceiling. On the outside walls are sunk-reliefs depicting his coronation, Thoth's declaration of welcome, and Amunet suckling the young pharaoh, some still brightly coloured.

Around to the left of the Sanctuary and further back is a wall inscribed with Tuthmosis III's victories, which he built to hide a wall of reliefs by Queen

Hatshepsut, now removed to another room **[m]**. **Hatshepsut's Wall** has reopened after lengthy restoration, as has the facing portion, where Tuthmosis replaced her image by offerings tables or bouquets, and substituted his father's and grandfather's names for her cartouches.

Beyond here lies an open space or **Central Court**, thought to mark the site of the original temple of Amun built in the XII Dynasty, whose weathered alabaster foundations poke from the pebbly ground.

The Jubilee Temple of Tuthmosis III

At the rear of this court rises the **Jubilee Temple of Tuthmosis III**, a personal cult shrine in Amun's back yard. As at Saqqara during the Old Kingdom, the Theban kings periodically renewed their temporal and spiritual authority with jubilee festivals. The original entrance **[n]** is flanked by reliefs and broken statues of Tuthmosis in *hed-seb* regalia. A left turn brings you into the **Festival Hall**, with its unusual tentpole-style columns, their capitals adorned with blue-and-white chevrons. The lintels – carved with falcons, owls, *ankhs* and other symbols – are likewise brightly coloured. During Christian times the hall was used as a church, hence the haloed saints on some of the pillars.

A chamber off the southwest corner **[o]** contains an eroded replica of the **Table of Kings** (the original is in the Louvre), depicting Tuthmosis making offerings to previous rulers – Hatshepsut is naturally omitted from the roll call. Behind the hall are further chambers, mostly ruinous. The so-called **Botanical Garden** is a roofless enclosure containing painted reliefs of plants and animals which Tuthmosis encountered on his campaigns in Syria **[p]**. Across the way is a roofed chamber decorated by Alexander the Great, who appears before Amun and other deities **[q]**. The **Chapel of Sokar** constitutes a miniature temple to the Memphite god of darkness **[r]**, juxtaposed against a (now inaccessible) shrine to the sun. A further suite of rooms is dedicated to Tuthmosis **[s]**.

Chapels of the Hearing Ear

Excluded from Amun's Precinct and lacking a direct line to the Theban Triad, the inhabitants of Thebes used intermediary deities to transmit their petitions. These lesser deities rated their own shrines, known as **Chapels of the Hearing Ear** (sometimes actually decorated with carved ears), which straddled the temple's enclosure wall, presenting one face to the outside world. At Karnak, however, they became steadily less approachable and were finally surrounded by the present enclosure wall.

Directly behind the Jubilee Temple is a series of chapels built by Tuthmosis III, centred upon a large alabaster statue of the king and Amun. On either side are the bases of another pair of obelisks erected by Hatshepsut, of which nothing else remains. Still further east lie the ruined halls and colonnades of a Temple of the Hearing Ear built by Ramses II. Behind this stands the pedestal of the tallest obelisk known (31m), which Emperor Constantine had shipped to Rome and erected in the Circus Maximus; it was later moved to Lateran Square, hence its name, the **Lateran Obelisk**. As the ancient Egyptians rarely erected single obelisks, it was probably intended to be accompanied by the Unfinished Obelisk that lies in a quarry outside Aswan, abandoned after the discovery of flaws in the rock.

Around the Sacred Lake

A short walk from Hatshepsut's Obelisk or the Cachette Court brings you to Karnak's **Sacred Lake**, which looks about as holy as a municipal boating pond,

with the grandstand for the Sound and Light Show at the far end. The main attraction is a shady (and pricey) **café** where you can take a break from touring the complex and imagine the scene in ancient times. At sunrise, Amun's priests would take a sacred goose from the fowl-yards which now lie beneath the mound to the south of the lake, and set it free on the waters. As at Hermopolis, the goose or Great Cackler was credited with laying a cosmic egg at the dawn of Creation; but at Karnak the Great Cackler was identified with Amun rather than Thoth. During the Late Period, Pharaoh Taharqa added a subterranean **Osireion**, linking the resurrection of Osiris with that of the sun. The **giant scarab beetle** nearby represents Khepri, the reborn sun at dawn.

The north–south axis

The temple's **north–south axis** is sparser and less variegated than the main section, so if time is limited there's little reason to go beyond the Eighth Pylon. The Gate of Ramses IX, at the southern end of the court between the Third and Fourth pylons, gives access to this wing of the temple, which starts with the Cachette Court.

The **Cachette Court** gets its title from the discovery of a buried hoard of statues early in the twentieth century. Nearly 17,000 bronze statues and votive tablets, and 800 figures in stone, seem to have been cached in a "clearance" of sacred knick-knacks during Ptolemaic times. The finest statues (dating from the Old Kingdom to the Late Period) are now in the Luxor and Cairo museums. The court's northwest corner incorporates a mass of hieroglyphics known as the *Epic of Pentaur* **[t]**, which recaps the battles of Ramses II depicted on the outside of the Great Hypostyle Hall. Diagonally across the court are an eighty-line inscription by Merneptah and a copy of the **Israel Stele [u]** that's in Cairo, which contains among a list of conquests the only known pharaonic reference to Israel: "Israel is crushed, it has no more seed". Rohl argues that the stele has been misread and really relates the achievements of Merneptah's father and grandfather, Ramses II and Seti I.

More proof of the complexities of Egyptology is provided by the **Seventh Pylon**, which was built by Tuthmosis III, but decorated and usurped during the XIX Dynasty, a century or so later, when the cartouches on its door jambs **[v]** were altered to proclaim false ownership. It is fronted by seven statues of

Middle Kingdom pharaohs, salvaged from pylon cores. On the far side are the lower portions of two **Colossi of Tuthmosis III**.

Although repair work has closed the **Eighth Pylon**, you might be able to walk around the edge for a distant view of its **four seated colossi**, or pay some *baksheesh* to be sneaked in for a closer look. The most complete figure is that of Amenophis I. Beyond a featureless court rises the **Ninth Pylon**, one of three erected by Horemheb and stuffed with masonry from the demolished Aten Temple, which is currently being rebuilt. Flanking the east wall of the final court is the ruinous **Jubilee Temple of Amenophis II**, which fulfilled a similar function to Tuthmosis III's temple in the main wing. The mud-brick houses of Karnak village are visible beyond the **Tenth Pylon**, from where an **Avenue of Sphinxes** once led to the Precinct of Mut.

The temples of Khonsu and Opet

Located in the southwest corner of Amun's Precinct are two smaller temples related to his cult. The **Temple of Khonsu** is dedicated to the son of Amun and Mut. Mostly built by Ramses III and IV, with additions by later kings, it is well preserved but crudely carved and dark inside. Many of the reliefs depict Herihor, first of Thebes' priest kings, who ruled Upper Egypt after the Ramessid pharaohs moved their capital to the Delta. This shift in power is also evident on the pylons, which show Pinundjem, another high priest, worshipping the gods as a king.

Alongside stands a smaller **Temple of Opet**, the hippopotamus-goddess traditionally believed to be the mother of Osiris. The temple is not always open, but if it is, check out the reliefs which are finer than Khonsu's and date from Ptolemaic and Roman times. The towering **Gateway of Euergetes I**, with its winged sun-disc cornice, was raised in Ptolemaic times and is currently shut.

The open-air museum

The northern sector of Amun's Precinct contains an **open-air museum**, for which a separate ticket (£E20) must be bought before entering Karnak. Its prime attractions are two early barque shrines, reassembled from blocks found inside the Third Pylon. From the XII Dynasty comes a lovely **White Chapel**, carved all over with bas-reliefs. While most depict *Djed* columns, *ankhs* and other symbols, it's the scenes of Senusert I embracing a priapic Amun-Min that one remembers. The plainer **Alabaster Chapel** of Amenophis I contains more innocuous scenes of the pharaoh making offerings to Amun and his barque. Along the way you'll pass rows of blocks from Hatshepsut's **Red Chapel**, which archeologists have been unable to reconstruct since each block features a self-contained design rather than a segment of a large relief. This hasn't deterred Egyptologists from trying the same feat with the **Shrine of Tuthmosis III**, with more success. You'll also notice some granite **statues of Sekhmet**, taken from a small **Temple of Ptah** alongside Karnak's enclosure wall, whose ruins aren't much reward for a 300-metre trek across broken ground, though the finest statues of Sekhmet are now in the Luxor Museum.

Other temples at Karnak

Beyond the Precinct of Amun is a host of other ruins, intermingled with canals and villages. None of them is readily accessible or officially open to tourists, and you need permission to visit them from the **Antiquities Office** in Luxor (behind the museum) or Karnak (outside the precinct), though staff here flit between offices, making it hard to catch them.

The Precinct of Mont

Dedicated to the falcon-headed Theban war-god of the Old Kingdom, who continued to be venerated after Amun gained primacy, the overgrown and ruinous **Precinct of Mont** is unusual for being oriented northwards rather than towards the river. Its main **Temple of Mont** (or Montu) dates from the XVIII and XIX dynasties, while the **Temple of Amun** was added in the XXX Dynasty. Both are currently being excavated by the French Institute of Archeology in Cairo.

Also worth noting are the **chapels of Amenirdis**, daughter of the Nubian king Kashta (honoured by another chapel at Medinet Habu in the Theban Necropolis), and **Nitocris**, daughter of Psammetichus I, who is said to have avenged her brother's murder by constructing a sunken festival hall near the Nile, inviting the suspects to party, then opening hidden sluices and drowning them all – the basis of a short story by Henry James.

The Aten Temple

The **Aten Temple** 100m east of Amun's Precinct was demolished by Horemheb during the Theban counter-revolution that followed the brief Amarna Period. The temple was constructed early in Akhenaten's reign, before he quit Thebes for Tell el-Amarna, and, like the Aten shrine at Luxor Temple, constituted his opening move towards a revolutionary monotheism. Its reconstruction from the thousands of blocks scattered around the site or used as pylon-filling is based on a computer program devised by a retired US diplomat in 1965. The Canadian Egyptologist John Redford, who spent more than a decade excavating here, reckons that Akhenaten was an indolent paranoiac with an Oedipal complex, who compelled his acolytes to worship beneath the burning sun, rather than in shadowy temples. Some blocks from here carved with reliefs, are on show in the Luxor Museum.

The Precinct of Mut

As Amun's consort, the goddess Mut rated her own temple complex, linked to her husband's by an Avenue of Sphinxes. The **Precinct of Mut** covers roughly twice the area of Mont's enclosure, and centres on a kidney-shaped **lake**. Locals informed Flaubert that Karnak's priests submerged all the gold and silver ornaments here when the Persian emperor Cambyses sacked Thebes, but so far the site has merely yielded masonry. Near the enclosure entrance is a headless granite **colossus** which has been matched with a serene head and mighty forearm held by the British Museum (attributed to Amenophis III, Tuthmosis II or Ramses II). It was Amenophis III who commissioned the grey diorite **statues of Sekhmet** that rise from the long grass, lie broken underfoot, or repose in museums. More than seven hundred exist, and they are thought to have formed a calendar where each day was represented by two statues that received offerings every morning and evening. The finest examples are in the Luxor Museum.

The Theban Necropolis

Across the Nile from Luxor, the **Theban Necropolis** testifies to the same obsession with death and resurrection that produced the Pyramids. Mindful of how these had failed to protect the mummies of the Old Kingdom pharaohs, later rulers opted for concealment, sinking their tombs in the arid Theban Hills while perpetuating their memory with gigantic mortuary temples on the plain below. The Necropolis straddled the border between the lands of the living and the dead: verdant flood plain giving way to boundless desert, echoing the path of the dead "going west" to meet Osiris as the sun set over the mountains and descended into the underworld.

Though stripped of its treasures over millennia, the Necropolis retains a peerless array of funerary monuments. The grandest of its tombs are in the **Valley of the Kings** and the **Valley of the Queens**, but there's also a wealth of vivid detail in the smaller **Tombs of the Nobles**. Equally amazing are the mortuary temples which enshrined the deceased pharaoh's cult: among them, **Deir el-Bahri** is timelessly magnificent and **Medinet Habu** rivals Karnak for grandeur, while the shattered **Ramesseum** and **Colossi of Memnon** mock the pretensions of their founders. On a humbler level, but still executed with great artistry, are the funerary monuments of the craftsmen who built the royal tombs, and the ruins of their homes at **Deir el-Medina**.

Beside its monuments, the west bank is interesting by way of contrast with Luxor: more rural than urban, and making fewer concessions to foreigners. Many of the Egyptians that you'll meet in Luxor actually come from villages on the west bank, and a lot of the money made in Luxor is invested there. The symbiosis between the two communities is underscored by the fact that, when speaking English, locals invariably refer to the west bank as "**the other side**" (in Arabic, *min Gharb*). People living there also jokingly liken it to "Palestine", living under the rule of "Israel", due to a land dispute between the villagers and Luxor City Council.

Visiting the Necropolis

Spread across *wadis* and hills beyond the edge of the cultivated plain, the Theban Necropolis is too diffuse and complex to take in on a single visit. Even limiting yourself to the Valley of the Kings, Deir el-Bahri and one or other of the major sites, you're likely to feel overwhelmed by the end of the day. Most people favour a series of visits, taking into account the climate and crowds – both major factors in the enjoyment of a trip. In **winter**, mornings are pleasantly hot, afternoons baking but bearable, and most coach tours are scheduled accordingly, making the Valley of the Kings crowded between 9am and 2pm (other sites are less overrun). As lots of people come early "to beat the crowds", the royal tombs are actually emptiest in the late afternoon. In **summer**, it's simply too hot throughout the afternoon, and you should get here as early as possible.

The **opening hours** of the sites may change with the season and security restrictions, but are generally from 7am to 5pm daily, except for the Valley of the Kings, which opens at 6am year round, and closes at 4pm in the winter. Making a full tour of the Necropolis is expensive – although a **student card** entitles you to a fifty percent discount. If you wanted to see all the sites in the Necropolis, you'd end up spending around US$70 on tickets (at the full rate) – but most people are satisfied to see far less than that.

Hotels and hustlers in Luxor sell **tours** which come in all shapes and sizes (see p.401). Even if you like the idea, don't sign up for the first one offered – at least, not without an idea of what's available elsewhere and the scope for **independent travel**. Virtually all tours include a visit to a papyrus or alabaster "factory" where your guide stands to earn a commission on **sales**; some agencies own the shops where they send their clients. There's no point in getting indignant about this unless you spend more time there than at the sites, but bear in mind that the asking price will initially be determined by the company you're keeping, since a busload of middle-aged tourists is patently wealthier than a few backpackers on donkeys.

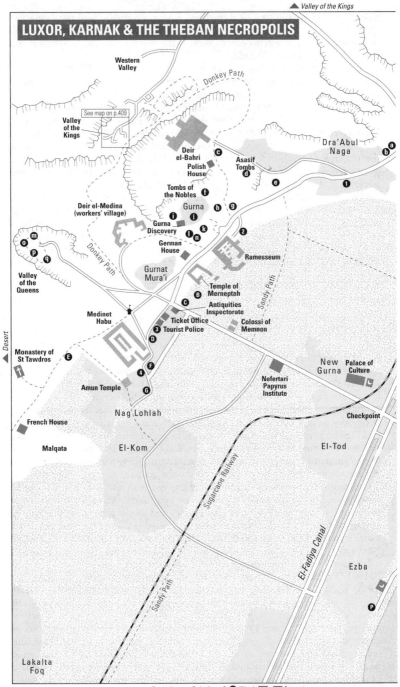

▲ *Valley of the Kings*

LUXOR, KARNAK & THE THEBAN NECROPOLIS

Western
Valley

Donkey Path

See map on p.409

Valley of the
Kings

Deir
el-Bahri

Polish
House

Asasif
Tombs

Dra'Abul
Naga

Tombs of
the Nobles

Deir el-Medina
(workers' village)

Gurna

Gurna
Discovery

German House

Valley
of the
Queens

Gurnat
Mura'i

Ramesseum

Temple of
Merneptah

Antiquities
Inspectorate

Medinet
Habu

Ticket Office
Tourist Police

Colossi of
Memnon

Monastery of
St Tawdros

New
Gurna

Palace of
Culture

Amun Temple

Nefertari
Papyrus
Institute

Nag Lohlah

Checkpoint

French House

El-Kom

El-Tod

Malqata

Sugarcane Railway

El-Fadiya Canal

Ezba

▲ *Desert*

Lakalta
Foq

Sandy Path

Esna, Haggar Daba'iyya & **Q** *(5km)* ▼ ▼*Armant*

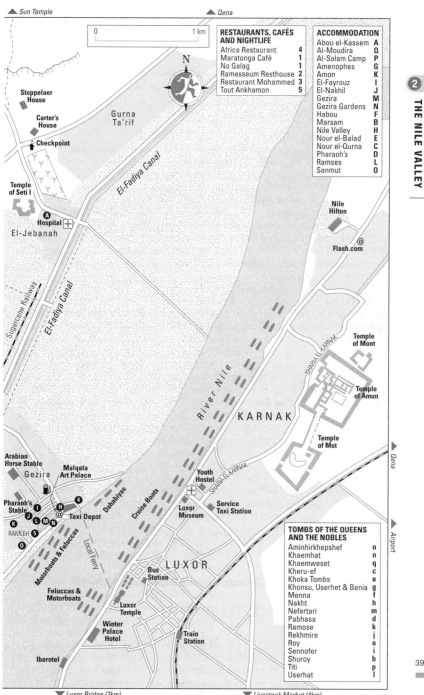

▲ Sun Temple   ▲ Qena

RESTAURANTS, CAFÉS AND NIGHTLIFE

Africa Restaurant	4
Maratonga Café	1
No Galag	1
Ramesseum Resthouse	2
Restaurant Mohammed	3
Tout Ankhamon	5

ACCOMMODATION

Abou el-Kassem	A
Al-Moudira	Q
Al-Salam Camp	P
Amenophes	G
Amon	K
El-Fayrouz	I
El-Nakhil	J
Gezira	M
Gezira Gardens	N
Habou	F
Marsam	B
Nile Valley	H
Nour el-Balad	E
Nour el-Qurna	C
Pharaoh's	D
Ramses	L
Senmut	O

Stoppelaer House

Carter's House

Gurna Ta'rif

Checkpoint

Temple of Seti I

Hospital ✚

El-Jebanah

A

Nile Hilton

Flash.com @

El-Fadiya Canal

Sugarcane Railway

El-Fadiya Canal

River Nile

SHARIA EL-KARNAK

Temple of Mont

Temple of Amun

KARNAK

Temple of Mut

▶ Qena

▶ Airport

Arabian Horse Stable

Gezira

Malqata Art Palace

Pharaoh's Stable

RAMLEH

Taxi Depot

Dahabiyas

Cruise Boats

Youth Hostel

Luxor Museum

Service Taxi Station

SHARIA EL-KARNAK

Motorboats & Feluccas

Local Ferry

Feluccas & Motorboats

Bus Station

LUXOR

Luxor Temple

Winter Palace Hotel

Train Station

Iberotel

TOMBS OF THE QUEENS AND THE NOBLES

Aminhirkhepshef	o
Khaemhat	n
Khaemweset	q
Kheru-ef	c
Khoka Tombs	e
Khonsu, Userhet & Benia	g
Menna	f
Nakht	h
Nefertari	m
Pabhasa	d
Ramose	k
Rekhmire	j
Roy	a
Sennofer	i
Shuroy	b
Titi	p
Userhat	l

▼ Luxor Bridge (7km)   ▼ Livestock Market (4km)

Useful **things to bring** include a torch, plenty of water and small change. If you're planning to cycle or donkey it, a hat and double rations of water are vital. A snack, too, is a good idea, as the choice of food and drink is limited, and prices are higher than in Luxor.

Photography is now prohibited in the tombs to protect their fragile murals, which are widely reproduced in print and on the Theban Mapping Project website (Ⓦ www.kv5.com) anyway. Dusk and early morning are the best times to capture the landscape and temples of the west bank.

Crossing the Nile

There are several ways of crossing **from Luxor** to the west bank. A shabby **local ferry** sails frequently during daytime and sporadically after midnight from the landing stage on the Corniche signposted "National Ferryboat", to dock near **Gezira village** on the west bank. Locals pay 25pt for the ride, tourists £E1. Crowded with villagers, bicycles and baggage, the ferry psyches you up for the day ahead. Alternatively, dozens of **motorboats** and **feluccas** inveigle for custom by the water's edge, charging £E5 per boatload after a brief haggle. Motorboats (called "lunches" in English or *zobak* in Arabic) are the fastest way to cross the river and may land or leave from anywhere along either riverbank, whereas crossing the Nile by **felucca** is more of a leisurely experience than a quick journey.

You should be able to take **bicycles** for free on all these vessels, but **motorbikes** can only be carried aboard the local ferry. Keep **safety** in mind: overcrowded boats or waterways at night are a recipe for disaster, as was proved during the festival of Abu el-Haggag in 2001, when 35 passengers drowned after a ferry hit their motorboat in the dark. During winter, when the Nile is at its lowest, ferries sometimes get stranded on sandbanks for hours, and irate passengers have been known to rip up the seats in a Nilotic version of road rage. Stepping across rickety wharfs after dark is a more mundane hazard – watch out for mooring lines and gaps in the planking.

Since the opening of **Luxor Bridge**, 7km south of town at Bogdadi, all coaches, minibuses and taxis from Luxor use this circuitous route, which can take an hour if traffic is heavy. Some operators get round this by sending the vehicle on ahead, to meet passengers taken across the Nile by motorboat – and crossing by boat remains by far the most pleasant option.

Getting around

Once across the Nile, how you choose to get around will depend on the time of year and what you plan to see, your budget and your sense of adventure. If you intend to visit the Necropolis more than once, try using various modes of transport. As most entail negotiating a price, it helps to know the ins and outs beforehand. Unless stated otherwise, none of the prices given below includes the cost of admission tickets, which have to be bought on the west bank (see p.402).

• One option that's often overlooked is exploring parts of the Necropolis **on foot**, having got there by public transport. From the taxi depot above the ferry landing stage in Gezira, covered **pick-ups** shuttle passengers to Old Gurna (known to drivers as *Gurna Foq*), bringing you within fifteen minutes' walk of Medinet Habu, the Valley of the Queens or the Ramesseum, for a mere 25pt. Many run on to Dra' Abu Naga, leaving you closer to the Tombs of the Nobles or Deir el-Bahri. The drawback is that the Valley of the Kings remains out of reach unless you're up to hiking over the hills and back again. In summertime it's really only feasible to walk in the morning over short distances.

- Assuming that you're reasonably fit, the cheapest way – after walking – to cover the Necropolis is by **cycling**. In winter, you'll feel cool when riding but start sweating once you stop. Guard against heatstroke and keep swigging water. A day's touring might involve cycling 30km: for example, 3km from the river bank to the main ticket kiosk, 8km from there to the Valley of the Kings (mostly uphill – beware of traffic), and 3km from Deir el-Bahri to Medinet Habu. The main drawback is that you can't walk over the hills from the Valley of the Kings to Deir el-Bahri. Cycling during summer is a lot more demanding, so it's imperative to take the long uphill stretch to the Valley of the Kings early in the morning, allowing you to coast back downhill in the afternoon heat. Roads vary from smooth tarmac to stony *pistes*. Bicycles (*ajila*) can be rented in shops and hotels in Luxor or on the west bank for £E10 a day. Test your bike before hiring; many have no gears, which makes any uphill stretch against a headwind murder.

Alternatively, you could drive a **motorbike**. Several bike shops in Luxor rent them by the day; after much haggling, you can probably get one for £E50. Be especially careful of children and livestock when riding on the west bank.

There are workshops for bicycle **repairs** on the road between the ticket office and Medinet Habu, near the *Nour el-Gurna Hotel*, and in the village of El-Jebanah.

- Getting around by **private taxi** is economical for groups, and the least tiring way of visiting a lot of sites, besides enabling you to set your own itinerary. Taxis are usually hired for four to six hours; expect to pay £E50-100, depending on your haggling skills and the current state of tourism. Arranging a taxi through your hotel in Luxor is pricey, so better to hire a taxi at Gezira on the west bank, where the competition is fiercest: Mohammed Ahmed Awad (mobile ☏010 3328041) is recommended. For one-off journeys, you can also use pick-ups (see opposite) as private taxis; if the vehicle is empty or it's after 10pm they'll take you to almost any village on the west bank for £E5 (group rate).

- Many visitors prefer organized, **guided tours**, bookable through any hotel or travel agency in Luxor. Some will tag you onto package tour groups travelling in a/c buses; others rely on a few **minibus** tour operators who take clients from everyone. The price per person depends on the size of the group and the agency or hotel's commission. Of the low-budget hotels, *Happy Land*'s rates (£E45 per person for twelve people; £E85 for two; £E150 for one person; admission tickets not included) are as good as any. Tours typically feature the Colossi of Memnon, the valleys of the Kings and Queens and Deir el-Bahri. If you want to hire an independent **guide**, the veteran Abu El Naga Gabrail, with a deep knowledge of Egyptology (☏&℻095/237-4594 or mobile ☏012 3772074, ⓦwww.naga-gabrail.com), is recommended. Coach tours booked through agencies like Misr Travel (☏095/237-3551) are pricier (from US$60 per person), but may reach sites, such as Medinet Habu or the Ramesseum, that minibus tours don't cover. Large tour groups get priority access to the royal tombs and a higher standard of commentary than is offered by unofficial guides, but lack atmosphere and spontaneity.

- Travelling by **donkey** offers the thrill of riding up the Theban Hills as mist cloaks the plain, skirting precipices and abandoned tombs before you descend into the Valley of the Kings, and returning via Deir el-Bahri and the Tombs of the Nobles – with fantastic views denied to other travellers. But it's a physically gruelling five-hour trip starting at 5am that's not for anyone with vertigo, nor children. Light relief is provided by the donkeys, which disobey commands of *Hoosh!* ("stop") or *Hatla!* ("faster") whenever they encounter another beast on heat, or anything edible. As "mountain" donkeys know the trail, mishaps are more comical than serious. Although few Luxor hotels offer donkey trips nowadays besides the *Venus* (£E55 per head, excluding tickets; mobile ℡012 1713599), they're popular with adventure holiday companies such as Explore, who rent donkeys from the Khalifa family in Gezira for around £E20 per person; contact Tayeb Khalifa if you're interested (℡095/231-0747 or mobile ℡012 3592468, ✉kingofluxor66@hotmail.com). A more laid-back donkey option is a **village tour** of Beirat, using farm trails and backroads, which can be lovely if it's not too hot.

• Though **horses** or **camels** aren't any use for exploring the Necropolis, they're great fun to ride in the desert beyond Medinet Habu, or through the west bank villages. They can be hired for about £E30 an hour from Pharaoh's Stables (℡095/231-2263 or mobile ℡010 6324961) or the Arabian Horse Stable (℡095/231-0024 or mobile ℡010 5048558) in Gezira, owned by rival brothers, Bakri and Nobi. Both will collect clients from hotels in Luxor.

• A **hot-air balloon flight** gives a majestic view of the whole Necropolis. This amazing experience is worth a splurge if you can afford it; the three balloon companies set prices on the basis of demand and exchange rates, at between £E85/US$110 and £E145/US$186 per person. See p.382 for details.

Buying tickets for the Necropolis

It's best to decide which sites in the Necropolis you wish to visit beforehand, since you really only get one chance to buy **tickets** for any particular site, at four separate ticket offices scattered across the west bank. Broadly speaking, tickets for all the mortuary temples (except Deir el-Bahri), Deir el-Medina and most of the Tombs of the Nobles are sold at the main office beside the tourist police HQ. The Valley of the Kings office sells tickets for itself and Ay's Tomb in the Western Valley; tickets for Tutankhamun's Tomb are sold at a separate kiosk within the Valley of the Kings. A third office at Deir el-Bahri sells tickets for Hatshepsut's Temple and some tombs in the vicinity, and there's yet another ticket office for the Valley of the Queens. See below for details of **prices**; card-carrying **students** get fifty percent discount on the rates given here. It's unlikely that you'll use more than six or seven tickets in a day's outing. Tickets are only valid for the day of purchase (with no refunds for unused ones).

Main office

#1	Medinet Habu (Temple of Ramses III)	£E20
#2	Ramesseum	£E20
#3	Tombs of Nakht and Menna	£E20
#4	Tombs of Rekhmire and Sennofer	£E20
#5	Tombs of Ramose, Userhat and Khaemhat	£E20
#6	Deir el-Medina (two tombs)	£E20
#7	Khokha Tombs	£E20
#8	Temple of Seti I	£E20
#9	Tombs of Khonsu, Userhet and Benia	£E12
#10	Tombs of Roy and Shuroy (Dra' Abul Naga)	£E12
#11	Tomb of Peshedu (Deir el-Medina)	£E10
#12	Temple of Merneptah	£E10

Deir el-Bahri office

Deir el-Bahri (Hatshepsut's temple)	£E21
Asasif Tombs (Kheru-ef, Ankh-hor)	£E20
Tomb of Pabhasa	£E20

Valley of the Kings office

Valley of the Kings (three tombs)	£E55
Tomb of Tutankhamun (sold inside the valley)	£E70
Tomb of Ay (Western Valley)	£E20

Valley of the Queens office

Valley of the Queens (excluding Nefertari's tomb)	£E20

Some suggested itineraries

If you're forced to cram the highlights into half a day, a **minimalist schedule** might run: **Valley of the Kings** (1hr 30min), **Deir el-Bahri** (20min), the **Tombs of the Nobles** (30min–1hr), **Medinet Habu** (30min), and/or the **Ramesseum** (30min).

If you have a full day: catch a taxi to the **Valley of the Kings** before 9am, spend a couple of hours there and then walk over the hills to **Deir el-Bahri**, arranging to be met there for another ride to **Medinet Habu** or **Deir el-Medina** and the **Valley of the Queens**. Alternatively, you could spend time at the **Tombs of the Nobles** and the **Ramesseum** before returning to the landing stage.

For those who like to linger over every carving, the tombs and temples on the west bank could easily fill three or four days.

The west bank villages

The **west bank villages** are incidental to most tourists visiting the Theban Necropolis, but integral to the landscape and atmosphere. Their fields stretch from the river banks to the temples on the desert's edge; their goats root amidst the Tombs of the Nobles. Though land remains paramount, almost every family is involved in tourism, either renting out donkeys or making souvenirs on the west bank, commuting to hotel jobs in Luxor, or sailing motorboats or feluccas on the Nile. Family and village ties bind them together and help them exploit the stream of rich visitors that flows across their land. Crafty, warm-hearted and proud, they are worth getting to know. Richard Critchfield's *Shahhat* (sold in most Luxor bookshops) gives a fascinating glimpse into their lives two generations ago, before tourism really changed things.

Your first encounter will be with **GEZIRA**, where ferries disgorge villagers returning from Luxor, and tourists arrive in motorboats. The depot for private and service **taxis** to villages on the west bank is up the slope; floodlit at night, it proclaims the urbanization of Gezira. During the last decade, the Luxor Council has been trying to claim all the land along the waterfront, but has met fierce resistance from locals who've built houses and hotels here as well as from foreigners who've bought apartments in the chic new district of **Ramleh**. Some of the waterfront buildings only escaped demolition after the matriarch of the Khalifa family lay down in front of the bulldozers. Traditionally Gezira's role in tourism was to ferry tourists about or guide them on donkeys through the Necropolis, but it now also has half-a-dozen hotels, flats for rent, an art gallery, Internet café, a dry-cleaners, bike shops and riding stables (see "west bank practicalities"). The village straggles to the El-Fadiya Canal, where **EL-TOD** begins. Its inhabitants call the canal "the Nile", and those residing on the El-Tod side of it regard themselves as superior to folks on the other, although they live similar lives and intermarriage is common. A police **checkpoint** ensures that no traffic goes up the road to the Necropolis before 6am.

Across the main road lies **NEW GURNA** (*Gurnat el-Jedid*), built in the 1940s with government funds to wean villagers away from old Gurna in the hills.

Designed by Hassan Fathy, a leading advocate of creating architecture suited to local conditions, the settlement contains two superbly proportioned public buildings – the **mosque** and **Palace of Culture** – made of Fathy's favourite material, mud-brick. However, the village failed to attract many Gurnawis, and others moved in instead, to find that Fathy's houses were too small for their extended families, obliging them to add breeze-block extensions.

Beyond the Colossi of Memnon, the barren, windswept foothills are pock-marked with the Tombs of the Nobles and the ramshackle dwellings of old **GURNA** (often spelt "Qurna", but pronounced with a "G"). Besides a sentimental attachment to their ancestral homes (many of them painted with splendid *Hadj* scenes), the villagers are loath to lose a traditional source of income – **tomb-robbing**. Over nine hundred tombs are dug into the hills, and undisclosed finds are still made. Once again, the government wants the Gurnawis out, and is pressuring people to move into a new settlement in a flood-prone *wadi*. In 1998 they sent in bulldozers backed by police; the ensuing violence left four dead and more than twenty injured. Wary of more bad publicity, they now insist that people demolish their old houses in Gurna before being given the title deeds for their new homes. Several tombs have been damaged due to the haphazard use of bulldozers. The village's history is related in the local Gurna Discovery exhibition (see p.426).

Skirting Gurna, the road runs on to **DRA' ABUL NAGA**, whose blue and yellow houses contrast with the arid moonscape all around, which glitters with light reflected off mica and alabaster dust. The village manufactures the statues and ashtrays sold in tourist shops throughout Egypt. Its **alabaster workshops** vie for attention with garish murals and craftsmen shaping vases and bowls with hand-grinders outside each showroom.

At Dra' Abul Naga, a spur road turns off towards Hatshepsut's temple, while the main one carries on to a crossroads beside a cemetery, where the road to the Valley of the Kings begins. The mud-brick complex on the hilltop was **Howard Carter's house** during his search for Tutankhamun's tomb. There's been talk of turning it into a museum, but nothing has happened yet. In the vicinity is another archeological residence called the **Stoppelaer House**, designed by Hassan Fathy. Japanese, French, German and Polish Egyptologists also have their residences on the west bank.

The wasteland at the crossroads is the site for the annual **Moulid of Abu Qusman** on the 27th of *Sha'ban*. It commemorates a local holy man known for his miracles and outspokenness, who died in 1984. On one occasion Abu Qusman supposedly crossed the Nile on his handkerchief after the ferry refused to take him because he lambasted the tourists on board for immorality. His moulid used to last all night, but nowadays the police wind it up at midnight.

West bank practicalities

You can find most things on Gezira's high street; **bicycle rental** (£E10 per day); **Internet** (£E10/hr) in the Nile Business Centre near the waterfront, and a **dry cleaners** further up the street. If you need medical treatment, go to Luxor's International Hospital rather than the **hospital** in El-Jebanah. Although there are no currency exchanges on the west bank, most hotels will change **money** unofficially.

Generally, the **police** leave tourists alone, but the checkpoint at the El-Fadiya Canal won't allow traffic to pass up the road to the Necropolis before 6am – which spoils things for donkey-groups hoping to catch the sunrise, unless they sneak through the fields – and service taxi drivers at Gezira's depot have been told not to take foreigners beyond the west bank **security zone**, which ends at

Haggar Daba'iyya (to the south) and Gurna Ta'rif (to the north). After dark, even travel to Haggar Daba'iyya is regarded with suspicion, as the village is reputedly a den of dope dealing. And plainclothes cops often visit bars and restaurants in all the west bank villages, to enjoy free hospitality, collect a bribe and keep an eye on the clientele.

Staying on the west bank

Staying on the west bank is increasingly popular. The village of **Gezira** is only five minutes by motorboat from Luxor Temple and is on the road to the Theban Necropolis, while other west bank localities are close to a variety of tombs and temples. In addition, you'll experience far less hassle and noise than in Luxor, and some places afford superb views of Luxor Temple or the Theban Hills. While the newest hotels are a/c and en-suite throughout, some of the older ones out **near the temples** are old-fashioned and basic – but the pleasure of staying beside an ancient ruin may outweigh the discomfort. See the **map** on p.398 for locations, and phone ahead to check there are vacancies before crossing the Nile with your baggage. Those hotels that aren't within walking distance of the ferry docks in Gezira village are accessible by pick-up (25pt) or private taxi (£E5–10) from the depot.

Some five hundred foreigners live on the west bank (about 400 of them British), so renting and selling **apartments** is big business – especially in the Ramleh district of Gezira. Mohammed Younis (mobile ☏010 6184321) owns five properties here – mostly blocks of a/c flats with nice bathrooms and simple kitchens, some sharing a rooftop with fine views, or a garden: a two-bedroom flat costs £E800 a week. Alternatively, Guy Mauviel of Egypt Rent a Flat in Luxor (see p.372) is an agent for many landlords on the west bank, and has two-bedroom apartments from €69 a week, €218 a month. The *Restaurant Mohammed* (see p.407) also rents out clean simple rooms (②) with a shared kitchen and bathroom.

The **hotels** below run the gamut from luxury to rough-and-ready. Though prices are higher than in Luxor, the view or ambience more than compensates. Unless stated otherwise, all the following have rooms with private bathrooms and include breakfast in the price. There's also a **campsite** in a rural setting, to the south of Gezira.

Abou el-Kassem Gurna Ta'rif, near Seti I's temple ☏095/231-3248, ℻231-2347, mobile ☏012 7387270. Quite a way from most of the sites (take an El-Jebanah- or Gurna Ta'rif-bound pick-up), this simple hotel near an alabaster workshop has dusty rooms with fans and showers (mainly used by Hungarian archeologists in the winter), and rents bikes and donkeys. ②

Al-Moudira Haggar Daba'iyya, 5km from Medinet Habu and 1km from Luxor Bridge, mobile ☏012 3251307, ℻012 3220528, ⓦwww .moudira.com. Imagine an Ottoman palace, with exquisite courtyards, vast gardens and pool, a Lebanese restaurant and bar. Its 54 individually styled suites feature antiques, mosquito nets, a/c, satellite TV and minibar; some contain a fountain and a Turkish hammam. Built by a Lebanese woman, Zeina Aboukheir, the hotel's only drawback is that it is miles from anywhere, so guests must

rely on taxis (£E15). There's a twenty percent surcharge at Christmas and New Year. ⑧

Al-Salam Camp By the Nile 1.4m from the ferry dock, mobile ☏010 6824067, ⓦwww.luxor -westbank.com/camp. A funky Dahab-style campground with a camper-bus serving as reception, six huts (£E20) and a clean washroom. Almost cut off by water when the Nile rises, it exists in a zonked-out world of its own. ①

Amenophes Nag Lohlah ☏ & ℻095/231-1228, ⓦwww.luxor-westbank.com. Pleasant a/c rooms with TV and balconies, a few minutes' walk from Medinet Habu; the view from its shady rooftop is marred by houses. Takes MasterCard and Visa. ③

Amon At the back of Gezira ☏095/231-0912, mobile ☏ 010 6394585, ℻095/231-1205. Two en-suite blocks flanking a lovely garden; the south-facing one has larger rooms with corner balconies. Guests may use the kitchen, and the hotel can fix transfers as far away as Hurghada. Sells beer. ❸

El-Fayrouz Gezira ☎095/231-2709, Ⓦwww .elfayrouz.com. A salmon-pink tower in the heart of the village. Spacious rooms with fans (some are a/c) and small balconies. There's also a gorgeous garden, and a rooftop overlooking the Theban Hills. Internet (£E7/hr). Sells alcohol. ❸

El-Nakhil On the edge of Gezira ☎ & Ⓕ095/231-3922, mobile ☎012 3821007. An attractive *qasr*-style cluster of comfortable a/c chalets (one equipped for disabled guests), backing onto fields beyond the *El-Fayrouz*. ❸

Gezira Gezira ☎095/231-0034, Ⓦwww.el-gezira .com. Down the first turning off the high street, this hotel has decent a/c rooms with balconies, an attractive rooftop and terrace; but mosquitoes are bad over summer and some women have reported problems with the owner. There's a book exchange, and guests get £E5 discount on the pool at *Gezira Gardens*. Meals, beer and wine served. ❷

Gezira Gardens Gezira, off the waterfront ☎095/231-2505, Ⓕ095/231-2506, Ⓦwww .el-gezira.com. Owned by the same family as the *Gezira*, this mini holiday village has a/c rooms or self-catering apartments sleeping up to four (US$45) with balconies overlooking the Nile or the swimming pool. Bar; restaurant; laundry service and satellite TV. ❹

Habou Nag Lolah, opposite Medinet Habu temple ☎095/231-1611, mobile ☎012 3580242. Immortalized in Critchfield's *Shahhat*, this seedy mud-brick labyrinth has stuffy barrel-vaulted rooms, but the shared bathrooms are clean and there's a fabulous view of the temple from the rooftop. Bike rental. ❷

Marsam Gurnat Mura'i, off the road to the Tombs of the Nobles ☎095/237-2403, mobile ☎010 3426471, Ⓔmarsam@africamail.com. Built for US archeologists and later owned by Sheikh Ali Abdul Rasoul, who helped discover the tomb of Seti I, this west bank institution is now managed by Czech-Australian Natasha. Its peaceful ambience and delicious vegetarian meals compensate for the simple mud-brick rooms with fans (a private shower costs £E40 extra) and lack of alcohol – there's also a decent library and the odd archeologist in residence. Reservations essential Dec–Feb. ❷

Nile Valley Gezira, near the motorboat and ferry docks ☎095/231-1477 or mobile ☎012 7964473, Ⓦwww.nile-valley.nl. The hotel's rooftop restaurant boasts the world's finest view of Luxor Temple. All rooms are a/c with small balconies; a low-budget floor with shared bathrooms and a swimming pool in the garden may come soon. Well managed and friendly, with live music and a buffet on Sunday evenings. Sells beer, wine and spirits. £E2 surcharge at Easter and Christmas time. ❸

Nour el-Balad On the edge of the desert out beyond Medinet Habu ☎095/242-6111, mobile ☎010 1295812. A mud-brick palace of chic "rustic" rooms with duvets, mosquito nets and tiled bathrooms. Rooms upstairs cost £E50–100 more, rooftop suites £E450–500 (which seems a lot for a view of the Theban Hills). Its isolation is its main drawback (or selling point). ❸

Nour el-Qurna Qurnat Mura'i, across the road from the Antiquities Inspectorate ☎095/231-1430 or mobile ☎010 1295812. Owned by the same family as the *Nour el-Balad*, this small hotel is secluded in a palm grove. Its eight mud-brick rooms have palm-frond beds with duvets, mosquito nets and tiled bathrooms – as featured in a French lifestyle magazine. The price varies according to the view. ❸

Pharaoh's Nag Lohlah, near Medinet Habu temple ☎095/231-0702 or mobile ☎010 6131436, Ⓔpharaohshotel@hotmail.com. Cosy rooms (most with a/c and bathrooms); the roof has a few larger ones costing £E60 more, and a side view of the temple. Serves beer and meals on a shady patio, plagued by mozzies in the summer. ❸

Ramses Gezira ☎231-2748, Ⓦwww .questfortheegyptianadventure.com. Across the street from the *Gezira*, this hotel has clean, mostly a/c rooms, and a fine view from its roof. It also owns a boat with three cabins, called the *Sindbad*, that sails between Aswan and Edfu. ❷

Senmut Ramleh, on the edge of Gezira ☎095/231-3077 or mobile ☎012 7369159, Ⓦwww.senmut-luxor.com. A Dutch-run B&B with a family ambience, in an upmarket villa quarter. Soothing rooms with or without a/c and bathrooms; the second-floor corner ones have the best views. Communal living room, kitchen and washing machine; meals are served when the hotel is full. ❷

Eating and drinking

You can get a **meal** of *kofta* or chicken with rice and salad at almost any of the **hotels** on the west bank for £E20–30. Two that deserve a special mention are the *Nile Valley* – which also has pizzas, fish and veggie options, a delicious buffet (£E35) at 7pm on Sundays, and a superb view of Luxor Temple – and the wonderful vegetarian cooking at the *Marsam*, which runs to all kinds of salads and tempura. Otherwise, check out the 24–hour *Restaurant Mohammed* near the main ticket office, which makes its own goat's cheese and has spotless toilets and a garden with a 600-year-old acacia tree. By the temples, the *Maratonga Café* does a mean *tageen* (not on the menu), while the *Ramesseum Resthouse* sells beer and wine and is popular with the local police. In Gezira, the *Africa Restaurant* near the taxi depot is good for fish and veggie dishes and has a nice patio, while *Tout Ankhamon*, owned by Hagg Mahmoud (who used to cook for the *Mövenpick*), serves vast set meals (£E35) of coconut curry or duck with rosemary, spicy lentil and vegetable stews, with *baklava* or watermelon for dessert.

The sale of **alcohol** is limited to the *Al-Moudira, Amon, El-Fayrouz, Gezira, Gezira Gardens, Nile Valley* and *Pharaoh's* hotels, the *Africa* restaurant and the *Ramesseum Resthouse*. The *Nile Valley* has the liveliest **nightlife**, especially on Tuesdays and Sundays when it features Saiyidi musicians and Dervish dancers; live *rababa* music can also be heard at Said Galag's Rastafied *No Galag* rooftop on Sunday evenings.

For a more restful scene, drop into the German-owned **Malqata Art Palace** (daily except Mon 11.30am–3pm & 5.30–10.30pm; Ⓦ www.luxor-westbank .com) in Gezira to look at vintage photographs of Egypt and contemporary Egyptian paintings over freshly brewed coffee, civilized conversation and foreign-language newspapers. They also serve tasty meals.

The Colossi of Memnon

A kilometre or so beyond New Gurna the main road passes the **Colossi of Memnon**, looming nearly 18 metres above the fields to the right. This gigantic pair of enthroned statues originally fronted the mortuary temple of Amenophis III, once the largest complex on the west bank, and possibly even larger than Karnak – which later pharaohs plundered for masonry until nothing remained but the king's colossi. Both have lost their faces and crowns, and the northern one was cleaved to the waist by an earthquake in 27 BC. Subsequently, this colossus was heard to "sing" at dawn – a sound probably caused by particles breaking off as the stone expanded, or wind reverberating through the cracks. The phenomenon attracted many visitors during antiquity, including the Roman emperors Hadrian (130 AD) and Septimus Severus, who gave orders to repair the statue in 199 AD, after which it never sang again.

Previously, the sound had been attributed to the legendary Memnon, whom Achilles killed outside the walls of Troy, greeting his mother, Eos, the Dawn, with a sigh. The Greeks identified the colossi with Memnon in the belief that his father, Tithonus, had been an Egyptian king. Before this, the colossi had been identified with Amenhotep, Steward of Amenophis III, whom posterity honoured as a demigod long after his master was forgotten. This association had some grounds in truth, since it was Amenhotep who supervised the quarrying of the monoliths at Silsilah, and their erection on the west bank. He was also probably responsible for Amenophis III's section of Luxor Temple.

Standing beside the barrier rope you can appreciate what **details** remain on the thrones and legs of the sandstone colossi. On the sides of the nearer one, the Nile-gods of Upper and Lower Egypt bind the heraldic plants of the Two Lands together. The legs of each colossus are flanked by smaller statues of Queen Tiy (right) and the king's mother, Mutemuia (left). As high as one can reach they are covered in graffiti, including Roman epigrams.

Behind them, the long-lost **Mortuary Temple of Amenophis III** is being excavated to form a new archeological park and is currently off-limits to the public.

The Valley of the Kings

Secluded amidst the bone-dry Theban Hills, removed from other parts of the Necropolis, the **Valley of the Kings** (daily: summer 6am–5pm, winter 6am–4pm; £E55) was intended as the ultimate insurance policy on life eternal. These secretive tombs of New Kingdom pharaohs were planned to preserve their mummies and funerary impedimenta for eternity. While most failed the test, their dramatic shafts and phantasmagorical murals are truly amazing. The descent into the underworld and the fear of robbers who braved the traps is still imaginable in the less crowded, darker tombs.

▲ Seal of the Valley of the Kings

Royal burials in the "Place of Truth" date from the early XVIII to the late XX dynasties. The first to be buried here was probably Tuthmosis I (1525–1512 BC). Until the time of Ramses I, queens and royal children were entombed here. **The tombs** were hewn and decorated by skilled craftsmen (known as "Servants at the Place of Truth") who dwelt at nearby Deir el-Medina. Work began early in a pharaoh's reign and never exceeded six years' duration; even so, some tombs were hastily pressed into service, or usurped by later kings. Broadly speaking, there are two types: the convoluted, split-level ones of early XVIII Dynasty rulers such as Tuthmosis I and Amenophis II, and the straighter, longer tombs of the XIX and XX dynasties.

The weaker rulers of the XX Dynasty were unable to prevent **tomb-robbing** on a massive scale. Both the vizier and police chief of Thebes were implicated in the disposal of treasure, while many of the robbers were the workmen who had built the tombs, embittered over arrears in pay. In desperation, the priests reburied many sarcophagi and objects in two **secret caches** that were only discovered in the late nineteenth century (see p.425).

The exploration of the Valley began in earnest with a series of **excavations** sponsored by Theodore Davis in 1902–14, when more than thirty tombs and pits were cleared. In 1922, the discovery of Tutankhamun's tomb made headlines around the world, while as recently as 1995 a **mass tomb for the sons of Ramses II** was uncovered beneath tomb KV5, long regarded as empty. Using clues from a papyrus codex in Turin, Professor Kent Weeks found a complex of one hundred and fifty tomb chambers, some as large as four hundred square metres. Though inscriptions suggest that fifty of Ramses' one hundred or so sons were meant to be interred here, only the remains of four adults in their twenties have been found so far, to be X-rayed for comparison with Ramses' mummy in the Cairo Museum (DNA testing has been ruled out). For the latest news from the dig and views of many of the tombs, visit the superb Theban Mapping Project **website** (Ⓦ www.kv5.com).

Sadly, the Valley of the Kings is acutely susceptible to mass **tourism** and changes in the local **geology**. During the 1990s, cracks appeared in three tombs and the ceiling of a fourth collapsed. To prevent further damage to the **reliefs** and pigments, caused by friction, carbon dioxide and moisture (the average visitor leaves behind 2.8g of sweat), the SCA has installed glass screens or dehumidifers. A graver threat is posed by a sub-stratum of grey shale, which has expanded upwards beneath the limestone, rupturing several tombs from below. Some blame this on 25 years of leaks from a (now demolished) tourist rest-house, while others contend that the water table has risen due to the High Dam (see p.480).

The upshot is that tombs may be **closed** for years or reopened after ages under wraps. Remember that the artwork is **fragile**, so help preserve it by not touching the walls. **Photography** is no longer allowed inside any of the tombs.

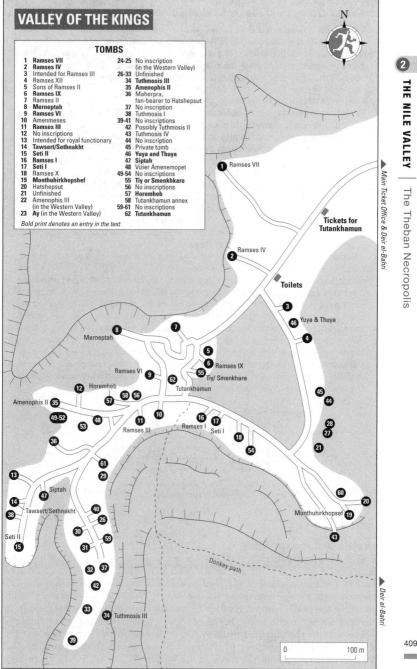

VALLEY OF THE KINGS

N

TOMBS

1 **Ramses VII**
2 **Ramses IV**
3 Intended for Ramses III
4 Ramses XII
5 Sons of Ramses II
6 **Ramses IX**
7 Ramses II
8 **Merneptah**
9 **Ramses VI**
10 Amenmeses
11 **Ramses III**
12 No inscriptions
13 Intended for royal functionary
14 **Tawsert/Sethnakht**
15 Seti II
16 **Ramses I**
17 Seti I
18 Ramses X
19 **Monthuhirkhopshef**
20 Hatshepsut
21 Unfinished
22 Amenophis III
   (in the Western Valley)
23 **Ay** (in the Western Valley)

24-25 No inscription
   (in the Western Valley)
26-33 Unfinished
34 **Tuthmosis III**
35 **Amenophis II**
36 Maherpra,
   fan-bearer to Hatshepsut
37 No inscription
38 Tuthmosis I
39-41 No inscriptions
42 Possibly Tuthmosis II
43 Tuthmosis IV
44 No inscription
45 Private tomb
46 **Yuya and Thuya**
47 **Siptah**
48 Vizier Amenemopet
49-54 No inscriptions
55 **Tiy or Smenkhkare**
56 No inscriptions
57 **Horemheb**
58 Tutankhamun annex
59-61 No inscriptions
62 **Tutankhamun**

Bold print denotes an entry in the text

Ramses VII

Tickets for Tutankhamun

Toilets

Yuya & Thuya

Merneptah

Ramses VI

Ramses IX

Tiy/ Smenkhare

Tutankhamun

Horemheb

Amenophis II

Ramses III

Ramses I

Seti I

Siptah

Tawsert/Sethnakht

Seti II

Monthuhirkhopshef

Donkey path

Tuthmosis III

0   100 m

▼ *Deir el-Medina*

Mummification and the Underworld

The **funerary beliefs** manifest in the Valley of the Kings derive from two myths, concerning Re and Osiris. In that of **Re**, the sun-god descended into the underworld and voyaged through the hours of night, emerging at dawn to sail his barque across the heavens until sunset, when the cycle began anew. **Osiris**, king of the underworld, offered hope of survival in the afterlife through his death and resurrection.

Mummification and burial

To attain the afterlife, it was necessary that the deceased's name (*ren*) and body continued to exist, sustaining the **ka** or cosmic double that was born with every person and inhabited their mummy after death. **Mummification** techniques evolved over millennia, reaching their zenith by the New Kingdom, when embalmers offered three levels of mummification. The deluxe version entailed removing the brain (which was discarded) and the viscera (which were preserved in canopic jars); dehydrating the cadaver in natron salts for about forty days; packing it to reproduce lifelike contours, inserting artificial eyes and painting the face or entire body red (for men) or yellow (for women); then wrapping it in gum-coated linen bandages, and finally cocooning it in mummiform coffins. On the chest of the mummy and its coffin were placed heart scarabs, designed to prevent the deceased's heart from bearing witness against him during the judgement of Osiris.

    Royal burials were elaborate affairs. Escorted by priests, mourners and musicians, the coffin was dragged on a sledge to the Valley of the Kings, where the sarcophagus was already occupied by a *sem* (death) priest, who performed the **Opening of the Mouth** ceremony, touching the lips of the mummy with an adze and reciting spells. As the mummy was lowered into its sarcophagus, priests slashed the forelegs of sacrificial animals, whose limbs were burned as the tomb was sealed. The tomb's contents (intended to satisfy the needs of the pharaoh's *ka* in the afterlife) included food, drink, clothing, furniture, weapons, and dozens of *shabti* figures to perform any task that the gods might require. Then the doors were walled up, plastered over and stamped with the royal seal and that of the Necropolis. To thwart robbers, royal tombs featured deadfalls and false burial chambers; however, none of these devices seem to have succeeded in protecting them.

The Journey of Re
From right to left: Sunset; Year; Eternity; Everlasting; Maat (justice); Re; Heka; Sunrise

Visiting the tombs

The main **approach** to the valley (known as *Biban el-Melouk*, "Gates of the Kings" in Arabic) is via a serpentine road that follows the route of ancient funeral processions. Before the road, when donkeys were the only means of travel, its silence and emptiness were striking ("White earth; sun; one's rump sweats in the saddle", noted Flaubert). Nowadays, you'll only get this feeling on the trail across the hills from Deir el-Medina, which is still travelled by donkeys (see p.401). At the entrance to the valley are a tourist bazaar, a cloakroom for stashing video-cameras (free of charge), and an office selling **tickets** for the Valley of the Kings and Ay's tomb in the Western Valley (see p.403 for prices).

The journey through the underworld and judgement of Osiris

Funerary artwork dwelt on the journey through the underworld, whose pictorial representation inverted the normal order, so that each register was topped by sand instead of sky. The **descent** into the underworld, or *Duat*, echoed that of a sarcophagus into its tomb, involving ramps, ropes and gateways. Each of the twelve **gates** was personified as a goddess and guarded by ferocious deities (for example, the "Lady of Duration" and the "Flame-eyed" serpent at the fifth gate). In the darkness between them lay twelve **caverns** inhabited by beings such as the jackal-headed gods who fed on rottenness at the first cavern, or the wailing goddesses with bloody axes who waited at the tenth. Voyaging through the twelve **hours** of the night in his solar barque, Re had to overcome the serpent Apopis and other lesser denizens of **primeval chaos**, which threatened the **righteous order** personified by the goddess Maat.

It was Maat's Feather of Truth that was weighed against the deceased's heart (believed to be the seat of intelligence) during the **Judgement of Osiris**. With Anubis on the scales and Thoth waiting to record the verdict, the deceased had to recite the **negative confession** before a tribunal of 42 **assessor gods**, each attuned to a sin. While the hearts of the guilty were devoured by crocodile-headed Ammut, the righteous were pronounced "true of voice" and led into the presence of Osiris to begin their **resurrection**, which paralleled Re's passage through the underworld. Helped by Anubis, Isis and Nephthys (often shown as serpents), Aker the earth-god (whose back bore Re's barque) and Khepri the scarab beetle, Re achieves rebirth in the fifth hour, and is fully restored to life by the tenth. Here the two myths part company, for whereas Re emerges from the body of the sky-goddess Nut to travel the heavens again, the Osirian journey concludes in an afterlife that is sometimes identified as the **Fields of Yaru**.

Since many of the scenes were supplemented by papyri buried with the mummy, funerary **artwork** is categorized in literary terms. The *Book of the Dead* is the name now given to the compendium of Old and Middle Kingdom Pyramid Texts and Spells, known in the New Kingdom as the *Book of Coming Forth*. Other **texts** associated with the New Kingdom include the *Book of Gates*, *Book of Caverns*, *Book of Hours*, *Book of Day and Night* and *Book of Amduat* (That Which is in the Underworld).

The Judgement of Osiris
From right to left: Anubis escorts the deceased and weights his heart before Ammut and Thoth; then Horus leads him to Osiris, Isis and Nephthys

Beyond this, you can walk or ride a *tuf-tuf* (£E1) 500m to the site entrance, just inside which is another kiosk selling tickets for Tutankhamun's tomb.

The valley is surrounded by limestone crags, the loftiest of which was the abode of Meretseger, snake-goddess of the Necropolis. The **site** (daily: winter 6am–5pm, summer 6am–4pm) is a natural suntrap, and is hot even in winter, the heat permeating the deepest tombs, whose air is musty and humid (drink lots of water).

One **strategy** is to head for peripheral tombs first such as Ramses IV or VII, Tawsert/Sethnakht, Seti II or Monthuhirkhopshef – while watching out for a chance to duck into others if there's a break between tour groups. Although we've listed the tombs in the order you'd encounter them in an anticlockwise circuit of the valley, it's better to select the most promising ones beforehand, and take whichever route makes sense. Most people find three to five **tombs** enough for one visit; of the 64 tombs (numbered in order of their discovery), barely a dozen are **open** at any one time – Luxor's tourist office knows which, even if the ticket kiosk at the entrance to the valley doesn't list them. At the time of writing most of the Ramessid tombs were open.

Tomb of Ramses VII (#1)

Set apart near the entrance to the valley, the short tomb of **Ramses VII** lay wide open for millennia, and is now glassed over. Greek and Roman graffiti mars its sunk-reliefs and vivid colours (red, yellow and blue on white), whose freshness is due to restoration. Amid the standard imagery are odd details like the figures entombed in cartouches on the walls of the final corridor, while the hippo-goddess Tweri is prominent in the nocturnal pantheon on the ceiling of the burial chamber, whose sarcophagus is veined with blue imagery. The tomb isn't visited much, so you can wander round in peace. However, other Ramessid tombs are finer, so visitors limited to three tombs should head elsewhere.

Tomb of Ramses IV (#2)

The next tomb, created for **Ramses IV**, is more of a crowd pleaser. Its cheerful colours make amends for the inferior sunk-reliefs and abundant Greek and Coptic **graffiti** (notice the haloed saints on the right near the entrance). The ceiling of the burial chamber is adorned with twin figures of Nut. On the enormous pink-granite **sarcophagus** are magical texts and carvings of Isis and Nephthys, to protect the mummy from harm. When these seemed insufficient, the priests stashed Ramses in the tomb of Amenophis II, whence the now empty sarcophagus has been returned. Notice the Coptic graffiti in the end storage room beyond the burial chamber. As for Ramses himself, his mummy in the Cairo Museum shows him to have been a short, bald man with a long nose. He became pharaoh in his forties after the failure of a conspiracy to usurp the throne (see p.437), and recorded the "testament" of his illustrious father, Ramses III, in the Great Harris Papyrus.

Tomb of Ramses IX (#6)

The tomb of **Ramses IX** belonged to one of the last rulers (1140–1123 BC) of the XX Dynasty, towards the end of the New Kingdom. It's indicative of waning majesty that the initial scenes in sunk-relief soon give way to flat paintings, akin to drawings. The walls of its stepped corridor (originally bisected by ramps, for moving the sarcophagus) depict Ramses before the gods and symbolic extracts from the *Book of Caverns*. Notice the solar barques bearing crocodiles, heads and other oddities, on the left-hand wall. The burial chamber is memorable for its *Book of Night* in yellow upon a dark blue background. Two sky-goddesses stretch back-to-back across the ceiling, encompassing voids swirling with creatures, stars and heavenly barques. While the king's sarcophagus pit gapes empty, his resurrection is still heralded on the walls by Khepri, the scarab incarnation of the reborn sun at dawn.

Tomb of Tutankhamun (#62)

One of the world's most famous tombs, the tomb of **Tutankhamun** is neither large nor imposing by the standards of the Valley of the Kings, reflecting Tut's short reign (c.1361–1352 BC; see p.329) as an XVIII Dynasty boy-pharaoh. Its renown stems from its belated discovery and its amazing hoard of treasures (now mostly in the Cairo Museum). After archeologist **Howard Carter** had dug in vain for five seasons, his financial backer, **Lord Carnarvon**, was on the point of giving up when the tomb was found on November 4, 1922. Fears that it had been plundered were dispelled when they broke through the second sealed door – officially on November 26, though in fact Carter and Carnarvon secretly entered the previous night, stole several items and resealed the door. Otherwise, the tomb was cleared meticulously. Each of its 1700 objects was documented, drawn and photographed *in situ* before being removed to an improvised laboratory in the tomb of Seti II, for stabilizing and cleaning by Arthur Mace. Unpacking everything took

△ Howard Carter opening the tomb of Tutankhamun

nearly ten years, the whole process being recorded in more than 1800 superb photographs by Harry Burton, who converted an empty tomb into a darkroom.

Carnarvon's death in Cairo from an infected mosquito bite in April 1923 focused world attention on a warning by the novelist Marie Corelli, that "dire punishment follows any intruder into the tomb". (At the moment of Carnarvon's death, all the lights in Cairo went out.) The **Curse of Tutankhamun** gained popular credence with this and each successive "mysterious" death. The US magnate Jay Gould died of pneumonia resulting from a cold contracted at the tomb; a famous Bey was shot by his wife in London after viewing the discovery; a French Egyptologist suffered a fatal fall; Carter's secretary died in unusual circumstances at the Bath Club in London; and his right-hand man Arthur Mace sickened and died before the tomb had been fully cleared. However, of the 22 who had witnessed the opening of Tut's sarcophagus, only two were dead ten years later. Howard Carter died in 1939 at the age of 64, while others closely involved lived into their eighties (not least Dr Derry, who performed the autopsy which suggested that Tut died from a blow to the head, aged about nineteen). Notwithstanding this, a new explanation for the "curse" was advanced by a scientist at Cairo University in 1991. Professor Thebat believes that Carnarvon and Mace were fatally weakened by radioactivity emanating from an unknown substance used as part of the mummification process, which had accumulated in the tomb over 3000 years; he also claims to have detected radioactivity in seventeen of the mummies in the Egyptian Museum.

As for the tomb itself, it is now glassed over to protect its paintings, and the number of visitors has been reduced by a steep admission charge. **Tickets** for Tut's tomb are available at a separate kiosk within the entrance to the Valley of the Kings – but at £E70 you might well decide that the tomb isn't worth it.

In 1922, Carter found the door at the bottom of the stairway **[a]** walled up and sealed with Tut's cartouche and the seal of the Necropolis, but signs of repairs, the detritus in the corridor **[b]** and another resealed door at the end indicated that robbers had penetrated the antechamber **[c]** during the XX Dynasty.

Most of the funerary objects now in the Cairo Museum were crammed into the undecorated chambers **[c, d** (now walled up) and **e]**. Another wall (now replaced by a barrier) enclosed the burial chamber, which was almost filled by four golden shrines packed one inside another, containing Tut's stone sarcophagus and triple-layer mummiform coffin, of which the innermost, solid **gold coffin** and **Tut's mummy** remain. In 2005 the mummy was CAT scanned in its tomb which revealed a broken leg that might have given rise to a fatal infection, and cast doubt on the theory that Tut died from a head injury that some scholars had attributed to murder.

The colourful **murals** run in an anti-clockwise direction, starting with the funeral procession where nine friends and three officials drag Tut's coffin on a sledge **[f]**. Next, his successor Ay performs the

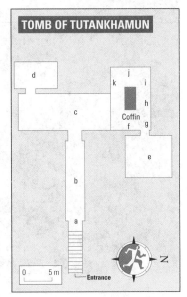

TOMB OF TUTANKHAMUN

Opening of the Mouth ceremony **[g]** and makes sacrifices to the sky-goddess Nut **[h]**. The deceased king embraces Osiris, followed by his *ka* (in the black wig) **[i]**. His solar boat and sun-worshipping baboons appear on the left wall **[j]**. On the hard-to-see entrance wall, Anubis and Isis escort Tutankhamun to receive life from Hathor **[k]**.

Tomb of Ramses VI (#9)

One reason why Tut's tomb stayed hidden for so long was that it lay beneath mounds of rubble from the tomb of **Ramses VI** (1156–1148 or 1151–1143 BC), which has been a tourist attraction since antiquity, when the Greeks called it the "Tomb of Memnon". The first two corridors have suffered from centuries of graffiti, but far worse occurred in 1992, when the ceiling fell down and had to be glued back on in nearly one thousand pieces.

It was begun by Ramses V but usurped and enlarged by his successor, whose offering of a lamp to Horus of the Horizon opens the *Book of Gates* **[a]**, which faces other sunk-reliefs from the *Book of Caverns* **[b]**. Like the astronomical ceiling, this continues through a series of corridors (note the winged sun-disc over the lintel and Ramses' cartouches on the door jambs **[c]**). Where the *Book of Gates* reaches the Hall of Osiris **[d]**, a flame-breathing snake and catfish-headed gods infest the *Book of Caverns* **[e]**. As Re's barque approaches the Seventh Gate, beyond which twelve gods hold a rope festooned with whips and heads **[f]**, the *Book of Caverns* depicts a procession of *ka* figures **[g]**. From here on, the astronomical ceiling features an attenuated sky-goddess and the *Book of Day and Night*.

The eighth and ninth divisions of the *Book of Gates* **[h]** and fifth division of the *Book of Caverns* **[i]** decorate the next chamber, originally a vestibule to the hall beyond, which

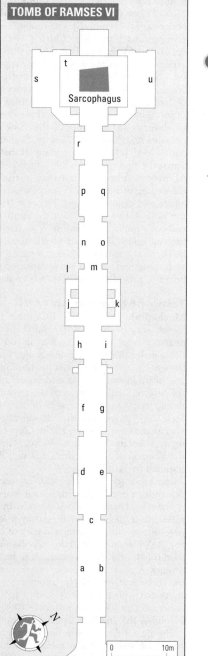

marked the limits of Ramses V's tomb. This contains the concluding sections of the *Book of Gates* **[j]**, the seventh division of the *Book of Caverns* **[k]** and a summary of the world's creation **[l]**. The rear wall also features a scene of Ramses VI making offerings and libations to Osiris. On the pillars, he makes offerings to Khonsu, Amun-Re, Meretseger, Ptah-Sokar, Ptah and Re-Herakhte **[m]**.

The descent to the next corridor is guarded by winged serpents representing the goddesses Nekhbet and Neith (left), Meretseger and Selket (right). On the corridor walls appear the introductory **[n]** and middle sections **[o]** of the *Book of Amduat*; on the ceiling, extracts from the *Books of Re* and the *Book of Day and Night*. Scenes in the next corridor relate the fourth and fifth **[p]** and eighth to eleventh **[q]** chapters of the *Book of Amduat*. The small vestibule beyond contains texts from the *Book of Coming Forth by Day*, including the "negative confession" **[r]**. On the ceiling, Ramses sails the barques of Day and Night across the first register, while Osiris rises from his bier in the second.

Lovely back-to-back versions of the *Book of Day* and *Book of Night* adorn the ceiling of Ramses VI's burial chamber, where his image makes offerings at either end of one wall **[s]**. The rear **[t]** and right-hand walls carry portions of the *Book of Aker*, named after the earth-god of the underworld who fettered the coils of Apopis, safeguarding Re's passage. Incarnated as a ram-headed beetle, the sun-god is drawn across the heavens in his divine barque **[u]**. The king's black granite **sarcophagus** was smashed open by treasure hunters in antiquity, and his mummy left so badly damaged that the priests had to pin the body to a board to provide the remains with a decent burial in another tomb.

Tomb of Merneptah (#8)

Merneptah (1236–1223 BC), the fourteenth son of Ramses II, didn't become pharaoh until his fifties, having outlived thirteen brothers with prior claims on the throne. On the evidence of his mummy, he was afflicted by arthritis and hardening of the arteries, and underwent dental surgery in old age. On the strength of his "Israel Stele" at Karnak and the identification of his father as the Pharaoh of the Oppression, many scholars hold that Merneptah was the Pharaoh of the Exodus (although this is disputed by Rohl; see p.669).

Like other tombs of the XIX Dynasty, his descends in corridors, with a total length of about 80m. Merneptah is welcomed by Re-Herakhte and Khepri **[a]**, the *Litany of Re* **[b]** unfolds opposite the sixteen avatars of Osiris **[c]**, Re's barque is pulled through the underworld **[d]**, and Nekhebkau leads his soul towards Anubis **[e]**. Beyond a pit watched by Thoth and Anubis **[f]**, another corridor decorated with the *Book of Amduat* **[g]** leads to an antechamber with images of Osiris and Nephthys **[h]**, and Merneptah as Imutef **[i]**.

The next hall is a false burial chamber (a trick that seldom fooled robbers) decorated with hymns to Osiris **[j]** and scenes from the

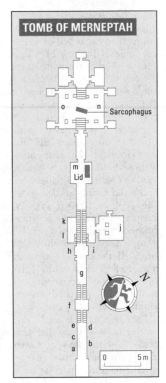

TOMB OF MERNEPTAH

Sarcophagus

0   5 m

Book of Gates. Notice the binding of the Serpents of Chaos **[k]**, a tug-of-war over a "rope" of human souls **[l]**, and the Osirian avatars above the lintel. The final corridors are largely bare, but for the outer **lid** of Merneptah's sarcophagus – left there by thieves – and the faint image of a monkey **[m]**.

In the real burial chamber, the gods voyage through the night across the ceiling, while murals show the metamorphosis of Khepri into Re, encircled by bird-men requesting the deceased's *ba* (soul) **[n]**, and Khnum piloting a boat with the pharaoh's mummy floating above **[o]**. There is a carving of the sky-goddess Nut inside Merneptah's massive granite **sarcophagus**.

Tomb of Ramses III (#11)

The grandest of the Ramessid tombs open at present is that of **Ramses III**. His 31-year reign (1198–1166 BC) marked the heyday of the XX Dynasty, whose power declined under the later Ramessids. Like his temple at Medinet Habu, the tomb harks back to the earlier glories of the New Kingdom. Uniquely for royal tombs, its colourful sunk-reliefs include scenes of everyday life. From another vignette derives its popular name, the Tomb of the Harpers.

Off the entrance corridors lie ten side chambers, originally used to store funerary objects. Within the first pair are fragmentary scenes of butchery, cooking and baking **[a]**, and ships setting sail, those with furled sails bound downriver **[b]**. Next, Hapy blesses grain-gods and propitiates snake-headed Napret, with her escort of aproned *uraei* **[c]**. The bull of Meri (right) and the cow of Hesi (left) coexist with armoury scenes **[d]**, while hermaphrodite deities bring offerings **[e]** to a treasury **[f]**. Ramses owns cattle and minerals **[g]**, and

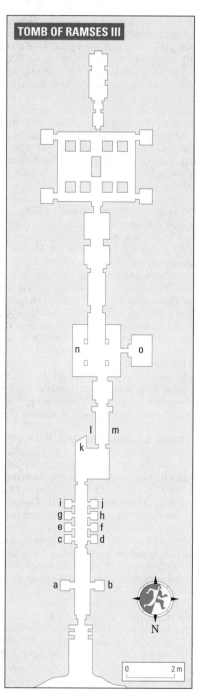

TOMB OF RAMSES III

0   2 m

from his boat inspects peasants working in the Fields of Yaru **[h]**. In a famous scene, two harpists sing to Shu and Atum, while Harsomtus and Anhor greet the king; the lyrics of the song cover the entrance wall **[i]**. The twelve forms of Osiris **[j]** are possibly linked to the twelve *decans* (divisions or hours) of the night.

The dead-end tunnel **[k]** shows where diggers accidentally broke into a neighbouring tomb, at which point the original builder, Pharaoh Sethnakht, abandoned it and appropriated Tawsert's (see opposite). When construction resumed under Ramses, the tomb's axis was shifted west. The corridor has scenes from the fourth **[l]** and fifth **[m]** hours of the *Book of Amduat*. Part of the *Book of Gates* specifies four races of men: Egyptians, Asiatics, Negroes and Libyans (along the bottom) **[n]**. On the facing wall, the pinioned serpent Apopis is forced to disgorge the heads of his victims, in the fifth chapter of the *Book of Gates*. In the side room **[o]** are scenes from the *Book of Amduat*. The rest of the tomb has been barred since its ceiling fell down.

Tomb of Horemheb (#57)

General **Horemheb** was the power behind the throne of Tutankhamun and his aged successor Ay, and finally became pharaoh himself. His reign (1348–1320 BC) marked the height of the Theban counter-revolution against the Amarna heresy and the last gasp of the XVIII Dynasty, and was spent shoring up the crumbling empire bequeathed by his predecessors. He died without leaving an heir (though Rohl thinks that he gave his daughter as a bride to King Solomon) and was succeeded by a military deputy called Paramessu, who took the throne name Ramses and founded the Ramessid dynasty.

Due to be reopened "next year", the tomb's layout prefigures Seti's (see p.420), with a long, steep descent through undecorated corridors to a well room which depicts Horemheb with deities, highly detailed and coloured. Hathor, Isis, Osiris, Horus and Anubis reappear in the anteroom before the burial chamber, whose entrance is guarded by Maat. Its unfinished scenes range from stick-figure drawings to fully worked carvings; the *Book of the Dead* begins to your left and runs clockwise round the chamber, whose huge sarcophagus is carved with a relief of Nut. In the second room to the left, Osiris appears before a *Djed* pillar.

Tomb of Amenophis II (#35)

One of the deepest tombs in the valley lies at the head of the *wadi* beyond Horemheb's tomb. Built for **Ameno-phis II** (1450–1425 or 1427–1400 BC) midway through the XVIII Dynasty, it has more than ninety steps and gets hotter and stuffier with each lower level. When the tomb was discovered in 1898, the body of the king was still in its sarcophagus and nine other royal mummies were found stashed in another chamber. The tomb's defences included a deep pit (now bridged) and a false burial chamber to distract robbers from the lower levels (which would have been sealed up and disguised).

From a pillared vestibule, steps descend into the huge chamber. On its six square pillars, Amenophis is embraced and

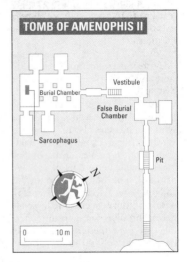

TOMB OF AMENOPHIS II

Vestibule

Burial Chamber

False Burial Chamber

Sarcophagus

Pit

0   10 m

offered *ankhs* by various gods. Beneath a star-spangled ceiling, the walls are painted pale beige and inscribed with the entire *Book of Amduat*, like a continuous scroll of papyrus. Notice the preliminary pen sketches to the left of the left-hand niche. When found in his quartzite sarcophagus (still *in situ*), the king's mummy had a floral garland around its neck. The second chamber on the right served as a cache for the mummies of Tuthmosis IV, Merneptah, Seti II, Ramses V and VI (hacked to pieces) and Queen Tiy, after their original tombs proved insecure.

Tomb of Tawsert/Sethnakht (#14)
Located en route to Seti II's tomb, this one is unusual for having two burial chambers. It originally held the mummy of Seti's wife, Queen **Tawsert**, but was usurped by Pharaoh **Sethnakht** (c.1200–1085 BC) after his own tomb (now Ramses III's) ran into difficulties. In the first corridor one finds Sethnakht making offerings to Horus and Isis, and Osiris enshrined. Further on, a ram-headed god with a knife is followed by Anubis and Wepwawet. Texts from the *Book of the Dead* cover what was meant to be Tawsert's tomb chamber beyond which steps lead down towards Sethnakht's vault.

At the bottom of the stairs, the pharaoh's soul attains harmony with Maat, cherishing the Papyrus and Lotus of the Two Lands; while Anubis embalms his mummy in a side chamber further on. A hall of texts from the *Book of Caverns* and the Opening of the Mouth ceremony precede the burial chamber, whose pillars show the gods greeting Sethnakht, while the walls depict the resurrection of Osiris and Re's journey through the night.

Tomb of Siptah (#47)
Siptah (1194–1188 BC) was the only son of Seti II, born not of Queen Tawsert, but of a Syrian concubine, Sutailja. Since he was only a boy, with an atrophied leg, Tawsert ruled as regent in alliance with an official named Bay (also of Syrian origin). After Siptah came of age, Tawsert married him; some believe that his death six years later was orchestrated by Tawsert and Bay. His one recorded achievement was to have led a campaign in Nubia, but it is more likely that he had it sent in his name. To complete his run of bad luck, Siptah's tomb was usurped by a later pharaoh, its contents smashed up in antiquity, and his mummy ended up in the tomb of Amenophis II. There it was found in 1905, when it was determined that he probably had cerebral palsy or polio as an infant. However, his tomb looks impressive, with a finely dressed Siptah mingling with the gods in the *Litany of Ra* and floating through scenes from the *Book of Amduat*.

Tomb of Seti II (#15)
At the end of the *wadi* lies the seldom-visited tomb of **Seti II** (1216–1210 BC), which Arthur Mace used as a storage and restoration area during the excavation of Tutankhamun's tomb. Its long, straight corridors are typical of the XIX Dynasty, decorated with colourful scenes. Due to Seti's abrupt demise, however, there was only time to carve sunk-reliefs near the entrance, and the rest was hastily filled in with paintings or outline drawings. The king's mummy was later hidden in tomb #35 and replaced by that of an anonymous dignitary, which was plundered by thieves, who left only the sarcophagus lid. His mummy indicates that he suffered from arthritis, but had good teeth, which was unusual for that time.

Tomb of Tuthmosis III (#34)
Likewise secreted in a separate *wadi*, high up in a cleft, the tomb of **Tuthmosis III** (1504–1450 or 1479–1425 BC) is one of the oldest in the valley. Its

concealment and (futile) defences make this tomb especially interesting, though some are disappointed by its artwork. Having ascended a wooden stairway to the cleft, you descend through several levels, crossing a pit by footbridge to reach a vestibule. Its walls depict 741 deities as stick figures, in imitation of the format used on papyrus texts from the Middle Kingdom onwards, which was favoured for murals early in the New Kingdom. Reduced to their essentials, the ramps and shafts that led into the underworld, and Khepri's role in pulling Re's barque, are clearly visible.

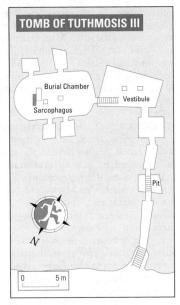

The unusual rounded burial chamber is also decorated with outline figures and symbols. Although the yellow background simulates aged papyrus, the texts were only painted after Tuthmosis had been laid to rest; there's a crossed-out mistake on the "instruction" fresco.

Elsewhere you'll notice double images (as at Abu Simbel), believed by some archeologists to have been meant to suggest motion, and others to be the result of overcarving. On one of the pillars, Tuthmosis's mother stands behind him in a barque; the register below shows three wives and a daughter, to the right of which a tree-goddess suckles the young king. By shining a torch inside the quartzite sarcophagus, you can admire a lovely carving of Nut, whose arms would have embraced his mummy before priests removed it to a safer hiding place near Deir el-Bahri.

Tomb of Seti I (#17)

The tomb of **Seti I** is the finest in the valley, but unfortunately closed to the public. Despite a decade spent restoring damage wrought by the rising water table and tourists, and the installation of dehumidifiers, it is still too fragile to expose. Discovered in 1817, it is the longest in the valley (over 120m) and has superlative carvings and gilded paintings comparable to those in Seti's temple at Abydos. It was Seti I (1318–1304 BC) who consolidated the XIX Dynasty, regained the colonies lost under Akhenaten, and paved the way for his second son, Ramses II, to reach new heights of imperialism. His tomb fared badly at the hands of European collectors: some of its reliefs are now in the Louvre and the Turin Museum, while Seti's sarcophagus lies in the Sir John Soane Museum in London.

Tomb of Ramses I (#16)

Buried next door to Seti is his father, **Ramses I**, founder of the XIX Dynasty, who was not of royal blood, but the son of a commander from Avaris. During his one-year reign (1320–1318 or 1295–1294 BC), Ramses campaigned in Asia, reopened the turquoise mines of Sinai, and married Sitre, the daughter of another soldier from the eastern Delta, siring an heir to continue the dynasty. His tomb has the shortest entrance corridor of any in the valley, leading to a small, finely painted burial chamber, the colours still bright against a blue-grey background. On the left wall are nine black sarcophagi in caverns, above twelve goddesses representing the hours of the night, from the *Book of Gates*. Elsewhere, Ramses appears with Maat, Anubis, Ptah, Osiris and other deities. In 1999, the royal **mummy** was traced to the Niagara Falls Museum, where it had supposedly lain, unidentified, since it was dubiously acquired in 1850. Since being returned to Egypt in 2004, it has been in the Luxor Museum, though the SCA is not convinced that it actually is Ramses.

Tomb of Monthuhirkhopshef (#19)

Sited high up a side-*wadi*, the seldom-visited tomb of **Monthuhirkhopshef** casts light on the life of princes – in this case, a son of Ramses IX, named "The Arm of Montu is Mighty". Monthuhirkhopshef died in his teens – before his father – for he wears the blue-and-gold sidelock of youth, a finely pleated linen skirt and elaborate make-up, as he makes offerings to deities in the entrance corridor of his tomb. Eye make-up was worn by both sexes in Ancient Egypt; it's thought that some of the ingredients helped to prevent eye diseases such as glaucoma.

Tomb of Queen Tiy/Smenkhkare (#55)

The undecorated tomb, designated **KV55,** has been a conundrum ever since its discoverer, Theodore Davis, failed to record its contents before removing the decrepit mummy in 1907, thus destroying crucial evidence. The mummy was initially attributed to **Queen Tiy** – the wife of Amenophis III – due to its pelvic shape and "feminine" position (left arm bound across the chest, right arm alongside the body), and a gilded panel that depicted her with Akhenaten. Later, however, the bones were identified as those of a man under 26 with signs of hydrocephalus, which seemed to fit Pharaoh Akhenaten instead. Yet another examination in 1933 found no signs of water on the brain (hydrocephalus), but diagnosed a platycephalic (abnormally flat) skull similar to Tutankhamun's – suggesting that this was the mummy of his mysterious predecessor, **Smenkhkare**.

Although new evidence has since been advanced for this being the mummy of Akhenaten, the Egyptian Museum remains unconvinced, and still attributes it to Smenkhkare.

Tomb of Yuya and Thuya (#46)

Another tomb with nothing to see (its contents are in the Cairo Museum) but a story attached is that of **Yuya and Thuya**, the parents of Queen Tiy. Though seemingly not of noble birth, Yuya was the highest official under Tuthmosis IV and Amenophis III. The latter's marriage to their daughter led to Thuya and Yuya becoming the grandparents of Pharaoh Akhenaten. In *Stranger in the Valley of the Kings*, Ahmed Osman argues that Yuya – whose mummy has a non-Egyptian appearance – was the Biblical Joseph (Genesis 41:39–40), whose talk of Yahweh subsequently inspired the monotheistic religion of Akhenaten (see Tell el-Amarna, p.328). However, others believe that Yuya and Thuya were of Nubian origin, as evinced by a famous bust of Tiy, whose face is indubitably African.

The Western Valley and the Sun Temple of Thoth

A neglected offshoot of the Valley of the Kings, the **Western Valley** (Biban el-Gurud) contains only four tombs (two of them royal), of which just one is open. The **Tomb of Ay** (#23) was built for Tutankhamun's successor, who had earlier been Akhenaten's vizier and prepared himself a tomb at Tell el-Amarna (see p.355). His crypt in the Western Valley is notable for the blend of royal and noble imagery in the burial chamber, where the *Book of Amduat* is juxtaposed

Hiking across the hills to Deir El-Bahri

This wonderfully scenic hike is easiest over winter but feasible at other times so long as you guard against heatstroke. Though **the hike** can be done in thirty minutes, it's worth taking it slowly once you've shaken off the souvenir vendors who wait above the start of the trail, where the donkey guides rest up. If you're tempted to be rude, remember that the vendors only come here because they can't afford to bribe the police to let them work in the Valley of the Kings.

When the path forks, take the left-hand track running flat along the top of a rock "loaf", before crossing the ridge to behold the Nile Valley. Directly beneath the sheer cliff lies Hatshepsut's temple; to see it, walk right for a bit before peering *carefully* over the edge. To descend, follow the path alongside the trampled fence till you reach a crag where the trail divides. Ignore anyone who tries to lure you down the steepest trail, to render "help" for *baksheesh* – the slightly less precipitous left-hand path is the one to take. Hiking along **other trails** in the Theban Hills is likely to be firmly discouraged by the police.

with a typical nobles' vignette of the deceased spearing fishes and birds. Given the distance by road off the main route to the Valley of the Kings (the Western Valley is clearly signposted), you can only get there by car or with a trail bike – **tickets** are sold at the entrance to the Valley of the Kings.

Locals call the valley "Wadi Monkey", after the caches of mummified baboons found there, probably connected with a remote **Sun Temple of Thoth** (to whom baboons were sacred). Uniquely for an Egyptian temple, this structure – which isn't open to tourists – is sited 400m above the Nile, on a spur of the Theban range that the ancients called the "Crown of Thebes". The mud-brick temple built by Mentuhotpe II in the XI Dynasty overlays a stone temple from the Archaic Period – the oldest known one in Upper Egypt. The temple is distantly visible at the start of the road to the Valley of the Kings, but can only be reached on foot or by donkey (1hr 30min–2hr) by a steep 5km path starting from near Howard Carter's house.

Deir el-Bahri

Of all the sites on the west bank, none can match the breathtaking panache of **Deir el-Bahri** (see p.402 for ticket details). Set amidst a vast natural amphitheatre in the Theban Hills, the temple rises in imposing terraces, the shadowed verticals of its colonnades drawing power from the massive crags overhead. Its great ramps and courts look modern in their stark simplicity, but in ancient times would have been softened and perfumed by gardens of fragrant trees. The reliefs that cover its colonnades and chapels bespeak of an extraordinary woman and dynastic intrigues. *Deir el-Bahri* ("Northern Monastery") is the Arabic name for the **Mortuary Temple of Hatshepsut** (pronounced "Hat-Cheap-Suit"), the only woman ever to reign over Egypt as pharaoh (1503–1482 BC). A daughter of Tuthmosis I, married to his successor Tuthmosis II, Hatshepsut was widowed before she could bear a son. Rather than accept relegation in favour of a secondary wife who had produced an heir, Hatshepsut made herself co-regent to the young Tuthmosis III and soon assumed absolute power.

To legitimize her position, she was depicted in masculine form, wearing a pharaoh's kilt and beard; yet her authority ultimately depended on personal willpower and the devotion of her favourite courtier, Senenmut, who rose from humble birth to the stewardship of Amun's estates, before falling from grace for reasons unknown. When Tuthmosis came into his inheritance after her death, he defaced Hatshepsut's cartouches and images, consigning her memory to oblivion until her deeds were rediscovered by archeologists.

In 1995, the temple was used to stage Verdi's *Aïda*, which was a financial flop due to poor promotion and colossal expenditure, not least on building a road to the Nile so that VIPs could arrive by boat from Karnak, which has hardly been used since. However, dozens of coach parties arrive along the road from Dra' Abul Naga, making this one of the busiest sites in the Necropolis.

Tragically, in November 1997 it made headlines when 58 tourists and four guards were shot or stabbed to death by Islamist extremists, on the temple's Middle Terrace. The terrorists might have escaped in a hijacked coach if the driver hadn't deliberately crashed it near the Valley of the Queens and if they hadn't been chased by villagers, for the police took an hour to reach the scene. The day is vividly remembered on the west bank, especially by the donkey guides who witnessed the **massacre** from the clifftop above. Ever since then, all the sites have been heavily guarded, and watchposts installed on the Theban Hills – a security regime that looks set to stay.

Hatshepsut's temple

Hatshepsut called her temple **Djeser Djeseru**, the "Splendour of Splendours". In ancient times an avenue of sphinxes probably ran from the Nile to its **Lower Terrace**, which was planted with myrrh trees and cooled by fountains (the stumps of a few 3500-year-old trees remain). At the top and bottom of the ramp to the next level stood pairs of stone lions (one of each pair is still *in situ*). Before ascending the ramp, check out its flanking **colonnades**, whose reliefs were defaced by Tuthmosis III, and later by Akhenaten. While Hatshepsut's image remains obliterated, those of Amun were

▲ Hatshepsut

restored after the Theban counter-revolution. Behind the northern colonnade (right of the ramp) are idealized scenes of rural life; reliefs in the southern (left) colonnade show the transport by river of two obelisks from Aswan – doubtless the pair that Hatshepsut erected at Karnak.

The **Middle Terrace** once also boasted myrrh trees, which Hatshepsut personally acquired from the Land of Punt in a famous expedition that's depicted along one of the square-pillared colonnades flanking the ramp to the uppermost level. Together with the Birth reliefs behind the other colonnade, and scenes in the chapels at either end, these are the highlights of her temple.

The Birth and Punt colonnades

To the right of the ramp is the so-called **Birth Colonnade**, whose reliefs assert Hatshepsut's divine parentage. Starting from the left, its rear walls show Amun (in the guise of Tuthmosis I) and her mother Queen Ahmosis (seated on a couch), their knees touching. Next, bizarre deities lead the queen into the birth chamber, where the god Khnum fashions Hatshepsut and her *ka* (both represented as boys) on his potter's wheel. Her birth is attended by Bes and the frog deity Heqet; goddesses nurse her, while Thoth records details of her reign. The sensitive expressions and delicate modelling convey a sincerity that transcends mere political expediency.

At the far end of the colonnade, steps lead back into a **Chapel of Anubis** with fluted columns and colourful murals. Tuthmosis III and a falcon-headed sun-god appear over the niche to the right; Hathor on the facing wall; offerings by Hatshepsut and Tuthmosis to Anubis on the other walls. As elsewhere, the images of Hatshepsut were defaced after her death by order of Tuthmosis.

On the other side of the ramp is the famous **Punt Colonnade**, relating Hatshepsut's journey to that land (thought to be modern-day Somalia). Though others had visited Punt to obtain precious myrrh for temple incense, Hatshepsut sought living trees to plant outside her temple. Despite the faintness of the reliefs, you can follow the story as it unfolds (left to right). Commissioned by Amun "to establish a Punt in his house", the Egyptian flotilla sails from the Red Sea Coast, to be welcomed by the king of Punt and his grotesquely fat wife (perhaps afflicted by elephantiasis). In exchange for metal axes and other goods, the Egyptians depart with myrrh trees and resin, ebony, ivory, cinnamon wood and panther skins; baboons play in the ships' rigging. Back home, the spoils are dedicated to Amun and the precious myrrh trees bedded in the temple gardens.

The Punt Colonnade leads into a larger **Chapel of Hathor**, whose face and sistrum (sacred rattle) form the capitals of the square pillars. In the first pillared chamber, the goddess appears in her bovine and human forms, and suckles Hatshepsut (whose image has not been defaced here) on the left-hand wall. The next chamber features delicate reliefs of festival processions (still quite freshly coloured) in a similar location. Peering into the gated sanctuary, you'll see another intact Hatshepsut worshipping the divine cow (left), and an alcove (right) containing a **portrait of Senenmut**, which would have been hidden when the doors were open. Apocryphally, it was this claim on the pharaoh's temple that caused his downfall. After fifteen years of closeness to Hatshepsut and her daughter Neferure (evinced by a statue in the Cairo Museum, which some regard as proof of paternity), Senenmut abruptly vanished from the records late in her reign. When archeologists excavated the sanctuary in the early twentieth century they found it stacked with baskets full of wooden penises, seemingly used in fertility rituals.

The Upper Terrace and sanctuaries

Reached by a ramp terminating in vultures' heads, the **Upper Terrace** has now emerged from decades of research and restoration work by Polish and Egyptian teams. Beyond its Osiride portico lies a courtyard flanked by colonnades and sanctuaries. In the **Sanctuary of Hatshepsut** (left) are stylish reliefs of priests and offerings bearers. On the other side is the **Sanctuary of the Sun**, an open court with a central altar.

The central **Sanctuary of Amun** is dug into the cliff, aligned so that it points towards Hatshepsut's tomb in the Valley of the Kings on the other side of the mountain. In Ptolemaic times the sanctuary was extended and dedicated to Imhotep and Amenhotep, the quasi-divine counsellors of Zoser and Amenophis III. Beneath it lies another burial chamber for Hatshepsut, presumably favoured over her pro forma tomb in the Valley of the Kings, since it was dug at a later date.

Other temples

From the heights of Hatshepsut's temple you can gaze southwards over the ruins of two similar edifices. The **Mortuary Temple of Tuthmosis III** was long ago destroyed by a landslide, but a painted relief excavated here can be seen in the Luxor Museum; more remains of the far older **Temple of Mentuhotpe II**, the first pharaoh to choose burial in Thebes (XI Dynasty). Unlike his XVIII Dynasty imitators, Mentuhotpe was actually buried in his mortuary temple; his funerary statue is now exhibited in the Cairo Museum.

Secret tombs and caves

Whereas Mentuhotpe's remains weren't discovered till modern times, many of the New Kingdom royal tombs were despoiled soon after their final burial in the Valley of the Kings. Towards the end of the XXI Dynasty, the priests hid forty mummies in a **secret cache** in the next hollow to the south above Mentuhotpe's temple, which the villagers of Gurna found in 1875 and quietly sold off for years until rumbled by the authorities, who forced them to reveal the cache's location. Amongst the mummies recovered were Amenophis I, Tuthmosis II and III, Seti I and Ramses II and III. Archeologists were baffled to find a XXII Dynasty coffin, beyond a passage blocked by royal mummies from an earlier period. As the steamer bore them downriver to Cairo, villagers lined the banks, wailing in sorrow or firing rifles in homage – a haunting scene in Shady Abdel Salem's film *The Mummy*, a classic of Egyptian cinema (1975).

Worth a look if you can persuade a guard at Deir el-Bahri to unlock it is the **Tomb of Senenmut**, just beyond the temple precincts. Its steep shaft descends past a bust of Senenmut into a chamber with a lovely astronomical ceiling; on its walls are extracts from the *Book of the Dead*. Why Senenmut should have built this tomb when he already had one at Gurna is uncertain; in any event, its unfinished burial chamber was never used.

Alas, the SCA is not willing to display a rare example of Ancient Egyptian lavatory humour in a **cave** to the north of Hatshepsut's temple. Amongst the doodles and inscriptions is a drawing of a man buggering a figure wearing pharaonic headgear and women's underwear. Theories suggest this could be Senenmut and Hatshepsut, or a fantasy of revenge by the juvenile Tuthmosis.

The Asasif Tombs

Midway between Deir el-Bahri and the Tombs of the Nobles lies a burial ground known as the **Asasif Tombs**, currently being studied by several archeological teams. While some of its 35 tomb chapels date from the XVIII Dynasty, the majority are from the Late Period (XXV–XXVI Dynasty), when Thebes was ruled by Nubian kings, and then from the Delta. **Tickets** for these tombs are sold at the Deir-el-Bahri ticket office (see p.402 for details).

The most likely to be open is the **Tomb of Pabasa (#279)**, the steward to a Divine Votaress of Amun during the XXVI Dynasty. His tomb reflects the Saïte Dynasty obsession with the Old Kingdom, having a similar design to tombs at Saqqara. Its massive gateway leads into a pillared court with scenes of hunting, fishing and viticulture (note the bee-keeping scene on the central column). A funeral procession and the voyage to Abydos appear in the vestibule.

Also worth noting is the **Tomb of Kheru-ef (#192)**, a steward of Queen Tiy during the Amarna period. His scenes depict a Jubilee Festival, Tiy and Amenophis III, musicians, dancers and playful animals – as lyrical as those in Ramose's tomb (see p.427).

The Tombs of the Nobles

The **Tombs of the Nobles** are a study in contrasts to their royal counterparts. Whereas royalty favoured concealed tombs in secluded valleys, Theban nobles and high officials were ostentatiously interred in the limestone foothills overlooking the great funerary temples of their masters and the city across the river. The pharaohs' tombs were sealed and guarded; the nobles' were left open, for their descendants to make funerary offerings. Whereas royal tombs are filled with scenes of judgement and resurrection, the nobles' chosen artwork dwells on earthly life and its continuation in the hereafter. Given more freedom of expression, the artists excelled themselves with vivid **paintings** on stucco (the inferior limestone on this side of the hills militates against carved reliefs). One detail found in all these tombs is the blue lotus, which one Swedish Egyptologist reckons was a drug used for sexual rituals, containing bioflavonoid compounds similar to gingko extract.

The **tombs' layout** marks a further evolution in funerary architecture since the Middle Kingdom tombs of Beni Hassan. Most are entered via a courtyard, with a transverse hall preceding the burial shrine with its niche containing an effigy of the deceased (or statues of his entire family). Strictly speaking, they are tomb chapels rather than tombs, since the graves themselves lie at the bottom of a shaft (usually inaccessible).

Excluding the Asasif Tombs nearer Deir el-Bahri (see p.425), all the tombs open to visitors cluster around the ramshackle village of old Gurna, where they're divided into four groups (each requiring a separate ticket from the main ticket office), namely: **Rekhmire and Sennofer**; **Ramose, Userhat and Khaem-hat**; **Nakht and Menna**; and **Khonsu, Userhat and Benia**. The first two lie furthest west and back from the road; the next trio downhill towards the Rames-seum; and the last two sets of tombs to the northeast, closer to Deir el-Bahri. Though signposting has improved, the uneven, littered **site** is still confusing; with houses interposed between sunken tombs, enclosed by low walls – so you may welcome directions. The car park down the hill from Rekhmire's tomb is a good place to start.

As visiting all the tombs plus the museum would take two hours or so, most people limit themselves to a single group or the highlights from each (marked ★ in the accounts following). Unlike at the Valley of the Kings, the guards might hassle for *baksheesh* or even play tricks with the lighting, so having a flashlight definitely helps.

Gurna Discovery

En route to Sennofer's tomb – head uphill from the car park and bear left at the mosque – the **Gurna Discovery** museum (daily except Tues 8am–noon & 2–5pm) relates how the village has changed over the centuries that it has been excavated by foreigners. Originally the Gurnawis were Bedouin who moved up from the plain to dig for treasure; but as European scholars sought papyri, potshards and other items formerly discarded as worthless, tomb-robbing became a wholesale business. Conflict with the authorities deepened the Gurnawis' mistrust of outsiders; while the trade in antiquities was deplored by archeologists, it was covertly upheld by museums and collectors abroad. In modern times, the Gurnawis have been denied a basic civic amenity – piped water – lest it leak into the bedrock and damage the tombs; only the mosque and the German House are supplied, so women and girls carry pails uphill every day. Illustrated with photographs and copies of drawings by Robert Hay (the originals are in the British Library), the exhibition was organized by Caroline Simpson, a longtime resident, and people from Gurna, whose hopes and fears for the future of their village are expressed in the final section. There is no admission charge, but donations are appreciated; for information see Ⓦwww.qurna.org.

Tomb of Rekhmire (#100)★

Located off to the right of the mosque, the richly decorated tomb of **Rekhmire** casts light on statecraft and foreign policy under Tuthmosis III and Amenophis II, whom Rekhmire served as vizier. The badly damaged murals in its trans-verse hall show him collecting taxes from Upper **[a]** and Lower **[b]** Egypt, and inspecting temple workshops, charioteers and agricultural work **[c]**. Around the corner from his ancestors **[d]**, grapes are trod in large tubs and the juice is strained and stored in jars **[e]**.

Along the rear wall are depicted a desert hunt **[f]** and a famous scene of Rekhmire receiving tributes from foreign lands **[g]**. Amongst the gifts shown are vases from Crete and the Aegean Islands (fourth row); a giraffe, monkeys and elephant tusks from Punt and Nubia (third row); and chariots and horses from Syria (second row).

Growing in height as it recedes towards the false door at the back, the long corridor is decorated with scenes of work and daily life. Slaves store grain in silos **[h]**, whence it was later disbursed as wages to armourers, carpenters, sculptors and other state-employed craftsmen **[i]**. An idealized banqueting scene with female musicians **[j]** merges into an afterworld with a lake and trees **[k]**. Also note Rekhmire's funeral procession and offerings to sustain him in the afterlife **[l]**.

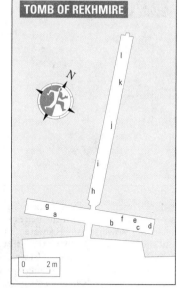

TOMB OF REKHMIRE

Tomb of Sennofer (#96)

From Rekhmire's tomb, slog 50m uphill to the left to find another colourful tomb, in better condition. Entered by a low, twisting stairway, the tomb of **Sennofer** is known as the "Tomb of Vines" after the grapes and vines painted on the textured ceiling of the antechamber. As mayor of Thebes and overseer of Amun's estates under Amenophis II, Sennofer's responsibilities included local viticulture. The walls of the burial shrine depict his funeral procession (left), voyage to Abydos (back, right) and mummified sojourn with Anubis (right). Its square pillars bear images of Hathor, whose eyes follow you around the room; a small tree-goddess appears on the inner side of the rear left-hand pillar.

Tomb of Ramose (#55)*

Down a dirt road to the southeast lies the tomb of **Ramose**, who was vizier and governor of Thebes immediately before and after the Amarna revolution. His spacious tomb captures the moment of transition from Amun- to Aten-worship, featuring both classical and Amarna-style reliefs, the latter unfinished since Ramose followed Akhenaten to his new capital. Besides its superb reliefs, the tomb is notable for retaining its courtyard – originally a feature of all these tombs.

Along the entrance wall of its pillared hall are lovely carvings that reflect the mellowing of classicism during the reign of Amenophis III, Akhenaten's father. Predictable scenes of Ramose and his wife **[a]**, Amenophis III and Queen Tiy **[b]** making offerings come alive thanks to the exquisite rendering of the major figures, carried over to their feasting friends and relatives **[c]**. The sinuous swaying of mourners likewise imparts lyricism to the conventional, painted funerary scene **[d]**, where Ramose, wife and priests worship Osiris.

The onset of Aten-worship and the Amarna style is evident in the reliefs at the back, despite their battered condition. Those on the left **[e]** were carved

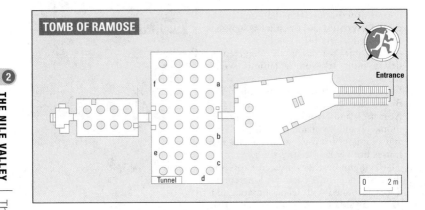

before Amenophis IV changed his name to Akhenaten and espoused Aten-worship, so the pharaoh sits beneath a canopy with Maat, the goddess of truth, receiving flowers from Ramose. (At the far end, note the red grid and black outlined figures by which the artist transferred his design to the wall before relief-cutting took place.) However, the corresponding scene **[f]** depicts the pharaoh as Akhenaten, standing with Nefertiti at their palace window, bathed in the Aten's rays. Ramose is sketched in below, accepting their gift of a golden chain; his physiognomy is distinctly Amarnan, but rather less exaggerated than the royal couple's (see p.328).

By a quirk of Egyptian security, a low wall bars access to Ramose's inner shrine, but there is nothing to prevent one from venturing into a dark tunnel leading off the hall, which suddenly plummets into his grave, 15m below – beware.

Tomb of Userhat (#56)

Immediately south of Ramose's tomb lies that of **Userhat**, a royal scribe and tutor in the reign of Amenophis II. Although some of the figures were destroyed by early Christian hermits who occupied the shrine, what remains is freshly coloured, with unusual pink tones. The tomb is also interesting in that it's still illuminated by means of a mirror reflecting sunlight inside, just as it was when the artists decorated the tomb.

Along the entrance wall of the antechamber are scenes of wine-making, harvesting, herding and branding cattle, collecting grain for the royal storehouse **[a]**, and the customary offerings scenes **[b]**. On the rear wall are reliefs of baking, assaying gold dust, and – lower down – a barber trimming customers beneath a tree **[c]**. The funerary feast scene **[d]** was extensively damaged by hermits, particularly the female figures. The inner hall contains paintings of Userhat hunting gazelles, hares and jackals from a chariot in the desert **[e]**; fowling and fishing amidst the reeds **[f]**; and funerary scenes **[g]**. In a niche at the end is a headless statue of the deceased's wife.

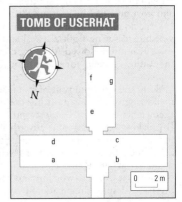

Tomb of Khaemhat (#57)

Next door is the tomb of **Khaemhat**, royal scribe and inspector of granaries under Amenophis III, which is reached via a forecourt off which two other tombs, now locked, once led. Flanking its doorway outside are battered reliefs of Khaemhat worshipping Re, and the complete set of instruments for the Opening of the Mouth ceremony (right). In the transverse antechamber with its red and black patterned ceiling, the best reliefs are on the left as you enter. Although Renenet the snake-headed harvest-goddess has almost vanished, a scene of grain boats docking at Thebes harbour is still visible nearer the niche containing statues of Khaemhat and Imhotep. In the bottom row to the left of the door into the corridor, Hathor breastfeeds a boy-king, surrounded by sacred cows.

Fishing, fowling and family scenes decorate the right-hand wall of the corridor, leading to a triple-niched chapel containing seated statues of Khaemhat and his family.

Tomb of Nakht (#52)*

Northeast of Ramose's tomb lies the burial place of **Nakht**, whose antechamber contains a small museum with drawings of the reliefs (which are covered in glass) and a replica of Nakht's funerary statue, which was lost at sea en route to America in 1917. Nakht was the overseer of Amun's vineyards and granaries under Tuthmosis IV, and the royal astronomer, but stargazing does not feature among the activities depicted in his tomb. The only decorated section is the transverse antechamber, whose ceiling is painted to resemble woven mats, with a *kherker* frieze running above the brilliantly coloured murals.

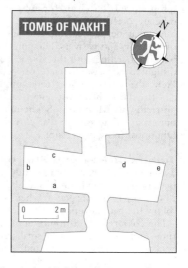

To one side, Nakht supervises the harvest in a scene replete with vivid details **[a]**. In the bottom register, one farmer fells a tree, while another swigs from a waterskin; of the two women gleaning in the row above, one is missing an arm. Beyond a stele relating Nakht's life **[b]** is the famous banqueting scene **[c]**, where sinuous dancers and a blind harpist entertain friends of the deceased, who sits beside his wife, Tawi, with a cat scoffing a fish beneath his chair; sadly, their figures have been erased.

The defacement of Nakht's image and Amun's name is usually ascribed to Amarna iconoclasm, but the gouging out of his eyes and throwing sticks in the hunting scene **[d]** suggests a personal animus. Happily, this has not extended to the images in the corner **[e]**, where peasants tread grapes in vats, and birds are caught in clap-nets and hung for curing (below). The plain inner chamber has a false door painted to resemble Aswan granite and a deep shaft leading to the (inaccessible) burial chamber.

Tomb of Menna (#69)

More scenes of rural life decorate the nearby tomb of **Menna**, an XVIII Dynasty inspector of estates. Accompanied by his wife and daughter, Menna worships the sun in the entrance passage. In the left wing of the first chamber, he supervises field labour (notice the two girls pulling each other's hair, near the far end of the third row), feasts and makes offerings with his wife. Across the way they participate in ceremonies with Anubis, Osiris, Re and Hathor. Though chiefly decorated with mourning and burial scenes, the inner chamber also features a spot of hunting and fishing, vividly depicted on the right-hand wall. The niche at the end contains the legs of Menna's votive statue.

Notice the finely painted **Hadj scene** on the outside of the house near the tomb.

Tombs of Khonsu, Userhet and Benia

This trio of small tombs near those of Nakht and Menna was opened to the public in 1992. The themes are standard, with scenes of offerings, hunting, fishing and funerary rites. In the tomb of Userhet (not to be confused with the Userhat in tomb #56), the guard will produce a mummified head for *baksheesh*.

Khoka Tombs

Set apart from the others – accessible by a track leaving the main road opposite the El Sheikh Abd El Gurna alabaster workshop – the **Khoka** (pronounced "Hookah") tombs were built for a trio of New Kingdom officials. **Neferonpet** (known as Kenro) was a treasury scribe; the tomb's inner chamber depicts him assessing deliveries of gold and food, and the work of sculptors and weavers. The golden-yellow, red and blue murals, the brightly patterned ceilings and the votive statues of the deceased and his wives (badly disfigured) are also characteristic of the tomb of **Nefersekheru**, next door. Here, the wives enjoy greater prominence, flanking Nefersekheru pictorially (to the right as you enter) and sculpturally (in niches), and known to posterity as Maatmou, Sekhemui and Nefertari. Their mummies were buried in a shaft off the rear corridor, which leads into the adjacent tomb of Dhutmosi (now inaccessible).

Tombs of Roy and Shuroy

Two new tombs have been recently opened on the edge of Dra' Abul Naga, just over 1km from the Khoka Tombs by road. You can get there by pick-up heading towards El-Jebannah; get off when you see a billboard with Mubarak's face, and follow the path beyond it to the left.

The colours in both tombs are remarkably fresh. High priest **Roy** from the time of Horemeheb has a small rectangular tomb (#255), whose scenes of wailing mourners, sacrificial bulls and funerary offerings are offset by a ceiling checkered with yellow, red, black and white crosses. His near namesake **Shuroy** was a brazier-bearer at Amun's temple during the XIX Dynasty and has a larger T-shaped tomb (#13). Here, the murals are fragmentary or merely sketched in, though there's a fine frieze of dwarves along the top of the wall to the left inside the transverse hall.

The Ramesseum

The **Ramesseum** or mortuary temple of Ramses II was built to awe the pharaoh's subjects, perpetuate his existence in the afterlife and forever link him to Amun-United-with-Eternity. Had it remained intact, the Ramesseum would doubtless match his great sun temple of Abu Simbel for monumental grandeur and unabashed self-glorification. But by siting it beside an earlier temple on land that was annually inundated, Ramses unwittingly ensured the ruination of his monument, whose toppled colossi would later mock his presumption, inspiring Shelley's sonnet *Ozymandias*:

I met a traveller from an antique land
Who said: Two vast and trunkless legs of stone
Stand in the desert ... Near them on the sand,
Half sunk, a shattered visage lies, whose frown,
And wrinkled lip, and sneer of cold command
Tell that its sculptor well those passions read
Which yet survive, stamped on these lifeless things,
The hand which mocked them, and the heart that fed.
On the pedestal these words appear:
'My name is Ozymandias, King of Kings:
Look upon my works ye Mighty, and despair!'
Nothing beside remains. Round the decay
Of that colossal wreck, boundless and bare
The lone and level sands stretch far away.

Nineteenth-century writers knew the ruins as the *Memnonium*. Their present name only caught on late in the nineteenth century, by which time the Ramesseum had been plundered for statuary – not least the seven-tonne head of one of its fallen colossi, now in the British Museum. Yet its devastation lends romance to the conventional architecture, infusing it with the pathos that moved Harriet Martineau to muse how "violence inconceivable to us has been used to destroy what art inconceivable to us had erected". As bus parties seldom intrude, the Ramesseum seems peaceful, its tranquillity enhanced by a group of trees near the First Pylon, which offer a pleasant contrast

▲ Ramses II

to the desolation of other sites in the Necropolis. Half an hour suffices to see the famous colossi and the best reliefs, but you may care to linger. The nearby **Ramesseum Rest-house** sells cold drinks and hot meals, and has toilets. Remember to buy a **ticket** for the site at the main ticket office before you come here (see p.402).

Exploring the Ramesseum

Like other mortuary temples in the Theban Necropolis, the Ramesseum faces towards the Nile and was originally entered via its **First Pylon**. Wrecked by the earthquake that felled the colossi, the pylon stands marooned in the scrub beyond a rubble-strewn depression that used to be the **First Court**. In 1983, Rohl found evidence for his "New Chronology" in an inscription on a block balanced atop the pylon, asserting that during the eighth year of his reign, Ramses plundered a city named "Shalem", which Rohl thinks was Jerusalem in the time of King Solomon (see p.807).

Visitors enter the temple via the northern flank of its **Second Court**, to be confronted by the awesome **fallen colossus of Ramses II**. This seated mega-lith once towered over the stairs from the first into the second court [a]; over 18m tall and weighing about 1000 tons, it was only surpassed by the Colossi of Memnon thanks to their pedestals. When it toppled some time after the first century AD, its upper half smashed through the Second Pylon into the court, where its head and torso lie today [b], measuring 7m across the shoulders; the cartouche on its bicep reads: "Ruler of Rulers". In the lower court are other fragments, notably feet and hands. As Dean Stanley wrote in 1852, "You sit on

THE RAMESSEUM

Sanctuaries

Magazines

Great Hypostyle Hall

Temple of Tuya

Deir el-Bahri

Ramesseum Resthouse

Second Court

Second Pylon

STATUES & RELIEFS (*)

Base of Ramses' Colossus	a
Head & torso of Colossus	b
Battle of Qadesh & Min festival *	c
Smaller fallen Colossus	d
Ramses before the gods *	e
Storming of Dapur *	f
Ramses receiving eternal life from Amun *	g
Belzoni & Salt	h
Amun's barque *	i
Barques of Mut and Khonsu *	j
Ramses with Sheshat, Atum & Thoth *	k

Royal Palace

First Court

First Pylon

0   20 m

his breast and look at the Osiride statues which support the porticos of the temple, and they seem pygmies before him".

Behind the chunky Osirian pillars rises what's left of the **Second Pylon**, whose inner face bears scenes from the second Battle of Qadesh, surmounted by a register depicting the festival of the harvest-god Min **[c]**. At the far end of the second courtyard, where three stairways rise to meet a colonnaded portico, is a **smaller fallen colossus** of Ramses **[d]**, more fragmented, though its face has suffered merely nasal damage. Originally there were two colossi, but the other – dubbed the "Young Memnon" – was acquired for Britain in 1816 by Belzoni. The name "Ozymandias" arose from the Ancient Greeks' misreading of one of the king's many titles, *User-Maat-Re*.

Beyond here, the core of the Ramesseum is substantially intact. The first set of reliefs worth noting occurs on the front wall of the **portico**, between the central and left-hand doorways **[e]**. Above a bottom row depicting eleven of his sons, Ramses appears with Atum and Mont (who holds the hieroglyph for "life" to his nose), and kneels before the Theban Triad (right) while Thoth inscribes his name on a palm frond (centre). The top register shows him sacrificing to Ptah and making offerings to an ithyphallic Min.

The **Great Hypostyle Hall** had 48 columns, of which 29 are still standing. The taller ones flanking the central aisle have papyrus shafts and turquoise, yellow and white lotus capitals, supporting a raised section of roof; while the lower side columns have papyrus-bud capitals. On the wall as you come in, reliefs depict Egyptian troops storming the Hittite city of Dapur, using shields to protect themselves from arrows and stones **[f]**. At the back of the hall, incised reliefs **[g]** show lion-headed Sekhmet (far right) presenting Ramses to an enthroned Amun, who gives him the breath of eternal life from an *ankh*; along the bottom are depicted some of the king's hundred sons. Notice the names of the treasure-hunter Belzoni and his patron, the British Consul Henry Salt, carved on the right-hand door jamb **[h]**.

Beyond this lie two **smaller Hypostyle Halls**. The first retains its astronomical ceiling, featuring the oldest known twelve-month calendar (whether lunar or solar months is debatable). Notice the barques of Amun, Mut and Khonsu (**[i]** & **[j]**), and the scene of Ramses beneath the persea tree with Atum, Sheshat and Thoth **[k]**. "Pukler Muskau" is the oddest of the many names scrawled on the columns over millennia. The ruined **sanctuaries** were presumably dedicated to Amun, Ramses the god and his glorious ancestors, for the edifice stood alongside an earlier temple of Seti I, which itself contained shrines to Seti and his father, Ramses I, both of whom were linked to Amun. Its scant remains lie to the northeast of the portico and Hypostyle Hall.

The whole complex is surrounded by mud-brick **magazines** that once covered about three times the area of the temple and included workshops, storerooms and servants' quarters, that has survived far better than the **royal palace** and **Temple of Tuya** that once adjoined the temple, of which only stumps of walls and columns remain.

Other mortuary temples

In ancient times, the Ramesseum was one of half a dozen mortuary temples ranged along the edge of the flood plain with no regard for chronological order. The **Temple of Merneptah**, built by Ramses' thirteenth or fourteenth son, lies just south of the Ramesseum, intruding onto the edges of, and reusing masonry from, the vast complex of Amenophis III that once spread to the Colossi of Memnon. Recently opened to the public after thirty years' study and restoration by Swiss Egyptologists, the site consists of fragments and portions of the temple, placed in their original positions and supported by modern stonework. The entrance is reached by walking past the *Marsam Hotel*, and represents the original position of the first pylon. An informative **museum** exhibits stone-carvings from the site (forty percent of them originally belonging to Amenophis III's temple or Deir el-Bahri) and records its excavation (1971–2001). Further in to the left stands a copy of the famous **Israel Stele** also replicated at Karnak, which features the earliest reference to Israel outside of the Bible (see p.394). Guards can unlock another section, containing the remains of a monumental gateway from Amenophis III's temple, clearly reused to build Merneptah's edifice.

While nothing remains of the temples of Tuthmosis IV, Tuthmosis II, Ay and Horemheb that once extended towards Medinet Habu, there is a substantial **Temple of Seti I** near the village of Gurna Ta'rif (accessible by pick-ups from old Gurna or Gezira). The site is still being excavated by German Egyptologists, but you can enter the temple, with its crude reliefs dedicated to Amun, Seti and Ramses I. Again, you must buy a ticket in advance at the main ticket office.

Deir el-Medina: the Workers' Village

Deir el-Medina, the **Workers' Village**, housed the masons, painters and sculptors who created the royal tombs in the Valley of the Kings. Because many were literate and left records on papyrus or *ostracae*, we know such details as who feuded with whom, their sex lives and labour disputes. As state employees, they were supposed to receive fortnightly supplies of wheat, dried meat and fish, onions, pulses and beer, corresponding in value to the price of a bull. When these failed to arrive (as often happened during the ramshackle XX Dynasty), the workers downed tools, staged sit-ins at Medinet Habu, or demonstrated in Luxor.

Normally they worked an eight-hour day, sleeping in huts near the tombs during their ten-day shift before returning to their families at Deir el-Medina – a pattern followed over generations, as most occupations were hereditary. In their spare time craftsmen worked for private clients or collaborated on their own tombs, built beneath man-size pyramids. Their own murals appropriated imagery from royal and noble tombs, which was parodied in the famous *Satirical Papyrus*, showing animals judging souls, collecting taxes and playing *senet,* and humans having sex (see box opposite).

Anyone taking the donkey trail to the Valley of the Kings can get a fine **overview** of the village from the hillside – but the real attraction is its tombs. Visitors should bear in mind that the "Deir el-Medina" **ticket** (#6) doesn't cover the tomb of Peshedu, which needs a separate ticket (#11) – both available only from the main ticket office. You can easily walk to Deir el-Medina from the main road; it's also feasible to do so from the Valley of the Queens or Medinet Habu.

The nearest pyramid to the entrance marks the **Tomb of Sennedjem** (or Sennutem), whose vaulted burial chamber is reached by steep flights of steps and two antechambers. Its colourful murals feature ithyphallic baboons (right end wall), Osiris and the Fields of Yaru, and Anubis ministering to Sennedjem's mummy (facing wall, far left). The **Tomb of Ankherha** (#359) has a similar design, with an antechamber whose ceiling is decorated with intricate abstract patterns. On the left wall of the burial chamber, Ankherha appears with Wepwawet and Khepri; Anubis breathes life into his mummy; his wife adores Horus as a falcon; and his naked daughters make libations. In the **Tomb of Peshedu** (#3), one can see the deceased praying beneath the tree of regeneration, below which flow the waters of the *Amuntit*, the "Hidden Region" where souls were judged. Unusually for Deir el-Medina, the **Tomb of Iphy** (#217) eschews ceremonial scenes and deities for tableaux from everyday life. The **Tomb of Iri Nefer** (#219) isn't officially open, but can be seen for £E5 *baksheesh.*

Sex in Ancient Egypt

While the pharaohs are known to have married their sisters, had multiple wives and dozens of concubines, our knowledge of the sex lives of the lower classes largely depends on murals, *ostracae* and papyri found at Deir el-Medina in the 1900s. Hushed up by prudish scholars of the time, this evidence has been re-examined by Professor Lynn Kersell of Columbia University, and suggests that sexual mores were very different from today. Apparently, the Ancient Egyptians had no concept of illegitimacy or virginity, and regarded fertility as so paramount that female servants would bear a child for the family if the wife proved infertile. There is also the recorded case of a serial adulterer who slept with many wives in Deir el-Medina, but went unpunished; nowadays, such behavior would incur death under the unofficial "honour code" of Upper Egypt. Yet even liberals would draw a line at some of the practices that Kersell believes were commonplace; one *ostraca* seems to show children assisting their parents in making love.

Just north of the village stands a **Ptolemaic temple** dedicated to Maat and Hathor, whose head adorns the pillars between the outer court and naos. Each of its three shrines is decorated with scenes from the *Book of the Dead*; near the back of the left-hand shrine, a hyena-like "Devourer of Souls" awaits those who fail the Judgement of Osiris. Ancient Greek graffiti is scrawled around the temple's entrance. Early in the Christian era, the temple and the workers' village were occupied by monks – hence the site's Arabic name of *Deir el-Medina* ("Monastery of the Town").

The Valley of the Queens

The **Valley of the Queens** is something of a misnomer, for it also contains the tombs of high officials (who were interred here long before the first queen was buried in this valley during the XIX Dynasty) and royal children. Polygamy and concubinage produced huge broods whose blood lines were further entangled by incestuous marriages between crown princes and their sisters, in emulation of Osiris and Isis. Princes were educated by priests and scribes, taught swimming, riding and shooting by officers, and finally apprenticed to military commands around the age of twelve. Less is known about the schooling of princesses, but several queens were evidently well versed in statecraft and architecture.

Originally named the "Place of Beauty", but now known in Arabic as *Biban el-Harem* ("Gates of the Harem"), the valley contains nearly eighty tombs, most of which are basically just pits in the ground. Although the finest murals rival those in the Valley of the Kings for artistry, many have been corroded by salt deposits or badly vandalized, and the tomb of Nefertari is so fragile that it has been closed to the public: small corporate or VIP groups can book in advance to see it at a cost of US$4000. **Tickets** for the other tombs are sold at the entrance to the valley, where there's a mini tourist bazaar; it takes 15 minutes to walk there from Deir el-Medina or the main ticket office.

Tomb of Amunhirkhepshef (#55)

After Nefertari's, the best tomb in the valley belongs to **Amunhirkhepshef**, a son of Ramses III who accompanied his father on campaigns and perhaps died in battle at the age of nine. He is shown wearing the royal sidelock of youth, in lustrous murals where Ramses conducts him through funerary rituals, past the Keepers of the Gates, to an unfinished burial chamber containing a granite sarcophagus. A glass case displays a mummified foetus that his mother aborted through grief at Amunhirkhepshef's death, and entombed with her son.

Tomb of Queen Titi (#52)

Sited along the well-trodden route to Amunhirkhepshef's tomb, this cruciform structure was commissioned by **Queen Titi**, wife of one of the Ramessid pharaohs of the XX Dynasty. A winged Maat kneels in the corridor (where Titi appears before Thoth, Ptah and the sons of Horus) and guards the entrance to the burial chamber with Neith (left) and Selket (right).

The burial chamber itself boasts jackal, lion and baboon guardians, plus three side chambers, the finest being the one to your right. Here, Hathor emerges from between the mountains of east and west in her bovine form, while the tree-goddess pours Nile water to rejuvenate Titi, who reposes on a cushion across the room. Sadly, most of these murals are faded or damaged.

Tomb of Prince Khaemweset (#44)

This colourfully painted tomb is reached via a separate path. **Prince Khaemweset** was one of several sons of Ramses III who died in a smallpox epidemic, and the murals in his tomb give precedence to images of Ramses, making offerings in the entrance corridor and worshipping funerary deities in the side chambers. In the second corridor, decorated with the *Book of Gates*, Ramses leads Khaemweset past the fearsome guardians of the Netherworld to the Fields of Yaru, bearing witness for him before Osiris and Horus in the burial chamber. Notice the four sons of Horus on the lotus blossom.

Tomb of Queen Nefertari (#66)

Queen Nefertari was the principal wife of Ramses II, with whom she had achieved almost equal status by the end of his reign. Her ascendancy was signified by the appearance of her image beside the king's on the pylon of Luxor Temple; the dedication of a shrine within the Ramesseum to Nefertari and the Queen Mother, Tuya; and finally by a massive temple at Abu Simbel, which identifies her with the goddess Hathor. After Ramses' death, Nefertari may have retired to a palace near the Fayoum or died herself, for no more is heard of her.

Her **tomb**, the most illustrious in the valley, was found in 1904 by an Italian archeologist, Ernesto Schiaparelli. Its extreme fragility and the damage caused by its plaster dehydrating, and salt crystals forming beneath its paintings, kept the tomb closed for decades while a solution was debated; eventually restoration began in 1986. It took five years and US$6 million to clean the murals and re-adhere paint and stucco to the walls, without altering or adding any colours. To avoid the humidity that causes salt crystallization, visitors were supposedly limited to 150 a day, but this was so often ignored that the murals visibly deteriorated within a few years – hence the new policy of restricting access to small numbers of big-spending VIPs and coporate groups.

Medinet Habu

Medinet Habu (Habu's Town) is the Arabic name for the gigantic **Mortuary Temple of Ramses III**, a structure second only to Karnak in size and complexity, and better preserved in its entirety. Modelled on the Ramesseum of his illustrious ancestor, Ramses II, this XX Dynasty extravaganza deserves more attention than it usually gets, being the last stop on most tourists' itineraries. The site itself was hallowed

▲ Ramses III

long before Ramses erected his "House of Millions of Years" and is still imbued with magical significance by the local *fellaheen*. Its massive brick enclosure walls sheltered the entire population of Thebes during the Libyan invasions of the late XX Dynasty and for centuries afterwards protected the Coptic town of *Djeme*, built within the great temple. You can get a fine **overview** of Medinet Habu from the top of the mound of earth near the southeast corner, or by drifting low over the temple in a hot-air balloon (see p.382).

The temple precincts

The entire complex was originally surrounded by **enclosure walls**, sections of which rise at intervals from the plain. Its front facade is quite asymmetrical, with a jutting **Ptolemaic Pylon** whose winged sun-disc glows with colour since its recent restoration, overshadowing the entrance to the temple precincts. This **Migdol Gate** is named after the Syrian fortress that so impressed Ramses with its lofty gatehouse that he built one for his own temple, and often relaxed with his **harem** in a suite above the gate, decorated with reliefs of dancers in slinky lingerie. As social conditions worsened during the latter years of his reign, a secondary wife, Tiy, hatched a harem conspiracy to murder him during the Optet festival, so that her son, Pentwere, could inherit – but the conspirators were discovered and forced to commit suicide, and Ramses' chosen heir eventually succeeded him. The two statues of Sekhmet by the gate's entrance may have served to transmit the prayers of pilgrims to Amun, who "dwelt" within the temple.

North of here stands a **Small Temple**, reputedly sited where the primeval mound arose from the waters of Chaos, preceding the creator-god Re-Atum of the Hermopolitan Ogdoad. The existing structure was built and partly decorated by Hatshepsut, whose cartouches and images were erased by Tuthmosis III. Akhenaten did likewise to those of Amun, but Horemheb and Seti replaced them. Some defaced reliefs [a] show Tuthmosis presiding over the foundation ceremonies, "stretching the cord" before the goddess Seshat, "scattering the gypsum" and then "hacking the earth" before a priapic Min.

Whereas the Small Temple antedates Ramses' work by three centuries, the **Chapels of the Votaresses** are Late Period additions. Several date from the XXV Dynasty of Nubian kings, who appointed these high priestesses of Amun and de facto governors of Thebes. The best reliefs are in the forecourt [b] and shrine of Amenirdis, sister of King Shabaka, whose alabaster funerary statue is now in the Cairo Museum. Ironically, these chapels remained objects of veneration long after Ramses' temple had been abandoned.

In the right-hand corner of the enclosure are the remains of a **Sacred Lake** where childless local women came to bathe at night and pray to Isis for conception. Behind this lies a ruined **Nilometer**, once fed by a canal from the river. Originally, this whole area was a garden.

Entering the Mortuary Temple of Ramses III

Like Deir el-Bahri and the Ramesseum, this mortuary temple was a focus for the pharaoh's cult, linking him to Amun-United-with-Eternity. The effigies of Amun, Mut and Khonsu paid an annual visit during the Festival of the Valley, while other deities permanently resided in its shrines. Ramses himself often dwelt in the adjacent palace, his Libyan and Sardinian bodyguard billeted nearby. Aside from its lack of freestanding colossi, the sandstone temple gives a good idea of how the Ramesseum must have looked before it collapsed.

Had it not lost its cornice and one corner, the **First Pylon** would match Luxor Temple's in size. For *baksheesh*, a guard may unlock a stairway to the top,

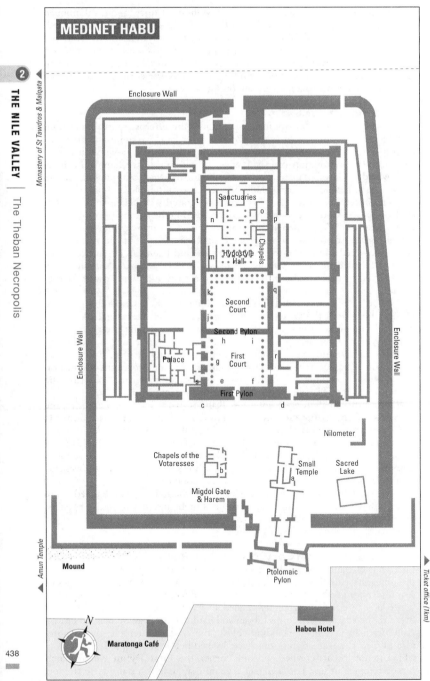

MEDINET HABU

Monastery of St Tawdros & Malqata

Enclosure Wall

t

Sanctuaries

n   o

p

Chapels

m   Hypostyle
Hall

k   q

Second
Court

j

Second Pylon

h   i

Palace   g   First
Court

s   e   f   r

First Pylon

c   d

Nilometer

Chapels of the
Votaresses   Small
Temple   Sacred
b   Lake

Migdol Gate
& Harem

a

Enclosure Wall   Enclosure Wall

Amun Temple

Mound   Ptolomaic
Pylon

Habou Hotel

Maratonga Café

N

Ticket office (1km)

▼ Amenophes Hotel

which offers a panoramic view of the temple, Theban Hills and Nile Valley. Reliefs on the outer walls (copied from the Ramesseum) show Ramses smiting Nubians **[c]** and Syrians **[d]**, though he never warred with either. Those on the inner wall relate genuine campaigns with Ramessid hyperbole. An outsized Ramses scatters hordes of Libyans in his chariot **[e]**. Afterwards, scribes tally the severed hands and genitals of dead foes (third row from the bottom) **[f]**.

Until the nineteenth century, the ruined houses of Coptic Djeme filled the **First Court**, now cleared to reveal its flanking columns. Those on the right bear chunky Osiride statues of the king, attended by knee-high queens. The other side of the court abuts the royal palace (now ruined and entered from outside). In the middle of this wall was a Window of Appearances **[g]** flanked by reliefs of prisoners' heads, whence the king rewarded loyal commanders with golden collars. Yet more scenes of triumph cover the outside of the **Second Pylon**, where Ramses leads six rows of prisoners to Amun and Mut **[h]** (those in the third row are Philistines) and a long inscription lauds his victories in Asia Minor **[i]**. The winged cobras and sun-discs on the ceiling of the pylon's gateway are still coloured.

Halls and sanctuaries

During Coptic times most of the Osiride pillars were removed to make room for a church, and a thick layer of mud was plastered over the reliefs in the **Second Court**. Now uncovered, these depict the annual festivals of Min **[j]** and Sokar **[k]**, with processions of priests and dancers accompanying the royal palanquin, the original colouring still intact. Elsewhere, the events of Ramses' fifth regnal year are related in a long text lower down the wall **[l]**.

The now-roofless **Hypostyle Hall**, beyond, once had a raised central aisle like the Great Hall at Karnak, and still has some brightly coloured pillars at the back. To the right lie five **chapels** dedicated to Ramses, his XIX Dynasty namesake, Ptah, Osiris and Sokar. On the opposite side are several (locked) treasure chambers whose reliefs show the weighing of myrrh, gold, lapis lazuli and other valuables bestowed upon the temple **[m]** – also visible on the outer walls.

Beyond this lie two **smaller halls** with rooms leading off. To the left of the first hall is the funerary chamber of Ramses III **[n]**, where Thoth inscribes his name on the sacred tree of Heliopolis. The other side – open to the sky – featured an altar to Re. On the lintels that once supported the roof **[o]**, Ramses and several baboons worship Re's barque. The central aisle of the next hall is flanked by statues of Ramses with Maat or Thoth. At the back are three **sanctuaries** dedicated to the Theban Triad of Mut (left), Amun (centre) and Khonsu (right). The false door behind the central one was for the use of Ramses' *ka*.

Along the outer walls

Some of the best reliefs at Medinet Habu are on the **outer walls** of the temple, involving a fair slog over broken ground. As most are quite faint, they're best viewed early or late in the day, when shadows reveal details obscured at midday. The famous **battle reliefs of Ramses II** run along the temple's northern wall, starting from the back. Although you'll encounter the last or middle scenes first, we've listed them in chronological order, as Ramses intended them to be seen. The first section **[p]** depicts the invasion of land-hungry Libyans, early in his reign. In the vanguard of the battle are Ramses, a lion, and the standard of Amun. Afterwards, scribes count limbs and genitals to assess each soldier's reward in gold or land. Yet despite this victory, Ramses was soon beleaguered on two fronts, as the Libyans joined with the Sea Peoples (Sardinians, Philistines and Cretans) in a concerted invasion of the Nile Delta. A giant Ramses fires arrows into a melee of grappling ships, in the only Egyptian relief of a sea battle **[q]**. A third invasion by the Libyans **[r]** was also thwarted, but their descendants would eventually triumph and rule Egypt as the XXIII and XXIV dynasties.

On the other side of the temple behind the First Pylon is a dramatic relief of Ramses hunting antelopes in the desert and impaling wild bulls in a marsh **[s]**, near a ruined **Palace** where he resided during visits. A calendar of festivals appears at the far end of the temple **[t]**, which is surrounded on three sides by mud-brick **storehouses**, eroded into worm-like shapes.

Other sites on the west bank

The village of **NAG LOHLAH** beside the temple will be familiar to readers of Richard Critchfield's *Shahhat* as the birthplace of its eponymous hero and the irascible Hagg Ali, owner of the *Habou Hotel* (which still exists, though Hagg is deceased). Most families have one foot in tourism and the other in farming, so that one finances the other as fortune allows. While Medinet Habu brings customers to their doorsteps – the *Maratonga Café* is ideal for cooling off – few visitors realise there's also an **Amun Temple** in someone's backyard (no set hours; admission free). Though small and knocked about, its reliefs are colourful, particularly the white background that has faded in other temples.

If it's not too hot, the Monastery of St Tawdros in the desert beyond Medinet Habu makes an interesting excursion. You can walk there in about twenty minutes, or cycle; even better, go riding in time for sunset. Be sure to cover your head and bring plenty of water; the unpaved track from Medinet Habu to the French House is easy going, but has no shade at all.

Monastery of St Tawdros

Roughly 200m right off the track into the desert, the **Monastery of St Tawdros** is easily identified by its beehive domes. Pharaonic, Greek and Roman masonry is incorporated into the low-vaulted church, whose shrines are dedicated to the Coptic martyrs Tawdros, Elkladius and Foktor. Tawdros (295–306 AD) was a leader in the Roman army before his conversion to Christianity, hence the monastery's alternative name, *El Muharrib* ("The Warrior"). The day of his martyrdom (January 20) and Easter see crowds of Copts descending on the monastery, but at other times the nuns who live there receive few visitors and seem pleased if anyone rings the bell.

Malqata

Further on, the **French House** stands guard over the scant **remains of Malqata**. This legendary pleasure palace built by Amenophis III had an artificial harbour linked to the Nile, for the royal family to arrive on its barge, *Aten Gleams*. Today the only visible remains are a depression flanked by parallel mounds and low foundation walls, but archeologists from Waseda University have analyzed thousands of flakes of paint and stucco, to visually reconstruct the paintings on the walls and ceilings of the king's bedroom and harem chambers (see Ⓦwww.waseda.ac.jp/projects/egypt).

Riziq

Travelling further afield is difficult, for police checkpoints seldom let tourists stray outside the security zone surrounding the Necropolis. However, many of the service taxis that carry pilgrims from Gezira to the **Moulid of St George** in the town of **RIZIQ** (also known as Razagat) – 15km south – travel by a desert track that avoids the checkpoints. Attended by Copts and Muslims alike, the moulid is certainly not for the squeamish, as the circumcision of infants and the slaughter of animals play a major role in events. Held in and around the town's **Monastery of St George** (*Mari Girgis*), it lasts for nearly a week, climaxing on November 11. Otherwise, the town is the start of the **road to Kharga Oasis** that is now open to tourists without restrictions, allowing rapid travel from Luxor to the oases for the first time (see p.384).

Esna

Small-town life and ancient stone are boldly juxtaposed at **ESNA**, where a huge pit in the centre of town exposes part of the **Temple of Khnum**. Some visitors are disappointed by what they find: the only part to have been excavated is the Hypostyle Hall, whose somewhat inferior reliefs detract from the forest of columns and lofty astronomical ceiling. That said, Esna is worth a stopover en route to the fabulous **temple at Edfu** if you can arrange it, but unless you care to visit the early Saturday morning **animal market**, there's no reason to linger after seeing the temple, which takes less than an hour.

Visible just north of Esna are two **barrages** that act as bridges over the Nile. The nearest was built by the British in 1906 as part of a grand scheme to tame the Nile, with barrages at four points along its length. In the 1990s, the river was further exploited by an Italian-built hydroelectric barrage, known to locals as the "Electricity Bridge". Both barrages have **locks** to allow vessels to pass through, while trucks and carts trundle across the top. Now that cruise boats no longer moor on the Esna's Corniche for passengers to visit the temple, salesmen throw their wares on to the decks for sunbathing tourists to inspect and hope that the cash doesn't fall in the water.

For overland travellers, Esna is the "border" between the Qena and Aswan governorates, whose respective **police** forces pass over the responsibility for escorting convoys here (hence the delay). Their reaction to independent travellers arriving in their midst or wanting to leave is hard to predict. It may depend on which direction you're travelling in, since Esna's police are more concerned with foreigners on their own territory than tourists entering the Aswan governorate.

If they make you wait for a convoy, it's diverting to read Gustave Flaubert's account of the courtesan Kuchuk Hanem entertaining him at her home in Esna by dancing "The Bee" (see "Books" in Contexts).

Practicalities

Esna lies on the west bank of the Nile 54km south of Luxor and 155km north of Aswan. Sadly for the local economy tourism tends to bypass Esna, as **cruise boats** merely pass through the locks, while travellers on **feluccas** from Aswan disembark 30km short of Esna to drive directly to Luxor, and low-budget hotels in Luxor no longer feature it on day excursions to Edfu and Kom Ombo **by private taxi**. If you're still determined, expect to pay about £E100 for a four-seater cab, and be sure to check beforehand which (if any) of the tourist convoys include a stop at Esna.

Getting there by **train** is awkward, as the station is on the east bank of the Nile, far from the temple, and not all trains stop at Esna anyway. **Buses** are handier, with four a day from Luxor and Aswan, which drop you in the centre of town, just under 1km from the temple. You're unlikely to be able to reach Esna by **service taxi** from Luxor or Aswan, but people sometimes manage it from Edfu or Kom Ombo. The taxi depot is situated around the curve of the canal from the bus station, but passengers are often dropped off on the main thoroughfare into the centre, where *caleche* drivers wait for customers, asking £E5 each way for the ten-minute drive to the temple.

To reach the temple on foot, you can either follow the Corniche south past the empty cruiser berths, or surrender yourself to the flow of the crowd through the souk, until you reach the sandbagged **police** station. Backtrack one block and turn right down a side street, which should bring you out by the temple. Another advantage of the riverside route is that it takes you past some old *mashrabiya* houses, a **bank** (daily except Fri 8.30am–2pm; during Ramadan 10am–1.30pm) and a **post office** (daily except Fri 7am–2pm). The **tourist police** are near the temple ticket booth, further down the Corniche.

With Luxor so close, there's no reason to stay in Esna, particularly as its only **hotel** is the filthy *El-Haramin* (no phone; ❶), 800m past a café near the cruise berths. A humble place on the corner by the temple serves **meals**, and street food is sold in the souk.

The Temple of Khnum

When Amelia Edwards visited Esna, the **Temple of Khnum** (daily 7am–5pm; £E20) was "buried to the chin in the accumulated rubbish of a score of centuries" and built over with houses.

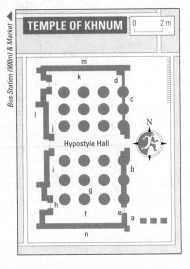

TEMPLE OF KHNUM

To minimize their destruction, only a portion was excavated in the 1860s. Now 10m below ground level, the temple resembles a pharaonic Fort Knox: its boxy mass fronted by six columns rising from a screen, the open space above them covered with wire mesh to discourage nesting birds. Tickets are sold at the riverside kiosk beyond the covered tourist bazaar, which runs between the temple and the river, five minutes' walk from the souk.

A Ptolemaic-Roman replacement for a much older structure dedicated to the ram-headed creator-god of ancient myth, the temple faced eastwards and probably rivalled Edfu's for size. Since what you see is merely the Roman section (dating from the first century AD), the **facade** bears the cartouches of Claudius **[a]**, Titus **[b]** and Vespasian **[c]**, and the battered sun-disc above the entrance is flanked by votive inscriptions to these emperors.

Entering the lofty **Hypostyle Hall**, your eyes are drawn upwards by a forest of columns that bud and flower in variegated capitals. Their shafts are covered with festival texts (now defaced) or hieroglyphs in the form of crocodiles **[d]** or rams **[e]**. One is a *Hymn of Creation* that acknowledges Khnum as the creator of all, even foreigners:"All are formed on his potter's wheel, their speech different in every region . . . but the lord of the wheel is their father too."

The hall's **astronomical ceiling** rivals Dendara's for finesse and complexity, but gloom, soot and distemper render much indiscernible. However, the zodiac register **[f]** visibly crawls with two-headed snakes, winged dogs and other

Khnum and Hapy

In Upper Egypt, **Khnum** was originally the ram-headed creator-god who moulded man on a potter's wheel and the guardian of the Nile's source (which myth assigned to the caves just beyond the First Cataract, although the Ancient Egyptians must have known better).

Later, however, Khnum was demoted to an underling of Amun-Re and shared his role as river deity with **Hapy**, god of the Nile in flood, who was also believed to dwell in an island cavern near the First Cataract. Shown with a blue-green body and a female breast, wearing a crown of lotus or sedge (the heraldic plants of Upper and Lower Egypt), he should not be confused with Horus's son, Hapi, the ape-headed deity of canopic jars.

▲ Khum

▲ Hapy

creatures. Notice the pregnant hippo-goddess Tweri (whom the Greeks called Thoeris), and the scorpion in the next aisle **[g]**. Registers on the walls below show Septimus Severus, Caracalla and Geta before the gods.

The last Roman emperor mentioned is Decius **[h]**, whose persecution of Christians (249–51) anticipated the "Era of Martyrs" under Diocletian. Further along **[i]** is the cartouche of Ptolemy VI Philometor (Mother Lover), whose father began the construction of Esna temple. To the right of the portal, Decius makes offerings to Khnum, including a potter's wheel **[j]**. The liveliest reliefs are near the foot of the northern wall **[k]**, where Khnum, Horus and Emperor Commodus net fish and malignant spirits. To the left of this tableau stands an ibis-headed Thoth; to the right, Sheshat, goddess of writing. Around the outer walls of the temple are texts dedicated to Marcus Aurelius **[l]** and stiffly executed scenes of Titus, Domitian and Trajan smiting Egypt's foes before the gods **[m** and **n]**. Several stone blocks from an early Christian church lie in front of the temple.

Edfu and around

The provincial town of **EDFU** boasts the best-preserved **cult temple** in Egypt, dedicated to the falcon-headed god **Horus** (see p.447). Though actually built in the Ptolemaic era, this mammoth edifice respects all the canons of pharaonic architecture, giving an excellent idea of how most temples once looked. In terms of sheer monumental grandeur, it ranks alongside Karnak and Deir el-Bahri as one of the finest sites in the Nile Valley. A "must see" for backpackers and package tourists alike – on every cruise boat or felucca itinerary – it has saved Edfu from the fate of Esna.

The same can't be said of other sites, which had few visitors even before travel restrictions made getting there more difficult, but if deserted ruins are your thing, **El-Kab** fits the bill; **Silsilah** makes an interesting stopover on felucca journeys between Aswan and Edfu; and **Kom al-Ahmar** deserves a mention even if visits aren't permitted.

Edfu practicalities

Situated on the west bank of the Nile, roughly equidistant from Luxor (115km) and Aswan (105km) and 65km north of Kom Ombo, Edfu is most easily

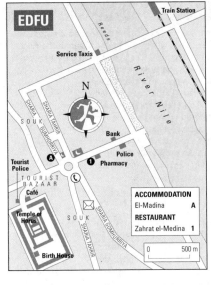

▲ *Cruise boat moorings*

reached **by taxi** in a convoy. The official rates from Luxor to Edfu and Kom Ombo are £E275 for a four-seater taxi, £E475 for a larger one, or £1100 for a minibus, but *Happy Land Hotel* (see p.369) can do a small car for £E180 and a minibus for £E330. While foreigners remain barred from using service taxis, the only other way of getting there is by bus or train. Awkwardly, the **train** station is on the east bank of the Nile, 4km from the temple, and **buses** travelling between Aswan and Luxor either drop passengers there or on the highway, from where you'll need to catch a covered pick-up to the bridge and then another into town (each costs 25pt), or rent one for the entire journey to the main square, five minutes' walk from the temple.

Arriving by river is a different story, as **cruise boats** moor far from the temple, to be met by *caleche*s. Since a branch of the Brooke Hospital was set up in Edfu, drivers have stopped whipping their horses to get there and back as fast as possible. The ride costs £E15–20, depending on your bargaining skills. **Feluccas** are also moored away from the centre, so their passengers may have to use *caleches* too.

Sharia al-Maglis, Edfu's main street, leads past a **police** station and a **bank** (Mon–Thurs & Sun 8.30am–2pm) to a circular junction named **Temple Square**. Further along, the temple lies off the tourist bazaar; the **tourist police** are based at the site entrance. Edfu's fruit and vegetable souk occupies an area of Tahrir and Gumhorriya streets, with the former continuing south into a textiles souk, while Gumhorriya carries on past the **post office** (daily except Fri 8am–2.30pm).

Avoid staying in Edfu, as the *El-Madina* **hotel** (☏097/471-1326; ❶) is quite filthy. The *Zahrat el-Medina* **restaurant** on Sharia al-Maglis serves basic chicken and vegetable dishes, or you can buy *fuul* and grilled fish in the fruit and vegetable market – ask the price first.

Leaving Edfu can be difficult. The police don't like foreigners waiting for buses on the highway, nor catching trains, and may insist that you hang around drinking tea with them until the next convoy is due, before putting you on a bus.

The Temple of Horus

The **site** (daily 7am–4pm; £E35) is a huge excavated compound overlooked by mud-brick houses and catcalling children. Ahead stretch the sandstone enclosure walls and towering pylon of the **Temple of Horus**, which lay buried to its lintels until the 1860s, when Auguste Mariette cleared the main building; a splendid drawing by David Roberts shows the courtyard full of sand and peasant houses built atop the Hypostyle Hall. Yet the mammoth task of excavation was nothing compared to the temple's construction, which outlasted six Ptolemies, the final touches being added by the twelfth ruler of that dynasty.

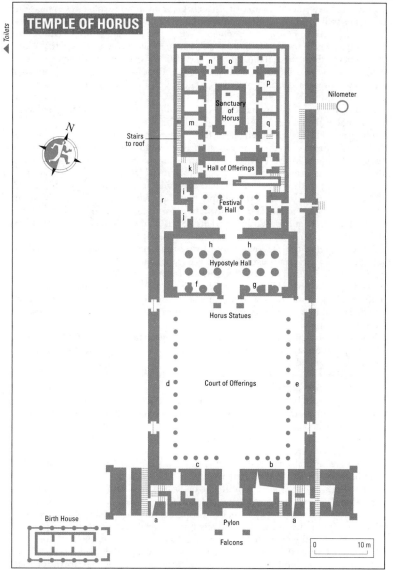

TEMPLE OF HORUS

▲ Entrance & Café

▲ Toilets

N

Stairs
to roof

Nilometer

n   o

p

Sanctuary
of
Horus

m   q

k   Hall of Offerings

i

r   Festival
Hall

j

h   h

Hypostyle Hall

f   g

Horus Statues

d   Court of Offerings   e

c   b

Birth House

a   a

Pylon

Falcons

0   10 m

Modern-day visitors approach the temple from the rear and have to walk its
full length in order to enter through a gate in the pylon, fronted by two giant
black-granite **falcons**. The **Pylon** was erected by Ptolemy IX before he was
ousted from power by his brother Alexander, who was later usurped by another
ruler, for its exterior reliefs show Neos Dionysos smiting foes before Horus the
Elder **[a]**.

Entering the immense **Court of Offerings**, you can study the festival reliefs on the inner walls of the pylon, which continue around the court along the bottom of the wall. In the *Feast of the Beautiful Meeting*, Horus's barque tows Hathor's to the temple, where the deities retire to the sanctuary after suitable rituals **[b]**. Later they emerge from the temple, embark and drift downstream to the edge of the Edfu nome, where Horus takes his leave **[c]**. Beneath the western colonnade, Ptolemy IX makes offerings to Horus, Hathor and Ihy **[d]**; his successor appears before the Edfu Triad across the way **[e]**. However, most visitors are content to photograph the pair of **Horus statues** outside the Hypostyle Hall **[f]**. One hawk stands higher than a man, the other lies legless in the dust.

The great **Hypostyle Hall** dates from the reign of Ptolemy VII (145–116 BC), known to his contemporaries as "Fatty". With a torch, you can examine two small rooms in the entrance wall: the Chamber of Consecrations, where the king or his priestly stand-in dressed for rituals **[f]**; and a Library of sacred texts adorned with a relief of Sheshat, the goddess of writing **[g]**. The reliefs showing the foundation of the temple and the deification of Horus **[h]** have been mutilated by iconoclasts. From here on you encounter the oldest section of the temple, begun by Ptolemy III in 237 BC and completed 25 years later by his son, who styled himself Philopator (Father Lover).

Try to imagine the shadowy halls during the annual festivals rhapsodized in temple texts, when the **Festival Hall** was decorated with faïence, strewn with flowers and herbs and perfumed by myrrh. Incense and unguents were blended according to recipes inscribed on the walls of the Laboratory **[i]**. Nonperishable offerings were stored in the room next door **[j]**, while libations, fruit and sacrificial animals were brought in through a passageway connected to the outside world.

The sacred barques of Horus and Hathor appear in glorious detail on either side of the doorway into the **Hall of Offerings**. During the New Year Festival, Horus was carried up the ascending stairway **[k]** to the rooftop; after being revitalized by the sun-disc, his statue was returned to the sanctuary via the descending stairway **[l]**. The ritual is depicted on the walls of both stairways, but you'll need a torch, and locked gates may prevent you from going far. Otherwise, carry on to the **Sanctuary of Horus**, containing a shrine of polished black granite and an offerings table. Reliefs on the lower half of the right-hand wall show Philopator entering the sanctuary and worshipping Horus, Hathor and his deified parents.

There are several chambers worth noting off the corridor surrounding the sanctuary. The Linen Room **[m]** is flanked by chapels to Min and the Throne of the Gods, while a suite nominally dedicated to Osiris contains colourful scenes of Horus receiving offerings **[n]**, a life-size replica of Horus's barque **[o]** and reliefs of his avatars **[p]**. Equally arresting is the **New Year Chapel**, with a blue-coloured relief of the sky-goddess Nut stretched across its ceiling **[q]**.

Returning to the Festival Hall, you can gain access to an external corridor running between the inner and outer walls, where the priesthood tallied tithes assessed on the basis of readings from the temple's own **Nilometer**. On the other side are tableaux from the Triumph of Horus over Seth, depicting Mystery Plays in which Seth was cast as a hippopotamus, lurking beneath his brother's boat **[r]**. At the end of the play, the priests cut up and ate a hippo-shaped cake, to destroy Seth completely.

Don't miss the colonnaded **Birth House**, a focus for the annual Coronation Festival re-enacting the divine birth of Horus and the reigning pharaoh. Around the back of the building are reliefs of Horus being suckled by Isis, both as a baby (low down on the rear wall) and as a young man (on the inside of the columns).

The cult of Horus

Originally the sky-god of the Nile Valley, whose eyes were the sun and moon, the falcon deity **Horus** was soon assimilated into the Osirian myth as the child of Isis and Osiris (see p.352 and p.486). Raised in the swamps of the Delta by Isis and Hathor, Horus set out to avenge his father's murder by his uncle Seth. During their titanic struggle at Edfu, Horus lost an eye and Seth his testicles. Despite this, Seth almost prevailed until Isis intervened on her son's behalf and Osiris pronounced judgement upon them from the netherworld, exiling Seth back to the wilderness and awarding the throne to Horus. Thus good triumphed over evil and Osiris "lived" through his son.

▲ Horus

All pharaohs claimed to be the incarnation of Horus the "living king" and reaffirmed their divine oneness in an annual **Festival of Coronation**. A live falcon was taken from the sacred aviary, crowned in the central court and then placed in an inner chamber where it "reigned" in the dark for a year as the symbol of the living king. Another event, sometimes called the **Festival of Triumph**, commemorated the Contendings of Seth and Horus in a series of Mystery Plays. At the equally lavish **Feast of the Beautiful Meeting**, his wet nurse and wife Hathor sailed from Dendara aboard the *Lady of the Lake* to be met near Edfu by his own barque, *The First Horus*. Public ceremonies preceded their conjugal encounters in the privacy of the temple's sanctuary. Besides these festivals, Horus also underwent a reunion with the sun-disc at New Year, similar to Hathor's at Dendara.

To complicate the cult of Horus still further, he was also associated with the Divine Ennead of Heliopolis and another variant of the Creation myth. Having distinguished the Osirian Horus from the Heliopolitan deity by terming the latter **Horus the Elder**, the Egyptians split him into archetypes such as **Herakhte** (often conjoined with Re), **Hariesis** (stressing his kinship to Isis) and **Haroeris** (see p.449). His priesthood asserted a place for Horus in the Creation myth by crediting him with building the first house amidst swamps at the dawn of the world, or even laying the Cosmic Egg whence the sun-god hatched. In rituals associated with the **Myth of the Great Cackler**, they launched a goose onto the sacred lake near Edfu temple, whose egg contained air and the potential for life – crucial elements in the world's creation.

Around Edfu: El-Kab, Kom al-Ahmar and Silsilah

Fifteen kilometres downriver from Edfu, the east bank road between Luxor and Kom Ombo passes the site known as **EL-KAB**, once the ancient city of *Nekheb*, dedicated to the vulture-goddess of Upper Egypt. Only opened to tourists in the late 1980s, the scattered ruins are meagre compared to other sites and you have to be pretty keen to bother. Tickets are sold from a kiosk by the highway, which bisects the site. Buses from Aswan or Luxor can drop you there on request, or you can catch a pick-up from Edfu.

The most conspicuous part of **the site** (daily 7am–5pm; £E20) lies towards the Nile, where the vast mud-brick **walls** that once enclosed the city stand, along with the conjoined **temples** of Nekhbet and Thoth, now reduced to stumps of painted columns and a series of **crypts** (notable for a scene of baboons dancing to the rituals of Mut). Across the road and up the slope from the ticket office, other ruins are scattered eastwards across the desert. You may not fancy hiking 3.5km to a small Chapel of Thoth and a Ptolemaic Temple of Nekhbet, but there are four **tombs** dug into the nearest ridge of hills. The best preserved is that of **Daheri**, royal scribe and tutor, and son of Tuthmosis I, which features ranks of lotus-sniffers and field workers. Next door are the lacklustre tombs of **Setau**, high priest of Nekhbet, and the commander **Aahmes**; superintendent **Renini** has a sprucer tomb, to the left.

On the far side of the Nile lies another site – **off-limits** to tourists – known as **Kom Al-Ahmar** (Red Mound), which the ancient Egyptians called *Nekhen* and the Greeks **Hierakonopolis** (City of the Falcon). As its names suggest, the city was closely associated with Horus and an earlier, local falcon-god, Nekheny. It flourished during the late predynastic and early dynastic periods (c.4000–2686 BC) and may have been the first administrative capital of the Two Lands, judging by such famous artefacts as the Palette of Narmer and the Scorpion Macehead – though vital evidence was lost during the first, poorly recorded excavation, which later generations of archeologists have tried to recover from other digs. Recent finds include Egypt's earliest cult-temple (a timber-framed structure fronted by cedar-wood pillars) and brewery (beer was one of the "four libations" offered to the gods). For news of current excavations by Renee Friedman of the British Museum, see Ⓦwww.hierakonopolis and Ⓦwww.archaeology.org.

Travelling between Edfu and Kom Ombo by felucca, you'll pass a succession of ancient quarries, most notably at **Silsilah**, where the river is constricted by sheer cliffs and the bedrock changes from Egyptian limestone to Nubian sandstone. The site's ancient name, *Khenu* (Place of Rowing), suggests that rapids once existed here during the season of inundation. If your boatman is willing to stop, the most imposing **quarries** lie on the east bank, approached by a narrow defile down which cut stones were dragged to waiting barges. Workmen's graffiti covers the rocks, while two formal inscriptions record the cutting of stone for Aten's temple at Karnak, and the reopening of the quarry early last century to provide stone for the Esna Barrage. Across the Nile are 32 rock-hewn **shrines** dedicated to officials, priests, and pharaohs Merneptah and Horemheb.

Kom Ombo

Thirty kilometres before Aswan, the arid hills of the Eastern Desert recede from the river banks and bumper crops of sugar cane are harvested on reclaimed land. Here, too, around the town of **KOM OMBO**, many of the **Nubians** displaced by Lake Nasser have settled. In ancient times this town stood at the crossroads of the caravan route from Nubia and trails from the gold mines of the Eastern Desert; under Ptolemy VI (180–145 BC), it became the capital of the Ombos nome and a training depot for African war elephants, which the Ptolemies required to fight the pachyderms of the Seleucid empire.

While modern-day Kom Ombo is known to the *fellaheen* for its sugar refinery and felucca-building yards, tourists associate it with the Ptolemaic **Temple of Haroeris and Sobek**. Unlike other temples in the valley, this still stands beside the Nile, making the approach by river one of the highlights of a felucca journey or Nile cruise.

Practicalities

Kom Ombo lies along the east bank "highway" between Luxor (170km) and Aswan (45km), roughly 60km south of Edfu. Since the temple is 4km from town, it's preferable to arrive on a felucca or cruise boat that moors nearby, rather than face the hassle of **getting there** by other means. Tourist coaches and private taxis must travel in a **convoy**, and foreigners can't use service taxis from Luxor or Aswan, so independent travellers must rely on buses (4–5 daily) or trains between Luxor and Aswan, which call at Kom Ombo. Coming from Aswan, ask the driver to drop you at the signposted turn-off before town, from where you can walk or hitch 1.5km to the temple. Otherwise, covered pick-ups (25pt) run from the town's service taxi depot to a ferry landing stage on the Nile, 800m walk from the temple, or you can get a private taxi directly to the site for about £E20.

The local **police** aren't keen on tourists wandering around town and try to confine boat passengers to the vicinity of the temple, so **staying** in Kom Ombo is out of the question. In town, the *Restaurant El-Noba*, south of the mosque, provides an alternative to **eating** at *fuul* and *taamiya* stands; near the temple is an outdoor café called *Rural Home*, with a herb garden, *shaduf* irrigation, henna-tattooing and other diversions. **Internet** and international phone lines are available in a kiosk near the Nile.

The Temple of Haroeris and Sobek

The **Temple of Haroeris and Sobek** stands on a low promontory near a bend in the river whose sandbanks were a basking place for crocodiles in ancient times. This proximity to the Nile has both preserved and damaged the **site** (daily 7am–5pm; £E20), covering the temple with sand which protected it from Coptic iconoclasts, but also washing away its pylon and forecourt, and undermining columns within the temple. What remains was aptly described by Amelia Edwards as a "magnificent torso"; truncated and roofless, it is still imposing, with traces of its original paint.

However, its main characteristic is its bisymmetry, with twin entrances and sanctuaries, and halls that are nominally divided down the middle. The left side is dedicated to the falcon-headed Haroeris, the "Good Doctor" (a form of Horus the Elder) and his consort Ta-Sent-Nefer, the "Good Sister" (an aspect of Hathor). The crocodile-god Sobek (here identified with the sun as Sobek-Re), his wife (another form of Hathor) and their son Khonsu-Hor are honoured on the right side of the temple.

Visitors approach the temple at right angles to its main axis, via an entrance by the **Gate of Neos Dionysos**. Only half of this gateway still stands and its provenance is obscure, as scholars disagree over the number, order and dates of the various Ptolemies, each of whom adopted a title such as Soter (Saviour), Euergetes (Benefactor) or Philometor (Mother Lover). Some identify Neos Dionysos as Ptolemy XII, others as Ptolemy XIII; however, there's general agreement that he fathered the great Cleopatra, had an interrupted reign (80–58 and 55–51 BC) and was nicknamed "The Bastard".

Before entering the temple you can pop into the **Chapel of Hathor** to see three **mummified crocodiles**, found nearby during roadworks in the 1970s.

The facade and Hypostyle Halls

With the forecourt (added by Trajan in 14 AD) reduced to low walls and stumps of pillars, your eyes are drawn to the **facade** of the Hypostyle Hall. Rising from a screen wall, its surviving columns burst in floral capitals beneath a chunk of cavetto cornice bearing a winged sun-disc and twin *uraei* above each portal. Bas-reliefs on the outer wall show Neos Dionysos being purified by Thoth and Horus **[a]**, and yet again in the presence of Sobek, whose face has been chiselled away **[b]**.

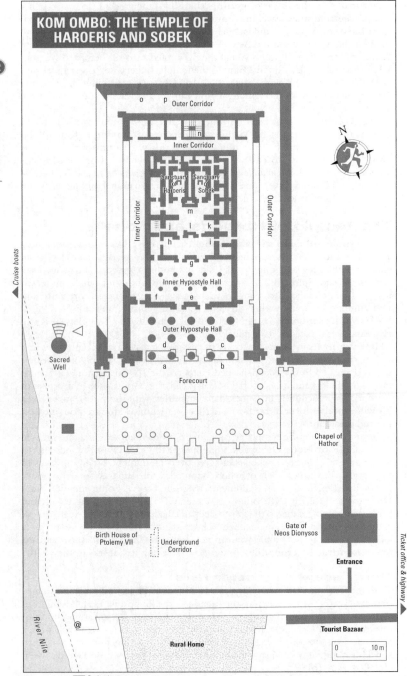

KOM OMBO: THE TEMPLE OF HAROERIS AND SOBEK

Outer Corridor

o   p

Inner Corridor

n

Inner Corridor

Sanctuary of Haroeris   Sanctuary of Sobek

Outer Corridor

m

j   l   k

h   i

g

Inner Hypostyle Hall

f   e

Outer Hypostyle Hall

d   c

a   b

Sacred Well

Forecourt

Chapel of Hathor

Cruise boats

River Nile

Birth House of Ptolemy VII   Underground Corridor

Gate of Neos Dionysos

Entrance

@

Rural Home

Tourist Bazaar

0   10 m

Ticket office & highway

▼ Cruise boats

N

Wandering amidst the thicket of columns inside the **outer Hypostyle Hall**, notice the heraldic lily of Upper Egypt or the papyrus symbol of the Delta carved on their bases. On the inner wall of the facade are splendid carvings of Neos Dionysos's coronation before Haroeris, Sobek, Wadjet and Nekhbet (the goddesses of the north and south) **[c]**, and his appearance before Isis, Horus the Elder and a lion-headed deity **[d]**. Neos Dionysos makes offerings to the same deities at the back of the hall, whose right side retains much of its roof, decorated with flying vultures.

Entering the older, **inner Hypostyle Hall**, you'll find a relief of Sobek in his reptilian form between the portals **[e]**. Ptolemy II receives the *hps* (sword of victory) from Haroeris (accompanied by his sister Cleopatra and his wife of the same name) in the southwest corner of the hall **[f]** and makes offerings to gods on the shafts of the pillars, while his elder brother does likewise to Haroeris at the back of the hall, where a list of temple deities and festivals appears between the doors **[g]**.

Vestibules and sanctuaries

Beyond lies the first of three, now roofless, **vestibules** (each of which sits a little higher than the preceding one) decorated by Ptolemy VI. Scenes at the back depict the foundation of the temple, with Sheshat, goddess of writing, measuring its dimensions **[h]**; and offerings and libations to Sobek **[i]**. To maintain the temple in a state of purity, these rituals were periodically repeated. Only priests were admitted to the next vestibule, which served as the **Hall of Offerings**. The ruined chamber to the right once held vestments and sacred texts, as at Edfu and Dendara. Offerings to Haroeris **[j]**, a description of the temple and an address to Sobek **[k]** appear on the southern wall, which also features a tiny relief of a woman giving birth, at roughly chest height **[l]**. Notice the painted vultures on the ceiling, too.

A fine relief between the doors of the sanctuaries **[m]** shows Ptolemy and his sister-wife being presented with a palm stalk from which hangs a *heb-sed* sign representing the years of his reign. Khonsu does the honours, wearing a blue crescent and red disc, followed by Haroeris and Sobek (representing air and water, respectively); Ptolemy himself sports a Macedonian cloak. Because so little remains of the **sanctuaries**, you can glimpse a secret corridor between them, whence the priests would "speak" for the gods; accessible via an underground crypt in one of the **shrines** behind the inner corridor **[n]**.

The outer corridor and precincts

In the **outer corridor** between the Ptolemaic temple and its Roman enclosure wall, pilgrims scratched graffiti on the pavements to while away the time before their appointment with the Good Doctor, who was represented by a statue in the small niche behind the central chapel. The carved ears heard their pleas and the eyes symbolized the health they sought. Though these carvings have been gouged away by supplicant fingers, other reliefs are in better shape. One shows Marcus Aurelius offering a pectoral to Ta-Sent-Nefer, the Good Sister (aka Sennuphis) **[o]**. The other testifies to sophisticated surgery nearly 2000 years ago, depicting instruments such as scalpels, suction cups, dental tools and bone saws **[p]**.

Finally, you can wander around the temple grounds, where other rituals were once enacted. The most intriguing structure is a finely built **Sacred Well** with two stairways descending to its depths (now out of bounds), which drew its water from the Nile. The small **pool** nearby was used for raising sacred crocodiles. Another curiosity is the partially exposed **underground corridor** leading to the **Birth House of Ptolemy VII** – or what's left of it since half the ruins fell into the Nile in the nineteenth century. A few reliefs are faintly visible, notably the scene of Ptolemy IX and two gods in a papyrus thicket, observed by an ithyphallic Min-Amun-Re clutching lettuces (which symbolize fertility).

Darow

Traditionally, **DAROW** (pronounced "De-*rau*") marks the point where Egypt begins to shade into Nubia: a distinction underlined by its **camel market**, attended by tribesmen from the northern deserts of the Sudan, and by a remarkable Nubian house called the **Beit al-Kenzi**. Darow itself is a ramshackle sprawl of mud-brick compounds either side of the highway and railway line.

Although Darow is not a stopover for convoys or most taxi excursions, **getting there** from Aswan (37km) is straightforward, as lots of buses and all trains except sleepers call here. At present, you can't use service taxis from Aswan (40min) or Kom Ombo (10min), but private taxis in Darow might agree to take you to Kom Ombo Temple and back for £E20–30.

Darow Camel Market

The **Camel Market** (Souk el-Gamal) happens every **Tuesday** throughout the year, and maybe also on Sundays or Mondays over winter. Although hours (7am–2pm) remain constant, with activities winding down after 11am, the location of the market changes seasonally. Over winter, it's often held in two dusty compounds on the eastern outskirts of Darow (fifteen minutes' walk from the main intersection; cross the bridge, walk on past the cane fields and turn right down a lane flanked by mud-brick walls). During summer, it may take place on the other side of town beyond the fruit, vegetable and poultry souk – just follow the crowds. The giveaway is truckloads of camels bumping hither and thither along a dusty lane.

At the end you'll find several hundred camels with their forelegs hobbled in the traditional manner, and scores of drovers and buyers drinking tea and smoking *sheeshas* beneath awnings. As the principal camel market between Dongola and Cairo, Darow is a good place to do business. The camels spend two days in quarantine before being sold to *fellaheen* who need a beast of burden, or merchants

---

The last Forty Days Road

The camel trail from northern Sudan to Upper Egypt is one of the last great desert droving routes still active. The camels are reared in Sudan's Darfur and Kordofan provinces and herded 300–400km eastwards across the Libyan Desert to Dongola on the Nile, whence they follow the river into Egypt. Herdsmen call this month-long route the **Forty Days Road** (*Darb al-Arba'in*), perhaps from folk memory of the old slave trail from Kobbe to Assyut (see p.572), which was even longer and harder.

Now, as then, the drovers are usually Bishari or Rizayqat nomads, who sometimes appear at Egyptian markets in their traditional garb of flowing trousers, woollen cloak, dagger and sword. For what amounts to three months' work in atrocious conditions, each drover receives the equivalent of £100 sterling, the guide about £150. The camel owners are town-dwelling Sudanese merchants who fly up to supervise the sale, on which they can expect to make a profit of 500 percent. Some traders manage to avoid paying import tax by smuggling camels into Egypt and feeding them marijuana to keep them quiet while sneaking past border patrols.

who plan to sell the camels for a profit at Cairo's Bilesh market. Many are destined to end up on the dinner tables of the poor, or in a knackers' yard. The Souk el-Gamal coincides with a **livestock market** where donkeys, sheep and cows jostle for space with people and trucks amidst trampled mud and dung. In summer, the two markets are often held side by side, with **handicrafts** (as well as saddlery) also sometimes sold at the camel market throughout the winter.

Beit al-Kenzi

A cooler attraction is the **Beit al-Kenzi** – a fabulous house in the traditional Nubian style, built of mud-bricks and dom palms, with beehive domes, inner courtyards and spacious rooms divided by reed-lattice partitions, to allow air to circulate. Its rooms are furnished with Nubian artefacts and the exterior decorated with geometric patterns and ceramic plates. The house was built in 1912 by the grandfather of its present occupant so that his descendants would retain something of the ancestral village that was sacrificed to the first Aswan Dam. Its owner, Aid Mohammed Hassanein, is happy to show visitors around and talk about Nubian culture – indeed, he regrets that more tourists don't come. The house is beside the Gar Rasoul Mosque on Sharia al-Kunuz; turn right outside the train station, walk along the road and head left to find it.

Aswan and around

Egypt's southernmost city (population 256,000) and ancient frontier town has the loveliest setting on the Nile. At **ASWAN** the deserts close in on the river, confining its sparkling blue between smooth amber sand and rugged extrusions of granite bedrock. Lateen-sailed feluccas glide past the ancient ruins and gargantuan rocks of Elephantine Island, palms and tropical shrubs softening the islands and embankments till intense blue skies fade into soft-focus dusks. The city's **ambience** is palpably African; its Nubian inhabitants are lither and darker than the *Saiyidis*, with different tastes and customs. Although its own monuments are insignificant compared to Luxor's, Aswan is the base for **excursions** to the **temples of Philae and Kabasha**, near the great dams beyond the First Cataract, and the Sun Temple of Ramses II at **Abu Simbel**, far to the south. It can also serve for day trips to Darow Camel Market, Kom Ombo, Edfu and Esna – the main temples between here and Luxor. But the classic approach is to travel upriver by felucca, experiencing the Nile's moods and scenery as travellers have for millennia – or on a luxurious cruise, as tourists have since the nineteenth century. The ins-and-outs of **felucca journeys** and **Nile cruises** are described on pp.474–475 and pp.476–477. However, Aswan itself is so laid-back that one could easily spend a week here simply hanging out, never mind going anywhere – though many people try to pack everything into two days. The local **tourism** scene is much the same as in Luxor (see box on pp.364–365).

Climate

The time of year is a major influence on people's level of activity. Situated near the Tropic of Cancer, Aswan is hot and dry nearly all the time, with average daily **temperatures** ranging from a delicious 23–30°C in the winter to a searing 38–54°C over summer. In late January and early February, hordes of Egyptians visit Aswan, block-booking hotels and seats on trains from Luxor and Cairo. Late autumn and spring are the perfect times to visit, being less crowded than the peak winter period, yet not so enervating as summer, when long siestas, cold showers and air conditioning commend themselves and the number of tourists dwindles.

Aswan in history

Elephantine Island – opposite modern Aswan in the Nile – has been settled since remotest antiquity, and its fortress-town of *Yebu* (or *Abu*) became the border post between Egypt and Nubia early in the Old Kingdom. Local governors, known as the "Guardians of the Southern Gates", were responsible for

Nubia and the Nubians

Nubia and Egypt have been neighbours since time immemorial. Some believe that Nubia was the cradle of the civilization that emerged in Egypt, for there's evidence of settlements in northern Nubia 10,000 years ago and archeologists have discovered the **world's oldest solar calendar** of standing stones, dating from around 6000 BC, at **Nabta Playa**, 100km from Abu Simbel. The two cultures seem to have evolved in similar ways until 3500 BC, when Egypt's unification raised the Old Kingdom to a level from which it could exploit Nubia as a source of **mineral wealth**, exotic goods and **slaves** – a pattern that was to last nearly 5000 years. The Egyptians called it *Ta-Seti* (Land of the Bow), after the weapons for which the Nubians were renowned, while its modern name is thought to derive from *nbw*, the ancient word for gold, which was mined there until Greco-Roman times. Although the collapse of centralized authority allowed Nubia to reassert its independence during the First Intermediate Period, the onset of the Middle Kingdom saw the annexation of Lower Nubia – the land between the First and Second Cataracts of the Nile – and a chain of mud-brick **fortresses** built to safeguard trade; while under the New Kingdom, Nubia was divided into nomes and ruled by a viceroy entitled the King's Son of **Kush** (Kush being its southern province), aided by the priesthood of cult-**temples**. It was only in the Third Intermediate Period that Nubia got its own back, as the local rulers of **Napata** took advantage of Egypt's disunity to invade and establish their own **Kushite Dynasty** (747–656 BC) of pharaohs, who reigned as their Egyptian predecessors had done until the Assyrian invasion of Egypt in 671 BC.

Thereafter the **Kingdom of Meroe** between the Fourth and Fifth Cataracts alternated between war with foreign conquerors like the Persians and amicable relations with most of the Ptolemies; some claim that Cleopatra (or *Kilu baba tarati* – "Beautiful Woman") was a Nubian born near Wadi Halfa. Relations with the Romans were stormy, as the Nubians supported the Egyptians' revolt against Emperor Augustus but then signed a treaty with Rome; towards the end of the first century AD another local principality, the **Blemmyes**, began raiding Egypt's southern border and occupied towns up until the reign of Diocletian – later breaking their peace treaty to ally themselves with the Nobatae tribes and revolt against Emperor Justinian (550 AD). The **Nobatae** were converted to **Christianity** by evangelical monks and became the chief bulwark against attacks by the Islamic rulers of Egypt during the twelfth and thirteenth centuries, until in 1315 the last Christian king was replaced by a Muslim one and most of the population accepted **Islam**.

Khalifs, sultans and Mamlukes made little attempt to control Nubia so long as it remained a "corridor to Africa" and supplied the ivory, slaves and exotica that they prized, until **Mohammed Ali** visited devastation on Nubia when he sent his son Ibrahim to enslave its male population as cannon fodder for his new army. Resentment smouldered through the reigns of khedives Abbas, Ismail and Tewfiq, drawing in the **British**, who began by supporting their forces and ended up underwriting an Anglo-Egyptian government in 1899, when the border between Egypt and Sudan was drawn 40km north of Wadi Halfa and Nubia was divided, yet again.

border security and trade with Nubia, for huge quarries for fine red granite, and mining in the desert hinterland of amethysts, quartzite, copper, tin and malachite. Military outposts further south could summon help from the Yebu garrison by signal fires and an Egyptian fleet patrolled the river between the First and Second Cataracts.

Besides this, Yebu was an important cult centre, for the Egyptians believed that the Nile welled up from subterranean caverns at the **First Cataract**, just upriver (see p.478). Its local **deities** were Hapy and Satet, god of the Nile flood

Meanwhile, the **Nubians** remained true to their ancestral homeland, extending from the First Cataract to Khartoum. Traditional life centred around **villages** of extended families, each with its own compound of domed houses. The people made a livelihood farming the verges of the river, planting date palms, corn and *durra* melons, as well as fishing and transporting trade goods. Socially and spiritually, the Nile formed the basis of their existence. The whole village celebrated births, weddings and circumcision ceremonies with Nile rituals, and, despite converting first to Christianity and then to Islam, they retained a belief in water spirits, petitioning them for favours. They also brewed beer and date wine.

This way of life – which had existed pretty much unchanged for five millennia – was shattered by the **Aswan Dams**. The first dam, built in 1902 and successively raised, forced the Nubians to move onto higher, unfertile ground: unable to subsist on agriculture, many of the menfolk left for Cairo and the cities, sending back remittances to keep the villages going. With construction of the High Dam, the Nubians' traditional homeland was entirely submerged, displacing the entire 800,000-strong community. Around half of them moved north, settling around Aswan and Kom Ombo, where the government provided homes and assistance with agriculture and irrigation. The rest were repatriated to Sudan, where many ended up in the Kassala/New Halfa area, a thousand miles to the south. Meanwhile the **ancient monuments** of Nubia were moved to higher ground or foreign museums, under a huge program co-ordinated by UNESCO.

In Egypt, the **Nubian community** has done well. Many have taken advantage of higher education and business opportunities, making their mark in government, commerce and tourism (85 percent of Nubian males in Aswan earn their living from tourism). Others from the first wave of emigration continue to provide the backbone of Cairo's janitors and servants; Nubians as a whole have always been noted for their honesty and reliability. Remarkably, the community has maintained its cultural identity, with the resettled villages (which took their old names) acting as guardians of tradition.

A few Nubian phrases
In the list below, accents indicate stress.

Er raigráy? or *er-minnabóu?*	How are you? (to a man or woman)
Ai raigérry	I'm fine
Ekináira?	What's your name?
Aigi ...	My name is ... (followed by *-era*)
Er fárdiray?	Are you busy?
Tégus	Sit down
Er wenáyseso	I am honoured
Asálgi	Tomorrow
Kattaháiruk	Thank you
Ena fiadr	Goodbye

and goddess of its fertility, though the region's largest temple honoured Khnum, the provincial deity (see p.443).

During settled periods, the vast trade in ivory, slaves, gold, silver, incense, exotic animal skins and feathers spawned a **market town** on the east bank (slightly south of modern Aswan, its linear descendant), but the island remained paramount throughout classical times, when it was known by its Greek appellation, *Seyene*. In the Ptolemaic era, the Alexandrian geographer **Eratosthenes** (276–196 BC) heard of a local well into which the sun's rays fell perpendicularly at midday on the summer solstice, leaving no shadow; from this he deduced that Seyene lay on the Tropic of Cancer, concluded that the world was round and calculated its diameter with nearly modern accuracy – being only 80km out. (Since that time, the Tropic of Cancer has moved further south.)

The potency of the **cult of Isis** at nearby **Philae** (see p.484) made this one of the last parts of Egypt to be affected by **Christianity**, but once converted it became a stronghold of the faith. From their desert Monastery of St Simeon, monks made forays into Nubia, eventually converting the local Nobatae, who returned the favour by helping them to resist Islamic rule through Fatimid times, until finally subjugated by Salah al-Din. However, Bedouin raiders persisted through to 1517, when Sultan Selim garrisoned an entire army here, by which time the town's name had changed from Coptic *Sawan* to its present form, and the population had embraced **Islam**.

From the early nineteenth century onwards, Aswan was the base for the conquest of the Sudan and the defeat of the Mahadist Uprising (1881–98) by Anglo-Egyptian forces. As British influence grew, it also became the favourite **winter resort** of rich, ailing Europeans, who flocked to Aswan for its dry heat and therapeutic hot sands, luxurious hotels and stunning scenery, spiced with the thrill of being "at the edge of civilization". Its final transformation into the Aswan of today owes to the building of the **High Dam**, 15km upriver, which flooded Nubia, compelling its inhabitants to settle in new villages built around Kom Ombo and Aswan itself, which is now predominantly Nubian.

To assert its identity, the city has established an **Africa University** for the study of African science and culture, and a **Nubia Museum** tracing the Nubians' history. The relationship between the Egyptian and Sudanese governments has been somewhat fragile, however, and the weekly ferry between Aswan and Wadi Halfa was suspended for a time in the mid-1990s because of tensions – at the time of writing, however, the ferry is running and inter-state relations are stable (see box on p.479).

Arrival, information and transport

Most tourists travel directly to Aswan from Cairo (889km) or Luxor (215km), as detailed in the introduction to this chapter; a few arrive by bus or train from Esna, Edfu or Kom Ombo (see the respective entries for details).

From **Aswan airport**, 23km south of town, you can get a taxi into the centre for about £E25 (agree the price first). The **train station** is in the north of town, five minutes' walk from the Corniche or the bazaar quarter. The inter-city **bus station** and main **service taxi** depot are both 3km north of town, near the Nile, a short ride by minibus (25pt) or taxi (£E5).

Information and assistance

The **tourist office** (daily 8am–2pm & 7–9pm; Ramadan 10am–2pm & 7–9pm, closed midday Fri; ⓣ & ⓕ097/231-2811) is housed in a domed Nubian-style building outside the station. The erudite and charming Shukri Sa'ad and

Hakeem Hussein can answer just about any question and will recommend good felucca captains, if asked beforehand – they won't pass judgement if you've already made a deal. They also provide current private taxi rates.

The **tourist police** (℡097/230-3436) are based near the Corniche beside Misr Travel, with a branch in the train station; both are open round the clock. In serious cases, try to deal with the boss, Sayed Abu Hamed (℡097/231-4393). The Aswan Governorate's **Police Department** occupies a grand modern tower on the Corniche, which also contains the passport office, and there's another, colonial-style police station on Sharia Abtal el-Tahrir.

Transport

Aswan is compact enough to get around on foot, but if you are burdened with luggage or bound for a distant hotel, you may want to rent a **taxi** or **caleche** (£E5; agree the price first), or take one of the **minibuses** that run from one end of the Corniche to the other for 25pt. All Aswan's nearby attractions are accessible by river – mostly by felucca – though you may want to rent a **bicycle** from the *Mona Lisa* on the Corniche, or the shop on the far side of the railway footbridge, for £E15 a day, to cycle out to the Unfinished Obelisk or the Sculpture Park.

For better or worse, **feluccas** are inseparable from the Aswan experience. It's wonderfully relaxing to drift downstream while egrets swoop overhead, or tack between rocky islands, but on the downside, it's all too easy to get irked by boatmen who fritter away time before demanding *baksheesh* for an unfulfilled itinerary; or get wearied of the persistent touts along the Corniche. Despite **rates** being set by the authorities per boatload (up to ten people), at £E25 for an hour's sailing or £E32 for two and a half hours with landfalls, market rules and haggling prevail. If big spenders abound, boatmen will sniff at official rates; if business is slack, they'll undercut each other. Unsurprisingly, prices are highest at the landing stage beneath the luxurious *Old Cataract Hotel*. (Longer felucca trips to Sehel Island, or downriver towards Luxor, are covered on p.477.)

Accommodation

As in Luxor, **accommodation** varies depending on the tourist trade and the season, and newly arrived tourists are importuned by **touts** (some board the train at Kom Ombo, to pre-empt their rivals). **Cruise boats** try to steal customers away from hotels by slashing their prices – and a week in a two- or three-star hotel can't compare with a week's cruise on the Nile. Though high season officially runs from October 1 to April 30, the squeeze is only felt (if at all) from mid-December to early February, when some hotels are booked up by Egyptian groups. The nadir of the low season (May 1–Sept 30) comes in the summer, when most places are empty and desperate for business. Many offer **reductions** of 15 to 50 percent at this time or will waive service charges and taxes after a bit of haggling.

In many mid-range and low-budget hotels guests may be subjected to **pressure** to sign up for taxi or felucca trips, whereby the hotel takes up to fifty percent of whatever you agree to pay the driver or boatman. Listen to their spiel, but don't let yourself be railroaded into a hasty decision.

Location counts for much in Aswan: hotels on the Corniche may have fabulous views, if not from the rooms, then from the rooftop. The poshest places are at the south end of the Corniche, or on private islands. Hotels in the bazaar tend to be cheaper, noisier, and often pitched at Egyptians rather than foreigners. The least attractive area is north of the train station, where the

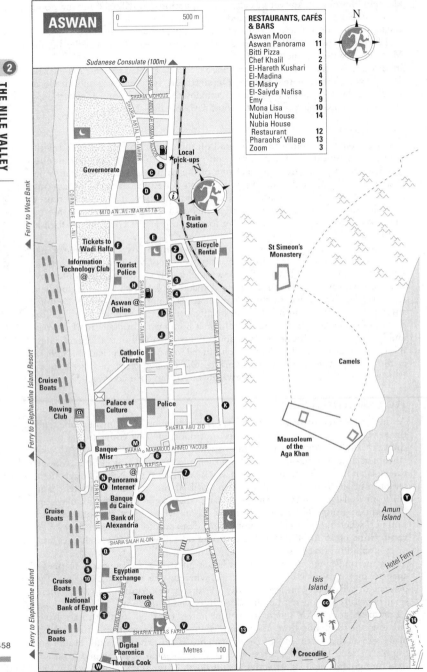

ASWAN

0 — 500 m

RESTAURANTS, CAFÉS & BARS

Aswan Moon	8
Aswan Panorama	11
Bitti Pizza	1
Chef Khalil	2
El-Hareth Kushari	6
El-Madina	4
El-Masry	5
El-Saiyda Nafisa	7
Emy	9
Mona Lisa	10
Nubian House	14
Nubia House Restaurant	12
Pharaohs' Village	13
Zoom	3

N

Sudanese Consulate (100m) ▲

Ferry to West Bank ◄

Ferry to Elephantine Island Resort ◄

Ferry to Elephantine Island ◄

SHARIA MOHOUS
SHARIA ABTAL EL-TAHRIR
SHARIA ABDUL RAHMAN YACOUB
CORNICHE EL-NIL

Governorate

Local pick-ups

MIDAN AL-MAHATTA

Train Station

Tickets to Wadi Halfa

Information Technology Club @

Tourist Police

Aswan @ Online

SHARIA AL-SOUK (SHARIA SAAD ZAGHLOUL)

Bicycle Rental

Catholic Church

Palace of Culture

Cruise Boats

Rowing Club

Police

SHARIA ABU ZID

Banque Misr

SHARIA MAHMOUD AHMED YACOUB

SHARIA SAYIDA NAFISA

Panorama Internet @

Banque du Caire

Bank of Alexandria

SHARIA SALAH AL-DIN

SHARIA ABBAS AL-AKAD

Cruise Boats

Egyptian Exchange

Tareek @

National Bank of Egypt

Cruise Boats

SHARIA ABBAS FARID

Digital Pharonica

Thomas Cook

0 — Metres — 100

St Simeon's Monastery

Camels

Mausoleum of the Aga Khan

Amun Island

Hotel Ferry

Isis Island

Crocodile

Sehel Island ▼

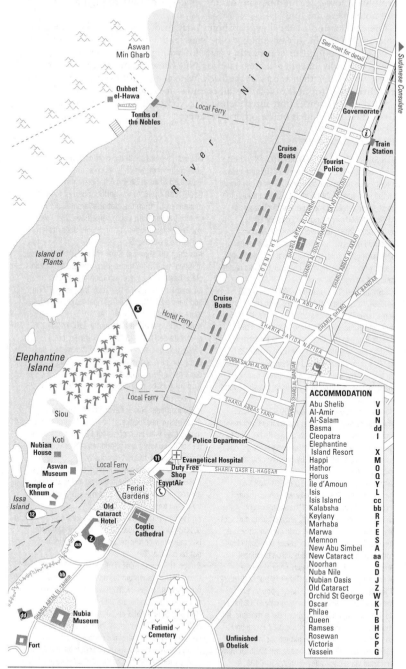

Bus Station (3km) & Kom Ombo ▲

Sudanese Consulate ▶

Aswan
Min Gharb

Qubbet
el-Hawa
Tombs of
the Nobles

Local Ferry

River Nile

See inset for detail

Governorate

Cruise
Boats

Tourist
Police

ⓘ Train
Station

Island of
Plants

CORNICHE

SHARIA ABTAL EL-TAHRIR

SHARIA AL-SOUK ISMAILIA

SA'AD ZAGHLOUL

SHARIA ABBAS AL-AKKAD

Cruise
Boats

Ⓧ Hotel Ferry

SHARIA ABU ZID

SHARIA SHARID AL-BANDAR

*Elephantine
Island*

SHARIA SAYIDA NAFISA

SHARIA SALAH AL-DIN

Local Ferry

Siou

SHARIA ABBAS FARID

SHARIA SHARID AL-BANDAR

Koti

Police Department

Nubian
House

Aswan
Museum

Ⓛ

Local Ferry

⓫ ✚ **Evangelical Hospital**
Duty Free
Shop   SHARIA QASR EL-HAGGAR

Temple of
Khnum

Issa
Island

⓬

EgyptAir

Ⓛ

Ferial
Gardens

Old
Cataract
Hotel

ⓐⓐ Ⓩ

✚ **Coptic
Cathedral**

ⓑⓑ

SHARIA ABTAL EL-TAHRIR

ⓓⓓ

**Nubia
Museum**

Fort

**Fatimid
Cemetery**

**Unfinished
Obelisk**

ACCOMMODATION	
Abu Shelib	V
Al-Amir	U
Al-Salam	N
Basma	dd
Cleopatra	I
Elephantine	
Island Resort	X
Happi	M
Hathor	O
Horus	Q
Ile d'Amoun	Y
Isis	L
Isis Island	cc
Kalabsha	bb
Keylany	R
Marhaba	F
Marwa	E
Memnon	S
New Abu Simbel	A
New Cataract	aa
Noorhan	G
Nuba Nile	D
Nubian Oasis	J
Old Cataract	Z
Orchid St George	W
Oscar	K
Philae	T
Queen	B
Ramses	H
Rosewan	C
Victoria	P
Yassein	G

Aswan Dams & Sculpture Park ▼   ▼ Northern Quarries

crumbling low-rise buildings are hardly what you'd want, though a couple of the hotels here are fine.

The devaluation of the Egyptian pound has made a lot more hotels afford-able, so you might as well enjoy a Nile view and a private bathroom, or even a swimming pool. But **standards** vary a lot within the same price band, and hotels generally charge a higher rate for Nile-view rooms, which tend to be larger and better than rooms at the back. With temperatures in the 50s°C, **air conditioning** (or at least a fan) is an essential in summer.

All the accommodation listed below is keyed to the **map** on pp.458–459. **Breakfast** is included unless otherwise stated.

Budget hotels

Abu Shelib Sharia Abbas Farid ☎097/230-3051. Clean-ish, shabby and cluttered; £E10 more gets a room with a/c and a bathroom. After a few beers on the roof you might be able to sleep through the noise from a nearby mosque and the bazaar. ❶

Al-Salam Midway along the Corniche ☎ & ☎097/230-2651, ✉mwahish@hotmail.com. Favoured by Egyptians for its breezy a/c rooms overlooking the Nile, this hotel is a bit shabby, but clean, with a great view of the river from its restau-rant and lounge. ❷

Happi Just off the Corniche ☎097/231-4115, ☎230-7572. Pleasant a/c rooms with bathrooms; some have TV, balconies and Nile views. Its restau-rant, which faces Elephantine Island, sells beer. Guests can use the *Cleopatra*'s pool for free. ❷

Hathor Midway along the Corniche ☎097/231-4580. A prime location and rooftop pool don't make up for shabby Nile-facing rooms and a manage-ment that shows little interest in its guests beyond selling tours. ❷

Horus Corniche el-Nil ☎ & ☎097/231-3313. Their renovated Nile-facing rooms have bathrooms and fans; the rest are much tattier. Its bar-restau-rant, nightclub and rooftop have great views, but you might be kept awake by bellydancing after midnight. ❷

Keylany Sharia Keylany ☎097/231-7332 or mobile ☎012 7866940, ☻www.keylanyhotel .com. This friendly hotel off the southern end of the bazaar has rooms with fans, a/c, soft beds and spot-less bathrooms; an Internet café and an attractive rooftop. They even serve pancakes and Columbian coffee for breakfast, and take online bookings. Associated with Luxor's *Happy Land Hotel.* ❷

Marwa Off Sharia Abtal el-Tahir ☎097/230-8532. This place and the *Victoria* (see opposite) are the cheapest in Aswan, charging only £E12 for a double. Located down an alley near a mosque, its rooms are tiny, with fans or a/c (£E2 extra) and a communal hot shower. Breakfast not included. ❶

Memnon Corniche el-Nil, above the National Bank; entrance via a back alley ☎097/230-0483. A

cleanish two-star, with a/c, soft beds and a small pool on the roof, which is its chief attraction. ❷

New Abu Simbel Sharia Abtal el-Tahrir ☎097/230-6096. In the northern part of town, 10 minutes' walk from the station. Carpeted a/c rooms with baths and hard beds; some have Nile views and balconies, fridges, TV or double beds. Its large garden is a bonus. ❷

Noorhan Off Sharia al-Souk ☎097/231-6069. Five minutes' walk from the station, this much-hustled place has shabby, clean-ish rooms with fans, or a/c and bathrooms (£E10 extra); Internet (£E15/hr) and beer (£E7.50); breakfast not included. Arranges tours, but not unduly pushy. ❶

Nuba Nile Off Midan al-Mahatta ☎097/231-3267 or mobile ☎012 7833786, ✉nobanile_hotel @hotmail.com. Very clean, a/c and carpeted, this is a good new option near the train station, if you don't mind the cramped bathrooms. ❷

Nubian Oasis Off Sharia al-Souk ☎097/231-2123 or mobile ☎012 2487175, ☎097/231-2124, ✉NubianOasis_Hotel_Aswan@hotmail.com. A multi-storey backpackers' haunt, with grungy a/c rooms (two with bathrooms for £E5 extra); Internet (£E8p/h), laundry service and tepid beer (£E7). Organizes trips, but not too pushy. ❶

Oscar Sharia Abbas al-Akkad ☎ & ☎097/230-6066. A quiet hotel behind the bazaar, with clean a/c rooms with bathrooms. Its management doesn't try to sell tours. ❷

Philae Corniche el-Nil ☎097/231-2090, ☎232-4089. This clean, faded a/c two-star hotel has rear-view or Nile-facing (£E10 extra) rooms, but no rooftop. ❷

Queen Off Sharia Atlas ☎ & ☎097/232-6069. Close to the station but far enough away to escape the noise. Its clean rooms have tiny bathrooms, TV, fridge and a/c; some are Nile-facing. ❷

Ramses Sharia Abtal el-Tahrir ☎097/230-4000, ☎231-5701. This centrally located tower-block covered in mock-pharaonic carvings has small, clean en-suite rooms with a/c and satellite TV (some overlooking the Tombs of the Nobles);

it also has a restaurant, bar and laundry service. ❷

Rosewan Off Sharia Atlas ☎097/230-4497. This aged place has dark, shabby rooms with erratic hot water, and a nice pizza café attached. ❶

Victoria Sharia Abtal el-Tahrir ☎097/230-3870. Aswan's cheapest, along with the *Marwa*, this old

bazaar hotel has a wonderful wonky staircase, shabby rooms with lumpy beds, and shared washrooms. ❶

Yassein Off Sharia al-Souk ☎097/230-7753. Small clean rooms with bathrooms and a/c (the best ones are on the third floor), within earshot of the train tracks. Laundry service. ❶

Mid-range hotels

Al-Amir Sharia Abbas Farid ☎097/231-4732, ⓕ230-4411. One street back from the Corniche, this small three-star hotel has partial Nile views and is mainly aimed at Gulf Arabs, who presumably don't mind being awoken by the mosque next door. The rooms are clean and comfy, with a/c and phone, but rather overpriced. ❸

Cleopatra Sharia al-Souk ☎097/231-4001, ⓕ231-4002, ⓦwww.cleopatraaswan.com. The smartest hotel near the bazaar, its clean, carpeted a/c rooms are often block-booked by Egyptian groups. Its best feature is the rooftop pool, though it is overlooked by taller buildings. ❻

Kalabsha Sharia Abtal el-Tahrir ☎097/230-2666, ⓕ230-5974, ⓔkalabshahotel@yahoo.com. Uphill

from the southern end of the Corniche, this tower-block is far less classy than its four-star neighbours, though it does have a small pool and some rooms with a superb view of the First Cataract of the Nile. ❻

Orchid St George Sharia Mohammed Khalid ☎ & ⓕ097/231-5997, ⓔhussein45@hotmail .com. A nice small hotel off the southern end of the Corniche. All rooms en-suite and a/c; book ahead if you want the family room (two doubles, three bathrooms and a terrace) or top-floor Honeymoon room (with a canopied bed). The rooftop has a small pool and hosts weekly Nubian parties. Guests can get a massage or use the Internet (£E10 p/h). ❹

Upmarket hotels

Basma On the hillside above the *Old Cataract* ☎097/231-0901, ⓕ231-0907, ⓦwww .basmahotel.com. This four-star complex has a large heated pool and a garden terrace with stunning views of the Aga Khan's mausoleum and the southern end of Elephantine, but is best avoided during the sculpture symposium, due to the noise outside. Disabled access. Free bus from the *Isis* at quarter past every hour. ❼

Elephantine Island Resort Elephantine Island ☎097/230-3455, ⓕ231-3538, ⓔresort.aswan @elephantine-island.com. It looks like an airport control tower, but the gardens and views are lovely, and the pool and spa worthy of its five-star rating. Lodgings range from cabins (US$100) to deluxe villas (US$485). Reached by a 24hr ferry done up like a pharaonic barge, from near the *Isis*. ❼

Île d'Amoun Amun Island, facing the *Old Cataract* ☎097/231-3850, ⓕ231-7190, ⓔreceptionamoun@hotmail.com. Small, chic Club Med resort of a/c bungalows in a lush garden with exotic birdlife. All the guests and staff speak French. Reached by a ferry from the EgyptAir docks. ❽

Isis Midway along the Corniche ☎097/231-5100, ⓕ231-5500. A mini-resort with cramped a/c bungalows in a small garden with a pool, it only

gets away with charging such high prices due to its prime location facing Elephantine. Italian restaurant; nightclub with bellydancing. ❼

Isis Island Upriver from Aswan ☎097/231-7400, ⓕ231-7405, ⓔnazab@rite.com. Owned by Allah Mubarak, the President's elder son, this five-star colossus was built beside a nature reserve containing the only primordial Nilotic vegetation left in Egypt. It has rooms and chalets; two pools, a health club, mini-golf and kids' zoo; rates are the same all year. Reached by a 24hr launch from the docks near EgyptAir. ❼

Marhaba Off the Corniche near Midan al-Mahatta ☎097/233-0102, ⓕ233-0105, ⓔmarhabaaswan @yahoo.com. A fancy mock-pharaonic pile with a/c rooms facing the Nile, a fab rooftop, and a large pool to come. Rooms cost only US$10 more in high season, and their buffet breakfast is a treat. ❼

New Cataract By the Ferial Gardens ☎097/231-6000, ⓕ231-6011. No longer sharing facilities with the *Old Cataract*, this refurbished a/c block (built by the Russians in the 1960s) features a disco, bar, restaurants and shops, tennis courts and a big pool. ❼

Old Cataract By the Ferial Gardens ☎097/231-6000, ⓕ231-8336, ⓔh1666-GM@accor-hotels .com.A splendid Edwardian-Moorish relic, tastefully refurbished and jealously guarded against interlopers. Its river-facing rooms have glorious views and the others overlook a fine garden, but some complain that the food and service don't match the high prices, ranging up to US$1200 for the Presidential suite. Buffet breakfast costs £E77 extra. ❽

The Town

Ignoring the residential and industrial suburbs (as every tourist does) greatly simplifies **orientation**. Although Aswan's sinuous **Corniche** follows the river bank for more than 4km, most things worth noting lie along the 1500-metre stretch between the Palace of Culture and **Ferial Gardens** (where the road swings inland), near Aswan's soaring concrete **Coptic Cathedral**, which was financed by Neyb Suwarez, owner of the El-Gouna transport company. Otherwise, the main focus of interest is **Sharia al-Souk** (aka Sharia Sa'ad Zaghloul), which runs two to three blocks inland as it snakes down from the train station to Sharia Abbas Farid. For most of the way it is paralleled by another busy thoroughfare, **Sharia Abtal el-Tahrir**, which runs ever closer to the Corniche but never quite touches it, and finishes up as a narrow backstreet. Note that not all the streets off the bazaar appear on our **map** of town (on p.459), and some areas are being demolished to create wider roads for traffic.

The bazaar and Corniche

Aswan's **bazaar** is renowned as the best in Egypt outside Cairo, and is not yet entirely corrupted by tourism. Traditional wares such as spices, ebony, basketwork and rugs are still in evidence, but souvenir shops are gradually forcing humdrum vendors into the alleys off Sharia al-Souk. Nonetheless, it's a pleasure to wander around, with its smells and colours evoking the Sudan and camel caravans across the Sahara. Fresh produce is chiefly sold around the junction of Sharia Saiyida Nafisa and Sharia al-Souk, and at the station end of the latter. Shop in the morning, since the quality drops as the temperature rises. Conversely, the spice, textiles and jewellery souks are barely active before 3pm, but thronged after sundown. The most attractive part is the stretch of tall wooden shopfronts to the north of Sharia Abdel Magid Abu Zid, mostly given over to souvenirs.

As in Luxor, going shopping with a guide or driver will mean paying a hidden commission. Popular buys include colourful **Nubian skullcaps** or long scarves; heavier, woven **shawls**; or **baskets** and **trays** in various sizes, some semi-antiques and others new. **Galabiyyas** and embroidered Nubian robes can be bought off the peg or tailored to order; try the shop of Metry Tawdros Mansour on Sharia Saiyida Nafisa. Pyramids or baskets of **spices** and dyes are another eye-catching feature of the bazaar; dried **hibiscus** (used to make *karkaday*), indigo dye and what is labelled as "saffron" (actually saf-saf flower) are common tourist purchases, and Aswan is also famous for the quality of its peanuts and its **henna** powder, sold in different grades. Local people are also proud of their salted fish, which comes in jars, but is something of an acquired taste.

Aswan's **Corniche** is the finest in the country, less for its architecture (which is mostly modern and undistinguished) than for the superb vista of Elephantine Island, and feluccas gliding over the water like quill pens across papyrus, with the tawny wastes of the Western Desert on the far bank. Unfortunately, you can't walk along the esplanade without being pestered by boatmen or their juvenile sidekicks; stay on the other side of the street and they'll leave you alone. Sunset is best enjoyed from the rockbound **Ferial Gardens** (daily 9am–11pm; £E5) or the terrace of the **Old Cataract Hotel** (featured in the movie *Death on the Nile*), which afford a sublime view of the southern end of **Elephantine Island** and the smaller islands beyond – although the *Old Cataract* now relegates non-residents to a lower terrace and levies a minimum charge of £E55 to discourage rubberneckers. If you're willing to walk further uphill past the Nubia Museum, the *Nubian House* restaurant (see p.470) commands an even finer vista of the **First Cataract**.

The Nubia Museum

Aswan's **Nubia Museum** (daily: 9am–1pm & 5–9pm; Ramadan 9am–4pm; £E35; camcorder permit £E20) has been widely acclaimed, delighting its sponsors, UNESCO, and posthumously crowning the career of its architect, the late Mohammed al-Hakim. Opened in 1998 after fifteen years on the

△ Aswan bazaar

drawing board, the museum is housed in an impressive modern building, loosely based on traditional Nubian architecture and faced in limestone, surrounded by landscaped grounds. It displays some 5000 artefacts, excellently organized and clearly labelled in English, making it a "must see" introduction to the history and culture of the Nubians; for a preview check out ⓦ www.numibia .net/nubia.

At the entrance to the main hall, a scale model of the Nile Valley shows the magnitude of the Nilotic civilizations and their architectural achievements. The exhibits lead you from prehistory through the kingdoms of Kush and Meroe into Christian and Islamic eras, until the drowning of Nubia beneath Lake Nasser and the salvage of its ancient monuments by UNESCO. Among the highlights are a quartzite statue of a Kushite priest of Amun, an eight-metre-high Ramses II, horse-armour from the Ballana tombs and frescoes from the Coptic churches of Nubia. There are also life-size models of traditional Nubian houses and photographs of the mud-brick fortresses, churches and cemeteries that were abandoned to the rising waters of Lake Nasser as the temples were moved to higher land.

In the grounds are further monuments and exhibits, including the mausoleum of 77 *wali* (Muslim sheikhs), a traditional Nubian house, and a cave containing prehistoric rock art removed from now inundated areas. An artificial water-course runs through the corner of the grounds nearest the main road, attractively spotlit at night.

The museum is about 500m uphill beyond the *Old Cataract* hotel, and about thirty minutes' walk from the town centre (£E15 return in a taxi). If you've still got some energy after the museum, you can trek uphill past the *Basma Hotel* to find a derelict mud-brick **fort** with a watchtower, built in Mohammed Ali's time (now off-limits as a military zone), and a vantage point overlooking the Fatimid Cemetery (see p.473).

Elephantine Island

Elephantine Island takes its name from the huge black rocks clustered around its southern end, which resemble a herd of pachyderms bathing in the river. Its spectacular beauty is marred only by the towering *Elephantine Island Resort*, reached by its own private ferry and cut off from the rest of the island by a lofty fence. (An even larger hotel lies abandoned at the far end of the island, after investors pulled out).

Further south, two **Nubian villages** – **Siou** and **Koti** - nestle amidst lush palm groves, their houses painted sky-blue, pink or yellow and often decorated with *Hadj* scenes. Chickens peck in the dust and goats chew garbage in mud-brick alleys twisting past walled gardens, where the only concession to tourism is a signposted **Nubian House,** whose owner sells tea and handicrafts and arranges live music, parties and henna-painting (see "Entertainments and activities", p.470). Public **ferries** (every 15min 6am–11pm; 25pt) sail to Elephantine from the landing stages near Thomas Cook and EgyptAir. Alternatively you can get there by felucca (negotiable rates), docking just below the Aswan Museum.

The Aswan Musuem

The small **Aswan Museum** (daily: winter 7am–4pm; summer 7am–5pm; £E10, ticket also valid for the Nilometer and ruins further south) casts light on the island's past, when its southern end was occupied by the town of *Yebu* or *Abu* (meaning both "elephant" and "ivory" in the ancient Egyptian language).

Most of the museum's best exhibits have been moved to the Nubia Museum, but a mummified gazelle and jewellery found at the island's Temple of Satet are worth a look, as is the new **Annex**, whose highlights include a life-size granite statue of a seated Tuthmosis III, a colobus monkey embracing a pillar, and a pre-nuptial agreement from the reign of Nectanebo II. The museum was originally the villa of Sir William Willcocks, who designed the first Aswan Dam, and is set amid fragrant subtropical **gardens**. Come back and enjoy them once you've visited the Nilometer and the ruins of Yebu.

The Nilometers

In ancient times the Nilometers at Aswan were the first to measure the river's rise, enabling priests to calculate the height of the inundation, crop yields over the next year and the rate of taxation (which peasants paid in kind). There are two on the island, built at the tail end of pharaonic civilization but based on far older practice and used for centuries afterwards.

The easier to find is the **Nilometer of the Satet Temple**, by the riverside; ninety enclosed rock-cut steps lead down to a square shaft with walls graduated in Arabic, Roman and (extremely faint) pharaonic numerals, reflecting its usage in ancient times and during the late nineteenth century. To get there from the museum, follow the path southwards for 300m to find a sycamore tree (the pharaonic symbol of the tree-goddess, associated with Nut and Hathor), which shades the structure. Should you approach it by river, notice the rock embankments to the south, which bear **inscriptions** from the reigns of Tuthmosis III, Amenophis III and the XXVII Dynasty ruler Psammetichus II.

The **Nilometer of the Temple of Khnum** is further inland amidst the remains of Yebu (see below). Built in the XXVI Dynasty, it consists of stairs leading down to what was probably a basin for measuring the Nile's maximum level; a scale is etched by the stairs at the northern end.

The ruins of Yebu

The southern end of the island is littered with the **ruins** of the ancient town, which covered nearly two square kilometres by Ptolemaic times. You can follow a trail from the Aswan Museum past numbered plaques identifying structures excavated or reconstructed by German and Swiss archeological teams, which are still working on Elephantine. A massive platform and foundation blocks (#6, #12 and #13) mark the site of the **Temple of Khnum**, god of the Aswan nome, founded in the Old Kingdom (when it accounted for two-thirds of the town's area) but entirely rebuilt during the XXX Dynasty. On its north side are the remains of pillars painted by the Romans, and Greek inscriptions; to the west stands the imposing gateway added by Alexander II, shown here worshipping Khnum.

Immediately to the north lies a Greco-Roman **Necropolis of Sacred Rams** (#11), unearthed in 1906, while further northwest stands the small **Temple of Hekayib**, a VI Dynasty nomarch buried in the Tombs of the Nobles (see p.467) who was later deified; the stelae and inscriptions found here by Labib Habachi in 1946 revealed much about Aswan during the Middle Kingdom.

Due east lies a **Temple of Satet** where excavations continue to produce discoveries. Built by Queen Hatshepsut around 1490 BC, it was the last of more than thirty such temples on this site, dating back four millennia, dedicated to the goddess who incarnated the fertile aspect of the inundation. Beneath the temples, German archeologists have found a shaft leading 19m into the granite bedrock, where a natural **whirl hole** is thought to have amplified the sounds of the rising water table (the first indication of the life-giving annual flood) and was revered as the "Voice of the Nile". Although the High Dam has since silenced its voice, a half-buried statue near the temple still draws new brides and barren women longing for the gift of fertility.

To the southwest of Khnum's temple, the layered **remains of ancient houses** have yielded Aramaic papyri attesting to a sizeable **Jewish colony** on Elephantine in the sixth century BC. A military order by Darius II permitting the Yebu garrison to observe Passover in 419 BC suggests that they defended the southernmost border of the Persian empire. Although nothing remains of their temple to Yahweh, the Germans used leftover blocks from Kalabsha (see p.489) to reconstruct a **Ptolemaic sanctuary** with decorations added by the Nubian Pharaoh Arkamani in the third century BC, at the southern tip of the island.

The other islands

The craggy strait between Elephantine and Amun islands looks its best from a felucca. If you're not already waterborne, the surrounding coves are frequented by lads who'll happily sail you across to any of the islands or the west bank. **Amun Island** is home to a reclusive Club Med, reached by private ferry from a landing stage near the telephone office. Further south, there's a grander hotel on **Isis Island**, likewise accessible by private ferry from one of the signposted landing stages across the road from the EgyptAir office. The jetty beside the Judges Club is used by boats to **Issa Island** – whose *Nubia House Restaurant* has a huge palm garden for sitting out in the summer – and to the *Pharaohs' Village* on the west bank of the river (see p.470 for details of both).

The shallows beyond Isis Island are home to Aswan's **crocodile**, the only one known to live downriver from the High Dam. It was purchased as a baby in Cairo by a German tourist, who released it into the Nile at Aswan. By all accounts it's a happy creature, which suns itself on a rock or lurks underwater waiting for fish to swim into its mouth.

The other side of Elephantine, and almost hidden from the town by its bulk, the lush **Island of Plants** (*Geziret an-Nabatat*) is still commonly referred to by tourists as "Kitchener's Island". Presented with the island in gratitude for his military exploits in Sudan, Consul-General Kitchener here indulged his passion for exotic flora, importing shrubs and seeds from as far afield as India and Malaysia. This beautiful island-wide **botanical garden** (daily 7am–sunset, until 5/6pm in summer; £E10) is an ideal place to spend a quiet afternoon, with colourful **birdlife** flitting through the trees. The island is accessible by rowing boat or felucca from the west bank or Elephantine Island; the price is negotiable.

The west bank

The main attractions on the **west bank** of the river are the **Mausoleum of the Aga Khan** (closed to the public) and the desert **Monastery of St Simeon**. When negotiating a price for a felucca, be sure to establish how long you plan to spend on the west bank. Unless you're prepared to hike for more than 2km across the hills, the more northerly **Tombs of the Nobles** are best visited as a separate excursion.

The Aga Khan's Mausoleum

Just uphill from the embankment is a walled estate comprising a private villa and riverside garden, and a stairway ascending the barren hillside to the **Mausoleum of the Aga Khan**. Outwardly modelled on the Fatimid tombs of Cairo, its open court culminates in a Carrara-marble *mihrab* and sarcophagus, enshrining Aga Khan III, the 48th Imam of the Isma'ili sect of Shi'ite Muslims, who was weighed in jewels for his diamond jubilee in 1945. After his death in 1957, his tomb attracted hordes of pilgrims, whose camps posed a health hazard until the government banned mass pilgrimages.

The Aga Khan was initially drawn to Aswan by its climate and hot sands, which relieved his rheumatism; subsequently he fell in love with its beauty, built a villa and spent every winter here. Until she was buried alongside him, his widow, the Begum, ensured that a fresh red rose was placed on his sarcophagus every day; legend has it that when none was available in Egypt, a rose was flown in by private plane from Paris on six successive days. The compound has been **closed** since the Begum's death in 2000, but is still an impressive sight on the hillside.

The Monastery of St Simeon

Unless you walk across the desert from the Tombs of the Nobles (see below), the ruined **Monastery of St Simeon** (daily 7am–4pm; £E12) must be approached from the valley below. You can either plod uphill through soft sand (30min) or hire a **camel** from the pack near the landing stage (£E25 return trip with half an hour's waiting time); the latter is more fun and less effort, but whichever way you approach, it's a good idea to bring water.

Founded in the seventh century and rebuilt in the tenth, *Deir Anba Samaan* crowns the head of a desert valley, which used to be cultivated down to the river's edge. Built like a fortress, it was originally dedicated to Anba Hadra, a local saint of the fourth century who encountered a funeral procession the day after his wedding and decided to renounce the world for a hermit's cave before the marriage was consummated. From here, monks made evangelical forays into Nubia, where they converted the Nobatae to Christianity. After the Muslim conquest, the Nobatae used the monastery as a base during their own incursions into Egypt, until Salah al-Din had it wrecked in 1173.

One of the custodians will show you around the split-level complex, whose lower storeys are made of stone, the upper ones of mud-brick. The now-roofless **Basilica** bears traces of frescoes of the Apostles, their faces scratched out by Muslim iconoclasts. In a nearby chamber with a font is the place where St Simeon (about whom little is known) used to stand sleeplessly reading the Bible, with his beard tied to the ceiling so as to deliver a painful tug if he nodded off. The central **Keep** has room for three hundred monks sleeping five to a cell, a tunnel-like refectory, bathhouse, ovens and bakeries (notice the millstones). Beware of sheer drops when exploring. At sunset the surrounding desert turns madder-red and violet; foxes emerge to hunt and hawks soar aloft.

For a real off-the-beaten-track experience, you could hire a guide and a camel to explore the far side of the hills between the monastery and the Tombs of the Nobles, where a huge **Unfinished Obelisk** lies abandoned in an ancient quarry, like the better known one in the quarries to the south of Aswan (see p.473).

The Tombs of the Nobles

Relatively few tourists bother with the **Tombs of the Nobles** (daily 7am–4pm; £E12), which are hewn into the hillside further up the west bank and whose artwork has an immediacy and concern for everyday life that makes a refreshing change from royal art. If you're curious, **local ferries** ply between the station end of the Corniche and the landing stage of the west bank village of **ASWAN MIN GHARB** (every 30min 6am–11pm). The fare is 25pt, but they'll try to charge £E1 (preferably each way). At the site kiosk, beware of being palmed off with used **tickets**. In order to combine a visit with the monastery and mausoleum, start early at the tombs, then ascend to the domed hilltop Muslim shrine known as **Qubbet el-Hawa** (Tomb of the Wind), and walk across the desert to St Simeon's (45min; bring plenty of water). Alternatively you could do the route in reverse, being dropped off below the monastery from which point you can hire a camel (£E45) to do the legwork between the sites for you.

The Tombs of the Nobles lie at different heights (**Old and Middle Kingdom** ones uppermost, **Roman** tombs nearest the waterline), and are numbered in ascending order from south to north. Taking the path up from the ticket kiosk you reach the high-numbered ones first.

Tomb of Sirenput I (#36)

Turn right at the top of the steps and follow the path downhill around the cliffside to find the tomb of **Sirenput I**, overseer of the priests of Khnum and Satet and Guardian of the South during the XII Dynasty. The six pillars of its vestibule bear portraits and biographical texts. On the left-hand wall he watches bulls fighting and spears fish from a papyrus raft, accompanied by his sandal-bearer, sons and dog. On the opposite wall he's portrayed with his mutt and bow-carrier, and also sitting above them in a garden with his mother, wife and daughters, being entertained by singers; the lower register shows three men gambling. Amongst the badly damaged murals in the hall beyond, you can just discern fowlers with a net (on the lower right wall), a hieroglyphic biography (left), and a marsh-hunting scene (centre). Beyond lies a chapel with a false door set into the rear niche; the corridor to the left leads to the burial chamber.

Tombs of Pepi-Nakht (#35) and Harkhuf (#34)

To reach the other tombs from Sirenput I, return to the top of the steps and follow the path southwards. Among a cluster of tombs to the left of the steps are two rooms ascribed to Hekayib (whose cult temple stands on Elephantine), called here by his other name, **Pepi-Nakht**. As overseer of foreign troops during the long reign of Pepi II (VI Dynasty), he led colonial campaigns in Asia and Nubia, which are related on either side of the door of the left-hand room.

A bit further south is the tomb of **Harkhuf** (#34), who held the same position under Pepi I, Merenre and Pepi II. An eroded biography inside the entrance relates his three trading expeditions into Nubia, including a letter from the eight-year-old Pepi II, urging Harkhuf to bring back safely a "dancing dwarf from the land of spirits" (thought to be a pygmy from Equatorial Africa), whom Pepi desired to see "more than the gifts of Sinai or Punt". The tiny hieroglyphic figure of a pygmy appears several times in the text.

Tombs of Sirenput II (#31)

The largest, best-preserved tomb belongs to **Sirenput II**, who held the same offices as his father under Amenemhat II, during the apogee of the Middle Kingdom. Beyond its vestibule (with an offerings slab between the second and third pillars on the right) lies a corridor with six niches containing Osiride statues of Sirenput, still vividly coloured like his portraits on the four pillars of the chapel, where the artist's grid lines are visible in places. Best of all is the recess at the back, where Sirenput appears with his wife and son (left), attends his seated mother in a garden (right), and receives flowers from his son (centre). Notice the elephant in the upper left corner of this tableau.

Tombs of Mekhu (#25) and Sabni (#26)

At the top of the double ramps ascending the hillside (up which sarcophagi were dragged) are the adjacent tombs of a father and son, which are interesting for their monumentality – a large vestibule with three rows of rough-hewn pillars, flanked by niches and burial chambers – and for their story. After his father **Mekhu** was killed in Nubia, **Sabni** mounted a punitive expedition that recovered the body. As a sign of respect, Pepi II sent his own embalmers to mummify the corpse; Sabni travelled to Memphis to personally express his thanks with gifts, as related by an inscription at the entrance to his tomb. Both tombs are crudely constructed and decorated, with small obelisks at their entrances, and twin vestibules that form a single rectangular room. Sabni's chapel has columns painted with fishing and fowling scenes.

Eating and drinking

Eating out in Aswan offers the pleasures of fresh fish and Nubian dishes such as okra in spicy tomato sauce, in riverside **restaurants** that are great on balmy nights but empty when it's cold. You won't find any Chinese food, and European cuisine is limited to a few big hotels. The bazaar is good for **street food**, with *fuul* and liver sandwiches sold near the station end of the street, and fruit and nuts on every corner. There are simple **cafés** for chicken and fish meals or *kushari*, and the usual array of juice bars and coffee houses. All the Corniche places are **open** till around midnight (or later if there is custom); the cafés in the bazaar may close an hour or two earlier. Phone numbers are only given where **reservations** are advisable.

Restaurants, cafes and bars

1902 Restaurant The *Old Cataract Hotel* ☎097/231-6000. The only restaurant in Aswan with a dress code, its palatial colonial décor beats its Euro-Levantine set menu (£E30 excluding drinks). Reservations for dinner (7.30–10pm) are obligatory; closed at other times.

Aswan Moon Corniche el-Nil, near the *Horus Hotel*. Distinguished by its floating extension hung with colourful fabric, this restaurant serves fish, chicken, vegetable dishes, pizzas and pasta for £E20–25, plus tax, but no alcohol.

Aswan Panorama Opposite Duty Free on the Corniche. A riverside place with similar prices to the *Aswan Moon* but also no alcohol. Their tageens are better than their *kofta* or kebabs – try the rice pudding with nuts and rosewater. Closes at 9pm.

Bitti Pizza Sharia al-Mahatta. On two floors, with a/c and a view of the square upstairs, *Bitti* (pronounced "Beatty") serves sweet and savoury *fiteer* (flaky Egyptian pizza) and Western-style pizzas for £E10–15. Soft drinks only.

Chef Khalil Sharia al-Souk, near the station. This small a/c café serves delicious fried and grilled

fish with rice, salad and *tahina* (£E25–35; crab £E50; mixed seafood platter £E100). No alcohol.

El-Hareth Kushari Sharia Mahmoud Ahmed Yacoub. An archetypal *kushari* joint in the bazaar, where you can fill up for £E4–5. Open till midnight or later.

El-Madina Sharia al-Souk. A share-a-table diner with set meals (£E20–25) of liver, chicken or kebab with salad, *tahina*, vegetable stew, rice and bread. No alcohol.

El-Masry Sharia Abu Zid. This simple a/c restaurant off the bazaar serves set meals (£E25–30) based around fish, kebab, pigeon or stuffed courgettes. No alcohol.

El-Saiyda Nafisa In the bazaar. Another good *kushari* place, on a side street off the like-named road, both so-called in honour of a Cairene saint (see p.186).

Emy Corniche el-Nil. Since the neighbouring *Aswan Moon* ceased selling booze, *Emy* (pronounced "Ee-me") has become the most popular hang-out. Indoors is warmer in winter, but the double-decker boat section has better views of Elephantine. Meals £E15–30; Stella beer (£E6) and Egyptian wine (£E37) are as cheap as you'll find in Aswan.

Mona Lisa Corniche el-Nil. A sweatbox during the summer, this shabby haunt of courting couples and solitary beer drinkers features worn-out music tapes and handpainted Cairo bazaar scenes, and rents out bicycles (inferior to those from the rental place behind the train station).

Nubian House On a hill behind the *Basma Hotel* ☎097/236-6226. Worth the journey for its amazing views over Elephantine Island and the First Cataract as well as its Nubian meals (£E35–40). Not to be confused with the Nubian House tea and handicrafts shop on Elephantine (see opposite) or the *Nubian Restaurant* on Issa Island (see opposite). No alcohol. Open 9am–1am, or from sunset on major holy days.

Nubia House Restaurant Issa Island ☎097/230-2465. Geared towards tour groups, for whom a buffet and folk show are laid on, it's lacklustre at other times, though its palm garden is a delightful place to relax on summer evenings. No alcohol. Free boat from the dock opposite EgyptAir.

Pharaohs' Village On the west bank of the Nile. This laidback restaurant by an orchard on the edge of the desert serves tasty Nubian food and can lay on live music if enough people are interested. No alcohol. Their motorboat leaves from beside the Judges Club near EgyptAir.

Zoom Sharia al-Souk. A no-frills sit-down patisserie with ice cream and sticky cakes.

Entertainments and activities

Traditional Aswani diversions include **promenading** along the Corniche and bazaar, meeting friends in riverside **restaurants**, and listening to Nubian **music**. Most tourists spend their days sightseeing or shopping, and when not attending the **Sound and Light Show at Philae** (see p.485), usually opt for an early night.

If you're craving some excitement, there's **bellydancing** at two seedy *baladi* venues on the Corniche, the Lalampola Disco in the *Isis Hotel* (12.30–4.30am) and the fifth-floor nightclub in the *Horus* hotel (midnight–4am). Alternatively, the *Isis Island* holds a fairly bland nightly Nubian show, dancer and band (10.30pm–1am). All three levy a minimum charge of £E41–45 for drinks (which are cheaper at the first two). Bellydancing is suspended during Eids, Sha'ban and other Muslim holy days.

Nubian music and weddings

Nubian music found a global audience in the 1990s, as the septuagenarian **Ali Hassan Kuban** hit the charts with *From Nubia to Cairo* and *Walk Like a Nubian*, and other musicians and vocalists teamed up to cut a series of CDs under the name **Samalat** (all on the Piranha label; ⓦ www.pirhana.de). Kuban grew up playing at weddings and parties and once earned his living as a tiller-man; many other Nubian stars have similar backgrounds. His soulful vocals and rhythmic backing-section are quite unlike the style of **Sayyed Gayer** (now retired), who sang poems and love songs to the simple accompaniment of a *douff* (drum), or the semi-classical compositions for the *oud* (lute) written by **Hamza ad-Din**, a Nubian composer born in Wadi Halfa, whose Sufi beliefs are expressed in such haunting compositions as *Escalay* (The Waterwheel).

While top stars rarely perform in Aswan you can hear their music playing in bazaars and cafés and performed by other musicians. If you like the sound, buy cassettes or CDs in Aswan's souk – salesmen will let you listen to a selection – as they're not widely available elsewhere (particularly in Cairo and Alex, which scorn the music of the south). Impromptu performances may occur at the Ferial Gardens, but live bands mainly appear at weddings, during the summer months.

Nubian weddings are celebrated on a lavish scale, with musicians costing as much as £E28,000. The bridegroom recoups the expense by inviting hundreds of guests and charging them £E10 each, which makes summer – the wedding season – an expensive time for locals. The wedding ceremony is followed by a week of celebrations, culminating in "pigeon nights" when guests devour quantities of pigeon to increase their sexual potency. (King Farouk was said to consume the juice of six birds a day.) As guests from foreign lands are held to be auspicious, tourists are often invited (but should never presume) to attend weddings in the villages around Aswan.

Over winter, Aswan's **Nubian Folk Troupe** sometimes performs wedding and harvest routines and the famous Nubian stick dance, at the Soviet-inspired **Palace of Culture** (☎097/231-3391) on the Corniche; tickets (£E10) are sold on a first-come, first-served basis. Alternatively, you can enjoy a **show with a meal** at the Nubian House on Elephantine (£E45 for dinner and music), the *Nubian Restaurant* on Issa Island (£E65; see opposite), or two delightful **houses** on Sehel Island (see p.478). The Kenzi House is run by Mohammed Hassan (☎097/230-1577), a cousin of the owner of the Beit al-Kenzi in Darow (see p.453), while the other residence belongs to Omar Abdel Aziz (☎097/230-1514), who can often be found at the felucca dock opposite EgyptAir. If enough people are interested, either can arrange food and entertainment for about £E45 per person, including transport to the island by boat.

Henna designs, spas and swimming

Elaborate **designs in henna** on the hands and feet of brides are a feature of Nubian culture. Several shops and hotels in the bazaar advertise "tattooing" – try Mahmoud Wahish (☎097/230-2651), the Nubian House (☎097/232-6226) on Elephantine Island, or Madame Rahmat (☎097/230-1465), who works from her home near the Brooke Animal Hospital on Sharia Sultan Abul Ela. A design costs £E20–50, depending on its size and complexity.

The *Elephantine Island Resort* does a three-day **spa** package (£E300) that includes the use of its sauna, gym and steam bath, massages and immersion in **hot sand** (good for arthritis and rheumatism) and a whirlpool bath. Similar facilities are available at the *Isis Island* resort, and you can also get a body (US$13–25) or facial (US$5) massage at the *Orchid St George Hotel*.

Several hotels let non-residents use their **swimming pools**: for £E20 you can use the heated and cold pools at *Isis Island*, or the rooftop pool at the *Cleopatra*; to rent a pool cabin for the day at the *Elephantine Island Resort* costs £E200 for up to three people. Though local boys happily bathe **in the Nile**, tourists seldom do for fear of bilharzia, which is a problem near the riverbanks and islands that impede the water's fast flow. If you're still keen, there are some lovely bathing spots out at the First Cataract.

Festivals

Aswan's main event is a six-week international **Sculpture Symposium** in late January or early February, when you can see sculptors at work on the terrace of the *Basma Hotel*, before their artworks are packed off to the Sculpture Park (see "Excursions from Aswan", p.476). On **Aswan Day** (January 15), the Corniche witnesses a good-natured parade of civic and military hardware; fire engines and ambulances follow jeep-loads of perspiring frogmen and rubber-suited decontamination troops. To appreciate the joke, catch the farcical orgy of drilling and polishing that takes place outside the Police Department and the Governorate Building the previous day.

Listings

Airlines EgyptAir on the Corniche (daily 8am–8pm; ☎097/231-5000) and at the airport (☎097/248-0568) near the High Dam, 23km south of town (£E25 by taxi), flies daily to Abu Simbel, Luxor and Cairo.

American Express Corniche el-Nil (daily except Fri 9am–5pm; ☎097/230-6983, ⓕ230-2909, ⓒaswan.tso.@aexp.com). Will exchange currency and travellers' cheques, hold client mail and organize travel.

Banks The Egyptian Exchange bureau (daily 8am–8pm) offers slightly better rates than the banks along the Corniche. There are ATMs outside Banque Misr (daily except Fri 8am–9pm) and the National Bank of Egypt (Mon–Thurs & Sun 8.30am–2pm). You can change travellers' cheques at Banque du Caire (daily except Fri 8.30am–2pm & 3–10pm) and Bank of Alexandria (Mon–Thurs & Sun 8am–2pm). MasterCard and Visa cash advances are available from Banque Misr.

Dry cleaners On the ground floor of the *Nubian Oasis Hotel* (£E2–5 per item).

Duty Free Southern end of the Corniche (daily 9am–2pm & 6–10pm). The only retail outlet in Aswan selling alcohol and cigarettes, it's poorly stocked and fusty. You can only buy imported booze within 48 hours of arrival in Egypt; domestic wine and spirits cost more than in Luxor. Takes Diners Club cards.

Foreign newspapers and books You'll find the *Egyptian Gazette, Al-Ahram Weekly* and the odd foreign paper on the Corniche near the *Horus* and *Philae* hotels. An expensive shop in the *New Cataract* offers the widest range of Egyptology books and novels; the Islamic Bookshop near the local taxi station and the Dar Al-Maaref in the arcade beside the tourist police stock a smattering of each at reasonable prices.

Internet The Information Technology Club on the Corniche has the cheapest rates (£E5/hr), but you'll get faster connections at the Internet café in *Keylany Hotel* (daily 9am–midnight; £E10/hr), or no-frills outfits in the bazaar like *Tareek, Panorama Internet* or *Aswan Online* (open till midnight or later).

Medical emergencies The Evangelical Mission Hospital off the Corniche (☎097/231-7176)

charges £E120 for a consultation (Mon–Sat 7am–noon & 4–6pm), but for serious problems you're better off at the Mubarak Military Hospital out towards the airport (☎097/231-7985; ambulance ☎123). The tourist office can recommend doctors or dentists.

Passport office Corniche el-Nil, on the 2nd floor of the Police Department ☎097/231-7006. Visa extensions only in the morning. Mon–Thurs & Sun 8am–2pm & 6–8pm.

Pharmacies El-Nile, next to the Banque du Caire on the Corniche (daily 8am–1am, closed 1–5pm on Fridays; ☎097/230-2674); Galal, next to the *Happi Hotel* (daily 7am–3pm & 6pm–midnight; ☎097/230-3011). Others are dotted all over town – ask at your hotel for the nearest.

Photo processing Photo Sabry on the Corniche near EgyptAir (Mon–Thurs, Sat & Sun 10am–1am, Fri 4pm–1am) prints photos and sells film. You can burn digital photos onto a CD at the Internet café in the *Keylany Hotel* (£E25) or Digital Pharonica on Sharia Abbas Farid (£E45).

Post office Main GPO (daily except Fri 8am–2pm) near the Rowing Club; the section for poste restante (same hours) is on Sharia Abtal el-Tahrir, one block inland behind the Bank of Alexandria. Outward-bound mail arrives quicker if posted from a major hotel.

Sudanese Consulate Off Sharia Abdullah Osman Yacoub, in the north of town (daily except Fri 9am–4pm ☎097/230-7231, ⓕ232-4563). Currently, Sudanese visas (US$50–100) can be issued here with a letter of recommendation from your embassy, which could be faxed from Cairo.

Telephone calls International calls can be made from the 24-hour telephone office near EgyptAir, or Menatel card booths all over town. It costs less to send a fax at the telephone office than at the BC Business Centre one block south of the Police Department, or in major hotels. Off-peak rates 8pm–8am.

Thomas Cook On the Corniche near the Police Department (daily 8am–2pm & 5–8pm; ☎097/230-4011, ⓕ230-6839). Changes money, sells cheques and arranges tours to Abu Simbel.

Excursions from Aswan

Aswan is a base for **excursions** to numerous sites, some of which can only be reached from here, though others are also accessible from Luxor. Providing you start early enough, it's possible to fit two or more sites into a **full day's itinerary**, though that won't allow you to linger at each place for long. Much depends on whether you engage a private taxi or rely on public transport, which is more time-consuming. Some tourists try to cram the highlights into two long day-trips: south to Abu Simbel and Philae; and north to Kom Ombo, Edfu and Esna.

The classic half-day excursion is to **Philae Island** with its lovely Temple of Isis, situated in the lake between the **Aswan Dams**. Typically, groups of tourists rent a private taxi to take them to the Philae launch dock, then the dams and back to Aswan, briefly visiting the **Unfinished Obelisk** and the **Fatimid Cemetery** on the outskirts of town (another short trip from town is to **Sehel Island**). For a four-hour tour (which suffices), four-seater taxis will charge £E30–40; larger Peugeot 504s, seating seven or eight, roughly £E65. For £E70–80, you can probably persuade them to extend the tour to include **Kalabsha Temple**, which otherwise entails a separate trip.

As for **Abu Simbel**, most tourists get there on a minibus or coach excursion in a convoy from Aswan, leaving at 4am and 11am. Thomas Cook and other agencies ask about £E550 for a ten-seater minibus, while budget hotels such as the *Nubian Oasis* charge £E35–40 per head for a more cramped vehicle. It's also possible to get there by bus, but you won't save any money; it does, however, allow you to travel outside of convoy hours and stay overnight if you wish. Alternatively – and much more expensively – you can reach Abu Simbel by **flying**, or a four-day **cruise on Lake Nasser**, departing from the High Dam (see box on p.483 for details).

The other main circuit takes in one or more of the **temples between Aswan and Luxor**. Relying on public transport, you could feasibly combine **Kom Ombo** with **Edfu**, but to see **Esna** as well really calls for a private taxi. Expect to pay about £E150–170 for a four-seater taxi, or £E230–275 for a larger vehicle to take you to each site for an hour and then on to Luxor. Taxis are obliged to travel in a **convoy** from Aswan; the one leaving at 8am is for sightseeing, while the 1.45pm convoy travels directly to Luxor without any stopovers. Alternatively, you could visit Kom Ombo and Edfu by felucca or a cruise boat.

Descriptions of the sites nearer town follow: for accounts of the Aswan Dams, Philae, Kalabsha Temple and Abu Simbel, see the subsequent sections.

The Fatimid Cemetery, the Unfinished Obelisk and the Sculpture Park

Some 500m from the grounds of the Nubia Museum, you'll see a green metal fence surrounding hundreds of mud-brick tombs ranging from simple enclosures to complex domed cubes. This veritable lexicon of Islamic funerary architecture is known as the **Fatimid Cemetery**, though the majority of tombs actually date from Tulunid times. Some of the domes are built on a drum with the corners protruding like horns, a design unique to Upper Egypt. Most tombs had marble inscriptions attached until a freak rainstorm washed them off, and they were taken to Cairo in 1887 without any record of their original locations, leaving the tombs starkly unadorned. While not as grand as the mausolea in Cairo's Cities of the Dead – or inhabited by squatters – they're an eerie sight, which might tempt you to explore the cemetery (open 24 hours; no admission charge). Its main gate is ten minutes' walk from the roundabout where the road to the airport forks off the Corniche. By aiming for the three-storey building on the far side of the cemetery, you can emerge from the necropolis to join the road to the Unfinished Obelisk and Northern Quarries 1km further on.

The **Northern Quarries** (daily 7am–5pm; £E20) are the best-known of the many quarrying sites in the hills south of Aswan, which supplied the ancient Egyptians with fine red granite for their temples and colossi. Its fame derives from a gigantic **Unfinished Obelisk**, roughly dressed and nearly cut free from

The Nile's timeless scenery is best appreciated on longer **felucca** journeys between Aswan and Luxor. While cruise boats are more comfortable and predictable, feluccas offer an unforgettable, uniquely Egyptian experience, which many travellers rate as the highlight of their trip – though tales of misery aren't uncommon either. Whether your felucca trip is blissful or boring, tragicomic or simply unpleasant, depends on a host of factors and your own expectations.

Firstly, bear in mind the time of year and **conditions on the river**. Feluccas are dependent on the wind, which nearly always blows south. Travelling downstream (towards Luxor) therefore involves constant tacking, unless you simply drift with the sluggish current, but there's no chance of being becalmed, unlike sailing upriver, where the cliffs between Esna, Edfu and Kom Ombo block the wind – which is why most tourists start from Aswan. The usual trips on offer are to Kom Ombo (two days, one night), or Kom Ombo and Edfu (three days, two nights); during winter, when daylight hours are short, it's likely that **schedules** will slip and you might not reach Edfu in less than three nights. As feluccas are prohibited from sailing after 8pm, most stop at sunset for an evening round a campfire, enlivened by Nubian singing and drumming. Each day will be different from the last: stow your watch and take things as they come.

Another factor is the **water level**. Between October and May, so little is allowed through the High Dam that feluccas must be careful near shore, and inexperienced pilots have come to grief on sandbanks in the Nile. While it's obviously vital to choose an experienced captain, some tourists urge pilots to go faster than is wise, and it's hard for them to disagree.

The point at which the **journey ends** often causes friction, as tourists who think they're going to **Edfu** find themselves 30km short of town (in the villages of Hammam, Faris or Al-Ramady) or even terminate at **Kom Ombo**, where minivans are on hand to drive them to Edfu temple and then on to Luxor and whichever hotel the captain has a deal with. (The proper fare is £E10 per person, payable on arrival in Luxor, but people are often gulled into paying the captain upfront and then face demands from the drivers for £E25.) Establish the drop-off point before you go, and refuse to hand over the rest of the cash if they cut the trip short while there's still sailing time left. But if nightfall is approaching and you've still got far to go, the crew's wish to finish the job is understandable and you might feel the same about the trip. Though in theory one could sail all the way to Luxor, nobody is likely to agree to go beyond Edfu.

Arranging a felucca trip

Assembling a group of six to ten people is easily done by asking around in Corniche restaurants or responding to messages posted in the tourist office. Since you'll be spending many hours in close proximity, the character and habits of your fellow travellers are a prime consideration. Women will benefit from teaming up with a couple of men for the duration: an all-female group is sure to have problems. Agree on the number of passengers before you go and don't be talked into accepting others later on, downriver, or food supplies and space will be more limited than you'd expected.

The **tourist office** can recommend good captains and where to find them, but won't deliver a verdict on guys with whom you've already started negotiations. Arranging things through a hotel will probably work out costlier than finding your own captain, and in the event of a dispute it will be harder to recover any cash, since the hotel will have taken a hefty commission. On the other hand, hotels usually vet their captains, minimizing the risk of you ending up with a baddie. Try socializing with a few before **choosing a captain** and opening negotiations. Would-be voyagers are entitled to a free cruise around Aswan "bay" to check out the boat and its crew in action. Typically, a vessel has an English-speaking Nubian captain and carries six passengers (the largest boats take ten) who sleep either ashore after the boat has tied up, or on mattresses aboard. Nights are chilly (and maybe damp) for much of the year, so a sleeping bag is essential, as the blankets supplied are insufficient. Ensure that the **boat** has a canvas awning to protect you from the sun (which doubles as a tent at night), adequate mattresses, a jerry can for water, a kerosene stove and lamp, proper cutlery and a padlocked luggage hold. It is unwise to travel on a felucca lacking any of these items. Some captains have been guilty of taking tourists for a jaunt on a smart boat, and then substituting an inferior vessel (or crew) on the day of departure. If this happens, refuse to set sail and report it to the tourist office, who'll act as an intermediary between you and the tourist police.

Payment and registration

Rates are calculated on the basis of six passengers, according to the duration of the journey, but also vary with fluctuating demand. The tourist office quotes £E31 per person for a trip to Kom Ombo, £E52 for Esna, £E56 for Edfu, and £E75 all the way to Luxor, which doesn't include the cost of food for the trip, nor registration. Though most captains will accept less in the summer, travellers who push the price too low risk being robbed by a crew bent on getting proper remuneration. Don't pay the whole amount until you reach your destination, lest the boat "break down" and curtail the trip prematurely, and be sure that all members of the group know what has been negotiated, to ensure solidarity in the event of a dispute with the crew.

Don't hand over your passport; captains or middlemen like to collect them as proof that they've got some passengers in the bag while they go hunting for more. A **photocopy** of the page(s) with your personal details and photograph suffices for **registration** with the River Police, which is mandatory for all travellers. This can be arranged by felucca captains or local travel agencies – all of which charge £E5 per person for the effort, though there is no official fee.

Food and hygiene

Meals, prepared on a campfire or primus stove, consist of *fuul*, rice, bread, feta cheese and salad, washed down with tea. The ingredients are easily found in the souk, along with crisps, biscuits, jam and other "luxuries". Some groups prefer to agree on a price without food and take the responsibility for their own **shopping**; others strike a deal that includes food, in which case it's wise for somebody to accompany the captain when he goes provisioning, to see what you're getting. Be sure to buy plenty of bottled water, or the crew may dip into the Nile for drinking or cooking purposes. There's a real risk of getting sick on a felucca journey if **hygiene** precautions aren't observed. Bring extra-strong sterilizing tablets to purify the jerry can of Nile water used for washing up (one tab per 25 litres); also purchase carbolic soap and be sure that everyone uses it (food is mostly eaten with fingers); burn rubbish and bury excrement (the Nile's banks are badly littered) – few captains will bother with any health precautions unless pressed. Also strongly **recommended** are a hat and sunscreen (the river feels cool but reflects sunlight with great intensity) and bug repellent (the shallows swarm with mosquitoes).

Recommended feluccas

Recommending good felucca captains is tricky, for once they appear in guidebooks they soon marry foreigners and move to Europe or Australia, leaving younger, inexperienced cousins to run the boats in their name – as has happened with the famous Jamaica family on Elephantine – or you get other captains pretending to be them. Shukri and Hakeem at the tourist office keep an eye on the situation and recommend boats rather than individuals by name: ask for the *Elizabeth*, *Lucky*, *Silver Moon*, *Sheraton* or *Washington*. Given that sexual harassment can be a problem and a few felucca men have drugged passengers, it pays to be careful; travellers can help by reporting offenders to the tourist police.

the bedrock, before being abandoned after a flaw in the stone was discovered. Had it been finished, the obelisk would have weighed 1168 tons and stood nearly 42 metres high. It's reckoned that this was the intended mate for the so-called Lateran Obelisk in Rome, which originally stood before the temple of Tuthmosis III at Karnak and is still credited as being the largest obelisk in the world. From chisel marks and discarded tools, archeologists have been able to deduce pharaonic quarrying techniques, such as soaking wooden wedges to split fissures, and using quartz sand slurry as an abrasive. A tourist trail runs through the quarries and a Visitors Centre is in the pipeline.

While it's just about feasible to walk to the Northern Quarries, you definitely need wheels to reach the **Sculpture Park** near the **Southern Quarries** out towards the Old Dam. The park displays sculptures by artists attending Aswan's international Sculpture Symposium, who spend a month on the terrace of the *Basma Hotel* creating works that are either judged fit to grace the streets of Aswan (the "Tottering Skyscraper" on the roundabout near the Coptic Cathedral), or join the others in the park. Besides the sheer variety and imaginativeness of the sculptures, the park enjoys a wonderful **view**, especially at sunset. Be sure to get a taxi whose driver knows what you mean by "*El Mathaf*

Nile cruises

No visitor to Aswan or Luxor can fail to notice the dozens of cruise boats moored along their Corniches. Though mainly used by prepaid package tourists, there's nothing to stop independent travellers from striking a deal and enjoying a cruise – and prices are so low that they compare favourably with staying in hotels. There are basically two kinds of **cruises**: seven nights there and back (always starting in Luxor) or a briefer cruise commencing at either end. Starting at Luxor will mean two nights' sailing time, with stopovers at the temples of Edfu and Kom Ombo, while from Aswan it's a one-night, two-day cruise only stopping at Kom Ombo or Edfu; in both cases, there's an indeterminate **wait** to pass through the locks at Esna, which makes it unwise to rely on getting back to Luxor or Cairo in time for a scheduled flight home. When the locks are closed for maintenance during June and the first half of December, boats can only sail to Esna, so passengers are bussed to sites further afield (up to 3hr).

You'll be told that all the **boats** rate five stars, which the Ministry of Tourism has indeed awarded them, though standards vary from bog-average three-star up to the truly palatial. Distinctions are best assessed in person; put on clean clothes, leave your luggage behind and go hopping from one boat to another, as far along the Corniche as you can walk. The boats are moored two to four abreast, and their lobbies give a fair idea of what the cabins are like. Even the average vessel will have decent cabins with en-suite facilities, a restaurant, bar, sun deck and swimming pool, but the superior boats have cabins with double beds, large bathrooms, patio doors and even balconies. The cruise schedule for each boat will be posted in the lobby.

Try to **deal** with the boat manager (*not* the captain, who'll be an old river-pilot speaking little English): the manager is more likely to quote a lower rate than travel agencies, whose commission is factored into the price. This is especially true if the boat is near its sailing time and only half full, or you have a bottle of Johnny Walker Black Label (the real thing, not the Egyptian rip-off) to throw into negotiations, which are invariably in US dollars (beware of being screwed on the exchange rate if you're using other currencies). **Prices** can go as low as $US40 per person per night, including all meals per 24-hour period, but not **drinks**, which are expensive. Many travellers smuggle booze aboard to stash in their cabin fridge, despite the ban on doing so on some boats. The **meals** provided range from mediocre catering food to sumptuous buffets, but snacks are rarely available.

el-Maftoua" and a rough idea of the route (about thirty minutes' journey). Take the road for the Old Dam, but turn off onto an uphill road rather than towards the Shellal docks (for ferries to Philae). Continue until you reach the top; the sculptures are on the right, the quarries to the left.

While **taxi tours** to Philae often briefly stop at the obelisk and the cemetery on the way back to Aswan, they ignore the park since few tourists ask to visit it. If your fellow passengers agree, it shouldn't be hard to persuade the driver to make the brief detour for £E10 extra. Otherwise, hire a taxi in Aswan for a few hours to visit all three sites in one trip (£E20–30).

Sehel Island and the First Cataract

Travellers enamoured of felucca journeys should visit **Sehel Island**, 4km upriver from Aswan. With a strong wind behind you, it can be reached in an hour or so; on calmer days, allow longer. The recommended rate for a three-hour felucca trip is £E50. Bring water and a hat, and come well shod: although the river is cool, the rocks and sand are scorchingly hot. Landing on the east side of the island, you'll be mobbed by kids wanting to take you to the **Nubian village** to the west, for *baksheesh*. Hospitality and handicrafts pervade the

Boats profit by charging passengers ludicrous sums for extra **offshore excursions**, such as £E150 to visit Karnak Temple from the nearby mooring berths in Luxor. While the management won't object if you find a cheaper way of doing things, they will *not* be happy if you let other passengers know about it, nor what you've paid for the cruise – which could be a fraction of what they've shelled out.

When it's time to leave the cruise, don't forget to **tip** the cabin cleaners, whose job includes folding bath-towels into the shape of crocodiles to amuse tourists. Cleaners and cooks share grotty bunk-rooms at the stern (whose oily patina contrasts with the pristine paintwork elsewhere on the boat) and get paid around £E10 a day, with breakfast and dinner thrown in.

Dahabiya cruises

Before the advent of organized cruise boats, adventurous travellers would rent a houseboat or **dahabiya** to journey up the Nile (Flaubert and Amelia Edwards left memorable accounts of their voyages). Most vessels went to the scrapyard in the 1960s, but a few have survived and been refurbished, with replicas now being built at Desouq in the Delta. A typical *dahabiya* has a spacious lounge and shaded upper deck, en-suite cabins ventilated by louvre panels, and lots of cushions and brass fittings. The boats tend to be hired by families or groups of friends who want to enjoy themselves in privacy, while still being waited upon hand and foot.

Such holidays aren't cheap and few **operators** cater to this niche-market. Mohammed Ahmed el-Saidi (mobile ☏106 993889, ✉Eniledongola@yahoo.com) owns the *Dongola* (built in 1856), *Omar Khayam*, *Ghazala* and *Sarafa* (the last two were seen on the Nile by Amelia Edwards), while Mandouh Khalifa (mobile ☏106 578322, ⊛www.nourelnil.com) owns the *Nour Aswan* and has another boat under construction. The *Nour Aswan* (with eight double cabins) can be rented for six days for £E1000 per person, while an eight-day cruise on the *Dongola* (sleeping 7–8) costs £E12,800 group-rate; meals and soft drinks included. When not cruising, they moor below the *Old Cataract Hotel* in Aswan, at Esna, or Luxor's west bank. *Dahabiya* cruises must be booked six months ahead, and may not run in July and August.

charming **Kenzi House** modelled on the Hosh al-Kenzi in Darow, and another house in the village, both of which offer **music** and **meals** in the evening (see "Entertainments and activities", p.470).

Village kids are also keen to lead you to the "ruins", two hills of jumbled boulders that dominate the island. Here are over 250 **inscriptions** from the Middle Kingdom until Ptolemaic times, "bruised" rather than carved into the weathered granite. Most record Egyptian expeditions beyond the First Cataract or prayers of gratitude for their safe return, but atop the eastern hill you'll find a Ptolemaic **Famine Stele** (#81). Backdated to the reign of Zoser, it relates how he ended a seven-year famine during the III Dynasty by placating Khnum, god of the cataract, with a new temple on Sehel and the return of lands confiscated from his cult centre at Esna, which had provoked Khnum to withhold the inundation.

The summit provides a superb view of the **First Cataract**, a lush, cliff-bound stretch of river divided into channels by outcrops of granite. Before the Aswan Dams, the waters foamed and boiled, making the cataract a fearsome obstacle to upriver travel. Until early last century, it was necessary to offload cargo and transport it overland while the lightened boats risked rowing against the rapids. Amelia Edwards described "the leap – the dead fall – the staggering rush forward", waves and spray flooding the boat and the oars audibly scraping the rocks on either side.

In ancient times the cataract was credited as being the source of the Nile (which was believed to flow south into Nubia as well as north through Egypt) and the abode of the deity who controlled the inundation (either Hapy or Khnum, or perhaps both working in tandem). The foaming waters were thought to well up from a subterranean cavern where the Nile-god dwelt. Offerings continued to be made at Sehel even after its putative location shifted to Biga Island during the Late Period or Ptolemaic times (see "Philae", p.484).

Moving on from Aswan

For foreigners, **travel restrictions** are an important consideration for onward travel, and rules in force at time of writing are subject to change. Aswan's tourist office is up to date with the current regulations.

Private and service taxis

The convoy rule definitely applies to **private taxis** to Kom Ombo and other points north of Aswan, so if you're renting a special taxi for an excursion, be prepared to start with the 8am convoy even if you quit it later. A second convoy leaves at 1pm, but this runs directly to Luxor without any stopovers. At the time of writing, foreigners were banned from using **service taxis**, which are the fastest way to get anywhere. The main service taxi depot beside the bus station serves **Darow** and **Kom Ombo** (£E1.50), **Edfu** (£E5), **Esna** (£E8), **Luxor** (£E10) and other points north. **Aswan environs, the Old Dam** (£E24) and the bus station itself are accessible by pick-ups from the "local" depot 50m north of the tourist office.

Buses

The unwritten **rule** is that tourists may only travel in buses outside of a convoy if there are no more than four tourists aboard the vehicle. This isn't likely to cause any difficulties when tourism is at a low ebb, but could make problems if more foreigners start wanting to travel, as places are allocated on a first-come,

By ferry to Sudan

For the truly adventurous there's a weekly **ferry from Aswan to Wadi Halfa**, in Sudan. The boat leaves from the High Dam Dock in Lake Nasser on Monday afternoon and takes 24 hours to reach Wadi Halfa; the return trip from Wadi Halfa departs Wednesday. One-way **tickets** (1st class £E650, 2nd class £E330) are sold at the Nile River Valley Transport Corporation (daily except Fri 8am–2pm) in the crumbling arcade behind Aswan's tourist police station, where just enough English is spoken to seal the transaction. The price includes an obligatory departure card, meals and drinks, though the portions are tiny, so you may want to bring your own extra food.

All foreigners will need a **Sudanese visa**, which must be organized in advance from the Sudanese Consulate in Aswan (see listings on p.472) or Cairo (see p.291 for details), as it can *not* be obtained on arrival in Wadi Halfa. You'll also need **vaccinations** for yellow fever, typhoid A and B, cholera and meningitis (available at clinics in Cairo), and start taking anti-malarial drugs before entering Sudan. Assuming that hasn't deterred you, after the boat journey from Aswan to Wadi Halfa it's fifty hours by train to Sudan's capital, Khartoum. The end of the decades-old civil war between the militant Islamic regime in the north and Christian or Anamist tribes in the south has encouraged many Sudanese to hope for a better future, but meanwhile a new conflict is ravaging the Darfur region of this vast country, about which it is said, "Allah didn't know whether to laugh or cry when he made it".

first-served basis, and seats on through-buses from other towns can't be booked in advance. The Upper Egypt Bus Co. runs five buses daily **between Aswan and Luxor** (3hr; £E10), which stop at each town en route (the 7am & 8pm services are most reliable), and a direct a/c bus to **Cairo** (13hr), leaving at 4pm (£E85). Travellers bound for the Red Sea Coast or Sinai can take the 3pm bus to **Hurghada** (7hr; £E25–35) and **Suez** (12hr; £E85), or the 6.30am service to **Mersa Allam** (5hr; £E20). Between 8am and 5pm there are five buses to **Abu Simbel** (4hr; £E20), some operated by the El Gouna Co., which has its own ticket office at the bus station. To reach the terminus (*mogaf*), catch a pick-up (25pt) from the local depot near the tourist office.

Trains

Trains are best used for long hauls. Tourists may catch six daily services to **Luxor** (3hr; 1st class £E30, a/c 2nd class £E21), stopping at Darow, Kom Ombo, Edfu and Esna en route. However, they can only buy tickets to **Cairo** (15hr; deluxe "Nefertiti" class £E81, 1st class £E73, a/c 2nd class £E38) on trains #981 (6am), #1903 (6pm) and #997 (8pm), plus the deluxe *wagons-lits* sleeper #85 (£E45 or US$51 for a bed in a double cabin, payment in euros or dollars only), leaving at 5.30pm. Most tourists economize by travelling on a regular train, as both 1st and a/c 2nd class have comfortable seating that makes an overnight journey quite tolerable, though the toilets are pretty awful.

Flights

For those with sufficient money, EgyptAir flies to **Luxor** (45min; £E359), **Cairo** (90min; £E987) and **Abu Simbel** (30min; £E658). The prices quoted are one-way fares – except for Abu Simbel, which is usually visited on a day-return ticket that includes transfers between the temple and the airport.

The Aswan Dams

Under a good administration the Nile gains on the desert; under a bad one the desert gains on the Nile.

Napoleon

The **Aswan Dams** attest that Egypt's fundamental dilemma is more intractable than suggested by John Gunther's pithy diagnosis: "Make more land. Make fewer people. Either solution would alleviate the problem, but neither is easy." Although each dam has brought large areas under cultivation, boosted agricultural productivity and provided hydroelectricity for industry, the gains have been eroded by a population explosion that again threatens to outstrip resources – impelling Egypt to undertake yet more ambitious irrigation projects.

Ever conscious of the dams' significance, Egyptians are inclined to view them as a tourist attraction, whereas most foreigners simply regard the edifices as a route to the temples of Abu Simbel, Philae and Kalabsha, which were reassembled on higher ground following the construction of the High Dam. Views from the top of the dams are spectacular, though, so don't begrudge tours' obligatory stopovers.

The Old Dam

Just upriver from the First Cataract stands the old **Aswan Dam**, built by the British (1898–1902) and subsequently twice raised to increase its capacity. Once the largest dam in the world, it stands 50m tall, 2km long, 30m thick at the base and 11m at the top. Driving across, you'll notice the 180 sluice gates that used to be opened during the inundation and then gradually closed as the river level dropped, preserving a semi-natural flood cycle. Now that its storage and irrigation functions have been taken over by the High Dam, it chiefly serves to generate hydroelectricity for the nearby Kima factory, producing chemical fertilizers. **Philae** (see p.484) is visible amongst the islands to the south of the dam.

Near the eastern end of the dam lies a former Reservoir Colony, now called **HAZAN**, where colonial villas nestle amidst verdant gardens. Service taxis and pick-ups run here from Aswan but won't carry foreigners at the time of writing.

The High Dam (Al-Sadd al-Ali)

By 1952 it was apparent that the Aswan Dam could no longer satisfy Egypt's needs nor guarantee security from famine. Nasser pledged to build a new **High Dam**, 6km upstream, which would secure Egypt's future, power new industries and bring electricity to every village. When the World Bank reneged on its promised loan under pressure from the US, Nasser nationalized the Suez Canal to generate revenue for the project and turned to the USSR for assistance. The dam's construction (1960–71) outlasted his lifetime, as well as the era of Soviet–Egyptian collaboration. When Egypt decided to install more powerful turbine generators in the late 1980s, they bought them from America – only to find that the Russian ones caused fewer problems. Today, Western European contractors are involved in a vast new project at Toshka, which one described as an "Engineer's Playground".

Lake Nasser and the environmental consequences

The most visible consequence of the High Dam is **Lake Nasser**, which backs up for nearly 500km, well into Sudan. Over 180m deep in places, with a surface area of 6000 square kilometres, the lake is the world's largest reservoir, and seems

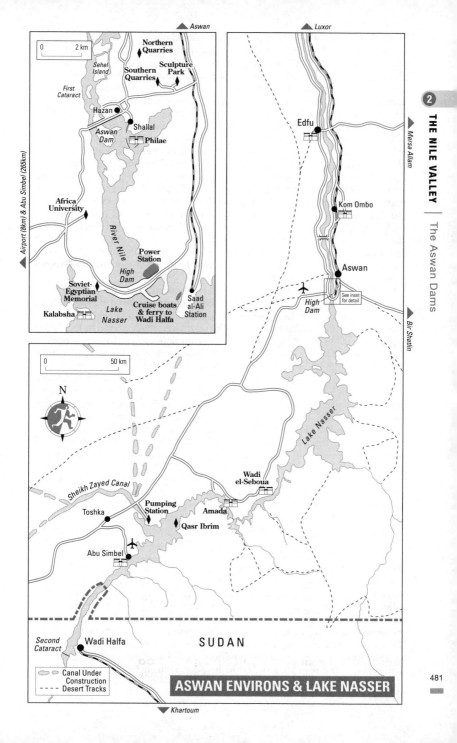

ASWAN ENVIRONS & LAKE NASSER

more like an inland sea. During the decade of drought that saw the Nile fall to its lowest level in 350 years, it saved Egypt from the famine that wracked Ethiopia and Sudan. When heavy rainfall caused the Nile to flood in 1988, the High Dam prevented Aswan from being inundated like Khartoum. Since a dam burst would wash most of Egypt's population into the Mediterranean, its security is paramount. The surrounding hills bristle with radar installations and anti-aircraft missiles; threats to bomb the dam made by Israel during the 1967 and 1973 wars, and by Gaddafi in 1984, have not been forgotten.

Although its human, cultural and environmental costs are still being evaluated, the dam has delivered most of its promised **benefits**. Egypt has been able to convert 700,000 *feddans* (a measurement of land slightly less than one acre) of cultivated land from the ancient basin system of irrigation to perennial irrigation – doubling or tripling the number of harvests – and to reclaim more than one million *feddans* of desert. The dam's turbines have powered a thirty percent expansion of industrial capacity, too; humming pylons carry megavolts to Aswan's chemical and cement factories, the Helwan Iron and Steel Mill, and the refineries of Suez. Fishing and tourism on Lake Nasser have developed into profitable industries, and the new Toshka pumping station and the Sheikh Zayed Canal are set to turn more desert into farmland as the **Toshka Project** progresses (see box on p.498).

While the main losers have been the **Nubians**, whose homeland was submerged by the lake (see pp.454–455), other **environmental consequences** are still being assessed. Evaporation from the lake has caused haze, clouds and even rainfall over previously arid regions and the water table beneath the Sahara has risen as far away as Algeria. Because the dam traps the silt that once renewed Egypt's fields, farmers now rely on *Nitrokima* fertilizers, and the soil salinity caused by perennial irrigation can only be prevented by extensive drainage projects, which create breeding grounds for mosquitoes and bilharzia-carrying snails. Ancient monuments have been affected by damp and salt-encrustation, blamed on the rising water table and greater humidity. Some even think that this has made Egypt more vulnerable to earthquakes. And with no silty deposits to replenish it, the Delta coastline is being eroded by the Mediterranean.

It's estimated that the lake itself will be filled by silt within five hundred years. But whereas some reckon that the Nubian desert may have reverted to its prehistoric lushness by then, others fear international conflicts over water resources in the not so distant future. When Ethiopia recently commissioned a study on damming the Abbai River (the source of the Blue Nile), the Egyptian government warned that any reduction of Egypt's quota of Nile water (fixed by treaty at 59 billion cubic metres annually) would be seen as a threat to national security, and that Egypt would, in fact, be needing a larger share in the future.

Visiting the High Dam

The High Dam is 13km from Aswan, and can be crossed anytime between 7am and 5pm. All vehicle passengers are charged a £E5 **toll** and may have to show their passports. Along the western approach stands the **Soviet-Egyptian Memorial**, a giant lotus-blossom tower built to symbolize their collaboration and the dam's benefits, as depicted in heroic, Socialist Realist bas-reliefs. A lofty **observation deck**, reached by elevator, allows four people at a time to see how the dam's concrete is crumbling and be stricken by vertigo. Off the road at the east end of the dam is a **visitors' pavilion** (daily 7am–5pm), which the curator will unlock for *baksheesh*. Exhibits include a fifteen-metre-high model of the dam, plans for its construction (in Russian and Arabic), and a photo narrative of the relocation of Abu Simbel.

However, unless you ask to visit the tower (*burg*) or "model" (*mekat*), taxis will only **stop midway across the dam** for a brief look. From this vantage point the dam's height (111m) is masked by the cantilever, but its length (3830m) and width at the top (40m) and base (980m) are impressive. From the southern side of the dam you can gaze across Lake Nasser to Kalabsha Temple. The **view** northwards includes the huge 2100-megawatt power station on the east bank and the channels through which water is routed into the Nile, rushing out amidst clouds of mist, sometimes crowned by a rainbow. **Philae** lies amongst the cluster of islands further downriver.

As foreigners may not use service taxis from Aswan, the only public transport to the High Dam is a 3rd-class train (hourly 6am–4pm; £E1) which terminates at **Sadd al-Ali Station**, 5km south of the eastern end of the dam, near the **docks** for the **ferry to Wadi Halfa** and Lake Nasser **cruise boats** (see the boxes on p.479 and below). However, tourists disembarking there are allowed to catch a service taxi from outside the station, into Aswan (£E1.50).

Cruises and fishing safaris on Lake Nasser

To appreciate the vastness of Lake Nasser and see the otherwise inaccessible sites known as **Wadi el-Seboua**, **Amada** and **Qasr Ibrim** (described on p.491), you really have to take a cruise. **Cruise boats** began operating on the lake in 1993 on the initiative of Mustafa al-Guindi, a Cairo-born Nubian who was responsible for the first two vessels, the *Eugénie* (modelled on an early twentieth-century hunting lodge) and the *Qasr Ibrim* (in 1930s Art Deco style), both operated by Belle Epoque Travel in Cairo (☎02/516-9649, ⊛www.eugenie.com.eg and ⊛www.kasribrim.com.eg).

There are now five other boats on the lake: *Prince Abbas* (☎097/231-4660 or mobile ☎012 2206747), *Queen Abu Simbel* (☎097/230-6512), *Nubian Queen* (✉Omar@nubianilecruises.com), *Nubian Sea* (mobile ☎012 3222065) and *Tania* (☎097/231-6393) – all rated 5-stars, except for the 4-star *Tania*. Each follows a similar **schedule**, departing on a four-day cruise from the High Dam or a three-day voyage from Abu Simbel, taking in the three sites mentioned above plus Abu Simbel and Kalabsha. Most passengers are package tourists who've pre-booked in their own country, but trips can be arranged through Belle Epoque in Cairo, or agents on the Corniche in Aswan such as Eastmar Travel (*Nubian Sea*) or Travco (*Tania*). Prices range from US$120–190 per person per day, including meals and admission to the sites; the *Nubian Sea* wins the prize for the finest food. As on Nile cruises, drinks are expensive, and some travellers choose to smuggle a supply aboard.

Lake Nasser is also a great place for **fishing** enthusiasts: among the fish that flourish here are Nile Perch (the largest caught weighed 176kg, just short of the world record); eighteen species of giant catfish, including the legendary Vundu; huge tilapia and pirhana-like tiger fish. Because tilapia (at the bottom of the food chain) spawns in April, other fish are most prolific in the summer months. The best fishing grounds are in the north, before you reach Amada – beyond Amada the fish get eaten by crocodiles.

Several operators in Aswan do **fishing safaris**. Try African Angler (☎097/230-9748 or mobile ☎101 0342410, ⊛www.african-angler.co.uk), run by former Kenyan safari guide Tim Bailey, which offers six- (£600–730) or thirteen-day (£1090–1315) packages (priced in sterling and including flights from Britain; land-only on request), or Lake Nasser Adventure (mobile ☎012 2405897, ⊛www.lakenasseradventure .com), set up by ex-*Eugénie* manager Pascal Artieda and a local fisherman, Negrashi. A third outfit, El-Temsah (☎097/231-5767 or mobile ☎012 3343203, ✉crocodile2004@hotmail.com), run by Ala Temsah, does fishing, **bird-watching** and **duck-hunting** for small groups for about £E600 per person a day.

Philae

The island of **PHILAE** and its **Temple of Isis** have bewitched visitors since
Ptolemaic times, when most of the complex was constructed. The devout and
curious were drawn here by a cult that flourished throughout the Roman
empire well into the Christian era. Although the first Europeans to "rediscover"

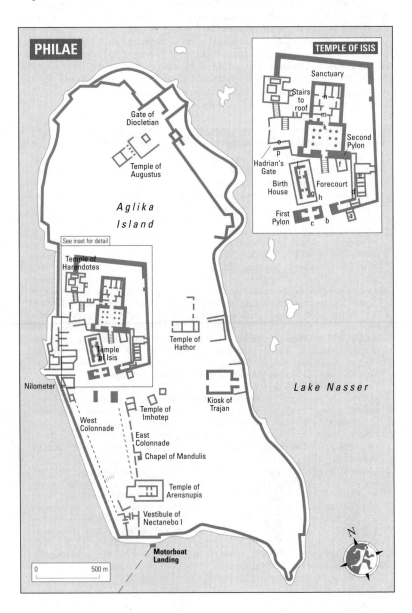

Philae in the eighteenth century could only marvel at it from a distance after their attempts to land were "met with howls, threats and eventually the spears of the natives living in the ruins", subsequent visitors revelled in this mirage from antiquity. "If a procession of white-robed priests bearing aloft the veiled ark of the God were to come sweeping round between the palms," mused Amelia Edwards, "we would not think it strange."

After the building of the first Aswan Dam, rising waters lapped and surged about the temple, submerging it for half the year, when tourists would admire its shadowy presence beneath the translucent water. However, once it became apparent that the new High Dam would submerge Philae forever, UNESCO and the EAO organized a massive operation (1972–80) to **relocate its temples** on nearby **Aglika Island**, which was landscaped to match the original site. The new Philae is magnificently set amidst volcanic outcrops, like a jewel in the royal blue lake, but no longer faces Biga Island, sacred to Osiris, whence its holiness derived.

Getting there

Most people visit Philae on **taxi tours from Aswan** (see p.473), which is the only easy way of getting there and back. Taxis drop you at the **Shallal** motorboat dock, 2km from the eastern end of the Old Dam, where you can buy site **tickets** (daily 7am–5pm; Ramadan 7am–4pm; £E35). Having agreed on a price for a motorboat to the island (officially £E25 return per boat-load or £E2.50 each for more than eight people), you shouldn't pay anything until you're back on shore, obliging the boatman to wait while you explore; if you linger more than an hour, *baksheesh* is in order. There's nowhere to buy food or drink on the island.

Sound and Light Show

Some reckon that Philae's **Sound and Light Show** is even better than the one at Karnak, due to its island setting. There are two or three performances nightly; check the schedules at the tourist office. As at Karnak, the show consists of an hour-long tour through the ruins, whose floodlit forms are more impressive than the melodramatic soundtrack. By manoeuvring yourself into the front row, you can enjoy a panoramic view of the entire complex without having to swivel your head during the second act. **Tickets** (£E55; no student reductions) are sold at the dockside just before the first show begins. You'll need to rent a **taxi** from Aswan to take you there and back; expect to pay £E20–25 for a four-seater cab (including waiting time), plus £E30–35 for the motorboat ride there and back.

The Temple of Isis

Philae's cult status dates back to the New Kingdom, when Biga Island was identified as one of the burial places of Osiris – and the first piece of land to emerge from the primordial waters of Chaos. Since Biga was forbidden to all but the priesthood, however, public festivities centred upon neighbouring **Philae**, which was known originally as the "Island from the Time of Re".

Excluding a few remains from the Late Period, the existing **Temple of Isis** was constructed over some eight hundred years by Ptolemaic and Roman rulers who sought to identify themselves with the Osirian myth and the cult of Isis (see above). An exquisite fusion of ancient Egyptian and Greco-Roman architecture, the temple complex harmonizes perfectly with its setting, sculpted pillars and pylons gleaming white or mellow gold against Mediterranean-blue water and black Nilotic rock.

The cult of Isis

Of all the cults of ancient Egypt, none endured longer or spread further than the worship of the goddess **Isis**. As the consort of Osiris, she civilized the world by instituting marriage and teaching women the domestic arts. As an enchantress, she collected the dismembered fragments of his body and briefly revived him to conceive a son, Horus, using her magic to help him defeat the evil Seth and restore the divine order. As pharaohs identified themselves with Horus, the living king, so Isis was their divine mother; a role which inevitably associated her with Hathor, the two goddesses being conflated in the Late Period. By this time Isis was the Great Mother of All Gods and Nature, Goddess of Ten Thousand Names, of women, purity and sexuality.

▲ Isis

By a process of identification with other goddesses around the Mediterranean, **Isis-worship** eventually spread throughout the Roman empire (the westernmost *Iseum* or cult temple extant is in Hungary). The nurturing, forgiving, loving Isis was Christianity's chief rival between the third and fifth centuries. Many scholars believe that the cult of the Virgin Mary was Christianity's attempt to wean converts away from Isis; early Coptic art identifies one with the other, Horus with Jesus, and the Christian cross with the pharaonic *ankh*.

Approaching the temple

Motorboats land near an ancient quay at the southern end of the island. In ancient times, on the original Philae, visitors ascended a double stairway to the **Vestibule of Nectanebo** at the entrance to the temple precincts. Erected by a XXX Dynasty pharaoh in honour of his "Mother Isis", this was the prototype for the graceful kiosks of the Ptolemaic and Roman era. Notice the double capitals on the remaining columns: traditional flower shapes topped with sistrum-Hathor squares that supported the architrave. The screens that once formed the walls are crowned with cavetto cornices and rows of *uraeus* serpents, a motif dating back to Zoser's complex at Saqqara, nearly three thousand years earlier.

Beyond the vestibule stretches an elongated trapezoidal courtyard flanked by colonnades. The **West Colonnade** is the better preserved, with finely carved capitals, each slightly different. The windows in the wall behind once faced Biga, the island of Osiris; the one opposite the first two columns is topped by a relief of Nero offering two eyes to Horus and Isis. The plainer, unfinished **East Colonnade** abuts a succession of ruined structures. Past the foundations of the **Temple of Arensnupis** (worshipped as the "Good Companion of Isis" in the Late Period) lies a ruined **Chapel of Mandulis**, the Nubian god of Kalabsha. Near the First Pylon, an unfinished **Temple of Imhotep** honours the philosopher-physician who designed Zoser's Step Pyramid and was later deified as a god of healing. Its forecourt walls show Khnum, Satis, Anukis, Isis and Osiris, and Ptolemy IV before Imhotep.

The Pylons and Forecourt

The lofty **First Pylon** was built by Neos Dionysos, who smites enemies in the approved fashion at either corner, watched by Isis, Horus and Hathor. Set at right angles to the pylon, the Gate of Ptolemy II **[a]** is probably a remnant of an earlier temple. The pylon's main portal **[b]** is still older (dating from the reign of Nectanebo II) and was formerly flanked by two granite obelisks; now only two **stone lions** remain. Inside the portal are inscriptions by Napoleon's troops, commemorating their victory over the Mamlukes in 1799. The smaller door in the western section of the pylon leads through to the Birth House and was used for *mamissi* rituals; the entrance depicts the personified deities of Nubia and the usual Egyptian pantheon **[c]**. On the back of the pylon are scenes of priests carrying Isis's barque.

Emerging into the **Forecourt**, most visitors make a beeline for the Birth House (see below) or the Second Pylon, overlooking the colonnade to the east. Here, reliefs behind the stylish plant columns show the king performing rituals such as dragging the barque of Sokar **[d]**. A series of doors lead into six rooms which probably had a service function; one of them, dubbed the Library **[e]**, features Thoth in his ibis and baboon forms, Maat, lion-headed Tefnut and Sheshat, the goddess of writing. At the northern end stands a ruined chapel **[f]**, which the Romans erected in front of a granite outcrop that was smoothed into a stele under Ptolemy IV and related his gift of lands to the temple.

Set at an angle to its forerunner, the **Second Pylon** changes the axis of the temple. A large relief on the right tower shows Neos Dionysos placing sacrifices before Horus and Hathor; in a smaller scene above he presents a wreath to Horus and Nephthys, offers incense and anoints an altar before Osiris, Isis and Horus. Similar scenes on the other tower have been defaced by early Christians, who executed the paintings in the upper right-hand corner of the pylon passageway, leading into the temple proper.

The Birth House

The western side of the forecourt is dominated by the colonnaded **Birth House** of Ptolemy IV, which linked his ancestry to Horus and Osiris. Most of the exterior reliefs were added in Roman times, which explains why the Emperor Augustus shadows Buto, goddess of the north, as she plays a harp before the young, naked Horus and his mother at one end of the central register, behind the Hathor-headed colonnade **[g]**. Further south and higher up, the Roman reliefs overlie inscriptions in hieroglyphs and demotic characters that partly duplicate those on the Rosetta Stone **[h]**. Inside the *mamissi*, a columned forecourt and two vestibules precede the sanctuary, which contains the finest scenes **[i]**. Although iconoclasts have defaced the goddess suckling the child-pharaoh on the left-hand wall, you can see Isis giving birth to Horus in the marshes at the bottom of the rear wall. Around the back of the sanctuary behind the northern colonnade is a corresponding scene of Isis nursing Horus in the swamp **[j]**.

Inside the Temple of Isis

Immediately behind the Second Pylon lies a small open court that was origi-nally separated from the **Hypostyle Hall** by a screen wall, now destroyed. A lovely drawing by David Roberts shows this "Grand Portico" in its rich original colours: the flowering capitals in shades of green with yellow flowers and blue buds; crimson and golden winged sun-discs flying down the central aisle of the ceiling, which elsewhere bears astronomical reliefs. The unpainted walls and column shafts show the hall's builder, Ptolemy VII Euergetes II, sacrificing to various deities. After the emperor Justinian forbade the celebration of Isis rituals at Philae in 550 AD, Copts used the hall for services and chiselled crosses into the walls. On the left-hand jamb of the portal **[k]** into the vestibule beyond, a piece of Roman graffiti asserts *B Mure stultus est* ("B Mure is stupid").

As at other temples, the **vestibules** get lower and darker as you approach the sanctuary. By a doorway **[l]** to the right of the first vestibule, a Greek inscrip-tion records the "cleansing" of this pagan structure under Bishop Theodorus, during the reign of Justinian. On the other side of the vestibule is a room giving access to the **stairs** to the roof (see below). The next vestibule has an interesting scene flanking the portal at the back **[m]**, where the king offers a sistrum (left) and wine (right) to Isis and Harpocrates. On the left-hand door jamb, he leaves offerings to Min, a basket to Sekhmet and wine to Osiris, with the sacred bull and seven cows in the background. In the partially ruined transverse vestibule, the king offers necklaces, wine and eye paint to Osiris, Isis, Hathor and Nephthys, outside the sanctuary **[n]**.

Dimly lit by two apertures in the roof, the **sanctuary** contains a stone pedestal dedicated by Ptolemy III and his wife Berenice, which once supported the goddess's barque. On the left wall, the pharaoh faces Isis, whose wings protectively enfold Osiris. Across the room, an enthroned Isis suckles the infant Horus (above) and stands to suckle a young pharaoh (below, and now defaced). The other rooms, used for rites or storage, contain reliefs of goddesses with Nubian features.

The Osirian Shrine

Try to persuade a guard to unlock the stairway to the roof, where a series of sunken rooms dwells on the resurrection of Osiris. After scenes of lamentation in the vestibule of this **Osirian Shrine**, you can see Isis gathering up his limbs, and the slain god lying naked and tumescent upon a bier (as always, the phallus has been vandalized). Mourned by Isis and Nephthys, Osiris revives to impregnate his sister-wife, while Selket and Douait reconstruct his body for its solar rebirth. Cast as the hawk-headed Sokar, Osiris is borne away to a papyrus swamp by the four sons of Horus, to be anointed with holy water with Anubis in attendance.

Hadrian's Gate

By leaving the temple through the western door of the first vestibule you'll emerge near **Hadrian's Gate**, set into the girdle wall that once encircled the island. Flanking your approach are two walls from a bygone vestibule, decorated with notable reliefs. The right-hand wall **[o]** depicts the origin of the Nile, whose twin streams are poured forth by Hapy the Nile-god from his cave beneath Biga Island, atop which perches a falcon. To the right of this, Isis, Nephthys and others adore the young falcon as he rises from a marsh.

Above the door in the opposite wall **[p]**, Isis and Nephthys present the dual crowns to Horus, whose name is inscribed on a palm stalk by Sheshat (right) and Thoth (left). Below, Isis watches a crocodile drag the corpse of Osiris to a rocky promontory (presumably Biga). Around the gate itself, Hadrian appears before the gods (above the lintel) and the door jambs bear the fetishes of Abydos (left) and Osiris (right). At the top of the wall, Marcus Aurelius stands before Isis and Osiris; below he offers Isis grapes and flowers.

North of the gateway lie the foundations of the **Temple of Harendotes** (an aspect of Horus), built by the emperor Claudius.

The Temple of Hathor and Trajan's Kiosk

To complete the cast of deities involved in the Osirian myth, a small **Temple of Hathor** was erected to the east of the main complex. Aside from two Hathor-headed columns *in situ* and fragmented capitals out back, the ruined temple is only notable for a relief of musicians, amongst whom the god Bes plays a harp. More eye-catching and virtually the symbol of Philae is the graceful open-topped **Kiosk of Trajan**, nicknamed the "Pharaoh's Bedstead". Removed from its watery grave by a team of British navy divers, the reconstructed kiosk juxtaposes variegated floral columns with a severely classical superstructure; only two of the screen wall panels bear reliefs.

Last in order of priority come the ruined **Temple of Augustus** and the **Gate of Diocletian**, which shared the northern end of old Philae with a mud-brick Roman village that was so eroded by repeated soakings that it was left to be submerged by the lake. The **toilets** lie in this direction.

Kalabsha

The hulking **Temple of Kalabsha** broods beside Lake Nasser near the western end of the High Dam, marooned on an island or strung out on a promontory, depending on the water level. Between the site and the dam lies a graveyard of boats and fishy remains, enhancing its mood of desolation. The main temple originally came from Talmis (later known as Kalabsha), 50km to the south of Aswan; in a German-financed operation, it was cut into 13,000 blocks and reassembled here in 1970, together with other monuments from Nubia. Strictly speaking, "Kalabsha" refers to the original site rather than the temple itself, which is named after the god Mandulis, and has no historic connection with two smaller monuments in the vicinity, relocated here from other sites in Nubia.

Getting there

Taxis are the best way of getting to Kalabsha and back. Official rates for a round trip from Aswan are £E25 for a four-seater taxi, £E35 for a seven-seater Peugeot. Better still, include Kalabsha in a half-day taxi tour taking in Philae, the dams and the Unfinished Obelisk (see p.473). Either is preferable to the penny-pinching alternative of taking a **train** to Sadd al-Ali Station (see p.483), then walking or hitching up to the dam and across to the other side of the lake (almost 10km in all).

Motorboats will take you over to Kalabsha and back for £E25 (for the whole boat; 6–8 people) with an hour at **the site** (daily 7am–5pm; £E20), which is sufficient; tickets are sold at the temple itself.

The Temple of Mandulis

The **Temple of Mandulis** is a Ptolemaic-Roman version of an earlier XVIII Dynasty edifice dedicated to the Nubian fertility god Marul, whom the Greeks called Mandulis.

By Ptolemaic times, Egypt's Nubian empire was a token one, dependent on the goodwill of the powerful Nabatean empire ruled from Merowe near the Fourth Cataract, about 400km south of Abu Simbel. Having briefly restored old-style imperialism, the Romans abandoned most of Nubia during the reign of Diocletian, falling back on deals with local rulers to safeguard Egypt's southern border. As the linchpin of the last imperial town south of Aswan, the temple bears witness to this patronage and the kingdoms that succeeded the Nabatean empire, which disintegrated under the onslaught of marauding Blemmye (c.550 AD), a group of nomadic tribes who were perhaps the ancestors of the modern Beja.

The causeway, court and facade

Approaching the sandstone temple from behind, you miss the dramatic effect of the great stone **causeway** from the water's edge, used by pilgrims in the days when Kalabsha was a healing temple, like Edfu and Dendara. For reasons unknown, its chunky **pylon** is skewed at a slight angle to the temple, a blemish rectified by having a trapezoidal **courtyard** whose pillars are set closer together along the shorter, southern side.

The first batch of reliefs worth a mention occurs on the **facade** of the Hypostyle Hall at the back of the court. While Horus and Thoth anoint the king with holy water in a conventional scene to the left of the portal, the right-hand wall bears a decree excluding swineherds and their pigs from the temple (issued in 249 AD); a large relief of a horseman in Roman dress receiving a wreath from the winged Victory; and a text in poor Greek lauding Siklo, the Christian king of the Nabatae, for repulsing the Blemmye.

The Hypostyle Hall and Sanctuary

The now roofless **Hypostyle Hall** is distinguished by columns with ornate flowered capitals, and some interesting reliefs along the rear wall. Left of the portal, a Ptolemaic king offers crowns to Horus and Mandulis, while Amenhotep II (founder of the XVIII Dynasty temple) presents a libation to Mandulis and Min. Across the way, a nameless king slays a foe before Horus, Shu and Tefnet.

Within the **vestibules** beyond, look for figures personifying the Egyptian nomes, below a scene of the king offering wine to Osiris and a field to Isis and Mandulis (near the stairs off the pronaos or outer vestibule); and a rare appearance by the deified Imhotep (low down on the left-hand wall of the naos or inner vestibule).

The **Sanctuary** is similar in size to the vestibules and, like them, once had two columns. Along its back wall you can identify (from left to right) the emperor offering lotuses to Isis and the young Horus, and milk to Mandulis and Wadjet; then incense to the former duo and lotuses to the latter. Although the god's cult statue has vanished, Mandulis still appears at either end of the scene covering the temple's **rear wall**: in his royal form, with a pharaonic crown, sceptre and *ankh* sign (right); and as a god whose ram's-horn crown is surmounted by a solar disc, *uraeus* and ostrich plumes (left).

From the temple's pronaos, you may be able to ascend a stairway to the **roof**, which features an abbreviated version of the Osirian shrines found at other complexes. The **view** of Lake Nasser and the High Dam, over the temple courtyards, is amazing. A passageway between the temple and its enclosure wall leads to a well-preserved **Nilometer**.

The Kiosk of Qertassi and Beit al-Wali

Re-erected near the lakeside at the same time as Kalabsha Temple, the **Kiosk of Qertassi** resembles a knocked-about copy of the "Pharaoh's Bedstead" at Philae, but actually came from another ancient settlement, 40km south of Aswan. Aside from its fine views of Lake Nasser, this Ptolemaic-Roman edifice is chiefly notable for two surviving Hathor-headed columns, which make the goddess look more feline than bovine. In the forecourt, notice the women pleading for mercy as Ramses seizes their menfolk, and the Nubians paying tribute in the form of gold, ivory, leopard skins, feathers, and even an ostrich.

The oldest monumental relic from Nile-inundated Nubia is a temple dug into the hillside behind Kalabsha Temple. Originally hewn under Ramses II, who left his mark throughout Nubia, this cruciform rock-cut structure is known by its Arabic name, **Beit al-Wali** (House of the Holy Man). The weathered reliefs flanking its narrow court depict the pharaoh's victories over Nubians and Ethiopians (left), Libyans and Asiatics (right). By contrast, scenes in the transverse hall are well preserved and brightly coloured. Here, Ramses makes offerings before Isis, Horus and the Aswan Triad (Hapy, Satet and Khnum), and is suckled by goddesses inside the sanctuary, whose niche contains a mutilated cult statue of three deities.

Wadi el-Seboua, Amada and Qasr Ibrim

As Lake Nasser rose behind the High Dam, flooding ancient Nubia, mudbrick fortresses and burial grounds were excavated and photographed before being abandoned to the rising waters, and half a dozen temples and tombs were salvaged, to be reassembled on higher ground or in foreign museums. At the time of writing, the three reconstructed sites known as **Wadi el-Seboua**, **Amada** and **Qasr Ibrim** can only be seen while **cruising on Lake Nasser** (detailed in the box on p.483), but spur roads to Wadi el-Seboua and Amada have been built so access might improve if security restrictions are ever eased. Meanwhile, cruise boats provide their passengers with motorboat rides to Wadi el-Seboua and Amada, moor tantalizingly close to Qasr Ibrim (where you can't land), and end or start their tours at Abu Simbel or Kalabsha.

Wadi el-Seboua

Cruise boats departing from the High Dam must sail nearly half the length of Lake Nasser before they reach **Wadi el-Seboua**. They usually moor there after dark for passengers to enjoy an awesome floodlit vista of three temples, joined by what appears to be a long processional avenue, which is revealed next morning to be a track across a desert of tan-coloured sand and grey rocks. The landscape is dotted with a few swathes of grass and a half-submerged crane that was used to transport the main temple from its original location, 4km away. **Admission** to the site costs £E35 (no student reductions).

Wadi el-Seboua means "Valley of the Lions" in Arabic and refers to the **avenue of sphinxes** leading to the **temple** of that name. It was built during the reign of Ramses II by his viceroy of Kush, Setau, using Libyan prisoners of war, who also worked on Abu Simbel. Like Abu Simbel, it was dedicated to Amun-Re, Re-Herakhte and the deified pharaoh, whose role as a conqueror is emphasized by images of Libyan and Asiatic captives carved on the pedestals of the statues of the king that flank its gateway. In the second court, the human-headed sphinxes give way to falcon-headed ones, representing the four forms of Horus, and archeologists have discerned a subtle attempt to "rehabilitate" Seth – the reviled murderer of Osiris – by using red sandstone for the steps and base of the temple proper. (Red was the colour associated with Seth, who was the patron deity of the Delta city of Avaris, whence the Ramessid dynasty originated.)

Beyond the temple **pylon** is an **open court** with columns fronted by Osiride statues of Ramses, notable for their thick legs. Scholars disagree whether this reflected his physique or was merely to make him look stronger, but this feature occurs on all statues of Ramses, whose virility is further attested to by images of his numerous progeny (53 princes and 54 princesses) below the offering scenes on the walls. The remainder of the temple is cut from rock and once served as a Christian church; its **reliefs** retain much of their scarlet, white and yellow paint due to being covered by plaster for centuries. The best-preserved ones are in the transverse vestibule, including an unusual portrayal of Hathor with a woman's body and a cow's head. You can also see Ramses making offerings to his own sphinx, above and behind the doorway into the sanctuary, where a votive niche contains remnants of the Christian murals that once covered the walls, resulting in a surreal tableau of Ramses offering flowers to St Peter.

Temple of Dakka

From Wadi el-Seboua, passengers can walk or ride a camel (£E35) 1.5km across the desert to the hilltop **Temple of Dakka** that once stood 40km north of its present site. Its most striking feature is an elegant freestanding **pylon**, which is over 12m tall; visitors are sometimes allowed to climb it, which affords them a fantastic view of the area. You may also see **hawks**, hovering on thermals above the pylon. There isn't much carving on the walls but the gateway is crowned by a winged sun-disc, and on its left-hand side is graffiti in Meroitic script thought to have been left by Nubian soldiers, retreating from Aswan in 23 AD.

The temple itself was started by **Arkamani**, one of the rulers (218–200 BC) of the Kingdom of Meroe – which at that time controlled Lower Nubia – and was added to by his contemporary, **Ptolemy IV**, and decorated by later Ptolemies. You can see the Hellenistic influence in the composite capitals (combining Greek and Egyptian forms) and scenes in the pronaos, where Isis sports big breasts in the Greek style. Also notice the four sacred cobras, carved in the corners of the entrance wall. On many of the reliefs in the temple the king performing the rituals is simply identified by a cartouche reading "Pharaoh", as the masons didn't know who was in power at the time in Alexandria, or didn't want to inscribe the name of a Ptolemy who wouldn't be on the throne for long – though this wasn't the case for Ptolemy IV and his sister-wife Arsinöe, who are shown offering a Maat (truth) figure to Thoth and Wepset on the lintel of the doorway into the vestibule.

At the back of the vestibule is a passageway and stairs leading to the **roof**, which affords a stunning view, while beyond lies the **Chapel of Arkamani** that originally served as the temple's sanctuary. Here, Arkamani makes offerings to the gods beneath a frieze of his cartouche interspersed with falcons and ibises, while on the rear wall is an interesting relief of Thoth as an ape adoring Tefnut, who is shown as a lioness. The temple was dedicated to a local form of Thoth called Thoth of Pnubs (literally, "sycamore-fig tree"), his consort Tefnut and their "offspring" Arensnupis, a Nubian god of the Meroitic era whom the Egyptians called "The Good Companion of Isis". A baboon worshipping a lion can also be seen in the side-passage leading off the chapel, while another ape consorts with a cow beneath a persea tree low down in the near right-hand corner of the sanctuary, which was built and decorated under the Roman emperors Augustus and Tiberius. Upon leaving the temple, walk around the east wall to see a **waterspout** in the shape of a lion's head, which shows that there must have been the occasional rainfall in ancient times.

Temple of Maharraqa

A short way downhill back towards the shore stands the small **Temple of Maharraqa**, taken from a site 50km north of its present location, which was the southern frontier of Egypt in Greco-Roman times. Its floral capitals and reliefs were left unfinished – in some places only roughly sketched in reddish-brown paint – and the temple's most interesting feature is the **spiral staircase** up to the roof, the only spiral staircase known in an ancient Egyptian building. The temple was probably dedicated to Seraphis.

Amada

Beyond Wadi el-Seboua, Lake Nasser describes an S-shaped curve that takes it past another set of temples in one of the loveliest parts of Nubia, where the rocky desert shoreline is fringed with acacia scrub. As at Wadi el-Seboua, cruise passengers are ferried to **Amada** by motorboat, and all three monuments are covered by one **ticket** (£E35; no student reductions). Bring a **torch** for examining the reliefs inside the temples.

Temple of Amada

The site is named after the **Temple of Amada**, which is the oldest surviving structure on Lake Nasser and contains some of the finest relief-carving to be seen on any of the Nubian monuments. It was built by the XVIII Dynasty pharaohs Tuthmosis III, Amenophis II and Tuthmosis IV, and restored and decorated during the XIX Dynasty. Like most of the Nubian temples, it was dedicated to Amun-Re and Re-Herakhte, who appear with various pharaohs in the usual offerings scenes. For archeologists, the temple is particularly interesting for two historic **inscriptions**: the first, carved on a stele on the left side of the entrance, describes the Libyan invasion of Egypt in the fourth year (1232 BC) of Merneptah's reign; while the other, on the back wall of the sanctuary, dates from the second year (1423 BC) of Amenophis II's reign, and relates how he dealt with seven leaders of a revolt in Syria, whose heads and limbs were hung on the gates of Thebes as a warning to other would-be rebels.

When Amelia Edwards visited Amada in 1873 she found the temple "half-choked" with sand, so that she had to crawl into the sanctuary on all fours; judging by the **camels** drawn by Bedouin and pilgrims on the cornice of the facade, it was buried so in medieval times. The inner part of the temple consists of a vestibule and sanctuary with a small cult-chamber on either side, whose **reliefs** are as lapidary as any produced during the XVIII Dynasty. The ones in the right-hand room depict the foundation and consecration of the temple; Tuthmosis III and Amenophis II make offerings to the gods in the other chamber. Amada Temple originally stood 2.6km from its present site, and was moved there on flatcars by French engineers in a race against the rising waters of the lake.

Temple of Derr

A few minutes' walk from Amada is the smaller **Temple of Derr**, once located on the east bank of the Nile (the only one in Nubia on that side of the river). With its gateway gone and its pillared forehall reduced to stumps, the temple now confronts visitors with a rugged portico featuring four square pillars and statues of Ramses II only roughed-out to waist-level. The interior of the temple was entirely hewn from rock, with few straight lines or right angles, and its sunk-reliefs finished in stucco with painted details. On the side walls of the pillared hall, Re-Herakhte's sacred barque is carried in a procession on the shoulders of priests, as Ramses walks alongside wearing a leopard-skin cloak; the white background and the yellow of the barque and cloak are still visible. More colours survive on the walls of the sanctuary, where Ramses burns incense and pours a libation to the barque before annointing Re-Herakhte with his little finger (right). At the back, the four cult-statues that originally represented Ramses, Amun-Re, Re-Herakhte and Ptah were hacked away by Christian iconoclasts.

Tomb of Pennut

Leaving Derr temple it's worth hurrying on ahead to get to the **Tomb of Pennut**, as it's only large enough to hold a few people. Pennut (or Penne) was a high official in Lower Nubia during the reign of Ramses VI, whose tomb was originally dug into a hillside at Aniba, 40km south of its present site.

Sunk-reliefs in the rectangular offerings chamber show Pennut and his wife before the gods, mourners at his funeral, and Pennut worshipping the cow-goddess Hathor in the Western Mountains. Upon leaving the tomb, its custodian delves into a bucket to extract a baby **crocodile**, which he offers to tourists for a photo opportunity. The shallows of Lake Nasser beyond Amada are home to many crocodiles (up to 5m long) and monitor lizards (up to 2.1m long), but they avoid the spots frequented by tourists and are mainly only seen by the 5000 fishermen who spend up to six months at a time in small rowing boats, collectively harvesting up to 50,000 tonnes of fish a year from the lake.

Qasr Ibrim

Qasr Ibrim – the last stop on the cruise before Abu Simbel – is unique for being the only one of the Nubian sites to remain *in situ*, albeit nowadays on an island rather than on the summit of a hill, since the lake rose 70m. This continuity has allowed the Egypt Exploration Society to carry out **excavations** every two years since 1961 and establish that Qasr Ibrim was occupied throughout successive periods from the late New Kingdom until the early nineteenth century, when it was inhabited by Bosnian mercenaries of the Ottoman empire, who married into the local Nubian community. Before their arrival in the sixteenth century, Qasr Ibrim was one of the last redoubts of Christianity in Lower Nubia, as it had previously been the last area to forsake paganism, abandoning the worship of Isis 200 years after the rest of Egypt. Its ruined sandstone **cathedral** dates back to the eighth century and overlies a temple of Isis built by the Nubian XXV Dynasty pharaoh Taharka; as many as six temples once have existed here. The cathedral's broken vaults rise amidst a muddle of dry-stone and cut-masonry walls, riddled with portals, niches and cavities, attesting to the age and complexity of the site. Due to its fragility and the ongoing excavations, tourists are not allowed to land here, but boats moor so close to the shore that the ruins can easily be seen, or closely examined with **binoculars**. Qasr Ibrim's unusual name is derived from the ancient *Pedme*, which became *Primis* in Greek, *Phrim* in Coptic and finally *Ibrim* in Arabic (which has no sound for "p").

Abu Simbel

The great **Sun Temple** of **Abu Simbel** epitomizes the monumentalism of the New Kingdom during its imperial heyday, when Ramses II (1304–1237 BC) waged colonial wars from the Beka'a Valley in Lebanon to the Fourth Cataract. To impress his power and majesty on the Nubians, Ramses had four gigantic statues of himself hewn from the mountainside, whence his unblinking stare confronted travellers as they entered Egypt from Africa. The temple he built here was precisely oriented so that the sun's rays reached deep into the mountain to illuminate its sanctuary on his birthday and the anniversary of his coronation. The deified pharaoh physically overshadows the sun-god **Re-Herakhte**, to whom the temple is nominally dedicated, just as his queen, **Nefertari**, sidelines **Hathor** in a neighbouring edifice, also hewn into the mountain.

The first European to see Abu Simbel since antiquity was the Swiss explorer Burckhardt, who found the temples almost completely buried by sand drifts in 1813. Although Belzoni later managed to clear an entrance, lack of treasure discouraged further efforts and the site was soon reburied in sand so fine "that every particle would go through an hourglass"; a process repeated throughout the nineteenth century. After Robert Hay took a cast of the face of the northern colossus, leaving it disfigured by lumps of plaster, Amelia Edwards ordered her sailors to remove the residue and tint the white stains with coffee, dismaying the vessel's cook, who had never "been called upon to provide for a guest whose mouth measured three feet and a half in width". Finally cleared, the temple became the scenic highlight of Thomas Cook's Nile cruises.

It was the prospect of losing Abu Simbel to Lake Nasser that impelled UNESCO to organize the salvage of Nubian monuments in the 1960s. Behind the temporary protection of a coffer dam, Abu Simbel's brittle sandstone was stabilized by injections of synthetic resin and then hand-sawn into 1041 blocks weighing up to thirty tons apiece. Precision was mandatory; the cuts had to be no more than 6mm wide. Two years after the first block was cut, Abu Simbel was reassembled 210m behind (and 61m above) its original site, a false mountain being constructed to match the former setting. The whole operation (from 1964 to 1968) cost US$40 million and is still being paid for; the cost of Egyptian tourist visas supposedly goes towards repayments.

Visiting Abu Simbel

Abu Simbel lies on the west bank of Lake Nasser, 280km south of Aswan and 40km north of the Sudanese border. A road runs there from Aswan, used by tourist vehicles travelling in a convoy, and public buses at other times. The site can also be reached by air or water – notably on the **luxury cruises** (p.483) that also visit other sites on Lake Nasser (see Wadi el-Seboua, Amada and Qasr Ibrim, on p.491). Although most tourists visit Abu Simbel on a **day-trip** from Aswan, it's quite feasible to spend a night there.

Getting there

From Aswan, Thomas Cook, Misr Travel and other agencies offer daily **excursions** by a/c coach for groups of ten (US$75), while low-budget hotels like the *Nubian Oasis* and the *Noorhan* offer trips in cramped minibuses for £E35 per head. Both travel in a **convoy** of tourist vehicles which leaves town at 4.30am, arrives at Abu Simbel three and a half hours later, and starts the return journey at 10am. This schedule makes sense given the heat of the desert, but means that hundreds of tourists arrive at the same time, packing out the temples. If you want to enjoy them in privacy and stay longer at Abu Simbel, there are five public **buses** (4hr; £E20) a day from Aswan, which tourists can use providing there aren't more than four of them aboard the vehicle. Services run by the Upper Egypt Bus Co. and the private operator El Gouna both leave from the main bus station.

For those with more cash, **flying** saves time and provides a unique view of Lake Nasser and Abu Simbel. EgyptAir flights from Aswan and Luxor are scheduled according to demand, with a dozen flights a day at busy times, and around

Photographing Abu Simbel

Abu Simbel is an awkward subject for **photography**. The immense facade should be snapped in the morning before it's cast into shadow, and needs a wide-angle lens to do it justice; details, however, are best captured with a telephoto lens (it also helps to underexpose the shot by 1–1.5 stops). To photograph Abu Simbel from the air, sit on the left side of the plane and use a telephoto (at least 200mm) lens with a haze filter. Depending on how many tour groups are visiting, it may be difficult to photograph the interior of the temples. There is **no charge** for cameras or camcorders, but flash photography is forbidden.

three when tourism is low. Most people opt for a same-day return flight from Aswan (£E658, including airport transfers); if you want to stay overnight you have to use the 11.15am flight. For those with more time and money, a luxury **cruise** to Abu Simbel is the best way to appreciate Lake Nasser and see the temples as the pharaohs did (see p.483 for details).

Abu Simbel town practicalities

Roughly 2km from the temple site, the new town of **ABU SIMBEL** (meaning "Father of the Ear of Corn" in Arabic) looks a desolate place as you roll in past the airport, but once beyond the main square it becomes quite picturesque as it straggles around rocky headlands dotted with beehive-domed houses and crimson oleander bushes. From the junction with its row of **cafés**, you can turn left and follow the main road as it curves around towards the temple, 1km away. This takes you past a **telephone office**, a **pharmacy** and three **banks** (none with ATMs; all closed Fri), followed by a **post office** with the **tourist police** around the corner, before you pass the town council and reach the stone-faced souvenir arcade that precedes the visitors' centre and ticket office for the temples – about fifteen minutes' walk in all.

Should you wish **to stay**, the only cheap option is the *Abu Simbel Village* (☎097/340-0092; ❷), a small, pink complex of a/c rooms with TV, fridges and bathrooms, 200m from the main intersection in the opposite direction from the temples, beyond the three-star *Noblah Ramses Hotel* (☎097/340-1118, ℗340-0106; ❺).Two pricier holiday villages lie out towards the temple: *Seti Abu Simbel* (☎097/340-0720, ℗340-0829, ⓦwww.setifirst.com; ❼), near the banks, has a/c rooms with fridge, TV and large bathrooms, in a lush garden with three pools, overlooking Lake Nasser; while *Nefertari* (☎097/340-0508, ℗340-0510; ❻), down a sidestreet between the town council and the tourist arcade, is similar, but older and shabbier. Both officially charge the same year-round, but summer discounts can be obtained through Eastmar Travel in Aswan (on the Corniche near Thomas Cook) or Cairo (13 Sharia Qasr el-Nil).

The small **hospital** en route to the *Abu Simbel Village* has a surgeon but no anaesthetist, and probably only exists because President Sadat had a holiday villa built at Abu Simbel (seldom used by Mubarak). Tourists on cruise boats may feel like VIPs themselves, insofar as it's hard to go far from the boats (which moor nearby, but just out of sight of, the temples) without an armed police escort.

The Sound and Light Show

Cruise-boat passengers provide most of the audience at the nightly **Sound and Light Show** (£E55; no student discounts), starting at 6.30pm, 7.45pm and 9pm in the winter and one hour later in summer. Don't worry about which language the show is in, as they provide headphones for simultaneous translation and, in any case, the images projected onto the temple facades are more arresting than the soundtrack. Tickets are sold at the temple ticket office.

The Sun Temple of Ramses II

Having checked out the **Visitors' Centre**, which relates how the temples were moved to their present location, visitors walk around the hill to be confronted by the great **Sun Temple** (daily 6am–5pm, later if planes land in the evening; £E55, student £E27, plus £E4 guide fee and £E2 local tax), seemingly hewn from the cliffs overlooking Lake Nasser. Having been depicted on everything from T-shirts to £E1 notes, its impact is perhaps a little diminished by familiarity: the technicolour contrast between red rockscape and aquamarine water is more startling than the clean-swept facade, which looks less dramatic than the sand-choked Abu Simbel of nineteenth-century engravings. For all the meticulous reconstruction and landscaping, too, it's hard not to sense its artificiality … but gradually the temple's presence asserts itself and your mind boggles at its audacious conception, the logistics of constructing and moving it, and the unabashed megalomania of its founder.

Although Re-Herakhte, Amun-Re and Ptah are also billed as patron deities, they're clearly secondary to Ramses, the pharaoh-god whom courtiers feared as "a powerful lion with claws extended and a terrible roar". He ruled for 67 years, dying at the age of 96, having sired scores of sons, most of whom predeceased him.

The colossi and facade

The temple facade is dominated by four enthroned **Colossi of Ramses II**, whose twenty-metre height surpasses the Colossi of Memnon at Thebes (though one lost its upper half following an earthquake in 27 BC). Their feet and legs are crudely executed but the torsos and heads are finely carved, and the face of the left-hand figure is quite beautiful. Between them stand figures of the royal family, dwarfed by Ramses' knees. To the left of the headless colossus is the pharaoh's mother, Muttuy; Queen Nefertari stands on the right of the colossus;

Cross-section of he Sun Temple

Prince Amunhirkhepshef between its legs. On the right leg of this same figure, an inscription records that Greek mercenaries participated in the Nubian campaign of the Saïte king Psammetichus II (c.590 BC).

The **facade** is otherwise embellished with a niche-bound statue of **Re-Herakhte**, holding a *was* sceptre and a figure of Maat. This composition is a pictorial play of words on Ramses' prenomen, *User-Maat-Re*, so the flanking sunk-reliefs of the king presenting the god with images of Maat actually signify Ramses honouring his deified self. Crowning the facade is a corvetto cornice surmounted by baboons worshipping the rising sun. On the sides of the colossal thrones flanking the temple entrance, twin Nile-gods entwine the heraldic papyrus and sedge around the hieroglyph "to unite". The rows of captives depicted beneath them are divided between north and south, so that Asiatics feature on the northern (right-hand) throne, Nubians on its southern (left-hand) counterpart.

The Hypostyle Hall and Sanctuary

This schematic division reappears in the lofty rock-cut **Hypostyle Hall**, flanked on either side by four pillars fronted by ten-metre-high statues of Ramses in the Osiris position, carrying the crook and flail (the best is the end figure on the right). Beneath a ceiling painted with flying vultures, the walls crawl with scenes from his campaigns, from Syria to Nubia. On the entrance walls, Ramses slaughters Hittite and Nubian captives before Amun-Re (left) and Re-Herakhte (right), accompanied by his eight sons or nine daughters, and his *ka*. But the most dramatic **reliefs** are found on the side walls (all directions as if you're facing the back of the temple).

The right-hand wall depicts the **Battle of Qadesh** on the River Orontes (1300 BC), starting from the back of the hall. Here you see Ramses' army marching on Qadesh, followed by their encampment, ringed by shields. Acting on disinformation tortured out of enemy spies, Ramses prepares to attack the city and summons his reserve divisions down from the heights. The waiting Hittites ford the river, charge one division and scatter another to surround the king, who single-handedly cuts his way out of the trap. The final scene claims an unqualified Egyptian triumph, even though Ramses failed to take the city. Notwithstanding this, the opposite wall portrays him storming a Syrian fortress in his chariot (note the double arm, which some regard as an attempt at animation), lancing a Libyan and returning with fettered Nubians. Along the rear wall, he presents them to Amun, Mut and himself (left), and the captured Hittites to Re-Herakhte, lion-headed Wert-Hekew and his own deified personage (right).

The eight **lateral chambers** off the hall were probably used to store cult objects and tribute from Nubia, and are decorated with offering scenes. Reliefs in the smaller **pillared hall** show Ramses and Nefertari offering incense before the shrine and barque of Amun-Re (left) and Re-Herakhte (right). Walk through one of the doors at the back, cross the transverse vestibule and head for the central **Sanctuary**. Originally encased in gold, its four (now mutilated) cult statues wait to be touched by the sun's rays at dawn on February 22 and October 22. February 21 was Ramses' birthday and October 21 his coronation date, but the relocation of Abu Simbel has changed the timing of these **solar events** by one day. Perhaps significantly, the figure of Ptah "the Hidden One" is situated so that it alone remains in darkness when the sun illuminates Amun-Re, Re-Herakhte and Ramses the god. Before them is a stone block where the sacred barque once rested.

The Hathor Temple of Queen Nefertari

A little further north of the Sun Temple stands the smaller rock-hewn **Temple of Queen Nefertari**, identified here with the goddess Hathor, who was wife

---

The Toshka and East Oweinat irrigation projects

Inaugurated by President Mubarak in 1997, the **Toshka Project** is a huge-scale twenty-year venture whose goal is to cultivate 1.5 million *feddans* (1.4 million acres) of desert northwest of Abu Simbel, and settle six million people there. The alluvial soil is potentially fertile and experimental farms have already successfully grown cotton, cucumbers, tomatoes, watermelons, bananas, grapes and wheat. To irrigate the land, the Egyptians have spent US$1 billion creating the world's largest **pumping station** to extract five billion cubic metres of water from Lake Nasser annually, and digging the **Sheikh Zayed Canal**. Named after the president of the United Arab Emirates (a big investor), the main canal – completed in 2002 – is 50km long, 30m wide and 6m deep. Work is now underway on four branch canals totaling 159km in length, as well as auxiliary pumping stations. The government plans to deliver water to the edge of each property, leaving the owner to distribute it across his land. A 49-year lease costs only £E50 per *feddan*, with the largest investor being Saudi Prince Alwaleed Bin Talal, whose farm is visible on the way to Abu Simbel.

Toshka's critics claim that the Egyptian government will end up footing most of the cost of the project – rather than twenty percent, as envisaged – and the total bill has been projected to be a staggering US$66 billion. Besides the pumping station and the canal, there is a network of new roads linking Toshka to another irrigation project at **East Oweinat**, using aquifer water. Some fear that these projects are too ambitious and may turn out to be white elephants, though supporters point out that the same was said of the High Dam, without which Egypt could not sustain itself today.

Birdwatching at Abu Simbel

Due to its location on a large body of water surrounded by desert, near the Tropic of Cancer, Abu Simbel sustains both indigenous African and migrant species of birds. Among the rarer species are pink-backed pelicans, yellow-billed storks, long-tailed cormorants, African Skimmers and pied wagtails, and pink-headed doves. While serious twitchers will haunt the coves with binoculars, casual birdspotters can see quite a few dazzling birds in the grounds of the visitors' centre or the *Nefertari* and *Seti Abu Simbel* hotels. The best time for birdwatching is during the **breeding season** in late January/early February.

to the sun-god during his day's passage and mother to his rebirth at dawn. As with Ramses' temple, the rock-hewn facade imitates a receding pylon (whose corvetto cornice has fallen), its plane accentuated by a series of rising buttresses separating six **colossal statues of Ramses and Nefertari** (each over 9m tall), which seem to emerge from the rock. Each is accompanied by two smaller figures of their children, who stand knee-high in the shadows. A frieze of cobras protects the door into the temple, which is simpler in plan than Ramses', having but one columned hall and vestibule, and only two lateral chambers; it runs 24m into the hillside.

The best **reliefs** are in the hall with square, Hathor-headed pillars whose sides show the royal couple mingling with deities. On the entrance wall Nefertari watches Ramses slay Egypt's enemies; on the side walls she participates in rituals as his equal, appearing before Anuket (left) and Hathor (right). In the transverse vestibule beyond, the portal of the sanctuary is flanked by scenes of the royal couple offering wine and flowers to Amun-Re and Horus (left), Re-Herakhte, Khnum, Satet and Anuket (right). The **Sanctuary** niche contains a ruined cow-statue of Hathor, above which vultures guard Nefertari's cartouches. On the side walls, she offers incense to Mut and Hathor (left), while Ramses worships his own image and that of Nefertari (right). The predominance of yellow in the paintings may allude to Hathor's title, "The Golden One".

The Western Desert Oases

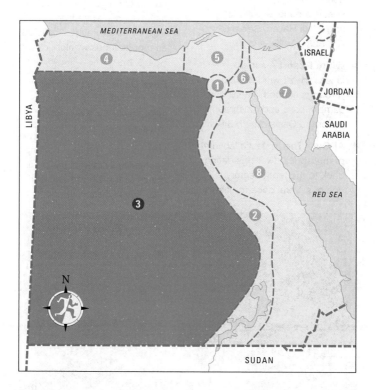

CHAPTER 3 # Highlights

* **Jeep or camel safaris**
  Whether you spend a night
  in the White Desert, or two
  weeks in the Great Sand Sea
  and the Gilf Kebir, you'll never
  forget the experience. See
  p.505 & pp.542–543

* **Bird-watching** Flamingoes,
  Senegal coucals and grey
  herons are only some of the
  species found at Lake Qaroun
  and Wadi Rayan. See p.521
  & p.523

* **White Desert** A surreal
  landscape of wind-eroded
  yardangs shaped like falcons,
  camels, lions and mushrooms,
  in Farafra Oasis. See p.544

* **Al-Qasr** This fantastic labyrinth
  of mud-brick dwellings dating
  back to the tenth century is
  one of several once-fortified

qasr villages in Dakhla Oasis.
See p.557

* **Prehistoric rock art** *The
  English Patient* cast a spotlight
  on the Cave of the Swimmers in
  the remote Gilf Kebir, and there
  are many other sites at Jebel
  Uwaynat. See p.578 & p.580

* **Dunes** Knife-edged *seif* dunes
  can run for over 140km, reform
  as crescents when they fall
  over an escarpment, or pile up
  as mountainous whalebacks.
  See p.583

* **Siwa Oasis** Its citadel, palm
  groves, rock tombs and salt
  lakes make Siwa a must for
  travellers. See p.584

* **Hot springs** The best bathing
  spot is Bir Wahed in the outer
  dunes of the Great Sand Sea,
  near Siwa Oasis. See p.597

△ *Yardangs* in the White Desert

The Western Desert Oases

For the Ancient Egyptians civilization began and ended with the Nile Valley and the Delta, known as the "Black Land" for the colour of its rich alluvial deposits. Beyond lay the "Red Land" or desert, whose significance was either practical or mystical. East of the Nile it held mineral wealth and routes to the Red Sea Coast; west of the river lay the Kingdom of Osiris, Lord of the Dead – the deceased were said to "go west" to meet him. But once it was realized that human settlements existed out there, Egypt's rulers had to reckon with the **Western Desert Oases** as sources of exotic commodities and potential staging posts for invaders. Though linked to the civilization of the Nile Valley since antiquity, they have always been different – and remain so.

Siwa Oasis, far out near the Libyan border (and covered last in this chapter as it is furthest away), is the most striking example: its people speak another language and have customs unknown in the rest of Egypt. Its ruined citadels, lush palm groves, limpid pools and golden sand dunes epitomize the allure of the oases.

The four "inner" oases of **Bahariya**, **Farafra**, **Dakhla** and **Kharga** lie on the "**Great Desert Circuit**" that begins in Cairo or Assyut – a Long March through the New Valley Governorate, where modernization has affected each oasis to a greater or lesser extent. While Bahariya and Farafra remain basically desert villages, living off their traditional crops of dates and olives, Dakhla and Kharga have become full-blown modern towns. The appeal of the latter two is stronger in the journeying – across hundreds of miles of awesome barrenness, most of it gravel pans rather than pure "sand desert".

Much nearer to Cairo (and suitable for day excursions) are two quasi-oases: the Fayoum and Wadi Natrun. The **Fayoum** is more akin to the Nile Valley than the Western Desert, with many ancient ruins to prove its importance since the Middle Kingdom. Though a popular holiday spot for Cairenes, it doesn't attract many foreign tourists except for hunters and ornithologists. **Wadi Natrun** is significant mainly for its Coptic monasteries, which draw hordes of Egyptian pilgrims but, again, comparatively few foreigners.

The desert

Much of the fascination of this region lies in the desert itself. It's no accident that Islam, Judaism and Christianity were forged in deserts whose vast

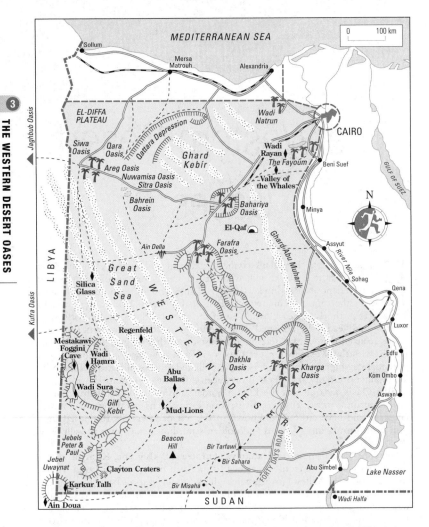

scarps and depressions displayed the hand of God writ large, with life-giving springs and oases as manifestations of divine mercy in a pitiless landscape. Although much of this landscape was once savannah, it was reduced to its current state millennia ago by geological processes and overgrazing by Stone Age pastoralists.

The **Western Desert**, which covers 681,000 square kilometres (over two-thirds of Egypt's total area), is merely one part of the Sahara belt across northern Africa. Its anomalous name was bestowed by British cartographers who viewed it from the perspective of the Nile – and, to complicate matters further, designated its southern reaches and parts of northwestern Sudan as the "Libyan Desert". Aside from the oases, its most striking features are the **Qattara Depression**, the lowest point in Africa, and the **Great Sand Sea** along the Libyan border, an awesome ocean of dunes that once swallowed up a whole army. Further south, the **Gilf Kebir** and **Jebel Uwaynat** feature some of the most magnificent prehistoric rock art in Egypt and were the setting for the events in the book and film *The English Patient*.

All the **practicalities** of visiting the oases (including the best times to go) are detailed under the respective entries in this chapter. The most comprehensive source of historical, ethnographic and geographical **information** is Cassandra Vivian's *The Western Desert of Egypt: An Explorer's Handbook* (last updated in 2000), which includes many useful maps and GPS (satellite navigation) waypoints, and is available from good bookshops in Cairo.

Visiting the desert: safaris

Organized desert safaris are the easiest and often the only way to reach some of the finest sites in and beyond the oases. There are **local operators** in all the oases, whose contact details appear in the relevent text. As more are based **in Bahariya** (see pp.542–543) than anywhere else, this is the best place to arrange safaris at short notice, particularly to the White Desert. Longer trips (4–19 days) to remoter sites such as El-Qaf, the Great Sand Sea, the Gilf Kebir or Jebel Uwaynat must be booked weeks or months ahead. Safaris to the Gilf and Uwaynat are restricted to spring and autumn and may sell out six months beforehand.

Sadly, some safari outfits fail to respect the **environment** by leaving rubbish behind or encouraging tourists to remove flint arrowheads or spray water on rock paintings so that they look clearer in photos. All those we recommend below have good environmental credentials and can be booked in advance from Cairo or from abroad.

Ancient World Tours ☎020/7917-9494, ⓦwww .ancient.co.uk. A British firm specializing in archeological and desert travel, which runs two trips a year to the Gilf Kebir and Jebel Uwaynat, starting from the UK, and has a solar-eclipse tour scheduled for 2006. Flights from Britain and deluxe accommodation in Cairo and Luxor are included in the package (£2000).

Badawiya Safari 22 Sharia Talat Harb, Cairo ☎02/575-8076, ⓦwww.badawiya.com. The sales office for an outfit in Farafra Oasis (see p.546), running 4WD, camel and walking treks all over the Western Desert. They visit Wadi Sura, Wadi Bakht, Karkur Talh and the Selima Sand Sheet over 14–19 days (US$150 per person per day).

Bedouin Camp El-Douhous, Dakhla Oasis ☎092/785-0480, mobile ☎010 6221359. A Bedouin family doing 4WD and camel safaris to Ain Amur, Qasr el-Labeka and Ain Umm Dabadib in Kharga Oasis, and the Gilf Kebir. They have GPS but not a satellite phone. Hagg Abdel Hameed and Yosef Zeydan run a 10–12-day Gilf safari costing £E2000 a day per car-load of tourists, plus £E200 a day for the guide.

Fliegel Jerzerniczky Expeditions ⓦwww .fjexpeditions.com. This Hungarian company, run by Sahara expert András Zboráy, mounts 15–16-day expeditions to the Gilf and Uwaynat starting from

Cairo (£E2400–2600 per person), and is scheduling an eclipse tour to Libya. András speaks English and German.

Khalifa Expeditions t02/847-3260, mobile ☎012 3215445, ⓦwww.khalifaexp.com. Safaris out of Bahariya (see also pp.542–543) featuring Wadi Hamra or the Mestakawi-Foggini Cave in the Gilf, silica glass in the Great Sand Sea, and Siwa.

Marzouk Desert Cruises 1 Midan Ibn Sandar, Hammamat al-Qubba, Cairo ☎ & ⓕ02/258-8083, ⓔmmarzouk2001@yahoo.com. The sales office of an outfit from Wadi Rayan (see p.523), which does 4WD safaris to the Valley of the Whales, and camel treks to Bahariya Oasis.

Pan Arab Tours 5 Saudi Egyptian Bldg, Sharia el-Nozha, Heliopolis ☎02/291-3502, ⓕ291-3506, ⓔpat@moussa.net. A highly experienced Cairo-based agency offering numerous 4WD tours and tailor-made safaris to the Gilf and Uwaynat and all over the Western Desert.

Zarzora Expedition c/o Minerva Travel & Tours, 18 Sharia al-Ahrar, Mohandiseen, Giza ☎02/761-8105, ⓦwww.zarzora.com. Cairene desert experts Wael Abed and former colonel Ahmed Mestekawi run a 19-day rock art tour including Wadi Hamra and the superb Mestekawi/Foggini Cave, and a 14-day Gilf, Sand Sea and Siwa safari. Has an eclipse tour in 2006.

Visiting the desert: driving

An increasing number of visitors are driving themselves, even to sites beyond the inhabited oases of the Western Desert. The following advice should be borne in mind even if you're going to stick to main roads. For motorists considering more ambitious trips, you'll need a much more detailed handbook: see "Books" in Contexts chapter for recommendations.

Permits

Motorists can drive to most places in the Western Desert without permission, with the following exceptions. Travel along the road **between Siwa and Bahariya** needs a permit which is easily obtained in Siwa but takes a day or more to arrange in Bahariya. Travel to **Ain Della** requires a permit (applications should be made at least two weeks before your intended departure date), as does travel to everywhere south of Dakhla or Kharga oases – specifically the **Gilf Kebir** and **Jebel Uwaynat** – where all expeditions must be accompanied by an Egyptian army officer; applications here should be submitted at least six weeks in advance. Permits for all these places can be arranged through Badawiya Safari in Farafra (see p.546) or Misr Travel in Cairo (1 Sharia Talaat Harb ☎02/393-0010, ⓕ392-4440, ⓔmisrtrav@link.com.eg), who are used to dealing with the branch of Military Intelligence responsible for the surveillance of foreigners (Section 26, Sharia Manshia el-Bakry, Heliopolis). You'll need to submit the names and passport numbers of everyone travelling, two photocopies of the main page and Egyptian visa in their passports, and the route and dates of travel.

Vehicles

The desert is a potentially lethal environment, so it's crucial to get the right vehicle. Many local safari operators swear by Libyan army-surplus Toyotas or Ford trucks, which are robust and easy to fix and handle well in the desert – though these don't have a/c or the other extras that are standard on the 4WD Landcruisers used by Cairo-based firms (or available for rental in Cairo). Mechanical reliability, high ground clearance and four-wheel-drive are vital; non-automatic gears, a water-cooled engine and an electrical fuel pump are strongly advised. Desert travel is extremely hard on tyres, so even if the car isn't fitted with the best Michelins, they must be in good condition and have inner tubes; always carry two spare wheels, a tyre pump and pressure gauge, levers and a jack. A fire extinguisher, vital spares and a full tool/repair kit are also essential.

Ideally, your vehicle should also have the following **modifications**: steel plates welded below the sump and fuel tank to prevent them being holed; fireproof lagging around the fuel lines where they pass the exhaust manifold; crossover seat belts; fabric-covered seats; an extra, false roof above the cab (painted gloss white for maximum cooling effect); and a mileometer for navigational calculations – but it's rare that you'll encounter a car with all of these.

If you're renting a car, weigh the pros and cons of **diesel or petrol** engines. Diesel fuel is roughly half the price of *benzin* – a significant difference if you're planning an expedition that requires hundreds of litres of fuel; but diesel pumps and ignition systems are much harder to repair if there's a breakdown, so you'll need to carry replacements for all the critical parts. Fuel purity is also an issue: fuel sold in the oases is often adulterated with water, so anyone planning a major expedition should fill their jerrycans in Cairo.

Equipment

You can never carry too much **water** (in metal or heavy-duty polythene jerry cans, securely fixed to brackets) or **fuel** – travelling off-track can reduce a car's normal mileage by half. Even staying within the limits of an oasis depression, it's vital to be able to orient yourself. A vehicle-mounted **compass** must be adjusted to the car's magnetic field, which will also distort readings on hand-held compasses if you stand too close (as do ferrous rocks in Bahariya Oasis).

An increasing number of expeditions rely on **GPS** (Global Positioning System) for **navigation**. GPS sets can be hand-held or mounted on a dashboard to give your exact position in latitude and longitude, your compass-bearing, and record "Waypoints" so that routes can be retraced. While GPS ensures that you know *where* you are and can plot a course to any given point, it doesn't take any account of obstacles that might prove insurmountable – so choosing the best route still depends on knowing the terrain, whether it's the lie of dune "lanes" or the fragility of saltpans.

For details of the best relevant **maps** for exploring the oases, see p.47.

Desert driving

Decide from the start whether you plan to travel on paved roads, unpaved tracks, or through trackless open desert. It's safe to travel alone by road, as the checkpoints at either end (and at intervals along major routes) will raise the alarm if you fail to arrive. Always **travel in pairs** of vehicles if you're going off-road (though locals often drive alone on familiar territory). Never set off – or keep going – during **sandstorms**; should you get caught in one, shelter in the lee of cliffs or palm trees and turn the car's rear end towards the wind, lest it sand-blast the front windscreen and headlights into opacity.

Driving at **night** is likewise taboo: potholes are vicious and it's easy to crash or get lost. The **best times for driving** are early morning and late afternoon, when there's less risk of overheating or misjudging the terrain. During the middle of the day, the details of the landscape are lost in the glare, making it harder to judge **distances and scale**. Both are distorted by the desert, where drivers often perceive near-vertical slopes as level ground, or discarded jerry cans as villages. These kind of optical illusions are commoner than **mirages** of shimmering "lakes".

If you are driving cross-country, stay alert for **changes in the desert's surface**, often indicated by a shift in colour or texture. Wheel ruts left by other vehicles can also yield clues: a sudden deepening and widening usually means softer sand (another sign of which is vegetation around the edges of dunes). Generally speaking, gravel plains provide a firm surface, while salt flats and dunes are the most unstable. Deflating one's **tyres** increases their traction on soft sand, but also their surface temperature and the car's fuel consumption, so keep a conservative speed.

Dunes

There's no substitute for experience of **dunes**, but a few points need making. Never crest a dune at high speed, in case the far side has collapsed, leaving a slipface. If you *do* go over, accelerate hard (which tends to lower the rear of the vehicle), charge down the slope and hope to butch it out. Braking or slewing sideways seems the natural reaction, but it's likely to somersault or roll the car over the edge. It's far safer to make a controlled descent in second gear and speed up as you reach the bottom.

When deflating tyres for better traction, do this just before you drive onto sand, and pump them up again before gaining firm ground. Shifting into a lower gear should also be done in advance. If stuck in soft sand, revving the engine will only dig you in deeper. Stop at once, change into low gear and try driving out slowly. If this fails, deflate the tyres as far as possible (or put traction mats, brushwood, rocks, etc beneath the rear wheels) and try again.

Health care and emergencies

Dehydration, heatstroke and sunburn are the main **health** hazards. You can monitor your own water-level by watching your urine, which should remain pale – if it starts to turn deep yellow, drink more water. Wear loose, light clothing and keep your head covered (a Bedouin *keffiyah* works far better than a baseball cap, and can be used to veil your face against dust or grit). Use sun block and skin cream, particularly if you're travelling to the super-arid Gilf Kebir. Some travellers find air conditioning a mixed blessing, since alternating between a chilled interior and a furnace-hot environment causes passengers to catch colds.

While the odds that you'll be sleeping out when a sandstorm strikes are remote (if so, hunker down behind your rucksack), getting stuck, breaking down or crashing in the desert can be fatal if you compound the misfortune by acting wrongly. Assuming you're driving solo, *never leave your own vehicle* unless you're within 5km of a plainly visible settlement or major highway. Otherwise, stay put, keep cool (literally) and try to attract attention. By day you can burn oil-soaked sand or bits of rubber to produce thick black smoke; at night, make a fire. A vehicle, smoke or fire are hard enough for search parties to locate; a person on their own is virtually impossible.

Other **emergencies** arise simply through drivers getting lost. The moment you suspect this, stop and try to get oriented using a compass or the sun; take your time calculating how much water and fuel remain, then decide on a course of action. The worst thing to do is simply drive on by instinct – it's a sure way of wandering even further in the wrong direction.

Although proper spares are obviously preferable, **improvised materials** can serve for vital **repairs**: nylon tights make a substitute fan belt and chewing gum can plug holes in fuel tanks or radiators.

Wadi Natrun

The quasi-oasis of **Wadi Natrun**, just off the Desert Road between Cairo and Alexandria, takes its name – and oasis stature – from deposits of natron salts, the main ingredient in ancient mummifications. Wadi Natrun's most enduring legacy, however, is its **monasteries**, which date back to the dawn of Christian monasticism, and have provided spiritual leadership for Egypt's Copts for the last 1500 years. Their fortified exteriors, necessary in centuries past to resist Bedouin raiders, cloak what are today very forward-looking, purposeful monastic establishments. Coptic monasticism experienced a revival during the 1980s, twenty years after an English writer dismissed the monasteries as "of little interest except to the specialist".

The area surrounding Wadi Natrun is known as **Liberation Province** (*Mudiriyat el-Tahrir*). In the 1950s, model villages, olive groves and vineyards were planted here to reclaim 25,000 hectares of land from the desert, a project initially financed by the sale of King Farouk's stamp collection and other valuables. After decades of patient land reclamation, palms, flowers and hothouse vegetables now grow beside the **Desert Road** to Alex, spreading further as you travel north. Not far beyond Giza you'll pass the glass pyramids and post-modern edifices of **MEDINET SADAT** (Sadat City), a dormitory suburb, science park and film studio that represents Egypt's high-tech aspirations for the twenty-first century. On the other side of the highway, motels have sprung up around the turn-off for Wadi Natrun, which runs via the ramshackle township of **BIR HOOKER** (named after Mr Hooker, an early manager of the Egyptian Salt & Soda Co.) into the Natrun Valley.

Getting there

Wadi Natrun makes a memorable day excursion from Alex or Cairo, with the easiest way to get there being to **rent a car**, or take a **taxi** (£E150–200 depending on how many monasteries you visit). By public transport, reaching the monasteries is a two-stage process. From Cairo, West Delta **buses** leave from the Turgoman terminal (hourly 6.30am–6.30pm; £E3) and terminate at Bir Hooker, where you should be able to hire a taxi to tour the monasteries for £E30–50. Otherwise, you can get a **service taxi** from Cairo (Aboud terminal) or Alex (Sidi Gaber) to the **Wadi Natrun Resthouse** at KM 95 on the Desert Road – a bunch of motels, gas stations and cafés where non-express inter-city buses also stop. From here, you can negotiate a private taxi ride to the nearest monastery, or hope to be offered a lift by one of the busloads of Coptic pilgrims that come this way.

Returning to Cairo or Alex by bus or service taxi from the Resthouse, you'll probably have to pay the full inter-city rate. There are hourly buses to Cairo until 7pm; departures for Alex are fewer and further between, with perhaps only two buses in the afternoon, when people are most likely to be leaving after having visited the monasteries.

The monasteries of Wadi Natrun

Christian monasticism was born in Egypt's Eastern Desert, where the first Christian hermits sought to emulate St Anthony, forming rude communities; however, it was at Wadi Natrun that their rules and power were forged. Peter Levi's study of monasticism, *The Frontiers of Paradise*, notes how this coincided with the persecution of Christians in urban areas, especially under Diocletian. Certainly, several thousand **monks** and hermits were living here by the middle of the fourth century, harbouring bitter grudges against paganism, scores which they settled after Christianity was made the state religion in 330 by sacking the temples and library and murdering scholars in Alexandria. E.M. Forster judged them "averse to culture and incapable of thought. Their heroes were St Ammon, who deserted his wife on their wedding eve, and St Anthony, who thought bathing was sinful and was consequently carried across the canals of the Delta by an angel". The Muslim conquest and Bedouin raids encouraged a siege mentality amongst the monks, who often lapsed into idle dependence on monastic serfs. Nineteenth-century foreign visitors unanimously described them as slothful, dirty, bigoted and ignorant – the antithesis of the monks here today.

The **four Wadi Natrun monasteries** have all been totally ruined and rebuilt at least once since their foundation during the fourth century; most of what you see dates from the eighth century onwards. Each has a high wall surrounding one or more churches, a central keep entered via a drawbridge, containing a bakery, storerooms and wells, enabling the monks to withstand siege, and diverse associated chapels. Their low doorways compel visitors to humbly stoop upon entry (don't forget to remove your shoes outside).

Their **churches** – like all Coptic chapels – are divided into three sections. The *haikal* (sanctuary) containing the altar lies behind the iconostasis, an inlaid or curtained screen, which you can peer through with your escort's consent. In front of this is the choir, reserved for Coptic Christians, and then the nave, consisting of two parts. *Catechumens* (those preparing to convert) stand nearest the choir, while sinners (known as "weepers") were formerly relegated to the back.

Practicalities: visiting the monasteries

Visiting hours vary from monastery to monastery, as does the extent to which each closes during the five seasons of **fasting**: 43 days before the Nativity, three days in commemoration of Jonah in the Whale, 55 days preceding Lent, the fast of the Holy Apostles (from Pentecost to July 12), and fifteen days marking the Assumption of the Virgin Mary (August 7–22). Deir Anba Bishoi alone is open every day of the year; Deir al-Suryani and Deir el-Baramus have regular opening times but close during most of the feasts; while Deir Abu Maqar will only admit those with a letter of introduction from the **Coptic Patriarchate** in Cairo (next to the Cathedral of St Mark, 222 Sharia Ramses, Abbassiya; ☏02/282-5374) or Alexandria (in the Cathedral of St Mark on Sharia al-Kineesa al-Kobtiyya; ☏03/483-5522). The Patriarchate can verify the opening dates of specific monasteries. Fridays, Sundays and public holidays are best avoided, as the monasteries are often swarmed by Coptic pilgrims from all over Egypt.

Male tourists wanting to **stay the night** in a monastery must get written permission from the appropriate "residence" in Cairo: Deir Anba Bishoi (☏02/591-4448); Deir al-Suryani (☏02/592-9658); Deir el-Baramus (☏02/592-2775). As other guests are devout pilgrims, you should make at least a token effort to attend prayers, and leave a donation in return for the tea and bread that's provided. Women are not allowed to sleep in any of the monasteries. Otherwise, there are several motels (❹–❺) along the Desert Road, near the turn-off for Wadi Natrun.

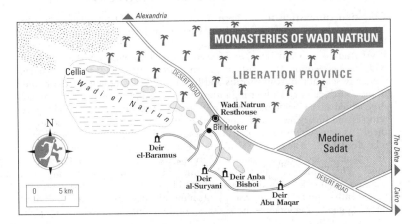

The monastic rule and working day

All Egyptian monasteries are cenobitic, meaning that the monks share food and possessions and unconditional submission to the rule of their abbot (a word that derives from the Arabic *abd*, "father").

The **monastic day** begins at 3am with an hour of silent prayer in individual *laura* (cells), before two hours of collective worship in the chapel, followed by unrelenting labour until the main meal of the day at noon. Afterwards, the monks work until 5pm, assemble for prayers and then return to their tasks until sheer exhaustion forces them to bed.

Work and prayer are seen as equal holy obligations, and many of the younger monks and novices are qualified engineers or scientists. High-tech coexists with spiritualism, which is clearly apparent during liturgies. Black garments symbolize their death to the world of bodily desires; their hoods (possibly representing the "helmet of salvation" in Ephesians 6) are embroidered with twelve crosses, after Christ's disciples.

Deir Anba Bishoi

The most accessible monastery is **Deir Anba Bishoi** (daily: winter 7am–6pm; summer 7am–8pm), 10km from the highway, with a signpost of sorts on the paved road. Over one hundred and fifty monks and novices live here, and the monastery of St Bishoi receives a stream of Coptic pilgrims. Foreigners are usually shown around by the English-speaking Father Shedrak.

The legend of **St Bishoi** suggests he was one of the earliest monks at Wadi Natrun. An angel told the saint's mother that he was chosen to do God's work even before his birth in 320; two decades later he moved here to study under St Bemoi alongside John "the Short". Adopting a rather imaginative chronology, the legend also recalls that Bishoi later met Christ as an old man, carried him to church, washed his feet and was allowed to drink the water as a reward. Whatever the truth, since Bishoi's death in 417 his body has reportedly remained uncorrupted within its casket, which is carried in procession around the church every year on July 17. Next to him lies Paul of Tammuh, who was revered for committing suicide seven times.

St Bishoi's is the oldest of the five **churches** in the monastery, and features three *haikals* dating from the fourth, ninth and tenth centuries. The **keep**, built three to four hundred years later, has chapels at ground level (around the back) and on the second storey, one floor above its drawbridge. There's also a fifth-century **well** where Berber tribesmen washed their swords after massacring the 49 Martyrs of the Monastery of St Makarius.

The multi-domed building furthest away from the entrance is the **residence of Pope Shenouda III**, the current Coptic pope. He uses it as an occasional retreat, though he was exiled here for some years by Sadat, and sometimes ostentatiously secludes himself here to protest at the mistreatment of Copts. Most of the Coptic popes have been chosen from the monks of Wadi Natrun, and Deir Anba Bishoi in particular.

Deir al-Suryani

A sixth-century dispute over the theological importance of the Virgin led dissenting monks to found another monastery, 500m from St Bishoi's. After they returned to the fold it was purchased for a group of Syrian monks, hence its name, **Deir al-Suryani** (winter Mon–Fri & Sun 9am–6pm, Sat 9am–3pm;

summer Mon–Fri & Sun 9am–7pm, Sat 9am–5pm). It was here that Robert Curzon came searching for ancient manuscripts (the ostensible reason for his tour of Balkan and Levantine monasteries in the 1830s), and found them lying on the floor or serving as covers for jars, all "well begrimed with dirt". The keep's oil cellar held a "mass of loose vellum pages", while the consistory of Abyssinian monks contained a library of Aramaic texts, hanging from pegs in individual leather satchels. Nowadays, the monastery's antique volumes are lovingly maintained in a modern **library**, and they have recently discovered a cache of manuscripts up to 1500 years old. The monastery also boasts the remains of some twelve saints and a lock of hair from Mary Magdalene.

Deir al-Suryani's principal **Church of the Virgin** (*al-Adhra*), built around 980, contains a *haikal* with stucco ornamentation and a superb ebony "**Door of Prophecies**", inlaid with ivory panels depicting the disciples and the seven epochs of the Christian era, culminating in the split with the Orthodox Church and the Coming of Islam. Some **murals** dating back to the church's foundation were recently discovered beneath the plaster, and can be seen through small apertures. A dark passageway at the back of the church leads to the **cave** where Bishoi tied his hair to a chain hanging from the ceiling to prevent himself sleeping for four days, until a vision of Christ appeared. The marble basin (*lakan*) in the nave is used by the abbot to wash the feet of twelve monks on Maundy Thursday, emulating Christ's act during Passion week.

The large **tamarind tree** in the grounds is said to have grown from the staff of St Emphram, who, as a monk, thrust it into the earth after his fellows criticized it as a worldly affectation. As Coptic pope, he established cordial relations with the Fatimid khalif in 997.

Deir el-Baramus

One of the more remote monasteries, **Deir el-Baramus** (daily: winter 9am–5pm; summer 9am–6pm) is accessed by a road running 4km north from the vicinity of Deir Anba Bishoi. The road has reduced the monastery's isolation amidst barren sands, but it still feels far from the madding crowd. Visitors are greeted outside by a picture of St Moses the Black, a Nubian robber who became a monk under the influence of St Isidore. The monastery itself was founded by St Makarius (see opposite) in 340, making it the oldest of the four that remain in Wadi Natrun. Its name, "Monastery of the Romans", honours Maximus and Domidus, two sons of the Roman Emperor Valentinus who died from excessive fasting; the younger one was only nineteen years old.

Their bodies are reputedly buried in a crypt below the **Church of the Virgin**, whose principal altar is only used once a day, since Mary's womb begot but one child. An adjacent altar, normally curtained off, serves the "Immaterial Fathers", the spirits of bygone saints and abbots who occasionally leave droplets of water sprinkled there. The relics of Moses and Isidore are encased in glass; pilgrims drop petitions into the bier. Notice the photo of a T-shirt bearing a bloody cross, the relic of an exorcism performed at the monastery in the 1980s, where the departing *afrit* (spirit) left a lurid sign as it was expelled from the body of the possessed victim.

Restoration work has revealed layers of medieval **frescoes** in the nave, the western end of which incorporates a fourth-century **pillar** with Syriac inscriptions. It was behind here that St Arsanious prayed with a pebble in his mouth, grudging every word that he spoke (including a statement to that effect). The ninth-century church (whose belfries of unequal height symbolize the respective ages of Maximus and Domidus) shares a vine-laden courtyard with a

keep and four other churches. Deir el-Baramus has eighty monks and novices, one of whom will show you around.

Cellia and birdlife

The monks may also tell you about **Cellia** (or El-Muna), the name given to the **ruins** of some five hundred **hermitages**, spread over a wide area 30km north of Deir el-Baramus. Cellia was founded by St Anthony, who is said to have told monks at Wadi Natrun who wished to live as hermits, "Let us take food at the ninth hour and then go forth and pass through the desert and consider the place." It's thought that Cellia maintained links with the pilgrim city of Abu Mina (see p.643) until their freshwater springs dried up. In 1995 American archeologists unearthed the Monastery of St John, plus traces of five subterranean monasteries that had been "lost" since their discovery by Prince Tousoum in 1930.

This remote part of Wadi Natrun has a melancholy beauty, its numerous **saline lakes** rimmed by crusts of **natron**, a mixture of sodium carbonate and sodium bicarbonate, which the Ancient Egyptians used for dehydrating bodies and making glass. Ducks, waterhens, jacksnipes and sandpipers are typical of the **birdlife** around these lakes, which also harbour Egypt's last surviving wild **papyrus**. Due to the salinity, it is a dwarf subspecies of the plant that once flourished throughout the Nile Valley, but gradually became extinct; the last large papyrus (which could reach 6m) was found by a Prussian soldier in the Delta in the mid-nineteenth century. Today it exists only on plantations, thanks to Dr Rageb, who rediscovered the lost technique of making papyrus paper and began to manufacture souvenirs from the stuff.

You'll need a **car** to explore the area.

Deir Abu Maqar

The oldest and furthest of the monasteries, **Deir Abu Maqar** lies 18km south-west of St Bishoi and can also be reached by an eight-kilometre spur off the Desert Road, midway between the main turn-off and Sadat City. It is **not open** to casual visitors, but will admit those with a letter of authorization from the Patriarchate (see p.510).

Enclosed by a circular wall ten metres high, the monastery requires visitors to pull a bell rope; in times past, two giant millstones stood ready to be rolled across to buttress the door against Bedouin raiders. Its founder, **St Makarius**, died in 390 "after sixty years of austerities in various deserts", the last twenty of which were spent in a hermit's cell at Wadi Natrun. He's said to have been so remorseful over killing a gnat that he withdrew for six months to the marshes, getting stung all over until "his body was so much disfigured that his brethren on his return only knew him from the sound of his voice". A rigorous faster, his only indulgence was a raw cabbage leaf for Sunday lunch.

Despite repeated sackings, Abu Maqar has hung onto the bodies of the numerous Coptic popes that have been buried here, plus the 49 Martyrs whom the Berbers killed in 444. In 1978, monks discovered what they believed to be the head of John the Baptist; however, this is also claimed to be held in Venice, Aleppo and Damascus. Since its nadir in 1969, when only six monks lived here, the monastery has acquired a hundred brethren, a modern printing press and a farm employing six hundred workers. The monks have mastered pinpoint irrigation systems and bovine embryo transplant technology in an effort to meet their abbot's goal of feeding a thousand laypersons per monk, revitalizing a landscape which "might be supposed to boast of nothing but the salt and natron for which it is indebted to its barrenness and its name" (*Murray's Handbook*, 1891).

The Fayoum

Likened in Egyptian tradition to a bud on the stem of the Nile and an "earthly paradise" in the desert, the **Fayoum** depends on river water – not springs or wells, like a true oasis. The water is distributed around the depression by a system of canals going back to ancient times, creating a lush rural enclave of palm trees dividing cotton and clover fields, orchards, and carefully tended crops of tomatoes and medicinal plants in the sandier outlying regions. Pigeons nest in mud-brick coops shaped like giant Victorian trifles, blindfolded cattle turn threshing machines and water buffalo plod home for milking. Along one shore of Lake Qaroun are fishing communities, while on the periphery are encampments of semi-nomadic Bedouin. Almost three million people live in the oasis, 500,000 in Fayoum City and the rest in four towns and 158 villages.

Despite the easy access from Cairo, foreign tourists are thin on the ground here. The main reason why is the governorate capital, **Fayoum City**, which has all of Cairo's drawbacks and few of its advantages. Avaricious drivers bedevil day excursions to the distant **antiquities**, whilst *baksheesh*-hungry locals pester visitors to **Lake Qaroun**, where wealthy Cairenes and foreigners come for shooting holidays. It is possible to experience the diverse **birdlife**, local **moulids** or **desert expeditions**, but you have to be determined. If you're only lukewarm, a brief day-trip will probably discourage further contact.

As for the **best time to go**, the Fayoum's winters are warmer and drier than Cairo's, its summers milder than in Upper Egypt; however, cold winds in spring – known as the *khamseen* – coat everything with dust. At other times, the clarity of the air causes the sun's rays to burn more strongly than you'd expect.

Getting there

The **road from Cairo** to the Fayoum starts near the Pyramids of Giza, whose silhouettes sink below the horizon as the road gains a barren plateau dotted with army bases, then (76km later) reaches the edge of the Fayoum depression. Here, you'll pass the Ptolemaic-Roman site of Kom Oshim (on the left) before you sight Lake Qaroun and cruise down through Sinnuris into Fayoum City, driving past the Obelisk of Senusert I.

Buses from Cairo's Aboud (every 15min 6am–8pm; £E8) and El Moneeb (every 30min 6am–7pm; £E4.50) terminals do the 100km journey in two to three hours; advance bookings are usually only necessary from midday Thursday till late on Saturday, or during Ramadan, Fayoumi moulids and public holidays. Alternatively, you can take a **service taxi** from Midan Orabi, Midan Giza or the El Moneeb terminal. These seven-seater Peugeots or pack-'em-in minibuses run practically non-stop from early morning to late at night, charging £E6–8 for a stomach-churning high-speed ride past the wrecks of previous crashes, reaching Fayoum City in about two hours – *inshallah*.

From the Nile Valley, catch one of the half-hourly buses or service taxis (£E2-4) **from Beni Suef**, which reach Fayoum City in an hour. The road runs through a cultivated strip beside the Bahr Yussef, so there's little sense of entering an oasis; en route it passes the start of tracks to the Lahun and Hawara pyramids. Buses and service taxis coming from this direction terminate at the Hawatim depot in the southwest of town.

Fayoum City

A kind of pocket-size version of Cairo, with the Bahr Yussef canal in the role of the Nile, **FAYOUM CITY** makes a grab at the wallets of middle-class Egyptians who come to bask beside Lake Qaroun during summertime. The few foreigners that venture here tend to be whisked through in buses and remain immured in luxury hotels, so independent travellers bear the brunt of local hustlers – and obnoxious teenagers, if you're a woman. Another major drawback is that mosquitoes swarm from every nook and waterway, making evenings a misery. Add makeshift buildings, weaving traffic and malodorous canals and you've got half a dozen reasons not to linger.

On the plus side, the city has the cheapest accommodation in the area and serves as the jumping-off point for almost everywhere you might consider visiting in the oasis. It also musters a pleasant **souk**, a couple of venerable **mosques** and some colourful **moulids** – the biggest of which is that of Ali er-Rubi (see p.518) in the middle of the month of Sha'ban.

The city's official title is **Medinet el-Fayoum**, but it is known as El-Fayoum or Fayoum in colloquial usage (not El-Medina, as some guidebooks say). The word "Fayoum" probably derives from Phiom, the Coptic word for "sea", although folklore attributes it to the pharaoh's praise of the Bahr Yussef: "This is the work of a thousand days" (*alf youm*).

Arrival and information

Trains from Cairo terminate at the **station** in the centre of town, while buses and service taxis end up at the **Kubri al-Misalla** depot beneath the bridge past the Gamal Abdel Nasser Mosque. Coming from Beni Suef you arrive at the **Hawatim** depot south of the old town, which is too far from town to walk – a taxi or horse-drawn cab (*hantour*) shouldn't cost over £E10. If you're feeling adventurous and can read Arabic numerals, take one of the green-and-white minibuses (25pt) that shuttle between outlying transport depots or suburbs and the centre of town (*wust al balad*), while motorbike taxis (£E1–3) weave around the downtown area. Minibuses #7 and #8 run from the Hawatim depot to the train station.

Once downtown, most things worth seeing can be reached on foot, with the Bahr Yussef canal facilitating **orientation** as an obvious landmark. Alas, the Fayoum's main **tourist office** (daily except Fri 8am–2pm; ☎084/343-044) at the rear of the governorate building, 2km north of the centre (accessible by #5 minibus from in front of the Banque Misr), has little to offer but an outdated brochure and a confusing map of town, and its staff speak little English: the more central tourist kiosk (daily except Fri 9am–2pm), near the four waterwheels, is no better. Even less English is spoken by the **tourist police** (☎084/347-298), who are usually on duty near the four waterwheels, and will send an officer to any hotel that reports having foreign guests, to explain the restrictions on travel within the oasis (see p.519).

You can **change money** at any of the four banks along the Bahr Yussef – the Banque du Caire and Banque Misr both have ATMs – but only the Bank of Alexandria on the north bank of the canal takes travellers' cheques or gives Visa cash advances (Mon–Thurs & Sun 8.30am–2pm; during Ramadan 10am–1.30pm). The main **post office** (daily except Fri 8am–2pm) on Sharia el-Bosta has EMS and poste restante, while for international calls you should head west along the canal to the 24-hour **telephone** exchange. Patients must pay cash up front at the **hospital** (☎084/342-249) on Sharia Sa'ad Zaghloul, 1km north of the centre, and would do better seeking treatment in Cairo.

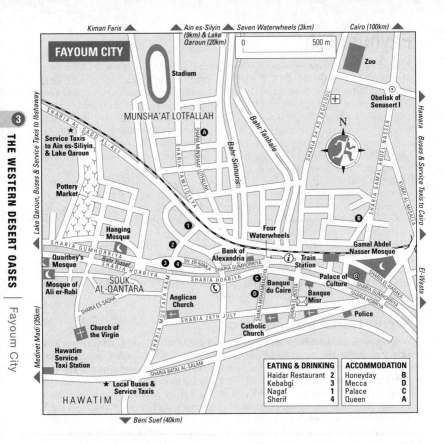

Accommodation

Outside of Er-Rubi's festival, there shouldn't be any difficulty **finding a room** in town, though none of the hotels are up to much. Other options exist at Ain es-Siliyin, Lake Qaroun, Wadi Rayan and Kom Oshim (see sections following).

Honeyday 105 Sharia Gamal Abdel Nasser ☎084/340-105, ℱ341-205. Ten minutes' walk from the centre, off the road to Senusert's obelisk, this two-star hotel has a/c rooms with TV and fridge, a restaurant and bar. Breakfast included. ❺
Mecca Sharia Mohammadiya ☎084/311-223. Under the same management as the Palace (see below), it has simple rooms with fans and shared bathrooms. ❶

Palace Sharia Horriya ☎084/351-222. Overlooking the Bahr Yussef downtown, it has fairly decent rooms with optional baths and a/c. The manager speaks good English and rents bicycles, motorbikes and cars. ❷
Queen Sharia Munsha'at Lotfallah ☎084/346-189, ☎346-233. Spacious en-suite rooms with satellite TV (a/c costs extra) in a quiet neighbourhood, fifteen minutes' walk from the centre. Breakfast included. ❹

The city

Fayoum City's most central landmark is the four large wooden **waterwheels**, symbolic of Fayoumi agriculture, that groan away behind the tourist kiosk. Because Nile water is introduced into the sloping depression at its highest point, gravity does half the work of distribution. Sluices at El-Lahun regulate the current, which is strong enough to power waterwheels for lifting irrigation water where needed – except during January, when the whole system is allowed to dry out for cleaning and maintenance.

Coptic and Muslim folklore ascribes the **Bahr Yussef** (River of Joseph) to its Biblical namesake, who's believed to have been the pharaoh's vizier and minister for public works. Originally a natural waterway branching off the Nile near Beni Suef, it was regulated from the XII Dynasty onwards, and since the building of the Ibrahimiya Canal in the nineteenth century, has drawn water from the Nile at Dairut, nearly 300km further south.

Walking west alongside the canal and crossing the fourth bridge from the tourist kiosk, you can follow a street with a wooden roof into the **Souk al-Qantara**, a labyrinth of alleys with stalls selling copperware and spices, grain and pulses, clothing and other goods – all without a hint of tourism. **Sharia es-Sagha**, the Street of Goldsmiths, is crammed with jewellers' shops, mostly owned by Christians. Like Beni Suef, Fayoum City has a substantial Christian minority – mainly Copts, but also Anglicans and Catholics – whose churches are ranged along Sharia 26th July. The oldest is the **Church of the Virgin**, dating from the 1830s, which contains an altar dedicated to the local saint Anba Abram (1829–1912), Bishop of Fayoum and Giza, who was reputedly able to transport himself across distances in a miraculous fashion.

Near the souk you'll also find three historic mosques. The **Mosque of Ali er-Rubi** is dedicated to a local sheikh whose renown among the Fayoumis eclipses even Anba Abram's. His mausoleum, down some steps from the mosque's courtyard, is surrounded by an enormous *darih* or carved box-frame, and people muttering supplications to the saint. Further west beside the canal, the **Mosque of Qaitbey** is the oldest in the Fayoum, built (or perhaps restored) by the Circassian Mamluke sultan Qaitbey (see p.189). Ancient columns from Kiman Faris (see box on p.520) uphold its dome, while the stone carving around the doorway, and the ebony *minbar* inlaid with Somalian ivory, are distinctly Mamluke. Qaitbey was also responsible for building the twin-arched **bridge** nearby, which was once named after his favourite concubine, Khwand Asl Bey (as was the mosque), but is now known as Bridge of the Gate of Farewells because it leads to a cemetery.

Crossing the bridge you can head along the riverside to find the **Hanging Mosque**, so called because its north frontage is upheld by five arches, once occupied by artisans' workshops. Alternatively, delve into the backstreets near the cemetery to visit the weekly **pottery market** off Sharia el-Mudaris (Tues only). Most of the red, pink or unglazed pots are made at the village of Nazla, south of Ibshaway.

The **Palace of Culture** is Fayoum City's newest landmark, a modernistic structure like an inverted pyramid, which houses a cinema, theatre and library. Behind it stands the **Gamal Abdel Nasser Mosque,** one of many that Nasser had built in provincial towns in the 1960s, and which bear his name. Another, earlier, hero of Egyptian nationalism is commemorated by Sharia Sa'ad Zaghloul, running out past the hospital and a modest **zoo** (daily 8am–5pm; £E2) to the governorate building, containing a small **museum** of local history and fauna, labelled only in Arabic (Sat–Thurs 8am–4pm; 25pt).

The Seven Waterwheels and the Obelisk of Senusert I

For a pleasant half-hour's walk in the morning or evening, follow the right bank of the Bahr Sinnuris northwards out of town for 3km to reach the **Seven Waterwheels** (not to be confused with the four by the tourist kiosk). First comes a single wheel near a farm; slightly further on, a quartet revolves against a backdrop of mango trees and palms; the final pair is a little way on, near a crude bridge. The Fayoum has about two hundred such waterwheels (introduced by Ptolemaic engineers in the third century BC), which have a working life of ten years if properly tarred and maintained. They act as pumps rather than powering machinery, using the flow of the stream to lift the water to a higher level, for irrigation.

Entering or leaving town by the Cairo road, you'll pass the thirteen-metre-high red-granite **Obelisk of Senusert I**, the only obelisk in Egypt to have a rounded tip. Senusert was the second king of the XII Dynasty, who displayed a special fondness for the Fayoum and was the first to regard it as more than just a hunting ground, building the Lahun and Hawara pyramids, Medinet Madi and Qasr es-Sagha. Following the XII Dynasty (1991–1786 BC), interest in the Fayoum declined and didn't properly revive until the advent of the Ptolemies, fourteen centuries later.

Eating and drinking

Eating out in the city is cheap, but don't expect to find any fancy **restaurants**. Perhaps the best choice is at the *Queen Hotel*'s restaurant, which is nicely decorated, with a longish menu – try the *shish tawouk* or *escalope panée*. Alternatively, try any of the cafés listed below, all of which are on Sharia Mustafa Kamil in the centre of town. The *Auberge du Lac-Fayoum* on Lake Qaroun (see p.521) and the *Honeyday Hotel* are the only places serving alcohol.

Haidar Restaurant One of the few cafés near the Bahr Yussef with signs in English, it serves stewed lamb, grilled chicken and salad, and is good value for money.

Kebabgi Another cheap eatery, offering a choice of kebab, *kofta*, chicken and rice, with side orders of spinach, zucchini, white beans or potatoes.

Nagaf A diner and takeway place that sells *fuul* and *taamiya*, macaroni, fried liver, lamb *tageen*, salads, sandwiches, and a kind of rice pudding called *ma'ammar*.

Sherif For ice cream, cakes and other sweets. On cold winter nights they offer *bilela*, a dish of hot wheat and milk topped with raisins, nuts and sugar.

Festivals

It's worth visiting Fayoum City purely for its **festivals**, as lots of local farmers do. Hotels overflow during **Ali er-Rubi's moulid** in Sha'ban, when the alleys around his mosque are crammed with stalls selling sugar dolls and horsemen, and all kinds of amusements can be tried, while the devout perform *zikrs* in the courtyard.

The other big occasion is the "viewing" (*Er-Ruyeh*) of the new moon that heralds **Ramadan**. This calls for a huge procession from the Gamal Abdel Nasser Mosque. Headed by the security forces, followed by imams and sheikhs, a parade of carnival floats "mimes" the work of different professions and bombards spectators with "lucky" prayer leaflets.

During the month of Ramadan, there's a small moulid at the domed white tomb of **Sheikha Mariam** (between the sluice of the Bahr Sinnuris and the four waterwheels). The **Great Feast** (starting on the tenth of *Zoul Hagga*) is a more private occasion, with most eateries closed, so avoid coming then.

On the Monday after the movable **Coptic Easter**, locals and day-trippers from Cairo picnic along the canalsides in the popular festival of "Smelling the Breeze" (*Sham el-Nessim*); many others celebrate it on the shore of Lake Qaroun.

Around Fayoum Oasis

The oasis's other populous centres – Sinnuris, Ibshaway, Itsa and Tamiya – hold little interest. However, there are enjoyable scenic spots easily accessible from Fayoum City in the form of the springs of **Ain es-Siliyin** and **Lake Qaroun**. Reaching the waterfalls of **Wadi Rayan** or the seldom-visited **ancient sites** on the periphery of the oasis is trickier, so don't undertake a jaunt lightly nor set off without adequate water and food for the day – you can't rely on finding either in the remoter places.

As in the Nile Valley, foreign visitors may find their freedom of movement impeded by the local **tourist police**, who may require that you use a private car or taxi to go any farther than Lake Qaroun. However, they don't keep a strict watch on **public transport** terminals, so it's just about feasible to get around by covered pick-ups (with fixed fares and routes) or local buses. There's no denying, though, that having your own transport makes life much easier; the *Palace Hotel* can supply a **car** (with or without driver) and also rents **motorbikes**, while Mohammed Ismail (☏084/820-306, mobile ☏010 6927621) is a reliable **taxi** driver who can take people around the oasis for about £E150 a day.

If you do **drive** yourself, stay alert for tractors, children and livestock, when visiting the remoter sites. You'll need a car with high ground clearance, if not 4WD; adequate water (for humans and radiators); and shovels and traction mats or boards (for digging cars out of soft sand). Always travel with at least one other car and heed local advice about the weather; and never travel during the *khamseen*.

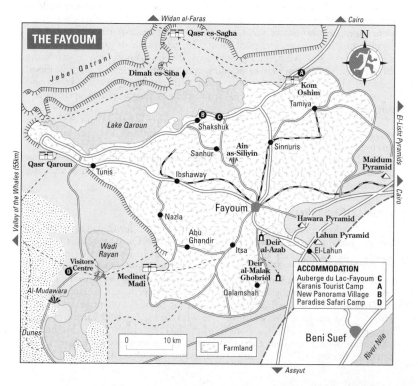

ACCOMMODATION
Auberge du Lac-Fayoum **C**
Karanis Tourist Camp **A**
New Panorama Village **B**
Paradise Safari Camp **D**

Sobek and Crocodilopolis

Kiman Faris (Horseman's Mounds) is the local name for a site on the northern outskirts of Fayoum City, rapidly disappearing beneath new colleges. Although nothing remains to justify a visit, it is the **site of Crocodilopolis** (later renamed *Arsinoë* after Ptolemy II's sister-wife), the Fayoum's ancient capital and centre of the **crocodile cult**. This supposedly began with Pharaoh Menes, the legendary unifier of Upper and Lower Egypt, whose life was saved by a croc while he was hunting in the Fayoum marshes. Crocodiles infested the lake beyond Kiman Faris (which was much larger in ancient times), so an urge to propitiate the creatures is understandable.

▲ Sobek

The crocodile deity, **Sobek**, was particularly favoured by Middle Kingdom rulers but assumed national prominence after he became identified with Re (as Sobek-Re) and Horus. He was variously depicted as a hawk-headed crocodile or in reptilian form with Amun's crown of feathers and ram's horns. At the Sacred Lake of Crocodilopolis, reptiles were fed and worshipped, and even adorned with jewellery, by the priests of Sobek.

Ain es-Siliyin

Fayoumis rate **Ain es-Siliyin** as a major beauty spot – and perhaps it was so in the days before the cafeterias, football pitch, pool and chalets were built in the hollow where the Siliyin **springs** bubbled forth. Nowadays they spurt from pipes, and hordes of picnickers (Fridays are busiest) have trampled the surrounding vegetation. The pool itself (25pt admission) is perennially packed with children and, whatever Egyptians say, it's *not* a good idea to drink the spring water, which is rich in titanium and supposedly good for low blood pressure. The road to the springs is lined with restaurants serving kebab and pigeon, and vendors selling seasonal fruit (mangos, guavas, plums, apricots and prickly pears).

To reach the springs, which are sited 9km north of town just before the village of the same name, ask for directions to the taxi and pick-up depot serving Sanhur, Shakshuk and other points north, located off the railway tracks several blocks west of Bahr Sinnuris. Public **transport** is cheap: to the springs or Sanhur by pick-up costs about 50pt; don't be fooled into renting a private taxi instead of a service taxi.

Lake Qaroun

Short of tankers gliding between the sandbanks of the Suez Canal, Egypt has no weirder juxtaposition of water and desert than **Lake Qaroun** (*Birket Qaroun*), where fishing boats bob against a backdrop of arid hills and the immensity of the Western Desert. Known to locals as "The Pond" (*El-Birka*), the lake's name may derive from the horn (*qorn*)-shaped peak on an island in the middle, but Fayoumis believe that it's named after a character in the Koran, who was swallowed up by the earth as a punishment for being "exultant in his riches". Folklore also has it that he was a sorcerer who turned the land barren, or a Jew whose treasure still lies at the bottom of the lake. Although "glassy and brooding, surrounded by beaches encrusted with salts, the recipient of all the drainage canals in the region" (as one nineteenth-century guidebook described it), the lake is favoured by Cairenes as a **bathing resort**, undeterred by the beach of broken shells and saline gunk (keen swimmers may be glad to note that, though foul-tasting, the water is at least free of bilharzia). The "season" runs year-round, but from January to April it's too cold to swim.

The view can be enjoyed at various establishments beside the shore, including the jutting *La Promenade Café* of the **Auberge du Lac-Fayoum**, a hotel that was once King Farouk's hunting lodge, where Allied and Arab leaders met after World War II to carve up the Middle East. If you ask nicely, they might let you see the suite used by Farouk, now faded and uncared-for. With a pair of binoculars, you can observe the lake's prolific **birdlife**: 88 species, including flamingoes, which have a colony on **Horn Island** (*Geziret el-Qorn*). If the ubiquitous tourist police raise no objections, you can rent **rowing boats** at the *Auberge* or *New Panorama Village*, and there are boatmen willing to row you out to the island or the far shore of the lake for a negotiable sum.

The lake itself covers 214 square kilometres, at 45m below sea level, a fraction of its size when the Nile first broke into the wind-eroded Fayoum depression seventy thousand years ago, forming a lake 40m above the current level. Egyptian mythology identified this with *Nun*, the waters of chaos and primeval life; from the Stone Age onwards people lived around the lake, which had shrunk considerably by Dynastic times.

Although the Middle Kingdom emerged at nearby Herakleopolis, it wasn't until Pharaoh Amenemhat I moved his capital from Upper Egypt to Lisht that the Fayoum became important. He had canals dug and the channel to the Nile deepened, draining parts for agriculture and submerging a greater area with what the ancients called **Lake Moeris**. It was this that the Ptolemies lowered to reclaim land for their settlements, whose decline by the end of the Roman period matched the lake's drop to 36m below sea level. Increasing salinity was a problem by medieval times, and after the lake came into equilibrium with the water sheet 40m beneath the Western Desert in 1890, it became too salty for its freshwater fish; since the 1970s, ten new marine species have been introduced, including eel, mullet, sole and shrimp. In recent years the water table has risen again, flooding houses, hotels and fields beside the lake.

Practicalities

Getting to Lake Qaroun without private transport involves taking a service taxi to Shakshouk, the main settlement beside the lake. Some vehicles join the lakeside road 3km east of the four-star hotel *Auberge du Lac-Fayoum* (see below) and then run west along the shore towards Shakshuk; others go directly there and then continue eastwards past the hotels.

Of the lakeside **eating** spots, the *Café Gabal el-Zinah*, 2km west of the *Auberge*, has children's play areas and serves fish, as does the cheaper *Qaroun Beach Café*, nearby, while *Café Louloua*, 3km west of the *Auberge*, serves pizzas and other Western dishes. The *Auberge* is known for its wildfowl dishes, but they don't live up to expectations or the price, though the surroundings are undoubtedly impressive.

As for **accommodation**, the *Auberge du Lac-Fayoum* (℡084/700-002, ℻710-730; **⑦**) is comfortable rather than luxurious, with a/c rooms, tennis and squash courts, two pools, three restaurants, a bar and a disco (closed over winter) – sadly, the view from the rooms is spoilt by the lakeside chalets in the garden. Off-season, the three-star *New Panorama Village* (℡084/701-314, ℻701-757; **⑥**) near Shakshuk, is worth a try as it often cuts its rates if trade is poor.

West of Shakshuk, the holiday villas of wealthy Cairenes spread out along the road that ultimately leads to **Qasr Qaroun** and **Wadi Rayan** (see p.522).

If you've got a car, keep going, since local women and children pester you remorselessly for *baksheesh*.

Qasr Qaroun and Tunis

QASR QAROUN (daily 8am–4pm; £E20), the best-preserved of the Fayoum's Ptolemaic temples, lies on the northwestern rim of the oasis. Though only 45km from Fayoum City, it takes ages to get there by service taxi to Ibshaway (1hr; £E1), and then another taxi to the village of Qaroun (1hr; £E2). It's worth hiring a car to explore the temple and visit Wadi Rayan on the same trip.

Not a palace as its Arabic name suggests, Qasr Qaroun is actually a temple – outwardly plain but inwardly labyrinthine. You'll need a torch to explore its warren of chambers, stairs and passageways at different levels; beware of scorpions, bats, snakes and lizards – the last resemble miniature crocodiles, as befits a temple dedicated to Sobek. Round about are the **ruins of Dionysias**, a Ptolemaic-Roman town believed to have been abandoned in the fourth century AD when the lake shrank (it's now 45 minutes' walk away), leaving desiccated stalks of vegetation. Early European travellers undertook nine-hour horse rides to this site, believing that it was the famous Labyrinth described by Herodotus and Strabo (see "Hawara", p.526). West of the temple is an even more ruinous **fortress**, constructed during the reign of Diocletian against the Blemmye (an indication of how far north these Nubian raiders went).

En route to or from Qasr Qaroun you'll pass through **TUNIS**, a farming village turned **artists' colony** of houses built in the vernacular style, using local materials. Among the first residents were Ahmed Abu Zed – one of Egypt's leading potters – and the Swiss couple Evelyne Porret and Michel Pastore, who set up a **pottery** school for local children to learn the craft. Phone to make an appointment to view the products of Ahmed's studio (☎084/820-357) or the school (☎084/820-405).

Wadi Rayan and the Valley of Whales

Wadi Rayan is a separate depression 15km outside the oasis, which has become a man-made wildlife haven and beauty spot. The idea of piping excess water from the Fayoum into the *wadi* was first mooted by the British but only put into practice in 1966, when three lakes and a waterfall were created, vegetation flourished and the area became a major nesting ground for birds. It has status as a **nature reserve**, harbouring the world's only known population of slender-horned gazelles (*gazella leptoceros*), eight other species of mammals, thirteen species of resident birds and 26 migrant and vagrant ones – not to mention the unique fossils in the **Valley of the Whales**. However, environmental problems have plagued the reserve: one lake has dried up and the others have become increasingly saline; the tourist board's promotion of Wadi Rayan as a major attraction doesn't always sit happily with its conservation aims; and the re-routing of the 2000 Paris–Dakkar–Cairo rally through Wadi Rayan disrupted the wildlife and littered the locality.

As no public transport goes anywhere nearby, you can only **get there** by car; bargain hard for a taxi from Fayoum City (about £E150) or Lake Qaroun (£E80–100). The route there is easy: leave the lakeside road at a signposted turning 28km west of the *New Panorama Village*, and follow it 8.5km to the entrance gate, where passengers are charged an **admission fee** of £E5 each plus £E5 for the vehicle. The open desert beyond gets sandier and lovelier the closer you get to the azure **lakes**, where a track leads down to the **waterfalls** (*shallalat*). The only ones in Egypt, they've appeared in countless videos and films despite being only a couple of metres high and shrinking as the level of the lower lake rises. Hordes of visitors descend here on Fridays and holidays, overwhelming its **visitors' centre**, cafeterias and **mosque** built of reeds, to sunbathe and play ghettoblasters on the beach around the falls.

Come at any other time to enjoy swimming, sunbathing and **bird-watching**. Besides the ubiquitous cattle egrets and grey herons, there are hard-to-spot wagtails, skylarks, kestrels, kites and coucals from Senegal. The reed beds developing here are being colonized by wetland species such as the little bittern, adding to the diversity of the habitat. As you continue south from the waterfalls turn-off, the beauty of the lower lake is offset by golden dunes (which sometimes encroach on the road), and you can hike up to the hill known as **Al-Mudawara** (The Lookout) for a spectacular **view** of the reed-fringed lake and the desert scarp beyond. At another point, 12.5km on, there's a signposted turning to a bird-watching site by the shore, followed 4km later by magnificent *seif* **dunes** 30m high. These parallel an inlet fringed by tamarisks, with three sulphur **springs** nearby. Thereafter, the road crosses a boring stretch of desert to return to the oasis. All of this route can be done in a 2WD car.

The Valley of the Whales

Fifty-five kilometres further into the desert is the amazing **Valley of the Whales** (*Wadi al-Hitan*). To get there, you'll need a 4WD vehicle as well as permission from the Egyptian Enviromental Affairs Agency (EEAA) office at Wadi Rayan (☎ & ℗084/830-535), which will send a guide to show you the way. The terrain is rugged so it's safer to have two cars. The *Paradise Safari Camp* (see below) can take you as a passenger, or you can bring your own 4WD and they will lead you in theirs.

The valley is extraordinary not only for its fossils, but for its surreal **boulders** like giant toasted marshmallows oozing syrup. Geologically, they belong to the Qasr es-Sagha Formation created by the ancient Tethys Sea, whose **fossils** consist of land mammals deposited by the swirling waters and marine life stranded when the sea receded during the Eocene era, 45 million years ago. The site was surveyed in 1877 by the geologist George Schweinfurth, who found 200 fossilized skeletons of what he thought was a reptile named Basilosaurus, which was later reclassified as a mammal with a slender body 20m long and small but fully developed hind feet. It's thought that this Zeuglodon was an evolutionary dead-end in the evolution of whales that began when some land mammals migrated into the sea; another, smaller whale found here, called Dorudon, may prove to be the ancestor of modern whales. At Wadi al-Hitan, one Zeuglodon lies prone beneath a promontory of fossilized coral, as if it had sought shelter as the waters shrank. New skeletons are being discovered all the time.

Due to the site's fragility and previous looting of fossils by souvenir-hunters, EEAA rangers now ensure that visitors respect the **rules**: look, photograph, but don't touch anything. Anyone breaking the rules can be heavily fined.

Accommodation and safaris

To get the most from Wadi Rayan you should stay the night. Run by the hospitable, multi-lingual Mohammed Marzouk and within walking distance of the falls, the Jannat or Paradise Safari Camp has large tents with beds with clean sheets, lit by candles, and a lovely outdoor restaurant serving meals of chicken or fish, where Bedouin parties are sometimes held. Beds (£E25 per person) can be reserved through Marzouk Desert Cruises, 1 Midan Ibn Sandar, Hammamat al-Qubba in Cairo (☎ & ℱ02/258-8083, ✉mmarzouk2001@yahoo.com), which specializes in 4WD safaris to the Valley of the Whales and camel treks to Bahariya Oasis via the Darb al-Rayan.

Medinet Madi

Medinet Madi (City of the Past) is another temple site in the desert, roughly 35km southwest of Fayoum City. **Getting there** entails catching the El-Qasmiya bus from the Hawatim depot and riding on through Itsa, El-Minia and Abu Gandir. Ask to be dropped off at Menshat Sef, roughly one hour later. From this bridge it's about an hour's walk to the temple. Turn right, follow the canal to the next bridge, cross over and take a narrower canal path past a small village on your left, aiming for a stone hut on the rise ahead, beyond which lies the site.

Squatting in a sandy hollow where excavations are revealing an avenue of sphinxes and lions (one of them ruffed and bearded like a Renaissance grandee), the **Temple of Medinet Madi** was built for the XII Dynasty pharaohs Amenemhat III and IV, and dedicated to twin deities. Sobek appears in relief on the outside of the rear wall, while Renenutet the serpent-goddess (also associated with harvests) can be seen in the left-hand room of the limestone edifice. Ptolemaic additions include two female winged sphinxes, and the **ruined town** of mud- and fired bricks to the southeast. Although legend attributes its destruction to a tribe of eleventh-century Nejd warriors enraged by the town's refusal of hospitality, the real cause of its blight was probably the shrinking of the lake. What looks like an embankment north of the temple was actually the storm beach of the lake in ancient times, 68m above its present level.

To return to Fayoum City, catch the bus from Menshat Sef (going in the same direction, as the route is circular).

Kom Oshim: ancient Karanis

The most accessible of the ancient sites in the Fayoum is **Kom Oshim** (daily 8am–4pm), 30km north of Fayoum City, where the Cairo road descends into the depression. Ask a bus or taxi driver to drop you at *Mat'haf Kom Oshim*, the small **museum** by the road, where admission **tickets** are sold (£E10 for the museum; £E20 for the site). Its curator speaks good English and is keen to explain details. Pottery and glassware, terracotta figures used for modelling hairstyles and two lifelike "Fayoum portraits" (see p.526) convey the wealth and sophistication of the ancient frontier town whose ruins lie behind the museum.

The **ruins of Karanis** clearly show the layout of this Ptolemaic-Roman town, founded by Greek mercenaries and their camp followers during the third century BC, which had a population of three thousand or so until the fifth century AD. Although the mud-brick houses have been reduced to low walls, two stone **temples** are better preserved – no thanks to the nineteenth-century Antiquities Department, which allowed contractors to destroy Roman buildings for their bricks. The larger one was built towards the end of the first century BC and dedicated to two local crocodile gods, Petesouchos and Pnepheros.

Professor Scott Woodward believes that the population of Fayoum Oasis was the most genetically diverse in ancient times and is reflected in the genetic make-up of Egyptians today. He reckons that over one million corpses are buried around the edges of the oasis, and at Karanis in particular, where 85 percent of the upper strata are blond-haired (northern Mediterraneans) and couples are genetically dissimilar; the lower layers, however, contain evidence of many brother-sister marriages. Scott attributes the change to the advent of

Christianity (with its taboo on incest) in the Fayoum, which seems to have happened in the first century AD, two hundred years earlier than was previously thought.

If you phone (☎084/501-825) a day ahead the museum can usually provide a **guide** for excursions to Qasr es-Sagha and Dimeh es-Siba (see below). Beside the museum, the *Karanis Tourist Camp* (☎084/501-825; ❶) serves simple **meals** in a shady garden, and has basic **chalets** should you care to stay. To return to Fayoum or Cairo, flag down any passing bus or service taxi.

Qasr es-Sagha, Dimeh es-Siba and Widan al-Faras

For those with a 4WD and a hankering to explore the desert, there are several satisfyingly remote sites to the **north of Lake Qaroun**. Though you don't need permission to visit them (they're unguarded), it's strongly advisable to take a guide from the Karanis museum, as the track to Qasr es-Sagha (40km) is not always apparent, and may have difficult patches of soft sand, though the initial stretch is clear enough and busy with trucks coming from a nearby quarry.

The small Middle Kingdom temple known as **Qasr es-Sagha** (Palace of the Jewellers) nestles inconspicuously halfway up an outlying scarp of the Jebel Qatrani. Although lacking any friezes or inscriptions, it's remarkable for its masonry, which is unlike that of any other Egyptian temple. The blocks are irregularly shaped, with odd angles and corners fitting together like a jigsaw; the overall effect is of an Inca edifice transplanted from the Andes. Notice the enigmatic dead-end **passage** built into the front wall of the temple. Lake Qaroun, which once lapped at the temple's base, now lies 11km away, beyond the ruins of Dimeh es-Siba, a Ptolemaic town that pegged out as the lake shrank.

To reach this you drive 9km south past hundreds of giant egg-shaped **boulders** that have fractured into halves or slices due to the baking heat. It's hard to imagine that a town of well-fed Greek soldiers and courtesans once flourished here. Starkly visible against the desert, the ruins of **Dimeh es-Siba** (Dimeh of the Lions) are ringed by a mud-brick wall up to 10m high and 5m thick. In the centre is a rough-hewn, ruined stone temple that was dedicated to Soknopaios, a form of Sobek (see p.520); the hill on which it stands was originally an island in the crocodile-infested lake. Approaching from that direction – a 2.5km walk – you'll come first to a 400-metre-long road (flanked by stone lions as late as the nineteenth century), running past ruined houses into the temple enclosure. The ruins are frequented by **owls**, and occasionally **jackals**.

Gung-ho 4WD types can also follow an ancient road (8km) from Qasr es-Sagha to the Old Kingdom **quarries** of **Widan al-Faras**. Here, the basalt used to make pots and statues simply fell off the hillside, to be loaded onto sledges and dragged down the escarpment to barges at Qasr. The quarry road, known as the *Rali Al-Farainah*, is perhaps the **world's oldest paved road**, made 4000 years ago from stones and chunks of fossilized wood (akin to the Petrified Forest in the Muqattam Hills outside Cairo). It has been used by scientists to measure the erosion of the desert, for where they once stood level, the road is now almost 1m above the desert's surface, meaning that the wind strips away 3cm per century. Widan al-Faras itself is a mountain extruded from the **Jebel Qatrani** range, whose fossil-rich sandstone and clay beds from the Eocene era are capped with a thick layer of black basalt. Guides who really know their stuff can navigate across the trackless desert from the Cairo–Baharia highway about 70km from Bawiti (the capital of Baharia Oasis), and descend the escarpment into the Fayoum.

Pyramids around the Fayoum

The Fayoum is associated with four separate **pyramid sites**, two of them beyond its limits, the other pair more conveniently sited off the Beni Suef road. The latter, at **Lahun** and **Hawara**, both date from the XII Dynasty, which governed Egypt – and ordered the waterworks that transformed the Fayoum – from its capital *Itj-tway* (Seizer of the Two Lands). This lay 30km to the northeast, near **El-Lisht**, where the dynasty's founder Amenemhat I built his own pyramid.

The fourth site, **Maidum**, is unconnected with the others (which it predates by seven centuries), but its dramatic-looking "Collapsed Pyramid" marks an evolutionary step between the pyramids at Saqqara and Giza.

Hawara Pyramid

Hawara (Great Mansion) may have stood on the shores of Lake Qaroun when it was built during the XII Dynasty, and later became the finishing point of a 100-kilometre **desert endurance race** instituted by Pharaoh Taharqa (690 BC) to train his troops (this was revived as an annual event in 2001). Aside from the race, held every November, Hawara gets few visitors, for its 54-metre-high **Pyramid of Amenemhat III** (daily 8am–4pm; £E20) has degenerated into a mud-brick mound since its limestone casing was removed in antiquity. Unlike most pyramids, its entrance was on the south side: one of many ruses devised to foil tomb-robbers. Alas, due to rising ground water, you

▲ Amenemhat III

can't go inside to examine such features as the stone portcullises that sealed the corridor or the roof block that was lowered into place once the sarcophagus was in the burial chamber, both operated by sand. None of them saved the body of the pharaoh (1842–1797 or 1855–1808 BC) from being looted and burned centuries before Petrie rediscovered his sarcophagus alongside that of his daughter, Nefru-Ptah, which was stored here while her own tomb was being constructed. It was found intact with her treasures in 1956. East of the pyramid (the direction from which visitors approach) lies a bone- and bandage-littered necropolis, with deep shafts to ensnare the unwary.

To the south, towards and beyond the canal, a few column stumps and masses of limestone chippings mark the **site of the Labyrinth**. All that's known about this fabled building comes from Strabo, Herodotus and Pliny. Herodotus wrote that it contained over three thousand chambers hewn from a single rock, surpassing all the "great works of the Greeks . . . put together", while Strabo maintained that it had as many rooms as there were provinces, so that each could be represented by officials at ceremonies. Most archeologists think that it was Amenemhat III's mortuary temple, although Rohl argues that it may have been an eternal representation of the bureaucracy and waterworks that Joseph devised to prepare Egypt for the seven years of famine foretold by the pharaoh's dream (Genesis 41:1–4).

During the early excavations at Hawara in the nineteenth century, Petrie unearthed 146 brilliantly naturalistic **"Fayoum Portraits"** (100–250 AD) in the Roman cemetery to the north of the pyramid. Executed in beeswax-based paint while their sitters were alive, they were cut to size and stuck on to the bandaged cadavers, whose mummification was perfunctory compared to the embalming of Dynastic times. One such portrait graces the Karanis museum (see p.524); others can be admired in Cairo's Egyptian Antiquities Museum (see p.138).

Getting to the pyramid involves a ten-kilometre bus or service taxi ride from Fayoum City's Hawatim depot to the village of Hawaraat al-Makta, where you cross the Bahr Yussef by a bridge, turn right at the T-junction beyond the village and walk on for about 3km until the pyramid appears. From its summit (easily reached by climbing the southwest corner) you should be able to see the Lahun Pyramid on the southeastern horizon.

Lahun Pyramid

Ten kilometres beyond Hawara, the incoming Nile waters pass through El-Lahun, where modern sluices stand just north of the **Qantara of Sultan Qaitbey**, the thirteenth-century equivalent of the regulators installed by Amenemhat III. (Photographing these installations is forbidden.) Lahun gets its name from the ancient Egyptian *Le-hone* ("Mouth of the Lake"), and gives it to the Pyramid of Senusert II sited 5km away. Most of the service taxis from the Hawatim depot to El-Lahun stop where the track leaves the main road; it's well over an hour's walk to the pyramids from there. Part of the route follows a massive **embankment**

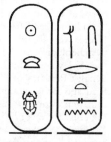

▲ Senusert II

thought to have been part of Amenemhat I's original barrage to divert water into the Fayoum. It ends at the desert's edge, where visitors buy an admission ticket for the site and pick up a police escort to walk the final kilometre to the pyramid.

Built seven or eight centuries after the pyramids at Giza, the **Pyramid of Senusert II** (daily 8am–4pm; £E25) employed a new and different technique, devised by the architect Anupy. The core consists of a rock knoll on which limestone pillars were based, providing the framework for the mud-brick overlay, which was finally encased in stone. Mindful of flooding, Anupy surrounded the base with a trench full of sand and rolled flints, to act as a "sponge".

The subsequent removal of its casing stones left the mud-brick pyramid exposed to the elements, which eroded it into its present mess. When Petrie entered the pyramid and found Senusert's sarcophagus it had been looted long ago; however, Brunton discovered the jewellery of Princess Sat-hathor, which is now divided between Cairo's museum and the Metropolitan Museum of Art in New York.

Senusert II (1897–1878 or 1880–1874 BC), Amenemhat III's grandfather, ordered eight rock-cut *mastabas* for his family to the north of his pyramid; east of them is the shapeless so-called **Queen's Pyramid**, apparently lacking any tomb.

Maidum Pyramid

Although technically outside the limits of the Fayoum, the **"Collapsed Pyramid" of Maidum** (daily 8am–4pm; £E25) can be reached from there (or from Cairo). Take an early-morning third-class train to El-Wasta from Fayoum (1–2hr), or from Cairo's Ramses Station (3hr), and then a service taxi to the village of Maidum (10–15min). From the far end of the village it's a short walk across the fields and two canals into the desert; beware of potholes and skulls underfoot. The pyramid is visible from the Nile Valley road, and during the last stage of the train journey. Tickets include admission to two *mastabas* and a ruined mortuary temple. Ask to see them or you won't get into either.

Standing isolated and truncated amidst the sands "with much of its outer layers collapsed into piles of rubble, it looks more like the keep of a medieval castle than a proper pyramid", as T.G.H. James observed. It rises in sheer-walled tiers above mounds of debris: a vision almost as dramatic as the act of getting inside used to be, when "visitors had to hang by their hands from the ledge above and drop into the entry guided by a guard". Nowadays you climb a 30m stairway on the north side, descend 75m to the bedrock by a steep passageway and then ascend to the airless **burial chamber** (bring a torch). Two new chambers were recently found using an endoscope; they have not been entered yet, but may have served to relieve the weight on the burial chamber. Round about the pyramid are unfinished *mastabas*, reduced to ruinous lumps, where the exquisite "Maidum Geese" frieze and the famous statue of Prince Ra-Hotpe and his wife Nofret were found (both can now be seen in the Cairo Egyptian Museum).

Archeologists ascribe the pyramid to **Snofru** (see p.252), the first king of the IV Dynasty (c.2613–2494 BC), or to **Huni**, the last ruler of the preceding dynasty. Partisans of Huni argue that Snofru is recognized as having built the Red and Bent pyramids at Dahshur, and would therefore not have needed a third repository for his *ka*. Mendelssohn's *The Riddle of the Pyramids* advances the contrary theory that Maidum was started by Snofru as a step pyramid (like Zoser's at Saqqara), and then later given an outer shell to make it a "true" pyramid. But the design was faulty, distributing stresses outwards rather than inwards, so that its own mass blew the pyramid apart. Mendelssohn argues that Snofru had already embarked on another pyramid at Dahshur, whose angle was hastily reduced (hence the Bent Pyramid), and that the Red Pyramid was a final attempt to get things right. Crucial to his argument is the idea that pyramids were built in production-line fashion, whether there were pharaohs to be buried in them or not; thus, kings who died before the completion of their own pyramid could be allotted one from the "stockpile".

El-Lisht Pyramids

The **Pyramids of El-Lisht** are the most inaccessible and ruined of the Fayoum collection, with little claim to anyone's attention. The larger of them, the **Pyramid of Amenemhat I** (1991–1962 BC), commemorates the founder of the XII Dynasty, whose capital, *Itj-tway*, was somewhere in the vicinity. Slightly to the south and harder to reach is the **Pyramid of Senusert I**, Amenemhat's son.

Fayoumi monasteries

Tradition has it that St Anthony personally inspired the first hermits in the Fayoum during the fourth century, and within two hundred years the depression held 35 monastic communities. As elsewhere in Egypt, Coptic monasticism gradually declined after the Muslim conquest, and only started to revive during the last century. But the habit of pilgrimage never faded, and still ensures visitors to monasteries that are virtually deserted except on holy days.

Deir al-Azab, the nearest monastery to Fayoum City, is reached by heading 5km out along the Beni Suef road, and turning left at a fork; the monastery is on the right after just over a kilometre. Founded during the twelfth century and recently rebuilt *sans* style, the "Bachelor's Monastery" no longer houses monks, but draws many Coptic visitors on Fridays and Sundays, and also holds the **Moulid of the Virgin** (August 15–22). It's the burial place of St Abram, the revered Bishop of Fayoum and Giza between 1882 and 1914, whose portrait is said to reach out and shake hands with blessed visitors.

The remoter, more picturesque **Deir al-Malak Ghobriel** (Monastery of the Archangel Gabriel) squats on a desert hillside overlooking the cultivated lowlands. Pilgrim buses may turn up for the **Moulid of Archangel Gabriel** (December 18), but otherwise it's very quiet. Wolves have been known to make their dens in the hillside caves; from the ridge you can see the Lahun gap, and sometimes the Lahun and Hawara pyramids. Service taxis for Qalamshah run past a yellow stone barn in the village of Qalhana, whence a dirt track leads to the monastery (5km; 1hr walk). Its **church** dates from the tenth or eleventh century and contains some superb medieval **frescoes** found during restoration work in 1991, plus the naturally mummified "**Naqlun Martyrs**" – unknown monks, women and children murdered at some time in the distant past. Their corpses aren't on show, but the monastery's shop sells gory photos.

The Great Desert Circuit

Only feasible for tourists since the 1980s, the **Great Desert Circuit** is one of the finest journeys Egypt has to offer. Starting from Cairo, Luxor or Assyut, it runs for over 1000km through a desert landscape pockmarked by dunes and lofty escarpments. En route, amid wind-eroded depressions, **four oases** are sustained: Bahariya, Farafra, Dakhla and Kharga. Unlike Siwa, these "inner oases" have been almost continuously under the control of the Nile Valley since the Middle Kingdom, ruled by the pharaohs, Persians, Romans, Mamlukes, Turks and British, who have left their mark in the form of temples, tombs, forts, mosques or roads. Since Nasser's time, an ambitious development programme known as the **New Valley** (see box overleaf) has transformed the oases.

Although each has a central focus, the differences between them are as marked as their similarities. **Bahariya** and **Farafra** both score highly on their hot springs and palm groves, but Bahariya is influenced by Cairene ways and a major centre for **desert safaris**, whereas Farafra is more rural and traditional. In **Dakhla** and **Kharga** the modern centres are less appealing than the ancient ruins and villages on their peripheries, redolent of historic links with the Nile Valley or caravan routes from Sudan. Staying overnight in the haunting **White Desert** between Bahariya and Farafra is a must; while for those with more time and money there are safaris to remoter sites like the **El-Qaf** stalactite cave, or the uninhabited oases along the desolate road to **Siwa Oasis**, which allows die-hard travellers to visit all the Western Desert oases in a mega-circuit of over 1400km. Due to red tape, however, this journey is far easier in the other direction, starting from Siwa.

Relying on **public transport**, it's likely to take the best part of a week to visit all four New Valley oases. If you only have a few days, Bahariya and Farafra are the obvious destinations to aim for, being just a day's journey from Cairo. Starting from Luxor and travelling in the opposite direction, it makes sense to ride straight on to Dakhla rather than stop in Kharga if you're pushed for time. But it would be a shame to rush the oases, when lazing around is part of their appeal.

The New Valley

The four "Great Desert Circuit" oases are situated along a dead, prehistoric branch of the Nile, and depend on springs and wells tapping the great aquifer beneath the Libyan Desert. In 1958 Nasser's government unveiled plans to exploit this, irrigate the desert, and relocate landless peasants from the overcrowded Nile Valley and Delta to the "**New Valley**" (*El-Wadi el-Jedid*). This was vital for social reasons, but also intended to forestall landless *fellaheen* from emigrating to Syria, which was at that time joined with Egypt in the United Arab Republic, and relatively underpopulated. Nasser set up a Desert Authority which found the oases to be isolated, with no roads or modern facilities, and many of their ancient wells and canals blocked. From this emerged a five-year plan and a New Valley Governorate to run Kharga, Dakhla and Farafra oases, in collaboration with the Giza Governorate, which administers Bahariya Oasis.

Since work began in the 1970s, the project has been through ups and downs, as investments proved costlier than expected and doubts surfaced about the subterranean water table. Previously it was thought to be replenished by underground seepage from Lake Chad and Equatorial Africa, whereas now it's believed to be a finite geological legacy, sufficient for between one and seven hundred years. Although the government has initiated **new projects** to bring Nile water to Kharga Oasis by the **Sheikh Zayed Canal** and exploit the groundwater beneath the desert at **East Oweinat**, many of the new settlements are still half empty, and advertisements urging farmers to settle there no longer appear on television. Hopes of prosperity and fears of decline still turn on the caprices of hydrology and the wits of the oasis-people, as they have since ancient times.

Visiting the oases

While it's possible to tour the oases in comfort, don't expect to find fancy restaurants or bright lights – though you can look forward to Bedouin parties round a campfire. All the oases have a range of **accommodation**, from air-conditioned hotels to thatched huts on the edge of the desert. Most double as safari operators, offering tours of other oases as well as their own. Getting around using public **transport** is manageable, though you may have to stand during long bus journeys. If you decide to rent your own vehicle, you'll have to contend with potholed roads and very few petrol pumps, hundreds of kilometres apart. Always keep your **passport** handy in case the police want to see it at checkpoints. There are **banks** in the "capitals" of Bahariya, Dakhla and Kharga oases (though only Kharga's has an ATM), and all the oases now have **telephone** (if not Internet) links with the outer world.

Broadly speaking, the oases share the **climate** of Nile Valley towns on the same latitude – Bahariya is like Minya, and Kharga like Luxor – but the air is fresher (although the dust sometimes causes swollen sinuses). Winter is mild by day and near freezing at night (bring a sleeping bag); in summer temperatures can soar to 50°C at midday and hover in the 20°s after dark. Spring and autumn are the **best times** to visit the oases, with the orchards in bloom or being harvested and enough fellow travellers around to make sharing costs easy.

Tourism is in the hands of local officials and entrepreneurs whose competence and honesty varies. In Bahariya there are numerous safari operators competing for business, whereas Farafra has far fewer outfits and no tourist office. Dakhla's tourist office will help visitors get a fair deal with local drivers or safari operators, while in Kharga, staff at the tourist office and museum run their own excursions as a sideline. As always, it pays to check out different sources and compare what they're offering. But don't let over-suspicion sour things, since you really need local help to get the best from the oases and will have to strike a deal with somebody in the end – preferably one that both sides feel happy with, as disgruntled guides or tourists can spoil even the most magical spot.

Visitors should respect local values by dressing modestly and observing the conventions on bathing in **outdoor springs** (mostly concrete tanks, fed by a pipe or water percolating up from below). The ones nearest town are always used by local men; if women bathe there, it is only after dark, never when males are present, and only fully covered by a *galabiyya*. Tourists can avoid these restrictions by bathing in more isolated spots, but most **women** cover up anyway to discourage lechery from guides and hangers-on. Women on their own should beware of entering palm groves or gardens – regarded here as an invitation to sex.

Transport to the oases

Starting **from Cairo**, you'll need to book seats a day beforehand at the Moneeb bus terminal in Giza. There are six **buses** daily to Bahariya (5-6hr; £E20), two of which continue on to Farafra (8–10hr; £E27) and Dakhla (14–16hr; £E40). Kharga (7-8hr; £E40) is served by two overnight buses, routed via the Desert Road that parallels the Nile Valley. The journey times given here are only estimates; it can take longer if the bus has a wheezy engine or bursts a tyre. All Upper Egypt and Superjet buses running these routes are a/c – whether it works is another matter.

Coming from Upper Egypt, the journey **from Luxor** to Kharga takes just two hours. Some hotels in Luxor can arrange a **car** (£E350–500) and safaris as far as Dakhla or the White Desert (see p.384). Finding other travellers to split the cost might take a few days, but is preferable to relying on a third-class **train** (7–12hr; £E10) that supposedly leaves Luxor every Thursday at 7am, but may not run for weeks due to sand on the line. Kharga is also accessible **from Assyut** in Middle Egypt, by bus or service taxi (4-5hr; £E8).

Travellers hoping to combine the Great Desert Circuit with Siwa are at the mercy of arbitrary rulings by the military in Cairo. Currently, fixing the paperwork in Siwa is simple, whereas it can take days in Bahariya – so it's easier to muster a group to split the cost of a **car** (at least £E1100) **from Siwa** to Bahariya than it is going the other way. However, this may change, so consult safari outfits in Bahariya (see p.542) and Siwa's tourist office (p.589) before deciding which direction to take.

Bahariya Oasis

Bahariya Oasis is the smallest of the four depressions, only 94km long and 42km wide; its desert floor and lower escarpments formed of Cretaceous sandstone, overlaid by limestone and basalt from the Eocene period. Despite having the highest elevation above sea level of the four oases, its water table is nearer the surface, making agriculture easier here. It is known to have been under pharaonic control by the Middle Kingdom, when *Zezes* (as the oasis was known) exported wine to the Nile Valley. During the Late Period Bahariya thrived as an artery between Egypt and Libya, while throughout Islamic times, Arab armies, merchants and pilgrims passed through. Today, it is tourists who come here to enjoy the hot springs and palm groves, or undertake safaris into the dunes and rock formations of the Western Desert.

As in most of the oases, people, springs and palm groves are scattered around a depression. Although Bahariya's covers 1200 square kilometres, less than one percent is actually cultivated, with date palms, olive and fruit trees, vegetables, rice and corn. Since a dramatic slump seventy years ago when 32 springs dried up, 63,900 palm trees died, and thousands emigrated to Cairo, the population has risen again to 60,000, including more than 5000 settlers from the Fayoum. In contrast, most of the original oasis families who have lived there for generations are of Saiyidi ancestory, or descended from Senussi refugees from Libya.

The **journey from Cairo** (360km) begins with the Pyramids of Giza visible as you enter the Western Desert. Not long afterwards you'll pass **6th October City**, one of the new satellite cities meant to reduce Cairo's congestion. To relieve the tedium of traversing flat, featureless desert, vehicles stop at a grubby halfway **resthouse** (with biscuits, *fuul*, soft drinks and toilets). Running alongside is a **railway** for transporting ore to the steel mills at Helwan, supplied by a vast open-cast iron **mine** that imparts a ferrous hue to the surrounding desert. Soon after entering Bahariya Oasis the road passes a gravel track to the outlying settlement of El-Harra, and subsequent side roads to the villages of Mandisha and Agouz. Don't get off if the bus calls at any of these places – wait for the end of the line at the oasis "capital", **Bawiti**.

Due to its proximity to Cairo the oasis comes under the Giza Governorate, which means that if you're **phoning from Cairo** you don't need to use the prefix ℡02. Some subscribers still have six-digit numbers instead of the more common seven digits. Mobile phone reception varies: MobiNil has widespread coverage in the oasis but Vodafone is limited to a 5km radius of Bawiti.

Bawiti

BAWITI harbours a picturesque nucleus of old houses on a ridge overlooking luxuriant palm groves, but that's not what you see on arrival. The lower ground beside the Cairo–Farafra road is littered with half-finished New Valley projects, disrupting donkey traffic but not the ramshackle shops and

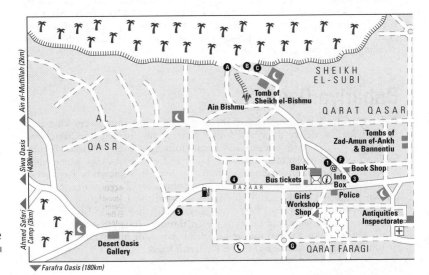

cafés that enliven Bawiti's **main street**. Almost everything of note from a practical standpoint can be found here, and buses from Cairo or Farafra drop you right in the centre. Battered 4WDs weave along the street between tractors and veiled women, past an array of coffee houses, hardware and grocery stores and, at the far end, a mosque. Raucous, dusty and making few concessions to tourists, the street is worth strolling along if the sun isn't too hot, though most tourists tend to focus on the few museums and sites that are peripheral to the locals – except for those with a financial interest in taking you there. Bawiti's tourist trade is as competitive as Luxor's, and you'll immediately be besieged by guys from rival outfits who'll try to get you to stay at their place or sign up for trips.

Bawiti's **shops** sell the usual knick-knacks and jewellery (made in Cairo), Bedouin carpets, robes and blankets (from Kerdassa), and woven baskets and platters, crystals and minerals from the oasis itself – the Girls' Workshop Shop near the cemetery is a good place for local products. It's also worth checking out the Desert Oasis Gallery, for naïve paintings, and the Farid Atiya Bookshop, for photo books, prints and posters relating to Egypt.

Arrival and information

Before terminating at the bus ticket kiosk, buses from Cairo are boarded by tourist police who ask foreigners where they are staying in the oasis – just give the name of any hotel or campground and they'll be satisfied. The **tourist police** (daily 8am–8pm; ☎02/847-3900) are based 1km up the main drag from the central, low-key **tourist office** on the ground floor of the government building (daily except Fri 8.30am–2pm and sometimes also 5–8pm; ☎02/847-3039, ✉mohamed_kader26@hotmail.com). At the tourist office, Mohammed Abd el-Qader can arrange local tours and desert safaris, which he claims are cheaper than those offered by the other operators (see p.542).

The National Bank for Development (Mon–Thurs & Sun 8am–2pm) is behind the post office: it can change **money** but not travellers' cheques, and doesn't have an ATM. When it's closed, Peter Wirth at the *International Hot Spring Hotel* changes money at good rates. The **post office** (daily except Fri

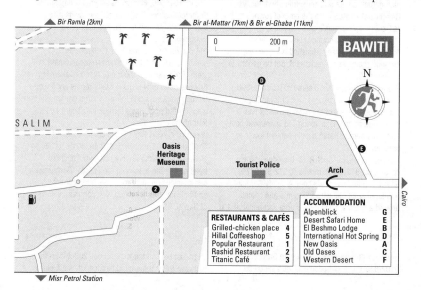

▲ *Bir Ramla (2km)* ▲ *Bir al-Mattar (7km) & Bir el-Ghaba (11km)*

0   200 m

BAWITI

N

SALIM

Oasis Heritage Museum

Tourist Police

Arch

Cairo

RESTAURANTS & CAFÉS
Grilled-chicken place	4
Hillal Coffeeshop	5
Popular Restaurant	1
Rashid Restaurant	2
Titanic Café	3

ACCOMMODATION
Alpenblick	G
Desert Safari Home	E
El Beshmo Lodge	B
International Hot Spring	D
New Oasis	A
Old Oases	C
Western Desert	F

▼ *Misr Petrol Station*

8am–2pm) is also on the main drag, around the corner from the InfoBox **Internet** (£E10/hr) kiosk, and there's a **telephone** office (daily 8am–midnight) near the *Alpenblick Hotel*. Bawiti has two **pharmacies** (open from morning till late evening) and a **hospital** (℡02/847-2390), but you'd be better off travelling to Cairo if there's a serious problem.

Accommodation

Hotels and campgrounds cater for every taste and budget and are rarely full, so it's a buyers' market. Decide whether you want desert seclusion or the "facilities" of Bawiti close at hand, and what kind of scene you fancy in the evenings. While locals make music and party on some of the campgrounds, the hotels tend to be devoid of nightlife. Also most campgrounds will provide free transport out from town, and usually into town too, while for some of the hotels you might have to rely on taxis or rent a bicycle.

The term **campground** here doesn't specifically refer to a place where you pitch a tent (though you can), but to a place that rents palm-thatch or mud-brick huts with sleeping platforms and mattresses – or proper rooms with beds and showers on the fancier sites. Most can rustle up a meal even if they lack a restaurant. If you are staying a long time, consider **renting a flat** – a one- or two-bedroom flat in the village of Agouz can be rented for £E50 or £E100 a night: contact Yehiya Kandil (mobile ℡012 3216790, ✉yahiakandil@yahoo .de) for details.

The hotels and campgrounds recommended below are arranged by **locality**, starting with Bawiti (see map on pp.532–533) and working outwards (see map on p.539). All rates quoted include **breakfast** unless stated otherwise.

Bawiti

Alpenblick Qarat Faragi ℡02/847-2184. Bahariya's oldest hotel, its dusty rooms have fans and sinks; don't pay extra for a bathroom as the shared facilities are cleaner. Its central location and nice garden are its only redeeming features. ❷

Desert Safari Home On the edge of town ℡02/847-1321, mobile 012 7313908, ✉khozamteego3@hotmail.com. Set amidst building sites, this semi-finished hotel has big en-suite rooms and a restaurant, but no garden to speak of. ❷

El Beshmo Lodge Ain Bishmu ℡02/847-3500, Ⓦwww.beshmolodge.com. One of three hotels with a superb view of the palm groves, it has cosy en-suite rooms, a spring-fed swimming pool, and a restaurant. Rates twenty percent lower in summer. ❸

International Hot Spring On the edge of town ℡ & Ⓕ02/847-2322, mobile ℡012 3212179, Ⓦwww.whitedeserttours.com. A comfy German-managed spa hotel with a/c rooms and chalets around a thermal pool; gym, sauna and restaurant;

plus a palm tree growing out of a deep hole in the ground. Rates include half-board (children under 5 free, 50 percent off for under-12s). ❼

New Oasis Ain Bishmu ℡02/847-3030, mobile ℡012 1044606, ✉max_rfs@hotmail.com. Similar to the *El Beshmo Lodge* across the ravine (see above), with its own garden and spring-fed swimming pool. ❸

Old Oases Ain Bishmu ℡ & Ⓕ02/847-3028, mobile ℡012 2324425, Ⓦwww.oldoasissafari.4t .com. The newest of the trio of hotels overlooking Bawiti's palm groves, its upstairs rooms are linked by rope walkways and there's a large garden and a spring-fed pool. Rates include half-board and a tour of the oasis. ❸

Western Desert Right in the centre ℡ & Ⓕ02/847-1600, mobile ℡012 4336015, ✉westerndeserthotel@hotmail.com. This new hotel across the road from the *Popular Restaurant* has spacious en-suite rooms with fans or a/c, TV and balcony, plus a rooftop with panoramic views of Bawiti. ❹

Agouz and the Black Mountain

Bedouin Village Agouz, 2km from Bawiti ℡02/849-6811, ✉bedouinvillage@yahoo.de.

Sited just beyond the local school, 200m from the highway, this campground has friendly staff, clean rooms with baths (£E20 per person, breakfast included), mud huts (£E10 per person), and a large tent for parties. Owner Abu Sa'ad is a fantastic *simseemeya* player. ❶

Oasis Panorama 2km from town, halfway up the Black Mountain ☎02/847-3354, ⓕ847-3896, mobile ☎012 7313908, ⓦwww.oasispanorama .com. An eyesore that locals call "The Hospital", which feels like a beach hotel whose sea has receded. Its en-suite rooms are cool and clean,

with fans or a/c (£E40 extra) and mosquito nets, but despite being well managed, the hotel feels rather soulless. ❺

Palm Village Between Agouz and Zabu, 5km from town ☎ mobile ☎012 4681024, ⓕ02/849-6271. Superior to the *Oasis Panorama* in its location and view of the Black Mountain, with larger, a/c rooms, plus some VIP rooms. Rates include half-board. Reductions between May and Sept. ❻

Ain al-Muftillah

Ahmed Safari Camp 4km from town ☎02/847-3399, mobile ☎012 4925563, ⓕ847-9090, ⓔahmed_safari@hotmail.com. The doyen of Bahariya's campgrounds has kept a few huts for old times' sake (£E10 per person), but mainly

consists of a/c rooms with fans and baths (£E60) around a lovely garden. They do beer, wine and meals, and promise free transport into town; the site is close to Alexander's Temple but otherwise remote. ❸

Towards Bir al-Mattar

Badr's Sahara Camp 3km from town on the Bir al-Mattar road ☎02/847-2955, mobile ☎012 7314966, ⓦwww.saharacamp.20m.com. Thatched huts with sleeping platforms (£E20 per person), clean shared bathrooms and a cafeteria, but little shade. Rents bicycles. ❶

Kasr el-Bawiti 2km from town on the Bir al-Mattar road, mobile ☎012 259256. A fancier complex of domed, en-suite chalets facing a terraced garden, near the hot spring of Bir el-Negba. Rates include full board and a tour of the oasis. ❼

Ain-Gufar

Eden Garden Camp 10km from Bawiti ☎02/847-3727, mobile ☎012 7311876, ⓦwww.edengardentours.com. Friendly, well-run site in a mini-oasis with a hot spring, cold pool, cosy huts (£E20 per person), two a/c en-suite

double rooms (£E50) and an outdoor lounge where you can sleep for £E5 (breakfast not included). Perfect for chilling out or partying, depending on how many people are around. ❶

Bir el-Ghaba

Bir el-Ghaba Camp 11km from town; no phone, contact through the *Alpenblick Hotel* in Bawiti. A primitive *kraal* of straw huts (£E5 per person) and mud-brick rooms (£E20 per person), near a hot spring. The site has no electricity or fridge, so guests should bring candles and food; getting a ride back into town may be hard if there are no visitors. ❶

Nature Camp 11km from town ☎02/347-3643, mobile ☎012 4504012, ⓔnaturecamps@hotmail.com. A better equipped campground in the vicinity, charging £E35 per person; some of the thatched huts have double mattresses. Tasty meals (£E25) cooked to order. ❷

Oasis Heritage Museum

Bawiti's most visible "sight" is the **Oasis Heritage Museum** created by Mohammed Eed, a 29-year-old self-taught artist, who was inspired by Badr in Farafra (see p.547). Some feel that his fired-clay statues are more expressive than Badr's but he has yet to enjoy the same success abroad. Both artists portray a way of life that's almost disappeared in the oases, for the men at least, whose job it once was to hunt gazelles and weave mats; clothes and bread were made

Bawiti's Antiquities Trail

All the **antiquities** officially open to the public (the tombs of Zad-Amun ef-Ankh, Bannentiu and Amunhotep Huy; the Temple of Alexander; the chapels of Ain al-Muftillah) are covered by a single **ticket** (£E30) and **photo permit** (£E25) sold at a kiosk downhill from the Antiquities Inspectorate in the centre of town. This also includes admission to the Inspectorate's makeshift museum, displaying three of the famous "Golden Mummies". However, as several of the sites are outside Bawiti, you'll need transport to realize the full value of the ticket – at least to reach Ain al-Muftillah and Alexander's Temple.

at home (women's roles haven't changed so much). A supine Bedouin drinking *arak* and a barber-doctor operating on a squirming patient are reminders that life wasn't so bucolic; old jewellery and robes hanging on the walls lend further authenticity. You can't miss the museum, as two nearly lifesize camels stand outside, flanked by women carrying water jars. Admission is free but donations are welcome. Mohammed has now embarked on a **new museum** which lies 1km beyond the town limits; a large stockade with a pigeon tower and beehive domes houses more statues, including one of a man shooting from a hide and another undergoing a traditional rheumatism cure with hot sticks, plus a 3D panorama of old Bawiti. If you want to visit, Mohammed can be found in the old museum or contacted by phone (☎02/847-3666). Otherwise, it's plainly visible beside the highway, near the turn-off for Agouz.

Antiquities Inspectorate

The unobtrusive **Antiquities Inspectorate** near the hospital displays three **mummies** from the huge cache found outside Bawiti. All are encased in gilded and painted *cartonage* (linen pasteboard) and have sculpted stucco masks – two of them gilded – hence their sobriquet "The Golden Mummies". Poignantly, the child was buried with its parents, and the female mummy had its head inclined towards her husband's. Her "chest plate" is sculpted with tiny triangular breasts – a funerary fashion in Greco-Roman times. In this era mummification was often perfunctory, as you can see from the sad, natron-soaked bundle that was once a child. Almost all the mummies removed from the earth have deteriorated – some previously on display here are no longer fit to be shown.

The tombs

From the Antiquities office you can walk downhill and cross the road to reach **Qarat Qasr Salim**, a dusty ridge harbouring two tombs that were opened to the public a few years ago. Both belonged to local merchants of the XXVI Dynasty, whose wealth enabled them to construct **tombs** of a kind previously reserved for high officials. **Zad-Amun ef-Ankh**'s is sunk in a steep-sided pit; its hall has rounded pillars (unusual for Bahariya) and is decorated with deities (notice the people bringing gifts, to the left), painted in ochre, brown and black upon a white background. Nearby is the tomb of his son, **Bannentiu**, at the bottom of a 10m shaft – mind your head on the steel grating and the low entrance to its votive hall. Here the pillars are square and the murals are in brick red, golden yellow, pale blue and black upon white, and some of the deities have only been sketched in, but there's a fine solar barque at the back, and the embalming process is shown on the right-hand wall.

Strange as it sounds, several tombs found by Fakhry in the 1930s were later lost, choked by sand and built over by villagers. That of **Zad-Khonsu ef-Ankh** was only rediscovered in 2000, beneath houses in the Sheikh el-Subi quarter. Bahariya's governor in the reign of the XXVI Dynasty pharaoh Amasis, he was buried in an alabaster sarcophagus enclosed within a limestone one, which are thought to have been quarried near Tell el-Amarna and Giza, shipped along the Nile and then dragged 200km overland to Bawiti. Since then, three more tombs have been found, belonging to the Badi-Isis family of oasis governors; two contain sarcophagi and mummies. While these tombs won't be accessible for some time yet, a new one has reopened another, belonging to **Amunhotep Huy**, a XVIII or XIX Dynasty governor. This lies on a ridge called **Qarat Hilwa**, 3km from town to the northwest of the Farafra road, though it's hard to find without a guide and not really worth the effort.

Bawati's old quarter, Ain Bishmu and Al-Qasr

Bawiti's **old quarter** is in the centre of town, a huddle of mud-brick homes and mausolea flanking a main street where elders sit and gossip on *mastabas*. To appreciate its commanding position, follow the alley winding off to **Ain Bishmu**, a craggy fissure in the bedrock where a spring was hewn in Roman times, gushing hot water (30°C) into a natural basin, to flow into the **palm groves** below. Sadly, the ravine is now disfigured by a pumping station, although the three hotels that have been built here try not to mar the breathtaking view of the palm groves. Mostly owned by the Dawawida family, the gardens look especially lovely when spangled with apricot blossom in spring. Nearby is the dovecote-shaped **Tomb of Sheikh el-Bishmu**, which local children will happily lead you into.

The old quarter's main street runs into **Al-Qasr**, an older village built directly over the capital of the oasis in pharaonic times and continuously inhabited since then – though many of the houses are now abandoned or used as livestock pens. Narrow alleys snake past secretive courtyards and walled gardens, abruptly ending or joining up with other lanes – making it easy to go astray. Some of the houses incorporate stones from a bygone XXVI Dynasty temple, and a Roman triumphal arch that survived until the mid-nineteenth century.

Ain al-Muftillah and the Temple of Alexander

The ancient town once extended 3km to **Ain al-Muftillah**, a spring that's nowadays almost lost on the outskirts of the desert. It's feasible to cycle but better to get there by car, as the route is not signposted or easy to explain. Look out for a barbed wire enclosure containing four **ruined chapels** excavated by Steindorff and Fakhry. Built during the XXVI Dynasty, they don't conform to the canons of temple architecture and are built of local sandstone, streaked with ochre and sienna, which makes them look unusually colourful but is liable to flake. One of the temples was dedicated to Bes, the patron deity of musicians and dancers, but all that remains of his image is a foot and a tail (though Bawiti's museum has a fine statue). By crossing the rise and a dune beyond, you can enjoy a **panoramic view** of Al-Qasr, Bawiti, and the springs and mountains described below.

Further out in the locality of Tibniya, ask at *Ahmed Safari Camp* for directions to the **Temple of Alexander**, 400m away via a sandy track. Built of the same stone as the chapels, its reliefs have suffered from being sandblasted by the wind for centuries, and nothing remains of the face and cartouche of Alexander the Great that archeologists recorded in the 1930s – though you can still discern Amun, receiving offerings from the pharaoh. This is (or was) the only temple in Egypt to bear Alexander's figure and cartouche, and it is thought to have been founded by Alexander when he passed through the oasis en route from Siwa to Memphis.

Valley of the Golden Mummies

In May 1996, a donkey owned by one of the guards at Alexander's Temple stumbled into a hole in the desert, thus alerting its master to what turned out to be the **largest cache** of mummies ever found in Egypt. Surveys have since shown that the necropolis covers ten square kilometres and may contain 10,000 mummies, stacked in family vaults. Whereas some were simply wrapped in linen, others were in terracotta coffins adorned with human faces, their bodies covered in gilded *cartonage* and their faces with stucco masks. The **Golden Mummies** caught the imagination of the public, and TV networks bid US$3 million to film the opening of a burial chamber in 1999. Coins and other artefacts buried with the mummies show that they date from Greco-Roman times, when the oasis was a thriving exporter of wine and wheat, ruled by an expatriate elite.

Hopes that DNA testing would reveal the mummies' ethnicity have been called into question by Dr Eskander – the first forensic examiner, later sacked – who claims that body parts were mixed up and double-counted, and that the cadavers were so poorly mummified that they have deteriorated into mere skeletons and organic dust, which is almost worthless from a scientific stand-point. Much has been learned, however, such as the average age of the deceased (35-40 years), and at the last televised tomb-opening (in 2004) another twenty mummies were unearthed, bringing the total found so far to 234. Since experience has shown that most of the mummies start decomposing once removed from their graves, they are now being preserved *in situ* – to respect the dead, according to Dr Hawass, who is supervising the further excavation of the valley. His book on the Golden Mummies (see p.847) remains the last word on the subject with fascinating descriptions of what it's like to excavate a site that reeks of mummified cadavers.

The main **excavation** site at "Kilo Setta" (KM 6) is off limits to tourists, though some hotels may be able to "fix" visits for a sum. You're better off, however, looking for free on the **websites** ⓦwww.guardians.net/egypt and ⓦwww.mummytombs.com.

Eating, drinking and nightlife

Eating out in Bawiti is wholesome but unexciting, as in most of the oases. Grilled chicken, salad and rice can be had at several of the hotels and camp-grounds, but most visitors gravitate to Bawiti's *Popular Restaurant*, which cooks one set meal a day of soup, vegetable stew, lamb, rice and salad (£E25), sells beer, and acts as the nerve centre of gossip and tourism in the oasis. The nearby *Titanic Café* serves only soft drinks, while the *Rashid Restaurant*, up by the Oasis Heritage Museum, is better for its desserts and *sheeshas* than its meals. The only other alternative is a nameless grilled-chicken place in the bazaar at the western end of the main street, where there are more tea and *sheesha* dens, including the overpriced *Hillal Coffeeshop* that doubles as a bus stop (see p.541). As well as the *Popular Restaurant*, you can buy **beer** at the *Oasis Panorama*, *International Hot Spring* and *Palm Village* hotels (which also sell wine and spirits) and *Ahmed Safari*, *Eden Garden* and *Bedouin Village* campgrounds.

Night-time entertainment consists primarily of **Bedouin parties**, which most campgrounds and hotels will arrange if enough tourists are staying. Held in a tent or round a fire, the singing, drumming and dancing are intoxicating even without beer (£E15-20) or hashish. Abu Sa'ad at the *Bedouin Village* charges £E25 to attend his parties, which happen several nights a week accompanied by the mellow, hypnotic sound of the *simseemeya*.

Around the oasis

Several outfits do **half-day tours** of the oasis, visiting the Black Mountain, Jebel el-Dist and Bir el-Ghaba to the northeast of Bawiti. Priced per jeep (four or five passengers), the cost ranges from £E120 at *Ahmed Safari Camp* to £E150-200 at the *Old Oasis Hotel* (whose tour is free for their guests). Alternatively, you could **rent a bicycle** for £E25 a day from New Newasha Handicrafts near the *Titanic Café*, and cycle out to Bir el-Ghaba – about 25km round-trip – or settle for exploring the palm groves, springs and villages nearer town.

Northeast of Bawiti

The hottest (45°C) and nearest spring to Bawiti is **Bir Ramla**, a nice 2km walk from Bawiti past palm and fruit orchards, but quite exposed. Males can bathe here in shorts; women only at night, in full-length opaque clothing. Similar rules apply to **Bir el-Negba**, 1km further on, and **Bir al-Mattar**, another concrete tank of warm (25°C) faintly sulphurous water, 7km from Bawiti. This "Well of the Airport" gets its name from an abandoned wartime airstrip, visible en route. Skirting palm groves, the road becomes a track leading on to **Bir el-Ghaba** (Well of the Forest), a hot and a cold spring in a eucalyptus grove. While kids or farmhands often bathe here by day, tourists can enjoy it at night (women

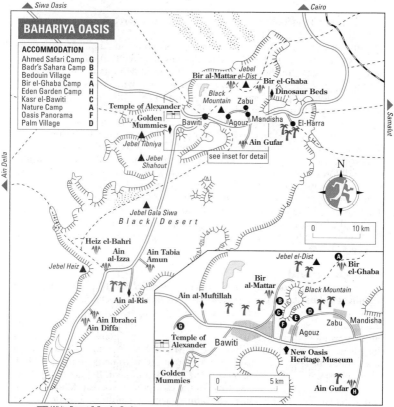

The Dinosaurs of Bahariya

In June 2001 a team from the University of Pennsylvania announced the discovery of a previously unknown type of dinosaur in Bahariya Oasis which, from the length of its forearm (1.69m), was the second-largest known to science (only surpassed by Argentinosaurus): 26–34m long and weighing 60–70 tonnes. This long-necked plant-eater lived 94 million years ago during the Late Cretaceous era when the local environment resembled the Florida Everglades, with mangrove swamps and tidal creeks – hence the title bestowed on it, **Paralititan** (Tidal Giant). Its full name, *Paralititan stromeri*, honours the Bavarian paleontologist **Ernst Stromer** (1870–1952), who first discovered dinosaur remains in Egypt between 1911 and 1915. He identified a giant herbivore, **Aegyptosaurus**, and three predators called **Spinosaurus** (Spine Lizard), **Carcharodontosaurus** (Shark-toothed Lizard) and **Bahariasaurus** – whose bones ended up in a Munich museum, where they were destroyed by an Allied air raid in 1944. When searching for Stromer's dinosaur beds, the Pennsylvania team only knew that they were somewhere near **Jebel el-Dist**; they wrote down the wrong GPS coordinates and got lost in the oasis, where by chance they found another site near **Jebel el-Fagga**, yielding the skeleton of Paralititan – with a tooth from a Carcharodontosaurus stuck in its pelvis – fossilized fish, turtles and ferns. The bones are now on show at the Geological Museum in Cairo; an impression of the creature appears on the **Bahariya Dinosaur Project website**, Ⓦ www.egyptdinos.org.

should wear a long T-shirt), and groups sometimes party at the campgrounds across the road (see p.535).

Visiting Bir el-Ghaba by day affords a view of mountains and hills that can be excursions in themselves. **Jebel el-Dist** (Mountain of the Pot) is more accurately described by locals in the tourist trade as "Pyramid Mountain", and the ever-changing play of light across it has inspired another name, "Magic Mountain". Alas, tours don't stop for long enough for you to reach the mountain, let alone go looking for **dinosaur remains** on the far side (see box above), but the fields and acacia groves nearer Bir el-Ghaba abound in **camels**, insects and **birdlife** – most noticeably wheatears, which semaphore to each other with their black-and-white tails, while birds of prey stay aloft, soaring on thermals.

En route to all these sites you'll pass the aptly named **Black Mountain**, whose dolomite and volcanic basalt mass is crowned by a ruined look-out post used by Captain Williams to monitor the Senussi in 1916, for which it is nick-named *Jebel el-Ingleez*, the "English Mountain". Most of the inhabited parts of the oasis are visible from its summit, whose rocks have an oddly sticky texture and smell faintly of biscuits. Cars usually halt in a *wadi* not far below the summit. There are several hotels and campgrounds in the locality of the Black Mountain (see pp.534–535).

East of Bawiti

Most tourists pay little heed to the **villages** outside Bawiti, whose people are friendly and hospitable. It's feasible to walk to **AGOUZ** (Old One), only 2km from town, off the Cairo highway. Agouz is reputedly inhabited by the descendants of families banished from Siwa Oasis for the loose morals of their womenfolk, but they would rather forget this slur on their ancestors. There's a campground in the village, and a hotel on the link road to **MANDISHA**, which lends its name to a field of **dunes** called Ghard Mandisha, that threatens neighbouring **ZABU**, where houses and palm groves have been drowned in sand. Behind the gardens at the back of the village, facing towards the escarpment, you can follow a track into a canebrake to find **Qasr el-Zabu** – a giant sandstone boulder where

Libyan nomads and other travellers have carved **inscriptions** since the twelfth century. Besides petroglyphs and sun symbols, you can see horses, a charioteer, a woman with her arms akimbo, and the name of the explorer Hyde.

South of Bawiti

The southern part of the oasis is generally seen by tourists bound for the White Desert on 4WD safaris. While some make a cursory detour off-road into the **Black Desert** (*Sahara Suda*) of charred outcrops and table-top rocks, others swing around the far side of **Jebel Gala Siwa** to see a lovely **dune** that has formed in the lee of the escarpment – which you can "ski" down. These tours sometimes stop for lunch at **Heiz el-Bahri**, where tamarisk-mounds and palms surround a cold spring, one of several fertile enclaves in the locality called "El-Heiz". Unfortunately tours seldom visit **Ain al-Ris**, to the south of the highway, where Roman and Christian ruins attest to its settlement in ancient times (Fakhry reckons that this was the "fourth oasis" described by texts in the temple at Edfu). This might be because the SCA made such a hash of "restoring" the **Church of St George** that they'd rather nobody saw the result; Copts believe that one of Christ's apostles, St Bartholomew, visited Bahariya before his martyrdom, and perhaps even died there. Ain al-Ris also harbours a mud-brick **Roman fortress** and remnants of an ancient **date-wine brewery**. Sticking to the highway, instead, you may notice a white **tomb** in the desert roughly 30km from Bawiti: a monument to Swiss man René Michel, a pioneer of tourism to Bahariya, who died here from heatstroke in 1986. At KM 56 are a checkpoint and the *Oasis Cafeteria*.

The Bahariya and Farafra depressions are separated by a limestone **escarpment** where gigantic drifts of sand flank the road as it traverses the **Naqb es-Sillum** (Pass of the Stairs), and two microwave masts relay signals between the oases (there's a first-aid post with an ambulance by the mast nearest Bahariya). From here on, many safari groups head off-road to reach Agabat and the White Desert, as described under Farafra Oasis (see p.542).

Moving on from Bahariya

Although there's a direct **road to Siwa Oasis** (420km), the practical obstacles can be formidable. All travellers need a **permit** (US$10 per person; US$100 for ten or more), which can currently only be obtained from Cairo by the safari operator that's taking them. Each person must submit a photocopy of their passport and visa, and the process takes at least 24 hours – maybe 2–3 days. Local drivers ask £E1100 or more for the journey (£E1500 to stay overnight in the desert), and it may be hard to find enough travellers to bring the **cost** down to an affordable level. People driving their own car (preferably 4WD) should exercise caution; there are no facilities (only checkpoints) along the road, 200km of which is in very poor condition. The drive takes at least seven hours, more if there's a lot of sand on the road. If you are intent on travelling this route, try and do it in the other direction, as the paperwork is done much more easily in Siwa: see p.600 for a description of the oases along the way.

If you've had enough of the desert, four buses daily run to **Cairo** (5 hr; £E20): you can book seats on the 6.30am and 10am services departing from the ticket kiosk (9am–1pm & 7–11pm) near the post office, but not on the buses from Farafra and Dakhla, which collect passengers from Bawiti's *Hillal Coffeeshop* between 11.30am and noon, and midnight and 1am.

Tourists not returning to Cairo invariably carry on to **Farafra Oasis**, maybe stopping for a night in the **White Desert** en route. While most people visit

Desert safaris out of Bahariya

Bawiti is the main **departure point for safaris in the Western Desert**, ranging from forays into Farafra's White Desert to long-range expeditions to the remote Gilf Kebir and Jebel Uwaynat (p.573). While local outfits and freelancers vie for business, price shouldn't be the only consideration, for the farther you go into the desert the more vital their competence becomes. Anyone offering **4WD** trips should provide at least one jeep as logistical support for the car carrying tourists (trips are usually priced on the basis of four passengers; more than that requires another car). In the case of **camel treks**, the supply-car stays out of sight and only appears to set up camp when needed, as trekkers alternate between riding and walking. While even local boys can handle the White Desert by 4WD (so they boast), trips to Siwa or Dakhla – never mind the Gilf or Uwaynat – require guides that know the route and how to travel off-road by 4WD or camel. Although **GPS** (satellite navigation) is invaluable, really expert guides don't need it, having memorized tracks and landmarks from experience.

For **overnight** trips to the White Desert, most safaris leave Bahariya in the morning, to visit the Black Desert and Crystal Mountain before reaching the White Desert in time to set up camp by nightfall. Most trips are priced on the basis of four passengers, but some firms quote a group-rate while others charge per person, in Egyptian pounds, US dollars or euros – a calculator is useful to compare rates. Desert safaris can also be organized from Farafra (see p.545 for details), but tend to be pricier, as there is less competition.

Ahmed Abd el-Rahim ☎ & ⓕ 02/847-2090, mobile ☎ 012 4925563, ⓔ ahmed_safari @hotmail.com. *Ahmed Safari Camp* offers the White Desert (£E600 for four people) and long-range destinations (US$110 per car per day) including the Gilf (US$120 per car, plus the cost of meals), and camel trekking (£E200 per person per day; minimum five people).
Ayman Aiadei ☎ 02/847-2232. Freelancer

offering overnight excursions to the White Desert for £E150-250 per person.
Desert Ship Safari ☎ 02/849-6754, mobile 012 3216790, ⓦ www.desertshipsafari.com. A long-time freelancer, Yehiya Kandil offers trips to the White Desert (1 night £E200 group-rate; 2 nights £E300; 4 nights £E420), El-Qaf and the Gilf; plus camel trekking (£E50 per person per day, minimum four people).

the White Desert on safaris (see above), it is possible to get there by **bus**, using the service that leaves between noon and 1pm. For a group aiming to reach Farafra directly it may be worth hiring an eight-seater **service taxi** (£E200). **Hitching** from Bahariya to Farafra is possible, but make sure your lift is going all the way; quiz drivers at the military checkpoint. The 180-kilometre journey takes about three hours; **motorists** hoping to reach the White Desert before sunset should allow time to set up camp. Fill up on **fuel** in Bawiti as there are no pumps until Farafra: use the Misr petrol station in the backstreets behind the hospital, whose *benzin* is less likely to be adulterated than at other filling stations in Bawiti. The journey requires about a hundred litres of fuel, of which twenty litres are consumed by the off-road section between Crystal Mountain, Agabat and the White Desert.

Farafra Oasis

Historically, **Farafra Oasis** was the least populous, most isolated of the four oases. When camels were the only means of travel, the Farafonis had

Eden Garden Tours ☎02/847-3727, mobile ☎012 7311876, ⊛www.edengardentours .com. Talat Mulah at *Eden Garden Camp* does off-road tours (£E150–200 per day per person), camel treks and walking tours as far south as Dakhla Oasis. His well-trained crew ensures that the food and music rocks and the logistics run like clockwork.

Karim El-Abed ☎02/847-2232. A freelancer also known as "Chocolate" or the "Desert Lion" who runs overnight excursions to the White Desert for £E150–250 per person.

Khalifa Expeditions ☎02/847-3260, mobile ☎012 3215445, ⊛www.khalifaexp.com. With three decades of experience between them, Khaled and Rose-Maria Khalifa do safaris to the Gilf, the Great Sand Sea and El-Qaf, camel trekking in the White Desert and painting tours to Ain Umm Dabadib in Kharga Oasis.

Lotfi Abd el-Sayed ☎ & ⨍02/847-3500, ⊛www.beshmolodge.com. Based at *El-Beshmo Lodge*, Lotfi does the White Desert (£E650 group-rate), El-Qaf and Wadi Rayan, and can arrange a car to Siwa (£E1100).

Mohammed Abdel Latif ☎02/847-2636. A great driver and all-round entertainer known as "Bodadi", his trips are sure to be fun but maybe not the most organized or fit to venture far beyond the White Desert. He can also be contacted through Guus Kruis in Holland (©gkruis@omni-trade.nl).

Reda Abd el-Rasoul ☎ & ⨍02/847-2934, mobile ☎012 7176318, ©redadesertfox @hotmail.com. A local history teacher and writer dubbed the "Desert Fox", who has led safaris for over twenty years and is highly knowledgeable and a great storyteller (often found at the *Bedouin Village* in Agouz). Reda charges £E250 per person a day for all destinations except the Gilf Kebir (US$150 per day).

Salah Abdallah ☎ & ⨍02/847-3038, mobile ☎012 2324425. From the *Old Oases Hotel*, Salah does the White Desert (£E1000 group-rate), a four-day trip to Wadi Rayan (US$100 per day per person) and expeditions to the Gilf Kebir (US$170 per person per day).

Western Desert Safari ☎ & ⨍02/847-1600, mobile ☎012 4336015, ©safari @westerndeserthotel.com. Does the White Desert overnight (US$35 per person) plus longer safaris to Wadi Rayan, El-Qaf, and other destinations.

White Desert Tours ☎02/847-2322, ⨍847-3014, ⊛www.whitedeserttours.com. Peter Wirth guides self-drive and tailor-made safaris all over the Western Desert. He's certainly not the cheapest (ask for a quote), but took the GPS readings for Cassandra Vivian when she was updating her *Explorer's Handbook*. Peter speaks English and German, and his wife, Miharu, speaks Japanese.

less contact with Bahariya (a journey of four days) than with Dakhla, which was tenuously connected to the Forty Days Road. Fakhry relates how the villagers once lost track of time and could only ascertain the right day for Friday prayers by sending a rider to Dakhla. Before the paved road was built in 1978 it took 4WD and a winch truck a whole day to climb the Bahariya escarpment. Yet the oasis had dealings with the Nile Valley as early as the V Dynasty, when it was called *Ta-ihw*, the "Land of the Cow". Even today, Farafra's cows are of the same breed as those depicted in ancient tombs and temples (though no pharaonic monuments have been found in the oasis), and are so valued that they are smuggled to Bahariya, using trails that avoid police checkpoints.

Qasr al-Farafra was the only village in the oasis before the New Valley scheme seeded a dozen hamlets across the depression, now inhabited by 15,000 settlers from the Assyut region. Qasr has remained a tight-knit community of four extended families and is noted for its piety, apparent during Ramadan, when the mosque overflows with robed imams and sheikhs. Compared to Bahariya few people are involved in **tourism** so there's almost no hustling – but little to do at night either. Farafra is the sleepiest of all the oases and few tourists stay longer than a night in Qasr.

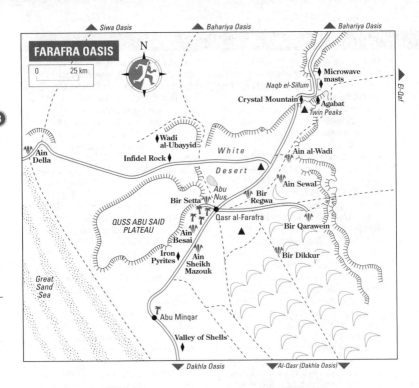

Crystal Mountain, Agabat and the White Desert

Coming from Bahariya, you'll enjoy a succession of fantastic views as you enter the Farafra depression. Many safaris stop at *Jebel al-Izaz* or the **Crystal Mountain**, sited beside the highway shortly before the Naqb es-Sillum starts its descent into the oasis. This ridge is entirely composed of quartz crystal and has a human-high natural arch through the middle, which is why locals call it *Hagar al-Makhrum*, the "Rock with a Hole". Small crystals lie all around, and there are lumps the size of footballs farther from the road. At this point, 4WDs may turn off onto tracks leading to Agabat, or continue along the highway, past the landmark **Twin Peaks** at the end of the range of hills on the left.

Agabat, "the Difficult" in Arabic, is the name given to scores of rock sugar-loaves surrounded by soft sand and powdered chalk. The sand can easily entrap vehicles that try to reach it from the direction of the highway, so it's easier to approach it off-road from the Crystal Mountain, whence a steep, dramatic descent into Agabat is possible.

This spectacularly rugged terrain merges into the famous **White Desert** (*Sahara el-Beida*) that stretches on either side of the highway. Here, the wind has eroded chalk monoliths into surreal forms resembling skulls, ostriches, hawks, camels, mushrooms and leopards, which loom above a dusty pan littered with shells, crystals and iron pyrites shaped like sea urchins or twigs. The chalk *yardangs* glint pale gold in the midday sun, turn violet and pink around sunset, and resemble icebergs or snowdrifts by moonlight – while **gazelles** may be glimpsed at daybreak as they forage for a few hours. Safari operators distinguish between the "Old" and "New" White Deserts to the east of the highway and the larger inselbergs near the western escarpment – but you're sure to be entranced whatever the locality. It can be hard to find a spot to camp out of sight of other groups at Christmas or Easter, when many people travel down from Cairo. Try to preserve this wonderful landscape by ensuring that no rubbish is left behind.

Although the White Desert is in Farafra Oasis, safari operators in Bahariya tend to offer the most competitive **excursions** (see pp.542–543 for details). However, if you want to take a trip from Farafra, the *El-Waha* and *Zwada* hotels charge £E150 per person for a trip ending in Bahariya; AquaSun Desert Safaris £E200 each, plus £E100 to continue on to Bahariya; while Badawiya Safari quotes US$55–60 per day to travel by jeep or **by camel**. If this is beyond your means, the alternative is to take a **bus** from Bahariya to Farafra (or vice versa) and ask to be dropped off in the White Desert, catching another bus out next day (bring plenty of water, a sleeping bag, food and firewood); or to hire a **taxi** or pick-up in Farafra to drive you there and back for £E80–100 (which only allows a brief look by day). It's worth noting that most of the White Desert is accessible by **2WD** vehicles, providing that the driver can distinguish between soft sand and firmer ground. **Mobile phones** only work within 25km of Qasr al-Farafra, unless you climb up on top of a *yardang* to get a stronger signal.

Qasr al-Farafra

As in Bawiti, the low ground in **QASR AL-FARAFRA** has been colonized by modern infrastructure, which obscures the view of the hilltop village, backing onto palm groves. Even there, development is apparent, with sewage mains being laid and old houses replaced by breeze-block homes with proper bathrooms. The traditional mud buildings have an austere beauty, their low windowless facades topped by flowing pediments or crenellations, but are disliked by locals for being dusty, shabby and old-fashioned.

Their new houses maintain the pattern of extended-family compounds but allow more privacy for newlyweds or grandparents – and dispense with the traditional *mastaba*, or street bench, for neighbours to gather. Yet everyone knows each other and their lineage: many of the villagers are of Libyan ancestry and bear the surname Senussi. The first census of the oasis in 1892 recorded only 542 inhabitants, and its population rose slowly while agriculture was limited to the nearby palm groves and a few outlying springs. Though Qasr's population has shot up to 5000 in the last twenty years due to better healthcare, its shops and market are still meagre and frugality is the order of the day, despite a few wealthy locals who've built villas on the edge of town.

Arrival, information and accommodation

While a triumphal arch welcomes traffic from Dakhla, buses from Bahariya pass the *Badawiya Hotel* on the outskirts before dropping passengers at the fuel station and shops down the road. On **arrival**, local police may enquire about your nationality, but shouldn't trouble you after that. The **post office** (daily 8.30am–2.30pm) and **telephone exchange** (24hr) are behind the Town Council. The **hospital**, on the main road to the *Badawiya* hotel (☎092/751-0047), is best saved for emergency use only. In the absence of a bank, you may be able to change small amounts of **cash** at the hotels.

As there isn't a tourist office, visitors rely on hotels and safari operators for **information**, with the Ali family being the main players: Farafra's Mayor Atif

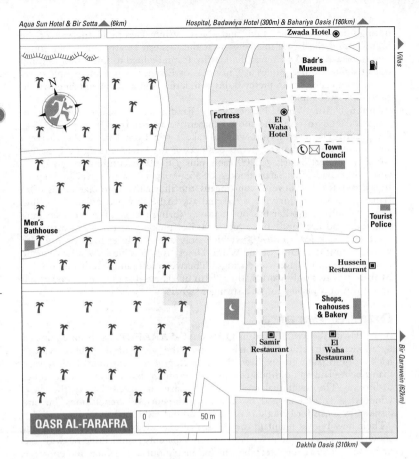

Aqua Sun Hotel & Bir Setta (6km) — Hospital, Badawiya Hotel (300m) & Bahariya Oasis (180km)

Zwada Hotel

Badr's Museum

Fortress

El Waha Hotel

Town Council

Men's Bathhouse

Tourist Police

Hussein Restaurant

Shops, Teahouses & Bakery

Samir Restaurant

El Waha Restaurant

Villas

Bir Qarawein (62km)

Dakhla Oasis (310km)

QASR AL-FARAFRA   0   50 m

Ali manages the *Badawiya* hotel; Sa'ad and Hamdy Ali run Badawiya Safari trips; while their artist brother Badr runs a local museum and gallery (see opposite). Your choice of **accommodation** may decide which safari operator you travel with (or vice versa), as the hotels expect their guests to sign up for safaris, and regard it as bad form for them to go elsewhere.

AquaSun Bir Setta, 6km from town ☎ & ℱ02/337-2898, mobile ☎ 012 2118632, ⒲www.eg-westerndesert.com. Accessible by taxi (£E7), this quiet hotel has a/c chalets with satellite TV and a warm pool, fed by a hot spring outside the grounds. The attached desert safari outfit is a respected firm from Sinai. Rates include half-board. ❺

Badawiya ☎092/751-0060, ℱ751-0400, ⒲www.badawiya.com. Located on the edge of town, this *qasr*-style complex has split-level rooms with raised beds and mosquito nets. Breakfast included; half-board optional. ❹

El-Waha ☎092/751-0040, mobile ☎012 7200387. A small hotel in Qasr, charging £E40 for single, double or triple occupancy of its basic rooms, with cleanish shared bathrooms. Women travellers have reported sexual harassment from the *El-Waha*'s safari crew. ❶

Zwada ☎092/751-0060. Larger, cleaner and friendlier than the *El-Waha*, with similar rates, though it closes when its staff are on safari in the White Desert – so phone ahead. ❶

The village

Behind the school you'll find **Badr's Museum**, the creation of a self-taught artist who has successfully exhibited in Germany, France and Britain. His museum resembles a *qasr*, with reliefs of camels and farmers decorating its walls, and an antique wooden lock on the door. Its dozen-odd rooms exhibit Badr's rustic sculptures and surreal paintings, stuffed wildlife, weird fossils and pyrites. The Farafonis find his desert garden incomprehensible, but relish his portraits of local people. The museum opens when Badr wishes; there's no admission charge, but donations are appreciated.

Previously, he painted *Hadj* **murals** of snarling lions and flying eagles on local houses. Sadly they have all vanished due to salt corrosion and only two more have been painted since – one for his brother Atif and one for their parents. Badr's "Fourth Dream" (as he puts it) is a studio-house embodying his ideas about architecture and creativity – if you're invited to visit, accept the offer. The brothers' **villas** are on the edge of the windblown desert, their high walls decorated with camels' heads and other symbols.

Otherwise, you can investigate the mud-brick **fortress** (*qasr*) that gives the village its name (though the full appellation is rarely used in everyday speech). Until early in the twentieth century, the Farafonis would retreat inside when invaders came; each family had a designated room, where, during normal times, provisions were stored and guarded by a watchman. Damaged by heavy rainfall, it began to crumble in the 1950s; the less damaged parts are now home to a few families, and blend into the surrounding houses.

You can also wander around the **palm groves** behind the village, which look especially lovely an hour before sunset. They are divided into walled gardens planted with olive and fruit trees as well as date palms (whose branches are used to fence the land). You can walk the paths freely, but shouldn't enter the gardens uninvited; for single women to do so is regarded as provocative. Likewise, avert your eyes from the **men's bathhouse** on the edge of the village, where youths splash around in a concrete tank fed by a pipe gushing warm water. Foreigners are expected to bathe at other springs.

Come nightfall, there's little to do but hang out in teahouses or maybe wallow in the hot spring at Bir Setta (see below), unless you happen to chance upon a *zikr* in somebody's home. **Zikrs** are a Sufi ritual where the participants seek to attain oneness with God by rhythmic swaying and chanting, which play an important role in the religious and social life of Farafra. The host throws his house open to male visitors; foreigners of both sexes are welcome, providing they respect that they are guests at a religious ritual, not spectators at a tourist attraction – which means modest dress and behaviour.

Local excursions

Besides the White Desert, there are many other beauty spots around Farafra, which are most easily seen on an organized trip: AquaSun Desert Safaris, based at the hotel of the same name (see above), charges £E250 (group rate) for three to fours hours exploring some of the sites. **Bir Setta** (Well Six) is a concrete tank of sulphurous hot water that's good for wallowing but stains clothes brown. Three kilometres away, the turquoise lake of **Abu Nus** is only recently formed, but draws all kinds of wildlife. Further afield are **Ain Besai**, a cold pool beside the rock tombs and chapels of a settlement abandoned in Christian times; the small, uninhabited oasis of **Ain el-Tanien**; and **Ain Sheikh Mazouk**, a hot sulphur spring feeding a tank where local men bathe. While Bir Setta is accessible by taxi from town, and Ain Sheikh Mazouk is close enough to the highway to be reached by bus, the others require private transport. This is also true of two sites of geological interest, namely an area of desert strewn with flower-shaped **iron pyrites**, and the **Valley of Shells** (*Wadi el-Khawaka*) out beyond Abu Minqar.

Eating and drinking

It doesn't take long to sample the culinary delights of Farafra. The *Badawiya* and *AquaSun* hotels serve decent spaghetti bolognese, *kofta*, kebab and salad, at higher prices than the humble **restaurants** in town which do omelettes, *fuul*, grilled chicken, salad, rice or soup, but sometimes run out of food by 7pm, and only sell soft drinks thereafter. The *Samir* and *El-Waha* (no connection with the hotel) are family-run, clean and friendly, while the *Hussein* is an outdoors, backpackers' favourite. For *sheeshas* and tea or Turkish coffee, there are a few teahouses (one of which doubles as a bus stop) among the shops on the main street, where you'll also find a **bakery**. Nowhere in Farafra sells **alcohol**, nor is *bango* to be found either.

Moving on from Farafra

If you're doing the circuit in reverse, **buses to Bahariya** (2–3hr; £E16) and **Cairo** (8–10hr; £E27) leave around 10am and 10pm daily, with an extra bus to Cairo on Monday, Wednesday and Friday at 9am. You buy tickets on board and there's usually no problem getting a seat, but be sure to arrive in good time, as the bus may leave before its scheduled departure time. Otherwise, there's a faint chance of **service taxis** to Bahariya, or lifts from cars that have just deposited tourists after a night in the White Desert. The going rate for a full taxiload is £E200.

 Buses to Dakhla Oasis (4hr; £E16) leave between 1pm and 2pm and 1am and 2am. Service taxis also cover the route, maybe once or twice a day. In a fully loaded vehicle passengers pay £E16 each; fewer individuals pay more. If you're planning to do this, spread the word so drivers know that you're interested. Buses both ways can be flagged down outside the *Badawiya Hotel* (the police there will do it for you) and also stop at the teahouse among the shops in town for a few minutes.

Between Agabat and Bir Regwa

There are endless ways of combining Agabat and the White Desert with springs and *wadis* to the east of the highway. One follows a track from Agabat to **Bir Regwa** (aka Bir al-Akhbar), a hot spring beside the highway, 33km from Qasr al-Farafra. Starting from Agabat, you pass through the desolate **Wadi Hinnis** (Valley of John) to enter a small depression called **Ain al-Wadi**, whose golden sand is dotted with shrubs and palms and has recently been used to grow watermelons. For geologists, the *wadi* is significant for containing the oldest exposed bedrock in the Farafra depression, dating from the Danian era. From there you travel to the ancient watering hole of **Ain Hadra**, recognizable by a single palm tree rising from a clump of fronds on a sandy hillock, surrounded by potsherds from Roman, Coptic and medieval times. Beware of camping here, as there are not only mosquitoes but **horned vipers**, which usually sleep in the winter but will wake up if disturbed. A short way beyond lies **Wadi Sunt**, otherwise known as "Acacia" after the venerable tree that shades the spot, whence the trail carries on past picturesque *yardangs* nicknamed the **Tents**, the **Ice Cream Cones** and the **Mushrooms**.

 Eden Garden Tours in Bahariya (see p.542) can organize three- to ten-day **walking** trips (£E175–200 per person a day) and up to fifteen days' **camel trekking** (£E200 per person a day) through this region.

El-Qaf (Gara)

Some safari operators in Farafra and Bahariya run trips to the remote **cave** called **El-Qaf** or **Gara**, 250km off-road from Farafra, shortly before the great sand barrier of the Ghard Abu Muharik that blocks any approach from the Nile Valley. Though doubtless known to Bedouin long before it was "discovered" by Rohlfs in 1873, its whereabouts were forgotten until it was rediscovered by Carlo Bergmann in 1991. Entered via a wide fissure in the ground that becomes a narrow corridor, the thirty-metre-deep cave has one large chamber and two small ones, full of white **stalactites**. Beware of the crack in the floor, harbouring snakes and scorpions. Although Rohlfs found El-Qaf while wandering off the caravan route to Assyut, it is nowadays reached by a track that leaves the highway near the southern microwave mast at Naqb es-Sillum. The cave can be reached in seven hours, but as the desert is flat and boring for most of the way, safaris include detours to Agabat or the White Desert that extend the excursion over two or three days.

Ain Della

Only 120km from Farafra by road, the humble **Ain Della** (Spring of the Shade) has played an epic part in the history of the Westen Desert as the last waterhole before the Great Sand Sea, used by raiders and smugglers since antiquity, motorized explorers in the 1920s and 1930s, and the Long Range Desert Group in World War II. It now has a small Egyptian army garrison that chases smugglers using 4WD instead of camels, as in the days of the Frontier Camel Corps, which once pursued a caravan of hashish all the way across the desert to Giza. Visiting Ain Della requires special **permission** from Cairo, which Badawiya Safari in Farafra can arrange with two weeks' notice. One of the routes through the Great Sand Sea runs via **Wadi al-Ubayyid**, where Italian archeologists are investigating a **prehistoric village** dubbed the "Hidden Valley" and a cave containing **rock art**. The road starts at a checkpoint in the White Desert, and has great rock formations for most of the way. At 53km into the journey to Ain Della, you'll pass the so-called **Infidel Rock** or "Church of the Spirits of the Lost Persian Army", an anthropomorphic rock formation on a hillock, that locals believe marks the last known location of the fabled Lost Army of Cambyses (see box overleaf).

The road to Dakhla

Relatively few vehicles follow the 310-kilometre road **between Farafra and Dakhla Oasis**. Once past Ain Sheikh Mazouk, the desert shifts from white stone to gravel and sand until you reach **Abu Minqar** (Father of the Beak). A green smudge in the wilderness, where wells have been sunk and houses built in an effort to attract settlers, it is the westernmost point on the Great Desert Circuit, and an obligatory tea-stop. Beyond lie more gravel pans, where golden orioles flit across the highway as it veers towards the escarpment that delineates Dakhla Oasis, where you'll pass through Al-Qasr and Mut Talatta before reaching Mut, Dakhla's main centre.

Off-road to Dakhla Oasis

Travelling off-road to Dakhla is an exciting journey. A paved road starting in Qasr al-Farafra runs out to **Bir Qarawein**, whose ancient well has now been supplemented by boreholes, allowing watermelons to be grown here (and *bango*, until the plantation was spotted by chance by an army helicopter). By

The Lost Army of Cambyses

One of the most famous tales in the *Histories* of Herodotus is of the Persian conqueror **Cambyses** (525–522 BC), son of Cyrus the Great, who sent an army across the desert to destroy the Siwan Oracle – which vanished in a sand storm. According to Herodotus, the 50,000-strong **army** marched from Thebes (Luxor) for seven days to an "oasis", and thence towards Siwa – which leaves room for doubt as to whether the oasis was Kharga or Farafra. Depending on which story you favour, their last watering hole was Ain Amur or Ain Della, beyond which the army ran out of water and perished in the Great Sand Sea after a sand storm blew up from the south, scattering and burying the weakened troops. Some ascribe this to the Persians' inability to calculate longitude, which led them to believe that Siwa was on a bearing of 289° from Kharga, instead of 310°; others to their ignorance of the environment. The mystery of where the army disappeared to tantalized explorers such as Almássy (see p.577), who claimed to have found the site but never disclosed its location.

In 2000 Dr Ali Barakat, a geologist from Helwan University, caused a sensation when he announced the **discovery** of bronze arrowheads and human skeletons north of Wadi al-Ubayyid. As later research by Tom Bown and Gaille McKinnon proved inconclusive, an SCA expedition foundered in the sands, and the results of forensic tests have yet to be published, all that can be theorized is that the army numbered far less than 50,000 (Persian sources routinely overestimated the size of armies, and Bown estimates that 50,000 troops would have needed 3000 tonnes of water and fodder), and may have been no larger than 5000 soldiers. Human bodies have been preserved by the desert for 5000 years, but no indubitably Persian corpse has been found yet – though Bown reckons that they exist in the lee of rock buttes, where the army might have camped or taken shelter.

Whatever the fate of his "Lost Army", Cambyses seems to have been a disastrously incompetent general, for while the Siwan expedition was marching towards its death, he was personally leading another army up the Nile to invade Ethiopia, which ran out of food in the Nubian Desert and had to resort to cannibalism to survive. News of these two disasters caused disaffected nobles in Persia to unite behind his son and stage a revolt, and it was en route to recover his throne that Cambyses accidentally stabbed himself in the thigh with his own dagger and died of gangrene in Syria. For an invader who had wantonly desecrated the Serapeum and sought to destroy the Oracle of Amun (said to control desert storms), these misfortunes must have seemed divine punishment for his arrogance.

turning off the road halfway to Qarawein, you can follow a track to the sweet-water spring of **Bir Dikkur**, marked by two palms and a camel's skeleton, and into the **dune lanes** that run parallel in a southeasterly direction. Some have trees protruding from their crests, where the dunes have buried whole palm groves on their relentless march towards Dakhla. Further on lie the **Black Valley**, whose floor is covered in iron pyrites, and the **Marble Labyrinth**, whose sharp stones are equally hard on tyres. Mobile phones don't work beyond Bir Dikkur, so a breakdown means serious trouble for cars travelling alone. The route ends with a steep **descent** from the plateau to Al-Qasr (see p.557) in Dakhla.

Eden Garden Tours in Bahariya combines this route with Agabat and the White Desert on a four-day jeep safari (£E175–200 per person per day), while Nasser in Dakhla (see opposite) can do it in reverse **by camel** in five to eight days.

Dakhla Oasis

Verdant cultivated areas and a great wall of rose-hued rock across the northern horizon make a feast for the eyes in **Dakhla Oasis**. Partitioned by dunes into more or less irrigated, fertile enclaves, the oasis supports 75,000 people living in fourteen settlements strung out along the Farafra and Kharga roads. Although it's the outlying sites that hold most attraction, the majority of travellers base themselves in or near **Mut**, Dakhla's "capital", which has better facilities. Mini-buses between Mut and the villages enable you to see how the Dakhlans have reclaimed land, planted new crops, and generally made the best of New Valley developments. Water is relatively abundant in the oasis, which has over 520 wells in its 410 square kilometres.

Most **villages** have spread down from their original hilltop maze of medieval houses and covered streets, into a roadside straggle of breeze-block houses, schools and other public buildings. Besides this exotic architecture, Dakhla has pharaonic, Roman and Coptic antiquities, dunes, palm groves and hot springs to explore. It was in this region that the *Breitling Orbiter 3*, the first balloon to circumnavigate the globe, touched down in 1999.

Mut

Dakhla's capital, **MUT** (pronounced "moot"), was branded a miserable-looking place by travellers early in the nineteenth century, but it has come on apace since the 1950s, as the Dakhlans have subverted or embraced planned modernity according to their needs and tastes. The architect of Mut's already crumbling low-rise flats is unlikely to have foreseen their balconies being converted into extra rooms or pigeon coops, and the four-lane Sharia al-Wadi that snakes through town rarely carries anything heavier than cyclists. Yet the locals welcome the hospital and schools and big capital investments such as the Fish Pond wastewater project.

Arrival and information

Arriving by bus you can get off at Midan Tahrir or Midan Gam'a, as buses run into the centre before winding up at the bus station near the hospital. Don't mistake Mut's conspicuous State Information Office on Midan Tahrir for the **tourist office** (daily 8am–2pm, and maybe 6–9pm; ☎092/782-1686), 250m west of Midan Tahrir, where energetic, conscientious Omar Ahmed is usually at his desk, and if not, can be contacted at home (☎092/782-0782). Well-informed and helpful, he is the best man to see about excursions. Besides Omar, **safari operators** include Nasser (who owns *Nasser's* camp in Sheikh Wali (see p.559) and whose brothers own the *Ahmed Hamdy*, *Hamdy* and *Abu Mohammed* restaurants; see p.554), the gofers at the *Anwar Hotel*, and Hagg Abd el-Hameed and Yosef Zeydan of the *Bedouin Camp* in El-Douhous. All of them are useful sources of information, as long as you bear in mind that they'll try to persuade you to sign up for an excursion (see p.554).

Mut's Banque Misr (daily except Fri 8am–2pm) can change **money** or travellers' cheques and give advances on Visa, and the tourist office also exchanges cash. Menatel card-phones all over town can be used for interna-tional calls if you can't be bothered to queue at the **telephone exchange** on Sharia es-Salam (24hr) or balk at paying premium rates at private exchanges or the *Mebarez Hotel*. There are **post offices** on Midan Gam'a and beside the telephone exchange (daily except Fri 8am–2pm), and **Internet** at the *Abu Mohammed* restaurant (£E15/hr) and *El-Forsan Hotel* (£E10/hr).

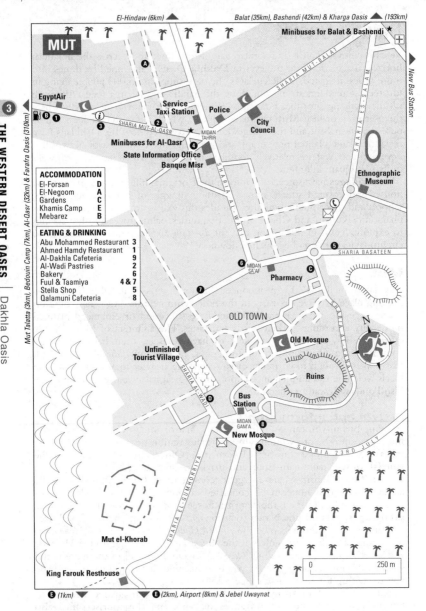

Mut's Central **hospital** (☎092/782-1555), 1.5km from Midan Tahrir along Sharia Mut-Balat, is well equipped by the standards of the Western Desert. You'll pass the **police station** (☎092/782-1500) en route to the hospital, and tyre-repair shops and a **fuel station** along the road to Mut Talatta. Anyone filling up for the Gilf Kebir should check the purity of their fuel before paying for it – adulteration has been reported.

Accommodation

As oases go, Dakhla offers a fair range of **accommodation** in Mut itself or at Mut Talatta springs (3km north). There's also decent accommodation further afield in the village of Sheikh Wali (5km; see p.559), in El-Douhous (7km; see p.556), Al-Qasr (32km; see p.557), and by the hot springs at Bir el-Gabel (37km). All except the last are fairly easily accessible by minibus.

Mut

El-Forsan Sharia al-Wadi ☎092/782-1343, ⓕ782-1347, ⓔelforsan1@yahoo.com. This central place has decent rooms with fans; en-suite costs £E20 more, and a/c another £E15. Internet (£E10 p/hr) and a hilltop garden with a playground and a coffee shop with a view. Breakfast not included. ❶

El-Negoom A few blocks behind the tourist office ☎092/782-0014, ⓕ782-3084. Perhaps the best choice in Mut: quiet, clean and welcoming, with a large garden and patio. Most rooms have a/c, phones and private baths, or share a bathroom and a TV lounge with two other rooms. ❷

Gardens Sharia Al-Ganain ☎092/782-1577, ⓔkhamis_camp@yahoo.com. This shabby, friendly hotel has mosquito-screened rooms with fans and lumpy beds (a double costs only £E16, or £E30 with a shower), and a dusty palm garden. ❶

Khamis Camp Off the airport road, 2km south of Mut, mobile ☎012 1078193, ⓔkhamis_camp @yahoo.com. Under the same management as the *Gardens*, this campground near a hot spring has mud huts (£E15 per person), or you can pitch a tent for £E5. The hot water is unreliable, meals are unlikely and you'll need a bike to get into town unless you take a short cut across the fields to King Farouk's Resthouse. ❶

Mebarez Sharia Mut-Al-Qasr ☎ & ⓕ092/782-1524. Clean a/c rooms with soft beds; a private bathroom costs £E20 extra. Its best feature is a tepid spring-fed pool at the back. Restaurant, international phone line, and satellite TV in the lobby. ❷

Mut Talatta

Sol y Mar Mut Inn In Mut Talatta, 3km from Mut ☎092/792-7982, ⓦwww.solymar-hotels.com. Small, clean en-suite chalets and rooms with shared facilities, around a large hot spring-fed pool; there's also a villa that can sleep thirty people (mostly used by tour groups) and a place to pitch tents. It's a nice place but rather overpriced. ❺

The town

With its low-rise blocks and whitewashed trees, the **New Town** presumably once looked good on a drawing board but has little appeal for visitors, and while locals are friendly, you can get tired of kids' incessant pleas for **pens**. Reputedly, this craze in Egypt originated in Mut back in the 1970s, when the first tourists to visit the oasis caused a sensation by not only wearing shorts, but handing out novelty "striptease" pens; tourists ever since have paid for their folly. It's also ironic that **Hassan Fathy**'s pioneering design for a **tourist village** in Mut remains unfinished, but later inspired similar complexes all over Egypt; whereas his social housing at Gurna and Baris Gedida proved a failure (see p.403 and p.571).

Behind the ridge where his buildings and the Islamic cemetery are located lies the **Old Town**, which is still inhabited by about 2000 people. Mut originated as a hilltop *qasr* or citadel of windowless facades and twisting passages, its interior divided into quarters separated by gates that were locked at night; and was still a fortified town when Harding-King saw it in 1909. Though the summit is in ruins, the lanes below are still bustling with life and fun to explore (though perhaps not for women on their own). You can enter from the north and exit on to Midan Gam'a (aka New Mosque Square), using the Old and New **mosques** as landmarks. **Midan Gam'a** used to be the hub of social life but is pretty sleepy nowadays, despite its role as a bus and service taxi terminus.

Off to the south you can glimpse the remains of **Mut el-Khorab** (Mut the Ruined), an ancient city dedicated to the Theban goddess Mut. Fennec foxes dwell in burrows in the sides of pits left by treasure-hunters, emerging to hunt at dusk, and can be seen on the way back from enjoying the sunset over the **dunes** that rise beyond the fields. This is the most accessible dune field in Dakhla, but not the finest. A bit further down the road to the airport is a modest colonial-style villa that was once **King Farouk's Resthouse**, which is now used to lodge visiting VIPs.

By arrangement with Omar at the tourist office, you can also visit Mut's **Ethnographic Museum** (£E3). Arranged like a family dwelling with household objects on the walls and a complex wooden lock on the palm-log door, its seven rooms contain clay figures posed in scenes from village life, by the Khargan artist Mabrouk. Notice the gazelle-hide receptacle for carrying fat on long camel journeys, and the spiked basket that Dakhlans hid beneath the sand to ensnare gazelles. Preparing the bride and celebrating the pilgrim's return from Mecca are two scenes that remain part of oasis life today.

Eating and drinking

Most **restaurants** in Mut offer similar menus of soup, pasta or rice, vegetable stew, chicken, *kofta* or kebab, for £E20–25 all in. Besides the *Gardens* or *Mebarez* hotels, you can eat in or outdoors at the *Abu Mohammed*, *Hamdy*, or, best of all, *Ahmed Hamdy*. The *Qalamuni Cafeteria* on Midan Gam'a does a few dishes, too, unlike the nearby *Al-Dakhla*, which just serves soft drinks. Otherwise, you can buy *fuul* and *taamiya* off Midan Tahrir and on Sharia al-Wadi; hot rolls from the **bakery** on Midan Sa'af; fruit at the **market** on Tahrir; or sticky desserts at *Al-Wadi Pastries* on Sharia Mut-Al-Qasr. Anyone buying supplies for an expedition should know that no meat is sold on Sundays. **Beer** is only available at the Stella shop on Sharia Basateen (open in the evening unless supplies have run out) and the *Abu Mohammed* restaurant (which charges £E20 a bottle) – though other hotels might order it in for tour groups staying there.

Transport within the oasis

Transport around Dakhla is hit and miss, depending on your destination. **Taxis** are the priciest option – bargain hard if you want the driver to wait at sites and then return to Mut, or try Omar at the tourist office, who can fix a taxi for a decent rate, with no hassle, or a **minibus** or **4WD**, with driver.

Public transport consists of green-and-white **minibuses**, running out towards both ends of the oasis. Minibuses to Al-Qasr (75pt) and other western villages pick up passengers near the corner of the Al-Qasr road and Midan Tahrir, while vehicles for Balat (£E1) leave from a depot near the bus station. Between 2 and 3pm, all the minibuses are full of schoolkids travelling home.

Local farmers get around in covered **pick-ups**, which usually charge minibus rates, though you may get a free lift or, conversely, be expected to pay "special" rates. Cycling is feasible in winter and **bikes** can be rented from the *Abu Mohammed Restaurant* or *Gardens Hotel* for £E15 a day. You need to be fit, though, since visiting outlying villages will involve a round trip of at least 60km.

Excursions and safaris

As some places are hard to reach, and it takes local knowledge of natural beauty spots to get the best from Dakhla, organized **excursions** can be a good idea. Omar at the tourist office can arrange half-day trips either to the east or the west (£E75 for the car) or a full day-trip to both (£E120–150), while other tours combine Al-Qasr and Muzawaka with the Magic Spring and some dunes: Nasser at Sheikh Wali's *Nasser Hotel and Camp* charges £E200/£E350 for a half-/full-day 4WD tour (group rate), or £E150 a day by camel (per person), while the *Anwar Hotel* and El-Douhous' *Bedouin Camp* (see p.556) both charge £E150 per person by jeep or camel for a full-day tour. All three also do **overnight** jeep excursions into the escarpment north of the oasis, or the dunes to the southwest: Nasser charges £E450 per night group rate (£E420 after five nights); the *Anwar* charges £E200 per person by jeep or £E250 by camel; and the *Bedouin Camp* offers camel treks and 4WD safaris for £E150 per person per night. Although the first two are fine for **Bir Dikkur** or the **White Desert**, the *Bedouin Camp* is the best bet for exploring the **Gilf Kebir**, though it's pricey – the ten- to twelve-day expedition costs £E2000 a day per jeep plus £E200 a day for the guide: it needs six weeks' notice to arrange the paperwork in Cairo.

Moving on from Mut

Upper Egypt **buses** leave Mut for **Kharga** (3hr; £E8) daily at 6am, 8.30am and 10pm, continuing on to **Assyut** (8hr; £E20–25). For **Farafra** (4hr; £E16), **Bahariya** (6hr; £E30) and **Cairo** (13hr; £E45) the bus departs at 6.30am and 6pm. There are also a/c Superjet buses to Cairo (13hr; £E45–55) at 7am and 8pm daily; both run via Kharga (3hr; £E8). Tickets to Cairo should be purchased the day before. All buses leave from Midan Gam'a, where tickets are sold; by buying them the day before you can board at Midan Tahrir or Al-Qasr if it's easier. **Minibuses and service taxis** also run from Midan Gam'a to the other New Valley oases and charge similar rates to the buses providing they are full. The tourist office or the *Anwar Hotel* can arrange a private minivan to **Luxor** (10hr) for £E400–500 (group rate). Before leaving Mut, **motorists** should fill up with fuel, as there's no more petrol until Kharga or Farafra. Though their local office has been closed since the weekly flight to Cairo was scrapped, bookings on **EgyptAir** flights from other airports can be confirmed through the tourist office.

North of Mut

Most visitors are initially drawn to the western part of the oasis by the village of **Al-Qasr**, which is deservedly renowned for its old town, an abandoned enclave of medieval mud-brick architecture, and easily reached by public transport. Should they ever reopen, the colourful **Muzawaka Tombs** are also within striking distance, as is the restored Roman temple of **Deir al-Hagar**, which lies further from the main road. To cover more ground than this requires days to spare or private transport. Shop around the various safari operators in Mut for trips to other villages, or **springs** and **dunes** you can reach by camel at sunset (staying overnight if desired) – then take the better deal.

The routes to Al Qasr

There are two **routes** to Al-Qasr via different villages, so, if you can, it's worth following one out and the other one back. Most traffic leaves Mut by the main road (and shorter route; 32km), with minibuses stopping at the villages of Rashda and Budkhulu; while along the secondary loop road (45km) they call at Qalamoun, Gedida and Mushiya. On the way you'll pass the **hot springs** and resort at **Mut Talatta** (3km; see p.553 for accommodation details) – which are open 24 hours, free of charge – and the drainage lake for irrigation water

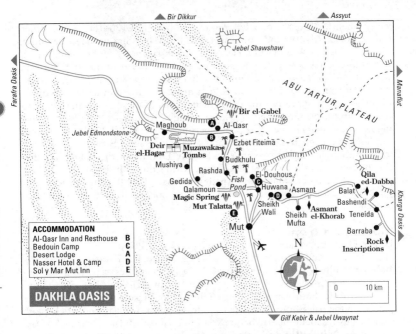

DAKHLA OASIS

ACCOMMODATION

Al-Qasr Inn and Resthouse	**B**
Bedouin Camp	**C**
Desert Lodge	**A**
Nasser Hotel & Camp	**D**
Sol y Mar Mut Inn	**E**

▼ *Gilf Kebir & Jebel Uwaynat*

known as the **Fish Pond** – a great spot for **bird-watching** (avocet, stilt and coot). With private transport, try a brief initial **detour** along the desert road via **Huwana**, to see the domed and coffin-shaped tombs of an **Islamic cemetery** between Huwana and the Bedouin village of **EL-DOUHOUS**, 1km from the junction where the desert road joins the highway and the loop road begins. El-Douhous is home to the *Bedouin Camp* (☎092/785-0480, mobile ☎010 6221359; ❶), a funky hillside retreat whose thatched huts have mattresses and mosquito nets (£E20 per person), while the spacious new "houses" have en-suite facilities: meals are served or you can bring your own food and cook.

The main road

Back on the main road beyond El-Douhous, olive groves and orchards presage the clifftop village of **Rashda**, set far back from the highway. The local custom that when he marries, a man must build a new house for his bride, accounts for Rashda's modern appearance. A nicer stopover is **BUDKHULU**, where new buildings flank an **old quarter** of covered streets and houses with carved lintels, surrounding a ruined **Ayyubid mosque** with a pepperpot minaret and a palm-frond pulpit. Visible on a hill as you approach the old quarter is a **Turkish cemetery** with scores of tombs shaped like bathtubs or grave markers in the form of ziggurats, plus a dozen *qubbas*: the freshly painted one belongs to a revered local sheikh, Tawfiq Abdel Aziz. During the Islamic era, Budkhulu was a customs post on the caravan routes between Kharga, Assyut and Farafra.

The loop road

Since the spring at Bir el-Gabel, near the escarpment, was trashed by thoughtless users, tourists have been taken to bathe at the so-called **Magic Spring**, a warm, deep pool in a pit fringed by palms, just off the **loop road** to Al-Qasr, which links three villages interspersed by stagnant pools and desert. **Qalamoun** dates back to pharaonic times, and many families are descended from Mamluke and Turkish officials once stationed here, whereas the next village is only 200 years old – hence its name, **GEDIDA** (New). Mut's tourist office can arrange a visit to the **mashrabiya factory**, a source of employment in a village whose men have traditionally worked in Cairo, taking it in turns to share the same job with a friend back home. Shortly before reaching **Mushiya**, the road passes **Bir Mushiya**, a keyhole-shaped tank fed by a tepid spring, where tourists are also taken to bathe.

The side road joins the highway between Al-Qasr and the turn-off for the Muzawaka Tombs, opposite a golden **dune field**. Originating as longitudinal dunes on the plateau above the escarpment, they cascade down the cliff to reform as crescent dunes below, and continue their way southwards. Tourists are brought here by jeep or camel to enjoy rolling down the dunes and to take in the view at sunset. The dunes have occasionally been heard to "sing" in a slow rhythm that locals have traditionally attributed to spirits, and scientists explain as the friction of one layer of sand slipping over another.

Al-Qasr

AL-QASR (or *'Asr*, as locals say) is a must – an amazing Islamic settlement built upon Roman foundations, that may be the longest continually inhabited site in the oasis and was indubitably Dakhla's medieval capital. Work on the site is being carried out by the SCA and the Dakhla Oasis Project – a multinational venture combining archeology and conservation that's been working in the oasis for 27 years: both bodies are taking pains to restore the town whilst maintaining its integrity. The old town crowns a ridge above palm groves and a salt lake, set back from sprawling New Qasr beside the highway. The "border" is marked by **handicrafts** sellers beside the New Mosque and a **tour centre** (daily 9am–5pm) where you can pick up a guide to lead you around and unlock certain houses. Pay him what you think is fair at the end – there's no set price.

Alternatively, for an agreeably spooky experience, you can go exploring alone, using the map overleaf. Beyond the twelfth-century **Nasr el-Din Mosque**, whose 21-metre-high **minaret** has a "pepperpot" finial typical of Ayyubid architecture, you enter a maze of high-walled alleyways and gloomy **covered passages**. Many of the houses here have acacia-wood **lintels** whose cursive or *kufic* inscriptions name the builders or occupants (the oldest dates from 1518): look out for the **doorway** featuring ornate carvings and brickwork, the **archway** with *ablaq* patterns, and the nearby **House of Abu Nafir** – built over a Ptolemaic temple – with hieroglyphics on its door jambs.

Another interesting feature is the rooftop *mala'af* or **air-scoop,** incorporated into an especially long T-shaped passage and designed to convey breezes into the labyrinth. Beyond here is a tenth-century **madrassa** (school and court), featuring painted *liwans*, niches for legal texts, cells for felons, and a beam above the door for whippings. The maze of alleyways also harbours a restored **blacksmith**'s forge, an antique **waterwheel** (*saqqiya*) and a donkey-powered **grain mill**. For more information on these and other facets of the old way of life, check out the **Ethnographic Museum**, (daily 10am–5pm; £E3) near the tour centre, founded by the anthropologist Aliya Hussein and containing artefacts and photos from all of the oases in the Western Desert.

If you fancy **staying**, the cheapest option is the fly-blown *Al-Qasr Resthouse* beside the main road (☎092/787-6013; ➊). Its few rooms have clean shared bathrooms and erratic water, or you can pay £E5 to sleep on the roof, where you'll get fantastic views of old Al-Qasr. On the opposite side of the road,

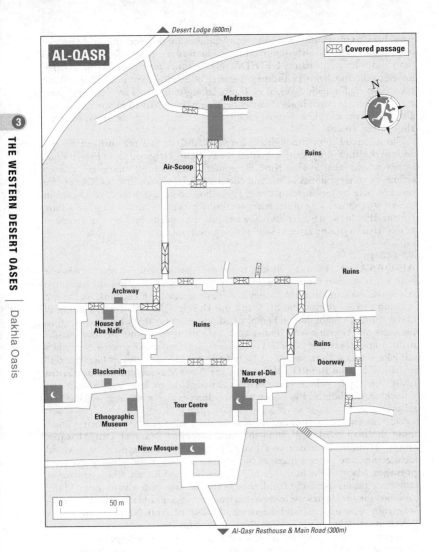

Desert Lodge (600m)

AL-QASR

▷◁ Covered passage

Madrassa

Ruins

Air-Scoop

Ruins

Archway

House of
Abu Nafir

Ruins

Ruins

Doorway

Blacksmith

Nasr el-Din
Mosque

Tour Centre

Ethnographic
Museum

New Mosque

0   50 m

Al-Qasr Resthouse & Main Road (300m)

200m beyond the old settlement, the *Al-Qasr Inn* (☎092/787-6802; ❹) is a fairly nondescript hotel with five rooms with baths, though it's often closed. The smartest choice is the classy *Desert Lodge* hotel (mobile ☎012 7345960, Ⓦwww.desertlodge.net; ❼) on a hilltop behind Al-Qasr, with superb views of the desert, a restaurant, Internet access, a library and outdoor chess. Rates include breakfast and dinner, but drinks are pricey and the staff could be more welcoming.

The Muzawaka Tombs

Five kilometres west along the highway from Al-Qasr, a signpost indicates the track to the **Muzawaka Tombs**, a twenty-minute walk or a slow drive through the silent desert, past rock buttes gouged with empty tombs. Of the three hundred or so recorded by Fakhry in 1972, two deserve his exclamation "Muza!" (Decorations), from which their name derives. Sadly, both have been **closed** for years as restoring them has proved far harder than anticipated due to their clay composition – but tour groups often come anyway to see the eerie-looking site, and the curator is ready to produce a pair of **mummies** from another tomb for a photo opportunity (*baksheesh* expected).

The **Tomb of Petosiris** is vividly painted with Roman-nosed blonds in pharaonic poses, curly-haired angels and a zodiac with a bearded Janus figure on the ceiling. In the back right-hand corner is a man standing on a turtle, holding a snake and fish aloft – a curious amalgam of Egyptian and Greco-Roman symbolism. Better-preserved, cruder murals in the **Tomb of Sadosiris** show Anubis (weighing the deceased's heart in one scene), Osiris judging on the rear wall, and another Janus – looking back on life and forward into the hereafter – just inside the entrance. Heading back, you can try hitching towards Al-Qasr, or cut across the desert towards the village. There's little risk of getting lost, since by climbing a table plateau you can always get oriented – and the views are splendid.

Deir al-Hagar

Unless you've rented a taxi, getting to **Deir al-Hagar** (daily 8am–5pm; £E20) demands commitment. The trail begins 2km further west along the highway, where an unmarked road runs south past some Roman ruins to a small, colourfully painted village (1km); beyond here a track crosses a ridge, whereupon the temple becomes visible on the right. Notwithstanding its Arabic name, "Stone Monastery", Deir al-Hagar is actually a Roman temple dedicated to the Theban Triad and the god of the oasis, Seth, and was originally called *Est Ah* ("Land of the Moon"). Its sandstone Hypostyle Hall, sanctuary and brick enclosure wall were built in the first century AD, under emperors Nero, Vespasian, Titus and Domitian (whose cartouches can be seen) and later served as a Coptic monastery (notice the mural of Christ, the lion and the lamb, in a niche to the left of the pylon), until a huge dune consumed it, collapsing the roof and leaving only the tops of the columns visible. One is inscribed with the names of almost every explorer who visited Dakhla in the nineteenth century, including Edmondstone, Drovetti, Cailliaud, and the entire Rohlfs expedition. It was they who named Dakhla's only mountain, **Jebel Edmondstone**, after the first European to reach the oasis since ancient times; Sir Archibald Edmondstone beat his French rival, Drovetti, by ten days, in February 1819, to "discover" it in the name of England. Such notions were incomprehensible to the oasis people, who attributed other motives to explorers; legend has it that Rohlfs sacrificed a servant to the spirits guarding the temple's treasury, in order to rob it. Trumpeting finches and other **birds** frequent the locality.

East of Mut

Villages on the east side of the oasis are more or less accessible from Mut by minibus; some halt at Balat or Bashendi, others go as far as Teneida. Unfortunately, most places of interest are some way off the main road, so to visit more than one or two you'll need your own transport, as well as food and water.

Heading out of town, you'll see where irrigation canals have enabled wheat, rice and peanuts to be grown on once barren land. **SHEIKH WALI** is on the verge of becoming a suburb of Mut, yet backs onto desert, with olive groves and goat-pens surrounding a Biblical **waterwheel**, while **dunes** swell in the distance. It is also home to the comfortable, ramshackle compound of the *Nasser Hotel & Camp* (☎092/782-2727, mobile ☎010 6826467; ❶), whose adobe

△ Madrassa, Al-Qasr

rooms, with fans and clean shared bathrooms, lie beneath a lukewarm rooftop pool fed by spring-water: solo travellers pay £E15 each, or £E10 to pitch a tent in the garden. **Asmant**, 6km on, has the usual sprawl of modern buildings by the roadside and a high-walled **old village** on the hill further back.

Asmant el-Khorab

Asmant lends its name to an ancient site 9km further east and 1km off the highway. **Asmant el-Khorab** ("Asmant the Ruined") is the local name for the **ruins of Kellis**, a Roman and Coptic town inhabited for seven centuries. Its two cult temples and three churches mark the shift from pagan Rome to Byzantine Christianity, with one of the **churches** dating back to the end of the first century AD. Kellis is one of several sites being studied by the Dakhla Oasis Project (see p.557). Besides temples and churches, they've unearthed the remains of aqueducts, farmhouses and tombs, including 34 mummies and wooden codices, casting light on religion and daily life in the third century AD. The site of Kellis is **off-limits** while excavations continue.

Balat and Qila ed-Dabba

After the swathe of desert beyond Asmant one welcomes the casuarina-tree-lined road through **BALAT**, whose teahouse is a *de facto* bus stop. Cross the road to explore the old village beyond the TV mast, with its 300-year-old **mosque** upheld by palm-trunks, and a maze of twisting **covered streets** that protect the villagers from sun and sandstorms and once prevented invaders from entering on horseback. Painted oxblood, salmon, terracotta or pale blue, with carved lintels and wooden peg-locks, its mud-brick **houses** are only slightly less impressive than the ones in Al-Qasr, with many still inhabited. Although the oldest dates from Mamluke times, Balat was a town and a governors' seat (its name means "Palace of the Lord") way back in the Old Kingdom, when it prospered through trade with Kush (ancient Nubia).

There's proof of this in Balat's ancient necropolis, known to the locals as **Qila ed-Dabba** (or "Ed-Dabba"), where five mud-brick *mastabas*, once clad in limestone but long ago reduced to lumps, mark the **tombs of VI Dynasty governors**. In 1977, French archeologists discovered an intact one from the reign of Pepi II (2292–2203 BC) by excavating a deep pit resembling an inverted step pyramid, to expose the burial chamber (daily 8am–5pm; £E20). Its painted reliefs are faint, but you can see the governor, Khentika, his wife and son; people ploughing, driving cattle and sailing boats; and Wadjet eyes. It took forty workers 763 days to construct the tomb. The ticket is also valid for the ruins at **Ain Asil** ("Spring of the Origin"), 1.5km east of the necropolis, where a fortress and farming community called "Our Root is Lasting in the Oasis" existed from the Old Kingdom until Ptolemaic times. Both sites are reached by a track 100m east of Balat's teahouse, and from Ain Asil a back road continues to Bashendi – about 5km in all.

Bashendi

Minibuses either terminate at or pass the turning for the village of **BASH-ENDI**, 2km off the main road. Its name derives from "Pasha Hindi", a medieval sheikh who is buried in the local cemetery, which dates back to Roman times. Tombs form the foundations of many of the houses, which are painted pale blue or buttercup yellow with floral friezes and *Hadj* scenes, merging into the ground in graceful curves.

The cemetery is at the back, where the desert begins. Some empty sarcophagi separate the domed tomb of Pasha Hindi (where locals pray for the recovery of lost items) from the square **Tomb of Kitnes**. While both structures are of Roman origin, the latter still retains its original funerary reliefs, depicting Kitnes meeting the desert-gods Min, Seth and Shu. Its key is held by a villager who can be fetched, but since admission costs £E16, you might settle for viewing its pharaonic lintels.

There is also a **carpet-weaving** factory, established with the help of Helwan University of Fine Arts, to train youths in making rugs and kelims: Mut's tourist office (see p.551) can arrange a visit (£E1.50 entrance fee).

Teneida and beyond

TENEIDA, on the eastern edge of the oasis, is a modern affair centred on a leafy square, whose only "sight" is a **cemetery** on the outskirts with weird tombstones resembling tiny houses. In desert lore, Teneida is known for the three Zwayah tribesmen who staggered out of the desert in 1931, alerting the authorities to a tragedy that was already weeks old. Bombed from their homes at Kufra Oasis in Libya by the Italians, five hundred Zwayah nomads had trekked 320km south over waterless desert to Jebel Uwaynat, where they found springs but no grazing. Faced with starvation, half the tribe struck out towards Dakhla without knowing the way, while the others remained to await their end. Thanks to the men's 21-day, 670km march (a feat of endurance with few parallels), search parties managed to rescue almost three hundred stragglers from the wilderness.

With a car you can press on to see some **rock inscriptions** off the highway 10km beyond Teneida. The carvings include an ostrich at the base of the sandstone outcrop beside the road, while beyond some fields another rock shaped like a seated camel is covered in prehistoric and Bedouin drawings of giraffes, camels and hunters, as well as the name of Jarvis (British governor of Dakhla and Kharga in the 1930s) and many other visitors. In olden times, this marked the intersection of two caravan routes, the *Darb al-Ghabari* ("Dust Road") between Dakhla and Kharga, and another track that linked Teneida to the Forty Days Road.

The road to Kharga

Beyond Teneida's last flourish of greenery, wind-sculpted rocks give way to dun table-tops and gravelly sand, persisting for most of the way from Dakhla to Kharga (193km). Following the ancient Darb el-Ghabari, the modern road skirts the phosphate-rich Abu Tartur Plateau that separates the two depressions. In the distance is a new township of 1500 flats, built by USAid, where almost nobody lives. The appearance of a phosphates factory and railroad 45km outside Kharga alerts you for a treat to follow. Golden **dunes** march across the depression, burying lines of telegraph poles and encroaching on the highway. Villagers faced with their advance have been known to add an extra storey to their house, live there while the dune consumes the ground floor, and move back downstairs once it has passed on. These dunes are outstretched fingers of the **Ghard Abu Muharik** ("Dune with an Engine") range, of the type known as "whalebacked". Folk wisdom asserts that the less common *barchan* or crescent-shaped dunes are always separate from whalebacks; you'll see a cluster of baby ones in the desert to the left, nearer town.

Kharga Oasis

Despite being the nearest of the oases to Luxor and the capital of the New Valley, **Kharga Oasis** gets far fewer tourists than the others. This may start to change now that tourists can use the direct road from Luxor – which takes only two hours as opposed to the day-long journey via Assyut – but other disincentives remain. **El-Kharga** is a 1970s' metropolis of 60,000 people with adequate facilities and a decent museum, but otherwise rather dull. While the oasis contains many ancient sites, most are only accessible by car, and the local **police** insist on accompanying tourists everywhere in town, even radioing

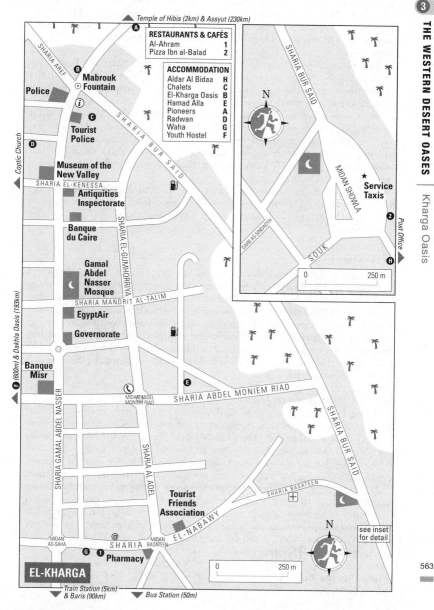

Temple of Hibis (2km) & Assyut (230km)

RESTAURANTS & CAFÉS
Al-Ahram   1
Pizza Ibn al-Balad   2

ACCOMMODATION
Aldar Al Bidaa   H
Chalets   C
El-Kharga Oasis   B
Hamad Alla   E
Pioneers   A
Radwan   D
Waha   G
Youth Hostel   F

SHARIA AREF

SHARIA BUR SAID

Police

Mabrouk Fountain

Tourist Police

Museum of the New Valley

SHARIA EL-KENESSA

Antiquities Inspectorate

Banque du Caire

Gamal Abdel Nasser Mosque

SHARIA MANDRIT AL-TALIM

EgyptAir

Governorate

SHARIA EL-GUMHORRIYA

Coptic Church

(600m) & Dakhla Oasis (193km)

Banque Misr

MIDAN ABDEL MONIEM RIAD

SHARIA ABDEL MONIEM RIAD

SHARIA GAMAL ABDEL NASSER

SHARIA AL-ADEL

Tourist Friends Association

EL-NABAWY

MIDAN AS-SAHA

MIDAN BASATEEN

SHARIA BASATEEN

@

SHARIA

Pharmacy

G 1

EL-KHARGA

0   250 m

Train Station (5km) & Baris (90km)   Bus Station (50m)

SHARIA BUR SAID

N

MIDAN SHOWLA

★ **Service Taxis**

DARB AS-SINDADYH

SOUK

Post Office

2

H

0   250 m

SHARIA BUR SAID

N

see inset for detail

HQ for permission before letting them step outside their hotel – which hardly makes for a comfortable atmosphere.

Submerged by the sea aeons ago, leaving fossils on the high plateau, the Kharga depression is hemmed in by great cliffs and broken up by massifs, with belts of dunes advancing across the oasis. It's thought that there were no dunes in Kharga during Roman times; myth has it that they erected a brass cow on the escarpment, which swallowed up the sand. Historically, Kharga's importance is due to the desert trade routes that converged on the oasis, notably the **Forty Days Road** (see p.572). Deserted Roman forts and entire villages that claim descent from Mamluke soldiers attest to centuries of firm control by Egypt's rulers, who have used Kharga as a place of exile since the fourth century. In modern times, the founder of the popular daily newspaper *Al-Akhbar* was banished here by Nasser, and since 1994, Islamists have been incarcerated in the maximum-security **Kharga Prison**, known as "The Scorpion" (visible from the highway as one enters the oasis from the north).

Kharga is also seen by some as a portent that the New Valley spells ruin for the oases. The influx of *fellaheen* from the Nile Valley has changed agricultural practices; **rice** cultivation has proved more water-intensive than expected, depleting aquifers and turning land saline. Social **life** has also changed; people stay indoors and watch TV more than socialize nowadays, and the once strong community spirit is disappearing.

It's indicative of the mixed antecedents of its citizens that the **name** Kharga may be pronounced "Harga" or "Harjah", depending on who's talking. Both the oasis and its capital are called Kharga; we've used the prefix "El-" to refer to the city.

El-Kharga

As the capital of the New Valley Governorate (comprising Kharga, Dakhla and Farafra oases), **EL-KHARGA** has grown into a sprawl of mid-rise buildings and highways, with the only reminder of its romantic oasis town origins being the souk. Banks and government buildings line the wide **Sharia Gamal Abdel Nasser**, which is too long and monotonous for pleasant walking, despite its ornamental obelisks, shrubs and green-and-white-striped kerbs. But **getting around** is easy, with similarly coloured minibuses shuttling along Sharia Gamal Abdel Nasser, between Midan Showla and the Mabrouk Fountain, at either end of town (25pt flat fare).

Arrival and information

Arriving by bus, it makes sense to decide on a hotel and get dropped off at the nearest point, rather than riding on to the bus station off Midan Basateen. Kharga's **tourist office,** on Sharia Gamal Abdel Nasser, by the Mabrouk fountain (Mon–Thurs & Sun 8.30am–2pm and maybe 7–10pm; ☏092/792-1206, ☏792-1205), has a boss who speaks little English, while his assistant Mohsen speaks far better English but is chiefly interested in promoting his own tours of the oasis (see p.567). For a free **guided tour** of the town, contact Adham Hassoun (mobile ☏010 1985569) at the Tourist Friends Association on Sharia el-Nabawy (daily 8am–2pm & 6–11pm). If you go with him, Kharga's police may agree to dispense with the otherwise obligatory police escort. The **tourist police** (☏092/792-1367; 24hr) are next door to the tourist office, with the regular **police** (☏122; 24hr) across the road.

You can change **money** and travellers' cheques at the Banque du Caire (which has the only **ATM** in the New Valley, taking Visa cards only) and

Banque Misr (both daily except Fri 8.30am–2pm & 5.30-8pm). For international calls, it's easier to use the Menatel card-phones on the streets than the 24-hour **telephone** exchange on Sharia el-Gumhorriya. The main **post office** (daily except Fri 8am–2.30pm) off Midan Showla has EMS post. **Internet** access is free at the Information Support Centre in the Governorate (daily except Fri 8am–3pm & 6pm–midnight), and costs £E5 an hour at the 24-hour cybercafé on Sharia el-Nabawy. The **hospital** (☎092/792-0777) and several **pharmacies** are also on this street.

There are **petrol** stations on Sharia Bur Said and off Sharia Abdel Moniem Riad, and a tyre-repair place off Sharia el-Nabawy.

Accommodation

There's no problem with finding **accommodation** in El-Kharga, though it's not always great value. Staying **outside town** is feasible with a car, and will be necessary if you're relying on local transport to visit far-flung sites. All the places listed here are in El-Kharga.

Aldar Al Bidaa Off Midan Showla ☎092/792-1717. Handy for the service taxi station but noisy, this hotel has shabby rooms, some with fans and baths – the *Waha* (see below) is similar, but half the price. ❶

Chalets (or *Villa*). A government resthouse behind the tourist office (which handles reservations), it has four carpeted chalets sleeping up to nine people with TV, bath, phone, fan or a/c. ❷

El-Kharga Oasis Sharia Aref ☎092/792-1500. Large a/c rooms with soft beds, bathrooms, and balconies overlooking a huge palm garden – it sounds great, but the hotel is always empty and the garden rife with mosquitoes. Breakfast included. ❷

Hamad Alla Off Sharia Abdel Moniem Riad ☎092/792-0638, ⓕ792-5017. Sited on a quiet backstreet, this small, dark hotel has clean a/c rooms with soft beds; some have bathrooms, fridges, TV, heaters and balconies. There's also a restaurant that sells beer. ❷

Pioneers ☎092/792-9751, ⓕ792-7983, ⓦwww.solymar-hotels.com. Out towards the

Temple of Hibis, Kharga's fanciest hotel has a/c rooms with satellite TV, around a pool, a garden with a *qasr*-style coffee shop, a restaurant and bar. Rates 30 percent lower over summer. Buffet breakfast and dinner included. ❽

Radwan Off Sharia Gamal Abdel Nasser mobile ☎010 3457230. By far the best choice in this price range, it has a/c en-suite rooms, Arabesque arches and a stuffed gazelle in the lobby. The rooftop has a great view of the mountains, with a pool table promised. ❷

Waha Off Midan as-Saha ☎092/792-0393. Within walking distance of the bus station, the *Waha* has basic rooms with grungy shared bathrooms; it's worth paying £E6 more for one with private facilities. ❶

Youth Hostel 600m west of Sharia Gamal Abdel Nasser ☎092/922-640. The *Beit es-Shebab* has beds (£E10) in clean dorms, each with their own bathroom, but is awkwardly located on the edge of town, and the police may object to foreigners staying there. ❶

The town

Prominently located on Sharia Gamal Abdel Nasser, the **Museum of the New Valley** (daily: winter 8am–5pm, summer 8am-6pm; £E20) is housed in a modern building modelled on the tombs at Bagawat, and contains artefacts from sites scattered across three oases. Of the exhibits on the ground floor (labelled in English), the most impressive are Greco-Roman: painted sarcophagi from Maks al-Qibli and Dakhla; death masks from Qasr el-Labeka; and mummified rams, eagles and ibises from the Muzawaka Tombs. The Old Kingdom is represented by an offerings tablet, scarabs and headrests from the tombs of the VI Dynasty governors in Balat. Look out for the *ba* birds, representing the soul of the deceased, unearthed by the French Mission at Dush. Upstairs you'll find Coptic textiles and pottery, and floral friezes from the Fatimid and Ottoman eras, mostly unlabelled.

While in the vicinity, check out the (dry) **Mabrouk Fountain**, just up the road at the main junction, created by a local artist in three days. Its lusty figures symbolize Mother Egypt dragging her unwilling child (the oases) towards its destiny. Aside from the **Gamal Abdel Nasser Mosque** (one of dozens that Nasser built in provincial towns in the 1960s), and a **Coptic Church** discreetly located off the high road, there's nothing else to see until you reach the lower part of town (it's best to take a minibus, rather than walk the 2–3km).

Here, dusty **Midan Showla** is abuzz with people and traffic, a lively **souk** running off into an old quarter of mud houses painted apricot or azure and daubed with the Hand of Fatima. Turn right at the crossroads and then left to find the **Darb as-Sindadyh**, a dark, twisting street roofed with palm trunks, which once extended over 4km; its oldest part dates from the tenth century. Only the initial renovated stretch remains nowadays.

The tourist office can arrange visits to El-Kharga's **pottery and carpet factory** and the **date factory** (both daily except Fri 8am–2pm; free) 50–100m south of Midan as-Saha. Dates play an important part in the city's calendar, and El-Kharga's **City Day** (October 3) celebrates the beginning of the date harvest with a parade of floats along Sharia Gamal Abdel Nasser. The marriage season is also timed to coincide with the flowering of the date crop (from July until harvest time). A more relaxing tourist activity is to chill out by the big swimming **pool** at the *Pioneers Hotel* (US$10 per person for non-residents).

Eating and drinking

The *Pioneers Hotel* **restaurant** features a lavish buffet supper when tour groups are staying, and otherwise offers an à la carte menu of continental and Egyptian dishes, a well-stocked bar, and a terrace overlooking the pool. You can eat well for about £E50 (excluding drinks). Other hotels offer variations on a set three-course meal (£E20–50) of soup, chicken or kebab, rice and salad, as do several of the cheap eateries on Sharia Basateen. The *Al-Ahram* café on Sharia el-Nabawy serves the usual set meals as well as *firik*, roasted green wheat served like rice or used as stuffing for chicken. Alternatively, you can scoff thin-crust pizza or sweet *fatir* at *Pizza Ibn al-Balad* on Midan Showla (open daily 7–11pm). The only places selling **alcohol** are the bar at the *Pioneers* (with beer, wine, spirits and cocktails) and the *Hamad Alla Hotel* (which just has Stella).

Moving on from El-Kharga

Overnight **buses** to Cairo (7–8 hr; £E40) leave the new bus station off Midan Basateen at 10pm and 11pm and take the Desert Road that bypasses the Nile Valley. On moonlit nights, try to get a seat on the left of the bus to see the magnificent escarpment en route to Assyut, one of the most dramatic vistas Egypt has to offer. It's almost worth travelling to Assyut (4–5 hr; £E8) by day just for the view; five buses depart between 6am and noon. Through-buses to Dakhla (£E8–9) leave Kharga at 2pm, 11pm and 1am. As a fallback, there are **service taxis** from Midan Showla to Assyut or Dakhla, though departures are irregular, and fares depend on how full the vehicle is when it finally leaves: you can wait for ages sometimes.

As yet there are no buses or service taxis along the **direct road to Luxor** (275km), which leaves the oasis at Baghdad (see p.571). However, Mohsen at the tourist office (see p.564) will take up to three people in his car for £E350, and taxi drivers on Midan Showla may agree to do the trip for £E350–400. The road is excellent and the journey takes only two hours. There are two first aid stations with water, but no fuel, en route. The road meets the Nile Valley at Riziq, 15km south of Luxor.

Excursions around the oasis

The size of the oasis, its minimal public transport and the sheer remoteness of many sites means that you really **need a car** to appreciate what Kharga has to offer. This can be arranged locally by a trio of moonlighting state employees – Mohsen at the tourist office (☏092/792-1026, mobile ☏0101 806127, ✉mohsen_di@yahoo.com); Mahmoud Youssef, director of the New Valley Museum (work ☏092/792-0084; home ☏092/793-4716); and Mansour Osman, the Inspector of Antiquities (mobile ☏012 3745279). Both Mansour and Mahmoud have access to the few 4WD cars in the oasis, and Mansour also owns a dirt-bike. Each can only take three passengers; the costs given below are the group rate.

Mahmoud charges US$200 for a twelve-hour 300km tour of all the sites accessible **by road**, from Deir el-Kashef in the north down to Dush in the far south. Mohsen quotes only US$30 but doesn't go beyond Qasr el-Zayan, and often fails to deliver all that's been agreed – so you'll do better paying more for the services of Mahmoud or Mansour (whose rates are similar), both of whom have expert knowledge of local archeology. All the tours end with a soak in a hot spring at sunset.

Excursions **off-road** to the remote northern sites of Qasr el-Labeka and Ain Umm Dabadib are only feasible in the winter, when snakes and scorpions go into hibernation. Mahmoud will drive you to both in a day for US$300 (or guide those with their own 4WD for US$200), while Mohsen offers separate half-day trips to Qasr el-Labeka (US$60) and Ain Umm Dabadib (US$150).

Otherwise there's a **train** that supposedly leaves for Luxor every Friday at 7am, from the train station 5km out along the road to Baris (see p.571). In reality, it may not operate for weeks, and when it does, the journey often takes far longer than the seven hours advertised.

North of El-Kharga

Two of the oasis' most evocative monuments lie just a few miles north of El-Kharga. Whilst the **Temple of Hibis** has suffered from poor restoration work in recent years, the nearby **Bagawat Necropolis** is more impressive – one of the oldest Christian cemeteries in Egypt, it's backed by an imposing ruined monastery, **Deir el-Kashef**. Further north, the depression is pockmarked with ruins of ancient towns and forts, with tunnels and other feats of Roman engineering waiting to be explored – these sites, however, such as **Ed-Deir**, **Qasr el-Labeka** and **Ain Umm Dabadib**, are difficult to reach and only really accessible by 4WD with a guide who knows the way (see above).

The Temple of Hibis

Although you can get there by catching a minibus from Midan Showla bound for El-Munira and asking to be dropped at *el-ma'abad* (the temple), it's more fun to walk from the Mabrouk Fountain (2km). En route, you'll catch sight of the ruined Ptolemaic **Temple of Nadura** atop a low hill in the desert to your right: its eroded sandstone wall and pronaos aren't worth the trek up to the top, though the view is.

Further on, billboards obscure the view of what remains of the **Temple of Hibis** after a US$20 million conservation fiasco. More accustomed to building bridges and factories, the contractors carrying out the restoration work damaged eighty percent of the stone blocks when dismantling the temple to move it to higher ground due to rising groundwater, and then

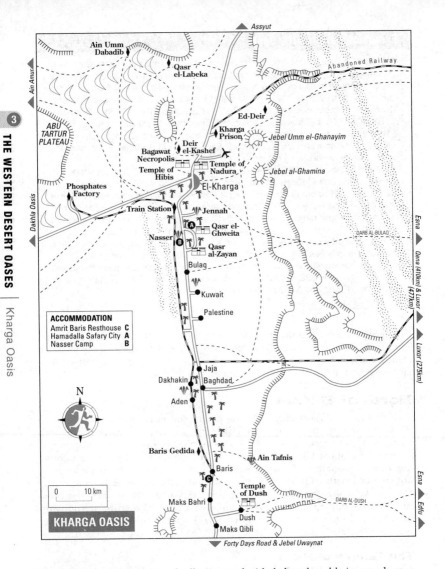

KHARGA OASIS

ACCOMMODATION
Amrit Baris Resthouse **C**
Hamadalla Safary City **A**
Nasser Camp **B**

botched reassembling it so badly it was decided that the old site was better after all.

The lush vegetation surrounding the remains of the temple covers the site of ancient Hibis, an XVIII Dynasty settlement that prospered under the Saïtes, Persians and Ptolemies. One of the few Persian monuments left in Egypt, the temple was raised in the sixth-century BC and dedicated to Amun-Re, though now you can barely see the carvings that once covered its walls. You don't need a ticket to see the temple itself, but the **kiosk** here is where you buy tickets for Bagawat and Deir el-Kashef (daily: summer 8am–6pm; winter 8am–5pm; £E20 for both sites).

The Bagawat Necropolis

Blocks from the temple are stacked beside the path that leads to the **Bagawat Necropolis**. The 263 mud-brick chapels were used for Christian burials between the third and seventh centuries, and display diverse forms of mud-brick vaulting or Roman-influenced portals, but are best known for their Coptic murals. A guard will unlock the **Chapel of Peace**, whose dome is decorated with images of Adam and Eve, the Ark, Abraham and Isaac, sadly defaced by Greek inscriptions. Flowery motifs and doves of peace can be seen inside **Tomb #25**, one of three adjacent family vaults on the ridge, where the guard usually asks *Shouf bebe?* If you reply affirmatively he'll produce a hideous mummified child, expecting male tourists to react with sang-froid and women tourists with dismay, not to mention *baksheesh* worthy of his efforts. Give him his due, but not until you've seen the frescoes in the **Chapel of the Exodus**. Crudely executed yet vivid, they depict Roman-looking pharaonic troops pursuing the Jews, led by Moses, out of Egypt, and other Biblical scenes.

Deir el-Kashef

From the ticket kiosk at the Temple of Hibis, a track curves around behind the hill on which the necropolis is built, past the ugly resthouse of the archeologist Fakhry and a series of rock-cut tombs, to reach the dramatic ruins of **Deir el-Kashef**, the Monastery of the Tax Collector. Named after a Mamluke governor, Mustafa, the five-storey monastery once housed hermits and travellers in its vaulted cells, nowadays choked by sand, and still commands a view of the point where the *Darb al-Ghabari* from Dakhla crossed the Forty Days Road. In the valley below you can see the ruins of a small **church** or hermitage, with Greek texts on the walls of the nave and the tiny cells where the monks slept. Beyond, four mighty crescent **dunes** to the north have spawned two infants downwind, either side of the Assyut road, near a crowd of whalebacks. Though disproving the notion that *barchan* and *seif* dunes don't mix, its physical causes are still explicable in terms of formulae devised by the explorer Bagnold, whose classic book *The Physics of Blown Sand and Desert Dunes* (1939) later helped NASA to interpret data from its Martian space probes. The book was written after five years' experimentation with a home-made wind tunnel and builder's sand; after his desert journeys of the 1920s, Bagnold felt "it was really just exploring in another form".

Other sights

For those with a **4WD car** (or dirt-bikes) and a local guide, there are many other sites to explore. The most rewarding area lies west of the Assyut road, where a track from Bagawat skirts the foothills of the bat- and snake-infested **Jebel el-Teir** (Bird Mountain), whose *wadis* contain prehistoric, ancient and Coptic **inscriptions**. It then diverges into two trails leading to the finest **Roman fortresses** in the oasis. Invariably built near springs, such structures once guarded, taxed and sheltered caravans on the road to Assyut. As a single caravan contained thousands of people and animals, they probably settled for the night in several forts; the bustle is unimaginable in the desolate ruins today.

Qasr el-Labeka is secluded in a *wadi* at the base of the northern escarpment, its twelve-metre walls enclosing sand-filled chambers. On an outcrop further north stands a ruined mud-brick temple, where one of the lintels still bears a painted vulture; another temple was dedicated to Hercules. Between the two buildings lies the spring that sustained the fort – a subterranean aqueduct (now silted up) of the kind found on a grander scale at **Ain Umm Dabadib**. Though it's only 18km from Labeka, the way is often blocked by dunes, and cars may have to backtrack as far as El-Kharga to find a corridor through the dune fields. The site covers 60,000 acres, including a ruined fortress, churches and tombs, plus a remarkable **underground aqueduct** that worked by liberating ground water, like the *qanats* of ancient Persia (Fakhry suggests that the system originated under Persian rule). Known as *manafis* in the oasis, this one runs for 15km with access holes every few metres, and part has recently been cleared by a local farmer and used to irrigate a patch of land to the southeast of the temple.

Further west of Ain Umm Dabadib, out beyond the limits of the Kharga depression, lies the totally isolated, windblown spring of **Ain Amur** ("The Lovely One"), situated 200m up the northwestern cliffs of the Abu Tartur Plateau. At 525m above sea level, this is the highest **spring** in the Western Desert and, like Ain Tafnis (see opposite), is fed by surface water trapped in the escarpment rather than water below the floor of the depression. Near the spring are the **ruins** of a Roman fortress with Coptic graffiti, one of which relates how an early Christian traveller was "faint from thirst" when the spring saved him. Some believe that Ain Amur was the last watering hole of the legendary Lost Army of Cambyses (see box on p.550). Travel to Ain Amur requires **permission** and a recognized guide (see p.567).

Far across the oasis near the eastern scarp wall, **Ed-Deir** once guarded the shortest camel route to the Nile, which climbs out of the depression at the Abu Sighawal ("Father of Underwear") Pass. The fort lies 1km beyond the end of a track starting near Munira (the checkpoint on the road as you enter Kharga Oasis from the north), which later turns into decrepit asphalt, so you could risk it in a regular car, walking over the dunes at the end. Its twelve rounded towers are connected by a gallery, surrounding a well, and the surviving rooms covered in **graffiti** drawn by generations of soldiers: Turks in fezzes, tanks, airplanes, and obscenities. The **abandoned railway** in the distance was built by the British in 1906–08 and once carried special carriages with double roofs and wide eaves to protect passengers from the heat. Trips to Ed-Deir do not require permission.

South towards Baris

Exploring the **southern spur of the oasis** means flitting between sites off a highway, which isn't a prospect to relish if you're reliant on buses. On the positive side, access roads have been improved to the point that the temples can be reached by 2WD car, so it's possible to negotiate with pick-up or **taxi** drivers on Midan Showla, who may agree to take you to the temples of Qasr el-Ghweita, Qasr al-Zayan and Dush for £E200–300. **Buses** bound for Baris (90km; 2hr; £E3) leave El-Kharga at 9am and 2pm; the morning bus begins the return journey at noon, while the later one leaves Baris at 6am next day.

Five kilometres south of town you'll pass Kharga's **train station**, an Islamic-style edifice whose marble interior aspires to a grander role than the terminus of a train from Luxor which seldom runs even once a week. Since a "tourist train" made its inaugural journey from Port Safaga in 1998, with celebrities like Michael Palin aboard, the reality has been a third-class train that hardly anybody uses, whose 477km journey can take up to twelve hours, especially if passengers have to clear sand-drifts from the tracks. It was moving sand dunes that scuppered the British-built railway from the Nile Valley (see above), and as the Ghard Abu Muharrik forges southwards, the new line is also in jeopardy.

Beyond the station, the palm groves east of the highway are irrigated by the **Jennah hot springs** (up to 45 °C), where tourists are taken to bathe at sunset. You can **stay** here at *Hamadalla Safary City* (☎092/798-2240; ❷), a complex of domed rooms with en-suite facilities and a/c, on the spur road to Qasr el-Ghweita, 17km from El-Kharga. It's is a far better bet than the nearby "villas" at *Nasser Camp* (℗092/792-7982; ❷), a dirty, arid bungalow site on the outskirts of **Nasser** village.

Qasr el-Ghweita and Qasr al-Zayan

Both these sites are reached by a signposted loop road to the east of the highway, which runs past *Hamadalla Safary City*. Named the "Palace of the Beautiful One" in Arabic, **Qasr el-Ghweita** (daily: summer 8am–6pm; winter 8am–5pm; £E20) is a fortified **hilltop temple** from the Late Period, with a commanding view of the area, which was intensively farmed in ancient times (its vineyards being mentioned in inscriptions in the Theban Necropolis). Ten-metre-high walls enclose a sandstone temple dedicated to the Theban Triad, built by Darius I on the site of an older shrine, and modified by the Ptolemies. Its Hypostyle Hall contains scenes of Hapy the Nile-god holding symbols of the nomes of Upper and Lower Egypt. Nearby you can see the adobe remnants of a Ptolemaic settlement.

The road continues 5km south to **Qasr al-Zayan** (daily: summer 8am–6pm; winter 8am–5pm; £E20), a Ptolemaic-Roman temple that lends its name to a village built over the ancient town of *Tkhonemyris*. This proximity to daily life helps you imagine it as a bustling settlement in antiquity. As at Qasr el-Ghweita, the temple is enclosed within a mud-brick fortress, together with living quarters for the garrison, a cistern and a bakery. Its portal bears the cartouches of Antonius Pius, who restored the temple in 138 AD. The plain hereabouts is 18m below sea level, the lowest point in Kharga Oasis.

As you return to the highway, the first large settlement, **Bulaq** ("to watch"), is divided into a picturesque old village to the west and a larger modern one to the east. Its **hot springs** are visible immediately before you enter town, on the right. Leaving Bulaq, you pass the whitewashed tomb of Sheikh Khalid shortly before the microwave tower that presages a string of New Valley settlements founded in the 1980s, named Kuwait, Palestine, Baghdad and Aden in a gesture of Arab solidarity. There's a checkpoint at the start of the **road to Luxor** (275km), near Baghdad.

Baris and beyond

Seventy kilometres south of El-Kharga, the township of **BARIS** (pronounced "Bar-ees") is named after the French capital, though its foraging goats and unpaved streets make a mockery of a billboard welcoming visitors to "Paris". Two kilometres before town, you'll pass the abandoned village of **Baris Gedida** (New Baris), begun in the early 1960s by architect Hassan Fathy and based on the principles of traditional oasis architecture, including wind shafts to cool the marketplace. Alas, work was halted by the Six Day War of 1967 and never resumed, so the initial settlers soon drifted away. Today, old Baris is set to develop further once the **Sheikh Zayed Canal** – drawing water from Lake Nasser (see p.498) – reaches Kharga, entering the depression at Baris.

Decent **accommodation** and simple **meals** are available at the laidback *Amrit Baris Resthouse* (℗092/796-3015, mobile ℗012 3766837; ❷), where staff can recommend a local **pick-up** driver to take you to the Temple of Dush, 23km away; expect to pay £E30 upwards for the return journey, including waiting time. Visitors with their own **4WD** can make a scenic detour via a track that leaves the highway to the east of Baris Gedida, leading to **Ain Tafnis** (14km). Tafnis is one of two springs in the oasis that's nearly 200m above the floor of the depression, located on the slope of a mountain protruding from

The Forty Days Road

Of all the trade routes between North Africa and the tropical south, the **Forty Days Road** (*Darb al-Arba'in*) was the one most involved in **slavery** – the only business profitable enough to justify the risks and rigours of the thousand-mile journey. The slaves, purchased at the Dongola slave market or kidnapped by the fierce desert tribes, were assembled at **Kobbé**, a town (no longer existing) 60km northwest of El-Fasher, the capital of Sudan's Darfur Province, once an independent kingdom.

After a few days' march from Kobbé, the slaves were unchained from their yokes, for there was no way to escape. With no permanent water source until Bir Natrun, 530km away, they could only survive on the ox skins of water that burdened the camels. From **Bir Natrun**, caravans trekked 260km northeast across waterless, open sands, vulnerable to attack by bandits from the Arab Kababish and Bedayatt tribes, or the black Gor'an from Nukheila Oasis. The next stop, **Laqiya al-Arba'in**, had water but scant grazing for camels, and with their reserves of fodder exhausted they could easily weaken and stumble along the rocky 280-kilometre journey to **Selima Oasis**. While human losses were erased by the sands, the road gained definition from its Bactrian casualties; a 1946 survey of northwestern Sudan noted "a track about one mile wide marked with white camel bones".

W.G. Browne, the first European to complete the route, estimated the slave caravan's value at £115,000 sterling – a huge sum for the time (1762). Egyptian customs posts taxed caravans arriving in **Kharga Oasis**, the last stage before their ultimate destination, Assyut. As the caravans approached, small boys were hidden in empty water skins to evade tax, but officials would beat them to thwart this ploy. The most valuable slaves were young Nubian women – prized as concubines because their skin remained cool whatever the heat. Having sold their chattels at **Assyut**, traders bought "fabrics, jewellery, weaponry and kohl" for the return journey.

Traffic along the Forty Days Road effectively ended in 1884, after the rise of the Dervish empire closed the Egyptian–Sudanese border. When it reopened slavery had been prohibited, so the caravans ceased. As the illiterate slave-drivers died off, memories of the *Darb al-Arba'in* faded, as Michael Asher discovered when he tried to retrace the route from Darfur in the 1980s. Yet its name lives on, as geographers have designated the region through which it once ran as the **Darb al-Arba'in Desert**.

---

the escarpment. Greek, Coptic and Arabic **inscriptions** can be found in caves nearby, and the area is strewn with potsherds.

Further south are two villages divided by a sand ridge and linked by history. For over five centuries, **MAKS BAHRI** ("Customs North") and **MAKS QIBLI** ("Customs South") lived off the caravans that passed along the infamous *Darb al-Arba'in* or **Forty Days Road** (see box above), taxing each slave that entered the oasis, selling supplies and pandering to the slavemasters. Today, there's no evidence of their slave-trafficking past in either village, though in Maks Qibli you can still see a small mud-brick fort, the **Tabid el-Darawish**, built by the British after the Dervish invasion of 1893. Nowadays, the Forty Days Road has been paved as far south as Bir Tafarwi, to link up with the new agricultural project at East Oweinat, but cars can't go beyond the **checkpoint** 5km south of Maks Qibli without a permit from Cairo.

In ancient times, another route led to Esna and Edfu in the Nile Valley, with a Roman fortress to protect trade and the community of **Kysis**, straddling the *Darb al-Dush*. Today, a spur road off the highway south of Maks Bahri leads to the ruins of Kysis and its dramatic hilltop **fortress**, whose walls are six metres high, with four or five storeys below ground. Abutting this is the **Temple of Dush** (daily: summer 8am–6pm; winter 8am–5pm; £E20), built by Domitian and enlarged by Hadrian and Trajan, who added a monumental gateway. Reputedly once partly sheathed in gold, it is covered in dedications to the last two emperors, and the gateway in **graffiti** by Cailliaud and other nineteenth-century travellers. The discovery of an elaborate system of clay **pipes** and a Christian church suggests that the town was abandoned when its wells dried up, some time after the fourth century AD. "Dush" is believed to derive from *Kush*, the name of the ancient Nubian kingdom with which the Egyptians traded along the Nile.

The Gilf Kebir and Jebel Uwaynat

Egypt's final frontier is the vast wilderness to the southwest of Kharga and Dakhla oases, where the Great Sand Sea gives way to the **Uwaynat Desert**. Unlike the flat sand-sheet of the Darb al-Arba'in Desert, this region is pockmarked with craters and outcrops and dominated by the huge plateau of the **Gilf Kebir**. Riven by *wadis* draining into lakes that dried out thousands of years ago, with colossal dunes leapfrogging each other to climb the 1000-metre-high escarpment, the Gilf is the closest environment on earth to the surface of Mars and has been studied by NASA since the 1970s. More recently, this obscure corner of Egypt was thrust into the limelight by the book and film *The English Patient*, dwelling on the exploits of the explorer Almássy and his discovery of the **Cave of the Swimmers** at **Wadi Sura**. This magnificent example of **prehistoric rock art** is only one of thousands of engravings, drawings or paintings in the *wadis* of the Gilf Kebir and **Jebel Uwaynat**, a massif straddling the borders of Egypt, Libya and Sudan. In ancient times Jebel Uwaynat was inhabited by cattle pastoralist cultures which left equally amazing rock art at **Karkur Talh** and Ain Doua. Their depictions of giraffes, ostriches, lions and cattle – and people hunting and swimming – suggests what the environment was like before the decisive shift from savannah to desert occurred at the end of the Holocene wet period, around 5000 BC.

Since then, the Uwaynat Desert has become the **driest desert on earth**, with an aridity index of 200 (meaning that the solar energy received could evaporate 200 times the amount of precipitation received). Rainfall is less than a millimetre a year, and may fall only once a decade at Uwaynat and every twenty years on the Gilf (torrential rainfall was recorded in 2000). Barring a fluke rainfall such as allegedly saved Rohlfs in the Great Sand Sea, the nearest **water** supply is at least 500km away at Bir Tarfawi, where an experimental farm called East Oweinat draws on fossil water and the road to civilization begins. Beyond Bir Tarfawi there are only tracks or trackless desert; no fuel, food nor means of communication with the outside world (unless you bring a satphone); nor any people except a few survey or **safari expeditions**. The **experience** of deep desert travel is fantastic – but not for everyone. The cost alone may be prohibitive, and if it isn't, you need to **reserve** at least six months ahead to be sure of getting a place; expeditions only run from February to March and

September to November, when the temperature is tolerable. Even so, **discomfort** is inevitable: sand gets into every crevice of your body, there's no water to spare for washing, and you start to stink – like everybody else in the vehicle. Unless you're willing to rough it and muck in when needed there's no point in coming at all. But if you do, you're sure to remember it for the rest of your life. For further information, the **websites** Ⓦ www.fjexpeditions.com, Ⓦ www .zarzora.com and Ⓦ www.khalifaexp.com feature extensive photogalleries of the Gilf and Uwaynat, and news of recently discovered rock art.

Getting there

Safaris to the Uwaynat Desert are a major logistical effort, involving tangles of red tape, tonnes of supplies, high-tech communications and navigation gear. Don't even think of going with less than three 4WD vehicles, or without a GPS set and satellite phone. Also essential is a **guide** who's done the trip enough times before to be confident; few of them use maps or compass bearings to chart the route, depending on their memory of landmarks, handed down from guide to guide. To prevent foolhardy ventures the authorities require all expeditions to have a permit from Military Intelligence in Cairo (see p.590), and since a 4WD ran over a landmine in 1999, have insisted that safaris are also **accompanied by an army officer** who knows where mines have been laid. They know lots about the desert, too, and often go into the safari business once their army careers are over, former colonel Mestekawi of Zarzora Expedition being the prime example.

Most of the safari outfits below are willing to take people in their own 4WDs providing they're able to handle the **driving**, which needs experience, skill and nerve. If you have doubts on any of these scores then you should come as a **passenger** and let the safari team handle all the practicalities; just sit back and enjoy the awesome natural beauty and isolation. Some safaris start from Cairo, others from Dakhla, Farafra or Bahariya oases; several firms are based in Europe and may organize package deals. Check that your travel **insurance** covers deep-desert journeys, and what (if any) back-up exists in case of **emergencies**; some outfits have contracts with an air-ambulance service whose light aircraft can land in the desert. Though the operator will supply meals, tents and bedding, you need to **bring** such personal essentials as sun block and skin cream and any luxuries like alcohol or cigarettes (the nearest supply is in Kharga or Dakhla oases). Binoculars are a must, too. See p.505 and pp.542–543 for details of recommended **safari outfitters** that specialize in the Gilf Kebir and Jebel Uwaynat.

The approaches

There are two classic **approaches** to this corner of Egypt. One takes the *Darb el-Tarfawi* south from Dakhla Oasis and then a track to **Abu Ballas**, en route to the Gilf and then Uwaynat. The other assumes a more easterly starting point, from Kharga Oasis or even Aswan or Abu Simbel, and uses the *Darb al-Arba'in* – recently paved as far south as Bir Kiseba – to reach **Bir Tarfawi**, from where the first motorized explorers approached Uwaynat in the mid-1920s, finding the desert easier to cross than they'd expected. Approaching the Gilf from the north was – and is – more difficult due to the Great Sand Sea, but some safaris do it, in which case Regenfeld is a mandatory stopover (see p.582).

From Dakhla

Abu Ballas ("Father of Pots") is 240km from Dakhla, before the southeastern tip of the Great Sand Sea. Named by Prince Kemal el-Din in 1916, this hill is an ancient water cache strategically located between caravan trails and springs. Once there were hundreds of **pots**, each able to hold about 30 litres of water, probably stashed by Tebu tribesmen to sustain their raids on Dakhla. Men from the oasis are said to have found their cache and smashed the pots; archeologists, explorers and tourists have removed most of the fragments, though a few remain photogenically posed. Ball suggested that the "lost oasis" of Zerzura might actually be Abu Ballas and refer to a *zir* or water jug rather than the Arabic name for a small black starling found in the Western Desert. There is **rock art**, too, halfway up the southeast face: a cow suckling its calf, a bearded hunter and his dog chasing an antelope with a bow and arrows, and a man's profile. An hour's drive beyond Abu Ballas is a spectacular field of sedimentary *yardangs* resembling basking sea lions, dubbed the **Mud-Lions** (or Red Lions). Thereafter, dunes slope imperceptibly to the top of the plateau, impeding the way to the Gilf.

From Kharga

Depending on how far south you follow the *Darb al-Arba'in* and which roads you use, you may pass the ancient spring of **Bir Tarfawi**, in a depression surrounded by palms, acacias and tamarisks, that was once filled by two lakes, ringed by Neolithic settlements. In 1981, radar imaging from the Space Shuttle revealed ancient riverbeds that convinced Farouk al-Baz that fossil water lay beneath the desert. His hypothesis proved to be correct, for the government has dug wells and established experimental **farms** at **Bir Sahara** and **El Ain**. Collectively named **East Oweinat** (the spelling differentiates it from Jebel Uwaynat, far away and unrelated to the project), they consist of circular fields irrigated by giant sprinklers, where high-value crops are grown for export to France from an airstrip. As the area is linked by road to Abu Simbel and Toshka and there are plans to extend the Sheikh Zayed Canal to Kharga Oasis, one can envisage a time when the middle of the Darb al-Arba'in Desert turns green – but not for a decade or two, perhaps.

The Gilf Kebir

For a hundred miles the great cliff went on. It seemed like the frontier of some "lost world" … unbroken except where the mouths of deep unlit gorges appeared as black slits, from the bottom of which an ancient debris of boulders spilled out fanwise for miles into the plain. It was tempting to go and explore one of those gorges. What might there not be far inland up the valleys which they drained? … But it was impossible to get close to the foot of the cliff without risking the cars.

Ralph Bagnold, *Libyan Sands: Travel in a Dead World*

Named the **Gilf Kebir** ("Great Barrier") by the first European to sight it, this 7770-square-kilometre limestone and sandstone plateau rises 1000m from the desert floor, an even more formidable obstacle than the Great Sand Sea. Early explorers only skirted its edges and it wasn't until the 1930s that they entered its valleys and found that the Gilf consists of two landmasses joined by an isthmus, almost cut through by a pass called Aqaba. Aeons ago in the late Tertiary age, the Gilf was a watershed draining water in all directions; its *wadis* were eroded by water and then by wind and sand over 100,000 years. The sheer cliffs on the south and southwest sides are the highest, while the north-easterly ones have been worn down by the Sand Sea: an unstoppable force meeting an unmovable object – and winning. **Dunes** have filled up the valleys and are climbing one on top of another to reach the plateau at Lama Pass; trillions of tonnes of sand on the march, white by the Sand Sea, or red around the middle of the plateau and its southern landmass. Despite being the "heart of aridity", the top of the plateau gets just enough rainfall for hardy **flora and fauna** to survive. While its Barbary sheep have been hunted to the verge of extinction by Libyan poachers, nobody is endangering the foxes and lizards seen by Misonne in 1969, nor the whittiers, butterflies and Rose of Jericho flowers that Samir Lama and Cassandra Vivian saw in 1998. And then there are the acacia trees that early explorers found, which were shrivelled when last seen but likely to survive until the next shower. Visitors may also find other surprises, too, like the wreck of a South African Air Force Blenheim bomber that turned up on the plateau in 2001 (thought to be one of five planes that took off from Kufra Oasis in 1942).

For many visitors the Gilf's allure has more to do with its fantastic **prehistoric rock art** – at Wadi Sura, Wadi Abd el-Malik and other sites – or the romance attached to the **explorers** who "discovered" it (though Tebu and Gor'an nomads were fully aware of it all along, since it was their ancestors who created it). Almássy gets all the limelight, naturally, but Michael Ondaatje's novel also mentions other explorers of the 1920s and 1930s, such as the Egyptian Prince Kemal el-Din, the Englishmen Ralph Bagnold, Douglas Newbold and Kennedy Shaw, and the Irishman Patrick Clayton. During World War II, they set up the Long Range Desert Group (LRDG: see p.579) that wreaked havoc behind Italian and German lines, while their former comrade Almássy served on the other side with the Afrika Korps. Since the 1960s the tradition of exploration has been revived by British, Belgian-Libyan, US, French and American-Egyptian expeditions, and by tourists from Germany, Italy, France, Hungary, Spain and Britain.

The "Zerzura" wadis

When Almássy and Lord Clayton took three cars and a plane to the Gilf in February 1932, the aim of their **Zerzura Expedition** was to find the legendary lost oasis of that name, which had obsessed Western explorers for generations (see p.582). Almássy was away visiting the Italians in Kufra when Clayton and Penderel flew over the northern Gilf and glimpsed "an acacia-dotted *wadi*" that they were unable to pinpoint on a map. After Almássy's return with a dozen bottles of wine to what was thereafter called Chianti Camp, they made further flights and spotted two such *wadis* from the air, but couldn't locate them on foot. Both Almássy and Clayton believed that these were two of the three valleys mentioned by Wilkinson in his 1835 list of unknown sites that set the European search for Zerzura rolling. But fate intervened in their plans, for Clayton died of polio on a visit to England, followed within a month by the expedition's sponsor, Prince Kemal el-Din, leaving Almássy to seek new sponsors and Clayton's widow to continue her husband's quest independently (see box opposite).

Returning next spring in cars with balloon tyres, Almássy's party explored **Wadi Abd el-Malik** ("Valley of the Servant of the King"), the longest of the deep fissures in the northern Gilf. They found lots of acacia trees and sites of Tebu encampments and a large cave with **drawings** of longhorn cattle, men, and a prehistoric dwelling. (Another grotto was later found by Peel and Bagnold, containing **paintings** of cattle and a dog.) It was a Tebu caravan guide who told Almássy the name of the *wadi* and its side-valley, **Wadi Talh** ("Acacia Valley"), and spoke of a third valley called Wadi Hamra. When asked if he knew

László Almássy – the real "English Patient"

While Michael Ondaatje's book *The English Patient* and the subsequent Oscar-winning film rescued Almássy's name from obscurity, both texts took liberties with the truth to cast "Count Ladislaus de Almasy" as a romantic hero whose love for another man's wife sealed their fates and left him dying of burns in an Italian villa. The real story is rather different – not least because Almássy was, in fact, homosexual.

Born in 1895, in Borostyánko, Hungary (now Bernstein, Austria), **László Ede Almássy** learned to fly while at boarding school in England. During World War I he was a fighter ace and then an aide to the last Hapsburg monarch (who once mistakenly called him "Count" – a title that stuck), serving as his driver during two farcical attempts to regain the throne in 1921. Almássy then became a salesman for the off-road-car manufacturers Steyr, for whom he won many races, and in 1926 took Steyrs into the desert on the first of his numerous Sahara expeditions, about which he wrote several books. The Bedouin called him Abu Ramleh – Father of the Sands.

In February 1932 he initiated the **Zerzura Expedition** to the Gilf Kebir, the first to combine cars with light aircraft. His co-explorers were **Lord Robert** and **Lady Dorothy Clayton East Clayton** (the fictional Geoffrey and Katherine Clifton), the Irish desert surveyor **Patrick Clayton** (no relation) and Squadron Leader Penderel. Unlike in fiction, Lord Clayton died of a sudden illness back home in England, and although his widow returned to the desert to continue searching for Zerzura, she didn't meet Almássy again or share his discovery of the Cave of Swimmers – nor did she perish there in 1939, but rather in a fall from her plane in England six years earlier. Thus the motive for Almássy's collaboration with the Germans in *The English Patient* is pure invention.

As a reserve officer in the Hungarian air force, Almássy could hardly refuse being posted to Rommel's **Afrika Korps**, which used his expertise as a spotter and his photos for their official handbook – to the fury of his old companions in Egypt, many of whom were now in the LRDG. Thanks to the codebreakers of Bletchley Park, the British knew of Almássy's infiltration of two German spies into Egypt, whom he guided through the Gilf to Kharga Oasis in 1941. He later made amends by visiting Patrick Clayton in an Italian POW camp and getting him moved to a better one. Almássy himself wound up in a Soviet camp where he lost his teeth from scurvy, before a Peoples' Court cleared him of being a Nazi sympathizer after testimony that he had sheltered Jewish neighbours in his flat in Budapest. His **final years** were spent in Africa, where he flew gliders and ran safaris. After catching dysentery in Egypt, he died in a clinic in Salzburg in 1951.

of Zerzura, he replied: "Oh, those silly Arab people, they do not know anything; they call these three *wadis* in the Gilf, Zerzura, but we local people know their real names." Almássy was sure that they had found Zerzura.

In 2002, an expedition exploring a valley to the west of Wadi Abd el-Malik climbed down three small canyons and found the largest cave yet discovered in the Gilf. Co-named after the expedition's leader and sponsor, the **Mestakawi-Foggini Cave** contains a peerless array of prehistoric art: **paintings** of humans and animals, **engravings** of cattle and ibexes, and the ghostly blown-outlines of dozens of **hands**. Some safari outfits now feature the cave on their itineraries (see p.505).

Another must-see is **Wadi Hamra** (Red Valley) on the eastern side of the plateau, named after its gorgeous **red dunes**, drifting down a black mountainside – a Martian landscape found nowhere else in Egypt. The sandstone rocks bear **engravings** of giraffes, oryx, ostriches, gazelles and Barbary sheep – the prey that hunter-gatherers killed with dogs, lassos, bows and arrows during the Early Holocene epoch (8000–6000/5000 BC). This rock art is centuries if not thousands of years older than the images in the Cave of the Swimmers. Wadi Hamra was found in 1931 by Patrick Clayton, who noted plenty of trees and Barbary sheep, while Almásy discovered that it led up to the Gilf plateau. During the war, he reputedly tried to persuade Rommel to land glider-troops on top of the Gilf and bring them down into Wadi Hamra. Today, the *wadi's* **vegetation** is relatively prolific, following a torrential downpour in 2000.

Wadi Sura and the Cave of the Swimmers

Although *The English Patient* transposes the Cave of the Swimmers to Ain Doua at Jebel Uwaynat, it actually lies in **Wadi Sura** (Picture Valley), where Almásy found it in October 1933, with the Frobenius expedition that was searching for rock art at Uwaynat and in the western valleys of the Gilf that had been explored by Patrick Clayton two years earlier. Clayton's son believes that his father found the *wadi* and its other caves first, but it was Almásy's privilege to discover the Cave of the Swimmers and name the valley. The film (shot in Tunisia) took liberties by making the cave where Katherine Clifton died a deep, convoluted passage: it is, in fact, a shallow hollow on the lip of the *wadi*, and shockingly exposed to the elements.

Inside, the **Cave of the Swimmers** harbours well over a hundred figures in diverse styles. The famous swimmers are 10cm long and painted in red; with small rounded heads on stalks, tadpole-shaped bodies and spidery arms and legs. Some are diving, implying that a lake once existed here (for which there's geological evidence). A second group of figures are depicted standing, with clumsy limbs, thick torsos and pea-shaped heads; hands only appear on the larger figures. Most are dark red, with bands of white around their ankles, wrists or waists, similar to the hunters at Karkur Talh. Still more intriguing are two yellow figures that seem to be stretching out their arms to welcome a third, smaller, red one, which may be a child and its parents. Cattle, giraffes, ostriches and dogs are also depicted on the walls.

Further along, the **Cave of the Archers** contains dark red and white figures of naked men clutching bows, some of them shooting at cattle – whose presence dates these pictures to the Cattle Period (5000–2500 BC) of North African rock art. Hans Winkler of the 1938 Monod expedition termed the style of the male figures "balanced exaggeration", for they all have wide shoulders and hips, tiny waists and tapering limbs; feet and hands are rarely shown, and heads often omitted too – unlike the spear-carrying hunters depicted in Karkur Talh at Jebel Uwaynat, which are otherwise similar in style.

On the sandy plain before the *wadi* a huge fallen boulder covers the **Giraffe Cave**, found by Clayton in 1931. Inside are giraffes, cattle and dogs painted in black or white.

Other wadis

The southern part of the Gilf is riddled with *wadis*, some easy to enter, others nearly impossible. **Wadi Mashi** ("Walking Valley") gets its name because the mountains vanish and reappear as you approach, but has yet to yield any finds, unlike **Wadi Dayyiq** ("Narrow Valley"), where a large area is covered by stone-chippings left by prehistoric people manufacturing knives, blades and arrow-heads from hard rocks; or **Wadi al-Bakht**, where four **prehistoric settlements** have been found. Besides ostrich eggs, grinding stones and bones there's heaps of pottery dating back to 6930 BC – as old as the pottery at

Nabta (see p.808) but different in style and colour. It's thought that people lived here for centuries, hunting ostriches and raising cattle around the shores of a lake until it disappeared by 5200 BC.

Nor is it just prehistory that has been preserved, for in 1991 a World War II ammunition truck was found in the desert to the east of Wadi Dayyiq. After being refuelled it started, and is now in the war museum at El-Alamein (see p.646). There are **relics of the Long Range Desert Group** (see box below) all over the region, from a Ford lorry and a GM stake-bed truck 10km southeast of the Gilf's southern tip, to hundreds of metal petrol cans with the Shell logo, laid out to form route markers. An evocative example is the **abandoned aerodrome** with a landing strip marked by concentric rings of petrol cans, near the *wadi* known as **Eight Bells**. This cluster of hills and depressions is the result of a vast prehistoric drainage system from around 5000 BC, which carried water south into an even larger one that fed a super-lake stretching from Lake Chad to within 600km of the Gilf Kebir.

Circumventing the southern Gilf, cars pass through **Wadi Wassa** ("Wide Valley"), another ancient drainage valley with dozens of side *wadis*, islands, and a wrecked **Chevy** used by the LRDG. On the *col* that divides Wadi Wassa from **Wadi Faragh** (Empty Valley), Shaw found a cave containing engravings of cows and more ancient giraffes; it was thereafter shown on maps as **Shaw's Cave**, despite being known to caravan guides as the Cave of the Arch (*Magarat el-Qantara*). It's here that a military escort is most appreciated, for there are **mines** on the plain where two tracks cross about 5km west of the mouth of Wadi Faragh – which wrecked a tourist 4WD in 1983 – and others are rumoured to have been laid at other strategic points. Only the Egyptian army knows which are mined and which are bluffs. Wadi Faragh is also distinguished by a **Monument to Prince Kemal el-Din**, erected by Almássy to commemorate his patron's expeditions to Uwaynat, the Gilf and Merga Oasis, using Citröen caterpillar-tracks in the 1920s.

The Long Range Desert Group (LRDG)

Founded by Ralph Bagnold in June 1940, to reconnoitre Axis forces and engage in "piracy on the high desert", the **Long Range Desert Group**'s motto was "Not by Strength, but Guile". Led by Bagnold and other pre-war explorers such as Patrick Clayton, Kennedy Shaw and Douglas Newbold, it consisted mainly of New Zealanders, who soon learnt the arts of desert warfare. As with Special Forces ever since, the emphasis was on self-reliance and mobility. Each patrol took all it needed for a cross-desert journey of 1500 miles (which could be doubled by establishing a forward supply dump), in stripped-down Chevy trucks fitted with sand mats and channels (doubling as air markers for supply drops) and a sun compass invented by Bagnold. Patrols operated for up to eleven weeks (without washing) as they espied convoys or delivered SAS commandos to attack airfields; destroying over 400 planes in ten months (more than the RAF). British Foreign Secretary Anthony Eden called them "my mosquito army", while the Italians dubbed them the Ghost Army. After Axis forces in North Africa surrendered in 1943, the LRDG were sent to the Balkans. They spoke a weird argot composed of English, Arabic, Hindi, German and Italian, and wore a mixture of uniforms, with a unit badge of a scorpion within a wheel, made by jewellers in Khan el-Khalili.

You can **read** about the LRDG's exploits in Bagnold's *Sand, Wind and War: Memoirs of a Desert Explorer*, Saul Kelly's *The Hunt for Zerzura*, Peter Clayton's *Desert Explorer* (about his father, Patrick), or on the LRDG Preservation Society's website ⓦ www.lrdg.org.

The Clayton Craters and Jebels Peter and Paul

The two main tracks towards Jebel Uwaynat pass the **Clayton Craters**, discovered by Patrick Clayton on the second Bagnold expedition in 1931. Measuring up to 1km across, the twenty craters have sandstone rims rising about 30m from the desert floor, enclosing domes of greenish igneous rock or cork-shaped basalt formations, with dry stream-beds. While the baked and fused sandstone suggests a volcanic origin, the geologist Rushdi Said argues that springs caused the ground to collapse, forming the craters. Elsewhere in the Libyan Desert, remote sensing satellites have identified craters formed by meteor strikes, near Kufra Oasis in Libya and amid the Great Sand Sea (see opposite).

Otherwise, the chief landmarks are the twin mountains named **Jebels Peter and Paul**, steep-sided quartz trachyte plugs in the Precambrian bedrock, like the northern part of Uwaynat. Safari groups give them a wide berth, as **mines** have reputedly been laid roundabouts.

Jebel Uwaynat

On a map of North Africa, the ruler-straight borders of Libya, Egypt and Sudan intersect at **Jebel Uwaynat**, the highest point in the Libyan Desert. Surrounded by sand-sheets, it rises through a "vertical battlement" to 1898m above the desert floor and 600m above sea level, just high enough to attract a little rainfall, which percolates down to eight small pools or "springs" at its base (after which Uwaynat is named). The valleys there are fertile if watered, sustaining communities from prehistoric times until the early 1930s. Yet Uwaynat's location remained a mystery to the outside world until 1923, when it was reached by Hassanein Bey by camel from Kufra Oasis in Libya. With its co-ordinates established, the next challenge was to find a route from Egypt, which was accomplished in 1925 by Prince Kemal al-Din and John Ball, who followed in half-tracks from Bir Tarfawi. They were followed by Shaw, Almássy, Bagnold *et al*, whose exploration of the Gilf was initally motivated by the desire to find a route to Uwaynat from the north.

After the Italians occupied Kufra and placed an outpost at Uwaynat, the possibility that it could be an unguarded back door into Egypt during wartime occurred to both Bagnold and the Italian commander Lorenzini – but not to the HQ staff-wallahs who turned down Bagnold's proposal for car patrols along the frontier. It wasn't until Italy declared war in June 1940 that the newly appointed General Wavell summoned him and learned that cars could easily drive from Uwaynat to Aswan in two days. The risk of a surprise attack that would cut links to Sudan and make all of Egypt hostage to a threat to blow up the Aswan Dam was too terrible to ignore, so Bagnold was authorized to set up long-range patrols to monitor any activity. In the event, the Italians never tried anything so bold, but Almássy later slipped through from Kufra via Uwaynat and the Gilf, to guide two German spies as far as Kharga Oasis, before returning to Libya.

Karkur Talh and other sites

Jebel Uwaynat covers 1500 square kilometres and consists of granite, sandstone and quartz trachyte formations. As in the Gilf, the northern slopes have borne the brunt of wind erosion and bizarre rock forms abound, while the *wadis* all around the base (called *karkurs*) contain engravings, drawings and paintings spanning thousands of years. One of the richest sites is **Karkur Talh** (Acacia Valley), where Hassanein Bey found images of lions, giraffes, ostriches, gazelles and cows engraved on the rocks at ground level – plus paintings of camels from a later epoch (camels reached Egypt in 525 BC). Higher up the valley, Shaw discovered ninety human figures drawn on the roof of a sandstone cave 1m high, whose figures were lither than the hunters in the Cave of the Archers at Wadi Sura but otherwise similar, leading Winkler to conclude that both were the work of the ancient Tebu ("Rock People") who once ranged across the Sahara from their mountainous homeland of Tibesti, in Chad. Besides the rock art in the main valley there are 200 paintings and engravings in a lateral *wadi*, and over 1000 other locations in the areas that the Belgian expedition of 1968 called **Wadi Talh I** and **II**.

All the other rock-art sites lie over the partly mined border in Sudan or Libya and are currently **inaccessible** (except on safaris via Libya with Ancient World Tours or Fleigel Jerzerniczky Expeditions; see p.505). These include **Karkur Murr**, where Clayton found starving refugees from Kufra in 1931, and the massif's largest "spring", **Ain Doua**, which was the fictional location of the Cave of the Swimmers in *The English Patient* – though the rock art here was actually discovered by Almásy's driver.

The Great Sand Sea and the "Lost Oasis"

Between the Gilf Kebir and Siwa Oasis lie 72,000 square kilometres of dune fields that the explorer Gerhard Rohlfs named the **Great Sand Sea**. Though maps still define parts as beyond the "limits of reliable relief information", its overall configuration is known. From thick "whalebacks" and a mass of transverse dunes near Siwa, it washes south in parallel *seif* dunes (oriented north–south, with a slight northwest–southeast incline) as far as the eye can see.

Although its general existence was known at the time of Herodotus, the extent to which it stretched southwards wasn't realized until the Rohlfs expedition of 1874 headed west from Dakhla, bound for Kufra Oasis in Libya. With seventeen camels bearing water and supplies, they soon met the *erg*'s outermost ranges: "an ocean" of sand-waves over 100m high, ranked 2–4km apart. Rohlfs estimated that their camels could scale six dunes and advance 20km westwards on the first and second days, but that their endurance would rapidly diminish thereafter, so with no prospect of water or an end to the dunes they were forced to turn north-northwest and follow the dune lanes towards Siwa. Their isolation was intense:

If one stayed behind a moment and let the caravan out of one's sight, a loneliness could be felt in the boundless expanse such as brought fear even in the stoutest heart ... Nothing but sand and sky! At sea the surface of the water is moved, unless there is a dead calm. Here in the sand ocean there is nothing to remind one of the great common life of the earth but the stiffened ripples of the last windstorm; all else is dead.

By the eighteenth day the expedition could no longer water every camel and the animals began dying. Then, according to the English version of his adventures, there was torrential rainfall in a spot where barely a drop falls for years, saving their lives and replenishing their water supply. Rohlfs called the spot **Regenfeld** ("Rainfield") and marked it with a cairn before he left, wondering "Will ever man's foot tread this place again?". However, in the German edition of his book, *Drei Monate in der libyschen Wüste*, he described a smaller expedition with no hint of supply problems – and whether or not a miraculous rainfall really saved their lives, Regenfeld has since been visited by scores of explorers and tourists. The message that he left in a bottle was removed by Hassanein Bey in 1923, who substituted a message of his own, followed decades later by Samir Lama and Jacques Monod. Now, all the messages, wine bottles and empty water tanks left by previous explorers have been taken by souvenir hunters.

Rohlfs' feat of trekking for 36 days over 675km (480km across the dunes) wasn't repeated until 1921–24, when Colonel de Lancey Forth entered the Sand Sea twice by camel from Dakhla and Siwa. Beneath a layer of sand he found campfires, charred ostrich eggs, flint knives and grinders from Neolithic times, when the desert was lush savannah.

Meanwhile, Ball and Moore had managed to round the Sand Sea's southeastern tip (near latitude 24) by car in 1917, while in 1923 Hassanein Bey circumvented its western edge as part of an extraordinary 3550-kilometre camel journey from Sollum on the Mediterranean to El-Fasher in Sudan's Darfur province. He also confirmed the existence of the hitherto legendary Jebel Uwaynat, whose water source encouraged motorized explorers to seek new routes to the southwest. For Prince Kemal el-Din in his fleet of caterpillar-tracked Citröens, and Bagnold and co – who found customized Model-T Fords more effective – the next obstacle was the Gilf Kebir (see p.575), which barred the way to remoter Libyan oases.

Zerzura: the "Lost Oasis"

With the "discovery" by motorized explorers of Selima, Merga and the Forty Day Road's water holes, the number of unlocated oases diminished until only the **"Lost Oasis" of Zerzura** remained. First mentioned in 1246 as an abandoned village in the desert southwest of the Fayoum, it reappeared as a fabulous city in the fifteenth-century treasure-hunters' *Book of Hidden Pearls*:

This city is white like a pigeon, and on the door of it is carved a bird. Enter, and there you will find great riches, also the king and queen sleeping in their castle. Do not approach them, but take the treasure.

Citing native sources in 1835, Wilkinson placed the oasis "five days west of the road from El-Hayiz to Farafra", or "two or three days due west from Dakhleh". *Murray's Handbook* (1891) reported an "Oasis of the Blacks . . . also called Wady Zerzura" to the west of Farafra, and described it quite matter-of-factly. But Zerzura was still unlocated, and the stories placing it west of Dakhla gained credibility after Europeans "discovered" Kufra Oasis in Libya, which the same tales had mentioned. However, both the Rohlfs and Harding-King expeditions heard accounts of black men who periodically raided Dakhla from an oasis seven or eight days' journey to the southwest.

Having weighed the evidence for various speculative locations in the last chapter of *Libyan Sands*, Bagnold demarcated three zones. The "northern" one – encompassing the whole Sand Sea, but rating the areas west of Dakhla and Farafra as likeliest – was propounded by de Lancey Forth, citing the story of a town with iron gates, seven days' camel journey to the south, in the *Siwan Manuscript*; plus tales of Bedouin chancing upon unknown oases while pursuing missing camels. Unfortunately, similar yarns also pointed towards the far south – that vast wilderness between Dakhla and the Selima and Merga oases in Sudan. Dr Ball and Newbold favoured this area, largely free of dunes and often low enough to approach the subterranean water table; in addition, Newbold thought he glimpsed an oasis during a flight over the desert.

Sand seas, dunes and silica glass

The true life of the desert is not made up of the marches of tribes in search of pasture, but of the game that goes endlessly on. What a difference in substance between the sands of submission and the sands of unruliness! The dunes, the salines, change their nature ... as the code changes by which they are governed.

Antoine de Saint-Exupéry, Wind, Sand and Stars

Though gravel plains, limestone pans and scarps account for ninety percent of the Sahara Desert, it's the **sand seas** or *ergs* that captivate the imagination. Covering hundreds of thousands of square kilometres of Algeria, Libya and Egypt, these dune fields are awesomely lifeless, yet shift and reproduce. Formed by wind and particles, vortices and accretion, their shapes, hues and textures are defined by light and shadow, a mutable reality. Venturers into this unearthly world must accept its whims and logic – this is elemental, not mortal terrain. Its sandstorms have buried armies and scoured paint from cars; soft spots and slip faces can trap the unwary, break limbs or axles; getting lost and dying of heat and thirst are real possibilities here.

While prevailing winds are the dominant factor, local geology and whatever precipitation or vegetation exists also determine the shape of **dunes**. Where sand is relatively scarce and small obstructions are common, windblown particles tend to form **crescent-shaped** *barchan* dunes, which advance horns first, moving over obstacles without altering their height. Baby dunes are formed downwind of the horns, which produces parallel lines of *barchans* with flat corridors between them, advancing up to 19m each year. *Barchans* can grow as high as 94m, extend for 375m, and weigh up to 450 million kilos. However, their mass is nothing compared to **parallel straight** dunes, or *seif* dunes (from the Arabic word for "sword"); some in the Great Sand Sea are 140km long – the longest dunes in the world. Formed by a unidirectional wind, they have slipfaces on both sides and a wavy, knife-edged crest along the top. When *seif* dunes fall over an escarpment they reform at the bottom as crescent dunes, which is why *barchans* are the prevailing form in Dakhla and Kharga. Occasionally, they pile one on top of another to create mountainous **whalebacks** or mega-*barchans*. When the wind direction alters constantly, it can even form **star-shaped** (*rhord*) dunes. These are rare in Egypt, but one has been recorded at Wadi al-Bakht in the Gilf Kebir. Another type of formation is the flat, hard-packed **sand-sheet**, found in the Darb al-Arba'in Desert.

Another mysterious feature of the Great Sand Sea are the surface deposits of pale-green translucent **silica glass**, found between latitudes N 25.02 and 26.13 and longitudes E 25.24 and 25.55. These are thought to have been caused by a prehistoric meteorite strike whose impact fused sand into glass; ground zero may have been the four-kilometre-wide **Al-Baz Crater** (named after its Egyptian-American discoverer, Farouk al-Baz, a pioneer in using satellites to search for water in arid areas), 150km southeast of the silica glass region. The Ancient Egyptians knew of silica glass (if not of its celestial origins), for it was from this unique material that the scarab on Tutankhamun's funerary pectoral cross was carved. **Shooting stars** are often visible in the sky above the Great Sand Sea.

The third, "central" zone extended southwest from Dakhla as far as Jebel Uwaynat and was championed by Harding-King, who cited native accounts of incursions by "strange cows", Tebu raiders and a "black giantess". When Ball discovered a cache of Tebu water jars at Abu Ballas, southwest of Dakhla, it supported the stories but argued against an oasis; for if a water source existed, why bother to maintain a depot in the middle of nowhere? Then came Almássy and Lord Clayton, who were sure that three *wadis* in the northern Gilf Kebir were the legendary Zerzura – but they failed to convince others.

Accepting Ball's theory of a consistent water level beneath the Libyan Desert, Bagnold argued that Zerzura could only exist in low-lying areas or deep, wind-eroded hollows. As the desert was surveyed, the possibility of such sites escaping notice diminished, and Bagnold doubted that an undiscovered oasis existed. Perhaps Zerzura might once have been a water hole or an area favoured with periodic rainfall, but the fabled oasis of palms and ruins must be a figment of wishful thinking: a Bedouin Shangri-la that tantalized foreign explorers.

Siwa Oasis

Isolated by hundreds of kilometres of desert, **Siwa Oasis** remained virtually independent from Egypt until the late nineteenth century, sustaining a unique culture. Yet despite – or because of – its isolation, outsiders have been drawn here since antiquity. The legendary Army of Cambyses was heading this way when it disappeared into a sandstorm; Alexander the Great journeyed here to consult the famous Oracle of Amun; and Arabic tales of *Santariyah* (as the oasis was known) were common currency into the nineteenth century. In modern times, Siwa has received visits from kings and presidents, anthropologists and generals. Tourism only really began in the mid-1980s but has gathered steam in recent years, as Siwa has become a firm favourite with independent travellers and adventure tour groups.

The oasis offers all you could ask for in the way of desert **beauty spots**: thick palm groves clustered around freshwater springs and salt lakes; rugged massifs and enormous dunes. Equally impressive are the **ruins** of Shali and Aghurmi, labyrinthine mud-built towns that once protected the Siwans from desert raiders. Scattered around the oasis are ruined **temples** that attest to Siwa's fame and prosperity during Greco-Roman times; some claim that the tomb of Alexander the Great lies here. Visitors are also fascinated by **Siwan culture** and how it is reacting to outside influences like TV, schooling and tourism. Nowadays, it is mostly only older women who wear the traditional costume, silver jewellery and complex hair-braids; younger wives and unmarried women dress much the same as their counterparts in the Nile Valley. But the Siwans still observe their own festivals and wedding customs; and among themselves they speak *Siwi*, a Berber tongue (see p.586). Though things are changing, the Siwans remain sure of their identity and are determined to maintain it.

Having weathered an invasion of 5000 rally cars and camp-followers when the Paris-Dakkar-Cairo rally was routed via Siwa in 2003, the Siwans are bracing themselves for a similar number of spectators on March 29, 2006, when a **total**

solar eclipse will occur over Siwa and Libya for four minutes and six seconds: rooms are already at a premium.

A little history

Beyond the fact that it sustained hunter-gatherers in Paleolithic times, little is known about Siwa Oasis before the XXVI Dynasty (525–404 BC), when the reputation of its **Oracle** spread throughout the Mediterranean world. Siwa's population seems to have been at risk from predatory desert tribes, so their first settlement was a fortified acropolis, about which Classical accounts reveal little about this beyond its name, **Aghurmi**, and its position as a major caravan stop between Cyrenaica and Sudan. The Siwans were related to the Berbers of Algeria, Tunisia and Morocco, and their language is just a variant of the Berber tongues, so their society may have originally been matriarchal. Their later history is detailed in the *Siwan Manuscript* (its whereabouts are a closely guarded secret), a century-old compilation of oral histories that relates how Siwa's rulers considered poisoning the springs with mummies in order to thwart the Muslim conquest (date uncertain), and how Bedouin and Berber raids had reduced Aghurmi's population to a mere two hundred by the twelfth century AD.

Shali and Siwan society

Round about 1203, seven families quit Aghurmi to found a new settlement called **Shali** (the Town). Their menfolk are still honoured as the "forty ancestors", and these pioneering families were probably the most vigorous of the surviving Siwans. Later, newcomers from Libya settled in the oasis, giving rise to the enduring distinction between the "Westerners" and the original, more numerous "Easterners", whose historic feud began after they disagreed over the route of a causeway that both had undertaken to build across the salt lake of Birket Siwa. Nonetheless, both coexisted within a single town built of *kharsif*: a salt-impregnated mud which dries cement-hard, but melts during downpours – fortunately, it only rains heavily here every fifty years or so. Fearful of raiders, Shali's *agwad* (elders) forbade families to live outside the walls, so as the population increased the town could only expand upwards. Siwan households added an extra floor with each generation, while the *agwad* regulated the width of alleys to one donkey's-breadth in an effort to ensure some light and air within the labyrinth.

Siwan bachelors aged between twenty and forty were obliged to sleep in caves outside town, guarding the fields – hence their nickname, the "club-bearers". Noted for their love of palm liquor, song and dance, these *zaggalah* shocked outsiders with their open **homosexuality**. Homosexual marriages were forbidden by King Fouad in 1928, but continued in secret until the late 1940s. Today, Siwans emphatically assert that homosexuality no longer exists in the oasis – whatever may be said on the website ⓦ www.gayegypt.com – and palm liquor has now been superceded by *arak* made from dates.

Another feature of Shali was the tradition of violent **feuds** between the Westerners and Easterners, in which all able-bodied males were expected to participate. Originally ritualized, with parallel lines of combatants exchanging blows between sunrise and sunset while their womenfolk threw stones at cowards and shouted encouragement, feuds became far deadlier with the advent of firearms, occasioning gun battles "on the slightest grounds". (Even now, Siwans know which clan they're descended from, and the town council is sited midway between the two neighbourhoods.) Yet they immediately closed ranks against outsiders – Bedouin raiders, *khedival* taxmen or European explorers.

Egyptian and British control

Visitors of the eighteenth and nineteenth centuries regularly experienced Siwan **xenophobia**. "Whenever I quitted my apartment, it was to be assailed with stones and a torrent of abusive language", Browne wrote in 1762. Having poked around the antiquities in Muslim guise, Frederick Hornemann was pursued into the desert, where "the braying of three hundred donkeys announced the arrival of the Siwan army", and only escaped thanks to his assistant's recitation of Koranic verses. Frederic Cailliaud was permitted to visit the gardens and ruins in 1819, but the town remained barred to strangers until six hundred troops sent by Mohammed Ali compelled the oasis to recognize **Egyptian authority** in 1820.

Although the Siwans subsequently revolted against their governor and defaulted on taxes (payable in dates) half a dozen times over the next sixty years, the oasis began to change. With the desert tribes suppressed, and Shali rendered unsafe by heavy rains, the *agwad* permitted families to settle outside the walls. From the 1850s onwards the great reformist preacher Mohammed Ibn Ali al-Senussi cast a spell over the desert peoples from Jaghbub Oasis just over the border, and Siwa – the site of his first *zawiya* – supported **Senussi** resistance to the Italian conquest of Libya (1912–30), until it became clear that their Senussi "liberators" would not restore Siwan independence. Thus in 1917, British forces were "welcomed by the cheering Siwans, who declared their loyalty as they always did with every new victorious conqueror" (Fakhry).

Anglo-Egyptian control of Siwa was maintained by the Frontier Camel Corps and Light Car Patrols. Agricultural advisors, a school and an orthodox imam were introduced following King Fouad's visit to the oasis in 1928. When the British withdrew as the Italians advanced across North Africa in 1942, the Siwans accepted Axis **occupation** with equal resignation. Unlike Rommel, who made a favourable impression during his flying visit, King Farouk dismayed the Siwans by wearing shorts and asking if they "still practised a certain vice" when he visited the oasis in 1945.

Modern Siwa

Paradoxical as it sounds, Siwa's biggest problem is an excess of fresh water, which gushes from springs and drains into salt lakes, increasing their volume and salinity. As Bagnold put it: "the air, hot and breathless, has a characteristic oasis smell, slightly sweet, of rank grass faintly charred, decaying through increasing saltiness". Smelly, mosquito-infested ponds all over town attest that the **water**

Siwi

Siwi is an unwritten Berber dialect that is the mother tongue of all native Siwans; children only start to learn Arabic from the age of six, in school. However, as Arabic is used in public life, visitors needn't deal with Siwi unless they want to. Here are a few useful phrases to get you started.

yes	*mashi*	Give me ...	*ooshi ...*
no	*oola*	donkey(s)	*yeizite (zitan)*
How are you?	*Tanta elhalenik?*	horse	*agmare*
What's your name?	*Bit in insmitinik?*	camel(s)	*alghum*
Where are you going?	*Imani tehab?*	dates	*tenii*
What do you want?	*Tanta ekhsitta'?*	olives	*azumour*
I want ...	*ehk sehk ...*	water	*aman*
What's this?	*Tanta wook?*		

table lies only twenty centimetres underground. **Land reclamation** projects have tried to tackle the problem since 1907, but creating drainage catchment areas in an oasis lying 18m below sea level has always proved hugely expensive. Foreign engineers are currently installing a system of pipes, but the water table is still rising.

While Egyptian military bases exist here on sufferance, the Siwans have welcomed developments in health care, education and communications. Two hospitals (one for women and children) treat patients who once had to travel to Mersa Matrouh. Over thirty Siwans have graduated from university and returned to live in the oasis. The road to Matrouh (completed in 1984) has encouraged exports of dates and olives, and tourism to the oasis, and during the 1990s the local **economy** was boosted by new factories producing olive oil, mineral water and carpets. More recently, some 500 Siwan **women** have been stitching traditional embroidery for an Italian couture house, earning twice the average Siwan wage for an agricultural labourer: the unmarried ones have saved so much money that they can be choosy about taking a husband.

Meanwhile, the Siwans' desire for **housing** with breeze-block walls and proper bathrooms rather than the traditional dusty mud-brick dwellings is alarming conservationists. Under pressure from Mounir Nematalla of the Ecolodge (see p.597) and the Friends of Siwa Association, the governor in Mersa Matrouh prohibited the building of new houses, but after public opposition ruled that they could go ahead providing the exteriors were faced with mud in the traditional oasis style. Currently, the only buildings to have complied are the bank and police station, which look like something out of a spaghetti western.

Visiting Siwa

The **best time** to come is during spring or autumn, when the Siwans hold festivals and the days are pleasantly warm. In winter, windless days can also be nice, but nights – and gales – are chilling. From May onwards, rising temperatures keep people indoors between 11am and 7pm, and the nights are sultry and mosquito-ridden. Even when the **climate** is mild you'll probably feel like taking a midday siesta or a swim.

Siwa is well known for its conservatism in matters of **dress** and **behaviour**. The tourist office requests visitors to refrain from public displays of affection or drinking alcohol, and women to keep their arms and legs covered – especially when bathing in pools. Women should also avoid wandering alone in places with few people around. Local people are generally more reserved than the Egyptians, and invitations home are less common.

Besides the official ban on **photographing** military installations (including the airport and sandbagged dugouts in unexpected locations), visitors should respect Siwan feelings on the issue. As a rule, local women are taboo subjects, whereas Siwan males – particularly the younger ones – don't mind being snapped (but always ask them first). For streetlife and visual clarity, take your pictures before 9am, or during the hour or so before sunset; people stay indoors when the sun is high, and its glare bleaches colours and textures from photographs.

Getting there: the routes

Unless you sign up with a desert safari – which might reach Siwa via the Qattara Depression – there are only two possible **approaches**. One is via road from Bahariya Oasis (see p.531); the other is from Alexandria or Mersa Matrouh – the route favoured by most visitors.

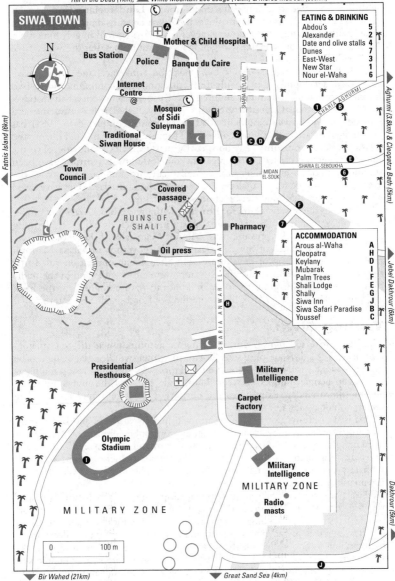

THE WESTERN DESERT OASES | Siwa Oasis

There are three **buses** daily from Sidi Gaber in Alexandria to Siwa (8.30am, 11am & 2pm; 9hr; £E27), which call briefly at Moharrem Bey and take on extra passengers at Mersa Matrouh, three to four hours later. Matrouh is the starting point for an additional bus (£E12) leaving at 7.30am. You may also be able to catch a service taxi or **minivan** from Matrouh to Siwa; the fare is £E12 per person, or £E150–200 to rent the whole vehicle.

The 300km **journey** from Matrouh to Siwa takes four hours by car or bus, with the Siwa road turning off the highway 20km west of Matrouh, at a checkpoint. There are minefields to the left for 50km into the desert, marked by triangular signs. About 100km further there is a tiny **resthouse** known as **Bir Nous** (Halfway Well), selling tea, soup and soft drinks. Its toilets are the nearest one gets to the horrors of this route before the road was built. Until the nineteenth century there was only a camel trail (eight days from Matrouh) across this flat desert, and the few landmarks might be obscured by dust clouds or sandstorms. The sharp limestone ridges and hollows beneath the powdery surface of this *shabak* (net) desert also made the route hazardous for early motorists, who followed the line of telegraph poles. Nowadays the monotonous vistas – interspersed with army camps – keep going until the last 40km, when rock outcrops presage the appearance of the oasis.

Siwa Town

Most visitors rate **SIWA TOWN** and the pools, rocks and ruins around as the oasis's main attractions, and not many bother to visit the outlying villages. Siwa Town has grown as its population has risen to 25,000 (at least 1000 of them from outside the oasis, mostly from two villages near Minya), and people have moved into breeze-block houses or low-rise flats, forsaking their traditional mud-brick dwellings – just as their ancestors had previously abandoned the fortified hilltop city of **Shali**, whose ruins overlook the modern town. A triumphal arch and broad roads debouch onto a central market area, but the town slips away into a maze of alleyways, and loses itself amidst the encircling palms. Boys driving donkey carts transport fodder and decorously wrapped Siwan women, and the braying of donkeys resounds from every quarter of town. After dark, a thousand stars emerge and Siwa's isolation from the world beyond the Great Sand Sea becomes almost palpable.

Arrival and information

Siwa's **tourist office** (daily except Fri 9am–10pm; in summer also Fri 6–8pm; ☎ & ℱ046/460-1338, mobile ☎010 5461992, ✉mahdi_hweiti@yahoo.com) is in the north of the town, directly opposite the flesh-pink Mother and Child Hospital, and close to the bus station. The office is run by the English-speaking Mahdi Hweiti, a native Siwan who knows everything about the oasis and can arrange trips to outlying villages. Should you have any trouble in Siwa, go to him rather than the police. There are two **pharmacies** in the centre and a fairly grungy public **hospital** on the outskirts. A gynaecologist and a paediatrician work alternate weeks at the Mother and Child Hospital near the tourist office. The **police** (☎046/460-1008) are next door to the **Banque du Caire** (Sun–Thurs 8.30am–2pm & 5–8pm, Fri & Sat 8–11am & 5–8pm, which has an ATM (Visa, MC, Maestro, Cirrus) and can cash travellers' cheques. A block from the bank is a new **Internet Centre** for Siwan youth, which tourists can also use (£E6/hr).

Accommodation

Siwa has both low-budget and upmarket **hotels**, including two lakeside ecolodges 13–16km from town. While it's worth reserving ahead if you're fussy about where you stay, the only time it's essential to do so is during Siwan festivals, when tour groups block-book hotels. On the whole, though, it's safe to assume that you'll find a bed. People wanting to stay for a long time can rent furnished **apartments** (from £E500 a month) through Mahdi at the tourist office. Providing you inform the tourist office first, **camping** is allowed throughout the oasis, but since any land that's cultivated or near a water source is sure to belong to somebody, you should ask their permission. A sleeping bag and bug repellent are advisable.

Unless stated otherwise, **breakfast** is not included at hotels. Places out of town are marked on the **map** of Siwa Oasis on p.595.

Siwa Town

Arous al-Waha Opposite the tourist office ☎046/460-0028. A state hotel whose name means "Bride of the Oasis", it has worn but clean, semi-carpeted rooms with fans, shower-cabins and fridges. **❷**

Cleopatra Sharia Anwar el-Sadat ☎ & ℱ046/460-0421. A range of clean, simple rooms, some with toilet, balcony and fan; those in the quieter "chalet" block have all three, but are plagued by mosquitoes. There's also an a/c suite with TV and fridge (£E130). **❶**

Keylany Midan el-Souk ☎046/460-1052, mobile ☎012 1057977. With its clean, carpeted en-suite rooms with fan and balcony, the *Keylany* is the best choice in this price range and is planning a rooftop café in the future. Reservations advised. **❷**

Mubarak In the Olympic complex ☎046/460 0883, ℱ460-0884. Antiseptic rooms with satellite TV, a/c and fridge; chalets (£E400) with large lounges and VIP suites (£E750) with multiple bedrooms and bathrooms. Jacuzzi and sauna for guests. Breakfast included. **❺**

Palm Trees Off Midan el-Souk ☎046/460-1703, ℱ460-0006, ✉salahali2@yahoo.com. Popular for its central location and palm garden, this place has basic rooms with fans (a private bathroom costs £E10 extra) and an erratic water supply. Manager Fahmy organizes safaris. **❶**

Shali Lodge Sharia el-Seboukha ☎046/460-1299, ℱ460-1799, ✉info@eqi.com.eg. A lovely small hotel built of *kharsif* and palm-logs in the traditional oasis style, with palm trees growing out its rooftop restaurant: it was the prototype for the *Ecolodge* (see opposite). **❺**

Shally Off Sharia Anwar el-Sadat ☎046/460-1203. Small, clean, low-budget place; all the rooms have fans (£E20), and some baths, and balconies overlooking Shali – the view from the roof is superb. **❶**

Siwa Inn Beyond the radio masts ☎046/460-1287, mobile ☎010 6176946, ✉siwainn@yahoo .com. A rustic-style place 25 minutes' walk from the centre of town, whose ten slightly musty rooms with fans and baths overlook a garden with a cold pool. Satellite TV and a restaurant. Breakfast included. **❸**

Siwa Safari Paradise Sharia Aghurmi ☎046/460-1590, ℱ460-1592, 🌐www.siwaparadise.com. A tourist village of a/c rooms with fridges and satellite TV (US$55), and bungalows with fan, heater and TV (US$49) around a large cold spring pool for swimming. Rates include half-board. **❺**

Youssef Midan el-Souk ☎046/460-0678. Siwa's cheapest hotel has small, clean rooms with fans (£E16), some with balconies and/or bathrooms (£E8 extra), and a rooftop with a great view of town. **❶**

East of Siwa Town: Aghurmi and Jebel Dakhrour

Fata Morgana Jebel Dakhrour, 4km from Siwa Town ☎ & ℱ046/460-0237, mobile ☎012 4175188, 🌐www.fatamorgana21.ch. Traditional-style rooms (some with fans and mosquito nets) with views of the Sand Sea or Dakhrour, and a garden with a small pool, in a remote, windswept setting. **❺**

Qasr el-Zeytuna Jebel Dakhrour, 3.5km from Siwa Town ☎ & ℱ046/460-0037, mobile ☎012 3722694. Nine spacious rooms backing on to gardens with a spring-fed pool, palm groves, goats and chickens. German and English spoken. Breakfast included. **❹**

Reem el-Waha 1km from Aghurmi, 3km from Siwa Town ☎046/460-0071, ℱ493-3608, mobile ☎010 3604941. Pleasant rooms with TV, fridge and balcony, overlooking a bleak yard with a small circular swimming pool. Breakfast included. **❸**

Siwa Shali Resort Jebel Dakhrour, 5km from Siwa Town, mobile ☎010 1119730, ℱ02/383-9242, 🌐www.siwashaliresort.com. Yet more windswept and remote, this classy holiday village of *kharsif*-style a/c rooms has a 200-metre-long serpentine pool, a Turkish bath, billiards, a piano and a desert library. **❼**

Adrar al-Milal Ecolodge 16km from Siwa Town ☎ mobile 010 538611, ⓔ info@eqi.com.eg. An amazing mud-brick complex with superb views over the lake, lovely rooms, a big pool and palm garden. Meals prepared from organic ingredients, a 24-hour bar and unlimited horse-riding included in the price. See p.597 for more about the *Ecolodge*. ⓥ

Taghaghien Touristic Island (aka *Safety Land*) 13km from town ☎ 046/460-0455, mobile 012 2155596, ⓦ www.Taghaghien-Island.com. Reached by a causeway, this island campground has cosy en-suite huts, a circular pool, fab views at sunset, and alcohol. On the downside, its palm trees are dying and no transport is provided. Breakfast included. ⓖ

Taziry 15km from town, mobile ☎ 010 6445881 or 010 1122519, ⓔ taziry@hotmail.com. Around the lake from the *Ecolodge*, this new hotel (whose name means "Moon" in Siwi) is similar in style but on a smaller scale and with less vegetation around its lakeside pool. Breakfast included; other meals to order. Free transfers on arrival and departure. ⓖ

The town

The **ruins of Shali**, looming above the centre and floodlit in the evening, are a constant invitation to explore. Until late last century this hermetic labyrinth attained a height of over sixty metres, with many levels of chambers, passages and granaries. Its surreal remains cover the entire saddle of rock below a **mosque**, which is said to have been the last one in Egypt where the muezzin still shouted out the call to prayer without the benefit of a loudspeaker. Down behind the hill around the back of Shali is a donkey-driven **oil-press** that dates back centuries (only used in December and January). From vantage points in Shali, you can see the whole modern town, its palm groves, the salt lakes and table-top rocks beyond; and providing you don't peer too obviously into the houses below, it's possible to glimpse the Siwans at home. Downstairs, women busy themselves with cooking (cockerels and goats roam the alleys) and childcare; a few mats and painted chests, used for storing the family valuables, constitute the only furniture.

You can get a closer look at home life at the sanitized **Traditional Siwan House** (Mon–Wed & Sun 10am–noon; £E1.50); enquire at the town council if the custodian isn't there. Set up with funds raised by the wife of the Canadian ambassador, who feared that few such mud-brick dwellings would survive another deluge and the trend towards breeze-block housing, it serves as a museum of traditional dress, jewellery and toys, resembling a handicrafts shop. There are numerous handicrafts shops in the vicinity of the **market** on Midan el-Souk, which is busiest on Fridays, when villagers come in to buy and sell. The other focus of life is the **Mosque of Sidi Suleyman**, built by King Fouad next to the whitewashed **tomb** of Siwa's patron sheikh (see box on p.592).

By following the Matrouh road out of town and then bearing right, you'll reach the unmistakable Jebel al-Mawta, or **Hill of the Dead** (daily 9am–2pm; £E20), also known as the Ridge of the Mummified. Amongst scores of XXVI Dynasty and Ptolemaic tombs reused by the Romans, who cut *loculli* for their own burials, four locked ones still retain murals or inscriptions. A custodian who lives nearby will unlock them if you make your presence known.

In the **Tomb of Si-Amun**, murals depict with great artistry a bearded, Greek-looking merchant and his family worshipping Egyptian deities; unfortunately, they were vandalized by Allied soldiers after the tomb's discovery in 1940, when the Siwans dug into the necropolis to escape air raids and also found the **Tomb of Mesu-Isis**. Another third-century BC creation, this was used for two burials although the decorators never got far beyond the entrance.

Whereas Si-Amun's tomb bespeaks of Cyrenaic influence, the **Tomb of the Crocodile** reflects Siwa's longstanding ties to the Fayoum, where the crocodile cult flourished – with a dash of Hellenistic style in the painting of gazelles nibbling at a tree.

Siwan festivals and weddings

Siwan festivals represent the most public side of a largely private culture, so it's worth making an effort to attend one. Since many Egyptians enjoy going to them, it is wise to reserve a room well in advance, and get there several days early, as buses to the oasis fill up nearer the time.

The largest and most famous is the **Siayha**, or **Tourism Festival**, which, despite its name, is a genuine event with a long tradition. Some 10,000 Siwans assemble at Jebel Dakhrour for three days of feasting, dancing and relaxation – acting as tourists in their own oasis. A sheikh from Sidi Barrani comes in to bless the feast, and local children enjoy a school holiday and a truckload of ice cream, sweets and sugar cane. Many non-Siwans and foreigners come too, and are made welcome. *Siayha* always occurs during the period of the full moon in October.

Two other festivals are celebrated by Muslims everywhere: the **Lesser Bairam**, at the end of Ramadan, occasioning festivities similar to those elsewhere in Egypt; and the **Corban Bairam** (Great Feast), which starts earlier in Siwa. The gathering of fuel and salt over the preceding nine days is reckoned to be as much a part of the event as the mass slaughter of sheep after festival prayers on the tenth day of Zoul Hagga. The sheep's hide is stewed together with its offal in an earthenware pot; its head and stomach are eaten the next day, when cuts of meat are distributed amongst relatives (new brides especially); and finally, any leftovers are preserved.

Ashura, on the tenth of Moharram, was once Siwa's principal feast, and fervently Shi'ite; the Fatimid Shia reached Egypt via the North African oases. Nowadays it's chiefly an event for children, who decorate their homes with palm stalks soaked in olive oil, and burn them at sunset, singing while the town is illuminated by torchlight. Afterwards the children go from house to house exchanging presents.

Throughout the year on Thursday evenings, a handful of Siwans perform **zikrs** at the **tomb of Sidi Suleyman** beside the mosque that bears his name. Tourists may attend if they dress and behave appropriately; women must cover their hair. Siwans still tell tales about this local saint, whose miraculous powers were manifest even before he was born, for when his pregnant mother craved fish, a pigeon dropped a fully cooked one at her feet. He is also said to have once conjured up a sandstorm to bury an army of Tebu raiders.

Weddings

Although you might be invited to join the tea-drinking crowd outside the bridegroom's family house, foreigners rarely witness the intricate ritual of **Siwan weddings**, which used to last a week but now take two or three days. Preceded by reciprocal visits of kinsfolk, and a ritual bath where the removal of an item of jewellery symbolizes her abandonment of maidenhood, the bride is "kidnapped" by her spouse's family, returned, and then delivered wrapped in a sheet. The traditional wedding dress of embroidered shawls and skirts is as flamboyant as the outdoor garb of married women is drab. Although urban Egyptian styles became popular in the 1990s, traditional attire is now making a comeback, along with dancing, singing and drinking homemade wine and spirits at wedding banquets in the villages.

Traditionally, a Siwan widow commanded the same *mahr* (dowry) as a virgin since both were "daughters of the forty ancestors", but could only remarry after one year of bereavement. The Siwans regarded newly bereaved widows as "devourers of the soul" (*ghulah*), and forced them to spend forty days in solitary confinement before they were "cleansed" – a taboo now largely lapsed.

The battered XXVI Dynasty **Tomb of Niperpathot** has a ruined court, side rooms, and a tiny burial chamber covered with red inscriptions, including praise of Niperpathot as "the straightforward one". For *baksheesh* the curator will unlock some other, unpainted tombs to show you **mummies** found at the Hill of the Dead, and a once-mummified skull, complete with hair.

Lastly, there's Siwa's incongruously pink and empty **Olympic stadium**, built within an army base to the south of town. With seating for 20,000, it could accommodate most of the population of the oasis, but is currently only used by a few army officers, as it awaits its place in Egypt's bid to host the Olympic Games some time in the future. The complex incorporates the *Mubarak Hotel* and a resthouse for the Minister of Defence; on an outcrop stands a **Presidential resthouse** originally built for King Fouad. Both can be seen on the road out towards Bir Wahed.

Crafts

Traditional **crafts** still flourish in the oasis, particularly pottery, basketmaking, and embroidery, with almost all the handicrafts made by women. They make traditional items such as black **robes** with orange or red piping, and embroidered **wedding dresses** embellished with antique coins, shells or beads, as well as cutting down old textiles into bags, tunics and waistcoats for the tourist market. Women also weave **carpets** and all kinds of **baskets** made from palm-fronds. The largest is the *tghara*, used for storing bread; smaller kinds include the red and green tasselled *nedibash* or platters like the *tarkamt*, traditionally used for serving sweets. They also mould **pottery** and fire it at home in bread-ovens: robust cooking and storage pots, delicate oil lamps, and a kind of baptismal crucible called the *shamadan en sebaa*. Popular buys include the *adjra*, used for washing hands, and *timjamait*, or incense burners; the smaller ones cost about £E5.

Unlike the gold-loving Egyptians, the Siwans have traditionally preferred **silver jewellery**, which served as bullion assets for a people mistrustful of banks and paper money. The designs are uniquely Siwan, influenced by Berber rather than Egyptian heritage. Local silversmiths once produced most of it, but in modern times it has largely come from Khan el-Khalili. Today, almost all the antique silver has ended up abroad and locals now prefer to buy gold jewellery from Alexandria, but Siwa Original Handicrafts, next to *Abdou's*, retains a few pieces (which you can't buy), and is one of several places selling modern replicas of traditional designs. Broad silver bracelets and oval rings wrought with geometric designs are the most popular items with visitors, while *Al-Salhat*, with its six pendants hung from silver and coral beads, is the easiest type of necklace to identify. You'll also recognize the *tiyalaqan*, a mass of chains tipped with bells, suspended from huge crescents; and an ornament for the head, consisting of silver hoops and bells suspended from matching chunks of bullion, called a *qasas*. Finally, there's the *aghraw*, a silver collar from which girls used to hang a decorative disc or *adrim*, that was removed on their wedding day – a custom that's no longer practised.

Eating and drinking

As the oases go, Siwa is good for eating, with several nice **restaurants** in the palm groves. *Kenouz*, on the rooftop of the *Shali Lodge*, has the fanciest menu, with spicy and sweet-and-sour dishes (£E15–20) as well as Egyptian staples, a menu-of-the-day (£E40–50), and stuffed goat, lamb or turkey by special order. Al-fresco alternatives where you can enjoy a full meal for £E25–30 include the *New Star*, which does a good beefsteak, and *Dunes*, whose chicken biryani is recommended. At all of these places you can recline on cushions and smoke a *sheesha*; *Nour el-Waha* also has backgammon. If you don't mind doing without a garden, *Abdou's* on Midan el-Souk is the place for soup, omelettes, *shish tawook* (chicken marinaded in yogurt and spices) and people-watching. The *East-West* (named after the rival clans of Shali) is good for breakfast, while *Alexander* is the most peaceful of the cafés off the bazaar. Providing there are customers, all are open till around midnight. **Alcohol** is only available at the *Taghaghien Touristic Camp* (which charges non-residents £E10 entry and sells lukewarm Sakkara beer and Egyptian wine), or to residents of the *Ecolodge* (who can consume unlimited imported liquor).

The shops on Midan el-Souk are well supplied with canned goods, sweets, juices and bottled water, with fresh bread available at the bakery, while the **market** stocks seasonal vegetables, dates and olives galore, which you can sample before buying. Look out also for the sweets made from dates – half a kilo stuffed with chocolate costs £E5.50, with almonds £E6.50.

Moving on from Siwa

Buses leave from a depot near the tourist office, where you should buy tickets the night before to be sure of getting a seat on the morning services (though standing passengers are seldom turned away). Daily buses to **Alexandria** (9hr; £E27) depart at 7am, 10am and 10pm, stopping en route at **Mersa Matrouh** (4–5hr; £E12), where a fourth bus, leaving Siwa at 1pm, terminates. Addition-ally, there is usually a **minivan** to Matrouh (£E12) in the afternoon, leaving from the Sidi Suleyman mosque.

The journey to **Bahariya Oasis** (420km) currently takes eight or nine hours, though the road is being upgraded, so should take five or six hours in future, depending on how much sand has blown across the road – having to dig cars out of sand drifts isn't uncommon, and traffic is so rare that a breakdown can leave you stranded for ages. **Permission** to use the road can be arranged within a day (except on Fri) by Mahdi at the tourist office, who will need a photocopy of your passport and visa to give to Military Intelligence, and a fee of US$10 plus £E11 per person.

Tourists seeking to split the cost of a **ride** to Bahariya (£E1300 to go directly, £E1500 to camp overnight in the desert along the way) can advertise for fellow travellers at the tourist office, but check first with the local safari operators how many they can take – some seat only three, others can pack in up to eight on benches. Those planning to **drive** themselves will need a 4WD with ample fuel and water, and be sure to register the licence number when obtaining military permission. The turn-off for Bahariya is 6km north of town on the right-hand side of the Mersa Matrouh road. With your own 4WD you can visit four unin-habited **oases** along the way, which are described on p.600.

Around Siwa Oasis

Although the **Siwa Oasis** depression is some 82km long and up to 28km wide, cultivated areas amount to less than 2000 acres and the total population is only 25,000; in some areas both population and cultivation have diminished since salination turned ancient gardens into barren *karshif*. Nearer town, dense **palm groves** and wiry olive trees are carefully tended in mud- and palm-leaf-walled gardens: dates and olives are the chief crops. Siwa has as many as 80,000 olive trees and over 310,000 palm trees, of which around 23,000 are male palms, valued only for the white heart at the top of the tree, a local delicacy.

Palms form the backdrop to most places that you're likely to go, especially the **pools** or **baths**, which for many visitors are the highlight of the oasis. The

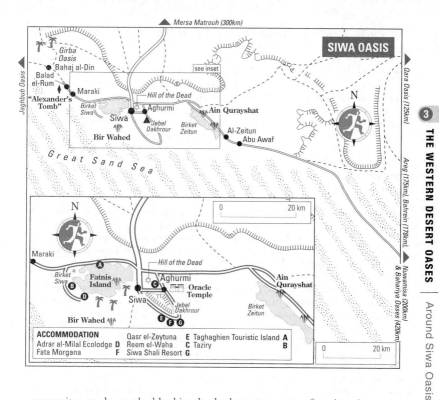

ACCOMMODATION

Adrar al-Milal Ecolodge	**D**	Qasr el-Zeytuna	**E**	Taghaghien Touristic Island	**A**
Fata Morgana	**F**	Reem el-Waha	**C**	Taziry	**B**
		Siwa Shali Resort	**G**		

nearer sites can be reached by bicycle, donkey *caretta* or on foot; just time your visit to avoid travelling in the hottest part of day. **Bicycles** can be rented from most hotels and handicraft shops for £E10 a day, but make sure you check the bike first before embarking on a long ride.

For remoter destinations such as Birket Zeitun or Bir Wahed, the tourist office can arrange half-day **excursions** by pick-up truck, while local safari operators can organize trips in 4WD vehicles. Recommended **safari outfits** that provide a decent service include Fahmy at the *Palm Trees* hotel (see p.590), Abu Bakr at the *East-West* restaurant (see opposite), Ali Abd Allah at Siwa Traditional Handicrafts (mobile ☏010 3041191, ✉el-daffasiwa@hotmail.com), and wild-life expert Ibrahim of Tash Tash & Abu Murai Safari, opposite the *Alexander Restaurant* (mobile ☏010 6170683). For those who fancy sand-boarding or need a sleeping bag, the Safari Adventure Company between the bank and the petrol station has a wide range of **equipment** for rent.

Be wary about accepting invitations to visit **private springs and gardens**. While financial motives aren't necessarily a deterrent – it's quite acceptable to pay for a good time – women without male escorts could find that intentions may well be lecherous.

Aghurmi and Jebel Dakhrour

This excursion is too far to walk in the heat, so it's best to hire a donkey *caretta* with a guide to ensure that you won't go astray on umarked roads and tracks. Just be sure to agree on a price beforehand; a two-hour circuit of the Oracle temple, the Tamusi Bath and Jebel Dakhrour should cost £E25 group-rate.

The road to Aghurmi begins at Siwa's main square and runs through the palm groves for 4km (a nice hour's walk if you're not going much further). Keep going straight on past the crossroads, and the modern village of **AGHURMI** appears shortly before the hill where the ancient Siwans built their first **fortified settlement** (daily 9am–4pm; £E20). Raised 12m above the plain and entered by a single gateway, Aghurmi had its own deep well (to the left, inside), making it impervious to sieges. The ruins are signposted as the "Alexander Crowning Hall", for it was here that the **Siwan Oracle** reposed in antiquity. Though some German architects have been criticized for crudely restoring the **temple** with concrete, it's no longer in danger of collapse and you can go inside again. There's a fabulous **view**, encompassing two salt lakes, Dakhrour and Siwa Town in the distance, and a great mass of palms.

Fakhry dates the existing temple to the reign of Amasis the Drunkard (570–526 BC) but reckons it evolved from a seventh- or eighth-century BC site dedicated to Amun-Re. Though others have attributed the primal shrine to the ram-headed Libyan god Ammon, experts agree that the **Oracle of Amun** was renowned from the XXVI Dynasty onwards.

Its history is subsequently much documented: a Persian army sent to destroy it was obliterated by the desert; emissaries sent by Cimon of Athens were told of his death as it happened; assured of success by the oracle, Eubotas of Cyrenaica took his own victory statue to the 93rd Olympiad; and Lysander tried bribery to win the oracle's endorsement of his claim to the Spartan throne.

But the most famous petitioner was **Alexander the Great**. Having liberated Egypt from its hated Persian rulers and ordered the creation of a city on the Mediterranean, Alexander hurried to Siwa in the spring of 331 BC. It's thought that he sought confirmation that he was the son of Zeus (whom the Greeks identified with Amun), but the oracle's reply – whispered by a priest through an aperture in the wall of the sanctuary – is unrecorded. Alexander kept it secret unto his death in Asia eight years later. Despite his personal wish to be buried near the oracle, he was probably interred in Alexandria, the capital he never saw – though two Greeks once claimed to have found his tomb in Siwa (see p.598).

From the ruins of Aghurmi you can gaze across thickets of palms to a cream-coloured pillar – part of a **ruined Temple of Amun** viewed side-on. To get there, continue along the road and take the signed turn to "Umm Ubayda". A painted bas-reliefed wall and giant blocks of rubble are all that remain of this once-substantial XXX Dynasty creation after it was dynamited by a treasure-hunting governor in 1897. Locally known as *Umm Ubaydah*, it was probably founded by Nectanebo II (360–343 BC), who also rebuilt the Temple of Hibis at Kharga Oasis.

Follow the path on to reach Ain Juba, known to tourists as the **Cleopatra Bath**, a deep circular pool of gently bubbling spring water, where local men bathe. Being fully visible to anyone passing along the trail, it's not a place where women can comfortably swim, and many prefer the **Tamusi Bath**, secluded 150m back along the path, where *Ali's Garden* serves tea and *sheeshas* as well as special meals and parties by arrangement.

Heading on from the Cleopatra Bath, bear left at the fork and take the first path on the right. A ten-minute walk through clover fields and groves of palms will bring you out in the desert near **Jebel Dakhrour**. This rugged massif is the site for the *Siyaha* **festival** in October, and affords stunning **views** from its summit. In contrast to the verdant oasis and the silvery salt lake, the southern horizon presents a desolate vista of crescent dunes and blackened mesas: the edge of the Great Sand Sea. The **hot sand** at Dakhrour is supposed to be good for rheumatic conditions and spinal problems, so sufferers come here to be buried up to their necks over three to five days during the summer months.

The loop road encircling Dakhrour runs past three hotels (see p.590) and leads back to Siwa Town via a military zone.

Bir Wahed

One of the best excursions Siwa can offer is a trip into the outer dunes of the Great Sand Sea, to **Bir Wahed** (Well One), 12km southwest of Siwa Town. Despite its prosaic name it's a magical spot: a **hot pool** the size of a large Jacuzzi, into which sulphurous water gushes; the run-off irrigates a garden around the pool. To soak up to your chest, puffing a *sheesha*, while the sun sets over the dunes and mesas all around, is a fantastic experience. You can climb outcrops or hunt for **fossils** in the vicinity, while on the way there or back you can plunge into a deep, jade-green **cold pool**, or sand-surf or roll down the sides of huge knife-edged **dunes**.

Most tourists visit Bir Wahed on a 4WD **excursion**, which can be organized by any of the safari operators on p.595. Expect to pay around £E80 per person for an overnight stay, including supper and breakfast, blankets and tents. Alternatively, you could **walk**, provided it's not too hot and you carry at least four litres of water. It takes four hours, following the road out past the Olympic stadium, fields and palm groves, and then jeep tracks into the dunes. Don't attempt this if a sandstorm has occurred in the last few days, or is forecast. You can sleep in a tent (£E10) and buy water, *fuul* and feta cheese at Bir Wahed, but anyone considering staying more than one night should bring supplies from town.

Whether you walk or go on an organized trip, you'll need a **permit** from the military to visit Bir Wahed, though if you are walking it is unlikely that this will ever be checked. Permits can be arranged by the tourist office for US$10 and £E10 per person, or your safari operator can do this for you.

Fatnis Island and Birket Siwa

Another popular destination is "Fantasy" or **Fatnis Island**, on the salt lake of Birket Siwa, 6km west of town. An easy bike ride, it can also be reached by *caretta* (£E20–25) or on foot (1hr). Take the road out past the town council, then the left-hand road at the first fork. En route you'll pass the Abu Alif Bath, where farmhands wash; beyond the palm groves, follow a causeway across salt-encrusted pans onto Fatnis Island, where palms surround a large circular tiled **pool**, fed by fresh water welling up from clefts in the rock 15m below. *Siwa Spa and Safari* sells tea and *sheeshas* and rents **snorkelling** or **diving** gear (£E50) if you fancy exploring the depths of the pool.

It's not hard to envisage a time when Fatnis will no longer be an island, for the **Birket Siwa** is receding as it becomes ever more saline, forming a thick crust that blackens the surrounding vegetation. Yet despite its faintly acrid smell the lake is extremely beautiful, with sculpted table-tops on the western horizon. The largest is **Jebel Beida** – the White Mountain – which the Siwans call in their own language *Adrar al-Milal*, and the Egyptians know as *Sidi Jaffar*.

On the far side of the mountain is the extraordinary **Adrar al-Milal Ecolodge** (see p.590), a vast, fantasy *qasr*-style hotel entirely built of *kharsif*, palm logs and translucent salt slabs (used instead of glass). The brainchild of Cairene environmental engineer Mounir Nematalla, the ecolodge uses local materials wherever possible, including olive wood and palm fibres for the furniture; and is designed to save energy and water and recycle waste products on its organic farm. Since it often has no guests at all, they don't mind the occasional visitor looking around, providing you get written permission from the *Shali Lodge* in town first. On the far shore of the lake is the similar but smaller *Taziry* hotel (see p.591). Both are reached by spur roads off the lakeside route to Maraki, which turns off the Matrouh highway 1km north of town. It's rather far to cycle (16km) so you'll need to take a car (£E30 return), or you could include it as a stopover on excursions to Balad el-Rum (see below).

Maraki and "Alexander's Tomb"

MARAKI is the collective name for several **villages** at the western end of the depression, separated from the main oasis by a rocky desert riddled with caves and tombs. The area was populous and intensively cultivated from Roman times until the fifteenth century, but is now mostly used for grazing by the **Bedouin** Al-Shihaybat tribe, which has settled at Bahaj al-Din. Most buildings are quite new as the old settlements were destroyed by the deluge of 1982, which forced residents to shelter in caves at Balad el-Rum.

In 1991, Maraki made news when Liana and Manos Souvaltzi announced their discovery of the "**Tomb of Alexander the Great**" beneath a ruined **Doric temple** near the village of **BALAD EL-RUM** ("Town of the Romans"). The Antiquities Council endorsed their claim, but backed off after the Greeks failed to refute criticism that they had misread vital inscriptions. The Souvaltzis then claimed that the tomb belonged to a Macedonian VIP and *might* shed light on the whereabouts of Alexander's tomb, which they still maintain is in Siwa Oasis, but SCA chief Dr Hawass halted excavations at the site (which remains guarded) and decreed that the Souvaltzis would never work in Egypt again. Check with Mahdi at the tourist office in case the site has reopened: in any case, he can arrange an **excursion** to the surrounding villages (from 1pm to sunset) for £E40 per person. If you're **driving** from Siwa, turn left off the Matrouh road 1km north of town and keep going.

To travel beyond the checkpoint at Bahaj al-Din requires a **permit** from the military, obtainable through the tourist office (US$10 and £E10 per person). At Bahaj al-Din, a track runs off to **Girba Oasis**, occupied by the Bedouin settlement of **Shiatta** and a detachment of soldiers. In olden times this was the *Masrab el-Ikhwan* ("Road of the Brotherhood") from Jaghbub Oasis in Libya, whereby Senussi preachers reached the Western Desert oases. (*Masrab* is the Siwan word for a camel route, called a *darb* in other oases.) Today the soldiers try to catch **smugglers** of hashish, electrical goods or videos; the punishment for capture may be summary execution.

Another hazard is the **minefields** along the Libyan border, sown by the British and Italians soon after they defined it in 1938 and by the Egyptians and Libyans since the 1970s. A corridor was cleared of mines to allow the passage of the 2003 Paris-Dakkar Rally, but nonetheless an Italian team was injured by a landmine. Beyond Shiatta is **off-limits** to outsiders, but should access ever be permitted there's an **underground river** waiting to be explored by divers.

Around Birket Zeitun

The largest salt lake in the oasis, **Birket Zeitun** is visible from Aghurmi and Jebel Dakhrour. Acres of mud the texture of dried cornflakes attest to the lake's slow recession. Only the far shore is inhabited, with villages that flourished in Roman times before centuries of slow decline set in, and US aid-built houses that nobody has ever lived in. The lake's increasing salinity is both the cause and result of depopulation: as fewer irrigation works are maintained, more of the warm water from the **Ain Qurayshat** spring flows unused into the lake, crystallizing mineral salts as it evaporates. The source is enclosed by an industrial-sized concrete tank where you can bathe, though beware of the underwater ledges.

Better bathing, however, can be found around 35km southwest of Siwa Town at **ABU SHUROUF**, where there's a large, kidney-shaped pool of cool, clear, azure water with bug-eyed fishes swimming about, opposite the Hayat mineral water bottling plant. The village beyond the pool is remarkable for harbouring all the female **donkeys** in the oasis, which are kept and mated here. In Siwan parlance, "Have you been to Abu Shurouf?" is a euphemism for "Have you had sex?"

Further south along the lake, the village of **AL-ZEITUN** was once a model Senussi community tending the richest gardens in the oasis, until it was abandoned following an Italian bombing raid in 1940. Near the eastern end of the ruins is a small smoke-blackened kiosk-**temple** where the locals once sheltered from bombs, which nowadays harbours bats. Two kilometres further on, the hillside is pockmarked with the eerie **Roman tombs** of **Abu Awaf**, overlooking the last **checkpoint** in the oasis before the *Darb Siwa* to Bahariya Oasis enters the deep desert (see p.600).

Siwa's tourist office can arrange a half-day **tour** of these sites for small groups, for £E40 per person including lunch.

Qara Oasis and the Qattara Depression

If you have the means and are seriously into desert travel, **Qara Oasis** has a compelling fascination. The smallest and poorest of the oases, populated by the descendants of runaway slaves, it has been described as "Siwa yesterday". Visitors are so rare that the villagers turn out to welcome them and serve a meal in their honour. Until flooding rendered it unsafe in 1982, the Qarawis occupied a Shali-like labyrinth atop "a solitary white mushroom of rock", edged by a "high smooth wall, impregnable to raiders, with one black tunnel for a street". Now, most families live in new houses on the plain. Legend states that Qarawi ancestors were once cursed by the Devil that their population would never exceed 317 – modern-day Qarawis deny this, pointing out that it currently stands at 370.

The shortest **route** from Siwa to Qara is the *Masrab Khidda* (125km), but its rough terrain and featureless mud flats make it essential to have someone who knows the way. Alternatively, you can head north towards Matrouh and turn off at the checkpoint just before the Bir Nous resthouse, on to a dirt road to Qara. Though not a regular destination for **safaris**, it's possible to find a pick-up to take you there and back for £E300, while the *Palm Trees Hotel* may do it for £E500 (group rates). Either way you'll require a **permit** from the tourist office (see p.589).

Northeast of Qara the land plummets into the **Qattara Depression**, which is seven times the size of all the Western Desert oases combined and may be the largest depression in the world. At 60–134 metres below sea level, it is one of the lowest places on earth, and the lowest point in Africa. Ever since Dr Ball first proposed it in the 1920s, Egyptian planners have dreamed of piping water 38km from the Mediterranean to the depression, utilizing the fall in height to generate hydroelectricity and run desalination plants and irrigation systems. But all attempts have foundered through lack of capital, and nothing seems likely to happen in the future. There is, however, exploration for **oil** at many points in the desert between Qattara and Mersa Matrouh, which explains the upgraded

Checkpoint Charlies

Travelling from Siwa to Bahariya or on other roads across the most desolate tracts of the Western Desert, spare a thought for the luckless **soldiers** at the **checkpoints**, marooned there for forty days at a stretch, with only each other and a pet cat or dog for company. Young conscripts, far from home and unused to the rigors of desert life, they are utterly bored and welcome any diversion that passing travellers can offer. They're not seeking *baksheesh*, but certainly appreciate Arabic newspapers or magazines (available in Cairo, Alex or Matrouh but not in Siwa or Bahariya), fresh fruit or candy – and such **gifts** will smooth your way through the inevitable licence- and permit-checks. Remember, these guys are here to ensure that if a car breaks down in the desert its passengers will be missed and a search launched – so it's only fair to look out for them, too.

tracks that crisscross the wilderness. With a permit, even 2WDs can use the **El-Alamein–Bahariya desert road** (273km) that dips into the depression at **Naqb Abu Dweis** (mined on both sides of the *wadi*; don't leave the road), and carries on past a series of checkpoints and turn-offs to drilling facilities, before joining the Cairo–Bahariya highway. While crossing the depression, it passes the uninhabited **Maghra Oasis**, where Jurassic **fossils** of mastadons, reptiles, fish and mammals have been found; petrified wood lies around, and there's a salt lake.

From Siwa to Bahariya: Areg, Bahrein, Nuwamisa and Sitra oases

The ancient *Darb Siwa* caravan route from Siwa to Bahariya has been upgraded to a **road** for some 200km, with the rest due to be finished by 2006. Six **checkpoints** en route provide assurance that vehicles which break down will be missed, but otherwise there are no sources of water, nor any fuel for 420km – and mobile phones are beyond signal range.

Safari operators in Siwa charge £E1300 to take a car-load of passengers to Bahariya, passing by a series of uninhabited oases off the road. Their beauty can only be appreciated by taking a longer 4WD excursion and camping **overnight** in one of the oases. Some outfits will take a group for £E1500 (meals included), and for £E1600-plus will tag another night in the White Desert (see p.544) on to the end of your trip.

Areg Oasis lies 1km off the road, about 175km from Siwa, girdled by an escarpment which 4WDs should only descend with caution and in pairs, though it's easy to scramble down on foot, providing you avoid the brittle overhangs of the cliffs that ring the depression. The eroded floor resembles shredded cloth, surrounded by striated buff and white chalk buttes looking like giant brioches that have sat in the oven for too long. The oasis was regarded as a haunt of bandits by nineteenth-century travellers, and its cliffs are riddled with **tombs**. A tablet from Alexandria records that the population of Siwa, Bahrein and other now-deserted oases numbered 400,000 in Persian times.

Bahrein Oasis lurks off the other side of the road, down a track from the third checkpoint. Just as you're wondering why you bothered to cross this dull stretch of desert, the oasis appears in all its glory. Named after its two azure salt lakes, Bahrein is awash with custard-coloured sand, hemmed in by giant croissant-like buttes, riddled with **tombs** whose *loculi* date them from Greco-Roman times, where you can still find bones. In 2004, Italian archeologists unearthed a ruined **XXX Dynasty temple** here. Seductive as they look, the

salt lakes are surrounded by mushy sand and salt crusts that can trap unwary vehicles, and if safari groups camp here, they usually do so in the palm groves on the far side, away from the mosquitoes and protected from sandstorms.

Nuwamisa Oasis looks equally lovely, with a salt lake rimmed by palms and crescent cliffs – but its name, Oasis of the Mosquitoes, is all too true. Literally millions of **mosquitoes** swarm as soon as the sun goes down, making camping a nightmare, even if you're all zipped up in your tent. For that reason, travellers often hasten on to **Sitra Oasis**, which isn't so badly infested and used to be a watering hole for Bedouin smugglers bringing hashish into Egypt. During the last 45km of the journey to Bahariya the road skirts the **Ghard Kebir** ("Great Dunes"), whose sandy crests were likened by Bagnold to "unclipped horses' manes". The dunes are slowly making their way south from the Qattara Depression, destined to arrive in Bahariya in a few hundred years.

Alexandria and the Mediterranean coast

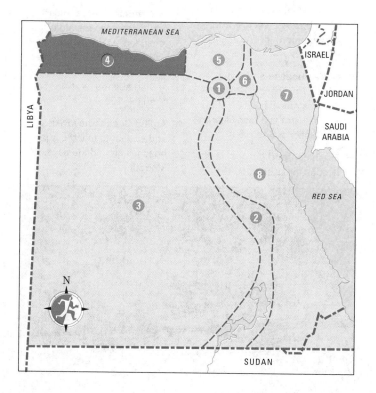

CHAPTER 4

Highlights

✳ **Bibliotheca Alexandrina** The city's new library is a stunning example of contemporary architecture, aimed at reviving the legendary "Mother Library" of antiquity. See p.627

✳ **Catacombs of Kom es-Shoqafa** This eerie subterranean Roman necropolis is full of bizarre carvings, with a dining room for mourners. See p.628

✳ **Coffee houses and patisseries** *The Trianon*, *Athineos* and *Pastroudis* have an old-world charm and many literary associations. See p.634

✳ **Fresh seafood** Alexandria is famous for its seafood restaurants, where customers select their meal from a mound of fish and crustaceans. See p.635

✳ **Diving** Explore the underwater remains of Cleopatra's Palace, Roman galleys, French warships and German U-boats. See p.638 & p.650

✳ **El-Alamein** The war museum and cemeteries are stark reminders of the decisive battle in 1942, and the hinterland harbours wrecked tanks and an abandoned field hospital. See p.644

✳ **Agiiba Beach** The loveliest and easiest to reach of the beaches around Mersa Matrouh. See p.652

△ War Museum, El-Alamein

Alexandria and the Mediterranean coast

For Ancient Egyptians, the **Mediterranean coast** marked the edge of the "Great Green", the measureless sea that formed the limits of the known world. Life and civilization meant the Nile Valley and the Delta – an outlook that still seems to linger in the country's subconscious. For, despite the white beaches, craggy headlands and turquoise sea that stretch for some five hundred kilometres, much of the Egyptian Med is eerily vacant and underpopulated.

Anywhere on the European side of the sea, mass tourism would have taken hold years ago. Here, though, in part due to a lack of freshwater sources, towns are few and generally small, and far outnumbered by military bases. Such tourism as exists is largely Egyptian and family-oriented; there is virtually no alcohol on sale and standards of dress verge on the puritanical. Foreign women, especially, could well find that the hassles far outweigh any pleasure to be gained here – in contrast to the much more relaxed beaches in Sinai. The chief resorts are **Mersa Matrouh** (a jumping-off point for Siwa Oasis) and **Sidi Abd el-Rahman**, while historical interest focuses chiefly on the World War II battle-field of **El-Alamein** and **wreck-diving** off Sidi Barrani and Sollum.

Alexandria, however, is an entirely different animal. Egypt's second city feels as Mediterranean and cosmopolitan as Athens or Marseille, its nineteenth-century architecture redolent of the colonial days immortalized by E.M. Forster, the poet Cavafy and, most famously, Lawrence Durrell. Its main sights, however, come from a different age, some dating from its time as the capital of Greco-Roman Egypt, and the seat of Cleopatra, the last of the Ptolemies; and others, such as the stunning modern library, the Bibliotheca Alexandrina, bringing the city bang into the twenty-first century. Antiquities from all eras can be viewed *in situ* underwater, as well as in local museums.

As for the **weather**, Egypt's Mediterranean coast gets hotter and drier the further west you travel, but Alexandria can be cold and windy in the winter, with torrential downpours and waves crashing over the Corniche for days on end. And should you happen to be there over New Year, beware of the blizzard of crockery that Alexandrians throw out of their windows at midnight. The Mediterranean Sea doesn't become warm enough for **swimming** till June, but you can be pretty sure of continuous sunshine from April until November. One date to note is March 29, 2006, when a **total solar eclipse** will take place over

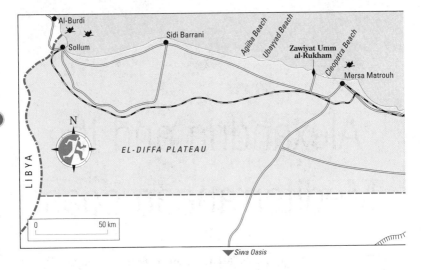

Mersa Matrouh, Siwa Oasis and Libya. Eclipse-watchers are already reserving accommodation, so if you plan to be here for the event, book ahead.

Alexandria (El-Iskandariya)

Alexandria, princess and whore. The royal city and the anus mundi.

Lawrence Durrell, *The Alexandria Quartet*

A hybrid city characterized by Durrell as the "Capital of Memory", Alexandria turns its back on the rest of Egypt and faces the Mediterranean, as if contemplating its glorious past. One of the great cities of antiquity, Alex slumbered for 1300 years until it was revived by Mohammed Ali and transformed by Europeans, who gave the city its present shape and made it synonymous with cosmopolitanism and decadence. This era came to an end in the 1950s with the mass flight of non-Egyptians and a dose of revolutionary puritanism, but Alexandria's beaches, restaurants and breezy climate still attract hordes of Cairenes during the summer, while its jaded historical and literary mystique remains appealing to foreigners.

Alexandria in history

When **Alexander the Great** wrested Egypt from the Persian empire in 332 BC at the age of 25, he decided against Memphis, the ancient capital, in favour of building a new city linked by sea to his Macedonian homeland. Choosing a site near the fishing village of **Rhakotis**, where two limestone spurs formed a natural harbour, he gave orders to his architect, Deinocrates, before travelling

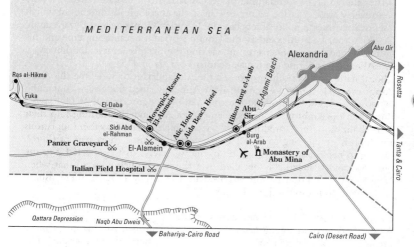

on to Siwa and thence to Asia, where he died eight years later. His corpse was subsequently returned to Egypt, where the priests refused burial at Memphis; its final resting place remains a mystery, although most archeologists believe it lies somewhere beneath Alexandria.

Thereafter Alexander's empire was divided amongst his Macedonian generals, one of whom took Egypt and adopted the title **Ptolemy I Soter**, founding a dynasty (323–30 BC). Avid promoters of Hellenistic culture, the **Ptolemies** made Alexandria an intellectual powerhouse: among its scholars were Euclid, the "father of geometry", and Eratosthenes, who accurately determined the circumference and diameter of the earth. Alexandria's great lighthouse, the **Pharos**, was literally and metaphorically a beacon, rivalled in fame only by the city's library – the **Bibliotheca Alexandrina** – the foremost centre of learning in the ancient world.

While the first three Ptolemies were energetic and enlightened, the latter members of the dynasty are remembered as decadent and dissolute – perhaps due to their brother-sister marriages, in emulation of the pharaohs and gods of Ancient Egypt – and relied on Rome to maintain their position. Even the bold **Cleopatra VII** (51–30 BC) came unstuck after her lover, Julius Caesar, was murdered, and his successor in Rome (and her bed), Mark Antony, was defeated by Octavian. The latter hated her and so detested Cleopatra's capital at Alexandria that he banned Roman citizens from entering Egypt on the pretext that its religious orgies were morally corrupting.

Roman rule and Arab conquest

Whereas Alexandria's Egyptians and Greeks had previously respected one another's deities and even syncretized them into a common cult (the worship of Serapis), religious conflicts developed under **Roman rule** (30 BC–313 AD). The empire regarded Christianity, which was supposedly introduced by St Mark in 45 AD, as subversive, and the persecution of Christians from 250 AD onwards reached a bloody apogee under Emperor Diocletian, when the Copts maintain that 144,000 believers were martyred. (The Coptic Church dates its chronology from 284 AD, the "Era of Martyrs", rather than Christ's birth.)

After the emperor Constantine made **Christianity** the state religion, a new controversy arose over the nature of Christ, the theological subtleties of which essentially masked a political rebellion by Egyptian **Copts** against Byzantine (ie Greek) authority. In Alexandria, the Coptic patriarch became supreme and his monks waged war against paganism, sacking the Serapis Temple and library in 391 AD and murdering the female scholar Hypatia in 415.

Local hatred of Byzantium disposed the Alexandrians to welcome the **Arab conquest** (641 AD), whose commander, Amr, described the city as containing "4000 palaces, 4000 baths, 400 theatres, 1200 greengrocers and 40,000 Jews". But while the Arabs incorporated elements of Alexandrian learning into their own civilization, they cared little for a city which "seemed to them idolatrous and foolish", preferring to found a new capital at Fustat (now part of Cairo). Owing to neglect and the silting up of the waterways that connected it to the Nile, Alexandria inexorably declined over the next millennium, so that when Napoleon's expeditionary force arrived in 1798, they found a mere fishing village with four thousand inhabitants.

Mohammed Ali and colonial rule

Alexandria's **revival** sprang from the sultan Mohammed Ali's desire to make Egypt a commercial and maritime power, which necessitated a seaport. The Mahmudiya Canal, finished in 1820, once again linked Alexandria to the Nile, while a harbour, docks and arsenal were created with French assistance. European merchants erected mansions and warehouses, building outwards from the Place des Consuls (modern-day Midan Tahrir), and the city's population soared to 230,000.

Nationalist resentment of foreign influence fired the **Orabi revolt** of 1882, in retaliation for which British warships shelled the city, whose devastation was completed by arsonists and looters. Yet such was Alexandria's vitality and commercial importance that it quickly recovered.

Having survived bombing during World War II, Alexandria experienced new turmoil in the postwar era, as anti-British riots expressed rising **nationalism**. The **revolution** that forced King Farouk to sail into exile from Alexandria in 1952 didn't seriously affect the "foreign" community (many of whom had lived here for generations) until the Anglo–French–Israeli assault on Egypt during the Suez Crisis of 1956. The following year, however, Nasser expelled all French and British citizens and nationalized foreign businesses, forcing a hundred thousand non-Egyptians to emigrate. Jewish residents also suffered after the discovery of an Israeli-controlled sabotage unit in the city, so that by the year's end only a few thousand Alexandrian Greeks and Jews remained. Foreign institutions, street names and suchlike were Egyptianized, and the custom of moving the seat of government to Alexandria during the hot summer months was ended.

Contemporary Alex – and the city in literature

Though "old" Alexandrians undoubtedly regret the **changes** since Suez, Durrell's complaint that they produced "leaden uniformity" and rendered Alexandria "depressing beyond endurance" seems jaundiced and unjustified. Egypt's second city (pop. 5,500,000) has become more Egyptian and less patrician, but it doesn't lack contrasts and vitality. The difference is that middle-class Egyptians set the tone, not Greeks, Levantines and European expats. If Cavafy, *arak* and child-brothels represented the old days, McDonald's, Coke and Nike symbolize a new and brasher kind of cosmopolitanism. Overcrowding, pollution and traffic have all worsened, but the Med still keeps Alex cool.

With few monuments to show for its ancient lineage and much of its modern heritage rejected, one finds Alexandria's past in faded coffee houses, minutiae such as old nameplates, the reminiscences of aged Arabs, Greeks and Jews, and in its **literary dimension**. E.M. Forster's *Alexandria: A History and a Guide* (1922) remains the classic source book, though Forster reckoned that the best thing he did was to publicize the work of Alexandrian-born Constantine Cavafy. Nostalgia, excess, loss and futility – the leitmotifs of Cavafy's poems – also pervade Lawrence Durrell's *The Alexandria Quartet*: indeed, Durrell used Cavafy as the basis for his character Balthazar. Generally, though, Durrell had little time for Egyptians, and his novels are not well-regarded in Egypt. Michael Haag's *Alexandria – City of Memory* evokes the world of three writers inspired by the city's history and society, though bearing in mind the ancient adage that "a big book is a big nuisance", you might prefer Naguib Mahfouz's *Miramar*, a concise evocation of post-revolutionary Alex from an Egyptian standpoint. For foreign views of Alex, check out Charlie Pye-Smith's *The Other Nile*, Douglas Kennedy's *Beyond the Pyramids*, and Paul William Roberts' *River in the Desert*.

Though travel writers have ignored Alex since the mid-1990s, books on the city's **archeology** and cultural heritage continue to be published. The French archeologist Jean-Yves Empereur of the Centre d'Etudes Alexandrines (Ⓦ www.cea.com.eg) has written two excellent guides to the city's sites and history, *Alexandria Revealed* and *Alexandria Rediscovered*, plus guidebooks to the Greco-Roman Museum and the Catacombs; while the Hungarian Egyptologist Győző Vörös touches on the city's maritime history in his book *Taposiris Magna: Port of Isis*. All these books are available in local bookshops (see p.639) or can be consulted in the library of the Archeological Society of Alexandria, 6 Sharia Mahmoud Mokhtar (Mon–Wed & Sun 4.30–7.30pm; ☎03/486-0650).

Approaches to Alex

Alex is easily reached **from Cairo**, with a choice of train, bus, service taxi or plane. Buses and service taxis offer two routes, travelling by the verdant Desert Road past the turn-off for Wadi Natrun (whose monasteries are covered in Chapter 3), or by the hazardous, congested Delta Road, which is much slower, though the distance is roughly similar (about 225km). Remember that transport can get booked up from mid-June to late September, so reserve seats unless you're prepared to use service taxis.

The best **buses**, which do the journey in three hours, are operated by Superjet from outside Cairo's *Ramses Hilton* hotel; slightly cheaper and less comfortable services, run by the West Delta bus company, leave from the Turgoman Garage and the Aboud Terminal. The fastest **trains**, a/c Spanish and Turbini services, both leave three times daily and take just over two hours. There is also the so-called French service that has nine daily departures, takes thirty minutes longer and costs thirty percent less. **Service taxis** do the run in about three hours, their advantage being that they leave all through the day, as soon as they're full; in Cairo both car- and minibus-taxis cluster outside Ramses Station and at the Aboud Terminal, their drivers bawling "*Iskandariya! Iskandariya!*". **Flying** from Cairo (50min; £E330 one-way) is not really worth it: it won't save you any time, once you take getting to and from the airports into account, and there are also safety concerns about Alex's airports. For full details of bus, train, taxi and flight schedules and terminals, see Cairo "Travel Details" at the end of Chapter 1 (p.298).

Getting to Alex **from other parts of Egypt**, buses and/or service taxis are your best bet. Transport from the Delta and the Canal Zone is quite regular;

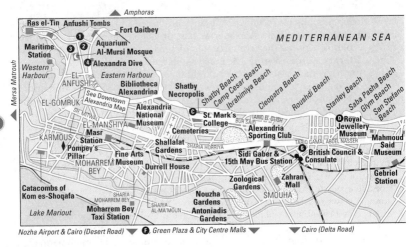

Amphoras

MEDITERRANEAN SEA

Nozha Airport & Cairo (Desert Road) ▼ **F**, Green Plaza & City Centre Malls ▼ ▼ Cairo (Delta Road)

from the Nile Valley, daily buses run from Beni Suef. See the relevant chapters for details.

Arrival, orientation and information

West Delta and Superjet **buses** drop passengers at the **15th May Station**, in Sidi Gaber, west of downtown; you can reach the centre by minibus #1, tram #2 or #4 (25pt), or taxi (locals pay £E5, foreigners around £E10). Trains from Cairo usually stop at Sidi Gaber Station (north of the bus terminal) before terminating at **Masr Station,** about 1km south of downtown Midan Sa'ad Zaghloul, which you can reach by walking up Sharia Nabi Daniel (10–15min). **Service taxis** are likely to wind up on **Midan el-Gumhorriya**, outside Masr Station, but might terminate at the outlying **Moharrem Bey** depot; from there, catch a minibus to Midan el-Gumhorriya (25pt) or a taxi into the centre (£E5).

Alexandria is currently served by two **airports**, neither of which lives up to its "International" status. **Nozha**, 5km south of the city (used by Lufthansa, Olympic and EgyptAir), has such decrepit runways and air-traffic control that other airlines use an ex-military airfield at **Burg al-Arab**, 60km west of Alex. Neither airport has any exchange facilities, ATMs or duty-free shops, so passengers arriving from abroad need to purchase Egyptian currency beforehand, to pay for getting into town. However, if you're planning to get a **visa** on arrival, this can only be bought with US dollars, pounds sterling or euros. Public **transport** into town is limited to bus #555 (£E6) from Burg al-Arab to Midan Sa'ad Zaghloul (scheduled to coincide with flight arrivals and departures); a taxi to Alex from Burg al-Arab costs £E80–100; from Nozha £E10–15.

Orientation, maps and street names

Alexandria runs along the Mediterranean for 20km without ever venturing more than 8km inland – a true waterfront city. Its great **Corniche** sweeps around the **Eastern Harbour** and along the coast past a string of city **beaches** to **Montazah** and **Ma'amoura**, burning out before the final beach at **Abu Qir**. Away from the beach, visitors hang around the downtown quarter of

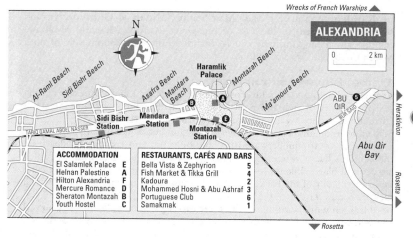

ALEXANDRIA

0   2 km

ACCOMMODATION		RESTAURANTS, CAFÉS AND BARS	
El Salamlek Palace	**E**	Bella Vista & Zephyrion	**5**
Helnan Palestine	**A**	Fish Market & Tikka Grill	**4**
Hilton Alexandria	**F**	Kadoura	**2**
Mercure Romance	**D**	Mohammed Hosni & Abu Ashraf	**3**
Sheraton Montazah	**B**	Portuguese Club	**6**
Youth Hostel	**C**	Samakmak	**1**

El-Manshiya, where most of the restaurants, hotels and nightclubs are within a few blocks either side, or inland, of **Midan Sa'ad Zaghloul**.

The Corniche (and breezes blowing inland) make basic orientation quite simple, but the finer points can still be awkward. Unlike Cairo, downtown Alex has yet to be properly mapped, and the standard Lehnert & Landrock *Map of Alexandria* omits whole streets and blocks. **Street names** are also problematic, for signs don't always square with the latest official designation or popular usage (usually one change behind). Other street names have simply been Arabicized: Rue or Place to Sharia or Midan; "Alexandre le Grand" to "Iskander el-Akbar". In the downtown area, most of the signs are in French and Arabic, and people may use either variant when giving directions. A historical map of *Archeological Sites of Alexandria*, published by the Alexandria Preservation Trust, is on sale at bookshops (see p.639).

Information

The main **tourist office** off the southwest corner of Midan Sa'ad Zaghloul (daily 8.30am–6pm; Ramadan 9am–4pm; ☎03/485-1556) is staffed by very helpful English-speakers, who can answer most questions as well as provide the free booklet, *Alexandria Night and Day*. It has branches at Nozha airport (daily 8am–8pm; ☎03/425-0528), Masr Station (daily 8am–8pm; ☎03/392-5985) and Sidi Gaber Station (daily 8.30am–3pm; ☎03/426-3953) and a part-time one at the Maritime Station (irregular hours; no phone). The university and foreign cultural centres are obvious sources of **contacts**; on Thursday nights you'll find half the expat community in the *Portuguese Club* or *Cap d'Or* (see p.636). There are also some useful **websites** relating to Alex – Ⓦwww.alexandriatour.com has a wide range of practical information and links, while Ⓦwww.houseofptolemy .org covers the city's ancient and modern history.

City transport

Downtown is compact enough to walk around, and along the Corniche to Fort Qaitbey makes a healthy constitutional (35–50min). However, you really need transport to reach other outlying areas. The main downtown terminals are **Ramleh**; the square outside Masr Station, **Midan el-Gumhorriya**; and **Midan Khartoum**, to the east of the Greco-Roman Museum. Minibuses running along the Corniche can be boarded from the seafront side of both Midan Orabi and Sa'ad Zaghloul.

Trams, buses and minibuses

Trams are integral to Alex life, conveying all classes at a snail's pace and rattling past the houses of rich and poor alike. Originally built in Britain, the trams currently in service were a gift from Denmark in the 1960s. Services run from 5.30am to midnight (1am in summer), with fares between 25pt and 75pt. Destinations and route numbers are in Arabic only, but you can get an idea from the vehicle's livery where it's heading, as all trams running east from Ramleh are painted blue, while those going west are yellow and red. More arcane clues lie in the colour of the background to the numeral(s) on the signboard, which identify routes #1 (blue), #2 (red), #3 (blue on yellow), #4 (white on blue) and #5 (black on white). On trams with three carriages, the middle one is **reserved for women**. Some have double-decker carriages, with a fab view from the top floor. Standing downstairs, you may have difficulty seeing the names of the tram stops, which are written in English on certain routes. All eastbound trams stop at the Sporting Club except for #4.

Run by the city and private operators, **buses** (50pt–£E1.50) are also numbered in Arabic and keep similar schedules to the trams, but are faster, with passengers boarding on the run between Sa'ad Zaghloul, Tahrir and El-Gumhorriya squares – the major terminals. City buses are often very crowded, and made worse by gropers and pickpockets. Whenever possible, it's best to use another form of transport. Fortunately, **minibuses** offer the chance of a reasonably comfortable ride and cover many of the same routes. Those run by the municipality are blue and white, while privately operated minibuses are blue. Both charge the same fares (50pt–£E2.25) and run similar hours to trams and buses.

Trams

#1 and #2	Ramleh to Victoria, via the Sporting Club and Roushdi
#4	Midan St Katerina to Moharrem Bey
#15	Ramleh to Ras el-Tin, via El-Gomruk and El-Anfushi (near Fort Qaitbey)
#16	Midan St Katerina to Pompey's Pillar and the Catacombs
#25	Midan Orabi (Unknown Soldier) to Sidi es-Sheikh (near Sidi Gaber station)
#36	Ras el-Tin to San Stefano

Buses

#3	Ramleh to Hannoville, via the Corniche
#11	Ras el-Tin to Montazah, via the Corniche
#460	Midan Khartoum to Hannoville, via the Corniche
#555	Midan Sa'ad Zaghloul to Burg al-Arab airport
#709	Midan St Katerina to Pompey's Pillar

Minibuses

#1	Midan Sa'ad Zaghloul to the 15th May bus station/Sidi Gaber station and on to Sidi Bishr
#2	Ramleh to Hannoville

#735	Ras el-Tin to Montazah, via the Corniche
#736	Midan St Katerina to Ma'amoura, via the Corniche
#736	Ramleh to Ma'amoura, via the Corniche
#765	Masr Station to El-Agami beach (Hannoville)
#766	Ras el-Tin to Abu Qir, via Sidi Gaber and the Corniche from Shatby onwards
#768	Masr Station to Abu Qir, inland

Taxis, caleches and car rental

Regular black-and-yellow (or orange) **taxis** never use meters and will charge whatever they can get away with (especially going to Masr Station or any other departure point). You should pay about £E4 for a ride across downtown (say, to Shatby), and £E20–30 for a trip to Montazah. The larger, blue Peugeots are a lot pricier than regular taxis, so don't take one by mistake.

Leather-hooded, brass-trimmed **horse-drawn carriages** solicit passengers with cries of "*caleche, caleche*" outside Masr Station and along the Corniche. Providing you don't get stuck in traffic jams or feel self-consciously "colonial", they can be a good way of touring the quieter parts of Alex and enjoying the sea breezes. You'll have to negotiate a price – reckon on roughly £E8–10 an hour.

Renting a car with a driver makes sense if you're going to visit El-Alamein or the remoter sites west of Alexandria. El Lord, 6 Sharia Goul Gamal in Roushdi (℡03/546-4316), charges £E130–195 a day depending on the type of car, with 120km mileage included; Avis in the *Hotel Cecil* (daily 8am–8pm; ℡03/480-7055), has Mercedes and Peugeots (three/six hours rental £E90/£E170) and charges £E450 for a day-trip to El-Alamein and St Mina.

Accommodation

Alexandria's **hotels** include old *pensions* and glitzy citadels of *Sheraton*-style internationalism, though there is little in the mid-range budget. A sea view is a big plus, and hotels charge accordingly – though in cheap hotels these rooms are freezing in wintertime. Two drawbacks that only later become apparent are **tram noise** and giant orange **cockroaches** – the twin banes of hotels near the waterfront. Basically, you either learn to live with them or move further inland. Bear in mind that the choice and availability of rooms is limited during high season, when **reservations** are advisable. The **price codes** quoted below are for the high season and refer to rooms without a sea view. You can count on hot water, and breakfast being included, unless stated otherwise. The downtown hotels are all marked on the map on pp.614–615.

Alexandria's **youth hostel** (℡03/592-5459) is on a main road opposite St Mark's College in Shatby, 1km east of the downtown area. Take tram #1 or #2 from Ramleh to the College and turn towards the Corniche; the hostel is at 32 Sharia Bur Said, next to some Greco-Roman tombs. Its triple-bed rooms (£E25) are no cheaper than a double room in some budget hotels in the centre, and the location is extremely noisy and only really convenient for the library.

If you're intending to stay a while, **renting a flat** makes sense. Most expats stay in the Roushdi district, a few kilometres east of the downtown area, where a two-bedroom flat costs £E1500–2500 a month. In downtown El-Manshiya, you can get the same for £E1500 a month.

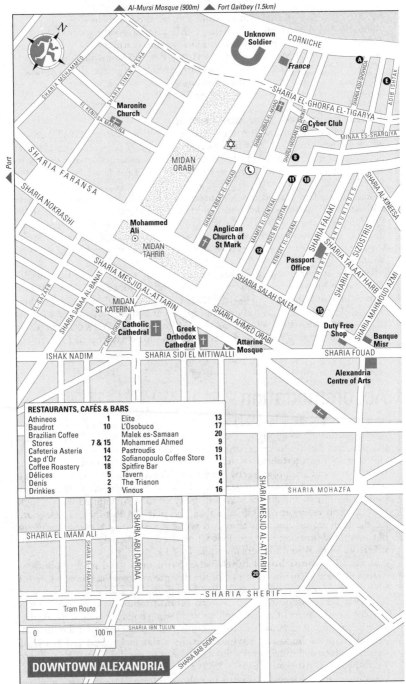

Al-Mursi Mosque (900m) ▲ Fort Qaitbey (1.5km)

RESTAURANTS, CAFÉS & BARS

Athineos	1	Elite	13
Baudrot	10	L'Osobuco	17
Brazilian Coffee		Malek es-Samaan	20
Stores	7 & 15	Mohammed Ahmed	9
Cafeteria Asteria	14	Pastroudis	19
Cap d'Or	12	Sofianopoulo Coffee Store	11
Coffee Roastery	18	Spitfire Bar	8
Délices	5	Tavern	6
Denis	2	The Trianon	4
Drinkies	3	Vinous	16

Tram Route

0   100 m

DOWNTOWN ALEXANDRIA

Pompey's Pillar & The Catacombs

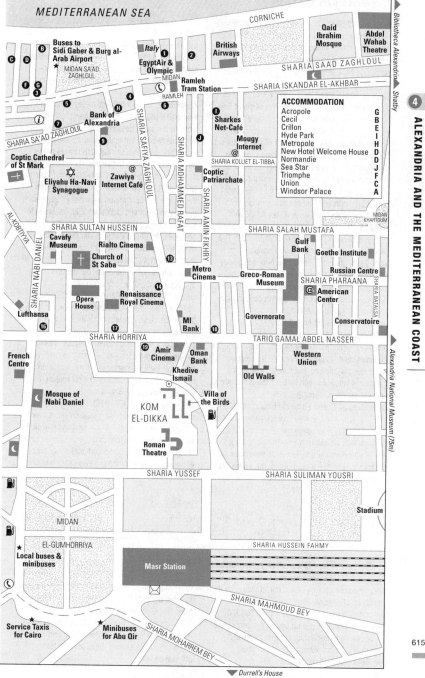

MEDITERRANEAN SEA

CORNICHE

Qaid Ibrahim Mosque

Abdel Wahab Theatre

Buses to Sidi Gaber & Burg al-Arab Airport

Italy

British Airways

EgyptAir & Olympic

MIDAN SA'AD ZAGHLOUL

Ramleh Tram Station

SHARIA SAAD ZAGHLOUL

SHARIA ISKANDAR EL-AKHBAR

RAMLEH

Bank of Alexandria

SHARIA SAFIYA ZAGHLOUL

Sharkes Net-Café

Mougy Internet

SHARIA SA'AD ZAGHLOUL

ACCOMMODATION

Acropole .... G
Cecil .... B
Crillon .... E
Hyde Park I
Metropole .... H
New Hotel Welcome House .... D
Normandie .... D
Sea Star .... J
Triomphe .... F
Union C
Windsor Palace .... A

Coptic Cathedral of St Mark

SHARIA KOLLIET EL-TIBBA

Coptic Patriarchate

AL-KOBITYA

Eliyahu Ha-Navi Synagogue

Zawiya Internet Café

SHARIA MOHAMMED RAFAT

SHARIA AMIN FIKHRY

MIDAN KHARTOUM

SHARIA SULTAN HUSSEIN

Cavafy Museum

Rialto Cinema

Church of St Saba

SHARIA SALAH MUSTAFA

Gulf Bank

Goethe Institute

Russian Centre

SHARIA NABI DANIEL

Metro Cinema

Greco-Roman Museum

SHARIA PHARAANA

SHARIA BATALSA

American Center

Opera House

Renaissance Royal Cinema

Lufthansa

MI Bank

Governorate

Conservatoire

SHARIA HORRIYA

TARIQ GAMAL ABDEL NASSER

French Centre

Amir Cinema

Oman Bank

Western Union

Khedive Ismail

Old Walls

Mosque of Nabi Daniel

KOM EL-DIKKA

Villa of the Birds

Roman Theatre

SHARIA YUSSEF

SHARIA SULIMAN YOUSRI

Stadium

MIDAN EL-GUMHORRIYA

Local buses & minibuses

SHARIA HUSSEIN FAHMY

Masr Station

Service Taxis for Cairo

Minibuses for Abu Qir

SHARIA MAHMOUD BEY

SHARIA MOHARREM BEY

Durrell's House

Bibliotheca Alexandrina ▶ Shatby

Alexandria National Museum (75m) ▶

4

ALEXANDRIA AND THE MEDITERRANEAN COAST

Downtown hotels

Acropole 27 Sharia Gamil el-Din Yassin ⓣ03/480-5980. Very central and within earshot of the trams, this old-fashioned hotel has dusty rooms with washbasins and clean bedding; there's a surcharge for a side sea view (£E10) or private bath (£E25). ➊

Cecil 16 Midan Sa'ad Zaghloul ⓣ03/4487 7173, ⓕ485-5655. Dead central, with fab views of the Eastern Harbour, the *Cecil* is an Alexandrian institution. Durrell, Churchill, Noël Coward and Somerset Maugham head the list of former guests, but modernization and *Sofitel* management has dispelled the old ambience. Regular rooms are cosy and a/c but nothing special; you'll pay U$50 extra for a sea view; a grand corner suite costs US$278. French and Chinese restaurants, nightclub, *Monty's Bar*, Avis desk. Takes Amex, MC and Visa. ➑

Crillon 5 Sharia Adib Ishtak ⓣ03/480-0330. The best-preserved of Alex's prewar *pensions*, with a lobby full of stuffed birds. Its 3rd floor has breezy Art Deco rooms with enclosed sea-view balconies and spotless shared bathrooms; don't bother with the small en-suite rooms on the 6th floor. In high season, half-board is obligatory. ➋

Hyde Park 21 Sharia Amin Fikhry, 8th floor ⓣ03/483-5667. A scruffy *pension* whose card promises "water inside the room", "beans services 24 hours" and "to lament to inside the Repubic" (whatever that means), but fails to mention the glassed-in balconies with harbour views that are its only redeeming feature. ➋

Metropole 52 Sharia Sa'ad Zaghloul ⓣ03/486-1467, ⓕ406-2040, ⓦwww.paradiseinnegypt.com. Centrally located on the corner of Midan Ramleh, this wonderfully ornate 1900s hotel has been refurbished to four-star standards. All rooms a/c with fancy bathrooms; the suites are furnished with antiques and have jacuzzis. It's worth paying US$35 extra for a sea view. French restaurant. ➑

New Hotel Welcome House 28 Sharia Gamil el-Din Yassin, 5th floor ⓣ03/480-6402. A shabby old doss-house boasting Alex's cheapest en-suite, sea-view rooms (£E35). The lift may not work. ➊

Normandie, 28 Sharia Gamil el-Din Yassin, 4th floor ⓣ03/480-6830, ⓔelrume4ever5@hotmail.com. In the same building as the *Welcome House*, and equally aged, but fairly clean. Its sea-view rooms are even cheaper, but with shared bathrooms (some lacking hot water). No breakfast. ➊

Sea Star 24 Sharia Amin Fikhry ⓣ03/480-5343, ⓕ487-2388. A few blocks from Midan Ramleh, this hotel's top-floor rooms have distant sea views; the rest are dark and claustrophobic, but en-suite and clean throughout. ➋

Triomphe 26 Sharia Gamil el-Din Yassin, 5th floor ⓣ03/480-7585. Attractively kitsch, fairly clean, and with side views of the sea from some rooms (£E30 extra), this is one of the better budget options on this popular street. No breakfast. ➋

Union 164 Sharia 26 Yulyu, 5th floor ⓣ03/480 7312, ⓕ480-7350. Reservations are essential at this bright, clean Art Deco hotel three blocks along the Corniche from Midan Sa'ad Zaghloul, with a cool lounge facing the Eastern Harbour. It's worth paying £E20 more for a large carpeted room with a harbour view, balcony and private bathroom. Breakfast (£E8) is obligatory in high season. ➋

Windsor Palace 17 Sharia ash-Shohada ⓣ03/480-8123, ⓕ480-9090, ⓦwww.paradiseinnegypt.com. This recently refurbished Edwardian hotel has three-star facilities (check out the Lady Spencer terrace and Prince Charles coffee shop), with soothing green and gold décor. Many of the rooms have fantastic views of the harbour. Takes MC and Visa. ➐

Outside the centre

If you don't mind being out of the centre, there are some **upmarket hotels** at Montazah (see p.632) or out near the malls and International Garden on Alexandria's southern edge.

El Salamlek Palace Montazah Gardens ⓣ03/547-7999, ⓕ547-3585, ⓦwww.sangiovanni.com. This grandiose pseudo-Alpine chalet was once the residence of Khedive Abbas's mistress and is decorated in period style (suites from $US370). Amenities include a private beach, the only casino in Alex (open to non-residents with passports), French and Italian restaurants (smart dress required). Takes all major cards. ➑

Helnan Palestine Near the Haramlik Palace ⓣ03/547-3500, ⓕ547-3378, ⓦwww.helnan.com. Originally built to house Arab leaders attempting to solve the Palestinian problem in 1964, this hotel has been refurbished as a five-star conference venue. Spacious rooms overlook the palace or a lagoon. Water sports and nightclub. Costs around thirty percent less off-season. ➑

Hilton Alexandria 14th of May Bridge, Smouha ☎03/490-9120, ℱ420-9140, ⓦwww.hilton.com. Opened in 2002, with first-rate amenities, though its motorway site on the outskirts (20min by taxi from the centre) is a big disadvantage. Takes all major cards. ⑧

Mercure Romance 303 Tariq el-Geish, Saba Pasha ☎03/584-0911, ℱ583-0526, ⓦwww .accorhotels.com. On the Corniche, between Montazah and the centre, this new four-star *Mercure* is worth checking out. Rooms booked through *Longchamps Hotel* in Cairo (see p.122) can cost as little as US$30 per person; rack rates are on par with the *Hilton*. Its Chinese restaurant and disco are also good. ⑧

Sheraton Montazah Montazah ☎03/548-1220, ℱ540-1331, ⓦwww.sheraton.com. Overpriced five-star tower on a busy junction outside the grounds of the palace. Nightclub, disco, small outdoor pool and tennis court. All rooms with a/c, minibar and satellite TV. Takes all major cards. ⑨

The city

I loved the shabbiness of the streets and cafés, the melancholy which hung over the city late of an evening, the slow decay (not destruction, mind you) of what the Europeans had left behind when they fled.

Charlie Pye-Smith, *The Other Nile*

Alex encourages nostalgia trips and random exploration, if only because "the sights" are limited and chance incidents often more revealing. Don't be afraid of following your nose and deviating from the usual itineraries, which could be completed in a day if done at the trot. While the Roman Theatre and the Catacombs of Kom es-Shoqafa are the monumental **highlights** of Alex – whose classical heritage is enshrined in the new library and Alexandria National Museum – it's the ambience of the former European and "native" quarters that sticks in your mind.

For convenience, these accounts start with the downtown area and work outwards, interweaving the ancient, remembered and existing cities. The **historical map** published by the Alexandria Preservation Trust helps make sense of the ancient city as you walk around, while anyone interested in **archeology** should check out the links on ⓦwww.houseofptolemy.org.

South and east of Midan Sa'ad Zaghloul

Since E.M. Forster wrote his guide to Alexandria in 1922, the city's centre has shifted eastwards from the former Place Mohammed Ali (now Midan Tahrir) to the seafront **Midan Sa'ad Zaghloul**, a square named after the nationalist leader (1860–1927) whose **statue** gazes towards the Mediterranean. His deportation by the British to Malta provoked nationwide rioting (1919) and guaranteed Zaghloul a hero's return, though the national independence he sought was denied for another generation. Zaghloul is referred to as "the Pasha" in Naguib Mahfouz's novel, *Miramar*.

With no trace of the Caesareum that stood here in ancient times (see overleaf), the square today looks post-colonial. Decrepit edifices that could have been lifted from Naples or Athens overshadow the **tourist office**. The dominant building is the pseudo-Moorish **Hotel Cecil**, where British Intelligence hatched the El-Alamein deception plan from a suite on the first floor. No longer the decadent and moribund establishment of *The Alexandria Quartet*, it now belongs to the *Sofitel* chain.

A similar mystique used to attend Alexandrian **patisseries**, of which there are three nearby. *Délices*, beneath a red awning, has followed the famous old *Trianon*, on the corner, in installing air conditioning and a doorman.

Athineos, by Ramleh tram station, used to be the grandest but now has gaping holes in its Art Nouveau décor: see p.634 for reviews of these and other patisseries.

The *Trianon* stands just behind the former site of **Cleopatra's Needles**, two giant obelisks that once marked the entrance to the Caesareum (see below). Nineteenth-century visitors enjoyed sketching and photographing the one still standing and its fallen companion (toppled by an earthquake in 1301) until both were removed in the 1870s, to be re-erected on London's Embankment and in New York's Central Park. Their popular name is a misnomer, for they originated at Heliopolis fourteen centuries earlier, and were moved to Alexandria fifteen years after Cleopatra's death.

Sharia Nabi Daniel: the Synagogue and Coptic Cathedral

Starting as an inconspicuous backstreet beside the tourist office, **Sharia Nabi Daniel** grows wider as it runs south along the route of the ancient **Street of the Soma**. Paved in marble and flanked by marble colonnades, this dazzled the Arabs in 641, even though its finest buildings had already vanished. Before its destruction by feuding Christians in the fourth century, the north end of the street was crowned by the **Caesareum**, a temple begun by Cleopatra for Antony, which Octavian completed and dedicated to himself. Full of "choice paintings and statues", the complex was entered by a gateway fronted by two huge obelisks ("Cleopatra's Needles"; see above) that he took from Heliopolis.

A short way down Nabi Daniel, high wrought-iron gates and clusters of police guard the **Eliyahu Ha-Navi Synagogue**, entered via an alley to the north (admission may be possible on Saturday mornings; bring your passport). Built in 1885 by Baron Jacques de Menasce, its columned Italianate interior features stained-glass windows, giant *menorahs* and a collection of Torah scrolls from bygone neighbourhood synagogues that once served a Jewish community of 70,000, tracing its ancestry back to the city's foundation. Nowadays only fourteen, mostly elderly, Jews remain, six of whom look after the synagogue and its extensive archives.

Across the road, another set of gates marked by crosses betrays the **Coptic Cathedral of St Mark**, in a compound enclosed by taller buildings, entered from Sharia al-Kineesa al-Kobtiyya (aka Rue de l'Eglise Copte), which joins Nabi Daniel further south. The cathedral is named after the Apostle martyred by pagans in 67 AD; kidnapped while giving Mass, he was dragged by horses through the streets of Alexandria, where his remains were held by a local church until 828, when the Venetians smuggled the body out of Muslim-ruled Alexandria in a barrel of salt pork, to reinter it at the Basilica di San Marco; the head was transferred to the custody of the Church of Mari Girgis in Cairo. In 1997, Pope John Paul II returned one of St Mark's fingers to Pope Shenouda III as a gesture of ecumenical reconciliation. The cathedral itself is an early twentieth-century Byzantine pastiche, whose interior was unfairly described by Forster as "fatuously ugly". Remains of some of the first 47 patriarchs of the Alexandrian See are buried in a chapel to the left of the iconostasis. Daily services are held from 6 to 8pm and 8 to 10pm.

This part of town is classic **Durrell** territory: the author himself lived with Eve Cohen (the model for Justine) in a flat at no. 40 Sharia Fouad, while several of his fictional characters were located nearby: Darley and Pombal on Nabi Daniel; Clea, Justine and Nessim on Rue Fuad Premier (now Sharia Fouad/Sharia Horriya).

The Cavafy Museum and the Church of St Saba

A more tangible relic of Alexandria's literary heritage can be found in a back-street just off Nabi Daniel, formerly called Rue Lepsius but now named Sharm el-Sheikh; to find it, turn onto Sultan Hussein and follow the alley running off between a luggage store and a lighting shop. At no.4, near the far end, a tiny sign in Greek identifies the **Cavafy Museum** (Mon–Wed, Fri & Sat 10am–3pm, Thurs & Sun 10am–5pm; £E10), which recreates the second-floor flat where **Constantine Cavafy** (1863–1933) lived at the zenith of his poetic talent, above a bordello around the corner from the Greek Orthodox Church of St Saba. "Where could I live better?" he asked. "Below, the brothel caters for the flesh. And there is the church which forgives sin. And there is the hospital where we die." He died there indeed, and was buried in the Greek Cemetery at Shatby, where his grave bears the simple epitaph, *Poet*.

The present museum was established by the Greek Consulate in 1992. Its custodian relates how "Cavafis" (as he is known) had nine brothers, loved candlelight, and died of throat cancer from drinking – but draws a veil over his homosexuality ("He never married"). Visitors can see his brass bed, icons, books and death mask, and the modest desk where he wrote *The Barbarians*, *Ithaca*, and his elegiac *The City*:

You won't find a new country, won't find another shore.
This city will always pursue you.
You'll walk the same streets, grow old
in the same neighbourhoods, turn grey in the same houses.
You'll always end up in this city. Don't hope for things elsewhere:
there's no ship for you, there's no road.
Now that you've wasted your life here, in this small corner,
you've destroyed it everywhere in the world.

There is also a room devoted to **Stratis Tsirkas**, a student of Cavafy's who wrote the trilogy *Drifting Cities*, about Greek underground politics in wartime Jerusalem, Cairo and Alexandria.

Across the road stands the Greek Orthodox **Church of St Saba** (daily 7.30am–12.30pm & 3.30–6pm), built over an ancient temple of Apollo. The seventeenth-century church contains a marble columnar tablet on which St Catherine is said to have been beheaded, a giant bronze bell, and relics of Patriarch Petros VII, killed in a helicopter crash on Mount Athos in 2004. While Alexandria's Greek population has shrunk from 300,000 (pre-1957) to about 1000 today, the Patriarchate of Alexandria encompasses all Africa and its congregation throughout the continent has risen to 250,000 – a number unseen since Roman times.

On to Midan el-Gumhorriya

Ancient Alexandria's crossroads lay near the modern-day intersection of Nabi Daniel, Fouad and Horriya streets. The last used to be the **Canopic Way**, lined by marble colonnades extending all the way from the Gate of the Sun, where visitors entered the city. Many scholars believe that this junction was the site of the **Mouseion** ("Shrine of the Muses"), an institution from which our word "museum" derives. Founded by Ptolemy I Soter (323–282 BC), it incorporated lecture halls, laboratories, observatories, and the legendary "Mother" Library (see p.627). Across the way stood the **Soma**, a temple where Alexander the Great was originally entombed, as were several Ptolemies. Here the victorious Octavian is supposed to have paid his respects to Alexandria's founder but disdained his heirs: "I wished to see a king, I did not wish to see corpses."

Part of the site is occupied by the nineteenth-century **Mosque of Nabi Daniel**, whose modern entrance is set back from the street. The mosque's crypt is popularly believed to hold the remains of the Prophet Daniel (in reality, it contains those of Mohammed Danyal al-Maridi, a Sufi sheikh, and one Lukman the Wise). Legends that Alexander's tomb lay deeper underground impelled the Egyptian Antiquities Organization to excavate in the early 1990s, but nothing was found; two Greeks later claimed to have found it near Siwa Oasis; while Professor Fakharani of Alexandria University believes that the Romans reburied him outside the Royal Quarter, where the Christian cemeteries are today.

Sharia Nabi Daniel ends at **Midan el-Gumhorriya**, a seething mass of bus and taxi ranks outside the neo-Baroque **Masr Station**, designed by a Greek and an Italian in 1927. You can beat a retreat into the Roman Theatre off Sharia Yussef.

Kom el-Dikka

Since 1959 Polish archeologists and staff from the Greco-Roman Museum have removed the Turkish fort and slums on **Kom el-Dikka** (Mound of Rubble), revealing a substratum of **Roman remains** beneath a Muslim cemetery (daily 9am–4pm; Ramadan 9am–3pm; £E10). During Ptolemaic times this was the Park of Pan, a hilly pleasure garden with a limestone summit carved into the shape of a pine cone, where Roman villas, baths and an amphitheatre were later built. The elegant **Roman Theatre** has marble seating for seven to eight hundred, cruder galleries for the plebs, and a forecourt with two patches of mosaic flooring. In Byzantine times, gladiatorial games were superceded by chariot races, with teams based on the Blues and Greens of Constantinople's hippodrome; some of the seats in the theatre bear graffiti supporting one of the teams (which were closely associated with political factions). Along the northern side of the theatre's portico are thirteen auditoria that might have been part of Alexandria's ancient **university**, with an annual enrollment of 5000 students.

A separate ticket, sold at the main entrance, entitles you to enter the newly opened **Villa of Birds** (£E5) – so called because of its mosaic floors, depicting nine different species of birds (and a panther). En route to the villa you'll pass a laboratory for cleaning antiques, with assorted masonry recently dredged from the sea bed laid outside.

Further north within the compound, excavation work is taking place on a **residential quarter** (closed to visitors) whose jumbled arches and walls resolve into streets, shops and houses at close quarters. Many of the buildings were constructed from alternating courses of brick and stone, a technique called *opus mixtum* ("mixed work"). Five centuries later, the Arabs used the same method to build a wall around the shrunken city, which was reinforced by the Turks. The **east gate** (Bab Sharq) of the Arab city is embedded in the Stadium beyond Masr Station.

Sharia Safiya Zaghloul and the Quartier Grec

Exiting Kom el-Dikka and turning northwards round the corner of the site, you'll come to a **statue of Khedive Ismail** that once stood by the Corniche. It was removed in 1956, when he became reviled by nationalists as a dupe of colonialism, and has only recently been granted a permanent home here. From the statue, cross over Sharia Horriya and head north along

Sharia Safiya Zaghloul. In Cavafy's day this was called the Rue Missala and known for its billiard halls and rent-boys; today it is named after the wife of the nationalist leader and noted for its shops and cinemas. The turning just beyond the Metro Cinema leads to the heart of what was once the **Quartier Grec**, or Greek Quarter, one of five urban zones allotted to different ethnic groups by Mohammed Ali, that became as rich and cosmopolitan as Alexandria itself. Many of its villas now house **cultural centres** (see p.639), along Sharia Batalsa (still identified by its old name of Rue de Ptolomees) and Sharia Phara'ana (signed Rue des Pharaons), including the American Center, previously owned by philanthropist and Zionist Georges Menasce.

The Greek Quarter's most famous building, however, is the **Greco–Roman Museum**, whose Classical facade by Leopold Deitrich Bey (1892) is visible at the far end of Rue du Musée. Home to Egypt's best collection of Classical antiquities, the museum is currently closed for refurbishment. Its reopening date and future lay-out are uncertain, but some of its extensive collection will be on display at other museums in the meantime. When it reopens you will be able to see such treasures as a mummified crocodile, human mummies dating from c.100–250 AD, relics of the Serapis cult promoted by Ptolemy I, and death masks, statues and busts of Roman emperors, including Julius Caesar. In the museum garden are some tombs cut from rocks and a giant head of Mark Antony.

The Alexandria National Museum

Back on Sharia Horriya (aka Tariq Gamal Abdel Nasser), head east beyond the governorate, passing en route a stratified section of the **old walls** behind some houses in an alley, and you'll reach the impressive **Alexandria National Museum**, at no. 110 near the corner of Midan Khartoum (daily 9am–4pm; £E30). Occupying an Italianate mansion once owned by a wood merchant, Assad Basily, the museum displays some of the amazing archeological finds made in and around the city during the past decade. Artfully lit and with English labelling, the museum also has an impressive art and history bookshop.

On the ground floor, pride of place is afforded to **artefacts from Herakleion** and Canopus (p.633). A diorite sphinx, a priest of Isis carrying a Canopic jar and a statue of the goddess share the spotlight with a granite stele of Nectanebo II that once stood at the mouth of the Canopic branch of the Nile. From **ancient Alexandria** come an effigy of Emperor Caracalla in pharaonic headgear, a **mosaic** of Medusa found beneath the Diana Cinema, a marble hand from an unknown colossus and the **head of Briniky**, the wife of Ptolemy II. Upper Egypt is represented by a life-size statue of Ben Menkh, lord of Dendara in Roman times.

Upstairs, splendid mother-of-pearl-inlaid doors and *mashrabiyas* precede **Coptic** stelae and friezes carved with lions, sheep or grapevines, followed by icons, priestly garments and accoutrements. The breadth of **Islamic** artefacts is even greater: sashes and capes of Persian or Turkish origin; gold coins minted under the Fatimid and Byzantine empires evincing trade between the two; and Mamluke and Ottoman weaponry (increasingly ceremonial and made in Europe as the balance of power tilted westwards). A final room upstairs entitled "Alexandria in the Twenty-First Century" juxtaposes photos of colonial street scenes and a satellite view of the city today with crystal tableware, bejewelled rings and medals from King Farouk's collection. Look out for the silver fish with a flexible body.

Around Midan Orabi and Midan Tahrir

The old heart of "European" Alexandria lies nine blocks west of Midan Sa'ad Zaghloul. To get there, you can catch a tram along Sharia el-Ghorfa el-Tigarya, or walk along **Sharia Sa'ad Zaghloul**, which starts as a busy shopping street aglow with neon, and ends as a shadowy alley. Along the way you may meet local characters like the stationer whose family escaped the Armenian genocide, arrived here penniless, got rich by founding a piano factory and then lost everything in 1957; or a seedy old guy who pimped for British soldiers in his youth and will regale you with sordid tales for the price of a drink in one of the backstreet **bars** (see p.636). Or you can delve into a warren of furniture and garment **workshops** across the square from the telephone exchange.

Emerging onto **Midan Orabi**, you'll see a Neoclassical **Monument of the Unknown Soldier** facing the seafront. No trace remains of the French Gardens where expatriates once strolled amongst the acacia trees and shrubs, but a derelict **synagogue** on the corner of Sa'ad Zaghloul and a **Maronite Church** off the square attest to the area's social complexion a century ago.

Midan Tahrir

South of the French Gardens lay "Frank Square", the European city's social hub; "There is nothing in Alexandria but the Frank Square and the huts of the Alexandrians", wrote Florence Nightingale in 1849. Originally the Place des Consuls, it was renamed in honour of **Mohammed Ali**, whose equestrian **statue** (by Jacques Mart; 1868) now barely stands out against the scabrous facades in the background. After the Orabi Revolt of 1882, rebels were tied to the acacias, shot and buried there by British forces. Not surprisingly, its name was changed to Liberation Square – **Midan Tahrir** – following the Revolution.

Midan Tahrir also witnessed two crucial events of the Nasser era. In October 1954, a member of the Muslim Brotherhood fired on Nasser during a public speech; the botched (perhaps staged) assassination gave Nasser an excuse to ban the Brotherhood and supplant General Naguib (who was falsely implicated in the conspiracy) as Egypt's acknowledged leader. Two years later, on the fourth anniversary of King Farouk's abdication, Nasser delivered a three-hour speech broadcast live from here on national radio, climaxing in the announcement that Egypt had taken possession of the Suez Canal; the repetition of the name "Lesseps" earlier in his peroration was actually the codeword for the operation to begin.

To the Attarine Mosque and beyond

A few streets around Midan Tahrir deserve a mention, if not a ramble. Leading off to the southeast, the erstwhile Bond Street of Alexandria, Rue Chérif Pacha, was Cavafy's birthplace; on the corner stood the Cotton Exchange that once echoed with the cries of European merchants. Renamed **Sharia Salah Salem** after a colleague of Nasser's, the street is less chic but still the place to find **antiques** and **jewellery**, much of it once owned by "foreigners" dispossessed by Nasser. Its main landmark is the Moorish-Gothic **Anglican Church of St Mark**, whose congregation includes many Sudanese. Six blocks further down at no.30 stands a copy of the Palazzo Farnese in Rome, built for an Italian bank and now housing the **Banque Misr**, whose lavish Gothic interior is worth seeing. In 1942, Durrell worked around the corner in a propaganda bureau at 1 Sharia Mahmoud Azmi. A plaque at no.2 marks the first trading company established by the **Al-Fayeds** – two poor lads born in Alex's Sharbangi Alley who became international business moguls.

Mohammed Al-Fayed is best known for his ownership of Harrods in London and the relationship between his son Dodi and Princess Diana. Al-Fayed's belief that they were killed by MI6 is widely shared in Egypt.

Jewellers also crop up in the backstreets north of Salah Salem and along two thoroughfares further south: Ahmed Orabi and Mesjid al-Attarin. The latter gets its name from the **Attarine Mosque**, which occupies the site of the fourth-century Church of St Athanasius, named after the rector who argued the "dual nature" of Christ against his theological opponent, Arius the Monophysite. The mosque has a lacey, multi-tiered minaret, reminiscent of Al-Nasir Mohammed's mosque in Cairo, and likewise dates from the fourteenth century. It was from here that Napoleon's forces removed a seven-ton sarcophagus, thought to be Alexander's, and later surrendered it to the British Museum, which attributed it to Nectanebo I.

Further west are two reminders of the city's multi-sectarian legacy. The **Greek Orthodox Cathedral** underpins a small Hellenistic enclave, while a huge **Catholic Cathedral** stands aloof from the bustling junction of Mesjid al-Attarin and Abu Dardaa streets. Northwest of Midan Tahrir, grandiose European architecture gives way to smaller-scale buildings that segue into the city's **souks**. Here, the main arteries are **Sharia Nokrashi** – heaving with fruit and vegetable stalls, butchers, bakeries and hardware stores – and **Sharia Faransa** (French Street), full of shops selling clothes, cloth and dressmaking materials. The network of alleys between the two thoroughfares is known as **Zinqat as-Sittat**, "The Women's Squeeze". Before the revolution, Nokrashi was notorious for its child bordellos. In *The Alexandria Quartet*, Justine sought her kidnapped daughter here, the diplomat Mountolive was mauled by child prostitutes, and Scobie (modelled on "Bimbashi" McPherson, the prewar head of the secret police) killed his neighbours with moonshine whisky.

Anfushi, Fort Qaitbey and the Pharos

Although the **Eastern Harbour** is no longer the busy port of ancient times, its graceful curve is definitely appealing. As it sweeps around towards Qaitbey's Fort, bureaucratic monoliths from the last decades of the twentieth century give way to stately palms and weathered colonial mansions, likened by Michael Palin to "Cannes with acne". Nearer the fort, fishermen cast rods and mend nets while the fresh catch is marketed and shipwrights work on hulls in a boatyard. Walking at least some of the way along the Corniche is highly recommended, but you may wish to use minibuses or trams for longer distances.

In ancient times, a seven-league dike – the **Heptastadion** – connected Alexandria with Pharos, then an island. Allowed to silt up after the Arab conquest, the Heptastadion gradually turned into a peninsula that the newcomers built over, creating the **Anfushi quarter**. Its Ottoman mosques and some old *mashrabiya*-ed houses are the only "sights" as such, but the variety of streetlife makes this an interesting area to explore. The best strategy is to hop on tram #15, running one block inland from the Corniche, which travels past most places of interest.

The **Terbana Mosque**, 700m along, is chiefly remarkable for its antique columns – no one knows where they came from. A huge pair with Corinthian capitals supports the minaret. Lesser columns are ranged eight to an arcade within and painted gloss white; there's also some fine tiling quietly going to pot – the mosque has been subject to slapdash "improvements" ever since it was built in 1685. The black-and-red-painted brickwork on the facade is a common Delta style.

The city's foremost religious building, the **Mosque of Abu al-Abbas al-Mursi**, is located the same distance again further north. It honours the patron saint of local fishermen and sailors, a thirteenth-century Andalusian sheikh. The existing structure was built in 1938 by an Italian architect, Mario Kossi, but its keel-arched panels, elaborately carved domes and cornices look as old as the sixteenth-century original. Women are only allowed into a room at the back of the mosque.

After a visit, have a drink in the arcade across the street and watch life go by. If you're feeling adventurous, you can investigate the maze of old houses behind the mosque; otherwise, press on to Qaitbey's fort.

Fort Qaitbey and the Pharos

One tram stop after Al-Mursi's mosque, then a short walk past the fishing port and repair yard full of brightly painted boats, will bring you to the promontory bearing Sultan Qaitbey's fort and the **Alexandra Yacht Club**, which holds an annual regatta in October.

Fort Qaitbey (daily 9am–5pm; £E12) is an Alexandrian landmark, a Toytown citadel buffeted by wind-borne spray, its flag forever rippling. Built during the 1480s and later beefed up by Mohammed Ali, it commands great views of the city and the spume-flecked Mediterranean. Within the keep there's a mosque whose minaret was blown away by the British in 1882.

△ Artist's impression of Alexandria

The fort occupies the site of the **Pharos**, Alexandria's great lighthouse, one of the Seven Wonders of the ancient world. A combination of aesthetic beauty and technological ambition, it transcended its practical role as a navigational aid and early-warning system, becoming synonymous with the city itself. Possibly conceived by Alexander himself, it was built during Ptolemy II's reign (c.279 BC) under the direction of an Asiatic Greek, Sostratus, and exceeded 125m – perhaps even 150m – in height, including the statue of Poseidon at its summit.

Its square base contained three hundred rooms, that, according to legend, once housed the seventy rabbis who translated the Hebrew scriptures into Greek for Ptolemy Philadelphus (c.200 BC), producing identical texts despite having worked alone. (In reality, this Septuagint version of the Bible wasn't completed until 130 BC, and the rabbis lived in huts on the island.) It is also thought to have housed hydraulic machinery for hauling the fuel up the second, octagonal storey; otherwise, this would have been accomplished by a procession of pack mules climbing a spiral ramp. The cylindrical third storey housed the lantern, whose light is thought to have been visible 56km away. Some chroniclers also mention a "mirror" that enabled the lighthouse keepers to observe ships far out at sea; a form of lens (whose secret was lost) has been postulated.

Around 700 AD the lantern collapsed, or was demolished by a treasure-hunting Khalif; the base survived unscathed and Ibn Tulun restored the second level, until an earthquake in 1303 reduced the whole structure to rubble. The northwest section of the fort's enclosure walls incorporates some huge red-granite pillars that might have been part of the Pharos. Since the 1990s, divers from the CEA have located over 2500 stone objects **underwater** at depths of 6–8m. These include the head of a colossus of Ptolemy as pharaoh and the base of an obelisk inscribed to Seti I, which have been brought to the surface, and several **monoliths**, weighing 50–70 tonnes apiece and embedded in the rock by the impact of their fall, that can only have belonged to the lighthouse. Five hundred metres offshore they've found **wrecks** of Greek and Roman trading vessels laden with **amphorae** of wine and fish sauce, and over fifty **anchors** of all eras – more pieces in the mosaic picture of ancient Alexandria that's emerging from surveys of the Eastern Harbour (see p.626). See p.638 of details of **diving** in the harbour.

The Anfushi Tombs, Ras el-Tin and the Western Harbour

Tram #15 runs on to the Ras el-Tin quarter, where you can alight at Sharia Ras el-Tin to find the rock-cut **Anfushi Tombs** (daily 9am–4.30pm; £E12), uncovered in 1901. Sited in pairs around a staircase leading to an open court, the four tombs are painted to simulate costly alabaster or marble and belonged to third-century BC Greek Alexandrians who adopted Ancient Egyptian funerary practices. The right-hand set has pictures of Egyptian gods, warships and feluccas; a Greek workman has also immortalized his mate's virtues in graffiti. Both the left-hand tombs have vestibules with benches for the deceased's relatives to eat and drink in their memory. Hang around and a keeper should appear to unlock the tombs.

It's possible that the necropolis extends beneath the gardens of **Ras el-Tin Palace**, overlooking the Western Harbour. In the days when Pharos was an island, a Temple of Neptune stood here. Now a Presidential residence and strictly off limits, the "Cape of Figs" palace was built for Mohammed Ali, its audience hall sited so that he could watch his new fleet at anchor while reclining on his divan. Rebuilt and turned into the summer seat of government under

Fouad I, it witnessed **King Farouk's abdication** on July 26, 1952. "What you have done to me I was getting ready to do to you", the king informed General Naguib, adding, "Your task will be difficult. It is not easy to govern Egypt." Wearing an admiral's uniform, Farouk departed on the royal yacht to a 21-gun salute; with him went the royal family, an English nursemaid, three Albanian bodyguards, a dog trainer and 244 trunks. For a vicarious glimpse of the palace's Moorish **interior**, visit Ⓦ www.presidency.gov.eg.

Egypt's main port and naval base since the mid-nineteenth century, the **Western Harbour** witnessed the boldest Italian commando raid of World War II. On December 18, 1941, three manned torpedoes penetrated the harbour to lay charges beneath the battleships HMS *Valiant* and HMS *Queen Elizabeth*. The British pretended that the ships were still afloat when their hulls were resting on the sea bed, but it took sixteen months' repairs before both were back in action.

Inland, blocks of *shoonas* or warehouses with their foreign names still faintly visible are given over to the **cotton industry**, "greasy fluff" and rags littering the streets as in Forster's day. Another major industry is smuggling, for which the **port** is notorious; its 62 quays handle over 5000 ships every year, carrying about 75 percent of Egypt's import and export trade.

On the way back you could enjoy lunch at one of the many **fish restaurants** on Sharia Safar Pasha, between Ras el-Tin and Anfushi, or *Kadoura* along the Corniche back towards the centre (see p.635).

The submerged Royal Quarters

The opposite jaw of the Eastern Harbour is formed by a narrow promontory called **Silsileh** ("the Chain"), that's occupied by the navy and out of bounds. Aside from being the site of Naguib Mahfouz's fictional *Pension Miramar*, its interest lies in the **underwater** discoveries made since 1996 by Franck Goddio and the National French Centre for Studies, whose survey of the sea bed five metres down has revealed extensive submerged **ruins** including granite columns, votive statues, sphinxes, pavements, ceramics and a pier from the **ancient Royal Quarters** of Alexandria. In 1998 they hauled up a sample to show the world: the largest and most striking objects were a metre-tall, black-granite figure of the goddess Isis holding a canopic jar, and an intact 380kg diorite sphinx with the face of what is thought to be Ptolemy XII, Cleopatra's father. Samples of their salvage can be seen on Goddio's website, Ⓦ www.underwaterdiscovery.org.

Goddio was quick to claim that they had found the site of **Cleopatra's palace** on the island of Antirrhodos (where she met her death), which had been plunged into the sea by a series of earthquakes and tidal waves some 1600 years ago. The Egyptians enthused about the idea of creating the world's first underwater museum – with Plexiglas tunnels that would allow visitors to stroll around five metres below the surface. However, many archeologists felt that the site of the palace and the provenance of the ruins had only been tentatively established, since several palaces existed there over a timespan of centuries. As a marine treasure-hunter rather than an archeologist by profession, Goddio has been criticized as a gadfly dashing from one project to another without completing any – yet still he turns up finds, not just in the Eastern Harbour, but also at Abu Qir (see p.633). His secret weapon is a nuclear resonance magnetometer that can detect likely antiquities by measuring the relative density of submerged objects against the earth's magnetic field, and plots them on a digital map fixed by GPS satellites. But as Goddio goes from triumph to triumph, the idea of an underwater museum has been quietly shelved after it was realized that the algae in the water that blooms in summer would render Plexiglas tunnels opaque.

Diving, however, is alluringly feasible, with visibility at its best (from 7–20 metres) from April to June and September to December. As well as seven or eight sphinxes, a giant obelisk and numerous columns, divers can see the wreck of an **Italian fighter** that was shot down and crashed on the ruins. Contact Alexandra Dive (see p.638) for all arrangements.

The Bibliotheca Alexandrina

On the mainland beyond Silsileh, another wonder of antiquity has been resurrected in a new form. The **Bibliotheca Alexandrina** (Mon, Wed, Thurs & Sun 11am–7pm, Fri & Sat 3–7pm; closed Tues ⓦ www.bibalex.gov.eg) resembles a giant discus embedded in the ground at an angle, representing a second sun rising beside the Mediterranean. Pictograms, hieroglyphs and letters from every known alphabet are carved on its exterior, evoking the diversity of knowledge embodied in the ancient library and the aspirations of the new one. Designed by a Norwegian-Austrian team of architects and built by Egyptian, British and Italian contractors, the complex includes a planetarium (the spheroid on the plaza facing the sea) and a cultural centre (in the block opposite the entrance to the library). The project to create a new Bibliotheca Alexandrina was approved by UNESCO in 1987 and cost some US$355 million, mainly met by Egypt, Saudi Arabia, the Emirates and Iraq. Repeated setbacks delayed its inauguration ceremony until 2002, but now that it is open, it is recognized as one of Alexandria's must-visits, in particular for its architecture and museums.

Meanwhile, scholars are pursuing a project to uncover the secrets of the **ancient library**. Founded shortly after Alexandria itself, on the advice of Ptolemy I's counselor Demetrius of Phalerum, it stood beside the Mouseion in the heart of the city (see p.619). Dedicated to "the writings of all nations", it welcomed scholars and philosophers and supported research and debates. By law, all ships docking at Alexandria were obliged to allow any scrolls on board to be copied, if they were of interest. By the mid-first century BC it held 532,800 manuscripts (all catalogued by the Head Librarian, Callimachus), and later spawned a subsidiary attached to the Temple of Serapis; the two were known as the "Mother" and "Daughter" libraries, and together contained perhaps 700,000 scrolls (equivalent to about 100–125,000 printed books today). As many as 40,000 (or even 400,000) were burned during Julius Caesar's assault on the city in 48 BC, when he supported Cleopatra against her brother Ptolemy XIII; as compensation, Mark Antony gave her the entire contents of the Pergamum Library in Greece (200,000 scrolls). It was Christian mobs that destroyed this vast storehouse of "pagan" knowledge, torching the Mother Library in 293 and the Daughter Library in 391, though medieval Europe later mythologized its **destruction** as proof of Arab barbarism. An apocryphal tale had the Muslim leader Amr pronouncing: "If these writings of the Greeks agree with the Koran they are useless, and need not be preserved; if they disagree, they are pernicious, and ought to be destroyed."

Visiting the museum

On the inland side facing Sharia Bur Said, a **colossus of Ptolemy II** dredged from the Eastern Harbour watches over a cloakroom (daily 11am–7pm) where all bags must be checked in, and kiosks selling **tickets** for the library (£E10), two museums inside it (£E20 each), and a combo ticket covering them all (£E45; no student discount). **Photography** is permitted in the Antiquities and

Manuscript museums (£E5, no flashes; video £E150), but not in the library itself. You can join a free **tour** in English just inside the entrance (at 11.15am, noon, 1.30pm, 2.15pm, 3pm, 3.45pm, 4.30pm and 5.15pm), or wander at will through the vast **reading area** – a stunning cascade of levels upheld by stainless-steel pillars suggestive of the columns in pharaonic temples. **Membership** (£E110 monthly; students £E55; disabled £E10) requires ID, a photo and proof of address. **Events** and **exhibitions** are advertised in the lobby.

Start with the permanent **Impressions of Alexandria** exhibit (free), whose maps, engravings and photographs from the Awad collection show how the city has evolved since antiquity and the ruins left after the British bombardment of 1882. Then move onto the intriguing **Antiquities Museum** in the basement (Mon & Fri 1–7pm, Tues 9am–4pm, Wed, Thurs & Sun 9am–7pm, Sat 11am–7pm). As well as a giant head of Serapis, a headless ibis statue and a black basalt Isis salvaged from Herakleion, it displays Thoth effigies from Tuna el-Gabel and Hermopolis, XI Dynasty model boats, and parts of two mosaic floors unearthed during the building of the present library, one depicting a dog beside a brass cup, the other a gladiator locked in combat. Back on the main entrance level, the **Manuscripts Museum** (same opening hours as the Antiquities Museum) is less intriguing, with its ancient scrolls and antiquarian tomes so dimly lit you can barely see any details. Lastly there's the Death Star-like **Planetarium**, whose shows *Cosmic Voyage*, *Human Body*, *Oasis in Space* and *Return to the Red Planet* (£E25) are the most child-friendly part of the complex (☎03/483-9999 ext. 1451 for details).

Pompey's Pillar and the Catacombs

The poor **Karmous quarter** in the southwest of the city contains two of Alex's best-known ancient monuments. **Pompey's Pillar** can be reached by taxi (£E5) or bus #709 or tram #16 from Midan St Katerina. From Pompey's Pillar you can either ride the tram or walk on to the **Catacombs of Kom es-Shoqafa**. If you've just arrived in Egypt, the poverty of the slums that lie between the two might seem shocking.

Pompey's Pillar

Pompey's Pillar towers 25m above a limestone ridge and garden, surrounded by the fruits and pits of excavations. Despite its name, the red-granite column was actually raised to honour the Roman emperor Diocletian, who threatened to massacre the dissenting populace "until their blood reached his horse's knees", but desisted when his mount slipped and bloodied itself prematurely. The column came from the ruined **Temple of Serapis**, which once rivalled the Soma and Caesareum in magnificence. Began by the Greek architect Parmeniscos in the reign of Ptolemy III (246–221 BC), and completed in the Roman era, the temple contained a "Daughter Library" of religious texts. Both were destroyed by Christian mobs on the orders of Bishop Theophilius in 391 AD.

Three subterranean galleries where the sacred Apis bulls were interred (see "Saqqara", p.247) are all that remain: you'll find them west of the ridge, which also features a Nilometer, three sphinxes (originally from Heliopolis) and some underground cisterns. Overall, however, the **site** (daily 9am–5pm, Ramadan 9am–3pm; £E10) is pretty disappointing considering what used to exist here.

The Catacombs of Kom es-Shoqafa

One of Alexandria's most memorable monuments, the **Catacombs of Kom es-Shoqafa** (daily 9am–5pm, Ramadan 9am–3pm; £E20), combine spookiness and kitsch, never mind their prosaic Arabic name, "Mound of Shards". To reach them, turn right around the corner after leaving Pompey's Pillar and follow the road uphill and straight on for about 500m; the entrance to the catacombs is on the left beyond a small square. Cameras must be left here, as photography is not allowed inside.

The triple-level complex, hewn 35m into solid rock, is reached via a spiral stairway, past the shaft down which bodies were lowered. From the vestibule with its well and scalloped niches, you can squeeze through a fissure (right) into a lofty **Caracalla** riddled with *loculi*, or family burial niches, each once sealed with a stone slab on which were painted the names and ages of the deceased. Even more arresting is the **Triclinium** (left), where relatives toasted the dead from stone couches. When the first archeologists entered the chamber they found wine jars and tableware, and recently murals, only visible under ultraviolet light. But the main attraction is the **Central Tomb** downstairs, whose vestibule is guarded by reliefs of bearded serpents with Medusa-headed shields. Inside are comically muscle-bound statues of Sobek and Anubis wearing Roman armour, dating from the second century AD when "the old faiths began to merge and melt" (Forster). Water has flooded the **Goddess Nemesis Hall** (still accessible) and submerged the lowest level, hastening the catacombs' decay. For more information, buy Jean-Yves Empereur's excellently illustrated *A Short Guide to the Catacombs of Kom es-Shoqafa*.

Moharrem Bey, Bab Sharq and Smouha

East of Karmous lies **Moharrem Bey**, a once-affluent suburb of mansions and villas, now derelict and slummy. The district grew up in the mid-nineteenth century as a result of the **Mahmudiya Canal** (dug at the cost of 20,000 lives), which revitalized commerce and created a mercantile elite who built palatial residences along its banks, described by *Murray's Handbook* as the "fashionable afternoon promenade". Its charm endured for a century, the final decades of which were embellished by the presence of residents like Cavafy (before he moved to the Rue Lepsius) and **Durrell**. In 1943, Durrell and Eve Cohen rented the top floor of a turreted **house** at 19 Sharia al-Ma'amoun, where he wrote *Prospero's Cell* and *The Dark Labyrinth* (the *Alexandria Quartet* came later). Subsequently leased to the painter and sculptor Effat Nagui and her husband and fellow artist Sa'ad el-Khadem, the house has been threatened with demolition for several years. To see if it's still standing, catch a taxi (£E5) from Masr Station down Sharia Moharrem Bey (about 3km).

Bab Sharq

Northeast of Moharrem Bey, the affluent **Bab Sharq** district can be easily approached from the Quartier Grec (see p.621) or en route to the Corniche beaches (see overleaf). Its nexus is **Midan Khartoum**, an L-shaped park whose Ptolemaic **column** (erected to celebrate Britain's recapture of Khartoum in 1898) is a local landmark at the junction of Sharia Horriya and the Suez Canal Road.

Flanking this on two sides are the hilly **Shallalat Gardens**, ablaze with scarlet flame trees over summer. Their nineteenth-century French designer utilized remnants of the west gate of the **Arab city walls** and the Farkha Canal to create rockeries and ornamental ponds. Here, E.M. Forster had his first date with Mohammed el-Adl, a tram conductor whom he met at Ramleh in the winter of 1916–17. Before then, Forster's sexual passions had never been reciprocated. The racial, class and sexual barriers that their relationship challenged underlie the finale of *A Passage to India*, which Forster was struggling with when he learned of Mohammed's death from tuberculosis in 1922. Near the northwest corner of the Gardens is the **Ibn el-Nabih Cistern**, whose three levels are upheld by antique columns salvaged from older structures. Of the 700 underground reservoirs reported by the historian El-Makrisi, this is the only one that's accessible today (dawn to dusk; free).

Beyond the Suez Canal Road lies a sprawling necropolis of high-walled **cemeteries** consecrated to diverse faiths. Though most of the tombs date from the nineteenth or twentieth centuries, burials have occurred here since ancient times. Professor Fakharani thinks that a marble chamber found beneath the Catholic cemetery near the crossroads may belong to a royal tomb, perhaps even that of Alexander himself. Like the Catholic compound, the Coptic, Greek Orthodox, Armenian, Maronite, Uniate, Protestant and Jewish cemeteries are full of lavish mausolea and sculptures, from the heyday of European supremacy. The necropolis extends nearly as far as St Mark's College in Shatby, in relation to which the Jewish cemetery is nearest.

During summer, affluent citizens hang out at the **Alexandria Sporting Club**, 1km east along Tariq Gamal Abdel Nasser. Its pool and tennis courts are the best in the city; polo and golf matches, or billiards and movies at night, are just some of the entertainments (see p.638). All eastbound trams stop at the Sporting Club.

Smouha

The **Smouha** district in the southern suburbs is a magnet for wealthy Alexandrians. The **Zahran and Smouha Malls,** 300–400m from Sidi Gaber station, and the **Green Plaza Mall** and **City Center** superstore (run by the French chain Carrefour) by the 14th May Bridge, are popular hang-outs. Smouha is also home to the **International Garden** and the **Jungle** theme park, full of attractions for children.

The district is named after the Baghdad-born Jewish architect Joseph Smouha, who moved to Egypt in the 1920s. His Smouha City (as it was originally called) was the local equivalent of Cairo's Heliopolis, a modern suburb for the upper-middle classes. Though all the "foreigners" were dispossessed by Nasser, their legacies – and names – survive in present-day Alexandria. The **Zoological Gardens** (daily: winter 9am–sunset; summer 9am–9pm; £E2) were opened in 1907 and cover 26 acres; among the many species of birds are macaws that swear like troopers, tutored by long-departed British soldiers. Next door, diverse trees planted by Khedive Ismail have grown to maturity in the **Nouzha Gardens** (same hours; £E1), where military bands once played.

Nearby, flocks of egrets nest in the vine-entangled trees of the **Antoniaidis Gardens** (same hours; £E1). Embellished with Classical statuary, they were once the private grounds of a wealthy Greek family. In ancient times, the Nouzha area was a residential suburb inhabited by the likes of Callimachus (310–240 BC), the Head Librarian of the Bibliotheca Alexandrina. It was around here, too, that Amr's Muslim forces camped before entering the city in 641 AD.

Corniche beaches

Alexandria's beaches are an overworked asset. Hardly a square metre of sand goes unclaimed during high season, when literally millions of Egyptians descend on the city. Before June the beaches furthest out are relatively uncrowded, with predominantly local users; however, Alexandrians alone can number hundreds on Fridays, Saturdays and public holidays – days to be avoided.

The popularity of the beaches doesn't imply Western-style beach culture. On most you'll rarely see any woman past the age of puberty wearing a swimsuit – they wander into the sea fully clad. The only place that Western women can swim without the hindrance of a *galabiyya*, or a lot of attention, is Venezia Beach at Montazah (see p.633). Most beaches have parasols and chairs for rent, and sometimes public showers, while fish restaurants, soft-drink and snack vendors are ubiquitous. Since 1991, the civic authorities have solved the image problem posed by the 47 sewage outlets that used to pollute the seaside from the centre of town to Montazah by pumping sewage into Lake Mariout instead, whence it finds its way into the Med more discreetly.

If that deters you, there are still three indisputable attractions: the **Royal Jewellery Museum** in Glym, the **Mahmoud Said Museum** in San Stefano and the extensive grounds of the **Montazah** palace, further along the coast. Many visitors go to **Abu Qir** for its seafood – though you can eat just as well in nicer surroundings in central Alexandria.

East to Montazah and Abu Qir

Travelling eastwards past the Corniche beaches looks simple on the map, but isn't so easy in practice. For the initial stretch as far as Cleopatra beach, minibuses #735, #736 and #768 run a block inland, and tram #2 three to five blocks in, leaving you with only the stops – mostly named after beaches – to go on. As most of the **city beaches** amount to an arc of sand overlooked by hotels and restaurants, they're hard to differentiate without a landmark in the vicinity. The following account includes some places a fair way inland.

Shatby to Roushdi

The district known as **Shatby** (or Chatby) is overshadowed by **St Mark's College**, a massive, red-brick, neo-Baroque edifice whose dome is visible from afar. Founded to educate the city's Christian elite, it now forms part of Alexandria University. On the far side of Sharia Bur Said is the grandly named **Shatby Necropolis** (daily 9am–4.30pm, Ramadan 9am–3pm; £E10), a small pit exposing some rock-cut ossuaries and sarcophagi from the third century BC, which can be viewed for free by peering over the wall of the nearby youth hostel. Shatby **beach** looks fit to spawn the "Swamp Thing", and subsequently mutates into **Ibrahimiya**, where Hitler's deputy Führer, Rudolf Hess, was born in 1896. When Alexandria was bombed in World War II, residents sheltered in the underground Roman cisterns between Ibrahimiya and Sidi Gaber.

Shortly before Cleopatra beach, tram #2 turns further inland, visiting **Sidi Gaber Station** and passing through the **Bacos** quarter where Gamal Abdel Nasser was born on January 15, 1918. He was eleven years old when he attended his first nationalist demonstration, got truncheoned and was jailed overnight. Tram #1 runs closer to **Cleopatra** beach, which has no connection with the lady herself, although the nearby **Roushdi** district was the site of Nikopolis, which Octavian (or Augustus Caesar, as he then styled himself) founded because he hated living in Alexandria. The British also built barracks and houses there, in the districts they named Stanley, Glym and San Stefano. Today, Roushdi is the centre of expat life in Alex, and many foreigners rent flats here – but a vestige of its origins remains in the form of the **Mustafa Kamel Necropolis** (daily 9am–4pm; £E12). Discovered in 1933, the four tombs date from the second century BC; two are upheld by Doric columns and one contains a mural of a horseman. To get there, catch tram #2 from Ramleh to Roushdi tram station and walk towards the Corniche along Sharia al-Mo'asker al-Romani.

The Royal Jewellery Museum

The **Royal Jewellery Museum**, at 27 Sharia Ahmed Yehia (daily 9am–5pm, Ramadan Mon–Thurs, Sat & Sun 9am–3pm, Fri 9–11.30am & 1.30–4pm, but check with tourist office first, as it may not have reopened after a recent refurbishment; £E35), is three blocks in from the Corniche, between Glym and San Stefano; a short walk from the El-Fenoun el-Gamila or Qasr el-Safa stop on the #2 tram line. The museum is housed in a mansion built for Mohammed Ali's granddaughter Princess Fatima el-Zaharaa (1903–83) and her husband Ali Heider, and is as splendidly vulgar as the treasures on display. Among the highlights are Mohammed Ali's diamond-inlaid snuffbox, King Farouk's gold chess set, a platinum crown with 2159 diamonds, and his diamond-studded gardening tools. The main gallery downstairs is lined with stained-glass cameos of courtly love in eighteenth-century France, while Provencal farmers, milkmaids and food decorate the service corridors. Upstairs are the wildest his 'n' hers bathrooms – hers with tiled murals of nymphs bathing in a waterfall, his with scenes of Côte d'Azur fishermen.

The Mahmoud Said Museum

Another treat in this part of town is the **Mahmoud Said Museum**, on Sharia Mahmoud Said Pasha (daily 10am–6pm; £E10): take tram #1 or #2 to Gianaclis (the stop after the Jewellery Museum), cross the tracks, head up the steps to the raised road and turn right. A judge who painted as a hobby, Mahmoud Said (1897–1964) was the first Egyptian artist to receive a state prize, yet disliked official commissions such as the wall-sized *Inaugural Ceremony of the Suez Canal* that greets visitors to the museum. He preferred to paint pensive, sensual women – *The Siren of Alexandria*, *Egyptian Country-Woman* and *Nabawiya with a flowered dress* – or landscapes of Alexandria, Lebanon and Stockholm.

Upstairs, six rooms are devoted to the brothers Seif (1906–79) and Adham (1908–59) Wanly, who founded the first Egyptian artists' studio in 1942 and taught Fine Arts at Alexandria University after the revolution. Seif was an Expressionist who depicted such bourgeois delights as casinos, nightclubs and horse-racing, with a prolific output including 3000 oil paintings, more than 80,000 sketches, and theatre and opera sets; while Adham was into Cubism, abstraction and Socialist Realism, producing such polemical works as *Hunger*, *Peace* and *Palestine*. There are also two rooms showcasing the work of contemporary local artists such as Myriam Abdel Alim, Magda Sa'd el-Din and Abdel Hadfi al-Gazzar, as well as the odd abstract by Farouk Hosni, Egypt's Minister of Culture since 1987.

Sidi Bishr to Montazah

Fourteen kilometres east of the centre is the suburb of **Sidi Bishr**, served by minibuses from Midan Sa'ad Zaghloul in the centre, or Sidi Gaber. Sidi Bishr's mosque stands between two beaches with the same name, and east of here, below the Automobile Club, are the "**Spouting Rocks**" of Bir Mas'ud, where the ancient Alexandrians placed water-powered horns and mills, delighting in gadgetry. It was here, too, that the geometrician Hero invented the world's first hurdy-gurdy and coin-operated vending machine (dispensing holy water) in the first century AD.

Beyond Sidi Bishr, the Miami Casino gives way to two more sandy inlets, **Asafra** and **Mandara**, and, a couple of kilometres beyond, **Montazah**, the city's walled pleasure grounds. You can enter the grounds (daily 9am–midnight; £E4, £E5 Fri and holidays) by the gates opposite the *Montazah Sheraton*. The 400 acres are well laid-out and tended, with brass lamps, a clock tower, a bowling alley, and the flamboyant Turko-Florentine **Haramlik Palace**. Commissioned by King Fouad and designed by Ernesto Verruchi Bey, the palace served as a Red Cross hospital during World War I, and it was here that E.M. Forster worked as a nurse. It was also from here that King Farouk fled to Ras-el Tin before abdicating. The building was restored by Sadat, at a cost of £E7 million, and is now a presidential residence and guesthouse, closed to the public.

The largest of Montazah's bays is rimmed by the sandy **Venezia Beach** (£E10.50 admission; £E20 with a beach chair and umbrella), where dress standards for Western women are relaxed (see p.631). A promontory ending in an ornate "Turkish" **Belvedere** and a **lighthouse** encloses the bay, providing a sheltered spot for **windsurfing** and **snorkelling** in summer.

Inland stands the smaller **El-Salamlek Palace**, built for the Austrian mistress of Khedive Abbas and now one of two luxury **hotels** in the grounds of Montazah (see p.616).

Ma'amoura and Canopus

Round the headland to the east, **Ma'amoura** is a private enclave of holiday flats and villas, charging visitors £E3 admission before they've even glimpsed the **beach**, access to which costs a further £E10. Its sands are cleaner than most, but modest dress is recommended for women. The main beach entrance is off a roundabout on the Abu Qir road, about 1km east of the *Sheraton*. The #736 minibus will deliver you to the residential *Ma'amoura Palace Hotel*, within the enclave, which has its own private beach (£E25 admission).

Past Ma'amoura, the road runs inland of a swathe of military and naval bases, occupying the ancient site of **Canopus**. Not that anything significant remains of this once-great Delta city, which flourished when a branch of the Nile reached the sea by the nearby "Canopic Mouth" but declined as this dried up and Alexandria arose. Classical mythology has it that Canopus was founded by a Greek navigator returning from the Trojan war, whom the locals later worshipped in the form of a jar with a human head. Nineteenth-century archeologists bestowed the title **Canopic jars** on similar receptacles used to preserve mummies' viscera. Each organ had its own protective deity (a minor son of Horus) whose visage adorned the stopper (human heads went out of fashion late in the XVIII Dynasty). Even after XXI Dynasty embalmers began replacing organs in the mummies, the practice of leaving Canopic jars in tombs continued. In 2004, marine archeologists found life-size statues of Ptolemaic rulers and thousands of bronze pots, chandeliers and incense burners on the sea bed off Canopus.

Abu Qir

When a straggle of jerry-built houses appears beyond the naval bases, you know you're entering **Abu Qir** (pronounced *Abu Ear*). This small fishing town can be reached by service taxi, or minibus #768 (from Masr Station); if you're coming from Montazah, the minibus stop is under the bridge and left around the corner of the palace walls from the *Sheraton* – look for knots of people waiting near the butchers. Abu Qir is garbage-strewn and ugly, and the raw sewage flowing down its **beach** should deter anyone from bathing; the only things going for it are itinerant vendors peddling everything from dolls to candelabras, and its **seafood restaurants** (see pp.635-636 for reviews).

Abu Qir is the site of two historic **battles**. Admiral Nelson's defeat of the French fleet at Abu Qir Bay (1798) effectively scuppered Napoleon's dream of an eastern empire and went down in British history as the Battle of the Nile, inspiring Mrs Hemans to write, "The boy stood on the burning deck …".

Though evenly matched in numbers, Admiral Bruey had his ships cabled together in shallow water when Nelson's fleet charged them amidships, inflicting carnage at close quarters. The French lost eleven ships and 17,000 men, the English two ships and 218 sailors. In 1998–99, Goddio's divers found the **wrecks** of the French flagship *L'Orient*, the *Sérieuse* and *Artémise* at a depth of 11m, 8km offshore. But Bonaparte had his revenge, when, in 1799, he personally led ten thousand cavalry against fifteen thousand Turks landed by the Royal Navy, pushing them back into the sea.

In 2001 Goddio's team announced the discovery of **Herakleion**, the fabled ancient entrepôt to Egypt that fell into the sea 1300 years ago. Buried by sediment for centuries in Abu Qir Bay, its identity was confirmed by a stele inscribed with the city's name, erected by Nectanebo I, and the pink-granite naos believed to belong to the temple of Heracles-Khonsu seen by Herodotus when he visited Herakleion in the fifth century BC. Divers also found three colossal statues of the Nile-god Hapy; in ancient times, the city stood at the mouth of a branch of the river.

Diving at these sites is a fantastic experience that Alexandra Dive (see p.638) can organize, though the bureaucracy involved requires 4–5 days' notice and at least four paying customers on each trip.

Eating and drinking

Alexandria can't match Cairo for culinary variety, but it beats the capital when it comes to **seafood and Greek restaurants** – and when these pall you can always fall back on Egyptian favourites like *shawarmas*, pizzas, *fuul* and felafel, or seek refuge in a few Oriental-ish places. **Coffee houses**, too, are an Alex speciality, and there are some good **bars** if you know where to look.

In addition, there are Western **fast-food outlets** all over town. *McDonald's* (daily 10am–11pm) is near the top of Sharia Safiya Zaghloul, around the corner from *Kentucky Fried Chicken* and *Baskin-Robbins* (both daily 10am–2am) on Ramleh; there's another *McDonald's* at Montazah, and a further branch of *KFC* on the Corniche in Roushdi.

Coffee houses and patisseries

Coffee houses and **patisseries** like *Athineos* and *The Trianon* have a certain mystique, and Cavafy or Durrell notwithstanding, their opulent interiors and cakes should not be missed. All of them are shown on the map on pp.614–615. For nocturnal types, there are expensive **24-hour coffee shops** in the *Cecil* and *Montazah Sheraton* hotels.

Traditional **Arab cafés** (*ahwas*) are another world from the European patisseries. If you're into sipping tea or *karkaday* surrounded by guys slapping down backgammon counters or dominoes between lung-charring tokes on *sheeshas*, there are loads of places around Midan el-Gumhorriya. You can always locate them by the sound of coughing, audible above Koranic recitals or Umm Kalthoum sobbing from the radio.

Athineos Midan Ramleh. Decorated with classical motifs and mirrors and frequented by eccentrics. Check out the gilded friezes and columns in the restaurant upstairs – the entrance is around the corner. Daily 8am–midnight.

Baudrot 23 Sharia Sa'ad Zaghloul. Walk through the newly refurbished rooms off the street to find a vine-trellised courtyard serving inexpensive cakes, coffee, chicken or fish meals and beer. Daily 7am–midnight.

Brazilian Coffee Stores Corner of Nabi Daniel and Sa'ad Zaghloul, near the tourist office. This stand-up breakfast spot features antique coffee mills, a glass map of Brazil and other period furnishings. There's also a sit-down branch on Sharia Salah Salem. Both daily 7am–11pm.

Délices Between Midan and Sharia Sa'ad Zaghloul. Less inviting since they smartened it up, junked the teak bar and installed air conditioning, but the tables outside have a nice view. Sells cakes, savouries, soft drinks and beer. Daily 7am–11pm.

Pastroudis 39 Sharia Horriya. This dark-panelled café features in *The Alexandria Quartet* (Durrell first met Eve Cohen here in 1943), but is now a sad parody of itself. The pavement tables on the south side overlook an outdoor antiques market; alcohol-drinkers must sit at the back indoors. Daily 9am–midnight.

Sofianopoulo Coffee Store 18 Sharia Sa'ad Zaghloul. Another vintage stand-up coffee shop with silver grinders and sacks of beans. On Mon–Sat they sell excellent cappuccino and croissants; on Sun you can only buy coffee beans. Daily 9am–11pm.

The Trianon Corner of Sa'ad Zaghloul and Ramleh. Redecorated and air-conditioned, the swankiest of Alexandria's patisseries boasts gilt columns and a splendidly ornate restaurant, not in use. The menu includes a Continental breakfast (£E7), pizzas (£E15–18), beer (£E13), cocktails (£E17) and wine (Egyptian £E77, French £E295, champagne £E715!). Try the flambé dishes. Daily 7am–midnight.

Vinous Corner of Nabi Daniel and Horriya. A very faded Art Deco salon, serving cakes and coffee. No alcohol. Daily 7am–midnight.

Restaurants and cafés

The following **restaurants and cafés** more or less represent the culinary and budgetary spectrum. Most of them are downtown, in the area delineated by Ramleh, Safiya Zaghloul, Nabi Daniel and Horriya streets (see map on pp.614–615), but there are also some recommendations far along the Corniche (marked on the city plan on pp.610–611). Phone numbers are only given where reservations are advisable. Unless indicated otherwise, credit cards are not accepted.

Abu Ashraf 28 Sharia Safar Pasha, Anfushi. Accessible by tram #15, this street is full of good-value fish and kebab restaurants, tempting passers-by with their outdoor charcoal grills. *Abu Ashraf* is devoted to fish and seafood, which is sold by weight and cooked in front of your eyes. Daily 24hr.

Bella Vista Abu Qir beach. The best place in Abu Qir to eat freshly caught seafood – the squid is particularly good – and enjoy the sea view and cool breezes over a beer or a *zibiba*. Daily noon–1am.

Cafeteria Asteria 40 Sharia Safiya Zaghloul. Sandwiches, macaroni, pizzas, ice cream and hot drinks at reasonable prices. Walk through the outer room to find a nice glass-roofed annexe, popular for romantic liaisons. Friendly, English-speaking Greek proprietor. Daily 8am–11pm.

China House *Hotel Cecil*, Midan Sa'ad Zaghloul ☎03/487-7173. The best of Alex's Chinese restaurants affords splendid views of the harbour. Try the delicious spring rolls, chicken dumplings, sweet-and-sour-shrimp, or grilled beef with garlic sauce – but leave room for the fried bananas with maple syrup and vanilla ice cream. Minimum charge (£E24) plus 22 percent tax. Takes all major cards. Daily 1pm–midnight.

Coffee Roastery 48 Sharia Fouad ☎03/483-4363. Come for the preppy MTV ambience and karaoke (Wed from 9.30pm; reservation required), as well as great smoothies and non-alcoholic cocktails, though the fajitas salads and melts are rather disappointing (£E5–9 minimum charge). Daily 7.30am–1am.

Denis 1 Sharia Ibn Basaam, off Ramleh. 1930s-style Greek fish bar where you select your *samak* or calamari from the freezer. Fish with chips, salad, tahina and beer costs around £E40. Daily 10am–midnight.

Elite 43 Sharia Safiya Zaghloul. Old-fashioned Bohemian place decorated with Chagall prints and articles about its owner Madame Christina and the artists she has known. Simple Greco-Levantine dishes: choose from the long menu on the wall rather than the short one given to tourists. Serves beer and *zibiba*. Daily 8am–midnight.

Fish Market Anfushi. 2nd floor of a waterfront complex that includes the *Tikka Grill* (see overpage). Spacious and snazzy, with a great view of the harbour and service verging on the obsequious. No menus; you choose from a mound of fish (£E45–80 per kilo) and crustaceans (£E105–160). The salad platter is a meal in itself. Wine and beer. Daily 1pm–1am.

Kadoura 33 Sharia Bairam al-Tonsi, off the Corniche in Anfushi ☎03/480-0405. Get off tram

#5 when it curves inland near the promontory to Qaitbey's Fort, and walk down a side street to find this famous fish restaurant. *Kadoura* (pronounced 'Adoura') is quite scruffy, with no menu. Diners choose from an ice-packed array of sea bass, mullet, bluefish, squid, shrimp and crab. All orders come with salad, rice and dips. Daily noon–midnight.

Malek es-Samaan Off Sharia Attarine. Look for the sign with a picture of a bird to find this humble open-air eatery in a yard that hosts a clothes market by day. Delicious spit-roast quail is all they serve (£E7 per bird). Daily 8pm–1am (or later).

Mohammed Ahmed 17 Sharia Shakor Pasha, off Sa'ad Zaghloul. One of the cheapest places for a takeaway or a quick meal downtown, it serves tasty *fuul*, felafel, and other vegetarian Egyptian dishes. Daily 6am–1am.

Mohammed Hosni 48 Sharia Safar Pasha, Anfushi. This semi-outdoor restaurant in a courtyard on the same street as *Abu Ashraf* (see p.635) serves seafood, kebabs and quail; two courses cost £E20–30. Daily till midnight or later.

L'Osobuco 14 Sharia al-Horriya ☎03/487-2506. Run by the same firm as *L'Aubergine* in Cairo,

this candlelit restaurant has an excellent menu that spans three continents and includes plenty of vegetarian dishes (£E35–50 for two courses), plus a bar featuring live jazz some evenings. Daily 11am–3am.

Samakmak 42 Qasr Ras el-Tin, Anfushi ☎03/481-1560. Fancier than *Kadoura* or *Abu Ashraf*, this fish restaurant is renowned for its crab tageen, crayfish, and spaghetti with clams, and belongs to a retired belly-dancer, Zizi Salem. In the summer you can eat outdoors in a large tent.

Taverna Opposite Ramleh tram terminal. Popular chain restaurant with a *shawarma* and kebab takeaway downstairs. Does Egyptian and Western-style pizzas, seafood and soup. Daily 8am–3am (2am in winter).

Tikka Grill Anfushi. Underneath the *Fish Market* ☎03/480-5114. Plush surroundings and great service, though the chicken tikka is nothing special. Serves alcohol. Daily 1pm–1am.

Zephyrion Abu Qir beach. Once the best seafood place at Abu Qir, *Zephyrion* (Greek for "sea breeze") has gone downhill since its former owner died, though its breezy terrace is still alluring. Daily noon–midnight.

Drinking

Although Alex is the centre of Egypt's wine and spirits industry (the vineyards are at Gianaclis, near Lake Mariout), **bars** have a low profile. *Monty's Bar* (daily 6pm–2am) in the *Hotel Cecil* is an anodyne place to sip beer or cocktails; if you're going to pay top prices, the *Fouad Bar* (daily 11am–2am) in the *El Salamlek Palace Hotel* at Montazah is plusher, with piano music in the evenings (smart dress required). But foreign residents and local drinkers tend to gather at the more characterful watering holes detailed below, where prices are lower. If you just want to buy booze, *Drinkies* (11am–midnight except Fri and Muslim holidays) on the corner of Sharia Gamil el-Din Yassin and Sharia el-Ghorfa el-Tigarya sells local wine, spirits, mixers and imported beer; other foreign brands can be purchased within 48 hours of arrival in Egypt at the **duty-free shop**, 31 Sharia Salah Salem (daily 11am–9pm, Ramadan 10.30am–2.30pm & 8–11pm). All the places below are marked on the map on pp.614–615 unless stated otherwise.

Cap d'Or Sharia Adib Ishtak, off Sharia Sa'ad Zaghloul. A real slice of old Alex, with Art Nouveau mouldings, carved teak and engraved mirrors. Intellectuals, bohemians and expats rub shoulders over grilled sardines and bottles of whisky or tequila. Its has a friendly atmosphere, and is popular with the gay community after midnight, when there may be live music. Daily noon–3am.

Elite 43 Sharia Safiya Zaghloul. Simple blue-painted extension to the restaurant of the same name. Frequented by tourists, writers and oddballs; a place to talk and meet people. Sells beer, *zibiba* and brandy. Usually open till midnight.

Portuguese Club (*Nady Portugali*) 42 Sharia Abd el-Qader Ragab, Roushdi ☎03/542-7599. A country club-cum-singles' bar, frequented by the expats of Roushdi, with pool or darts competitions (Tues), a disco (Thurs) and monthly party nights. Non-members must buy a drinks card to the value of £E60. Located 3km from the centre, off Tariq Gamal Abdel Nasser (see map on p.610); catch tram #2 to the Egyptian-American Center and walk two blocks inland to find the first side street off Sharia Kafr Abdou – which is the name to give if you take a taxi (£E5). There's no sign outside the club. Daily 3pm–till the last customer leaves; open for breakfast from 10am on Fri.

Spitfire Bar Off Sharia Sa'ad Zaghloul. Small hang-out covered in stickers from oil companies, warships and overland travel groups (the kind of foreigners that frequent the place), with Western pop and sports on TV. Mon–Sat noon–midnight.

Nightlife and entertainment

Thursday and Friday are the big nights out in Alex, but there's something happening all week. Several hotel **nightclubs** offer bellydancing and/or a "Russian Show" and DJ. It's wise to phone ahead and book a table at the ones in Montazah. At the *Helnan Palestine* (June–Sept daily 11.30pm–4.30am; Oct–May 3–4 nights weekly) they only admit mixed-sex groups and have a minimum charge of £E100 per person, while the *El-Salamlek Palace* has a nightly programme (10.30pm–3am) in the summer (£E120 per head with dinner). The *Montazah Sheraton's* thirty-minute show at midnight is hardly worth catching (minimum charge £E45 per person). In the centre, the *Hotel Cecil's* nightclub (daily 11.30pm–4am) has four bellydancers from midnight onwards (minimum charge £E60 per person).

Though most four- and five-star hotels have **discos**, they're moribund outside of summer, except for the *Mercure's*, which is busy on Thursday nights throughout the year. All the discos restrict entry to mixed-sex groups, so if you're on your own, hang out at the *Portuguese Club* (see opposite) until a decent sized group of people there decides to go dancing at the *Mercure* and tag along – don't bother with the club's own disco, upstairs. If you prefer **karaoke**, there's a Wednesday-night bash at the *Coffee Roastery* (p.635), though without any alcoholic drinks to loosen inhibitions.

Arts and festivals

After decades in the doldrums, Alexandria's cultural scene has seen a recent renaissance. The new library is naturally at the forefront, but money has also been spent on the city's historic opera house and other venues. The tourist office has details of their monthly programmes, also advertised *in situ* and at the *Elite* restaurant (see p.635).

The Cultural Centre at the **Bibliotheca Alexandrina** (see p.627) stages **classical music** (Arabic as well as European), modern **dance** and **drama**. Larger orchestral works and **ballet** are performed at the **Opera House** (☏03/486-5106) off Sharia Horriya. Originally called the Theatre Mohammed Ali and now better known as the **Sayed Darwish Theatre**, this Beaux Arts building – fusing elements of the Odeon Theatre in Paris and the Vienna Opera House – has recently been restored to its original splendour.

A few blocks west of the opera, the one-time Mohammed Ali Club, where the city's elite mingled in colonial times, houses the **Alexandria Centre of Arts** (☏03/495-6633), whose blue-and-gold auditorium hosts concerts by guest musicians from Egypt and abroad. Another, smaller venue for music is the **Conservatoire de Musique d'Alexandrie** at 90 Sharia Horriya (☏03/487-5086).

In August you can see **bellydancing and folk dances** by the Rida Troupe (*Ballet Rida*) or the National Troupe (*El-Fir'a el-Qawmiyya*) at the outdoor **Abdel Wahab Theatre** (☏03/486-3637), on the Corniche east of Ramleh. During summer there's also a **circus** (☏03/592-3251), which sets up either at Azarita near the Abdel Wahab Theatre, or at St Marks College in Shatby: check performance times with the tourist office.

In September, Alexandria's annual **International Film Festival** gives Egyptians a rare opportunity to see foreign movies in an uncensored state: the Convention Hall en route to the library is the main venue, but every cinema in town screens a few. Film-going is popular throughout the year, with extra showings at all **cinemas** during Ramadan. Downtown, the three-screen Royal Renaissance (℡03/485-5725) by the Sayed Darwish Theatre and the six-screen Amir (℡03/392-7693) on the corner of Sharia Horriya and Safiya Zaghloul each screen two or three English-language films you might have seen last year. These are trumped by first-releases at the scruffy old Rialto (℡03/486-4694) on Safiya Zaghloul, which far outclass the awful B-movies at the faded Art Deco Metro (℡03/487-0432) down the road. Out in Smouha, the four-screen Renaissance (℡03/424-5899) in the Zahran Mall and the five-screen Osman Group Cinema (℡03/444-5898) in the Smouha Mall vie to show the latest Hollywood blockbusters.

Other cultural events include the two-week **Alexandria Biennial**, an exhibition of art from Mediterranean countries staged in November in odd-numbered years; a **long-distance swimming** festival each July, and an annual **International Yachting Regatta** in October.

During Ramadan, the Egyptian, Islamic side of Alex revels in five **moulids** over five consecutive weeks, starting with *zikrs* outside the Mosque of Al-Mursi. The day after its "big night", the action shifts to Sidi Gaber's mosque, then Sidi Bishr's; these are followed by the moulids of Sidi Kamal and Sidi Mohammed al-Rahhal.

Sport and activities

For those qualified to go **diving**, there are many **ancient ruins and wrecks** to be seen five to eighteen metres beneath the waters around Alexandria. Few other cities boast such a wealth of historic underwater sites, with blocks from the Pharos littering the sea bed near Qaitbey's fort, and Roman trading vessels lying 500m offshore. Some 11,000 artefacts and pieces of masonry remain from what was once the Royal Quarter in the Eastern Harbour, while Napoleonic wrecks and an ancient port lie beneath Abu Qir Bay.

Visibility in the Eastern Harbour declines as the water gets warmer, whereas other, less sheltered sites are best dived in the summer, when the sea is calm. **Alexandra Dive** (℡ & ℻03/483-2045, ⓦwww.alexandra-dive.com), beside the *Tikka Grill* on the Corniche, can usually forecast conditions for the next 24 hours, and offers diving for a minimum of three people at two different sites for US$90 each (including lunch and the fee to Underwater Archeology Department; equipment costs another US$20 per person). They also offer PADI, CMAS or SSI open-water (from £E150), dive master and specialist (US$90–150) **courses**; **windsurfing** (£E80/hr) and **water skiing** (£E200/hr); half-day **fishing trips** (minimum four persons; US$50 each) and one-day **boat safaris** for groups of ten, to Abu Qir and Nelson's Island (£E100 per person). In summer, their dive centre at Mersa Matrouh (see p.651) also offers World War II wreck-diving. It's worth contacting them in advance to discuss the feasibility of specific sites, as some require a permit that takes 4–5 days to obtain.

Other activities can be pursued at the **Sporting Club** (℡03/543-3627). Dr Ashraf Sabri (mobile ℡010 6666514) can sign you in as a guest (£E25), after which you pay to use the **swimming pools** (£E25), tennis and squash courts, 18-hole **golf** course (£E250), or riding stables. Non-residents may use the tennis courts at the *Montazah Sheraton* (£E25/hr plus £E8 for each item of equipment). If you'd rather watch **football**, check who's playing at the Municipal Stadium, the home ground of **Al Ittihad**. Founded by students from Ras el-Tin in the 1920s, the club has won the Egyptian cup six times.

Listings

Airlines EgyptAir (3 weekly flights to Cairo; ☎03/482-5701); BA (3–4 flights weekly to London; ☎487-6668) and Olympic (2–3 weekly to Athens; ☎03/486-1014) are on Midan Ramleh; Air France (☎03/487-8901) at 22 Sharia Salah Salem; Lufthansa (3 weekly to Frankfurt; ☎03/487-7031) at 6 Sharia Talaat Harb. Most are closed Fri. Other airlines represented by travel agents, mostly open daily except Fri 9am–4pm.

American Express 34 Sharia al-Mo'asker al-Romani, Roushdi (☎03/541-0177). Based in a travel agent out near Sidi Gaber Station, it's a nuisance to reach. Daily 9am–5pm.

Arabic language courses Alexandria Centre for Languages, 11 Sharia Mahmoud Khattab, Bab Sharq (☎03/393-1506, mobile ☎012 3480745, ⊛www.aclegypt.com). Normal and intensive level (16hr/20hr tuition per week) thirteen-week courses (£E800/£E1000) in autumn, winter and spring, and three-week courses (£E350/£E450) in the summer.

Banks Bank of Alexandria, 59 Sharia Sa'ad Zaghloul, 23 Sharia Talaat Harb and 26 Sharia Salah Salem (Mon–Thurs & Sun 8.30am–2pm, Ramadan 10.30am–1pm); National Bank of Egypt in the *Montazah Sheraton* (daily 10am–2pm; ATM accepts MasterCard) and the *Hotel Cecil* (Mon–Thurs & Sun 8.30am–8pm, Fri & Sat 9am–noon & 4–7pm); HSBC, 47 Sharia Sultan Hussein (ATM accepts Visa, Cirrus, Electron, Plus and MC); Banque Misr, 1 Sharia Talaat Harb (Visa, MC, Cirrus and Plus).

Bookshops The best for non-fiction and novels in English are Dar el-Mustaqbal, 32 Sharia Safiya Zaghloul (Sat–Thurs 9am–4pm, Sun 9am–1pm); Al-Ahram, on the corner of Sharia Horriya and Talaat Harb (Sat–Thurs 9am–4pm, Sun 9am–1.30pm); and in the Alexandria National Museum (see p.621). You can rummage through second-hand novels (abridged for students of English) on the pavement near the French Centre on Sharia Nabi Daniel, which has a French bookshop in its grounds. Foreign newspapers are sold outside Ramleh telephone exchange and the *Metropole Hotel*.

Consulates Britain, 3 Sharia Mena, Roushdi (Mon–Thurs & Sun 8am–1pm; ☎03/546-7001); Ireland, 9 Sharia El-Fawateem (Mon–Thurs & Sun 8am–1pm; ☎03/484-3320); Israel, 10 Sharia Mena, Roushdi (Mon–Thurs & Sun 9.30am–3.30pm;

☎03/544-9501); USA, 3 Sharia Phara'ana (one day a month 9am–3pm ☎02/797-2301 for details). Australia, New Zealand and Canada have no consular representation; other consulates are listed in *Alexandria Night and Day*.

Cultural centres American Center, 3 Sharia Phara'ana (Mon–Thurs & Sun 10am–4pm, Ramadan Mon–Thurs & Sun 10am–3pm; ☎03/486-1009, ⓔAmericanCenterAlexandria @yahoo.com); British Council, 11 Sharia Mahmoud El Ela, Roushdi (Mon–Thurs 10am–8pm, Fri–Sun 1–8pm; ☎03/545-6512, ⓦwww.britishcouncil .org.eg); Cervantes Institute, 101 Sharia Horriya (daily 5–8pm, ☎03/392-0214, ⓦwww.elcairo .cervantes.es); French Centre, 30 Sharia Nabi Daniel (Sun–Thurs 9am–noon & 5–7.30pm; ☎03/492 0804, ⓦwww.ambafrance.eg.org/cfcc /alexandrie); Goethe Institute, 10 Sharia al-Batalssa (Mon & Wed noon–6pm, Tues & Sun 10am–4pm; ☎03/483-9870, ⓔgialex@internetalex.com); Russian Centre, 5 Sharia Batalsa (Mon–Thurs & Sun 10am–1pm & 5–8pm; ☎03/486-5645).

Dentist Medhat Naga, above the Bank of Alexandria on Sharia al-Kinessa al-Kobtiyya (☎03/487-5551); or Dr Samuel, 51 Sharia Omar Lotfi, Camp Cesar (☎03/592-7216).

DHL 5 Sharia Salah Salem, beside the Banque du Caire (Sat–Thurs 9am–4.30pm).

Film processing Kodak film is sold and developed opposite the Rialto Cinema on Safiya Zaghloul; other places can be found on Sharia Sa'ad Zaghloul.

Hospital The Al-Almani (German) Hospital, 56 Sharia Abdel Salaam Aref, in Saba Pasha (☎03/585-7682), is well-equipped and holds day clinics with specialized doctors for non-emergency cases.

International calls There are Menatel booths all over town. The 24hr exchange on Midan Ramleh has direct-dial phones and sells phonecards; the exchanges on Midan el-Gumhorriya and Sharia Sa'ad Zaghloul (both daily 8am–11pm) work on the pre-booking system. Speedy connections can be obtained at any of the top hotels, which charge 50–70 percent above the normal rate.

Internet New places are opening all the time. Downtown are Cyber Club, Sharia Hassan el-Sheikh, off Sharia Sa'ad Zaghloul (daily 24hr); Mougy Internet, 18 Sharia Kolliet el-Tiba (Sat–Thurs 8am–1am,

Fri 3pm–1am); Sharkes Net Café, Sharia Amin Fikhry (Sat–Thurs 11am–10pm); Tantan Internet Centre, 18 Sharia Dr Ahmed Badawy, 200m west of the library (daily 9am–1am); and Zawiya Internet Café, Sharia Dr Hassan Fadaly, off Safiya Zaghloul (Mon–Sat 11am–11pm). Smouha's Zahran Mall has Click-It (daily 10.30am–1am) on the ground floor, and Access Cybercafé (daily 9am–midnight) on the floor above. Hourly rates range £E4–10.

Passport office To renew your visa (£E12.50), go to kiosk #6 on the first floor of 25 Sharia Talaat Harb (Mon–Thurs, Sat & Sun 8am–3pm; ☎03/484-7873), with one photo and a copy of the relevant pages of your passport (there's a photocopier on the street outside). No applications accepted after noon.

Pharmacies Khalil, on Sharia el-Ghorfa el-Tigarya, off Midan Sa'ad Zaghloul (Mon–Thurs, Sat & Sun 9am–midnight; ☎03/480-6710); Strand, by the

intersection of Safiya and Sa'ad Zaghloul streets (daily 9am–1am; ☎03/486-5136), and others on Safiya Zaghloul and Nabi Daniel streets.

Post offices Midan Ramleh (daily 8am–3pm), Sharia el-Ghorfa el-Tigarya (same hours) and Masr Station (daily 8am–5pm). *Poste restante* is unreliable, so ask if you can have mail sent c/o the *Hotel Cecil*. Express Mail Service is open till 2pm at all the main post offices.

Thomas Cook 15 Midan Sa'ad Zaghloul ☎03/484-7830, ⊕487 4073, ✉tcalex@thomascook .com.eg. Cashes and sells travellers' cheques, and deals with stolen ones. Daily 8am–5pm.

Tourist police Above the tourist office (☎03/487-3378); in the Maritime Station (☎R03/480-4633); and at the entrance to Montazah gardens (☎03/547-3814). All except the last are open 24 hours.

Moving on from Alexandria

Most of the places covered in the remainder of this chapter can be reached from Alexandria by public transport. It's also feasible to make **day excursions** to Rosetta and Tanta in the Delta (see Chapter 5) or the Monasteries of Wadi Natrun (see Chapter 3). Moving on from the city, there are also direct services to Port Said in the Canal Zone.

Buses

The **15th May Terminal** behind Sidi Gaber Station (accessible by tram #2, and then an underpass) is the city's main bus station. It has two separate booking offices and terminals 50m apart, used by the Superjet (5.30am–10.30pm; ☎03/428-9092) and West Delta (5.30am–10.30pm; ☎03/427-0916) companies. From 7am till midnight, both run hourly a/c services to **Cairo** (£E20–25) and its airport (£E25–31). Hourly West Delta buses to **Mersa Matrouh** (£E15–23) run all year, supplemented by more comfortable Superjet services (daily 7.15am & 4pm; £E24) in the summer. Matrouh is a stopover for West Delta buses to **Siwa Oasis** (£E27) leaving Alex at 8.30am, 10.30am and 2pm; and a/c and non-a/c services to **Sollum** (12 daily; £E23–27). Other destinations are **Port Said** (Superjet 6.45am; £E22; West Delta 6am, 8am, 4pm & 6pm; £E17–22); **Ismailiya** (West Delta 7am, 9am & 2.30pm; £E20); **Suez** (West Delta 6.30am, 9am, 2.30pm & 5.30pm; £E22); **El-Arish** (West Delta 9am; £E28); **Hurghada** (Superjet 8pm; £E80; West Delta 6.30pm; £E60); **Tanta** (West Delta hourly 6am–6pm; £E6) and **Zagazig** (West Delta 8am, 9am & 2pm; £E13–15). Tickets for West Delta buses can also be bought at their office (☎03/480-9685) on the corner of Midan Sa'ad Zaghloul and Sharia el-Ghorfa el-Tigarya, provided the computer isn't down, which it frequently is.

Trains

Train services between Alex and Cairo are detailed on p.298. At **Masr Station**, tickets for 1st and 2nd class a/c trains are sold from the office beside the tourist information booth on platform one, while ordinary 2nd class and 3rd class tickets are sold in the front hall. Services to Tanta and Cairo can also be boarded at **Sidi Gaber Station**.

Service taxis

The vast, shade-less **Moharrem Bey Terminal** (known as *El-Mogaf Gedida*, the "New Terminal") on the city's outskirts can be reached by minibus from the western side of Midan el-Gumhorriya (25pt) or by taxi (£E5). Its ranks of Peugeots, Toyota minibuses and minivans run to almost everywhere that's worth mentioning within 250km of Alexandria, including **Cairo** (£E12), **Abu Sir** (£E3), the **Monastery of Abu Mina** (£E3), **El-Alamein** (£E4), **Mersa Matrouh** (£E12), **Port Said** (£E15), **Rosetta** (£E6), **Tanta** (£E5) and **Zagazig** (£E13). Listen for the drivers shouting out destinations, or ask for directions to the right clump of service taxis.

The Mediterranean coast

Egypt's 500-kilometre-long **Mediterranean coast** has beautiful beaches and sparkling sea all the way to Libya. However, many stretches are still mined from World War II (see below) or off limits due to military bases, or simply hard to reach – while all the most accessible sites have been colonized by holiday villages. Unlike in Sinai and Hurghada, these cater almost exclusively to Egyptians, whose beach culture is significantly different from Westerners'. Whilst the beach scene here may lack the atmosphere and the coral reefs found in the Red Sea, the Med is wonderful for **wreck-diving,** with numerous warships and submarines to explore without the scrum of divers that you get at wrecks off Sinai. Just be sure to contact local dive centres well in advance, as some of the wrecks require special permission to dive.

Most foreign travellers heading this way aim for Siwa Oasis (see p.584) rather than the disappointing resort town of **Mersa Matrouh**. Aside from the **beaches** near Matrouh, other coastal sites are awkward to reach (or leave) without private transport, though you may consider it worth making the effort to get to the famous World War II battlefield of **El-Alamein**, which is also within taxi range of several luxurious beach hotels. In general, though, even the sea can seem reclusive here, hidden from sight of the "coastal" highway by **holiday villages** or barren ridges, while the B-road and railway along which many of the region's villages are located run still further inland.

It's worth noting that sections of the Mediterranean coast and the desert inland are still littered with **unexploded shells and minefields**. Never stray into wired-off areas or anything that resembles an abandoned camp or airfield, even if local goatherds seem unfazed by the risk. Stick to well-worn paths and regular beaches and you'll be quite safe.

Between Alexandria and El-Alamein

The "sights" **between Alexandria and El-Alamein** are relatively neglected by tourists, in some cases deservedly so. Getting there can involve much toing and froing around unsignposted crossroads miles from anywhere and, without your own transport, none of the places below is easy to reach as stops en route to El-Alamein or Mersa Matrouh. If you're using public transport, it's better to consider them as day excursions from Alex.

There are many new **holiday villages** along the highway to Matrouh. Some are reserved for elite sections of Egyptian society such as the army, navy and diplomatic corps, while others cater to anyone wealthy enough to afford an apartment there. If you have a car and loads of money, their gorgeous beaches and middling to luxurious facilities could be worth investigating. Otherwise, they're simply blights on the landscape that induce a numbing fatalism, as one succeeds another, for mile after mile. By contrast, the colonial-era beach resort of **El-Agami** (20km from downtown Alexandria and serving as a commuter suburb of the city) seems almost historic.

Abu Sir and Burg al-Arab

Thirty kilometres beyond El-Agami the coastal highway passes the site called **Abu Sir**, better known to archeologists by its Roman name, **Taposiris Magna**. Here, the limestone ridge to the south of the road bears the ruins of an ancient **port city** that the Egyptians called *Per Usiri* ("Dwelling of Osiris") and the Greeks, *Busiris*. There were actually two ports: one on the Mediterranean and the other on Lake Maryut, to the south, which was linked to the Nile until the twelfth century AD. Egypt's agricultural wealth was shipped by barge to Maryut and transferred to seagoing vessels, while imported luxuries travelled the other way; customs posts levied duties on both. In Roman times, the Maryut region produced as much grain as the Fayoum and the Nile Valley, which went to appease the potentially riotous plebs in the imperial capital.

Vital to this commerce was a chain of lighthouses from Alexandria to Cyrenacia (Libya), which warned mariners of the abrupt change from sea to sand, along a low-lying coastline largely devoid of landmarks but plagued by reefs and shoals. While Alexandria's Pharos has disappeared, you can get an idea of its shape from the sole surviving **lighthouse** in the chain, at Abu Sir. Most Egyptologists believe that this was a one-tenth scale replica of the Pharos, although Győző Vörös (excavator of the sun temple on Thoth Hill; see p.422) thinks it was the prototype for the Pharos, rather than a scaled-down copy. The triple-tiered structure rises above several natural caves amidst an ancient cemetery where both humans and sacred animals were buried. The latter were probably related to a ruined **temple of Osiris**, surrounded by fourth-century BC enclosure walls; its gutted interior was used as a Christian church at the end of the fourth century, and later as a fortress by the Arabs, a hideout by Bedouin caravan-robbers, and a coastguard station by the British.

On the slopes to the south of the temple lies the partially excavated **ruined city**, including a winery and a public bathhouse from the time of Justinian. Lower downhill was once a busy harbour on Lake Maryut, where pilgrims bound for the Osiris temple disembarked, followed centuries later by Christians on their way to Abu Mina (see opposite), and then by Muslims travelling to Mecca. The lake became ever more saline as the Canopic branch of the Nile silted up and the British dug canals to flood it with sea water, to create a defensive barrier to the west of Alexandria. Nowadays, parts often dry out entirely in summer and others are used as drainage basins for industrial effluents or excess water from Alex – but the **view** from the ridge is still beautiful.

Unfortunately, **getting there** offers lots of scope for getting lost, as the drivers of minibuses from the Moharrem Bey terminal in Alex either confuse Abu Sir with Abu Qir (see p.633) or with Burg al-Arab, 4km inland from

Abu Sir. It's better to hire a taxi (£E150–200), but be sure that the driver understands exactly which site you have in mind.

Confusion arises because the lighthouse is often referred to as the **Burg al-Arab** ("Arab's Tower"), the name given to a coastal watchtower destroyed by the British in 1882, which was later bestowed on a model village designed by Wilfred Jennings-Bramly in 1915, on the opposite side of the lake from Abu Sir. Burg al-Arab served as RAF headquarters during the battle of El-Alamein and was later graced with a villa where President Sadat planned the October War of 1973. It still occupies a guarded enclave on the edge of the sprawling community.

To confuse things further, at KM 52 on the highway there's also a turn-off to the five-star **Hilton Burg al-Arab** (☎03/374-0730, ⑤374-0760, ⓦwww .hilton.com; ❸) on the coast, whose amenities include a private beach, a large pool and a children's splash pool, a gym and sauna. Rates are heavily discounted online and over winter, when foreign tour operators charge as little as US$55 for a double room, including breakfast. Package tourists fly straight into **Burg al-Arab airport**, an ex-military airfield that currently serves as Alexandria's international terminal.

The Monastery of Abu Mina

If you're hiring a car to visit El-Alamein or Abu Sir, consider a side-trip to the Coptic **Monastery of Abu Mina**, 15km inland from Abu Sir. It can also be reached from Alexandria by minibus from the Moharrem Bey terminal (£E3-4), and there are enough pilgrim coaches heading for the site to make hitch-hiking feasible – though not the best strategy to adopt at the outset.

Deir Mari Mina (as it's known locally) honours **St Menas**, an Egyptian-born Roman legionary who was martyred in Asia Minor in 296 after refusing to renounce Christ. His ashes were buried here when the camel that was taking them home refused to go any further. Miraculous events on the spot persuaded others to exhume Menas in 350 and build a church over his grave, later enclosed within a huge basilica. A pilgrim city grew up as camel trains spread his fame (Menas is depicted between two camels), and "holy" water from local springs was exported throughout Christendom. But when these dried up in the twelfth century, the city and its vineyards were abandoned and soon buried by sand, only a small community of monks remaining.

While its belfry towers are visible from far away, high walls enclose the concrete buildings of the modern monastery, erected in 1959, which is outwardly graceless and luridly decorated within, like all modern Coptic architecture. Not that monks and believers would agree, or even think it relevant; what counts is the spirit of devotion, most evident on November 11, when pilgrims celebrate **St Menas's Day**. (A Coptic encyclical of 1943 asserted that it was Menas, the "wonder-worker of Egypt", who ensured the Allies' victory at El-Alamein.)

In addition to Menas, the crypt houses the body of Pope Kyrillos VI (1959–71), whom Copts regard as a saint, writing petitions on his marble grave. With permission from the monks, you may be allowed to explore the nearby **ruins** of the ancient monastery and pilgrim town. Fragments of marble paving, granite and basalt columns and mosaics of semi-precious stones give some idea of how large and lavishly decorated the basilica of St Menas was, at a time when Christian churches in Europe were primitive structures, if they existed at all. Until its water dried up, the pilgrim town even featured a hospice with hot and cold baths.

Beach resorts near El-Alamein

The coastal road to El-Alamein is flanked by wall-to-wall **holiday villages** built during the 1990s. These gigantic eyesores were reputedly to blame for the devaluation of the Egyptian currency. Speculators borrowed billions of pounds to construct resorts whose projected value was pledged as security for the loans but turned out to be grossly overestimated, leaving banks with a massive liquidity crisis. Worse, over 80km of unspoilt beaches and wildlife habitats disappeared under shoddy apartments and construction debris, ruining the coastline forever. Each resort is presaged by an ostentatious gateway, guarded by armed security men. Mostly moribund over winter, they come alive as BMW-borne families move in for the summer.

While most are open to non-residents for a day-charge, their **beach scene** is staid by Western standards, and bikinis, cocktails and **nightlife** are only on offer at the four-star *Aida Beach Hotel* (☎ & ℻046/410-2818; ➐) at KM 77, or the new five-star *Mövenpick Resort El-Alamein* (☎046/419-0060, ⓦwww .mövenpick-hotels.com; ➑) at Ghazala Bay, KM 130, which has a vast swimming pool (heated in winter), a dive centre and white beach, with all rooms facing the sea. UK tour operators offer seven-night packages from £389, and online agencies quote huge discounts on rooms. You may also find good online deals at the sprawling, three-star *Atic Hotel* (☎03/950-718; ➐) at KM 90, which has a lovely beach, too.

El-Alamein

Before Alamein we never had a victory. After Alamein we never had a defeat.

Winston Churchill, *The Hinge of Fate*

EL-ALAMEIN ("Two Worlds") is an apt name for a place that witnessed the turning point of the North African campaign, determining the fate of Egypt and Britain's empire. When the Afrika Korps came within 111km of Alexandria on July 1, 1942, the city and the capital experienced "The Flap": documents were burned, civilians mobbed railway stations, and Egyptian nationalists prepared to welcome their Nazi "liberators". Control of Egypt, Middle Eastern oil and the Canal route to India seemed about to be wrested from the Allied powers by Germany and Italy. Instead, at El-Alamein, the Allied Eighth Army held, and then drove the Axis forces back, to ultimate defeat in Tunisia. Some 11,000 soldiers were killed and 70,000 wounded at El-Alamein alone; total casualties for the North African campaign (September 1940–March 1943) exceeded 100,000.

Travellers who wish to pay their respects to the dead or have an interest in military history should find the **cemeteries** and the **war museum** worth the effort of getting there. Commemorative **services** are held at El-Alamein each October; contact the British, Italian or German embassies in Cairo for details.

Getting there – and leaving

The utterly misnamed "City" of El-Alamein squats on a dusty plain 106km west of Alexandria, situated along a spur road that turns inland from the coastal highway. Anyone driving past could blink and see nothing except construction debris until they pass the Italian War Cemetery 9km down the highway. If you can afford it, the easiest way of visiting El-Alamein is by **renting car** with a driver, through Avis or El Lord in Alex (see p.613), for £E450. Alternatively, you may be able to rent a **taxi** for the day in Alex, for upwards of £E200 return, depending on your bargaining skills. Though comparatively expensive, a car enables you to reach the far-flung cemeteries and leave El-Alamein without difficulty – a major advantage over public transport.

Hourly West Delta **buses** from Alex to Mersa Matrouh can drop you at the police checkpoint by the turn-off for the Allied War Cemetery, or 1km further west along the highway, closer to the War Museum (see below); you'll pay £E6–7 for the journey. The other way is to catch a **minibus** (£E4) from the Moharrem Bey terminal in Alex. While getting there is straightforward enough, leaving can be harder. Basically, you walk back to the highway and flag down any bus or minibus heading in the right direction – but be sure they're going all the way to your destination (whether it's Alex or Mersa Matrouh), otherwise you risk being stranded if they turn off the highway to settlements such as Bahig or Ras al-Hikma, from which there may be no onward transport unless you fork out for a private taxi.

Staying in the vicinity boils down to a choice between the grotty *Al-Amana Hotel* (☏046/493-8324; ❹) opposite the museum, or the more distant, luxurious resorts along the coast – see opposite for details.

The Battle and its legacy

Rather than the single, decisive clash of forces that people generally imagine, the **Battle of El-Alamein** alternated between vicious fighting and relative lulls over four months (July–November) in 1942. The **Afrika Korps'** initial advance on El-Alamein was stymied by lack of fuel and munitions and stiff Allied resistance organized by Auchinleck. Once resupplied, however, Field Marshal Erwin **Rommel** was able to press the advantage with 88mm cannons that outranged the Allies' guns, as well as faster, better-armoured tanks.

At this time General Bernard **Montgomery** ("Monty") took over the Allied **Eighth Army**, and his first command was that it would retreat no further. He negated his army's weaknesses by digging his tanks into pits with only the gun turrets poking out above ground, protecting them until the German Panzers came within range. Aware that the Allies were being quickly resupplied, Rommel now launched a huge offensive, attacking Alam Halfa ridge with ten divisions. Suffering heavy losses (August 31 to September 6) and desperately short of fuel, the Afrika Korps withdrew behind a field of 500,000 landmines. Monty patiently reorganized his forces, resisting pressure from his superiors to attack until he had amassed 1000 tanks.

Having cracked the Enigma code, the Allies were now able to exploit a huge tactical advantage – Rommel was absent sick in Italy, and the Allies knew it. When they punched a corridor through the minefields of the central front on October 23, the Germans, who had expected the main assault on their southern flank, were taken unawares. Rommel managed to return two days later, but was obliged to concentrate his mobile units further north, stranding four Italian divisions in the south. The Allies had established a commanding position at Kidney Hill, from which point Monty launched the decisive strike on November 2, using air power and artillery and leaving Rommel with only 35 operational tanks by the end of the day. The Eighth Army broke out on November 5 and surged west, and the Afrika Korps fought rearguard actions back through Libya until its inevitable surrender six months later.

The War Museum and cemeteries

Whilst you can be sure of finding all the **cemeteries** open (daily: summer 8am–5pm; winter & Ramadan 9am–4pm), it's worth phoning ahead to check about the museum (☎046/410-0021), as it tends to close now and again for some reason or another. All the Allied memorials lie beside a spur road off the highway, which begins just after the turn-off for the Qattara Depression (see opposite). First comes the **Greek Memorial**, followed 400m later by the **South African Memorial**, and then the **Allied War Cemetery** secluded on the reverse slope of a hill. Planted with trees and flowers, it is a tranquil site for the graves of 7367 Allied soldiers (815 of them nameless, only "known unto God"), with memorial cloisters listing the names of 11,945 others whose bodies were never found. Though over half were Britons, the dead include Australians, New Zealanders, Indians, Malays, Melanesians, Africans, Canadians, French, Greeks and Poles. If you want to find a particular headstone, the Commonwealth War Graves Commission in London can tell you exactly where to look. Walking down to the cemetery, you'll pass the **Australian Memorial**, honouring the 9th Australian Division that stormed Point 29 and Thompson's Post during the penultimate phase of the battle.

If you're coming by bus or service taxi, you're likely to be dropped further west along the highway, where a Sherman tank (not of World War II vintage, but captured from the Israelis) near a gas station marks the start of an uphill turn-off leading to the museum ("*El Mathaf*", in Arabic). Follow this to a T-junction and turn left; the museum is 200m ahead, past a telephone exchange. The **War Museum** (daily: summer 8am–5pm; winter & Ramadan 9am–4pm; £E5) is well presented, with photos and models conveying the harsh conditions in the field. Due weight is given to the experience of both sides, and Egypt's role in the Allied struggle is deservedly credited. Notice the section on the explorer Almássy (of *The English Patient*) and his role in guiding two German spies through the desert. Outside are two dozen tanks, cannons and trucks, including a lorry belonging to the Long Range Desert Group that was found in the desert in 1991 (see p.579). There's also a restored **Command Bunker** that was used by Monty during the battle, which you'll have to ask a guide to unlock.

On the highway west of El-Alamein is a **plaque** marking the furthest point of the Axis advance, which asserts: *Manco la Fortuna, Non Il Valore* ("Lacking Fortune, Not Valour"), *1.7.1942, Alessandria 111km*. Further out you'll glimpse the **German Cemetery**, which overlooks the sea from a peninsula to the north: a squat octagonal building that houses the remains of 4280 German soldiers. An elegant white tower marks the **Italian Cemetery**, 3km further along the highway, which contains a small museum, and a chapel with the dedication: "To 4800 Italian soldiers, sailors and airmen. The desert and sea did not give back 38,000 who are missing." Do not wander around between these cemeteries; while the grounds themselves have been cleared, the intervening strips of land are still mined.

The battlefield

The battlefield itself is generally far too dangerous to explore, due to the **minefields** laid by both sides. A staggering 17.2 million landmines are estimated to remain in the Western Desert, which still kill and maim local Bedouin to this day. Casualties were highest in the 1950s, when a foreign scrap-metal dealer taught locals to make bombs from unexploded shells and blow derelict tanks into portable chunks. Germany, Britain and Italy have always rejected Egyptian and Libyan demands that they fund landmine clearance programmes – the current excuse is that Egypt hasn't signed up to the Ottawa Convention banning the manufacture of landmines. Although a few Bedouin with 4WDs are prepared to take people to such strategic strongpoints as **Kidney Ridge** and **Tell el-Issa**, you would be foolish to rely on assurances that they know safe routes through the minefields.

However, at least two relics of the struggle can be seen without any risk from the road to the Qattara Depression that starts near the Greek Memorial. To the east of the road, **El-Alamein Station** looks much as it did in 1942, albeit no longer thronged with Allied troops (who dubbed the station "Heaven") and supplies; while 24km further south, the ridge on the western side is honey-combed with trenches and tunnels belonging to the **Italian Field Hospital** and defensive positions that were stormed by the Allied 30th Corps in "Operation Lightfoot". This road is well surfaced and eventually dips down into the Qattara Depression to meet up with the Cairo–Bahariya highway (see p.600) but you do need a **permit** to use it – and whatever you do, don't stray off the tarmac road, as the verges and surrounding areas are heavily mined.

Sidi Abd el-Rahman

Nine kilometres past the last of the battlefield memorials, a spurt of new housing anounces **SIDI ABD EL-RAHMAN**, which is used as a pit-stop by buses going to Matrouh and Siwa. There's no point in lingering here unless you're going to use the stunning white **beach** at the *El-Alamein Hotel* (☎046/492-1228; ❼), a fancy resort where the rooms and villas are often reserved up to a year in advance. It lies about 3km past a township established to settle Awlad Ali **Bedouin** who moved in from Libya onto the lands of the weaker Morabiteen tribe a couple of centuries ago. Many have abandoned their traditional goat's-hair tents for stone houses, but they still maintain flocks, which they graze on scrubland or pen behind their now-immobile homes. Ten kilometres into the desert behind them lies a **graveyard of Panzers**, destroyed in the final rout of the Afrika Korps from the battlefield; it was here that Von Thoma, the commander of the nearly obliterated 15th and 21st Panzer divisions, surrendered. Earlier in the campaign, the Afrika Korps' heaquarters and tank repair depot were located at Sidi Abd el-Rahman, behind a belt of minefields and gun emplacements 8km in depth.

Mersa Matrouh

Although **MERSA MATROUH** has grown phenomenally and sees itself as a sophisticated resort, it remains a hick town at heart, which in summer is clogged with Egyptian and Libyan holidaymakers. The town's beaches are scrappy, with the best options being far from town at the magnificent cove at Agiiba and the neighbouring Ubbayad beach. Social norms here are conservative: more women wear yashmaks than headscarves, and sermons are broadcast from mosques every day, not only on Fridays. By no stretch of the imagination does Matrouh fit the tourist board's promise of a hedonist's playground. The only people likely to think so are the Libyans who've been coming here since the border was reopened; Egyptians go the other way, seeking work in Libya, while Western visitors are generally more interested in reaching Siwa Oasis (see p.584) or heading underwater to **dive** Matrouh's World War II **wrecks** (see p.651).

A grid of mould-poured low-rise blocks housing eighty thousand people, the **town** spreads up from the coast towards a ridge festooned with radar dishes. As Matrouh has gone from being a quiet fishing port to the booming capital of the Mediterranean governorate, immigrants have poured in from other parts of Egypt, inspiring mixed feelings amongst the locals.

Despite appearances, Mersa Matrouh ("Sheltered Anchorage") has a long **history**. Founded by Alexander the Great on his way to Siwa, it was here that

Mark Antony and Cleopatra sought solace after their defeat at Actium, and that her fleet put out to sea for its final battle against Octavian. During the Islamic era, Matrouh was a busy trading port with a sideline in smuggling; its other main industry (dating back to Roman times) was harvesting sponges. Divers came from as far away as the Cyclades – up to two thousand of them per year in the early twentieth century. To pluck the sponges from the sea bed 60–90m below, they used a stone to make themselves sink faster, which they jettisoned at the bottom. Sponge-harvesting ceased in the early 1980s. Today, cut-price Chinese goods at the Souk Libyani ("Libyan Market") outside town, and a record consignment of 300 tonnes of hashish seized by the coastguard, suggest that cross-border trading and smuggling are flourishing again.

Getting there

The 209km journey **from Alex** is best accomplished **by bus**. There are hourly West Delta services (£E15–23) throughout the year, augmented from June to September by comfier Superjets (7.15am & 4pm; £E24) that likewise depart from the Sidi Gaber terminal and take about three hours. Both are faster and a lot less scary than **service taxis** from the Moharrem Bey depot (£E12; 3hr 30min). The only **trains** from Alex are filthy third-class services, used by conscripts en route to or from their postings in Mersa Matrouh, which take between six and nine hours (£E3.50).

Matrouh can be reached directly **from Cairo** in about six hours by West Delta buses from the Turgoman Terminal (4 daily; £E28–37). Book seats a day beforehand. Mornings are the best time to catch sporadic **service taxis** (£E20) from Ahmed Helmi and Koulali squares, near Ramses Station, which take about seven hours; an alternative is to ride to Alex and pick up another service there. There are three sleeper **trains** a week from Cairo's Ramses Station (US$62) to Matrouh, leaving at 11pm and arriving at 6am next morning, as well as a summer-only daily a/c service leaving early in the morning. EgyptAir **flights** run on alternate days (1hr; about £E450 one-way).

Tourists intent on travelling to **Siwa Oasis** without staying in Matrouh should catch either one of the direct services from Alex, or an early morning bus from Cairo to Matrouh, and then the afternoon bus on to Siwa. Since Matrouh's bus station is far from the centre of town, you won't have much time to look around before returning to board the bus at 5pm. Advice on travelling on to Siwa appears on p.653.

Arrival and information

On **arrival**, you can catch a microbus (25pt) or taxi (£E3–5) into the centre of town from Mersa Matrouh's bus and service taxi station, train station or airport. Blue-and-white taxis are the mainstay of **transport** around town (£E3) and to the nearer beaches, or you can rent a bike from one of the stands along Sharia Iskandariya (£E10 per day).

The municipal **tourist office** (daily 9am–2.30pm; ☎046/493-1841) near the Corniche has friendly, English-speaking staff who can answer most questions. The **tourist police** (☎046/493-5575) are next to the tourist office on the Corniche, while the regular **police** (☎046/493 3015) are just inland on Sharia ash-Shatta. Both are open 24 hours, though little English is spoken at either, so if you have a problem, try to get one of the women at the tourist office to act as interpreter. On the same street are the **post office** (daily except Fri 8.30am–2pm) and 24-hour **telephone exchange**, but the latter is so crowded and unreliable for international calls that it's worth paying extra for a direct

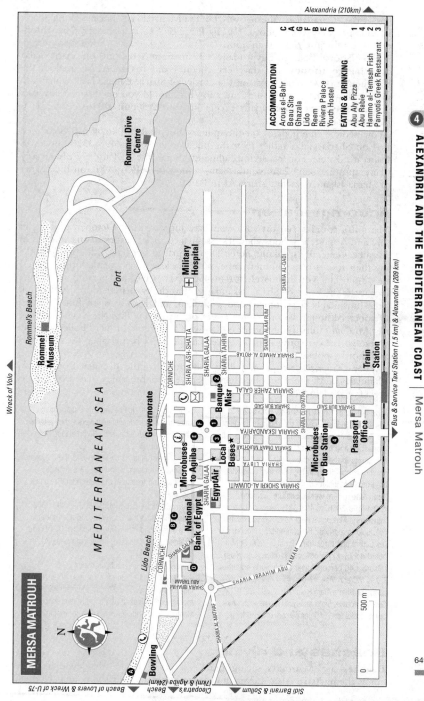

MERSA MATROUH

ACCOMMODATION
Arous el-Bahr   C
Beau Site   A
Ghazala   G
Lido   F
Reem   B
Riviera Palace   E
Youth Hostel   D

EATING & DRINKING
Abu Aly Pizza   1
Abu Rabie   4
Hammo al-Temsah Fish   2
Panyotis Greek Restaurant 3

Alexandria (210km)

MEDITERRANEAN SEA

Wreck of Volo
Rommel's Beach
Rommel Museum
Rommel Dive Centre
Port
Lido Beach
Governorate
Military Hospital

CORNICHE
SHARIA ASH-SHATTA
SHARIA GALAA
SHARIA TAHRIR
SHARIA AHMED AL-ROTAB
SHARIA AL-QADI
SHARIA ALAM RUM
SHARIA ZAHER GALAL
SHARIA BUR SAID
SHARIA CLEOPATRA
SHARIA BUR SAID
Banque Misr
Train Station
Passport Office
SHARIA ISKANDARIYA
SHARIA OMAR MUKHTAR
SHARIA LIBYA
SHARIA SHOKRI AL-QUWATLI
SHARIA AL-DUWATI
SHARIA IBRAHIM ABU TAMAM
SHARIA IBRAHIM ABU TARAM
SHARIA AL MATHAF

Microbuses to Agiiba
Local Buses
EgyptAir
National Bank of Egypt
Microbuses to Bus Station

Bowling

Bus & Service Taxi Station (1.5 km) & Alexandria (209 km)

Sidi Barrani & Sollum
Cleopatra's Beach
Beach of Lovers & Wreck of U-75
Beach of Lovers (1km) & Agiiba (24km)

N

0   500 m

line at the *Rivira Palace*. Alternatively, use the Menatel card-phones along Sharia Iskandariya. Speed.Net, above *Abu Aly Pizza* on Sharia Iskandariya, has **Internet** access for just £E2.50 an hour.

The National Bank of Egypt (daily 8.30am–5pm & 6–9pm) on Sharia Galaa can **change money** and travellers' cheques and has an ATM, as does the Banque Misr, five blocks east on the corner of Sharia Zaher Galal, which also gives cash advances on MasterCard and Visa. Should you need to extend your visa, the **passport office** (daily except Fri 9am–2.30pm; ☎046/493-5351) is near the train station.

For medical emergencies, try the military **hospital** (☎046/493-5286; closed Fri) on Sharia Galaa rather than the public one (☎046/493-3370), or go to Cairo if possible. For less serious ailments, there's the Al-Farghaly **pharmacy** (daily: summer 8am–2am; winter 8am–9pm; ☎046/493-9390), on the corner of Sharia Iskandariya and Sharia Alam Rum.

Accommodation

Matrouh's **tourist season** runs from late June to early October, peaking in July and August, a period when it's essential to make **reservations** months in advance. Generally speaking, hotels are overpriced but have little problem filling their rooms over summer; some of them close down (or slash their prices) in winter. The **youth hostel** (☎046/493-2331; £E12 per person), in a dingy locality 600m west of Sharia Iskandariya, has dinky shared rooms with bunk beds (unsuitable for women) and a kitchen, and is only open from May to October. Although you can pitch a tent on beaches within the town limits for free, you *must* inform the tourist office (who'll notify the tourist police) exactly where you're **camping**. Unauthorized campers risk being taken for smugglers and shot by police patrols.

Where distances are given below, they refer to the distance from Sharia Iskandariya. All the places listed are open year-round; unless stated otherwise, breakfast is included.

Arous el-Bahr Corniche ☎046/493-4420, ⓕ493-4419. The recently refurbished "Bride of the Sea" has pleasant sea-facing a/c rooms with fridges, TV and bathrooms, plus billiards, gym and sauna in the basement. Half-board (£E62 per person) is obligatory in high season; otherwise breakfast not included. ❹

Beau Site 1.5km west along the Corniche ☎046/493-2066, ⓕ493-3319, ⓦwww.beausite .masr.com. Matrouh's best hotel has a/c rooms overlooking a private beach and blue lagoon; a restaurant and three bars. From June to Sept half-board (£E75–87) is obligatory; off-season room rates are 40 percent lower and include breakfast. Takes MC and Visa. ❼

Ghazala Sharia Alam Rum ☎046/493-3519. Spartan double, triple and quad rooms with sinks but no locks for £E15 per person, or £E20 for a

room to yourself. No hot water, and no running water in the shared toilets/showers – they provide a bucket of water for guests. No breakfast. Honest management. ❶

Lido Sharia Galaa ☎ & ⓕ046/493-2248. Rooms are small but clean, with fans, TV, balconies, and soap and towels in the bathroom. Breakfast optional. ❷

Reem Corniche ☎046/493-3605, ⓕ493 3608. Less fancy than the *Beau Site*, but a lot cheaper for a sea-facing room with a balcony. Half-board included in high season; off-season rates 30 percent lower. ❺

Riviera Palace Sharia Iskandariya ☎ & ⓕ046/493-3045. Central three-star hotel with a fake stuffed tiger in the lobby, pleasant carpeted rooms with fridges, and a good restaurant (no alcohol). Block-booked from July to September. ❻

Beaches and diving

Beaches are Matrouh's saving grace, so it's a shame that women can't enjoy them. As in Alex, Egyptian women sunbathe and swim fully clothed, accompanied by male relations; a foreigner acting differently can be subject to persistent staring and pestering. Only residents at the *Beau Site* can use its private beach, free from hassle.

For qualified divers, the coastal waters from Matrouh to the Gulf of Sollum are as rewarding for **wreck-diving** as the Red Sea (for details, see Ⓦwww .sportesport.it/wrecks.htm and Ⓦwww.ubootwaffe.net), with visibility usually superb. Trips can be arranged by the **Rommel Dive Centre** (daily mid-April to Nov; mobile ℡010 6666514, ℮alxdiv@dataxps.com.eg) near the port, an offshoot of Alexandra Dive (see p.638). Call a few days in advance to discuss the feasibility of specific sites.

The nearby municipal beaches and the dive centre are accessible by bicycle, which can be rented from hotels and shops along Sharia Iskandariya. **Transport** to the western beaches varies with the season: from June onwards you should be able to catch a microbus from the corner of Sharia Galaa (£E3 to Agiiba), or an open-sided *tuf-tuf* bus (50pt) that shuttles back and forth along the Corniche every hour or so from 6.30am to sunset, to Cleopatra and Agiiba beaches. Additionally, local buses leaving from Sharia Tahrir run to Zawiyat Umm al-Rukham.

The town beaches

The three beaches around Matrouh's crescent-shaped bay are separated by breakwaters and a small port further east. Beyond this, a spit of land curves around to face the town, rimmed on the landward side by **Rommel's Beach**. The Desert Fox supposedly bathed here in between plotting the Alam Halfa offensive from a nearby cave, now turned into a small **Rommel Museum** (daily 9am–5pm; £E5). His maps, desk and leather greatcoat (donated by his grandson, Manfred) are among the exhibits, which carry amusing captions like: "Rommel was the professor of contemporary military leaders to the extent that he was in every place at the same time." Rommel's Beach is a popular sunbathing spot for Egyptians.

Less than 100m off Rommel's Beach lies the stern half of the **Volo**, a 1567-tonne British freighter torpedoed en route from Torbruk to Alexandria by a German U-boat in December 1941; 28 of the 34 crew died. Soon after sinking the *Volo*, U-boat **U-75** was holed by depth-charges from *HMS Kipling*; 14 submariners drowned but thirty were rescued. The sub lies 600m off what is now the **Beach of Lovers** (*Shahata al-Gharam*), on the far side of Matrouh bay. A mile out in deeper water are **U-577**, sunk by a British Swordfish torpedo-bomber in 1942, and the destroyer **HMS Kipling**, crippled by Junkers-88s in May that year. As they are war graves, it is illegal to remove objects from any of these wrecks.

Back on land, you'd do better sunbathing at **Cleopatra Beach**, roughly 7km west of town, which drops away sharply a metre offshore. Across the dunes on its far right-hand side is **Cleopatra's Bath**, a hollow rock whirlpool bath where she and Mark Antony reputedly frolicked. Outside of the bath, heavy surf and sharp, slippery rocks make this a dangerous spot to swim.

Ubayyad and Agiiba beaches

Ubayyad Beach, 14km from town, is a vast expanse of silvery sand where the sea is calm and shallow up to 200m out. As you'd expect, it has been colonized: besides the Badr Tourist Village (open to the public) there is a private resort for army officers. Five kilometres further on, near the village of Umm Abraham, the sands have disgorged a tiny **ruined temple-fort** dedicated to Ramses II by his general Nebre, which marked Ancient Egypt's westernmost port. **Zawiyat Umm al-Rukham** (its local name) isn't signposted from the coastal road, and is currently off-limits while excavations continue. One find so far is a magnificent funerary statue of Nebre, now on display in the Luxor Museum (see p.376).

From the next headland, 24km from town, a path slopes down to **Agiiba Beach**. Agiiba ("Miraculous") is an apt name for this stunningly beautiful cove, but "beach" is rather a misnomer. To swim in the calm, crystal-clear turquoise water, you can dive off rocky shelves protruding into the sea or wade in off a tiny beach gunked up with algae. From July onwards, you'll have to walk around the headlands and along the shore to find an uncrowded site. Bring food and drink as there's no guarantee of stalls operating on the cliff top, which overhangs some caves.

Eating

Matrouh's high street overflows with grocery stores and bakeries, and a fruit and veg **market** on nearby Sharia Omar Mukhtar – though many places are open year-round, they have longer hours in summertime. Of the hotel **restaurants,** the *Beau Site* and the *Riviera Palace* are the swankiest: otherwise, you're better off choosing one of the more local places listed below. The opening hours given are for summertime; over winter, most places close before midnight, though coffee houses on the main drag and around the market stay open till the small hours.

Abu Aly Pizza Sharia Iskandariya. This two-storey diner three blocks from the Corniche offers fresh pizza (£E11–20), *shawarma*, sandwiches, soups and desserts. Open daily 9am–2am, 9am–3am in summer.

Abu Rabie Sharia Iskandariya. Sit-down and takeaway diner offering *fuul, taamiya*, shrimp (*gambari*) or calamari sandwiches, or any of those served with rice and salad as a meal. Open till midnight year-round.

Hammo al-Temsah Fish Sharia Tahrir. Select your seafood from the freezer or wall-menu, specify grilled or fried, and sit back to await a delicious meal with all the trimmings. You can eat well for £E20–30, if you don't splurge on shrimp (£E140 per kilo).

Panyotis Greek Restaurant Sharia Iskandariya. Established in 1922, by one of the two families of Greek descent still living in Matrouh, it dishes up tasty fried fish or calamari with salad in the summer. Out of season no food is served, but alcohol is available year-round. Daily 8am–1am.

Drinking, nightlife and entertainment

Matrouh is not exactly a metropolis, but it has a fair spread of restaurants and a few entertainments – in summer, at least. The **Governorate Festival** (August 24) catches the season in full swing, with a folkloric parade of dancers, horses and camels down the main street and along the Corniche, and films and plays in the evening. In July and August, there's also **live music** in the pleasure gardens en route to the *Beau Site Hotel*, which also hosts a **disco**. Out of season, there's not much to do – the **bowling** alley across the road from the *Beau Site* is open all year, and non-residents can play **billiards** (£E10 p/hr) and use the women-only **gym** and **sauna** (£E5 per person) at the *Arous el-Bahr Hotel*. Otherwise, you can watch TV in coffee houses, or **drink:** you can have an inexpensive beer downstairs at the *Panyotis Greek Restaurant,* though *zibiba* and brandy must be consumed upstairs or taken away wrapped, while the bars at the *Beau Site* are nice but pricey and a long walk from the centre.

Moving on

Matrouh's **EgyptAir** office on Sharia Galaa (Tues–Sun 9am–2pm & 6–9pm; ☏493-6572) is only open from June to September, when there are flights to Cairo (Wed, Fri & Sun at 11am).

To Siwa

There are three a/c **buses** daily from Matrouh to **Siwa Oasis**, leaving at 7.30am, 1.30pm and 5pm (£E12) – or you could catch the last through-bus from Alex, between 6.45 and 7.30pm. Allow half an hour to reach the bus station from the centre of town (by microbus from the junction of Omar Mukhtar and Cleopatra streets). There shouldn't be any problem getting a seat except around major Muslim or Siwan festivals, and tickets can normally be bought on the bus. There may also be the odd **minibus** (£E12 per person for a full load) from the bus depot, but this should be used only as a last resort. Bring food and water for the four-and-a-half-hour journey.

Motorists should avoid travelling in the midday heat and fill up before leaving Matrouh, as there is only one petrol station along the 300km route. The Siwa road is reached by following the Corniche west out of town, turning inland and passing the airport turn-off, and then heading south at the next junction, 20km from Matrouh. There's a police checkpoint, so you can't miss it. Don't stray far from the road if you stop for a leak; there are minefields on either side for miles into the desert.

Sidi Barrani, Sollum and on to Libya

The **road to Libya** reflects relations between the Arab Republic of Egypt and the Libyan *Jamahiriyah* ("State of the Masses"). During the 1960s, when Gaddafi regarded Nasser's Egypt as the vanguard of revolutionary Arab nationalism, people and goods flowed both ways, encouraging the Libyan leader to propose that the two countries unite in 1973 – an ambition that came to nought as President Sadat cultivated the Western powers and finally signed a peace treaty with Israel. In response, Libya severed relations, closed the border and began agitating for the overthrow of the Egyptian government; a cold war ensued, with sporadic incursions by Libyan warplanes and saboteurs during the 1980s.

It wasn't until the end of the decade that relations were restored and the border was reopened. Despite an upturn in civilian traffic, there's still an overwhelming military presence along the 120km to **SIDI BARRANI** – a small port named after the Senussi missionary Sidi Mohammed el-Barrani, which was ferociously contested during the Western Desert campaign. In December 1940, the Eighth Army took 37,000 Italian prisoners for the loss of 600 of their own troops, only to be driven back by the Afrika Korps in 1942. At several sites along this coast, further remnants from the war can be seen underwater. The Rommel Dive Centre in Matrouh (see p.651) offers **wreck-diving** trips to see the Royal Navy destroyer **HMS Defender,** which hunted four Italian submarines off the Libyan coast before being holed by a Junkers-88 in July 1941; the cruiser **HMS Niad** (torpedoed by a U-boat in 1942); the destroyer **HMS Gurka** (also sunk in 1942); and the German submarine **U-79** (depth-charged in 1941).

Sixty kilometres beyond Sidi Barrani, **SOLLUM** (pronounced "Sa-loom") overlooks the sea from a 180-metre cliff with a harbour at the bottom. A small **Allied War Cemetery** at the eastern entrance to town recalls the toll exacted at "Hell Fire Pass" (Halfaya), where five waves of British tanks were destroyed by German guns dug into the ridge. Offshore lies an exciting dive site, the Italian submarine **Gondar**, containing three manned torpedoes of the type used against warships in Alexandria's Western Harbour (see p.626). The sub was forced to surface by depth charges and was scuttled by its own crew in 1940: again, Rommel Dive Centre (see p.651) can organize dives. Back on shore, the town boasts little more than a **bank**, a telephone office, a few grubby eateries and the new *Sert* **hotel** (☎046/480-1113; ❷), which has en-suite rooms: its **restaurant** is the best place to eat in town.

The **border** crossing beyond the Halfaya Pass is officially open 24 hours, but its lethargic customs officials and sweltering queues of vehicles suggest otherwise. While Egyptians and Libyans cross over regularly, foreign tourists are only just beginning to visit Libya, which hardly encourages impulse visits. Libyan **visas** must be obtained beforehand in Cairo (see p.291), and frankly it's far easier to travel directly to Benghazi or Tripoli on a Superjet from the capital (see p.301), than catch the twice-daily **bus** from Matrouh to Sollum (leaving at 11am and 2pm; £E8; 4hr) and then a service taxi to the border crossing (£E4). On the Libyan side of the border, local service taxis run to Al-Burdi, whence buses go to Tobruk and Benghazi. If you're planning to **drive** your own vehicle along the coast and into Libya, be sure to have your passport and car papers ready to show at the innumerable checkpoints along the way.

The Delta

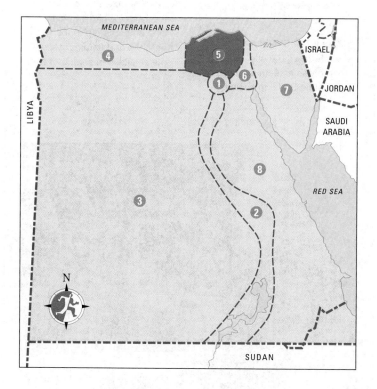

CHAPTER 5 **Highlights**

* **Rosetta's Delta Style Architecture** The little town of Rosetta has been busy restoring its legacy of highly distinctive eighteenth- and nineteenth-century mansions, making it a very worthwhile stopover en route from Alexandria into the Delta. See p.661

* **Moulid of Saiyid Ahmed el-Bedawi** The city of Tanta becomes a seething mass of chanting Sufis, musicians, vendors, circus acts and spectators in the Delta's biggest festival of the year, held in October. See p.664

* **Tanis** The region's most interesting archeological site. See p.668

* **Lake Manzala** One of Egypt's top sites for birdwatching, where herons, spoonbills, pelicans and flamingoes wade the shallows in search of fish. See p.673

△ Sarcophagus lids, Tanis

The Delta

While the Nile Valley's place in Ancient Egypt remains writ large in extraordinary monuments, the **Nile Delta**'s role has largely been effaced by time and other factors. Although several pharaonic dynasties arose and ruled from this region – Lower Egypt – little of their twenty provincial capitals remains beyond mounds of debris known as *tell* or *kom*. The pharaohs themselves set the precedent of plundering older sites of their sculptures and masonry – hard stone had to be brought to the Delta from distant quarries, so it was easier to recycle existing stocks – and nature performed the rest. With a yearly rainfall of nearly 20cm (the highest in Egypt, most of it during winter) and an annual inundation by the Nile that coated the land in silt, mud-brick structures were soon eroded or swept away. More recently, farmers have furthered the cycle of destruction by digging the mounds for a nitrate-enriched soil called *sebakh*, used for fertilizer; several sites catalogued by nineteenth-century archeologists have all but vanished since then.

Of the Delta's show of ancient monuments, the ruins of **Tanis**, **Avaris** and **Bubastis** are certainly worth knowing about, if not visiting. As for Islamic architecture, there's a sprinkling of "Delta Style" mansions and medieval mosques in the coastal towns of **Rosetta** and **Damietta**. Practically everywhere else on the map is an industrialized beehive or a teeming village, only worth visiting for **moulids** or popular festivals, of which the region has dozens. Combining piety, fun and commerce, the largest events draw crowds of over a million, with companies of *mawladiya* (moulid people) running stalls and rides, while the Sufi *tariqas* perform their *zikrs*. People camp outdoors and music blares into the small hours. Smaller, rural moulids tend to be heavier on the practical devotion, with people bringing their children or livestock for blessing, or the sick to be cured.

The great **Moulid of Saiyid el-Bedawi**, held at **Tanta** just after the cotton harvest in October, starts a cycle of **Muslim** festivals lasting well into November. At one- to two-week intervals, pilgrims and revellers congregate for week-long bashes at **Basyouni**, **Dasuq**, **Mahmudiya**, **Fuwa** and **Rosetta**. The Muslim month of Shawwal (following Ramadan) also occasions moulids at **Bilbeis** and **Zagazig**. During May, the remote **Monastery of St Damyanah** witnesses one of Egypt's largest **Christian moulids** and, come August, another event take place at the village of **Mit Damsis**. In January a unique **Jewish moulid** is held at **Damanhur**.

The Delta's other possible attraction is its flat, intensely green **landscape**, riven by waterways where feluccas glide past mud-brick villages and wallowing buffalo. The northern **lakes** are a wintering ground for herons, storks, great crested grebes and other water birds, while doves and pigeons – reared for

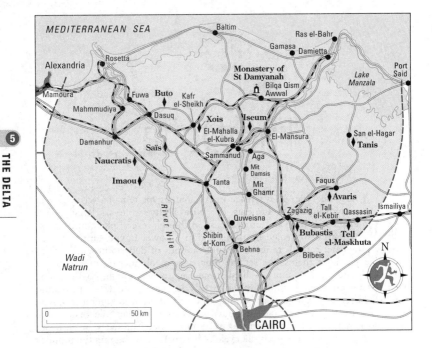

human consumption in cotes shaped like Khmer temples – join other **birdlife** pecking around the cotton-, rice- and cornfields. In ancient times, wealthy Egyptians enjoyed going fowling in the reeds, using throwing sticks and hunting cats; their modern-day counterparts employ shotguns. The Delta is also still a habitat for wildcats and pygmy white-toothed shrews, but boars have been driven out and the last hippopotamus was shot in 1815.

More sombrely for the ecology, the Delta is one of the world regions most vulnerable to the effects of **global warming**. Oceanographers predict that a one-metre rise in the sea level would swamp Alexandria and submerge the Delta as far inland as Damanhur, destroying six percent of Egypt's cultivable land and displacing 3.3 million people. The freshwater Delta lagoons, which provide much of the nation's fish, would also be ruined. A more immediate threat is **erosion** by the Mediterranean. Now that the Delta is no longer renewed by silt from the Nile, its coastline is being worn away.

Visiting the Delta

As few visitors have time for more than one moulid or site, we've dealt with the region in less detail than other parts of Egypt. Depending on where you're aiming for, it might be better to start from Alex, Cairo or the Canal Zone: Rosetta and Damanhur are easiest to reach from Alex; Tanta from Cairo; and Zagazig from Ismailiya.

From Cairo, buses and service taxis to all parts of the Delta leave from Aboud terminal in Shubra (see p.300). There are direct buses from Cairo to the Delta resorts over summer. In some cases, a shortage of local **accommodation** makes day-trips more feasible than overnight stays. Trains are OK for reaching major towns, but service taxis and buses are the best way of **getting around**. Renting a car isn't necessarily a good idea: it's easy to have accidents on the Delta roads, and the unsurfaced ones are legally off limits to foreign drivers – a hangover from 1960s spy-phobia. Should the police decide to make a fuss, you could conceivably spend a night in jail.

Rosetta, Damanhur and the Western Delta

The broader Rosetta branch of the Nile delineates one edge of the **Western Delta**, whose other flank fades into desert. Its cottonfields and mill towns are visible enough from the Delta Road or the Cairo–Alexandria railway, and few places merit closer inspection. **Rosetta** makes a nice day excursion from Alex (there's no tourist accommodation), and **Damanhur** hosts two remarkable moulids, but you have to be pretty keen on archeology to bother with the *koms* off the Tanta road.

Rosetta (Rashid)

The coastal town of **ROSETTA** (*Rashid* in Arabic) has waxed and waned in counterpoint to the fortunes of Alexandria, 65km away. When Alex was moribund, Rosetta burgeoned as a port, entering its heyday after the Ottoman conquest of Egypt in the sixteenth century, only to decline after Alexandria's revival. The modern-day town is still "surrounded by groves of orange and lemon trees", as Eliza Fay wrote home in 1817, but its "appearance of cleanliness ... so gratifying to the English eye" has dissipated, and these days few tourists come to wander through its run-down, littered streets in search of once-elegant Ottoman mansions. It's certainly a far cry from the early nineteenth century, when E.D. Clarke saw "English ladies from the fleet and the army" wearing "long white dresses", riding "the asses of the country".

This earlier European fascination is due to the discovery of the **Rosetta Stone** by French soldiers in 1799. Their officer realized the significance of this second-century BC basalt slab inscribed with ancient hieroglyphs and demotic Egyptian and Greek script, which was forwarded to Napoleon's savants in Cairo. Although their archeological booty had to be surrendered in 1801 – which is how the Stone, "Alexander's Sarcophagus" and many other objects wound up in the British Museum – it was a French professor, Jean-François Champollion (1790–1832), who finally deciphered the hieroglyphs by comparison with the Greek text, and unlocked the secret of the Ancient Egyptian tongue.

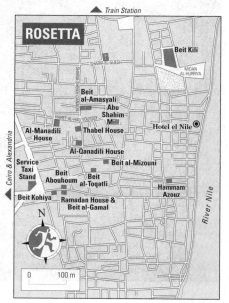

△ Ramadan House, Rosetta

Getting there

The quickest way to reach the town is by **service taxi** (1hr; £E3) from Alexandria's Midan el-Gumhorriya. There is also one **train** a day from Alex, which takes two hours. From Cairo, there is no direct transport, and the best way to get here is by train or service taxi to Damanhur, from where you can take a taxi (£E1) across town to pick up a service taxi to Rosetta; the journey from Damanhu r takes 1hr 15min and costs £E2.25. There are no longer any train services between Rosetta and Dasuq, Damanhur, Tanta or Cairo.

The Town

Rosetta's main appeal lies in its **"Delta Style" architecture** dating from the Ottoman period of the eighteenth and nineteenth centuries. Many of the Delta Style mansions have recently been restored, their hallmarks being pointed brickwork (usually emphasized by white or red paint), inset beams and carved lintels, and a profusion of *mashrabiya*-work. Some also incorporate ancient columns. Though many of the Delta Style houses have been restored and look great from the outside, only one house, plus a Delta Style mill, are currently open to the public. **Tickets** to visit those, and Rosetta's other sights, are available from the Abu Shahim Mill (see below).

Almost opposite the service taxi station where you arrive, you'll see some fine Delta-style houses, all dating from the eighteenth century. **Beit Kohiya** stands next to the mosque, while two doors further on is **Ramadan House,** part of which is under restoration. **Beit al-Gamal** stands next to that, with **Beit Abouhoum** just across the street.

Further examples of Rosetta's Delta Style architecture lie on, or just off, Sharia Sheikh Qanadili, which runs north, parallel to the river, and is the second turning on your left past Beit Abouhoum. Just down the first turning on the right off Sheikh Qanadili is **Beit al-Toqatli**, held up by a recycled ancient column. Look upwards here to check out the *mashrabiya* window screens on the upper floors. Down the second right off Sheikh Qanadili are two more Delta Style residences, of which **Beit al-Mizouni**, built in 1740, is currently open to the public, though its interior isn't very exciting. The first house worth investigating along Sharia Sheikh Qanadili itself is **Al-Qanadili House**, on the left after 200m. It is currently undergoing restoration, but you may be able to pop in for a quick look, although the outside is more impressive. **Thabel House**, 50m farther on the left, is one of the oldest of the Delta Style houses, built in 1709. Just around the corner, at the end of the next turning on the left (Haret al-Hag Youssef) is **Al-Manadili House**, its portico supported by two ancient columns of pharaonic or Greco-Roman origin. Inside, it boasts some wonderful ceilings, but is currently closed for restoration.

Fifty metres further along Sheikh Qanadili is **Beit al-Amasyali** (currently closed for restoration), its upstairs reception room ennobled by a superb wooden ceiling and mother-of-pearl-inlaid *mashrabiyas*. Like the **Abu Shahim Mill** next door, it was built around 1808 for the Turkish Agha, Ali al-Topgi, who bequeathed them both to his servant Al-Amasyali. The mill, with its huge wooden grinders and delicately pointed keyhole arches, is open to the public, and it is here that you can buy tickets to visit all Rosetta's sights (all daily 9am–4pm, closing an hour earlier during Ramadan). Among them, a £E12 ticket (£E6 for students) allows you to visit the mill, the Beit al-Mizouni House (see above) and the Hammam Azouz bathhouse (see overleaf).

Continuing along Sharia Sheikh Qanadili from here, a right turn after 100m takes you onto Sharia el-Guesh, with its small church. A left just before the church leads 500m to the train station, served by one morning train to Alex and four trains a day to Mamoura (some connecting for Alexandria). Continuing straight ahead along El-Guesh past the church, you come to **Beit Kili** off Midan al-Hurriya, an eighteenth-century house containing a small **museum**, whose only notable exhibit is a diorama showing British soldiers being trounced by the locals. The museum is currently closed for restoration, but when it reopens tickets (£E12, students £E6) should be available at Abu Shahim Mill.

Straight ahead of you at this point is the river, and if you continue along the Corniche for 500m or so, and then take a right, you'll find a nineteenth-century bathhouse, **Hammam Azouz** (tickets from Abu Shahim Mill, see p.661). The marble interior, with its marble floors and fountains, has been lovingly restored, enabling you to see a fine example of a traditional bathhouse, though it is not in use today.

Seven kilometres out of town is the **Fort of Qaitbey** (daily 9am–4pm, Ramadan 9am–3pm; £E12, students £E6; tickets available only at Abu Shahim Mill). Built in 1479 to guard the mouth of the Nile, it served as the first line of defence against the Crusaders and was later reinforced by the French, whose use of masonry imported from Upper Egypt led to the discovery of the Rosetta Stone. The fort can be reached from town by green-and-white taxi (£E30 round-trip) or fishing boat (£E50 after bargaining). For an alternative river trip, you can visit the tranquil old **Mosque of Abu Mandar**, 5km upriver from Rosetta; taxi-boats leave from the docks near Midan al-Horriya – expect to pay £E20–30 after haggling.

Around mid-November, the chain of festivals that started in Tanta the previous month should reach Rosetta. Don't despair if you come a few weeks earlier, since similar **moulids** occur at Fuwa, Mahmudiya and Dasuq, further inland. Salted fish (*fisikh*) and hummus are the traditional snacks at these events.

If you need to stay the night in Rosetta, there's a trio of cheap **hotels** 200m along the Corniche south of the Beit Kili museum. The best is the *Hotel el Nile* (☎045/292-2382; ❶), which is simple, clean and very cheap, and some rooms have balconies overlooking the river.

Damanhur and around

Most of the land between Alex and Tanta is given over to **cotton**, Egypt's major cash crop, whose intensive cultivation began under Mohammed Ali. His French hydroengineer's scheme to regulate the flood waters by means of barrages across the Rosetta and Damietta branches of the Nile was ultimately realized by Sir Colin Scott-Moncrieff in 1880–90. The shift from flood to perennial irrigation enabled three or four cotton crops a year to be grown in the Delta, as is still the case.

Hardly surprising, then, that local towns are heavily into textiles, particularly the Beheira governorate capital, **DAMANHUR**, once *Tmn-Hor*, the City of Horus. This is also the main **transport** hub for the Western Delta, with regular trains and service taxis to Cairo and Alex, plus service taxis to Tanta from Kubra Helu station, and to Rosetta or Dasuq (change there for Kafr el-Sheikh) from Kubra el-Felah station. A £E1 taxi ride will get you from either of the two service taxi stations to the other or to the train station.

Although much of Damanhur is drably functional, this city of 170,000 people gains a dash of colour from green-shuttered houses and bougainvillea-laden archways, and blossoms during its festival, **Moulid of Sheikh Abu Rish**, when turbaned Sufis perform *zikrs* and *munshids* to enthusiastic crowds. This occurs in late October or early November, a week after the festival at Dasuq, across the river. With venues so close together, the *mawladiya* (moulid people) can easily move on to the next event: barbers, circumcisers and all.

Egypt's only **Jewish moulid**, held over two days in January, is a very different scene. The shrine of **Abu Khatzeira** ("Father of the Mat"), a nineteenth-century mystic, is cordoned off by security police who rigorously exclude non-Jewish Egyptians, fearing a terrorist attack. Within the cordon a few thousand mostly French or Israeli visitors bring sick relatives or bottled water to be blessed, and "bid" for the key to Abu Khatzeira's shrine; the money raised supports its upkeep.

Two moulids: Dasuq and Fuwa

A week or so after Tanta's festival (see below), the agricultural town of **DASUQ** (the "q" usually pronounced as a glottal stop) holds the **Moulid of Ibrahim al-Dasuqi** (in mid- to late October), drawing almost as many people. Al-Dasuqi (1246–88) was the only native-born Egyptian to found a major Sufi order, the Burhamiya (whose chosen colour is green): the other brotherhoods originated abroad, or were started here by foreigners.

Should you decide to attend the eight-day event, Dasuq is probably easiest to reach from Damanhur by bus or service taxi. You can also get to it by service taxi from Kafr el-Sheikh and Rosetta, and there are two very slow daily trains from Cairo via Damanhur. Service taxis from Dasuq also serve **FUWA**, 13km northwest, where another **festival** occurs in late October or early November.

Between Damanhur and Tanta

A couple of **ancient sites** reduced to *kom* lie off the road **between Damanhur and Tanta** (64km). Roughly 23km out of Damanhur, a track leads three kilometres left off the main road to the village of El-Nibeirah, near two low mounds marking the site of **Naucratis**. During the XXVI Dynasty, when Egypt was ruled from the Delta, King Amasis (570–26 BC) granted this Greek colony a monopoly of trade between Egypt and Greece. Excavating the site for the British Museum in the nineteenth century, Flinders Petrie found it littered with shards of Greek pottery, and imagined that he was "wandering in the smashings of the Museum's vase-room".

At Itai El-Baroud, the last town before crossing the Rosetta branch of the Nile, another turn-off runs fourteen kilometres south to El-Tud, by the "Mound of the Fort", *Kom el-Hisn*. This used to be **Imaou**, which became the capital of the Third Nome (an administrative district) during the New Kingdom, and was turned into a necropolis by the Hyksos pharaohs. A temple enclosure and numerous tombs are still evident.

Tanta and the Central Delta

Tanta, Egypt's fifth largest city, hosts the country's greatest moulid, which is worth experiencing for at least a day. The city also serves as a jumping-off point for practically everywhere else in the **Central Delta**, with several other moulids and a host of ancient sites scattered around the region. With regular trains and service taxis to Alex (roughly a 2hr journey) and Cairo (1hr 30min) running from early morning till nigh on midnight, you don't have to stay in Tanta; indeed, you'd be lucky to find a vacant room during the moulid. Elsewhere, tourist accommodation is virtually nonexistent anyway. Because the northwestern corner of this part of the Delta is easier to reach from Damietta or El-Mansura, we've allocated sites there to the "Eastern Delta" section (see p.666).

Tanta

A bustling industrial city with strong rural ties, **TANTA** marks the end of the cotton harvest in October with Egypt's largest festival, the **Moulid of Saiyid Ahmed el-Bedawi**. Tanta's population jumps from 250,000 to nearly three million as visitors pour in from the Delta villages, other parts of Egypt and the Arab world. Streets and squares fill with tents and stalls; Sufis prepare for *zikrs*, while musicians test their amps ("Allah, two, three"). Thousands camp out amidst heaps of blankets and cooking pots, though sleep seems impossible. With music and chanting, vendors and devotees, a circus with lions and tigers and a levitation act, Tanta becomes a seething cacophony. If you plan to attend the week-long festival, it is best to leave all your valuables somewhere safe. Pickpocketing is rife and injuries may result from crushing or fist-fights in the dense crowd.

The moulid honours the founder of one of Egypt's largest Sufi brotherhoods. Born in Fès in Morocco in 1199, **Saiyid Ahmed el-Bedawi** was sent to Tanta in 1234 by the Iraqi Rifaiyah order, and later established his own *tariqa* ("brotherhood"), the Ahmediya. His name is invoked to ward off calamity – "*Ya saiyid, ya Bedawi!*" – but his moulid is anything but angst-ridden. "Although a religious festival, pleasure is the chief object of the pilgrims, and a few *fatahs* at the tomb of the saint are sufficient to satisfy every pious requirement", noted *Murray's Handbook* in 1891. The climax to the eight-day festival occurs on a Friday, when the Ahmediya – whose banners and turbans are red – parade with drums behind their mounted sheikh. Events focus on the triple-domed, Ottoman-style **mosque** wherein Bedawi and a lesser sheikh, Abd el-Al, are buried, which is located some 300m east of the railway station.

Tanta is known for its roasted chickpeas or garbanzo beans (*hummus* in Arabic, though it does not necessarily mean that they are mashed with garlic and tahini). They can be bought at any of the multitude of sweet shops surrounding the mosque.

Practicalities

Should you wish **to stay** in the vicinity during the moulid book a room as far in advance as possible. The *New Arafa Hotel* on Midan al-Mahata, almost opposite the train station (☎040/340-50401, 2 or 3, ⊛www.arafahotel.com; ❺), is conveniently located and good value, its good-sized rooms equipped with a/c, TV and a minibar. Alternatively, the *Green House Hotel* on Sharia el-Borsa, off Midan el-Gomhurriya, about 600m east of the station (☎040/333-0761 or 2, ℱ333-0320; ❺), has similar facilities but smaller rooms and is not quite as comfortable, though its friendly staff can organize most things for you on request. Diagonally opposite the *Green House*, the Delta **Bank** cashes travellers' cheques, and there's an ATM for Visa and MasterCard outside the bank next door.

As the **transport** hub of the Delta region, Tanta is well served, with regular buses to Cairo's Aboud terminal (half-hourly 6am–10pm; 1hr 30min). These serve the **Gomla bus station**, 2km north of the city centre (£E1–2 by taxi, or 30pt by minibus from opposite the rail station), where you will also find buses to Damanhur and Alexandria (every 45min till 7pm), and to Mansura and Port Said (3 daily, all in the morning), and Suez (4 daily), plus service taxis to Cairo (1hr 15min), Damanhur (1hr) and Alex (2hr 15min). Buses to Mahalla el-Kubra leave every fifteen minutes from **Mura Shaha station**, which is connected with Gomla by microbus (25pt), and where you will also find service taxis to Mahalla (30min), Sammanud (40min), Mansura (1hr), Ismailiya (2hr) and Zagazig (1hr). Service taxis to Kafr el-Sheikh (1hr) leave from a place called Staad, which is on the microbus route between Gomla and Mura Shaha. From the handsome railway station in the city centre, there are six air-conditioned **train** services a day to Benha, Cairo, Damanhur and Alexandria, plus innumerable slow ones to the above destinations, as well as fourteen to Mansura (1hr 30min), three to Damietta (2hr) and fifteen to Zagazig (1hr 30min).

Sites around Tanta

Some of the places below are directly accessible from Tanta; to reach others you might have to change once or twice. For the committed, renting a private **taxi** gives the greatest scope for excursions.

As a footnote to bygone rulers, it's worth mentioning (but not visiting) the village of **Mit Abu el-Kom**, near the small town of Quweisna to the south of Tanta, as the **birthplace of Anwar Sadat**. Born in 1908, he escaped rural life by joining the army, became a nationalist and conspired with like-minded officers to overthrow King Farouk. As Nasser's heir, President Sadat waged war against, and then signed a peace treaty with, Israel; opened Egypt to Western capitalism – generating a consumer boom and massive corruption; and was ultimately assassinated by Islamic militants in 1981.

Buto and Xois

Only those with private transport and a consuming passion for **ancient sites** will bother trying to reach **Tell al-Faraoun** ("Mound of the Pharaoh"), on the edge of some marshes north of Ibtu village, itself 5km north off the Dasuq–Kafr el-Sheikh road. The site appears on maps as **Buto**, the Greek name for a dual city known to the Ancient Egyptians as *Pr-Wadjet*. **Wadjet**, the cobra-goddess of Lower Egypt (and whom the Greeks called Buto) was worshipped in the half of the city known as Dep. The other city, known as Pe, was dedicated to Djbut, the heron-god, who was later supplanted by Horus. Nothwithstanding all this, the 180-acre site had been obliterated down to its paving stones by the time Petrie excavated it.

Should you carry on to **KAFR EL-SHEIKH** and follow the Tanta road south, you'll pass the village of Sakha, occupying the site of **Xois**, ancient capital of the Sixth Nome.

Saïs

Nothing but a few pits filled with stagnant water remains of the once great city of **Saïs**, near the modern village of **Sa el-Hagar**, beside the Rosetta branch of the Nile. Founded at the dawn of Egyptian history, it was always associated with the goddess of war and hunting, **Neith**, whose cult emblem appeared on predynastic objects. In Egyptian cosmology, she was also the protectress of embalmed bodies; the Greeks identified her with Athena.

The city became Egypt's capital during the **Saïte Period**, when the XXVI dynasty (664–525 BC) looked back to the Old Kingdom for inspiration, refurbishing the pyramid tombs and reviving archaic funerary rituals. In 525 BC the dynasty was overthrown by the Persian emperor Cambyses, who is said to have had the body of the penultimate Saïte king, Amasis "the Drunkard", removed from its tomb, whipped and burnt.

El-Mahalla el-Kubra and Sammanud

EL-MAHALLA EL-KUBRA, 24km northeast of Tanta, is Egypt's fourth largest city and a taxi staging-post for journeys to the riverside town – almost a suburb, these days – of **SAMMANUD**. Should you wish to stay in El-Mahalla, the town's top **hotel** is the *Omar Khayyam* on Midan Setta w'Ashreen Yulyu,

300m north of the train station along 26th July Street (℡040/223-4299, ⓦwww.omarkhaiam.com; ❶), which is good-value, clean and well-kept, with a choice of smaller rooms with shared bathrooms or larger en-suite rooms with a/c. Service taxis to Mansura, Damietta and Alexandria, along with frequent local buses to Tanta, leave from a depot round the corner from the train station, while service taxis for Tanta and Cairo leave from 500m south on 26th July Street, by a clock in the form of the Eiffel Tower: intercity buses also stop here.

Immediately west of the Sammanud taxi depot, near the hospital, a large mound and a scattering of red and black granite blocks mark the site of the Temple of Onuris-Shu, rebuilt by Nectanebo II to grace **Tjeboutjes**, the capital of the Twelfth Nome. Another city, **Busiris**, occupied a bluff overlooking the river further south, along the road out of Sammanud. However, part of a XXVI Dynasty basalt statue and fragments of a monumental gateway are all that remain of this reputed birthplace of Osiris.

The H8 road, which runs northeast from Sammanud to El-Mansura (see p.671), takes you past the site of ancient *Pr-Hebeit*, 10km to the west, better known by its Roman name, **Iseum**. Here, the great **Temple of Isis** which Nectanebo began and Ptolemy II completed has been reduced to an enclosure wall, some carved granite blocks and Hathor-headed capitals.

The Eastern Delta and the Delta resorts

The **Eastern Delta** scores on several counts. **Tanis**, **Avaris** and **Bubastis** are the best **pharaonic ruins** that Lower Egypt can offer; there are **moulids** aplenty, both Christian and Muslim; and if you include the places on the Central Delta coast, which are easier to reach from here, the region can also claim three low-key **beach resorts** and some fine **birdwatching**.

Bastet

The feline goddess **Bastet** was originally depicted as a lioness, her head surmounted by a solar disc and *uraeus* serpent. As the daughter of Re, she was associated with the destructive force of the sun-god's eye. This aggressive side of Bastet can be seen in texts and reliefs describing the pharaoh in battle. Her epithet, "Lady of Asheru", also linked her to the goddess Mut at Karnak, where temple reliefs show the pharaoh running ritual races in front of Bastet.

▲ Bastet

After about 1000 BC, however, this aspect of Bastet became subsumed by Sekhmet (see p.394), and the goddess herself was portrayed more commonly as a cat, often with a brood of kittens, and carrying a sacred rattle. The *Coffin Texts* of the Middle Kingdom frequently invoke her protection as the first-born daughter of Atum (another aspect of the sun-god). In return, the Egyptians venerated cats and mummified them at several sites, including Bubastis and Memphis.

The Greeks later identified Bastet with Artemis, the Virgin Hunter, who was believed to be able to transform herself into a cat. The Egyptian association with cats remained strong even after the arrival of Christianity, and it was from Egypt that cats are thought to have arrived in Europe during or before the fourth century AD.

For some of these destinations it might be simpler to approach the Eastern Delta from Port Said or Ismailiya, rather than from Alex.

Zagazig and the ruins of Bubastis

The charmingly named **ZAGAZIG** (usually pronounced "Za'a'zi") is less appealing in reality, blighted by fumes from a soap factory. Only founded in 1830, it boasts of being the home town of Colonel **Ahmed Orabi** (1839–1911), leader of the 1882 revolt against British rule, whose statue stands outside the station. As a provincial capital with a thriving university, Zagazig is reticent about being the source of most of the **papyri** sold in tourist shops throughout Egypt, which are manufactured in sweatshops and sold to dealers for as little as £E3–4 apiece. From a tourist's standpoint, its attractions are the **Moulid of Abu Khalil**, held outside the main mosque sometime during the month of Shawwal, and the paltry ruins of Bubastis, to the southeast of town.

Whatever its shortcomings, Zagazig has the merit of being readily accessible. You can travel the 80km from Cairo by **bus** (every 20min; 1hr 30min; £E5) or **service taxi** (1hr 15min; £E3.50) from the Aboud terminal; coming back, service taxis for Cairo leave from just by the railway station. To find the bus station, cross the tracks via the pedestrian underpass, then turn left, and it's 200m ahead on the right. Buses from here also serve Benha (half-hourly; 45min), Alexandria (2 daily; 3hr 30min), Ismailiya (3 daily; 2hr) and Port Said (1 daily; 4hr). To find service taxis for Ismailiya and Port Said, you'll have to go the Ismailiya service taxi station, 5km from the town centre, reached by microbuses (50pt) from outside the train station. Buses and service taxis for Tanta, Mansura and Faqus leave from the Mansura bus station, which you can also get to by microbus from in front of the station (25pt). **Trains** from Zagazig serve Cairo (13 daily; 1hr 30min), Benha (13 daily; 40min), Faqus (5 daily; 1hr), Ismailiya (20 daily; 1hr 15min) and Port Said (6 daily; 2hr 30min).

Should you need to stay in Zagazig, there are two cheap **hotels** opposite the train station. The better of the two by far is the *Opera* (☎055/230-3718; ❶), though it's slightly hidden away, with its entrance tucked away down a side alley and its sign in Arabic only. For something a little bit classier, try the three-star *Marina* at 58 Sharia Gamal Abdel Nasser (☎055/235-4975; ❸).

Bubastis

To reach the site of **Bubastis** (daily 9am–3pm; £E10, camera £E10, no student reductions), take the underpass on the left-hand side of the station and continue straight ahead (southeast) along Sharia Farouq for just under a kilometre, either on foot, or by microbus from the beginning of Farouq (25pt), or by taxi (£E1). The site is about 100m to your right at the end of the street. You are likely to get a thorough grilling on entry from the guards, who are not really used to foreign visitors, and may even follow you around the site, and there's little to see beyond the few displayed artefacts but scattered blocks and gaping pits. Nonetheless, archeologists have found here Old and New Kingdom cemeteries and vaulted catacombs full of feline mummies. The city was known to the Ancient Egyptians as *Pr-Bastet* ("House of Bastet"), after the cat-goddess whom they honoured with licentious festivals. Pilgrims sailed here in high spirits, saluting riverside towns with music, abuse and exposed loins. In the fifth century BC, Herodotus noted that 700,000 revellers consumed more wine than "during the whole of the rest of the year", and described how the city lay on raised ground encircling a canal-girt temple, "the most pleasing to look at" in all of Egypt. Begun by the VI Dynasty pyramid-builders, Bubastis was enlarged and embellished for over 1700 years, attaining its apogee after its rulers established the XXII Dynasty, though the capital in this period was probably still Tanis (see p.668).

Bilbeis and Benha

To the south and southwest of Zagazig a couple of minor towns are worth a passing mention. **BILBEIS**, 10km away by road or rail, hosts a couple of festivals during Shawwal: its **moulids** of Abu Isa and Abu Alwan predate Abu Khalil's in Zagazig. Further west, beside the Damietta branch of the Nile, **BENHA**, at the junction of the Cairo–Alexandria and Cairo–Ismailiya train lines, is near another ancient site. To the northeast of town, 150m off the road, *Kom el-Atrib* is what remains of **Athribis**, once the capital of the Tenth Nome. This was the birthplace of Psammetichus I (664–610 BC), who restored pharaonic authority over Upper and Lower Egypt, replacing the so-called *Dodekarchy* with centralized government by the Saïte dynasty. Benha is served by six air-conditioned fast trains a day, plus numerous slower ones, and there are buses every twenty minutes from 6am to 9pm from Cairo's Aboud terminal, plus service taxis from Aboud.

Tanis, Avaris and the "Land of Goshen"

Early archeologists were drawn to the eastern marches of the Delta in search of clues to the Israelites' Biblical sojourn, but what they found proved more important to knowledge of Ancient Egypt. Fragmented statues and stelae, papyrus texts and layers of debris have shed light on dynastic chronologies and religious cults, the movement of Delta waterways and imperial borders, invasions and famines. Fresh discoveries are still being made – particularly at Avaris, a site associated with the Hyksos "Shepherd Kings" who seized control of the Delta after the collapse of the Middle Kingdom, and which could also have been inhabited by the Israelites during their sojourn in Egypt. The following accounts simplify a mass of contradictory evidence and theories thrown up by archeologists.

Tanis

One of the oldest-known sites is a huge *kom* near the village of **San el-Hagar** ("San of the Stones"), 167km northeast of Zagazig. Barring a stint by Petrie, the excavation has mostly been in French hands since the 1860s. Although best known by its Greek name, **TANIS**, the city was called *Zoan* in the Bible and known to the Ancient Egyptians as *Djanet*. It originally stood beside the Tanite branch of the Nile, which has long since dried up. In the film *Raiders of the Lost Ark*, it is here that Indiana Jones uncovers the Ark of the Covenant.

The **age and identity** of Tanis have been much debated, as scholars have frequently conflated it with Avaris, the capital of the Hyksos, or the much later city of Pi-Ramses, supposedly the "City of Bondage" from which the Israelites fled. In recent decades, however, both have been firmly identified with other sites (see below), and Tanis is now thought to have come into existence long afterwards, during the Third Intermediate Period. Some theorize that the XXI Dynasty founded Tanis as their capital at the same time as they abandoned the traditional cult of Seth in favour of the Theban Triad.

The desolate **site** looks as if the huge Ramessid **Temple of Amun** was shattered by a giant's hammer, scattering chunks of masonry and fragments of statues everywhere. Confusingly for scholars, the founders of Tanis plundered masonry from cities all over the Delta (some predating the Hyksos, who had earlier usurped it). In 1939, Pierre Montet discovered the **tombs of Psusennes II and Osorkon II**, containing the "Treasure of Tanis", which is now in the Cairo Museum. Perplexingly, it was soon noted that the tomb of the XXI

Dynasty ruler Psusennes seems to have been built *after* that of Osorkon, who is supposed to have lived well over a century later, during the XXII Dynasty. Rohl argues that the two dynasties were actually contemporary, and that by assuming that they were sequential, archeologists have overestimated the duration of the Third Intermediate Period by at least 140 years – thus distorting the whole chronological basis of Egyptology. Rohl's views, which are hotly debated, are outlined in detail in his book *A Test of Time* (see p.849). Criticism of them can be found on a number of websites, best accessed through the Waste of Time homepage at Ⓦmembers.aol.com/lan/20Wade/Waste/Index.htm.

While the site at Tanis can be wandered at will, **getting there** is awkward. The best jumping-off point is **FAQUS**, 37km to the south, which can be reached by service taxi from Ismailiya, Cairo or Zagazig, by bus from Zagazig or from Cairo's Aboud terminal (every 45min 7.30am–8.15pm; 2hr), or even by train (5 daily) from Cairo and Zagazig. From Faqus, you can catch a local bus or service taxi to San el-Hagar, or rent a private taxi for the round trip.

Avaris

Since 1966, excavations by Manfred Bietak at **Tell ed-Daba** ("Mound of the Hyena") have yielded many discoveries that have confirmed it as the site of **AVARIS**, the long-vanished **Hyksos** capital. The most sensational find, in 1991, were **Minoan–style frescoes** in a Hyksos-era palace on the western edge of the site, evincing strong links with the Minoan civilization on Crete, 500 miles away, even if not disproving the idea that the Hyksos originated in Palestine or Syria. (The term Hyksos derives from *hekau-khasut*, "princes of foreign lands".) Painted as Cretan civilization reached its zenith, the murals feature Cretan mountain landscapes and acrobats vaulting over bulls, as in the Minoan frescoes at Knossos. Both the Minoans and the Hyksos are thought to have associated bulls with the worship of storm gods.

However, the Hyksos finds are only half the story, for Avaris existed long before their invasion, and may hold the key to early Biblical history. Before finding the frescoes, Bietak's team excavated what had been a hilly residential quarter, uncovering grave goods that suggested that the bulk of the population originated from Palestine and Syria. This lay above a stratum of evidence for an older, more sophisticated community of non-Egyptians, where 65 percent of the burials were of children below the age of two. Rohl argues that this represents the **Israelites** during their sojourn in Egypt and the culling of their male newborn by the "pharaoh who did not know Joseph", which places the events of Exodus in the reign of Djudmose of the XIII Dynasty, c.1447 BC – two or three centuries earlier than is commonly accepted. The plagues that struck Egypt, followed by the Exodus, left the Delta exposed to invasion by the warlike nomads later known as the Hyksos. Having been taken over by these newcomers, Avaris remained the Hyksos capital until its destruction by Ahmosis I, the founder of the New Kingdom.

Tell ed-Daba is only 7km from Faqus, and although the site is not yet officially open to tourists, those with a special interest can get permission to visit from the Supreme Council of Antiquities in Cairo.

The "Land of Goshen"

Many archeologists have striven to uncover the **"Land of Goshen"** where, according to the Biblical book of Exodus, the Israelites toiled for the pharaoh before Moses led them out of Egypt – though some shrewdly plugged the Biblical connection to raise money for digs with other aims (notably Petrie at Tanis). Public opinion was fixated on the Biblical "store cities of Pithom and Raamses", speculatively assigned to many locations between Avaris and the Bitter Lakes (the area through which the Suez Canal runs). "Raamses" has usually been identified as Pi-Ramses, the royal city of the XIX Dynasty pharaoh Ramses II – which is why his successor, Merneptah, regularly gets fingered as the pharaoh of the Exodus. Conversely, Rohl argues that the Bible was really referring to Avaris, but using the name of the Ramessid city that existed at a later date, which would have been familiar due to Ramses II's wars in Palestine.

It is now certain that **Pi-Ramses** was centred on the modern-day village of **Qantir**, 3km northeast of Tell ed-Daba, but extended far enough to cover most of Avaris, which had been laid to waste centuries earlier. A mud-brick palace dating to the earliest phase of the city was discovered in 1929, and Bietak's excavations have revealed barracks and workshops, also from the Ramessid era. Unfortunately for those who believe that this was the "City of Bondage", no evidence of a foreign population was found in any of the strata associated with the New Kingdom – whereas at Tell ed-Daba, there are extensive traces from the Middle Kingdom, and even mass graves that fit the Biblical account of a calamity. Rather, Pi-Ramses was a parvenu city founded by Seti I and turned into a royal capital by Ramses II, which had dwindled in significance by the end of the New Kingdom. Much of its stonework was later taken to Tanis or Bubastis during the XXI and XXII dynasties; the most notable bits still *in situ* are the feet and one arm of a colossus of Ramses II, lying 50m apart in a field.

If the Israelites did flee from Avaris, what of the other cities mentioned in the book of Exodus – Pithom and Succoth? Here, the evidence is less conclusive, but they could well have been somewhere around **Tell el-Maskhuta**, an enormous *kom* off the road between Zagazig and Ismailiya. If Tell el-Maskhuta was really Pithom, then another *kom* a few kilometres to the west may have been Succoth.

To reach Sinai, the Israelites presumably went through Wadi Tumaylat, nowadays the route for traffic between Zagazig and Ismailiya (hourly buses). Before Tell el-Maskhuta, it passes **Tell el-Kebir**, where Orabi's rebellion was finally defeated by the British in September 1882. In the 1920s, the government sponsored a reforesting project in what was then virgin desert, and now supports plantations and orchards all the way to Ismailiya.

Mit Damsis and El-Mansura

Trains and inter-city buses take the shortest route **between Zagazig and El-Mansura**, and for most of the year that's a sensible option. In August, however, you might consider the alternative Mit Ghamr–Aga road in order to visit **Mit Damsis** village near the Damietta branch of the Nile, site of the Coptic **Moulid of St George**. Buses and service taxis **from Cairo** to El-Mansura, Zagazig and Faqus go mainly from the Aboud terminal; some minibus service taxis depart from outside Ramses train station, but these leave town by a more roundabout route and end up taking longer.

Mit Damsis

The **Moulid of St George** (August 2–28) is notable primarily for its **exorcisms**. Copts attribute demonic possession to improper baptism or deliberate curses, and specially trained priests bully and coax the *afrit* ("demon") to leave through its victim's fingers or toes rather than via the eyes, which is believed to cause blindness.

Egyptian Muslims likewise believe in possession, but don't always regard it as malign; in some cases they try to harmonize the relationship between the spirit and its human host rather than terminate it. Egyptians of both faiths take precautions against the Evil Eye. Christians put store in pictures of St George and the Virgin, while Muslims display the Hand of Fatima – literally hand-printed on the walls of dwellings – and perhaps the legend "*B'ismallah, masha' Allah*" ("In the name of God, whatever God wills").

Because the **moulid** is well attended there's a fair chance of lifts along the seven-kilometre track that turns west off the main road, 15km south of Aga. Mit Damsis rarely appears on maps; don't confuse it with Damas, which does.

El-Mansura

EL-MANSURA was founded as the camp of Sultan al-Kamil's army during the 1218–21 siege of Damietta, though its name ("The Victorious") was a premature boast, since the Crusaders reoccupied Damietta in 1247. Weakened by cancer and tuberculosis, Sultan Ayyub was unable to dislodge them, and died here in 1249 – a fact concealed by his widow, Shagar al-Durr, who issued orders in Ayyub's name, buying time until his heir could return from Iraq. Encouraged by the Mamlukes' withdrawal, France's Louis IX (later canonized as Saint Louis) led a sortie against the enemy camp, slaying their general in his bath. But with victory in sight, the Crusaders fell sick after eating corpse-fed fish, just before a devastating counterattack launched by Beybars the Crossbowman. Louis was captured and ransomed for Damietta's return, and later met a similar fate on his Tunisian crusade.

The medieval house where Louis was imprisoned, **Beit Luqman**, still stands near the Mwafi Mosque (20m north of the train station), but much of the rest of today's El-Mansura is modern, with tree-lined avenues, a university, and a central mosque whose twin minarets are visible from far away. For outsiders, the town's most interesting feature is its delicious buffalo-milk **ice cream**.

Buses to Cairo (daily every 45 minutes 8.30am–9.30pm; 2hr) and Zagazig (daily every 30 minutes; 1hr 30min) run from the international bus station, which is 500m east of the train station down Sharia Gamal el-Din el-Afghani at the junction with Sharia el-Guesh. Buses from here also serve Sinai and the Canal Zone, with six a day to Sharm el-Sheikh (7hr) and nine to Suez (3hr 30min). Service taxis to Zagazig and Cairo leave from a station 1km further to the southeast. For Tanta, Alexandria, Mahalla el-Kubra, Kufr el-Sheikh, Damietta and Port Said, service taxis run from Talkha station across the river. **Trains** from Mansura are all pretty slow, and serve Cairo (4 daily; 3hr), Zagazig (10 daily; 2hr–2hr 30min), Damietta (10 daily; 2hr), Tanta (15 daily; 1hr 30min) and Mahalla el-Kubra (15 daily; 40min).

El-Mansura has several **hotels** to choose from. The *Marshal el-Gezirah*, 2km west of the town centre on the Corniche (T & F 050/221-3000, 1, 2 or 3; ❻), is the ritzest place in town, but there are several other decent choices that are both cheaper and more centrally located. The *Marshal Hotel* opposite the station (T 050/233-3920; ❷) has very comfortable, carpeted rooms – ask for a big one, as they all cost the same – and a café and pastry shop downstairs. The *Cleopatra*, 1km west at 13 Souk el-Toggar el-Gharby, off Sharia el-Habasy (T 050/223-6789 or 224-6789, F 224-1234; ❷) has cosy rooms off its rather sombre wood-panelled corridors. Between the two, the *Abou Shama*, 300m west of the station on Sharia Bank Misr (T 050/225-5810, F 225-5811; ❶) is more modest, but still perfectly presentable.

The Monastery and Moulid of St Damyanah

Normally difficult to reach without private transport, the **Monastery of St Damyanah** becomes accessible during its namesake's **moulid** (May 15–20), when service taxis and private buses convey pilgrims across to the small town of Bilqas Qisim Awwal, whence it's 3km by track to Deir Sitt Damyanah.

The monastery – whose four churches date from the nineteenth and twentieth centuries – is, in fact, rather less interesting than **Damyanah's story** and **festival**, which is one of the largest Christian moulids in Egypt. The daughter of a Roman governor under Diocletian, Damyanah refused to marry and insisted that her father build a palace into which she and forty other virgins could retire. All refused to worship Roman gods, and their example eventually converted her father – enraging Diocletian, who had the lot of them executed.

As with the Church of St George at Mit Damsis, Copts ascribe the building of Damyanah's shrine to St Helena, the mother of the Roman emperor Constantine. Pilgrims bring sick relatives (or livestock) to be blessed, and believe that Damyanah manifests herself at night as a pigeon, which can be distinguished from other birds by the trajectory of its flight. Icons and special pottery (inscribed "Happy returns, Damyanah") are popular buys at the fair, where Muslim tattooists do a brisk trade in St George, Christ on the cross, snakes, birds and other motifs, which punters select from display boards.

Damietta (Dumyat)

Sited near the mouth of the eastern branch of the Nile, the port city of **DAMIETTA** became prosperous in medieval times, through its trade in coffee, linen, dates and oil. However, it was always wide open to seaborne invasions and was seized by the Crusaders in 1167–68 and 1218–21, on the latter occasion accompanied by St Francis of Assisi – who ignorantly imagined that the Sultan al-Kamil knew nothing of Christianity, although he numbered Copts amongst his advisors. The main function of the Crusaders in Egypt, however, was pillage, and Damietta suffered heavily during its occupations. When Louis "the Pious" returned with a further crew in 1247, the inhabitants fled or deliberately sold the Crusaders contaminated fish – one cause of their defeat at El-Mansura (see p.671). Unfortunately, Damietta suffered a far worse attack under the Mamlukes, who razed the town and rendered its river impassable as a punishment for suspected disloyalty and a precaution against future invasions.

The town was revived by the Ottomans whose last pasha surrendered to the Beys here just before the rise of Mohammed Ali. With the opening of the Suez Canal, Damietta had to reorient its trade towards Port Said, some 70km away. Nowadays it's a thriving port city of 120,000 inhabitants, with the status of a provincial capital, and is known as a centre for the manufacture of furniture, which is the local cottage industry.

The only real reason to stay in Damietta is as a base for bird-watching or beachcombing. If this is the case, there are several modest **hotels** on the Nile-side Corniche, including the cheap but basic *Emad* near Doumiat el Ra'esy post office, where the river bends (℡057/322-533; ❶). Just 200m away is the three-star *Soliman Inn* on Sharia el-Gala' (℡057/376-050, ℻377-050; ❺), with a/c, TV and fridge in every room, and the less well-equipped but friendly and comfortable *El-Manshy*, just off el-Gala' on Sharia el-Nokrashy (℡057/323-308; ❸), which also has a decent restaurant. As for **transport**, Damietta is linked by rail to Tanta, Zagazig, Alex and Cairo, and by hourly buses (6am–5pm) or service taxis to Cairo. Closer at hand are Port Said (30min drive along the causeway between Lake Manzala and the Med) and the beach resorts of the Central Delta.

Lake Manzala

East of Damietta lies **Lake Manzala**, a great place for **birdwatching** if you can find a boatman to take you through the reeds. In the nineteenth-century, European visitors tended to be more interested in shooting wildfowl than observing it. "Their compact mass formed living islands upon the water; and when the wind took me to these, a whole island rose up with a loud and thrilling din to become a feathered cloud in the air", wrote one hunter.

Winter is the best time to see herons (*balashon* to locals), spoonbills (*midwas*), pelicans (*begga*) and flamingoes (*basharus*). Along the Nile, these last are called "water camels" (*gamal el-bahr*).

Three Delta resorts

Ranged along the coast of the Central Delta are three beach resorts popular with middle-class Egyptians: **Ras el-Bahr**, **Gamasa** and **Baltim**. Transport to all of them is better during summer than out of season, when they are all rather dead.

RAS EL-BAHR, where the eastern branch of the Nile flows into the Med north of Damietta, is a pleasant beach resort with several restaurants and **hotels**. Try the *Abo Tabl* in the centre of town at 4 17th St (℡057/528-166; ❷), the *El-Salam* on the sea front 1km north at 6 44th St (℡057/529-156; ❸), or the smaller and more modest *El-Mobasher* six blocks further north and three east at 1 56th St (℡057/527-097; ❷). Across the river lies the busy fishing port of **Ezbet el-Bourg** (unmarked on most maps), named after an abandoned nineteenth-century **coastal fort** that's fun to explore. Hidden beneath a section of the walls is the **command bunker** (code-named Centre #10) containing seven small rooms in which Sadat's generals directed the October War of 1973. In summer (June–Sept), Ras el-Bahr is readily accessible by **service taxi** and **bus** (every 45min; 3hr 30min) from Cairo's Aboud terminal. Otherwise, it is easily accessible year-round by frequent service taxi from Damietta, and less frequently from El-Mansura.

GAMASA, a much smaller resort, further along the coast, is rather miserable out of season, when all its **hotels** are closed. In summer, try the *Hanoville* (℡057/760-750; ❸), and the *Beau Rivage* (℡057/760-268 or 9; ❸), both at the far end of town from the market and the main road in. Hourly **buses** run to Gamasa from Cairo's Aboud terminal (summer only; 8am–3pm); otherwise, there are **service taxis** year-round from El-Mansura, while infrequent service taxis travelling between Baltim and Damietta will drop off, and usually pick up, passengers at the Gamasa turn-off on the coastal highway, from where it's a 4km walk to the town.

The third resort, **BALTIM**, is actually halfway to Rosetta, and sometimes accessible from there by service taxi. Baltim town, which is 5km from the resort, connected to it by frequent **service taxis**, can also be reached year-round by service taxi from Cairo's Aboud terminal, and there are infrequent service taxi pick-ups along the coastal highway between Baltim and Damietta. The resort has a couple of **hotels**, both with pretty spacious rooms: the *Dahab* (℡047/421-641; ❷) at one end of the resort, has a restaurant, café and pool tables on the first floor, while the *Cleopatra* (℡047/240-541; ❸), at the other, has a *fatir* joint out front. Rooms in both hotels can be noisy in summer, so try and get one as near to the top as possible.

The Canal Zone

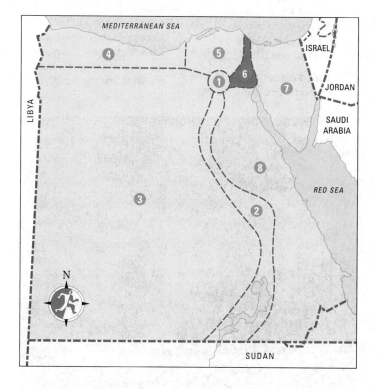

CHAPTER 6   # Highlights

* **Birds of prey** Migrating vultures and eagles fly over Suez in spring. See p.684

* **Garden city** A European-style Ismailiya constructed for the builders of the Canal. See p.685

* **Umm el-Khaloul** Try the local shellfish special-ity, popular in Suez and Ismailiya. See p.689

* **Limbo Festival** A doll-burning festival held annually in Ismailiya a week after Easter. See p.690

* **Mediterranean air** The fresh sea breeze, shopping and pleasant street cafés are a particular attraction of Port Said. See p.691

* **Ship-watching on the Suez Canal** International ferries are among the many giant ships that ply the Canal, still a crucial trade link between the West and the East. See p.694

△ The Suez Canal

The Canal Zone

Once feted as a triumph of nineteenth-century engineering and regarded as the linchpin of Britain's empire, the **Suez Canal** nowadays seems as Joseph Conrad described it: "a dismal but profitable ditch", connecting the Red Sea and the Mediterranean. Except around the harbour mouths or where ships are glimpsed between sandbanks, it's a pretty dull waterway, too, relieved only by the Canal cities of Port Said and Ismailiya.

With its evocative waterfront, prosaic beaches and duty-free shopping, **Port Said** feels like Alexandria minus its cultural baggage – and a place that's somehow more authentic as a maritime city. By contrast, the Canal scarcely impinges on the leafy, villa-lined streets of **Ismailiya**, once the residence of the Suez Canal Company's European staff and now a popular honeymoon destination. Foreigners generally overlook both cities, prejudging them on the basis of **Suez**, a neglected city but a vital transport nexus between Cairo, Sinai and the Red Sea Coast.

Heading to south Sinai, bus passengers (or car drivers) cross the Suez Canal at either the **Ahmed Hamdi Tunnel** (12km north of Suez City) or the **car ferry** 7km north of Ismailiya. Destinations in **north Sinai** are served by a passenger ferry, at **Qantara**, and the new **Ferdan Suspension Bridge** nearby, both to East Qantara. Built in cooperation with Japan, and opened in October 2001, the 4.1km bridge, also known as the Salaam or Peace-Mubarak Bridge, is intended to accommodate the expected increase in traffic caused by several major development projects on the north coast. A couple of kilometres to the south is the Ferdan Railway Bridge, built on the site of an old track hastily built to transport army troops to Gaza during World War I, but dismantled by the Israelis in 1968. The largest retractable bridge in the world, it was planned during a period of optimism in the Middle East, when a rail network running the Orient Express was planned, linking Egypt to Turkey and Europe via Palestine, Israel and Lebanon. This has been put on hold, but you can still see the bridge – which sits alongside the canal when not in use – closing daily from 9am to 11am and again from 9pm to 1am, a process which takes twenty minutes, to allow trains and cars to cross the canal. Buses and service taxis run direct from Ismailiya to El-Arish in Sinai. Drivers should be aware that stretches of the canal are **off-limits** and should stick to main routes to avoid questioning by the military.

The canal's history

The **first attempts** to link the Red Sea and the Mediterranean by means of a canal are usually attributed to Necho II (610–595 BC) of the XXVI Dynasty. Herodotus claims that 120,000 workers had died before the project

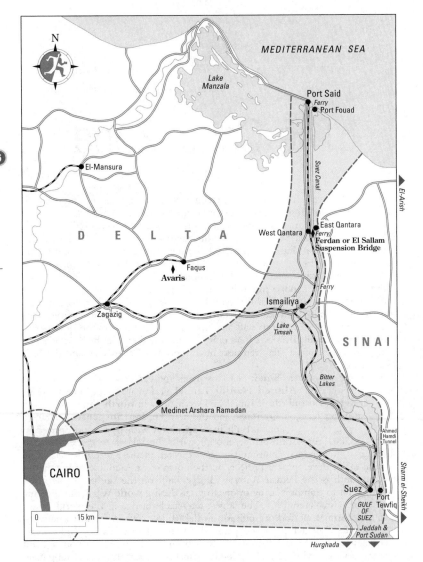

was abandoned after an oracle predicted that only Egypt's foes would benefit from it. Sure enough, it was the Persian emperor **Darius**, around 500 BC, who completed the first canal in the region, linking the Red Sea and the Great Bitter Lake, whence an older waterway created by Ramses II connected with Bubastis on the Nile and thence to the Mediterranean.

Refined by the Ptolemies and Trajan (who added an extension leading to Babylon-in-Egypt), this system of waterways was restored by **Amr** following the Muslim conquest and was used for shipping corn to Arabia until the eighth century, when it was deliberately abandoned to starve out rebels in Medina. Although the Venetians, Crusaders and Ottomans all considered renewing the old system, the idea of a canal running direct between the Red Sea and the Mediterranean was first mooted – and then vetoed – by Napoleon's engineers, who miscalculated a difference of ten metres between the two sea levels.

The discovery of their error, in the 1840s, encouraged a junior French consul, **Ferdinand de Lesseps**, to present his own plan to Said Pasha, who approved it despite British objections. ("It cannot be made, it shall not be made; but if it were made there would be a war between England and France for the possession of Egypt", Palmerston asserted.)

Work began at the Mediterranean end in 1859 and continued throughout the reign of Said's successor, Ismail (hence the names of Port Said and Ismailiya). Of the twenty thousand Egyptians employed in the **construction of the Suez Canal**, a great many died from accidents or cholera, while Ismail himself went bankrupt attempting to finance his one-third share of the £19 million sterling investment, most of which went on bankers' charges.

In 1875, Ismail was forced to sell his shares to Britain for a mere £4 million sterling and the Suez Canal effectively became an imperial concession. By appealing to the Rothschilds for a loan over dinner, Prime Minister Disraeli bought Ismail's shares before France could make an offer, and reported to Queen Victoria: "You have it, Madam". When the Canal finally opened in 1888, its vast profits went abroad with the **Suez Canal Company**, which acted as a state within a state, while two world wars saw the **Canal Zone** transformed into the largest military base on earth.

Following the end of World War II nationalist protests against the British presence grew, and guerrilla attacks in the Zone led to the British assault on Ismailiya's police barracks that sparked "Black Saturday" in Cairo (see p.685). After the 1952 Revolution, Egypt's new leaders demanded the withdrawal of British forces and a greater share of the Canal's revenue, and when the West refused to make loans to finance the Aswan High Dam, Nasser announced the Canal's **nationalization** (July 26, 1956). Britain and France tried to hamper this process, smearing Nasser as an "Arab Hitler". Israel's advance into Sinai that October became the agreed pretext for them to "safeguard" the Canal by bombarding and invading its cities. But by standing firm and appealing to outraged world opinion, Nasser emerged victorious from the **Suez Crisis**.

The battered Canal cities had hardly recovered when the **1967 War** with Israel caused further damage and blocked the Canal with sunken vessels. The Canal was closed and Suez was evacuated during the "War of Attrition" that dragged on until 1969, while Israel fortified the **Bar-Lev Line** along the east bank, which the Egyptians stormed during the **October War** of 1973 (known as the *10th Ramadan* or *Yom Kippur* war, respectively, to Arabs and Israelis). Although the Canal was reopened to shipping in 1975, both sides remained dug in on opposite banks until 1982, when Israel withdrew from Sinai. While the Canal was closed, supertankers were built to travel around Africa – and were too large to pass through Suez once it reopened.

Despite this, the Canal today handles up to ninety ships a day, carrying fourteen percent of the world's trade; the direction of traffic is alternated, with an average transit time of fifteen hours. At 167km long, it's the third longest canal in the world and the longest without locks, though are plans afoot to deepen the Canal and double its width.

Suez (El-Suweis) and Port Tewfiq (Bur Tewfiq)

Since its devastation by Israeli bombardments and the evacuation of almost the entire population between 1967 and 1973, **SUEZ** has risen from the rubble to reclaim its inheritance. Unlike Port Said and Ismailiya, th e city's history long predates the Canal, going back to Ptolemaic *Klysma*. As Arabic *Qulzum*, the port prospered from the spice trade and pilgrimages to Mecca throughout medieval times, remaining a walled city until the eighteenth century, when Eliza Fay described it as "the Paradise of Thieves". The Canal brought modernization and assured revenues, later augmented by the discovery of oil in the Gulf of Suez.

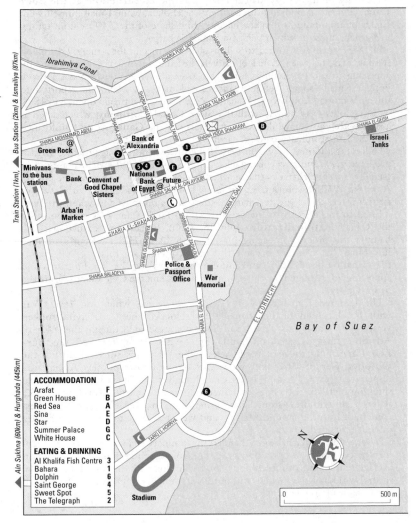

ACCOMMODATION
Arafat	F
Green House	B
Red Sea	A
Sina	E
Star	D
Summer Palace	G
White House	C

EATING & DRINKING
Al Khalifa Fish Centre	3
Bahara	1
Dolphin	6
Saint George	4
Sweet Spot	5
The Telegraph	2

All this was lost during the wars with Israel, requiring a massive reconstruction programme financed by the Gulf states. While noxious petrochemical refineries, cement and fertilizer plants ring the outskirts, most of the city's 300,000 inhabitants have been rehoused in prefabricated estates or the patched-up remnants of older quarters.

What Suez lacks in looks is made up for to some degree by the friendliness of the local people. For the foreign visitor, however, it's best to dress for the city wherever you are, saving your shorts and skimpy tops for the beaches of Sinai. The paucity of things to do in Suez is perhaps most keenly felt by the city's young people, many of whom spend their evenings hanging out, puffing on *sheesha* – the monotony broken only by their home team playing football in the city's stadium. Despite its important contribution to the Egyptian economy,

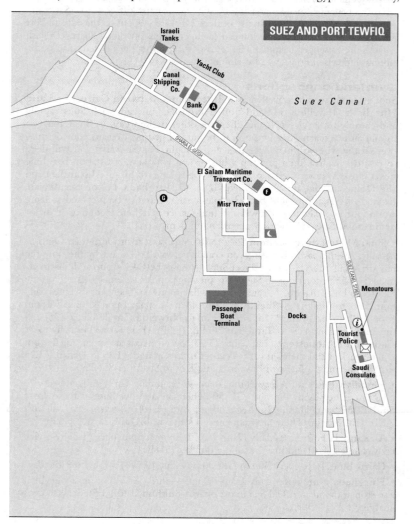

SUEZ AND PORT TEWFIQ

Israeli Tanks

Yacht Club

Canal Shipping Co.

Bank Ⓐ

Suez Canal

SHARIA EL-GEISH

El Salam Maritime Transport Co. Ⓕ

Ⓖ

Misr Travel

SUEZ CANAL STREET

Menatours

Passenger Boat Terminal

Docks

ⓘ

Tourist Police

Saudi Consulate

Suez has yet to see significant investment in its infrastructure. Its residents seem to feel they have been largely forgotten by their government.

Arrival – and moving on

Like the other Canal cities, Suez has regular connections with **Cairo** by bus (half-hourly 6am–6.30pm; £E7–8) and **service taxi** (£E6), from either Turgoman station (see map p.106) or the Al-Mazah terminal in Heliopolis. Both cover the 134km in under two hours. Both buses and service taxis arrive at Suez's new bus terminal on the outskirts of town on the Cairo–Suez road. From here you can take a taxi (£E5) or a microbus (50pt) into the town centre. The **train** station is 1.5km west of the city centre's Arba'in market (50pt by minibus) and is served by six daily uncomfortable trains from Cairo, which run on to Ismailiya (6–7hr).

For the benefit of people arriving by ship, the **tourist office** (Mon–Sat 8am–3pm ☎062/333-1141) and **tourist police** (24hr) are way out on the edge of Port Tewfiq, on Suez Canal Street; you can catch a minibus out along Sharia el-Geish as far as the Passenger Terminal. The tourist office can supply a decent map of the city, but little else in the way of useful information.

Overland connections

Suez is mainly seen by travellers as an **interchange between Cairo, Sinai and Hurghada**. Travelling overland from Hurghada, you can reach Suez rapidly and cheaply by service taxi, and then get other transport on to Sinai, but you should aim to reach Suez by noon to be sure of getting a bus to your destination – otherwise you may have to stay overnight. For **El-Arish** you will need to get to Ismailiya, then pick up a bus or taxi. The new bus station has three ticket kiosks: one for **Cairo**, one for East Delta buses to **Sinai**, **Alexandria** and **the Delta**, and one for Upper Egypt buses to **Hurghada**, **Luxor** and **Aswan**. Each kiosk has a timetable, but schedules change often so be prepared to hang around for a connection. You will also find service taxis here that go to all major destinations. Fares vary widely, according to demand.

• **Sinai** Most of the buses from Suez to the Sinai start their journey in Cairo or Ismailiya. In the past this meant you couldn't always find a seat by the time the bus arrived in Suez. However, direct Superjet buses between Cairo and Sharm el-Sheikh – which don't stop in Suez – are proving popular, lessening demand on the East Delta buses that do, so seat availability has improved. There are six buses daily from Suez to **Sharm el-Sheikh** (8.30am, 11am, 1.30pm, 3pm, 4.30pm 5.15pm & 6pm; 4hr; £E30). The 11am bus goes on to **Nuweiba** (5hr 30min; £E35) and the 3pm bus continues to **Taba** (6hr 30min; £E32). There is one bus daily to **St Catherine's Monastery** (2pm; 6hr; £E25). Service taxis are often quicker but will be packed and there's no a/c – expect to pay around £E35 to Dahab, £E25 to St Catherine's, £E27 to Nuweiba and £E27 to Sharm el-Sheikh.

• **Ismailiya** Buses run every 30min (6am–4pm; 45min–1hr; £E5), and service taxis just as frequently (45min; £E4.50). There are also five buses daily to **Port Said** (7am, 9am, 11am, 12pm & 3.30pm; 2hr; £E10); a service taxi will cost £E10 (1hr 50min). There are frequent service taxis to **Qantara** (see p.690).

• **Alexandria** Four buses daily (7am, 9am, 2.30pm & 5pm; 6hr; £E25). Service taxis charge £E20 and may be a little quicker (5–6hr).

• **Cairo** Buses leave every 30min (1hr 30min–2hr; £E7–8) throughout the day.

• **Hurghada** Nine buses daily (6am–10pm; 4–5hr; £E33–43), most of which also stop at the nearer Red Sea resort of **Ain Sukhna** (1hr; £E5). Service taxis charge £E25 (4–5hr).

- **Upper Egypt** Buses leave for Luxor (8am, 2pm & 8pm; 10hr; £E46–55) and Aswan (5am, 11am & 5pm; 8hr; £E54–62). You can also get buses to Assyut (7am & 7pm; 7hr; £E37–40) and Qena (hourly 6am–6.30pm; 8hr; £E43–50).

International ferries

Suez is the point of departure for passenger **boats to Saudi Arabia and Sudan**; the former are used by migrant workers or pilgrims, the latter by a few determined travellers. Ferries to the Saudi port of **Jeddah** sail every day, and there are additional sailings during the *Hadj* season (six weeks either side of the Muslim month of Zoul Hagga). Boats leave around 2pm and arrive in Jeddah around 10am three days later. Prices start at £E230 for deck space and £E400 per person in a four-berth, second-class cabin (first class is £E460). Providing there's not a storm, sleeping on deck is fine. Boats to **Port Sudan** currently leave on Thursday, Friday and Sunday (tickets cost £E300 for deck space), though schedules change from month to month. The ferry takes a week to get to Port Sudan, so take enough food and drink for the journey. Contact Telstar in Cairo (☎02/794-4600) for up-to-date details, or in Port Tewfiq enquire at El Salam Maritime Transport Co. (☎062/332-6251 or 332-6252) or Menatours (☎062/322-8821 or 322-0269).

Be warned that you can't buy a **ticket** unless you already have the right visa(s). The Saudi consulate in Port Tewfiq has sections for work and *Hadj* **visas** but tourist visas can be harder to obtain, so it might be a better idea to get a transit visa in Cairo, where you can also obtain a Sudanese visa – *inshallah*.

Accommodation

Outside the *Hadj* season, **finding a room** in Suez should be easy. Except where indicated, breakfast is not included in the rates given below.

Arafat Hotel Off Sharia el-Geish in Port Tewfiq ☎062/333-8355. Clean, small rooms with balconies and fans, some with bathrooms. The only budget option if you need to stay in the Port area. The manager has information about passenger ships for Saudi Arabia etc. ❷

Green House Hotel Corner Sharia el-Geish and El Nabi Mousa St ☎062/333-1553, ℻333-1554. Smarter sister of the *White House* (see below) though still a little rundown. Clean a/c rooms with Gulf views. Swimming pool. No bar, but serves Stella (£E8). Popular with foreign engineers based in the area. ❻

Red Sea 13 Sharia Riad, Port Tewfiq ☎ & ℻062/333-4302. Clean and comfortable a/c rooms with bath, phone, balcony and satellite TV – the smartest hotel in Suez. Sixth-floor *Mermaid Restaurant* has great views of the canal. Breakfast included. ❼

Sina 21 Sharia Banque Misr ☎062/333-4181. Small rooms with fans, TV and clean shared bathrooms, with a fridge on each floor. A good, central, low-budget option. ❷

Star 17 Sharia Banque Misr ☎062/322-8737. A mixture of large and small rooms with fans and balconies; some have baths. Another good budget option, a little cheaper than the *Sina*. ❷

Summer Palace Port Tewfiq ☎062/322-4475, ℻332-1944. Run-to-seed three-star hotel, chiefly notable for its Gulf views and freshwater pool. Overpriced, but worth a visit to its al fresco café to enjoy the views. ❼

White House 322 Sharia el-Geish ☎062/333-1550. Two-star hotel with clean, slightly shabby rooms with a/c, TV and bathroom: avoid those that face the noisy street. There's a restaurant and international phone and they serve local beer; breakfast included. ❹

The city

Should you decide to stay (or simply pass a few hours between buses), Suez City is readily accessible by microbus from the bus terminal (50pt) or taxi (£E5). The main street, **Sharia el-Geish** ("Army Street"), is a two-kilometre-long swathe where cruising minibuses drop and collect passengers along the way to

Port Tewfiq. Dusty palms and decrepit colonial-era buildings (including several churches) are followed by a strip of hotels, restaurants and currency exchanges. The stadium, on Tariq el-Horriya in the south of the city, is home to Suez FC, enthusiastically supported by the local residents.

The backstreets to the south of El-Geish harbour cheap cafés, while **Sharia Sa'ad Zaghloul** runs past consulates and a fun park towards the governorate. North of El-Geish, a tawdry souk overflows **Sharia Haleem**, presaging a quarter of workshops and chandlers, crumbling century-old apartments with wooden balconies interspersed by modern government-built low-rises. There's a better **bazaar** to the northwest in Arba'in.

Along El-Geish itself, you'll find the **Convent of the Good Chapel Sisters**, an imposing colonial-style building given to the international sisterhood in 1872 by the Suez Canal Company after one of its directors recovered from a mystery illness while in their care. A decline in their numbers (from 45 down to around five) led the nuns to give their chapel over to the Coptic church, but they still run a primary school and a dispensary for the poor and provide a home for around fifteen underprivileged children. The convent's most notable feature, however, is its **Statue of Our Lady**, which draws pilgrims from all over Egypt and beyond, particularly cancer patients and women with fertility problems. The statue's miraculous properties date back to its discovery by a group of fishermen in the Gulf of Suez in 1882; the men took it back to their village and presented it to the most respected family, but by morning it had disappeared. The fishermen searched the village to no avail; only when they returned to sea did they find the statue in exactly the same place they first saw it. They decided it should be kept somewhere more holy and took it to the sisters, who have looked after it ever since.

Should you happen to be by the Canal in spring, migratory **birds of prey** provide a more arresting sight. Griffon vultures and Imperial and Steppe eagles overfly Suez to avoid crossing the Red Sea, which lacks the rising thermals on which they depend for flight. A more permanent resident is the Indian House crow – recognizable by its ear-splitting *caaarrrr* – which is thought to have arrived from India on ships during the course of the nineteenth century.

Eating, drinking and other practicalities

Eating out in Suez is limited but adequate. Your best bet for seafood is the *Al Khalifa Fish Centre* (☎064/333-7303) at 320 Sharia el-Geish, 100m west of the *White House Hotel*: there's no menu; just wait for the proprietor to bring out a platter of fish and simply point to what looks best. Another good choice is the *Dolphin* restaurant on Tariq El-Horiya. For good-value *shawarma*, sandwiches or baked macaroni, check out the *Sweet Spot*, also on Sharia el-Geish, west of the *White House*, or *Bahara* on Sharia el-Geish, opposite the *White House*.

Drinking is even more limited, with only one bar, the *Saint George* on Sharia el-Geish (next to *Sweet Spot*), where you can find Suez's expat community gathered in the evening. For non-alcoholic beverages, try *The Telegraph* coffee shop on Sharia 23rd July.

You can **change money** at the Bank of Alexandria on Sharia el-Geish (daily: summer 9am–2pm & 5–8pm; winter 8am–2pm & 6–9pm); the National Bank of Egypt on Sharia Sa'ad Zaghloul (Mon–Thurs & Sun 8.30am–2pm & 5–8pm); the Banque du Caire in Port Tewfiq (Mon–Thurs & Sun 8.30am–2pm & 5–8pm), or private exchanges in the souk. Also in Port Tewfiq is Menatours (☎069/322-8821), the agents for **American Express** (beside the tourist police) and a branch of the **post office** – the main one is on Sharia Hoda Sharawi, in the centre of town (both daily except Fri 8am–3pm).

You can make international calls from the **telephone exchange** (daily 8am–midnight) on the corner of Sa'ad Zaghloul and El-Shahada. For **Internet access**, try *Future* Internet café on Sharia Salah al-din and Sharia Haleem, or *Green Rock* Internet Café, about 200m northwest of the north of the Convent of Good Chapel Sisters.

Visa extensions can be made at the **passport office** (daily except Fri 8am–2pm) inside **police** headquarters on Sharia Horriya; as always, arrive early with your passport and photo, a pen, something to read and a sense of humour.

Ismailiya

ISMAILIYA's schizoid character is defined by the rail line that cuts across the city. South of the tracks lies the European-style **garden city** built for foreign employees of the Suez Canal Company, extending to the verdant banks of the Sweetwater Canal. Following careful restoration, its leafy boulevards and placid streets of colonial villas look almost as they must have done in the 1930s, with bilingual street signs nourishing the illusion that the British empire has just popped indoors for cocktails.

The Muslim Brotherhood and the Battle of Ismailiya

Ismailiya – one of the most Europeanized of Egyptian towns – was the birthplace of the **Muslim Brotherhood** and its founder, **Hassan el-Banna**. As a child, el-Banna nailed up leaflets calling on Muslims to renounce gold and silks, and awoke his neighbours before dawn prayers. When older, he campaigned against female emancipation, delivering fiery sermons in rented cafés. He founded the *Ikhwan el-Muslimeen* in 1928 and within fifteen years the Brotherhood had spread throughout Egypt and spawned offshoots across the Middle East, articulating an Islamic response to modernization on Western terms.

From campaigning for moral renewal it went on to organize paramilitary training and terrorist cells, and was outlawed by King Farouk (whose agents assassinated el-Banna) in 1949. Despite this, the Brotherhood mounted attacks against the British and an economic boycott in the Canal Zone. The British suspected that they received arms from sympathizers in the Egyptian police and tried to disarm the main barracks outside Ismailiya, whose garrison was ordered to resist by their superiors and only surrendered after fifty of them had been killed. The **Battle of Ismailiya** (January 25, 1952) outraged Egyptians and provoked an orgy of rioting in Cairo the following day – **"Black Saturday"** – when the police stood by as Brotherhood activists sped around in jeeps, torching foreign properties.

Legalized after the 1952 Revolution, the Brotherhood was soon suppressed again for trying to kill Nasser in Alexandria. Hundreds of Brothers spent years in concentration camps, until amnestied by President Sadat, who sought to co-opt them as a counterweight to the left. Eventually, their growing influence and criticism of his policies led Sadat to jail them *en masse*, whereupon his assassination by *Al-Jihad* proved that other groups had grown up in the Brotherhood's shadow and surpassed it in radicalism. To isolate these new militants, Mubarak, too, wooed the Brotherhood with all kinds of concessions short of legalization. In **recent years** he has followed a less clear policy. While he has ordered the arrest of scores of Brothers and the closure of their headquarters in Cairo, associates or sympathizers of the Brotherhood currently form the second largest bloc in the National Assembly after the NDP, and the government appears to view them as a moderating influence within the Islamist movement.

North of the train tracks you move into another world of hastily constructed flats grafted onto long-standing **slums**, and a quarter financed by the Gulf Emirates that provides a *cordon sanitaire* for the wealthy suburb of **Nemrah Setta** (Number Six). This Janus-profile reflects the city's twentieth-century **history**, when two disparate sons of Ismailiya had a lasting effect on Egyptian society. **Hassan el-Banna** created the Muslim Brotherhood that was the bane of the British and has vexed Egypt's rulers since independence (see box on p.685). Two generations later, Ismailiya became synonymous with **Osman Ahmed Osman**, a self-made millionaire contractor whom Sadat appointed as Minister of Housing and Reconstruction in 1975. As Gulf investments poured into the Canal Zone, billboard-size pictures of Osman began to outnumber those of his patron, who finally agreed to opposition demands for an audit. By the time it was discovered that millions had been stashed in Swiss banks, Osman had fled the country. Subsequent investigations into his political connections proved inconclusive and he is now back in business.

Arrival, information and accommodation

Although Ismailiya can be reached by train (6 daily; 3–5hr), buses or taxis are a quicker way of **getting there from Cairo**. Buses (every 30min 6.30am–6.30pm; £E7.50) and service taxis (£E6.50) both leave from the Turgoman Garage, in Bulaq, stopping at the Al-Mazah terminal in Heliopolis thirty minutes later, and take two to three hours. The 120-kilometre desert road runs through two places worth noting. **Khanka** contains Egypt's main asylum for the criminally insane, which has made its name a popular synonym for "totally crazy". Further out, a spate of country clubs presages **Medinet Ashara Ramadan** (10th of Ramadan City), a satellite city for the new breed of Cairene commuters, complete with quasi-American suburban homes and steak houses.

All buses and service taxis wind up at the new **bus station** on the ring road outside Ismailiya, opposite the massive Suez Canal University building. From here take a taxi (£E3) or microbus (50pt) into the town centre.

The old town's grid-plan and clearly named streets make **orientation** easy. The **tourist office** is inside the new Governorate Building on El-Togari Street, in the north of the city 2km from downtown (daily except Fri 9am–2pm; ☎064/332-1070 or 332-1072); as usual, it's an inconvenient location and does little other than supply a booklet with some information and a map. Hotel staff are likely to prove more informative and helpful.

Accommodation

Apart from a couple of smart hotels, most of Ismailiya's accommodation has seen better days. However, the majority of the hotels are safe, reasonably clean and cheap, and Ismailiya only really gets busy during festivals and the summer season – May to September – when it's a popular honeymoon destination for Egyptian couples. Finding accommodation at other times should be easy, with some hotels likely to be empty – a fact reflected by a general lack of atmosphere in town. Breakfast is included in rates given below unless indicated otherwise.

Crocodile Inn 172 Sharia Sa'ad Zaghloul ☎064/391-2555, ℱ391-2666. The only reasonably smart hotel in the town centre, with a restaurant and 24-hr coffee shop. Nice a/c rooms with balconies, and breakfast included, but overpriced. ❺

Isis Midan Orabi ☎064/392-2821. A range of rooms with fans. Friendly, helpful staff. Reductions for long-staying guests. A low-budget option. No breakfast. ❷

Mercure Forsan Island 2km east of town ☎064/391-6316, ℱ391-8043. Leafy four-star resort set in fifty acres of grounds. a/c rooms and villas with satellite TV, minibar and international phone. Swimming pool and watersports. Half-board only. ❽

Nefetari 41 Sharia Sultan Hussein ☎064/391-5555. A good choice with agreeable, albeit very pink, rooms, some with a/c and private baths. No breakfast. ❷

Palace Midan Orabi ☎064/391-6327, ℱ391-7761. A wonderfully pretentious nineteenth-century

pile with a/c rooms, satellite TV and private baths. Popular with honeymooners, so often full. A good-value option, especially for those travelling on their own, with single rooms just £E50 including breakfast. ❺

Traveller's Hotel Sharia Ahmed Orabi ☎064/362-3304. Also called *Hotel des Voyageurs*. Colonial-style flea pit that's stronger on atmosphere than creature comforts. Nice rooms with balconies, but no restaurant, breakfast or anything much else. Fans on request. ❶

Youth hostel at Sharia Imhara Siyahi, 1km from the centre and £E2 by taxi ☎064/392-2850, ℱ392-3429. Overlooks Lake Timsah with its own beach. It has 26 double, triple or six-person rooms with private baths. Double £E44 with breakfast; dorm bed £E23. Non-members pay £E1 extra. It's just past the bridge on the left as you head south out of town. ❶

The town and around

Shaded by pollarded trees, Ismailiya's carefully restored old town is a pleasure to walk or bike around. Most of the sights can be reached on foot within ten minutes, although a couple of places outside town warrant renting a bicycle in the backstreets off Mohammed Ali Quay, or catching a service taxi from the turn-off near Mallaha Park.

Starting on Mohammed Ali Quay, first on the trail is the large, vaguely Swiss-looking **House of Ferdinand de Lesseps**, who lived here during the Canal's construction. Disappointingly, you can only visit the interior if you're a VIP, since the house now serves as a private hotel for guests of the Suez Canal Authority. In de Lesseps' study, books and photographs are scattered around his desk and bed as if the Frenchman had been reviewing his life's work, while his carriage stands outdoors, encased in glass. Lone visitors might chance a peek inside if the rear gate is open; otherwise, you could try presenting yourself at the Suez Canal Authority and bluffing the press officer into fixing a visit – though this could well prove a waste of time.

A pleasant fifteen minutes' walk down the street from the de Lesseps' House, the **Ismailiya Museum** (Mon–Thurs & Sat–Sun 9am–4pm, Fri and during Ramadan 9.30am–noon & 1.15–4pm; £E6, students £E3) leans towards ancient history, devoting a section to the waterways of Ramses and Darius. The highlights of its collection of four thousand Greco-Roman and pharaonic artefacts is a lovely mosaic from the fourth century AD, depicting Phaedra, Dionysos, Eros and Hercules. Other sections cover the canal in modern history, the Battle of Ismailiya and the "Crossing" of October 1973.

With permission from the museum, you can also visit some plaques and obelisks from Ramses II's time, in the **Garden of Steles** just west of the museum. However, it's nicer to wander amid the 500 acres of exotic shrubs and trees of **Mallaha Park**, or stroll alongside the shady **Sweetwater Canal** that was dug to provide fresh water for labourers building the Suez Canal. Previously, supplies had to be brought across the desert by camels, or shipped across Lake Manzala to Port Said.

Lake Timsah

Notwithstanding its name, "Crocodile Lake", there are several nice **beaches** around **Lake Timsah**, which you can reach by taking a taxi or walking 1km out along Sharia Talatini. You can dine outside near picturesque fishing boats, or pay £E5–10 to use the manicured lawns and beaches of the private resorts and clubs (which may include snacks and drinks in the deal), though many of these places close outside high season. Wealthier citizens patronize the *Mercure Forsan Island* with its **waterskiing**, **windsurfing** and **tennis** facilities; you can use the beach and swimming pool for £E15 (Mon–Thurs), or £E25 (Fri–Sun).

The Bar-Lev Line and other excursions

Service taxis turning off near Mallaha Park are usually bound for "Ferri Setta" (50pt), outside town, where locals use a **ferry crossing** to the east bank of the canal. Here, a vast sand rampart breached by deep cuts marks the former **Bar-Lev Line**, named after the Israeli general who designed it. Intended to stall any attack on Sinai for 48 hours, this 25-metre-high embankment was defended by forty mined strongpoints. In the event, they were totally surprised by Egypt's assault on **October 6, 1973**. As hidden artillery opened up at 2pm, eight thousand commandos dragged launches to the water's edge, roared across the 180-metre-wide canal and scaled the ramparts with ladders. Within hours, high-pressure hoses ordered from Bavaria "for the Cairo Fire Department" were blasting gaps for the Egyptian armour massing behind pontoon bridge layers.

However, although "The Crossing" was an Egyptian triumph (still remembered with pride), the war subsequently turned against them. An Israeli force under Ariel Sharon counterattacked across the canal between Lake Timsah and the Great Bitter Lake, wheeled inland to cut the Cairo–Suez road, and had virtually encircled the Egyptian army in Sinai by the time the superpowers imposed a ceasefire. Disengagement on the ground began with UN-sponsored talks at **Kilometre 101** – the nearest Israeli tanks came to Cairo.

A more scenic but distant view of the Canal can be had from **Nemrah Setta**, an exclusive suburb of French colonial-style villas on a hilltop outside town, where, in 1969, an Israeli shell killed the Egyptian Chief of Staff, General Abdul-Monaim Riad. To get there costs £E2–3 by private taxi, or take a service taxi from Midan Orabi to "Ferri Setta" (50pt) and walk up the hill.

The surrounding countryside also has its charms. By taking a service taxi (£E2) from Sharia Talatini (just past the rail line) to **El-Mahsama**, and alighting at Dr Hassan's Hospital, you can walk along the Nile tributary past fields irrigated by archaic water-pumps and old men on donkeys – a scene redolent of the Biblical land of Goshen.

Eating, nightlife and other practicalities

Ismailiya is good for **eating out**. When the weather's fine, citizens dine al-fresco near the fishing port on Lake Timsah; it's worth the cost of a taxi (£E2–3) out along Sharia Talatini to eat fish straight from the lake. You might even risk the local speciality, *Umm el-Khaloul* – a kind of shellfish that's best avoided during hot weather when there's a greater risk of it going off. Otherwise, there are several decent restaurants in the centre. The most popular **drinking** spots are *King Edward* (see listings below and overleaf) and the bar at the *Mercure Forsan Island*, both of which attract an interesting crowd as the night wears on. Alternatively, most of the evening streetlife can be found around Sharia Talatini, Sharia Sa'ad Zaghloul and Sharia el-Geish, where shops, cafés and juice bars are open late into the night.

The **post office** (daily except Fri 9am–4pm) and the 24-hour **telephone exchange** are both just off Midan Orabi, while the **passport office** (daily except Fri 8am–2pm) is nearby on Midan Gummhorriya. You can **change money** at the Bank of Alexandria or the National Bank of Egypt, both just off Midan Orabi (both Mon–Thurs & Sat–Sun 8.30am–2pm, 5–8pm, Fri 8.30am–noon; the latter takes Visa and MasterCard), though you might get a slightly better rate for cash at the exchange at 22 Ahmed Orabi, near the *Traveller's Hotel*. For **Internet** access, try the *Bahgat Internet café* (☎064/391-2428, £E2/hr) on the southeast corner of Midan Orabi, or the *Easy Café* (☎064/392-3823, £E1.50/hr) on Sharia Tahrir, near Midan Gummhorriya.

Restaurants

Fabiola's off Sharia Sa'ad Zaghloul. Inexpensive pizza joint, but don't bother if it's empty as this could mean a long wait for mediocre food. Daily 11am–11pm.

George's Sharia Sultan Hussein. Quiet, a/c Greek restaurant specializing in seafood and kebabs. Has a well-stocked bar, the only one in town. £E14–38 for a full meal. Daily 11am–1am.

King Edward 171 Sharia Tahrir ☏ 064/332-5451. Air-conditioned haunt of expats and affluent natives, offering tasty Continental and Egyptian food (main dishes £E10–30), wine and beer. DJ plays Western and Middle Eastern music, but don't expect it to get going till after 11pm.

Mona Pizza Sharia Sultan Hussein ☏ 064/392-3232. Another pizza place right next to *Nefertiti's*, trendier than *Fabiola's* and with better food.
Nefertiti's Sharia Sultan Hussein ☏ 064/391-0494. Specializes in fish (£E20–25) and shrimps (£E40), but does meat dishes, too. Sells beer and wine. Daily noon–midnight.

Festivals

Should you happen to be here around Easter, Ismailia is a good place to witness the spring festival of **Shams el-Nessim**, when families picnic in the park between the Sweetwater Canal and Lake Timsah, and a **Flower Festival** adds colour to the occasion.

Even better is the "**Doll-Burning**" or **Limbo Festival**, held a week later. Its curious title refers to a hated nineteenth-century local governor – Limbo Bey – effigies of whom were torched by the citizenry. Ever since then, it has been customary to burn dolls resembling one's pet hate: footballers are popular targets whenever Ismailiya's soccer club does poorly. The dolls are burned on the streets after dark.

Moving on

To get anywhere from Ismailiya, it's back to the bus station on the ring road opposite the new Suez Canal University building. Private taxis (£E2–3) or service taxis (50pt) to the bus station leave from the rank on Sharia Talatini just north of the railway tracks.

• **North Sinai** Buses leave eight times a day for **El-Arish** (8.30am, 9am, 9.30am, 10am, 11am, 1pm, 2pm, 3pm & 5pm; 3hr; £E10); service taxis cost £E6. There are also service taxis to **Rafah** (£E10).

• **South Sinai** Buses leave throughout the day and night to **Sharm el-Sheikh** (6.30am–midnight; 6hr; £E33), two of which carry on to **Dahab** (2.30pm & 12.30am; 7–8hr; £E34). A service taxi to Sharm el-Sheikh costs £E34. There's also a nightly bus to **Nuweiba** (9pm; 7–8hr; £E48).

• **Canal cities** Buses travel regularly via Ismailiya between **Port Said** (hourly 6.45am–6.45pm; 1hr; £E5) and **Suez** (hourly 6.30am–6pm; 1hr; £E5) and there are also service taxis (Port Said £E4.50; Suez £E4.50). A service taxi to **Qantara** is £E1.50.

• **Lower Egypt** There are two buses daily to **Alexandria** (7am & 2.30pm; 4hr; £E22) and frequent departures for **Cairo** (every 45min 6.30am–7pm; 2hr; £7). Outside of these hours service taxis go to Cairo (£E5) and to the Delta town of **El-Mansura** (£E6).

North of Ismailiya – canal crossings

Seven kilometres north of Ismailiya, a **car ferry** crosses the canal more or less non-stop during daylight hours. Together with the Ahmed Hamdi Tunnel outside Suez, it used to carry almost all the traffic between mainland Egypt and Sinai until the opening of the Salaam (or Ferdan) Suspension Bridge in October 2001, which is now the most direct route from Cairo to Israel.

The only other crossing point is at **QANTARA**, 44km from Ismailiya and 80km from Port Said. As its name ("Bridge") suggests, this was the route used by pilgrims and armies to cross the marshy Isthmus of Suez before the canal was built. Since then, it has been spanned by pontoon bridges in wartime, but

The New Kingdom war machine

Recent excavations in the Eastern Delta and Northern Sinai have cast light on the revolution in Egyptian warfare during the New Kingdom. The Hyksos invasion forced the Egyptians to adopt the weapons of their enemy – horses, chariots, composite bows, edged swords and bronze armour – and master cavalry tactics, hitherto unknown. **Chariots** became the key to their success, allowing rapid movement on the battlefield and over long distances. Light enough to be lifted over obstacles by their crew, they were kept on the road by mobile repair units and stables at the rear; one for 400 horses has been found at Tell ed-Daba in the Delta. Twelve **fortresses** along the **Great Horus military route** across Northern Sinai (depicted on Seti I's reliefs in the columned court at Karnak) provided defence in depth and stores for major campaigns; one at Tell Habouh, near Qantara, covers 12,000 square metres. Armies were supplied by donkeys or by galleys in coastal waters. Such logistics enabled Tuthmosis III to move 20,000 troops 400km in nine days – without being detected – while Ramses II extended Egypt's strategic reach to 2000km by pioneering the use of oxen (the mainstay of military logistics for the next thousand years). This formidable war machine made imperialism inevitable, and was fed by the spoils of war: 894 chariots, 2000 horses and 25,000 pack animals were taken at the battle of Meggido alone.

The fortresses lie within what is still a sensitive military area, not yet open to tourists. Anyone with a serious interest should contact the **Centre for Sinai Studies** at the Archeological Institute in West Qantara (☎064/334-2713 or 333-3718).

is now negotiated by a small passenger ferry, carrying locals, bikes and donkeys from one side of Qantara to the other. Most of the town is on the west bank, whose unpaved main drag has a busy souk and lines of service taxis going to Cairo and the Canal cities; the battered, poorly rebuilt houses are a reminder that armies clashed here in 1973. On the east bank of the canal there's a cafeteria and service taxis for El-Arish (2hr 30min; £E5), but it's easier to take one direct from Ismailiya.

Port Said (Bur Said)

Founded at the start of the canal excavations, **PORT SAID** was long synonymous with smuggling and vice, boasting an "even larger stock of improper photos than Brussels or Buenos Aires". The adventurer De Monfreid was amused by the Arab cafés where "native policemen as well as coolies" smoked hashish in back rooms, supplied by primly respectable Greeks. "If anyone had even had the bad taste to pronounce the forbidden word, I believe that they would have all turned into pillars of salt. All the same, every single one of them got his living from trafficking in hashish, either as a retail seller, or as a small-scale smuggler who haunted the liners."

Nowadays, this bustling city of 420,000 people earns its living as a free port and beach resort, yet a faintly raffish atmosphere lingers around its old streets of timber-porched houses, vaguely resembling the French Quarter of New Orleans. Prior to the current downturn in tourism caused by the unrest in Israel and the Occupied Territories, which has rather halted development in the region, *Bur Said* had been attempting to lure tourists away from Alexandria by promising better shops and less crowded beaches, cheap hotels and good restaurants. Aside from day-trippers off cruise liners, foreign tourists seldom visit the city and hustlers are rare, making it an agreeable place to relax for a day or two

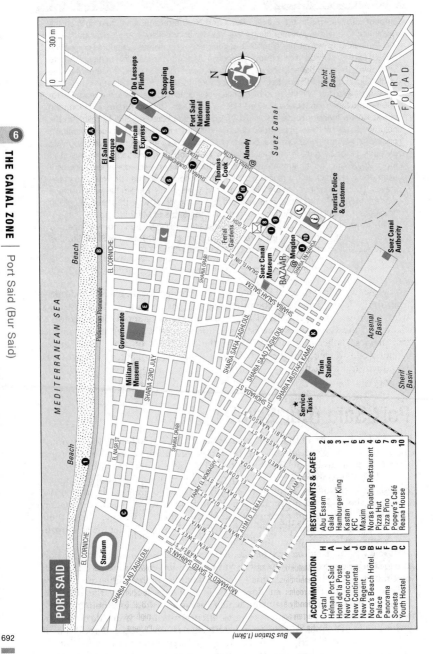

PORT SAID

Stadium

MEDITERRANEAN SEA

Beach

Beach

Pedestrian Promenade

EL CORNICHE

EL CORNICHE

EL CORNICHE

EL CORNICHE

EL MASRY ST

Military Museum

Governorate

SHARIA 23RD JULY

SHARIA DRABI

SHARIA DRABI

SHARIA SAAD ZAGHLOUL

MOHAMED EL SAYED SABHAN ST

SHARIA SAAD ZAGHLOUL

SHARIA SAFA ZAGHLOUL

SHARIA SAFIA SALEM

SHARIA SALAH EL DIN ST

DIST ST

El Salam Mosque

American Express

SHARIA EL GUMHOURIYA

SHARIA EL GUMHOURIYA

SOMOL ST

Port Said National Museum

De Lesseps Plinth

Shopping Centre

Suez Canal

N

PORT FOUAD

Yacht Basin

Thomas Cook

Afandy

SHARIA PALESTINE

Ferial Gardens

Suez Canal Museum

BAZAAR

Megdon

SHARIA EL NAHDA

Tourist Police & Customs

Suez Canal Authority

Arsenal Basin

Sherif Basin

Train Station

Service Taxis

EL SHOHADA ST

SHARIA MUSTAFA KAMEL

ABU EL HASSAN NABIL MANSUR ST

HAMED EL ALYS ST

FAWZY EL NOBRASHY ST

61RA ST

DAKHLIA ST

EL RODA ST

ASHMAUN ST

ASWAN ST

BEN SWEF ST

EL MINYA ST

NABEH ST

EL SABAH ST

SHARIA SAFIA ZAGHLOUL

SHARIA SAAD ZAGHLOUL

ISMAIL ST

EL SALAM ST

▲ Bus Station (1.5km)

0   300 m

ACCOMMODATION

Crystal	H
Helnan Port Said	A
Hotel de la Poste	I
New Concorde	K
New Continental	J
New Regent	G
Nora's Beach Hotel	B
Palace	E
Panorama	F
Sonesta	D
Youth Hostel	C

RESTAURANTS & CAFÉS

Abu Essam	2
Galal	8
Hamburger King	3
Kastan	1
KFC	6
Maxim	5
Nora's Floating Restaurant	4
Pizza Hut	6
Pizza Pino	7
Popeye's Café	9
Reana House	10

if you don't mind the lack of "sights" and diversions and are content to hang out on the beach or one of the European-style street cafés.

Arrival, information and accommodation

Trains **from Cairo** (six daily) take at least four and a half hours to reach Port Said via Ismailiya, and are grimy to boot, making it more appealing to do the 220km journey by bus (3hr). Regular a/c East Delta buses depart from Cairo's Turgoman Garage (hourly 7am–8pm; 4hr; £E13–16). There are no direct trains **from Alexandria**, and seats on buses (4 daily; 6hr; £E18–22) should be reserved the day before, at the East Delta kiosk on Midan Sa'ad Zaghoul. All buses, including those from Suez (4 daily; 2hr 30min; £E9.50) and Ismailiya (hourly 6am–7pm; 1hr 30 min; £E5.50) terminate at Port Said's bus station at the entrance to the city. Service taxis provide the fastest transport **from Suez and Ismailiya** and augment buses **from the Delta**, where Damietta and El-Mansura have the best connections. Coming **from El-Arish** in north Sinai, you can catch a service taxi (£E9–10) direct to the city.

Because Port Said is a **duty-free port**, visitors are supposed to pass through **customs** upon entering and leaving the city. You may not have to, but if you do pass through customs, it is advisable to declare any cameras or other gadgets, which they might think you bought at a discount here, or you may be subject to a twelve percent levy as you go out (ships' passengers are exempt). Simply request a paper (£E1) and fill it in with details of your belongings, keeping it to show when you leave. The main **point of arrival** is the bus station, which is on the outskirts of Port Said just off the main road from Ismailiya, from where you can catch a taxi (£E2) downtown (along and around Sharia el-Gumhorriya). **Orientation** is straightforward, as most things of interest or use to tourists can be found on three thoroughfares: the waterfront Sharia Filastin (Palestine Street); Sharia el-Gumhorriya (Street of the Republic), two blocks inland; or Sharia 23rd July.

The **tourist office** (Sat–Thurs 9am–6pm & Fri 9am–2pm; ☎066/323-5289) on Sharia Filastin can supply a useful map of the town with listings of hotels and services and some historical background, a second tourist booth is located at the train station, while the **tourist police** (☎066/322-8570) is at the back of the main customs building.

Accommodation

Most of Port Said's accommodation is very good value, with Sharia el-Gumhorriya offering the widest range of **hotels**, from modern tower blocks to old-style *pensions*. Be aware, however, that rooms can be hard to find on Thursday and Friday nights, when many Egyptians come here to do weekend duty-free shopping. The **youth hostel** on Sharia al-Amin (☎066/322-8702, ☎322-6433; £E8), near the stadium, has clean but gloomy dormitory rooms; it admits non-members (£E2 extra). Rates given below include breakfast unless stated otherwise.

Crystal Hotel 12 Mohamed Makhmud ☎066/322-2747. A big complex which resembles a youth hostel, with large en suite a/c rooms at very low prices. The management is friendly enough, but the building itself is somewhat barren and dreary. ❶

Helnan Port Said El Corniche St ☎066/332-0890, ☎332-3762, ✉reshps@helnan.com. A five-star hotel right on the beach, with amenities including a pool, gym, sauna, coffee shop, nightclub, and Port Said's only bowling alley. ❼

Hotel de la Poste 46 Sharia el-Gumhorriya ☎066/322-9655, ☎322-8898. Rambling 1940s-style place offering high-ceilinged rooms with fans and baths. Overall it's very good value, though TVs and fridges and breakfast cost extra. Recommended. ❷

New Concorde Sharia Mustafa Kamel ☎066/323-5342, ⓕ323-5930. Carpeted rooms with baths, fans and TV, near the train station. Some of the rooms on the upper floors have views of the canal. ❺

New Continental 30 Sharia el-Gumhorriya ☎066/322-5024, ⓕ333-3088. Pleasant enough, though a bit shabby; a/c rooms with satellite TV, international phone and balconies. ❹

New Regent off Sharia el-Gumhorriya ☎066/322-3802, ⓕ322-4891. Small but comfortable hotel offering a/c rooms, all with TV and fridge. ❻

Nora's Beach Hotel El Corniche ☎066/332-9834, ⓕ332-9841. Huge beachside complex with 200 apartments and suites – a bit frayed at the edges but still comfortable – with a/c, private bathroom, satellite TV, minibar, balcony or terrace. With its three swimming pools and a health club, it's popular with Egyptian families. ❺

Palace 19 Sharia Ghandi, opposite the governorate building, near the beach ☎066/323-9450, ⓕ323-9464. Pleasantly furnished rooms with a/c and private bathrooms. ❻

Panorama Hotel Shari el-Gumhorriya ☎066/332-5101, ⓕ332-5103. A/C rooms with satellite TV, private bathrooms and big balconies. Great views especially from the billiard room on the eleventh floor. A bit worn, but clean and comfortable. ❺

Sonesta Sharia Sultan Hussein, off Sharia Filastin ☎066/332-5511, ⓕ332-4825, ⓦwww.sonesta.com/Egypt_portsaid. Air-conditioned rooms have private bathrooms, satellite TV and a minibar, and overlook the canal entrance and fishing harbour. There's also a nice pool, but no beach. Breakfast costs extra. ❽

The city

Sharia el-Gumhorriya reflects Port Said's metamorphosis from a salty entrepôt to a slick commercial centre, plate-glass facades superseding early twentieth-century balconies as the street progresses from the Arsenal Basin to Sharia 23rd July.

The adjacent **bazaar** quarter is a microcosm of Egyptian consumer aspirations, ranging from humble stalls on Salah El Din Street to the smart boutiques on Sharia en-Nahda. These have been joined by designer shops such as Hugo Boss and sports stores like Nike and Reebok at the junction of Sharia el-Gumhorriya with Sharia 23rd July. There is even a Clark's shoe shop downtown and a Marks and Spencer in the shopping centre opposite the *Sonesta*.

The **Military Museum** on Sharia 23rd July (daily 9am–4pm; £E5) gives a strong sense of the Canal's embattled history. The 1956 Anglo-French-Israeli invasion is commemorated by lurid paintings and dioramas, while another room is dedicated to the October War of 1973. This gives pride of place to the storming of the Bar-Lev Line (see p.688), a heroic feat of arms ultimately wasted by the high command's failure to exploit Egypt's breakthrough in Sinai. Curiously absent from the large display of weaponry are the Soviet-made *Strella* and *Molutka* rockets that enabled Egyptian infantrymen to destroy Israeli jets and armour, rated by strategists as a minor revolution in modern warfare.

From here, it's about 15–20 minutes' walk to the **Port Said National Museum** on Sharia Filastin (daily except Fri 9am–5pm, Fri 9am–noon & 2–5pm; £E20, students £E10, camera £E10), which runs the gamut of Egyptian history. Highlights of its well-displayed collection include two mummies, an exquisitely worked faïence shroud and painted coffin, Ptolemaic funerary masks, Islamic tiles and *mashrabiyas*, Coptic textiles (especially a tunic adorned with images of the Apostles) and the coach of Khedive Ismail, used during the Canal's inauguration ceremonies. Cool and uncrowded, the museum makes a pleasant retreat from the heat and hubbub around this part of the waterfront.

Come evening, townsfolk and holidaymakers **promenade** along the Corniche, or near the National Museum, watching dozens of vessels at anchor, their bulky hulls dwindling to lights bobbing far offshore. At the far end of the quay is a massive sandstone plinth that used to bear a huge **statue of de Lesseps,** before it was torn down following the 1952 Revolution. For an idea of the Canal's workings, take a cruise on the *Noras* floating restaurant or catch the free **ferry** (every 15min) across to Port Fouad (see below). There's also a new **Suez Canal Museum** being built behind the fire station on Sharia Safia Zaghloul.

You can rent chairs and parasols for £E5 on Port Said's shell-strewn **beach,** which has public showers at 100m intervals. For calmer water and more relaxed sunbathing, consider paying £E20 to use the **pool** at the *Sonesta* hotel. The pool at the *Helnan* costs a hefty £E50 but this includes use of the gym and sauna.

Port Fouad

Founded as a suburb for Canal bureaucrats in 1927, **PORT FOUAD** is quieter than its sister city. Residents boast of commuting between Asia and Africa – an enjoyable ride in a battered ferry reeking of everything but interContinental status. The suburb's decrepit but stylish **1930s architecture** can be appreciated by making a tour of Port Fouad's Art Deco flats, colonial villas and well-tended gardens. Travellers hoping to work their passage to the Med or the Indian Ocean could ask around at the **yacht basin,** although success is far from assured.

Eating and drinking

Eating out in Port Said is enjoyable, as fresh seafood abounds and most places have tables outdoors, allowing you to savour the bustling streetlife, while Sharia el-Gumhorriya has plenty of **patisseries** and **coffee houses** to relax at. If you fancy cruising the Suez Canal while you eat, make a reservation at *Nora's* **floating restaurant** on the waterfront near the National Museum. *Nora's* sails at least twice daily (3.30pm and 9.30pm) but schedules change, so check times at the *Nora's Beach Hotel* where you can also reserve tickets. The ninety-minute cruise costs £E15 including a soft drink, or £E36–60 including lunch or dinner. The spit-and-sawdust *Cecil Bar* beneath the *Reama House* restaurant is where to go **drinking** if you want to imbibe an atmosphere redolent of the olden days, in the company of aged Greeks. The bar is open till midnight or later. There is also the standard duo of *KFC* and *Pizza Hut*, both on Sharia 23rd July, if you're feeling homesick.

Abu Essam El-Corniche St, diagonally opposite the *Helnan*. Excellent fish restaurant with moderate prices. A full meal costs £E20–30.

Galal On the corner of Gaberti and el-Gumhorriya. A nice place to sit outside, drink beer and eat *kofta* sandwiches or seafood (£E15–20). They also do *shawarma* takeaways. Daily 7am–1am; closed during Ramadan.

Hamburger King Corner of Sharia el-Gomhorriya and Sharia Tarh el-Bahr ☎066/322-4877. Burger bar popular with young Egyptians. Hamburgers (£E5), sandwiches, *shawarma* (£E4–8) and pizza (£E10–20). Also serves fresh fruit juice (£E3) and does home delivery.

Kastan El-Corniche St, towards the stadium. Large and very busy 24-hr seafood and fish restaurant on the beach. Around £E40 for a full meal. Recommended.

Maxim In the shopping centre on the corner of el-Gumhorriya and el-Corniche. Port Said's most expensive fish restaurant, with splendid views of ships entering the Canal. A full meal costs £E40–60.

Pizza Pino On the corner of el-Gumhorriya and 23rd July streets. Popular joint with slick decor and a seductive range of Italian dishes and ice cream.

Popeye's Café Sharia el-Gumhorriya, opposite the Hotel de la Poste. A pleasant Mediterranean-style street café serving a wide selection of food, including huge banana splits. Daily 9am–2am.

Reana House 5 Sharia el-Gumhorriya, diagonally across from the *New Continental Hotel*. Tasty Korean and Chinese food including vegetarian dishes, at reasonable prices. Serves alcohol. Open till midnight or later.

Listings

Currency exchange Numerous private exchanges around Sharia en-Nahda and the shopping malls at the northern end of Sharia el-Gumhorriya can change money with less hassle than banks and sometimes at a slightly better rate. Travellers' cheques can be cashed at Thomas Cook, at 43 Sharia el-Gumhorriya (daily 8am–5pm; ☏066/322-7559, ℱ323-6111). An American Express office is on the northern end of Sharia el-Gumhorriya, in the Medina Tower (daily except Fri 8am–2pm; ☏066/334-1108, ℱ334-1087). Several of the banks along Sharia el-Gumhorriya now have ATMs which accept Visa and MasterCard.

Hospitals The best equipped and newest hospital is Al-Soliman near the sports stadium (☏066/333-1533). Emergencies can also be treated at the Al-Mabarrah (☏066/322-0560) or El-Tadaman (☏066/323-1790) hospitals.

Internet Afandy Internet Café is located opposite Nasco Tours on Sharia Filastin. The Megdon Internet Café (daily 10.30am–3am; ☏066/322-8881) is on Sharia el-Nahada.

Passport office In the governorate building on Sharia 23rd July (Thurs & Sat 8am–2pm).

Pharmacy The 24-hr Hussein Pharmacy on Sharia el-Gumhorriya (☏066/333-9888) is diagonally opposite the *Hotel de la Poste*.

Post office The main branch (daily except Fri 9am–2pm) is near the southeast corner of Ferial Gardens.

Telephone exchange Just along from the tourist office on Sharia Filastin (24hr).

Moving on

East Delta **buses** to Cairo or Alexandria, Superjet a/c services to Cairo and buses to Ismailiya or the Delta all leave from the main bus station at the edge of town on the road to Ismailiya, about 3km from downtown. East Delta Bus Company (☏066/372-9883) has daily buses to Cairo (hourly 6am–10pm; 3hr; £E16), Alexandria (7am, 11am, 3.30pm & 7pm; 3hr; £E22), Ismailiya (hourly 6.30am–6.30pm; 1hr; £E5), Suez (hourly 6.30am–6.30pm; 2hr; £E10), and Luxor (1 daily; 8hr; £E53) via Hurghada (5hr; £E37). Superjet (☏066/322-9018) has one bus daily to Alexandria (4.30pm; 4hr; £E22) and several throughout the day to Cairo (3hr; £E17). All buses and **service taxis** stop at the customs station outside the city, though foreigners may well get waved through.

To get to **Cyprus**, the *Princess Marissa* **ferry** departs around 7.30pm every Tuesday and Saturday in the summer (Tues & Fri in the winter), arriving in Limassol the next morning around 10am. At time of writing the onward journey to Haifa had been suspended. The fare to Limassol is US$120 per person one-way for a cabin (4 persons max). Tickets are available from Nasco Tours on Sharia Filastin, north of the tourist office (☏066/332-9500, ℱ323-8850).

Sinai

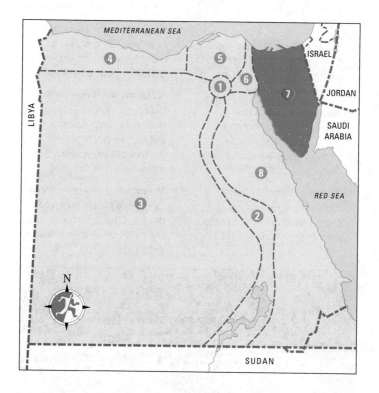

CHAPTER 7 # Highlights

* **Reefs and wrecks** Check out the infamous blue hole, or go wreck-diving round the Thistlegorm. **See p.709**

* **Ras Mohammed** Egypt's first national park, sited at the tip of the Sinai peninsula, offers some world-class diving. **See p.714**

* **Na'ama Bay** By night, the bars and clubs of Egypt's premier resort are teeming with revellers. **See p.721**

* **Nabeq** Check out the spectacular scenery and the world's most northerly mangroves in Nabeq National Park. **See p.730**

* **Dahab** Chill out in Asilah, renowned for its diving, laid-back beach cafés and cheap accommodation. **See p.731**

* **Bedouin culture** Moulids and weddings are held at full moon in the desert. **See p.741**

* **Sandy beaches** Between Nuweiba and Taba stretch miles of beautiful beaches, peppered with budget-priced camps for travellers. **See p.743**

* **Desert safaris** Take a camel or jeep safari to secluded palm-fringed *wadis* with Bedouin hosts. **See p.748**

* **St. Catherine's monastery** Built by Byzantine Empress Helena to commemorate the sight of the burning bush at the foot of Mount Sinai. **See p.750**

* **Mount Sinai** Climb the mountain where Moses received the Ten Commandments and see dawn break over the Sinai desert. **See p.753**

△ St Catherine's monastery

Sinai

The **Sinai** peninsula has been the gateway between Africa and Asia since time immemorial and a battleground for millennia. Prized for its strategic position and mineral wealth, Sinai is also revered by disparate cultures as the site of God's revelation to Moses, the wanderings of Exodus and the flight of the Holy Family. As Burton Bernstein wrote, "It has been touched, in one way or another by most of Western and Near Eastern history, both actual and mythic", being the supposed route (there's no archeological proof) by which the Israelites reached the Promised Land and Islam entered North Africa, then a theatre for Crusader-Muslim and Arab-Israeli conflicts, and finally transformed into an internationally monitored demilitarized zone.

Though mostly wilderness, Sinai looks far too dramatic – and too beautiful – to be dismissed as "24,000 square miles of nothing". The interior of southern Sinai is an arid moonscape of jagged ranges harbouring **Mount Sinai** and **St Catherine's Monastery**, where pilgrims climb the Steps of Repentance from the site of the Burning Bush to the summit where God delivered the Ten Commandments. Further north, the vast **Wilderness of the Wanderings** resembles a Jackson Pollock canvas streaked with colour and imprinted with tank tracks. The Sinai is also home to a remarkably high number of plants and wildlife; over sixty percent of Egypt's plant life thrives in this area, and 33 species are unique to the Sinai. Among a number of mammals that inhabit the region are the hyena, ibex and the rabbit-like hyrax. Venture into this "desert" on a **camel trek** or **jeep safari** and you will also find remote springs and lush oases, providing some insights into **Bedouin culture**.

Above all, however, the south has the lure of exquisite coral reefs and tropical fish in the **Gulf of Aqaba**, one of the finest **diving** and **snorkelling** grounds in the world. The beach resorts at **Sharm el-Sheikh** (which includes **Na'ama Bay**), **Dahab** and **Nuweiba** cater to every taste and budget. From Sharm el-Sheikh you can also make expeditions to Egypt's deepest reefs and most diverse aquatic life at **Ras Mohammed**, a mini-peninsula at the southern tip of Sinai, and the **Tiran Strait**, scattered with the wrecks of ships that have floundered on the reefs of this narrow passageway connecting the Red Sea to the Gulf of Aqaba. Northwest of here, the **Gulf of Suez** pales by comparison with its eastern counterpart – though year-round winds make it a great destination for diehard windsurfers, there are no reefs and few sites to interest the general visitor.

Northern Sinai is visited by almost no Western tourists, although in summer it fills up with Egyptian holidaymakers. With a barren coastline, which you scarcely glimpse from the road, it has a single town and focus in **El-Arish**, a laid-back if conservative place with a palm-fringed beach and a weekly Bedouin market.

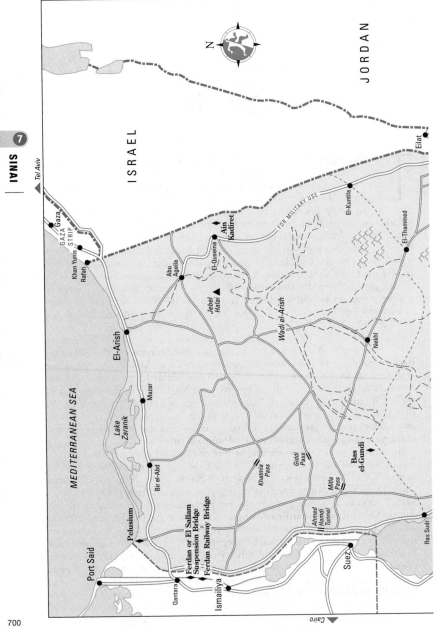

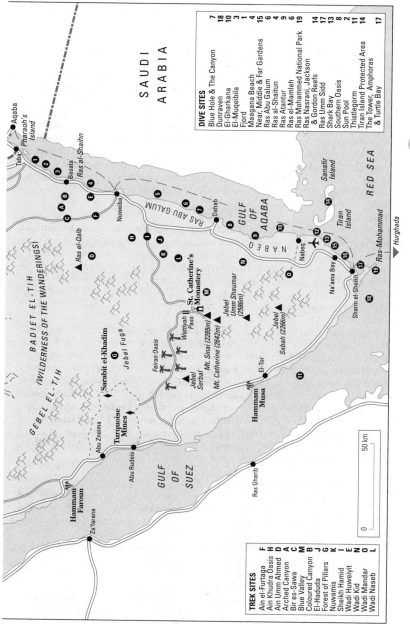

DIVE SITES

Blue Hole & The Canyon	7
Dunraven	18
El-Gharkana	10
El-Muqeibila	3
Fjord	1
Maagana Beach	15
Near, Middle & Far Gardens	6
Ras Abu Galum	4
Ras al-Shaitun	9
Ras Atantur	6
Ras el-Mamleh	19
Ras Mohammed National Park	
Ras Nasrani, Jackson	14
& Gordon Reefs	
Ras Umm Sidd	17
Shark Bay	13
Southern Oasis	8
Sun Pool	2
Thistlegorm	11
Tiran Island Protected Area	14
The Tower, Amphoras	
& Turtle Bay	17

TREK SITES

Ain el-Furtaga	F
Ain Khudra Oasis	H
Ain Umm Ahmed	A
Arched Canyon	D
Bir es-Sawa	C
Blue Valley	M
Coloured Canyon	B
El-Haduda	G
Forest of Pillars	J
Nuwamis	K
Sheikh Hamid	I
Wadi Huweiyit	E
Wadi Kid	N
Wadi Mandar	O
Wadi Naseb	L

7

SINAI

701

Some history

Fifty million years ago the Arabian Plate began shearing away from the African landmass, tearing the Sinai peninsula from the mainland while the Red Sea inundated the gap. Hot springs on the sea bed indicate that the tectonic forces which created Sinai are still active – the Gulf of Suez is widening by three inches each year. In **prehistoric times** the climate was less arid and Sinai supported herds of gazelles which Stone Age people trapped and slaughtered in stone enclosures.

Bronze Age Semites from Mesopotamia were the first to exploit Sinai's lodes of copper ore and turquoise, foreshadowing the peninsula's colonization by the III Dynasty pharaohs, who enslaved its Semitic population to work the mines and build roads and fortresses. According to Egyptian mythology, it was in Sinai that Isis sought the dismembered body of Osiris; and Hathor, also associated with the region, was called "Our Lady of Sinai". **Pharaonic rule** continued until the invasion of the Hyksos "Shepherd Kings", whose occupation of northern Egypt lasted well over a century, till Ahmosis I drove them out and finally destroyed their last bastion in Gaza. This was subsequently the route by which Tuthmosis III and Ramses II invaded Palestine and Syria.

The Exodus

Enshrined in the Old Testament and by centuries of tradition, the **Exodus of the Israelites** is a historical conundrum, as no archeological evidence of their journey through Sinai has ever been found – though excavations at Avaris in the Delta (see p.669) suggest that this was the "City of Bondage" from which they fled. This is generally thought to have happened during the reign of the XIX Dynasty pharaoh, Merneptah (1236–1223 BC), although Egyptologist David Rohl argues that it occurred two centuries earlier (c.1447 BC), under Dudimose of the XIII Dynasty (see p.811).

To identify their route and various crucial sites, scholars have compared Biblical descriptions with physical features and tried to reconcile myths with realities. The **"Red Sea"** found in the King James Bible is a mistranslation of the Hebrew *Yam-suf*, or **Sea of Reeds**, which fits the salt lakes and marshes to the north of Suez, known today as the Bitter Lakes. From there, the Israelites proceeded down the coast to **Ain Musa** and followed **Wadi Feiran** inland towards **Mount Sinai**, although an alternative theory has them trekking across northern Sinai and receiving the Ten Commandments at **Jebel Halal**. Either way, the subsequent forty years in the wilderness are only explicable in terms of a lengthy stay at "Kadesh Barnea", identified as the oasis of **Ain Kedirat**, where there are extensive ruins.

Christianity and Islam

Over the next millennium or so, Sinai was invaded by Assyrians, Hittites and Babylonians, recaptured by Egypt, and conquered in turn by the Persians and Greeks. While the Ptolemies built ports along the Mediterranean coast, Semitic tribes from Petra established themselves between Aqaba and Gaza, both ultimately succumbing to the **Romans**. Whether or not the **Holy Family** had previously crossed Sinai to escape Herod's massacre, the region had begun to attract hermits even before Emperor Constantine legalized **Christianity**, which rooted itself in cathedrals and **monasteries** under Justinian's patronage.

In 639–40 the **Arabs** swept into Sinai, fired with the zeal of **Islam**. The new faith suited local tribes, which turned to plundering the desert monasteries while the Arabs sacked the cathedral cities. Northern Sinai eventually became a pawn in the **Crusades**, the area between Aqaba and Rafah belonging to the Frankish Kingdom until its collapse at Acre.

After the Crusades, the victorious Mamlukes reopened Sinai's trade routes but the peninsula remained Egypt's Achilles heel, as the Ottoman Turks and Mohammed Ali demonstrated with their conquests of 1517 and 1831.

Twentieth-century Sinai

Sinai's strategic importance increased with the completion of the **Suez Canal**, and in 1892 Britain compelled Turkey to cede it as a buffer zone. Backed by Germany, the Turks retook it in 1914, laying roads and water pipelines along the northern coast and across the interior. Anglo-Egyptian forces only dislodged them – and went on to take Jerusalem – after a prolonged campaign.

During World War II Sinai witnessed little fighting, but the **creation of Israel** brought the territory right back into the front line. In 1948 the Israelis repulsed Arab attacks from all sides and took the **Gaza Strip** and **El-Arish** before an armistice was signed, only withdrawing under British pressure. By closing the Gulf of Aqaba to Israeli shipping and nationalizing the Suez Canal, however, Nasser brought together British and Israeli interests. It was Israel's advance into Sinai in October 1956 that was the agreed pretext for Anglo-French intervention in the **Suez Crisis**; though militarily successful, the three states were compelled to quit by international opposition, UN peacekeeping forces establishing a buffer zone in Gaza and guaranteeing free passage through the Gulf of Aqaba.

But further **Arab–Israeli wars** were inevitable. When Egypt ordered the UN to leave and resumed its blockade in **1967**, Israel launched a pre-emptive strike and captured the entire peninsula, which it retained after the **Six Day War** and fortified with the Bar-Lev Line along the east bank of the Suez Canal. In the **October War of 1973**, Egypt broke through into Sinai but then suffered a devastating counterattack across the canal.

US-sponsored peace negotiations culminated in President Sadat's historic visit to Jerusalem, the **Camp David Accords** and a peace treaty signed in 1979, which led to Egypt's decade-long expulsion from the Arab League. Under its terms Israel evacuated all settlements founded during the occupation of Sinai and the territory reverted to Egypt; a phased transition completed in 1982, except for the disputed enclave of Taba, finally resolved in 1989. The Multinational Force and Observers (**MFO**) based at Na'ama Bay monitors Sinai's "banded" demilitarized zones from orange-flagged outposts around the peninsula.

Introduced to Sinai by the Israelis, **tourism** initially suffered from the hand-over, as the Camp David Accords forbade any development for five years. Since 1988, however, its recovery has shifted into overdrive: where the Aqaba coast once had just five hotels it now has more than 150, with more in the pipeline. While the areas of Ras Mohammed, Abu Galum and Nabeq are protected by their status as nature reserves, the entire coastline north of Nuweiba, and from Sharm el-Sheikh to Nabeq National Park, are highly developed. With plans to extend hotel development further into the desert, and ever more direct charter flights arriving from Europe to Sharm el-Sheikh, Sinai's days as a wilderness may well be numbered.

The mercurial nature of Middle Eastern politics, however, means that tourism along the Sinai coast is a fickle business. Since 2000, the Palestinian Intifada has slowed tourist traffic from Israel to a near standstill, while the 2004 terrorist attacks in Taba worsened the situation further. Whilst the Sharm el-Sheikh resorts remain busy, plans for a "Red Sea Riviera" – encompassing Taba, Eilat in Israel and Aqaba in Jordan – have been put on hold for the time being; the airport at Taba is rarely used nowadays, and the tourist camps along the coast around Nuweiba are now

The Bedouin

Most of Sinai's population are **Bedouin** who claim descent from the tribes of the Hejaz on the Arabian Peninsula, and thus rate themselves amongst the purest Arab genealogies. Only the Jebeliya tribe is anomalous, tracing its origins to the Caucasus.

Traditionally, each tribe roamed its own territory in search of grazing and settled around local oases. The Mizayna claimed the land between El-Tor and Nuweiba; the Tarabeen a swathe from Nuweiba to El-Arish; the Jebeliya the St Catherine's region, and so on. The number of **tribes** in Sinai is uncertain, ranging from 14 to 27 depending on which of their subdivisions are counted. Other tribes include the Sawalha, Alekat, Walad Shaheen and Tiyahah. Collectively, they are known as the *Tawarah* ("Arabs of Tor"), after the ancient name of the peninsula, or simply as *Al-Arab*. But for all the tribes, tribal and family honour were paramount, raids and camel-rustling a perpetual cause for blood feuds that might persist for generations. Agriculture or fishing was a hand-to-mouth activity, secondary to herding goats and camels – the latter being the measure of a tribe's wealth, with racing camels esteemed above all. Though devout Muslims, the Bedouin retained pagan superstitions and practices from the "time of darkness", with their own common law (*'urf*) instead of regular Islamic jurisprudence.

Unsurprisingly, the Bedouin took advantage of discarded weaponry to resist outside authority, attempts to settle the nomads having little success until the 1970s, when Israel constructed water tanks, schools and clinics at various sites. By providing employment and exposing the Bedouin to Western comforts, the coastal resorts had an equally profound effect on traditional lifestyles. Nowadays, many earn their living through tourism, taxi driving or construction work, and stone huts with corrugated iron roofs and TV antennae are more common than black tents. Although relations between the Bedouin and Egyptians are generally peaceful, grievances do arise; they are usually focused on administrators and entrepreneurs from mainland Egypt whom many Bedouin regard as here on sufferance, but who are steadily growing in numbers.

For more on traditional Bedouin culture see p.759.

mostly empty. The Bedouin camps at Tarabeen have been particularly hard hit and are almost completely devoid of life.

Visiting Sinai

The differences between Sinai and mainland Egypt can induce culture shock. For those accustomed to Egyptian towns and beaches, Sinai will seem amazingly uncrowded, laid-back and hassle-free – especially so for women. If you arrive from Israel or Jordan, of course, spending some days on a Sinai beach and then heading on to Cairo, you experience the reverse. Native Bedouin and recent settlers from the mainland both assert Sinai's distinctive character and disparage Egyptian government, often comparing it unfavourably with the period of Israeli rule. Even the customary salutation is different: *"Kif halak"* ("How is your health/situation?") instead of *"Izzayak"*.

For the purposes of this guide, the peninsula divides into three zones – the **gulf coasts of Suez and Aqaba**, the **interior**, and **northern Sinai**. Communications between the resorts along the coastal strip of the Gulf of Aqaba and the interior around St Catherine's are well established (these two areas make up the administrative region of **South Sinai**), but northern Sinai is effectively sundered from both, despite the upgrading of a route between El-Arish and Nekhl, inland. Transport to each zone **from mainland Egypt** is described at the start of each section, while the **approaches from Israel and Jordan** are covered in Basics – see p.39.

Unlike elsewhere in Egypt, you can visit part of the peninsula on a free **Sinai-only visa**, valid for two weeks, which can be obtained at Taba (on the border with Israel), the port of Nuweiba (where boats arrive from Jordan), or Sharm el-Sheikh airport, 10km north of Na'ama Bay, where charter flights from Europe land. This is *only* valid for the Aqaba coast down to Sharm el-Sheikh and the immediate vicinity of St Catherine's Monastery (effectively it's a visa for South Sinai); if you wish to visit Ras Mohammed, other parts of Sinai's interior or mainland Egypt, you'll need a **regular Egyptian visa**, which *cannot* be issued at Nuweiba or the Taba border crossing, but can be obtained upon arrival at Sharm el-Sheikh airport (US$15). It is possible to pay in sterling, but the exchange rate will not be favourable so use dollars if you can.

Climate, activities and maps

Sinai's **climate** is extreme. On the coast, daytime temperatures can reach 50°C (120°F) during summer, while nights are sultry or temperate depending on the prevailing wind. In the mountains, which receive occasional snowfall over winter and the odd rainstorm during spring, nights are cooler – if not chilly or freezing. Outside of winter, you should wear a hat, use high-factor sunscreen and drink four to six litres of water a day (more if you're trekking) to avoid sunburn and heatstroke.

The climate is obviously a factor affecting tourist **activities** in Sinai. During summer, the heat is likely to make you spend less time on the beach and more time in the water, and to forgo trekking or camel riding entirely. Happily, **diving** or **snorkelling** (see pp.707–709) can comfortably be done at any time of the year and constitute Sinai's greatest attraction. Details of dive centres, courses and trips are given under each resort as appropriate. There's a general rundown on **camel** and **jeep safaris** on pp.747–748, with specifics in each relevant location. As a rule, sites near the coast can be visited at any time of the year by jeep, and between October and April by camel. **Trekking** in the High Mountain Region (see p.748) is possible in winter if you are prepared to face chilly nights and possible snow flurries; in summer, it's only a matter of being fit enough to stand the heat.

While the **map** at the start of this chapter indicates the main diving and safari sites, serious divers or trekkers should acquire the 1:250,000 *Sinai Map of Attractions*, an English-language tourist map based on Israeli army surveys, which is sold at the Taba border and most resorts. At a pinch, divers could make do with one of the maps produced by dive centres or travel agents, which outline the chief dive sites and Ras Mohammed National Park. For local information, pick up a copy of *Mix*, a free bimonthly **listings magazine**, or better still *H2O* magazine, a free quarterly publication by the Red Sea Association; both are available in Sharm el-Sheikh hotels, but harder to find in Nuweiba and Dahab.

Transport, accommodation and costs

All the main tourist spots are accessible by well-paved roads and some form of public transport. Most travellers find it easy to get around, as **buses** are frequent and cheap and **service taxis** run to and from every resort. The sole exception is the **border at Taba**, which has only a couple of buses a day waiting to take people further south – as well as a few service taxis, whose drivers are notorious for taking financial advantage of the shortage of buses. Foreign **motorists** are restricted to main roads; given the baking heat and huge distances, **hitchhiking** is a dubious proposition unless your destination is nearby or you're certain of a ride all the way (or at least to somewhere with shade and buses). Women should *never* hitch alone. MFO personnel are forbidden to give lifts.

The type of **accommodation** varies from place to place, ranging from costly holiday villages at Na'ama Bay to cheap "campgrounds" at Nuweiba – not campgrounds in the usual sense, these consist of huts of stone, concrete, bamboo or palm leaves, and may or may not have electricity and bathrooms. Although tourism is a year-round business, there are definite peak periods when hotels charge higher prices and are liable to be full. To some extent this depends on the resort: Sharm el-Sheikh receives a surge of European package tourists over spring, autumn and Christmas. Before the political situation between Israel and the Palestinians deteriorated, the Bedouin-run camps between Taba and Dahab, especially those at Tarabeen and to the north, were flooded with Israelis during Jewish holidays. Also bear in mind **Egyptian holiday periods** – December 22–February 2, March 1–May 3 and July 19–October 31 – when you should try to book in advance.

Aside from accommodation, the **cost** of everyday items, meals and transport is higher in Sinai than anywhere else in Egypt, but still cheaper than in Israel or Europe. The tap water is not drinkable in Sinai, so you'll need to buy bottled water, which is cheap so long as you buy it from shops rather than hotels. There are **banks** in all the main resorts, while US dollars can be exchanged in many shops. Many dive centres and hotels will also take payments in euros now, while Israeli shekels (NIS) are also accepted in many Aqaba resorts.

The gulf coasts

Sinai rises and tapers as the peninsula runs towards its southern apex, red rock meeting golden sand and deep blue water along two gulf coasts. Even the **Gulf of Suez**, as E.M. Forster noted, looks enticing from offshore – "an exquisite corridor of tinted mountains and radiant water" – though it's nowadays transformed after dark into a vision of Hades by the flaming plumes of oil rigs.

For most travellers, however, Suez is merely an interlude before the **Gulf of Aqaba**, whose amazing coral reefs and tropical fish have given rise to a number of popular resorts. The beach scene here is the best Egypt can offer and should aquatic pursuits pall – if such a thing is possible – there are opportunities for making trips into the wild **interior** by jeep or camel. Even from the beach, the view of the mountains of Sinai and Saudi Arabia is magnificent.

Approaches to the gulf coasts

Aside from those arriving from Israel or Jordan, most travellers approach the gulf coasts from **Cairo**, **Suez** or **Hurghada**. Note, however, that most services to Taba and Nuweiba travel across the interior of the peninsula, avoiding both gulf coastlines for much of the way.

• **From Cairo,** Superjet **buses** to **Sharm el-Sheikh** (3 daily; 5hr; £E68) leave from the **Turgoman Garage** behind the *Ramses Hilton* (see p.299 for details). Check schedules and reserve seats the day before (earlier during Ramadan). Ten East Delta buses run daily from the **Sinai Terminal** (*Mahattat Seena*) in the Abbassiya district to **Sharm el-Sheikh** (5hr; £E42–60); four to **Dahab** (9hr; £E62–75) and **Nuweiba** (8–10hr; £E62–75), three of which carry on to **Taba** (9hr; £E75); and one to **St Catherine's Monastery** (8hr; £E55). All services are a/c, offer on-board snacks and halt at one or two resthouses en route; refreshments are expensive.

Rapid access to Sinai and great views of the peninsula might entice those with plenty of cash onto EgyptAir **flights**. There are four daily from Cairo to Sharm el-Sheikh airport (£E735 one-way; 1hr).

• **Suez City** is the interchange for numerous buses coming from Hurghada, Cairo or northern Sinai. **Buses** leave from the new bus terminal on the Ismailiya Road, going to **Sharm el-Sheikh** (5 daily; 5–6hr; £E25), **Dahab** (daily at noon; 7–8hr; £E30), **Nuweiba** (daily at noon & 3.30pm; 6–7hr; £E30), **St Catherine's** (daily at 7am & 11am; 6hr; £E25) and **Taba** (daily at 7am; 7–8 hr; £E35). **Service taxis** also leave from the bus terminal for Dahab (£E35), St Catherine's (£E20), Nuweiba (£E25) and Sharm el-Sheikh (£E25).

• **From Hurghada** you can take a **catamaran** to **Sharm el-Sheikh** (Mon, Tues, Thurs & Sat at 8am); 90min; one-way £E250) or charter a seven-seater **taxi** for the 750km drive (£E700 shared among passengers).

• There are also three or four EgyptAir **flights** per week to **Sharm el-Sheikh from Luxor** (currently Tues, Thurs & Sat; one-way £E531), plus one a week **from Hurghada** (£E359), with more in peak season. Service **from Alexandria** is sporadic, departing only in peak tourist periods.

Diving and snorkelling

The Red Sea offers some of the finest **diving** and **snorkelling** in the world, accessible to most travellers at a fraction of the cost of getting to the Seychelles or the Great Barrier Reef. Much of the diving here is easy to reach and relatively sheltered from harsh winds and currents, making it a popular destination for those who have little or no experience.

It's a cheap place to **learn open-water diving** and gain a PADI, BSAC or CMAS certificate, entitling you to dive anywhere in the world (NAUII, SSI or MDEA are less widely accepted); indeed, many people visit Sinai simply to acquire their certificates on one of the scores of diving **courses** available. The initial step is a five-day **open-water** (OW) course, costing €405–470/US\$525–610 (plus €30–35 or US\$40–47 for the certificate). Most centres offer a supervised introductory dive (€35–50 or US\$47–67) for those uncertain about shelling out for a full course. Qualified divers can progress through **advanced open-water**, **dive master** and **instructor** certification, and take **specialized courses** in underwater rescue, night or wreck diving (to name but a few that are available).

When **choosing a dive centre**, the main considerations should be the quality of the instructors and the state of the equipment. Linguistic misunderstandings can be dangerous, so you need an instructor who speaks your **language** well. Ask to see a card proving that he or she is qualified to teach the course (PADI, BSAC or whatever), and not merely a dive master. Amazingly, dive centres in Egypt were virtually unregulated until 1996, and there is still some question over how well the new laws are being enforced. Though centres associated with big hotels are safer bets than outfits on their own, smart premises are less important than the **equipment**. If left lying about, chances are it'll also be poorly maintained. Also notice the location of the compressor, used to fill the tanks; if it's near a road or other source of pollution, you'll be breathing it in underwater. Ask around and then stick to the dive centres that have been there the longest and have proper links with organizations like PADI. Remember that with diving, there is no substitute for a good training and safety record.

Broadly speaking, most dive centres in Sharm el-Sheikh and Nuweiba are very good. In Dahab, however, regulations are less likely to be adhered to and competition between dive centres is cut-throat, encouraging some divers to simply go for the cheapest option. One famous Dahab dive site, the **Blue Hole**, is entirely unsuitable for inexperienced divers – having claimed the lives of several people in recent years. Note that if you're certified but haven't logged a dive in the past three months, you might have to take a "check dive" as a refresher before you can go on a sea trip.

Dive centres are detailed under each resort, while **dive sites** are summarized opposite. The type of diving and the degree of experience required are mainly determined by underwater topography and currents. Around Sharm el-Sheikh the chief activity is **boat diving** (you enter the water offshore) at sites ranging from novice-friendly to demanding. Up the coast past Dahab and Nuweiba this gives way to **shore diving**, where you wade or swim out to the reefs. Some slope gently out to sea while others drop off sharply; the deeper the drop-off the richer the variety of corals and fish. **Liveaboards** (also called safari boats) are vessels that allow you to spend days or weeks at sea, cruising the dive sites and shipwrecks of the north Red Sea around Ras Mohammed and the Tiran Strait or the more southerly reefs beyond Hurghada. During quiet periods, bookings can be arranged at short notice either directly on the boat at the marina or through a dive centre, but to be sure of what you're getting it's best to book in advance through an agent (see Basics for details). Some operators offer a discount if you book by email or telephone.

Snorkelling is also great fun and costs much less. If you're planning to do a lot, it's cheaper to buy your own gear in Cairo or Israel than to rent it from dive shops in Sinai (you might be able to sell it when you leave). Coral reefs and spiny urchins can rip unprotected feet to shreds; in all events you should only walk in designated "corridors" to protect the corals – if the water is too shallow to allow you to float above them. However cool the water may feel, the sun's rays can still burn exposed flesh (water magnifies the effects of ultraviolet), so always wear a T-shirt and use waterproof sunscreen.

Protecting the reefs

As far as the **environment** goes, the position of divers is ambiguous. While the sport enables millions of people to witness the marvel of tropical coral reefs and learn about the fragile ecosystem that maintains them – Egypt's marine national parks alone attract two million tourists each year – divers also pose one of the most serious **threats** to the reefs existence. Boat diving is now so popular in Sharm el-Sheikh that many sites are now considered to be "over-dived". Meanwhile, hundreds of divers happily stay in hotels built directly overlooking the sea that through construction pollution and badly managed beach policies have irreversibly damaged the reefs below. Perhaps it is understandable that the most environmentally aware resort in the Sinai – Basata (see p.744) – doesn't welcome divers.

Always **remember** that reefs are very fragile, so the fundamental rule is: **look but don't touch**. In areas protected by law, you are forbidden to feed the fish or remove anything from the sea. Don't buy **aquatic souvenirs**, the export of which is illegal. Tourists can help by boycotting stores selling them and telling the shopkeepers why. Even shells from the beach shouldn't be collected as souvenirs; they will be confiscated at the airport or border when you leave Egypt, with a US$1000 **fine**.

Sinai dive sites

The following sites are all marked on the map on pp.700–701.

Amphoras Between Ras Um Sidd and Na'ama Bay. Named after a Turkish galleon laden with amphoras of mercury that lies on the reef – the site is also known as "Mercury".

Blue Hole 8km north of Dahab. The challenge of this 80-metre-deep hole in the reef is to swim through a passage 60m down and come up the other side – which is highly risky even for expert divers. You can safely snorkel around the rim of the hole, however.

Canyon Near the Blue Hole. A narrow reef crack, 50m deep, which is only for experienced divers.

Dunraven En route from Bombay to Newcastle, the *Dunraven* steered onto a reef in fine weather on April 25, 1873 and sank 25m. Though its 25 crew escaped, the captain was found negligent (he fatuously remarked, "Twenty-five is my lucky number!").

El-Gharkana A luxuriant reef, offshore from mangroves and lagoons with rare waterfowl and flora. Part of the Nabeq protected area.

El-Muqeibila 25km south of Taba. A lovely diving beach stretching 15km from Mersa el-Muqeibila to Ras el-Burqa, often within walking distance of the main road.

Fjord 10km south of Taba. A picturesque cleft with underwater reefs.

Gordon Reef Off the coast of Ras Nasrani, in the shipwreck-littered Tiran Strait. Sharks and strong currents. Popular with experienced divers; not for beginners.

Jackson Reef A large reef between Tiran Island and the mainland, with a 70-metre drop-off, sharks and pelagic fish, and the shipwreck *Lara*. Strong currents; dangerous for beginners.

Maagana Beach 5–10km north of Nuweiba. The reef falls sheer around the "Devil's Head" to the north, getting shallower and less impressive further south.

Near, Middle and Far gardens 1–5km north of Na'ama Bay. A series of lovely coral reefs, good for easy diving and snorkelling. The Near Gardens are within walking distance of Na'ama.

Pharaoh's Island Near Taba. Superb underwater scenery and strong currents; a diving guide is recommended. Israelis call it "Coral Island". Easy access by boat.

Ras Abu Galum 50km south of Nuweiba. A protected area with a deep virgin reef wall and great fish. Access by 4WD or boat.

Ras Atantur Between Dahab and Nabeq. Colourful, abundant reef, with a shipwreck – the *Maria Schroeder* – 10km further south. Access by 4WD.

Ras el-Mamleh 20km south of Nuweiba. Another slab of virgin reef wall on the northern edge of the Ras Abu Galum protected area. Access by 4WD or boat.

Ras Mohammed National Park 25km southwest of Sharm el-Sheikh. Wonderful corals, mangrove lagoons, anemone gardens and crevice pools, with shark reefs offshore. Also site of the *Yolanda* shipwreck (see below).

Ras Nasrani Sheer reef wall riddled with shark caves; the Light and the Point are notable spots. Beware of sharks and strong currents. Not for inexperienced divers.

Ras Um Sidd Within walking distance of Sharm el-Sheikh. Exquisite fan corals and fish. Up the coast towards Na'ama are other popular sites like Turtle Bay, Amphoras and The Tower.

Shark Bay Colourful reef just off the beach of a small resort, 10km north of Na'ama Bay. Good for novices and experienced divers alike; snorkellers too.

Southern Oasis Gently sloping reef to the south of Dahab. Easy diving and snorkelling.

Sun Pool 10–15km south of Taba. A gorgeous diving beach extending as far north as the Fjord.

Thistlegorm Near El Tor in the Gulf of Suez. Sunk by German bombers in 1941, this British ship, discovered by Jacques Cousteau, was laden with rifles, uniforms, trucks and jeeps. It was also packed full of ammunition, which exploded, ripping the ship apart and killing most of the crew. Tubeworms grow out of the bathtub in the captain's cabin. A popular dive from Sharm el-Sheikh.

Tiran Island Protected Area An archipelago with over 20 dive sites, all amazing. Sharks and strong currents; only for experienced divers unless explicitly stated otherwise.

The Tower South of Na'ama Bay. Sheer reef pillar dropping 60m. Easy access from the beach and mild currents; good for novice divers.

Turtle Bay Between Ras Um Sidd and Amphoras. Shallow bay with turtles, easy to enjoy. Access by boat.

Yolanda Off Ras Mohammed. A Cypriot freighter that struck a reef during a storm in 1981; its cargo includes a BMW and scores of porcelain lavatories.

Coral reefs and tropical fish

Created by the same tectonic stresses that formed the Dead Sea and East African Rift Valley, the **Red Sea basin** is more than 3km deep in places, yet effectively separated from the Indian Ocean by an underwater "sill" at Bab el-Mandab, roughly 100m below the surface. Circulation between the Red Sea and the Gulf of Aqaba is similarly limited by the 200-metre-deep Tiran Strait, although the gulf itself attains depths of 1830m. As neither is fed by rivers and their rate of evaporation far exceeds any rainfall, both are exceptionally warm and salty – providing an ideal environment for tropical fish and coral reefs.

It's the warmth of the Red Sea water that is responsible for the Sinai's particular brilliance of coral – a revelation if you have previously snorkelled in such places as Hawaii or the Caribbean, whose reefs will ever after seem dull by comparison.

Coral reefs

The **coral reefs** that fringe the Sinai coastline from El-Tor to Taba have been created by generations of minuscule polyps extracting calcium from the sea water and depositing limestone exoskeletons on the remains of their ancestors. Fossilized reefs form the bedrock for living ones, which can grow 4–5cm a year, but are easily bruised or killed; if snapped off, coral loses its colour within hours of being removed from the sea.

Reefs come in all shapes and sizes, some more encrusted with coral growths than others, but the idealized representation given below should give you an idea of where different species might be found. Some corals live 300 metres down, but you'll find most corals within 20–30 metres of the surface. The presence of sharks is usually a sign of a reef's good health.

Just below the shoreline, the warm water and eroded, sand- and rubble-covered bottom of the **lagoon** attract starfish, sea slugs and stinging anemones. Clams and sea urchins hide in crevices, while small yellow anemone fish and schools of viridian and carmine damselfish flit about. Other species include azure and opal blennies, tentacled clownfish and multitudes of butterfly fish.

Beyond lies the **reef flat**, a barren, fossilized shelf curving up towards the **reef crest**, overgrown with organ-pipe corals and anemones. Damselfish, angelfish, snappers and parrotfish are ubiquitous, while sea worms and eels emerge from deep **caves** below the crest. Mountain and stag-horn corals encrust the upper **slope**, whose lower section merges into bare terraces or sandy shelves overgrown with **sea grass**, the habitat of sea horses and pipefish.

Close to the surface further out are **pillars**; their own richly developed coral formations attract damselfish, basslets, wrasses and grunts, to name but a few. The **forereef** tends to draw larger fish, octopuses and squids, with stingrays and mantas (whose wingspans can reach nearly 5m) gliding along the sea bed.

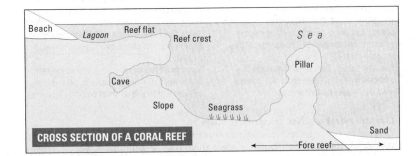

Beach　Lagoon　Reef flat　Reef crest　*S e a*

Pillar

Cave

Slope　Seagrass

Sand

CROSS SECTION OF A CORAL REEF　　Fore reef

Tropical fish and other creatures

The Red Sea's flora and fauna are related to tropical Indo-Pacific species, with no observable migration from the Mediterranean, although blue-speckled parrotfish have travelled the other way. The following are the most basic notes for identification – and for avoiding the odd dangerous species.

Wherever soft, stinging anemones cling to the reef you're likely to see yellow **anemone fish**, recognizable by their twin vertical stripes. Equally commonplace are **angelfish**, with their long dorsal fins diminishing to filaments. Crescent angelfish are blue at the front, with a yellow vertical stripe and black hindquarters, while Emperor angelfish are horizontally pinstriped in blue and yellow, and the larger Arabian angelfish (up to 50cm long) is blue all over but for a yellow splotch. The same colour scheme in reverse appears on **butterfly fish**, which favour sunny slopes and forereefs; around lagoons, pillars and crests you'll also see racoon butterfly fish, striped in yellow and black, with a black and white eye patch.

Slopes and forereefs are the habitat of small **goatfish** (red mullet) with horizontal stripes of blue and yellow (or yellow and black in the case of Forsskal's goatfish). Diverse types of **parrotfish** and **snappers** frequent deeper water alongside crests and pillars. Parrotfish are easily recognizable by their beaky mouths and vibrant colours; snappers are similarly sized, with silvery scales striped and spotted in red, green or electric blue. Likewise bulky and diversely hued are **wrasses**, related to the bigger **Napoleon fish**, which can dwarf a person. Dugongs or **sea cows** are equally large and harmless, unlike small, sharp-toothed and armoured **triggerfish**, **filefish** and **porcupine fish**, more commonly found in deeper water.

Dangers of the deep

Considering all the **dangerous creatures**, it's remarkable that most visitors get nothing worse than the odd cut from sharp coral. Poisonous species include spiny **scorpion fish**, wildly coloured **turkeyfish** and **dragonfish**, and the oddly finned **lionfish**. By not touching anything remotely fitting their description you should avoid danger from these sources.

The lethal **stonefish**, camouflaged as a gnarled rock, is harder to spot but fortunately rare. You're more likely to be at risk from stinging **purple anemones** and burning **fire coral**, or **black sea urchins** with needle-like spines, which nestle in crevices. Dark caves sometimes harbour razor-toothed **moray eels**, which may bite if they feel threatened. **Stingrays** can deliver a painful dose of venom, and at certain times of the year **jellyfish** arrive in hordes, contact with which can cause mild irritation.

Although makos, hammerheads and other **sharks** frequent the deep waters around Ras Mohammed and the Tiran Strait, they're seldom found near the coast. However, blood in the water can attract them from afar, so never enter the sea with an open wound. Hammerheads and white-tip reef sharks have been known to attack with little provocation, though some divers consider **barracuda** more aggressive. Sighting either predator near shore, climb out quickly but calmly and spread the word; if you're diving in deeper water, keep still and you'll almost certainly be ignored.

Between Suez and Sharm el-Sheikh

The 338km journey between **Suez** and **Sharm el-Sheikh** takes only a few hours by bus or service taxi, and there's little point in stopping unless you've got private transport or you are an avid windsurfer. Such attractions as exist along (or off) the route are otherwise awkward to reach (or leave), so most travellers pass them by. Beyond **El-Tor**, the area's administrative capital, there's little of interest until you reach the diving grounds of **Ras Mohammed**.

Although the resort of **Ras Sudr** is essentially an oil town, its proximity to Cairo means it is becoming increasingly popular with Cairenes as a weekend get-away, while its year-round wind draws windsurfers from further afield. Further south, and inland, the pharaonic ruins at **Serabit el-Khadim** are also starting to attract larger numbers of visitors, most of them arriving from Sharm el-Sheikh or Dahab by jeep. For simplicity's sake, we've covered them here rather than later.

If you're not already booked on a through-service to Sinai, Suez is the place to catch a bus or service taxi. Most traffic uses the **Ahmed Hamdi Tunnel** – named after an Egyptian general killed in the October War – 17km north of Suez. Though there has long been a ferry at **Qantara,** access to **north Sinai** has been improved with the construction of a 4km-long suspension bridge at **Ferdan,** 49km south of Port Said near Qantara.

South along the Gulf of Suez

As you head south by road, the **Gulf of Suez** is sensed before it appears as a glint on the horizon, beyond the sands that rim the west for much of the way. Roughly 50km past the Ahmed Hamdi Tunnel, a dirt road turns off towards the coast to **AIN MUSA**, the **"Springs of Moses"**. According to scholastic conjecture and local legend, it was here that the Israelites halted after crossing the Red Sea, and Moses threw a tree into the bitter spring of Marah, which miraculously became drinkable (Exodus 15). Ain Musa is recognizable from the highway by the deposits of calcium and magnesium salts that surround the oasis, where only one of the twelve springs mentioned in Exodus remains, yielding water that has a strong chemical odour and acts as a powerful laxative. Many of the palm trees in the oasis were decapitated during various Sinai conflicts; an Israeli battery stationed here shelled Suez and Port Tewfiq during the War of Attrition, until Egypt recaptured Ain Musa in 1973. Camping is possible, although limited by the lack of food, water, and transport out. Ask at the village if you're interested, and you may find a Bedouin willing to guide you round.

Ras Sudr and Hammam Faraoun

Famed for the variety of seashells washed up on its beach, the resort of **RAS SUDR** is marred by a reeking oil refinery that doesn't seem to bother the middle-class Cairenes who patronize its holiday villages and **hotels**. North of town, *Sama Larish Village* (☎069/333-2120; ⑥) offers functional but tired-looking red-roofed chalets, with breakfast, while the nearby *Banana Beach village* (☎069/338-0698; ⑥ half-board) is similar. The town itself offers little more than a few fly-blown **restaurants**, such as the *Manta Fish Market,* next to the bus station, 300m south of the main road, a handful of shops and an **Internet café** (per hour £E2), two blocks south of the main street.

This part of the coast is so windy it is often overlooked by travellers who seek the calmer reef-fringed shores of Sharm el-Sheikh, but the year-round and day-long cross-shore gusts make it a paradise for **windsurfers and kite-boarders** who head for *Moon Beach*, 40km south of Ras Sudr (mobile ☎010 5810088, ☎069/340-1501, ☎069/340-1503, ✉moonbeachresort@hotmail .com; ⑥). The cheapest way is to book in advance through the small, friendly, British-run Gybemasters Windsurfing Company (UK mobile ☎015 80753824,

ⓔgybemasters@btinternet.com, ⓦwww.moonbeachretreat.com), which offers windsurfing and kiteboarding lessons here for beginners including boards and rigs (£E80 per hour) and rental of kit for intermediate and advanced surfers (£E60 per hour or £120 per week if booked in the UK), as well as yoga instruction. To get to *Moon Beach* from Sharm el-Sheikh, take a taxi from Ras Sudr (around £E40). From Cairo, there's a direct bus that leaves Al Maza, close to Heliopolis, three times a week (Thurs, Fri & Sat 8am, returning 5pm; 3hr; £E15).

The coast improves 55km south of Ras Sudr, where a turn-off leads to **HAMMAM FARAOUN** ("Pharaoh's Bath"), several near-boiling **hot springs** which Arab folklore attributes to the pharaoh's struggles to extricate himself from the waves that engulfed his army as he chased Moses and the Israelites. Local Bedouin use the springs for curing rheumatism, and it is possible to bathe; a cave in the hill beside the shore leads into "the sauna", a warren of chambers awash with hot water, but it's more comfortable to bathe where the springs flow into the sea. There are plans to build a hotel nearby, but in the meantime the only option if you want to stay is to **camp**. You must inform the soldiers posted nearby, who enforce a ban on visiting the beach after 6pm.

Serabit el-Khadim and the turquoise mines

Built upon a 755-metre-high summit reached by a tortuous path, the **rock-hewn temple** known as **Serabit el-Khadim** ("Heights of the Slave" in Arabic) is the only pharaonic temple in Sinai, surrounded by some of the region's grandest scenery. Erected during the XII Dynasty, when turquoise mining in the area was at its peak, it is an enduring symbol of pharaonic power over the nameless thousands who toiled in the mines of Sinai. Though Bedouin still glean some local turquoise by low-tech methods, the amount that remains isn't worth the cost of industrial extraction.

The temple itself consists of open courts and sanctuaries dedicated to the goddess Hathor in her aspect as "Mistress of Turquoise", and the god Soped, "Guardian of the Desert Ways". Both deities are invoked on rock-cut and free-standing stelae relating to mining expeditions. These were only possible for half of the year due to the heat and scarcity of water, and thus a permanent colony was never established. The temple (whose precincts were segregated from the mining area by a crude stone wall) was abandoned during the reign of Ramses VII. Known to the Bedouin for centuries, it was first "discovered" by Reinhold Niebuhr in 1792, but not excavated until early in the nineteenth century.

Serabit el-Khadim is becoming a popular stop on **jeep safaris**. From Sharm el-Sheikh, they approach Serabit from the south, via a track leading off the road from St Catherine's into **Wadi Mukattab** – the Valley of Inscriptions. Here you can find dozens of hieroglyphic texts carved into the rocks, alongside Proto-Sinaitic **inscriptions** that continue into Wadi Maraghah, where ancient mine workings and stelae were damaged when the turquoise mines were revived by the British and before going bust in 1901. Most desert outfitters in Na'ama Bay, such as Sun 'n' Fun (see p.725), can organize a trip out here for around €235 or US$320 for a group of seven people.

El-Tor

There's little to see along the coastal highway – which often veers inland, giving a wide berth to airstrips and oil terminals – besides a scattering of holiday resorts all the way to **EL-TOR**, the administrative capital of South Sinai. Originally, the Egyptian government based its administrators at Abu Rudeis, near the fledgling oilfields that were their prime concern – not realizing that this lay outside the territory of the main Bedouin tribal confederation and thus limited their influence over the tribes. After capturing South Sinai in 1967, the Israelis used ethnographic data to devise a system that exploited tribal allegiances, under a military governor in Sharm el-Sheikh, then called Ofira. The Egyptians took note and, once they had recovered the region, established their own South Sinai Governorate at El-Tor, just within the territory of the powerful Mizayna tribe.

The main reason to come to El-Tor is for the **windsurfing and kiteboarding**. The town itself consists of a mass of housing, a number of construction sites and a scattering of government buildings, including the governorate office where you can get **visa extensions** (Mon–Thurs & Sun 8am–2pm). Most kiteboarders and windsurfers **stay** at *Moses Bay* (T069/377-4343, W www .mosesbayeltur.com; ❻), 2km north of the centre on the coast. It's the most attractive hotel in the area with a/c rooms with baths, satellite TV and a large sandy beach, as well as an aqua sports centre that rents out windsurf boards and kiteboards. Otherwise, the *Delmoun*, on the edge of town just back from the coast (T & F069/377-1060; ❹), has a/c rooms with bath, while *Tur Sinai* (T069/377-0059; ❸) is conveniently located next to the bus station.

A couple of kilometres up the coast from *Moses Bay* are the **hot springs** of **HAMMAM MUSA**, which lie in the shadow of the looming hill named after them. A path leading halfway up the hill affords spectacular views. Entry to the baths is £E20, and there's a cafeteria nearby selling snacks and drinks.

Ras Mohammed

At Sinai's southernmost tip is the not-to-be-missed **RAS MOHAMMED** peninsula, fringed with lagoons and reefs. Declared a nature reserve in 1983, then Egypt's first marine **National Park** in 1989, it is home to a thousand-odd species of fish as well as 150 types of corals: see "Coral reefs" and "Tropical fish and other creatures" on pp.710–711 for further details. The age of this amazing ecosystem is evinced by marine fossils in the bedrock dating back twenty million years; on the shoreline are newcomers only 75,000 years old. Though chiefly for **divers**, there are enough calmer reefs for **snorkellers** to have a great time as well.

You can **visit** the national park any day from sunrise to sunset, providing you have a full Egyptian **visa** and not just a Sinai-only one (they check). The €5 (US$6.70) entry charge is usually included in the cost of excursions by jeep or boat from Sharm el-Sheikh (bear in mind that as the number of dive boats allowed each day is limited, you can't be certain of a place on a boat at short notice). Alternatively, if you just plan to snorkel you could rent a taxi (about £E120) or car (US$45–85) for the day. There are two perimeter gates on the road between El-Tor and Sharm el-Sheikh, leading to a main entrance, whence it's 20km to the nearest reefs.

Various trails – accessible by regular car – are marked by colour-coded arrows. The blue one leads to **Aqaba Beach**, the **Eel Garden**, the **Main Beach** and a **Shark Observatory** 50m up the cliffside, which affords distant views of the odd fin. Purple and then red shows the route to the **Hidden Bay**, **Anemone City** and **Yolanda Bay**, while green signifies the way to the **Crevice Pools** and the **Mangrove Channel**, where children can safely bathe in warm, sandy shallows. Divers prefer the deeper sites that can only be reached by boat, such as the **Shark Reefs** off Yolanda Bay (the place to see sharks, barracuda, giant Napoleon fish and manta rays); and **The Mushroom** or the **wreck** of the *Dunraven*, out towards **Beacon Rock**.

A **visitor centre** (10am–sunset) off the road between the Sharm gate and the main entrance shows videos in English and Arabic on alternate hours and contains

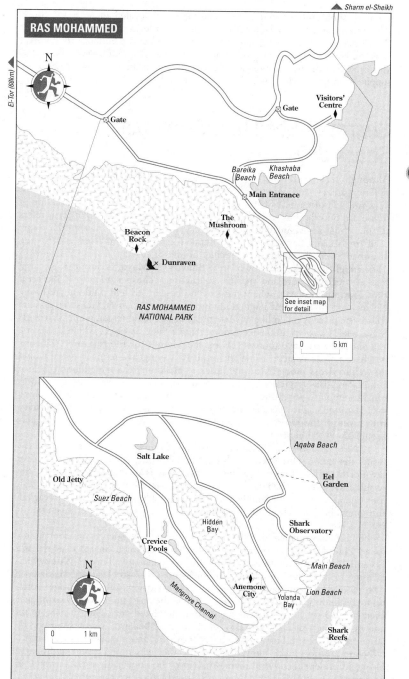

RAS MOHAMMED

Sharm el-Sheikh

El-Tor (68km)

N

Gate

Gate

Visitors'
Centre

Bareika
Beach

Khashaba
Beach

Main Entrance

The
Mushroom

Beacon
Rock

Dunraven

RAS MOHAMMED
NATIONAL PARK

See inset map
for detail

0   5 km

Salt Lake

Aqaba Beach

Old Jetty

Eel
Garden

Suez Beach

Hidden
Bay

Shark
Observatory

N

Crevice
Pools

Main Beach

Mangrove Channel

Anemone
City

Lion Beach

Yolanda
Bay

0   1 km

Shark
Reefs

a library, shop and restaurant. Free **telescopes** are located there, at the Shark Observatory, and at Suez Beach. You can pick up a form for a **camping** permit (US$5 per person per night; children under 12 free) at the entrance to the park, or at the National Protected Lands office in Hadaba (☏069/366-0668). Note that you can't rent diving equipment at Ras Mohammed, and the nearest **shop** for supplies is in Sharm el-Sheikh, about thirty minutes away by car.

Sharm el-Sheikh, Na'ama Bay and Shark Bay

Although technically one destination, **Sharm el-Sheikh** comprises several different areas – and constant development means there are more added each year. You will often hear Sharm el-Sheikh referred to simply as **Sharm**, though if you are outside the resort (Dahab, say, or Cairo, or the UK) that term refers to the whole resort, including Na'ama Bay, while if you are within the resort itself (in Na'ama Bay, say, or Ras Nasrani) the term Sharm refers only to the area that covers the downtown precinct of Sharm el-Maya.

Sharm el-Sheikh's downtown area, **Sharm el-Maya**, is home to a large market area, the port and marina. It can be a cheaper base than **Na'ama Bay**, 7km up the coast, where most of the best hotels and nightlife are based. Na'ama has an excellent wide sandy beach and top-class facilities; the general feel of the place is much like any Mediterranean coastal resort, while Sharm el-Maya retains a *baladi* ambience reminiscent of Suez or Cairo, which can come as a shock to package tourists leaving their hotels for the first time. Whereas beachwear is de rigueur at Na'ama, tourists staying in Sharm el-Maya would do well to **dress** modestly off the beach to avoid unwelcome attention. Sharm and Na'ama Bay tragically hit the headlines on July 24 2005, when the resort's usual tranquillity was shattered by a series of co-ordinated bomb attacks, which killed over eighty people and injured more than two hundred. **Security measures** in the resort have been heightened since the attack, but travellers should always be vigilant.

Southeast of Sharm el-Maya bay, a string of hotels and villas have sprouted along the coast. This stretch, which extends from the Ras Um Sidd dive site north to The Tower dive site, is known as **Ras Umm Sidd**. With the swankiest resorts perched close to the coast, cheaper hotels favoured by British tour operators fill up the land behind. It's a pretty bleak area, with poor beaches, and guests have to rely on shuttle buses to get them to the better amenities of Na'ama Bay.

The cliff above Sharm el-Maya bay is home to a prosperous residential area called **Hadaba**; further north, roughly halfway between Sharm el-Maya and Na'ama Bay, you come to another largely residential area, **Hay el-Nur,** which is home to the main bus station, a hospital and a well-stocked supermarket.

Hotel development has not stopped at Na'ama Bay, and tourist villages, some up to a million square meters in size, now line the coast up to **Ras Nasrani** and even beyond to the borders of the **Nabeq** protected area. The once-beautiful and isolated retreat of **Shark Bay**, 8km north of Na'ama, is now swamped by large resorts – it still boasts a fine beach, however, and a view of Tiran Island.

Divers are no longer allowed to explore the reefs near Na'ama and Sharm el-Sheikh independently; all diving must now be done with a guide, which in practical terms means sticking with trips run by the dive operators.

Getting to Sharm and Na'ama

East Delta and Superjet **buses from Cairo and Suez** terminate at the Hay el-Nur bus station behind the Mobil station. The **port** where the catamaran arrives from Hurghada is 600m south of Sharm el-Maya. Sharm el-Sheikh **airport**, 10km north of Na'ama, is busy with charter flights from Europe, whose passengers are driven off to their holiday villages by bus; arriving on your own you'll be dependent on costly taxis to get anywhere.

Transport between Sharm el-Maya and Na'ama is frequent, with regular **minibuses** carrying local workers between the two resorts (£E1 per person, possibly more if you have luggage). You can pick these up by flagging them down at any point along the road, but bear in mind you won't be sharing space with cosmopolitan Egyptian holidaymakers, so it's advisable to be modestly dressed. Private **taxis** demand £E15–20 per carload.

Sharm el-Sheikh

A hunk of sterile buildings on a plateau commanding docks and other installations, **SHARM EL-SHEIKH** was developed by the Israelis after their capture of it in the 1967 war. Their main purpose was to thwart Egypt's blockade of the Tiran Strait and to control overland communications between the Aqaba and Suez coasts. Tourism was an afterthought – though an important one, helping to finance the Israeli occupation and settlements, which Egypt inherited between 1979 and 1982. Since then, Sharm's infrastructure seems to have expanded in fits and starts, without enhancing its appeal much. Despite some plush hotels and reams of propaganda about it being a slick resort, Sharm el-Sheikh is basically a **dormitory town** for the Egyptian workers who service neighbouring Na'ama

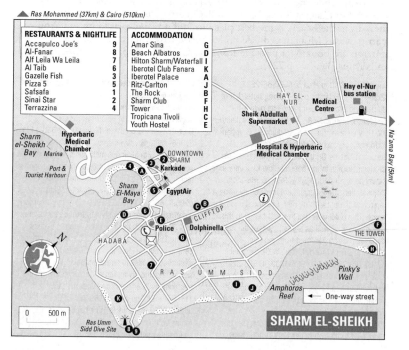

Ras Mohammed (37km) & Cairo (510km)

RESTAURANTS & NIGHTLIFE
Accapulco Joe's	9
Al-Fanar	8
Alf Leila Wa Leila	7
Al Taib	6
Gazelle Fish	3
Pizza 5	5
Safsafa	1
Sinai Star	2
Terrazzina	4

ACCOMMODATION
Amar Sina	G
Beach Albatros	D
Hilton Sharm/Waterfall	I
Iberotel Club Fanara	K
Iberotel Palace	A
Ritz-Carlton	J
The Rock	B
Sharm Club	F
Tower	H
Tropicana Tivoli	C
Youth Hostel	E

Sharm el-Sheikh Bay
Marina
Hyperbaric Medical Chamber
Port & Tourist Harbour
DOWNTOWN SHARM
Karkade
Sharm El-Maya Bay
EgyptAir
CLIFFTOP
Police
Dolphinella
HADABA
RAS UMM SIDD
Amphoras Reef
Pinky's Wall
THE TOWER
Hay el-Nur bus station
HAY EL-NUR
Medical Centre
Sheik Abdullah Supermarket
Hospital & Hyperbaric Medical Chamber
Na'ama Bay (5km)
One-way street

0   500 m

Ras Umm Sidd Dive Site

SHARM EL-SHEIKH

Bay. Aside from package tourists conned by brochures, the only foreigners here are divers – drawn by the proximity of **Ras Um Sidd** and other **reefs** – and a few backpackers who take advantage of its cheapish accommodation and commute into Na'ama Bay. Sharm has a beach, but its small bay doesn't match that of Na'ama, and the seedy downtown area also detracts from the hotels' "luxury" pretensions. In its defence, however, **Sharm el-Maya** is the cheapest place in the area to go shopping for food and has some good restaurants, snack bars and souvenir shops. Sharm also has a great attraction for children in the **Dolphinella**, opposite the *Cliff Top Hotel* in Hadaba (℡069/366-4855, daily 10.30am–6am), which holds dolphin displays (US$15) throughout the day. In addition, between 3 and 4pm daily, you can swim with the dolphins: it costs a hefty US$90 for thirty minutes, but that can be split by up to six people.

Arrival and information

While there is a **bank** at *Iberotel Palace*, other facilities are concentrated on the Hadaba clifftop where an arcade contains three banks (daily 8am–2pm & 6–8pm) that change travellers' cheques, a **post office** (daily except Fri 8am–3pm), and a **pharmacy** (daily 9am–3pm & 6–11pm). The **police** and **tourist police** (both open 24hr) share a building nearby, beyond the mosque. Further inland is a 24-hour **telephone** exchange that sells international phonecards for public telephones. The very isolated and largely worthless **tourist office** (℡069/366-4721; daily except Fri 9am–3pm) is located a couple of kilometres northeast of the banks.

Accommodation

Most **accommodation** is either deluxe and costly or simple and relatively inexpensive. The former enables package tourists to ignore Sharm's general lack of charm, while the latter serves as a fallback if the *Pigeon House* in Na'ama or *Shark's Bay Camp* at Shark Bay are full. Otherwise the windswept **clifftop** area, away from the beach, is the best place to look for mid-priced options. You can **camp** at Ras Mohammed (see p.716) if you have your own transport.

If you are booking a package from the UK, you are best off picking a hotel in Na'ama Bay (see p.721).

Amar Sina Clifftop area ℡069/366-2222, ℻366-2233. Eclectic, good-looking hotel, full of domes and arches, designed by its owner-in-residence. More than 85 a/c rooms with satellite TV. They've also created a "traditional" Egyptian farm and veterinary clinic around the back. ❻

Beach Albatros On the cliff overlooking Sharm el-Maya, access to the beach below by a very long staircase or lift ℡069/366-3924, ℻366-3925. Construction of the beach here involved in-filling a stretch at the back of the reef, causing the latter's death. This hotel now has the best beach in this part of town, as well as a great view of the mountains and Ras Mohammed from the pool. ❼

Hilton Sharm Waterfall Resort On the beach at Ras Um Sidd ℡069/366-3232, ℻366-3228. *Hilton*'s latest addition to Sharm has 401 a/c rooms with all the trimmings, including an impressive waterfall feature and a small cable car to an even smaller beach. ❽

Iberotel Club Fanara On the beach at Ras Um Sidd, next to the lighthouse ℡069/366-3966, ℻366-3819. Well-designed all-inclusive on one of the few good beaches in the area, especially for snorkelling. A/c rooms with satellite TV and terrace, pools and the latest in resort facilities. ❽

Iberotel Palace Sharm el-Maya ℡069/366-1111, ℻366-1293. ⓦwww.iberotel-eg.com/palace. Over 240 rooms with luxurious mod-cons. There's a large section of beach, and lots of restaurants and sports facilities, including bicycle rental and a bank. ❽

Ritz-Carlton By the beach at Ras Um Sidd ℡069/366-1919, ℻366-1920, ⓦwww.ritzcarlton.com/resorts/sharm_el_sheikh. Trumpeted as the first *Ritz* in Africa, this hotel has Internet access via the TV in each of the huge a/c rooms, a fitness centre, beauty salon and a spa. There is a beach with direct access to a reef (meaning it is good for snorkelling and diving but bad for swimming) and two pools with a "river" and waterfall. ❾

The Rock Clifftop area ℡069/366-1765, ℻366-0203, ⓔtherock@sinainet.com.eg. a/c rooms with TV and bath. *On the Rocks* bar, swimming pool and shuttle bus. ❻

❼

Tropicana Tivoli Clifftop area ☎069/366-1381, ℱ366-1380. Rooms with a/c and kitchenette, sited around a large pool. Also runs a shuttle bus to its sister hotel in Na'ama Bay and the beach at Ras Um Sidd. Breakfast included. ⑥

Youth hostel Clifftop area ☎ & ℱ069/366-0317. Cramped a/c triples and doubles, and cleanish bathrooms. Facilities include a basketball and soccer court. May be full of young Egyptians or otherwise virtually empty. Non-members admitted (£E2 extra). Breakfast included. ②

Diving courses and excursions

Most **dive centres** are firmly attached to hotels, but the majority of them are happy to take non-guests for courses and daily boat diving. Before signing up for anything, ask where you'll be doing your training; the water in Sharm el-Maya is less pleasant than in Na'ama Bay due to its proximity to the marina. You're better off looking there or at the dive centres around **Ras Um Sidd**. Prices for most dive trips and courses mirror those offered by dive centres in Na'ama (see p.724 for details).

Sharm el-Sheikh dive centres

All Sharm el-Sheikh's **dive centres** are open daily (mostly 8.30am–6pm). Dive boats set off (at around 9am) from the marina in Sharm el-Maya; most centres will collect you and drop you off again if necessary. (This is crucial if you're marooned at one of the hotels on the cliff in Ras Um Sidd.) Most of Sharm and Na'ama Bay's major dive centres are members of the **Sharm Diving Union** (☎ & ℱ069/366-0418, ✉info@southsinai.org), which organizes regular clean-ups of the sea. For dive centres based in **Na'ama Bay** and **Shark Bay**, see p.724 and p.729.

African Divers *Seti Sharm Hotel*, Ras Um Sidd mobile ☎012 33131712, ⓦwww.africandivers .com. PADI, CMAS, NAUI, SSI.
Colona Dive Club *Amar Sina*, Hadaba ☎069/366-3670, ℱ366-0546, ⓦwww.colona.com/sharm. Caters primarily for Scandinavian clients. Liveaboards available. PADI Gold Palm resort, SSI, Nitrox.

New Waves *Tropicana Tivoli* ☎069/366-3399, ℱ366-2211, ✉info@oceanq.com. ⓦwww .divenewwaves.com. Five-day packages and liveaboards available. SSI, BSAC, NAUI.
Rasta Divers Ras Um Sidd ☎069/366-3328, mobile ☎012 2133881, ✉rasta@sinainet.com.eg. Rather exclusive, catering mostly to private groups. Liveaboards available. PADI, CMAS, SSI.

Liveaboards

Some of the dive centres listed above and on p.724 offer **liveaboards.** Alternatively, you can book directly with one of the operators or boats listed below. They all have offices in Hadaba, and set off from the marina in Sharm el-Maya.

Blue Bubbles ☎ & ℱ069/366-3458, mobile ☎012 3103755, ⓦwww.bluebubbles.info. Liveaboards on a number of boats of varying standards; from €95–120 per person per day.
King Snefro Boats mobile ☎012 3150612, ℱ069/366-1201, ✉boats@kingsnefro.com. Four boats and sixteen years' experience in the Red

Sea, specializing in the waters from Abu Nuhas to the Tiran Strait. The cost, €90–105 per person per day, includes transfers and full board. Children under 7 go free.
Sea Queen I, II and III mobile ☎012 2186669, ⓦwww.seaqueens.com. Managed by Karim Fayed, this is liveaboard in style.

Eating, drinking and nightlife

Aside from **eating and drinking** in hotels, Sharm el-Maya offers a wide range of restaurants, coffee shops and *fuul* and *taamiya* stalls. **Seafood** is especially good; *Al Taib* (mobile ☎010 1557686), set in the gardens on the hill leading up to Hadaba from Sharm el-Maya, serves excellent and good-value fish, shrimps and calamari. They also do takeaways and home delivery. Two good seafood restaurants in the main market area are the *Sinai Star* and the more intimate *Safsafa*, both popular with tour groups, and both charging £E30–60 for a meal. Across from the *Sinai Star*, *Gazelle Fish* serves reasonably priced calamari at £E20 or a lobster for £E70. Next to the *Iberotel Palace* is the *Terrazzina* beach restaurant, which is popular with local residents and serves the catch-of-the-day in a relaxed atmosphere. The stunningly located *Al-Fanar* at Ras Um Sidd lighthouse dishes up excellent Italian food and has a vast sea view taking in Ras Mohammed. The trendier *Accapulco Joe's*, next door, shares its view.

The cheapest **snacks** are egg or *taamiya* sandwiches, sold in the main market area. *Yara*, next to Al Shaikh bakery, sells sandwiches and a good selection of typical Egyptian desserts like *rozz y laban* (rice pudding) and *om Ali* (a kind of bread pudding). There are also a couple of pizza joints; *Pizza 5*, at the foot of the cliff (☎069/366-3436), also does delivery.

For picnics, the best **supermarket** in Sharm el-Maya is Sharm Express, though Sheikh Abdullah's, a minibus ride away in Hay el-Nur, has more choice. **Fruit** and **vegetables** are cheaper from the stalls in the main market.

Nightlife is somewhat limited to Ras Um Sidd's *Alf Leila Wa Leila* (☎ & ℱ069/366-3110), a tacky Oriental show with bellydancers and a "sound and

Moving on from Sharm el-Sheikh

Sharm el-Sheikh is the transport hub of South Sinai, with overland bus services to Cairo, the Canal Zone and most points in the peninsula, boats to Hurghada, and flights to domestic and international airports.

All Sharm's **buses** leave from the Hay el-Nur bus station (☎069/366-1622), halfway between Na'ama Bay and Sharm el-Sheikh. The direct a/c Superjet nightbus leaves for **Cairo** at 11pm (£E68), though you'll need to buy your ticket in advance in person at the bus station to be sure of getting a seat. The Superjet bus makes fewer stops and tends to be quieter than the East Delta buses to Cairo (8 daily; £E55; also evening buses at 10pm, 11pm & midnight; £E65), for which you have to reserve seats in person at the bus station in advance.

The bus to St Catherine's Monastery (£E25) leaves daily at 8.30am, though it's worth turning up early. This bus, however, won't get you there in time to see the monastery on the same day, as it closes at midday. The daily 9am service to **Taba** (£E26.50) stops at **Dahab** which can also be reached by daily direct buses at 8.30am, 9am, 12.30pm, 2.30pm and 5pm (£E11). Daily services to **Nuweiba** (9am, 2.30pm & 5pm; £E22) can be crowded. Buses also run daily to the Canal cities of **Suez** (7am, 9am [a/c], 10am, 1.30pm, 4.30pm, 6pm & 7pm; £E30) and **Ismailiya** (5 daily; £E40); as well as to **Luxor** (6pm; £E100) and **Alexandria** (9am; £E80).

In the absence of a bus you'll be thrown back on **service taxis**, whose rates are negotiable. The usual destinations on offer are Suez, Dahab and St Catherine's, though others can be agreed if the price is right. The larger the group, the less each person pays.

Tickets for the two-hour **catamaran** journey from Sharm to **Hurghada** across the Gulf of Suez (Mon, Tues, Thurs & Sat at 6pm; £E250) can be bought at Mena Tours (10am–10pm, except Fri 1–10pm; ☎069/360-0190) in the *Marriot Hotel* in Na'ama Bay. You can also buy tickets at the port one hour before departure.

The EgyptAir office in Sharm el-Sheikh (daily 9am–2pm & 6–9pm; ☎069/366-1058, ℱ366-1057) sells tickets for regular **flights** from Sharm el-Sheikh airport, 10km north of Na'ama, to **Cairo** (four daily) and **Luxor** (Tues 7am & Thurs 5.35pm). There are also sometimes flights to **Hurghada** and **Alexandria** in peak season. For **flights to Europe**, check with the representatives of UK tour operators such as Explorers (☎069/360-1406) and Goldenjoy (☎069/360-1600).

light show". The English-language version (Mon 9.30pm; US$15 or US$30 with dinner) is followed by a disco that lasts till the early hours.

The reefs between Sharm and Na'ama

The fabulous array of **dive spots** around Sharm and Na'ama is the chief attraction of both resorts, offering endless scope for boat or shore diving. The most accessible site is **RAS UMM SIDD**. The area is basically all coral reef without any natural sandy beaches – what sand there is has been imported by the hotels to create their own beaches. The endless construction has inevitably increased the debris many divers now encounter underwater in this area.

From Ras Umm Sidd, a paved road lined with holiday villages and hotels runs to **THE TOWER**, a fine diving beach colonized by the *Tower* (☎069/360-0231, ℱ360-0230; ❾) and *Sharm Club* (☎069/360-0260, ℱ360-0733; ❽) **hotels**. The *Tower's* beach café is a good place for people-watching but the real lure is a huge **coral pillar** just offshore, which drops 60m into the depths.

It's easy to get to The Tower by taxi from either Sharm or Na'ama, but it is no longer possible to access most of the reefs between Ras Umm Sidd and The Tower from land, as hotels along this stretch of coast now effectively block public access to the sea. Diving these reefs by boat, in order of appearance after Ras Um Sidd, you come to Fiasco, Paradise, Turtle Bay, Pinky's Wall and Amphoras. **Turtle Bay** has warm sun-dappled water that's lovely to swim in, even if there are fewer **green turtles** (*Chelonia myades*) than you'd wish for. **Amphoras** gets its name from the cargo of clay jars aboard an Ottoman ship that sunk on the reef; as the jars contain mercury, it's lucky that they remain sealed. Diving down to the **wreck** is safe enough for novices.

Na'ama Bay

With its fine beach and upmarket facilities, **NA'AMA BAY** has transformed itself so rapidly even the residents have trouble keeping up. In a few short years the bay has grown from a few huts on the beach and one lone hotel to what looks like a mini-city, especially at night when the electric lights blaze in the desert sky. The **diving** and **snorkelling** are still the main draws, with dive centres, hotels and malls being the only points of reference along the beachfront strip. The **beach** is divided into hotel-owned plots that are supposedly open to anyone providing they don't use the parasols or chairs – though hippy-looking types may be hassled and topless bathing is not only illegal, it is highly unadvisable. There are two public beaches (£E5), though they can be hard to find, squeezed in next to the *Novotel* and the *Hilton*.

Accommodation

Luxurious **holiday villages** featuring acres of marble floors and lush landscaped gardens are the norm here, so independent travellers on a **tight budget** either stay in downtown Sharm and commute by microbus, or roost at the

---

Diving emergencies

In case of **diving emergencies**, contact Dr Adel Taher at the Hyperbaric Medical Centre near the Sharm el-Sheikh marina (☎069/366-0922, mobile ☎012 2124292). There is also a decompression facility at the pyramid-shaped International Hospital in Hay el-Nur (☎069/366-0272). The 24-hour hotline for emergencies is mobile ☎012 3331325.

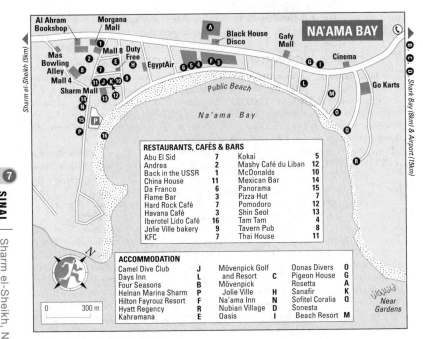

RESTAURANTS, CAFÉS & BARS

Abu El Sid	7	Kokai	5
Andrea	2	Mashy Café du Liban	12
Back in the USSR	1	McDonalds	10
China House	11	Mexican Bar	14
Da Franco	6	Panorama	15
Flame Bar	3	Pizza Hut	7
Hard Rock Café	7	Pomodoro	12
Havana Café	3	Shin Seol	13
Iberotel Lido Café	16	Tam Tam	4
Jolie Ville bakery	9	Tavern Pub	8
KFC	7	Thai House	11

ACCOMMODATION

Camel Dive Club	J	Mövenpick Golf		Oonas Divers	O
Days Inn	L	and Resort	C	Pigeon House	G
Four Seasons	B	Mövenpick		Rosetta	A
Helnan Marina Sharm	P	Jolie Ville	H	Sanafir	K
Hilton Fayrouz Resort	F	Na'ama Inn	N	Sofitel Coralia	Q
Hyatt Regency	R	Nubian Village	D	Sonesta	
Kahramana	E	Oasis	I	Beach Resort	M

Pigeon House or next door *Oasis*, Na'ama's budget options. Bargains can be had at the luxury hotels, if booked as a **package** from the UK, but make sure you're not booked into one of the hotel "extensions", which offer a lower standard of accommodation and an awkward highway crossing to get to the sea.

Alternatively, a few of the **diving colleges** rent out rooms to divers on their courses. The central *Red Sea Diving College* (☎069/360-0145, ℉360-0144, Ⓦwww.redseacollege.com; ➏) is on the beach with clean, en-suite a/c rooms, as well as dorm beds with a/c and breakfast for US$20 per person; while *Oonas Divers* (☎069/360-0581, ℉360-0582, Ⓦwww.oonasdiveclub.com; ➏), at the northern end of the bay, also has a/c rooms, all with balconies and views, and guests are allowed to use the beach and pool at the nearby *Sonesta* (see opposite). Attached to one of Na'ama's best dive centres, *Camel Dive Club Hotel* (☎069/360-0700, ℉360-0601, Ⓔreservation@cameldive.com, Ⓦwww.cameldive.com; ➐) is a small, well-designed, four-star hotel right in the heart of Na'ama, on the main strip one block from the beach. Its a/c rooms have satellite TV, and the rooftop *Camel Bar* is popular with divers.

If you have your own transport, you might consider **camping** at Ras Mohammed (see p.716).

Days Inn Na'ama Bay ☎069/360-0210. This middling resort does not aspire to be Na'ama Bay's classiest, but it does get you right on the beach for a reasonable rate. ➐

Four Seasons 9km north of Na'ama ☎069/360-3555, ℉360-3550, Ⓦwww.fourseason.com /sharmelsheikh. Glitzy hotel designed for the jet set. Expect six-star treatment and facilities. ➒

Helnan Marina Sharm At the southern end of Na'ama Bay, on the main strip ☎069/360-0751, Ⓔmarinasharm@helnan.com. Na'ama's first (Israeli-built) hotel. Some disabled-friendly rooms. Showing its age but notable mainly for having one of the better beaches in Na'ama. ➑

Hilton Fayrouz Resort On the beach ℡ 069/360-0140, ℻ 366-0040, ✉ yasser.avdelhamid@hilton .com. Comfortable and spacious a/c chalets set in pretty landscaped gardens. One of the largest beaches in Na'ama Bay and home to one of the locals' favourite pubs, *Pirates Bar*. Children under 12 stay free. ❽

Hyatt Regency Just north of Na'ama Bay ℡ 069/360-1234, ℻ 360-3600, ⓦ www.sharm .hyatt.com. Expensively bedecked hotel overlooking the coral gardens – this means a poor beach, but beautiful landscaping, along with good management, disabled rooms, non-allergenic sheets and towels, and an excellent if pricey Thai restaurant. ❾

Kahramana Hotel Three blocks back from the beach ℡ 069/360-1071, ⓦ www.kahramana.com. Centrally located four-star complex built around a pool with a nice bar and pool table. Worth considering if booking a package from the UK. ❽

Mövenpick Golf and Resort 7km north of Na'ama ℡ 069/360-3200, ℻ 360-3225, ⓦ www.mövenpick-sharmgolf.com. 270 luxurious a/c rooms, high-quality gym and health club, the best swimming pool in the area and of course, an 18-hole championship golf course. The beach, however, is disappointing. ❽

Mövenpick Jolie Ville In the middle of Na'ama ℡ 069/360-0100, ℻ 360-0111, ⓦ www .mövenpick-sharmresort.com. This hotel is so large that it utilizes golf carts to shuttle occupants from one end to the other. Popular beach bar and nightly cabaret entertainment. Also home to the first casino in the area and the *Cactus Disco*. ❽

Na'ama Inn Two blocks back from the beach ℡ & ℻ 069/360-0805, ⓦ www.naamainn.net. Not the quietest of places, but conveniently located for clubbers or shopaholics. ❻

Oasis On the edge of the desert, 400m from the beach ℡ & ℻ 069/360-1602. Next to the better *Pigeon House* (see below) and only worth considering if the latter is full. Similar prices and accommodation, but no atmosphere and not particularly welcoming. ❹

Pigeon House At the north end of Na'ama Bay, 400m from the beach ℡ 069/360-0996, ℻ 360-0995, ✉ pigeon@access.com.eg. This Bedouin-owned and -run hotel is the most popular budget option in Na'ama, with a choice of rooms with fans and shared bathrooms, or en-suite and a/c. Good for solo travellers. Pre-booking is a must as the cheaper rooms are almost always full. Arranges safari trips, and guests get a ten percent discount at the on-site Anemone Dive Centre. A reasonable breakfast buffet is included. ❹

Rosetta Opposite the *Hilton*, on the other side of the highway ℡ 069/360-1888, ℻ 360-1999, ⓦ www.tropicanahotels.com. Large a/c rooms with satellite TV; there are two pools, a nice outdoor Egyptian restaurant, and the *Black House* disco. It's the base for Emperor Divers. ❽

Sanafir One block back from the beach on the main strip ℡ 069/360-0197, ℻ 360-0196, ✉ reservation @sanafirhotel.com. One of the first hotels in Na'ama, with a much-imitated white-domed compound of a/c rooms. There's a pool, and several restaurants and bars, which make it a popular evening venue. It's especially lively after midnight when *The Bus Stop*, Na'ama's coolest club, gets going, so things can be noisy. Good buffet breakfast included. ❻

Sofitel Coralia On the north hill overlooking Na'ama Bay ℡ 069/360-0081, ℻ 360-0085, ⓦ www.sofitel .com, ✉ h1970@accor.com. Impressive-looking resort with 300 a/c rooms with terraces. One of the largest pools in Sharm, a beach, and on-site stables for horse riding expeditions to the desert. ❾

Sonesta Beach Resort At the northern end of Na'ama on the beach ℡ 069/360-0725, ℻ 360-0733, ⓦ www.sonesta.com, ✉ reservations @sonestasharm.com. Beautifully designed place with 520 rooms, which manages to make you feel as if it were the only hotel on the beach. Facilities include tennis courts, two restaurants, seven swimming pools and a casino set around gardens. Each chalet is designed in traditional Arabic manner, with whitewashed archways, domed roofs and spacious interiors. Nightly entertainment show with buffet dinner. Recommended. ❽

Diving courses and excursions

Much of Na'ama's appeal lies in its plethora of **dive centres** (see overleaf), which offer an extensive range of courses, trips and equipment rental. Though generally good, their prices and operating styles vary, so it's worth shopping around.

Total novices can make a supervised **introductory dive**; most places charge €50 including equipment. Five-day open-water **diving courses** progress from classroom theory to your first dives in the hotel swimming pool or from the shore at Na'ama Bay or Shark Bay, finishing with a few boat-dives at the end. Anemone Dive Centre offers one of the cheapest **open-water PADI** courses in Na'ama (€300 + €30 for the certificate, or US$405 + US$40), while

Emperor charges €330 or US$445 (plus €35 or US$46 for certificate). At the other end of the skill spectrum, you can be trained as an instructor or pursue **specialized courses** like night diving or underwater navigation (€200–400 or US$270–540).

Nearly all diving, except on the courses, is done from a boat, with dive centres offering a variety of daily **boat trips** to the sites. One day's diving at "local" sites like **Ras Nasrani** costs €40–50 (US$53–67, which includes two dives, tanks and weights, while trips further afield to the **Gordon** and **Jackson reefs** in the Tiran Strait (see p.730) or **Ras Mohammed** (p.714) will set you back €50–60 (US$67–80). (Remember that entry to Ras Mohammed costs €5 (US$6.70) extra and requires a full Egyptian visa, so visitors with Sinai-only visas are not permitted to dive there.) A one-day **Thistlegorm** trip (see p.709) with two dives costs €110 (US$148) with Anthias, or €160–200 (US$215–270) for a two-day trip (including equipment). Space permitting, **snorkellers** can join any boat for about €25 (US$34).

If you want to do lots of boat diving, **dive packages** can be a good deal. These cost around €240 (US$188) for a five-day package (ten dives), which is discounted if booked in advance. Rates do not include lunch on the boat (£E30). Some outfits include the price of **equipment rental** in the deal, while others don't. If not, count on an extra €25 (US$34) per day.

For many divers, **liveaboards** are the best way to get the most out of the Red Sea, giving them the opportunity to get to less-visited sites out of "peak hours" and to make up to five dives a day rather than the two dives offered by daily boats. They can also work out cheaper than staying in a hotel and buying a dive package separately, averaging around €100 (US$135) per person per day full-board for a boat with 4–8 a/c cabins: airport transfers, diving equipment and alcohol are usually extra.

Na'ama dive centres

All the dive centres are open daily (mostly 8.30am–6pm). Dive boats leave (at around 9am) from the marina in **Sharm el-Maya**, and most dive centres will collect you from your hotel and drop you off again. For a list of dive centres based in **Sharm el-Sheikh** and **Shark Bay**, see p.719 and p.729. And for more **liveaboards**, see p.719.

Anemone Dive Centre *Pigeon House* ☏ & ⓕ069/360-0999, ✉anemone@sinainet.com .eg. Laid-back and good value, offering discounts for those staying at *Pigeon House* and for anyone carrying a *Rough Guide*. PADI, NAUI, SSI. Recommended.

Anthias *Sonesta Beach Resort* ☏069/360-0725, ⓦwww.anthiasdivers.de. Austrian-run outfit that delivers proven service and options for just about any dive in the area including liveaboard. Offers Open Water diving courses for €240 (US$325) and a 2-day trip to the Thistlegorm for €160–200 (US$215–270). Recommended.

Camel Dive Club Next to the *Sanafir* ☏069/360-0700, ⓕ360-0601, ✉info@cameldive.com, ⓦwww.cameldive.com. Good facilities with its own accommodation and lots of daily dive trips. Popular with UK tourists. Recommended.

Dive Africa *Sharm Holiday Hotel* ☏069/360-1388, ⓦwww.diveafrica.com. Liveaboards available. PADI and SSI.

Divers International Near Gafy Mall ☏069/360-1939, ⓦwww.diversintl.com. PADI, NAUI, SSI. Open Water course €325 + €30 (US$440 + US$40) for the certificate.

Easy Divers *Na'ama Inn* ☏069/360-0802, ⓦwww.sharm.easydivers.com. A good-value place offering Open Water PADI course for €300 (US$405), and trips to the Thistlegorm from €90–120 (US$120–160).

Emperor Divers & Red Sea Scuba Schools *Rosetta* ☏069/360-1734, ⓦwww.emperordivers .com. Liveaboards available. PADI. Open Water course €325 (US$440) plus €35 (US$46) for the certificate. Day-trip to the Thistlegorm is €115 (US$155) plus €25 (US$34) for equipment hire.

Ocean College *Na'ama Inn* ☏069/360-0581, ✉ocean@sinainet.com.eg. PADI, BSAC.

Oonas Divers Near the *Sonesta* ☎069/360-0581, Ⓕ360-0582, ⒺΞcaroline@oonasdiveclub.com, ⓦwww.oonasdiveclub.com. Five-star PADI dive centre with its own accommodation.
Red Sea Diving College Na'ama beach ☎069/360-0145, Ⓕ360-0144, Ⓔoperations@sinai-services.com. Fine facilities and tuition, its own accommodation and liveaboards available. PADI; sells PADI books. Recommended.

Sinai Dive Club *Hilton Fayrouz Resort* ☎069/360-0136, Ⓕ360-1040, Ⓔinfo@dive-club.com, ⓦwww.dive-club.com. Liveaboards available. PADI, CMAS, SSI and NRC Nitrox courses.
Sinai Divers *Ghazala Hotel* ☎069/360-0697, Ⓕ360-0158, Ⓔinfo@sinaidivers.com, ⓦwww.sinaidivers.com. Efficient and experienced. Liveaboards available. PADI, CMAS, SSI.

Snorkelling and watersports

While diving is the main pursuit, Na'ama is also great for **snorkelling** – a less demanding but equally pleasurable activity. If you've never snorkelled before and find breathing through a tube unsettling, start with the baby reefs just off the beach, where the sea is only waist deep. By the time you've circled a reef and seen its profusion of rainbow-hued fish, snorkelling should feel like fun and you'll be ready to move on to bigger things. Unfortunately, unless you're going to join a dive boat to get to further-flung sites (which is a very relaxing way of doing things; see p.719), visiting the local reefs involves some walking: drinking water, a hat and proper footwear are essential. It's wise to start early as the sea is usually calmest in the morning, an important factor when you've got to swim over serrated reefs.

The best **reefs** – aptly known as coral gardens – run for several miles **north of Na'ama Bay**. They don't get many divers (being deemed inferior to The Tower or Shark Bay) but are ideal for snorkelling. Just look for a safe descent from the rocks and the shortest, smoothest reef flat, with dark water beyond its edge. Bear in mind that these reefs are regularly visited by glass-bottom boats, so you will need to take care while you're in the water. The **Near Gardens** can be reached on foot by following the coast beyond Oonas Dive Centre. Plummeting to unseen depths beyond its crest, the reef has spawned offshore pillars and fantastic encrustations, swarming with angelfish, parrotfish and blue snappers. From here you can swim to the equally amazing **Middle and Far gardens**, further up the coast.

If you're willing to pay to reach **other sites**, several agencies run overland snorkelling trips to the mangrove forests of **Nabeq** (see p.730), or boat trips to the less demanding reefs at **Ras Mohammed**, **Ras Nasrani** or **Shark Bay**. Sun'n'Fun, which has branches in many hotels in Na'ama and beach kiosks by the *Hilton* (☎069/360-1623, ⓦwww.sunnfunsinai.com), offers a full-day boat trip to Ras Mohammed or Tiran for €20 (plus €5 entry fee), while Fanous Moto Safari (☎069/360-3059) runs snorkelling trips to the Near and Far gardens and White Knights. A full-day overland trip to Nabeq, including Shark Bay and Dahab, costs US$80.

Apart from snorkelling, there's a wide variety of **watersports** on offer from most beachfront hotels, including sailing, windsurfing (instructors for both are available), water skiing, parasailing, jetskiing and pedalos. There are also, of course, **glass-bottom boats** to view the depths without getting wet: Sun'n'Fun has boat trips leaving every two hours throughout the day (1hr 30min; £E60, children £E35).

Overland trips and safaris

Should the wonders of the deep pall, safari companies (see overleaf) and travel agencies (see p.729) can arrange tours by jeep, camel, motorbike or quads. Some of the most popular day excursions by jeep are a mangrove-and-snorkelling visit to **Nabeq** (Sun'n'Fun does a half-day trip for US$35); a 4WD trip to the **Coloured Canyon** followed by snorkelling at either Dahab or Nuweiba; and **St Catherine's Monastery** (overnight trip including climbing **Mount Sinai** for US$60). Nearer to Na'ama lies **Wadi Mandar**, visited on sunset trips by jeep (US$35) or camel (US$25 with tea, US$35 with dinner). If you see trips advertised for less, they probably involve travelling by bus rather than jeep. A bit further up the road is **Wadi Ain Kid**, a long fertile canyon culminating in an oasis of palm trees, a well and Bedouin farm; overnight excursions cost around US$60 including a Bedouin dinner. Several companies also offer excursions to **Serabit el-Khadim** (see p.713) and **Hammam Faraoun** (p.713).

For longer desert trips, the experienced guiding company **Desert Safari**, at the *Pigeon House* (T & F 069/360-0999, mobile T 010 1436127, E anemone@sinainet.com.eg), offers jeep safaris for around US$65 per person per day; Khaled Liston (T 069/366-2068, mobile T 010 1850305, E khaledliston@hotmail.com) runs tailor-made desert and diving safaris, with excellent personal service, for around US$75 per person per day; Madian Adventure (T 069/366-0593, F 360-0594, E peninsula@menanet.net), one of the most experienced guides in the area, offers jeep safaris and mountain trekking from US$80 per person per day; while **Hussein Abu Ahmed** (mobile T 010 6145071) is a long-standing, excellent-value Bedouin guide who can also be contacted via the *Pigeon House*. All these companies also offer the day-trips detailed above, though many of the sites, except for Nabeq, Wadi Mandar and Wadi Ain Kid, are cheaper to reach from Nuweiba or Dahab.

Horse-riding in the desert can be arranged at the *Sofitel* Equestrian Centre (T 069/360-0081), where desert trips cost US$25 per hour and overnight trips start from US$100. The most authentic **camel rides** with Bedouin guides can be booked through the *Pigeon House* for around US$40 for a couple of hours.

"Quads" or **quadrunners**, also known as ATVs (All-Terrain Vehicles), are another popular way of getting into the desert. Canyon Safari at the *Pigeon House* (T 069/360-0997, mobile T 012 3158121) rents quads (US$30 for two people per hour; US$20 for one person) and also runs a popular guided sunset trip (US$40 for two people; US$28 for one) which takes two hours with a stop for Bedouin tea. Other quad excursions include a six-hour trip to Nabeq with lunch (US$130 for two people; US$110 for one) and a Bedouin dinner trip (US$65 for two people; US$45 for one).

If you fancy venturing out on your own **by car**, a Jeep Cherokee can be rented for US$90 a day from Avis in Morgana Mall (T 069/360-0979). Prices for a smaller car such as a Ford Fiesta start from US$35 a day; try Bita Car Rental (T 069/360-0826) at the *Falcon Hotel*; Hertz (T 069/366-2299) opposite the Bank of Cairo in Hadaba; or, if you are over in Shark Bay and beyond, Budget (T 069/360-1610) at Coral Bay, past the airport. If you just need a **moped** to get around Na'ama, these are available for US$15 per hour or US$50 per day from Red Sea Star Sports Centre (mobile T 012 22260432), behind the *Hilton*. They also rent **push bikes** for £E20 per hour.

Bear in mind that it is illegal for unaccompanied foreigners to go **off-road**; there are still many unexploded landmines in Sinai and you won't know where they are.

Other activities

Thrill-seekers can try **go-kart racing** at the state-of-the-art *Ghibili Raceway* (T 069/360-3939, F 602-323) on the Airport Road just before the entrance to the *Hyatt Regency*. For US$25 during the day or US$35 at night (until 1am), you can have ten laps racing round one of the four circuits, including one for children over 7: all first-timers have to undergo a training session. If you still have energy to burn, head for the **bungee rocket** and **trampolines** at the nearby *Sinai Extreme Park* (mobile ☎010 6696968), or the MAS **bowling alley** (☎069/360-2220, daily 7pm–1am; £E25 per game), a few hundred metres south of the *Hard Rock Café*. Children will also enjoy the **dolphin shows** at the Dolphinella in Sharm (see p.718 for details).

Shopping

A number of **malls** and recreated "**souks**" compete to attract the attention of tourists, but there's little here you can't find in Cairo or Luxor – at lower prices. However, there are a few interesting shops: Aladdin at the **Camel Dive Club Hotel** (which has another branch at the **Falcon El-Diar** further down the street on the opposite side), and Bashayer, in Sharm Mall behind Red Sea Diving College, are worth taking a look at for arts and crafts, mostly from Upper Egypt; nearby, Karkade, opposite the **Cataract Hotel** (☎069/360-2855), sells a huge selection of oils, spices and herbs, plus an interesting collection of antiques. They have another, larger shop in Sharm el-Maya.

Restaurants and cafés

There are no really cheap places to eat or drink in Na'ama, so what passes for inexpensive is relative. On the plus side, the quality of the **food** is high if you like hotel-style cuisine which ranges from Egyptian, Italian and seafood to Japanese and Thai; prices tend to be higher along the **beach promenade** where every hotel offers at least one beachside restaurant, and along the inland strip outside the *Sanafir* and *Camel Dive Club* hotels – both these stretches are busy with holiday-makers and a handful of Egyptian touts. If you fancy eating on the beach, try the *Hilton*'s Italian restaurant, or the fish restaurant at Shark Bay Bedovin Camp (see p.729).

For **snacks and deserts**, head to the *Jolie Ville* bakery, at the northern end of the strip near *McDonald's,* for sweet and sticky delicacies and an espresso (£E9).

Abu El Sid On the roof of the *Hard Rock Café.* Atmospheric Egyptian restaurant with soft lighting and decorated with tiles and Oriental musical instruments fixed to the walls. Reasonably priced grilled meat dishes including a T-bone steak for £E32.

Andrea In the mall 200m northwest of the *Hard Rock Café.* Mostly chicken-based dishes, but also good-value Egyptian food; from £E20–25 for a meal.

Back in the USSR On the side of Morgana Mall near the highway. A throwback to the Soviet Union, with Marx, Engels and Lenin looming over a blood red decor while patrons dine on European-Russian dishes. Obviously, the best place in town for a vodka shot.

China House and Thai House Na'ama Centre, 2nd floor. Two restaurants, side-by-side under one ownership, that attempt to recreate the Far East on the Na'ama Bay strip. Main dishes at both cost around £E35–55.

Da Franco *Hotel Ghazala*, on the promenade between the *Mövenpick* and *Hilton*. Excellent pizza and pasta restaurant; reasonably priced main dishes (£E30–50).

Hard Rock Café Just around the corner from the main strip. Serves hamburgers with all the trimmings; hugely popular nightspot. Daily 12.30pm–2am (till 3am Sat).

Kokai *Hotel Ghazala* next to *Da Franco*. Japanese restaurant, slightly cheaper than *Kona Kai* at the *Marriott*.

Mashy Café du Liban *Sanafir*. Al fresco Lebanese cuisine. Good value, especially if you're a meat lover. Open daily for lunch and dinner; dishes £E25–70.

Pomodoro *Sanafir*. Good, basic Italian restaurant, run by Italians, with pasta in the range of £E20–80. Some dishes attempt an Egyptian-Italian fusion, such as the *kofta* casserole (£E33).

Shin Seol Sharm Mall. Reasonable Chinese restaurant with roof garden. About £E25 for a three-course meal.

Tam Tam *Hotel Ghazala* ☎069/360-0150. Tasty Egyptian food near the beach with rooftop seating and live music. Excellent *karkade*, lentil soup and Egyptian sweets. Does takeaway. Daily until 1am.

Tavern Pub In a small mall behind Mall 4, mobile ☎012 7676580. Tucked inside a pedestrian mall, this authentic British pub serves as a hang-out for expats and football fans who come to watch the sport on several big screen TVs. Classic English pub grub including a daily 'Sunday roast' (£E40), curry and chilli.

Nightlife

Alcoholic drinks are widely available at European prices, perhaps more so than anywhere else in Egypt; the **duty-free shop** in front of the *Kahramana* (daily 11am–2pm & 6–11pm) sells cheap booze, though you can only buy duty-free within the first 24 hours of your arrival in Egypt. A favourite starting point for the evening is the *Camel Dive Bar* at the Camel Dive Club, a friendly pub decorated with flags and soccer jerseys, strewn with peanut shells on the floor. The main hang-outs for British expats are the *Tavern Pub* (see above), which turns into a **bar** at night then a disco later on, and *The Mexican Bar* (1pm–midnight), next to the *Na'ama Inn*, under the cliff at the end of the main strip, with a resident DJ. Locals prefer to gather at the nautically themed *Pirates Bar* in the *Hilton* (happy hour 5.30–7.30pm), which also serves food, while the café at the *Iberotel Lido* is a good spot for watching the sun set over Na'ama Bay. The beach pathway is also lined with **cocktail bars** attached to the resorts – the *Havana Café* and the *Flame Bar*, both behind the *Hilton*, are worth trying.

Na'ama's premier **nightspot** is the *Sanafir*, which hosts a range of nightlife. From 9.30pm there is an Oriental show featuring mainly Russian bellydancers, with a cover charge of £E50 unless you eat at one of their restaurants, while the rooftop bar *Star Talks* is popular with holiday romancers. *Sanafir* also hosts Na'ama's hippest club, the *Bus Stop* (£E50, includes one drink), which gets going around midnight and goes on to 3am. On Fridays, the *Bus Stop* organizers run *The Echo Temple*, at the foot of the Sinai mountains in the desert (£E145; details from ⓦ www.pachasharm.com). The equally popular *Pacha* (£E190) shares a venue with the *Bus Stop*, but has a separate entrance and boasts pools and foam parties. *Sanafir's* main competition, particularly popular with Italians, is the *Hard Rock Café*, just round the corner from the main strip (disco daily 8pm–2/3am; ☎069/360-2665), with other **discos** including the *Black House Disco* at the *Rosetta*, *Cactus* at the *Mövenpick* – both of which are popular with hotel staff – and the Latin-themed *Salsa* next to *Hard Rock Café*; none is likely to be very lively before midnight. There are **pool tables** in many of the hotel bars, including the *Kahramana* and the *Sanafir*.

For a more Egyptian evening, the main strip outside the *Sanafir* is lined with countless coffee shops offering **sheeshas**, Oriental drinks and people-watching. The best *sheesha* in town, however, can be found at the outdoor café, the *Panorama*, with steps that climb up the hillside leading to private alcoves with tables, couches and great views: *sheeshas*, here, come in various flavours and cost £E10.

Na'ama Bay also has several **casinos** that open late into the night, including the *Casino Royale* at the *Mövenpick*, and one at the *Sonesta*: you'll need to show your passport before entering. There's also a **cinema** at the *Safir* hotel, on the edge of town on the Airport Road, where you can watch relatively new Hollywood films for £E20.

Listings

Banks and exchange Most hotels in Na'ama have banks that open daily (8.30am–2pm & 6–9pm). The National Bank of Egypt has branches in the *Ghazala*, *Mövenpick* and *Hilton*. You can get cash advances on Visa and MasterCard at Banque Misr (9am–1.30pm & 5–8pm) in the Sharm Mall.

Several banks now have ATMs; one that usually works is at the HSBC Bank next to *McDonald's*. For changing cash, Swiss Exchange in Morgana Mall (daily 9am–midnight) may offer slightly better rates than the banks.

Books and newspapers Most of the four- and five-star hotels have small bookshops and can provide international newspapers for their guests. Several have a "library" where you can pick up books left behind by past guests, though English-language books can be hard to find.

Dentist Dr Hassan El Saarkawy, at Mall 8, 2nd floor (mobile ☎012 1206078).

Doctor Dr Wael Habib, at the Mount Sinai Clinic in the *Mövenpick* (☎069/360-0100, 24hr mobile ☎012 2189889). For diving emergencies, Dr Adel Taher at the Hyperbaric Medical Centre in Sharm el-Sheikh (☎069/366-0922, emergency mobile ☎012 2124292).

Hospitals The nearest hospitals are in Sharm El-Sheikh, in Hay el-Nur: Sharm International Hospital (☎069/366-1624) and Sharm Medical Centre (☎069/366-1744).

Internet cafés Na'ama Bay is probably the most expensive place in Egypt to use the Internet, with cafés charging a standard £E20 per hour, and hotels £E30 or more. Connections, however, tend to be pretty fast. Try *Cyber Disco* at the *Hilton Fayrouz* (☎069/360-0136; £E30 per hour) or *Camel Cyber* at *Camel Dive Club* (☎069/360-0700, ✉info@cameldive.com; £E20 per hour). *Sinainet*

has cafés at the *Ghazala* and *Ghazala Gardens* (on either side of the main highway between the *Hilton* and *Mövenpick*), the *Mövenpick* and the *Kahramana*, all charging £E20 per hour. There's also *GlobalLink* in Mall 8 (daily 10am–midnight; £E20 per hour) and *Speed* (£E20 per hour) opposite the *Mashy Café du Liban*.

Pharmacy Towa, in the Sharm Mall (daily 10am–1am; ☎069/360-0779), offers free home delivery if you're too sick to go there in person. Another is Na'ama Bay Pharmacy (☎069/366-0338). The best-stocked pharmacy is next to the hospital in Hay el-Nur in Sharm el-Sheikh.

Supermarkets Cherry, Sharm Mall (daily 9am–midnight); Shamandoura, next to the *Sanafir* (daily 9am–midnight); and Sheikh Abdullah's in Hay el-Nur (see p.716), the cheapest with the most variety.

Telephone exchanges Sharm No. 2 is opposite the entrance to the *Sheraton*, about 1km north of Na'ama Bay (daily 10am–10pm).

Travel agents Abu Noub, Morgana Mall (☎069/360-0066, ⓦwww.abanoub.com) is an established, reliable agent; Nass Tours, Mall 8 (☎ & Ⓕ069/360-1258), can help with booking trips to Petra; Thomas Cook, Gafy Mall (daily 9am–2pm & 6–10pm; ☎069/360-1808), is a friendly agent that offers the usual range of travel services, plus Visa cash advances.

Western Union At the DHL office in the *Rosetta* (Mon–Thurs & Sun 9am–9pm; ☎ & Ⓕ069/360-2222).

Shark Bay

Ten kilometres up the coast from Na'ama, the once tranquil and secluded resort of **SHARK BAY** is now overlooked and overwhelmed by large holiday villages, and the sandy track that used to lead there has been replaced by a variety of tarmacked roads servicing the hotels. But that hasn't deterred its many visitors, particularly the scores of day-visitors from Na'ama. Despite the bay's forbidding name (*Beit el-Irsh*, "House of the Shark" in Arabic), all the sharks have been scared away by divers, leaving a benign array of tropical fish and coral gardens just offshore, with deeper reefs and bigger fish further out. There's a £E10 charge to use the beach, which includes the use of showers and a soft drink.

If you want to **stay**, Sheikh Embarak's **Shark Bay Bedouin Home** (☎069/360-0947, ⓦwww.sharksbay.com; ❹) is a pleasant mix of bungalows and beach huts, with its own jetty and **dive centre** (✉umbi@sinainet.com.eg) that runs boat trips to the Tiran Strait (day-dive US$55; liveaboard US$100 a day), while Bedouins who hang out there can arrange jeep safaris into the interior. Its restaurant and Bedouin café are quiet nightspots that close around midnight; guests wanting more action can club together for a taxi into Na'ama. Package tourists generally stay at the nearby *Holiday Inn*, 1km south (☎069/360-2131, ⓦwww.holidayinnsharm.com; ❽), which boasts the usual luxury facilities, though its architecture is some of the least appealing in the area.

The Tiran Strait and Nabeq

The headland of Ras Nasrani beyond Shark Bay marks the onset of the **Tiran Strait**, where the waters of the Gulf of Suez flow into the deeper Gulf of Aqaba, swirling around islands and reefs. In 1992, the Tiran archipelago was declared a protected area, and it may one day become a fully fledged national park. Meanwhile, there's no admission charge or facilities and the only access is by boat from Sharm el-Maya or Shark Bay. This is *not* an excursion for novice divers, as the sea can be extremely rough and chilling (bring high-calorie drinks and snacks to boost your energy).

Sharks, manta rays, barracuda and Napoleon fish are typical of the deepwater sites around the **islands of Tiran** and **Sanafir**, though there are also shallow reefs like the Small Lagoon and Hushasha. The multitude of **shipwrecks** in the Gulf is due to treacherous reefs and currents, insurance fraud, and Egypt's blockade of the Strait in the 1960s. The **Jackson Reef** has a spectacular 70m drop-off and the wreck of the *Lara* to investigate, while the **Gordon Reef** boasts the hulk of the *Lucila*. Two notable sites at **Ras Nasrani** are the **Light**, with a 40m drop-off and pelagic fish; and the **Point**, with a dazzling array of reef fish.

Nabeq

Beyond the mouth of the Gulf of Aqaba, a 90km swathe of the coast as far north as Dahab City has been designated another protected area, named after the small oasis and **Bedouin village** of **NABEQ**. As few dive boats come here from Na'ama, the **reefs** are quieter than at Tiran or Ras Mohammed. Most visitors are on half-day trips to see Nabeq's mangrove forests – the most northerly in the world. **Mangroves** can filter salt from sea water and thus survive in tropical coastal areas. As sediment traps, they reduce erosion and provide a habitat for mating fish and migratory birds (in summer and autumn), acting as the ecological interface between the coast and the interior, whose flood-prone *wadis* sustain ibex, hyrax, foxes and other **wildlife**.

All approaches to Nabeq are best made by someone who knows the way; wander off the track and you might inadvertently encounter **mines** left over from Israeli-Egyptian wars, which killed a jeepload of tourists in 1995. Admission to the protected area costs €5 (US$6.70); the only facilities are a **cafeteria** and visitors' centre.

Anyone considering **staying** in the Nabeq area should bear in mind that it is much windier here than in Na'ama, transport connections are limited to shuttle buses and the beaches can be poor. However, development is encroaching slowly, with the southern reaches having new roads and hotels, and plans for a marina being mooted. One of the best of the beachfront **hotels** is the *Radisson* (☎069/371-0315, ☏069/360-2141; ❽), a luxurious resort 17km north of Na'ama, with six restaurants, three pools and a spa centre, while the beautiful *Nubian Village*, next door (☎069/371-0200; full-board only ❻), is designed to resemble a Nubian village.

Dahab and Asilah

Jagged mountains ranged inland of Na'ama Bay accompany the road 95km northwards, providing a magnificent backdrop for **Dahab**'s tawny beaches, from which its Arabic name – "gold" – derives. The resort divides into two localities: a cluster of holiday villages catering for affluent visitors, and the Bedouin settlement of **Asilah** 2.5km up the coast, where younger travellers hang out in a kind of "Goa by the Red Sea" – though as Asilah moves upmarket, the distinction between them is blurring. A third area north of Asilah, near the dive sites of the Canyon and Blue Hole, is tipped for future development should the tourist numbers rebound after the recent downturn.

Dahab City

Don't be discouraged by **DAHAB CITY**, the colony of municipal housing and government offices next to the holiday villages. The only reason to go there is to use its facilities: a **post office** (daily except Fri 8am–3pm) and 24-hour **telephone exchange** (international calls with phonecards); a **supermarket** (daily 8am–10pm); and a **bank** which accepts travellers' cheques and Visa (Sun–Thurs 8.30am–2pm & 5–8pm, Sat 9am–2pm, closed Fri). The nearby *Swiss Inn Golden Palace Resort* has a bank that opens on Fridays (9am–noon & 6–9pm). The **tourist police** are located opposite the *Coralia Dahab*, while the nearest **hospital** is in Sharm el-Sheikh (see p.716).

Most tourists arrive at Dahab City's East Delta **bus station** and then head straight onto Asilah; every bus is met by **taxis** and **pick-ups** that charge £E1–2 per person to Asilah, £E5 for solo travellers. Few places are more than ten minutes' walk from the taxi drop-off point.

The **holiday villages** around Dahab Bay are self-contained, with private beaches and access to a coral reef on the headland. Whilst there is no need to leave the complex at all, those who wish to can head to Asilah to shop, eat and drink. At the eastern end of the string of resorts is the opulent **Hilton Dahab** (℡069/364-0310, ℮dahab@hilton.com; ❼), whose beach is open to non-residents for £E40 a day. Next door, the **Swiss Inn Golden Palace Resort** (℡069/364-0471, ℻364-0470, ℠www.swissinn.net; ❼) has its own dive and windsurfing centres, while the **Ganet Sinai Hotel** (℡069/364-0440, ℻364-0441; ❻ including buffet breakfast), has a/c rooms with TVs and sea views, a private beach without coral (£E15 for non-guests, including a soft drink) and also a windsurfing centre. The most lavish hotel is the Greek-inspired **Iberotel Dahab** (℡069/364-1264 or 5 ℻364-1265, ℠www.iberotel-eg.com/dahabeya; ❽), a 145-room palace with windsurfing and diving centres, plus a kids' club. Further round the bay, the somewhat isolated **Helnan Dahab Hotel** (℡069/364-0425, ℻364-0428; ❼) has the usual luxury facilities along with a good beach. Back at the eastern end of the bay, but accessed by a separate road near the lagoon, the charming **Coralia Dahab** (℡069/364-0301, ℠www .accor-hotels.com; ❼), monopolizes a windswept bay enclosed by a sandbar – a fabulous spot if you want to learn how to windsurf.

Asilah

With its breathtaking views, quiet ambience and string of good beachside restaurants and hotels, the gentrified hippie colony of **ASILAH** is now the Red Sea coast's best backpacker hang-out. Its reputation as *the* place for hippy travellers emerged in the 1960s, when Israeli troops started coming here for a bit of R & R, introducing the Bedouin to a different way of life. Nowadays, the Bedouin village of tin shacks and scrawny goats has changed beyond recognition: concrete buildings stretch back behind scores of restaurants, small inns and bungalows while local children wander beneath the palm trees selling Bedouin trousers (made in China), friendship bracelets and camel rides. Most of the palm huts were long ago replaced by hotels (some of which are very smart), while a section of the beach has been paved to create a pedestrian "corniche" – yet

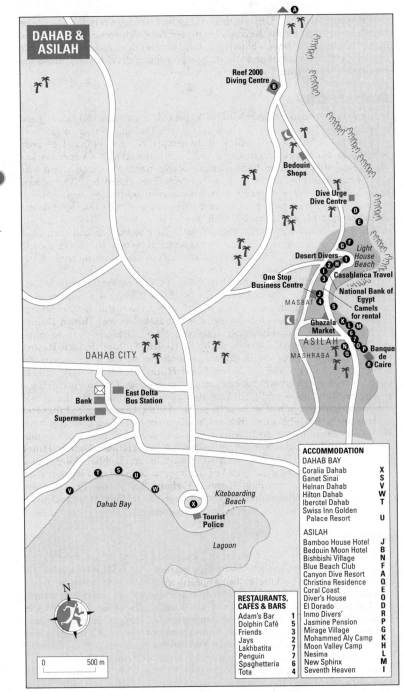

DAHAB & ASILAH

Reef 2000
Diving Centre — **B**

Bedouin
Shops

Dive Urge
Dive Centre — **D**
E

Desert Divers
Light
House
Beach
G **F**
2 **H** **1**
3

One Stop
Business Centre
Casablanca Travel

National Bank of
Egypt

J
4
Camels
for rental
5

MASBAT

K **L** **M**
Ghazala
Market
6 **7** **O**

ASILAH

N **Q** **P**
Banque
de
Caire
R

MASHRABA

DAHAB CITY

Bank

East Delta
Bus Station

Supermarket

T **S** **U**

V

W

Dahab Bay

X

Kiteboarding
Beach

Tourist
Police

Lagoon

N

0   500 m

ACCOMMODATION

DAHAB BAY

Coralia Dahab	X
Ganet Sinai	S
Helnan Dahab	V
Hilton Dahab	W
Iberotel Dahab	T
Swiss Inn Golden Palace Resort	U

ASILAH

Bamboo House Hotel	J
Bedouin Moon Hotel	B
Bishbishi Village	N
Blue Beach Club	F
Canyon Dive Resort	A
Christina Residence	Q
Coral Coast	E
Diver's House	O
El Dorado	D
Inmo Divers'	R
Jasmine Pension	P
Mirage Village	G
Mohammed Aly Camp	K
Moon Valley Camp	H
Nesima	L
New Sphinx	M
Seventh Heaven	I

**RESTAURANTS,
CAFÉS & BARS**

Adam's Bar	1
Dolphin Café	5
Friends	3
Jays	2
Lakhbatita	7
Penguin	7
Spaghetteria	6
Tota	4

Asilah manages to live on as a travellers' ghetto offering time-out from all that cultural immersion. Such is the lure that visitors often stay longer than they'd expected, getting stuck in a daily routine of café life, or if they are more active, working at one of the dive centres (mostly in return for food, accommodation and some diving).

Given Asilah's reputation, it's important to stress the limitations on pure hedonism. Women can generally sunbathe here without any hassle, but **going topless** violates Egyptian law, and there are periodic crackdowns on **dope**: if you consume, it's at the risk of the police deciding they need to make up numbers on their arrest forms (see box below). While stories abound of duplicitous locals, beware also of being ripped off by resident **con-artists** from Israel or Europe, who exploit the naive, and unpleasant, travellers' belief that it's only natives who "can't be trusted". Stick to bottled water to avoid the risk of **hepatitis** from contaminated cisterns; a dozen or so cases of infection occur every year.

Arrival and information

Arriving in Asilah, you'll be dropped at the parking lot in front of the bridge that divides **Masbat** to the north from **Mashraba** to the south. Both neighbourhoods extend for about one kilometre in each direction, strung out with restaurants and hotels along a pedestrian walkway, before petering out into the dust. **Lighthouse Beach**, at Masbat's northern headland, is the usual first stop for sunbathers and snorkellers.

There are a number of **Internet cafés** up and down the walkway, some doubling as **second-hand bookstores**. Most charge around £E5 per hour for Internet access, and usually have **telephone, fax** and photocopying facilities too. There are a couple of **ATM** machines, one by *Jay's* restaurant and another outside Ghazala Market. A Banque de Caire is opposite *Star of Dahab* (daily 9am–12.30pm & 6–9pm), with a smaller branch at the *Sabry Palace*. The One Stop Business Center (℡069/364-0466) at *Bamboo House* has safety deposit boxes (£E20 per week or £E3 per day, £E10 key deposit), a Western Union money transfer service, and international calls for £E7 per minute to most countries.

Drug smuggling and cultivation in Sinai

The Sinai Bedouin have a long tradition of **smuggling** hashish into Egypt. During colonial times the route followed the Mediterranean coast, until the militarization of El-Arish and the Canal Zone compelled smugglers to seek new routes across the interior. When this also became militarized due to war with Israel, they switched their attention to the mountains of South Sinai and the Aqaba coast. Under Israeli rule their activities were tolerated so long as the dope was bound for Egypt, but the emergence of an Israeli market caused a clampdown in the 1970s, at a time when hash supplies from Lebanon were drying up.

Meanwhile, however, foreign hippies were flocking to Sinai and asking the Bedouin for grass (using the Indian term *ganja*, from which *bango*, the Egyptian word for marijuana, derives). Thus was planted the seed of a local **cultivation** industry, which really got going once Sinai was returned to Egypt and its police chief took a hand in the business for a decade. Today, Sinai is one of Egypt's main sources of *bango*, as cultivators can't be prosecuted owing to a loophole in the Camp David Accords – unlike dealers, who risk long-term imprisonment or even hanging, and rely on bribery to get off the hook. But the police must make *some* arrests, so it's rather like an auction where the lowest bidders are cast as scapegoats. This applies equally to foreigners – especially those who bring heroin or ecstasy to sell in Asilah.

Accommodation

Asilah's accommodation ranges from simple, budget **campgrounds**, with basic concrete cells, usually with padlocks and electricity, and with showers, sinks and toilets in the yard, to the more upmarket versions that are closer to **hotels** with en-suite facilities, sea views and a/c. Factors to consider when choosing a site are: whether, and when, they have hot showers, how they're rigged up to deal with mosquitoes, and noise levels (watch out for anywhere near the main strip at Masbat).

Bamboo House Hotel Masbat ☏ 069/364-0263. A hotel with a/c rooms and a Western Union money transfer service. ❺

Bedouin Moon Hotel 3km north of Masbat ☏ 069/364-0695, ✉ bedouinmoon@menanet .net. Good for beach combing and diving: attached to the Reef 2000 dive club. They also have dorms (€12 per bed). ❹

Bishbishi Village Mashraba ☏ 069/364-0727, mobile ☏ 010 5488708, ⊛ www.bishbishi.com. Operated by the indefatigable Jimmy (who also runs the *Penguin* restaurant), this popular backpacker hang-out has a range of rooms from basic cells to a/c rooms with private bath. It's a good place to meet other travellers looking to organize a desert trek. ❷

Blue Beach Club 200m north of Lighthouse Beach ☏ 069/364-0411, ⊛ www.bluebeachclub.com. Friendly place with a hip, young European staff. The easy-going atmosphere and range of activities (including yoga, Arabic language lessons, reiki, horseback riding, diving and heavy drinking at the *Furry Cup* bar) more than makes up for the unspectacular rooms. ❻

Canyon Dive Resort 11km north of Mashbat ☏ 069/364-0197. Attractive two-star place next to the Canyon dive site. Worth considering if all you want to do is dive, but otherwise a bit far from town. ❺

Christina Residence Mashraba ☏ 069/364-0390, ⓕ 364-0406, ⊛ www.christinahotels.com. This hotel is in two parts: one on the beach and another, less expensive place on the main road. Both buildings have smart, clean rooms. Breakfast included. ❻

Coral Coast 300m north of Lighthouse Beach ☏ 069/364-1195, ✉ coralcoasthotel@link.net. Large concrete hotel block on the beach, past the *Blue Beach Club*. Has a branch of Fantasea Divers attached. ❻

Diver's House Tucked away in the south of Mashraba ☏ & ⓕ 069/364-0451, ⊛ www .divershouse.com. Small rambling hotel run by an Egyptian-British couple. A variety of quirky rooms on offer, including a dorm room and a dungeon-like double with a domed ceiling. ❷

El Dorado 350 metres north of Lighthouse Beach ☏ & ⓕ 069/364-1027, ⊛ www.eldoradodahab.com.

Immaculate but basic cabins with toilet and shower, and its own dive centre. Excellent restaurant. ❻

Inmo Divers' Home Mashraba ☏ 069/364-0370, ⓕ 364-0372, ⊛ www.inmodivers.de. Stylish lodgings around a dive centre. Free Internet, swimming pool and children's play area. All rooms have double beds and bathrooms; discount for longer stays, divers and advance bookings. ❸

Jasmine Pension On the beach next to *Diver's House* ☏ 069/364-0370, ⊛ www.jasminepension .com. One of the best budget places around, with a welcoming staff and clean, good-value rooms. ❷

Mirage Village Near Lighthouse Beach ☏ 069/364-0341, ⊛ www.mirage.com.eg. Tucked away behind a walled compound; pleasant rooms, clean bathrooms and mosquito-free due to its windy position. Friendly, laid-back management, too. Recommended. ❸

Mohammed Aly Camp On the beach where Masbat meets Mashraba ☏ 069/364-0268, ⊛ www.clubred.com. Although it is very central with 128 rooms, only a few of them have much appeal. The best overlook the sea and have fans and their own bathrooms. Run in association with the popular Club Red dive centre. ❷

Moon Valley Camp Masbat, mobile ☏ 010 3719903, ⊛ www.ghazala-hotels.com. Located about 75m north of *Jays*, this is a quiet spot with a/c rooms. ❷

Nesima Mashraba ☏ 069/364-0320, ⓕ 364-0321, ⊛ www.nesima-resort.com. Possibly the most beautiful hotel in Asilah, with a great pool setting. Used by British dive operators Regal and Crusader Travel. Discounts on rooms with fans in quiet periods. ❻

New Sphinx Mashraba ☏ & ⓕ 069/364-0032. Forty rooms with bath, a/c and satellite TV, plus a pool. The older annexe next door is cheaper but shares the same facilities. ❺

Seventh Heaven Masbat ☏ 069/364-0080, mobile ☏ 012 3612964, ⊛ www.7heavenhotel.com. Another good backpacker hang-out, this one has a good location between the bridge and Lighthouse Beach. There is a restaurant, though the breakfast is nothing to write home about. ❶

Eating, drinking and nightlife

A score of **restaurants** by the beach vie for customers. House, trance and chill-out music fill the air; floor cushions and posters reflect the mix of Bedouin and hippie influences. Cold drinks are always available, though not all places have alcohol licences, and you can sit around for hours without being required to eat (dishes take a long time to prepare, in any case). With menus displayed outside, it's easy to compare prices. Ask other visitors where they've eaten (and not got sick) – everyone has their favourite place.

Pancakes with bananas, apples, ice cream or honey are popular for **breakfast** or late-night munchies, while main **meals** consist of pizzas, pasta or **fish**. Many places display a tempting heap of fresh fish and crustaceans outside; just check the price before ordering. Unless you splash out on lobster, you can eat quite well in Asilah for £E20–35 a meal, including drinks and dessert. Most places are open until midnight (or later), though the choice of food diminishes after 9pm. There are also numerous **supermarkets** (daily 7.30am–midnight), **fruit stalls** and *taamiya* stands.

Of the **restaurants**, *Jays*, run by an English woman, is popular with resident divers for its safe food (only open in the evenings), as is *Friends* nearby, one of a run of similar beachside grills that stretch to the bridge. South of the bridge, the scene quietens down a bit until you get to the very popular *Penguin* restaurant, good for a game of backgammon, a *sheesha*, and a decent fish platter, accompanied by great milkshakes. Closeby, the *Lakhbatita* restaurant is worth a visit for its décor and atmosphere, though the food can be hit-and-miss - the *cioppino* (seafood stew) at £E15 is the house speciality. It's decorated with tiles from old Coptic churches and doors from medieval warehouses from the Delta region, while the shelves are lined with giant jars of pickled vegetables and antiques collected from all over Egypt. Nearby, the *Spaghetteria* on the main road north of the *New Sphinx* serves decent pasta, while the *Dolphin Café*, just up from the police station, has reasonable Indian vegetarian baltis and noodles.

Nightlife is generally based in the hotels and restaurants that sell alcohol – both *Nesima* and the *New Sphinx* have popular bars with happy hours 7–9pm. The main place for the diving set is the *Furry Cup* bar at the *Blue Beach Club*, which has a happy hour 6.30–8.30pm, while backpackers tend to hang out at the *Penguin* restaurant, or *Adam's Bar*, near Lighthouse Beach. The biggest bar in town is *Tota*, recognizable by its ship-like façade, with satellite TV and a large, attractive beer garden in the back. Those who prefer quieter entertainment can enjoy yoga and meditation at the *Blue Beach Club* and *Nesima*, or borrow a book from the library at the Arabesque Bazaar on the beachfront near Lighthouse Beach.

Diving, snorkelling and windsurfing

In recent years aquatic pursuits have begun to be taken as seriously in Dahab as in Na'ama. Here, however, **shore diving** is the norm, with the reefs reached by pick-ups. The nicest reefs are to the north of Dahab Bay just past the lagoon; at Asilah the reefs are meagre, except for the area around the lighthouse, and much of the sea bed is covered in rubbish. Most divers head 7–8km up the coast where you can find the Eel Garden, Canyon and Blue Hole dive sites. Daily trips to these sites are arranged by most dive centres (see overleaf), or get there by taxi (£E40 per carload).

The **Canyon** is a dark, narrow fissure that you reach from the shore by swimming along the reef and then diving to the edge of a coral wall. It can be frightening for inexperienced divers, as it sinks to a depth of 50m, but there's plenty to see at the top of the reef. Further north lies the notorious **Blue Hole**, which has claimed several lives (usually experienced divers who dive too deep for too long). This spectacular shaft in the reef plunges to 80m; the challenge involves descending 60m and swimming through a transverse passage to come up the other side. Divers who ascend too fast risk getting "bent"; inexperienced divers should not attempt this dive under any circumstances. Fortunately, the Hole can be enjoyed in safety by staying closer to the surface and working your way round to a dip in the reef known as the Bridge, which swarms with colourful fish and can even be viewed using snorkelling gear.

The main destination for day-long **dive safaris** is the Ras Abu Galum protected area, a 30km stretch of coast with three diving beaches, accessible by jeep or camel (see opposite). **Naqb Shahin** – closest to Dahab – has fantastic coral and gold fish, but the sea is very turbulent, so many divers prefer **Ras Abu Galum** or **Ras el-Mamleh**, further north. All three sites have deep virgin reefs with a rich variety of corals and fish. Club Red does a one-day, two-dive trip by camel to Ras Abu Galum for €75 (US$100) including all equipment, while Fantasea offers two standard shore dives near Dahab for €50 (US$70), including tanks, weights and lunch. Trips to the **Thistlegorm** (see p.709) are also available from Club Red for €90 (US$120) including transport, food and three dives.

Diving courses

While **renting equipment** is costlier here than in Na'ama, **diving courses** are generally cheaper. Competition means cut-price deals, especially when business is quiet, but you should keep a sense of perspective – the rockbottom outlets are not necessarily going to be rigorous about your safety. Stick to the long-established centres like Club Red (open-water course €180, plus €30 for the certificate, or US$240 plus US$40), Nesima (open-water course €300 including equipment, plus €30 for certification, US$405 + US$40), INMO, Dive Urge or Divers International.

Windsurfing

The wind blows at least two hundred days each year at Dahab, making this area a haven for windsurfers and kiteboarders. Both the *Hilton* and the *Swiss Inn* have windsurfing centres and rent boards for about €25 (US$34) per hour. Kiteboarding is also popular and enthusiasts can usually be found at the lagoon near the *Coralia*, although currently no one rents out equipment, so you'd have to bring your own.

Dive centres

Adventure Divers Club On Lighthouse Beach ☎ & ℱ 069/364-0161. PADI.

Canyon Dive Club Masbat, and at The Canyon mobile ☎ 012 2225601, ⊛ www.canyondiveresort.com. PADI.

Club Red *Mohammed Aly Camp* ☎ 069/364-0380. PADI.

Dahab Divers Lighthouse Beach ☎ 069/364-0487, ✉ ddlodge@menanet.net, ⊛ www.dahab-diverslodge.com. PADI.

Dive Urge Masbat ☎ 069/364-0957, ⊛ www.dive-urge.com. PADI.

Divers House Mashraba ☎ 069/364-0885, ⊛ www.divershouse.com. PADI.

El Dorado Masbat ☎ 069/364-1027, ⊛ www.eldoradodahab.com. PADI.

Fantasea Dive Club Lighthouse Beach ☎ & ℱ 069/364-0043. PADI, SSI.

INMO Mashraba ☎ 069/364-0370, ℱ 364-0372, ⊛ www.inmodivers.de. PADI.

Nesima Dive Centre *Nesima Hotel* ☎ & ℱ 069/364-0320. PADI, BSAC.

Nirvana Dive Centre Near Lighthouse Beach ☎ 069/364-1261, ⊛ www.nirvanadivers.com. PADI, BSAC.

Planet Divers *Planet Oasis Hotel*, near Lighthouse Beach ☎ 069/364-1090, ⊛ www.planetdivers.com. PADI, CMAS, IANTD.

Red Sea Relax *Neptune Hotel,* just south of the footbridge between Mashbat and Masraba ☏069/364-1309, ℻364-1308, ⓦwww.red-sea -relax.com. CMAS, SSI, PDIC.
Reef 2000 *Bedouin Moon Hotel* ☏069/364-0087, ⓦwww.reef2000.com. SSI.

Sinai Dive Club *Coralia Dahab* ☏069/364-0301. PADI.
Sub Sinai Khaled Amin, Mashraba ☏ & ℻069/364-0317, ⓦwww.subsinai.com. PADI.

Jeep and camel safaris

If you fancy **riding on the beach** at Asilah, look out for the boys who rent out horses (£E50 for one hour) or camels (£E10–15 per hour); they hang out by the restaurants on the beach near the palm trees in Masbat. Alternatively, the *Blue Beach Club* offers horse trips down the beach for £E80 per hour.

A more exciting option, however, is to sign up for trips into the rugged interior, which can be organized at most campgrounds, through safari agencies, or by negotiating directly with guides. The most popular **day excursions** are by jeep to the **Coloured Canyon** (see p.714), which costs £E75 per person for a group of six; by camel to **Wadi Gnay**, a Bedouin hamlet with palms and a brackish spring (£E35 per person); or by camel to the mangrove forest of **Nabeq** (£E50–70). Some outfits, including Reef 2000 dive club, also organize rock-climbing trips in combination with their desert safari.

Most campgrounds and hotels have their own Bedouin contacts for trips to the desert, but itineraries and prices can vary widely so shop around. Hamid at *Crazy Camel* camp (☏069/364-0662, mobile ☏012 2708230, ⓦwww .crazy-camel.de) arranges camel and jeep safaris from US$50–60 per person per day, while Said Kader at Desert Divers (mobile ☏010 1888906, ⓦwww .desert-divers.com) can arrange camel and jeep safaris with either diving, windsurfing or yoga themes. Embah Safari near Lighthouse Beach (☏ & ℻069/364-1690, ⓦwww.embah.com) offers diving, camel or jeep safaris from US$60 per person per day, as well as excursions to St. Catherine's and the Coloured Canyon.

Ras Abu Galum

The coast between Dahab and Nuweiba is hidden from view as the road veers inland, but this remote area, the **Ras Abu Galum** Protectorate, harbours some of the richest wildlife in the Sinai. Access is limited to a coastal track (walking or camel only) from Dahab or an unpaved road (4WD) that branches off from the main road 20km short of Nuweiba. There are huts on the beach (£E20 per person) and a couple of small shops and restaurants, but it is wise to bring extra food if you plan on staying a while. It is possible to walk from Dahab (Ras Abu Galum is approximately two hours from the Blue Hole) or you can rent a pick-up truck (£E20–30). For more in-depth exploration, the Dahab-based eco-tourism outfit, Centre for Sinai (☏069/364-0702, mobile ☏010 6660835, ⓦwww.centre4sinai.com.eg), can introduce you to a Bedouin guide familiar with the area.

Moving on from Asilah and Dahab

Buses leave from Dahab City's East Delta bus station. Of the buses to **Sharm** (9 daily; 1hr 30min; £E11), seven continue on to **El-Tor** (3hr; £E22), and there are four buses daily to **Cairo** (7–8hr; £E62; £E75 for 10pm bus), with the 8am Cairo bus stopping at **Suez** (4–5hr; £E35). There is also a bus to **Luxor** (4pm; £E110). Two buses daily go to **Zagazig** (10am & 8.30pm 6–7hr;

£E45) and **Ismailiya** (10am & 8.30pm; 6–7hr; £E42). There are three daily buses to **Nuweiba** (10.30am, 3pm & 4pm; 1hr; £E11), with the 10.30am bus continuing on to **Taba** (3hr; £E22). The daily bus to **St Catherine's** (1hr; £E16) leaves around 9.30am, but you will miss the monastery if you take this bus, so unless you want to stay overnight it's best to go on an organized trip (see p.749).

Shared taxis can be booked in advance at any of the safari agencies and at most camps; it's worth asking around, as prices can vary for the same trip. Embah Safari, near Lighthouse Beach in Masbat, offers a good-value overnight trip to St. Catherine's Monastery and Mount Sinai (£E40 per person) with a guide in a comfortable minibus. It also runs a **microbus** to Cairo (8am £E45; 11pm £E55).

Nuweiba and Tarabeen

NUWEIBA is another resort on the Gulf of Aqaba, consisting of a **port** with nearby tourist complexes, followed 4km up the coast by **Nuweiba "City"**, an administrative and commercial centre grafted on to a former Israeli *moshav* (co-operative village). During the late 1970s, thousands of Israeli and Western backpackers flocked here to party and sleep on the beach – a heyday remembered fondly by shop and campground owners. Today, tourism comes in fits and starts, picking up when Israeli students go on holiday, though much of the year the campgrounds lie dormant. For most travellers, Nuweiba serves primarily as a stepping stone for onward travel by bus to Eilat in Israel or by ferry to Aqaba in Jordan.

Nuweiba's neighbouring Bedouin settlement is called **TARABEEN**, after the local Bedouin tribe, and tends to attract younger, low-budget travellers. Before relations with Israel soured, there were more than twenty campgrounds and a few hotels on its wide and sandy beach, buzzing with restaurants and tourist bazaars; now the place is eerily empty, with only a few camps still working, waiting for the situation to improve and tourists to return. For complete peace and quiet, with only the stars overhead and the sound of the waves, undisturbed by bright lights or loud music, head to the **DUNAS**, just south of Nuweiba City, or further north to the campgrounds and cafés around **RAS AL-SHEITAN** and **BIR SWAIR**.

Arrival and information

Nuweiba's main **bus station** is at the port, though the Taba bus also stops on the highway close to Nuweiba City. **Taxis** charge £E15–20 from the port to Tarabeen, and £E10 from Nuweiba City to Tarabeen. You can walk from Nuweiba City to Tarabeen in twenty minutes along the beach; it takes slightly longer by road. Package tourists usually fly into Sharm el-Sheikh **airport**, from where shuttle buses take them to their hotels.

Accommodation

Accommodation is concentrated in three main locations: near the port, along the beach south of Nuweiba City, and in Tarabeen, a couple of kilometres north. Tarabeen is the place to find cheap **campgrounds** (❶–❷), though these tend to come and go, many evolving into hotels. If you really want to get away from it all, head south of Nuweiba City to the sand dunes of **Dunas**,

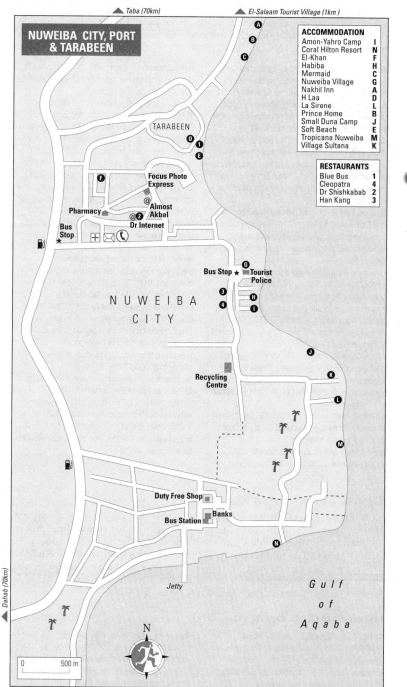

NUWEIBA CITY, PORT & TARABEEN

Taba (70km)

El-Salaam Tourist Village (1km)

TARABEEN

Focus Photo Express

@ Almost Akbal

Pharmacy

@ Dr Internet

Bus Stop

NUWEIBA CITY

Bus Stop Tourist Police

Recycling Centre

Duty Free Shop

Banks

Bus Station

Dahab (70km)

Jetty

Gulf
of
Aqaba

N

0   500 m

ACCOMMODATION

Amon-Yahro Camp	I
Coral Hilton Resort	N
El-Khan	F
Habiba	H
Mermaid	C
Nuweiba Village	G
Nakhil Inn	A
H Laa	D
La Sirene	L
Prince Home	B
Small Duna Camp	J
Soft Beach	E
Tropicana Nuweiba	M
Village Sultana	K

RESTAURANTS

Blue Bus	1
Cleopatra	4
Dr Shishkabab	2
Han Kang	3

where a couple of camps provide complete peace and quiet. Most camps do not include breakfast in the price and rates may rise dramatically during Israeli holidays.

Amon-Yahro Camp Nuweiba City, the last camp before Dunas ☎069/350-0555, mobile ☎012 7115883 ⓦwww.amonyahro.net. This clean camp has raised huts with electricity. It's run by Egyptologist Murad Said, who also takes visitors on reliable and informative trips into the desert. ❶

Coral Hilton Resort East of the port ☎069/352-0320, ⒻＧ352-0327 ⓦwww.hiltonworldresorts .com. Luxury holiday village with two heated pools and lots of sports facilities. Home to the Emperor dive centre. Non-residents can use the beach for £E45. ❽

El-Khan East of the road between Nuweiba City and Tarabeen ☎069/350-0316. Bungalows, rooms, a good restaurant, and a Bedouin handicrafts exhibition and shop. Also arranges camel and jeep safaris. ❶

La Sirene Between Nuweiba City and the port ☎069/350-0701, Ⓕ350-0702. Attractive a/c bungalows dotted along a beautiful stretch of beach, with an on-site dive centre. ❻

Habiba Nuweiba City ☎069/350-0770. Comfortable a/c bungalows and huts. Very good restaurant. Breakfast included. ❻

H Laa Central Tarabeen ☎069/350-0679. The best of several similar camps in Tarabeen: the rooms are basic, fan-cooled concrete boxes, but somewhat nicer than what's on offer in neighbouring camps. ❶

Mermaid North Tarabeen ☎069/350-0871. A mix of concrete huts and bamboo shelters on a quiet stretch of private beach. ❷

Nakhil Inn North Tarabeen ☎069/350-0879, Ⓕ350-0878, Ⓔsurf@sinainet.com.eg. Smart,

tastefully designed rooms, all with a/c, satellite TV, bath and international telephone. Children under 12 stay free. On-site dive centre. ❻

Nuweiba Village Nuweiba City ☎069/350-0402, Ⓕ350-0407. ⓦwww.nuweibaresort.com. Very comfortable a/c bungalows with TV, as well as a disco, dive centre and private beach. Free Internet access. The closest hotel to central Nuweiba City – a five-minute walk. An adjacent compound (*Red Rocks*) has beach huts sleeping three (❸), with electric lighting but no other facilities. Booking online can cut the price by half. Recommended. ❼

Prince Home North of Nuweiba City ☎069/350-0068, mobile ☎010 5385215. Perhaps Nuweiba's best value budget guesthouse, with clean, a/c rooms, on a quiet stretch of beach next to the larger *Nakhil Inn*. Recommended. ❸

Small Duna Camp South of Nuweiba City ☎069/350-0198. Basic huts and a fish restaurant, run by Mgbul Abdalla from the Mzeina tribe. ❶

Soft Beach Tarabeen, mobile ☎010 3647586. Classic Sinai beach bungalow with a dozen or so straw shacks on the sand. Located at the southern end of the main street in Tarabeen. ❶

Tropicana Nuweiba 3.5km south of *Nuweiba Village* ☎069/350-0056, Ⓕ350-0022, Ⓔtropicananuweiba@hotmail.com. Comfortable four-star branch of *Tropicana* chain. ❻

Village Sultana 2.5 km south of the *Nuweiba Village* ☎069/350-0490, ⓦwww.sinai4you .com/sultana. One of the better beach bungalows in the Dunas area, with stylish stone huts all with bathroom and a/c. ❼

Diving and snorkelling

Nuweiba has several shallow **reefs** offshore, the best of which is the **Stone House**, beyond the southern promontory; though fine for **snorkelling**, they're not so great for **diving** unless you're still a novice, so the divers that come here usually travel to Ras Abu Galum (p.737) or sites north of Nuweiba (see p.743). These trips can be arranged by any of Nuweiba's four **dive centres**: Scuba Divers at the *La Sirene* hotel, for example, has a jeep dive trip to Ras Mamleh for €60 (US$80), and an SSI Open Water course for €310 (US$415).

Nuweiba dive centres

Diving Camp Nuweiba *Nuweiba Village* ☎069/350-0403, Ⓕ350-0260, Ⓔdcn@sinainet .com.eg. PADI, CMAS.

Emperor *Coral Hilton Resort* ☎069/352-0320, Ⓕ352-0327, ⓦwww.emperordivers.com. PADI.

Trips to Ras Mamleh for €65 (US$86).

Scuba Divers *La Sirene* ☎069/350-0705, Ⓕ350-0701, ⓦwww.scuba-divers.de. SSI.

Sinai Dolphin *Nakhil Inn*, mobile ☎012 3341064, Ⓔsinaidolphin@yahoo.com. PADI.

Jeep and camel safaris

Local Bedouin guides offer a wide range of **camel or jeep safaris** into the interior. Their duration depends on your destination and mode of transport; it usually takes two or three times as long by camel as it does by jeep. Most guides charge £E100–150 per person per day (camel journeys are more expensive than jeep), which should include meals and the cost of registering the trip with the police. Drinking water may cost extra and be more expensive the further you get from shops, so it's wise to buy plenty to take along.

The nearest destinations are the palmy oasis of **Ain el-Furtaga** (which can be reached by regular car) and the colourful sandstone canyon of **Wadi Huweiyit** (by camel or 4WD). Slightly further north lies **Moyat el-Wishwashi**, a large rainwater catchment cistern hidden in a canyon between imposing boulders. All these sites can be reached by camel in a day. The most popular day excursion by jeep is to the **Coloured Canyon** (about £E50 per person) via a trail from Ain el-Furtaga. Its name comes from the vivid striations on the steep walls of the canyon, which is sheltered from the wind and eerily silent. Having got there by 4WD, you can hike through the canyon in either direction. Other destinations include **Wadi Ghazala**, with its dunes and acacia groves where gazelles may be glimpsed; **Ain Umm Ahmed**, whose deep torrent fed by snow on the highest peaks of the Sinai shrinks to a stream as the seasons advance; and the oasis of **Ain Khudra**, supposedly the Biblical Hazeroth, where Miriam was stricken with leprosy for criticizing Moses.

Recommended **guides** include Anis Anisan at *El Khan* camp (☎ & 🖷 069/350-0316), who can arrange trips for small or large groups and will try to include a Bedouin wedding, camel race or a full moon *zwara* (traditional Bedouin meeting). The all-night **Bedouin weddings** are worth seeing as they provide a rare opportunity for young Bedouin men and women to mingle; the women wear beautiful wedding shawls decorated with sequins that catch the light of the full moon while the men perform dances to impress them. Also recommended is Morad Said at *Amon-Yahro Camp* (☎069/350-0555, mobile ☎012 7115883), an English-speaking Egyptologist with plenty of insight into the Bedouin life, and Hassan Hamid at *Sun Beach Camp* (☎069/350-0889), who takes jeep tours of up to six people to Ain Khudra, Ain el-Furtag and the Coloured Canyon (£E80 per person excluding food), and also offers the same itinerary by camel (£E100 per person including food). Camel and jeep trips are also available from the *Nakhil Inn* for a similar rate, or from any of the backpacker camps around Tarabeen and Dunas. Other guides can be contacted at a kiosk near the highway at Ras al-Shaitun, 10km up the coast, which is the starting point for many excursions (see p.744).

Eating and nightlife

As an established backpacker hang-out, Tarabeen is home to a number of **budget cafés**, whose menus feature familiar dishes such as pizza, pasta and apple pancakes. Nuweiba City has less to offer, though its small shops are good for self-caterers to stock up on fresh fruit and the like. **Nightlife** boils down to a disco in the *Nuweiba Village* (£E20 admission), or playing guitars, drums or backgammon and getting stoned at Tarabeen. There are no **bars** as such; if you want a beer, try the liquor store near the shops northwest of the *Nuweiba Village*.

Restaurants

Blue Bus Tarabeen. Camp and restaurant serving reasonable fish, pasta and pizza. Nice position on the beach.

Cleopatra Nuweiba City, 220m south of *Nuweiba Village*. Egyptian-themed restaurant serving good seafood and chicken dishes. There's outdoor seating around a fountain strung with drying shark and various crustaceans.

Dr Shishkabab Nuweiba City. Sandwiches (£E10–20) and meat and vegetarian (£E15) dishes in the bazaar area. A favourite with budget travellers. The gracious Dr Shishkabab, usually around in the evenings, is happy to talk to tourists, lend travel advice, and put you in contact with guides for a desert safari. Daily 7am–1am.

Habiba Nuweiba City. Well-prepared food at this camp's beachfront buffet restaurant, which gets very busy at lunchtimes serving tourists on day-trips from Sharm el-Sheikh and Na'ama. Daily 11am–midnight.

Han Kang Nuweiba City, close to *Nuweiba Village*. Excellent Chinese-Korean restaurant. Daily 11am–2pm & 6–10pm.

Listings

Banks and exchange There's a bank in the *Nuweiba Village* (daily except Fri 9am–1pm & 6–9pm), at the *Hilton*, and in the port area.

Doctor There is a doctor on call at the *Nuweiba Village*. The hospital in Nuweiba is poorly equipped, so head for Sharm el-Sheikh if you're seriously ill; see p.721.

Film and processing Fuji Focus Photo Express on the main street in Nuweiba City sells slide and Advantix film.

Internet café Almost Akbal (daily 10am–midnight; £E6 per hour) is on the main street, and Dr Internet (daily 10am–midnight; £E6 per hour) is next to *Dr. Shishkabab*, though the former has the better connection.

Pharmacy Gasser, near *Dr Shishkabab* (daily 10am–10pm; ☏069/350-0605).

Police Near the Town Council ☏069/350-0242; the tourist police office is beside the parking lot outside the *Nuweiba Village*; both are open 24 hours.

Post office North of the 24-hour mall (daily except Fri 8am–3pm).

Telephone office Next to the post office, with international phones which take phonecards.. For local calls there is a stall with phones near *Dr Shishkabab* that also sells international newspapers.

Moving on

Some intercity **buses** trundle through Nuweiba City, but the only sure way of getting a bus south is to take a taxi to the main bus station (☏069/352-0370) at the port. Buses leave daily at 6.30am, 10am and 4pm for Dahab (1hr; £E11) and Sharm el-Sheikh (3hr; £E22), though schedules change from winter to summer and they often run late or early – call first to double check the times. Services to Taba depart daily from the bus station at 6am, 9am and 11.30am (1hr; £E10), and 5–10 minutes later from the bus stop on the highway near Nuweiba City.

Of the two buses to **Cairo**, the 10am service (7hr; £E75) runs via St Catherine's Monastery, while the 2.30pm service (£E80) travels further north across the interior of the peninsula via Nekhl. There is sometimes a 5pm Cairo bus, which has a better chance of having seats. There are other, less comfortable buses to Cairo that leave directly from Nuweiba Port; these have no fixed schedule and leave when they're full.

You might also find **service taxis** hanging around Tarabeen, bound for Taba, Dahab, Sharm el-Sheikh or St Catherine's. Prices are negotiable, so bargain hard.

Boats to Aqaba in Jordan

From Nuweiba's port (☏069/352-0427) you can catch a **ferry** or the **high-speed catamaran to Aqaba** in Jordan. For both services, it's advisable to turn up at the port two hours before the scheduled departure time, and you'll have to pay a departure tax of £E50.

The **ferry** leaves daily at 12.30pm (an extra trip is put on in the afternoon during busy periods such as the *Hadj* season) and takes 3–5 hours, depending on the weather. Foreigners must buy a first-class **ticket** (US$32 one-way), and can *only* pay in US dollars. During Ramadan or the *Hadj* season, it's a definite advantage to have access to the first-class lounge, as the boat is crowded with Egyptian workers returning home or pilgrims bound for Mecca. The ferry also carries **vehicles** (US$100). Tickets are sold inside the port's entrance; you'll need to show your passport to go through the gates, and once inside you're not allowed to leave. Foreigners are assigned an official to guide them through customs and immigration and onto the boat. Don't be surprised if it leaves much later than scheduled. On boarding you'll be asked to hand over your passport, which will be returned at Aqaba customs or, if you go searching for it, on the boat.

The **catamaran** also operates daily, departing at 2.30pm and taking about an hour. **Tickets** cost US$46 (one-way) and are definitely worth shelling out for as this vessel is far more comfortable than the ferry, though it doesn't carry cars. Formalities at Nuweiba's port are identical to those for the ferry.

Jordanian visas (valid for one month) are issued on board, or immediately after disembarkation. Things go more quickly if you've already obtained one in Cairo, but British, Canadian, US, Australian and New Zealand citizens shouldn't have any trouble getting one on the spot. Visa fees are around US$15 (payable in US$ or dinars) but can cost more depending on nationality.

If there are five or more of you travelling, you can ask for a **group visa**, which is free of charge for a minimum four-night stay. It is no longer a problem if your passport shows **evidence of a visit to Israel**, though this will still preclude entry to Syria.

If you just want to visit Petra and return, you can book trips through *Habiba* camp (T069/350-0770, W www.sinai4you.com/habiba).

Between Nuweiba and Taba

The 70km of coastline **between Nuweiba and Taba** (the border crossing into Israel) was for a long while relatively untouched, scattered with just a few appealing low-key resorts. During the 1990s, these were joined by plenty of new holiday villages and a massive tourist development called **Taba Heights**. However, since September 11, 2001 many of these resorts have been virtually empty due to the dearth of Israeli visitors, with some closing down completely. Visitor numbers took a further knock after the events of October 7, 2004, when two massive car bombs destroyed a portion of the *Taba Hilton* hotel, killing 31 people and injuring more than 120. The attack coincided with a second bombing at Ras Al-Shaitun that left three dead. The alleged ringleader, a Palestinian named Ayad Said Salah, and his Bedouin assistant were killed during the attacks, while two other bombers escaped but were later arrested. A police dragnet in El Arish (where the attacks were organized) led to the arrest of some 2400 people, many of whom are still in custody, though only five have actually been charged in connection with the incident.

It seems inevitable that business will pick up again, but in the interim, independent travellers who venture this way will get long stretches of beautiful beaches more or less to themselves. The nicer places are signposted and may be visible from the highway, depending on the terrain. **Buses** can drop you at any point along the way if you ask the driver, but bear in mind that there are no **banks** until Taba, nor anywhere to buy **food** except the pricey resort restaurants.

The first spot worth noting is **MAAGANA BEACH**, whose southern end – called **Lami Beach** – begins 8km from Tarabeen. Though its reefs are quite shallow and unimpressive, the beach itself is nice, with public showers and toilets and striking rock formations. There's a **campground** with huts (❷) and a cafeteria frequented by Bedouin who run **camel and jeep trips** to Wadi Huweiyit (see p.741) and other sites. Two kilometres further on lies the picturesque headland of **RAS AL-SHAITUN**, where the **reef** drops off sharply to the north, making it ideal for shore diving and snorkelling. *Castle Beach* resort (☏069/350-0926, mobile ☏012 7398495; ❸) has **beach bungalows** with verandahs, a good restaurant, and a shop selling souvenirs. There is a good reef for divers, and you can **rent camels** and guides for excursions to Moyat el-Wishwashi (see p.741). Several other camps nearby have a variety of accommodation, including *Ras Satan* camp (mobile ☏010 5756064; ❶), a basic place of tents and bungalows run by the affable Ayash.

If you are interested in **exploring the desert,** Ayash at *Ras Satan* can put you in contact with guides who take three- to four-day camel trips to places such as Ain Hudra and Wadi Ghazala for £E80 per person per day, or who will take you to a traditional village near Gebel Gunna in the St Catherine's Protectorate. Otherwise, try the guides who hang out on the beach or at the kiosk beside the highway.

A further 8km up the coast is the upmarket beach resort of *Bawaki* (☏069/350-0470, ⓦ www.bawaki.com; ❻), boasting a/c rooms with hot showers, a restaurant, bar and pool. It also has a few triple-bed huts (❸). Breakfast is included in the price of accommodation, but other meals are expensive.

Just beyond Bawaki, there are several more camps at **MAHASH**, which occupies a particularly fine stretch of white sandy beach with a cool breeze even on the hottest summer days. Camps here include *Yasmina*, *Ma'ayan* and *Eden*, with a small supermarket (all ❶–❷ per person). A bit further north you will find *Ananda* (mobile ☏012 2212042; ❷), a more upmarket camp with very comfortable, spacious huts, beautiful domed rooms, and a good restaurant. It is popular with groups on yoga, Tai Chi, Qi Gong and meditation holidays from Europe.

Basata

The trendiest resort in these parts is **BASATA** (Arabic for "Simplicity"), which lies by the headland of Ras el-Burqa. Created by the German-educated Sherif el-Ghamrawy, it is Egypt's most eco-friendly resort, with its own greenhouse, generator, bakery, desalination plant and school for local Bedouin children. Organic waste is fed to Basata's donkeys, goats, pigeons and ducks, or used to fertilize the fruit and vegetables. The huts are made entirely from natural materials; empty Baraka bottles are shredded and sent back to the company for recycling, and children can earn treats by collecting cigarette butts from the beach. Alcohol, drugs, television and loud music are forbidden lest they spoil the ambience, which is family-oriented with a New Age ethos. There's a communal vegetarian or fish dinner each night, and guests may help themselves in the kitchen and bakery: write down what you've taken and pay when you leave. You can store your own food in the fridge.

Such is Basata's popularity that it's advisable to **reserve ahead** (☏ & ⒻE069/350-0481, ⓦ www.basata.com; ❹). There are sixteen huts, some of them mud-brick, or you can pitch a tent on the beach. Guests can sign up for **inland safaris** (£E70 per person per day by jeep, £E100 by camel) or rent

snorkelling gear (£E24), but divers aren't welcome. You'll either feel at home with Basata's New Agers or find them unbearably cliquey.

Bir Swair and around

Five kilometres beyond Basata is *Aquasun* (☎069/530-391, ⓕ530-390; ❹), a less eco-conscious mix of bungalows with a/c and bathrooms. The quiet sandy beach has a lovely **reef**, good for **snorkelling**, although there is no dive centre. **Jeep or camel trips** can also be arranged to Wadi Quseib and other destinations. A couple of kilometres further on is *Sallyland* (☎069/353-0380, ⓕ353-0381; ❺), an a/c three-star hotel of little note except that it has one of the few **bars** in the area. Others can be found at the newish hotels along the coastal road, such as the *Sonesta* and *Safari Beach*.

Next to *Sallyland* is the Bedouin settlement of **BIR SWAIR**. Few of its camps have survived the economic downturn, but *Antica*, *Bir Swir*, and *Alexandria* will all open their doors should a tourist arrive. They all have basic but comfortable huts on one of Sinai's nicest beaches, as well as friendly staff and atmosphere (❶–❷). Guests here can visit the Bedouin village behind the camps in the mountains; you will be graciously received with tea and hospitality, but it is recommended you give them a few Egyptian pounds in return and, as ever, always ask before taking photographs.

Travellers with their own car and scuba gear can explore several wonderful **reefs** within walking distance of the highway, notably **El-Muqeibila**, 25km before Taba. Another great beach lies 3km north of Taba Heights (see below) called the **Sun Pool**, which begins with a gentle slope and then plunges as it nears the **Fjord**, a beautiful inlet in the hills by the shore. Here, you can stay at *Salima* (❹), a few rooms with communal showers, behind a nice café overlooking the Fjord.

Taba Heights

Eighteen kilometres south of Taba, the purpose-built **TABA HEIGHTS** development (ⓦwww.tabaheights.com) covers 4.5 million square metres of land and boasts 5km of beach. Dubbed the "Red Sea Riviera", this huge resort complex is based around a "village", which features a casino, watersports, dive centre, restaurants, bars, cafés, shops, bazaars and a medical centre. The resort's **hotels** are all luxurious and tend to be much cheaper if booked as part of a package in the UK. The beautifully designed *Marriott* ☎069/358-0100, ⓕ358-0109, ⓦwww.marriotthotels.com/tcpeg; ❻) is well-landscaped, with 240 rooms, most overlooking the Gulf of Aqaba, and an Arabian spa. It also has children's facilities and a travel agency. The huge five-star *Hyatt Regency Acacia* (☎069/358-0234, ⓕ358-0235, ⓦwww.taba.hyatt.com; ❽) has 426 a/c rooms with balconies, disabled rooms, six restaurants and bars, shops, three pools, a private beach, kids' club, health centre, tennis courts, shuttle bus and car rental, while the slightly smaller *Sofitel* (☎069/358-0800, ⓕ358-0808, ⓦwww.sofitel .com; ❽) has 294 a/c rooms with satellite TV, shops, laundry, health club, tennis and squash, and a dive-centre.

Pharaoh's Island

Seven kilometres before Taba you'll see **Pharaoh's Island** (*Gezirat Faraun*), known to Israelis as "Coral Island". Its barren rocks are crowned by the renovated ruins of a **Crusader fort** built in 1115 to levy taxes on Arab merchants while ostensibly protecting pilgrims travelling between Jerusalem and St Catherine's Monastery. The fort was subsequently captured by Salah al-Din but abandoned by the Arabs in 1183. Being only 250m offshore, it can be admired just as well from the mainland if you'd rather not pay US$4 for the boat ride (leaves from the *Salah al-Din* hotel; see below) and another £E20 to tour the fort, which retains several towers and passageways along with a large cistern. There's also an expensive cafeteria that only opens when there are lots of tourists around. Actually, the main reason to come is to dive or snorkel in the maze of **reefs** off the northeastern tip of the island, though, as the currents are strong and the reefs labyrinthine, it's best to be accompanied by a guide. This can be arranged at the *Salah al-Din* **hotel** (℡069/353-0340, ℻353-0343, ℮mstc@ritsec3.com.eg; ⑥, including breakfast) by the road on the mainland opposite the island (children under 12 stay free).

Taba and the border

Hugging the Gulf of Aqaba's northernmost reaches, the unassuming border town of **TABA** consists of little more than a handful of hotels, cafés, shops and a bus terminal. Its history, however, has been turbulent. Following its withdrawal from the Sinai, Israel claimed that Taba lay outside the jurisdiction of the Camp David Accords, and demanded US$60 million compensation for its return to Egypt. It took ten years of bitter negotiations until international arbitration finally returned the town to Egypt in 1989. After a period of relative calm, Taba's peace was further shattered on October 7, 2004 when a massive car bomb (see p.703) tore away a side of the *Hilton Taba Hotel*, killing 32 people. An annexe of the hotel, also known as *Nelson Village* (℡069/353-0140, ℻02/578-7044, ⓦwww.hiltonworldresorts.com; ⑧), remains open while the main building is being rebuilt, though a better **accommodation** option is the new *Tobya Boutique Hotel* (℡069/353-0275, ℻353-0269, ⓦwww .tobyaboutiquehotel.com; ⑥), on the highway 1km south of Taba. With a swimming pool and a private beach, this stylish complex is decked out in Egyptian–African themed hand-woven wool carpets, while the rooms are embellished with local crafts.

Buses from Taba run daily to **Nuweiba** (6.30am, 9am, 2pm & 3pm; £E11), **Dahab** (3pm; £E22), **Sharm el-Sheikh** (3pm; £E26.50), **Cairo** (8am, 10am & 2pm; £E55–75) and **Suez** (7am; £E40). If there are other passengers around willing to share the cost, you could get a **service taxi** to Tarabeen (around £E30), Nuweiba (£E30), Dahab (£E50) or Sharm (£E75). Alternatively, **cars** can be rented from Max, opposite the entrance to the *Hilton Taba* (mobile ℡010 5452382), for around US$60 per day.

Crossing the border

Despite recent political troubles, the **border with Israel** is still currently open 24 hours, year-round except during Yom Kippur and Eid el-Adha. Avoid crossing after mid-morning on a Friday or any time on Saturday, however, as most public transport and businesses in Israel shut down over *shabbat*. The whole process can be very quick – unless you get caught behind a large group. There's an **exit tax** of £E2 payable on leaving Egypt. The Israelis issue free three-month **visas** to EU, US, Australian and New Zealand citizens. However, if you plan on travelling to Syria or other Arab countries that do not recognize Israel, ask immigration on both sides of the border to leave your passport unstamped. Travellers must walk across a no-man's land between the Egyptian and Israeli checkpoints; from the Israeli checkpoint you catch a shared taxi or a #15 bus into Eilat.

Coming from Israel there is an NIS68 exit tax and a £E30 entry tax into Egypt. Visas can be obtained from the Egyptian Embassy in Basel Street, Tel Aviv, or the consulate on Efroni Street in Eilat (both Mon–Thurs & Sun

9–11am, allowing you to pick up the visa the same day after 2pm). Visas for UK nationals cost NIS75. If you are planning only to go to Nuweiba, Dahab, St Catherine's or Sharm el-Sheikh, you can opt for a fourteen-day **Sinai-only visa** (see p.705), issued free at the border. Don't listen to any taxi drivers who tell you that you need to take a taxi to the bus stop – it is less than five minutes' walk.

If you need to **change money**, the exchange rate on the Egyptian side, at Bank Misr, is better than the Israeli bank where you pay your exit tax. If this is closed there is another branch nearby at the *Taba Hilton*.

The interior

The **interior of Sinai** is a baking wilderness of jagged rocks, drifting sand and wind-scoured gravel pans, awesome in its desolation. Yet life flourishes around its isolated springs and water holes, or whenever rain falls, renewing the vegetation across vast tracts of semi-desert. Hinterland settlements bestride medieval pilgrimage routes, which the Turks transformed from camel tracks into dirt roads, then the Egyptians and Israelis improved and fought over. Both sides also built and bombed the airstrips which the MFO now use to monitor the Sinai's demilitarized zones.

As a result, the only readily accessible part of the interior is **St Catherine's Monastery**, **Mount Sinai** and **Feiran Oasis**, although some other, smaller oases can be reached by jeep or camel from the Aqaba coast or St Catherine's (see below). That said, most buses from Cairo to Nuweiba traverse the **Plateau of El-Tih** (The Wanderings) via **Nekhl** and the **Mitla Pass**, allowing you to see something of the peninsula's interior. Because of the unexploded ordnance lying around, **independent motoring** is officially restricted outside the St Catherine's Feiran Oasis area.

Inland safaris and treks

Though most tourists are initially attracted by Sinai's beaches and reefs, even a brief trip into the interior should prove a memorable experience that'll whet your appetite for more.

Inland safaris range from half-day excursions by jeep or camel to fully fledged treks lasting up to two weeks. Travelling **by jeep** is obviously faster and makes few or no demands on your physique, but tends to distance you from the landscape and at the worst can reduce the experience to a mere outing. This is rarely the case if you travel **by camel**, which feels totally in keeping with the terrain. If you've never ridden a camel before, try a half-day excursion before committing yourself to a longer trip. Even a few hours in the saddle can leave you with aches in muscles that you never knew existed, so it is advisable to alternate between walking and riding. It's easy to get the hang of steering: pull firmly and gradually on the nose rope to change direction; a camel should stop if you turn its head to face sideways. Couching the animal – thrusting one's face close to its muzzle and growling "*kkhhurr, kkhhurr*" – is best left to the Bedouin guides. See "Camels" in Basics chapter for advice on posture.

Safaris can be organized at any of the resorts on the Aqaba coast; you'll find details and prices listed under each resort. For those with more time and stamina, the most rewarding option is to go **trekking on foot**. Treks can be arranged at the village of St Catherine's (where you can also obtain maps for one-day walks in the area from the protectorate) or at certain points along the roads into the interior – such as the village of Sheikh Hamid – and also through many of the Bedouin who run trips from the coastal resorts. The list of destinations below is by no means all-inclusive, but should give an idea of what's on offer.

Practicalities depend on one's destination and mode of travel. Day excursions from the coast can be made on a Sinai-only visa, but to travel for any longer or explore the High Mountain Region beyond the immediate vicinity of St Catherine's Monastery and Mount Sinai you must have a proper **Egyptian visa**. To climb mountains you must also have a **permit** from the police, which can be obtained by your Bedouin guide. It is illegal – and highly risky – to go trekking without a guide. To help you select destinations and plot routes, buy the 1:250,000 *Sinai Map of Attractions*, which is sold at the main resorts on the coast. Other things to **bring** are listed in the "High Mountain Region and Feiran Oasis" section (p.755).

Finally, **respect the landscape** and leave it unspoiled. Bring plastic bags to remove your rubbish when you go and burn any toilet paper left behind. Gathering firewood should be left to your guide, and gardens should never be entered without permission from the owners.

Safari destinations

The following are all shown on the map on pp.700–701.

Ain el-Furtaga 16km from Nuweiba by road. Palmy oasis at the crossroads of trails to the Coloured Canyon, Wadi Ghazala and Ain Khudra Oasis.

Ain Khudra Oasis One of the loveliest oases in Sinai. Reached by hiking from the St Catherine's road, with help from local Bedouin, or from the south by 4WD.

Ain Kid Oasis 14km off the road between Sharm el-Sheikh and Dahab; reached via Wadi Kid, a red-walled canyon where a spring appears in rainy years. The oasis has a freshwater well.

Ain Umm Ahmed Another beautiful oasis, accessible by 4WD or camel from Bir es-Sawa. Can serve as a base for climbing expeditions to Ras el-Qalb (see below).

Arched Canyon Sinuous gorge that's only accessible on foot; drop-off and pick-up by 4WD from Ain el-Furtaga or Bir es-Sawa.

Bir es-Sawa Small oasis with a spring issuing from a cave, beside the El-Thammed road.

Blue Valley 12km from St Catherine's. Canyon painted blue by a Belgian artist in 1978.

Coloured Canyon 17km north of Ain el-Furtaga. Two rainbow-hued canyons, great for walking or rock-climbing (no water). One of the most popular day-trips from Nuweiba.

El-Haduda The biggest sand dune in eastern Sinai, reached from Sheikh Hamid (see below).

Feiran Oasis Over 12,000 palm trees, monastic remains, and access to Jebel Serbal. Wadi Feiran may have been the route taken by the Israelites to reach Mount Sinai.

Forest of Pillars Unique natural phenomenon on the cliffs of Jebel el-Tih, 15km northeast of Serabit el-Khadim (see below). Access by 4WD or camel only; guide essential.

Jebel Sabah A 2280m peak from which Saudi Arabia and mainland Egypt are visible on clear days. Experienced hikers only, with abundant food and water. Permit required.

Jebel Serbal Near Feiran Oasis. One of the loveliest mountains in Sinai, with ruined chapels lining the trail to the summit (2070m). No climbing skills needed, but guide and permit required.

Jebel Umm Shaumar The second-highest peak in Sinai, whose summit (2854m) affords a view of the entire southern horn of the peninsula. Experienced climbers only. Permit required.

Nuwamis Prehistoric site with 5550-year-old graves and inscriptions 6km from Ain Khudra. Reached on foot (2hr 30min) from Sheikh Hamid, by appointment only.

Ras el-Qalb Isolated mountain (999m) associated in Bedouin folklore with the monster Ula. For climbers only; no water. Permit required.

Serabit el-Khadim Hilltop temple overlooking the Gulf of Suez, with ancient turquoise mines and inscriptions in the surrounding valleys. Access by 4WD, then on foot.

Sheikh Hamid Bedouin settlement on the road to St Catherine's, 7km from the Dahab–Nuweiba road. Starting point for walking or camel treks to Ain Khudra, Nuwamis, El-Haduda, and remoter destinations (up to two weeks).

Wadi Ghazala Links Ain el-Furtaga and Ain Khudra Oasis. Acacia groves, dunes and gazelles.

Wadi Huweiyit North of Nuweiba. Colourful canyon with typical desert flora; easy hiking.

Wadi Mandar 40km north of Sharm el-Sheikh. Bedouin camel races occur here on January 1.

Wadi Naseb Running down from Mount Catherine towards Dahab, the verdant upper reaches of the *wadi* are inhabited by Bedouin. 4WD essential.

St Catherine's Monastery and Mount Sinai

Venerated by Christians, Jews and Muslims as the site of God's revelation of the Ten Commandments, **Mount Sinai** overlooks the valley where Moses is said to have heard the Lord speaking from a burning bush.

The bush is now enshrined in **St Catherine's Monastery**, nestling in a valley at the foot of the Mount, surrounded by high walls and lush gardens. As tourists have followed pilgrims in ever greater numbers the sacred mount has witnessed unseemly quarrels between Bedouin over the shrinking amount of sleeping space for the climbers at the peak, and the monastery itself shows signs of strain. Yet for most travellers it remains a compelling visit, while other seldom-visited peaks offer equally magnificent views if you're prepared to make the effort to reach them.

Getting there – and moving on

Despite its isolated location, St Catherine's is one of the most accessible parts of South Sinai. You can visit on **organized tours** from Na'ama Bay, Dahab, Nuweiba, Cairo, Hurghada or Eilat, or you can make your own way by bus, car or service taxi.

The main drawback to **buses** are their variable schedules and the fact that they rarely get to St Catherine's Monastery before it shuts at noon. If you want to visit, you should consider **staying** at least one night. A daily bus leaves Cairo's Abbassiya terminal at 11am for St Catherine's village via Feiran Oasis (7hr; £E55). Services from the Aqaba resorts turn off the highway between Dahab and Nuweiba; they start from Sharm el Sheikh's Hay el–Nur bus station (9.30am), Dahab (9.30am), Nuweiba (10.30am) and Taba (10am). All buses stop about 10km before the monastery at a petrol station/police checkpoint/ticket office for the Saint Catherine protectorate, where foreigners must purchase a **ticket** (US$3) to enter the area.

If you are coming by bus and just want to climb Mount Sinai, ask to be dropped at the turn-off for the monastery, 1.5km before St Catherine's village. Alternatively, you could take a **guided overnight trip** from Dahab or Sharm el-Sheikh, which includes a moonlit ascent of Mount Sinai, sleeping at the peak and returning to the monastery in the morning after sunrise. The village's restaurants are pick-up points for people **leaving** by bus; most depart between noon and 1pm, except for the Suez bus, which goes at 6am.

For a group of travellers, another option is to engage a **service taxi** at Suez, Dahab, Nuweiba or Taba and split the cost. Taxis usually run in the morning and afternoon if enough customers are interested, raising their fares once the last bus has left. The same goes for taxis leaving St Catherine's, which run to Dahab and other places, depending on demand.

The Monastery of St Catherine

The **Monastery of St Catherine** is a Greek Orthodox – rather than Coptic – foundation. Its origins date back to 337 AD, when the Byzantine **Empress Helena** ordered the construction of a chapel around the putative **Burning Bush**, already a focus for hermits and pilgrimages. During the sixth century, the site's vulnerability to raiders persuaded Emperor Justinian to finance a fortified enclosure and basilica, and to supply two hundred guards – half of them Greeks or Slavs – from whom the Jebeliya Bedouin claim descent.

Although the Prophet Mohammed is said to have guaranteed the monastery's protection after the Muslim conquest, the number of monks gradually dwindled until the "discovery" of St Catherine's relics (see p.756), which ensured a stream of pilgrims and bequests during the period of Crusader domination (1099–1270). Since then, it has had cycles of expansion and decline, on occasion being totally deserted. There are currently 22 monks, most of whom came here from the monasteries of Mount Athos in Greece.

Visiting the monastery

The monastery is **open** to visitors from 9am till noon. It's officially closed on Fridays, Sundays and on all Greek Orthodox holidays, but will sometimes open from 11am to noon on these days, in order to accommodate tourist demands. There is no admission charge, but visitors must be modestly dressed.

You enter through a small gate in the northern wall near **Kléber's Tower** (named after the Napoleonic general who ordered its reconstruction) rather

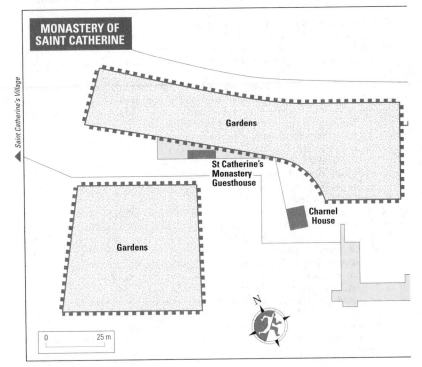

MONASTERY OF SAINT CATHERINE

Saint Catherine's Village

Gardens

St Catherine's Monastery Guesthouse

Charnel House

Gardens

0   25 m

than the main portal facing west, which has a funnel that was used for pouring boiling oil onto attackers. Built of granite, 10–15m high and 2–3m thick, St Catherine's **walls** are essentially unchanged since Stephanos Ailisios designed them in the sixth century.

As you emerge from the passage, a right turn takes you past **Moses' Well**, where the then-fugitive from Egypt met Zipporah, one of Jethro's seven daughters, whom he married at the age of 40. Walking the other way and around the corner, you'll see a thorny evergreen bush outgrowing an enclosure. This is the transplanted descendant of the **Burning Bush** whence God spoke to Moses: "Come now therefore, and I will send thee unto Pharaoh, that thou mayest bring forth my people the children of Israel out of Egypt" (Exodus 3:10). Sceptics may be swayed by the fact that it's the only bush of its kind in the entire peninsula and that all attempts to grow cuttings from it elsewhere have failed. The bush was moved to its present site when Helena's chapel was built over its roots, behind the apse of St Catherine's church.

A granite basilica, **St Catherine's Church** was erected by Justinian between 542 and 551; the walls and pillars and the cedarwood doors between the narthex and nave are all original. Its twelve pillars – representing the months of the year and hung with icons of the saints venerated during each one – have ornately carved capitals, loaded with symbolism. At the far end, a lavishly carved and gilded iconostasis rises towards a superb mosaic depicting Jesus flanked by Moses and Elijah, with Peter, John and James kneeling below – unfortunately it's roped off and hard to see behind the ornate chandeliers suspended from the

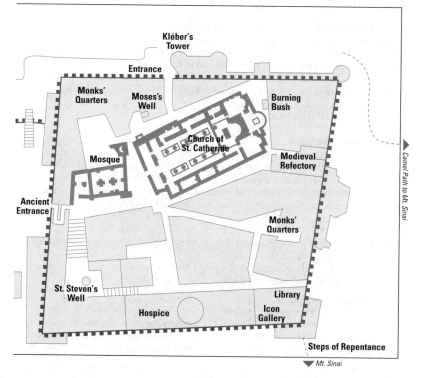

coffered, eighteenth-century ceiling. Behind the iconostasis is the **Chapel of the Burning Bush**, only viewable by special dispensation. The narthex displays a selection of the monastery's vast collection of **icons**, running the gamut of Byzantine styles and techniques, from encaustic wax to tempera. The church's **bell** is rung 33 times to rouse the monks before dawn.

Other parts of the monastery are often closed to laypersons. Amongst them are an eleventh-century **mosque**, added to placate Muslim rulers; a **library** of over 3000 manuscripts and 5000 books, surpassed only by the Vatican's; and a **refectory** with Gothic arches and Byzantine murals. You can usually enter the **charnel house**, however, which is heaped with monks' skeletons; the cemetery itself is small, so corpses have to be disinterred after a year and moved into the ossuary. The cadaver in vestments is Stephanos, a sixth-century guardian of one of the routes to the Mount.

St Catherine's village

While the monastery and Mount Sinai are the focus of interest, most of the facilities of use to tourists are in the **village of St Catherine**, 3km away. Shared taxis provide **transport** between the two, charging £E5. The road terminates at the village's main square, which acts as the bus station. On one side is an arcade containing a **bank** (Mon–Thurs & Sun 8.30am–2pm & 6–9pm), several supermarkets and restaurants; on the other side are the **tourist police** and a small **hospital**. In the vicinity of the mosque are a **post office** and **telephone exchange**.

There's little to choose between the **restaurants** (6am–10pm), which do simple meals of chicken and rice or spaghetti Bolognese – the *Panorama* also serves soup and pizzas (£E20–25). A **bakery** opposite the mosque sells pitta bread.

For **short walks** in the area, guide maps can be purchased from the St Catherine Protectorate visitor centre and Bedouin museum at the end of the road before the monastery If you're planning to do any trekking in the High Mountain Region, ask locals to point you towards **El-Milga**, uphill past the main square of the village (about 150m northwest of the Co-Op petrol station), where you'll find **Sheikh Mousa** (☎069/347-0457, mobile ☎010 6413575, ✉sheikmousa@yahoo.com), the chief of the Bedouin guides who lead expeditions. For more details, see "The High Mountain Region and Feiran Oasis", p.755.

Accommodation

Most people on tours arrive in the early hours to climb Mount Sinai and **catch the sunrise** before descending again. Independent travellers, however, can leave their packs in the monastery's storeroom (£E2) and ascend the camel path to **sleep out**. With nighttime temperatures around 10°C during summer and near zero over winter (when frosts and snow aren't uncommon), a sleeping bag is essential if you plan to do this; you can also rent blankets on the summit. Note, however, that with so many people wanting to sleep out, there is often little room at the top, and you may have to sleep further down the mountain at Elijah's Hollow (see p.755) and complete the journey before sunrise. The best bet for budget travellers is one of the two **campgrounds** near St. Catherine's village, though most of those that are further away will arrange transport.

Daniela Village St Catherine's village ☎ & ℱ069/347-0379. a/c rooms with baths; plus a restaurant, cafeteria and bar. ❼

El Malga Bedouin Camp 150m past the Co-Op gas station in St. Catherine's village

☎069/347-0457, mobile ☎010 6413575, ✉sheikmousa@yahoo.com. Welcoming lodge with basic double rooms and dorms (£E15), with mattresses on the floor. Very clean bathrooms. Ask for Salah, if you want to do some desert trekking. ❷

El Wadi El Mouqudus Between *Katherine Plaza* and *Daniela Village* ℡ 069/347-0225. Friendly management and spacious three-star rooms with fridge and TV, plus a swimming pool in summer. Half-board only. ❻

Fox Desert Camp 800m from the village, near the main intersection ℡ 069/347-0344, mobile ℡ 010 5659399. This backpacker hang-out is the cheapest place in the area, with basic stone cabins and moth-eaten mattresses. You can camp for £E7 and use the communal showers and restaurant. ❶

Katherine Plaza Just outside the village ℡ 069/347-0289. Smart four-star place with a/c rooms, restaurant and bar. ❼

Morgen Land Village 5km from the monastery ℡ 069/347-0700, ℉ 347-0331. Dorm beds (US$10) or large rooms with showers; there's also a restaurant. ❺

Safary Camp and Hotel 500m from the village behind *Katherine Plaza*, also known as 'Moonland.' ℡ 069/347-0085, mobile ℡ 069 3470162, ✉ mnland2002@yahoo.com. The only budget place around where you can sleep on a bed rather than a mattress on the floor. Its doubles and triples are popular with backpackers and overlanders, or you can camp for £E10. Recommended in this price range. ❷, including breakfast.

St Catherine's Monastery Guesthouse St Catherine's Monastery ℡ 069/347-0353. Located just outside the monastery walls, and sheltered by the towering red cliffs of Mt Sinai, this hotel has a dramatic setting unmatched in the Sinai. Such glorious views do not come cheap, however, and the ensuite twin-bedded rooms are small and basic. ❻

St Catherine Tourist Village By the main road, 500m from the monastery ℡ 069/347-0333, ℉ 347-0323. The smartest hotel in the area, with comfortable a/c apartments; breakfast and dinner included. ❼

Ascending Mount Sinai

Whilst some archeologists question whether **Mount Sinai** was really the Biblical mountain where Moses received the Ten Commandments, it's hard not to agree with John Lloyd Stephens that "among all the stupendous works of Nature, not a place can be selected more fitting for the exhibition of Almighty power". A craggy, sheer-faced massif of grey and red granite "like a vengeful dagger that was dipped in blood many ages ago", its loftiest peak rises 2285m above sea level. Strictly speaking, it's only this that the Bedouin call *Jebel Musa* ("Mount Moses"), though the name is commonly applied to the whole massif. Some Biblical scholars reckon that Moses proclaimed the Commandments from Ras Safsafa, at the opposite end of the ridge, which overlooks a wide valley where the Israelites could have camped.

Walking to the summit

Neither of the two **routes to the summit** requires a guide, but you shouldn't attempt the walk at night without a torch, and certainly not in winter – accidents are not uncommon.

The longer but easier route is via the switchback **camel path**, starting 50m behind the monastery. It's possible to rent a camel for most of the ascent from Bedouins hanging out at the foot of the mount (£E40; £E15 at midday; 2hr), but it's really worth the effort of walking, which takes around two to three hours. You can stock up on water at the monastery shop before setting off, and there are refreshment stalls along the way. Their prices are higher the higher you go, but it will save you carrying extra weight. Bedouin entrepreneurs at the peak rent out blankets and mattresses for the night (£E5–10).

Beyond the cleft below the summit, the path is joined by the other route, known as the *Sikket Saiyidna Musa* ("Path of Our Lord Moses") or **Steps of Repentance**. Hewn by a penitent monk, the 3750 steps make a much steeper ascent from the monastery (1hr 30min), which is hell on the leg muscles. Some of the steps are a metre high.

△ A trader on Jebel Musa, Mount Sinai

Two buildings top the summit, a mosque and a Greek Orthodox church, both usually locked. Next to the mosque is the cave where God sheltered Moses: "I will put thee in a cleft of the rock, and will cover thee with my hand while I pass over" (Exodus 33:22). A little lower down the slope, a bunch of semi-permanent structures have sprung up, offering weary travellers a place to sleep.

Many people ascend by the camel path and descend by the steps. Start your ascent around 5pm (earlier during winter) to avoid the worst of the heat and arrive in time to watch the spellbinding sunset. With a torch, you could also climb the camel path (but not the steps) by night, though not during winter. Descending the steps you'll enter a depression containing a 500-year-old cypress tree, known as the Plain of Cypresses or **Elijah's Hollow**, where pilgrims pray and sing. Here Elijah heard God's voice (I Kings 19:9–18) and hid from Jezebel, being fed by ravens. One of the two chapels is dedicated to him, the other to his successor, Elisha.

The High Mountain Region and Feiran Oasis

The area around St Catherine's is sometimes termed the **High Mountain Region**, as it contains numerous peaks over 2000 metres (6500 feet). Snow frequently covers the ground in winter and flash floods can occur at any time of the year. The scenery is fantastic, with phalanxes of serrated peaks looming above *wadis* full of tumbled boulders and wiry fruit trees; springs that are mere trickles in summer turn into waterfalls over winter. This harsh but beguiling land is the stamping ground of the Jebeliya and Aulad Said tribes, some of whom act as guides for **treks** on foot or by camel; with a few exceptions, the terrain is too rough for vehicles, even with 4WD. The trekking season runs from March to October. By law, foreigners are forbidden to embark on such expeditions without a Bedouin guide.

The main **starting point** for treks is the village of **El-Milga** near St Catherine's (see p.752), where Sheikh Mousa will get things organized. He'll take your passport, register it with the police, purchase food and water, and work out all the details of the expedition. An all-inclusive trek, including guide, food and transport, costs around US\$30 per day. Even if you're going to walk, you'll need a camel to carry your baggage; surplus gear can be left at the sheikh's house. The ideal number of trekkers is three to five people; larger groups travel more slowly. You'll need comfortable hiking boots, warm clothes, a sleeping bag, sunglasses, sunscreen, lip salve, bug repellent and toilet paper. Though Sheikh Mousa can provide eating utensils, you'll need to bring water purification tablets unless you're willing to drink from springs. To make sense of the landscape, it's essential to have a good map of South Sinai (see p.748) and a compass.

Mount Catherine, Blue Valley and other walks

Egypt's highest peak, **Mount Catherine** (*Jebel Katerina*; 2642m), lies roughly 6km south of Mount Sinai, and can be reached on foot in five to six hours. The path starts behind St Catherine's village and runs up the Wadi el-Leja on

Mount Sinai's western flank, past the deserted Convent of the Forty and a Bedouin hamlet. Shortly afterwards the trail forks, the lower path winding off up a rubble-strewn canyon, Shagg Musa, which it eventually quits to ascend Mount Catherine – a straightforward but exhausting climb. On the summit are a chapel with water, a meteorological station and two rooms for pilgrims to stay overnight. The **panoramic view** encompasses most of the peninsula, from Hammam Faroun and the Wilderness of the Wanderings to the Arabian mountains beyond the Gulf of Aqaba.

According to tradition, it was on this peak that priests found the remains of **St Catherine** during the ninth or tenth century. Believers maintain that she was born in 294 AD in Alexandria of a noble family, converted to Christianity and subsequently lambasted Emperor Maxentius for idolatry, confounding fifty philosophers who tried to shake her faith. Following an attempt to break her on a spiked wheel (hence Catherine Wheels), which shattered at her touch, Maxentius had her beheaded; her remains were transported to Sinai by angels. Others doubt that she ever existed and regard her cult as an invention of Western Catholicism, validated by "the land of her supposed sufferings" because of medieval France's demand for "holy oil" and other relics.

If climbing Mount Catherine seems too ambitious, consider visiting the **Blue Valley**, 5km southeast of the intersection of the roads to St Catherine's, Nuweiba and Feiran Oasis. You can do this as a day-trip from Dahab or in half a day from St Catherine's village by renting a jeep and guide. The canyon's name derives from a Belgian who in 1978 painted its rocks a deep blue in emulation of the Bulgarian artist Christo, who hung drapes across the Grand Canyon and wrapped up the Reichstag in Berlin.

Longer treks

The two **four-day treks** outlined below give an idea of what can be done; some other possibilities are mentioned under "Feiran Oasis" (see opposite).

Starting off in **El-Milga**, the **first trek** begins by taking the path through the **Abu Giffa Pass** down into Wadi Tubug, passing walled gardens en route to Wadi Shagg, where you'll find Byzantine ruins and huge boulders. From there you proceed to a grove of olive trees reputedly planted by the founder of the Jebeliya tribe, where you spend the night. The next day you follow the trail through Wadi Gibal and climb one of two peaks offering magnificent views, before descending to Farash Rummana, a camping spot with showers. On the third day you strike north through a canyon to the water holes of Galt al-Azraq, pushing on to camp out at Farsh Umm Sila or Farsh Tuweita. The final day begins with an easy hike down towards Wadi Tinya, before climbing Jebel Abbas Pasha (2383m), named after the paranoid ruler who built a palace there (now in ruins). Having retrieved your gear at the foot of the mountain, you follow a path down through the Zuweitun and Tubug valleys, back to Abu Giffa and El-Milga.

The **second trek** starts at **Abu Sila** village, 3km from El-Milga, where there are some rock inscriptions. You'll probably camp out near the sweetwater spring of Bustan el-Birka. Day two involves descending into Wadi Nugra, below Jebel el-Banat, where you can relax and bathe in pools fed by a twenty-metre-high waterfall. You then press on along the path through Wadi Gharba to the tomb of Sheikh Awad, where the Aulad Gundi tribe holds an annual feast in his honour. Having spent the night here, you have a choice of three routes to Farsh Abu Tuweita, the final night's camping spot. On the fourth day you follow the same route as the final leg of the other hike, visiting Abbas Pasha's ruined palace before returning to El-Milga.

Feiran Oasis

It's thought that the ancient Israelites reached Mount Sinai by the same route that buses coming from the west use today, via Wadi Feiran and Wadi el-Sheikh. Travelling this road in the other direction, you might glimpse the **Tomb of Nabi Salah** near the **Watiyyah Pass**, where Bedouin converge for an annual **moulid** on the Prophet Mohammed's birthday. Celebrants smear themselves with "lucky" tomb dust, sacrifice sheep, race camels, bury their dead and pray, before enacting a rodeo and feasting on roast camel stuffed with lamb. Beyond the pass lies El-Tafra, a small and dismal oasis village.

Roughly 60km from St Catherine's the road passes a huge walled garden marking the start of **FEIRAN OASIS**. A twisting, granite-walled valley of palms and tamarisks, the oasis belongs to all the tribes of the *Tawarah*, who have houses and wells here. (Elsewhere, intertribal law permits the grazing of animals and pitching of tents on any land, but not the cutting of wood or building of stone houses.) Feiran was the earliest Christian stronghold in the Sinai, with its own bishop and **convent**, ruined during the seventh century but now rebuilt. Further back in time, this was reputedly the *Rephidim* of the Amalakites, who denied its wells to the thirsty Israelites, causing them to curse Moses until he smote the Rock of Horeb with his staff, making water gush forth. Refreshed, they joined battle with the Amalakites the next day, inspired by the sight of Moses standing on a hilltop, believed to have been the conical one that the Bedouin call **Jebel el-Tannuh**, with ruined chapels lining the track to its summit (1hr).

Other **hiking** possibilities in the area include **Jebel el-Banat** (1510m), further north, and the highly challenging ascent of **Jebel Serbal** (2070m), south of the oasis. This is approached via the rugged Wadi Aleyat, with a few springs at its upper end. From here you can either follow a goat track up a steep, boulder-strewn ravine called Abu Hamad (5hr), or take the longer but less precipitous *Sikket er-Reshshah* ("Path of the Sweaty") to the summit. From the main peak on the ridge there's a wonderful view of the oasis, countless mountains and *wadis*, with a narrow ledge jutting over a 1200m precipice.

As for finding a guide, make arrangements in El-Milga; a service taxi to Feiran costs £E70 for a group. Although Feiran Oasis lacks any tourist **accommodation**, you could probably camp out somewhere in the palm groves with local consent.

The Wilderness of the Wanderings

Separating the granite peaks of South Sinai from the sandy wastes of the north is a huge tableland of gravel plains and fissured limestone, riven by *wadis*: the **Wilderness of the Wanderings** (*Badiet el-Tih*). Life exists in this desert thanks to sporadic rainfall between mid-October and mid-April; two or three down-pours are enough to send yellow torrents surging down the *wadis*, rejuvenating the hardy vegetation that supports wildlife and refilling the cisterns that irrigate groves of palms and tamarisks. During Byzantine times, these cisterns sustained dozens of villages along the Sinai–Negev border; nowadays, the largest irrigated gardens are in Wadi Feiran and Wadi el-Arish.

Crossing the Wilderness via Nekhl and the Mitla Pass

The shortest route between Nuweiba and Cairo (470km; 6–7hr) crosses the great Wilderness via Nekhl and the Mitla Pass, more or less following the old *Darb el-Hadi* pilgrimage trail between Suez and Aqaba. By day the heat-hazed plateau is stupefyingly monotonous and it's hard not to fall asleep, which would mean missing a glimpse of several historic locations.

The road from Nuweiba heads north to El-Thammed before cutting west across Wadi el-Arish. **NEKHL**, at the heart of the peninsula, features a **derelict castle** built by Sultan al-Ghuri in 1516 and a big MFO observation post. South of one of the *wadi's* many tributaries lies **Qalat el-Gundi** ("Fortress of the Soldier"), a **ruined fort** built by Salah al-Din, which can also be reached by a track from Ras Sudr, on the Gulf of Suez. The fort stands atop a small mountain about one hour's climb from the road; be extremely careful when ascending the path, as there's a sheer drop on either side.

Moving west, the road descends through the 480-metre-high **Mitla Pass**, one of three cleavages in the central plateau. When Ralph Bagnold attempted this route, from Cairo, by Model-T Ford in the early 1920s, it was choked with "yellow undulating cushions" of sand that buried the wire-mesh road laid by the British during World War I. The outcome of three Arab-Israeli conflicts was arguably determined at the Mitla Pass in some of the bloodiest **tank battles** in history. During the war of 1956, an Israeli parachute battalion seized and held the road until the arrival of armoured columns from El-Thammed, which dominated the interior. Having deployed their tanks in expectation of a similar strategy, the Egyptians were wrongfooted during the 1967 War, when the Israelis advanced from Abu Ageila (in the northeast), captured the passes and then systematically annihilated their encircled foes, leaving the roadside littered with charred remains. In the October War of 1973, Egyptian forces failed to exploit their breakthrough along the Bar-Lev Line by rapidly seizing the Mitla and Giddi passes; many blamed their subsequent defeat on the cautiousness of the commander-in-chief, General Ismail.

Northern Sinai

While jagged mountains dominate the gulf coasts and interior of the peninsula, **northern Sinai** is awash with sand: pale dunes rising from coastal salt marshes and lagoons to meet gravel plains and *wadis* far inland. A succession of water holes along the coastal strip between Egypt and Palestine has made this *Via Maris* the favoured route for trade and invasions since late pharaonic times. However, few of the settlements have ever amounted to much, nor deserve a visit nowadays. Although the palmy beaches at **El-Arish** have spawned a popular domestic holiday resort, most foreigners just zip through on direct buses between Cairo and Tel Aviv or Jerusalem, crossing the border at **Rafah**. This divided frontier town has been the subject of heated political tensions since 2003, when Egypt discovered thirty tunnels dug beneath its side of the border, which were widely regarded as the main conduit for smuggling contraband weapons and drugs between Egypt and Gaza. The discovery led to a stepping up of patrols and arrests of alleged smugglers and tunnel diggers, many of whom had been operating since the 1980s.

No north–south transport is available to foreigners across the Sinai peninsula, so the only way to travel **between the Mediterranean and Aqaba coasts** is via Cairo and Suez. It's quickest to do this by **service taxi**, changing at Ismailiya and then again at Suez (or vice versa).

The road from Suez to El-Arish

The dominant impression of the road to El-Arish is of a string of **new towns** consisting of huge apartment buildings and named after hitherto insignificant villages based around wells. Whereas nineteenth-century guidebooks compared the merits of vital watering holes like **Bir el–Abd** ("brackish water and some telegraph-men's huts") and **Mazar** ("it is better not to camp near the well on account of the camel ticks"), modern travellers can drive past without a qualm. Between these towns lie ramshackle villages where the local Bedouin are being induced to settle (see box below), interspersed by golden **sand dunes** up to 50m high and 200m long.

Bedouin culture

Although the provision of schools, medical posts and water tanks has enticed many **Bedouin** to forsake nomadic lives, others still roam the desert with their flocks. From the El-Arish road you can glimpse girls in peacock robes with hennaed tresses, aloof boys and men, and black-garbed women in veils or leather masks spangled with coins – the colour of the cross-stitched embroidery on their robes and hoods indicates whether they are married (red) or not (blue). On the horizon you may see black tents pitched in the desert; women are responsible for weaving the goat-hair *beit shaar* ("house of hair") and striking, unloading, packing and erecting them whenever the family moves on. In Bedouin divorces the husband gets the domestic animals while the woman keeps the tent.

The Bedouin are keen observers of the Sinai's furtive **wildlife**. Hares and foxes can lead them to water holes; desert sandgrouse, gazelles and the rare mountain ibex (*bedan*) make good hunting; and flocks must be guarded against the depredations of the jackal (*taaleb*), wolf (*dib*) and hyena (*dhaba*). The last has a mythological counterpart, the *dhabia*, believed to have the power to mesmerize solitary travellers into entering its lair. Other creatures imbued with supernatural significance are the dreaded horned viper, known as *Abu Jenabiya* ("Father of Going Sideways"), and the fox – personifying wisdom and cunning – who is a favourite character in children's tales.

Plants are even more important to the Bedouin, who feed their camels on a prickly tribulus called *ghraghada* and make extensive use of **herbal medicine**. Among the many remedies, *rabla* is an aromatic flower made into an essential oil that's used as a general pick-me-up; while *handl* seeds are ground into a paste, cooked in olive oil and applied in a bandage to aching joints, or mixed with garlic to treat snake or scorpion bites.

Storytelling holds a special place in Bedouin culture, where poetic imagery and Koranic rhetoric sprang naturally from the lips of shepherds exposed to a rich oral heritage since childhood. When food is lacking for guests, hospitality can still be rendered in words: "Had I known that you would honour me by walking this way, I should have strewn the path between your house and mine with mint and rose petals!". Although professional reciters of Arabic poetry are now rare, most Bedouin can reel off folk tales, which usually begin with the phrase *"Kan ma kan . . ."* ("There was, there was not").

Conversation is the expected reward for Bedouin **hospitality**, which traditionally stretched to three days, each named after a stage in the ritual: *salaam* ("greeting"), *ta'aam* ("eating") and *kelaam* ("speaking"). Before the rising of the morning star on the fourth day, hosts helped their guests prepare for departure; those who lingered beyond the drying of the dew were as welcome "as the spotted snake". Honour can now be satisfied by three servings of tea or coffee, and it's no longer mandatory to slaughter an animal.

Pelusium

Roughly 40km along the road to El-Arish from Qantara you pass a signposted turn-off for **PELUSIUM**, a fortress town that guarded Egypt's eastern border for many centuries, named after the Pelusiac branch of the Nile that once watered its surroundings. Many stories are attached to what the Bible records as the "Strength of Egypt". The Assyrian king Sennacherib lost 185,000 soldiers after swarms of rats ate their bows and quivers, while the army of Cambyses is said to have induced Pelusium's garrison here to surrender without a fight by driving cats (the sacred animal of the goddess Bastet) before them. Here the Roman general Pompey was murdered on the orders of Ptolemy XII, and the Crusader king Baldwin I died of ptomaine poisoning after eating putrid fish.

Although the Pelusiac branch of the Nile started to dry up in the third century AD, the city remained inhabited well into the Islamic era, before being abandoned to the sands. In recent years, moves to bring 400,000 *feddans* of land under cultivation by digging the **Al-Salaam Canal** through this region have spurred a rash of **excavations** to recover archeological evidence before it is destroyed. The sites range from Qantara by the Suez Canal to Tell el-Mahraf near El-Arish. At Pelusium, they have uncovered parts of the pharaonic town and a **Roman amphitheatre** that can now be visited by tourists (daily 9am–5pm) – though since you need a car to get there, and official permission to tour the site, it seldom receives visitors.

El-Arish

Originally a Roman garrison town named *Rhinocolorum* ("Noses Cut Off") after the fate of dissidents exiled there, **EL-ARISH** has experienced more than its fair share of invasions. Until recently this was a popular resort for domestic tourists, attracted by the palm-shaded beaches and bracing rollers, but events over the border in Gaza and the souring of relations between Israel and Egypt have meant that many Egyptians are eschewing El-Arish for other Mediterranean resorts such as Alexandria. Westerners have been slow to sample the life here, which is why the tourist poster advertising El-Arish superimposes their images on the beach.

Whether through cause or effect, El-Arish is more **conservative** than the Aqaba coast resorts, with restrictions on booze and dress and a relatively subdued nightlife. However, for a group of travellers prepared to rent a beach apartment and provide their own entertainment, El-Arish could be the place. Its most attractive feature is a mass of **palm groves** on the outskirts, which are unfortunately being whittled away as more and more holiday villas are built. Considered the back of beyond even by Egyptians, the quiet town was thrust into the spotlight in October 2004, when it was discovered that the terrorist attacks in the southern Sinai were masterminded from here. This revelation led to a wave of arrests, though the vast majority of these alleged perpetrators languish in prison without charge.

Arrival and accommodation

El-Arish is served by **buses** from Cairo's Turgoman terminal (6 daily; 5hr; £E16–22) and Ismailiya's main terminal (6 daily; 3hr; £E7), as well as **service taxis** from Ismailiya (£E7), and from the east bank of Qantara (2hr 30min; £E7). EgyptAir **flights** from Cairo to El-Arish (Thurs & Sun; 1hr; US$109 one-way) run in summer only.

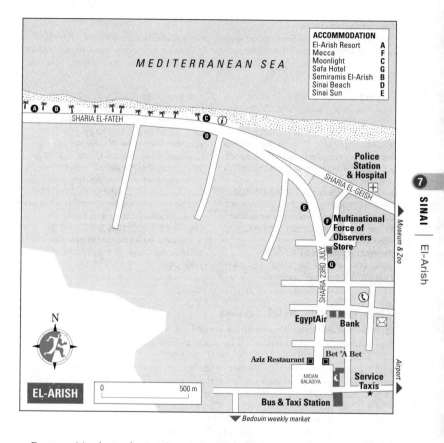

Bedouin weekly market

From a visitor's standpoint there are really only two streets in town. Arriving from the west, you'll cruise along **Sharia El-Fateh** – parallel to the beach – until it swings inland and downhill to become **Sharia 23rd July**. This eventually turns into a **souk** of wooden-shuttered stores that look like a set from a Wild West movie, and terminates in **Midan Baladiya**, with its raucous mosque and fuming **bus station**. Minibuses (50pt) and service taxis (50–75pt) constantly shuttle between the souk and the beach, sparing you the 2–3km walk and stopping at any point along the way.

The **tourist police** (☎068/335-3400) and a largely useless **information** kiosk (☎068/336-3743; Sat–Thurs 9am–2pm) share a building on El-Fetah, in front of the *Sinai Beach Hotel*; the main **police** station (☎122) and **hospital** (☎068/336-1077) lie east along Sharia el-Geish, which forks off inland. There is a better equipped **Mubarak Military Hospital** (☎068/332-4018) near the North Sinai Governate in Dahiya. One block north of Sharia 23rd July, a side street leads to a **bank**, **post office** (daily except Fri 8am–2pm), 24-hour **telephone exchange** (international calls possible, but no card-phones), and the EgyptAir office.

Accommodation

Outside of the July–September season there shouldn't be any problem **finding somewhere to stay**. The string of beachside hotels tend to be either overpriced or dirt-cheap hovels, so check out the town itself for good-value options.

El-Arish Resort Across from the beach on Sharia El-Fateh ☎068/335-1321, ⓕ335-2352. Well-kept singles, doubles and triples, with a nightclub, pool, tennis courts and the only bar in El-Arish. Non-residents can pay £E25 to use the beach and pool. The rooms are expensive in peak season, but you can usually get a discount of up to 40 percent out of season. ❽

Mecca Sharia El Salam ☎ & ⓕ068/335-2632. Welcoming hotel on a quiet street, one block east of Sharia 23rd July. Its clean rooms are probably the best value budget accommodation in town. ❷, including breakfast.

Moonlight Mobile ☎012 7022516. Passable rooms within earshot of the lapping waves. It's not a bad option, though rather scruffy. ❷

Safa Hotel Sharia 23rd July ☎068/335-3798. Friendly staff, and reasonable rooms with showers and fans. Has a rooftop restaurant with nice views, and a laundry service. Look for the green 'hotel' sign, 150m north of the Mr. Kodak store. ❷

Semiramis El-Arish Sharia El-Fateh ☎068/336-4166, ⓕ336-4167. Singles and doubles far from the beach, as well as pricier Med-facing suites. ❻

Sinai Beach Sharia El-Fateh ☎068/336-1713. Doubles and triples with private bathrooms and a/c, some with balconies overlooking the sea. ❺

Sinai Sun Sharia 23rd July ☎068/336-1855, ⓕ336-3855. Decent rooms of all sizes with balconies, bathrooms, a/c and TV. A good mid-range choice. ❹

The beach and town

Despite the huts and chalets lining several kilometres of **beach**, you can still find uncrowded stretches shaded by palm trees, the odd wrecked anti-aircraft gun adding a surreal touch. With cooler, rougher seas than the Aqaba coastline, and no reefs, El-Arish's beach is better for bracing dips and idle sunbathing than snorkelling or diving (there's no dive shop, anyway). Foreigners often get invited to join family gatherings, and for women travellers this can be a good way to avoid hassle from lecherous youths. Visitors are exhorted to stay off the beach after dark and dress modestly when in town – rules enforced by the police.

For a town of 50,000 inhabitants, El-Arish offers few sights or entertainments. On Thursdays a **Bedouin market** sells fruit, vegetables and Bedouin handicrafts: the latter are also available in tourist shops such as the **Multinational Force of Observers** store on Sharia 23rd July (☎068/335-1206). The only other attraction is a **Sinai Heritage Museum**, just beyond the UN post along the coastal road to Rafah (catch a bus or service taxi). The museum is open daily (Sat–Wed 9am–2pm summer 8am–8pm; £E4) and contains mostly stuffed wildlife and Bedouin handicrafts. Next door is a small and miserable **zoo** (same hours).

Eating and nightlife

The cheapest places to eat are the *fuul* and *taamiya* joints around Midan Baladiya or the simple **restaurants** along Sharia 23rd July. *Aziz* (below the *El-Salaam Hotel*, beside Midan Baladiya) and *Bet 'A Bet* across the street do good *kofta* and salad, or chicken and chips, at reasonable rates. On the beach try *Basata*, beyond the *El-Arish Resort*, for good seafood. With the exception of the well-stocked but expensive bar in the *El-Arish*, you'll be hard pressed to find any **alcohol**. If desperate for hard liquor, you could take a service taxi to the border and use the duty-free shop outside Egyptian customs and immigration.

Smoking **sheeshas** over backgammon in a café on Sharia 23rd July is usually all that El-Arish can offer in the way of **nightlife** – and that's an exclusively male pursuit. Otherwise, in the summer the **El-Arish Resort** has a **nightclub** with live music and bellydancers, while the outdoor restaurant opposite the **El-Arish**, an unmarked dance hall on the beach nearer town, and the disco on Sharia 23rd July occasionally host **entertainers**.

Moving on

Direct **buses** run from the terminal beside Midan Baladiya to Cairo (£E16–22) and Ismailiya (£E7), while **service taxis** leave from opposite the terminal also to Cairo (£E14) and Ismailiya (£E7). In summer, there are also EgyptAir **flights** to Cairo (Thurs & Sun).

The Red Sea Coast and Eastern Desert

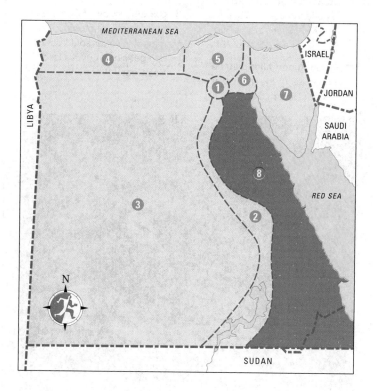

CHAPTER 8

Highlights

* **Red Sea monasteries** Deep in the desert, St Paul's and St Anthony's were the world's first monasteries. See p.769

* **Dive safaris** Book a "liveaboard" for access to the more remote reefs and wrecks of the south Red Sea. See p.783

* **Camel and jeep safaris** Experience the *wadi's* & Bedovin culture of the Red Sea Mountains. See p.791

* **Trekking and hiking** In the mountains of the rarely visited Eastern Desert. See p.792

* **Prehistoric rock art** Join a survey expedition to map sites in the Eastern Desert. See p.798

* **Mersa Alam** Camps and hotels here give access to some of the best, least-visited and most southerly dive sites in Egypt. See p.801

* **Camel market at Shalateen** The village's photogenic daily market is as far south as you can get along Egypt's Red Sea Coast. See p.804

△ Diving in the Red Sea

8

The Red Sea Coast and Eastern Desert

or 1250 kilometres, from Suez to the Sudanese border, turquoise waves lap rocky headlands and windswept beaches along a coastline separated from the Nile Valley by the arid hills and mountains of the **Eastern Desert**. Like Sinai, the region's infertility and sparse population belie its mineral wealth and strategic location, and there are further points in common in the wildlife, Bedouin nomads and long monastic tradition. Tourism, too, is developing along similar lines, with holiday villages proliferating along the coast, and dive boats ranging down the Red Sea as far south as Eritrea.

An entrepôt since ancient times, the **Red Sea Coast** was once a microcosm of half the world, as Muslim pilgrims from as far away as Central Asia sailed to Arabia from its ports. Though piracy and slavery ceased towards the end of the nineteenth century, smuggling still drew adventurers like Henri de Monfried long after the Suez Canal had sapped the vitality of the Red Sea ports. Decades later, the coastline assumed new significance with the discovery of oil and its vulnerability to Israeli commando raids, which led to large areas being **mined** – one reason why tourism didn't arrive until the 1980s. It's worth being aware that large areas of the coastline and many *wadis* are still mined, and that any area with barbed-wire fencing (however rusty) is suspect. Never wander off public beaches or into the desert without a guide.

While Cairenes appreciate the beaches at **Ain Sukhna**, south of Suez, the real lure consists of fabulous island reefs off the coast of **Hurghada** – a booming, bold and brash resort town – and the less touristic settlements of **Port Safaga**, **El-Quseir** and **Mersa Alam** to the south. So far the international airport at Mersa Alam has only opened to charter flights from Italy, so access to points further south remains difficult unless you have your own transport. This looks likely to change in the near future, with the coast south of Quseir now subject to ambitious development plans. Dive companies are also establishing supply bases for their dive boats along the southern coastline, opening up "virgin" reefs in the south to divers, whose only option previously was a long journey by sea from Hurghada or Sharm el-Sheikh in the Sinai.

Crossing the Eastern Desert by bus gives little idea of its spectacular highlands. Apparently devoid of life, the granite ranges and limestone *wadis* harbour ancient rock art, temples and quarries, gazelles and ibexes, and Bedouin. While you might not have the inclination, stamina or money for long excursions into

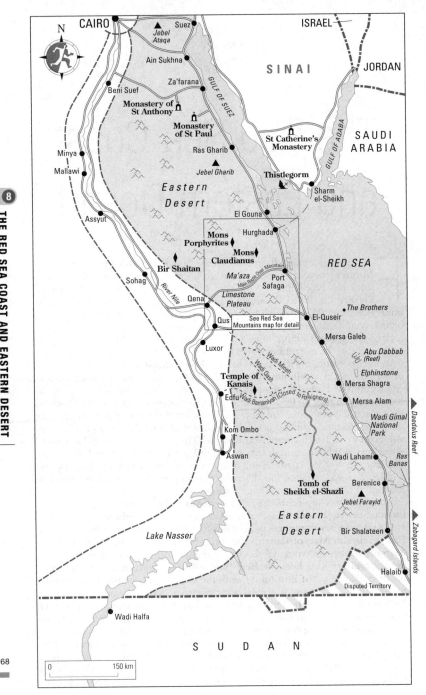

the interior, thousands of Copts visit the **Red Sea monasteries**, and further south, amid the **Red Sea Mountains**, truckloads of dervishes converge on **Wadi Humaysara** for the **Moulid of Al-Shazli**. If totally off-the-beaten-track destinations are your thing, the Eastern Desert has more to offer than at first appears.

The Red Sea monasteries

Secreted amidst the arid Red Sea Hills, Egypt's oldest **monasteries** – dedicated to **St Paul** and **St Anthony** – trace their origins back to the infancy of Christian monasticism, observing rituals that have scarcely changed over sixteen centuries. This tangible link with the primitive church gives them a special resonance for believers, but you don't have to be religious to appreciate their tranquil atmosphere and imposing setting – there's also scope for **bird-watching** in the vicinity.

Transport, tours and accommodation

Though neither monastery is directly accessible by public transport, they can still be reached in several ways. The main thing to realize is that a quick visit is impossible, and no one is in any hurry once you get there. If you feel OK about travelling with devout believers, it's best to join the **pilgrim tours** arranged from Cairo by the Coptic Patriarchate (22 Sharia Ramses, Abbassiya; ☏02/960-025) or the YMCA (27 Sharia al-Gumhorriya; ☏02/917-360), which dispatches a minibus every week. Coptic churches in Luxor or Hurghada may also run tours on a non-profit basis.

Commercial **tours** from Cairo or Hurghada are another possibility. Misr Travel does a tour from Hurghada to both monasteries for US$30 per person; other agencies charge less but visit only one. Depending on your starting point and number, it could work out cheaper to negotiate a **rented taxi**. A six- to eight-hour excursion should cost about £E300 from Suez, £E400 from Cairo; taxis from Za'farana might do a four- to five-hour jaunt for around £E170. To drive from one monastery to the other (82km) takes about ninety minutes.

The cheapest method combines **public transport, hitching and walking**. Outside of the hottest months, this shouldn't be dangerous providing you bring ample water and minimal luggage. Any bus from Cairo or Suez to Hurghada can drop you at the **turn-off for St Paul's Monastery** (26km south of Za'farana and 152km south of Suez), recognizable by its plastic-roofed bus shelter. Young Copts alight here, confident of hitching to the monastery, 13km uphill, for there's a fair amount of traffic along the well-paved road. If pilgrims visiting both sites don't offer you a lift, St Anthony's Monastery can be approached via service taxis running between Beni Suef and Za'farana. From the signposted turn-off 33km west of Za'farana, it's 15km uphill to the monastery, with some hitching prospects.

There are **dormitories** at the monasteries, though to stay in them you need written permission from the "residence" in Cairo (26 El-Kenisa El Morcosia St Kolet Beck, Cairo; ☏02/590-6025), which is often refused, particularly if you are not part of a religious group. Both monasteries have **cafeterias**, and St Paul's has a shop selling basic foodstuffs, but you might want to bring your own supplies. Smoking and drinking alcohol are forbidden here, and you should respect the monasteries' conventions on dress and behaviour.

The Monastery of St Anthony

West of Za'farana a wide valley cleaves the Galala Plateau and sets the road on course for the Nile, 168km away. Called **Wadi Arraba**, its name derives from the carts that once delivered provisions to the monastery, though legend attributes it to the pharaoh's chariots that pursued the Israelites towards the Red Sea. Turning off the road and south into the hills, it's possible to spot the monastery sited beneath a dramatic ridge of cliffs, known as Mount Qalah. If in doubt, ask anyone you encounter to point you towards *Deir Amba Antonyos* or *Deir Qaddis Antwan*.

Lofty walls with an interior catwalk surround the **Monastery of St Anthony** (daily 8am–5pm; closed during Lent and Christmas), whose lanes of two-storey dwellings, churches, mills and gardens of vines, olive and palms basically amount to a village. Formerly self-sufficient, the community now gets most of its food either from Cairo or its own farm near Beni Suef, but remains dependent on water from its **spring**, where Arab legend has it that Miriam, sister of Moses, bathed during the Exodus.

An English-speaking monk will give you a partial tour, which varies with each visitor; don't expect to see everything, especially as the monastery is currently undergoing a major restoration program. Highlights include the **keep**, a soot-blackened **bakery** and a **library** of over 1700 manuscripts. The oldest of the five **churches** is dedicated to the monastery's namesake, who may be buried underneath it. Be sure not to miss the wall paintings, some of which date back to the seventh century and have recently been restored to their former glory after years hidden under layers of soot, candle grease and grime. During Lent (when the gates are locked and deliveries are winched over the walls), monks celebrate the liturgy in the twelve-domed Church of St Luke, dating from 1776. Some of the churches date from the early twentieth century and there are new ones under construction. There is a well-stocked bookshop which sells books about the monastery and the Coptic Church in Egypt, as well as souvenirs and postcards. There's a small **museum** detailing the monastery's history next to the bookshop.

All of these buildings are recent compared to the monastery's foundation, shortly after Anthony's death in 356. A sojourn by St John the Short (whose body was later stolen by other monks) is all that's recorded of its early **history**, but an influx of refugees from Wadi Natrun, and then Melkite monks, occurred

St Anthony

To many, **St Anthony** (251–356) is considered the "father of monasticism", and his life certainly coincided with a sea-change in Christianity's position. When Anthony was orphaned at the age of 18, he placed his sister in a convent, sold his possessions and became a hermit. Christians at the time faced growing persecution – the "Era of Martyrs" from which the Coptic calendar is dated – but the transformation of Christianity into a state religion in 313 caused many believers to view the Church as tainted by worldliness and foreign influences, and the hermit's life as a purer alternative. Admirers pursued Anthony ever deeper into the wilderness, camping out beneath Mount Qalah, where he dwelt in a cave until his death at the age of 105.

Icons depict the saint clothed in animal skins, barefoot and white-bearded, with an escort of lions. A century later, the Greek scholar Athanasius recounted his privations and visions in that prototypical work of Christian hagiography, the *Life of Anthony*, basis for the depictions of Anthony in the Wilderness throughout the next millennia of Coptic and Western art.

△ The Eastern Desert

during the sixth and seventh centuries. Subsequently pillaged by Bedouin and razed by Nasr al-Dawla, the monastery was restored during the twelfth century by Coptic monks, from whose ranks several Ethiopian bishops were elected. After a murderous revolt by the monastery servants, it was reoccupied by Coptic, Syrian and Ethiopian monks.

Headed by Bishop Yustus, today's 110 permanent brethren are university graduates and ex-professionals – not unlike the kind of people drawn to monasticism in the fourth century AD. A typical day at the monastery begins at 4am, with two hours of prayer and hymns followed by communion and Mass, all before breakfast.

St Anthony's Cave

Early morning or late afternoon is the best time to ascend to **St Anthony's Cave** (*maghara*), 2km from, and 276m above, the monastery (bring water). After passing a sculpture of St Anthony carved into the mountain rock, you'll face 1200 steps (45min) up to the cave, but the stunning views from 680m above the Red Sea reward your effort. Technicolour *wadis* and massifs spill down into the azure gulf, with Sinai's mountains rising beyond. The cave where Anthony spent his last 25 years contains medieval graffiti and modern *tilbas*: scraps of paper bearing supplications inscribed with "Remember, Lord, your servant", which pilgrims stick into cracks in the rock. **Birdlife** – hoopoes, desert larks, ravens, blue rock thrushes and pied wagtails – is surprisingly abundant, and you might glimpse shy **gazelles** in the early morning.

The Monastery of St Paul

The **Monastery of St Paul** (daily 6am–4pm; closed during Lent and Christmas) has always been overshadowed by St Anthony's. Its titular founder (not to be confused with the apostle Paul) was only 16 and an orphan when he fled Alexandria to escape Emperor Decius' persecutions, making him the earliest known hermit. Shortly before his death in 348, Paul was visited by Anthony and begged him to bring the robe of Pope Athanasius, for Paul to be buried in. Anthony departed to fetch this, but on the way back had a vision of Paul's soul being carried up to heaven by angels, and arrived to find him dead. While Anthony was wondering what to do, two lions appeared and dug a grave for the body, so Anthony shrouded it in the robe and took Paul's tunic of palm leaves as a gift for the pope, who subsequently wore it at Christmas, Epiphany and Easter.

The monastery (called *Deir Amba Bula* or *Deir Mari Bolus*) was a form of posthumous homage by Paul's followers: its turreted walls are built around the cave where he lived for decades. To a large extent, its fortunes have followed those of its more prestigious neighbour. In 1484 all its monks were slain by the Bedouin, who occupied St Paul's for eighty years; rebuilt by Patriarch Gabriel VII, it was again destroyed near the end of the sixteenth century.

The monastery is much smaller than St Anthony's and a little more primitive looking. It boasts four churches, but the **Church of St Paul** is its spiritual centre, a cave-church housing the remains of the saint. The walls of the church are painted with murals generally thought to be inferior to those of St Anthony's, though they have been well preserved. A monk will show you round the chapels and identify their icons: notice the angel of the furnace with Shadrach, Meshach and Abednego, and the ostrich eggs hung from the ceiling – a symbol of the Resurrection. The southern sanctuary of the larger **Church of St Michael** contains a gilded icon of the head of John the Baptist on a dish. When

Bedouin raided the monastery, its monks retreated into the five-storey **keep**, supplied with spring water by a hidden canal. Nowadays this is not enough to sustain the 75 monks and their guests, so water is brought in from outside.

There is a small shop selling supplies and a reasonably priced cafeteria just outside the monastery grounds.

Ain Sukhna

Without private transport or a firm intention to visit the Red Sea monasteries (see p.769), it's hardly worth stopping **between Suez and Hurghada**. Heading south past the oil refineries and natural gas refineries that appear at intervals all along the coast, you'll see parched highlands rising inland. The **Jebel Ataqa** is the northernmost range in the Eastern Desert and an old Bedouin smuggling route by which hashish reached Cairo; Henri de Monfried sent his cargo this way.

Roughly 50km south of Suez, a series of beaches and coves marks **AIN SUKHNA**, where middle-class Cairenes come to picnic at weekends. Ain Sukhna's name derives from the **hot springs** (35°C) that originate in the Jebel Ataqa, but it's the sea that attracts people. Light patches offshore indicate **coral reefs**, ideal for snorkelling, while rusty barbed-wire fences delineate areas sown with land mines (beneath the cliffs). There are paying **beaches** (£E20–40) in front of the *Ain Sukhna* and *Mena Oasis* hotels; other stretches are free. If you haven't got a car, Ain Sukhna is best reached by **bus from Suez** (see p.582; last bus back 3.30pm).

There are a growing number of **hotel** resorts in the area that attract plenty of affluent Egyptians, but hardly any foreigners. Twenty kilometres north of Ain Sukhna is the welcoming *Palmera* resort (☎062/341-0816 or 341-0817, ⓦwww.palmerabeachresort.com; ➐), with the *Ramada* a further 13km at the southern end of Ain Sukhna (☎062/329-0500, ⓕ329-0515; ➑). Other luxury resorts in the area include the *Mena Oasis* (☎062/329-0850, ⓕ329-0855; half-board only ➎) and *Portrait* (☎062/332-5560, ⓕ333-2003; ➌): all the resorts offer accommodation and, in some cases, golf. The only budget accommodation in the area is the *Sahara Inn* motel (mobile ☎012 12363445; no a/c; ➍), along the desolate, windblown highway: its cafeteria is a good place to ask around for a lift to the monasteries. The next bus stop beyond Ain Sukhna is at **Ras Gharib**, an oil town buffeted year-round by winds – the place holds little appeal, except perhaps to mountaineers interested in tackling **Jebel Gharib** (1757m).

El Gouna

Approximately 22km north of Hurghada lies the vast tourist resort of **El Gouna** (ⓦwww.elgouna.com). Built on a series of islands linked by purpose-built bridges and canals, it covers 17,000 square kilometres of land, supports 10,000 staff and includes a hospital, four power plants, an international airport and several factories. The infrastructure includes a brewery that makes Sakkara and Löwenbrau beer, a winery producing Obelisque wine, a cheese factory making mozzarella, a state-of-the-art hospital and decompression chamber (mobile ☎012 2190383), plus an eighteen-hole golf course and a casino. There are two shopping centres, with the main one having an open-air **cinema**, cafés, restaurants, bars, nightclubs, a school, banks, two travel agencies, a **museum**, **aquarium** and a post office. For those staying in Hurghada, there is a free shuttle bus to the resort's **disco** (£E20; 10pm), the *Palladium*. There are **dive centres** attached to four of the hotels, while other activities include horse-riding, go-karting, tennis, squash, and even flights in a microlight plane. If you fancy a quick nip and tuck to complete your holiday, El Gouna even has its own plastic surgery centre. The resort is already popular with the Egyptian jetset, although its Western clientele is not quite as well-heeled, being more of a middle-class package-tour crowd who get good deals by booking in advance.

Accommodation

There are some fifteen **hotels** in the resort, ranging from three- to five-star, as well as several clusters of private villas. Most of El Gouna's hotels offer parasailing, water skiing and windsurfing facilities.

Mövenpick Resort ☎065/354-4501, ℻354-5160, ℮resort.elgouna@moevenpick.com. Luxurious a/c rooms with bath, balcony or patio overlooking sea, pool or gardens, and satellite TV. Has four swimming pools, a dive centre (🅦www.divetribe.com), kitesurfing and a 3km stretch of beach. ❽
Sheraton Miramar ☎065/354-5606, ℻354-5608, 🅦www.sheraton.com/elgouna. Built on nine islands, its 338 a/c rooms have terraces, sea views and satellite TV. Two main swimming pools, three for children, with a kids' club and a dive centre. Wheelchair friendly. ❽

Steigenberger Golf Resort ☎065/358-0140, ℻358-0149, 🅦www.steigenbergergolf-elgouna .com. German-owned plush hotel with 18-hole championship golf course. ❽
Three Corners Rihana Inn ☎065/358-0025, ℻358-0030, ℮rihana@hurghada.ie.eg.com. A/c studios for two or four people, terraces with pool or mountain views, kitchenettes and satellite TV, and access to the beach and better facilities of its four-star sister hotel *Three Corners Rihana Resort* (all-inclusive only; ❽). Home to the recommended Colona Dive Centre. ❻

Eating and drinking

Whilst most people eat and drink in their own hotels, there are a few options worth considering if you fancy a change.

Barten Abu Tib Marina. This small red-lit bar is the best place in El Gouna for an after-hours drink. It opens at 9pm and closes late.
El Taybeen Café A popular meeting place serving a good variety of sandwiches, soups, pizza and pasta. Local bands play here on Thursday nights.

Peanuts Bar in the *Three Corners Rihana Resort*. A popular, centrally located bar.
Waves ☎065/354-9702 ext 19, *Sheraton Miramar*. Seafood restaurant serving excellent grilled fish and calamari. Live music and the pool-side setting add to the atmosphere. A special seafood barbeque is prepared on Saturdays.

Hurghada (Ghardaka)

In the course of two decades, **HURGHADA** has been transformed from a humble fishing village of a few hundred souls into a booming town of over 100,000 people, drawn here from all over Egypt by the lure of making money. This phenomenal growth is almost entirely due to **tourism**, which accounts for 95 percent of the local economy. Yet it's worth taking Hurghada's claims to be a seaside resort with a handful of salt. Unlike Sinai, where soft sand and gorgeous reefs are within easy reach and women can bathe unhassled, Hurghada's public beaches are distant or uninviting, while the best marine life is far offshore. If you're not into diving or discos, you'll soon find that Hurghada lacks charm – though you have to admire its commercial gusto; many of the townsfolk come from Luxor's west bank, where tourism has been a way of life for generations.

While package tourists laze in their resorts, independent travellers often feel hard done by. Paying for boat trips and private beaches is unavoidable if you're to enjoy Hurghada's assets, and although conditions for diving, windsurfing and deep-sea fishing are great, the **cost** is high, with real bargains limited to accommodation. Nor will you save much by self-catering; everything in the shops is more expensive than in Cairo or the Nile Valley. As tour groups come all year

Russians in Hurghada

Hurghada's popularity with **Russian tourists** began in 1994, and was initially greeted with joy by hoteliers, whose occupancy rates had plummeted following terrorist attacks in the Nile Valley. Being inured to chaos and inflation back home, the Russians weren't deterred by bomb scares and proved to be big spenders. Sadly, however, cultural differences soon soured things, and many locals now regard them all as drunks or whores, while the Russians reciprocate with equal contempt. It doesn't help that some of the Russians really *are* mafiosi or prostitutes (the latter ply their trade in hotels as "personal assistants") – nor that the Egyptians are irked by the lack of a common language in which to hustle them.

Aside from filling up the holiday villages and replacing Egyptian bellydancers in the Oriental shows, the Russians haven't had much effect on other tourists – except perhaps for the bewilderment when they first see restaurant signs advertising *borsch* and *pelmeni*. As the Russians generally have little interest in diving (being content to make descents in the *Sindbad Submarine* (see p.786), or snorkelling trips to Giftun Island), not much mixing occurs, except in Hurghada's discos.

round, there's no "off" season for holiday villages, whose **peak times** are the European Christmas and Easter holidays and the Russian vacation period of August and September. Low-budget hotels are most in demand over winter, when backpackers use Hurghada as a transit point between the Nile Valley and the Sinai.

The town itself is a hotchpotch of utilitarian structures, garish hotels, gaudy boutiques and sporadic patches of waste ground. Most of the coastline from Ed-Dahar down to New Hurghada is shielded from view by the line of holiday resorts, so if you've come for the beach, be prepared to pay for the pleasure. While some may be put off by the city's out-and-out commercialism, other tourists will take solace in what they can discover underwater: a score of coral islands and reefs within a few hours' reach by boat, and many other amazing dive sites that can be visited on liveaboards.

Approaches to Hurghada

Hurghada's multiplicity of **approaches** makes it more accessible than its location suggests. Vehicles go flat out along the coastal highway and desert roads, but a full tank of petrol is essential – there are few pumps en route. Some of the desert routes from the Nile are described in more detail later on.

• **From Alexandria** There are no flights from Alexandria, but Superjet (£E75) and Upper Egypt (£E65) both have one **bus** daily to Hurghada (9hr).

• **From Cairo** EgyptAir has four **flights** a day (1hr; US$131 one-way), which will need to be booked several days ahead over winter. There are around eleven **buses** daily from the Turgoman terminal (7hr 30min), four of them a/c Superjets (£E47–60), the others Upper Egypt (£E45). During the morning there may also be **service taxis** to Hurghada (6hr); £E35 from Ataba Square. El Gouna Transport Company (☎02/574-1533) also runs comfortable a/c buses (9am, 1pm, 2.30pm, 4pm, midnight, 1am, 2am; 6hr; £E55 including snacks and drinks) from Cairo's Midan Tahrir. You can also catch these buses half an hour later at Nasser City Station (Autostrad Road).

• **From Suez** The 410km from Suez can be covered in five hours by **service taxi** (£E30 per person), or at a less perilous speed by one of the fourteen daily **buses** (6hr; £E33–43), most with a/c. Service taxis and buses leave from the

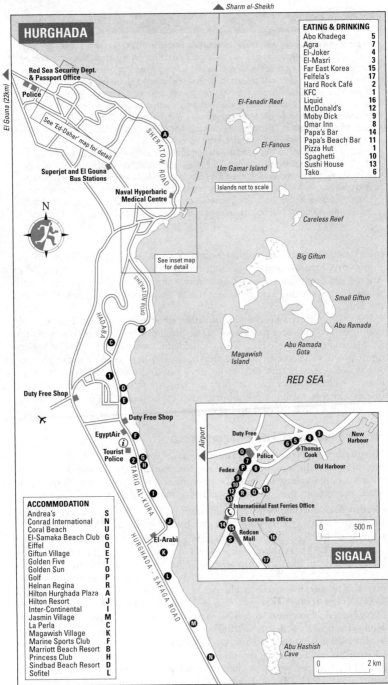

▲ Sharm el-Sheikh

HURGHADA

Red Sea Security Dept. & Passport Office

Police

See 'Ed-Dahar' map for detail

Superjet and El Gouna Bus Stations

Naval Hyperbaric Medical Centre

See inset map for detail

N

Duty Free Shop

EgyptAir

Tourist Police

Duty Free Shop

El-Arabi

EATING & DRINKING

Abo Khadega	5
Agra	7
El-Joker	4
El-Masri	3
Far East Korea	15
Felfela's	17
Hard Rock Café	2
KFC	1
Liquid	16
McDonald's	12
Moby Dick	9
Omar Inn	8
Papa's Bar	14
Papa's Beach Bar	11
Pizza Hut	1
Spaghetti	10
Sushi House	13
Tako	6

El-Fanadir Reef

El-Fanous

Um Gamar Island

Islands not to scale

Careless Reef

Big Giftun

Small Giftun

Abu Ramada

Abu Ramada Gota

Magawish Island

RED SEA

SHERATON ROAD

HADABA

TARIQ AL-KURA

HURGHADA - SAFAGA ROAD

El Gouna (22km)

ACCOMMODATION

Andrea's	S
Conrad International	N
Coral Beach	U
El-Samaka Beach Club	G
Eiffel	Q
Giftun Village	E
Golden Five	T
Golden Sun	O
Golf	P
Helnan Regina	R
Hilton Hurghada Plaza	A
Hilton Resort	J
Inter-Continental	I
Jasmin Village	M
La Perla	C
Magawish Village	K
Marine Sports Club	F
Marriott Beach Resort	B
Princess Club	H
Sindbad Beach Resort	D
Sofitel	L

SIGALA

Airport

Duty Free

Police

Fedex

Thomas Cook

New Harbour

Old Harbour

International Fast Ferries Office

El Gouna Bus Office

Redcon Mall

0   500 m

Abu Hashish Cave

0   2 km

▼ T, U & Port Safaga (45km)

bus station on the Cairo–Ismailiya road. You should be able to get a bus ticket at an hour's notice, except during the *Hadj* season or major Muslim festivals.

• **From Sinai** EgyptAir runs one **flight** a day to Hurghada from Sharm el-Sheikh (departing Sat 6.10pm; £E359), though more are put on at peak times. The ninety-minute **catamaran** trip from Sharm el-Sheikh across the Gulf of Suez (US$43/£E250) currently departs on Mon, Tues, Thurs & Sat at 6pm, though schedules vary according to the season. Tickets can be bought through Mena Tours in Sharm el-Sheikh (daily except Fri 10am–10pm, Fri 1–10pm; ☏069/360-0190), in the *Marriot Hotel* in Na'ama Bay, and at Sharm el-Sheikh port one hour before departure, though this is risky if you have a vehicle, as space is limited.

• **From the Nile Valley** During winter, hordes of travellers come from Luxor, whence there are seven daily **buses** (4–5hr; £E25) via Qena and Safaga. Alternatively, take a service taxi to Qena, walk to another taxi depot and catch a service taxi on to Hurghada (4hr; £E20). There are three buses a day from Aswan (8hr; £E40) via Safaga, while a few service taxis cross the desert between Beni Suef and Za'farana, or Qift and El-Quseir. At the time of writing there are no **flights** from Luxor, but EgyptAir sometimes runs them during peak travel periods.

Orientation

Although Hurghada stretches for nearly 40km along the coast, it's easily divisible into three zones, whose salient features are mapped on p.776 and p.780.

The **town** proper – known as **Ed-Dahar** ("The Harbour") – is separated from the coast by a barren rock massif, so you rarely glimpse the sea. Coming in from the north, its evolution is apparent as administrative buildings give way to hotels, shops and a maze of mud-brick homes at the feet of Jebel el-Afish. Its amorphous downtown embraces the bazaar quarter and a flourishing strip of restaurants, shops and hotels known as "Hospital Street", which spreads from Sharia Abdel Aziz Mustafa to the Aquarium on the Corniche. The main thoroughfare is **Tariq El-Nasr** (aka El-Nasre Way), whose busiest stretch lies between the bus station and Ed-Dahar's boarded-up telephone exchange (known as the *centraal*), which acts as a terminus for local public transport. The coastal Corniche is widely known as the Sheraton road, in reference to the now-closed landmark hotel that has long been its northernmost feature.

From Ed-Dahar, two main roads run 2–4km south to **Sigala** (pronounced "Si-*gala*"), which contains the modern **port** of Hurghada and a mass of restaurants and hotels, squeezed in wherever the terrain allows. Beyond Sigala is nothing but desert and an endless array of **coastal holiday villages** and construction sites, linked by slip roads to the Hurghada–Safaga road and dignified with the name of **New Hurghada**. This extends more than 30km south of Sigala and there seems nothing to prevent it from ultimately linking up with the resorts at Port Safaga, 50km south.

Arrival, information and transport

Most independent travellers **arrive** in Ed-Dahar at the **bus station** on the southern edge of the downtown area, though coming by Superjet or El Gouna buses, you'll arrive at a terminal 1km further south. Service taxis from the Nile Valley wind up at the **taxi station** on Tariq El-Nasr, near the Police Station. If you're planning to stay in Ed-Dahar it should be possible to find accommodation within walking distance of the bus station or the taxi stand, but from the

Superjet terminal, you might want to hop into one of the ubiquitous white minivans (£E1) that ply Tariq El-Nasr.

People arriving by boat from Sinai will disembark at the **harbour** in Sigala, whence you could walk to several mid-range places or catch a minivan (£E1) or taxi (£E10) to the centre of Ed-Dahar.

Most package tourists who fly into the **airport** off the Hurghada–Safaga road are whisked to their resorts in buses; arriving independently, a taxi into Ed-Dahar will cost £E15.

Hurghada's **tourist information** centre is located in New Hurghada (daily 8.30am–8pm; ☎065/346-3221) next to the tourist police and opposite the faded *Grand Hotel*. Large and airy with helpful staff, it is let down by a lack of practical information. A second tourist information office in Ed-Dahar, close to Esh-Shahid Mosque, is virtually useless. Much more helpful is the *Connect Hurghada & Red Sea Guide*, a monthly magazine with a **listings guide** and area map; it's free from most hotels. The free colour magazine *Red Sea Bulletin* (Ⓦwww.redsea-bulletin.com) comes out twice a month with articles and information about Hurghada in three languages (English, German and Russian), and can be picked up at hotels and dive centres, while *The Complete Map of Hurghada* shows the location of all the coastal resorts and can be bought from most souvenir shops for a negotiable £E25.

In addition, private agencies, hotels, dive centres and individual fixers are all ready to help – for a price. Any information you're given in Hurghada should be regarded as suspect, since everyone earns a commission on whatever you can be induced to spend. Normally this doesn't matter too much – except when they steer you towards dodgy, potentially lethal dive centres.

Transport

While **walking** is fine for getting around Ed-Dahar, transport is needed to reach Sigala or anywhere further south. **Private minibuses** run up and down the coast along the Corniche/Sheraton Road, as well as Tariq El-Nasr to the airport and beyond. You'll pay £E1 for most rides between Ed-Dahar, Sigala and New Hurghada, or £E2 for a trip as far south as the *Jasmin Village*, 21km away. The minibuses run 24 hours a day (though after midnight you may pay prices similar to that of a taxi), and can be flagged down at any point along their route. **Private taxis** charge around £E5–10 for a ride in Ed-Dahar, £E10 to Sigala, and £E20–35 to the furthest holiday villages. To rent a taxi for the day, £E170 is the going rate for five or six hours, provided you don't drive any further than Safaga.

Some tourists scoot around on rented **bicycles**, which are OK in town if you can handle the traffic but are not up to trips down the coastal highway, which is often buffeted by strong crosswinds. There are lots of places around the bazaar renting bikes for £E15–25 per day; rates in Sigala are slightly higher. If you want to go further afield, you could **rent a car**: local firms are the cheapest, though their deals tend to be for limited mileage on poorly maintained cars. For expeditions into the desert, Aziz Tours at the *Grand Hotel* rents out US Hummers with drivers.

Accommodation

Much of Hurghada consists of **hotels and holiday villages**, with well over a hundred in operation and more being built: demand is currently so high that most villages boast occupancy rates of 80–100 percent. If you're coming for the diving, a **package deal** is the cheapest option, and you won't have to do the rounds of the dive centres. Hotels catering to **independent travellers** get £E150 commission for each guest that they sign up for a diving course, so if you book with your hotel when you get here, you may well be able to negotiate a discount on the price of a room. As in Luxor and Aswan, many hotels make more on trips and commissions than on rooms – not to mention other transactions, at places with a liberal attitude toward selling dope.

Arriving at Hurghada's bus station, you'll be mobbed by **hotel touts**, offering free transport to their establishment (see opposite). Otherwise, £E10 is absolute tops for a ride to anywhere in Ed-Dahar – which is where most visitors stay if they haven't already booked into a holiday village. If you're bent on locating a hotel on your own, bear in mind that few streets are named, and there are effectively no house numbers.

Hurghada's **water** has to be piped from the Nile Valley, so depending on your hotel's storage capacity it might be cut off for several hours a day. Profligate consumption means that others go short. Foreigners who live here strongly advise against **drinking** the tap water, and if the thought of cooling down by standing under the sprinklers that irrigate the gardens of some of the upmarket hotels appeals, think again: this (barely) treated sewage is largely responsible for the stink that blankets the town.

Downtown Ed-Dahar

Most **low-budget places** cluster around the bazaar or the "strip" of cafés and shops between Sharia Abdel Aziz Mustafa and the Corniche, while **mid-range hotels** are sited off the main road near the Esh-Shahid Mosque and the coastal **holiday villages**. In general hotels are not as "luxury" as they claim to be – a good guide would be to subtract one star from their rating. All the following places are marked on the map on p.780: breakfast is included unless stated otherwise, and you can generally count on hot water.

El-Arosa On the Corniche ☎ & ℱ 065/354-9190, ℮ elarosahotel@yahoo.com. Nice, clean a/c rooms with baths; indoor pool and music bar. Guests can use the beach at the pricier *Geisum Village*, across the road. ❻

El-Gezirah Off Sharia al-Bahr ☎ 065/357-785, ℱ 354 8708. Spacious a/c rooms with TV. Bar, restaurant and disco, plus free use of the pool and disco at the *Sand Beach*. Mainly German, Dutch and Russian groups. ❸

Empire Hospital Street ☎ 065/354-9200 or 9, ⓦ www.threecorners.com. Large hotel that dominates the skyline, with comfortable a/c en-suite rooms, satellite TV, balconies with sea views. Sister hotel to the *Village* on the Corniche round the corner giving guests access to the beach. ❻

Four Seasons Near the Corniche end of the strip ☎ & ℱ 065/354-5456, ℮ forseasonsshurghada @hotmail.com. Simple, cleanish rooms, all with baths, balconies and partial sea views; a few have a/c (£E5 extra). ❸

Happy House Between the Ed-Dahar Mosque and Tariq El-Nasr, mobile ☎ 012 3585016. Small, friendly, low-budget hotel of long standing. Clean rooms with fans; one hot shower; kitchen. Inquire with Mustafa at the shop downstairs. ❷

Happy Land Sharia Sheikh Sebak ☎ 065/354-7373. Slightly shabby rooms with private bathrooms, in the noisy tourist bazaar. Mostly used by Egyptians, and within earshot of a mosque. ❷

Hilton Hurghada Plaza South end of the Corniche ☎ 065/354-9745, ℱ 354-7597, ⓦ www.hilton.com. Massive but isolated five-star resort perched on an arid hill between Ed-Dahar and Sigala; if you're going to stay here, you probably won't bother leaving its confines. ❽

Pharoes Behind the *Snafer Hotel* ☎ 065/354-7577. Cheap but acceptable backpacker joint, with double rooms for just £E30. ❶

Sand Beach On the Corniche ☎ 065/354-7992, ℱ 354-7822. Four-star holiday village with three pools, a beach and diving centre, billiards room and disco. Popular with Russians. ❼

Sea Horse Off Sharia al-Bahr ☎ 065/354-8704. Comfortable rooms with private baths, a/c and balconies. Restaurant, bar, disco, billiards, backyard pool and sea views. Residents can use its beach, and the one at the *New Sea Horse*, by *Hilton Hurghada Plaza*. ❻

Sea View On the Corniche ☎ 065/545-959, ℱ 546-779. Modern, clean a/c rooms with baths and satellite TV. Tiny swimming pool. Seafood

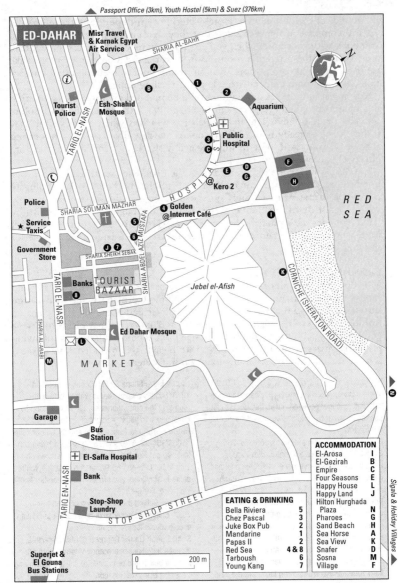

Passport Office (3km), Youth Hostel (5km) & Suez (376km)

ED-DAHAR

Misr Travel & Karnak Egypt Air Service

SHARIA AL-BAHR

Tourist Police

Esh-Shahid Mosque

Aquarium

Public Hospital

HOSPITA STREET

@ Kero 2

Golden @ Internet Café

Police

SHARIA SOLIMAN MAZHAR

Service Taxis

Government Store

SHARIA SHEIKH SEBAK

TARIQ EL-NASR

SHARIA ABDEL AZIZ MUSTAFA

Banks

TOURIST BAZAAR

Jebel el-Afish

RED SEA

CORNICHE (SHERATON ROAD)

Ed Dahar Mosque

MARKET

SHARIA AL-ARABI

Garage

Bus Station

El-Saffa Hospital

Bank

Stop-Shop Laundry

STOP SHOP STREET

TARIQ EN-NASR

Superjet & El Gouna Bus Stations

0   200 m

EATING & DRINKING

Bella Riviera	5
Chez Pascal	3
Juke Box Pub	2
Mandarine	1
Papas II	2
Red Sea	4 & 8
Tarboush	6
Young Kang	7

ACCOMMODATION

El-Arosa	I
El-Gezirah	B
Empire	C
Four Seasons	E
Happy House	L
Happy Land	J
Hilton Hurghada Plaza	N
Pharoes	G
Sand Beach	H
Sea Horse	A
Sea View	K
Snafer	D
Sosna	M
Village	F

Sigala & Holiday Villages

Sigala & New Hurghada Holiday Villages

restaurant and free use of the *Sea Horse*'s beach for residents. ④

Snafer On the Corniche ☎ & ℻ 065/354-0260, ⓔashrafhurghada@hotmail.com. A pleasant hotel with courteous staff and clean rooms – probably Ed-Dahar's best value mid-range hotel. If you can

manage the stairs (there's no elevator) the upper floors have good sea views. ④

Sosna Off Tariq El-Nasr ☎065/354-6647. Clean, carpeted rooms with fans and bedside lamps; private bathrooms are optional. Mainly used by Egyptians. Liberal atmosphere. ②

Village On the Corniche ☏ 065/354-8816, ℱ354-7514. Similar in standard to its sister hotel, *Empire*, with comfortable a/c en-suite rooms with satellite TV, some with sea views. Less opulent than some of the other hotels on this part of the beach, but the rooms are a shade cheaper. ➏

Sigala

Despite a relatively good choice of places to eat, it's hard to see why anyone would want to stay in Sigala, since there are better mid-range options in Ed-Dahar and ritzier holiday villages in New Hurghada. However, if everywhere else is full, you could try the following options:

Andrea's ☏ 065/344-2251, ℱ344-3388. Pleasant Italian-owned place, home to Bubbles dive centre. a/c rooms, three bars and a swimming pool. Popular with young English, German and French tourists. ➎

Eiffel ☏ 065/344-4570, ℱ344-4572. Clean, comfortable rooms, a great location near Papa's Beach, a roof-top swimming pool and low rates make this a good choice for independent travellers. ➏

Golden Sun ☏ 065/344-4403, ✉ malky_dawood@rediffmail.com. Basic place with funky décor (check out the stuffed goat and fox in the lobby) and a welcoming staff. Tucked into an alley opposite Misr Travel. ➎

Golf ☏ 065/344-2828, ℱ344-4328. Located on main road by Misr Travel, with rambling dim hallways that open up to decent rooms, some with sea views. ➎

Helnan Regina ☏ 065/344-2276. On the beach with three pools and a jetty. a/c rooms and chalets. Half-board. ➐

New Hurghada

New Hurghada is the name given to the array of **holiday villages** that have proliferated for 30km south along the coast. Each is fully self-contained, so there's zero incentive to leave the complex. Though geared to package tourists, they'll take independent travellers if trade is slack. Where the clientele is mainly from certain countries, you could feel at a disadvantage if you don't speak the right language. Unless stated otherwise, all of the holiday villages are a/c, with a pool, diving centre, beach and disco. We've calculated their distance from the bus station in Ed-Dahar; for their exact locations, see the map on p.776.

Conrad International 22km ☏ 065/346-0020, ℱ344-3258, ⊕ www.conradhotels.com. Five-star resort with an onyx-floored lobby and an outsized pool; largely German guests but also some English. ➑

Coral Beach 28km ☏ 065/346-1610, ℱ346-1616, ⊕ www.rotana.com. Stylish rooms with satellite TV and minibar. Two pools, tennis, squash and horse-riding. Large beach with reef. Mainly caters to Italians. ➐

El-Samaka Beach Club 16km ☏ 065/346-5143, ℱ346-5142, ⊕ www.elsamakabeachclub.com. Bungalows (a/c midday and evenings only) with a small beach and windsurfing lagoon. Used by German and Russian tour groups. ➏

Giftun Village 14km ☏ 065/346-3040, ℱ346-3050, ⊕ www.giftunbeachresort.com. Spanish-style chalets with fans, fronting a good beach and windsurfing lagoon. All-inclusive. ➐

Golden Five 25km ☏ 065/344-6300. A Vegas-style combination of theme park and hotel complex, with daily shows, a replica Egyptian village and a cable-car lift. ➑

Hilton Resort 17km ☏ 065/346-5020, ℱ346-5035, ⊕ www.hilton.com. The same five-star rating as its sister *Plaza* hotel (see p.779), but a bit older and less pricey. ➑

Inter-Continental 17km ☏ 065/346-5100, ℱ346-5101. Opulent complex of rooms with bath, bidet, satellite TV and sea views. Very large marina, health club and tennis courts. ➑

Jasmin Village 21km ☏ 065/346-0460, ℱ346-0459. Simple rooms with satellite TV and fridge. Small beach with reef and windsurfing lagoons. Playground, zoo and aviary. Disabled access. Half-board only. ➐

La Perla 6km ☏ & ℱ065/344-3280. Pleasant and well-managed, with a/c rooms and a swimming pool. A bit far from the action and the beach, but still popular with English groups. ➏

Magawish Village 19km ℱ065/346-4633, ℱ346-4620, ✉ magawish@link.net. A former Club Med, with a big beach and good sports facilities, especially for windsurfing, plus a children's play-ground. Half-board only. ➏

Marine Sports Club 16km ⓕ065/346-3004, ⓕ343-6007. Good-value a/c rooms with TV and fridge. Popular with Egyptian sports fishermen. ❻
Marriott Beach Resort 11km ⓕ065/344-6950, ⓕ344-6970, ⓦwww.marriott.com\hrgeg. Five-star complex with a large pool and a small sandy beach, a marina and residents-only disco. ❼
Princess Club 16km ⓕ065/346-5000, ⓕ346-5007, ⓔprincesshurghada.net.com. Spacious a/c rooms with satellite TV and fridge; also has three-storey villas equipped for self-catering. Small pool and windsurfing lagoon. ❼

Sindbad Beach Resort 13km ⓕ065/344-3261, ⓕ344-3267, ⓦwww.sindbad-group.com. Efficiently managed and family-oriented four-star complex with lots of nightlife, a huge waterchute on the beach and an entertainment complex called 'Splash Park' that offers dolphin shows. Also home to *Sindbad Submarine* (see p.786). Half-board only. ❽
Sofitel 20km ⓕ065/346-4646, ⓕ346-4640, ⓦwww.sofitel.com. Classy pseudo-Moorish complex and the best hotel in town. The ex-Club Med management runs events like themed dinners for which guests are encouraged to dress up. Used by Hayes & Jarvis tours. Half-board only. ❽

Hostelling, camping and apartment rental

Hurghada's **youth hostel** (ⓣ065/354-4989 or 350-0054; HI members £E30, non-HI £E32) is on the beach 5km north of town, next to the Marine Institute of Oceanic Studies. It has separate blocks for men and women, containing spartan rooms with fans, bunk beds, and clean shared bathrooms: there's a three-day maximum stay. Although **camping** on the beach is legal for one night, it isn't encouraged in Hurghada, and you could find yourself being moved off by local authorities – there's also the problem of actually finding any public beach available.

If you're hoping to stay and work, **renting an apartment** may make sense. Most rentals are arranged through diving centres or hotels that employ foreigners, but if you put the word out, prospective landlords – and housemates – should come forward. It's also worth checking the classifieds in the *Connect Guide* (see p.778). Expect to pay about £E800–1500 per month (excluding bills) for a two-bedroom apartment near the beach, and about £E700 in the Amal district, between Ed-Dahar and Sigala.

Diving

It is **diving** that really put Hurghada on the map, kick-starting tourism along the Red Sea Coast. The marine life here is broadly similar to that found off the coast of Sinai (see p.711), but the topography favours island corals over coastal reefs, with sharks, giant moray eels and manta rays in its deeper, rougher waters. The tide here is more dramatic, too; it drops by up to five metres from high to low tide, compared with a one-metre change in Sinai. Many islands have sheer-sided coral *ergs* (pillars) that are fantastic for drift diving, while others are shallow enough for snorkelling. There are about ten islands within day-trip range and over a score of sites that can be visited on extended dive safaris, or "liveaboards".

As ever, dive **tourism** is its own worst enemy: once-rich coral and shell-fish grounds have been devastated by the sheer weight of visitors. Hurghada welcomes hordes of tourists each week, and is home to more than one thousand tour boats. Anchoring on the reefs does irreparable damage to fragile corals, and those closest to the port have been hit especially hard. To help combat the problem, the Underwater National Parks of the Red Sea and Protected Islands (aka Marine Park) has introduced a new daily "environmental tax" for all divers (£E3.50), snorkellers (£E2) and those on diving safaris (£E5), the proceeds of which are being ploughed back into Red Sea environmental projects, as well as clean-air projects in Cairo; this is in addition to the standard per-person charge of €4 (US$5) per day to dive the Giftun Islands and the nearby reefs and €5 (US$6.70) per day for sites further south such as Brothers and Zabargad. The problem is also being tackled by **HEPCA** (Hurghada Environmental Protection and Conservation Association), which is installing mooring buoys and trying to raise ecological awareness – but few of the local dive centres show much interest. Tourists can help by favouring centres that belong to HEPCA and display a certificate from the Egyptian Underwater Sports Federation – and by refusing to buy marine curios like clamshells (whose export is illegal) or stuffed sharks. You can make a difference simply by minimizing your own impact upon the dive sites you visit; don't touch the coral, don't remove anything from the sea bed, don't throw anything in the water (particularly cigarette butts) and don't feed the fish.

Your life may depend on **choosing the right diving centre**; some outfits are dangerously incompetent (past accidents have seen divers marooned at sea or lost in caves). Always check that the instructor is qualified, with valid ID and insurance, not merely photocopies. Many are freelancers who frequently change jobs, so even the best centres sometimes get bad ones (or vice versa). As a rule of thumb, however, it is safer to dive with the large outfits attached to holiday villages than with backstreet operators taking clients sent by low-budget hotels (whose recommendations *can't* be trusted). Of the 150 dive centres in Hurghada, thirty are run by Europeans and tend to have higher standards than the local outfits. In 2001, the Red Sea Association for Water Sports and Diving was formed to increase levels of safety and service and to help market Hurghada as a dive destination; however, as membership is compulsory for all diving operators, it is not a sign of reputability.

The **courses** on offer are similar to those in Sinai. A four- or five-day PADI open-water course costs €300–350 (US$405–470) including the dive certificate; a two-day advanced course is €200–230 (US$270–310). Beginners can expect to pay €45–60 (US$60–80) for an introductory lecture followed by two supervised dives. Scuba **equipment** is included in the price of courses, but otherwise costs €15–25 (US$20–33) extra; renting snorkelling gear for a day costs about €4-8 (US$5–11). The average rate for a day's **boat diving** is €40–60 (US$53–80); most trips comprise two dives, separated by lunch, which is normally included in the price. Never hand over cash to someone on the street who promises to arrange a trip; book through a dive centre, where you can complain if things go wrong. You'll need to sign up and surrender your passport the night before; check that details are correctly noted, since wrongly documented passengers may be prevented from boarding. See overleaf for a list of reliable dive centres.

For longer trips, the Colona Dive Centre, based at *Magawish Village* (see p.781) can arrange **liveaboards** and diving packages taking you further south to sites in Safaga, Mersa Alam, Wadi Gimal and Wadi Lahami. The cost depends on the amenities of the vessel and the quality of the meals provided; expect to pay at least €80–100 (US$110–135) per person per day, though extra diving fees (see opposite) can also add €15–70 (US$20–94) to the final cost depending on where you dive. Most safaris last for a week, though you could stay out longer if you have the interest and the money.

Even if you're only going to Giftun Island, check that the boat has a radio, lifejackets, oxygen and a first-aid kit. Many of the dive boats lack **safety equipment**. In case of emergency, there are decompression chambers in the Hurghada area: in El-Gouna's hospital (see p.773) and the Mubarak Naval Hyperbaric & Emergency Medical Centre, near the harbour (☎065/354-9525 or 354-4195). Thirty or so dive centres are members of the Diving Emergency Centre Organization (DECO; mobile ☎012 2187550, ✉info@deco -international.com); those diving with them are encouraged to pay €6 (S$8) for three weeks' cover, which includes free use of the decompression chambers in El-Gouna or Mersa Alam.

Diving centres

Of the 150 centres currently operating, the only ones subject to any serious monitoring are those affiliated to **HEPCA**, which are listed below. We'd advise that in general you should avoid those that aren't members. Should you have specific marine safety or environmental concerns, contact HEPCA at PO Box 144, Hurghada, Red Sea, Egypt (☎065/344-6674, 344-5035, ⑤344-5035, ⓔhepca@hepca.org).

Aquanaut *Shedwan Golden Beach* ☎065/354-9891, ⑤354-7045, ⓦwww.aquanaut.net.

Aquarius Diving Club *Marriott Beach Resort* ☎065/344-6950, ⑤344-6970, ⓦwww.aquarius-redsea.com.

Blue Heaven Divers *Regina Hotel* ☎ & ⑤344-5920, mobile ☎010 1141745, ⓦwww.blueheaven-divers.com.

Blue Water Dive Resort *Arabia Beach Hotel*, Sigala ☎065/354-8790, ⑤354-4888, ⓔinfo@blue-water-dive.com.

Colona *Magawish Village* ☎065/346-4632, ⑤346-4632, ⓦwww.colona.com. Also in El Gouna at the *Three Corners Rihana Inn*.

Deep Blue Diving Centre *Calimera Golden Beach Hotel*, 10km north of Hurghada. mobile ☎012 2280630.

Dive In Red Sea *Melia Pharaoh*, New Hurghada ☎065/344-6720, ⑤344-6724.

Divers International *Hilton Hurghada Plaza* ☎065/354-9745 ext 5507.

Easy Divers Academy El Gouna ☎ & ⑤065/358-0027, ⓔeasydive@intouch.com.

Easy Divers *Village*, Ed-Dahar ☎065/354-8816, ⑤344-3300, ⓦwww.easydivers-redsea.com.

El-Samaka *El-Samaka Beach Club* ☎065/344-6532, ⑤344-6530.

Emperor Divers *Hilton Resort* ☎ & ⑤065/344-4854, ⓔinfo.hurghada@emperordivers.com.

James & Mac *Giftun Village* ☎065/344-2665, ⑤344-2300, ⓔinfo@james-mac.com.

Jasmine Diving Center *Jasmin Village* ☎065/346-0665, ⑤344-6441, ⓔjasmindc@intouch.com.

Orca Tariq El-Nasr, between Ed-Dahar and Sigala ☎ & ⑤065/344-4150.

Sharm El-Naga Diving Centre Sharm El-Naga mobile ☎010 1234540.

Sub Aqua *Sofitel* ☎ & ⑤065/344-2473.

Subex Downtown, off the Corniche ☎065/354-7593, ⑤354-7471, ⓔredsea@subex.org, ⓦwww.subex.org.

Dive sites

Most sites within day-trip range are to the east and northeast of Hurghada. Inexperienced divers should be wary of the northerly reefs, where the currents are strongest. While many liveaboards go as far north as Ras Mohammed, sites to the south are regarded as more prestigious. Though mentioned under other towns, they are only accessible on liveaboards from Hurghada, or via dive centres further south. All of the following are within day-trip range unless stated otherwise.

Abu Hashish Cave An underwater cave in the reef, once used as a dope smugglers' cache.

Abu Ramada Three coral blocks covered in psychedelic-hued soft corals, off Giftun Island.

Abu Ramada Gota (aka "Aquarium") Amazing standing *ergs* and 1500-year-old stony corals, with a profusion of bannerfish, sweetlips and spotted groupers.

Brothers Several *ergs* emerging from the deeps of the Red Sea, 80km northeast of El-Quseir. A popular liveaboard destination, now open only to boats with permits.

Dolphin House A horseshoe-shaped reef 15km south of Mersa Alam, widely used by dolphins as a nursery for their young. HEPCA has recently installed buoys to prevent boats from entering. An excellent site for snorkelling.

El-Fanadir Beautiful reef slope and large table corals, to the north of Sigala.

El-Fanous Coral gardens just off Big Giftun Island, good for snorkelling as well as diving.

Giftun Island Most of the reefs on the Big and Small Giftun have been ruined by years of dive boats dropping their anchors onto the coral, and are now mostly visited by craft packed with snorkellers

(£E40–50 per person; £E100 overnight; equipment and food included). If you want to go on one of the less crowded boats used by divers, it'll cost £E10–20 extra. Two notable spots are the Small Giftun Drift (fine reef wall and lovely fan corals) and the Stone Beach on the northeast side of Big Giftun.

Shadwan Island Halfway to Sinai, so out of day-trip range. Sheer walls and deep trenches attract reef and oceanic sharks. Its lighthouse was of keen interest to de Monfried, when he navigated his boat through these waters in the early 1920s, with 600 kilos of hashish secreted in its hold.

Thistlegorm Sunken cargo ship full of jeeps, found by Jacques Cousteau off the coast of Sinai. A very popular four-day safari, albeit cheaper to make from Sharm el-Sheikh (see p.724).

Umm Gamar Island Sheer walls and caves, brilliant for drift diving. You can swim through a cave filled with thousands of silvery glassfish.

Zabargad Island Deep reefs teeming with oceanic fish and corals, 100km southeast of Berenice. A favourite long-haul destination, only open to boats with permits.

Beaches, pools and watersports

While diving is the main activity (see above), Hurghada presents itself as an all-round beach resort. Whilst the **public beach** in Sigala (daily 8am–sunset; £E3.50) has at last been transformed from a wasteland where no foreign tourist would be seen dead to a tidy shore with sunshades and a small refreshment kiosk, to sunbathe without unwanted attention, you'll have to go for the **private beaches**. In Ed-Dahar, the *Shedwan Golden Beach*, *Three Corners*, *Geisum Village* and *Sand Beach* open their beaches to outsiders for £E30 (you can also use the pools at the *Shedwan* and *Sand Beach*). Interlopers who slip past security usually get caught on the beach because they lack the distinctive bathing mats that are issued to residents and paying guests.

Further down the coast is the cheaper option of *Shellghada Beach*, just north of the *Sheraton*, where £E5 buys a day on the sand, volleyball and use of the freshwater showers. Eat at the restaurant and there is no entry charge. *El Saqiaa Restaurant and Beach* near the *Eiffel Hotel* offers a similar deal (£E15 including a free drink) and has a larger beach. Slightly more expensive is *Liquid* (£E30), a trendy beach bar opposite the *Roma Hotel* in Sigala, which has hammocks and sells beers. Other holiday villages allow outsiders to use their beaches and **swimming pools** for a charge that ranges from £E35 at the *El-Samaka Beach Club* to £E60 at the *Magawish Village* (which has the nicest beach). Admission policies may change, so phone ahead to avoid a wasted journey. Small coral reefs offshore from the *Shedwan Golden Beach* in Ed-Dahar, and the *Jasmin Village* in New Hurghada, offer a taste of the colourful array of fish and corals further out to sea. Buying beach or camping gear in Hurghada can be expensive; the Abu Ashara supermarket near *Papa's Bar* has a good selection at low fixed prices.

Powerful gusts make Hurghada a great place for **windsurfing**, especially the beaches at the *Magawish* and *Hurghada Beach*. Several holiday villages have lagoons and centres where you can rent boards (for around €10/US$13.50 per hour) and wetsuits, and some places offer windsurfing instruction. Happy Surf has branches at *Three Corners* (☎065/354-7816), the *Sofitel* (☎065/344-7261) and *Magawish Village* (mobile ☎012 7018500); Pro Center is based at *Jasmin Village* (☎065/344-6450); Habri/Friendly Surfing Center is at the *Hurghada Beach Resort* (☎065/344-3710); while Sam Surf Centre (mobile ☎010 5781351) is at Regina beach in Sigala.

If you book one or two days ahead, *Marine Sports Club* (☎065/344-4861, 2 or 3) can arrange **deep-sea fishing** day trips for £E400 per boat (6–8 people) including equipment. For a few hours' **snorkelling**, try Prince Sea Trips (☎065/354-1182, ⊛www.prince-diving.com) at the *Four Seasons* in Ed-Dahar. It's run by friendly Bedouin brothers who grew up in Hurghada, and costs

£E30 if you book direct, rather than the £E50–60 charged by most of the operators and agents around town.

The Aquarium, Sindbad Submarine and Aquascope

If you want a glimpse of the Red Sea's wonders without getting wet, visit the **Red Sea Aquarium** (daily 9am–10pm; £E5, camera £E2) on the Corniche. Its tanks are labelled in English, with diagrams of where to find each species on the reef. You can learn to recognize wrasses, triggerfish, sailfintangs, angelfish and many other types, but it's sad to see them in such cramped conditions when you know that millions of others are swimming freely not far away.

Alternatively, there's the much-hyped **Sindbad Submarine** (US$50, children US$25), which can take you to depths of 22m in comfort. Disappointingly, however, half the time is spent getting to and from the sub's mooring offshore from the *Sindbad Beach Resort*, and after submerging a diver swims alongside trailing bait to attract wrasses, groupers and parrotfish past the portholes. You'd do better to go on an introductory dive – but if the sub still appeals, bookings can be made at the *Sindbad* (☎065/344-4688) or other holiday villages.

Another window on the underwater world can be seen from on board **Aquascope** (US$40), a sort of New Age glass-bottom boat. The two-hour trip leaves from the *Royal Palace Hotel* (☎065/346-3657) near the tourist information office in New Hurghada and includes a fifty-minute tour of the coral reefs. A more traditional glass-bottom boat experience can be had on the **Red Sea Dolphin** (10am & 3pm; 2hr; US$39 including drinks), which is based at the *Inter-Continental* 3km south of the tourist information office in New Hurghada on Tariq Al-Kura.

Eating and drinking

Hurghada is good for **eating out**, with a wide choice of cuisine suited to all budgets. There are dozens of restaurants in holiday villages, mostly upmarket and with **music** in the evenings, while for a cheap meal, you can check out the many (sometimes nameless) fish restaurants and pizza parlours in Ed-Dahar and Sigala. **Opening hours** are generally mid-morning until 11pm or midnight (maybe later in high season), though the choice of food dwindles after 10pm. Almost everywhere adds 10–12 percent in **service taxes** to the bill – at some holiday villages they bump things up by as much as 21 percent.

If you're keen on saving money it's worth tracking down some **street stalls**. There are two good *fuul* and felafel stands on the street running south of, and parallel to, Sharia Sheikh Sebak; juice bars and nut stalls are scattered around the bazaar, and there are *kushari* stands near the bus station. In Sigala, there's a pair of felafel stands on Sigala Square near the police station, and a place with refrigerated carcasses outside that does tasty kebab, *kofta* and pizzas. Don't miss the two excellent cake shops inside The Market mall, on the strip. For the less adventurous there's the ubiquitous *Pizza Hut* and *KFC* near *Sindbad Beach Resort*, *McDonald's* in downtown Sigala, and a new *Hard Rock Café*, across from the *El-Samaka* hotel in New Hurghada.

Unless otherwise stated, all the places below are in Ed-Dahar, and are marked on the maps on p.776 or p.780.

Abo Khadega In Sigala. Small workers' café where you can get a tasty meal of soup, rice, salad, beans and grilled meat for £E8.

Agra In Sigala, near the *Golf Hotel*. Excellent Indian restaurant serving a variety of dishes including lamb biryani (£E28) and Tandori Murgh (£E28).

Bella Riviera Near *Shakespears Hotel*. Friendly café serving tasty lentil soup, spaghetti Bolognese, lasagne and salads at low prices. No alcohol.

Chez Pascal In Three Corners Empire shopping centre. Good food and service in a soothing atmosphere – try the lobster thermidor (£E50) or black pepper steak (£E44). Sells alcohol.

El-Joker Near the police station in Sigala square. Excellent seafood restaurant with generous portions at very good prices (£E25–35) – try the calamari soup. Open 11pm–1am.

El-Masri Near the police station in Sigala square. Offers kebabs, traditional Egyptian food and chicken at very reasonable prices (around £E15).

Far East Korea Redcon Mall, Sigala ☎ 065/445-207. Good-value Chinese-Korean restaurant with friendly staff; also does takeaway.

Felfela's Sigala, between the *Holiday Inn* and *Sheraton* hotels ☎ 065/344-2410. Branch of the famous Cairo restaurant chain serving decent Egyptian food at reasonable rates. Lots of space, nice atmosphere and great view of the harbour. Sells beer. Good for vegetarians. Does takeaway.

Mahyma Giftun Island. A bar and restaurant for tourists visiting the island, open till 10pm. As you might expect, not terribly cheap and a limited menu. Pizza £E20, Stella £E12, coffee £E7.

Mandarine Hospital Street. Excellent but pricey Lebanese restaurant with a pleasant street-side patio. Serves decent mixed grill (£E55), and mixed seafood (£E120).

Moby Dick, 150m north of *McDonalds* in Sigala. Popular with tour groups, this restaurant serves both Egyptian and Western food, with very good falafel, as well as pizza and pasta.

Omar Inn In Sigala, opposite the *Golf* hotel ☎ 065/344-6166. A coffee shop that serves decent food, including pizza, seafood, snacks and fruit juice. Good place for people-watching. Does takeaway.

Red Sea In the bazaar, off Tariq El-Nasr. One of Hurghada's classiest seafood places, with a rooftop garden and a/c downstairs. Main dishes cost £E20–50. Sells alcohol. A second branch is located on the strip near the *Empire Hotel*.

Spaghetti Near *McDonald's* in Sigala. Steak and seafood restaurant with large outdoor seating area. Good value and popular with families.

Sushi House Next to *McDonald's* in Sigala. Reasonably priced sushi; also does takeaway. Open daily 9am–10pm

Tako In Sigala, 500m north of *McDonalds'*. Popular Egyptian fast-food outlet, famous for its *shawarma*.

Tarboush Sharia Abdel Aziz Mustafa. Small, simple pizzeria, with about fifteen not so different-tasting varieties (£E8–23) on the menu. No alcohol.

Young Kang Sharia Sheikh Sebak. Reasonable Chinese-Korean restaurant, with fair-sized portions at moderate prices. Sells beer.

Drinking

As you'd expect in a major resort, lots of **drinking** goes on in discos, restaurants and hotels – though the number of actual bars isn't that large. Most restaurants don't sell alcohol during Ramadan and before 1pm on Fridays, but holiday villages are exempt from these restrictions. There are **duty-free shops** in the AKA mall near the EgyptAir office in New Hurghada, and next to the *Ambassador Hotel* on the road to the airport. **Smoking** is less popular in Hughada than in Luxor or Dahab – which isn't surprising given that *bango* costs at least £E50 a *talga*. The following **bars** are open till midnight.

Juke Box Pub On the Corniche in Ed-Dahar. Tacky bar but good views from the rooftop beer garden. Serves food and stages sporadic Oriental belly-dance shows.

Liquid Sheraton Road, opposite the *Roma Hotel*. This beach bar has become the hang-out of choice for Hurghada's diving fraternity and other foreign residents, with different styles of music played each night, plus dance nights at weekends. Plays a good selection of alternative music, a welcome break from the techno played at *Papa's Beach Bar*.

Papa's Bar Next to *Rossi's* in Sigala. mobile ☎ 010 5129051, ⓦ www.papasbar.com. Another of Hurghada's popular bars for foreigners, mainly because it's Dutch-run and full of diving instructors.

Papas II Below the *Juke Box Pub* on the Corniche, Ed-Dahar. Mobile ☎ 010 2641992. Similar to its older sister bar in Sigala, with live music on several nights a week.

Papa's Beach Bar 350m south of the harbour, Sigala. Easily the most popular nightclub in Hurghada, where most people end up for late-night dancing (it doesn't really get going until after midnight). Entry is £E50, which includes two drinks.

Nightlife

Hurghada has some of the liveliest **nightlife** in mainland Egypt, as hotels strive to outdo each other's discos and floor shows – but none are wild raves and the music is mostly mainstream. Posh places baulk at shorts or trainers; smart-casual **dress** is universally acceptable. Most discos have a **minimum charge**, sometimes paid up front in return for a card that gets punched whenever you buy a drink – don't lose it. Drink **prices** vary from £E8 to £E14 for a Stella, Sakkara Gold or Meister, £E20–25 for an imported beer or a cocktail. Few discos get going before 11pm, and while most are advertised as staying open till 4am, they may close earlier if things are quiet.

Discos wax and wane in popularity, with the current most popular hangouts being *Papa's Beach Bar*, which attracts both tourists and young Egyptian men, and *Liquid*, a more laidback option with better music (see p.787 for both). Other favourites are in holiday villages; try the *Dome* (10pm–4am) at the *Inter-Continental* or the discos at the *Sand Beach*, *Princess Club* and *Sindbad Beach Resort*. Although £E20 minimum charge is standard almost everywhere, the *Giftun Village* charges £E15, while the disco at the *Sofitel* is free.

Occasionally you can see **bellydancing** at some clubs, with *Elf Leila Wa Leila* ("1001 Nights"), on the southern outskirts of Hurghada, having one of the best shows. Tickets including transport can be bought at most hotels (US$15–18 including dinner, $10 with soft drinks only; 8–10.30pm). Some of the resort discos also put on 'Russian shows', with tawdry dance troupes tumbling onto the dance floor to perform between songs. Slightly less exotic and less expensive is the **bowling alley** at the *Aqua Fun Hotel* (℡065/344-3262) in Sigala.

Listings

Banks Of the two close together on Tariq El-Nasr, the Banque Misr (daily 9am–9pm) has an ATM outside and gives cash advances on Visa and MasterCard, while the National Bank of Egypt (Mon–Thurs & Sun 8.30am–2pm & 6–9pm, Fri 9–11am & 2–5pm) takes travellers' cheques. There is also an ATM in the *Empire* and *La Pacha Cataract* in Sigala. In New Hurghada there are ATMs at the HSBC near *KFC* and *Pizza Hut* near *Sindbad Beach Resort*; at the *Inter-Continental* in New Hurghada and Banque Misr just north of the tourist office which also gives cash advances on Visa and Mastercard. Money transfers can be arranged through Federal Express or Thomas Cook (see overpage).

Car rental CRC Rent-a-Car (℡065/344-4885; @crc_hurghada@yahoo.com), near the *Grand Hotel*, charges US$45 a day for a Peugeot 106; Limo 1, at the *Inter-Continental* (℡065/346-5100, ℻346-5101), has Mazdas from US$30 per day or a 4WD Lada Niva at US$45. Hertz (℡065/344-2884), opposite EgyptAir in New Hurghada, usually rents Hyundais. Other companies worth considering are Europcar (℡065/344-3660) based at the *Royal Palace Hotel* in New Hurghada; Avis (℡065/344-7400) opposite Waves Resort, which has a good range of 4WDs; and Thrifty at the *Melia Pharoah* in New Hurghada (℡065/344-6723).

Federal Express In Sigala (daily 8am–6pm; ℡065/344-2444). Costly, fast and reliable worldwide express mail service. Can also wire money.

Hospitals The general hospital in Ed-Dahar (℡065/335-4670) and the private El-Saffa on El-Nasr St (℡065/354-0665) have improved, but the best medical treatment is available at the private hospital in El-Gouna (℡065/354-9709 ext 2201/2, emergencies ext 2200), or El-Salam Hospital (℡065/354-8787) in the *Arabia Village Hotel*. Less serious complaints can be treated by physicians on call at holiday villages, or check the listings in the *Connect Guide*. Diving emergencies can be dealt with either at El Gouna Hospital or Hurghada's new Naval Hyperbaric & Emergency Medical Centre (℡065/344-9150 or 354-4195) near the harbour.

Internet cafés These are sprouting up all over Hurghada and usually charge around £E10 per hour, though you can sometimes bargain this down to £E5. In Ed-Dahar, on the strip near the *Empire Hotel*, is Kero 2 (daily 9am–2am; ℡065/355-5309). About 50m west of here, and down a side alley, is the friendly and cheaper *Golden Internet Café* (24 hrs; mobile ℡012 7449660).

Laundry Stop-Shop (daily 8am–8pm; ℡065/344-6609), off Tariq El-Nasr, 300m south of the bus station, charges 50pt–£E4 an item. Most hotels can have your washing sent out for £E2–8 per piece.

Passport office Entrance on the left side of the prominently signposted Red Sea Security Department building, 3km past the Esh-Shahid Mosque (Mon–Thurs & Sun 8am–2pm; ☎065/344-6727).

Pharmacies There are several on Sharia Abdel Aziz Mustafa and Tariq El-Nasr. You can also find well-stocked pharmacies outside the hospitals.

Post office On Tariq al-Nasr, 200m north of the bus station (daily except Fri 8am–2pm). Has direct-dial phones and Express Mail Service.

Telephone calls Direct-dial phones in the 24-hour *centraal* in Sigala, just south of *McDonald's*, as well as at several points on the street; phonecards are sold at the *centraal*. If you're prepared to pay premium rates, many hotels and shops in the bazaar advertise international lines that may result in speedier connections.

Thomas Cook In Sigala (daily 9am–2pm & 6–9pm; ☎065/344-3338, ℱ354-1870). Offers all the usual services including Moneygrams, and also handles MasterCard emergencies.

Tourist police Next to the tourist office in New Hurghada (24hr; ☎065/346-3300). To contact the police in Ed-Dahar, call ☎065/354-3365 or ☎122.

Working Distinctly feasible if you have diving qualifications (Divemaster upwards) or foreign languages (especially Japanese or Russian). Hotels and dive centres need people to work at reception or drum up clients. Ask other foreigners working here which firms are dodgy, and don't hand over your passport lightly. Whatever you do, do not invest any money in Hurghada – the biggest sharks aren't found in the Red Sea.

Moving on

Scores of travel agencies offer **excursions** to Luxor, Sinai or Cairo as day-trips or overnight packages. Terms and prices vary, so shop around. Among the contenders it's worth mentioning Misr Travel (daily 8.30am–10pm; ☎065/344-1699, mobile ☎010 5418079) for its day-trips to the **Red Sea Monasteries** (US$55), **Mons Claudianus** (US$42) and **Wadi Hammamat** (US$25, $30 with barbecue). Other long-established agents in Hurghada include Abu Noub Travel (☎065/344-2843) and Eastmar (☎065/344-4581): as well as local trips, they handle tours to **Cairo** (two days; US$140) and day-trips to **Luxor** (6am–11pm; US$80), and to **Sinai** by catamaran, including taking in **St Catherine's Monastery** and **Dahab** (US$165).

Moving on by **public transport**, you've the usual choice between buses, service taxis and the odd flight, plus a sea link across the Gulf of Suez to Sharm el-Sheikh in Sinai.

Buses

For travel by **bus** to Cairo and Luxor, it's a good idea to buy your tickets in advance from the main bus station (☎065/354-7582). East Delta runs six a/c buses daily to Cairo (10am, 11am, 5.30pm, 11.30pm, 1am & 2am; 6–8hr; £E55). Suez is served by a dozen buses daily (9.30am–1am; 5–8hr; £E30) and tickets are sold on the bus. Buses to Luxor (10.30am, 1pm, 7pm, 10.30pm, 12.30am, 1am & 3am; 5hr; £E25) are routed via Safaga and Qena; those to Aswan (10.30am, 12.30pm, 12.30am; 8hr; £E40) also go via Safaga, which is also accessible by buses bound for El-Quseir (5am, 5.30am, 6am, 3pm, 5.30pm, 8.30pm, 1am, 3am; £E20) and Mersa Alam (4hr; £E30). Other buses travel to Safaga hourly (7am–2am; £E10). Buses to Assyut (£E20) and Sohag (£E16) in Middle Egypt run frequently but are unlikely to have a/c.

Besides the above, a/c **Superjet** buses with toilets and "in-flight" snacks and movies depart four times a day for Cairo (12pm, 2.30pm, 5pm & 12am; 6hr 30min; £E57) from the Superjet station (☎065/355-3499), 1km south of the main bus station; the 2.30pm bus carries on to Alexandria (£E85). There is also a daily Superjet bus to Sharm el-Sheikh, via Suez (9pm; £E70). Buy tickets in advance to be sure of a seat.

Alternatively, the **El Gouna Transport Company** (☎065/354-1561 or mobile ☎010 2593889) runs seven buses from Hurghada, via El Gouna, daily to Cairo's El-Munib bus station in Giza (9am, 1pm, 2.30pm, 4pm, 12am, 1am, 2am; 30min later at El-Gouna; 7hr; £E55).

Taxis

Mornings are the best time to catch seven-seater **service taxis** to Suez (5hr; £E25), Cairo (6–7hr; £E35), Port Safaga (45min; £E5) or El-Quseir (1hr 30min; £E10). Whatever the time of day, you shouldn't have to wait more than half an hour for a service taxi to Qena (4hr; £E12), whence buses run on to Luxor (see p.282). Don't believe anyone who says there's a "convoy charge" for foreigners. Groups of travellers can consider taking their own **taxi** all the way to Sharm el-Sheikh (about £E700) – which is one way to avoid a tedious interlude at Suez (see p.682). Plenty of taxis are prepared to take tourists to Luxor; £E180 for seven people is a fair price.

Flights

If you've got the money and book early, EgyptAir **flights** are the quickest way of reaching **Cairo**, with four daily departures (6.30am, 10.30am, 5pm, 12am; US$130). In peak season there is also usually a Saturday flight to **Sharm el-Sheikh** (US$62) and sometimes two flights per week to **Alexandria** (approx US$160). You can book flights at the EgyptAir office (daily 8am–8pm ☏065/346-3034) in New Hurghada, or with Karnak EgyptAir (☏065/354-7891 mobile ☏012 2200026) in Ed-Dahar; both are open daily 8am–8pm. The **airport** is 15km south of Ed-Dahar, off the Hurghada–Safaga road (£E25 by taxi, plus £E4 for an airport entry tax).

By sea

Links with Sinai have been transformed by the introduction of a high-speed catamaran that cuts the journey to Sharm el-Sheikh to ninety minutes – as opposed to five or six hours by the old ferry, or 12–18 hours overland. The **catamaran** runs to Sharm four times a week (Mon, Tues, Thurs & Sat at 8am; £E250), though it is out of service for several weeks in the late spring for annual maintenance. Tickets can be bought from International Fast Ferries (☏065/344-7571; ⊛www .internationalfastferries.com) in Sigala, close to *McDonalds*. Fantasia Shipping (☏065/344-1118) also runs a **ferry** three times a week **to Duba** in Saudi Arabia (3hr; 9am; US$100). Advance bookings can also be made for both the catamaran and the ferry through Sherif Tours at the *Sand Beach* (☏065/354-5147) or El-Shaymaa Sea Trips (☏065/354-6907), near the tourist bazaar in Ed-Dahar.

The Red Sea Mountains

Inland of Hurghada the barren plains erupt into the **Red Sea Mountains**, which follow the coast southwards towards Ethiopia. This geologically primitive range of granite, porphyry and breccia contains Egypt's highest mountains outside Sinai, rearing up to 2187m (over 7000ft) above sea level. During winter, peaks exceeding 1500m draw moisture from rising masses of air, while in summertime they precipitate brief, localized storms accompanied by violent lightning and flash floods. Hardy desert plants flourish in their wake, providing grazing for feral ruminants and the flocks of a few thousand nomads. Roaming their vast tribal lands, these Bedouin are perfectly at home in the wilderness – unlike isolated groups of miners and soldiers, who feel almost as exiled as the slaves who quarried here in ancient times.

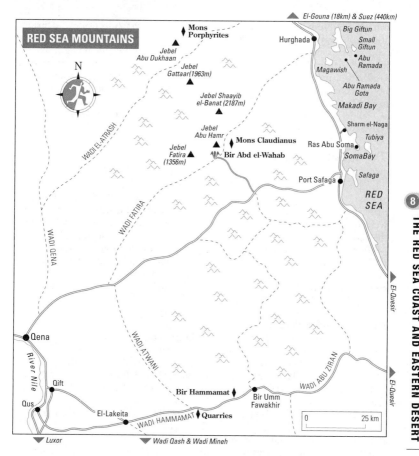

As far as Europeans are concerned, the Red Sea Mountains were first climbed in the 1920s and 1930s, and have hardly been scaled since; as Sinai becomes increasingly commercialized, this may become the next wilderness to attract tourists.

Exploring the mountains

Short of befriending some Bedouin and tagging along with them, the Red Sea Mountains are most easily accessible via **day excursions from Hurghada**. Most companies offer a half-day camel or jeep safari at sundown including a barbecue and Bedouin entertainments for around US$35. Prince Safari Trips (☎065/354-1182, ✉info@prince-diving.com), at the *Four Seasons* hotel, offers a sunset "safari" (£E100), with a thirty-minute Landcruiser journey to a Bedouin village for a camel ride, followed by tea and some Bedouin music, which makes a good introduction to the Bedouin and the majestic landscape they live in. It also runs longer desert camping trips (£E180 per person per day, minimum five people) for the more adventurous.

The government is trying to promote **adventure tourism** in the Eastern Desert, so the opportunities for organized treks and mountain-climbing are improving. From October to March, Red Sea Desert Adventures in Shagra Village, Mersa Alam (mobile ☎012 2467826, 🌐www.redseadesertadventures .com), for example, offers jeep and camel safaris and hikes, including a six-day jeep safari from Hurghada to Mons Claudianus and Mons Porphyrites with a visit to the prehistoric rock art in Wadi Qattar (€850 or US$1145, including hotel accommodation, transport, safari, food and drink), and a six-day safari from Mersa Alam taking in Berenice and Wadi Sakait (from €400 or US$540), as well as half-, full-day and overnight camel or jeep trips starting from €30 (UD$40) per person.

Two Roman quarries

Twenty kilometres north of Hurghada, a piste quits the highway and climbs inland towards **Jebel Abu Dukhaan**, the 1161-metre-high "Mountain of Smoke". Anciently known as **Mons Porphyrites**, this was the Roman Empire's main source of fine red porphyry, used for columns and ornamentation. Blocks were dragged 150km to the Nile, or by a shorter route to the coast, whence they were shipped to far-flung sites such as Baalbek or Constantinople.

Round about the extensive quarries lies a **ruined town** of rough-hewn buildings with two large cisterns and an unfinished Ionic temple. Rock hyraxes (a kind of large rodent) lived in dens around Jebel Abu Dukhaan until all its trees were cut down for fuel. From the ruins, the piste follows Wadi el-Atrash and Wadi Qena down to the Nile Valley.

Mons Claudianus

Although **Mons Claudianus** is only 50km distant from Mons Porphyrites as the crow flies, lofty massifs necessitate more roundabout approaches. Coming from Hurghada, you need to follow a piste that starts between the port and Magawish Village. There are also two routes off the Port Safaga–Qena road: a well-surfaced one, 41km from the coast, and a longer, rougher piste nearer Qena.

Under the emperors Trajan and Hadrian, the pale, black-flecked granite quarried at Mons Claudianus was used to construct the Pantheon and Trajan's Forum in Rome. Around the **quarries**, beneath Jebel Fatira and Jebel Abu Hamr, you'll find numerous unformed capitals and abandoned columns. Wadi Fatira contains a cracked, 200-tonne monster, dubbed the "**Mother of Columns**" by the Arabs, while in the quarries of Hydreuma lies a giant unfinished **sarcophagus**. There's also a sizeable ruined town, **Fons Trajanus**.

Mountains and water sources

Between the two quarries rise the highest mountains in the Eastern Desert: Jebel Gattaar and Jebel Shaayib el-Banat.

Jebel Gattaar and Jebel Shaayib el-Banat

Jebel Gattaar (1963m) is esteemed by the Bedouin for its permanent springs and comparatively abundant vegetation. Umm Yasar and other *wadis* draining from Gattaar contain hundreds of acacia and ben trees, a remnant of once-extensive forests that were ravaged by charcoaling. As late as the 1880s, E.A. Floyer found Wadi Gattaar "thickly studded with big mimosa trees, some twenty and thirty feet high", whose reckless felling compelled the Bedouin to cut down live acacias for fodder when drought struck in the 1950s.

Further south, the loftier **Jebel Shaayib el-Banat** (2187m) rises to a summit that the geographer and mountaineer George Murray likened to a "monstrous

> ## The Ma'aza Bedouin, gazelles and ibexes
>
> From St Anthony's Monastery to the Qift–El-Quseir road, 90,000 square kilometres of highland form the stamping ground of the **Ma'aza** ("Goat") tribe of **Bedouin**, who migrated here from Arabia in the 1700s. As their name suggests, goats form the basis of their livelihood, although gathering plants and hunting are also important. Herbalists buy wormwood, henbane, argel and ben-tree seeds from the nomads, while hunters from the Gulf Emirates used to rent them as guides until the Ma'aza grew disgusted with their wanton slaughter of Barbary sheep (now almost extinct), ibexes and gazelles.
>
> Traditionally the Ma'aza only hunt with dogs, rocks and knives, sprinting after their prey. Whereas **gazelles** are regarded as everyday food, ibex meat is prized because it supposedly enables them to run up mountains without tiring. The sound of rutting **ibexes** locking horns in September attracts the foul **botfly**, which squirts its larvae into their mouths and nostrils. Smashing dead branches with rocks makes the same noise – something to remember should you camp out in these mountains, as botfly can also live as parasites in humans.

webbed hand of seven smoothed fingers". The highest mountain in mainland Egypt, its peak was first climbed by Murray in 1922. In Bedouin folklore, Shaayib harbours a "Tree of Light" whose leaves can cure blindness; the world's only other one is believed to be in Lebanon.

Wadi Naggaat and the Ma'aza Limestone Plateau

Early Christian hermits made their home in **Wadi Naggaat**, between Jebel Abu Dukhaan and Jebel Shaayib. *Naggaat* means "dripping place", a Bedouin term applied to a particular type of water source that falls from cliffs to irrigate maiden-hair ferns, reeds and mosses, and fills pools where ibexes and people drink.

But with only four *naggaat* in the Eastern Desert and not enough rope to plumb the fifty-metre-deep well of Bir Gattaar, the Bedouin must also use surface springs and gravel seeps. These are far more common in the granite Red Sea Mountains than on the **Ma'aza Limestone Plateau** that separates the range from the Nile Valley, one reason why Bedouin dislike this "Place of Stray-ings". Its mysterious **Bir Shaitan** ("Pool of Satan") is popularly believed to be replenished by Nile water via an underground passage but is actually dependent on rainfall; the shade from the overhanging rocks prevents evaporation.

South of Hurghada

Down the coast from Hurghada, the stream of holiday resorts becomes less dense until two belated spurts of development on the outskirts of **Port Safaga** (58km) and **El-Quseir** (a further 85km). Little more than an overgrown, grubby port, Safaga has few charms though it is within boat range of some stunning offshore reefs, while El-Quseir retains a sleepy quality unlike anywhere else on the Red Sea. From both points, connections with the Nile Valley are assured, via roads that cut across the Eastern Desert following old camel routes.

Further south, communications become tenuous and bureaucratic obstacles loom as you head **towards the Sudanese border**. From Shalateen, you need military permission to proceed further south, or into the mountains, and the allure of the far south depends primarily on its reefs, which can be reached by dive boats operating out of Hurghada, Safaga, El-Quseir and Mersa Alam.

The highway initially runs several kilometres inland before regaining the coast. About 40km after Hurghada and 18km before Safaga, a signpost indicates the turn-off for **SHARM EL-NAGA**, a wide bay where *Sharm El-Naga Camp* (mobile ☎010 1513615; ❹) has 26 pastel-coloured tents furnished with beds, wardrobes and 24-hour electricity. The site also has hot-water showers, and you can sometimes bring your own tent. The main attraction here is the **beach-diving** and **snorkelling**, and day-trippers from Hurghada often come here to use the beach (£E15 fee for non-stayers), which makes a quieter alternative to overcrowded Hurghada.

The luxury development of **Soma Bay** (2km further on from Sharm El-Naga) boasts, among other things, an 18-hole golf course. There are several hotels offering similar facilities, of which the *Sheraton Soma Bay* (☎065/354-5845 or 354-5915, ☏354-5885 ⓦwww.sheraton-somabay.com; ❽) is the most appealing. Further south, just before Safaga is **Makadi Bay**, a similar-style complex with a *Meridien* and several four- and five-star *Iberotel*, of which the *Iberotel Makadi Beach* (☎065/359-0000, ☏359-0000, ⓔgm@iberotelmakadibeach .com; ❽) is the one to choose.

Port Safaga and the road to Qena

Once known for the restorative health properties of its sandy beaches, **PORT SAFAGA** (*Bur Safaga*) now amounts to very little. Coming in from the north you pass a slip road curving off to six holiday villages on a headland, which cater to groups on diving holidays. The town begins 3km later and consists of a single windswept avenue running straight on past concrete boxes with bold signs proclaiming their function, until the bus station and a final mosque, 4km south. Silos and cranes identify the port, which runs alongside (but out of bounds) for most of this distance. Safaga's only attraction is the **reefs** to the north, and if you're not going to see them, there's not much reason to hang around. As buses and taxis travelling between Hurghada and Luxor use the desert highway that turns off at Safaga, passengers can see all there is to see as they drive through town.

Accommodation

In Safaga itself, accommodation includes several pricey **hotels** near the beach, a few mid-range options on the Corniche, a cheaper budget hotel on the main road and a couple of very basic places near the port. If you're diving, you'll probably be staying at one of the cluster of holiday resorts with dive centres, all of which are around 3–5km north of town unless otherwise stated; minibuses (£E1) run out to the *Shams Safaga*, the furthest of the resort complexes.

Amira El Corniche ☎065/325-3821, ⓔamirahotel@hotmail.com. Has decent amenities, including sauna, gym, and swimming pool. Breakfast included. ❺

Cleopatra Opposite EgyptAir, in town ☎065/253-926. Reasonably clean, carpeted rooms with TV and baths, off dingy corridors. Caters mainly for Egyptians. ❷

El-Ezz Near the port entrance and bus station ☎065/325-2312. Basic rooms, mostly used by arrivals at the port rather than foreign travellers. No breakfast. ❷

Holiday Inn Resort ☎065/326-0100, ⓔreservation@holidayinnsafaga.com. Safaga's most stylish tourist village, with an outsized pool

and fine sea views; rooms have a/c, fridge and satellite TV. Happy hour 8–10pm for cocktails in the *Windsurf Bar*. ❼

Lotus Bay Resort & Gardens ☎065/325-1040, ⓔlotusbay@yahoo.com. Also called *Lotus Bay Club Villas*. Spacious array of villas in a nice garden. All mod cons. Italian/Swiss clientele. Half-board only. ❻

Maka Near the Bank of Alexandria and port entrance ☎065/325-1866. Basic and ramshackle, this is the cheapest place around the port, with shared bathrooms and unreliable hot water. There's no breakfast, which is just as well given the lack of sanitation. ❶

Menaville Village ☎065/326-0064, ☏326-0068. A decent place that's not too flashy, and reasonably priced. Mainly Swiss, Italian and French clientele. ❻

Nemo Mobile ☎010 3648708, ☂www.nemodive
.com. This European-owned, Disney-themed hotel,
located on El Corniche (take the first left before
entering town), has an eager management, bright
rooms and sea views. Breakfast included. ❺
Solymar Resort Paradise ☎065/326-0017,
☏326-0016, ☂www.solymar-hotels.com. Located
4km north of town, this was Safaga's first resort.
It's been renovated and attracts a largely Slavic
clientele. Half-board only. ❻
Shams Safaga ☎065/325-1781, ✉shamshotels
@hotmail.com. Has a private reef, good sports
facilities and a children's playground. Popular with
British tour groups. Half-board only. ❻

Sun Beach Next to the *Lotus Bay Resort*
☎065/326-0055, ☏326-0054. This rather run
down resort accepts only tour groups in its beach
chalets, but independent travellers are allowed to
camp on the beach for about £E30, with use of the
showers and café. It's also home to the Orca dive
centre. ❹
Three Corners Amira On the coast between the
port and the town ☎065/325-3821, ☏325-3825.
Smart upmarket hotel, part of El Gouna's *Three
Corners* chain, with its own beach. Good value
though far from the rest of the tourist villages.
Half-board only. ❻

Diving and snorkelling

Boats and instructors at the main **diving centres** tend to be committed to
groups, though they will take on independent travellers if they have space:
expect to pay around €260 (US$350) for a four-day open-water course, or
€50 (US$67) for two boat dives. If you have your own equipment, the *Sun
Beach* resort runs **snorkelling** day trips to Tubiya Island for £E30 per person
including lunch. As in Hurghada (see p.782), an additional **environmental fee**
of €2.20 a day is levied on all diving and snorkelling trips.

The main diving grounds lie 6–8km offshore from the holiday villages,
between Safaga Island and Ras Abu Soma. **Tubiya Island** is ringed with corals
only just off its beach, while dive boats drop their clients directly over the
sunken **North and South Fairway Reefs** or the twin pairs of sites known
as **Tubiya Kebir**, **Tubiya Soraya**, **Gamul Soraya** and **Gamul Kebir**. Other
sites include the **Seven Pillars** off Ras Abu Soma, and the **Panorama Reef**
and **Shark Point**, 10km east of Safaga Island. Most of them are notable for their
coral pillars and strong currents.

Among the big fish prevalent in these waters are aggressive **hammerhead
sharks**. Research suggests that they track their victims with two forms of
biological sensor. At long range and when closing in on its kill, the hammerhead
senses vibrations in the water, but in the final seconds it tunes into electromag-
netic fields "bounced" off its target. It was hammerheads that caused many of
the fatalities of Egypt's greatest maritime disaster, in December 1991, when
the Salem Express ferry, on its return from Jeddah, hit a reef only a few miles
offshore and sunk in three minutes. Around 1300 of the 1600 passengers on-
board perished, many from attacks by the hammerheads.

Dive centres

Alpha Red Sea *Amira Hotel* ☎065/325-3229,
☂www.alpharedsea.com.
Barakuda *Lotus Bay* (☎065/325-1041,
☏325-1476) and *Menaville Village* (☎065/344-
6950, ☏344-6970).
Ducks *Holiday Inn Resort* ☎065/326-0100,
☏065/325-2825, ✉ddredsea@t-online.de.

Menadive *Menaville Village* ☎065/326-0064.
Orca *Sun Beach* ☎065/326-0111, ☂www
.orca-red-sea.com.
Shams Safaga *Shams Safaga* ☎065/251-782,
☏251-780, ✉shams@internetegypt.com.
Volkert/Paradise Dive *Solymar Resort Paradise*
☎065/326-0017, mobile ☎010 2514061.

Other practicalities – and leaving Safaga

Most of Safaga's facilities are along the main drag, including the **police** station
and EgyptAir, 200m south of the City Council, followed by a **hospital** 500m

on. There's a **petrol station** beyond the next turn-off, across the main road from the Bank of Alexandria; further south on the other side are Banque Misr and the National Bank of Egypt, and a **telephone exchange**. Tourists staying at the holiday villages can more conveniently change money at **banks** inside *Safaga Marina* and the *Shams Safaga* or the Banque du Caire in the shopping arcade near the *Holiday Inn*. The arcade also has a Fuji photographic shop.

Aside from the **restaurants** at the holiday resorts, there are several **cafés** offering sandwiches or *shawarmas* on the main drag. For grilled meat, pasta, salads and pizzas, however, you're better off at the *Aly Baba restaurant* (daily noon–10pm), 2km north of the town centre, or the *El-Joker restaurant* (☎065/326-0575), 3km north of town opposite the *Lotus Bay*.

There are a couple of **internet cafés** in Safaga: *Yasmin Internet* (☎065/326-0575 or mobile ☎012 7523236) opposite the *Lotus Bay*, and the *Internet Café* (mobile ☎012 7962800) next to *Aly Baba restaurant*; both charge £E10 per hour.

Safaga's **bus station** is near to the port, with around nine **buses** daily to Hurghada (6am–11.30pm; £E10) and Suez (6am–11.30pm; £E23–35), seven to Cairo (6am–11.30pm; £E55), seven to Qena (8am–midnight; £E20), six to Luxor (8am–midnight; £E25), three to Aswan (at 1am, 2am & 11.30am; £E45), two to Alexandria (7am & 6pm; £E70) and one to Sharm el-Sheikh (8.30pm; £E75). Sticking to the Red Sea Coast, two buses a day (6pm & 7pm; £E10) run down to El-Quseir, while three others (9.30pm, 3am & 4am; £E15–20) carry on to Mersa Alam. **Service taxis** leave from the depot 500m south of the port entrance and run in between buses to Hurghada and Qena for similar rates, though it can take a long time to muster enough passengers for El-Quseir.

The road to Qena and off to the quarries

Safaga is primarily a commercial port for shipping out phosphates and importing US grain sent as food aid. The reopening of a long-abandoned freight railway has ended a windfall for the Ma'aza Bedouin, who used to feed their flocks on grain spilt along **the desert road to Qena** (161km). However, elders still spend their final years here: the pickings are good and they get to meet everybody. It's a harsh landscape of fissured rocks and canyons, with a beautiful dune cascading down the hillside shortly before you pass a small cafeteria, 85km from Qena. There are no petrol stations en route, but passengers can refresh themselves at wayside stands planted with trees, irrigated by the pipeline that conveys water from the Nile to Safaga and Hurghada.

Those with 4WD vehicles might consider two routes leading off **towards Mons Claudianus** (see p.792). The turn-off west of Safaga gets there in 25km via Bir Abd el-Wahab, whereas the rougher piste outside Qena follows its eponymous *wadi* to El-Heita before forking right up Wadi el-Atrash towards Jebel Abu Dukhaan (roughly 150km).

El-Quseir and the route to Qift

EL-QUSEIR, 85km from Safaga, is also a phosphates extraction centre, though with fewer inhabitants and more appeal. In pharaonic times, it was from here that boats sailed to the "Land of Punt" (thought to be Yemen or Somalia), as depicted in reliefs within Hatshepsut's temple at Deir el-Bahri. The Romans knew it as *Leukos Limen* ("White Harbour"), while under Arab rule El-Quseir was the largest port on the Red Sea until the tenth century, and remained a major transit point for pilgrims until the 1840s, when Flaubert caught its last flickers of exoticism. Crude pearl-fishers' *pirogues* resembling dug-out tree trunks shared the harbour with graceful Arab *dhows*, whose outsize sterns and high prows mimicked calligraphic flourishes, while Arabs and Africans jostled with Tartars from Bukhara and Crimea.

Today, El-Quseir is a sleepy place that seems mostly unaffected by tourism, despite the presence of three holiday villages on its outskirts. The town retains a charm all of its own, and locals are happy to help with directions if you get lost – not that it's necessary, as you'll soon find everything. The main **orientation** point is a traffic roundabout where service taxis drop and wait for passengers, near a Co-op garage and the *Sea Princess Hotel*. The road bearing off to the right leads to a small **harbour** where you can watch men building boats on the beach, or stroll past shuttered and balconied houses to reach a **mosque** dating back to the thirteenth century and a **quarantine hospital** built to screen pilgrims in the nineteenth century.

Smack in the centre of town, just past the main traffic roundabout, sits El-Quseir's most impressive landmark, the sixteenth-century crumbling **walled fortress** (daily 9am–5pm; £E10), now housing a museum. Designed to protect trade routes used by the Ottomans, the fortress fell into decline after trade was diverted around the Cape of Good Hope. Napoleon's army raised the French flag here in 1799, only to attract the attention of British warships, the HMS Daedalus and HMS Fox, which were sailing off the coast. The French survived a brief assault by the British, but abandoned the fort two years later for engagements elsewhere in the country. The fort's most recent occupant was the Egyptian army, who were stationed here until 1975.

The fortress entrance is through a gate on the southern side of the building, where you can buy a ticket for a guided tour, which lasts about forty minutes. The cistern, the watchtower (which you can climb for excellent views), and rooms built into the walls of the fortress each contain small exhibits on the history and traditions of the Red Sea coast, including displays on Bedouin life, the Coptic monasteries, Roman mines and ship building.

Aside from the fortress, El-Quseir's main diversion is strolling along the beach-side **promenade** where cafés serve snacks and cold drinks. Life moves at a pretty slow pace, except on Fridays, when Ma'aza and Ababda Bedouin flock into town for the weekly **market**. The best **dives sites** near the town are the Brothers, east of El-Quseir, and the Elphinstone and Abu Dabbab reefs, down towards Mersa Alam, although the Quei and Wizr reefs are closer. All the **dive centres** are attached to the resort hotels, who may not allow outside divers to join their trips. If you want to dive here, it's best to book a package deal from the start.

Practicalities

Accommodation is limited to two hotels in the centre and three holiday villages outside town. The central *Sea Princess* (☎065/333-1880; ❷) is an odd little hotel decorated with film posters and vintage banknotes, whose friendly staff and clean shared bathrooms just fail to make the rabbit-hutch rooms tolerable. A far better option is *El Quseir Hotel* (☎065/333-2301; ❸), a refurbished period home with charming rooms, all with separate toilet. This hotel is a real treat and a welcome break for mid-range travellers tired of boxy concrete bungalows. It's a bit more expensive than you'd normally pay for non-en-suite rooms, but the ocean views from the balcony make up for it: there's no sign, just look for the "Diving world – Red Sea Egypt" emblem. At the luxury end, it's hard to beat the *Mövenpick Resort El Quseir* (☎065/332-100, ☎332-128; ❽), a spacious five-star resort 7km north of town (£E15–20 by taxi) with every facility imaginable, including a dive centre. The European-managed, Nubian-style resort is one of the few in this part of Egypt that has managed to blend with the local environment and native culture, whilst contributing to local community development projects like computer training. The other two resorts are the nearby three-star *Flamenco Beach Resort* (℡065/335-0200, ℻335-0211, ✉gm@flamencohotels.com; ❼), a garish pink complex 500m north of the *Mövenpick*, and the modest *Fanadir* (℡065/333-1414, ℻333-1415; ❻), 2km south of town, with a/c chalets and three-person villas, a smallish pool, a dive centre and little shade.

Among the handful of **places to eat** around El-Quseir, the best is the *Old Restaurant*, a popular Bedouin-themed place some 50m north of the *El-Quseir Hotel*: try the grilled chicken (£E7) or a seafood platter (£E60). *The*

Rock art of the Eastern Desert

The **rock art of the Eastern Desert** is one of Egypt's best-kept secrets, overlooked due to the abundance of pharaonic monuments in the Nile Valley and the difficulty of reaching many of the sites, spread over 24,000 square kilometres of desert to the east of Luxor and Edfu. Though small by comparison with the Western Desert, the dangers of this terrain shouldn't be underestimated: it's easy to get lost in the labyrinth of waterless *wadis*, and at least one 4WD group has died there. The **sites** vary from a single boulder to swathes of cliff-face dotted with pictures of people and animals, flotillas of boats and herds of giraffes, ostriches and elephants. While pharaonic and Roman inscriptions have revealed much about mining and trade, it is the rock art created before the unification of Egypt (c.3100 BC) that's really intriguing for the light it sheds on the origins of Egyptian civilization.

Dating predynastic rock art is highly speculative, involving stylistic comparisons and analysis of patination (the extent to which inscriptions and rock faces darken with exposure to sunlight, dew and other factors). Since *wadis* often subside, some scholars date art by its height above the valley floor, assigning **spirals** to the earliest phase (7000–6000 BC), followed by **wildlife** and hunting scenes. Giraffes, crocodiles, hippos and ibexes plainly belong to a time when the region was moister than today (c.4000–2700 BC), and camels didn't reach Egypt until 625 BC; whereas elephants lived here in predynastic times and were later imported by the Romans, so their presence can be ambiguous. **Cattle** reflect the pastoralism that took hold between 5500 and 4000 BC, and probably inspired the bovine iconography of pharaonic civilization.

The oldest **human figures** are gods or chieftains in ostrich-feather headdresses, brandishing maces; intriguingly similar to the "Conquering Hero" motif in pre- and Early Dynastic art at Hierakonpolis in the Nile Valley. They often appear standing in **boats**, which come in four types and are frequently surrounded by ostriches, elephants or cattle. Both Hans Winkler, who did seminal research in the 1930s, and David Rohl, who recently studied the rock art, believe that the oldest boats represent **"Eastern Invaders"** from Mesopotamia, who reached Egypt by the Red Sea and conquered the indigenous people of the Nile Valley, kick-starting Egyptian civilization. Boat motifs were employed throughout the pharaonic era.

In pharaonic times the Eastern Desert was an important source of gold, porphyry and breccia, so one finds plenty of **hieroglyphs**, cartouches of great pharaohs, and images of Min (the local deity of Coptos, and god of the desert). For the Romans, the road to Berenice was an important trade route, well protected with forts and scribbled with diverse **graffiti**, while Bedouin filtering in from Sinai and up from Sudan left their own tribal markers.

Citadel Restaurant, (☎065/333-3981, mobile ☎012 1018553), on the main road near the fortress, is more of a local place but serves excellent meals. For **drinks and snacks**, head down to the Corniche where a string of cafés line the beach. Alcohol and **nightlife** are confined to the holiday villages, which sometimes feature a bellydancer; non-residents may attend at the management's discretion.

El-Quseir's **bank** is on Sharia el-Gumhorriya, 150m north of the roundabout, while the road that turns right at this point leads to an old-fashioned **telephone exchange**. For **Internet cafés**, *Hotline* is about 100m east of the *Sea Princess*, just south of the roundabout, with a fast ADSL connection (£E8 per hour), while *Crazy Net* is just off the main roundabout near the *Centraal*, but has a slow dial-up connection (£E3 per hour).

Broadly speaking there are three areas of interest. Two are partially accessible by 2WD, using the roads between El-Quseir and Qift or Mersa Alam and Edfu, but all of the *wadis* between them require 4WD.

Wadi Hammamat. The El-Quseir-to-Qift road passes lots of rock art and inscriptions, especially from pharaonic times. The quarries at Wadi Hammamat are full of beautiful **hieroglyphs**, some overlaying dancing goddesses and ibexes. Predynastic boats and pharaonic inscriptions appear on the rocks either side of the road between Wadi Hammamat and El-Lakeita. Both these localities mark the start of trails to predynastic sites in **Wadi Qash** and **Wadi Atwan**, that require a 4WD and a guide who really knows the way.

Wadi Mineh. Accessible by 4WD from either main road, this ravishing terrain of broad *wadis* and dunes is impenetrable without GPS, and contains the greatest wealth of petroglyphs and rock art in Egypt. At the northern end of Wadi Mineh is everything from pharaonic boats and **Horus figures** to Roman graffiti extolling the virtues of a prostitute. Farther south in Wadi Abu Wasil, a secluded area that Winkler called **Site 26** is covered with pictures of **chieftains**, boats, ostriches and cattle. One appears to show a man bleeding a cow, a practice found among pastoralist tribes even today.

Wadi Barramiyah. The Mersa Alam to Edfu road runs straight through this wadi, where the rock-cut **Temple of Kanais**, 50km from Edfu, contains scenes of Seti I smiting Shasu (sand-dweller) and Nubian foes, and inscriptions lauding the well that he had dug along this desolate route. East of the temple, predynastic **boats** appear on both sides of the road; some are huge, with up to seventy crewmen. Notice the pictograms of a hippo, an elephant, and a pharaonic standard resembling the hieroglyph "to bore", appropriate for a mining area. There are more boats and animals within walking distance of the road, and up side *wadis*. **Wadi Umm Salam** has been dubbed the "Canyon of the Boats" and also contains lines and squiggles that match up to modern maps of the *wadi* systems – a **predynastic map** of the area, some believe.

Practicalities

For climatic reasons, the rock art of the Eastern Desert is best explored from mid-September till mid-May. Vehicles must travel in pairs and carry all water and fuel needed for the journey. Due to gold mining in the area and the need to protect vulnerable sites, access is only allowed from the Red Sea Coast (not the Nile Valley), and Military Intelligence and SCA **permits** for off-road travel are only issued to a single foreign operator, Ancient World Tours, in conjunction with the Egyptian firm Pan Arab Tours. Ancient World Tours has been working with Russ Ruthe and David Rohl of the Eastern Desert Survey to run "Followers of Horus" **tours** to record all the rock art in the region. For details, visit ⊛www.ancient.co.uk, or contact ©mra@dial.pipex.com.

The **bus station** and the **service taxi stand** are side-by-side in the heart of town, a ten-minute walk from the main roundabout. There are five a/c buses daily to **Cairo** (10.30am, 12.30pm, 9pm, 10.30pm, 12am & 5am; 10hr; £E60) and two non-a/c (5am & 8pm; 10hr; £E35); all services stop at Safaga and Hurghada. Heading south, there are five buses daily to **Shalateen** via the coastal route (7.30am, 12pm, 5.30pm, 8.30pm, 10.30pm, 3.30am; 4hr; £E20), while buses daily head inland to **Qena** (5am, 3pm & 5pm; 2hr; £E8–10). **Service taxis** depart when full for Cairo (£E40), Hurghada (£E8), Safaga (£E5), Mersa Alam (£E10) and Qena (£E15). Alternatively, you could get a group together and hire a **minibus** and driver from one of the tourist agencies in town. Koshar Tourist Services (☎065/333-1666, ℉333-1695) will take up to eleven people to Cairo (£E600), Hurghada (£E150), Safaga (£E100), Qena (£E250), Mersa Alam (£E150), Berenice (£E300) or Shalateen (£E500).

The desert road to Qift

The modern road from **El-Quseir to Qift** (216km) follows the earliest known route across the Eastern Desert, via Wadi Hammamat ("Valley of the Pigeons"). Mysterious drawings of boats, humans and animals have been tentatively dated to predynastic times, while hieroglyphic inscriptions attest to quarrying and mining from the I Dynasty onwards. Near **Bir Umm Fawakhir** (92km from El-Quseir), gold mines marked on a pharaonic survey map of c.1400 BC have been recently reopened by a Canadian mining company. Further west, the great well at **Bir Hammamat** was dug by eight thousand men for Ramses IV, to enable quarrying to continue year-round at **Wadi Hammamat**, the source of the hard dark breccia prized for statues and sarcophagi. The **quarries**, south of the road, are covered in cartouches and inscriptions, overlaying **Predynastic rock art**; hieroglyphs and boats occur at intervals as far as **El-Lakeita**. Rock art and inscriptions exist at many other places in the Eastern Desert, but access is restricted (see box on pp.798–799).

For Bedouin, the road marks the boundary between **Ma'aza** tribal land and **Ababda** territory. Though traditional rivals, they may graze and water their flocks on each other's preserves should their own land be drought-stricken. Tribal politics are conditioned by the harsh environment and long memories; the names of wells and landmarks are often historically specific. For example, Bir Umm Howeitat, near the Umm Rus gold mine inland of Mersa Umbarak, is named after the Saudi Bedouin who harried the Ma'aza in their original homeland and later in Sinai.

South to Mersa Alam

The coastal road south of El-Quseir (sections of which are currently being moved slightly further inland to protect the coast and wildlife) runs through some of the most amazing landscape and desert in Egypt. It's sprinkled with holiday resorts all along the 132km stretch to Mersa Alam, while an international airport 50km north of the town receives three charter planes a week from Europe in low season and many more during peak times.

Although the southern Red Sea Coast is growing in popularity with travellers and divers, its tourist infrastructure is far from developed – telephone use is limited and some resorts have to rely on expensive satellite communications, though mobile phone coverage is reasonable in the area. A few of the **resorts** along the coast, such as *Helio* and *Utopia*, won't take independent travellers, but many of the others will, such as the huge *Akassia*, 26km south of El-Quseir (mobile ☎012 7455049, ℗www.akassia.com; half-board only ➏), with 360 rooms and five swimming pools, including a wave pool. Alternatively, there's the three-star *Mangrove Bay Resort*, 30km south of El-Quseir (T02/748-6748, F02/760-5458, mobile T010 2581250, Emangrove@menanet.net; ❻), with its own beautiful white sandy beach. Twenty-four kilometres north of Mersa Alam is the five-star *Kahramana* (mobile T127 454105, Wwww.kahramana .com; half-board ❽, all-inclusive if booked as a package from the UK), whose Mexican-inspired architecture is set against beautiful and empty sandy beaches, with its own dive centre.

A ten-minute walk beyond the *Kahramana*, at **Mersa Shagra**, is the north-ernmost of three "ecolodges" run by Red Sea Diving Safari. *Shagra Village* (T02/337-1833, F719-4219, Einfo@redsea-divingsafari.com; ❻) is a beach-side dive centre with environmentally friendly accommodation, ranging from tents on the beach to smart bungalows, both with shared-bath facilities, as well as more luxurious en-suite chalets. Rates include all meals and unlimited soft drinks (beer costs US$3 a bottle). Mersa Shagra is also home to Red Sea Desert Adventures (mobile T012 2449073, Edesert@red-sea.com), whose jeep and camel safaris run from October to March (see p.792), as well as Egypt's most southerly decompression chamber, the Hyperbaric Medical Centre (mobile T122 187550); divers are encouraged to take out cover in case they have to use it (US$6 for three weeks).

Mersa Alam

The town of **MERSA ALAM** itself is undistinguished, consisting of a large army base, some government buildings and new apartment blocks constructed for the expected influx of hotel staff to the area, grafted onto a fishing port where liveaboards now moor. Opposite is a coffee shop patronized by local divers. The **bus station** is on the edge of town, 800m west of the traffic circle, with irregular buses and **service taxis** to Hurghada (£E30) and Shalateen (£E20). There is also regular transport to Edfu and Aswan in the Nile Valley, but the road through the mountains is closed to foreigners so you may be sent back at one of the checkpoints. Travellers heading for the tomb of Sheikh el-Shazli risk being turned back, too – Red Sea Desert Adventures (see above) is the best source of information on this route.

Mersa Alam's **accommodation** options include the new two-star *Sahara Hotel*, 2km north of the town centre on the west side of the highway (T065/372-0181, mobile T012 7745973, Ebelalelkholy@amhi.com.eg; ❺), though the small *Riff-Villa Guesthouse*, 1km south of the traffic circle (T065/372-0001, mobile T012 4624933, Wwww.riff-villa.ch; ❺), is better. Run by a welcoming German/Swiss couple who provide all the comforts of home, it can also organize all manner of desert and diving trips. For budget travellers, there's the rather scruffy *Mersa Alam Star Hotel*, 300m west of the traffic circle, just past the petrol station (mobile T012 7761017; ❶), which has basic fan-cooled double rooms without bathroom.

South of Mersa Alam

South of the town are three other camps offering basic **accommodation** for the keen divers that have made it this far. Twelve kilometres south, *Awlad Baraka Diving Camp* (mobile T010 5851189, Wwww.aquarius-redsea .com; full-board only ❼), has twenty comfortable "African" huts, a restaurant and café. It is run in association with Deep South Diving Centre on the beach side of the road (mobile T012 7923336, Einfo@deep-south-diving.com), which organizes day-trips (€35 or US$47 for two dives including lunch) to some of the best and most remote dive sites in the south Red Sea, such as **Samaduy**, **Abu Dabab**, **Elphinstone** and **Fury Shoal**; they also offer open-water diving courses (€300 including certification). There's another Red Sea Diving Safari "ecolodge" at *Nakari Village*, 18km south of Mersa Alam (☏02/337-1833, 🖷719-4219, ⓦwww.marsanakari.com; ⑤), while 32km further south is *Shams Alam Hotel and Beach Resort* (mobile ☏012 2444932, ⓦwww.shamshotels.com; half-board only ⑥), home to the European-run Wadi Gimal Diving Centre (mobile ☏012 2367010, ⓦwww.shams-dive.com).

A hundred metres beyond the *Shams Alam Hotel* is the entrance to **Wadi Gimal National Park**, a unique protected area covering 6000 square kilometres of land and 4000 square kilometres of sea. Inside its borders, three ranger stations, built to look like ancient Roman domiciles, are used as base camps by scientists surveying the land and studying plant and animals species. Spring (March–April) and autumn (September–October) are particularly good times to observe bird migrations, including osprey, falcons, white-eyed gulls and the occasional flamingo. The park headquarters, next to the Wadi Gimal Diving Centre, is not yet equipped for travellers, but there are plans to build an on-site information centre. To **camp** in the park, foreigners need permission from the Coast Guard in Mersa Alam – Red Sea Desert Adventures (mobile ☏012 2467826) may be able to help – or contact Mohamed Abbas (🖃tahoon82@hotmail.com), a researcher at the park.

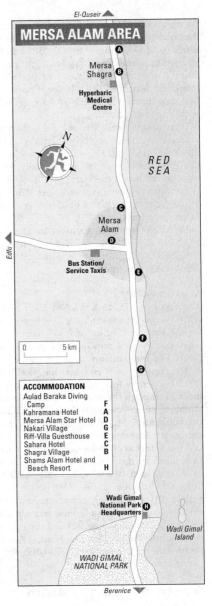

MERSA ALAM AREA

El-Quseir ▲

Ⓐ

Mersa Shagra Ⓑ

Hyperbaric Medical Centre

Edfu ◄

Ⓒ

Mersa Alam

Ⓓ

Bus Station/ Service Taxis Ⓔ

RED SEA

Ⓕ

Ⓖ

0   5 km

ACCOMMODATION

Aulad Baraka Diving Camp	F
Kahramana Hotel	A
Mersa Alam Star Hotel	D
Nakari Village	G
Riff-Villa Guesthouse	E
Sahara Hotel	C
Shagra Village	B
Shams Alam Hotel and Beach Resort	H

Wadi Gimal National Park Headquarters Ⓗ

WADI GIMAL NATIONAL PARK

Wadi Gimal Island

Berenice ▼

Around 80km south of the park, and 9km south of the village of Hamata, is the third of the Red Sea Diving Safari "ecolodges", *Wadi Lahami Village* (☏02/337-1833, 🖷719-4219; ⑥), which caters for experienced divers only and has accommodation in tents. Just beyond the turnoff for the *Wadi Lakhmi Village* is the southernmost resort on the Red Sea Coast, the five-star *Lakhmi*

Bay (mobile ☎012 3173344, ✉info@lahamibay.com; ❼), which offers excellent amenities despite its remote location, including an Italian restaurant, pool bar, tennis courts, sauna and fitness centre, as well as a branch of the Orca Diving Centre. Its dive area is a further 50km south at the port of **Ras Banata**, whose island reefs are home to one of the few undisturbed breeding grounds for **sea turtles** on the Red Sea Coast. Its 235m-high hill was mined until 1959 for its leaf-green coloured gems, called peridotites.

The far south: Berenice to the Sudanese border

As the coast road heads southwards to the Sudanese border the seemingly endless coastline is almost completely empty except for the occasional mangrove, herd of grazing camels or cluster of tanks left by the military. One hundred and forty-five kilometres south of Mersa Alam is the town of **BERENICE**, named after the wife of Ptolemy II, on whose suggestion a trading port was established here in 275 BC. Abandoned during the fifth century AD, the site was excavated in 1818 by Belzoni, who found a Temple of Semiramis and other ruins. Nowadays, Berenice amounts to a few characterless buildings clustered together in a wind-swept bay, with little to interest tourists except a Bedouin museum apparently instigated by the wife of the Belgian ambassador to Egypt.

With tourism increasingly being encouraged, however, the hinterland of Berenice has several would-be attractions. For climbers, there is the challenge of Egypt's "most aggressive peaks", **Jebel Farayid** (whose highest point was reached by Murray in 1925) and the **Berenice Bodkin** – one of the largest rock spires in the whole of North Africa and the Middle East. Here, too, are the ancient **Emerald Mines of Wadi Sakait**, worked from pharaonic to Roman times and under the khalifs; Mohammed Ali had them reopened, but few gems remained to be found and the mines were soon abandoned. Nearby is a small Ptolemaic rock temple, dedicated to Isis and Serapis.

The reasons why this area has long been off limits are geopolitical. Following the Iranian Revolution, the **Ras Banas air base** was earmarked for use by the US Rapid Deployment Force and war games were held in the Eastern Desert, simulating an Allied response to an Iranian attack on the Saudi oil fields. Such manoeuvres waned after Iran was embroiled in war with Iraq, and the US

The Moulid of Abul Hassan al-Shazli

Outside Egypt, **Abul Hassan al-Shazli** (who died in 1258) is known as al-Shadhili, hence the name of his Sufi order, the *Shadhiliyya*. According to believers, al-Shazli asked God to let him die in a place where nobody had ever sinned, and the Prophet Mohammed buried him deep in the mountains at **Wadi Humaysara**. The remoteness of his grave has never deterred pilgrims, for whom the journey has become much easier since a local entrepreneur built a road to the site as a gift. It turns off the Edfu road at the tomb of another Sufi sheikh, Salim, which pilgrim trucks circle three times to avoid incurring his jealousy, before driving on to Wadi Humaysara (100km).

Al-Shazli's **moulid** starts ten days before the Muslim feast of Eid al-Adha and reaches its climax the day before the Eid. Twenty thousand Sufis from all over Egypt gather to perform *zikrs* outside his tomb, and hundreds of tents and snack stalls are pitched for the occasion. Arranging a ride there will require much palaver, but you shouldn't have any problem identifying the pilgrim trucks, festooned with banners and loudspeakers. At other times of the year, Red Sea Desert Adventures (see p.801) can sometimes organize trips for around £E80 per person.

"forward base" withdrew to Diego Garcia – so that when Iraq invaded Kuwait in 1990, the only unit available for immediate airlift into Saudi Arabia was a single battalion of Egyptian commandos.

More recently, the **far south** has been a bone of contention between Egypt and Sudan, whose common border was arbitrarily set by the British in 1899 on the basis of the 22nd parallel. After independence, both agreed that this was unfair on the Bishari nomads whose tribal grounds straddled the border, so a slice of Egyptian territory was placed under Sudanese administration – a compromise that worked fine until Sudan granted a Canadian oil company offshore exploration rights, and Egypt responded by sending in troops to reassert its sovereignty. Since 1992, the region from **Bir Shalateen** down to **Halaib** has been under military rule, and Egypt has launched a crash programme of "development" to cement its hold on this previously neglected, potentially oil-rich region.

In 1999, some restrictions were lifted and tourists can now travel at least as far as **Shalateen**, which has a daily camel market that attracts plenty of Sudanese traders. A lot of haggling goes on between the traders, but it won't make much sense without a local guide: with some advance warning, Red Sea Desert Adventures (see p.801) will run a very informative day-trip to the village. As yet there is no tourist accommodation in the area, and official permission must be obtained from police in Berenice or Shalateen if you wish to **camp**. Your best chance for a camping permit is through Red Sea Desert Adventures. The area is still a very sensitive military zone and anyone not obtaining permission is likely to be treated with extreme suspicion.

Contexts

Contexts

The historical framework

The present borders of Egypt are almost identical to those in pharaonic times, territories such as Sinai and Nubia being essentially marginal to the heartland of the Nile Valley and its Delta, where Egyptian civilization emerged some five thousand years ago. The historical continuity is staggering: the pharaonic era alone lasted thirty centuries before being appropriated by Greek and Roman emperors.

Egypt's significance in the ancient world was paramount, and the country has never been far from the front line of world history. Although neither Christianity nor Islam was born in Egypt, both are stamped with its influence. In modern times, when the Arab world sought to rid itself of European masters, Egypt was at the forefront of the anti-colonial struggle, while its peace treaty with Israel altered the geopolitics of the Middle East.

Uncertainties ...

Any attempt to précis this vast span of history inevitably runs the risk of obscuring social dynamics and ordinary people amid a roll call of dynasties and great men and women. While the continuity of so many aspects of Egyptian life supports this conservative view, dramatic watersheds and subtle fluxes are also a feature of Egyptian history. Nor are the facts graven in stone. Egyptology is riddled with uncertainties, not least in its chronology of dynasties and kingdoms (not an Egyptian concept, but a modern invention enabling scholars to get a handle on three thousand years of history). Two critics have assailed conventional chronology from opposite directions. Their arguments deserve to be read in full, but can be summarized as follows.

In *A Test of Time*, **David Rohl** examines the "Four Pillars" of synchronicity between Ancient Egyptian and Biblical history and judges only one to be impeccable. Anomalies such as the royal burials at Tanis and Deir el-Bahri, Israelite chariots on the Ashkelon Wall at Karnak, and evidence of their sojourn at Avaris call for a revision of the chronology of the Third Intermediate Period, with knock-on effects on earlier times. Rohl's **New Chronology** puts the Exodus in the XIII rather than the XIX Dynasty, and makes Akhenaten a contemporary of David and Saul. The sceptical response from other archeologists can be read on ⓦhttp://members.aol.com/IanWade/Waste/Index.html.

Unlike Rohl, **Anthony West** is not a professional Egyptologist, and his *Serpent in the Sky* – propounding that the Egyptian temples embody the legacy of an older, greater civilization dating back to Atlantis – was laughed off until two geologists agreed that the erosion in the bedrock of the Sphinx shows that it was created at least 2600 years earlier than had hitherto been assumed. Egyptologists failed to refute their evidence in a showdown at the 1992 conference of the American Association for the Advancement of Science, but have since taken comfort from a study by the Getty Institute, which concludes that the erosion proves nothing of the kind.

As both debates are unresolved, we've stuck to **orthodox chronologies**, about which even mainstream Egyptologists differ and acknowledge margins of error. These are up to a hundred years in the period around 3000 BC, seventy-five years around 2000 BC, and between ten and fifteen years around 1000 BC. From 500 BC onwards, dates are fairly precise until the Ptolemaic era, when the chronology gets hazy, only firming up again in Roman times.

The beginnings

Stone tools from the gravel beds of Upper Egypt and the Uwaynat Desert attest to the presence of **hunter-gathering hominids** in the area over 250,000 years ago, when the Sahara was a lush savannah that supported zebras, elephants and other game. Between the **Late Middle Paleolithic** (c.70,000 BC) and **Upper Paleolithic** (c.24,000 BC) eras there were fluctuating wet and dry periods, when lakes rose or shrank and grasslands expanded or receded, and tribes are assumed to have moved backwards and forwards between the Nile and the oases. While most still lived by hunting and fishing, herding cattle emerged even before cereal cultivation, sheep and goat herding filtered through from the Near East (c.7000 BC).

During the **Neolithic** era, Middle Egypt and the Delta had **settled communities** that cultivated wheat and flax, herded flocks and wove linen. Although some reverted to a nomadic lifestyle after the rains of the Neolithic era checked the process of desertification, others remained to develop into agricultural societies. It was during the **Middle and Late Neolithic periods** (6600–5100 and 5100–4700 BC respectively) that human occupation of the Western Desert reached its peak, giving rise to the rock art in the Cave of the Swimmers and other sites at the Gilf Kebir and Jebel Uwaynat.

Predynastic Egypt

The impetus for development came from southern Egypt. At **Nabta Playa**, 100km west of Abu Simbel, archeologists have identified the world's **oldest calendar** of standing stones and sculpted monoliths – dating from around 6000 BC – that attests to a Neolithic culture with a knowledge of astronomy and the resources and organization to create such a site. And then there are the mysterious **boats** drawn in the Eastern Desert perhaps a thousand years later, which Rohl believes represent "Eastern Invaders" who conquered the indigenous people of the Nile Valley. However, evidence of later agricultural societies is less impressive, and there is disagreement over the categorization of cultures. The earliest is known as the **Badarian**, after the village of El-Badari where Brunton carried out excavations in the 1920s. The Badarians were farmers, hunters and miners; they made fine pottery, carved bone and ivory, and traded for turquoise and wood.

The **Naqada I** period, from about 4000 BC onwards, was characterized by larger settlements and a distinctive style of pottery: burnished red clayware with black rims or white zoomorphic decorations. Clay and ivory figurines show Naqada menfolk sporting beards and penis shields, raising a possible ethnic connection with their Libyan neighbours. More extraordinary are the narrow-necked vases carved from basalt, which can't be reproduced by twentieth-century technology but were supposedly made by the Stone Age Naqada I culture.

In the conventional scheme of things, graves from the **Naqada II** period contain copper tools and glazed beads that signify advances in technology, and extraneous materials such as lapis lazuli, indicating trade with Asia. The graves themselves evolved from simple pits into painted tombs lined with mats and wood and, later still, brick. The development of extensive irrigation systems (c.3300 BC) boosted productivity and promoted links between communities.

The Two Lands

By this time, the communities of Upper and Lower Egypt existed in two loose **confederations**. As power coalesced around Naqada in the south and Behdet in the Delta, each confederation became identified with a chief deity and a symbol of statehood: Seth and the White Crown with **Upper Egypt**, Horus and the Red Crown with the **Delta**.

Later, each acquired a new capital (Hierakonpolis and Buto, respectively) and strove for domination over the entire region. The eventual triumph of the southern kingdom resulted in the **unification of the Two Lands** (c.3100 or 2090 BC) under the quasi-mythical ruler **Menes** (aka Narmer), and the start of Egypt's Dynastic period. Some identify him as pharaoh Aha, whose tomb is the earliest found at Saqqara, but if the Greek name "Menes" is derived from the Egyptian *mena* ("Establisher"), it may not refer to any actual individual.

The Archaic Period

The **Early Dynastic** or **Archaic Period** was the formative epoch of Egyptian civilization. Its beginnings are a mix of history and myth, relating to the foundation – supposedly by Menes – of the city of **Memphis**, located at the junction between Upper and Lower Egypt: the first imperial city on earth.

From this base, Djer and Den, the third and fifth kings of the **I Dynasty** (c.3100–2890 or 2920–2770 BC), attempted to bring Sinai under Egyptian control. Writing, painting and architecture became increasingly sophisticated, while royal tombs at Saqqara and Abydos developed into complex *mastabas*, thought to have been modelled on the palaces of living kings. At this time, royal burials were accompanied by the deceased's servants – a practice that later dynasties abandoned.

Also indicative of future trends was the dissolution of the unified kingdom as centralized authority waned towards the end of the dynasty. Although this was restored by **Raneb** (or Hotepsekhemwy), founder of a new line of rulers, regional disputes persisted throughout the **II Dynasty** (c.2890–2686 or 2770–2645 BC).

These disputes probably inspired the **contendings of Seth and Horus**, a major theme in Egyptian mythology. The Stele of Peribsen shows a temple facade surmounted by the figure of Seth, rather than Horus, the traditional symbol of kings. However, the rivalry between the two regions and their respective deities apears to have been resolved under **Khasekhemwy**, the last king of the dynasty – paving the way for an era of assurance.

During the **III Dynasty** (c.2686–2613 or 2649–2575 BC), advances in technology and developments in culture raised Egypt to an unprecedented level of civilization. The main figure of the III Dynasty was **King Zoser** (or Djoser), whose architect, **Imhotep**, built the first **Step Pyramid** at Saqqara in the 27th century BC. The pyramid's conception and construction were a landmark and later generations deified Imhotep as the ultimate sage. On the economic and political front, the III Dynasty also sent expeditions into Sinai, to seek turquoise and copper and to subjugate the local Bedouin.

The Old Kingdom

Pyramid-building and expansionism were likewise pursued during the **IV Dynasty** (c.2613–2494 or 2575–2465 BC). The Dynasty's first king, **Snofru** (aka Sneferu), raised two pyramids at Dahshur and made incursions into Nubia and Libya. His successors, **Cheops** (Khufu), **Chephren** (Khafre) and **Mycerinus** (Menkaure), erected the **Pyramids of Giza**, expanded trade relations with the Near East, and developed mining activities in Nubia, where a copper-smelting factory was established at the Second Cataract. Though Snofru's line expired with the death of **Shepseskaf**, his widow Queen **Khentkawes** is believed to have married a high priest to produce an heir.

This trend continued during the **VI Dynasty** (c.2345–2181 or 2465–2323 BC), when nobles were buried in their own **nomes** (provinces). While punitive expeditions carried the pharaoh's banner deep into Nubia, Libya and Palestine, domestic power ebbed to the nomarchs, reaching the point of no return under **Pepi II** (aka Neferkare), whose death heralded the **end of the Old Kingdom**.

The First Intermediate Period

After Pepi's death, decades of provincial rivalry and chaos ensued, with petty dynasties claiming the mantle of the Old Kingdom. The Greek historian Manetho records seventy rulers during the brief **VII Dynasty** (c.2181–2173 or 2150–2134 BC), while an unknown number of kings vainly asserted their claims from Memphis during the **VIII Dynasty** (c.2173–2160 or 2150–2134 BC).

When rains failed over the Ethiopian highlands, famine struck Egypt, exacerbating civil disorder. Weak principalities sought powerful allies such as **Herakleopolis**, the dominant city of the Twentieth Nome, whose ruler, **Achthoes**, gained control of Middle Egypt, assumed the throne name Meryibre, and founded the **IX Dynasty** in 2160 or 2154 BC.

Whereas most of the north came under the control of the IX and **X Dynasty** (c.2130–2040 or 2154-2040 BC) kings of Herakleopolis, Upper Egypt was contested by the rulers of Edfu and Thebes. After vanquishing his rival, the Theban ruler Inyotef Sehertowy tried to extend his power beyond Upper Egypt, founding the **XI Dynasty** (c.2133–1991 or 2134–2040 BC). The struggle between north and south was only finally resolved by **Nebhepetre Mentuhotpe II**, who reunited the whole country under one authority in 2055 or 2050 BC, establishing the Middle Kingdom.

The Middle Kingdom

During Mentuhotpe's fifty-year reign the mines and trade routes were reopened; incursions into Libya, Nubia and Sinai resumed; and arts and crafts flourished again. His successors, Mentuhotpe III and IV, were most notable for their expeditions to the Land of Punt. Inscriptions from Wadi Hammamat name the vizier in charge of the second expedition as **Amenemhat** (or Ammenemes), who subsequently founded the **XII Dynasty** (c.1991–1786 or 1985–1955 BC).

Amenemhat returned the capital to Memphis and safeguarded the Nile Delta from raiders by constructing the Walls of the Prince, a fortified *cordon sanitaire*. Northern Nubia was annexed, and trade extended further into Palestine and Syria.

Under Amenemhat's son, **Senusert I** (aka Sesostris I), the administrative capital was transferred to the **Fayoum**, where massive waterworks were undertaken. Amenemhat II curbed the power of the nomarchs, while Senusert III may have abolished the office completely. These kings also built **the last pyramids**, at Lahun, El-Lisht and Hawara, where the final pyramid was erected by Amenemhat III, alongside the Labyrinth described by Herodotus.

According to Rohl's New Chronology, it was **Amenemhat III** who took **Joseph** as his vizier and let the **Israelites** settle in the Delta (c.1662 BC). Graves at Avaris suggest a large Semitic population stricken by calamities, akin to the Biblical account of the events leading up to the Exodus, which Rohl assigns to the reign of the XIII Dynasty pharaoh **Dudimose** (c.1447 BC). Both these dates are utterly at variance with the conventional chronology, which places the Exodus two centuries later, during the New Kingdom.

However, there is no disagreement that the late XII Dynasty was a **troubled time**, with the Nile flooding at record levels, bringing poor harvests and famine in its wake. The faces of the statues of pharaohs of this era are uniquely stern and careworn. Whether or not Egypt was also smitten by plagues and disrupted by an exodus from the Delta, it was obviously in poor shape to resist an invasion.

The Second Intermediate Period

Under the **XIII Dynasty** Egypt slid towards an era of disorder that archeologists term the **Second Intermediate Period**, when the pharaohs lost control of Nubia and the Delta. For the first time, Lower Egypt fell into the hands of "rulers of foreign lands" or *heka kaswt* – later rendered by Manetho as **Hyksos**. While Manetho relates that "peoples of an obscure race" appeared "like a blast of God" in the reign of Dudimose, most archeologists believe that they filtered into the eastern Delta as immigrants or slaves during the late Middle Kingdom, and only took over later. There's less doubt that they had weapons and technology which gave them an edge over the Egyptians: chariots, bronze armour, helmets and swords, and recurved bows that outranged the Egyptian ones.

For a time, the western Delta remained independent, under the **XIV or Xois Dynasty**, which was contemporaneous with the **Hyksos XV Dynasty** until about 1650 BC. After capturing Memphis, the Hyksos established relations with Thebes and traded up and down the Nile, but continued to rule from the Delta city of **Avaris** and maintain links with Palestine, Crete and Persia. Relations deteriorated after the **Theban XVII Dynasty** began harassing their caravans and ships, and the Hyksos king **Apophis** sent an insult to Sekenenre Tao II of Thebes, who used it as a pretext to declare war (c.1560 BC). Sekenenre Tao's son **Khamose** continued the struggle on two fronts (after the Hyksos forged an alliance with Nubia) and was within striking distance of Avaris when he died, whereupon his brother, **Ahmosis I**, finally expelled the Hyksos from Egypt (in 1567 or 1550 BC), ushering in a new era.

Although Egyptian chronicles describe their rule as anarchic, evidence such as the *Rhind Mathematical Papyrus* suggests that the Hyksos fostered native culture, took Egyptian names and ruled as pharaohs, while their introduction of the *shaduf* irrigation device proved of lasting benefit to Egyptian agriculture. Many think that their dismissive sobriquet, the "Shepherd Kings", is a mistranslation by Josephus of Manetho's rendering of the original Egyptian name.

The New Kingdom

The **XVIII Dynasty** (c.1567–1320 or 1550–1307 BC) founded by Ahmosis inaugurated the **New Kingdom**, a period of stability, wealth and expansion, whose rulers include some of the most famous names in Egyptian history. During this era **Nubia** was brought under Egyptian control, yielding gold, ivory, ebony, gems and, most importantly, slaves. The professional armies of the pharaohs also invaded the Near East, Syria and Palestine, establishing colonies governed by Egyptian viceroys or local satraps. One result was an influx of immigrants into Egypt, bringing new customs, ideas and technology.

The effects are evident at **Thebes**, capital of the New Kingdom, where a spate of temples and tombs symbolize the pre-eminence of the god **Amun** and the power of the pharaohs. While **Tuthmosis I** (c.1525–1512 BC) built the first tomb in the Valley of the Kings, his daughter **Hatshepsut** raised the great mortuary temple of Deir el-Bahri, ruling as pharaoh (c.1503–1482 BC) despite her stepson's claim on the throne. Having belatedly assumed power, **Tuthmosis III** embarked on imperial conquests, extending Egyptian power beyond the Fourth Cataract in Nubia, and across the Euphrates to the boundaries of the Hittite empire. His successor **Amenophis II** (c.1459–1425 BC) penetrated deeper into Nubia, and **Tuthmosis IV** (c.1425–1417 BC) further strengthened the empire by marrying a princess of Mitanni, a state bordering the Hittites.

The zenith of Egyptian power coincided with the reign of **Amenophis III** (c.1417–1379 BC). With the empire secure and prosperity at home, the king devoted himself to the arts and the construction of great edifices such as Luxor Temple. During the same period, a hitherto minor aspect of the sun-god was increasingly venerated in royal circles: the **cult of Aten**, which the pharaoh's son would subsequently enshrine above all others.

The Amarna Revolution

By changing his name from Amenophis IV to **Akhenaten** and founding a new capital at Tell el-Amarna, the young king underlined his commitment to a new **monotheistic religion** that challenged the existing priesthood and bureaucracy. Since the story of Akhenaten and **Nefertiti** is related in detail on p.327, it suffices to say that the **Amarna Revolution** barely outlasted his reign (c.1379–1362 BC) and that of his mysterious successor, **Smenkhkare**, who died the following year.

The boy king **Tutankhamun** (1361–1352 BC) was easily persuaded to abjure Aten's cult and return the capital to Thebes, heralding a **Theban counter-revolution** that continued under **Ay** and **Horemheb**. Though Horemheb (c.1348–1320 BC) effectively restored the *status quo ante*, his lack of royal blood and, more importantly, an heir, brought the XVIII Dynasty to a close.

The XIX Dynasty

The **XIX Dynasty** (c.1320–1200 or 1307–1196 BC) began with the reign of Horemheb's vizier, **Ramses I** (c.1320–1318 BC), whose family was to produce several warrior-kings who would recapture territories lost under Akhenaten. **Seti I** (c.1318–1304 BC) reasserted pharaonic authority in Nubia, Palestine and the Near East, and began a magnificent temple at Abydos. His son **Ramses II** (c.1304–1237 BC) completed the temple and the reconquest of Asia Minor, commemorating his dubious victory at Qadesh with numerous reliefs, but later concluding a treaty with the Hittites. At home, Ramses usurped temples and statues built by others, and raised his own monumental edifices – notably the Ramesseum at Thebes and the sun temples at Abu Simbel.

His son **Merneptah** (c.1236–1217 BC) faced invasions by the "Sea Peoples" from the north and Libyans from the west, but eventually defeated the latter at Pi-yer in the western Delta. He is also popularly believed to be the pharaoh of the **Exodus**, though the only known pharaonic reference to the Israelites describes an Egyptian victory against these "nomads". The XIX Dynasty expired with **Seti II** (c.1210 BC), to be followed by a decade without a ruling dynasty.

The XX Dynasty

The **XX Dynasty** (c.1200–1085 or 1196–1070 BC), begun by Sethnakhte, was the last of the New Kingdom. His successor **Ramses III** (c.1198–1166 BC) repulsed three great invasions by the Libyans and Sea Peoples, and built the vast temple-cum-pleasure palace of **Medinet Habu**. But strikes by workmen at the royal necropolis and an assassination plot within the king's harem presaged problems to come. Under the eight kings who followed (all called Ramses), Egypt lost the remains of its Asiatic empire, and thieves plundered the necropolis. **Ramses XI** (c.1114–1085 BC) withdrew to his residence in the Delta, delegating control of Upper Egypt to **Herihor**, high priest of Amun, and Lower Egypt to Vizier **Smendes**.

The Third Intermediate Period

This division was consolidated under the **XXI Dynasty** (c.1069–945 BC), the successors of Herihor and Smendes ruling their respective halves of Egypt from **Thebes** and **Tanis**. The two ruling houses (both designated as the XXI Dynasty) seem to have coexisted in harmony, with the Theban priest-kings acknowledging the Tanite pharaohs' superiority. Towards the end of this era, a powerful new dynasty of **Libyan** extraction was founded by **Shoshenk I**. This **XXII Dynasty** (c.945–715 BC) ruled Egypt from Bubastis in the Delta until a rival line seized power in Upper Egypt, precipitating civil war between the Bubastite monarchs and the Theban **XXIII Dynasty** (818–720 BC), which was further complicated by a brief **XXIV Dynasty** (727–715 BC) of Ethiopian kings.

The lifespan of these four dynasties – termed the **Third Intermediate Period** (TIP) – is one of the murkiest eras of Egyptian history, yet crucial to the New Chronology hypothesis, as the accepted dates for the New Kingdom hinge on the length of the TIP. Rohl contends that the XXI and XXII dynasties overlapped for generations, and that the duration of the TIP should therefore be reduced accordingly – with knock-on effects down the line. Even mainstream Egyptologists differ over the next significant dynasty, which some assign to the final phase of the TIP, and others regard as the start of the Late Period – but at least they all more or less agree on dates from this point onwards.

The Late Period

In 747 BC, Egypt's prolonged instability was brought to an end by the intervention of neighbouring Nubia. The Nubian king Piankhi advanced as far north as Memphis, while his brother Shabaka went on to conquer the Delta and reunite the Two Lands. The **XXV Dynasty of Nubian Kings** (c.747–656 BC) was marked by a revival of artistic and cultural life and renewed devotion to Amun (as evinced by reliefs at Karnak and Luxor). The dynasty's later, Ethiopian, rulers had to contend with the Assyrians, who were thrown back from the gates of **Thebes** in 671 and eventually sacked the city in 664 BC.

Egypt became a province of the Assyrian empire, ruled by local princes who paid tribute to the Assyrians until they withdrew from Egypt to defend their empire from the Babylonians, leaving a vacuum that was filled by **Psammetichus I**, the fourth ruler of the **XXVI Dynasty** (664–525 BC). Known as the Saïte Dynasty after its capital at **Saïs** in the Delta, this was the last great age of pharaonic civilization, harking back to the glories of the Old Kingdom in art and architecture, but also adopting new technologies and allowing colonies of Greek merchants at Naucratis and Jewish mercenaries at Elephantine.

Necho II (610–595 BC) defeated Josiah, King of Judah, at Megiddo, but was routed by the Babylonians. He is also credited with starting to build a canal to link the Nile with the Red Sea. Though **Psammetichus II** (595–589 BC) enjoyed several victories, his successor **Apries** was overthrown following defeat in Cyrenacia, the throne passing to **Amasis** "the Drunkard", who relied on Greek allies to stave off the Persian empire.

Persian rule

The **Persian invasion** of 525 BC began a new era of rule by foreigners that essentially lasted until Nasser eventually overthrew Egypt's monarchy in 1952.

Mindful of the Assyrians' mistake, the Persian emperors **Cambyses** and **Darius I** kept a tight grip on Egypt. Besides completing Necho's canal and founding a new city near Memphis, called **Babylon-in-Egypt** (today's "Old Cairo"), they built and restored temples to enhance their legitimacy. But **rebellions** against Xerxes and Artaxerxes testified to Egyptian hatred of this foreign **XXVII Dynasty** (c.525–404 BC).

Ousted by Amyrtaeus, sole ruler of the XXVIII Dynasty, the Persians constantly assailed the native rulers that followed. Though **Nectanebo I** of the **XXX Dynasty** (c.380–343 BC) managed to repulse them with Greek help, his successor's campaign in Phoenicia failed. Finally, bereft of allies, **Nectanebo II** (360–343 BC) was crushingly defeated by Artaxerxes III, and fled to Nubia. Egypt remained under Persian control until 332 BC, when their entire empire succumbed to **Alexander the Great**.

The Ptolemies

Alexander's stay in Egypt was brief, though long enough for him to adopt local customs. He offered sacrifices to the gods of Memphis and visited Amun's temple at Siwa; reorganized the country's administration, installing himself as pharaoh; and founded the coastal city of **Alexandria**; he then went off to conquer what remained of the known world. Upon his death in 323 BC, Alexander's Macedonian generals divided the empire, Ptolemy becoming ruler of Egypt and establishing the **Ptolemaic Dynasty** in 332.

Under Ptolemy I, **Greek** became the official language, and Hellenistic ideas had a profound effect on Egyptian art, religion and technology. Although Greek deities were also introduced, the Ptolemies cultivated the Egyptian gods and ruled much like Egyptian pharaohs, erecting great cult temples such as Edfu and Kom Ombo. They also opened new ports, established the great Library of Alexandria and had Hebrew scriptures translated into Greek by Jewish rabbis. The first synagogue in Egypt was founded at Leontopolis in the Delta.

It was dynastic disputes that led to the loss of Ptolemaic control. **Roman intervention** in Egypt grew until, under Ptolemy XII Auletes (80–51 BC), Egypt was almost totally dependent on Rome. **Julius Caesar** attacked Egypt in 54 BC, taking Alexandria by force.

The most famous queen of Egypt, **Cleopatra VII** (51–30 BC), was also the last of the Ptolemies. Under the protection of Julius Caesar – by whom she bore a son, Caesarion – Cleopatra managed to prolong her family's rule. After Caesar's death, she formed a similar alliance with **Mark Antony** to preserve Egyptian independence. Their joint fleets, however, suffered disaster against **Octavian** at the Battle of Actium, and both committed suicide rather than face captivity. Subsequently Egypt was reduced to the status of a province of the Roman Empire (30 BC).

Roman rule and the rise of Christianity

The **Roman emperors**, like the Ptolemies, adopted many of the Egyptian cults, building such monuments as Trajan's kiosk at Philae and temples at Dendara and Esna. Their main interest in the new colony, however, lay in its potential as grain supplier to Rome. With this end constantly in mind, trade routes were ensured by Roman garrisons at Alexandria, Babylon (Old Cairo) and Syene (Aswan). In terms of culture, language and administration, **Hellenistic influence** barely diminished and Alexandria continued to thrive as an important centre of Greek and Hebrew learning.

Although the **Holy Family's flight to Egypt** from Palestine cannot be proven, Egypt's Jewish colonies would have been a natural place of refuge, and many sites remain associated with the episode. According to Coptic tradition, **Christianity** was brought to Egypt by **St Mark**, who arrived in the time of Nero. Mark converted many to the new underground faith, founding the Patriarchate of Alexandria in 61 AD.

Politically, the most significant ruler was **Trajan** (98–117), who reopened Necho's Red Sea Canal. Trade flourished with the export of glass, linen, papyrus and precious stones. But the *fellaheen* were growing increasingly discontented with heavy taxation and forced recruitment into the Roman army.

The Copts

First-century Egypt was fertile ground for the spread of Christianity. The religion of the old gods had lost its credibility over the millennia of political manipulations and disasters, while the population – Egyptians and Jews alike – was becoming increasingly anti-Roman and nationalistic in its outlook. The core of Christianity, too, had a resonance in ancient traditions, with its emphasis on resurrection, divine judgement and the cult of the great mother.

Inevitably, as Egypt's Christians – who became known as **Copts** – grew in political confidence, there was conflict with the Roman authorities. In 202, **persecutions** began, reaching their height under **Diocletian** (284–305), when thousands of Coptic Christians were massacred. Copts date their calendar from the massacres in 284.

The legalization of Christianity and its adoption as the imperial religion by **Constantine** in 313 did little to help the Copts. The Roman leaders, from their new capital at **Byzantium**, embraced an orthodox faith that differed fundamentally from that of their Egyptian co-religionists – and persecutions continued. An attempt to reconcile differences at the **Council of Nicaea** (325) failed, and the split had become irrevocable by the time it was formalized at the **Council of Chalcedon** (451), following which the Copts established their own completely separate Patriarchate at Alexandria.

The same period also saw the emergence of **monasticism**, which took root in the Egyptian deserts. The monasteries of St Catherine in the Sinai, those of Wadi Natrun and Sohag, and St Anthony's and St Paul's in the Red Sea Mountains, all originated in these years.

The coming of Islam

Apart from a brief invasion in 616, Egypt remained under **Byzantine rule** until the **advance of Islam** in the seventh century. Led by the Prophet Mohammed's successor, Abu Bakr, the Muslim armies defeated the Byzantine army in 636. General Amr Ibn al-As then advanced towards Babylon-in-Egypt, which surrendered after a brief siege, to be followed by Heliopolis (640) and finally the imperial capital of Alexandria (642).

Amr built his capital, **Fustat**, north of the fortress town of Babylon-in-Egypt, in what is today Old Cairo. However, Egypt was merely a province in the vast Islamic empire that was governed from Damascus and Baghdad. As in Roman times, Egypt's primary role was as a bread basket for the empire.

Arabization and Islamicization was a gradual and uneven process, with intermittent periods of religious toleration and discrimination. Much depended on the character of the khalifs and their own power struggles, whose impact was felt throughout the Islamic empire. In 750, the empire's ruling **Umayyad** dynasty was defeated by the armies of Abu al-Abbas (a descendant of Abu Bakr), and an **Abbassid** khalifate came to power in Baghdad, administering Egypt, along with its other territories, for the next two centuries.

The Tulunids (868–905) and Ikhshidids (935–969)

In 868, **Ahmed Ibn Tulun**, sent to administer Egypt on behalf of Khalif al-Mu'tazz, declared the territory independent. He and his successors, the **Tulunids**, ruled for 37 years, during which time economic stability and order were restored. Like previous rulers, Ibn Tulun built a new capital city, **Al-Qitai**, whose vast mosque still remains. The dynasty did not long outlive him, however. His spendthrift son, Khomaruya, was assassinated, as were his heirs, and by 905 Abbassid rule was reimposed.

Egypt remained under the direct control of Baghdad until 935, when Mohammed Ibn Tughj was appointed governor and granted the title Ikhshid (ruler or king) by the khalif. Like the Tulunids, the **Ikhshidid dynasty** functioned virtually independently of the khalifate. Severe taxation, though, led to popular discontent, and the death in 965 of Tughj's second son, Ali, combined with famine, drought and political instability, opened the way for an invasion of the **Shi'a Fatimids** from Tunisia.

The Fatimid Era (969–1171)

The early **Fatimid khalifs** ruled half the Muslim world, with Egypt forming the central portion of an empire that included North Africa, Sicily, Syria and western Arabia. **Gohar**, commander of the khalifal forces, built the city of **Al-Qahira** (the Triumphant) as a new capital in 969, its walls containing opulent palaces and the prestigious mosque-university of Al-Azhar. **Khalif al-Muizz** installed himself in the city and from there ruled the empire. Trade with India, Africa and Europe expanded, the burdensome tax system was abolished, and a vast multi-racial army that included Europeans, Berbers, Sudanese and Turks was formed.

Whereas Al-Muizz and his successor Al-Aziz were efficient and tolerant rulers, under whom Egypt's economy prospered and the arts flourished, the third khalif – **Al-Hakim** (996–1021) – was a mad and capricious despot. His laws outraged the population, while his support of Byzantine against Latin Christians, and destruction of the Church of the Holy Sepulchre in Jerusalem, later provided a pretext for the First Crusade. His mysterious disappearance (see p.162) was taken by his followers – he championed Shi'a against Sunni Islam – as proof of messianic stature.

By the long reign of Al-Hakim's grandson, **Al-Mostansir** (1035–94), decay had set in. The empire was largely controlled by army commanders, administration was chaotic and famine added to the troubles. A series of governors imposed control over the army and restored peace and prosperity to Egypt for a further hundred years, but the loss of Syria to the Seljuk Turks, and new forces in Europe, left the empire increasingly vulnerable.

The **First Crusade** (1097–99), and those that followed, were motivated as much by the desire to acquire estates as to restore Christian dominance to the Holy Land. Egypt, however, was not attacked until 1167, by which time the Crusader kingdom held the former Fatimid coastal area of Palestine. Outraged at the fraternization between Franks and Fatimids, the Seljuk Sultan, Nur al-Din, sent an expedition to Cairo to repel them. The sultan's deputy, Shirkoh, occupied Upper Egypt, while his nephew, Salah al-Din al-Ayyubi – known to Europe as Saladin – took possession of Alexandria.

The Ayyubids (1171–1250)

On the death of the last Fatimid khalif in 1171, **Salah al-Din** became ruler of Egypt. To this day he remains a hero in the Arab world, a ruler renowned for his personal modesty, generosity, culture and political acumen. Having no pretensions to religious leadership, Salah al-Din chose for himself the secular title of *Al-Sultan* ("The Power") rather than that of khalif, giving his family's name – Ayyub – to the dynasty that succeeded him. Of his 24-year reign, he spent only eight years in Cairo, the rest being spent in liberating Crusader-held territory. By 1183, Syria had been won back and in 1187 Jerusalem was recaptured.

In Cairo, Salah al-Din built a fortress – today's Citadel – and expanded the Fatimid walls to enclose the city. In order to propagate Sunni orthodoxy, he also introduced the Seljuk institution of the **madrassa** or teaching mosque, thus turning Cairo into a great centre of learning. Hospitals were endowed, too, and the pharaonic canal at Fayoum was reopened.

Following his peaceful death in Damascus in 1193, Salah al-Din's eastern territories fragmented into principalities, though Egypt remained united under the Ayyubids. His nephew, **Al-Kamil** (1218–38), repulsed the Fifth Crusade. The last of the dynasty, **Ayyub** (1240–49), built up a formidable army of Turkish-speaking Qipchak slaves from the Black Sea region, and he himself married a slave girl, **Shagar al-Durr** ("Tree of Pearls").

It was Shagar al-Durr who took power following Ayyub's death, ruling openly as sultana until the Abbassid khalifs insisted that she take a husband, quoting the Prophet's words: "Woe to the nations ruled by women." Jealous of her power and warned by astrologers that he would die at a woman's hands, her husband, Aybak, planned to take a second wife, whereupon she had him murdered. She herself was assassinated soon afterwards, but her henchman, **Beybars the Crossbowman**, clawed his way to power, inaugurating the Mamluke era.

The Mamlukes (1250–1517)

Beybars was a commander among the foreign troops – the Mamlukes – on whom the later Ayyubids depended. Following his accession, **Mamluke amirs** (military leaders) retained control of Egypt for the next three centuries, each sultan intriguing his way up the ranks to assume the throne by *coup d'état* or assassination.

Bahri Mamlukes (1250–1382)

The **Bahri** ("River") **Mamlukes**, named after their garrison by the Nile and predominantly Turkic, formed the first of these military dynasties. The dynasty was founded by **Qalaoun**, who poisoned Beybars' heirs to inherit the throne. He sponsored numerous buildings in Cairo, and established relations as far afield as Ceylon and East Africa, concluding treaties with the Hapsburg Emperor Rudolph and other European princes. His son, **Khalil**, forced the remaining Crusaders from their stronghold in Acre in 1291.

Qalaoun's son **Mohammed al-Nasir** (1294–1340) was another great builder and power-broker. He concluded treaties with the Mongols, after defeating them in Syria, and strengthened political and trade ties with Europe. After his death a series of weak relatives were barely able to hold the throne in the face of conflicts between rival Mamluke factions.

Burgi Mamlukes (1382–1517)

In 1382 the sultanate was seized by **Barquq**, one of the Circassian **Burgi** ("Tower") **Mamlukes** from the garrison below the Citadel. To finance his campaigns against the **Mongols**, who by 1387 were on the borders of Syria, he had to impose punitive taxes that beggared the economy.

Hardships were exacerbated by famine and plague during the reign of his son, **Farag** (1399–1405), and it was only under Sultan **Barsbey** (1422–37) that Egypt regained some of its power. Barsbey established friendly relations with the new power in the north, the Ottoman Turks, and expanded trade in the Indian Ocean. But although the next hundred years saw relative peace and security, the Egyptian economy remained shaky.

The country experienced a brief revival under the rule of **Qaitbey** (1468–95), though his lavish building programme imposed a huge burden. The 46th, and penultimate sultan, **Qansuh al-Ghuri** (1501–16), suffered the loss of customary revenues after Vasco da Gama discovered the Cape of Good Hope, dealing a crippling blow to Egypt's spice trade monopoly. Worse was to come, as the **Ottoman Turks** consolidated their northern empire, defeating the Shi'ite Persians and then attacking Mamluke territory in northern Syria. In 1516, Al-Ghuri was killed in battle and his successor, Tumanbey, was executed in Cairo by the Ottomans in 1517.

Ottoman Egypt (1517–1789)

Even after the Turkish conquest, the Mamlukes remained powerful figures, running the administration of what was now a province of the vast Ottoman Empire. Government was provided by a series of **pashas**, career officials trained in Istanbul. As long as taxes were received, the Ottomans interfered little with Egyptian affairs and Cairo retained its importance as a religious, if not cultural or commercial, centre.

The Mamluke army continued to grow with the import of Caucasian slaves and by the end of the sixteenth century had become powerful enough to depose a pasha, although the Ottomans still held overall control. The growing power of the highest rank of the military corps – the **Beys** – posed a challenge to that of the pashas. Their arbitrary taxes, profligate ways and internal rivalry dominated events.

Meanwhile, economic decline, accelerated by changes in European shipping routes, and an outbreak of plague in 1719, left the country in a sorry shape. The French traveller Volney, visiting around 1784, described a depopulated country, whose capital was crumbling and surrounded by mounds of rubbish.

French Occupation 1798–1802

At the end of the eighteenth century, Egypt became a pawn in the struggle for power between France and Britain. **Napoleon** saw Egypt as a means to disrupt British commerce and eventually overthrow their rule in India. In 1798, his fleet landed at Alexandria, where he issued a proclamation that began with the Islamic *bismillah* ("In the name of God . . ."); stated his aim of liberating Egypt from the "riffraff of slaves"; and concluded that he respected Allah, his Prophet and the Koran more than the Mamlukes did.

Although Napoleon routed the Mamlukes at Imbaba and occupied Cairo, he left his fleet exposed at Abu Qir Bay, where it was attacked and destroyed by the British under Nelson. With his grand vision in tatters, and facing a declaration of war from the Ottoman sultan, Napoleon returned secretly to France. General Kléber, whom he left in charge, had a victory over the Ottomans, but was then assassinated. When his successor, General Menou, took charge, declared his conversion to Islam, and proclaimed Egypt a **French protectorate**, the British invaded from Abu Qir and occupied Alexandria. Combined Ottoman-British forces then took Damietta and Cairo, and the French were forced to surrender. Under the Capitulation Agreement, the archeological treasures gathered by Napoleon's savants were surrendered to Britain – which is why the **Rosetta Stone** ended up in the British Museum rather than the Louvre.

Mohammed Ali and his heirs (1805–92)

After the expulsion of the French a power struggle ensued, which was won by **Mohammed Ali**, an officer in the Albanian Corps of the Ottoman forces. Widely regarded as the founder of modern Egypt, his dynasty was to change Egypt more radically than any ruler since Salah al-Din.

The Ottomans confirmed Mohammed Ali as **Pasha** in 1805, whereupon he proceeded to decapitate – literally and figuratively – what remained of the Mamluke power structure. The first time was on the occasion of his accession, where he tricked them into a coup attempt; six years later, he dispensed with the rest of the Mamluke leadership, inviting 470 Beys to a feast at the Citadel and slaughtering the lot.

Though nominally a vassal of the Ottoman sultan, Mohammed Ali's control was absolute. He confiscated private land for his own use and set about modernizing Egypt with European expertise, building railways, factories and canals. Meanwhile, his son Ibrahim led a murderous campaign to subjugate northern **Sudan**, of which the only positive result was the introduction of a special kind of **cotton** – henceforth Egypt's major cash crop.

When Mohammed Ali died insane in 1849, his power greatly reduced after disastrous adventurism in Greece and Syria, he was succeeded by **Abbas** (1848–54), who closed the country's factories and schools and opened Egypt to free trade, thus delaying the country's industrial development for the next century.

Abbas's successor, **Said Pasha** (1854–63), granted a concession to a French engineer, **Ferdinand de Lesseps**, to build the **Suez Canal**. The project was completed in 1869, by which time **Khedive Ismail** (1863–79) was in power. An ambitious and enlightened ruler, Ismail transformed Cairo, spending lavishly on modernization. However, exorbitant interest rates had to be paid on loans from European lenders. Egyptian indebtedness spiralled and, to stave off bankruptcy, Ismail sold his Suez Canal shares to the British government in 1875.

He was deposed and succeeded by his son **Tewfiq** (1879–92), whose own financial control was limited by the French and British, to the disgust of patriotic Egyptians. A group of army officers forced him to make power-sharing concessions and to appoint their leader, **Ahmed Orabi**, as Minister of War. France and Britain responded by sending in the gunboats, shelling Alexandria and landing an army at Ismailiya, which subsequently routed Orabi's forces at Tell el-Kebir and restored Tewfiq as a puppet ruler under British control.

British occupation... and nationalism

Britain's stated intention was to set Egyptian affairs in order and then withdraw, but its interests dictated a more active and permanent involvement. From 1883 to 1907, Egypt was controlled by the British Consul-General, Sir Evelyn Baring, later **Lord Cromer**, who coined the term "Veiled Protectorate" to describe the relationship between the two countries.

The emergence of the **Mahdi** in Sudan accelerated the trend towards direct British involvement in military and civil affairs. Sudan was nominally an Egyptian *khedival* possession – a status quo which the British, ostensibly, moved to protect. However, Britain was clearly pursuing its own interests and dominating Egyptian government to the extent of replacing its key officials with British colonial personnel. Egyptian resentment at this usurpation of authority found expression both under Tewfiq's son, **Abbas II**, who came to power in 1892, and in a nationalist movement led by a young lawyer, **Mustafa Kamel**. To ameliorate the situation, the British made a series of reforms and allowed Orabi to return from exile in Ceylon.

Economically, however, Egypt was effectively a colony, with Britain supplying all the country's manufactured goods, and in turn encouraging Egyptian dependence on cotton exports. In order to grow cotton, the *fellaheen* had to take out loans; when prices fell, many were forced to sell up to large landowners.

Towards independence

Politically, things came to a head when Turkey entered **World War I** on the side of Germany, in November 1916. Egypt was still nominally a province of the Ottoman Empire, so to protect its interests – the Suez Canal and free passage to the East – Britain declared Egypt a protectorate. By 1917, **Fouad**, the sixth son of Ismail, was *khedive* of Egypt, with Sir Reginald Wingate its High Commissioner.

The **nationalist movement** flourished under wartime conditions. In 1918, its leader, **Sa'ad Zaghloul**, presented the High Commissioner with a demand for autonomy, which was rejected. The request to send a delegation (*Wafd*) to London led to Zaghloul's arrest and deportation to Malta, a decision rescinded after nationwide anti-British riots. In 1922 Britain abolished the protectorate and recognized Egypt as an independent state, but kept control of the legal system, communications, defence and the Suez Canal. In March 1922, Fouad assumed the title of king.

The years between independence and World War II saw a struggle for power between the king, the British and the nationalist **Wafd Party**. Backed by the masses, the Wafd won landslide elections, but King Fouad retained power and the backing of the British. His son, **King Farouk**, succeeded him to the throne in 1935 and a year later signed a twenty-year **Anglo-Egyptian treaty**, which ended British occupation but empowered British forces to remain in the Suez Canal Zone. In 1937, Egypt joined the League of Nations, but the outbreak of World War II halted its move to complete independence.

World War II

During **World War II**, Egypt served a vital strategic role as a British base in the Middle East. The Wafd leadership went along with support for the Allies – on the tacit understanding that full independence would be granted after the war – keeping internal tensions controlled. Cairo became a centre of international power-broking, with its British political-military command and exiled Balkan royals.

Rommel's **Afrika Korps** came within 111 kilometres of Alexandria, but was repulsed by the **Eighth Army** under General Montgomery at the **Battle of El-Alamein** in October 1942. Thereafter the tide of war turned in the Western Desert Campaign and the Allies continued to advance across North Africa, through Libya and Tunisia.

Postwar manoeuvrings

On **conclusion of the war**, the Wafd demanded the evacuation of British troops and unification with Sudan – in opposition to British plans for the latter's self-government. Popular resentment was expressed in anti-British riots and strikes, supported by the **Muslim Brotherhood**, which led to clashes with British troops. In January 1947, British troops were evacuated from Alexandria and the Canal Zone.

Following the declaration of the state of **Israel** in May 1948, Egypt joined Iraq, Syria and Jordan in a military invasion. The defeat of the Arab forces was followed by a UN-organized treaty in February 1949 that left the coastal **Gaza Strip** of Palestine under Egyptian administration. Many of the Egyptian officers who fought in this war were disgusted by the incompetence and corruption of their superiors: it was from the officers' ranks that many of the leading lights of the 1952 Revolution were to emerge.

The 1952 Revolution

For the time being, the country experimented with democracy, holding its first **elections** in ten years. The Wafd won a majority and formed a government with Nahas Pasha as prime minister. A course for crisis was set, as the **Suez Canal** – which the British still controlled – loomed increasingly large. In 1952, Nahas was dismissed by King Farouk after abrogating the 1936 treaty with Britain, and the army was sent out onto the streets to quell anti-British protests.

Reaction was swift. On July 23, 1952, a group of conspiratorial **Free Officers** seized power and forced the **abdication of King Farouk**. General Naguib, the official leader of the group, was made commander of the armed forces and became prime minister, but real power lay in the hands of the nine officers of the **Revolutionary Command Council** (RCC), foremost amongst whom was Colonel **Gamal Abdel Nasser**.

Under RCC direction, the constitution was revoked, political parties dissolved, the monarchy abolished and Egypt declared a **republic** (July 26, 1953). Meanwhile, a struggle for power was taking place behind the scenes, as Naguib attempted to step beyond his figurehead status and moderate the revolutionary impulses of the RCC. After being implicated in an attempt on Nasser's life at Alexandria in 1954, Naguib was placed under house arrest. Nasser became acting head of state and in June 1956 was confirmed as president.

The Nasser Era (1956–70)

President Nasser dominated Egypt and the Arab world until his death in 1970, his ideology of Arab nationalism and socialism making him supremely popular with the masses (if not always their governments) from Iraq to Morocco. Under his leadership, Egypt was at the forefront of **anti-colonialism**, lending support to liberation struggles in Algeria, sub-Saharan Africa and other regions. Nasser also helped to set up the Non-Aligned Movement with Yugoslavia, India and Indonesia in 1955.

Diplomacy and war

Nasser's most urgent priority, from the start, was to assert Egyptian control over the **Suez Canal**. In 1954 he reached agreement for the withdrawal of British troops from the Canal Zone, though the Canal's management and profits were to remain in foreign hands. At the same time he was seeking credits from the World Bank to finance construction of the Aswan High Dam and weapons to rearm Egyptian forces, depleted from the 1948 war.

When the Soviet Union offered to supply the latter, the United States vetoed loans for the dam. Committed to the Aswan plan, Nasser had little alternative but to **nationalize the Suez Canal**, in order to secure revenue. This he did in July 1956.

His action was regarded by the West, and especially by Britain, as a threat to vital interests, and an unholy alliance was formed to combat the "Arab Hitler". Britain and France concluded a secret agreement with Israel, whose **invasion of Sinai** in October 1956 was to provide the pretext for their own military intervention. Following massive bombardment of the zone and British paratroop landings in Port Said, the United States stepped in to impose a solution, threatening to destabilize the British economy unless their forces were withdrawn. The American motivation was to keep Britain and France from gaining control of the Middle East, and the Arabs from moving en masse into the Soviet camp. In the event, the canal was reopened under full Egyptian control and Nasser emerged from the **Suez Crisis** as a champion of Arab nationalism.

On a wave of **pan-Arab** sentiment, Egypt and Syria united to form the **United Arab Republic** (UAR) in 1958: an unworkable arrangement that foundered within three years. Nasser also intervened in the **Yemen civil war**, supporting the revolutionary faction, to the extent of authorizing the use of poison gas against royalist forces. On a broader political front, he moved closer to the Soviet Union, accepting technical and military assistance on a massive scale, to help build the Aswan Dam and to counter an increasingly well-armed, US-supplied Israel. Meeting in Cairo in 1964, the **Arab League** set aside funds for the formation of the **Palestine Liberation Organization**.

War was again on the horizon. When Israel threatened to invade Syria in 1967, Nasser sent Egyptian forces into Sinai, ordered UN monitors to withdraw, and blockaded the Tiran Straits, cutting shipping to the Israeli port of Eilat. Israel responded with a pre-emptive strike, destroying the Egyptian air force on the ground and seizing the entire Sinai. This **Six Day War** resulted in permanent Israeli occupation of Sinai and the Gaza Strip, the West Bank and the Golan Heights. It was a shattering defeat for the Arabs, and Nasser in particular, who proffered his resignation to the public, only resuming the presidency after vast demonstrations of support on the streets.

The Six Day War had no official resolution, merely subsiding into a **War of Attrition**, which was to drag on for the next two years. From their positions in Sinai, Israeli forces bombarded Egypt's Canal cities, and even Cairo and Middle Egypt suffered bombing raids. Egypt, meanwhile, was rearming with Soviet assistance and struggling to deal with millions of refugees from the Canal Zone and the newly occupied Gaza Strip.

Progress and repression

Amid the political drama of Suez and the wars with Israel, it is easy to overlook the **social achievements** of the Nasser era. One of the first acts of the Revolutionary Command Council was to break up the old feudal estates, transferring **land** to the *fellaheen*. As a result of the **Aswan Dam**, the amount of land under cultivation increased by fifteen percent – exceeding Egypt's population growth for the first time. The dam's electricity also powered a huge new **industrial base**, which was established virtually from scratch.

Similarly radical progress was made in the fields of **education and health care**. The number of pupils in school doubled, and included both sexes for the first time. As a result of a huge programme of local health centres and the doubling of the number of doctors, average life expectancy rose from 43 to 52 years.

The downside of Nasserism was a heavily bureaucratic, Soviet-modelled system. Political life was stifled by the merging of all parties into the **Arab Socialist Union** (ASU). Opponents of the regime were not tolerated: censorship, torture, show trials and political internment were widespread.

Nevertheless, **Nasser's death** – from a heart attack – in September 1970 came as a profound shock to the whole Arab world. His funeral procession in Cairo was the largest the country has ever seen.

Egypt under Sadat (1970–81)

Nasser's successor was his vice president, **Anwar Sadat**, whom the ASU hierarchy confirmed as president in October 1970. His role was to reform an Egypt demoralized by defeat in the 1967 war, economic stagnation and austerity. His first significant act was to announce a "**corrective revolution**", reversing the policy of centralized economic control and expelling over a thousand Soviet advisors.

Again, however, domestic affairs were overshadowed by military developments. In concert with Syria and Jordan, Egypt launched a new campaign against Israel. On October 6, 1973, Egyptian forces crossed the Suez Canal, storming the "invincible" Bar-Lev Line to enter Israeli-occupied Sinai. This **October War** (aka 10th Ramadan/Yom Kippur War) ultimately turned against the Arabs, but enhanced their bargaining position and dealt a blow to Israeli self-confidence. In addition, Egypt regained a strip of territory to the east of the Suez Canal.

The open door policy

After the war, extensive changes took place in Egypt. An amnesty was granted to political prisoners, press censorship was lifted and some political parties, including the Muslim Brotherhood, were allowed. Equally important was Sadat's economic policy of *infitah* or "**open door**", designed to encourage private and foreign investment and to reduce the role of the state in the economy.

Helped by Gulf Arab investments – a reward for the October War – and stimulated by the reconstruction of the Canal cities, the economy boomed. However, the benefits were distributed unevenly: while the number of millionaires rose from 500 to 17,000 between 1975 and 1981 and an affluent middle class developed, the condition of the urban poor and *fellaheen* worsened. Some five million families subsisted on less than US$30 a month, and one and a half million Egyptians migrated to work in the Gulf states.

In 1977, when the International Monetary Fund insisted on the removal of subsidies on basic foodstuffs, there were nationwide **food riots**. Sadat saw the crunch coming and needed a major injection of Western capital.

Camp David and afterwards

In 1977 Sadat went to Jerusalem, the first Arab leader to visit Israel. This dramatic step, accompanied by a total realignment of Egyptian foreign policy towards the United States, reflected Sadat's need for US investment and his belief that Israel's acquisition of nuclear weapons made a military solution to the conflict impossible.

Under the US-sponsored **Camp David Agreement** of 1978, Egypt recognized Israel's right to exist and Israel agreed to withdraw from Sinai. This independent peace treaty, which failed to resolve the Palestinian issue, outraged Arab opinion. Meeting in Baghdad, the Arab League Council decided to withdraw their ambassadors to Egypt, sever economic and political links, and transfer the League's headquarters from Cairo to Tunis.

At home, Sadat encouraged the rise of Islamic political forces to counter leftist influences. But as the Muslim Brotherhood grew stronger and protested against the economic slump and the Camp David accord, Sadat clamped down, ordering wholesale arrests of his critics. This resulted in a highly charged atmosphere, and ultimately **Sadat's assassination** by Islamic militants in October 1981.

Mubarak's Egypt – from 1981 until the present

Sadat's policies have for the most part been continued, with rather more caution, by his successor **Hosni Mubarak**, who took office in 1981 and remains in power at the time of writing. While sheer survival counts for something, the country's situation is almost as precarious as it was in the early 1970s, when the writer Naguib Mahfouz likened Egypt to a group of drowning men struggling to reach the water's surface.

The economy

The **economy** was left in dire straits at the end of the Sadat era, and its root problems seem intractable. Only three percent of Egypt's land is useable for agriculture, while the **population** rises by a million every nine months (it currently stands at 75 million). Since the mid-1980s, Egypt has had to import half the food it needs, and its **foreign debt** has reached over US$33 billion. Without US$2 billion a year in **US aid** (Egypt is the largest recipient after Israel), the economy would collapse. It is this situation that has led to such schemes as the Toshka Project, which aims to make 500,000 acres of desert fertile by irrigating it with water pumped from Lake Nasser (see p.498).

Domestic revenues depend on a narrow base vulnerable to regional instability: remittances from Egyptians working abroad, crude oil production, tolls on shipping through the Suez Canal, and tourism. All were badly hit by the **Gulf War** of 1990–91, which led to over a million refugees returning from Kuwait and Iraq and wiped out the tourist industry for a year. The government's support for US action against Iraq was rewarded by the writing-off of US$7 billion in debts, further military and economic aid, and the promise of contracts and jobs for Egyptians in the Gulf States, but prospects had hardly begun to improve when terrorist attacks on tourists exposed another aspect of the economy's vulnerablity. **Tourism** had only just recovered from the crippling effects of the 1997 Luxor massacre when the September 11, 2001 attacks in the US sent it plunging again.

Even before this, the economy's fragility was evident, as speculation against the Egyptian pound and a liquidity crisis in the banking system led to a six percent **devaluation** of the national currency in 2001, and its flotation in 2003. Things could have been worse had Egypt not been attracting new investments from foreign and domestic sources since the mid-1990s, while the prospect of Egypt becoming a major exporter of **natural gas** over the next decade offers some hope to economists.

For most ordinary Egyptians, however, living standards are no higher than in Nasser's time, and the need for housing, jobs and land is greater than ever. Discontent is also fostered by widespread **corruption**, extending from local government to central ministries and the private sector. In 2002, the ex-governor of Giza was sentenced to sixteen years' hard labour for taking over £E1 million in bribes, and charges were brought against two MPs from the ruling National Democratic Party and nine senior officials from the Irrigation Ministry, alleged to have wasted £E45 million of public funds and taken £E30 million in kickbacks. While cases of buildings collapsing due to contractors cutting corners have become all too familiar, the whole nation was shocked by a catastrophic **train fire** in February 2002 that killed 363 third-class passengers – exposing the ramshackle state of Egypt's railways and officialdom's indifference to the lives of the poor.

Domestic politics and foreign affairs

Mubarak's pseudo-liberalization of the media and parliamentary politics has given a democratic gloss to an authoritarian system, essentially unchanged since Nasser's time. In 1999, he was endorsed as president for a fourth six-year term, in a national referendum that was widely believed to be rigged, though opposition complaints were muted. Under the **emergency laws** passed after Sadat's murder – still in force today – demonstrations are illegal unless licensed by the police (who violently suppress unauthorized ones), and **censorship** of the media extends to the removal of "atheist" works from the Cairo Book Fair. Torture and other abuses of power by the police and security forces go unpunished, while human rights activists and political opponents are arrested. In 2002, Sa'ad Eddin Ibrahim of the Ibn Khaldun Centre for Developmental Studies was jailed for seven years for receiving funds from the European Union and issuing reports that "tarnished Egypt's reputation abroad"; sixteen candidates for the local elections in Alexandria received prison terms for membership of the outlawed Muslim Brotherhood; and a student was shot dead during a protest about Palestine.

As the third president to have emerged from the armed forces, Mubarak is even more beholden to them than his predecessors. Ex-military and police officers hold top jobs in civilian life, and **internal security** is a constant preoccupation. Between 1992 and 1998, **Islamic militants** and the security forces fought a vicious, low-level war in Middle Egypt. Human rights organizations estimate that over 1200 people were killed and 10,000 wounded during the six-year insurgency, and about 20,000 detained under the emergency laws in 1993 alone. Ironically, the Luxor massacre that made headlines around the world proved to be the swansong of the *Gamaat Islamiya* – whose imprisoned leaders denounced the massacre and announced a ceasefire – while the other militant group, Islamic Jihad, had by this time decamped to Afghanistan, where they forged an alliance with Osama Bin Laden's Al-Qaida (see p.833).

Mubarak's **foreign policy** involves a delicate balancing act, as Egypt remains impaled on the contradictions of its relationship with America, Israel and the Arab world. The US is Egypt's prime financial underwriter and arms supplier, yet consistently favours Israel, which Arab states and peoples universally regard as the main source of instability and danger in the Middle East. While Mubarak managed to restore ties with other Arab states (which readmitted Egypt to the Arab League in 1990 and later returned the League's headquarters to Cairo) whilst maintaining a "cold peace" with Israel, the tensions and frustrations implicit in this policy are obvious. To a large extent, the regime's stability hangs on the decisions of other governments and the outcome of US and Israeli elections – as the tortuous **peace process** in the Middle East has faltered or revived.

Following the election of the left-leaning Ehud Barak as Israeli prime minister and the signing of the Wye Accords in 1999, hopes were high for a comprehensive peace, but within months the deal had collapsed, Syria's presidency changed hands and impetus was lost. In September 2000, Israeli hardliner **Ariel Sharon** sparked a new Palestinian uprising by intruding on Jerusalem's Haram ash-Sharif, the third holiest shrine in Islam. Within weeks Sharon had won the Israeli elections and the so-called **Al-Aqsa intifada** had become a far bloodier reprise of the *intifada* of the 1980s.

Prospects for fresh negotiations receded as the new US president George W. Bush announced America's disengagement from the peace process. Although the rising death toll compelled a US volte-face, it was clear that the new administration was far less sympathetic to the Palestinians than Clinton had been. The terrorist attacks of **September 11** crystallized their view of world affairs as a struggle between good and evil, with the Palestinians cast as terrorists unless proven otherwise, while the identification of two of the hijackers as Egyptians and most of the rest as Saudis – not to mention the nationality of Al-Qaida's leaders – further undermined relations between the US and its closest Arab allies, Egypt and Saudi Arabia. While both regimes managed to keep a lid on domestic opposition to America's war in Afghanistan and the invasion of **Iraq**, the stress was increasingly apparent.

What next?

The US overthrow of Saddam Hussein's dictatorship and Bush's urgings for reform and democracy within the Arab world angered Egypt's elite and the population at large, who regard all the rhetoric about freedom as a cover for US imperialism. Yet although Egyptians are hungry for change – the younger generation especially – there is widespread cynicism about Mubarak's recent reforms and Egypt's future.

Many are fatalistic, resigned to Mubarak and the "Menoufi Mafia" (from his home province in the Delta) rigging the 2006 presidential election while ostensibly opening it to other candidates (hitherto, only Mubarak could stand). It's widely believed that the ailing 77-year-old wants his son, **Gamal Mubarak**, to succeed him, despite assertions that "Egypt is not Syria". A small Westernized minority may consider Gamal a modernizer like King Mohammed VI of Morocco, but most people view him as a playboy set to inherit the family fortune, and favour his father to continue in power, if only because "He's already eaten all he can" and now cares about Egypt's well-being and his place in history – whereas newcomers to power would start their looting from scratch.

At the time of writing, Mubarak had not yet announced if he would be standing for a fifth term in September 2006, but there is rising **opposition** to the referendum to approve new rules for presidential elections, which impose tough conditions on independent candidates. In spring 2005, Cairene lawyer **Ayman Nour** gained the halo of martyrdom when he was jailed (and later freed) on charges of forging signatures as MP of a new liberal party, al-Ghad ("Tomorrow"); feminist Nawal el-Saadawi nominated herself to stir things up; over 1000 judges threatened to boycott the election unless they were given control over the process; and the Muslim Brotherhood joined the three legal opposition parties and the reformist alliance **Kifaya** ("Enough") in urging a boycott. The Brotherhood has since been at the forefront of demonstrations, dispersed by the police (who shot dead a student in El-Mansura) – while armed gangs of government supporters have attacked Kifaya protesters.

Another concern is the resurgence of **terrorism**. In October 2004, car bombs killed 34 tourists at the Sinai resorts of Taba and Ras al-Shaitun. The government blamed it on a local Palestinian angered by events in Gaza, but the interrogation of 2500 North Sinai residents caused protests in El-Arish. In April 2005, Cairo suffered three attacks in a week, by a husband, wife and sister who died in the process. The authorities pointed to their amateurism as proof that no terrorist network was involved – but some analysts fear that one has already taken root.

In short, the next year or so is likely to be the most uncertain time since Mubarak took power in 1981 – if not the most critical.

Islam

It's difficult to get any grasp of Egypt without first knowing something of Islam. What follows is a very basic background: some theory, some history and an idea of Egypt's place in the modern Islamic world.

Beginnings: practice and belief

Islam was a new religion born of the wreckage of the Greco-Roman world around the south of the Mediterranean. Its founder, a merchant named **Mohammed** from the wealthy city of Mecca (now in Saudi Arabia), was chosen as God's Prophet; in about 609 AD, he began to hear divine messages, which were later transcribed into the **Koran**, Islam's holy book. This was the same God worshipped by Jews and Christians – Jesus is one of the minor prophets in Islam – but Muslims claim He had been misunderstood by both earlier religions.

The distinctive feature of this new faith was directness – a reaction to the increasing complexity of established religions and an obvious attraction. In Islam there is no intermediary between humans and God (**Allah**) in the form of an institutionalized priesthood or complicated liturgy; and worship, in the form of prayer, is a direct and personal communication with God. Believers face five essential requirements, the so-called "**Pillars of Faith**": prayer five times daily, the pilgrimage (*Hadj*) to Mecca, the Ramadan fast, a religious levy, and – most fundamental of all – the acceptance that "there is no God but Allah and Mohammed is His Prophet".

The Pillars of Faith

The Pillars of Faith are still central to Muslim life, articulating and informing daily existence. Ritual **prayers** are the most visible. Bearing in mind that the Islamic day begins at sunset, the five daily times are sunset, after dark, dawn, noon and afternoon. Prayers can be performed anywhere, but preferably in a mosque. In the past, and even today in some places, a muezzin (prayer crier) would climb his minaret each time and summon the faithful.

Nowadays, the call is likely to be pre-recorded; even so, this most distinctive of Islamic sounds has a beauty all of its own. The message is simplicity itself: "God is most great (*Allahu Akbar*). I testify that there is no God but Allah. I testify that Mohammed is His Prophet. Come to prayer, come to security. God is great." Another phrase is added in the morning: "Prayer is better than sleep."

Prayers are preceded by ritual washing and are spoken with the feet bare. Facing Mecca (the direction indicated in a mosque by the *mihrab* or niche), the worshipper recites the *Fathah*, the first chapter of the Koran: "Praise be to God, Lord of the worlds, the Compassionate, the Merciful, King of the Day of Judgement. Only thee do we worship and thine aid do we seek. Guide us on the straight path, the path of those on whom thou hast bestowed thy grace, not the path of those who incur thine anger nor of those who go astray." The same words are then repeated twice in the prostrate position, with some interjections of *Allahu Akbar*. It is a highly ritualized procedure, the prostrate position symbolic of the worshipper's role as servant (Islam literally means "submission"), and the sight of thousands of people going through the same motions simultaneously in a mosque is a powerful one. On Islam's holy day, Friday, all believers are expected to attend prayers in their local grand mosque. Here the whole community comes together in worship led by an *imam,* who may also deliver the *khutba,* or sermon.

Ramadan is the name of the ninth month in the lunar Islamic calendar, the month in which the Koran was revealed to Mohammed. For the whole of the month, believers must obey a rigorous fast (the custom was originally modelled on Jewish and Christian practice), forsaking all forms of consumption between sunrise and sundown; this includes food, drink, cigarettes and any form of sexual contact. Only a few categories of people are exempted: travellers, children, pregnant women and warriors engaged in a *jihad,* or holy struggle. Given the climates in which many Muslims live, the fast is a formidable undertaking, but in practice it becomes a time of intense celebration.

The pilgrimage, or **Hadj**, to Mecca is an annual event, with millions flocking to Mohammed's birthplace from all over the world. Here they go through several days of rituals, the central one being a sevenfold circumambulation of the Ka'ba, before kissing a black stone set in its wall. Islam requires that all believers go on a *Hadj* as often as is practically possible, but for the poor it may well be a once-in-a-lifetime occasion, and is sometimes replaced by a series of visits to lesser, local shrines – in Egypt, for instance, to the mosques of Saiyida Zeinab or El-Hussein in Cairo.

Based on these central articles, the new Islamic faith proved to be inspirational. Mohammed's own Arab nation was soon converted, and the Arabs then proceeded to carry their religion far and wide in an extraordinarily rapid territorial expansion.

Development in Egypt

Islam's **arrival in Egypt**, in 640, coincided with widespread native resentment of Byzantine rule and its particular version of Christianity. By promising to respect Egyptian Christians and Jews as "people of the Book", the Muslim leader **Amr** got acquiescence, if not immediate support, from the population, in the wake of the Arab conquest. For many Egyptians who had found Christianity a more valid religion than the old pagan, polytheistic theology, Islam must have seemed a logical simplification, capturing the essence of human relationships with an all-powerful god.

Early on, the spread of Islam was accompanied by a practical conflict of interest. The Arabs wished to spread the faith, yet their administration depended on finance raised by a poll tax (*jizia*) levied on non-Muslims. A balance was maintained for a while, but towards the end of the ninth century, rulers began to use the tax as a punitive measure, alongside a series of repressive acts directed against the Christian and Jewish faiths. Khalif al-Hakim, in particular, embarked on a programme of destroying churches and synagogues. However, it was not until the eleventh century that Cairo attained a **Muslim majority**, and not until the thirteenth century for Egypt as a whole.

The original Arab dynasties of Egypt subscribed to **Sunni Islam** – the more "orthodox" branch of the religion, dominant then, as now, in most parts of the Arab world. However, the Fatimid dynasty, which took control of Egypt in 969, signalled a shift to **Shi'ite Islam**, which was to continue (among the rulers, at least) until late in the twelfth century. Under the Ayyubid dynasty that followed, Egypt reverted, permanently as it turned out, to Sunni adherence, with orthodoxy propagated through the new institution of the **madrassa** – a theological college attached to a mosque.

Orthodoxy, by its very nature, has to be an urban-based tradition. Learned men – lawyers, Koranic scholars and others – could only congregate in the cities where, gathered together and known collectively as the **ulema**, they regulated the faith. In Sunni Islam, the *ulema* divide into four schools (*madhahib*): *Hanbali, Maliki, Hanafi* and *Shafi'i* – the last two of which predominate in Egypt. The *ulema* of Cairo's great **Mosque of Al-Azhar** is regarded as the ultimate theological authority by most Sunnis outside the Gulf Arab states, and issues *fatwas* (opinions) on a range of questions submitted by believers, from family matters to financial affairs – in person, by post or email (📟www.alazhar.org, 📧info@alazhar.org).

Sheikhs and Sufis

Alongside this formal religious establishment, Egypt also developed **a popular religious culture**, manifested in the veneration of sheikhs and the formation of Sufi brotherhoods – both of which remain important today.

Sheikhs are basically local holy men: people who developed reputations for sanctity and learning. There is no set process for their sanctification in Islam – only acclamation – so the names change with the locality. Similar to sheikhs are individuals revered simply as **saiyid** ("lord") or **saiyida** ("lady"), often due to their direct descent from the Prophet's line. Important Egyptian examples include Saiyid el-Hussein, Mohammed's grandson and the son of Ali, and the Prophet's granddaughters, Saiyida Zeinab and Saiyida Nafisa.

Although the Koran explicitly prohibits monasticism and isolation from the community, Islam soon developed religious orders dedicated to asceticism and a mystical experience of God. Collectively known as the **Sufis**, these groups generally coalesced around a charismatic teacher, from whom they derived their name. The largest of these brotherhoods (*tariqas*) in Egypt are the **Rifai**, the **Ahmediya** and the **Shadhiliyya** – who can be seen at moulids ("saint's day" festivals) parading with their distinctive banners.

Towards crisis

With all its different forms, Islam permeates almost every aspect of Egyptian society. Unlike Christianity (or at least Protestant Christianity), which has accepted the separation of church and state, Islam sees no such distinction. Civil law was provided by the *sharia*, the religious law contained in the Koran, and intellectual life by the *madrassas* and Al-Azhar University.

The religious basis of Arab study and intellectual life did not prevent its **scholars and scientists** from producing work that was hundreds of years ahead of contemporary "Dark Age" Europe. The medical treatises of Ibn Sina (known in Europe as Avicenna) and the piped water and sewage systems of Fustat are just two Egyptian examples. Arab work in developing and transmitting Greco-Roman culture was vital to the whole development of the European Renaissance.

By this time, however, the Islamic world was beginning to move away from the West. The **Crusades** were one enduring influence towards division.

Another was the Islamic authorities themselves, who were increasingly suspicious (like the Western church) of any challenge and actively discouraging of innovation. At first it did not matter in political terms that Islamic culture became static. But by the end of the eighteenth century, Europe was ready to take advantage. Napoleon's expedition to Egypt in 1798 marked the beginning of a century in which virtually every Islamic country came under the control of a **European power**.

Islam cannot, of course, be held solely responsible for the Muslim world's material decline. But because it influences every part of its believers' lives, and because East–West rivalry had always been viewed in primarily religious terms, the nineteenth and twentieth centuries saw something of a **crisis in religious confidence**. Why had Islam's former power now passed to infidel foreigners?

The Islamist response

Reactions and answers veered between two extremes. There were those who felt that Islam should try to incorporate some of the West's secularism and materialism; on the other side, there were movements holding that Islam should turn its back on the West, purify itself of all corrupt additions and thus rediscover its former power.

The earliest exponent of the latter view was the **Muslim Brotherhood** (*il-Ikhwan il-Muslimeen*), founded in Ismailiya by **Hassan el-Banna** in 1928. The Brotherhood preached a moral renewal of Islam, established a network of schools and training centres, and later set up clandestine paramilitary groups. It was aimed as much against the corrupt feudal and *khedival* institutions as against Western imperialism.

Within fifteen years, the Brotherhood had spread through Egypt and spawned offshoots through the Middle East. Its terrorist activities prompted a violent state response, with its banning by King Farouk, whose bodyguards assassinated El-Banna in 1949.

After Egyptian independence and the Revolution of 1952, the legitimized Brotherhood rapidly became disillusioned with Nasser's secular nationalism. In 1954, two Brothers attempted to assassinate him during a public meeting in Alexandria. Mass arrests followed and the Brotherhood went underground again, not surfacing in public until the Sadat era, when the government regarded it as a useful counterweight to the left.

By this time the Brotherhood had moderated its strategy, if not its aims, and its tacit cooperation with the state led to the emergence of more radical groups. One such group, *Al-Taqfir w'al-Higrah* ("Repentance and Holy Flight"), gained notoriety for attacking boutiques and nightclubs in Cairo during the food riots of 1977. Another faction, established within Egypt's Military Academy, planned a *coup d'état* but was nipped in the bud. Most famous – and effective – was the organization known as **Al-Jihad** (Holy Struggle), which assassinated Sadat and attempted to launch a revolution in Assyut in 1981.

Under Mubarak, the mainstream Islamic opposition was allowed to establish clinics and schools for the poor, achieving a greater influence over cultural life. During the late 1980s, **Gamaat Islamiya** (Islamic Societies) captured the professional unions, and thousands of Egyptians put their savings into Islamic investment houses, which offered higher returns than ordinary banks. When these went bankrupt amid accusations of fraud, the Islamic movement's credibility was badly dented, but its prompt distribution of aid after the 1991 Cairo earthquake redeemed its reputation amongst the urban poor.

The following year, **Islamic militants** began a terrorist campaign in Middle Egypt, attacking tourists, policemen and Copts. The *Gamaat Islamiya* (not to be confused with the Islamic Societies, despite their overlapping membership and ideology) and the smaller *Jihad Islami* (Islamic Jihad) both claimed Sheikh Omar Abdel Rahman and Al-Jihad as their exemplars, and divine sanction for attacks on the "Pharaonic regime", "infidel" tourists, and Copts who refused to pay *jizia* – the tax that non-Muslims had to pay under the Khalifate. In practice, this involved local groups of extortionists, some of them traditional criminal families, or simply one clan revenging itself on another under the guise of terrorism.

While Copts complained that the security forces were riddled with Islamist sympathizers, Muslims in Middle Egypt were subjected to curfews, roadside searches, arbitrary arrest and torture by the security forces, badly straining communal relations. In other ways, however, the authorities deferred to the Islamist agenda, by jailing 300 Egyptians for the "crime" of converting to Christianity, and ruling that a Cairo professor found "guilty" of apostasy must separate from his wife. In 2000, nineteen Copts and two Muslims were killed in clashes at El-Qusiya that the police inexplicably ignored for two days.

However, the *Gamaat Islamiya* has not officially been implicated in any violence since its imprisoned leadership announced a ceasefire in 1998. Cynics reckon that they were simply fed up after nearly twenty years in prison, and their repudiation of past acts of violence in 2002 was a ploy by the government to deflect suspicion that terrorism is still latent in Egypt. As for the *Jihad Islami*, its leaders **Ayman al-Zawahiri** and Mohamed Atef had long ago since fled Egypt for Europe and the US before joining Bin Laden in Afghanistan (where they first met during the *jihad* against the Soviets). Having masterminded attacks against US targets in Africa and the Middle East, they stunned the world with their attack on the Twin Towers on September 11, 2001.

Although the government has variously accused Iran, Sudan and Al-Qaida of fomenting terrorism, more profound causes lie in Egypt and the wider world. Egypt's stagnant economy breeds despair, and its corrupt elite provokes anger among the vast majority of Egyptians who are struggling to get by. The appeal of Islam as a radical solution gains strength from its historic stature – by returning to the "pure" Islam of the Prophet, it is argued, Muslims can reunite and pursue their destiny, free of the arbitrary nation-states and parasitical regimes bequeathed by imperialism. While many people doubt that Islam offers a solution for *everything* – and the lifestyle-aspirations of Egyptian youth are far from fundamentalist – the Islamists' view of world events is broadly shared at every level of society, from janitors to generals.

The Muslim Brotherhood (led by 84-year-old Mahdi Akef) has a large following in universities and legal associations, with activists willing to risk arrest and torture. Besides intimidation, the authorities have tried to marginalize them by changing the law on professional syndicates and attempting to introduce a unified nationwide **azan** (call to prayer) in place of the cacophony of individual muezzins (which critics fear would silence dissenting voices). The training of **women imams** at Al-Azhar University is another aspect of the strategy to "modernize" Islam and move it away from radicalism.

Monumental chronology

The chronology below is designed for general reference of monuments and dynasties or rulers. For simplicity, only the **major figures of each dynasty** or era are listed, likewise the monuments and artefacts.

The following **abbreviations** are used: EAM (Egyptian Antiquities Museum in Cairo), IAM (Islamic Arts Museum in Cairo) and BM (British Museum in London).

c.250,000 BC ▶ **Hunter-gathering hominids** roam the savannahs. Stone tools have been discovered in gravel beds of Upper Egypt and Nubia.

c.25,000 BC ▶ **Late Paleolithic era**. Onset of desertification, until rains of Neolithic era. Ostrich eggs and flints have been found beneath dunes of Great Sand Sea.

c.6000 BC ▶ **Middle Neolithic era**. Intensive occupation of the Western Desert by hunter-gatherers. Rock art at the Gilf Kebir; solar calendar at Nabta Playa.

Predynastic Egypt

c.5000 BC ▶ Pastoralism becomes widespread in the Eastern and Western deserts, while **Badarian culture** takes root in the Nile Valley. Pottery, jewellery and ivory excavated at village of El-Badari in Upper Egypt.

c.4000 BC ▶ **Naqada I culture** Burnished pottery and granite mace heads have been found near Qus in Upper Egypt.

Early Dynastic or Archaic Period (c.3100–2686 or 2920–2575 BC)

c.2920–2770 BC ▶ **I Dynasty** *Aha; Djer, Den.*

c.2920 or 3100 BC ▶ **Unification of the Two Lands** (Upper and Lower Egypt) by **Menes**. Foundation of Memphis; Palette of Narmer (EAM); Stele of Peribsen (BM); Scorpion Macehead (Ashmolean Museum).

2686–2613 or 2469–2575 BC ▶ **III Dynasty** *Zoser; Sekhemkhet; Huni.* Step Pyramid and Unfinished Pyramid built at Saqqara; Collapsed Pyramid at Maidum.

Old Kingdom (c.2686–2181 or 2575–2134 BC)

2613–2494 or 2575–2465 BC ▶ **IV Dynasty** *Snofru; Cheops; Chephren; Mycerinus.* Bent Pyramid at Dahshur; Great Pyramids of Giza.

2494–2345 or 2465–2323 BC ▶ **V Dynasty** *Userkaf; Sahure; Neferefre; Nyuserre; Unas.* Sun Temples and Pyramids at Abu Sir; several further pyramids at Saqqara.

2345–2181 or 2323–2150 BC ▶ **VI Dynasty** *Teti; Pepi I; Pepi II.* More pyramids at Saqqara.

First Intermediate Period (c.2181–2050 or 2134–2040 BC)

2181–2160 or 2150–2134 BC ▶ **VII and VIII dynasties** Period of anarchy and fragmentation of power.

2160–2130 or 2154–2040 BC ▶
IX and X dynasties *Achthoes.* Capital at Herakleopolis, near Beni Suef.

2133–1991 BC ▶ **XI Dynasty**
Inyotef Sehertowy; Nebhepetre

Mentuhotpe II reunites Two Lands in 2050 BC. Ruined mortuary temple at Deir el-Bahri; Mentuhotpe's statue (EAM).

Middle Kingdom (c.2055–1650 or 2050–1786 BC)

1991–1786 or 1985–1955 BC ▶
XII Dynasty *Amenemhat I; Senusert I and II; Amenemhat III.* Pyramids at Lahun, Lisht and Hawara; rock tombs

at Beni Hassan and Aswan; site of Medinet Madi.

1955–1650 BC ▶ **XIII Dynasty**

Second Intermediate Period (c.1786–1567 or 1650–1950 BC)

1786–1603 or 1650–1550 BC ▶
XIV Dynasty

1674–1567 BC ▶ **XV and XVI (Hyksos) dynasties** *Khyam; Apophis I and II.* Capital at Avaris in the Delta

(with Minoan frescoes); *Rhind Mathematical Papyrus* (BM).

1684–1567 BC ▶ **XVII Dynasty** Expulsion of the Hyksos by Ahmosis. Tombs at Qarat Hilwah.

New Kingdom (c.1567–1085 or 1550–1070 BC)

1567–1320 or 1550–1307 BC ▶
XVIII Dynasty Two Lands reunited; period of imperial expansion. *Ahmosis; Amenophis I; Tuthmosis I and II; Hatshepsut; Tuthmosis III; Amenophis II and III; Akhenaten; Smenkhkare; Tutankhamun; Ay; Horemheb.* Temple of Deir el-Bahri; site of Tell el-Amarna; royal tombs in the valleys of the Kings and Queens at Thebes; Luxor and Karnak temples; Tutankhamun's gold (EAM).

1320–1200 or 1307–1196 BC ▶
XIX Dynasty *Ramses I; Seti I; Ramses II; Merneptah; Seti II.* Serapeum at Saqqara; temples at Abydos and Abu Simbel; Ramesseum and royal tombs at Thebes.

1200–1085 or 1196–1070 BC ▶
XX Dynasty *Sethnakhte; Ramses III (and eight other minor and hopeless Ramses).* Temple of Medinet Habu and further royal tombs at Thebes; some are plundered by workmen.

Third Intermediate Period (c.1069–747 BC)

1069–945 BC ▶ **XXI Dynasty** Authority divided between Tanis and Thebes. *Smendes; Herihor; Psusennes I and II.* Capital at Tanis; Treasure of Tanis (EAM); *Book of the Dead* (BM).

945–715 BC ▶ **XXII Dynasty** *Shoshenk; Osorkon.* Ruins at Tanis; Shoshenk's relief at Karnak.

818–715 BC ▶ **XXIII and XXIV dynasties**

Late Period (747–332 BC)

747–656 BC ▶ **XXV (Nubian) Dynasty** *Piankhi; Shabaka; Taharqa; Tanutamun.* Reliefs at Luxor; Kiosk

of Taharqa at Karnak; statue of Amenirdis (EAM).

664–525 BC ▶ **XXVI (Saïte) Dynasty** *Psammetichus I; Necho II; Psammetichus II; Apries; Amasis.* Ruins of Naucratis; steles at Ismailiya.

525–404 BC ▶ **XXVII (Persian) Dynasty** Persian invasion. *Cambyses; Darius I; Xerxes; Artaxerxes I.* Temple of Hibis at Kharga Oasis; completion of Nile–Red Sea canal; foundation of Babylon-in-Egypt (Cairo).

404–380 BC ▶ **XXVIII and XXIX dynasties** *Amyrtaeus; Amasis "The Drunkard".* Temple of El-Ghweeta, Kharga Oasis; tomb of Amunhotep Huy, Bahariya Oasis.

380–343 BC ▶ **XXX Dynasty** *Nectanebo I and II.* Additions to Philae and Karnak; ruined temple of Amun at Siwa Oasis.

Ptolemaic Era (332–30 BC)

332–30 BC ▶ Alexander the Great conquers Egypt and founds Alexandria. His successors, the Ptolemies, make the city a beacon for the Mediterranean world, where Hellenistic and Judaistic culture mingle. Their line expires with Cleopatra VII (51–30 BC), vanquished by the power of Rome. In Nubia, the kingdom of Meroe reaches its apogee. Construction (or modification) of temples of Edfu, Esna, Kom Ombo, Dendara and Philae; catacombs in Alexandria; Sanctuary of Amun at Siwa Oasis; ruins of Karanis and Qasr Qaroun in the Fayoum; Valley of the Mummies at Bahariya Oasis; temple of Dakka, Lake Nasser.

Roman and Byzantine Period (30 BC–640 AD)

30 BC ▶ Octavian (Augustus) annexes Egypt to the **Roman Empire**. Tomb of Kitnes and Temple of Dush in Kharga Oasis.

45 AD ▶ St Mark brings **Christianity** to Egypt. Muzawaka Tombs in Dakhla Oasis.

249–305 ▶ **Persecution of Coptic Christians** under Decius and Diocletian. "Pompey's Pillar" at Alexandria.

313 ▶ Edict of Milan **legalizes Christianity**. Foundation of monasteries of Wadi Natrun, St Anthony, St Paul and St Catherine.

395 ▶ Partition of Roman Empire into East and West; Egypt falls under Eastern, **Byzantine**, sphere. Necropolis of El-Bagawat at Kharga Oasis.

451 ▶ Council of Chalcedon leads to **expulsion of Copts from Orthodox Church**. Numerous objects in Coptic Museum (Cairo).

Arab Dynasties (640–1517)

640–642 ▶ **Arab conquest** of Egypt; **introduction of Islam**. Mosque of Amr and ruins of Fustat in Cairo.

661–750 ▶ Egypt forms part of **Umayyad Khalifate**, ruled from the dynasty's capital at Damascus. Ceramics and pottery (IAM).

750–935 ▶ **Abbassids** depose Umayyads and form new dynasty, ruling from Baghdad. In 870 Egypt's governor, **Ibn Tulun**, declares independence, founding a dynasty which rules until 905. Mosque of Ibn Tulun in Cairo.

935–969 ▶ **Ikhshidid dynasty** takes power in Egypt.

969–1171 ▶ **Shi'ite Fatimid dynasty** conquers Egypt and seizes the Islamic Khalifate, which it rules from Cairo. Mosques of Al-Azhar, Al-Hakim and Al-Aqmar, Mausoleum of Imam Al-Shafi'i, and various fortified gates, in Cairo.

1171–1250 ▶ **Salah al-Din** founds **Ayyubid dynasty** and liberates land conquered by the Crusaders. Egypt returns to **Sunni Islam**. Intrigues of **Shagar al-Durr** open the way to **Mamluke** takeover. Madrassa-Mausoleum of Al-Silah Ayyub and the Aqueduct in Cairo; ruins of Shali in Siwa Oasis. Mausoleum of Shagar al-Durr in Cairo.

Mamluke Dynasties (1250–1517)

1250–1382 ▶ **Bahri Mamlukes** *Qalaoun; Khalil; Mohammed al-Nasir.* In Cairo: Qalaoun's Maristan-Mausoleum-Madrassa, Mosques of Al-Nasir, House of Uthman Katkhuda, and Qasr Bashtak.

1382–1517 ▶ **Burgi Mamlukes** *Barquq; Farag; Barsbey; Qaitbey; Qansuh al-Ghuri.* In Cairo: Barquq's Mausoleum, Madrassa and Khanqah of Barsbey, Mosque of Qaitbey, and the Ghuriya. Also, Fort Qaitbey in Alexandria.

Ottoman Period (1517–1798)

1517 ▶ **Selim the Grim conquers Egypt**. For the next three centuries the country is ruled as an Ottoman province from Constantinople. In Cairo: Mosques of Suleyman al-Silahdar and Suleyman Pasha; Sabil-Kuttab of Abd al-Rahman Katkhuda. Terbana Mosque in Alex.

1798–1802 ▶ French occupation of Egypt. Capitulation Agreement of 1802 leaves British in effective control of the country. Treasures shipped off to Louvre/British Museum. European graffiti left on numerous temples.

Pashas, khedives and kings (1805–1952)

1805 ▶ **Mohammed Ali** seizes power and begins a programme of ruthless **modernization**. Mohammed Ali Mosque in Cairo; Ras el-Tin Palace and Mahmudiya Canal in Alexandria. Belzoni, Mariette and others pioneer digs at pharaonic sites in the Nile Valley and Delta.

1848–54 ▶ Reign of **Abbas I**.

1854–63 ▶ Reign of **Said Pasha**. Suez Canal begun.

1863–79 ▶ Reign of **Khedive Ismail**. Completion of Suez Canal; Central Cairo boulevards constructed.

1879–92 ▶ Reign of **Khedive Tewfiq**. British crush the **Orabi Revolt** (1882–83). Tewfiq reinstated as a puppet ruler under British control. Howard Carter discovers Tutankhamun's tomb at Thebes (1922) at the tail end of a period of intensive excavations throughout Egypt.

1935–52 ▶ Reign of King Farouk; during World War II Egypt stays under British control.

1952–53 ▶ Farouk overthrown by Free Officers. Egypt declared a republic. Construction of Midan Tahrir in Cairo.

Modern Egypt (1952–)

1956 ▶ **Nasser** becomes President; **Suez Crisis**. Major industrialization programme, and construction of schools, hospitals and public housing.

1967 ▶ **Six Day War** with Israel; massive damage to Canal cities.

1970 ▶ **Nasser dies** and is succeeded as president by **Sadat**. High Dam at Aswan completed (1970).

1973 ▶ **October War** with Israel.

1977–78 ▶ Food riots. Sadat's trip to Jerusalem leads to **Camp David** agreement. Mohandiseen district of Cairo built, along with hundreds of new hotels, shops, etc. First line of Cairo metro completed.

1981 ▶ **Assassination of Sadat**. Presidency assumed by **Mubarak**.

1990 ▶ **Gulf War**.

1991 ▶ **Cairo earthquake** Many buildings damaged, but the second metro line is pushed to completion.

1994 ▶ **Underwater finds at Alexandria** Divers and archeologists begin exploration of the ruins of the ancient Lighthouse of Pharos and the royal quarters in the harbour at Alexandria.

1995 ▶ Tomb of Ramses II's sons found in the Valley of the Kings.

1996 ▶ **Valley of the Mummies** Egypt's largest cache of mummies is discovered in Bahariya Oasis.

1997 ▶ 58 foreigners killed by Islamic militants at Hatshepsut's Temple, near Luxor. **Toshka Project** inaugurated.

2000 ▶ The interior of the **Red Pyramid** at Dahshur is reopened after many years.

2001 ▶ Discovery of the underwater city of **Herakleion** at Abu Qir on the Mediterranean coast.

2002 ▶ Inauguration of the **Bibliotheca Alexandrina**, and the completion of the main branch of the **Sheikh Zayid Canal** at Toshka.

2004 ▶ Opening of the Alexandria National Museum. Bombing of *Taba Hilton* in Sinai.

2005 ▶ **Referendum** held on changing the electoral law ahead of the 2006 presidential election, which opposition parties urge the public to boycott.

Music

As with other cultural spheres, Egypt's musical traditions date back to pharaonic times, though the primary influences are Arab and Islamic. Given Egypt's status in the Arab world, it is no surprise that Cairo is the centre of the Arab recording industry – a dominance partly acquired by the collapse of its rivals in Lebanon, Libya and Kuwait. Egypt's vast population makes it the most important market for Arab music, and the amazingly high proportion of youth (over thirty million Egyptians are under 25) has ensured a big demand for contemporary sounds. What follows is the briefest of introductions to the various major musical genres.

Ancient Egyptian music

You won't hear **Ancient Egyptian music** played anywhere – indeed, nobody is sure what it sounded like – but enough is known about the instruments for musicologists to have tried to recreate the hymns and processional songs that accompanied religious rituals and court life in ancient times. Flutes and clarinet-type instruments go back to the Old Kingdom (if not predynastic times), as do harps (which evolved from hand-held instruments to large, free-standing ones), trumpets, cymbals and castanets. By the Middle Kingdom, harps were accompanied by the sistrum (a kind of rattle associated with the goddess Hathor and often carved with her face), tambourines, clappers and a type of guitar. The lute and lyre appeared during the Second Intermediate Period and were probably introduced by the Hyksos, while other instruments came into Egypt as a result of the various foreign invasions after the fall of the New Kingdom.

Religious music

During Ramadan and other major festivals you'll encounter **religious music** – renditions of **Koranic verses**, or praises to Allah, teased out in any number of ways.

Performers may be **munshids** – professional reciters who move from one festival to another – or simply the **muezzin** or **imam** of the local mosque. In everyday religious life, all muezzins have their individual styles of phrasing, and the government's proposal to replace diverse voices with a single nationwide **azan** has been fiercely resisted (though many city-dwellers would welcome a ban on amplifiers). The superstar in this genre is **Mohammed Gabriel**.

Recitals at **moulids** are often more participation than performance, with dozens of Sufi devotees chanting and swaying to the accompaniment of a drum. These recitals, known as **zikrs**, can last for days.

Classical Arabic music

Antecedents of **classical Arabic music** can be traced back to the **Bedouin** reciters and singers of the Arabian peninsula, but also to the more refined **court music** of the great khalifal cities of Baghdad and Damascus, and Ottoman Constantinople.

During the last century, the form has been characterized by oriental scales, passionate rhetoric, bravura soloists, massed orchestras and male choirs. The most famous twentieth-century exponent was **Umm Kalthoum** (aka Oum Khalsoum); until her death in 1975, she was the most popular singer in the Arab world. Her career coincided with the advent of long-distance broadcasting and she was the first Arab music star. In Egypt, she was a national institution, known as "The Mother of Egypt" and accorded a weekly concert on radio (and, later, TV). Almost as revered was **Mohammed Abdel Wahab**, who will be forever associated with the nightclubs of Cairo's Tawfiqiyya district and who also composed Egypt's national anthem, *Biladi, Biladi*. Another superstar was the actor/singer **Abdel Halim Hafez**, whose film recordings are still widely loved long after his death in 1977. Fears that the genre had become ossified have been dispelled by its recent revival at the hands of **Hany Shaker**, while the Iraqi megastar **Kazem Al-Saher** (now living in Cairo) collaborated with the poet Nizar Qabbani (Umm Kalthoum's lyricist) to produce *Al Hob-Al-Mustaheel* – a massive hit that won a new generation of fans.

Regional/ethnic music

The different types of folk or popular music you'll come across vary greatly with the region and environment: Cairo, the Nile Valley, the Delta and the desert all have their own characteristic sounds, rhythms and instruments. Often their songs reflect the rituals of everyday life: weddings, moulids, harvest festivals, old stories of village life or triumphs.

Saiyidi

The music of Upper Egypt – known, like its people, as **Saiyidi** – has a characteristic rhythm, which horses are trained to dance to. It is based upon two instruments: the *nahrasan*, a two-sided drum hung over the chest and beaten with sticks; and the *mismar saiyidi*, a kind of wooden trumpet. Performances often involve monologues, ripe with puns and wit. One of the famous names of the genre, **Omar Gharzawi**, is known for his rebuttals of the stereotyped image of stupid, hot-headed Saiyidis, while the late **Shoukoukou** has a special instrument (a joke clapping doll, sold at festivals) named after him. On a more official standing is *Rais* ("Boss") **Met'al al-I'nawi**, often chosen by the government to represent Egypt at foreign music festivals. The current popular favourite is **Mohammed El-Agouz**.

Fellahi

The northern counterpart to Saiyidi music, found in the Delta, is known as **fellahi** (peasant) music. It is generally softer, with a fondness for the *matsoum* (one and a half) rhythm, and use of instruments like the *rababa*, a two-stringed viol, and the *mismar*, a kind of oboe.

Sawaheeli

Found along the Mediterranean coast and in the Canal Zone, **Sawaheeli** music is characterized by the use of a banjo-like stringed instrument, the *simseemeya*. Another form, specific to Alexandria, also features the accordion, the result of the city's Greek and Turkish influences.

Bedouin

There are two kinds of **Bedouin** music: one found in the Western Desert, towards Libya, the other in the Eastern Desert and Sinai. Both have songs recounting old intrigues, activities and stories to a strong rhythmic accompaniment. This has been a major influence on *Al-Jeel* music (see p.843).

Nubian

Performed in its own language, in the southern reaches of the Nile Valley, **Nubian** music has more African than Arab roots. It relies a lot on handclapping and the *duf*, a kind of tambourine. More urbanized versions – found in Aswan or Khartoum – have opted for brass sections and female choruses, while **Ali Hassan Kuban** overlays the traditional percussion and *oud* framework with Western instruments such as the guitar, violin and accordian, tuned to Arabic scales. Conversely, the Nubian composer **Hamza ad-Din** has written music for classical orchestral performances.

Pop music

In Cairo and other cities, rural traditions have mixed with the more elite classical styles and adapted to reflect urban preoccupations and the faster pace of life. By the mid-1980s two main types of music had developed: **Shaabi** and **Al-Jeel**. Nowadays, some would say that the distinction between them is moot, and artists such as Hakim can rightfully claim to have a foot in each camp, while pop idol Amr Diab has spearheaded attempts to stake a claim on the world market. In Egypt, *Shaabi* and *Al-Jeel* stars release their latest hits at peak sales periods such as Ramadan and St Valentine's Day. News and audioclips of *Shaabi* and *Al-Jeel* stars can be found on the website ⓦwww.mazika.com.

Shaabi

Shaabi ("people") music was born in the working-class quarters of Cairo, where millions of second- and third-generation rural migrants live. It blends the traditional form of the *mawal* (plaintive vocal improvisations) with a driving beat. Its lyrics are often raunchy or satirical, politically and socially provocative. You will rarely hear this music via the media. It is not so much banned as beneath the contempt of the middle classes and respectable society, who see its rudeness and social criticism as coming from another Egypt. It is to be heard, however, at weddings and parties throughout working-class Cairo and at some

Although CDs are catching on in Egypt, **cassettes** remain the medium of choice for recorded music, being robust, cheap and very easy to copy – piracy is such a problem that it has its own special police division in Cairo. Outlets are street-corner kiosks, small shops and market stalls, most of which tend to specialize in either Shaabi or Al-Jeel, or the old oriental musics, traditional and modern. There are no charts as such, though you will soon know when a song is the city's "number one". If it's big, producers can expect to sell up to a million copies.

The following is a highly **selective list of artists and recordings** to start you off in Cairo cassette browsing. In Britain or North America, you can find a limited range of records, too – mostly Umm Kalthoum and the like, though with a few more contemporary releases on world music labels such as Mondo Melodia, Piranha, Axiom or Mango/Island. David Lodge's *Yalla: Hitlist Egypt* collection (Mango/Island) devotes a side each to *Shaabi* and *Al-Jeel*.

Ancient Egyptian music

Michael Atherton *Ankh: The Sound of Ancient Egypt* (available abroad as a CD on the Celestial Harmonies label).

Religious music

Mohammed Gabriel Anything by the superstar of Koranic recitation.

Classical Arabic music

Umm Kalthoum *Al-Atalaal* and *Enta Omri*. Two of her greatest live recordings – among dozens of releases.

Mohammed Abdel Wahab *The Music of Abdel Wahab* (available abroad on the Axiom label).

Kazem Al-Saher *Al-Hob Al-Mustaheel*. The Iraqi-born pop star's collaboration with Umm Kalthoum's lyricist.

Saiyidi music

Ahmed Ismail and Sohar Magdy Anything by this duo is worth acquiring.

Nubian music

Ali Hassan Kuban *From Nubia to Cairo* or *Walk Like a Nubian* (both available abroad on the Pirhana label).

Hamza ad-Din *Escalay*. Classical music inspired by Nubian sounds and Sufism.

Khedr *Ya Sahabba*. Sung in an obscure Nubian dialect – and popular mainly among Nubians.

Bedouin music

You won't find cassettes in Cairo but may strike lucky in Sinai or Mersa Matrouh.

Al-Jeel music

Amr Diab *Ya Tareek*; *Awedony*; *Ya Omnena*; *Tamaly Ma'ak*; *Caravelle*. Egypt's first international crossover star, often likened to Ricky Martin. *Habibi*, the English version of his *Nour el Ain*, was a hit in Europe and the US in 1998.

Hisham Abbas *Gowa Fe* or *Habibi Da*. One of the new hot talents on the *Al-Jeel* scene.

Mohammed Mounir *Ana Qalbi Masaken Sha'abiya*. Plaintive songs of life and the city, by the master of the genre.

Shaabi music

Ahmed Adaweer *Al-Tareek* or *Adaweat*. The father of it all at his best.

Hakim *Yaho* or *Al Nazra*. Today's hardcore *Shaabi* favourite. *Shakl Tani/Remix* is a compilation of his earlier songs remixed by the British worldbeat dance group Transglobal Underground (available abroad on Mondo Melodia).

Hassan el-Asmar *Mish Hasheebak*. Classic *Shaabi* lyrics of hard urban life.

---

of the nightclubs along Pyramids Road – and played on battered cassettes in taxis, buses and cafés everywhere.

The original *Shaabi* singer was **Ahmed Adaweer**, who, from 1971 on, introduced the idea of street language and subsequently broke every rule in the book. Later exponents introduced elements of rap and disco into the *Shaabi* sound, in the manner of Algerian *Raï* music. The genre is still frowned upon in official cultural circles, but commands a wide following. **Sha'ban Abdel Rahim** was a laundry ironer until a television appearance catapulted him to stardom. His earthy persona infuriated Egypt's cultural arbiters (leading the chief censor to propose that only singers with university degrees should be allowed to appear on TV), while his song *I hate Israel* was cited in the Knesset as proof of anti-Semitism in the Egyptian media. After his next bestseller, *Don't Hit Iraq*, Sha'ban was embraced by the government and recorded *The Word of Truth*, a paean to Mubarak crediting him with making running water and mobile phones readily available to the masses. Meanwhile, rival *Shaabi* superstar **Hakim** has tried to reach an international crossover audience with a remix of his hits by Transglobal Underground, following the example of Amr Diab (see below).

Al-Jeel

Al-Jeel means "the generation" and followed hot on the heels of *Shaabi*, in the early 1980s. It takes disco elements a step further, using drum tracks and synthesized backing, and mixes these with Nubian and Bedouin rhythms. The latter came in large part through the influence of Libyan musicians, who had fled to Cairo in the late 1970s after Gaddafi's "cultural revolution", where he clamped down on Western musical influences. Some fans and critics now call it "Mediterranean Music", acknowledging the crosscurrents of influences within the Arab world and its European diaspora – while others simply see it as classic Arabic pop.

Whatever the name, it's big business – though not exactly as in the West. Artists receive hardly anything from sales of tapes and CDs; they earn their money from appearances at weddings and concerts. That said, Egypt's foremost pop idol, **Amr Diab**, broke into the international market after he won the 1998 World Music Award for *Nour el Ain* (released in English as *Habibi*), to become the bestselling Arab singer ever. He was also the first Egyptian artist to release a pop video and make collaborative recordings with a Spanish flamenco group, the *Raï* star Khaled and the Greek singer Angela Dimitriu. **Mohammed Mounir** is almost as popular, and rated ahead of the rest of the pack for his plaintive songs of city life.

Several female singers have a big following, especially **Ruby**, whose pop videos are brazenly sexual by Egyptian standards, going far beyond the soft-focus romanticism of **Hanan** or **Samire Saieed**. Ruby was born in the Islamist stronghold of Assyut, though its inhabitants are quick to point out that she grew up in Cairo.

Al-Jeel lyrics, in contrast to *Shaabi*, are usually about love or the country and rarely stray into sensitive areas. However, performances remain a focus for discontented youth, and stars are increasingly courted by politicians and allowed to express popular feelings. **El-Magmoaa** ("The Clique") is a group of pop singers, film and TV stars, whose benefit song *Jerusalem will come back to us* is a bitter attack on Israel's treatment of the Palestinians.

Books

Most of the books listed below are in print; those that are out of print (o/p) should be easy to track down in second-hand bookstores. Books that are only published in Egypt are most easily available in Cairo; we have identified these by giving the publisher's name after the book title (the American University in Cairo Press is abbreviated to AUC).

Travel

General

Karl Baedeker *Egypt: Handbook for Travellers* (o/p). The classic guide-book, used by generations of tourists from the 1870s until World War II. Of the numerous editions, the 1929 revision – which includes the discovery of Tutankhamun's tomb – is the one to hunt for in second-hand bookshops (it sells for about £100/US$160; a facsimile edition, published in the 1980s, is also out of print but can often be found for £20/US$30 or so).

Jonathan Cott *The Search for Omm Sety: A Story of Eternal Love* (Olympic). A biography of Dorothy Eady, who believed herself to be the reincarnation of a temple priestess and lover of Seti I at Abydos (see p.349).

Robert Curzon *Visits to Monasteries in the Levant* (E. Mellen). Famed account, by a man later made Viceroy of Egypt, of youthful adventurings in Egypt, Palestine and Greece in the 1830s. Several chapters deal with Egyptian monasteries, where Curzon got the monks drunk and stole their antiquarian manuscripts.

Amelia Edwards *A Thousand Miles up the Nile* (Darf). Verbose, patronizing classic from the mid-nineteenth century. All books on Egypt have their Amelia quotes – the *Rough Guide* included.

Gustave Flaubert *Flaubert in Egypt* (Penguin). A romp through the brothels, baths and sites by the future author of *Madame Bovary*, who cared little for monuments but delighted in Egyptian foibles and vices. Skilfully edited by Francis Steegmuller.

Amitav Ghosh *In an Antique Land* (Granta). Wry tales of contemporary life in a Delta village, interspersed with snippets of less absorbing historical research.

Michael Haag *Egypt Chronicle* (Rough Guides). A pocket-size guide to Egypt's five-thousand-year civilization, with timelines on each page and sidebars on significant figures from Cheops to Nasser. Also covers topics such as Egyptian movies, Arab music, irrigation and the Suez Crisis.

Douglas Kennedy *Beyond the Pyramids* (Abacus). A dour, Paul Theroux-ish jaunt around Egypt in the late 1980s; the Alex and Assyut sections stand out.

E.W. Lane *Manners and Customs of the Modern Egyptians* (East-West). Facsimile edition of this encyclopedic study of life in Mohammed Ali's Cairo, first published in 1836. Highly browsable.

★ **Deborah Manley** *The Nile: A Traveller's Anthology* (o/p). A good anthology to go for: nicely illustrated and with selections gathered from some very obscure sources.

Bimbashi McPherson *The Man Who Loved Egypt* (o/p). Discreetly edited letters of the prewar head of Cairo's secret police, interesting for the light they cast on moulids and low-life. A serial paedophile, McPherson was portrayed as Scobie in *The Alexandria Quartet*.

Henri de Monfreid *Hashish* (o/p). A latter-day swashbuckler who followed a spell in Djibouti jail by smuggling hash on the Red Sea during the 1920s. The second half relates his dealings with the Suez underworld.

Murray's *Handbook for Travellers in Egypt* (o/p). A worthy rival to Baedeker, likewise replete with footnotes, engravings and colonial attitudes. Later editions distinguished by their coverage of Sinai sell for around £30/US$50.

Gerard de Nerval *Journey to the Orient* (o/p). Stoned on hash, de Nerval thrilled to Mohammed Ali's Egypt: splendour and squalor, eroticism and cruelty – the Orientalist fantasy that still colours perceptions today. A wacky read.

Florence Nightingale *Letters from Egypt* (Parkway). A stuffier view of Egypt, by a 29-year-old Englishwoman who had yet to make herself famous in the Crimean War. Illustrated with paintings and drawings by David Roberts, Edward Lear and other artists of the period.

Christopher Pick *Egypt: A Traveller's Anthology* (J. Murray). Mixed bag of observers from the eighteenth and nineteenth centuries, including Disraeli, Mark Twain, Vita Sackville-West, Flaubert, E.M. Forster and Freya Stark.

Charlie Pye-Smith *The Other Nile* (o/p). Witty and insightful account of a tour in the early 1980s, interwoven with recollections of trips into Sudan and Ethiopia, before coups and famine made them inaccessible.

Paul William Roberts *River in the Desert* (Random House). Chiefly interesting for its eyewitness account of a *zaar* (exorcism) and a chapter on the Kushmaan Bedouin of the Eastern Desert.

★ **Anthony Sattin** *The Pharaoh's Shadow* (Phoenix). Fascinating discourse on the "survival" of Ancient Egyptian religious beliefs and practices in modern-day Egypt. Sattin's earlier book on British colonial society in Egypt is sadly out of print (see "Medieval and Modern History", p.852).

Stanley Stewart *Old Serpent Nile: A Journey to the Source* (Flamingo). Stewart managed to travel from the Nile Delta to the Mountains of the Moon in Uganda in the late 1980s, and relates his adventures in spare, taut prose.

Cairo

James Aldridge *Cairo* (o/p). Highly readable history of the city from ancient times until the mid-1960s, including several fine maps and photographs. Only found in second-hand bookshops.

Artemis Cooper *Cairo in the War* (o/p). Excellent account of a febrile era, with vignettes of Evelyn Waugh, Olivia Manning and other postwar luminaries.

★ **Maria Golia** *Cairo: City of Sand* (Reaktion Books). Focuses on the domestic life, housing and nitty-gritty of contemporary Cairo, including criticism of the satellite cities, ring road and other prestige projects.

Trevor Mostyn *Egypt's Belle Epoque: Cairo 1869–1952* (o/p). Expat high-life and diplomatic intrigue, from the time of Ismail to the revolution that overthrew King Farouk.

★ **Richard Parker** *Islamic Monuments of Cairo: A Practical Guide* (AUC). Excellent and detailed handbook to the monuments and history of seventh- to nineteenth-century Cairo.

★ **Max Rodenbeck** *Cairo: The City Victorious* (Picador). This superb history of Cairo includes the best anecdotes from earlier histories by Aldridge and Stewart (see p.845 and below), and follows events up until 1999.

Desmond Stewart *Great Cairo, Mother of the World* (AUC). Entertaining and erudite history of the city, from pharaonic times through to the Nasser era. Available in Cairo.

Alexandria

★ **Jean-Yves Empereur** *Alexandria Revealed*; *Alexandria Rediscovered* (AUC). As director of the Centre d'Etudes Alexandrines, responsible for excavating the Pharos, the Catacombs and lesser-known sites, Empereur has unearthed a mass of evidence about the ancient city. In *Alexandria Rediscovered* he writes about the problems of working in a city whose buried past is all too fragile. Both books are very readable and profusely illustrated.

E.M. Forster *Alexandria: A History and a Guide* (o/p UK). A foreword by Lawrence Durrell and erudite notations by Michael Haag enhance Forster's 1922 guidebook. Forster's companion piece was *Pharos and Pharillon* (o/p), a diverse collection of essays on Alexandrian life.

★ **Michael Hagg** *Alexandria: Capital of Memory* (Yale University Press). An evocative and beautifully written account of the city as experienced by Forster, Cavafy and Durrell, illustrated with many rare photographs from the 1920s, 1930s and 1940s.

Roy MacLeod *The Library of Alexandria: Center of Learning in the Ancient World* (AUC). A history of the legendary library that delves into the city's Greek heritage, the book trade in antiquity, Neoplatonist philosophers, Mystery Schools and many other topics. An introduction by the director of the new Bibliotheca Alexandrina brings the story full circle.

Jane Lagoudis Pinchin *Alexandria Still: Forster, Durrell and Cavafy* (AUC). A rather dry study of the influence of the city and its three most famous writers on one another, strictly for people seriously into these writers.

The desert

★ **Wael Abed** *The Other Egypt: Travels in No Man's Land* (Zarzora Expedition). A *tour d'horizon* of the natural wonders of the Western Desert by one of Egypt's leading safari guides and desert ecologists. Illustrated with eighty colour photos,

plus rare black-and-white photos taken by explorers in the 1920s and 1930s. Sold in Cairo for about £E75.

★ **Michael Asher** *In Search of the Forty Days Road: Impossible Journey* (o/p). Only peripherally related to Egypt, but well worth reading. Asher's camel journeys, in the Sudanese desert and from Mauritania to the Nile, evoke all the hardships and magic of the desert.

★ **R.A. Bagnold** *Libyan Sands: Travels in a Dead World* (Immel); *Sand, Wind and War: Memoirs of a Desert Explorer* (Tucson). One of a band of motorized explorers of the Western Desert during the 1920s and 1930s, Bagnold later wrote the seminal work on dune-formation (a book continuously in print since 1939 and used by NASA to interpret satellite photos of Mars) and led the Long Range Desert Group. Despite Bagnold's restrained prose, his exploits are compelling and the sheer range of journeys – to all the oases, Uwaynat, the Great Sand Sea and the Forty Days Road – make them essential reading.

★ **Burton Bernstein** *Sinai: The Great and Terrible Wilderness* (o/p). Mixture of travel writing and history, describing Sinai on the eve of its handover to Egypt in 1979. Dated but still the best book on the region.

Alain Blottiere *Siwa: the oasis* (Harpocrates). Slim, idiosyncratic book blending history, reportage and personal musings.

Peter Clayton *Desert Explorer* (Zerzura). A biography of the author's father, Patrick Clayton, who mapped the Western Desert at the same time as Bagnold and was likewise active in the LRDG until his capture by the Italians.

Ahmed Fakhry *The Oases of Egypt* (AUC; 2 vols.). Fakhry's unfinished trilogy is still the last word on the Western Desert Oases. Volume I, covering Siwa, is fascinating; Volume II, on Bahariya and Farafra, is heavier going, while Fakhry's death in 1973 aborted the volume on Dakhla and Kharga. Volume I has been republished in paperback; Volume

II remains out of print, but can be found in Cairo bookshops.

Zahi Hawass *Valley of the Golden Mummies: The Greatest Egyptian Discovery since Tutankhamun* (Abrams). Written by the chief of Egypt's Supreme Council for Antiquities, who is currently excavating the Greco-Roman necropolis in Bahariya Oasis, with superb photos of the mummies. Its omission of others' doubts about his methodology is perhaps forgivable. Available in Cairo bookshops.

Saul Kelly *The Hunt for Zerzura: The Lost Oasis and the Desert War* (Murray). A detailed account of the real drama that inspired *The English Patient*: it's likely to remain the last word in English until somebody translates Almássy's own account from German, or his biography from Hungarian.

George Murray *Dare Me to the Desert* (o/p). Despite its awful title, this is an interesting account of Murray's climbing expeditions in the Red Sea Mountains during the 1920s and 1930s.

David Rohl (ed.) *Followers of Horus Eastern Desert Survey Vol. 1* (ISIS). Profusely illustrated study of the rock art of the Eastern Desert, by the Followers of Horus (see p.799). Order by post from Mike Rowland, ISIS Treasurer, 127 Porter Rd, Basingstoke, Hants RG22 4JT, England. The editor is better known for his controversial books and TV series *A Test of Time* and *Legend* (see "Ancient History", below).

★ **Cassandra Vivian** *The Western Desert of Egypt: An Explorer's Handbook* (AUC). The best guidebook on the subject, ranging from geology to folklore and petroglyphs to safaris. It covers all the oases and off-the-beaten-track sites, complete with maps and GPS waypoints, last updated in 2000. Fits the dashboard of a 4WD, but too heavy for a rucksack. Sold in Cairo and Bahariya Oasis for £E65–80.

Ancient history

General works

Martin Bernal *Black Athena* (Vintage). These dense, provocative works assert the "Africanness" of Ancient Egyptian civilization and its contribution to Greek and Roman culture. The first two volumes (1987 and 1991) show a formidable breadth of enquiry, though Egyptologists and Classicists nit-pick holes everywhere.

Margaret Bunson *Encyclopedia of Ancient Egypt* (Facts on File). Over 1500 entries, with useful subject indexes, charts and chronologies – though not as comprehensive as the *British Museum Dictionary of Ancient Egypt* (see below).

★ **Mark Collier & Bill Manley** *How to Read Egyptian Hieroglyphics: A step-by-step guide to teach yourself* (British Museum Press). Just what the title says – and an unexpected bestseller, thanks to its clarity and the exciting sense of knowledge that it confers.

★ **Peter France** *The Rape of Egypt* (o/p). Interesting background on the characters and personalities of the early "archeologists", and a no-holds-barred indictment of imperialist looting.

Nicholas Grimal *A History of Ancient Egypt* (Blackwell). The first detailed, reign-by-reign account since Gardiner's *Egypt of the Pharaohs* (1961), which synthesizes a mass of recent revisions, particularly chronological.

★ **George Hart** *A Dictionary of Egyptian Gods and Goddesses* (Routledge). Indispensable guide to the deities and myths of Ancient Egypt, profusely illustrated with line drawings. Hart's *Egyptian Myths* (Routledge) is equally informative, covering similar ground.

Colin J. Humphreys *The Miracles of Exodus: A Scientist's Discovery of the Extraordinary Natural Causes of the Biblical Stories* (Continuum). With a title like that, who could resist a look? You might not finish it, however.

T.G.H. James *An Introduction to Ancient Egypt* (o/p); *Egypt: The Living Past*; *Ancient Egypt: The Land and Its Legacy*; *Egyptian Painting*; *Egyptian Sculpture.* James was the keeper of the Egyptian Antiquities department of the British Museum until the mid-1980s. His *Introduction* is a serious text for beginners; *The Land and Its Legacy* and *The Living Past* are coffee-table books, good for pre-visit reading; while the *Painting* and *Sculpture* volumes are accessibly written and lavishly illustrated.

Jaromir Malek *The Cat in Ancient Egypt* (British Museum Press). A charming monograph with delightful illustrations.

Geoffrey T. Martin *The Hidden Tombs of Memphis* (Thames & Hudson). A detailed account of discoveries at Memphis, most notably the Tomb of Maya, a contemporary of Tutankhamun.

Dimitri Meeks and Christine Favard-Meeks *Daily Life of the Egyptian Gods* (J. Murray). Scholarly study of the rituals and beliefs surrounding the gods; a TV spin-off focused on the more salacious bits.

Richard Parkinson *Voices from Ancient Egypt: An Anthology of Middle Kingdom Writings* (o/p UK; University of Oklahoma). All kinds of literature, from spells and curses to state propaganda. The material for once brings to life people rather than monuments.

Stephen Quirke and Jeffrey Spencer (eds.) *The British Museum Book of Ancient Egypt* (British Museum Press). A good general survey, lavishly illustrated with material from the museum's Egyptian collection.

Gay Robins *Women in Ancient Egypt* (British Museum Press). Interesting study of a subject largely ignored until a decade ago, focusing on queens and priestesses, fertility rituals and much else.

★ **David Rohl** *A Test of Time: The Bible – From Myth to History*; *Legend: Genesis of Civilisation* (Arrow). The former is a stimulating argument for revising the chronology of Ancient Egyptian and Biblical history; the latter advances an unusual theory of Egypt's predynastic era. Both are closely argued and worth reading even if you're sceptical (as most Egyptologists are).

★ **Ian Shaw** *The Oxford History of Ancient Egypt* (Oxford University Press). An excellent survey taking in the latest theories and discoveries up until 2000 – though Rohl doesn't even rate a mention. Contains many fine illustrations and site plans.

★ **Ian Shaw and Paul Nicholson** *British Museum Dictionary of Ancient Egypt* (British Museum Press). Richly illustrated, paperback-sized dictionary, especially good for site plans and assessments of recent discoveries.

Robert Sole and Dominique Valbelle *The Rosetta Stone* (Profile). Relates the discovery of the crib that enabled Champollion to decipher Ancient Egyptian hieroglyphs – without which, their civilization would still be a mystery.

John Taylor *Egypt and Nubia* (British Museum Press). Covers the history of Nubia from 4000 BC to the dawning of the Christian era, focusing on ancient Nubian art and relations with Egypt.

★ **Joyce Tyldesley** *Hatchepsut: The Female Pharaoh* (Penguin). Examines the life and achievements of the woman who ruled as pharaoh (depicted with male genitalia) and the sexual politics of the XVIII Dynasty. Fascinating reading.

Jean Vercoutter *The Search for Ancient Egypt* (Thames & Hudson). Pocket-size account of Egypt's "discovery" by foreigners, packed with drawings, photos and engravings.

★ **Kent Weeks** *The Lost Tomb*; *Atlas of the Valley of the Kings* (AUC). The former describes Weeks' discovery and excavation of the mass tomb of the sons of Ramses II, while the latter is the first volume of an ongoing magnum opus. Both are showcased on the Theban Mapping Project's website, ⓦ www.kv5.com.

★ **John Anthony West** *Serpent in the Sky: The High Wisdom of Ancient Egypt* (Quest); *The Traveler's Key to Ancient Egypt: A Guide to the Sacred Places of Ancient Egypt* (Quest). West's New Age interpretation – postulating a connection with the mythical civilization of High Atlantis – has been greeted with derision by mainstream Egyptologists. *The Traveler's Key* is a lively on-site guide that points out inconsistencies in orthodox Egyptology and presents alternative theories.

Karl-Theodore Zauzich *Discovering Egyptian Hieroglyphs: A Practical Guide*. Profusely illustrated guide to the subject, revealing how to read hieroglyphs and their symbolic nuances.

Pyramidology

Guillemette Andreu *Egypt in the Age of the Pyramids* (Murray). Nicely illustrated study of the pyramids' evolution in the context of Egyptian life and culture, by a French Egyptologist.

Robert Bauval *The Orion Mystery* (Mandarin). Postulates that the Giza Pyramids corresponded to the three stars in Orion's Belt as it was in 10,500 BC. Archeologists are unconvinced, but at least the theory isn't as preposterous as Hancock's extrapolations (see below).

I.E.S. Edwards *The Pyramids of Egypt* (Penguin). Lavishly illustrated, closely argued survey of all the major pyramids, recently updated to take account of new discoveries and theories, though Mendelssohn (see below) is conspicuously absent.

Graham Hancock *Fingerprints of the Gods* (Mandarin); *The Message of the Sphinx*; *The Mars Mystery* (Heinemann); *Heaven's Mirror* (Penguin).

Picking up where Bauval left off, Hancock asserts that the Egyptian and pre-Columbian pyramids, Angkor Wat temple and the stone figures of Easter Island were all created by a lost civilization propagated by Martians. Bestselling codswallop.

Peter Hodges *How the Pyramids were Built* (Arris & Phillips). As a professional stonemason, Hodges has practical experience, rather than academic qualifications, on his side. An easy read, and quite persuasive.

Britta Le Va and Salima Ikram *Egyptian Pyramids* (Zeitouna). Slim booklet of evocative sepia photos and brief accounts of the major pyramids. Available in Cairo.

Kurt Mendelssohn *The Riddle of the Pyramids* (o/p). An attempt to resolve the enigma of the Maidum and Dahshur pyramids, which postulates a "pyramid production line" and caused a stir in the world of Egyptology during the 1980s.

The Amarna Period/Tutankhamun

Cyril Aldred *Akhenaten, King of Egypt* (Thames & Hudson). Conventional account of the Amarna period by one of Britain's leading postwar Egyptologists.

Christiane Desroches-Noblecourt *Tutankhamen: Life and Death of a Pharaoh* (Penguin). Brilliantly illustrated, detailed study of all aspects of the boy-pharaoh and his times.

Thomas Hoving *Tutankhamun: the Untold Story* (o/p). Lifts the lid on archeological backbiting and the tomb thefts by Carter and Carnarvon.

Ahmed Osman *Stranger in the Valley of the Kings*; *The Secret History of Egypt at the Time of the Exodus* (Bear & Co.). Osman believes that Yuya,

Akhenaten's grandfather, was the Biblical Joseph, that Atenism inspired Jewish monotheism, and otherwise substantially revises the Exodus story.

Nicholas Reeves and John H. Taylor *Howard Carter Before Tutankhamun* (British Museum Press). Original photographs and drawings and first-hand accounts of excavations bring the irascible Carter to life.

Julia Samson *Nefertiti and Cleopatra* (Rubicon). Fascinating account of Egypt's most famous queens, by the Petrie Museum's expert on Amarna civilization. Samson concludes that Smenkhkare, Akhenaten's mysterious successor, was actually Nefertiti; her coverage of Cleopatra is rather less controversial.

Ptolemaic, Roman and Coptic Egypt

Alan Bowman *Egypt After the Pharaohs* (British Museum Press). Scholarly, nicely illustrated study of an often overlooked period.

★ **Lucy Hughes-Hallet** *Cleopatra: Histories, Dreams and Distortions* (Pimlico). Arresting deconstructive analysis of Cleopatra in history and myth down through the ages.

Otto Meinardus *Monks and Monasteries of the Egyptian Desert* (AUC). A rather turgid history and guide to Egypt's Coptic monasteries.

Dominic Montserrat *Sex and Society in Graeco-Roman Egypt* (Kegan Paul).

In-depth study of sexual mores and practices in a famously licentious era.

Gyozo Vörös *Taposiris Magna: Port of Isis*. Many scholars disagree with his theories about this ancient port, such as the notion that its lighthouse was the prototype of the Pharos at Alexandria, not a scaled-down copy (see p.642).

Barbara Watterson *Coptic Egypt* (Scott Academic Press). Covers Coptic history and culture from ancient times to the present.

Claudia Yvonne *Coptic Life in Egypt* (AUC). A concise historical and contemporary narrative, illustrated with some superb photos.

Medieval and modern history

The Crusades

Amin Maalouf *The Crusades through Arab Eyes* (Al Saqi Books). Lebanese writer and journalist Maalouf has used the writings of contemporary Arab chroniclers of the Crusades to retrace two centuries of Middle Eastern history. His conclusion is that present-day relations between the Arab world and the West are still marked by the battle that ended seven centuries ago.

★ **Steven Runciman** *A History of the Crusades* (Penguin). Highly readable three-volume narrative, laced with anecdote and scandal. Runciman's hero is Salah al-Din, rather than Richard the Lionheart, who is depicted (like most of the other traditional Western good guys) in all his murderous ferocity.

Colonial Era

George Annesley *The Rise of Modern Egypt* (Pentland). A readable survey of the period from Napoleon's invasion to the Suez Crisis, marred by Annesley's colonialist attitudes.

Corelli Barnett *The Desert Generals* (Cassell Military). An iconoclastic study concluding that Montgomery was a less assured general than his predecessors, let alone Rommel. Still, he did win the North African campaign.

★ **John Bierman & Colin Smith** *Alamein: War Without Hate* (Penguin). A superb account of the North African campaign, quoting extensively from the recollections of soldiers on all sides, and conclusively laying the myth of Italian cowardice to rest.

George Greenfield *Chasing the Beast* (R. Cohen, US). Evocative memoirs of the Western Desert campaign, by a Cambridge graduate who joined the infantry.

Peter Mansfield *The British in Egypt* (o/p). Interesting account of how Egypt passed from being the "veiled protectorate" to an outright imperial possession. Mansfield is also author of *The Arabs* (Penguin), a clear, perceptive and wide-ranging introduction to the Arab world from the arrival of Islam to the 1970s.

★ **Anthony Sattin** *Lifting the Veil: British Society in Egypt 1768–1956* (o/p). A fascinating slice of social history, charting the rise and fall of British tourists and expatriates in Egypt. Classic photographs, too.

Post-Independence

Raymond William Baker *Sadat and After* (J. B. Tauris). Heavyweight but fascinating critique of Egyptian society from six different perspectives, including those of the Muslim Brotherhood, Nasserists, Marxists and Osman Ahmed Osman, each presented sympathetically. A *tour d'horizon* of Egyptian political thought.

A.J. Barker *Arab-Israeli Wars* (o/p). An illustrated account of the 1948, 1956, 1967 and 1973 wars, by a military historian. Photographs (and sympathies) come largely from the Israeli side.

Mohammed Heikal *Cutting the Lion's Tail*; *The Road to Ramadan*; *The Autumn of Fury* (all o/p). These three books cover, respectively, the Suez Crisis, the 1973 War, and Sadat's rise and fall. As a confidante of Nasser's since the Revolution, one-time editor of *Al-Ahram* and Minister of Information, Heikal provides a genuine inside view.

David Hirst and Irene Beeson *Sadat* (o/p). Revealing political biography of the man whom Kissinger described as "the greatest since Bismarck", but which stops short of his assassination.

★ **Derek Hopwood** *Egypt: Politics and Society 1945–90* (Routledge). Accessible and useful survey of the modern era, now in its third edition.

Human Rights Watch *Hostage-Taking and Intimidation by Security Forces*; *Violations of Freedom of Religious Belief and Expression of the Christian Minority*. Two sobering reports of human rights abuses in Egypt during the 1990s.

Anwar Sadat *In Search of Identity* (Buccaneer). An anodyne, ghosted autobiography that reveals less about the character of Egypt's assassinated president than either Heikal or Hirst and Beeson.

Robert St John *The Boss* (o/p). Racy, anecdotal biography of Nasser, written a decade before his death. Interesting, albeit dated since its publication in 1960.

Anthropology, sociology and feminism

★ **Nayra Atiya (ed.)** *Khul-Khaal: Five Egyptian Women Tell Their Stories* (Syracuse University Press, US). Gripping biographical accounts by women from diverse backgrounds, revealing much about contemporary Egyptian life. Essential reading.

★ **Nicholas Biegman** *Egypt's Side-Shows*. Engaging colour photos of moulids, weddings and other rituals of Egyptian life. For a slightly academic treatment of the former, see Biegman's *Egypt – Moulids, Saints and Sufis*.

★ **R. Critchfield** *Shahhat: An Egyptian* (AUC). A wonderful book, based on several years' resident research with the Nile Valley *fellaheen*, across the river from Luxor. Moving, amusing and shocking, by turn.

Joseph Hobbs *Bedouin Life in the Egyptian Wilderness*. Fascinating, albeit academic account of the Khushmaan clan of Ma'aza Bedouin living in the Jebel Galala of the Eastern Desert.

★ **Rana Kabbani** *Europe's Myths of Orient* (o/p). An easier read than Edward Said's heavyweight *Orientalism*, this book unravels the erotic fantasies and myths which Western travellers, painters and poets built up about the East. Starting with the Crusades and continuing on through the Victorians, Kabbani shows how the East was portrayed as sexually voracious and thus intellectually and morally inferior.

Smadar Lavie *The Poetics of Military Occupation: Mzeina Allegories* of Bedouin Identity under Israeli and Egyptian Rule* (University of California Press, US). Interesting study of the Bedouin tribe most affected by the changes in Sinai under both regimes, by an Israeli anthropologist.

Lila Abu Lughod *Veiled Sentiments: Honour and Poetry in a Bedouin Society* (University of California Press, US). Another anthropological study, devoted to the Awlad Ali tribe of the Western Desert.

★ **Nawal el-Saadawi** *The Hidden Face of Eve* (Zed). Egypt's best-known woman writer, Saadawi has been in conflict with the Egyptian authorities most of her life. This is her major polemic, covering a wide range of topics – sexual aggression, female circumcision, prostitution, divorce and sexual relationships. Her website (ⓦwww.naw alsaadawi.net) embraces literature, sociology and politics (see also Egyptian Fiction, p.855).

Huda Shaarawi *Harem Years: Memoirs of an Egyptian Feminist 1879–1924* (Virago). A unique document from the last generation of upper-class Egyptian women who spent their childhoods and married lives in the segregated world of the harem.

Islam

★ **A.J. Arberry (trans.)** *The Koran*. This translation by Oxford University Press is the best English-language version of Islam's holy book, whose revelations and prose style form the basis of the Muslim faith and Arab literature. Arberry's scholarship is also evident in *Sufism: An Account of the Mystics of Islam* and *The Koran Interpreted*.

★ **Karen Armstrong** *Muhammed: A Biography of the Prophet* (Harper). A widely acclaimed biography which illuminates the Prophet's world and faith, and dispels many Western falsehoods and misconceptions about them.

★ **Titus Burckhardt** *Art of Islam: Language and Meaning* (o/p). Superbly illustrated, intellectually penetrating overview of Islamic art and architecture.

H.A.R. Gibb *Islam* (in the US: *Studies on the Civilization of Islam*) (o/p). Concise exposition of the historical development and nature of Islam.

Wildlife

★ **Bertel Bruun** *Common Birds of Egypt* (AUC). Slim illustrated guide, ideal for birdwatching your way around the country.

★ **Guy Buckles** *Dive Guide The Red Sea* (New Holland). An illustrated guide to over 125 diving and snorkelling sites from Sinai to Eritrea, with notes on access, visibility and diving conditions as well as the species that you'll see.

David Cottridge & Richard Porter *A Photographic Guide to Birds of Egypt and the Middle East* (New Holland). This ornithology guide is better illustrated than Brunn's, but heavier to carry around.

Richard Hoath *Natural Selections: A Year of Egypt's Wildlife* (AUC). Enlightening and charming study of Egypt's birds, land and sea creatures, illustrated with the author's drawings.

Edward Lieske & Robert F. Myers *Coral Reef Guide* (Collins). A full-colour guide to more than 1200 species in the Red Sea, with brief details of a few dive sites.

Egyptian fiction

André Aciman *Out of Egypt: A Memoir* (Harvill). Wry, affectionate tale of a flamboyant Jewish family who emigrated to Alex at the turn of the century and left three generations later. Aciman himself came of age in Italy and France.

Alaa Al-Aswany *The Yacoubian Building* (AUC). Four entwined stories about the tenants of a Cairo apartment block. A pious doorkeeper's son with a chip on his shoulder, a gay newspaper editor and a fallen aristocrat seeking their own kind of love, and a power-hungry politician provide an insight into the joys and frustrations of Cairene life.

★ **Salwa Bakr** *The Golden Chariot* (Garnet). Absorbing novel set in a women's prison near Cairo, seen through the eyes of an Alexandrian aristocrat jailed for murder. The inmates' stories represent a microcosm of women's oppression in contemporary Egypt.

André Chedid *The Sixth Day*; *From Sleep Unbound* (Swallow). Another émigré author, whose metaphor-laden plots and clinical prose are not exactly beach reading.

★ **Gamal al-Ghitani** *Incidents in Zafraani Alley* (Egyptian Book Organization – only available in Egypt); *Zayni Barakat* (Penguin). *Incidents* is a highly accessible, darkly humorous read, which could be interpreted as a satire on state paranoia and credulous fundamentalism. Its ending is confused by the fact that the page order has been scrambled in the English-language edition. *Zayni Barakat* is a convoluted, elliptical drama set in the last years of Mamluke rule, which reached a wider audience at home when it was adapted for Egyptian television in 1994.

Nabil Naoum Gorgy *The Slave's Dream and Other Stories* (Quartet). The amorality of man and nature is the main theme of this collection of tales, apparently influenced by Borges and Bowles.

Gamil Attiyah Ibrahim *Down to the Sea* (Quartet). Stumbling translation mars what is – in the original

– a fascinating exploration of life in Cairo's Cities of the Dead.

★ **Yusuf Idris** *The Cheapest Nights; Rings of Burnished Brass* (P. Owen). Two superb collections by Egypt's finest writer of short stories, who died in 1991. Uncompromisingly direct, yet ironic.

★ **Naguib Mahfouz** *Adrift on the Nile; Arabian Days and Nights; Miramar; Midaq Alley; Palace Walk; Palace of Desires; Sugar Street; The Thief and the Dogs; Respected Sir; The Search; Wedding Song; The Beggar; The Beginning and the End; Autumn Quail; War in the Land of Thebes.* Awarded the Nobel Literature Prize in 1989, Mahfouz was the Grand Old Man of Egyptian letters. His novels have a rather nineteenth-century feel, reminiscent in plot and characterization of Balzac or Victor Hugo; most are set in Cairo or Alexandria. Favoured themes include the discrepancy between ideology and human problems, hypocrisy and injustice, and taking personal responsibility.

Yusuf al-Qa'id *War in the Land of Egypt* (Arris). A Gogol-esque satire of corruption and hypocrisy in 1970s rural Egypt, which was first published in a Russian translation and only later in Arabic.

Alifa Rifaat *Distant View of a Minaret* (Heinemann). A well-known writer in her fifties expresses her revolt against male domination and suggests solutions within the orthodox Koranic framework.

★ **Nawal el-Saadawi** *Woman at Point Zero* (Zed); *The Fall of the Imam* (Minerva); *God Dies by the Nile* (Zed); and others. Saadawi's novels are informed by her work as a doctor and psychiatrist in Cairo, and by her feminist and socialist beliefs, on subjects that are virtually taboo in Egypt. *Point Zero*, her best, is a powerful and moving story of a woman condemned to death for killing a pimp. You will find very few of her books on sale in Egypt, though *The Fall of the Imam* is the only one officially banned (see also p.853).

Adhaf Soueif *Aisha; In the Eye of the Sun; The Map of Love* (all Bloomsbury). Born in Cairo and educated in Egypt and England, Soueif's semi-autobiographical novels are acclaimed for their sensibility. *In the Eye of the Sun* is a 790-page novel exploring love and destiny in the Middle East during the 1960s and 1970s; while *The Map of Love* is even richer in its historical detail and interpretation, and was shortlisted for the 1999 Booker Prize.

★ **Bahaa Taher** *Aunt Safiyya and the Monastery* (University of California Press). Beautifully crafted novella set in a village in Upper Egypt, where the imperatives of a vendetta are challenged by a Muslim farmer and a Coptic monk. Taher's lapidary prose is sensitively translated by Barbara Romaîne.

Anthologies

Margot Badran and Miriam Cooke (eds.) *Opening the Gates: a Century of Arab Feminist Writing* (Virago). Mix of fiction and polemic, including a fair number of Egyptian contributors.

★ **Marylin Booth** (ed./trans.) *My Grandmother's Cactus: Stories by Egyptian Women* (Quartet). Short stories by the latest generation of women writers, including Radwa Ashour, Salwa Bakr, Etidal Osman, Neamet el-Biheiri, Ibtihal Salem and Sahar Tawfiq.

Inea Bushnaq *Arab Folktales* (Pantheon). Great collection of folk stories from across the Arab world, including many from Egypt, with interesting thematic pieces putting them in context. Highly recommended.

W.M. Hutchins (ed./trans.) *Egyptian Tales and Short Stories of the 1970s & 80s* (AUC). Includes various stories by Nawal el-Saadawi, Amira Nowaira, Gamal al-Ghitani and Fouad Higazy.

Poetry and biography

C.P. Cavafy *Collected Poems*. Elegiac evocations of the Alexandrian myth by the city's most famous poet. An excerpt from *The City* appears under "Alexandria" in this book.

Tawfiq al-Hakim *The Prison of Life* (AUC). An autobiographical essay by one of the formative figures of modern Egyptian literature, covering the first thirty years of Al-Hakim's life.

Foreign fiction

Michael Asher *The Eye of Ra*; *Firebird* (HarperCollins). An explorer (see "The desert", p.846) with an SAS background, Asher is strong on outlaw tribes, secret elites and real mysteries like the lost oasis of Zerzura, but the paranormal twist to his thrillers lacks the chill of Easterman's *Name of the Beast* or the ingenuity of Smethurst's *Sinai* (see opposite).

Noel Barber *A Woman of Cairo* (o/p). Ill-starred love and destiny amongst the Brits and Westernized Egyptians of King Farouk's Cairo, interwoven with historical events and characters. From that perspective, a good insight into those times.

Gillian Bradshaw *The Beacon at Alexandria* (o/p). A woman learns medicine in secret, disguises herself as a man and practises it in sectarian strife-ridden Alexandria, and later in barbarian-haunted Thrace.

Moyra Caldecott *Daughter of Amun* (Bladud). Romanticized account of the rise and fall of Queen Hatshepsut.

Agatha Christie *Death Comes at the End*; *Death on the Nile* (Collins). The latter is a classic piece of skullduggery solved by Hercule Poirot aboard a Nile cruiser, which Christie wrote while staying at the *Old Cataract Hotel* in Aswan. *Death Comes at the End* is a lamer effort, set around Luxor and the Valley of the Kings.

Robin Cook *Sphinx* (o/p). Humdrum thriller about a secret tomb in the Valley of the Kings.

Len Deighton *City of Gold* (Arrow). Hard-boiled thriller set in 1941, when vital information was being leaked to Rommel. Follet's *The Key to Rebecca* (see below) concerns a later phase in the war, involving another spy.

Paul Doherty *The Mask of Ra* (Headline). Set at the time of Hatshepsut's accession, this pharaonic whodunit is in a similar vein to Gill's trilogy (see opposite).

Lawrence Durrell *The Alexandria Quartet* (Faber). Endless sexual and metaphysical ramblings, occasionally relieved by a dollop of Alex atmosphere or a profound psychological insight.

★ **Daniel Easterman** *Name of the Beast* (o/p). If you can swallow the notion of the Antichrist masterminding an Islamic fundamentalist coup, this fantasy-thriller grips from the beginning. The ending is a letdown, however.

Ken Follet *The Key to Rebecca* (Pan). Fast-paced thriller based on the true story of a German spy, Eppler, who operated in Cairo during 1942. Follet exercises artistic licence when describing the outcome, but the bellydancer Sonia, and Sadat's involvement, are largely faithful to history.

Anton Gill *City of the Horizon*; *City of Dreams*; *City of the Dead* (Bloomsbury). Gill's trilogy pits the scribe Huy against diverse conspirators during the reigns of Tutankhamun and Horemheb, in the aftermath of the Amarna era.

★ **Robert Irwin** *The Arabian Nightmare* (Dedalus). Brilliant, paranoid fantasy set in the Cairo of Sultan Qaitbey, where a Christian spy contracts the affliction of the title. As his madness deepens, reality and illusion spiral inwards like an opium-drugged walk through a *medina* of the mind.

Christian Jacques *Ramses the Great*; *The Battle of Kadesh*; et al (Simon & Schuster). This over-hyped series of historical novels makes Jeffrey Archer seem like Scott Fitzgerald. Not worth reading, never mind buying.

Robert Liddell *Unreal City*; *The Rivers of Babylon* (Peter Owen). Two ironic novels of expat life, the first set in wartime Alexandria, the second in Cairo prior to the Suez Crisis.

Penelope Lively *Oleander, Jacaranda* (Penguin). Fond memories of growing up in Cairo in the 1930s–40s, by a British novelist whose childhood perceptions were often at odds with those of her adult contemporaries.

Norman Mailer *Ancient Evenings* (Abacus). Set in the reign of Ramses II like Jacques' stories, but far more prolix, tedious and rambling. Only enlivened by its sex scenes.

Olivia Manning *The Levant Trilogy* (Penguin). The second half of this six-volume blockbuster of love'n'war finds the Pringles in Egypt, and is based on the experiences of Manning and her husband Reggie.

Glenn Meade *The Sands of Sakkara* (Coronet). *The Eagle Has Landed* transplanted to Egypt, with a plot to kill Roosevelt and Churchill at the *Mena House* near the Pyramids.

★ **Michael Ondaatje** *The English Patient* (Picador). The novel takes liberties with the truth when portraying Almássy and his co-explorers (see p.577) but its brilliance is undeniable, and its equal focus on Kip and Dorothy make it richer and more multi-layered than the film.

Michael Pearce *The Mamur Zapt and the Donkey-vous*; *The Mamur Zapt and the Girl in the Nile*; *The Mamur Zapt and the Men Behind*; *The Mamur Zapt and the Return of the Carpet*; *The Mamur Zapt and the Spoils of Egypt* (Fontana/ Harper Collins). A series of cracking yarns set in *khedival* Egypt, featuring the chief of Cairo's secret police.

★ **William Smethurst** *Sinai* (Headline). Political skullduggery, ancient history and the paranormal keep you hooked and baffled till the end. Mostly set in Sinai, so an ideal read for the beach at Dahab.

Wilbur Smith *River God*; *The Seventh Scroll*; *Warlock* (Pan). A blockbuster trilogy that crams the Hyksos invasion and liberation of Ancient Egypt into one volume, before its hero, the royal eunnch Taitha, undertakes a quest into the Dark Arts in the deserts of North Africa. Enjoyable, if lines like "By the festering foreskin of Seth ...." don't make you snort with derision.

Paul Sussman *The Lost Army of Cambyses* (Bantam). An archeological-cum-terrorist thriller that centres on the legendary Persian army which vanished in a sandstorm (see p.550).

Journals

Ancient Egypt Magazine Easy-to-read articles by academics from museums and universities, plus listings of lectures, conferences and events held by Egyptology societies in Britain. A subscription for six issues costs £21 in the UK. Articles from back issues appear on the magazine's website, ⊛www .ancientegyptmagazine.com.

Journal of Egyptian Archeology; Egyptian Archeology Published by the Egyptian Exploration Society, the *Journal* is the world's leading forum for all matters Egyptological: all the new theories and discoveries get printed here first. *Egyptian Archeology* magazine, illustrated and with a popular slant, is also published by the Society. Membership of the society costs £30 or £40 per annum (depending on whether you wish to receive one or both publications). For details contact: The Secretary, Egyptian Exploration Society, 3 Doughty Mews, London WC1N 2PG (☎020/7242-1880, ☎020/7404-6118, ⊛www.ees.ac.uk).

Language

Language

Language

Egyptians are well used to tourists who speak only their own language, but an attempt to tackle at least a few words in Arabic is invariably greeted with great delight and encouragement and as often as not the exclamation "You speak Arabic better than I do!" Whatever else you do, at least make an effort to learn the Arabic numerals and polite greetings. Although most educated and urban Egyptians will have been taught some English and are only too happy to practise it on you, a little Arabic is a big help in the more remote areas. French may also come in handy in some cities, such as Alexandria, where Greek is also spoken by older folk; German, too, is increasingly understood in tourist-related spheres.

Egyptian Arabic

Although Arabic is the common and official language of 23 countries, the spoken dialect of each can vary considerably. Egyptian Arabic, however, because of the country's vast film, television and music industry, is the most widely understood in the Arab world.

Pronunciation

Transliteration from Arabic script into English presents some pronunciation problems, since some letters have no equivalents. The phonetic guide below should help: everything is pronounced.

ai as in *eye*	**ey/ay** as in *day*
aa as in *bad* but lengthened	**ee** as in *feet*
'a as when asked to say *ah* by the doctor	**kh** as in Scottish *loch*
a' a glottal stop as in *bottle*	**gh** like the French r (back of the throat)

Note that double consonants should always be pronounced separately.

Basics

aiwa (or) **na'am**	Yes	**itfaddal (m)** /	
la	No	**itfaddali (f)**	Come in, please (to m/f)
shukran	Thank you	**an iznak (m)** /	
afwan	You're welcome	**'an iznik (f)**	Excuse me
min fadlak (m) /		**aasif (m) / asfa (f)**	Sorry
fadlik (f)	Please (to m/f)	**inshallah**	God willing

Greetings and farewells

ahlan w-sahlan	Welcome/hello	**assalaamu aleikum**	Hello (formal)
ahlan bik (m) /		**wa-aleikum**	
biki (f) / bikum (pl)	(response)	**assalaam**	(response)

marhaba (or) sa'eeda	Greetings	izzayak (m) / izzayik (f)	How are you (m/f) ?
fursa sa'eeda	Nice to meet you	qwayyis (m) /	
sabah il-kheer	Good morning (morning of goodness)	qwayyisa (f)	I (m/f) am fine
		(f) il-hamdu lilla	Thanks be to God
sabah in-nur	(response–morning of light)	tisbah (m) / tisbahi (f) 'ala kheer	Good night
masa' il-kheer	Good evening (evening of goodness)	wenta (m) / wenti (f) bikheer	And to you (m/f)
masa' in-nur	(response–evening of light)	ma'a salaama	Goodbye

Questions and directions

ismak (m) / ismik (f) ey?	What is your (m/f) name?	... el-mogaf?	... the service taxi depot?
ismi ...	My name is ...	... il-mataar?	... the airport?
titkallim (m) /		... il-twalet?	... the toilet?
titkallimi (f)	Do you (m/f) speak	... mat'am?	... a restaurant?
'Arabi?	Arabic?	shimaal/yimeen/	Left/right/straight
ingleezi?	English?	alatool	ahead
fransawi?	French?	areeb/ba'eed	Near/far
ana batkallim		hinna/hinnak	Here/there
ingleezi	I speak English	il-autobees yissafir	When does the bus
ana ma-batkallimsh		imta?	leave?
'arabi	I don't speak Arabic	il-atr yissafir imta?	When does the train leave?
ana fahem (shwaiya)	I understand (a little)		
ya'ani ey bil-		... yoosal?	... arrive?
ingleezi?	What's that in English?	issa'a kam?	What time (is it)?
feyn funduk il ... ?	Where is Hotel ... ?	il-awil/il-akhir/	
... mahattat il-		et-tani	First/last/next
autobees?	... the bus station?	wallahagga	Nothing
... mahattat il-atr?	... the train station?	lissa	Not yet

Requests and shopping

fi 'andak (m) /		(wa-laakin)	(but)
'andik (f) ... ?	Do you (m/f) have ...?	akbar/asghar	bigger/smaller
... sigara/sagayir	... cigarette(s)	bi-kam (da)?	How much (is it)?
... kibreet	... matches	da ghaali awi	It's too expensive
... gurnal	... newspaper	kebir awi	big
ayyiz (m) / ayyza		sughayyar awi	small
(f) haga ...	I (m/f) want something ...	maashi	That's fine
		fi/fi?	There is/is there?
tanya	... else	di/da	This/that
... ahsan min da	... better than this	mish ayyiz (m) /	
... arkhas min da	... cheaper	ayyza (f) ...	I (m/f) don't want ...
... zay da	... like this		

Accommodation

fi 'andak (m) / 'andik (f) ouda?	Do you (m/f) have a room?	fi ... ?	Is there ...?
ayyiz/ayyza ashuf il-owad	I (m/f) would like to see the rooms	... mayya sukhna?	... hot water?
		... doush?	... a shower?
mumkin ashuf il-owad?		... balcona?	... a balcony?
	Can I see the rooms?	... takyeef hawa?	... air conditioning?
		... telifoon?	... a telephone?
		kam il-hisab?	How much is the bill?

Useful phrases

ana mish fahem (m) / fahma (f)	I (m/f) don't understand	mish shorlak	It's not your business
ana mish 'arif (m) / 'arfa (f)	I (m/f) don't know	sibni le wadi!	Don't touch me!
		yalla	Let's go
ana ta'aban (m) / ta'abana (f)	I (m/f) am tired/ unwell	baranah	Slowly
		khalás	Enough! Finished!
ana gawa'an (m) / gawa'ana (f)	I (m/f) am hungry	maalesh	Never mind
		mush muhim	It doesn't matter
ana 'atshaan (m) / 'atshaana (f)	I (m/f) am thirsty	ma feesh mushkila	There's no problem
ana (mish) mitgawwiz (m) / mitgawwiza (f)	I (m/f) am (not) married	mumkin?	May I/is it possible?
		mish mumkin	It's not possible

Calendar

youm	day	bahdeen	later
leyla	night	youm is-sabt	Saturday
usbu'a	week	youm il-ahad	Sunday
shahr	month	youm il-itnayn	Monday
sana	year	youm it-talaata	Tuesday
innaharda	today	youm il-arb'a	Wednesday
bukkra	tomorrow	youm il-khamees	Thursday
imbaarih	yesterday	youm il-gum'a	Friday

Money

feyn il-bank?	Where's the bank?	giney	Egyptian pound
ayyiz/ayyza aghayyar ...	I (m/f) want to change ...	nuss giney	half pound
		robah giney	quarter pound
... floos	... money	irsh	piastre
... ginay sterlini	... British pounds	irshayn	2 piastres
... dolar amrikani	... US dollars	khamsa irsh	5 piastres
... euro	... Euros		
... shikaat siyahiyya	... travellers' cheques		

Numbers and fractions

sifr	0	wahid wa 'ashreen	21
wahid	1	talaateen	30
itnayn	2	arb'aeen	40
talaata	3	khamseen	50
arb'a	4	sitteen	60
khamsa	5	sab'aeen	70
sitta	6	tamaneen	80
sab'a	7	tis'een	90
tamanya	8	miyya	100
tes'a	9	miyya wa-khamseen	150
ashara	10	mitayn	200
hidarsha	11	talaata miyya	300
itnarsha	12	khamsa miyya	500
talatarsha	13	alf	1000
arb'atarsha	14	alfayn	2000
khamastarsha	15	talaat alaaf	3000
sittarsha	16	arb'at alaaf	4000
sab'atarsha	17	nous	1/2
tamantarsha	18	robah	1/4
tis'atarsha	19	tumna	1/8
ashreen	20		

Egyptian food and drink terms

Basics

'Aish	Bread	Sukkar	Sugar
Zibda	Butter	Skhudaar	Vegetables
Beyd	Eggs	Salata	Salad
Samak	Fish	Fawakih	Fruit
Gibna	Cheese	Zabadi	Yoghurt
Gibna rumi	Yellow cheese	Shurba	Soup
Gibna beyda	White cheese	Izzaza	Bottle
Murabba	Jam	Kubbaya	Glass
'Asal	Honey	Showka	Fork
Lahma	Meat	Sikkeena	Knife
Firakh	Chicken	Mala'a	Spoon
Zeit	Oil	Tarabeyza	Table
Zeitun	Olives	Garson	Waiter
Filfil	Pepper	Lista/menoo	Menu
Melh	Salt	El-hisaab	The bill (check)

Drinks

Shai	Tea	'Ahwa fransawi	Instant or filter coffee
Shai bi-na'ana	Tea with mint	Mayya	Water
Shai bi-laban	Tea with milk	Mayya ma'adaniyya	Mineral water
Shai kushari	Tea made with loose-leaf	Beera	Beer
		Nibeet	Wine
Shai lipton	Tea made with a tea bag	'Asir	Fruit juice
		'Asiir burtu'an	Orange juice
Laban	Milk	'Asiir limoon	Lemon juice
'Ahwa	Coffee (usually Turkish)	'Asiir manga	Mango juice
Ziyaada	very sweet	Karkaday	Hibiscus
Maazboot	medium	Tamar hindi	Tamarind (cordial)
'Ariha	little sugar	'Asiir 'asab	Sugar cane juice
Saada	no sugar		

Soups, salads and vegetables

Shurba	Soup	Fasuliyya	Beans
Shurbit firakh	Chicken soup	Gazar	Carrots
Shurbit 'adas	Lentil soup	Bamya	Okra (gumbo, ladies' fingers)
Shurbit khudaar	Vegetable soup		
Salata	Salad	Bisilla	Peas
Salatit khiyaar	Cucumber salad	Batatis	Potatoes
Salatit tamatim	Tomato salad	Ruz	Rice
Salatit khadra	Mixed green salad	Torshi	Pickled vegetables
Basal	Onion	Baytingan	Eggplant (aubergine)

Main dishes

Kofta	Mincemeat flavoured with spices and onions, grilled on a skewer	Hamam mashwi	Grilled pigeon
		Lahm dani	Lamb
		Kibda	Liver
Kebab	Chunks of meat, usually lamb, grilled with onions and tomatoes	Kalewi	Kidney
		Mokh	(Sheep) brains
		Dik rumi	Turkey
Molukhiyya	Jew's mallow, a leafy vegetable stewed with meat or chicken broth and garlic to make a slimy, spinach-like dish	Samak mashwi	Grilled fish served with salad, bread and dips
Firakh	Chicken grilled or stewed and served with vegetables	Gambari	Prawns
		Calamari	Squid

Appetizers and fast food

Fuul	Fava beans served with oil and lemon, sometimes also with onions, meat, eggs or tomato sauce	Taamiya	Balls of deep-fried mashed chickpeas and spices
		Shawarma	Slivers of pressed, spit-roasted lamb, served in pitta bread

Tahina	Sesame seed paste mixed with spices, garlic and lemon, eaten with pitta bread	Shakshouka	Chopped meat and tomato sauce, cooked with an egg on top
Hummus	Chickpea paste mixed with tahini, garlic and lemon, sometimes served with pine nuts and/or meat (but also just the Arabic for chickpeas/garbanzo beans; indeed, more commonly used with that meaning in Egypt)	Makarona	Macaroni "cake" baked in a white sauce or mincemeat gravy
		Mahshi	Literally "stuffed", variety of vegetables (peppers, tomatoes, aubergines, courgettes) filled with mincemeat and/or rice, herbs and pine nuts
Babaghanoug	Paste of aubergines mashed with tahina	Wara einab	Vine leaves filled as above and flavoured with lemon juice
Kushari	Mixture of noodles, lentils and rice, topped with fried onions and a spicy tomato sauce	Fatir	Sort of pancake/pizza made of layers of flaky filo pastry with sweet or savoury fillings

Desserts, sweets, fruits and nuts

Mahallabiyya	Sweet rice or cornflour pudding, topped with pistachios	Tuffah	Apples
Balila	Milk dish with nuts, raisins and wheat	Mishmish	Apricots
		Mohz	Bananas
Baklava	Flaky filo pastry, honey and nuts	Balah	Dates
		Tin	Figs
Basbousa	Pastry of semolina, honey and nuts	Tin shawqi	Prickly pear (cactus fruit)
Umm (or Om) Ali	Corn cake soaked in milk, sugar, raisins, coconut and cinnamon, served hot	Shammam	Melon
		Battikh	Watermelon
		Farawla	Strawberries
		Fuul sudani	Peanuts
Gelati or ays krim	Ice cream	Lib battikh	Watermelon seeds
'Ishta	Cream	Loz	Almonds

Some phrases

Ayyzeen el-menu min fadlak	We'd like the menu please	... taza	... fresh
Sukkar aleel	With little sugar	... lahm	... meat
Ihna ayyzeen ...	We'd like to have ...	... mistiwi kwaiyis	... cooked enough
Bidoon sukkar	Without sugar	... beyd	... eggs
'Ey da?	What is this?	Da laziz aawi	This is very tasty
Ma'alabtish da	I didn't order this	Iddini/iddina ...	Give me/us ...
Ihna mush ayyzeen da	We don't want this	El-hisab, minfadlak (m) / minfadlik (f)	The bill, please
Da mish ...	This is not ...	... taba'	... a plate
Ana makulsh ...	I can't/don't eat ...	... futa	... a napkin
		Shokran	Thank you

Glossary of Egyptian terms

This is a glossary of basic Egyptian terms in everyday use, plus Islamic and architectural terms; for pharaonic symbols and terms used in temple architecture, see p.312 and p.348. Common alternative spellings are given in brackets.

Ablaq Striped. An effect achieved by painting, or laying courses of different coloured masonry (the costlier method); usually white with red or buff. A Bahri Mamluke innovation, possibly derived from the Roman technique of *opus mixtum* – an alternation of stone and brickwork.

Abu "Father of"; a term of respect.

Ain (Ayn, Ein) Spring.

Amir (Emir) Commander, prince.

Bab Gate or door, as in the medieval city walls.

Bahr River, sea, canal.

Baksheesh Alms or tips.

Baladi National, local, rural or countrified.

Bango Marijuana.

Baraka Blessing.

Beit House. Segregated public and private quarters, the *malqaf*, *maq'ad* and *mashrabiya* are typical features of old Cairene mansions.

Bey (Bay) Lord or noble; an Ottoman title, now a respectful form of address to anyone in authority.

Bir (Beer) Well.

Birka (Birqa, Birket) Lake.

Burg (Borg) Tower.

Cadi (Qadi) Judge.

Caleche Horse-drawn carriage.

Corniche Seafront or riverfront promenade.

Darb Path or way; can apply to alleyways, thoroughfares, or desert caravan routes.

Deir Monastery or convent.

Egyptian Environmental Affairs Agency (EEAA) The agency responsible for Egypt's nature reserves.

Ezba A hamlet or village.

Fellaheen (sing. Fellah) Peasant farmers who work their own land or as sharecroppers for wealthier farmers.

Felucca Nile sailing boat.

Finial Ornamental crown of a dome or minaret, often topped by an Islamic crescent.

Galabiyya Loose flowing robe worn by men.

Gezira Island.

Ghird (Ghard) Sand dune.

Gam'a Large congregational mosque, as opposed to a *masguid*.

Gumhorriya Republic.

Hadj (Haj) Pilgrimage to Mecca.

Hagg/Hagga One who has visited Mecca.

Haikal Sanctuary of a Coptic church.

Hammam Turkish bathhouse.

Hantour A Middle Egypt term for *caleche* (see above), or horse-drawn carriage.

Haramlik Literally the "forbidden" area; ie women's or private apartments in a house or palace.

Ikhwan Familiar name for the Muslim Brotherhood (*il-Ikhwan il-Muslimeen*), Egypt's oldest Islamic organization (founded in 1928 and banned since 1954).

Islamist (s) Groups aiming to replace secular with Sharia law (see p.869) and re-align Egypt's foreign policy – some by peaceful means, others violently. The term is preferred to "fundamentalist", since almost all Muslims believe in the literal truth of the Koran, and are thus fundamentalist by definition.

Ithyphallic Decorous term for a god with an erection; Min, Amun and Osiris were often depicted thus by the Ancient Egyptians.

Jebel (Gebel, Gabal, etc) Hill or mountain.

Jihad Often translated as "Holy War", the word can also describe non-violent striving in the cause of Islam, or a believer's inner, spiritual battle with temptation or moral weakness.

Karkur Gorge.

Khalif (Caliph) Successor to the Prophet Mohammed and spiritual and political leader of the Muslim empire. A struggle over this office caused the Sunni–Shia schism of 656 AD. Most khalifs ruled from Baghdad or Damascus and delegated control of imperial provinces like Egypt.

Khalig Gulf or canal.

Khan Place where goods were made, stored and sold, which also provided accommodation for travellers and merchants, like a *wikala*. It's from *khan* that we get the word caravanserai.

Khanqah Sufi hostel, analagous to a monastery.

Khedive Viceroy.

Kom Mound of rubble and earth covering an ancient settlement.

Kubri Bridge.

Kufic The earliest style of Arabic script; Foliate *kufic* was a more elaborate form, superseded by *naskhi* script.

Kuttab Koranic school, usually for boys or orphans.

Liwan Arcade or vaulted space off a courtyard, commonly found in mosques and madrassas. Originally, the term meant a sitting room opening onto a covered court.

Madrassa Literally a "place of study" but generally used to designate theological schools. Each madrassa propagates a particular rite of Islamic jurisprudence.

Mahwagi Local laundryman or woman.

Malqaf Wind scoop for directing cool breezes into houses; in Egypt, they always face north.

Maq'ad Arch-fronted "sitting place" on the second floor of old Cairene houses, overlooking the courtyard.

Maristan The medieval term for a public hospital.

Mashrabiya An alcove in lattice windows where jars of water can be cooled by the wind; and by extension, the projecting balcony and screened window itself, which enabled women to watch streetlife or the *salamlik* without being observed. Although flat latticework partitions are strictly termed *mashrafiya*, *mashrabiya* loosely covers both types of work.

Masguid A small local mosque, as opposed to a *gam'a*.

Masr (Misr, Musr) Popular name for Egypt, and Cairo.

Mastaba Stone or mud-brick benches at the entrance to buildings. In Cairo, Mohammed Ali had them removed to reduce idling and speed up the traffic.

Merlons Indentations and raised portions along a parapet. Fatimid merlons were angular; Mamluke ones crested, trilobed (like a fleur-de-lys) or in fancier leaf patterns.

Mida'a Fountain for the ritual ablutions that precede prayer, located in a mosque's vestibule or courtyard.

Midan Open space or square; originally, most were polo grounds.

Mihrab Niche indicating the direction of Mecca, to which all Muslims pray.

Minaret Tower from which the call to prayer is given; derived from *minara*, the Arabic word for "beacon" or "lighthouse".

Minbar Pulpit from which an address to the Friday congregation is given. Often superbly inlaid or carved in variegated marble or wood.

Mit Village or hamlet.

Mosque A simple enclosure facing Mecca in its original form, the mosque acquired minarets, *riwaqs*, madrassas and mausolea as it was developed by successive dynasties. Large congregational mosques are called *gam'a*; smaller, local "places of prostration" are known as *masguid* – a very old distinction. Very small mosques, often associated with Sufi orders or fundamentalist groups, are known as *zawiyas*.

Moulid Popular festival marking an event in the Koran or the birthday of a Muslim saint. The term also applies to the name-days of Coptic saints.

Muezzin A prayer-crier (who nowadays is more likely to broadcast by loudspeaker than to climb up and shout from the minaret).

Muhazafat Governorate, or province; Egypt is divided into 26 of them.

Munshid Professional reciter of Koranic verses and praises to Allah.

Murqanas Stalactites, pendants or honeycomb ornamentation of portals, domes or squinches.

Mustachfa The modern Egyptian term for a public hospital.

Naskhi Form of Arabic script with joined-up letters, introduced by the Ayyubids.

National Democratic Party (NDP), Hizb il-Watani il-Dimuqrati in Arabic The ruling party since 1978, when it was created by Sadat to replace the Arab Socialist Union.

Pasha (Pacha) Ruler – a lord or prince. Nowadays, a respectful term of address for anyone in authority, pronounced "basha".

Qala Fortress, citadel.

Qarat Peak, ridge.

Qasr Palace, fortress, mansion.

Qibla The direction in which Muslims pray, ie the wall where the *mihrab* is located.

Qubba Dome, and by extension any domed tomb.

Raïs Boss, chief.

Ras Cape, headland, peak.

Riwaq Arcaded aisle around a mosque's *sahn*, originally used as residential quarters for theological students; ordinary folk may also take naps here.

Sabil Public fountain or water cistern. During the nineteenth century it was often combined with a Koranic school to make a *Sabil-Kuttab*.

Sahn Central courtyard of a mosque, frequently surrounded by *riwaqs* or *liwans*.

Salamlik The "greeting" area of a house; ie the public and men's apartments.

Sanctuary The *liwan* incorporating the *qibla* wall in a mosque, or the shrine of a deity in an Ancient Egyptian temple.

Sharia Street (literally "way"). Also laws based on Koranic precepts, which Islamists wish to see applied in Egypt.

Sharm Bay.

Shorta Police.

Soffits Undersides of arches, often decorated with stripes (*ablaq*) or formalized plant designs (an Ottoman motif).

Squinch An arch spanning the right angle formed by two walls, so as to support a dome.

Sufis Islamic mystics who seek to attain union with Allah through trance-inducing *zikrs* and dances. Whirling Dervishes belong to one of the Sufi sects.

Supreme Council for Antiquities (SCA) The state organization responsible for Egypt's ancient monuments.

Tabut A cenotaph or grave marker, sometimes embellished with a "hat" indicating the deceased's rank.

Tariqa Sufi order or brotherhood.

Tell Another word for kom (see opposite).

Tir Canal.

Thuluth Script whose vertical strokes are three times larger than its horizontal ones; *Thuluth* literally means '"third".

Tuf-tuf A form of transport in some tourist areas, consisting of an engine pulling open-sided carriages, but running along roads; similar to a Noddy train.

Wadi Valley or watercourse (usually dry).

Wahah Oasis.

Waqf The endowment of some religious, educational or charitable institution in perpetuity. In Egypt, thousands of such bequests are overseen by the Ministry of Awaqf.

Wikala Bonded warehouse with rooms for merchants upstairs. Here they bought trading licences from the *Muhtasib* and haggled over sales in the courtyard. *Okel* is another term for a *wikala*.

Yardang Freestanding, wind-eroded rock formations, typical of the White Desert.

Zaar Exorcism.

Zawiya Originally a *khanqah* centred around a particular sheikh or Sufi order (*tariqa*), but nowadays used to mean a very small mosque.

Zikr Marathon session of chanting and swaying, intended to induce communion with Allah.

Ziyada Outer courtyard separating early mosques from their surroundings; literally "an addition".

Zuqaq Narrow cul-de-sac, from the Turkish word for "street".

Travel store

Rough Guides travel...

TRAVEL STORE

UK & Ireland
Britain
Devon & Cornwall
Dublin DIRECTIONS
Edinburgh DIRECTIONS
England
Ireland
Lake District
London
London DIRECTIONS
London Mini Guide
Scotland
Scottish Highlands &
    Islands
Wales

Europe
Algarve DIRECTIONS
Amsterdam
Amsterdam
    DIRECTIONS
Andalucía
Athens DIRECTIONS
Austria
Baltic States
Barcelona
Barcelona DIRECTIONS
Belgium & Luxembourg
Berlin
Brittany & Normandy
Bruges DIRECTIONS
Brussels
Budapest
Bulgaria
Copenhagen
Corfu
Corsica
Costa Brava
    DIRECTIONS
Crete
Croatia
Cyprus
Czech & Slovak
    Republics
Dodecanese & East
    Aegean
Dordogne & The Lot
Europe
Florence & Siena
Florence DIRECTIONS
France

French Hotels & Restos
Germany
Greece
Greek Islands
Hungary
Ibiza & Formentera
    DIRECTIONS
Iceland
Ionian Islands
Italy
Italian Lakes
Languedoc &
    Roussillon
Lisbon
Lisbon DIRECTIONS
The Loire
Madeira DIRECTIONS
Madrid DIRECTIONS
Mallorca & Menorca
Mallorca DIRECTIONS
Malta & Gozo
    DIRECTIONS
Menorca
Moscow
Netherlands
Norway
Paris
Paris DIRECTIONS
Paris Mini Guide
Poland
Portugal
Prague
Prague DIRECTIONS
Provence & the Côte
    d'Azur
Pyrenees
Romania
Rome
Rome DIRECTIONS
Sardinia
Scandinavia
Sicily
Slovenia
Spain
St Petersburg
Sweden
Switzerland
Tenerife & La Gomera
    DIRECTIONS
Turkey
Tuscany & Umbria

Venice & The Veneto
Venice DIRECTIONS
Vienna

Asia
Bali & Lombok
Bangkok
Beijing
Cambodia
China
Goa
Hong Kong & Macau
India
Indonesia
Japan
Laos
Malaysia, Singapore &
    Brunei
Nepal
The Philippines
Singapore
South India
Southeast Asia
Sri Lanka
Taiwan
Thailand
Thailand's Beaches &
    Islands
Tokyo
Vietnam

Australasia
Australia
Melbourne
New Zealand
Sydney

North America
Alaska
Boston
California
Canada
Chicago
Florida
Grand Canyon
Hawaii
Honolulu
Las Vegas DIRECTIONS
Los Angeles
Maui DIRECTIONS

Miami & South Florida
Montréal
New England
New Orleans
    DIRECTIONS
New York City
New York City
    DIRECTIONS
New York City Mini
    Guide
Orlando & Walt Disney
    World DIRECTIONS
Pacific Northwest
Rocky Mountains
San Francisco
San Francisco
    DIRECTIONS
Seattle
Southwest USA
Toronto
USA
Vancouver
Washington DC
Washington DC
    DIRECTIONS
Yosemite

Caribbean
& Latin America
Antigua & Barbuda
    DIRECTIONS
Argentina
Bahamas
Barbados DIRECTIONS
Belize
Bolivia
Brazil
Cancùn & Cozumel
    DIRECTIONS
Caribbean
Central America
Chile
Costa Rica
Cuba
Dominican Republic
Dominican Republic
    DIRECTIONS
Ecuador
Guatemala
Jamaica

...music & reference

TRAVEL STORE

Small print and

Index

A Rough Guide to Rough Guides

In the summer of 1981, Mark Ellingham, a recent graduate from Bristol University, was travelling round Greece and couldn't find a guidebook that really met his needs. On the one hand there were the student guides, insistent on saving every last cent, and on the other the heavyweight cultural tomes whose authors seemed to have spent more time in a research library than lounging away the afternoon at a taverna or on the beach.

In a bid to avoid getting a job, Mark and a small group of writers set about creating their own guidebook. It was a guide to Greece that aimed to combine a journalistic approach to description with a thoroughly practical approach to travellers' needs – a guide that would incorporate culture, history, and contemporary insights with a critical edge, together with up-to-date, value-for-money listings. Back in London, Mark and the team finished their Rough Guide, as they called it, and talked Routledge into publishing the book.

That first *Rough Guide to Greece*, published in 1982, was a student scheme that became a publishing phenomenon. The immediate success of the book – with numerous reprints and a Thomas Cook Prize shortlisting – spawned a series that rapidly covered dozens of destinations. Rough Guides had a ready market among low-budget backpackers, but soon also acquired a much broader and older readership that relished Rough Guides' wit and inquisitiveness as much as their enthusiastic, critical approach. Everyone wants value for money, but not at any price.

Rough Guides soon began supplementing the "rougher" information about hostels and low-budget listings with the kind of detail on restaurants and quality hotels that independent-minded visitors on any budget might expect, whether on business in New York or trekking in Thailand.

These days the guides – distributed worldwide by the Penguin Group – offer recommendations from shoestring to luxury and cover more than 200 destinations around the globe, including almost every country in the Americas and Europe, more than half of Africa, and most of Asia and Australasia. Our ever-growing team of authors and photographers is spread all over the world, particularly in Europe, the USA, and Australia.

In 1994, we published the *Rough Guide to World Music* and *Rough Guide to Classical Music*, and a year later the *Rough Guide to the Internet*. All three books have become benchmark titles in their fields – which encouraged us to expand into other areas of publishing, mainly around popular culture. Rough Guides now publish:

- Travel guides to more than 200 worldwide destinations
- Dictionary phrasebooks for 22 major languages
- History guides ranging from Ireland to Islam
- Maps printed on rip-proof and waterproof Polyart™ paper
- Music guides running the gamut from Opera to Elvis
- Restaurant guides to London, New York, and San Francisco
- Reference books on topics as diverse as the Weather and Shakespeare
- Sports guides from Formula 1 to Man Utd
- Pop culture books from *Lord of the Rings* to Cult TV
- World Music CDs in association with World Music Network

Visit **www.roughguides.com** to see our latest publications.

Rough Guide credits

Text editor: Amanda Tomlin
Layout: Jessica Subramanian
Cartography: Animesh Pathak
Picture editor: Simon Bracken
Production: Katherine Owers
Proofreader: Margaret Doyle
Cover design: Chloë Roberts
Editorial: London Kate Berens, Claire Saunders, Geoff Howard, Ruth Blackmore, Polly Thomas, Richard Lim, Clifton Wilkinson, Alison Murchie, Sally Schafer, Karoline Densley, Andy Turner, Ella O'Donnell, Keith Drew, Edward Aves, Nikki Birrell, Helen Marsden, Alice Park, Sarah Eno, Joe Staines, Duncan Clark, Peter Buckley, Matthew Milton; **New York** Andrew Rosenberg, Richard Koss, Steven Horak, AnneLise Sorensen, Amy Hegarty, Hunter Slaton, April Isaacs
Design & Pictures: London Dan May, Diana Jarvis, Mark Thomas, Jj Luck, Harriet Mills; **Delhi** Madhulita Mohapatra, Umesh Aggarwal, Ajay Verma, Amit Verma, Ankur Guha
Production: Julia Bovis, Sophie Hewat

Cartography: London Maxine Repath, Ed Wright, Katie Lloyd-Jones; **Delhi** Manish Chandra, Rajesh Chhibber, Jai Prakash Mishra, Ashutosh Bharti, Rajesh Mishra, Jasbir Sandhu, Karobi Gogoi
Online: New York Jennifer Gold, Suzanne Welles, Kristin Mingrone; **Delhi** Manik Chauhan, Narender Kumar, Shekhar Jha, Rakesh Kumar, Lalit Sharma, Chhandita Chakravarty
Marketing & Publicity: London Richard Trillo, Niki Hanmer, David Wearn, Demelza Dallow, Louise Maher; **New York** Geoff Colquitt, Megan Kennedy, Katy Ball; **Delhi** Reem Khokhar
Custom publishing and foreign rights: Philippa Hopkins
Manager India: Punita Singh
Series editor: Mark Ellingham
Reference Director: Andrew Lockett
PA to Managing and Publishing Directors: Megan McIntyre
Publishing Director: Martin Dunford
Managing Director: Kevin Fitzgerald

Publishing information

This sixth edition published November 2005 by
Rough Guides Ltd,
80 Strand, London WC2R 0RL
345 Hudson St, 4th Floor,
New York, NY 10014, USA
14 Local Shopping Centre, Panchsheel Park,
New Delhi 110017, India
Distributed by the Penguin Group
Penguin Books Ltd,
80 Strand, London WC2R 0RL
Penguin Putnam, Inc.,
375 Hudson St, NY 10014, USA
Penguin Group (Australia)
250 Camberwell Road, Camberwell,
Victoria 3124, Australia
Penguin Books Canada Ltd,
10 Alcorn Avenue, Toronto, ON,
M4V 1E4 Canada
Penguin Group (New Zealand),
Cnr Rosedale and Airborne roads,
Albany, Auckland, New Zealand

Typeset in Bembo and Helvetica to an original design by Henry Iles.
Printed at Legoprint in Italy
© Dan Richardson

888pp includes index
A catalogue record for this book is available from the British Library.

ISBN: 1-84353-463-0

Help us update

We've gone to a lot of effort to ensure that the sixth edition of **The Rough Guide to Egypt** is accurate and up to date. However, things change – places get "discovered", opening hours are notoriously fickle, restaurants and rooms raise prices or lower standards. If you feel we've got it wrong or left something out, we'd like to know, and if you can remember the address, the price, the time, the phone number, so much the better.

We'll credit all contributions, and send a copy of the next edition (or any other Rough Guide if you prefer) for the best letters. Everyone who writes to us and isn't already a subscriber will receive a copy of our full-colour thrice-yearly newsletter. Please mark letters: **"Rough Guide Egypt update"** and send to: Rough Guides, 80 Strand, London WC2R 0RL, or Rough Guides, 4th Floor, 345 Hudson St, New York, NY 10014. Or send an email to **mail@roughguides.com**.

Have your questions answered and tell others about your trip at **www.roughguides.atinfopop.com**.

SMALL PRINT

Acknowledgements

The authors would like to jointly thank Amanda Tomlin for her superb editing.

Thanks from **Dan Richardson** to Hagg Ibrahim, Hamada, Karin and Tayeb el-Khalifa for their hospitality and friendship in Luxor; and the assistance of outstanding tourist officials, namely Mrs Hafza (Luxor), Shukri Sa'ad and Hakeem Hussein (Aswan), Hussein Farag and Mahmoud Abd el-Samir (Minya), Ramadan Abdou (Assyut), Hassan Rifat (Sohag), Mahdi Hweiti (Siwa), and Omar Ahmed (Dakhla). Also thanks to Mahmoud Youssef of the Museum of the New Valley in Kharga Oasis, Talat Mulah of *Eden Garden Camp* in Bahariya, and the staff of the *Crillon Hotel* in Alexandria. In Britain, thanks to Bruce Lyons at Crusader Travel for sorting out the flights; Ros Ford for her knowledge of Cairo galleries, Abydos and Aswan; Terrence DuQuesne for details of the Assyut Tombs; and Michael Ackroyd at Ancient World Tours for filling in the gaps.

Daniel Jacobs: Big thanks to Hisham Youssef at the *Berlin Hotel* in Cairo, and also to Caroline Evanoff, Mahdi Mohammed el-Batram, Salah Mohammed, Hamdi Shora, Humphrey Davies, and above all to the people of Cairo for their warmth, kindness and hospitality.

Michael Kohn: First and foremost, at Rough Guides, thanks to Geoff Howard for sending me off to Egypt, and to Amanda Tomlin for editing my text. Cheers also to fellow RG scribes Dan Richardson and Dan Jacobs. In Egypt, a mighty debt of gratitude to Werner in Sharm el-Sheikh, Roberta in El-Quseir, Karen and Thomas far down the Red Sea coast and Christina and Karsten in Mersa Alam. As always, thanks to Baigal, for waiting.

Readers' letters

Thanks to all the readers who took the trouble to write in with their comments and suggestions (and apologies to anyone whose name we've misspelt or omitted).

Vipin J. Adhia; Simon Allen; Sue Allum; Marino Perez Avellaneda; Ulrike Bender; Nils Bindha; Frederico Botana; Simon Brown; Jenny Caldwell; Julie Dean; Osman Durrani; Margaret Evans; John Fanning; Saffia Farr; Egil Fossum; Chris Frean; Gary Goldfinch; Paul Gregory; Pete Griffith; Becci Henderson; Frank Hsin; John Jordan; Roshdy Khattab; Jem Kime; Raymon Kondos; Annette Kwan-Terry; Brian Leek; Carl Mandabach; Nick Moore; John C. Myles; Veronica Ng; Joanna Nibler; Emma Phillips; Dr Abdelsalam Ragab; Barry Ramdhani; Dorothy-Ann Reimer; Charles Robertson; Gopa Roy; Andrzej Sidorowski; Christine Spencer; Keri Thomas; Sarah Tibbatts; Deborah & Xavier Vrigneau; Mark Weston; Kesley Williams; P. Windley.

Photo credits

All photos © Rough Guides except the following:

Cover

Main front picture: Mosque of Sultan Hussan at sunset, Cairo © Getty
Small front top picture: Hawksbill turtle © Alamy
Small front lower picture: Market, Cairo © Alamy
Back top picture: Sphinx, Giza © Getty
Back lower picture: Feluccas on the Nile © Alamy

Title page

Lahun Pyramid © Sandro Vannini/CORBIS

Full page

Eastern Desert © Jean-Pierre Pieuchot/GETTY

Introduction

King Tutankhamun's death mask © Elvele Images/ALAMY
Islamic Cairo © f1 online/ALAMY
Corals and diver, the Red Sea © F. Jack Jackson/ALAMY
Camels in Luxor © Frans Lemmens/GETTY
Sign © Sylvain Grandadam/ROBERT HARDING
Statue of Ibis and the goddess Maat © Roger Wood/CORBIS
Cinema hoardings, downtown Cairo © Abbie Enock/TRAVEL INK
Egyptian man drinking tea and smoking pipe © Peter Adams/GETTY
Donkey, Siwa Town © Luca Trovato/GETTY
Bakers © Chris Caldicott/AXIOM
Camel caravan © Jim Erickson /CORBIS

Things not to miss

01 Abu Simbel © Richard Passmore/GETTY
02 Bellydancing © Roger Ressmeyer/CORBIS
03 Abydos © James Morris/AXIOM
04 Dunes © Sylvain Grandadam/GETTY
05 Monastery of St Paul © Bojan Brecelj/CORBIS
06 Jeep safari © Hugh Sitton/ALAMY
07 Bedouin weavers, Western Desert © Sarah Errington/HUTCHINSON
08 School of Batfish in Red Sea near Ras Mohammed © Ivor Fulcher/CORBIS
09 An Egret in the wildlife haven of Wadi Rayan © Amjad el-Geoushi/ALAMY
10 The Sphinx, Giza © Guy Midkiff/ALAMY
11 Juice bar © Michael Juno /ALAMY
12 Feluccas on the Nile, Aswan © Ellen Rooney/GETTY
13 *Fuul* seller in Old Cairo © Rachel Ziemba
14 View of Aghurmi across palm groves, Siwa Oasis © James Morris/AXIOM
15 Tourist cruise boat © Christine Osbourne - Worldwide Picture Library/ALAMY
16 Bedouins seated on camels © Simon Miles/CORBIS

17 Tawaret © Roger Wood/CORBIS
18 Alexandria © Sandro Vannini/CORBIS
19 Mount Sinai © Joerg Hardtke/GETTY
20 Khan el Khalili market in Cairo ©Richard T. Nowitz/CORBIS
21 Gold jewellery © Carlos Freire/HUTCHINSON
22 Diver at the wreck of the *Giannis D* © Paul Ives/ALAMY
23 Valley of the Kings © Bojan Brecelj/CORBIS
24 Catacombs of Kom es Shoqafa © Stuart Franklin/MAGNUM
25 Meze food © Jean Dominique DALLET/ALAMY
26 Karnak Temple ©Jean Dominique DALLET/ALAMY
27 Feluccas © Christine Osbourne - Worldwide Picture Library/ALAMY
28 Mount Sinai © Jon Arnold/ALAMY
29 Floorshow at Na'ama Bay © Sanafir Hotel/Sanafir Hotel
30 Karkaday seller © Sylvain Grandadam/ROBERT HARDING
31 Dahshur © Peter Wilson/Dkimages

Black and whites

p.100 View across Cairo to the pyramids © Hugh Sitton Photography/ALAMY
p.257 Interior of *Naguib Mahfouz Café* at Khan el Khalili bazaar © Eddie Gerald
p.306 Ancient ruins at Philae © Hans Georg Roth/CORBIS
p.413 Opening the tomb of Tutankhamun © Hulton-Deutsch/CORBIS
p.463 Aswan bazaar © John Hatt/Hutchison
p.502 Sand formations in the White Desert © Sandro Vannini/CORBIS
p.560 Inside the mud brick madrassa of Al Qasr Dakhla Oasis © Miamnuk Images/ALAMY
p.604 Al Alamein war cemetary © Gary Cook/Alamy
p.624 Engraving of the Pharos of Alexandria © Fischer von Erlach Historical Picture Archive/CORBIS
p.656 Two stone coffin lids in Tanis © Ian M Butterfield/ALAMY
p.660 Rosetta, Delta-style buildings, Beit Ramadan © Daniel Jacobs
p.676 Fishing boat and cargo ship, Suez Canal © Dorian Shaw/HUTCHINSON
p.698 St Catherine's Monastery © Hanan Isachar/CORBIS
p.754 Arab trader on top of Gebil Musa © Ian M Butterfield /ALAMY
p.766 Diving in the Red Sea © BE&W agencja fotograficzna Sp.zo.o./ALAMY
p.771 St Anthony's Coptic Monastery © BennettPhoto/ALAMY

Index

Map entries are in colour

I

INDEX

INDEX

U

V

W

X

Y

Z

INDEX

I

INDEX